Law and Medical Ethics

516373

'It would not be correct to say that every moral obligation involves a legal duty; but every legal duty is founded on a moral obligation.'

LORD CHIEF JUSTICE COLERIDGE
in *R v Instan* [1893] 1 QB at 453

Law and Medical Ethics

Sixth Edition

J K Mason CBE MD LLD FRCPath FRSE

Regius Professor (Emeritus) of Forensic Medicine
at the University of Edinburgh

R A McCall Smith LLB PhD FRSE

Professor of Medical Law
at the University of Edinburgh

G T Laurie LLB PhD

Senior Lecturer in Law
at the University of Edinburgh

 LexisNexis™ UK

Members of the LexisNexis Group worldwide

United Kingdom	LexisNexis Butterworths Tolley, a Division of Reed Elsevier (UK) Ltd, Halsbury House, 35 Chancery Lane, LONDON, WC2A 1EL, and 4 Hill Street, EDINBURGH EH2 3JZ
Argentina	LexisNexis Argentina, BUENOS AIRES
Australia	LexisNexis Butterworths, CHATSWOOD, New South Wales
Austria	LexisNexis Verlag ARD Orac GmbH & Co KG, VIENNA
Canada	LexisNexis Butterworths, MARKHAM, Ontario
Chile	LexisNexis Chile Ltda, SANTIAGO DE CHILE
Czech Republic	Nakladatelstvi Orac sro, PRAGUE
France	Editions du Juris-Classeur SA, PARIS
Hong Kong	LexisNexis Butterworths, HONG KONG
Hungary	HVG-Orac, BUDAPEST
India	LexisNexis Butterworths, NEW DELHI
Ireland	Butterworths (Ireland) Ltd, DUBLIN
Italy	Giuffrè Editore, MILAN
Malaysia	Malayan Law Journal Sdn Bhd, KUALA LUMPUR
New Zealand	LexisNexis Butterworths, WELLINGTON
Poland	Wydawnictwo Prawnicze LexisNexis, WARSAW
Singapore	LexisNexis Butterworths, SINGAPORE
South Africa	Butterworths SA, DURBAN
Switzerland	Stämpfli Verlag AG, BERNE
USA	LexisNexis, DAYTON, Ohio

© Reed Elsevier (UK) Ltd 2002
Reprinted 2003

A CIP Catalogue record for this book is available from the British Library.

Typeset by Doyle & Co, Colchester
Printed in England by Clays Ltd, Bungay, Suffolk

Visit Butterworths LexisNexis *direct* at www.butterworths.com

Preface

Six editions in 20 years testify to the almost explosive growth of the disciplines of medical law and bioethics which continues unabated. Once again, we have to acknowledge an increase in the size of the book; try as we might, we found that inevitable – despite the fact that we have tried to confine ourselves to those aspects of medical law that have an ethical component.

As a result, the current edition has been no easier to write than were its forebears. Not only has medical law widened its scope, it has also become very much more complex. In keeping with this, the relevant case reports seem to be getting longer as the days go by; 87 pages on the difference between an abortifacient and a contraceptive seems a lot by any standards – yet they reflect no more than the never-ceasing need for the law to keep an eye on the evolution of modern morality.

There has been no shortage of causes célèbres in the past three years – nearly all of them having developed in the shade of the Human Rights Act 1998. Ms B and Mrs Pretty have pled their causes with varying success, the conjoined twins have been separated and the House of Lords has decided that Mr and Mrs McFarlane wanted another child anyway. Even so, recognisable patterns of acceptable medical law and behaviour are beginning to emerge from the haze.

Perhaps above all since we last went to press, we have been witnessing a sea-change in centralised control of medical practice that has been enacted against a background of unprecedented attack on the medical profession by way of ministerial obiter dicta and by the media. One can sympathise with the President of the Royal College of Pathologists when he writes of 'the winter of our discontent'. But Bristol, Alder Hey and Yorkhill *did* happen and have had profound effects on medical ethics and medical practice. Some of these have been good, others not so good; we can only hope that the former will come to prevail as the dust settles.

It is said that the opera diva Dame Nellie Melba gave no fewer than 11 final performances. She happened to be godmother to the father of the senior author of this book and the tradition seems to have passed down the line;

nevertheless, this really is the last time *(premature and unlikely: RAMcS, GTL).* Meanwhile, it is a pleasure to welcome Graeme Laurie to full co-authorship.

We would like to thank Ms Lorna Fleming for assisting us in our research and the Faculty of Law for making this possible. Finally, and once again, we thank our publishers for their support in yet another turbulent gestation.

Edinburgh,   JKM
September 2002   RAMcS
                                                                                                  GTL

Contents

Contents

Table of statutes

Table of foreign enactments

Table of cases

B

H

K

L

PARA

N

O

P

X

Introduction

1 Introduction

1.1 This book is concerned with a vital debate which has captured the imagination of people throughout the world – that is, as to how we should deal with the remarkable advances in medicine and human biology that bid fair to change the way in which we see ourselves as human beings. But the debate is also concerned with the more day-to-day issues of the role of law in medical practice and with the moral and legal contours of the doctor/patient relationship. It has an academic side to it – bioethics and medical law are recognised components of the curricula of many universities and colleges – but is also a public debate involving legislators and, increasingly, national bioethics commissions or committees. It is, of course, inevitable that such an issue should give rise to a burgeoning literature consisting of both general and specialised material.[1]

1.2 The importance and intensity of the public moral conversation about bioethics and medical law are explained in part by the very nature of its subject matter. This is an area of concern which touches upon people's most intimate interests. It deals with matters of human reproduction and human mortality – or sex and death – both of which have traditionally involved our religious convictions and have provoked intense emotions. In addressing these issues, the debate raises many fundamental questions. What is it to be a person? What is the value of human life? How, if at all, should we attempt to influence the future biology of the species through the use of new genetic knowledge?

1.3 There is no shortage of conviction on any of these issues. Most major religious traditions have firm views on such matters and are frequently prepared to assert them as being valid for all. Those who approach these matters from

---

1   The literature on bioethics is now greater than its counterpart in any other area of applied ethics. Constraints of space prevent more than a few examples of the genre but, of the general works available, T L Beauchamp and J F Childress *Principles of Biomedical Ethics* (5th edn, 2001) has established itself as a classic. Other well-known works include J Harris *The Value of Life* (1985), a thought-provoking work by a philosopher who has made a major contribution to the subject. A useful starting point for many readers will be the various compilations which have been made, including J Harris (ed) *Bioethics* (2001) and P Singer and H Kuhse (eds) *A Companion to Bioethics* (2001).

the viewpoint of individual freedom, or of human rights, are just as vigorous in their assertion of values, arguing that moral issues of this sort lie clearly within the confines of privacy. The antagonism between these two positions is sometimes intense and it often seems as if there is little prospect of common ground. Yet, in so far as we have to live in a community, we are obliged to identify what is permissible and what is not – and this implies the involvement of the law. So we do need, for example, a law concerning artificial reproduction because, unless the law pronounces on the issue, society can be seen to be endorsing a non-interventionist approach which allows for unrestricted freedom of choice. In some cases, this may be what society actually wants but, in others, it will not represent the communal position, which also deserves protection. To take another example, the possibility of embryo stem cell research requires a legal response unless the human embryo is to be considered as a mere artefact. In fact, there are very few people who would argue for no regulation of such a form of research; the majority of supporters of a liberal attitude to this issue would accept that *some* level of regulation is vital in this area even if it is only in respect of the type of research permitted and the period during which it can be carried out.

1.4 Inevitably, then, the law is drawn into the debate and this is especially so when there is a conflict of individual interests. A dispute involving the parents and hospital authorities or social workers as to the medical treatment of a child provides an example. Such an issue arose in dramatic form in the recent conjoined twins case decided by the Court of Appeal in England. The courts were clearly uncomfortable about being drawn into this tragic matter but, ultimately, the judges had to reach a decision.[2] The law cannot avoid taking a view in such cases; the alternative is an irrational and inconsistent approach to their solution. In a liberal society, however, the legislature and courts may seek to limit legal intervention in medically-related matters. Such a society may take a positivist stance and view the function of the law as being that of the neutral adjudicator – a role in which the moral content of legal decisions is kept to a minimum. This concept of the legal role has proved largely unrealistic in the area with which we are concerned. Medical law is catalysed by moral issues. The debate on embryonic stem cell research, for example, is essentially an exposition of different moral views; yet, in practice, it becomes one concerning what the law should be. It is pointless to attempt to disengage the moral from the legal dispute – when we talk about legal rules, we are inevitably drawn into a discussion of moral rules.

1.5 Thus, we often find ourselves engaged in debating not what the law is but what it should be. This requires us to engage in moral evaluation and this, in turn, raises the question of how we are to identify what is right. More specifically, we are confronted with a need to identify an ethical basis for the practice of medicine and its regulation by the law. And this is no easy task, living, as we do, in a pluralist, secular age.

---

2 *Re A (children) (conjoined twins: surgical separation)* [2000] 4 All ER 961, (2000) 57 BMLR 1. Fully discussed below at para 16.65 et seq.

A BASIS FOR MEDICAL ETHICS

1.6 There is a plethora of theories on hand that are designed to help us decide what is morally right. These range from authoritarian, revelatory theories at one extreme to subtly nuanced visions of existential ethics at the other. In between these options – each of which, in its own way, discourages meaningful moral debate – there is a range of categories to which moral responses might be allocated. Of course there is always the possibility of eclecticism; morality, it seems, is sometimes not so much a maze as a smorgasbord.

Religious theories

1.7 Many accounts of medical ethics are strangely silent as to the importance of religious theories of medical ethics – the element of surprise stemming from the fact that medicine and religion have been intertwined from the earliest times, when priests were also recognised as physicians. As a direct result, religious theories historically constitute a major element of thinking in medical ethics and their influence continues to be felt in all corners of the subject. The common feature of such theories is a vision of man as involved in a dialogue with a divine creator, or possibly a spiritual force, as to the way in which the human body should be treated. This vision may manifest itself in an insistence on ritualistic practices, for example, in relation to burial. Such examples should not, however, be dismissed as an exercise of power based on superstitious reverence – many religious practices, especially those of orthodox Judaism, are, in fact, based on sound principles of public health. It may, on the other hand, be expressed at a higher level of abstraction, fashioning a view of the sanctity of human life which is capable of resolving a whole raft of practical issues. The Judaeo-Christian religious tradition has had the greatest impact in the Western world and is one which continues to influence much of the contemporary debate.

1.8 Religiously-based medical ethics have a clear sense of fundamental values. In the Christian tradition, these include not only a belief that human life is a divine gift which cannot be disposed of by mortals but also include a strong attachment to the importance of monogamous, enduring marriage. These values are translated into practical rules in the shape of an antipathy to abortion and euthanasia – an antipathy that amounts to prohibition in orthodox Roman Catholic thinking – and of a belief that various forms of intervention in human reproduction are morally wrong. Inherent in many of these traditions is a strong sense of the *natural*, which proposes a teleology for man. In the light of this, it is often seen as wrong to interfere with the manifest destiny which has been prepared for man. This may result in the rejection of an everyday medical issue such as sterilisation just as much as it might lead to a blanket refusal to contemplate interference in the genetic endowment of mankind.

1.9 It would be wrong to assume that those who approach medical ethics from a religious viewpoint are uncritical and authoritarian in their moral thinking. Indeed, many of the more sensitive contributions to the literature of medical ethics have been made by those who approach the subject from this background. And sometimes it is only such a voice which will raise awkward,

5

and yet very important, questions. The debate on euthanasia provides an instance of this in the form of the serious and persistent questioning provided by John Keown.[3] An historic example is the Protestant theologian, Paul Ramsey, whose work anticipated many of the questions which have since become the staple of contemporary debate in medical ethics.[4]

The currents of medical ethics

1.10 Ethical discourse is concerned with the search for justification for our actions. An ethical dilemma arises when two or more courses of conduct may be justifiable in any given set of circumstances, possibly resulting in diametrically opposed outcomes. How, then, do we know what is the 'right' thing to do? Various means may be employed to argue for an ethical resolution to a dilemma and morality is but one such means. Morality may be individual or communal, in that it reflects a core set of values by which individuals or communities abide. As we discuss below, morality may even be a simple question of intuition and, on this criterion alone, it is difficult to argue that an individual's personal value system is 'wrong'. Ethics, on the other hand – while they may be informed by moral debate and argument – usually operate within an established framework of values which serves as a reference from which to conduct the debate about the rightness or wrongness of an action. Thus, for example, Beauchamp and Childress have long championed the utility of 'principlism' as a means to this end.[5] In brief, this view holds that ethically appropriate conduct is determined by reference to four key principles which must be taken into account when reflecting on one's behaviour towards others. These are:

(i) the principle of respect for individual autonomy (ie – individuals must be respected as independent moral agents with the 'right' to choose how to live their own lives),

(ii) the principle of beneficence (ie – one should strive to do good where possible),

(iii) the principle of non-maleficence (ie – one should avoid doing harm to others), and

(iv) the principle of justice (ie – people should be treated fairly, although this does not necessarily mean that everyone should be treated equally).

While principlism is by no means universally accepted as the lingua franca of ethics,[6] it does, nonetheless, provide a very good example of how ethical discourse requires reflection and justification of our actions by reference to accepted values and mores.

1.11 At a broader level of abstraction, contemporary medical ethics can be seen as a tapestry in which an array of philosophical theories interweave with

---

3 In particular by way of *Euthanasia Examined* (revised 1997) and *Euthanasia, Ethics and Public Policy* (2002). See the discussion of euthanasia, chapter 18, below.

4 See eg P Ramsey *The Patient as Person* (1970).

5 Para 1.1 above.

6 Cf B Gert, C M Culver and K D Clouster *Bioethics: A Return to Fundamentals* (1997).

one another. The two strands of deontological and utilitarian thought are, however, particularly evident. Deontological theories focus on the rightness or wrongness of an act in itself. They are not concerned with the consequences which that act will have; rather, they are concerned with identifying those features of the act which mark it as morally acceptable or otherwise. The classical exposition of such a theory is that by Kant, who stressed that every person must be treated as an end in him- or herself, rather than as a means to an end. Thus, the essential message of Kantian moral teaching is that we should not use others but should respect their integrity as individuals. Modern theories of autonomy find their roots in this background and, as we shall see later, autonomy has come to be associated closely with the liberal individualism which has exerted a massive influence on the philosophical climate at the turn of the twentieth century.

1.12 Critics of deontological theories of morality, particularly of those in the Kantian mould, often stress what is seen as a rigidity of approach. The 'strict' Kantian does not give sufficient weight, it is said, either to human intuitions as to what is right at the time or to the virtues. An alternative, and more flexible, approach might be one which was more sensitive to the human feelings involved in any moral dilemma and one which also paid more attention to the consequences which flow from our actions. One such approach is that adopted by utilitarianism, a philosophy which has played a major role in the medical debate and which is regarded by many as underpinning modern ethical medicine.

1.13 Utilitarians are accustomed to being misrepresented by those who believe that utilitarianism is a philosophical theory which started, and ended, with the work of Jeremy Bentham. Classic utilitarianism of the Benthamite school held that the test of the morality of an action was the extent to which it promoted good consequences (pleasure) or bad (pain). The utilitarian measure of good is, therefore, the maximisation of happiness, although modern utilitarians, in particular, would stress that this does not necessarily lead to unrestricted hedonism. Modern utilitarianism acknowledges the importance of rules in identifying moral goals and, in this way, prevents the happiness of the many from overshadowing the rights of the few. Preference utilitarianism, a further modification of the classical theory, allows for the judging of the good of individuals according to their own values, a position perhaps best expressed in modern bioethics through the work of Peter Singer.[7]

1.14 Liberal individualism leans towards a utilitarian or consequentialist approach, in that it measures the effect of a decision on individuals. To the liberal individualist, the good which society should pursue is the fulfilment of the individual. The ideal society is, then, one in which each person makes his own decisions as far as is possible and 'creates himself'. In this way, the individual exercises and enhances his autonomy – how autonomy is used is not a major concern to the liberal individualist, so long as it is not used in a way which restricts others from exercising their own autonomy.

---

7 Singer's contribution to contemporary applied ethics has been considerable. In the field of bioethics, he is associated with challenges to the traditional sanctity of human life view; on which, see his *Rethinking Life and Death* (1994).

1.15 Autonomy is by far the most significant value which has been promoted by contemporary medical ethics.[8] The concept which has dominated medical ethics more than any other in the last half-century is the insistence that individuals should have control over their own bodies, should make their own decisions relating to their medical treatment and should not be hindered in their search for self-fulfilment. The acknowledgment of autonomy has served to discredit medical paternalism and has led to the promotion of the patient from the recipient of treatment to being the partner in a therapeutic project – and this change has been reflected in the development of the legal regime by which medical treatment is regulated.

1.16 In one sense, the philosophical apotheosis of autonomy has brought liberation. It has enhanced the freedom of those whose vulnerability, physical or mental, may have exposed them to insensitive treatment or even to exploitation; it has imparted dignity to the lives of those who might, otherwise, have felt themselves to be powerless in the face of the articulate and the professional. Yet, from another view, the acceptance of autonomy as the benchmark of the good has led us to ignore other values, and this may have negative effects. Even if self-fulfilment does shine through the development and the exercise of autonomy, there is a social dimension to life which is potentially equally enriching. Autonomy must be qualified by the legitimate interests and expectations of others, as well as by economic constraints. In the medical context, the claims of autonomy must be moderated so as to accommodate the sensitivities of others, including those of the doctor – who is, after all, also an autonomous agent. It may be that respect for individual autonomy points in the direction of allowing voluntary euthanasia – but another moral agent has to administer the drug that ends life, and that person may be affected by the task. There are also the interests of others in being protected against involuntary euthanasia; it is possible that, in providing such protection, we may have to deny self-determination to those who are truly volunteers. Personal autonomy must also be measured against the needs of society as a whole. In an ideal world, a sick person should be able to demand the treatment of his or her choice. A moment's reflection, however, is enough to show us that this is an impossible goal. Society itself demands a just distribution of resources and this cannot be achieved in an ambience of unrestricted 'rights' – put another way, we can only realise our autonomy within the framework provided by society.[9]

1.17 Even so, the concept of rights has many proponents and, like autonomy, rights theory plays an important part in contemporary moral debate. Yet the language of rights may also become unduly assertive and combative and may hinder, rather than promote, moral consensus.[10] This is not to suggest that rights are unimportant. Many of the central moral positions defended in

---

8 For a recent contribution, see O O'Neill, *Autonomy and Trust in Bioethics* (2002).
9 See A V Campbell 'Dependency: the foundational value in medical ethics' in K V M Fulford and G J M Gillett (eds) *Medicine and Moral Reasoning* (1994).
10 In the view of some philosophers, rights can be reduced to principles which form the real content of morality. For a sceptical view, see R Frey *Rights, Killing and Suffering* (1983); to be contrasted with L W Sumner *The Moral Foundation of Rights* (1987) and with the outstanding contribution of K Cronin *Rights and Christian Ethics* (1992).

this book can be couched in terms of rights. Once again, however, rights-talk is peculiarly suited to an individualistic moral tradition and conflicts of rights tend to lead to moral impasse. Most discussion centres on the rights of the patient – but has the doctor no rights when choosing treatment in accordance with his Hippocratic principles and his training? The law, itself, is prepared to recognise this as a de facto situation. The one-time Master of the Rolls, Lord Donaldson, expressed this unequivocally when he said:

> [I cannot, at present, conceive of any circumstances] in which the court should ever require a medical practitioner to adopt a course of treatment which in the bona fide clinical judgment of that practitioner is contraindicated as not being in the best interests of the patient.[11]

In the same passage, Lord Donaldson described the fundamental duty of the doctor as being to treat the patient in accordance with his own clinical judgment – which opens the way to an alternative dialogue through the language of obligations. The way to a satisfactory doctor/patient relationship is not through the confrontational profession of rights but, rather, through a realisation of the obligations incumbent upon each side to work towards the ideal.[12]

Autonomy and paternalism

1.18 The paternalist acts for the benefit of another, or in the other's best interests, without the specific consent of the person for whom he acts. Until a few decades ago, the practice of medicine was unquestionably paternalist – at least in parts – and many of those involved might have been surprised to discover that their practices could be considered morally objectionable. Thus, patients were often treated without any adequate explanation of what was involved or significant facts about their illness were kept from them. It was, for example, common not to pass on information if it was thought that the knowledge would cause them distress, and psychiatric patients could be subjected to treatments without any concern as to their views or preferences. Such practices are now regarded as unethical in modern Western medicine,[13] and are consequently rare. Yet they still occur and have surfaced, for example, in disclosures of the unauthorised retention of tissues from paediatric post-mortems examinations. It may be that the pathologists involved in these practices did not ask for the permission of the parents, but at least some of them failed to do so because they wished to protect the parents from distressing facts. To quote from the President of the Royal College of Pathologists:

> No one ever had enthusiasm for discussing the detailed autopsy process with recently bereaved relatives, and it was always more comfortable to draw a veil over it. But that veil meant that relatives did not know what was going on ...

11 For a useful discussion in depth, see H Teff *Reasonable Care* (1994) and, in particular, his discussion of medical models in ch 3.
12 In *Re J (a minor) (wardship: medical treatment)* [1992] 2 FLR 165 at 172, (1992) 9 BMLR 10 at 17.
13 Compare a Western view: R J Sullivan, L W Menapace and R M White 'Truth-telling and Patient Diagnoses' (2001) 27 J Med Ethics 192 with: D F-C Tsai 'Ancient Chinese Medical Ethics and the Four Principles of Biomedical Ethics' (1999) 25 J Med Ethics 315.

Strip away [the extraneous factors] and there remains the inescapable and uncomfortable fact that in the past post-mortem organ retention has been a prime example of professional paternalism.[14]

Even so, while an unqualified rejection of paternalism in medicine might satisfy some proponents of autonomy, it would undoubtedly, at the same time, cause avoidable harm. Paternalism is acceptable in principle where the person who is the object of such action is incapable of making his or her own decision.[15] An intervention in such a case will be justifiable if the disabling condition is either permanent or cannot be expected to lift in time for the person in question to be able to do so. Any intervention must, however, be necessary, which means that the advantages it brings significantly outweigh the disadvantages which would otherwise accrue. This is essentially a test of reasonableness, which involves a careful assessment of motives for action and a balancing of interests. To achieve this balance, it may be necessary to consider what is likely to be the future view of the patient.

1.19 The principal subjects of medical paternalism are likely to be children, the psychiatrically ill, and the unconscious. The medical treatment of children who are too young to make up their own minds provides a common and clear case of justified medical paternalism. At the same time, the paternalist must take into account in this context the fact that capacity increases with growing maturity, and that caution must, therefore, be exercised in acting paternalistically towards teenagers. Paternalism in relation to the psychiatrically ill may be justified on the grounds that there is a mental disability which incapacitates the patient to the extent that he or she cannot understand that treatment may be required; it is, then, reasonable to assume that the patient will endorse what has been done once recovery has occurred. This latter justification – the appeal to subsequent consent – may also be invoked in the treatment of the unconscious. Anticipated consent may be forthcoming in the vast majority of cases, but the treatment of those who are unconscious after an attempt at suicide may be more difficult to justify. The doctor who treats such a person is clearly acting paternalistically and could either argue that the attempt at suicide may have resulted from a mental illness (and therefore be treatable without consent), or that the patient will later endorse the treatment. But what about the case where the patient has made it clear in advance that suicide is what he or she wants and is the result of rational consideration?[16] In practice, such patients are often treated, although it is difficult to fit that into the category of justified paternalism.

1.20 As in all areas of medical practice, room must remain for clinical discretion to be exercised by the doctor. There will be cases where minor acts of paternalism aimed at preventing distress to those who are anxious will be the ethically right thing to do. The law ought to recognise this at the same time that it recognises and protects the right of individual autonomy.

14 J Lilleyman 'From the President' (2001) Bull R Coll Path No 114, p 2.
15 For a detailed account of paternalism in all its forms, see E Buchanan and D W Brock *Deciding for Others: The Ethics of Surrogate Decision Making* (1990).
16 We will see later that there is also a hazard that the patient's life may be reprieved but only in a disabled state.

Paternalism and autonomy are not, therefore, mutually exclusive: the task of medical ethics and of medical law is to balance the two in a way which enhances individual dignity and autonomy but which does not inhibit the exercise of discretion in the marginal case.

Intuitions, experience and morality

1.21 There are grounds, then, for doubting the practicality or effectiveness of applying a broad deontological brush to medical ethics. Each case is unique, and its individual features may change with each consultation. Recent moral philosophy supports this approach, stressing the importance of imagination as a means of navigating our way through the moral landscape.[17] This moral imagination may, to an extent, rely on metaphors rather than on rules – all of which points to a role, even if a circumscribed one, for moral intuitions. Intuition may have a limited appeal as a basis for moral philosophy but it should not be wholly discounted and this, for the reasons given above, is especially so in the field of health care.[18] Intuitions may point in the direction of a value which may not always be articulated formally but which may none the less be very important

1.22 Our own view is that medical ethics is perhaps not best served by a rigid attachment to an undiluted vision of patient autonomy – but neither was it well served by the paternalistic philosophy of the past. What is required is an openness to the complexity of moral decisions, and an awareness of the sensitive, contextual nature of the doctor-patient relationship. An understanding of the demands of this relationship is not necessarily something that philosophers can teach or lawyers prescribe. The insights of cognitive science, and of psychology in general, increasingly recommend a model of moral reasoning which gives a large role to learned moral responses. These moral abilities – if one might call them that – are acquired through education within a particular ethos and through hands-on experience in dealing with people and their suffering. There is all the difference in the world between, say, the experienced nurse who has spent years working in a hospice setting and the lay person who approaches the issue of end-of-life decisions from an entirely theoretical perspective. A moral response which discounts the validity of the insights of the former would be unlikely to be helpful. Those involved in caring for patients are moral beings who must be encouraged to develop and express their sense of the moral demands of a particular situation. There is not necessarily one right answer to the dilemmas which they encounter, and this should perhaps be recognised more extensively than it is today. There may be two right answers, or even more, depending on the people involved and the circumstances. A moral straitjacket is hardly helpful. Having said which, we should, perhaps go on to examine the practical environment in which health carers set about their work.

17 See M Johnson *Moral Imagination: Implications of Cognitive Science for Ethics* (1993); L May, M Friedman and A Clark (eds) *Mind and Morals: Essays on Ethics and Cognitive Science* (1996).
18 For expression of this view, see T B Brewin 'How Much Ethics Is Needed to Make a Good Doctor?' (1993) 341 Lancet 161. Also G Gillett 'Euthanasia, Letting Die and the Pause' (1988) 14 J Med Ethics 61.

The Hippocratic influence

1.23 For the origins of our current medical practice – with its emphasis on the one-to-one relationship between doctor and patient within the confines of the home, surgery or hospital – we must look to Greece where, by 500 BC, the originally strong influence of the priest/physician had waned; a predominantly religious discipline had been taken over by the philosophers who, through the processes of logical thought, observation and deduction, transformed the concepts of medicine. Inevitably, this led to the formation of schools involving the close association of practitioners, paternalism and the elements of the 'closed shop'; a code of intraprofessional conduct evolved, heralding the dawn of what has become known as medical etiquette. In addition, the new concepts dictated that the physician went to the patient rather than the patient to the temple. A standard of practice relevant to the new ideals was required and has survived as the Hippocratic Oath.[19]

1.24 While Hippocrates remains the most famous figure in Greek philosophical medicine, he was not alone and it is probable that the Oath predates his own school. It therefore indicates a prevailing ethos rather than a professorial edict and it is still regarded as the fundamental governance of the medical profession. Much of the preamble relates to medical etiquette and is clearly outmoded – very few ageing medical professors now anticipate social security by way of the generosity of their students! This, however, is not our concern here – and it is to be distinguished clearly from medical ethics. As to the latter, the Oath lays down a number of guidelines. First, it implies the need for co-ordinated instruction and registration of doctors – the public is to be protected, so far as is possible, from the dabbler or the charlatan. Secondly, it is clearly stated that a doctor is there for the benefit of his patients – to the best of his ability he must do them good and he must do nothing which he knows will cause harm. Thirdly, euthanasia and abortion are proscribed; the reference to lithotomy probably prohibits mutilating operations (castration) but has been taken by many to imply the limitation of one's practice to that in which one has expertise. Fourthly, the nature of the doctor-patient relationship is outlined and an undertaking is given not to take advantage of that relationship. Finally, the Oath expresses the doctrine of medical confidentiality.

1.25 In fact, the Hippocratic Oath did not become an integral part of ethical teaching until well into the Christian era; it lapsed with the decline of Greek civilisation and was restored with the evolution of university medical schools. It is doubtful if any British medical school now requires a reiteration of the Oath at graduation – although most Scottish universities require assent by students to a modified version – but, avowed or not, all doctors would admit to its persuasive influence. The language of the Oath is, however, archaic and a modernised version was introduced by the World Medical Association as the Declaration of Geneva. This was last amended at Stockholm in 1994[20] and provides the basis for an International Code of Medical Ethics.[21]

19 See Appendix A.
20 See Appendix B.
21 See Appendix C.

1.26 We have seen that Greek medicine was essentially a private matter and, indeed, its mode of practice was scarcely attuned to the needs of public health. For the origins of this, we must turn to the Judaeo-Christian influence which, certainly in the Israeli tradition, expressed itself most powerfully in accepting that the rights of the individual must sometimes be sacrificed for the good of the community – there was strong emphasis, for example, on the isolation of infectious cases, including those of venereal disease, the regulation of sewage disposal and the like – and the principles of public health medicine were born. As we have already noted, the fact that medicine was dominated by religion turned out to be mutually advantageous. Much of this attitude passed to the Christians, who were also forced into the group life-style, and were fortified by the concepts of equality, charity and devotion to the less fortunate – concepts which still underlie the ethical practice of medicine in Christian countries. It is unsurprising that, during the Dark Ages, medicine was virtually kept alive in the monasteries which provided the template for the voluntary hospitals of later years.

THE ORGANISATION OF MODERN MEDICINE

1.27 Probably the single most important feature which distinguishes 'modern medicine' is the importance attached to experimentation and research and it was this change in emphasis which dictated most urgently that medical practice should be subject to central control.

1.28 The age of medical research can be said to have begun with the Renaissance and, since that time, the practice of medicine has become increasingly scientifically based. New dimensions are, thus, introduced and new dilemmas posed. It is obvious that scientific medicine cannot improve without extensive research while, on the other hand, that process tends to turn medical practice into a series of problem-solving exercises – a diversion which, even now, stimulates some of medicine's severest critics.

1.29 Perhaps the first practical effect of the scientific approach was to convince doctors that they have an expertise worth preserving and, as early as the sixteenth century, we find the establishment of the Royal College of Physicians of London, together with a general tightening of the rules governing the practice of surgery. The early Royal Colleges had considerable powers of examination and registration. The latter function has now gone and the major purpose of the colleges – which now represent some eight specialities with additional faculties – is to maintain a standard of excellence among specialised practitioners – a matter of current importance to which we return below.

1.30 As organisation proceeded, fortune began increasingly to depend upon fame, and fame in its turn upon academic superiority over one's colleagues – from all accounts, British medicine in the eighteenth and early nineteenth centuries was not the happiest of professions. Even so, it was not so much medical ethics, as they are understood today, that were found wanting but, rather, medical etiquette. Something had to be done to ensure the status of the profession and this need was first met by the formation of the British Medical Association (BMA) in 1832. The BMA has always been deeply concerned with the way medicine is practised but its present main function is the protection of doctors' interests – today, it is a non-affiliated registered trade union.[22]   Clearly, an interested party could not represent the public need for control of a profession with such power and it was largely due to the lobby of the BMA itself that the General Medical Council (GMC) was established by the Medical Act 1858.[23]   The current statutory regulation of the medical profession is found in the Medical Act 1983 which is about to be substantially amended.[24]

1.31 It is emphasised that, while the GMC remains the governing body of the medical profession,[25] its most significant public function from now on will be encapsulated in ensuring that medical professionals are up to date and fit to practise.[26]   Whatever may be the overall standard of fitness – and there is little or no reason to suppose that it has deteriorated in recent years – there is no doubt that the number of high profile, individual instances of alleged misconduct that were exposed at the end of the 20th century caused considerable public disquiet. How far this was fanned by the increasingly aggressive news media or was dictated by political expediency remains open for argument;[27] the fact remains that sufficient evidence accrued to provide solid grounds for review – and revision – of the current system of control of

22 Trade Union and Labour Relations (Consolidation) Act 1992. The distinction between a trade organisation and a regulatory body such as the GMC has recently been emphasised in *General Medical Council v Cox* (2002) Times, 16 April, in which it was held that the GMC was not a trade organisation for the purposes of the Disability Discrimination Act 1995, s 13.
23 The General Medical Council at present consists of 102 members. The new General Council will consist of 35 members of which it is probable that 19 will be elected by the medical profession (elected members must form a majority of the Council). The Academy of Medical Royal Colleges and the Council of Heads of Medical Schools will each nominate one member and there will be 14 lay members nominated by an independent commission. The President will be elected by the Council which will be responsible for the strategic management of the delivery of its statutory functions. There will, of course, be a large number of persons working with or on behalf of the Council; these will be recruited through open selection or appointment.
24 Discipline within the National Health Service is additionally regulated within a complex framework of disciplinary committees: see National Health Service (Service Committees and Tribunal) Regulations 1992, SI 1992/664. Incompetence by hospital practitioners is investigated under the terms of Ministry of Health Circular HM(61)112(1961) as amended by HC(90)9(1990). Personal misconduct is dealt with by a system of internal inquiry but the distinction may be difficult to make: *Skidmore v Dartford and Gravesham NHS Trust* [2002] EWCA Civ 18, [2002] ICR 403. The actions of a disciplinary inquiry are subject to judicial review (*R v Department of Health and Social Security, ex p Darnell* (1986) 293 BMJ 322).
25 The increasing status afforded to 'alternative medicine' is to be noted. These practitioners have their own controlling bodies: see, for example, Osteopaths Act 1993; Chiropractors Act 1994. A practitioner of any form of alternative medicine will be judged by the standards of that particular art but must recognise that he is practising alongside orthodox medicine: *Shakoor v Situ* [2000] 4 All ER 181, (2001) 57 BMLR 178.
26 A function that was introduced only as recently as 1995 by way of the Medical (Professional Performance) Act 1995. The whole attitude to regulation of the health care professions is being changed with the publication of: Department of Health *Reform of the General Medical Council* (May 2002) www.doh.gov.uk/gmcreform.pdf and, at the time of writing, the draft Medical Act 1983 (Amendment) Order 2002 www.doh.gov.uk/medicalact1983.doc. Modern governments seldom publish consultation documents that they do not propose to enact; for the purposes of this chapter, we will assume that the Order is a fait accompli.
27 For a cynical appraisal, see T Jackson 'Gods and Monsters' (2001) 322 BMJ 371.

the medical profession.[28] It has also to be said that the public reaction was such as to significantly tie the hands of the profession's leaders – although they now express themselves as well satisfied with the proposed changes.[29]

1.32 Maintaining the official register of medical practitioners will remain a basic function of the GMC. The function of the register has, up till now, been to protect the public from those who have not undergone recognised training; unlike the practise of dentistry, no specific offence lies in an unqualified person practising medicine in the United Kingdom – the offence has always been that of pretending to be a registered medical practitioner[30] or of usurping functions which are statutorily limited to registered practitioners – such as prescribing 'prescription only' medicines. Registration will, however, not be sufficient in the future when a registered medical practitioner will also require a licence to practise. This will be granted on first registration but, thereafter, will be subject to revalidation – a procedure whereby the practitioner's continuing fitness to practise is evaluated, presently suggested as being every five years. One technical result is that one must now read 'registered practitioner with a licence to practise' wherever the words 'registered practitioner' arise in a legal sense.

1.33 The disciplinary function of the GMC has, perhaps, always been its activity which has occasioned the most interest and, here, the Amendment Order 2002 has caused a sea change in attitude.[31] The overriding factor is now the doctor's fitness to practise and misconduct is but one possible cause of unfitness; the changing emphasis is exemplified by the relevant title in the Medical Act 1983 being altered from 'Professional Conduct and Fitness to Practise' to 'Fitness to Practise and Medical Ethics'. As a result, the traditional Professional Conduct Committee will be abolished along with those others that are currently operative – only the Education Committee survives (see below). The power to co-opt committee members is a prominent feature of the new regulations. Some or all of the members of Committees may be persons who are not members of the Council[32] – which suggests that there

---

28 Aside from regular reports of individual errors, a number of major incidents were disclosed which resulted in public investigations. Among these are to be included the standards of paediatric cardiac surgery at Bristol: *Report of the Public Inquiry into Children's Heart Surgery at Bristol Royal Infirmary 1984–1995* (Cm 5207, 2001) www.bristol-inquiry.org.uk; the retention of organs at Alder Hey Hospital: *The Royal Liverpool Children's Inquiry Report* (HC12, 2001) www.rlcinquiry.org.uk; the retention of organs in Scotland: *Final Report of the Independent Review Group on Retention of Organs at Post-mortem* (Scottish Exec, 2001) www.show.scot.nhs.uk/scotorgrev/Final%20Report/ropm-00.htm.
29 Even so, a leading article in the BMJ has it that 'the independence of the medical profession in the United Kingdom is under unprecedented attack through these government proposals': D P Gray 'Deprofessionalising Doctors?' (2002) 324 BMJ 627.
30 Medical Act 1983, s 49. The Council has occasionally lapsed in this respect. An example is that of an unqualified person from overseas who managed to obtain registration with the GMC; he received £450,000 in salary from the NHS before being detected through the vigilance of a pharmacist: J Ironside 'Five Year Sentence for Fake General Practitioner' (1992) 304 BMJ 1652. It will, in future, be a similar offence to hold a licence to practise (Medical Act 1983, s 49A inserted by the 2002 Order).
31 Major modification of the Medical Act by way of an Order in Council is empowered by Health Act 1999, Pt III, s 60.
32 Medical Act 1983, Sch 1, Article 25(2A) inserted by 2002 Order.

will be greater lay-person control at all levels – and, indeed, a member of the Council will not be allowed to sit on several committees, including the most significant Fitness to Practise Panels.[33]

1.34 We make no attempt here to consider in detail the administrative law concerning medical practice.[34] Indeed, such is the speed with which new codes and regulations appear, that it would be a fruitless task.[35] Suffice it to say that, as currently proposed, a doctor's fitness to practise can be questioned before a Fitness to Practise Panel on the grounds of misconduct, deficient professional performance, a conviction for or caution following a criminal offence, his or her mental or physical health and, finally, a determination by any body responsible for the regulation of the health or social care professions in the United Kingdom that his or her fitness to practise is impaired.[36] The doctor whose fitness to practise is found to be impaired may be subject to erasure from the register (except in a 'health case'[37]), to suspension for up to 12 months, to conditional registration in accordance with the Panel's directions for up to three years or, in the case of misconduct, criminal conviction or of a determination by another body, to reprimand. Any of these restrictions can be imposed when an original suspension order is reviewed and, in the case of indefinite suspension, the doctor may request a review not more often than every two years. An appeal against a decision of the Fitness to Practise Panel is available to the High Court in England and Wales, the Court of Session in Scotland and the High Court in Northern Ireland.[38] Finally, it is to be noted that the name of a doctor that has been erased can be restored to the Register but not within five years of erasure; subsequently, applications for restoration can be made yearly.

1.35 The effect of the transfer of the existing appellate function of the Privy Council to the High Court and its equivalents in Scotland and Northern Ireland will be watched with interest – particularly, perhaps, as to whether it will lead to different standards in judging appeals. Even as things stand, the attitude of the

33 Medical Act 1983 (Amendment) Order 2000, SI 2000/1803, Article 4.
34 For that, the reader is referred to the seminal work by J Montgomery *Health Care Law* (2nd edn, 2002). It is to be noted that the conduct of the GMC is open to judicial review both as to its 'advice' (*Colman v General Medical Council* [1989] 1 Med LR 23, QBD; sub nom *R v General Medical Council, ex p Colman* (1989) 4 BMLR 33, CA) and as to the actions of its Committees (*R v General Medical Council, ex p Gee* [1987] 1 All ER 1204, CA. While exercising a judicial power, the GMC is not part of the judicial system of the state: *General Medical Council v BBC* [1998] 3 All ER 426, (1998) 43 BMLR 143.
35 For example, the National Health Service Reform and Health Care Professions Act 2002 alters the composition and powers of the Commission for Health Improvement (CHI); at the same time, it is proposed to merge CHI with part of the Audit Commission to form a new Commission for Healthcare Audit and Inspection (CHAI) (Department of Health *Delivering the NHS Plan* (April 2002)) www.doh.gov.uk/about/nhsplan/index.htm.
36 Medical Act 1983, s 35C(1). An interim suspension order can be imposed for a period of up to 18 months in the event that it is considered that protection of the public is a matter of urgency (s 41A). The relationship between the GMC and the newly constituted National Clinical Assessment Authority (see para 1.37 below) (http://www.ucaa.nhs.uk), which is intended to advise employers on doctors' efficiency, is, as yet, uncertain: S Dewar and B Finlayson 'Dealing with Poor Clinical Performance' (2001) 322 BMJ 66.
37 Suspension in a 'health case' can only become indefinite if the original suspension has been in force for at least two years (s 35D(6) inserted by 2002 Order).
38 National Health Service Reform and Health Care Professions Act 2002, s 29. Judgments on appeal from decisions related to health and performance are no longer limited to points of law (a limitation that the Privy Council found frustrating: *Hall v General Medical Council* [2001] UKPC 46, (2001) 65 BMLR 53).

Privy Council has been changing over the years. Traditionally, the Council has been reluctant to alter the view of the facts taken by the disciplinary committee.[39] Times, however, have changed, perhaps particularly with the advent of the Human Rights Act 1998. Indeed, it is only the availability of an appeal to an independent tribunal that saves the disciplinary function of the GMC and its equivalents from incompatibility with the 1998 Act.[40] As a result, there has been something of a steady flow of cases in which the findings of the committees of the GMC have been modified on appeal[41] and it is to be expected that the High Court, being closer to the 'coal-face', may be even more interventionist in the future.

1.36 It is clear that the disciplinary function of the GMC will be altered very considerably and it would be unfortunate if that of maintaining the standards of conduct of the profession were to assume a relatively small part of the Council's remit. So far as this book is concerned, one of the most important roles of the GMC has been to fill the gap in constraining such actions as are not actionable yet which would not be expected of the ethical practitioner. For example, the law on medical confidentiality is in many ways unclear, but few doctors would have wished to tangle with the GMC on the issue of professional secrecy. There is nothing criminal in adultery; yet the public cannot expect family relationships to be destroyed as a result of the doctor's privilege to enter the bedroom.

1.37 The future must, however, be indefinite as one of the most far reaching legislative intentions is the establishment of a Council for the Regulation of Health Care Professionals,[42] the main function of which is to promote the interests of patients and other members of the public in relation to the performance of the individual professional 'regulatory bodies'[43] – in common parlance, to dictate their policies; a regulatory body must comply with any directions given by the new Council[44] which will have the power to investigate complaints as to the regulatory bodies' exercise of their functions. This policy change has been described as 'facing the medical profession with its greatest assault in 150 years',[45] a statement which may carry a ring of hyperbole. Nevertheless, all

---

39 *Libman v General Medical Council* [1972] AC 217, [1972] 1 All ER 798.

40 *Preiss v General Dental Council* [2001] UKPC 36, [2001] 1 WLR 1926, [2001] Lloyd's Rep Med 491. For a similar Scottish decision, see *Tehrani v United Kingdom Central Council for Nursing, Midwifery and Health Visiting* 2001 SC 581, 2001 SLT 879.

41 *Krippendorf v General Medical Council* [2001] 1 WLR 1054, (2001) 59 BMLR 81 (wrong assessment tests – Professional Performance); *Bijl v General Medical Council* [2001] UKPC 42, (2001) 65 BMLR 10 (unnecessarily draconian penalty – PCC); *Manzur v General Medical Council* [2001] UKPC 55, (2001) 64 BMLR 68 (disproportionate penalty for fraud – PCC); *Srirangalingham v General Medical Council* (2002) 65 BMLR 65, [2002] Lloyd's Rep Med 77 (inappropriate suspension – PCC); *Hossain v General Medical Council* [2001] UKPC 40, (2001) 65 BMLR 1, [2002] Lloyd's Rep Med 64 (unreasonable erasure – PCC). A significantly larger number and proportion of appeals has been allowed since the turn of the 21st century and the coming into force of the Human Rights Act 1998.

42 National Health Service Reform and Health Care Professions Act 2002, s 25. For critical assessment, see S Dewar and B Finlayson 'Regulating the Regulators' (2002) 324 BMJ 378.

43 Currently, the General Medical, Dental, Optical, Osteopathic and Chiropractic Councils, the Royal Pharmaceutical Societies of Great Britain and Northern Ireland and, so long as they subsist, the Council for Professions Supplementary to Medicine and the UK Central Council for Nursing, Midwifery and Health Visiting.

44 Although 'it may be that changes to the rules of the regulatory bodies will only be made with the agreement of both Houses of Parliament.

45 Chairman of the Academy of Medical Royal Colleges quoted in (2002) BMA news, 16 March, p 1.

but nine of the Council's members will be appointed by a devolved Parliament or by the Secretary of State; one would surely need rosy spectacles of the deepest hue not to see this as raising the spectre of overt political control of the health care professions. Supervisory regulation of the 'regulators' seems to be a feature of modern governance and is currently moving out of the administrative sphere into that of clinical health care.[46] Thus, we have the Commission for Health Improvement,[47] responsible in the main for providing advice and information to, and reviewing and reporting on NHS and Primary Care Trusts; the National Institute for Clinical Excellence,[48] which provides information on what is the best practice and, significantly, on the effective use of available resources (see para 11.22 below); and the National Clinical Assessment Authority,[49] which provides a service to NHS bodies who are concerned at the performance of individual doctors. Medical education has not been neglected. Undergraduate education and examination and the supervision of those undertaking their year of provisional registration remain within the ambit of the Education Committee but we now have a proposal for a Medical Education Standards Board[50] which will be responsible for monitoring post-graduate training in the NHS and elsewhere; this looks very like a body set up to regulate the Royal Medical Colleges with the consequent demise, not only of their current Specialist Training Authority,[51] but also of qualifications such as Membership or Fellowship of the Colleges having any real meaning.

1.38 On the other side of the coin one must also note the regulatory arrangements that are specifically directed to public participation in health care delivery. The most important of these is the establishment of the Commission for Patient and Public Involvement in Health,[52] the main function of which is to advise on all aspects of public involvement in, and consultation on, matters relating to the health service in England. A prominent component of this will include advising and monitoring the success of Patients' Forums which are to be established for each NHS Trust or Primary Care Trust[53] in England under s 15 of the same Act. On a more general note, Health Authorities, Primary Care Trusts and NHS Trusts are under a duty to involve and to consult with the public on any aspect of the services they provide while, at the same time, the Secretary of State must now make arrangements for the provision of an independent Advocacy Service which will assist the public in making complaints under procedures operated by a health service body.[54]

46 K Walshe 'The Rise of Regulation in the NHS' (2002) 324 BMJ 967.
47 Health Act 1999, s 19. Soon to have its powers increased: National Health Service Reform and Health Care Professions Act 2002, s 12.
48 National Institute for Clinical Excellence (Establishment and Constitution) Order 1999, SI 1999/220 and 1999/2219.
49 National Clinical Assessment Authority Regulations 2000, SI 2000/261.
50 Department of Health *Postgraduate Medical Eduction and Training: The Medical Education Standards Board*, Consultation Paper (2001) www.doh.gov.uk/medicaltrainingintheuk/mesb-consultation/index.htm.
51 Post-graduate training for general practitioners is now controlled by the Joint Committee on Postgraduate Training for General Practice.
52 National Health Service Reform and Health Care Professions Act 2002, s 20.
53 Primary Care Trusts were established by the Health Act 1999, s 2 which inserts s 16A into the National Health Service Act 1977.
54 Health and Social Care Act 2001, ss 11 and 12. Community Health Councils will now be abolished (2002 Act, s 22) by reason of increased powers of scrutiny of the health services that is given to local authorities in the Heath and Social Care Act 2001, ss 7–10.

1.39 The main purpose of this long and arguably incomplete[55] survey of recent legislation is to emphasise the burden of regulation thereby imposed on the pattern of medical practice. Many of the bodies established have yet to find their feet and it would be premature to attempt to praise or criticise their function. None the less, it would be idle to deny that the plethora of regulation could represent a tidal wave of political control not only of health administration but also of clinical practice – and, while the needs and aspirations of the public must have priority, comparable legislation designed to protect the independence and integrity of the medical profession is conspicuous in its absence. Doctor/patient relationships are changing in a changing world and this shift is not confined to the United Kingdom.[56] We can only hope that the change will be for the better.

1.40 A major criticism of the GMC has been that it has very little power to institute disciplinary proceedings itself; effectively, the Council has been able to act only by way of information received – a little understood fact which has resulted in some grossly unfair criticism of its efficiency. Very often, the only likely informants will be fellow doctors – for example, in the important circumstances when treatment of doubtful validity is being provided.[57] Most professional men and women are inherently unwilling to denounce their colleagues and this reticence was severely criticised in the Bristol inquiry.[58] Even so, the distinction between disparaging the skill of another doctor, which the GMC would regard adversely, and informing of behaviour which raises a question of patients' well-being, which is rightly approved,[59] may be tenuous and it is the uncertainty of the dividing line that often deters those who have an equal understanding of the problems at issue. The same reservations may not, however, apply when health care professionals of other disciplines are involved and, indeed, a large proportion of reports of dubious behaviour on the part of doctors stem from outraged nursing staff.[60] Many such protests are based on grounds of conscience, these being related especially to life or death decisions, and the probability is that the great majority are motivated by the genuine belief that they are protecting the public against undisclosed violations of the moral, professional and criminal codes. An employee who discloses in good faith, inter alia, that the health or safety of an individual has been, is being or

---

55 We could, for instance, add the NHS Modernisation Agency which is designed to bring together improvements in health care and the development of leadership in the NHS. Somewhat controversially, the Agency will be able to reward those institutions that have 'done well' with increased decision making autonomy.

56 See N Edwards, M J Kornacki and J Silversin 'Unhappy Doctors: What Are the Causes and what can be Done?' (2002) 324 BMJ 835.

57 R Smith 'Doctors, Unethical Treatment, and Turning a Blind Eye' (1989) 298 BMJ 1125. See also criticism of the management of a case of doubtful practice associated with advertising: A B Kay 'Alternative Allergy and the General Medical Council' (1993) 306 BMJ 122; R Smith 'GMC in the Dock Again' (1993) 306 BMJ 82.

58 Para 1.31 above.

59 General Medical Council *Good Medical Practice* (1998) para 24. See also Appendix C.

60 A survey of community nurses recently indicated that only some 61% would certainly have reported a general practitioner whose performance was thought to put patients at risk: J Burrows 'Telling Tales and Saving Lives: Whistleblowing – the Role of Professional Colleagues in Protecting Patients from Dangerous Doctors' (2001) 9 Med L Rev 110. Interestingly, as many would have been more likely to report fellow nurses than report doctors. Very clear guidance is now provided in the new Nursing and Midwifery Council *Code of Professional Conduct* (2002), section 8 (www.nmc-uk.org/cms/conduct/Publications/Code%20of%20professional%20conduct.pds).

is likely to be endangered is now protected from recrimination by the Employment Rights Act 1996, ss 43A–J[61] – protection of the individual is, of necessity, subject to a number of qualifying conditions which include following a prescribed procedure. Clearly, the practice of what is popularly known as 'whistle blowing' is open to abuse or misconception – defects in the system may be real or imaginary and no more than indirectly associated with patient safety; nevertheless, the great majority would now approve the spirit of the regulations, particularly having regard to the fact that the reasonableness of the disclosure will be judged specifically on a 'need to know' basis – that is, on the identity of the person to whom the disclosure is made. Not only is frankness in the investigation of both ethical and clinical error to the advantage of the patient[62] but it is also important that the spectre of 'closed ranks' does not undermine the public's faith in the health care professions.[63]

PUBLIC RELATIONS

1.41 The importance of the overall relationship between the medical profession and the public cannot be overstated. The growing primacy of the cult of patient autonomy and self-regulation has carried with it a parallel claim to a right to personal assessment of one's doctor's expertise and quality – aided by a surfeit of 'league tables' and mortality records. This has added a new dimension to the GMC's traditional attitudes to advertising by the medical profession. Time was when, for example, a doctor discussing medical matters of public interest on the radio had to do so anonymously for fear of disciplinary action on the part of the GMC. There is little doubt that such restrictions were based on a fear of competitive doctors 'touting' for patients; the advent of the National Health Service virtually eliminated any need for such behaviour and the antipathy of the GMC was steadily relaxed.

1.42 Solution of the matter was, however, catalysed by the reference of the GMC's ban to the Monopolies and Mergers Commission who held that the rule forbidding advertising in the press by general practitioners was against the public interest.[64] At the same time, the Commission recommended considerable restraint – including a ban on disparaging other doctors and on claiming special aptitudes. The Commission, fearing exploitation, declined to extend its recommendations to advertising to the general public by specialists. This rule has now been relaxed, subject to the proviso that information about specialist services should include advice that patients cannot usually be seen or treated by specialists, either in the NHS or private practice, without a referral, usually from a general practitioner.[65]

61 Inserted by Pubic Interest Disclosure Act 1998, s 1.
62 This is the purpose behind the recently established National Patient Safety Agency (National Patient Safety Agency (Establishment and Constitution) Order 2001, SI 2001/1743), the function of which is to set up a system for mandatory reporting and collation of incidents and 'near-misses' on a national scale.
63 The case of Dr Chapman, whose allegation of wrongful dismissal for questioning a colleague's research was rejected after eight years' investigation, is in point: H Spencer '"Never again" says NHS whistleblower' (1997) 314 BMJ 623.
64 Interestingly, the Court of Appeal subsequently upheld that the recommendation did not render the GMC's position unreasonable (*Colman* para 1.34 above).
65 GMC *Good Medical Practice* (1998), para 46.

1.43 The recommendations of the MMC, which were designed for the benefit of patients and for the improvement of specialist services, have now been accepted by the GMC,[66] whose advice currently reads:

> If you publish or broadcast information about services you provide, the information must be factual and verifiable ... The information you publish must not make claims about the quality of your services nor compare your services with those your colleagues provide. It must not, in any way, offer guarantees of cures, nor exploit patients' vulnerability or lack of medical knowledge.[67]

The GMC's general opposition to covert and overt elitism on the part of 'specialists' has been overtaken and overruled by the Council of Europe.[68] As a result, a Specialist Register, referring to 53 medical specialties, is now held and constitutes the bench-mark for those claiming a particular expertise and who have qualified for a Certificate of Completion of Specialist Training conferred by the Specialist Training Authority.[69] Thus, the traditional secrecy surrounding specialism no longer exists.

Legal intervention in medicine

1.44 The early twenty-first century picture of medical practice is one of rapidly advancing technology which is effected in a strongly research orientated environment and which exists within an increasingly hedonistic and materialistic society. Society, for its part, demands more and more esoteric methodology, and personal involvement in medicine is encouraged at all levels. The law, however, moves more slowly than either medicine or the public mores. Thus, the general rules of doctoring are being developed within a moral framework which is constantly being restructured by contemporary society while, at the same time, doctors frequently find themselves operating in an atmosphere of legal uncertainty. All of this promotes confrontation within the triangular relationship of medicine, society and the law;[70] a major purpose of medical jurisprudence as it evolves is to break down the barriers of latent hostility.

1.45 Whether the law has a right to impose morality is a well-known and controversial issue in jurisprudence[71] but, for present purposes, we argue that the public conscience, as embodied in the law, provides a useful foundation for medical ethics. This, however, is not to say that the law should dictate to the profession and, particularly, not that it should dictate by means of restrictive

---

66 The history of the GMC's change of attitude was outlined in D H Irvine 'The Advertising of Doctors' Services' (1991) 17 J Med Ethics 35.
67 N 65 above, paras 44-45.
68 Directive 93/16/EEC (OJ No L 165,7.7.1993), Title II and III.
69 European Specialist Medical Qualifications Order 1995, SI 1995/3208. A number of additions and amendments to the list of specialties have since been effected but these are generally of a semantic nature.
70 Lord Woolf, now Lord Chief Justice, identified 5 main areas of dissatisfaction involving all three parties in 'Clinical Negligence: What is the Solution? How Can We Provide Justice for Doctors and Patients?' (2000) 4 Med L Internat 133.
71 There are still few better discussions than the rather elderly text by S Lee *Law and Morals* (1986).

statute. Effectively, we are suggesting that medicine must operate within broadly stated legal rules – such as those embodied in the common law – and, as Lord Scarman classically indicated,[72] the law must be flexible in the absence of parliamentary direction.

1.46 The crucial question, then, is that of determining the *extent* to which medical decisions should be the object of legal scrutiny and control. At one extreme there are those who hold that the medical profession should be left to regulate itself and that it alone should decide what is acceptable conduct. According to this view, intervention by the law is too blunt a way of tackling the delicate ethical dilemmas which doctors have to face: the individual, guided by personal experience and by prevailing public and professional standards, must confront and resolve the day-to-day ethical issues of medical practice – and it is a truism that no two patients present precisely the same problems in diagnosis and management.

1.47 The contrary view, frequently expressed just as firmly, denies that there is any reason why doctors alone should regulate their relationship with their patients. In this view, reserving to the medical profession the right to decide on issues, say, of life and death is an improper derogation from an area of legitimate public concern and an encroachment by clinicians into what is, properly, social policy. According to the proponents of this opinion, the law, even if it is an imperfect and often inaccessible weapon, is at least one means of controlling the medical profession in the interests of the community as a whole.[73] In the event, modern conditions are such that the courts cannot avoid involvement in decisions that are essentially matters of medical ethics rather than law; as a result, they are increasingly prepared 'to adopt a more proactive approach to resolving conflicts as to more traditional medical issues'.[74]

1.48 We will see as we go through the various problem areas discussed in this book that the relationship between the law and medicine has, effectively, settled into a classical domestic state in which mutual trust is, occasionally, interspersed with outbursts of disaffection. Certainly, the law has, traditionally, been content to allow doctors as free a hand in carrying out their duties as is possible. Nonetheless, as Lord Woolf has cogently pointed out in a non-judicial capacity,[75] times change – including as to the distribution of domestic chores – and can change rapidly if the conditions are ripe. Thus, we have, again, Lord Brandon holding, only a decade ago:

> The application of the principle which I have described means that the lawfulness of a doctor operating on, or giving treatment to, an adult patient disabled from giving consent will depend not on any approval or sanction of

---

72 In *Gillick v West Norfolk and Wisbech Area Health Authority* [1986] AC 112, [1985] 3 All ER 402, HL.
73 'I would expect medical ethics to be formed by the law rather than the reverse': *Airedale NHS Trust v Bland* [1993] 1 All ER 821 at 858, (1993) 12 BMLR 64 at 103 per Hoffmann LJ.
74 Lord Woolf 'Are the Courts Excessively Deferential to the Medical Profession? (2001) 9 Med L Rev 1.
75 Para 1.47 above.

a court but on the question whether the operation or other treatment is in the best interests of the patient concerned.[76]

By 2000, however, we have the Court of Appeal unanimously limiting the powers of the doctor beyond matters of clinical judgment and, at the same time delineating the relative powers and responsibilities of the doctors and the judges:

> [I]n determining the welfare of the patient the *Bolam*[77] test [of the acceptability of a doctor's actions] is applied only at the onset to ensure that the treatment proposed is recognised as proper by a responsible medical opinion skilled in delivering that particular treatment ... In deciding what is best for the disabled patient the judge must have regard for the patient's welfare as the paramount consideration. That embraces issues far wider than the medical ... In my opinion *Bolam* has no contribution to make to this second and determinative stage of the judicial decision.[78]

In effect, this retreat from *Bolam* is but part of a steady shift of judicial and societal concern away from the duties of the medical profession and its relocation under the umbrella of patients' rights – though whether or not this serves to harmonise doctor/patient relationships is open to discussion. We return to the issue later in this chapter.

1.49 It has to be said, however, that the courts are also willing to recognise their position in relation to the legislature in face of the speed of evolution of modern technology – as Lord Browne-Wilkinson put it: 'Existing law may not provide an acceptable answer to the new legal questions [raised by the ability to sustain life artificially].'[79] He went on to question whether judges should seek to develop new law to meet a wholly new situation and to suggest that it was a matter which required society, through the democratic expression of its views in Parliament, to reach its decisions on the underlying moral and practical problems and then reflect those decisions in legislation – and, in this, he was strongly supported by Lord Mustill.[80] In other words, the House of Lords, at least, is anxious that society, as the third point in the triangle of policy decision-makers, should take its full share of responsibility for the ethico-legal directions we are following.

1.50 The fact that the courts are prepared to assist doctors in coming to their ethical decisions – and have shown this by the steadily extended use of their

---

76 *Re F* [1990] 2 AC 1 at 56, sub nom *F v West Berkshire Health Authority* (1989) 4 BMLR 1 at 8, HL.
77 *Bolam v Friern Hospital Management Committee* [1957] 2 All ER 118, (1957) 1 BMLR 1. We discuss the *Bolam* test, which judges the propriety of a doctor's action by way of the standards of the medical profession itself, in detail in chapter 9 below. Suffice it to say here that it appears to be becoming the fulcrum on which the delicate medico-legal relationship is balanced. Both the Lord Chief Justice of England (paras 1.44 and 1.47 above) and the Lord Chancellor (Lord Irvine of Lairg 'The Patient, the Doctor, their Lawyers and the Judge: Rights and Duties' (1999) 7 Med L Rev 255) see its modification as central to the development of a medical jurisprudence.
78 *Re SL (adult patient) (medical treatment)* [2001] Fam 15, (2000) 55 BMLR 105 at 119 per Thorpe LJ.
79 In *Airedale NHS Trust v Bland* [1993] 1 All ER 821 at 878, (1993) 12 BMLR 64 at 124.
80 (1993) 12 BMLR 64 at 135.

declaratory powers[81] – is laudable and helpful. But it does not compensate in toto for the fact that doctors often still have to work in a 'legal vacuum' in which, without such pre-emptive assistance, they may be uncertain as to whether or not they face the prospect of a civil action or, again in the words of Lord Mustill, they take the risk of having to validate their conduct after the event in the context of a trial for murder. For these reasons, some may see it as preferable to have certain general rules set out clearly by way of statute and we have, in fact, concrete examples of the benign effect of legislative involvement in medical issues – it is through statute, for example, that the legal uncertainties which once surrounded the new reproductive technologies have been largely dispelled.[82] The way in which this has been achieved varies according to the jurisdiction. The common British approach is for Parliament to state its general aims and to demit their refinement to officially appointed Authorities on which the profession and the public are adequately represented.[83] This approach serves to circumvent one of the most cogent arguments against introducing legal rules into human affairs – which is, that once rules acquire a specific meaning, they allow little room for manoeuvre and can turn out to be more restrictive than was originally intended by the framer of the rule. An effect of this can be to distort people's behaviour through the fear of litigation or prosecution. One may then be concerned, not with doing what one feels to be right, but with what one feels to be the legally safest thing to do.

1.51 Doctors in the United Kingdom may be particularly fortunate in this respect as, notwithstanding the subtle changes of direction that we have discussed, the courts remain inherently reluctant to interfere in clinical matters. While they will accept the absolute right of a patient to refuse treatment,[84] they will, at the same time, refuse to dictate to doctors what treatment they should give.[85] Indeed, the fear could be that, if anything, the pendulum has swung too far in favour of therapeutic immunity. [86]

1.52 Moreover, one must question whether the adversarial system is the right route to follow if there is to be a decision in the event of disagreement between doctor and patient or, more often, between doctor and surrogate decision maker. The concept of winners and losers provides an uneasy foundation for the solution of sensitive and complex ethico-legal problems but one looks in vain for a suitable alternative. Certainly, the vision of a bed-side consultation, as evidenced in *Re B*,[87] has its attractions but it would be ingenuous in the extreme to suppose that it could take the place – or even partly take the place – of a full court hearing in every similar case. The resolution of allegations of medical negligence is a particular source of societal dissatisfaction with the legal process; it is, however, a problem of completely different nature that is considered in detail in chapter 9 below.

81 See, for example, *Practice Note (Family Division: Incapacitated Adults: Declaratory Proceedings)* [2002] 1 All ER 794, [2002] 1 WLR 325.
82 Human Fertilisation and Embryology Act 1990.
83 Eg the Human Fertilisation and Embryology Authority established under the 1990 Act.
84 *Re T (adult: refusal of medical treatment)* [1992] 4 All ER 649, (1992) 9 BMLR 46.
85 *Re J (a minor) (wardship: medical treatment)* [1992] 2 FLR 165, (1992) 9 BMLR 10.
86 For a general overview of the seminal decisions, see J K Mason 'Master of the Balancers: Non-voluntary Treatment Decisions under the Mantle of Lord Donaldson' [1993] JR 115.
87 *Re B (adult: refusal of medical treatment)*, sub nom *Ms B v An NHS Hospital Trust* [2002] EWHC 429, (2002) 65 BMLR 149.

THE DOCTOR'S POSITION

1.53 There is no doubt, too, that the intrusion of the law into the doctor/ patient relationship, essential as it may be in some instances, leads to a subtle but important change in the nature of the relationship. Trust and respect are more likely to flourish in one which is governed by morality rather than by legal rules and the injection of formality and excessive caution between doctor and patient cannot be in the patient's interest if it means that each sees the other as a potential adversary.

1.54 Where, then, does the doctor stand today in relation to society? To some extent, and perhaps increasingly, he is a servant of the public, a public which is, moreover, widely – though not always well – informed on medical matters. The competent patient's inalienable rights to understand his treatment and to accept or refuse it are now well established and society is conditioned to distrust professional paternalism. The talk to-day is of 'producers and consumers' and the ambience of the supermarket is one that introduces its own stresses and strains.

1.55 It is, moreover, in many ways extraordinary that the provision of a national health service, which one would have thought should, above all other services, be free of bias, has, in recent years, become perhaps the main political issue that determines the voters' intentions in the United Kingdom.[88] As a result, more and more extravagant claims – and, more significantly, promises – are made with little regard for the fallibility and limitations of those who must implement them. Like it or not, only one person can be the best thoracic surgeon in Startown; the rest can only carry on doing their personal best which no amount of 'hype' or sanction can improve.

1.56 Unless the humanity of both health carers and patients is appreciated by both sides and is not exploited in the political arena, the resulting disappointment, again on both sides, may well lead to a relationship of conflict – or of mutual suspicion – which is in the interests of neither doctor nor patient. What is needed is one of mutual understanding in which doctors acknowledge the interests of patients and patients, for their part, reciprocate this respect while appreciating the pressures, both physical and mental, under which a health carer must work. The public has also to understand the broader issues in medicine. The profession must experiment and research if it is to improve its art and many would hold that a slight loss of autonomy on the part of patients is a small price to pay for a useful advance in therapeutic skills. The profession must also teach, or there will be no doctors to serve future generations; some loss of confidentiality can be looked upon as a return for the best treatment and the best investigative facilities. Clearly, these opposing attitudes cannot be reconciled so long as they are polarised or if the claims of one party are accepted to the exclusion of the other.[89] A middle way,

---

88   The Chairman of the BMA believes the NHS has become 'the Punch and Judy show of British politics': L Eaton 'Politicians Must Stop Exploiting Patients' (2002) 325 BMJ 6.
89   Do documents such as *Your Guide to the NHS* (2001) (http://www.nhs.uk/nhsguide/ start.htm) assist in this or do they serve to amplify the potential for conflict? Certainly, the 2001 Guide is a marked improvement on its predecessor, *The Patient's Charter*, in that it also emphasises patients' responsibilities. Going a stage further, should the conditions set out in such guides be legally enforceable? See M H W Silver 'Patients' Rights in England and the United States of America' (1997) 23 J Med Ethics 213.

based on respect and trust, must be found and this is the function of medical jurisprudence which we attempt to express in the chapters which follow.

THE DARKER SIDES OF MEDICINE

1.57 Even so, society itself occasionally demands questionable practices of doctors. The extreme of the medico-ethical problems of the late twentieth century related to what are described as cruel, inhuman or degrading treatments or punishments. Political violence is all around us and the doctor cannot wholly dissociate himself from this; an international attempt to define his position is to be found in the Declaration of Tokyo,[90] which shows well the difficulties of drafting ethical codes of an academic nature – definitions of principle can only be interpreted in the mind of the individual. Who is to define a degrading procedure? Whether or not a caning is ethically preferable to deprivation of liberty is a matter of personal opinion. Is it self-evident that the well-being of an indiscriminate terrorist bomber is as valuable as is that of his potential victim? Granted that unethical biological measures are to be used in interrogation, could it not be that a doctor's presence, although disapproving, might be to the benefit of the victim? And, one might ask, by what right can the doctor command complete clinical independence when, in some circumstances, he may be ignorant of the widespread effect his decision may have on others? The motivation of the Declaration of Tokyo is impeccable in condemning the excesses of politically motivated punishment and torture, but it fails in its general purpose because it was drafted with that rather narrow end in view. Clause (8) states that the doctor 'shall in all circumstances be bound to alleviate the distress of his fellow men and no motive ... shall prevail against this higher purpose'. Carried to its logical conclusion, this would ostracise all those who assist in bringing criminals to justice and punishment – yet, surely, forensic medicine must be seen as providing an ethical service to the community.[91]

1.58 Reverting to a more prosaic level of forensic medicine, there has always been something of an armed truce between the medical profession and the police as to confidentiality. The anxiety engendered here has been summed up: 'Although doctors in general wish to co-operate with the police, they must be sure that any information divulged *in confidence* will not be used in court unless they are aware at the time of interview that that information might be so used.'[92]

1.59 The matter of the professional relationship between doctors and the police has, to a large extent been solved in the Police and Criminal Evidence Act 1984. The major contentions centred not only on confidentiality but also on the problems associated with intimate body searches. The resulting controversy exemplifies the difficulties exposed when relying on individual conscience as a

---

90 See Appendix D. It is to be noted that the spirit of the Declaration of Tokyo is now expressed in the Human Rights Act 1998, Sch 1, Article 3 and the European Convention on which it is based allows for no derogation.
91 The death penalty is now outlawed throughout the European Union. Its last vestiges were removed from UK statute law in the Crime and Disorder Act 1998.
92 The problem is discussed further in chapter 8 below.

guide to ethical medical practice. As regards confidentiality, the BMA – and other interested groups – succeeded in protecting medical records from the powers of police search by way of having them classified as excluded material.[93] The doctor, however, remains the holder of the records and is, therefore, at liberty to disclose them if he so wishes;[94] on the other hand, he may withhold them, in the absence of a court order, even in the face of serious crime.[95] As to searches, the leadership of the BMA agreed with those politicians who regarded the legal permit to make searches as 'an oppressive and objectionable new statutory power [which was] a serious affront to a person's liberty'.[96] Many others, including ourselves, would consider drug peddling, with its potential catastrophic effect on people of all ages, as being a crime which merits draconian preventive methods. In the event, the 1984 Act retained the legal right of the authorities to ask for an intimate search (s 55) and/or for the taking of an intimate sample (s 62) but stipulated that the latter must be performed by a medical practitioner or, now, a registered nurse.[97] So far as we know, these provisions of the 1984 Act have not been challenged in the European Court of Human Rights.[98]

1.60 The small cadre of police surgeons, or forensic medical examiners, comes into closest contact with the police[99] but it is, perhaps, the prison medical service which most magnifies and brings into focus many of the problems associated with codified ethics. Given an abnormal population, is it possible to apply to it normal methods? One would have hoped that this would be so, but there is little doubt that prison doctors are under considerable stress which results, in summary, from attempting to answer the question: are they there to serve the prisoners or the prison?[100] Smith believed that those in the service who regard their problems as exaggerated delude themselves; there is no reason to suppose that conditions have changed greatly[101] and the frequent allusions to prisoners made in this book – particularly as to consent to examination and treatment – testify to the strength of this view. The number and proportion of mentally disordered prisoners has increased steadily over the years and is swelled by those who find themselves unable to live in the community by virtue of mental illness. It is not at all uncommon for such persons to end up in prison where access to psychiatric care may be inadequate and, at the same time, transfer to a psychiatric hospital is very difficult in

---

93 Police and Criminal Evidence Act 1984, ss 11, 12.
94 *R v Singleton* [1995] 1 Cr App R 431, [1995] Crim LR 236.
95 *R v Cardiff Crown Court, ex p Kellam* (1993) 16 BMLR 76. It is to be noted that Evans LJ made this ruling 'with considerable reluctance'.
96 W Russell 'Intimate Body Searches – for Stilettos, Explosive Devices, et al' (1983) 286 BMJ 733.
97 S 62(9) as amended by the Criminal Justice and Police Act 2001, s 80. There have been a number of amendments to the 1984 Act which include increased powers of the police to retain samples and records in certain circumstances. These have survived a challenge by way of the European Convention on Human Rights: *R (on the application of S) v Chief Constable of South Yorkshire Police* (2002) Times, 3 October, CA.
98 Comparable powers are available in Scotland by way of the Criminal Procedure (Scotland) Act 1995, ss 18 and 19 or by obtaining a Sheriff warrant. Further amendments, similar to those in England, are pending in the Criminal Justice (Scotland) Bill 2002.
99 For a critical editorial comment, see The Lancet 'Three-faced Practice: Doctors and Police Custody' (1993) 341 Lancet 1245.
100 R Smith 'Prison Doctors: Ethics, Invisibility, and Quality' (1984) 288 BMJ 781.
101 J Reed and M Lyne 'The Quality of Health Care in Prison: Results of a Year's Programme of Semistructured Inspections' (1997) 315 BMJ 1420.

practical terms. This may have tragic consequences – as was demonstrated in a study from New Zealand which showed that the prison suicide rate escalated by some 500% when arrangements for such transfer deteriorated.[102] This has clear implications as to human rights and in respect of the prison authorities' duty of care towards mentally disordered inmates. While the courts are reluctant to extend the task of an already overburdened service still further, it is clear that there is a certain minimal level of care that prisons must meet. In *Kirkham v Chief Constable of the Greater Manchester Police*,[103] liability was imposed on the police for failing to inform a remand centre that a prisoner being transferred to their care was a suicide risk. By contrast, the Court of Appeal in *Knight v Home Office*[104] took the view that a prison hospital could not be expected to meet the same standard of care as a psychiatric hospital in the treatment of a potentially suicidal prisoner. The limitations placed on prison authorities are an inevitable consequence of the overcrowded conditions. It is undesirable enough to house ordinary offenders in such conditions; it is unconscionable to treat in this way those who may only be there because of mental illness. Such injustices should be every bit as much a matter for the concern of civil libertarians as are the rights of those who do not seek treatment. It must be a matter for general satisfaction that the present government has announced a positive policy designed to empower and improve co-operation between the prison medical service and the NHS.[105]

The impact of human rights on medical law

1.61 We have already noted that rights discourse is not without its problems, and in some circumstances the assertion of 'patients' rights' may be antithetical to the establishment and maintenance of a healthy and productive therapeutic relationship. Nonetheless, the relatively young discipline of medical law has emerged against a background of universal human rights, as embodied in a wide range of international treaties, covenants, agreements and laws.[106] Taken

102 K Skegg and B Cox 'Impact of Psychiatric Services on Prison Suicide' (1997) 338 Lancet 1436.
103 [1990] 2 QB 283, [1990] 3 All ER 246. Liability cannot be avoided by a claim that the suicidal act of the deceased amounted to a novus actus interveniens: *Reeves v Metropolitan Police Comr* [1998] 2 All ER 381, (1998) 41 BMLR 54, CA. At the same time, the obligation on the police to prevent a prisoner taking his own life arises only if they knew, or ought to have known, that he presented a suicide risk: *Orange v Chief Constable of West Yorkshire Police* [2001] EWCA Civ 611, [2002] QB 347, [2001] 3 WLR 736, CA.
104 [1990] 3 All ER 237, (1989) 4 BMLR 85.
105 National Health Service Reform and Health Care Professions Act 2002, s 23. Also recently published is the Recommendation of the Council of Europe on *Ethical and Organisational Aspects of Health Care in Prison*, Recommendation R(98)7 which sees the prison medical officer as doubling as clinician and public health officer (paras 22–25).
106 For example, the Universal Declaration of Human Rights (10 December 1948), the Convention for the Protection of Human Rights and Fundamental Freedoms (4 November 1950), the European Social Charter (18 October 1961), the UN Convention on the Elimination of All Forms of Racial Discrimination (21 December 1965), the International Covenant on Civil and Political Rights and the International Covenant on Economic, Social and Cultural Rights (16 December 1966), the Convention for the Protection of Individuals with regard to Automatic Processing of Personal Data (28 January 1981), the UN Convention on the Rights of the Child (20 November 1989), and the Universal Declaration on the Human Genome and Human Rights (UNESCO, 11 November 1997).

together, these measures endorse a particular view of the world which has as its central focus the primacy of the human being, and flowing from this are a number of direct and collateral rights which, it is declared, all human beings are possessed of. In the health care context, it is frequently asserted that these include:

- The right to be respected and treated with dignity
- The right to the highest attainable standard of physical and mental health and associated right to health care
- The right to consent and to refuse medical interventions
- The right not to be subjected to medical or scientific experimentation without consent
- The right to equality under the law
- The right to protection against arbitrary interference with privacy or with the family
- The right to enjoy the benefits of scientific progress and its application
- The protection of the rights of vulnerable persons

This list reflects an impressive array of rights when seen together, although it is important to note that not all of these rights are of the same genre. Rights of non-interference (*negative rights*), such as the right to consent and refuse and the right to protection for privacy, rank alongside rights of entitlement (*positive rights*), such as the right to the highest attainable standard of health. The difference between such categories of right is more than a mere matter of classification. The consequences of giving effect to positive rights are generally thought to be more far-reaching than respecting negative rights, especially in economic terms, and this has a direct correlation to the likelihood of such rights being respected or protected by states in practice. Although the rhetoric of rights has been a powerful motivator for international bodies such as the Council of Europe to produce instruments such as the *Convention on Human Rights and Biomedicine*,[107] many states, including the United Kingdom, do little more than pay lip-service to these measures,[108] while continuing to implement domestic laws in flagrant breach of their provisions.[109] The problem is that instruments such as the Council of Europe Convention represent an ideal of circumstances. They are ethically justified and contain sound principles and provisions (at least from a western perspective), but for the lawyer who is concerned with turning rights into realities, they are largely vapid documents containing only aspirational rights. States which agree to their provisions and sign up to their terms rarely do so with a view to making substantive changes in domestic law. Either it is argued that laws are adequate as they stand, or reservations are taken if the consequences of signing are too great yet political expediency requires a show of commitment. Moreover, not only is there a substantial lack of *volonté* to be bound by their terms to any serious

---

107 Council of Europe *Convention for the Protection of Human Rights and Dignity of the Human Being with Regard to the Application of Biology and Medicine: Convention on Human Rights and Biomedicine* (1997).

108 Only 13 of the 44 member states of the Council of Europe had ratified this Convention by August 2002. The UK was not one of them.

109 For example, the UK passed the Human Fertilisation and Embryology (Research Purposes) Regulations 2001, SI 2001/188 widening the circumstances in which human embryos can be created for research purposes in flagrant contravention of Article 18(2) of the Council of Europe Convention.

extent, but there is a pitiful absence of effective mechanisms to ensure enforcement against aberrant states.

1.62 None of this is to decry the efforts of the drafters of these instruments, and it is certainly not to state that they are without value, for they can influence to a large extent the form of further measures and can guide a path through the ethical and legal mire that must be negotiated if further developments are to be instituted. Further assistance comes for other quarters. For example, in 1993 the Director-General of UNESCO created the International Bioethics Committee (IBC) to respond to the major concerns raised by the progress made in the life and health sciences, but, as the first chair of the Committee (Noelle LeNoir) stated:

> 'The International Bioethics Committee is to be designed first and foremost as a forum for the exchange of ideas and debate. It will also incite concrete action to be taken in the field. Far from setting itself up as an inspection authority, its basic task will be to facilitate understanding of the upheavals in progress.'

At the present time, then, the most effective impetus for change remains the implementation of laws at the national level, and this is most clearly demonstrated by the passing of the Human Rights Act 1998 which incorporated the Articles of the European Convention on Human Rights (ECHR, 1950) into UK domestic law in October 2000.

THE HUMAN RIGHTS ACT 1998

1.63 The terms of the Human Rights Act protect citizens against the acts or omissions of a public authority in contravention of their rights, and the institutions of the NHS are paradigm examples of such authorities.[110] Other examples include the Human Fertilisation and Embryology Authority and similar statutorily-based bodies. Moreover, it is easy to envisage how the Articles of the ECHR might have an influence on patient rights and the practice of medical law, perhaps significantly so. Key provisions of the Convention embody rights that affect areas at the core of the discipline. These include Article 2 (the right to life), Article 3 (the prohibition on torture, and cruel and inhuman treatment), Article 5 (the right to liberty of the person), Article 8 (the right to respect for private and family life), Article 9 (the right to freedom of thought, conscience and religion), Article 10 (freedom of expression, especially where this is likely to conflict with other rights such as those to privacy), Article 12 (the right to marry and found a family), and Article 14 (the prohibition on discrimination in the protection or exercise of these rights). Throughout this book we examine the jurisprudence to date and assess the ways in which these rights have, or have not, changed this area of law. It is telling, however, to note that initial predictions of wide-sweeping changes have not been borne out in practice.[111] Already it has been established, for

---

110 See generally, J Wadham and H Mountfield *Blackstone's Guide to the Human Rights Act 1998* (1999).
111 See, for example, British Medical Association *The Medical Profession and Human Rights* (2001).

example, that the right to life does not imply a correlative right to die,[112] that the withdrawal of feeding and hydration from severely incapacitated patients can still be justified in their best interests,[113] and that so-called dangerous persons can continue to be subjected to a medical control system which can do nothing for them, all in the name of the public interest.[114] Equally, this is not to imply that the 1998 Act has had no influence whatsoever. Indeed quite the contrary is true in the realm of judicial review, where procedural safeguards have been subjected to very close scrutiny, and strengthened as a result in many cases.[115]

1.64 Ultimately, however, the overall impact of human rights discourse on the discipline of medical law will turn on the willingness of the courts to adopt an openness towards an *ethos* of human rights. If they assume a narrow, legalistic interpretative approach to the individual rights contained in the ECHR and consider themselves constrained by existing case-law – both domestic and European – then there is little prospect of considerable change. Alternatively, there is the option of taking a step backwards to consider the bigger picture – that is, to assess the *values* more fundamental still than the particular rights articulated in the Convention and the 1998 Act, and which underpin these instruments. This calls for a more holistic approach to the role of giving effect to human rights. From such a moral ambience values such as respect for human dignity and self-determination emerge as guiding principles in the interpretation of individual rights.[116] Medical lawyers spend much of their time calling for the courts to take responsibility away from the medical profession and to assume it themselves, yet in the context of the debate about the role of the Human Rights Act many fear that the system will 'lead to a major shift in power from the Executive and Legislature to the Judiciary'.[117] We suspect, however, that in the context of medical law, domestic precedents and a lack of refinement in Strasbourg jurisprudence will mean that the likely approach of the courts will be to continue to give responsibility for the protection and development of patient rights to the medical profession.[118] We predict that the Big Questions in medical law concerning life and death will not be addressed through the interpretation of the Human Rights Act or the European Convention on Human Rights. The focus of change is at the margins of medical law, such as in the field of judicial review. This, of course, is not to suggest that this is a marginal area of the discipline, but the point remains that we are simply tinkering at the edges.

112   *R (on the application of Pretty) v DPP* [2001] UKHL 61, [2002] 1 AC 800, [2002] 1 All ER 1; confirmed in the European Court of Human Rights as *Pretty v United Kingdom* (Application 2346/02) [2002] 2 FCR 97, [2002] 2 FLR 45.
113   *NHS Trust A v M, NHS Trust B v H* [2001] 1 All ER 801, (2000) 58 BMLR 87.
114   *A v The Scottish Ministers* 2001 SC 1, confirmed by the Privy Council at 2001 SLT 1331.
115   See, for example, *R (Wilkinson) v RMO, Broadmoor Hospital Authority* [2001] EWCA Civ 1545, [2002] 1 WLR 419, (2001) 65 BMLR 15 (procedural requirements regarding forced treatment of detained persons).
116   See D Beyleveld and R Brownsword *Human Dignity in Bioethics and Biolaw* (2001).
117   See, Sir Nicholas Lyall 'Whither Strasbourg? Why Britain Should Think Long and Hard Before Incorporating the European Convention on Human Rights' [1997] EHRLR 132 at 136.
118   See further, G T Laurie 'Medical Law and Human Rights: Passing the Parcel Back to the Profession?' in A Boyle et al (eds) *Human Rights and Scots Law: Comparative Perspectives on the Incorporation of the ECHR* (2002).

Reproductive medicine

2 Aspects of sex law

2.1 Sex law is one of those wide-ranging areas of the law which crosses the boundaries of, amongst others, the criminal law, family law and human rights law. It also clearly has a medical dimension, as the debate about sex is, in one sense, a debate about what can be done with the human body – and this is something in which doctors, and medical lawyers, may claim a legitimate and functional interest.

SEXUAL FREEDOM

2.2 Possibly the most frequently quoted reference in jurisprudence is to Mill,[1] who said:

> The only purpose for which power can rightfully be exercised over any member of a civilised community against his will is to prevent harm to others. His own good, either physical or moral, is not a sufficient warrant. He cannot rightfully be compelled to do or forebear because it would be better for him to do so, because it would make him happy or because, in the opinion of others, to do so would be wise, or even right.

2.3 This libertarian sentiment is now widely endorsed in an age in which the notion of interfering with others for their own good is deeply distrusted. Sexual behaviour is regarded as a private matter in our society and, even if there is still some room for an ethics of sex, the role of the law in regulating sexual conduct is significantly constrained. In this non-paternalistic climate, the guiding principle is that of consent: the law seeks to distinguish those sexual acts which are mutually consensual from those in which one of the parties is an objector or is, at least, non-consenting. In the former situation, the law should only intervene if it is believed that autonomous consent cannot or, as a matter of public policy, should not be

---

1   J S Mill *On Liberty and Representative Government* Blackwell's Political Texts (1948) p 8.

given. It is clear that these criteria may open the doors to jurisprudential conflict – a dilemma which was well demonstrated in the dramatic, and unsavoury, case of *Brown*.[2]

2.4 Here, a group of homosexual men indulged in a series of sado-masochistic sessions and were indicted – and convicted – under the Offences Against the Person Act 1861, ss 20 and 47.[3] By the time the matter reached the House of Lords, the issue had become essentially that of the role of consent in legitimating what were agreed to be injurious sexual practices – injurious, that is, short of killing or inflicting grievous bodily harm.[4] In the event, the House of Lords held that, although a prosecutor had to prove absence of consent in order to secure a conviction for mere assault, it was not in the public interest that a person should wound or cause actual bodily harm to another for no good reason and that, in the absence of such a reason, the victim's consent afforded no defence to the charges. All the defendants had admitted causing hurt or injury calculated to interfere with the health of another party and the gratification of sado-masochistic desires did not constitute a legitimate excuse for so doing. It is to be noted that this rejection of an appeal against conviction was on the basis of a 3:2 majority, the dissenting opinions, effectively, maintaining that it was a matter for Parliament rather than the courts to legislate for what was seen as a new offence.

2.5 *Brown* is not an easy decision to analyse. The activities of the accused had generated no complaints, they involved adults only, the incidents took place on private property where it was unlikely that they would ever be seen by the public – as a result, the decision was hotly debated in the academic literature.[5] In so far as it purports to restrict the freedom of adults to pursue sexual satisfaction in private, it is hardly consonant with the prevailing endorsement of that freedom. It is, however, easier to justify if one treats it as a decision which sets out to affirm the general principle that the physical integrity of the human body should be respected. Much will depend upon one's view of the role of the criminal courts as declarors of moral rules. If one believes that the criminal law should act as the guardian of certain moral values, then *Brown* is no more than an example of a court being prepared to do just that. If, on the other hand, one feels that it is no business of the criminal courts to make general statements about violence and the symbolic degradation of the human body – even if consensual – then *Brown* becomes an example of unacceptable moral judgment.

2.6 On the face of things, the decision strikes at the heart of Millian philosophy – and it was, in many ways, surprising that it was upheld in the European

---

2   *R v Brown (Anthony)* [1994] 1 AC 212, [1993] 2 All ER 75, HL. For one of several critiques of this judgment, see E Edwards 'No Defence for a Sado-masochistic Libido' (1993) 143 NLJ 552.
3   A charge of indecent assault being time-barred: Sexual Offences Act 1967, s 7.
4   The majority in the House of Lords accepted that consent does not elide the unlawfulness of inflicting such injuries: *R v Donovan* [1934] 2 KB 498; *A-G's Reference (No 6 of 1980)* [1981] QB 715, [1981] 2 All ER 1057.
5   Although mainly as to the role of consent as a 'defence' to the charges: L Bibbings and P Alldridge 'Sexual Expression, Body Alteration, and the Defence of Consent' (1993) 20 JLS 356; S Hedley 'Sado-masochism, Human Rights and the House of Lords' (1993) 52 CLJ 194.

Court of Human Rights,[6] which accepted that, despite the evident interference with their privacy, national authorities were entitled to consider the prosecution and conviction of the applicants as being necessary in a democratic society for the protection of health.[7] Clearly, it was the 'protective' exception, as related to the extreme nature of the activities in *Brown*, that held sway. The European Court could not apply the principle in a later case of homosexual activity involving up to four adult men in conditions of privacy. Despite the simultaneous video-taping of the scene, the Court was satisfied that it was most unlikely that others would become aware of what was going on and that there was no threat to either public health or morals. Prosecution based on the Sexual Offences Act 1956, s 13, as affected by the Sexual Offences Act 1967, s 1(2), was, therefore in breach of the European Convention on Human Rights, Article 8; the complainer was awarded substantial damages.[8]

2.7 *Brown* must, therefore, be looked on as a special case and it seems unlikely that s 1(2) of the 1967 Act will survive the passing of the Human Rights Act 1998 for long in its present form.

INCEST

2.8 Incest – defined in the *Concise Oxford Dictionary* as 'Sexual commerce of near kindred' – is, perhaps, the most illogical of sexual offences.

2.9 The primary difficulty lies in its scope – 'near kindred' must be interpreted before any law is applied. Most jurisdictions which maintain the concept limit the offence to intercourse between three generations of relations in the direct line of descent or ascent and between siblings; the relationship persists in the illegitimate state and siblings of half blood are included. This is the situation in England and Wales – with a curious dispensation for grandmothers and grandsons.[9] But around this norm there are variations ranging from an absence of the offence as such in France to the relatively wide relationships which are proscribed in Scotland.[10] No one can be happy when a relationship is legal south of the River Tweed but attracts a potential sentence of life imprisonment to the north. In the face of such variations, it is reasonable to question the rationale of the offence for which there is, undoubtedly, an innate public distaste.

2.10 Few of the common reasons adduced for the so-called 'incest-taboo' provide good grounds for legislation in modern times. Socio-anthropological theories depend, in many ways, on the supposed advantages to the tribe or clan of 'breeding out'; such imaginings have no place in modern society, with its easy access to the opposite sex outside the immediate family. More often, the case against incest is based on genetic grounds; this, we suggest, is a

---

6 *Laskey, Jaggard and Brown v United Kingdom* (1997) 24 EHRR 39.
7 As a result, the court did not find it necessary to consider whether the interference could also be justified on the ground of protection of morals.
8 *ADT v United Kingdom* [2000] 2 FLR 697, (2001) 31 EHRR 33.
9 Sexual Offences Act 1956, ss 10, 11.
10 Criminal Law (Consolidation) (Scotland) Act 1995, s 1.

fundamental misunderstanding. In the first place, genetics can have no place in the historic development of an incest taboo because genetic considerations would only have been apparent to those communities who regularly practised in-breeding and, therefore, suffered from no restrictive 'horror'. Secondly, genetics are related to procreation, while incest is a matter of sexual intercourse; genetic considerations are more properly directed at the marriage laws. Thirdly, there is no certainty that an isolated incestuous pregnancy will result in congenital abnormality. In the worst imaginable case – that of father/daughter incest with both carrying a deleterious recessive gene – the chances of a manifestly affected offspring are 1:4. Even so, this, taken with the intermediate possibility of multi-factorial disease,[11] would, in any case, be sufficient to render an incestuous pregnancy legally terminable under s 1(1)(d) of the Abortion Act 1967 – in addition to the obvious indications under s 1(1)(a); many jurisdictions specifically include pregnancy arising from rape or incest as a justification for legal termination but the wide scope of the 1967 Act makes this unnecessary in Great Britain. Far more cogently in relation to the present era, incest must be disruptive of the family; the same can, however, be said about adultery, yet we do not judge it as a criminal offence. Many wives to husbands indulging in incest will say that they are quite prepared to resume normal family relationships 'if only he will stop it'. Here, the argument is edging towards what must be the family's and society's basic revulsion to incest – that it exemplifies the exploitation of those in the care of, or under the authority of, the perpetrators. Not even apparent consent can be truly autonomous in such circumstances; effectively, incest is often an insidious form of rape.

2.11 Once that is accepted, the way to modernising the law becomes very much clearer. Age becomes a significant factor; the seniority of the offender increases the degree of subordination and, thus, the severity of the offence. But this is not the only feature bearing on authority. A father, in effect, has inherent authority which persists through life; a ban on father/daughter intercourse should, therefore, be absolute. Similar authority, albeit only until approximately school-leaving age, rests in the stepfather or the mother's partner; the same can be said of the foster father, while the authority of an adopting father corresponds closely to that of the genetic father. None of these is related in blood to the child, yet intercourse is, in every case, within the family and the effect on the child is the same – she is being sexually abused by someone she trusts.

2.12 Scottish legislation[12] provides an example of how some of these principles may be effected. Prohibited relationships are now defined and are restricted, as regards the offence of incest, to those which are consanguineous and adoptive – sexual intercourse between a man and his adopted daughter or former adopted daughter is now characterised as incest, as are the other permutations of the adopting state; half-blood and illegitimate relationships are now included. A separate offence of having intercourse with a step-child is created when the step-child is either under the age of 21 or has, at any time before attaining the

---

11 See chapter 6.
12 See para 2.9 above. Prohibitions under Scots law still include uncle/aunt and great-grandparent relationships.

age of 18, lived in the same household and been treated as a child of the step-parent. A further offence of having intercourse with a child under the age of 16 who is a member of the same household and over whom a position of trust or authority exists is also enacted, provided that the person concerned is over 16 years old; neither 'a position of trust' nor 'a member of the same household' are defined but the section clearly envisages at least a loose form of intra-familial application. A number of defences, including that of ignorance as to relationship or age, are specified for each scenario.

2.13 Although it is, to an extent, peripheral to the present discussion, it is worth noting the introduction, throughout the United Kingdom, of the offence of an adult man having sexual intercourse, whether vaginal or anal, or engaging in any other sexual activity with a minor in relation to whom he is in a position of trust.[13] Section 4 of the 2000 Act defines a position of trust effectively in terms of supervisors and minor residents of institutions – including residential homes, hospitals and schools, where the last includes non-residents. The legislation is, therefore, very much concerned with the abuse of power but is far removed from the control of incest.

2.14 The provisions as to incest, on both sides of the border, are a compromise between strict logic and public policy, perhaps the outstanding anomaly being that the potential right of adult brothers and sisters to behave themselves in private as they please is not yet recognised. Equally importantly, the legal obsession with defloration is perpetuated. We cannot help feeling that to force anal sex on a young girl or homosexual acts upon a young boy is as offensive as it is to enforce penetrative heterosexual sex; once the overall importance of trust and authority is recognised, they all become of the same nature and they should, accordingly, be treated as a group.[14] The use of the word 'incest' to cover a wide spectrum of relationships – as it does, particularly in Scotland – may also be considered inappropriate; it should, if retained, be limited to that act which is objectionable on any rationale – a sexual relationship between parent and child. Otherwise, we will continue to argue in favour of an all-embracing concept of assault with sexual intent to cover those sexual offences that are governed, directly or indirectly, by the concept of consent.

HOMOSEXUALITY

2.15 We have hinted above at the apparent illogicality in using the criminal law to constrain the private lives of adult siblings while, at the same time, acknowledging the virtually unrestricted sexual autonomy of other adults, particularly as related to their sexual orientation. Indeed, it is probably fair to say that the increasingly liberal attitude to sex in the United Kingdom has been driven by the rapidly changing attitudes to homosexuality that have

13 Introduced by the Sexual Offences (Amendment) Act 2000, s 3.
14 Anal intercourse would certainly not be incest in Scotland. But, since the Criminal Justice and Public Order Act 1994, s 142, which applies to England and Wales only, extends the meaning of sexual intercourse to include anal intercourse in relation to rape, we wonder if this might be extended also to incest. However, we doubt that it could be so absent a specific amendment to the Sexual Offences Act 1956, s 10.

developed over the last half-century. The Sexual Offences Act 1967, permitting male homosexual practices by two consenting adults in private, was passed amid considerable public concern; 27 years later, the age of consent was lowered from 21 to 18 years and, by the turn of the century, this had been further reduced to 16 in England, Wales and Scotland and to 17 in Northern Ireland.[15] The Sexual Offences Acts are, however, primarily concerned with actual sexual activity. In the present context, interest centres on the effects of homosexual orientation on a person's social well-being and, here, the law remains somewhat ambivalent – although, decreasingly, less so.

2.16 First, as to earning one's living, it is not illegal in the United Kingdom to refuse employment on the grounds that a person is homosexual,[16] but to refuse to employ male homosexuals while, at the same time, to accept lesbians would almost certainly contravene the Sex Discrimination Act 1975, s 1(1)(a).[17] Once employed, however, the fairness of dismissal on the grounds of homosexuality would be a matter of proof which would be governed by the Employment Rights Act 1996, s 98(1) and (4) which, today, would be unlikely to succeed save in exceptional circumstances. A marked advance in the recognition of the homosexual's status has been seen in the field of family law. Most significantly, the House of Lords has held that a same-sex partner can be regarded as a 'member of the family' where this is in accord with social justice; for this purpose, however, the relationship must be more than superficial and of long standing.[18] Equally importantly, it has been established both in England and in Scotland that there are no statutory or public policy reasons why a single person should be barred from adopting a child simply because he or she was living in an established homosexual relationship.[19] In so far as it is 'the court's duty to give first consideration to the need to safeguard and promote the welfare of the child'[20] and that, therefore, the interests of the adopters fall to be considered also, these cases go a long way to vindicating the homosexual family in the eyes of the law.[21]

2.17 Having said which, the question of whether or not homosexual marriage should be admitted follows inevitably. The simple argument in its favour, which scarcely needs definition, is that people in homosexual partnerships should be given the same legal protection as is accorded to those in a marriage. There is a strong case for this, just as there is a strong case for the giving of such protection to heterosexual partnerships outside marriage. Yet recognition of the case for such a degree of protection does not, of itself, make the case for homosexual marriage. If a sufficient number of people wish to preserve the

---

15 Sexual Offences (Amendment) Act 2000, s 1(1), (3) and (4).
16 B W Napier 'AIDS, Discrimination and Employment Law' (1989) 18 ILJ 84. In many common law jurisdictions – eg Australia, United States – homosexuals are specifically protected by the anti-discrimination laws.
17 *James v Eastleigh Borough Council* [1990] 2 All ER 607, HL.
18 *Fitzpatrick v Sterling Housing Association Ltd* [2001] 1 AC 27, [1999] 4 All ER 705. The issue lay in the Rent Act 1977, Sch 1, para 3. The House would not allow a same sex partner to be regarded as a 'surviving spouse' for the same purpose.
19 *T Petitioner* 1997 SLT 724, 1996 SCLR 897; *Re W (a minor) (adoption: homosexual adopter)* [1997] 3 All ER 620, [1997] 3 WLR 768.
20 Per Singer J in *Re W* [1997] 3 All ER 620 at 627, [1997] 3 WLR 768 at 775.
21 See C Barton 'Will gays get their way?' *The Times*, 27 May 1997.

heterosexual nature of marriage – and there is probably a fairly substantial majority in favour of this approach – then it could be argued that even a pluralist society should recognise this entitlement. A liberal society, however, should at the same time recognise that there are those who wish to enter into publicly-acknowledged same-sex partnerships which have legal ramifications. This is a legitimate desire and, in that it will allow those involved to feel more accepted, it is churlish to stand in their way. A possibly acceptable solution lies in the creation of a form of 'registered partnership' or 'union' which, although not a marriage, has similar legal effects – such a system operates in many countries of the European Community and it may not be all that far away in the United Kingdom.[22]

2.18 Kennedy,[23] in putting the case for legalising converted transsexual marriage which we discuss briefly below, went on to extrapolate this to the authorisation of homosexual marriages – 'I have no doubt it will occur', he said, 'later if not sooner'.[24] And he has been proved right in the case of at least one member state of the European Community where same-sex marriage has been assimilated into the national structure without cataclysmic effect.[25] Whether such legislation will spread depends very much on how the principles outlined above are accepted or rejected.

2.19 Meantime, we can return from the future to the present and note that a number of United Kingdom cases related to more general discrimination against homosexual men and women have been heard in the European jurisdiction; the results have not been as consistent as might have been anticipated although a trend is discernible. In *S v United Kingdom*,[26] the applicant, who had been living in a lesbian relationship 'as man and wife', appealed against an eviction order from her council accommodation that was issued on the death of her partner – an order which could not have been made had she been of the opposite sex. The European Commission found that the relevant housing legislation was designed to protect the family; the difference in the treatment of the applicant from that which would have been given to a person of the opposite sex could, therefore, be justified reasonably and objectively. *B v United Kingdom*[27] was an immigration case concerning the repatriation of a homosexual partner who could have remained lawfully in the United Kingdom had he been a woman. The Commission held that a state whose immigration laws provided better treatment for heterosexual couples did not practise discrimination; again, it was decided that the difference in treatment had a

22 A Civil Partnerships Bill 2002 has been introduced in the House of Lords. This follows the lines of several European Registered Partnership Acts: Denmark (1989), Norway (1993), Sweden (1995), Belgium (1999), France (1999), Finland (2002), Germany (2001, acknowledgment of relationship), Portugal (2001, de facto marriage).
23 I M Kennedy 'Transsexualism and Single Sex Marriage' (1973) 2 Anglo-Am LR 112.
24 An irony would be that, unless UK law recognises a change of sex in law, this would fail to satisfy the one group that has been most in favour of recognition of marriage – that is the converted transsexuals.
25 The Dutch Act on the Opening up of Marriage 2000 amends the Civil Code, Book 1 so that Article 30 reads baldly: 'A marriage can be contracted by two persons of different sex or of the same sex'. For general discussion, see K Norrie 'Sexual Orientation and Family Law' in J Scoular (ed) *Family Dynamics: Contemporary Issues in Family Law* (2001).
26 European Commission for Human Rights Application 11716/85, DR 47, p 274.
27 European Commission for Human Rights Application 16106/90, DR 64, p 278.

legitimate aim – the protection of the family – and the resultant action was proportionate to that aim.

2.20 A more recent case in point demonstrated the somewhat grey area that is apparently developing in relation to the rights of homosexuals on the one hand and of transsexuals on the other. *Grant v South-West Trains Ltd* [28] touched on the rather mundane subject of concessionary fares for railway employees. The applicant drew heavily on the case of *P v S and Cornwall County Council*,[29] the judgment on which, as we will see below, was, essentially, based on the claim that equality for all was a fundamental principle of European Community law. The ruling in *P v S* is clearly subject to open-ended interpretation and it is unsurprising that it was relied on to underpin the proposition that, if discrimination was to be avoided, homosexual couples were entitled to the same industrial benefits as were heterosexuals when the benefit in question was payable to those involved in a meaningful common law opposite sex spousal relationship. The European Court of Justice would, however, not go that far – a surprising withdrawal in that it was contrary to the recommendation of the Advocate General concerned. In reaching its conclusion, the Court observed that, in the present state of the law within the Community, stable relationships between two persons of the same sex are not regarded as equivalent to marriages or stable relationships outside marriage between persons of opposite sex. Consequently, an employer was not required to treat the two situations as similar – it was for the legislature alone to adopt measures that might affect the position. Most importantly in the present context, the court firmly distinguished discrimination on the ground of gender reassignment from differences of treatment based on a person's sexual orientation.[30] Thus, it seemed that the European Courts would not press the United Kingdom into legislation in respect of sexual orientation alone; at the same time, the language of the opinions left a strong impression that they would regard it as desirable.

2.21 The key issues in any relevant legislation lie, first, in privacy and, secondly, in its effect, if any, on the health and morals of the society concerned. The United Kingdom's – and the European – response to the former has already been outlined and is discussed in rather more detail in chapter 7. The sexual privacy of those in the enclosed worlds of the armed forces and the merchant navy provides a cogent example of the principles involved. These have, to an extent, been recognised by Parliament,[31] which is not only equitable but, given the increasing integration of women within the core structure of the forces, also appears logical. It is to be noted, however, that the 1994 Act still allowed for a homosexual act to be a ground for discharge from the armed forces or, where it occurred in conjunction with other acts or circumstances, to constitute an offence under the Service Discipline Acts.[32] It is, however, a long step to include under this head the power to discharge persons from the armed forces who have not committed any offence but whose sexual orientation

28 Case C-249/96, [1998] All ER (EC) 193, [1998] 1 FLR 839.
29 [1996] All ER (EC) 397, [1996] 2 FLR 347.
30 But the court did not rule out the possibility that discrimination on the basis of sexual orientation might be proscribed when the Treaty of Amsterdam (2 October 1997) came into force.
31 Criminal Justice and Public Order Act 1994, s 146.
32 Section 146(4).

is homosexual; this has been the subject of two important interweaving referrals to the European Courts.

2.22 The first of these provided, in the main, an interesting exercise in semantics – how, in effect, is the word 'sex' to be interpreted? In *Smith*,[33] the Court of Appeal refused judicial review of the discharge of a lesbian and three homosexual men from the Armed Forces as part of administrative policy – the grounds being that, on *Wednesbury* principles,[34] the Secretary of State had not acted unreasonably; moreover, the Court was unable to find any substance in the suggestion that discrimination on the grounds of sexual orientation was recognised as improper discrimination in European Community law. Meantime, *Perkins*[35] was also challenging the Ministry's policy by way of the EU's Council Directive on equal treatment.[36] *P v S*[37] had now been decided and this led to some doubt as to whether 'sex discrimination' was, in fact, as limited in scope as the Court of Appeal had held in *Smith*. Accordingly, *Perkins* was referred to the European Court. By another strange twist, however, the hearing of *Grant v South West Trains*[38] was interpolated and, in that case, 'sex' for the purposes of the Equal Pay Directive[39] was interpreted as excluding sexual orientation. Lightman J then concluded that, this being an essential part of the reasoning of the European Court, it must, also, apply to the Equal Treatment Directive; *Perkins'* reference to that court was, accordingly, withdrawn.[40]

2.23 It is to be noted that both these decisions were taken in the British courts with reluctance; it is probable, therefore, that everyone breathed a sigh of relief when *Smith* eventually progressed to the European Court of Human Rights[41] where the solution to the problem, if not to the semantics, was put beyond doubt. Effectively, the Court held that, while some difficulties could be anticipated if the Ministry's policy was abandoned, these were not insuperable; moreover, the Court considered it could not ignore the widespread and consistently developing views and the legal changes in the domestic laws in favour of the admission of homosexuals to the Armed Forces of other member states of the Community. By a majority of 6:1, the Court found that both the investigations of the cases and the consequent discharge of the applicants constituted grave infringements of the European Convention on Human Rights, Article 8. The fact that the policy was of a 'blanket' type that could not be varied in individual cases was also a determining factor. Interestingly, the Court also determined that the *Wednesbury* standard adopted in judicial review proceedings was set so high in favour of the administration that the applicants in the case had, effectively, been deprived of a domestic remedy in relation to the violation of their right to respect for their private lives.

---

33 *R v Ministry of Defence, ex p Smith* [1996] QB 517, [1996] 1 All ER 257, CA.
34 *Associated Provincial Picture Houses Ltd v Wednesbury Corporation* [1948] 1 KB 223, [1947] 2 All ER 680.
35 *R v Secretary of State for Defence, ex p Perkins* [1997] IRLR 297.
36 76/207/EEC (OJ 1976 L39/40).
37 Para 2.51 below.
38 Para 2.20 above.
39 Council Directive 75/117.
40 *R v Secretary of State for Defence, ex p Perkins (No 2)* [1999] 1 FLR 491, [1998] IRLR 508.
41 *Smith and Grady v United Kingdom, Lustig-Prean and Beckett v United Kingdom* (Applications 33985/96 and 33986/96) (2000) 29 EHRR 493, [1999] IRLR 734.

2.24 This decision was, we feel, inevitable in so far as the ECtHR had, some time before, confirmed that it regards any legislation restricting the rights of adults to act as they please in private as an infringement of Article 8 of the Convention. The mere fact that prosecutions have not been taken in recent years under such legislation is considered immaterial – the threat is sufficient to affect peoples' private lives and is disproportionate to any aims that might be sought to be achieved.[42] *Smith* does little more than underline the fact that the Armed Forces cannot plead a special case. Legislative disapproval of homosexual privacy now appears to be a thing of the past.[43]

2.25 The question of the age at which homosexual sexual activity is lawful has been settled since the last edition of this book was published. The intense argument as to whether the age at which it is lawful to engage in homosexual activity should be reduced to 16 years has been waged at two levels – first, on grounds of discrimination between the sexes and, second, on the capacity of young men and women to consent to sexual activity. Informed medical opinion in the United Kingdom was undoubtedly opposed to an age differential between lawful hetero- and homosexual activity. A leading article in the Lancet argued the case for equality very strongly[44] and both the Royal College of Psychiatrists and the British Medical Association supported the view that homosexual activity in men should be legal from the age of 16. Pressure from members of the House of Commons was intense and, in 1997, the European Commission on Human Rights found, by a majority of 14:4, that there was no objective or reasonable justification for the maintenance of a higher minimum age of consent to male homosexual than to heterosexual acts and that, in imposing such a differential, the United Kingdom was in breach of the applicant's right to respect for his private life under Article 8 of the European Convention on Human Rights.[45] The matter has now been put to rest by way of the Sexual Offences (Amendment) Act 2000 which amends the existing legislation in England, Wales and Scotland by substituting the age of 16 for 18 wherever it is appropriate.[46]

TRANSSEXUALISM

2.26 Although the civil law in the United Kingdom currently takes little note of sex, the problems of transsexualism – or the gender dysphoria syndrome – arise with increasing frequency and carry serious issues in medical jurisprudence in their wake. Transsexuals are not necessarily homosexual; the great majority are heterosexual – the basic issue being that they have, so

---

42 *Modinos v Cyprus* (1993) 16 EHRR 485. Confirming *Dudgeon v United Kingdom* (1982) 4 EHRR 149.
43 The Government has made it clear that it intends to abide by this ruling subject to the introduction of a suitable code of conduct: *Official Report*, 18 November 1999, vol 339, c 684.
44 Editorial Comment 'Legislating Fairly for Consenting Homosexuals' (1994) 343 Lancet 185.
45 *Sutherland v United Kingdom* (1997) 24 EHRR CD 22.
46 Sexual Offences Acts 1956, ss 12, 13; Sexual Offences Act 1967, ss 1, 8; Criminal Law (Consolidation) (Scotland) Act 1995, s 13. The relevant age is reduced from 18 to 17 in Northern Ireland by way of amendments to the Homosexual Offences (Northern Ireland) Order 1982.

to speak, been dressed in the colours of the opposing team. The transsexual does not necessarily demonstrate any anatomical or physiological abnormality but, nevertheless, suffers from an intense wish to be, and be accepted as being, of the opposite sex. A proportion of transsexuals may pass through a phase of homosexuality, but the two states differ in that, while homosexuals are content with their own sex but prefer to express it in their own way, transsexuals are convinced that nature has made a mistake in their case and they are intent on rectifying it. It follows that homosexuality and transsexualism pose distinct ethical and sociological questions.

2.27 The fully developed syndrome must lead to severe distress. Nevertheless, living with a problem is a personal matter and, in the absence of identification cards, National Service and the like, society is scarcely concerned to regulate the outward trappings of transsexualism such as transvestism. But when it comes to rectification, public morality is concerned at three heads: the treatment of the condition; the acceptance of that treatment; and, most particularly, the final legal status of the transsexual with its multiple ramifications.

2.28 Psychiatric treatment of the fully fledged syndrome is generally ineffective; the patients need to change their sexual function and this goal can be achieved only by radical surgery. This includes castration in both males and females which, in some jurisdictions, may be unlawful in itself without judicial approval.[47] An artificial vagina can be fashioned in the male but, for obvious reasons, surgery is more likely to satisfy such a male-to-female convert than the female-to-male.[48] None the less, at least in the former case, the cosmetic results can be very good – the patient can finish up, as did two of the principals in reported British court cases, as a pin-up beauty or a 'Bond girl';[49] as it has been put: 'the pastiche of femininity can be very convincing'.[50]

2.29 As we will see later, some countries have wide-ranging legislation in place, but it is by no means uniform.[51] Elsewhere, the legality of consent to sex reassignment is generally based on a tacit understanding between medicine and the law. Operations are, nowadays, nearly everywhere justified under the doctrine of 'necessity' or of 'genuine medical treatment'. The ethical problem then becomes that of case selection and, in practice, a comparatively small number of applicants are, in fact, recommended for operation. Nevertheless, while some foreign national centres have a very high turnover – of anything up to 800 cases per year – something over 2,000 total cases, including some 400 females, have been operated upon within the British National Health Service and the threat of judicial review proved sufficient to cause a change of heart in health authorities which originally refused funding

47 S Gromb, B Chanseau and H J Lazarini 'Judicial Problems Related to Transsexualism in France' (1997) 37 Med, Sci & L 27.
48 The surgery is well described for the non-medical by J J Hage 'Medical Requirements and Consequences of Sex Reassignment Therapy' (1995) 35 Med, Sci & L 17.
49 April Ashley in *Corbett v Corbett (otherwise Ashley)* [1971] P 83, [1970] 2 All ER 33 and Caroline Cossey in *Cossey v United Kingdom* (1990) 13 EHRR 622, [1991] 2 FLR 492.
50 Paraphrased from Professor Dewhurst in *Corbett v Corbett (otherwise Ashley)* [1971] P 83 at 104.
51 For a resumé, see A Rogers 'Legal Implications of Transsexualism' (1993) 341 Lancet 1085.

for the purpose even before the threat materialised.[52] There is, therefore, no question as to the lawfulness of sex reassignment in the United Kingdom.

The diagnosis of sex

2.30 We must be clear as to the terminology if we are to speak of a person's 'sex'. Ormrod's four criteria[53] are well known but are worth recapitulating briefly. A person's sex can be identified in a number of ways or, more often, in a combination of ways:

(a)   *External genitalia* – which is the way sex is diagnosed at birth and is, therefore, the basis on which a person is registered. The appearance of the external genitalia is, however, subject to developmental abnormality and to maternal or fetal hormonal dysfunction. There are also a number of genetically controlled biochemical disorders related to the synthesis of the sex hormones which may cause confusion. Such errors are often discovered only at puberty and they constitute the majority of reasons for correction of the register.[54]

(b)   *Gonads* – this is clearly a poor test in practice. In the absence of exploratory surgery, it may be impossible to distinguish between the internal gonads of the female and undescended testes in the male.

(c)   *Chromosomes* – As is well known, the normal female carries XX sex chromosomes and the normal male XY. The sex chromosomes are, however, notorious for trisomies or deletions – that is, numerical variations on the normal number of two corresponding genes – and such abnormalities are responsible for a number of cases of difficulty in defining sex. Conceptual difficulties also arise. It is usually said that the possession of a Y chromosome indicates maleness; it might, equally, be said that the possession of XX chromosomes indicates femaleness. Where, then does one place the trisomy XXY? It will be seen later that such problems have greatly influenced the courts of the European Community.

(d)   Finally, we can look at the person's *gender* – a concept which is difficult to define and one which means different things to different people. Ormrod, whose influence has been so surprisingly profound, probably hit the nail on the head when, speaking of the treatment of 'intersex' – or the presence of characteristics of both sexes – he commented that doctors would ask which gender should the patient be *encouraged* to assume.[55] In short, gender is, first, the expression of one's sex within the social construct and this is, to an extent, fashioned by the individual's psyche. Transsexualism represents the ultimate in the 'assumption' of a sexual identity and, as a result, gender has come to be identified as

---

52 C Dyer 'Transsexuals Challenge Rationing Decision' (1996) 313 BMJ 319. A 'blanket' prohibition of gender reassignment surgery was finally declared unlawful in *R v North West Lancashire Health Authority, ex p A* [2000] 1 WLR 977, (2000) 53 BMLR 148, CA.
53 R Ormrod 'The Medico-legal Aspects of Sex Determination' (1972) 40 Med-leg J 78.
54 Births and Deaths Registration Act 1953, s 29; Registration of Births, Deaths and Marriages (Scotland) Act 1965, s 42.
55 Ormrod (1972) 40 Med-leg J 78.

the sex to which the individual thinks he or she does or ought to belong.[56] The condition of transsexualism is, therefore, more descriptively named the gender dysphoria syndrome. It is, however, a *positive* mental state – the individual *wants* to be of the opposite sex and actively seeks a coincidence between his/her physical and psychological sex; thus, we can distinguish, say, the 'tomboy' who is simply not fond of the sex she has been given.

2.31 Sexual orientation is simply the way in which an individual prefers to practise his or her sexuality. Accordingly, it does not come into the diagnosis of that person's sex[57] – a distinction which, as we have already seen (and to which we will revert), has been of major significance – and a source of some confusion – in interpreting European law.

Seeds of a medico-legal conflict

2.32 Faced with a conflict of evidence, the medical solution is to 'assign' a person to the sex which they are most likely to be able to support in society[58], the function of the chromosomal sex being then relegated to that of an indicator of the direction in which to steer an infant's upbringing. In later life, the one characteristic of sex or gender which is apparent to no one, including the principal, is the state of a person's chromosomes. Unfortunately, because of its immutability, that is the feature which appeals most to the lawyer.

2.33 The law, both in England and Wales and in Scotland[59] has resolutely turned its face against 'sex change'; only a genuine mistake at birth can justify an alteration on one's birth certificate – and even this is sufficiently uncommon as to be reported in quality newspapers when it occurs.[60] Intersex is said to occur in anything from 0.1 % to 2 % of births depending, inevitably on the classification of abnormality adopted.[61] Surgical and psychiatric treatment may be employed in order to guide the subject along the better path but, in general, United Kingdom policy is to regard the birth certificate as documentation of an immutable historical fact. In practice, this matters surprisingly little. United Kingdom law is relatively unconcerned with sex and the registration of 'corrected' transsexuals in their 'new' sex for National Insurance and employment purposes is relatively common.[62] The ultimate test, however, lies in marriage, which is the union between a man and a

---

56 The definition of gender has been discussed by A C Loux 'Is he our sister? Sex, Gender and Transsexuals under European Law' [1997] 3 Web J of Current Legal Issues 1 (http://webjcl.ncl.ac.uk).
57 *Smith v Gardner Merchant Ltd* [1998] 3 All ER 852, [1998] IRLR 510, CA.
58 S Creighton and C Minto 'Managing Intersex' (2001) 323 BMJ 1264.
59 *X Petitioner* 1957 SLT (Sh Ct) 61.
60 Eg A Lee 'Joella is Classed as a Girl at Last' *The Times*, 2 December 1998, p 1.
61 Creighton and Minto, para 2.32 above.
62 In *White v British Sugar Corpn* [1977] IRLR 121, for example, a woman who was treated as a 'man' for national insurance needs was regarded as a woman for the purposes of the Sex Discrimination Act 1975. The UK Government's attitude was reaffirmed in *I v United Kingdom*, para 2.50 below at paras 48–49.

woman.[63] The leading British case in this context is *Corbett v Corbett*,[64] in which it was held that:

(a)   marriage is a relationship which depends on sex and not on gender;
(b)   sex is determined by the consideration of the chromosomal pattern, the original gonadal status and the pre-operative genitalia; and
(c)   if these are not congruent – as they were in *Corbett* – the genitalia will be preferred to the other two.

2.34 It is very widely supposed that Ormrod J held that a person's sex depended on his/her chromosomes but he did *not* say that. He *did*, however, add:

> The biological sexual constitution of an individual is fixed at birth and cannot be changed either by the natural development of organs of the opposite sex or by medical or surgical means.[65]

2.35 Since the organs and the genitalia of a converted transsexual *have* been changed, the chromosomes are the last immutables and have, therefore, assumed an importance which Ormrod J probably never intended. The other inherent difficulty within the *Corbett* framework is that it failed to define genitalia – which, in a woman, can run from the fallopian tubes to the vulva. This particular aspect has to be stressed because it leads directly to consideration of the testicular feminisation syndrome (TFS) – a condition in which, as Ormrod J virtually admitted later,[66] the *Corbett* criteria disintegrate. The genetically controlled defect in the TFS lies in the inability of the male hormones to activate their 'target' organs. The defect may be partial or total and, in the latter event, we are presented with an apparently normal woman, but one who has an undeveloped vagina, no uterus, undescended testes and a male chromosomal pattern. Thus, in calling such a person a woman, we are pitting the possession of a vulva against all the other *Corbett* criteria which, surprisingly, take little or no account of personal appearances. Yet, these days, no one would dream of attempting to impose a 'true' sex on someone who is by upbringing, self-assessment and popular acclaim clearly a woman. The practical importance of the testicular feminisation syndrome in the context of this text is that the TFS patient is, effectively, a *naturally converted transsexual*. If, therefore, we accept such persons in their apparent sex without demur – as we must on both medical and social grounds – we are providing considerable logical ammunition to those who press for acceptance of the *artificially converted transsexual*. And this is a point which has been taken up by the European Court of Human Rights.

---

63 A homosexual 'marriage' is void: Matrimonial Causes Act 1973, s 11(c); a marriage that cannot be consummated is voidable: Matrimonial Causes Act 1973, s 12(a). The position is similar in Scotland where the fact that the parties are of the same sex constitutes a legal impediment to marriage (Marriage (Scotland) Act 1977, s 5); irreversible impotence is the only ground for finding a marriage voidable.
64 [1971] P 83, [1970] 2 All ER 33. The 'marriage' took place in Gibraltar. An unreported case, *Franklin v Franklin (otherwise Jones)*, is said to have been the first involving a 'marriage' in England; it was annulled: Scotsman, 9 November 1990, p 2.
65 [1971] P 83 at 104, [1970] 2 All ER 33 at 47.
66 Para 2.30 above.

2.36 As something of a collateral issue – but of major significance to the present discussion – it was held in *Corbett* that, notwithstanding the validity of the marriage or of the sex of the 'wife', she was physically incapable of consummating a marriage by the use of an artificial cavity. The case was thus distinguished from *SY v SY*,[67] in which a decree of nullity had been refused on the grounds that a vestigial vagina could have been corrected by forming an artificial passage; Wilmer LJ commented:

> If a woman with an artificial vagina is incapable of true sexual intercourse she cannot be raped or commit adultery. I would regard such a result as bordering on the fantastic.[68]

2.37 The irony of the distinction between the two cases is that it would seem to have been made on the basis that SY was an imperfect woman – today, it is almost certain that she would have been diagnosed as a case of testicular feminisation and, accordingly, as a chromosomal male.

2.38 These aspects of the *Corbett* test have now been addressed in the High Court with what appear to us to be significant results. *W v W*,[69] concerned a woman whose genital sex was indeterminate at her birth in 1947 and who had been reared, almost forcibly, as a boy – very largely on the grounds of her male chromosomal pattern. Her sexual orientation became progressively more female, her vagina was reconstructed and, eventually, she married a man. Despite the fact that they were now divorced, the husband sought a decree of nullity on the grounds that the parties had not been male and female respectively at the time of the marriage. Charles J emphasised that Mrs W was not a transsexual. Rather, he classified her as suffering from a partial androgen insensitivity syndrome – effectively, an incomplete form of the testicular feminisation syndrome. The limitations of the *Corbett* criteria for establishing a person's sex were, thereby, exposed – and particularly because Ormrod J's last refuge, the external genitalia, were indeterminate in Mrs W's case. The judge was, therefore, free to alter the *Corbett* terms – and he made a thorough job of it in the course of a very long judgment.

2.39 In coming to his conclusion, Charles J found, in particular, that the capacity of a person to consummate a marriage as a male or female was a factor, *although not a decisive factor* [our emphasis] in the assessment of his or her sex; that the appearance of the genitalia could not be the defining criterion when it was, itself, ambiguous; and that all six factors mentioned in *Corbett* – including psychological, hormonal and secondary sex characteristics – should be taken into account when considering the issue. Most significantly, regard had to be paid to:

> the respondent's development which led her to making a final choice to live as a woman well before she started taking oestrogen and before she had surgery.[70]

67 [1963] P 37, [1962] 3 All ER 55, CA.
68 [1963] P 37 at 60, [1962] 3 All ER 55 at 63.
69 *W v W (physical inter-sex)* [2001] Fam 111, (2001) 58 BMLR 15.
70 At BMLR 51.

It was concluded that Mrs W had been wrongly certified at birth and that she was a female for the purposes of marriage to the applicant.[71]

2.40 Clearly, the major result of this judgment is to establish the position of the TFS subject in relation to marriage which has, hitherto, been equivocal. There is, however, little reason why Charles J's analysis should not, also, be modified and extrapolated to transsexualism. Indeed, *W v W*, in virtually relegating the status of the person's karyotype – or chromosomal constitution – to that of an incidental observation, may help to counteract the attraction of the expediency of the chromosomal test, recourse to which has led to some unfortunate consequences – in particular, the application of *Corbett* to the criminal law. This arose in *R v Tan*,[72] in which a converted male to female transsexual who was living as a woman was considered to be a man for the purposes of the Sexual Offences Act 1956, s 30; the case, however, does no more than demonstrate the dangers of extrapolating a judicial decision from its true ambience. It was left to the Australians to re-emphasise that criminal activity is to be judged by behaviour. This was demonstrated in two cases which interact almost as scientific controls.[73] In *Cogley*, the converted transsexual complainant was considered to possess a vagina and the circumstances were very similar to those envisaged by Wilmer LJ in *SY v SY*. The trial judge found that the conformity of the current genitalia and the 'core' identity constituted the essential ingredient for establishing the 'sex' of a person. The Court of Appeal, however, in an obiter opinion, thought that judges' expressions in such cases laid down no legal principles and that the determination of disputed sex was a matter for the legislature.[74] In *Harris*, two male to female transsexuals were accused of attempting to procure an act of indecency by a male. One had undergone reassignment surgery and was held to be a female within the meaning of the Crimes Act 1900 (NSW); the other, although psychologically a female, had not had surgery and was considered male. The importance of the existing genitalia was, thereby, emphasised, Mathews J saying:

> The criminal law is concerned with the regulation of behaviour ... I cannot see that the state of a person's chromosomes can or should be relevant ... in the determination of his or her criminal liability ... How can the law sensibly ignore the state of [the external] genitalia ... simply because they were artificially created or were not the same at birth?

71 A further remarkable case in which a female to male transsexual 'married' a somewhat naïve woman has also been reported. Its major import lies in the threat of a charge of perjury arising from such deception: *S-T (formerly J) v J (transsexual: void marriage)* [1999] Fam 103, [1998] 1 All ER 431.
72 [1983] QB 1053, [1983] 2 All ER 12.
73 *R v Cogley* [1989] VR 799; *R v Harris, R v McGuinness* (1988) 35 A Crim R 146: discussed in H Finlay 'Transsexuals, Sex Change Operations and the Chromosome Test: *Corbett v Corbett* not Followed' (1989) 19 UWAL Rev 152 and in R Bailey-Harris 'Sex Change in the Criminal Law and Beyond' (1989) 13 Crim LJ 353 – which includes the appeal stage in *Cogley*. For a comparison of the cases with *Tan* (above), see J Taitz 'The Law Relating to Consummation of Marriage when One of the Spouses is a Post-operative Transsexual' (1986) 15 Anglo-Am LR 141. See also the same author: 'Confronting Transsexualism, Sexual Identity and the Criminal Law' (1992) 60 Med-leg J 60.
74 For pioneer Commonwealth legislation in the field, see the South Australian Sexual Reassignment Act 1988. Section 7(8)(b) states that a recognition certificate may be issued to an adult who has been reassigned.

2.41 Although the New South Wales Court of Appeal conceded that there was some doubt as to whether a similar test would be applied in civil litigation, the implications always were that the Australian courts would apply the same reasoning to family law when asked – and this has happened recently in a case of transsexual marriage where the biological criteria defining males and females, as elaborated in *Corbett*, were flatly rejected in favour of definition based on social acceptance and self-perception.[75]

2.42 It cannot be overemphasised that *Corbett*, itself, was about marriage – and only about marriage. But, even when it is so limited, its rigidity exposes the principles to severe criticism and it was, of course, marriage that brought UK transsexualism into the European amphitheatre. *Corbett* has, however, been further criticised on the general grounds that it is unfeeling and fails to take into account the total sexual ambience of an individual.[76] Thus, in the American case of *MT v JT*[77] the transsexual partner to a marriage was held to be capable of acting within marriage as a female. In rejecting *Corbett*, Handler J could perceive:

> ... no legal barrier, no cognisable social taboo, or reason founded in public policy, to prevent that person's identification, at least for the purposes of marriage, to the sex generally indicated.

2.43 This reasoning cannot, however, be so readily applied to the female to male transsexual and 'marriages' involving them have been annulled in the United States.[78] Even in the event of the law being changed so as to validate a marriage between a converted transsexual and a person of the same chromosomal complement, such a 'marriage' between a female to male transsexual and a woman would, in the absence of additional legislation, be voidable in both England and Scotland on the grounds of incurable impotency.[79] In any event, the rather bizarre result remains that, whereas a marriage between a resultant female and a normal man is void, an apparently homosexual marriage between a post-operative female and a normal woman would be perfectly legal in the United Kingdom.[80]

2.44 Meantime, the United Kingdom ship sails on although it is becoming progressively more battle-scarred in the process. Thus, the inviolability of the British birth certificate was restated in *P and G*[81] but there were significant

---

75 *Re Kevin* [2001] Fam C 1074: 'For the purpose of ascertaining the validity of a marriage under Australian law the question whether a person is a man or a woman is to be determined as of the date of marriage' per Chisholm J.

76 For criticism along these lines, see S Whittle 'An Association for as Noble a Purpose as Any' (1996) 146 NLJ 366.

77 355 A 2d 204 (NJ, 1976).

78 *B v B* 355 NYS 2d 712 (1974).

79 See K McK Norrie 'Transsexuals, the Right to Marry and Voidable Marriages in Scots Law' 1991 SLT 353. Although the government statement in *I v United Kingdom* (1997) 23 EHRR CD 66 suggested that a decree of nullity would not be granted on the basis of approbation.

80 It has been suggested that, if public policy is against such marriages, the logical conclusion is that a converted transsexual should not only be entitled to alter his or her birth certificate but should be obliged to do so: C Mcafferty 'Gays, Transsexuals and the Right to Marry' [2002] Fam Law 362.

81 *R v Registrar General, ex p P and G* [1996] 2 FCR 588.

suggestions that 'new research' and the like might affect judicial attitudes in the future. The most recent contribution to the saga is to be found in *B v B*.[82] Here, a male to female converted transsexual sought a declaration that her marriage to a man was valid. Johnson J, while certainly not unsympathetic, disposed of the petition fairly rapidly – in essence, he held that the current law was represented by *Corbett* and that any change would be a matter for the legislature. Importantly, however, *B v B* went to appeal[83] which was dismissed by a majority, the gist being that the status of a person was defined by registration at birth – how that status was to be recognised by society was a question of public policy and not one to be answered by the courts. Perhaps the most significant aspect of the case, however, was the very strong dissent expressed by Thorpe LJ who held that times were changing rapidly and that the family justice system must be sufficiently flexible to accommodate major social developments. In his view, there were now insufficiently compelling reasons, having regard to the interests of society as a whole, on which to deny Mrs B legal recognition of her marriage. The learned judge must have been considering the domestic effect of the ECHR decision in *I v United Kingdom*[84] with some anticipatory pleasure.

2.45 The problem of marriage, and the application of Article 12 of the European Convention on Human Rights – which defines the right to marry and to found a family – underlies the running conflict that has been waged over the past 15 years between the United Kingdom and the European courts in relation to transsexualism.[85] We can consider, next, whether or not the gap is widening and what are the chances of a full reconciliation.

Transsexualism in Europe

2.46 There are at least twenty countries of those constituting the current Council of Europe in which the legal definition of sex is sufficiently wide to include the possibility of transsexual marriage in the 'converted' sex.[86] The fact that the United Kingdom is not among them leads to anomalous situations – as Norrie has pointed out, a German transsexual could be legally married in Britain but, with domicillary law applying, a British transsexual would be unable to marry in Germany[87] – and, in many ways, it is surprising that the United Kingdom was not challenged in Europe until 1986. Since then, however, there has been a gathering swell of applications to the European Court of Human Rights and to the Court of Justice of the European Communities

---

82 *B v B (Validity of Marriage: Transsexual)* [2001] 1 FLR 389, (2001) 58 BMLR 52.
83 *Bellinger v Bellinger* [2002] 1 All ER 311, [2001] 2 FLR 1048.
84 Para 2.50 below, where the case is discussed.
85 For previous discussion, see J K Mason 'United Kingdom *v* Europe: Current Attitudes to Transsexualism' (1998) 2 Edin LR 107.
86 Austria, Belgium, Denmark, Estonia, Finland, France, Germany, Greece, Iceland, Italy, Latvia, Luxembourg, the Netherlands, Norway, Slovakia, Spain, Sweden, Switzerland, Turkey and Ukraine. The list is that provided by the organisation 'Liberty' in: *I v United Kingdom*, para 2.50 below at para 40 Gender re-assignment is recognised to some extent in several anglophone countries outside Europe including Canada, Australia, New Zealand and the majority of the United States.
87 K McK Norrie 'Reproductive Technology, Transsexualism and Homosexuality: New Problems for International Private Law' (1994) 43 ICLQ 757.

covering many aspects of the transsexual's life. The main point of contention has been to the effect that, in refusing to alter a converted transsexual's birth certificate, that person has been precluded from marrying in the sex of his or her choice; more recently, however, controversy has spilled over into the fields of industrial and discrimination law.

RESPECT FOR PRIVACY AND THE RIGHT TO MARRY

2.47 The seminal case is that of *Rees v United Kingdom*,[88] in which the court noted the relatively relaxed attitude taken in the United Kingdom outside marriage – where one rarely has to produce a birth certificate and where there is no documentation comparable to the continental civil status certificate; accordingly, it dismissed the application under Article 8 (the right to respect for one's private and family life) by a majority of 12:3. The application under Article 12 (the right to marry and found a family) was dismissed unanimously since marriage was clearly a matter of union between two persons of opposite biological sex. The court also bowed to the seemingly inevitable in so far as the right to marry under Article 12 is subject to this being 'according to the national laws governing the exercise of this right'.

2.48 However, five years later the court was, effectively, asked to overturn the *Rees* decision in *Cossey v United Kingdom*.[89] It did not do so, but, this time, the majority in respect of Article 8 was reduced to 10:8, while the previous unanimity in respect of Article 12 was reduced to a count of 14:4. Some of the difference may be due to the fact that *Cossey* involved a male to female conversion which is generally more acceptable to those who are physiologically minded.[90] We believe, however, that the fundamental reasons for the shift in opinion are to be found in the dissenting opinion of Martens J who based his opinion largely on the changing societal attitudes to activities that are essentially private. He drew attention to the fact that the court in *Rees* had left the door open to accommodate scientific and societal changes in the future and suggested that 'treatment' of the syndrome was incomplete without full recognition of the new status.

2.49 The regulation of sex reassignment operations in France is stricter than it is in the United Kingdom. It is not surprising, therefore, that the French government fared even worse the next year. *B v France*[91] concerned an appeal to the ECHR against a refusal of the Cour de Cassation, first, to declare that, following surgery, B was now of female sex and, second, to alter her documentation accordingly. The refusal was based largely on the grounds that she was still biologically male; any changes in her lifestyle and anatomy that had come about had come about by her own choice and had been achieved without the safeguards that French law insisted upon.[92] In summary, B's appeal

---

88 (1986) 9 EHRR 56, [1987] 2 FLR 111.
89 (1990) 13 EHRR 622, [1991] 2 FLR 492.
90 The result might have been even closer had it not been for Ms Cossey's unusual social history – including the use of her male identity for her own purposes.
91 (1992) 16 EHRR 1, [1992] 2 FLR 249.
92 For discussion of French law, see S Gromb, B Chanseau and H J Lazarini 'Judicial Problems Related to Transsexualism in France' (1997) 37 Med, Sci & L 27.

was upheld by a majority of 15:6. Article 8 had been violated, largely on the grounds that, in the French system, a person's sex is being constantly publicised by way of his or her social security number and that, as a result, B found herself in a position that was incompatible with the respect due to her private life. In a somewhat sophistic argument, the court maintained, on the one hand, that new elements in the debate – including recognition of the testicular feminisation syndrome and suggestions of a genetic background to transsexualism – were now apparent but that, on the other hand, the transsexual question was in a state of flux – legally, morally and socially. The court concluded that there was insufficient evidence to induce them to overturn the *Rees* and *Cossey* judgments, which had favoured the United Kingdom. As a result, France was forced to mend its ways – though it seems that only a requirement to alter the civil status to accord with the person's appearance has been accepted. Intuition strongly suggested that the United Kingdom would lose the next case brought against it under Article 8, but, once again, the European Court of Human Rights, surprisingly, overturned its Commission and decided in favour of the United Kingdom in relation to a violation of that article – albeit by the narrow margin of 11 to 9 votes.[93] In some ways, the applicants had a stronger case than those heard previously – one, for example, who had been married as a man and had a daughter by that marriage, was a pilot and was unable to obtain employment in her new sex. None the less, the court held that there had been no later developments in the field which would induce them to overturn *Cossey*. The United Kingdom was, however, firmly rapped over the knuckles for not having kept its legal measures in this area under review and even the domestic courts have been critical of governmental inactivity in respect of the report of its own inter-departmental working party which reported in 2000.[94]

2.50 The European courts may grind slowly but they are tenacious. In our previous edition, we wondered whether the long outstanding case of *I v United Kingdom*, which was heard by the Commission in 1997, might have provided the watershed. The case has resurfaced in the European Court as we go to press and it does, indeed, make interesting reading.[95] I was a converted male to female who complained that failure to alter her birth certificate made it difficult for her to obtain professional advancement as a nurse, that she could not obtain employment in the prison service without disclosing her change of sex and that, under existing law, she could not marry a man. In a unanimous judgment which is remarkable for the absence of original thought, the Court found the United Kingdom was in breach of both Articles 8 and 12 of the Convention. In effect, the Court reiterated that times were changing and that the United Kingdom was out of step with the majority of Europe – and with parts of the wider world; that the United Kingdom had been repeatedly warned of its tardiness; that the Court had lost patience; and that the United Kingdom had used up its margin of appreciation. As to marriage, the Court could not be persuaded that it must still be assumed that the terms 'man' and 'woman'

93 *Sheffield and Horsham v United Kingdom* [1998] 3 FCR 141. A plea of violation of Article 12 was dismissed by a majority of 18 to 2.
94 Per Butler-Sloss P in *Bellinger*, para 2.44 above at All ER 335.
95 *I v United Kingdom* (Application 25680/94) [2002] 2 FCR 613, sub nom *Goodwin v United Kingdom, I v United Kingdom* (2002) Times, 12 July 2002.

must refer to a determination of gender by purely biological criteria. In general, while not underestimating the difficulties imposed or the important repercussions which any major change in the system of birth certification might have (para 71), the Court would not take the view that to make an exception in the case of some 2000 to 5000 transsexuals would pose the threat of overturning the entire system (para 67). Which may well be so; the concern remains, however, that it might seriously undermine it.

LABOUR LAW AND DISCRIMINATION

2.51 The issue of the status of the birth certificate involves some fundamental domestic administrative law; the relatively cautious approach of the Court of Human Rights in its dealings with the United Kingdom is, therefore, understandable. Labour and discrimination law is, however, more open to interpretation and the United Kingdom has, as a result, been criticised more readily in the European Court of Justice. For this, we must turn to *P v S and Cornwall County Council* [96] – a case which has had far-reaching implications.

2.52 The facts of the case are, briefly, that P was taken on as manager of an educational establishment run by Cornwall County Council. A year later he announced his intention of undergoing a sex-change operation and a dismissal notice was served while he was on sick leave following a preliminary operation. When he was asked to complete some of his tasks, he said he would do them dressed as a female but was told to do so at home. P completed gender reassignment before the actual date of her dismissal and appealed to the Industrial Tribunal, claiming discrimination on the grounds of sex.

2.53 The tribunal could find no discrimination based on the Sex Discrimination Act 1975, but then asked the European Court of Justice whether there was any further instruction to be obtained from Council Directive 76/207/EEC, which deals with equal treatment for men and women: did this, in fact, cover the dismissal of a transsexual for a reason related to a gender reassignment?

2.54 The opinion was delivered by Advocate General Tesauro, who started from the premise that:

> ... in a society as it is to-day, in which customs and morals are changing rapidly, citizens are guaranteed ever wider and deeper protection of their freedoms and social and legal studies are increasingly taking on present-day – and, for that very reason, real – values.[97]

2.55 The law, he said, must not fail to adjust to society as quickly as possible – and he pointed out that full rights of sex change, including marriage, are now available by virtue of special legislation in four countries of the European Union and a change of civil status is allowed in eight more by way of the

---

96   [1996] IRLR 347, [1996] 2 FLR 347.
97   Opinion of Advocate General Tesauro, Case C-13/94, *P v S and Cornwall County Council* transcript para 9.

courts or the administration.[98] The problem of distinguishing *Rees* and *Cossey* from *B v France* was solved by the fact that attitudes had changed and science had progressed in the interval. The Advocate General admitted that the EC directive referred to the traditional man/woman dichotomy; the problem was to decide whether it is *only* discrimination between men and women that is covered by the directive or whether it refers to *all* unfavourable treatment connected with sex.

2.56 Sex, he said, was to be regarded as a continuum between man and woman, so that it would not be right to refuse to protect those who are treated unfavourably precisely because of their sex and/or sexual identity or because they fall outside the traditional man/woman classification. Again, however, he had to admit that there was no discrimination as such because male and female transsexuals were treated in the same way.[99] But one thing, he thought, was certain: P would not have been dismissed had she remained a man – how, then, could it be denied that the cause of discrimination was precisely, and solely, sex?

> To maintain that the unfavourable treatment suffered by P was not on grounds of sex ... because in such a case it is not possible to speak of discrimination between the two sexes would be a quibbling formalistic interpretation and a betrayal of the true essence of that fundamental and inalienable value which is equality.[100]

And, again, Advocate General Tesauro said:

> I note that the directive is nothing if not an expression of a general principle and a fundamental right.[101]

2.57 The Advocate then called on the court to make a courageous decision in the profound conviction that what is at stake is a universal fundamental value: the irrelevance of a person's sex with regard to the rules regulating relations in society. The court accepted his advice.

2.58 It seems to us that the court, in so doing, is depending on doubtful logic which runs on the lines: transsexualism is to do with sex, therefore sex was involved in the dismissal and, therefore, she was dismissed on the grounds of sex – which is discrimination. It is wholly desirable that the status of transsexuals should be settled in law, but it is less than satisfactory that it should depend upon semantic juggling.[102] Nor does it seem right that the terms of a Council directive should be significantly extended to representing 'an expression of a general principle' without reference to the Council. We have seen that the

---

98 These figures are now outdated, see para 2.46 above.
99 It is to be noted, however, that three times as many men wish to become women as the reverse.
100 Case C-13/94 at para 20.
101 Ibid at para 22.
102 The court might, for example, have stated firmly that discrimination on the ground of cross-dressing was discrimination within the meaning of the Sex Discrimination Act 1975. For discussion, see R Wintemute 'Recognising New Kinds of Indirect Sex Discrimination: Transsexualism, Sexual Orientation and Dress Codes' (1997) 60 MLR 334.

European Court of Justice is, currently, unwilling to follow this through to its logical end.[103]

2.59 Even so, *P v S* was rapidly accepted in the United Kingdom by way of an interesting tribunal case involving a converted male to female transsexual who wanted to be a police woman.[104] Her application was rejected as a matter of policy in that she would be unable to carry out certain police duties since her legal sex was male. She appealed to the industrial tribunal under both the Sex Discrimination Act 1975 and the EC directive.

2.60 The tribunal first considered M's legal sex and, having pointed out that the European Court never considered whether P in *P v S* was *legally* female, it applied *ex p P and G*[105] and concluded that she had male status. But, as regards the law, they followed *P v S* and found that the applicant had been discriminated against on the grounds of sex within the meaning of the EC directive and that this was in breach of the directive.

2.61 This is no place to discuss the submission of the Chief Constable in detail. Suffice it to say that the police relied on Article 2(2) of the directive – which acknowledges the right of member states to exclude from its application those occupations for which the sex of the worker constitutes a determining factor. They also contended that there was a genuine occupational qualification which excluded the applicant in so far as the terms of the Police and Criminal Evidence Act 1984 (PACE) dictated some gender-specific duties such as the searching of suspects.[106] After long discussion, the tribunal found that the Chief Constable had justified the discrimination and had satisfied the derogation provided by Article 2(2) – including the demands of proportionality.[107] They also looked at the gender-specific duties dictated under the various codes of practice and under the Police Manual and concluded that the investigation of crime was likely to be jeopardised if the officer was unable to search suspects lawfully.[108] When it came to the Sex Discrimination Act 1975, the tribunal held that the basic comparison required by the statute, namely that between a man and a woman, is not present in the case of a converted transsexual. The tribunal was satisfied that the Act did not apply in this situation.

2.62 This, however, was not sustained for long. In *Reed*,[109] a male to female transsexual convert was subjected to persistent harassment by male colleagues to such an extent that she became ill and was discharged on the grounds of

---

103   See *Grant v South West Trains Ltd* Case C-249/96 [1998] All ER (EC) 193, [1998] 1 FLR 839, para 2.20 above.
104   *M v Chief Constable of the West Midlands Police* (1996) IT Case 08964/96, unreported.
105   *R v Registrar General, ex p P and G* [1996] 2 FCR 588, [1996] 2 FLR 90.
106   Interestingly, it was debated whether PACE itself is discriminatory. This prompted the tribunal to consider sending the case to the European Court but they decided not to, as the *Corbett* test, on which they relied, has already been upheld both in the European and domestic courts and has, therefore, already overcome the discriminatory hurdle.
107   See also *Sirdar v Army Board and Secretary of State for Defence* [1999] All ER (EC) 928, [2000] IRLR 47 in which refusal to transfer a female cook to the Royal Marines was considered justified.
108   A Chief Constable is entitled to refuse employment of a transsexual for similar reasons: *Chief Constable of West Yorkshire Police v A* [2002] IRLR 103, [2002] ICR 552.
109   *Chessington World of Adventures Ltd v Reed, ex p News Group Newspapers Ltd* [1997] IRLR 56, [1998] ICR 97.

incapability. Ms Reed then contracted a peculiarly British marriage with her female partner giving her *Corbett*-tested sex as male – an eventuality we have discussed above. Even so, her complaint of discrimination under the Sex Discrimination Act 1975 was upheld by the industrial tribunal and her employers appealed. The Employment Appeal Tribunal held that there was no clear indication in the 1975 Act that it excluded an action by a transsexual; moreover, the test for establishing a person's legal sex in the context of marriage was to be distinguished from that applying under the 1975 Act. Discrimination on the basis of gender reassignment was sex based, was covered by the 1975 Act and *P v S* was to be followed – and this is now enshrined in statute law.[110]

APPLICATION TO FAMILY LAW

2.63 We have yet to look at that aspect of transsexualism which is most intimately connected to *medical* law – that is, its application to family law and, here, the European bandwagon has taken a surprising turn.

2.64 *X, Y and Z v United Kingdom* [111] concerned a female to male transsexual who had enjoyed a stable relationship with a woman for 15 years. During this time, the couple had had three children by way of artificial insemination by donor (AI). X now put in an application to the Registrar General not to have his birth certificate altered but, rather, to be recognised as the father of the eldest child for the purposes of registering her birth. The Registrar believed that only a biological man could be regarded as a father for the purposes of registration but conceded that there was nothing unlawful in the daughter bearing her 'father's' surname. The European Commission on Human Rights then, predictably, decided that there had been a violation of Article 8 of the European Convention on Human Rights – that is, of respect for a person's private and family life, home and correspondence.

2.65 The European Court of Human Rights, however, noted that the application raised very different problems from those it had addressed in previous cases concerning transsexuals – these included the granting of parental rights to transsexuals and the manner in which the social relationship between a child conceived by AI and the person acting in the role of father should be defined in law. The majority opinion retreated behind the defences that there was, as yet, no clear consensus among member states, that the law was in a transitional condition and that to make an exception in national law of this type could lead to inconsistencies and confusion in family law – that is, they applied a wide margin of appreciation. On the other side of the coin, the court found that refusal to allow the application resulted in little, if any, disadvantage to the principals and held, by 14 votes to six, that there had been no violation of Article 8.

2.66 Somewhat strangely, both the Commission and the court felt that its decision in respect of Article 8 rendered further discussion as to a violation of

---

110 Sex Discrimination (Gender Reassignment) Regulations 1999, SI 1999/1102.
111 *X, Y and Z v United Kingdom* (1997) 24 EHRR 143, [1997] 2 FLR 892.

Article 14 redundant. Since this was the only area in which the question of sex discrimination arose, it is only in the dissenting judgments that this important aspect of the application – and its relationship to the Human Fertilisation and Embryology Act 1990 – was reasonably well aired. The 1990 Act is discussed in detail in chapter 3. For the present, we can say that the effect of s 28(3) is to allow that, when an unmarried woman is artificially inseminated in the course of treatment services provided for her and a man together, then that man will be regarded 'for all purposes' as the father of the child. X was, however, unable to rely on the 1990 Act once pure *Corbett* principles were applied – s 28(3) makes no provision for a converted transsexual. Here, there is a suggestion of what might be considered a significant misconception creeping into the ECHR for both the judgment (at para 21) and two dissenting opinions – those of Judges Foighel and Vilhjálmsson – translate 'man' in s 23(3) as 'the male partner' – a phrase which is notably absent from the Act. It is well-nigh impossible, either legally or physiologically, to see X as a man; but it is far less difficult to see him as a 'male partner' – particularly as the 'pastiche' was particularly good in his case.[112] The dissenting opinion that, as a result, the United Kingdom's stance constituted discrimination on the grounds of sex, then has some force – if the Act supports the fiction of fatherhood in the case of a man, is it not sex discrimination to refuse it in the case of a woman carrying out the social functions of a man? The determining factor would seem to be the welfare of the child involved – and the Court was markedly ambivalent as to how this would be influenced by its decision.[113] But, whether or not one sees the need for or the desirability of the remedy sought, the solution should lie in changing the Act rather than in distorting the use of language.

Conclusion

2.67 What, then, is the current position of transsexualism in a United Kingdom that is subject to European Community law?

2.68 There are now very few who would deny that transsexualism is a recognisable psychiatric abnormality, that it causes considerable suffering to those afflicted and that it deserves to be treated. A converted transsexual is doing no public harm and is entitled to operate within his or her chosen sex. Reviewing the cases that have been reported, it is difficult to resist the conclusion that the opposition to transsexualism they demonstrate results not so much from the appearance as from a *change* of appearance in the subjects. Current legal thinking in this area, however, suffers from the assumption that the end-state will always be satisfactory – and this is not always so. There are few reports in this respect but the results of a small Portuguese study are interesting: of seven persons treated, the result was considered good in three, reasonable in three and bad in one – not an over-impressive testimony to current therapy.[114]

---

112 Many years ago, Thomson hinted at the same semantic distinction in respect of the Marriage Acts. J M Thomson 'Transsexualism: a Legal Perspective' (1980) 6 J Med Ethics 92.
113 At paras 47 and 51.
114 J Costa-Santos and R Madeira 'Transsexualism in Portugal: the Legal Framework and Procedure, and its Consequences for Transsexuals' (1996) 36 Med, Sci & L 221.

Before accepting sex conversion as beneficent and as something of an individual right, it is important to appreciate that the result may be social non-acceptance and, ultimately, a disaster for the patient. That may be a risk the individual is willing to accept and can be seen as insufficient grounds on which to base a restrictive public policy when the popular and judicial thrust is to accept the legal as well as the social consequences of a change of sex.

2.69 Certainly, there are, at best, very doubtful grounds for extending and maintaining the *Corbett* standard outside administrative and family law. There can be very little support for the notion that the nature of sexual offences should be based on chromosomes rather than on gender and there are few, if any, tenable reasons why people should not work and behave in their chosen sex. A certificate of change of sex would offend no historian's sensitivities and legislation could cover its applicability to cases like that of *M*. But can we extend this essentially laissez-faire attitude to marriage?

2.70 The proposition that a transsexual marriage should be valid if the transsexual is found to be capable of fulfilling the essential role of the sex he or she has assumed has been widely canvassed – and, as a corollary, it is suggested that the role should be founded on the ability of the two partners to love and understand one another.

2.71 We have already discussed the question of homosexual marriage and it might well be supposed that the same arguments apply in the case of transsexuals. In many ways this is so, yet it is also possible to formulate a case for the latter based on wider considerations. Marriage is defined as the union between a man and a woman but, problems of consummation excepted, the anatomic/physiologic completeness of either partner is seldom of major importance. A man with infantile or undescended testes is still capable of a legal marriage with his sexual opposite. Similarly, a woman without a uterus and who is unable to bear a child would rightly expect to be treated as a woman for the purposes of marriage to a man. It is at least arguable that the gap between such situations and that involving the converted transsexuals is not unbridgeable. That having been said, we would still suggest that the preferable proportionate response to stable transsexual relationships is, once again, by way of their official registration as partnerships. The debate is, however, by no means closed.

DELIBERATE TRANSMISSION OF SEXUALLY TRANSMITTED DISEASE

2.72 The liability for deliberately infecting another person with sexually transmissible organisms remains a live issue, particularly in view of the conviction in *HM Advocate v Kelly*.[115] Although the principles would be the same in respect of any such disease, the problem is amplified in the case of HIV infection as, here, the scenario includes the real possibility of causing death and of unlawful killing.

115 23 February 2001, unreported, High Court of Judiciary, Glasgow. Discussed from the public health aspect in S M Bird and A J Leigh Brown 'Criminalisation of HIV Transmission: Implications for Public Health in Scotland' (2001) 323 BMJ 1174. See also J Chalmers 'The Criminalisation of HIV Transmission' (2002) 28 J Med Ethics 160.

2.73 Aspects of medical law which are of particular significance to HIV infection are discussed at several points in this book. Here, we are concerned only with issues surrounding the knowing possibility of transmission of disease from one individual to another; these can be viewed from the perspective either of the criminal law – the purpose of which is to deter by way of threatened punishment – or of the civil law – which is primarily concerned to compensate individuals for injury done to them.

2.74 There are a number of existing criminal offences which might be used as vehicles by which to prosecute the person who knowingly subjects another to a risk of HIV infection. These range from relatively minor nuisance-based offences, through assault to attempted murder. The criminal law should experience little difficulty in treating the act as a serious assault or, indeed, as attempted murder when the exposure is deliberate and arises outside the context of sexual intercourse. Thus, deliberately stabbing a person with a syringe filled with infected blood, with the intention of infecting the victim with HIV, would appear to satisfy the requirements of attempted murder, even though a lesser offence could be easier to charge. The same might be said of throwing infected blood or, possibly, spitting at another with the intention of transmitting the virus. There has been a legislative response to this type of assault in a number of jurisdictions. The high incidence of syringe attacks in the Irish Republic – usually as incidental to robbery – led to legislation which imposes a penalty similar to that for attempted murder.[116] In New South Wales, the Crimes Act 1900 has been amended to include a new offence of causing grievous bodily disease,[117] this response again being prompted by highly-publicised incidents in which blood-filled syringes were used as weapons.

2.75 A very much more difficult situation arises when a person who is aware of his HIV-positive status has unprotected sexual contact with a person to whom he has not disclosed that status. The questions are then posed: should this be a criminal offence, and if so, what offence might it be? Unsurprisingly, there has been considerable discussion of this issue and various responses have been advocated and adopted. The major division lies between those jurisdictions that are prepared to introduce the concept of criminality into what is, essentially, a matter of public health and those that believe that the adverse consequences of doing so are such as to outweigh any potential advantages.

2.76 The argument in favour of punishing the knowing sexual transmission of HIV depends on the fact that such behaviour amounts to the infliction of substantial harm on another; it is, therefore, indistinguishable from other forms of assault or, in the case of English law, from the range of offences currently prosecuted under the Offences Against the Person Act 1861[118] – an aspect to which we return, briefly, below. There may, of course, be no actual

116   Non-Fatal Offences Against the Person Act 1997.
117   Crimes Act 1900, s 36.
118   For discussion of the possible offences committed, see S H Bronitt 'Spreading Disease and the Criminal Law' [1994] Crim LR 21; D Ormerod and M Gunn 'Criminal Liability for the Transmission of HIV' [1996] 1 Web J of Current Legal Issues (http://webjcl.ncl.ac.uk); H Power 'Consensual Sex, Disease and the Criminal Law' (1996) 60 J Crim L 412.

intention to harm – indeed, one assumes that such an intention is absent in most cases. What there is, however, is recklessness in relation to the risk of serious harm. Provided that he knows of his own infection, an HIV-positive man who engages in unprotected sex is willingly subjecting his partner to a risk of infection and, ultimately, of death – and the same is true of the infected woman. There is probably broad agreement that such conduct is reprehensible and, indeed, this view has been sufficiently widely held in some jurisdictions to prompt a specific legislative response. Over 20 of the United States have amended existing statutes or have introduced new laws to make it a criminal offence to have sexual contact with another when one knows of the fact that one is HIV-positive and when this fact is unknown to one's partner.[119] Some such statutes are narrow in their scope and require that there be an intention to transmit the infection; others are prepared to punish the reckless exposure to risk which such action implies. Legislative action has also been taken in Australia: in South Australia, for example, it is now an offence for an HIV-infected person to fail to take all reasonable precautions to prevent transmitting the disease to another.[120]

2.77 There have, however, been a number of examples of prosecution in the absence of specific legislation of HIV-positive persons who have transmitted, or risked transmitting, the infection to an unsuspecting partner. Some of these attracted considerable media attention, not least because of the severity of the sentences imposed; one such example is that of a sentence of 14 years' imprisonment being imposed by a Finnish court on an HIV-positive man who had sexual relations with over 100 women whom he had not informed of his infected status.[121] Prosecutions have also been reported in other European countries, including Denmark[122] and Germany. In Germany, a charge of attempted manslaughter might be competent but would probably fail on the grounds of an insufficient degree of intention or on proof of causation; a conviction for a life-endangering assault or for attempting to endanger a person's life could then be appropriate. A charge of assault would be precluded in the event of a valid consent to intercourse (Penal Code, ss 223, 223a).[123]

2.78 The most useful discussion of the problem in the ambience of the common law has been in Canada, where there have been relatively numerous decisions

---

119 An example of the American legislative response is the Illinois Statute of 1989 (Ill Rev Stat 1989, ch 38; 720 ILCS 5/12-16.2 (West, 1992)). This statute has survived constitutional challenge: *People of the State of Illinois v Russell* 630 NE 2d 794 (Ill, 1994).

120 Public and Environmental Health Act 1987.

121 J Acher 'HIV man jailed for unsafe sex' Scotsman, 11 July 1997, p 12. Other prosecutions which attracted particular attention included that brought under s 190 of the Cyprus Criminal Code. This section makes it an offence to transmit (culpably) a disease dangerous to life, an offence originally introduced in order to combat the spread of typhoid and cholera: M Kelly 'Cypriot knowingly gave lover AIDS virus' Scotsman, 30 July 1997, p 5.

122 C Csillag 'Prison Sentence for Exposing Women to Risk of Infection' (1993) 341 Lancet 751 (23 women were involved with the accused: the sentence imposed was 18 months' imprisonment).

123 L G Nurenberg-Fürth, NJW 1988, 2311; A G Kempten, NJW 1988, 2313; AG Hamburg, NJW 1989, 2071; BGH, NJW 1989, 781; BGH, NJW 1990, 129. The issue is covered by A J Szwarc *AIDS und Strafrecht* (1996).

on the point. There is no specific section of the Canadian Criminal Code that establishes an offence to communicate a disease through recklessness; prosecuting authorities have, therefore, turned to charging common nuisance, criminal negligence, assault, administering a noxious thing or attempted murder – with mixed results. Nuisance convictions, brought under the Canadian Criminal Code, s 180, were sustained in *R v Summer*,[124] *R v Kreider*,[125] and *R v Thornton*[126] (reckless blood donation), but an attempt to prosecute for common nuisance was unsuccessful in *R v Ssenyonga*,[127] even though the court was prepared to entertain a prosecution for criminal negligence. The latter crime was successfully prosecuted in *R v Wentzell*[128] and *R v Mercer*,[129] both of which demonstrate the sort of irresponsible, not to say heartless, behaviour which attracts criminal attention in this context. In *Mercer* the accused continued to have sexual intercourse with, and infected, a 16-year-old girl, despite having tested positive for HIV and having been advised by a doctor as to the risk of transmission. His original sentence of 27 months' imprisonment was increased to 11 years on appeal by the Crown.

2.79 The Canadian experience of using the assault provisions of the Criminal Code to prosecute in such cases demonstrates the theoretical difficulty which commentators have long identified as being a particular stumbling block to conviction in such cases – that is, consent. In essence, consent to intercourse on the part of a sexual partner would appear to cover the very act which is alleged to constitute the assault. The court in *Ssenyonga* held that there had, in fact, been consent to the application of that degree of force which was inherent in sexual intercourse and, moreover, that this consent was not vitiated by fraud. It is not surprising that the court should have reached this view; fraud in the context of rape has always been interpreted restrictively and has been taken to relate only to misrepresentations as to the nature of the act of sexual intercourse rather than to its implications. The issue arose once more in *R v Cuerrier*,[130] in which the accused began a sexual relationship with a woman after he had been notified that he had tested positive for HIV; he did not tell her of this fact, nor did he seek to minimise the risk to her. He was charged with aggravated assault after he began a relationship with another partner. On appeal by the Crown against Cuerrier's acquittal at trial, the Court of Appeal of British Columbia concluded that the fact that a partner is not informed of HIV infection does not vitiate consent.[131] The case, however, was taken to the Supreme Court of Canada, where it was decided that the concealment of HIV status constituted fraud of a sufficiently serious nature to invalidate consent. In these circumstances, a conviction for aggravated assault is possible under Canadian criminal law.[132] The nature of consent to sexual intercourse is, therefore, central to the problem and this largely accounts for

124 (1989) 73 CR (3d) 32.
125 (1993) 140 AR 81.
126 [1993] 2 SCR 445, 82 CCC (3d) 530.
127 (1993) 81 CCC (3d) 257.
128 (8 December 1989, unreported), NS Co Ct.
129 (1993) 84 CCC (3d) 41.
130 [1996] BCJ No 2229, BCCA.
131 (1996) 111 CCC (3d) 261, BCCA.
132 (1998) 2 SCR 371. The Court, however, distinguished between fraud in relation to rape and fraud related to assault; the law as to the former was left unchanged.

the fact that the criminal law had not been used to prosecute people for the reckless sexual transmission of HIV in England and Wales.[133] There has been some doubt as to what offence could be charged in those countries given that the Offences Against the Person Act 1861, s 20 (infliction of grievous bodily harm) probably necessarily involves an assault and s 47 (occasioning actual bodily harm) certainly does. Assault will be vitiated by consent and the question arises as to whether or not the iniquitous case of *Clarence*[134] – in which it was essentially held that consent to sexual intercourse was not limited by conditions – still represents the law in England and Wales.[135] The probability is that it does not and any distinction between causing and inflicting injury now seems irrelevant.[136] An alternative approach, should one be needed, is that ss 23 and 24, which define liability for 'unlawfully and maliciously' administering to another 'any poison or other destructive or noxious thing' might provide a route to conviction though it involves a certain amount of semantic licence.

2.80   The criminal law of Scotland is somewhat more elastic and, in *Kelly*,[137] a man who had intercourse with a girl when knowingly infected with HIV was successfully prosecuted for culpably and recklessly engaging in sexual intercourse to the danger of a woman's health and life.[138] The conditions for conviction laid down by Lord Mackay in his charge to the jury included: that the accused knew he was HIV positive; that he knew the virus could be transmitted by way of sexual intercourse; that he pretended that he was not infected; that intercourse took place and that, as a result, the woman became infected; and that he acted culpably and recklessly, conditions which demanded a higher objective test than did carelessness or negligence. Kelly was sentenced to imprisonment for five years.[139]

2.81   The English Law Commission has recommended that it should be an offence to transmit HIV recklessly,[140] but this view was not shared by the government which, early in 1998, announced its intention of drafting proposed

133   The nearest approach seems to be *R v Gaud*, where a surgeon who was suffering from Hepatitis B knowingly put hundreds of patients at risk. He was sentenced to one year's imprisonment, having been charged with the common law offence of causing a public nuisance. See C Dyer 'Surgeon jailed for infecting patients' (1994) 309 BMJ 896. The case is discussed in detail in M Brazier and J Harris 'Public Health and Private Lives' (1996) 4 Med L Rev 174.

134   *R v Clarence* (1889) 22 QBD 23.

135   Power, para 2.76 above, suggested that *R v Brown*, para 2.4 above, overrules *Clarence* but the proposition has not been tested in the precise conditions of sexually transmitted disease.

136   See *R v Ireland, R v Burstow* [1998] AC 147, [1997] 4 All ER 225, in which psychiatric harm was 'inflicted' over the telephone.

137   Para 2.72 above.

138   This and other possibilities were foreseen: G T Laurie 'Aids and Criminal Liability under Scots Law' (1991) 36 J Law Soc Scot 312. Brazier and Harris, para 2.29 above, suggested that such an offence is almost available in England under the Public Health (Control of Disease) Act 1984, s 17 but this applies only to notifiable diseases (which do not include HIV infection or AIDS) which are spread in a public place.

139   *Kelly* has been criticised for opening a Pandora's box in respect of liability. For discussion of culpable recklessness and reckless endangerment see V Tadros 'Recklessness, Consent and the Transmission of HIV' (2001) 5 Edin LR 371.

140   *Legislating the Criminal Code: Offences Against the Person and General Principles* (Law Com No 218) (Cm 2370, 1993). For discussion, see R Bennett, H Draper and L Frith 'Ignorance is Bliss? HIV and Moral Duties and Legal Duties to Forewarn' (2000) 26 J Med Ethics 9 and response by Chalmers, para 2.72 above.

reforms of the law relating to non-fatal offences against the person so as to allow for prosecution where the transmission of serious disease is intentional but not where it is reckless.[141] In taking this view, the government signalled its acceptance of a philosophy of non-coercion in this area[142] – a view which has been consistently advocated by many organisations working with those infected with HIV or with those in high-risk groups. A decision to treat the reckless transmission of a fatal condition to another as being beyond the scope of the criminal law may be justifiable on grounds of such pure public health expediency. At the same time, it undoubtedly represents a calculated, politically-motivated failure on the part of the criminal law policy-makers to acknowledge, and act upon, the profound wrong which is done to those whose life expectancy may be drastically shortened by the deception involved.[143]

2.82 The failure of the state to prosecute does not leave the injured person without any remedy: it is possible that an action in tort might be brought against one who infects another with HIV. There are several heads under which a claim for damages might lie,[144] of which negligence seems to be the most appropriate for discussion. A claim would be based either on a failure to conform to the standards of reasonable conduct or on the consent being flawed as a result of having been given on the basis of inadequate information as to the risks involved;[145] in either event, an action would depend upon a duty of care being owed by and to each partner in the course of sexual connection. Such a duty is established in the United States[146] but, surprisingly, the issue is by no means settled in the United Kingdom. The nearest 'authority' we have found is an extra-judicial opinion given by Lord Brandon to the effect that such a duty does exist[147] – and we feel confident that the courts would follow such a line. The infection of another with HIV is an undoubted harm, which is clearly foreseeable in *Donoghue v Stevenson*[148] terms. Even so, the plaintiff would face many hurdles, perhaps the most difficult of these being to establish causation – particularly in the case of AIDS, with its long incubation period and the shadowy nature of exposure to the virus.[149] It is possible that a defence

141 Home Office *Violence: Reforming the Offences Against the Person Act 1861* (1998).
142 The question of whether the criminal law should be used at all to prevent the transmission of HIV through risky sexual behaviour is one on which there are, not surprisingly, divergent views. There appears to be a strong consensus amongst medical commentators that the criminal law should not be invoked: R Porter 'History Says No to the Policeman's Response to AIDS' (1986) 293 BMJ 1589; P Old and J Montgomery 'Law, Coercion and the Public Health' (1992) 304 BMJ 891. Will the introduction of the criminal law have much of an impact on the behaviour of those who might spread the infection? On this, see D E Woodhouse et al 'Restricting Personal Behaviour – Case Study on Legal Measures to Prevent the Spread of HIV' (1993) 4 Int J S AIDS 144.
143 There are news reports of a rather similar case coming to trial in England: S Lister 'Doctor is Charged with Giving Lover Herpes' *The Times*, 12 January 2002. The charge is apparently one of causing grievous bodily harm.
144 See J Taitz 'Legal Liability for Transmitting AIDS' (1989) 57 Med-leg J 216.
145 'Informed consent' is discussed in detail at para 10.99 below.
146 Eg *Long v Adams* 333 SE 2d 852 (Ga, 1985). A short news item indicates that damages of $18m have been awarded in Florida to a man who was infected with HIV by his fiancée: *Financial Times*, 27 August 1993, p 1.
147 K Litton and R James 'Civil Liability for Communication of AIDS – A Moot Point' (1987) 137 NLJ 755.
148 *M'Alister (or Donoghue) v Stevenson* [1932] AC 562, 1932 SC (HL) 31.
149 Tadros, para 2.80 above, points out that that it is unclear how this obstacle was overcome in *Kelly*.

of volenti non fit injuria might be attempted in such an action, but this would be unlikely to be successful, given the clear knowledge of risk which the modern interpretation of that defence entails. Thus, the nature of the consent would be fundamental to the outcome and could find expression by way of contributory negligence – a concept which could be used to redress the balance of responsibility for transmission of any infectious disease.[150]

2.83   The question of whether there is a duty to warn of HIV infection is one which has caused some concern to doctors.[151] There is a major issue of confidentiality here,[152] but there is also the question of whether an injured third party has a right to seek compensation from a doctor who could have warned him or her of the threat posed by a sexual partner. There has been no litigation on this issue in the United Kingdom but it has been addressed in the United States, first, in relation to hepatitis. In *DiMarco v Lynch Homes-Chester County*[153] a blood technician had accidentally infected herself with the hepatitis virus. Her doctor did not warn her to refrain from sexual contact with others for six months, with the result that she transmitted the infection to the plaintiff. The Supreme Court of Pennsylvania agreed that, in such a case, the doctor owed a duty of care which extended to anybody who was foreseeably physically intimate with the patient. It did not matter that the identity of the plaintiff was not known at the time.

2.84   This reasoning was extended to HIV infection in the Californian case of *Reisner v Regents of the University of California*.[154] Here, a girl of 12 had been infected as a result of the use of contaminated blood products. Her doctor, who was aware of the fact that infection had taken place, did not inform the family that this had happened, with the result that she grew to maturity in ignorance of her plight. She engaged in a sexual relationship with the plaintiff, who sought damages from the doctor in respect of his infection with HIV, arguing that he had been owed a duty of care by the doctor. The California Court of Appeal, like the Supreme Court of Pennsylvania, sustained this argument, ruling that a doctor's duty of care might extend to those with whom he was not in a direct relationship and whose identity he might not know. Such liability would not be potentially too broad as claims by distant fourth or fifth persons could be limited by considerations of causation. This decision might be taken as creating a whole new range of duties to warn but, in fact, it does not. The negligence consists in the doctor's failure to warn *his patient*; had he done that, then she would have been in a position to avoid communicating the infection to others.[155] The decision does not, then, create a general duty to warn all those who might be at risk.

---

150   See Old and Montgomery, para 2.81 above.
151   In a number of American states specific statutory provisions impose a duty of disclosure on HIV positive persons to disclose their status to their partners, see J W Rose, 'To Tell or Not to Tell: Legislative Imposition of Partner Notification Duties for HIV Patients' (2001) 22 J Legal Med 107.
152   Which is discussed at greater length at para 8.23 et seq below.
153   583 A 2d 422 (Penn, 1990).
154   37 Cal Rep 2d 518 (1995).
155   See discussion by A Grubb 'HIV; Doctor's Liability to Future Partner' (1997) 5 Med L Rev 250.

2.85 It is uncertain whether this jurisprudence is immediately transferable to the United Kingdom, where we are left in an unsatisfactory situation. There is little doubt that we have a moral duty not to infect others if it can be avoided[156] but moral obligations are of little moment to a person who is harmed but can find no means of redress. The uncertainty of the civil law suggests that there is a place for retaining, or initiating, some criminal sanction in cases where infection is deliberately or recklessly transmitted through sexual activity. Certainly, it is interesting to observe that the majority of comparable jurisdictions do, in fact, adopt such a policy. We have seen that the opposition to this is apparently not so rigid as it has been in the past – at least in relation to deliberate infection – and that the British government may be following that line.[157] We have consistently expressed our doubts as to the medical benefit of separating HIV infection from other forms of communicable disease and it may well be that, ultimately, the preferred approach to the specific problem will be through the amendment and application of the Public Health Acts. This would mean that, rather than using the sledgehammer of the law of assault, the courts could identify the protected interest as being that of community health. Such an approach would remove the stigma of conviction for assault while, at the same time, providing a measure of protection for the innocent victims of reckless behaviour.

156 J Harris and S Holm 'Is there a Moral Obligation not to Infect Others?' (1995) 311 BMJ 1215.
157 R Ford and P Webster 'Straw Seeks Jail for Spreading AIDS' *The Times*, 6 March 1998, p 1.

3 The management of infertility and childlessness

3.1 The title of this chapter draws attention to a distinction which we believe to be of practical, as well as semantic, importance. Primary infertility is a problem of the production of gametes or of implantation of the embryo. This may be susceptible to hormone therapy – a matter which we barely consider here; ovum or sperm donation then becomes a secondary treatment of childlessness due to unsuccessful treatment of the primary condition. Similarly, the basic in vitro fertilisation (IVF) technique is most commonly used as a treatment of childlessness due to blockage of the fallopian tubes which cannot be corrected by recanalisation therapy. The distinction between infertility and childlessness appears to be narrow but it may be significant in relation to resource allocation. Thus, it could be held that, whereas the treatment of infertility is clearly a medical matter, childlessness can be seen as a social problem which should be funded from a different source.[1] While we do not subscribe to this theory, it might serve to justify the relative scarcity of the latter facilities in the National Health Service.[2]

3.2 Some 10% of marriages are said to be infertile and the couple desire children in, at least, a high proportion of these.[3] In addition, there are couples who should give special thought to producing children naturally for genetic reasons, either because one may carry a dominant deleterious gene or because both are known to bear recessive characteristics (see chapter 6, below). Again, a couple may be able to conceive a child but the woman is unable to carry it

---

1 For discussion, see S Redmayne and R Klein 'Rationing in Practice: the Case of In Vitro Fertilisation' (1993) 306 BMJ 1521.

2 The *Ninth Annual Report of the Human Fertilisation and Embryology Authority* (2000) indicates that there are now 75 licensed centres offering IVF treatments, with an additional 29 providing donor insemination only. 45 of the IVF clinics accept both fee paying and non-fee paying patients; 27 are fully fee paying and only 3 are exclusively non-fee paying. It is said that almost 25% of health authorities refused to purchase IVF facilities in 1994: D Evans 'Infertility and the NHS' (1995) 311 BMJ 1586.

3 This notional figure, which must be extremely hard to validate, has its basis in *Report of the Committee of Inquiry into Human Fertilisation and Embryology* (Dame Mary Warnock, chairman, 1984), para 2.1. It may be an underestimate in modern terms: M Freeman 'Medically Assisted Reproduction' in I Kennedy and A Grubb (eds) *Principles of Medical Law* (1998), para 10.02.

for medical reasons. Opportunities for adoption are now meagre and, for many years, attention has focused on the elaboration of methods designed either to substitute the gametes of one or other person or to bypass the natural process in other ways.

3.3 The legal and moral issues involved have been considered at governmental level in many countries.[4] Overall, it is remarkable how similar have been the conclusions of the various committees of inquiry which have reported throughout the English-speaking world – assisted reproduction is now well-established and there is little new to say.

THE CONTROL OF ASSISTED REPRODUCTION

3.4 The legal response of the United Kingdom is to be found in the Human Fertilisation and Embryology Act 1990.[5] The main thrust of the Act is to establish a Human Fertilisation and Embryology Authority (HFEA) (s 5) which is mandated to supervise and provide information and advice to the Secretary of State about embryos and about treatment services governed by the Act.[6] The Authority maintains a Licence Committee through which only three forms of licence can be issued to clinics approved for the purposes of the Act – these authorise activities in the course of providing treatment services (s 13), the storage of gametes and/or embryos (s 14), and reproductive research (s 15); the activities governed and limited by the licences are detailed in Schedule 2. In respect of assisted reproductive treatment provided for the public – with which we are primarily concerned in this chapter – the Act, in broad practical terms, prohibits the use, or storage, of gametes and the creation of embryos outside the body unless the clinic is in possession of a licence to do so.[7] Thus, in general, it allows for a flexible development of reproductive art under the control of peer and lay review.[8] Sections 3 and 4, however, define activities which *cannot* be licensed. These include: placing in a woman any live gametes or embryos other than those of human origin; placing a human embryo in any animal; replacement of an embryonic nucleus by a nucleus taken from a cell of any other person or embryo; and, of particular significance, keeping or using an embryo after the appearance

---

4   For a précis of European attitudes, see S Goldbeck-Wood 'Europe is Divided on Embryo Regulations' (1996) 313 BMJ 512.

5   Hereafter 'the 1990 Act'. The Act is, in many ways, a complex piece of legislation and we feel it would be superfluous to attempt a detailed analysis. A very complete commentary is to be found in R G Lee and D Morgan *Human Fertilisation and Embryology* (2001).

6   For details, see L Hagger 'The Role of the Human Fertilisation and Embryology Authority' (1997) 3 Med L Internat 1.

7   It will be noted that intra-fallopian transfer of gametes is not subject to licensing unless either the sperm or eggs are donated. Even so, the HFEA is maintaining a watchful eye on the process which carries its own hazards.

8   The Chairman of the Authority may not be a registered medical practitioner or directly associated with the provision of treatment services; such persons must, however, constitute at least one third but not more than one half the total membership (Sch 1, para 4). The current Chairman is a senior academic administrator and, aside from medical scientists, the membership includes appointments from such varied professions as the religious ministry, the law and broadcasting.

of the primitive streak – by definition, later than 14 days from the day the gametes were mixed but excluding any time for which the embryo was stored (s 3(4)).

3.5 Section 1 of the Act contains some important definitions, the most significant of which include that, except where otherwise stated, an embryo means a live human embryo where fertilisation is complete – that is, following the appearance of a two-cell zygote – and that, in so far as the Act governs the creation, keeping or use of an embryo, it applies only to an embryo outside the human body.

3.6 Finally, it should be mentioned that the Authority must prepare and maintain a Code of Practice about the proper conduct of activities carried on under licence (s 25). As with all such mandated codes, the code is not legally binding per se. Nevertheless, the fact that it had been disregarded would count heavily in any criminal or civil actions brought against the offending clinic. Of perhaps greater practical importance, the licence committee is empowered to vary, revoke or refuse to renew a licence in the light of any deviations from the provisions of the code.

3.7 With that précis completed, we can go on to consider the practical applications of the Act.

INSEMINATION

3.8 Donor insemination (DI)[9] may provide a solution to male infertility, a condition which accounts for roughly 50% of cases of involuntary failure to conceive. In this procedure, semen obtained from a donor is injected into the woman; this results in conception in a proportion of cases which is surprisingly low.[10] The husband's or male partner's semen may similarly be introduced into the uterus by artificial means (AIH or AIP) – a need which might arise from impotence, from inadequate formation of spermatozoa or from a hostile vaginal reaction to constituents of the semen; treated semen would be used in the last two instances. Many couples who have recourse to DI are loath to abandon all hope of their own offspring. In such circumstances, the semen of the apparently infertile male partner is mixed with that of the donor so that the couple can still believe that the ovum may have been fertilised by the male partner's sperm. This form of artificial insemination is sometimes known as AIHD.

---

9 In so far as insemination by donor will virtually always be artificial, we feel that the time has come to adopt the modern terminology in preference to the traditional acronym AID. The same does not apply to insemination by husband or partner where we will continue to use the common abbreviations.

10 The national clinical pregnancy rate per treatment cycle has risen from 6.6 % in 1991/92 to 12.1 % in 1998/9: HFEA *Ninth Annual Report* (2000) Table 4.18. These figures include GIFT using donated gametes. Interestingly, the number of treatment cycles administered has more than halved between 1992 and 1999. GIFT, or gamete intra-fallopian transfer, involves the introduction of the sperm to the ovum in their natural habitat – the fallopian tube – rather than in the Petri dish. The process is, therefore, one of in vivo fertilisation. By contrast, in ZIFT, or zygote intra-fallopian transfer, the preformed zygote is placed in the tube; fertilisation is, therefore, in vitro.

Artificial insemination by the husband or male partner

3.9 In general terms, both AIH and AIP lie beyond the scope of the 1990 Act. This derives from the terms of s 4(1)(b) which are that no person shall use the sperm of any man in the course of providing treatment services for a woman except in pursuance of a licence *unless* the services are being provided for the woman and the man together. The meaning is perfectly clear so long as the man and woman are husband and wife; it is less so in the event of AIP. This is so because, first, the Act does not use the word 'partner' which, as a result, remains undefined and, second, because the phraseology is very similar to that used in s 28(3) which deals with paternal status and which has provoked considerable legal confusion. We return to the matter below where it will be seen that, for the purposes of the Act, 'together' is to be interpreted as implying a stable, heterosexual relationship – which, in turn, of course, begs the definition of 'stability'.[11] The Act is, also, at best veiled as to its attitude to donor insemination within an unmarried partnership and, again, we return to this at para 3.26.

3.10 Finally in this context, it is to be noted that AIH has been refined in recent years by the introduction of micromanipulative techniques – in particular, those of intracytoplasmic sperm injection (ICSI) or sub-zonal insemination (SUZI). In these methods, a single spermatozoon is injected directly into an egg. The sperm can, thus, be preselected and the technique is a valuable adjunct to the management of male infertility due to poor quality of the semen. It is, perhaps, self evident that such sophisticated methods which involve in vitro fertilisation[12] must be conducted in a licensed clinic in accordance with the Act. Looked at from the ethical standpoint, their success depends to a great extent on the specific expertise of the operator; currently, only 13 of the 75 clinics are licensed to provide treatment services by way of ICSI. Moreover, the opportunities for pre-implantation genetic selection – a technique which, itself, poses a number of moral issues (discussed further below at para 6.26) – are greatly reduced; a matter of particular concern when the quality of the sperm, which is now enjoying a non-competitive existence, is, itself, suspect. As a result, most academic embryologists have been adopting a cautious attitude to the new techniques.[13]

3.11 Leaving aside any aspects of family law which depend upon marital status, and excluding any consideration of the moral value of marriage, it is tempting to conclude that uncomplicated AIH and AIP give rise to no major legal, status or ethical problems of themselves; the procedures will only be regarded as questionable if there is objection to *any* interference with nature in this area. This, however, is something of a simplistic view as AIH can be used for reasons other than compromised fertility in the male and its morality may then be questionable. Pre-eminent among these is the use of AIH as a preliminary to selection of the sex of the conceptus and we discuss this as a separate matter below.

---

11 Six months cohabitation has been suggested as the minimum for the purposes of the current Civil Partnerships Bill 2001 – but this is a retrospective assessment whereas, in the present context, it is the future which matters to a resultant child.
12 For which see para 3.42 below. The techniques can be combined with ZIFT (zygote intrafallopian transfer).
13 See S Mayor 'Technique for Treating Infertility may be Risky' (1996) 313 BMJ 248.

3.12   Otherwise, the major issue raised by AIH lies in the possibility of 'sperm banking' for use by a woman after her husband's or partner's death. There are obviously times when a woman whose partner is in a high-risk profession might wish to have this done, while semen may be available from 'banking' prior to testicular ablation, say, during treatment of malignant disease. The process has a specific moral relevance as to the effect on the child born into a single parent family.[14] Legally, it could lead to complex problems in relation to probate and succession.[15] The dilemma has been only partially resolved by the Human Fertilisation and Embryology Act 1990, s 28(6)(b) of which states baldly that where the sperm of a man, or any embryo the creation of which was brought about with his sperm, is used after his death, he is not to be treated as the father of the child.[16] It is to be noted that the process is not prohibited – indeed, Sch 3, para 2(2) allows for the relevant consent from the man prior to his death; however, the original government White Paper[17] made it clear that it was to be discouraged and both the statutory authority and the clinics themselves will take this into account in any cases that come within their ambit – the indications are that a significant proportion of clinics disapprove the process.[18]

3.13   That, however, is not the end of the story as the proactive procedure of sperm banking can be extended to the retroactive, and rather more macabre, practice of sperm recovery from a partner who is either dead or is irreversibly comatose. The major relevant case in the United Kingdom is that of Mrs Blood,[19] a case which has wide implications and one that merits consideration in some depth.[20] In essence, Mr Blood was the victim of

---

14 Posthumous insemination would not be lawful in France where both the donor and the recipient must be in stable partnerships at the time consent is given – Loi no 94-564, Article 10. For discussion, see M Latham 'Regulating the New Reproductive Technologies: A Cross-Channel Comparison' (1998) 3 Med L Internat 89.
15 Although these do not seem insuperable in the United States: *Woodward v Commissioner of Social Security* 435 Mass 536 (2002).
16 The 1990 Act leaves open the related questions of the man who is reported missing but is, in fact, dead and of the woman who reasonably believes her dead partner to be alive – we think it is likely that legal paternity could be established in either case.
17 *Human Fertilisation and Embryology: A Framework for Legislation* (Cm 259).
18 E Corrigan, S E Mumford and M G R Hull 'Posthumous Storage and Use of Sperm and Embryos: Survey of Opinion of Treatment Centres' (1996) 313 BMJ 24. In an unusual recent case, which is also of interest as to the meaning of 'undue pressure', a clinic actually put pressure on a man to withdraw his consent to posthumous use of his sperm; the court found, with regret, that he had done so: *Centre for Reproductive Medicine v U* [2002] EWHC 36 (Fam), (2002) 65 BMLR 92, [2002] Lloyd's Rep Med 93; the decision was upheld on appeal: [2002] EWCA Civ 565. It seems that there is far less opposition in, say, the United States: S M Kerr, A Caplan, G Polin et al 'Postmortem Sperm Procurement' (1997) 157 J Urol 2154. The process is forbidden under the generally positivist legislation of Victoria: Infertility Treatment Act 1995 (Vict), s 43.
19 *R v Human Fertilisation and Embryology Authority, ex p Blood* [1997] 2 All ER 687, (1997) 35 BMLR 1, CA.
20 For a very readable account of the case, see D Morgan and R G Lee 'In the Name of the Father? *Ex Parte Blood*: Dealing with Novelty and Anomaly' (1997) 60 MLR 840. For retrospective consideration in depth, see S A M McLean 'Creating Postmortem Pregnancies: A U.K. Perspective' (1999) Juridical Rev 323. The less satisfactory aspects of the case are examined in S J Treece and D Savas 'More Questions than Answers? R v Human Fertilisation and Embryology Authority, ex parte Blood *The Times* 7th February 1997' (1997) 3 Med L Internat 75.

meningitis. When he was in terminal coma, his wife requested, and obtained, a specimen of semen, which she hoped to use for insemination after his death.[21] There was some confusion – particularly in the expert evidence – as to whether he was or was not 'brain stem dead' at the time the specimen was taken[22] and, although it is, perhaps, not strictly germane to the present issue, the point has some general significance. If he were alive, removal of the specimen would, for example, have been treatment for a husband and wife together and, thus, beyond the requirements of a licence – aside from the difficulty of establishing that it was in 'his best interests' that it should be done,[23] there would have been nothing to stop his wife's immediate AIH.[24] Such an argument could not, however, be deployed once he was dead. In short, Mrs Blood's major hurdle was that her husband's semen was stored – ironically for the main purpose of establishing the legality of removing it – and this was unlawful in the absence of the consent of the sperm donor. The latter, to be 'effective', had to be given in writing and was subject to prior counselling – neither of which condition could be fulfilled. Accordingly – and in the face of something of a public outcry[25] – the HFEA held that the storage of the specimen was, and its use would be, unlawful; furthermore, the Authority declined to exercise its discretion to allow the gametes to be exported to another country where treatment could be given in the absence of the donor's written consent.

3.14 Mrs Blood applied for judicial review of this decision but her application was dismissed, Sir Stephen Brown P holding that the HFEA was, effectively, following the will of Parliament; more specifically, he judged that EC law did not assist the applicant. The Court of Appeal agreed with the High Court decision in so far as treatment in the United Kingdom was concerned. It did, however, conclude that, in failing to exercise its discretion to facilitate treatment abroad, the HFEA had not been properly advised as to the importance of EC law in relation to cross-border treatment and had been over-concerned with the creation of an undesirable precedent – something which was impossible given the ruling that the original storage was illegal in the absence of written consent. The case was, therefore, remitted to the Authority, who exercised their discretion in the light of the further evidence adduced in the Court of Appeal.[26]

3.15 In the end, then, *Blood* does nothing to alter or to ease the effect of existing domestic law and the almost palpable anxiety of the court to support Mrs Blood's quest for reproductive freedom has been the subject of considerable

21 As already noted, requests for posthumous *recovery* of sperm are not all that uncommon. Something of the order of 4% of American and Canadian fertility clinics were found to have undertaken the procedure: (1997) 125 Bull Med Ethics 5.
22 See chapter 13 for discussion of 'brain stem death'. It is generally agreed that Mr Blood was *not* dead when his sperm was extracted.
23 It is an assault to touch a person who is incapable of consenting unless, among other possibilities, it is in his or her best interests to do so: *Re F (mental patient: sterilisation)* [1990] 2 AC 1, sub nom *F v West Berkshire Health Authority* [1989] 2 All ER 545. The law's ability to recognise best interests in an ever widening circle of circumstances is a continuing theme in this book.
24 Accepted by Lord Woolf in the Court of Appeal [1997] 2 All ER 687 at 696, (1997) 35 BMLR at 23.
25 Well described by P R Ferguson 'Posthumous Conception: Blood and Gametes' 1997 SLT 61.
26 Following some minor administrative hiccups, Mrs Blood was delivered of a son by caesarian section on 11 December 1998.

academic criticism.[27] One positive result of the case was the setting-up of a review of the consent provisions in the Human Fertilisation and Embryology Act 1990 which reported in 1998.[28] In general, the report recommended the retention of the status quo. Two major alterations to the Act were, however, suggested – first, that the Authority should have the power to waive the consent restrictions on storage of gametes when it was in the best interests of an incompetent donor that they should be removed[29] and, second, that s 28(6) of the Act should be amended so as to allow the child to acknowledge its deceased father – albeit while retaining the existing law as to inheritance.[30] No action has, however, been taken at the time of writing.[31]

3.16 Yet a further legal problem could arise were nullity of the marriage to be mooted – as it could well be in some circumstances calling for AIH. Use of the procedure does not, however, constitute consummation of marriage and a decree of nullity can still be obtained if a woman conceives in this way; any children would still be regarded as legitimate on the grounds that the parents were married at the time of conception. Approbation might, however, preclude the granting of such a decree.[32]

3.17 A somewhat bizarre application of AIH relates to long-term prisoners whose wives may wish, or need on the grounds of age, to conceive before their release. A relevant case has recently been heard in the Court of Appeal[33] in which it was held that the justifiable withdrawal of conjugal rights which was inherent in imprisonment could include a denial of access to artificial insemination. However, the principle of proportionality applies and it was held that exceptional circumstances could require the consequences of imprisonment to yield to the European Convention on Human Rights;[34] the policy whereby the Secretary of State judges each case on its merits was considered to be neither in breach of the Convention nor irrational or unlawful.[35] In an interesting obiter opinion, Lord Phillips thought that the starting point for exceptional circumstances could be when the founding of a family was prevented absolutely rather than delayed by a refusal to grant facilities for insemination.[35a]

---

27 For example, M Brazier 'Hard Cases Make Bad Law?' (1997) 23 J Med Ethics 341.
28 S A M McLean *Review of the Common Law Provisions Relating to the Removal of Gametes and of the Consent Provisions in the Human Fertilisation and Embryology Act 1990* (1998).
29 C Strong 'Ethical and Legal Aspects of Sperm Retrieval after Death or Persistent Vegetative State' (1999) 27 J Law Med & Ethics 347 argues that the practice could be acceptable given it was in accord with reasonably inferred autonomous agreement during life. Interestingly, Strong noted that there had been at least 90 reported relevant cases in the United States.
30 For a comparative analysis, see R Atherton '*En Ventre sa Frigidaire*: Posthumous Children in the Succession Context' (1999) 19 LS 139.
31 The Human Fertilisation and Embryology (Amendment) Bill 2000 lapsed with the dissolution of Parliament. The Human Fertilisation and Embryology (Deceased Fathers) Bill 2001 was 'talked out'.
32 *REL v EL* [1949] P 211, [1949] 1 All ER 141 (see also *G v G* 1961 SLT 324).
33 *R (on the application of Mellor) v Secretary of State for the Home Department* [2001] EWCA Civ 472, [2001] 3 WLR 533, (2001) 59 BMLR 1.
34 Per Lord Phillips MR at [45]. See now Human Rights Act 1998, Sch 1, Articles 8 and 12.
35 The Court noted that the European Commission on Human Rights had already approved this possibility in *ELH and PBH v United Kingdom* (1997) 91A D & R 61.
35a At [68].

Primary sex selection

3.18 Public concern has been aroused in recent years by the entry into the market place of preconception sex selection of children. Most methods claiming scientific respectability depend upon altering the proportion of male- and female-bearing spermatozoa in the ejaculate and artificial insemination with the processed specimen. Opinions differ as to whether such methods are efficient and to what extent they can be relied upon but interest in the topic has been galvanised by recent claims of accuracy of the order of 90 % – together with the forecast of a clinic opening in Scotland.[36] The efficiency of the method is not, however, our main concern. What calls for analysis is the ethical position in the event that a reasonably efficient method of sex selection at conception becomes available.[37] Discussion is then at two levels – the practical and the deontological. The fact that both are highly culture-dependent – with a very evident east/west divide – deserves emphasis. Thus, at the practical level, it is probably fair to say that preconception sex selection would have, at most, a negligible effect on the distribution and status of the sexes in the United Kingdom. But this is essentially a Western view and one which might well not be true of countries in the Far East – indeed, the gender balance has become dangerously unstable in parts of India where health carers who practise a post-conception sex determination service are now liable to have their licences revoked.[38] On the ethical plane, very few, it is supposed, would oppose primary sex selection for the prophylaxis of X-linked disease.[39] Similarly, even those concerned to minimise embryonic and fetal rights would see 'sperm sorting' as being morally preferable to secondary sex selection by way of embryo selection or abortion.

3.19 Beyond this, sex selection for non-medical or social reasons has been classed as anything from 'playing God' to offering an acceptable new dimension to family planning.[40] The latter view cannot be rejected out of hand – it is difficult to see why family design should not be refined in this way when so much family planning of other sorts is practised and encouraged. This, however, presupposes that the method is perfected and, whatever proportion of choice is ultimately effected, it can never be 100 %. There is bound to be a residue of couples who have been to considerable expense and discomfort to select the sex of their child and who will be bitterly disappointed when their wishes are unfulfilled; thus, we foresee a possibly disastrous outcome for some 30% of children currently born using this technique. It follows that, in contrast to other

36 Scottish views, in the form of media interviews, are given in S McLean and K Mason 'The Great Baby Debate ... Viewed from Both Sides' *Sunday Herald*, 8 July 2001, p 11.
37 The Lancet 'Jack or Jill?' (1993) 341 Lancet 727 – which indicates that responsible UK medical opinion is not wholly dismissive of the practice.
38 G Mudur 'Indian Medical Authorities Act on Antenatal Sex Selection' (1999) 319 BMJ 401. A ban has also been imposed in Turkey: B Arda 'Ethics and the Commercial Use of Genetics' (1995) 111 Bull Med Ethics 19. In Bihar, the current female:male ratio of 600:1000 is probably the lowest in the world: K Kusum 'Sex Selection' in C Sureau and F Shenfield (eds) *Ethical Aspects of Human Reproduction* (1995).
39 See para 6.5 below.
40 This seems to be the view of the Dutch Health Council – the reproductive freedom of parents should be respected: 'Sex Selection for Non-medical Reasons' (1996) 119 Bull Med Ethics 8.

forms of reproductive liberty,[41] primary sex selection poses a real threat of harm to a resultant child; an equally distasteful increase in the number of 'social' abortions might also result. For these reasons alone, we advocate a legal limitation of 'gender clinics' to those licensed to undertake the practice; the potential consequences for individual children – and, perhaps, for society by way of a 'eugenic wedge'[42] – are too serious for the process to be left unsupervised.[43]

Donor insemination

3.20 Donor insemination introduces two additional concepts into the management of infertility. First, the procedure escapes the confines of a private matter between two persons in a close emotional relationship; rather, it involves a third party whose contribution lies at the heart of the enterprise. Secondly, sperm donation inevitably results in the production of a gross excess of gametes and, consequently, to the creation of options for their storage and later use. Ideally, therefore, all forms of DI should be subject to control but, effectively, this is as impossible as is the control of natural insemination. Once again, there has been some concern as to how the 1990 Act recognises this fact. In this respect, we have seen already that the wording of s 4(1)(b) clearly excludes the need for a licence when carrying out simple AIH or AIP; whether or not it also excludes DI undertaken within a stable relationship is, however, less obvious. The solution seems to lie in the fact that the section must be interpreted along with the meaning of treatment services which are defined in s 2(1) as 'services provided to the public or a section of the public'. It is not immediately apparent – at least to one of the authors – why an individual should not be regarded as 'a section of the public'. Nevertheless, it is widely agreed that, taken together, ss 2(1) and 4(1)(b) combine to exclude 'do-it-yourself' or 'private' inseminations from the strictures of the Act and that this is irrespective of whether the sperm used is that of a husband, a partner or a donor.

3.21 Control of a public insemination programme is, however, both desirable and possible and, to this end, the use of a man's sperm – and, conversely, the use of a woman's eggs – has been classed as one of the two *treatment services*, as defined in s 2, which are permitted only in pursuance of a licence – the other includes, broadly, any treatment which involves the creation of an embryo outside the human body and, hence, is almost entirely a matter of management of childlessness due to abnormality in the woman.[44] Ultimately, the legality and morality of donor insemination and ovum donation[45] depend on the consent of the owners of the gametes to their use; consent provides the plinth on which control is based and its form is detailed in the 1990 Act, Sch 3.

41 D McCarthy 'Why Sex Selection should be Legal' (2001) 27 J Med Ethics 302 makes a powerful case for the onus being with those who oppose sex selection to show that its restriction would be a restriction of liberty that could not reasonably be rejected.
42 A phrase borrowed from T Marteau 'Sex Selection' (1993) 306 BMJ 1704.
43 The Human Fertilisation and Embryology Authority has no control so long as the sperm is not stored and the process is carried out in private for the benefit of a man and woman together. Licensed clinics should not, however, select the sex of embryos for social reasons, nor should they use sperm sorting techniques in sex selection: HFEA *Code of Practice* (2001, 5th revision) paras 9.9 and 9.10.
44 1990 Act, ss 1(2), 3(1)(a) and 4(1)(b).
45 See para 5.46 below.

3.22 In summary, so-called 'effective consent' must be in writing and can apply to the use, storage and/or disposal of gametes. Thus, gametes cannot be used or received other than in accordance with the terms of an effective consent (Sch 3, para 5) and this extends to the use of any embryo created from those gametes (Sch 3, para 6); a consent to storage of gametes – which is, itself, governed by the clinic's possession of a 'storage licence' (s 11(b)) – must specify the maximum period of storage[46] and, again, this applies to any embryo so formed (Sch 3, para 8); and, thirdly, the person giving consent must specify what is to be done with the gametes or created embryos in the event that he or she dies or becomes incapacitated (Sch 3, para 2(b)). In addition, the donor must be given adequate information and must be counselled before consenting (Sch 3, para 3).

DI and the marital bond

3.23 Notwithstanding the restrictions imposed by the consent requirements, there are those who object strongly to DI on the grounds that the basis of the marriage bond is compromised by the wife's pregnancy through another man. It is supposed that the privity of marriage is invaded and that, in this respect, DI is little different from adultery.

3.24 The question of whether DI constitutes adultery in legal terms was debated in the Scottish case of *MacLennan v MacLennan*,[47] where it was determined that adultery could not be held to have taken place because there was no sexual contact between the woman and the donor. This approach to the question would probably be acceptable now throughout the common law jurisdictions. DI without the consent of the husband may, however, be taken as constituting cruel and unreasonable conduct for divorce purposes. Given the consent of both parties, the acceptance of DI can be seen as the fulfilment of the perfectly legitimate desire to have a child to care for. The very fact of agreement to the process testifies to the strength of the bond between the parties – and this is confirmed by the comparatively low incidence of divorce in couples who have chosen DI. The marital bond is disturbed by the procedure only in a metaphysical sense and this disturbance is, in any event, actively sought by the couple.

3.25 This is not to recommend that DI be undertaken lightly. Ill considered donation can lead, inter alia, to unfortunate anatomic incompatibilities between the social parents and the resulting child and to the transmission of both genetic and sexually transmitted disease; in addition, it may promote some aspects of eugenic selection that are, at least, of questionable morality.[48] In the United Kingdom, it is now illegal to provide a public treatment service involving the use of a man's sperm without a licence to do so; counselling as to its psychological and legal implications is an integral part of the process.

---

46 They cannot, normally, be stored for longer than ten years (1990 Act, s 14(3)). An exception may be made if the person seeking storage was under 45 years of age when the gametes were placed in storage and the other conditions laid down in regulation have been satisfied. These include the fact that the special circumstances arose *after* storage began (Human Fertilisation and Embryology Act (Statutory Storage Period) Regulations 1991, SI 1991/1540).
47 1958 SC 105.
48 These risks have, of course, been recognised for some time: C L R Barratt and I D Cooke 'Risks of Donor Insemination' (1989) 299 BMJ 1178.

Major ethical problems

3.26 It is probably fair to say that the major ethical problems associated with DI have been eliminated from the standard husband and wife or heterosexual partnership situations. It can, however, happen that a single woman requests DI or the request may come from a lesbian couple. Since there is no legal regulation of the matter, a doctor will have to decide on ethical grounds alone whether or not to proceed in these circumstances.

3.27 The Royal College of Obstetricians and Gynaecologists gives some answer to this in the guidelines it has laid down for its members. These recommend that DI be performed only on a married woman and, then, with the consent of her husband in writing. Some would say that this is excessively conservative; a single woman may feel precisely the same desire for a child as a married woman and should have the same access to a child as has her married counterpart. The same argument may be put forward on behalf of the homosexual woman, whether she is living by herself or with a partner. Should the experience of giving birth and raising a child be denied in either case because of the absence of a husband? Why should society exclude the possibility of conception in this way when it allows such women to conceive by normal means and permits them to keep their children as a normal right of parenthood?[49]

3.28 Artificial insemination is not, however, a natural process and it usually involves the medical profession. In participating in the process of procreation, the doctor is performing an act which is not morally neutral. Even if the principal objective of DI is to satisfy the desire for a child, thought has to be given to the child who is the end result; most would hold that the child's interests should be considered paramount – and that this holds throughout the spectrum of assisted reproduction.[50] The doctor must, therefore, question whether he should play a part in the deliberate creation of a child who could be disadvantaged as compared with his peers who have fathers. Whether or not such disadvantage – including any disadvantages of lesbian parenthood – are real or imaginary is undecided[51] and is, perhaps, indeterminable, for there are probably proportionately as many good and bad homes regularised by church or state as there are occupied by single parents.

3.29 The 1990 Act, s 13(5) emphasises the importance of this particular problem by specifying consideration of 'the need of the child for a father' as

---

49 A comprehensive survey of lesbian claims to DI, including empirical evidence as to the effect on children of being raised in a lesbian ambience is to be found in P Baetens and A Brewaeys 'Lesbian Couples Requesting Donor Insemination: An Update of the Knowledge with Regard to Lesbian Mother Families' (2001) 7 Human Repro Update 512. Some have cast doubt on the motivation of single women seeking DI: eg S Jennings 'Virgin Birth Syndrome' (1991) 337 Lancet 559.
50 D Giesen 'Developing Ethical Public Policy on Reproduction and Prenatal Research: Whose Interests Deserve What Protection?' (1989) 8 Med Law 553.
51 For review, see S Golombok and J Rust 'The Warnock Report and Single Women: What About the Children?' (1986) 12 J Med Ethics 182. In general, see M B King and P Pattison 'Homosexuality and Parenthood' (1991) 303 BMJ 295. The Committee of Inquiry into Human Fertilisation and Embryology (Dame Mary Warnock, Chairman) (Cmnd 9314) (hereafter referred to as Warnock) was unable to conclude any more firmly than that it is, as a general rule, better for children to be born into a two-parent family (at para 2.11).

one of the welfare principles to be satisfied before treatment is given under licence. In support of this, HFEA's *Code of Practice*[52] lists four major factors which clinics should take into account when people seek treatment using donated gametes – including such vagaries as the possible attitudes of other members of the family to the resulting child. The onus on the doctor is, therefore, considerable. We, ourselves, would fall back on the distinction we have already made between social and medical treatments. It is open to a fertile single woman, whether hetero- or homosexual, to have a child by natural means. Professional intervention in such circumstances, if any, is unarguably a matter of social, rather than medical, expedience; we doubt if a doctor ought to confuse his role as a therapist with that of a social worker or political economist – despite the manifestly interventionist attitude adopted by HFEA, the decision and its solution should be left to the woman herself.[53] On the other side of the coin, s 38 of the 1990 Act now relieves the doctor who conscientiously objects to such procedures of a duty to act. The discussion is, however, more germane to those forms of assisted reproduction which depend wholly upon medical expertise.[54] HFEA's *Code of Practice* has no legal force per se but, in the event of litigation, its terms would almost certainly be taken to represent 'good medical practice' and renewal of a licence would undoubtedly be prejudiced were its recommendations to be flouted (1990 Act, s 25(6)). As a result, clinics are likely to be restrictive rather than liberal in their acceptance of unattached or homosexual patients.

Legal considerations

3.30 The legal position of the child born as a result of AID has been established in the United States and in many parts of the Commonwealth for some time.[55] The situation in the United Kingdom is now governed by the 1990 Act which repeals the Family Law Reform Act 1987, s 27 and, at the same time, resolves the anomalies previously extant between England and Wales and Scotland.

3.31 Section 28(2) covers the case of the married woman. In essence, the rule is that, given she has been inseminated with the sperm of a man other than her husband, and provided that her husband has consented, he will be treated as the father of the child; s 28(4) emphasises that, in these circumstances, no other person is to be treated as the father of the child and the donor is covered against withdrawal of consent by the husband by s 28(6)(a).[56] The s 28(2) rule is voided if the husband can show that he did not, in fact, consent to the procedure. The frankly confusing terms of s 28(5) do, however, retain the

---

52 See para 3.6 above at para 3.14.
53 This is clearly the situation in the United States. There was apparently no difficulty in recruiting 26 single women without partners who were willing to undergo a definite research project involving pregnancy by DI: A J Peters, B Hecht, A C Wentz and R Jeyendram 'Comparison of the Methods of Artificial Insemination and the Incidence of Conception in Single Unmarried Women' (1993) 59 Fertil Steril 121.
54 See para 3.40 below.
55 Eg Artificial Conception Act 1985 (W Australia); Status of Children (Amendment) Act 1984 (Vict); Artificial Conception Act 1984 (NSW). See also Children's Status Act 1987 (RSA); Uniform Parentage Act (1973) (USA).
56 This section also applies to inseminations done privately (or 'DIY' inseminations). There is, of course, nothing to prevent a man claiming paternity under the common law: *X v Y* (2002) GWD-344, 29 March, Glasgow Sheriff Court.

common law principle of *pater est quem nuptiae demonstrant*; thus, the husband who does not consent to DI will still have to rebut that presumption by way of accepted methods of paternity testing. It is to be noted that the statutory provisions will prevail in the event of disagreement between the partners.[57] Section 29(4) preserves the somewhat archaic exclusion of hereditary titles, honours and the like from the general principles attaching to the AID child – although where the onus of proof or disproof of patrilinearity then lies or, indeed, how it can be discharged is a matter for speculation. An exception of greater practical importance is that, by virtue of Sch 4, para 8, ss 27–29 of the 1990 Act do not apply for the purposes of restricting live organ transplants between persons not genetically related (Human Organ Transplants Act 1989, s 2).

3.32 Section 28(3) extends the responsibilities and privileges of fatherhood to the woman's partner subject, first, to the insemination being carried out in a licensed clinic and, secondly, to their seeking treatment 'together' – a matter we have already touched upon in relation to unlicensed treatment. Despite the similarity of the wording in ss 4(1)(b) and 28(3)(a), its use in the latter carries rather more practical significance. Although it may be the result of no more than selective publicity, it is, in many ways, surprising how many of these cases result in acrimony. The question of 'fatherhood' then becomes central to the dispute and its solution may depend upon the interpretation of 'treatment together'. It is unsurprising that the matter has been debated in the courts. Does it mean 'together' in a spatial sense – ie that the woman and the man are physically present in the clinic? – or does it, perhaps, mean that both the woman and the man are receiving treatment? – in which case, it is reasonable to ask what 'treatment' the man is being given other than emotional support. The latter interpretation was clearly in the mind of Johnson J when he said:

> It seems plain to me that the subsection envisages a situation in which the man involved himself received medical treatment, although ... I am not sure what treatment is envisaged.[58]

3.33 This, however, seems an improbable Parliamentary intention and the question was aired more thoroughly by Wilson J in *U v W*.[59] In this bizarre case, a woman conceived and bore twins as a result of micromanipulation of her ova and the sperm of an anonymous donor, the process having failed when using the semen of her partner. U applied to have her partner declared the father of the twins by virtue of the 1990 Act, s 28(3)(a).[60] In the process of deciding the meaning of the suspect wording, Wilson J rejected the tentative interpretation offered in *Re Q* and opined:

> [W]hat has to be demonstrated is that, in the provision of treatment services with donor sperm, the doctor was responding to a request for that form of treatment made by the woman and the man as a couple, notwithstanding the absence in the man of any physical role in such treatment.[61]

---

57 *Re CH (contact: parentage)* [1996] 1 FLR 569.
58 In *Re Q (parental order)* [1996] 1 FLR 369 at 371.
59 *U v W (A-G intervening)* [1997] 2 FLR 282, (1997) 38 BMLR 54.
60 See para 3.32 above.
61 (1997) 38 BMLR 54 at 66. Wilson J also drew attention to the terms of the optional acknowledgment of paternity suggested in what is now Annex E of the HFEA *Code of Practice*.

3.34 In short, this judgment confirms the generally held view[62] that the purpose of the words 'treatment … together' is, as we have already seen, in s 4(1)(b) to exclude AIH or AIP from the restrictive terms of the 1990 Act and, in s 28(3), to ensure legal paternity of the child born to a woman and her bona fide partner as a result of DI conducted in a licensed clinic.[63] In conferring parenthood on a man who, otherwise, has neither genetic nor legal claim to that status, s 28(3) represents a remarkable advance in legislation and it is, in many ways, surprising that the Act makes no simultaneous attempt to define a 'partner' – indeed, it does not mention the word.[64] *U v W* suggests that whether or not a couple 'qualify' for s 28(3) status is a matter to be determined on the facts[65] – although there is nothing to stop responsible bodies fixing their own arbitrary limits in other situations.[66] Clearly, however, considerable responsibility devolves to the clinic which has wide discretion as to the choice of 'suitable' parents.[67]

3.35 It will be seen, therefore, that, in normal circumstances, the child conceived by DI within the married state is spared the potential, even if vestigial, disadvantages of illegitimacy and the position of the child born out of wedlock is secured. The 1990 Act makes no specific mention as to the registration of the birth of the child but, again, this appears to be clarified by implication. Section 29(1) states that the treatment in law of a woman's husband as the father of a child resulting from consensual donor insemination is 'for all purposes' – and this must include the registration of births and marriages. At the same time, it is clear that the consent provisions of the Act, in particular, are capable of creating a class of children who are legally fatherless and this must be a matter for criticism.[68]

3.36 This is compounded by the near absolute freedom from parental responsibility conferred on the donor by s 28(6)(a) of the 1990 Act, which specifically excludes him from paternity.[69] Anonymity of the donor is now

---

62 And that expressed by Bracewell J in *Re B (parentage)* [1996] 2 FLR 15.

63 U, in fact, failed in her bid to impose paternity on W because the procedure was not carried out in a clinic licensed in the UK. The restriction was held not to constitute an infringement of the European Convention on Human Rights, Article 59. A comparison of *Blood* (see para 3.13) and *U v W* provides a nice example of the juggling which can accompany attempts to harmonise domestic and European Community law. The topic is, however, beyond the scope of this book.

64 This obviously concerned the Lord Chancellor during the debate on the Bill when he referred to 'the difficulty in distinguishing partners to stable relationships from more transitory ones': Official Reports, HL, 20 March 1990, col 209-10.

65 [1997] 3 WLR 739 at 749, (1997) 38 BMLR 54 at 66.

66 One railway company, for example, laid down two years as a period of partnership qualifying for family rebates: *Grant v South-West Trains Ltd* [1998] All ER (EC) 193, [1998] 1 FLR 839.

67 HFEA *Code of Practice* (2001) Part 3.

68 For case law, see *Re Q (parental order)* [1996] 1 FLR 369.

69 It will be seen from what has already been said that the donor could, for example, be seen as the legal father if he provides a specimen for insemination of an unmarried couple by an unlicensed practitioner. Anonymity in Europe ranges from absolute in France to a child's right to identify his or her father on reaching maturity in Sweden. For an interesting review of Swedish donors' attitudes, see K R Daniels, H L Ericsson and I P Burn 'The Views of Semen Donors Regarding the Swedish Insemination Act 1984' (1998) 3 Med L Internat 117. Surprisingly, opposition to lifting the veil was found as much, if not more so, among the families and doctors as among the donors.

subject to the licensing authority keeping a register of identifiable individuals who have been treated, whose gametes have been stored or used and who were, or may have been, born as a result of treatment services (s 31(2)). As a corollary to this, a person over the age of 18 years, or a person over 16 years old and intending to marry, may now require the licensing authority to establish whether he or she might have been born as a result of treatment services and, if so, to provide such information as to parentage as is required by regulation. The regulations cannot require the licensing authority to give any information as to the identity of a person whose gametes have been used and that prohibition will have retrospective force should it be revoked (s 31(5)).[70] We imagine that the type of available information will be limited to include, say, information as to the donor's ethnic type and genetic health.

3.37 Thus, on paper, anonymity for those who seek it seems to be adequately protected. Nevertheless, we have reservations as to the retention of names on the register. Apart from the fact that clandestine breach of confidentiality now seems to be an accepted feature of public administration, the mere fact that a list of names exists will be a source of inspiration to zealots in the cause of freedom of information. From the more specific aspect, a nominal register is held to be important to guard against the possibility of incest or of marriage within the prohibited degrees in later generations; the HFEA's *Code of Practice* dictates that, save in exceptional circumstances, no more than ten children should be fathered by one donor. The dangers, both real and imaginary, of such matings as a result of DI may be overstated; the disclosure provisions in the event of marriage are theoretically sound but may be an example of using a sledgehammer as a nutcracker. Outwith the intermarriage factor, claims are made that children have a right to know their true parentage and also that they have a strong psychological urge to do so;[71] much of the evidence for the latter is, however, anecdotal and no comparable study of children born by way of adultery has been, nor can be, made. If there *is* such pressure, the compromise of allowing access to limited information can only lead to frustration.[72] The frequently drawn analogy with adoption – in which there is a statutory right to discover a true genetic relationship[73] – is flawed. In the latter situation, some bonding with the true parents may have occurred; there is, at least in the 'stranger' process, no necessary genetic affiliation with either

70 Personal data relating to treatments under the 1990 Act are exempt from the subject access provisions of the Data Protection Act 1998, s 7 except in so far as their disclosure is made in accordance with s 31. Disclosure can, however, be ordered by the courts in the interests of justice (s 34) and in the case of proceedings under the Congenital Disabilities (Civil Liability) Act 1976 or of comparable actions for damages in Scotland (s 35). The limited access to the records of a deceased person afforded to his or her personal representatives by the Access to Health Records Act 1990, s 3(1)(f) is unaffected.

71 See eg G D Mitchell 'In-vitro Fertilisation: The Major Issues – a Comment' (1983) 9 J Med Ethics 196. From Australia, L Waller 'The Law and Infertility – The Victorian Experience' in S McLean (ed) *Law Reform and Human Reproduction* (1991). A full review is in K O'Donovan 'What Shall We Tell the Children? Reflections on Children's Perspectives and the Reproduction Revolution' In R Lee and D Moran (eds) *Birthrights: Law and Ethics at the Beginning of Life* (1989).

72 Almost inevitably, the extent of the information to be provided is under challenge by way of the European Convention on Human Rights, Article 8 at the time of writing: *R (on the application of Rose) v Secretary of State for Health* [2002] EWHC 1593 (Admin), [2002] All ER (D) 398.

73 Adoption Act 1976, s 51; Adoption (Scotland) Act 1978, s 45(5).

adopting parent; and, pragmatically, disclosure of status is almost certain once the child requires to see his or her birth certificate. The *need* for the DI child to have the same discovery rights as the adoptee is, therefore, by no means self-evident.

3.38 Even so, as we have already noted,[74] the right to discover the identity of the donor has been recognised in some countries. Such a legal right was established in Sweden in 1985 but the legislation does not *require* children to be informed that they were conceived in this way. As a result, the 'right' depends on parental discretion and it seems that a considerable proportion of parents either choose not to tell their children the facts or claim to be putting the matter off until later.[75] Parents who have not revealed the fact of DI to their children may claim that this is to protect the child from hurt or distress, a motive that is supported by at least some evidence as to the psychological consequences of receiving this information.[76] The Government in the United Kingdom has now issued a consultation document with a view to deciding whether the existing provisions for donor anonymity should be abandoned.[77] Whatever decision is reached, any changes would apply only after the regulations had been altered; retrospective changes to the regulations are expressly prohibited by statute.[78]

3.39 Very few of us ever question our paternity and still fewer will doubt their maternity – for the same regulations apply to ovum donation[79] as to sperm donation; it seems to us that the almost inevitable result of regulating for a few to question their parentage will be to encourage the majority to do so. It is doubtful if the statutory creation of children anxiously awaiting their eighteenth birthday in order to exorcise an implanted suspicion can be to the overall benefit of family relationships. Occasionally – and particularly in the event of the reason for DI lying in a genetic abnormality in a woman's husband or partner – disclosure of true parentage may be highly desirable; such situations are, however, better met by good counselling within a responsible family environment.[80]

THE INFERTILE OR CHILDLESS WOMAN

3.40 Although we appreciate that treatment for childlessness is available to unmarried women[81] – whether or not they are single or living in a partnership

---

74 Para 3.36 above.
75 C Gottlieb, O Lalos and F Lindblad 'Disclosure of Donor Insemination to the Child: The Impact of Swedish Legislation on Couples' Attitudes' (2000) 15 Human Reproduction 2052. In Germany, a need for knowledge of the truth of one's heredity is so much ingrained in the national psyche that laws provide for compulsory examinations in order to obtain the evidence from reluctant parties:§372a of the German Civil Procedure Code (ZPO).
76 A J Turner and A Coyle 'What Does It Mean to be a Donor Offspring? The Identity Experiences of Adults Conceived by Donor Insemination and the Implications for Counselling and Therapy' (2000) 15 Human Reproduction 2041.
77 Department of Health *Providing Information about Gamete or Embryo Donors* (2001).
78 1990 Act, s 31(5).
79 See para 3.46 below.
80 For a novel approach to the dilemma, see S Wilson 'Identity, Genealogy and the Social Family: the Case of Donor Insemination' (1997) 11 Int J Law Pol Fam 270.
81 HFEA *Code of Practice*, paras 3.10 and 3.15a.

– the majority of requests for appropriate treatment are likely to come from married couples. It is in this sense that we speak of 'husband and wife' in what follows.

3.41 Childlessness due to abnormalities in the man is, as we have seen, largely a matter of the defective formation of spermatozoa. A woman may also suffer from primary infertility. In addition, however, she may be beset by anatomical problems which prevent her having children by natural means – of which, blockage of the fallopian tubes is the most important. The proportion of cases due to anatomical abnormality and to infertility resulting from faulty ovum production is about equal. We do not, here, discuss the purely medical treatment of the latter; its incidental legal and ethical significance is noted briefly below.[82] However, when hormonal treatment has failed, the anovular woman is in the same position as the azoospermic man and may be able to parent a child by way of gamete replacement; despite the fact that ova are far more scarce and are more difficult to handle than are spermatozoa, ovum donation is now a practical routine procedure. Even so, it is, perhaps fortunately, still impossible to develop a full-term fetus in a laboratory environment. Ovum donation is, therefore, pointless without, at the same time, providing a womb. Both may be contributed by the same woman or they may be available independently. These form the bases of the legal and moral problems complicating the treatment of the infertile woman. By contrast, childlessness due to various anatomic or physiological abnormalities must be treated according to its specific cause; the nature of the available procedures will become apparent as the chapter progresses.

In vitro fertilisation (IVF)

3.42 Many modern reproductive techniques involve the fertilisation of the ovum in laboratory – or in vitro – conditions and the subsequent transfer of the embryo[83] from the petri dish to the uterus. Strictly speaking, therefore, IVF and embryo transfer (ET) are technical terms. Nevertheless, popular usage equates IVF with the standard treatment for childlessness due to blockage of the fallopian tubes and ET with the implantation of an embryo which has no genetic relationship either to the recipient or to her husband. This apparently semantic distinction is, we believe, of practical importance. If damage is to be done to the embryo, one would anticipate it being most likely while being manipulated in transit – and this is a matter of general technique rather than of a specific therapy.

3.43 Standard IVF treatment involves collection of ova from the wife's abdomen, fertilisation of these with her husband's sperm in the laboratory

82 See para 3.69.
83 The *First Report of the Voluntary Licensing Authority for Human In Vitro Fertilisation and Embryology* (1986) p 8, recommended the use of the term pre-embryo to distinguish the organism before differentiation into fetal and placental cells has occurred. There is, thus, physiological justification for this. We, however, prefer not to use the term as, despite protestations to the contrary, it smacks of an attempt to make a moral distinction between the pre-embryo and the embryo – which we suggest is spurious and unnecessary. The interjection of pre-embryo as a stage in development is also inconsistent with the definition of an embryo as a two-cell zygote given in the 1990 Act, s 1(1).

and transfer of the resulting embryo to her uterus; the treatment is, therefore, essentially one designed to bypass diseased fallopian tubes. The actual collection of ova is now relatively simple through a laparoscope; the treatment cycle does, however, involve complex hormonal priming to ensure superovulation. This is important to the process as the success rate is greatly improved when more than one embryo is implanted; moreover, an excess is needed so as to ensure that the embryos inserted are normal. The mean live birth rate depends to an extent on the size and expertise of the treatment centre but is currently in the order of 21% of treatment cycles; clinical pregnancy rates vary from 9.5% when one embryo is transferred to 26% when three are implanted.[84] Thus, while IVF may well be the optional treatment for one of the commonest female causes of childlessness, the expectations of success are relatively low – an important point to be made when counselling childless couples. The pregnancy and live birth rates following IVF show no significant differences when related to the underlying reason for the treatment.

3.44 The rationale of the process corresponds closely to that of AIH and, as such, presents no problems in the field of family law. The genetic and natural parentage of the resulting infant are not disputed. All that has occurred is that a technique has been substituted for a natural process; if any would protest that this is in some way immoral, they would, at the same time, have to contend that the surgical treatment of any disease is similarly immoral. It is, however, apparent that IVF, by definition, involves the creation of an embryo outside the human body and is, therefore, unlawful if performed by a person who is not licensed to do so.

3.45 There is, of course, no technical reason why the sperm must be those of the husband and, in the event of combined male infertility and an impassable female genital tract, donor semen could be used in the same way. In such circumstances, the legal problems would be comparable to those of DI, which have been discussed above.[85]

Ovum donation

3.46 An alternative situation is that the ovum is donated by another woman. The need might arise as being the only way in which a woman with, say, abdominal adhesions could have children and it might be desirable in the event of a potential mother carrying an X-linked genetic disease; (see chapter 6) about 16% of childlessness for female reasons is due to ovarian failure and the ovaries may be destroyed during, say, treatment for cancer. The scenario is now that the donated egg is fertilised by the husband's semen and the embryo then transferred to the wife's womb. The process can, therefore, be looked upon as the female variant of DI. The obvious practical difference is that, whereas spermatozoa are plentiful and easily harvested, ova are scarce and

---

84 HFEA *Ninth Annual Report* (2000) Tables 4.7 and 4.8. There is no significant difference in pregnancy or birth rates when either 2 or 3 embryos are implanted but the triplet rate is unacceptably high in the latter event. As a result, the HFEA has limited the number of embryos inserted to 2 per cycle (press release 8 August 2001).
85 All of which presupposes that there are no errors. An interesting case in which black twins were born to a Caucasian couple is due to be litigated during publication of this book: O Dyer 'Black Twins are Born to White Parents after Treatment Mix-up' (2002) 325 BMJ 64.

their recovery involves some discomfort and inconvenience to the donor. Thus, the donor must be stimulated hormonally in order to coincide with the recipient's optimal menstrual state and, in many cases, a laparoscopy will be required. The difficulties, then, associated with ovum donation lie not only in the technique but, also, in finding the donors – the process is such that pure altruism generally provides not more than a fraction of the overall requirement. Ova may be obtained from women in the course of other surgery – in particular, during sterilisation. There is, however, some concern lest their consent may be flawed in that a measure of coercion in the form, say, of free treatment is often used; the International Federation of Gynecology and Obstetrics has, in fact, declared that the process is unethical.[86] Nevertheless, centres in the United Kingdom may still pursue such arrangements provided that very strict criteria as to counselling, management and consent are met. The policy is currently under review, as is that associated with the more common practice of 'egg sharing' – in which women who are, themselves, undergoing infertility treatment involving ovarian stimulation donate a proportion of their surplus ova for others to use; the HFEA has been persuaded of the value of the method and has, somewhat grudgingly, given its approval.[87] The difficulties associated with ovum donation or the delayed use of the patient's own ova are compounded by the fact that, in contrast to the storage of spermatozoa and early embryos, cryopreservation of ova is not proven to be entirely risk free in respect of induced chromosomal abnormality;[88] the HFEA has, however, sanctioned the use of stored ova in strictly controlled conditions.[89] An alternative, presently experimental, approach to the preservation of a woman's procreative capacity is to remove, store and, later, graft a portion of ovarian tissue; however, since the gametes within the ovary are immature, control of their use is outwith the remit of the HFEA.

3.47   Once fertilisation by the husband and implantation of a donated ovum has been achieved, however, the natural – though not the genetic – parentage will be reasonably clear. It is difficult to see any circumstances in which motherhood would be challenged[90] and, in a patrilineal society, there are fewer objections to an admixture of ovum-derived genes in the family than to those which arise as a result of DI. The matter is now put beyond legal doubt; s 27(1) of the 1990 Act follows pioneering Australian legislation[91] in holding

---

86 *Recommendations on Ethical Issues in Obstetrics and Gynecology* (1997) 133 Bull Med Ethics 8. See also the stringent restrictions in Canada under the Human Reproductive and Genetics Technologies Act 1996. The main problem is that of the woman developing the ovarian hyper-stimulation syndrome including the formation of ovarian cysts and the so-far unproven risks of more serious sequelae.

87 HFEA *Ninth Annual Report* (2000) p 28. Their reluctance derives, of course, from the implication of payment in kind when the treatment is given at reduced cost by way of recompense. Currently, direct payments of more than £15 (plus reasonable expenses) for gamete donation are disallowed.

88 Though it has to be noted that IVF using frozen embryos results in significantly lower pregnancy and live birth rates than when using fresh embryos: HFEA *Ninth Annual Report* (2000), Tables 4.1 and 4.13.

89 Currently, only two clinics are licensed to use frozen human eggs: HFEA Press Release 25 January 2000.

90 See *Ampthill Peerage* [1977] AC 547, HL, per Lord Simon at 577.

91 Status of Children (Amendment) Act 1984 (Vict). See also the Artificial Conception Act 1985 (W Aust) ss 5(1) and 7(1).

that a woman who carries a child as a result of the placing in her of an embryo or of sperm and eggs, and no other woman, is to be treated as the mother of the child.

3.48 But what of the similar wife with an infertile husband? Although such a combination might be regarded as too rare for consideration, it could, theoretically, arise in about one in every 400 marriages seeking children. Such a state can be managed by embryo donation whereby an embryo preformed from donated ovum and donated sperm is implanted in the infertile woman. The resultant complications then lie somewhere between those of in vitro fertilisation and those surrounding surrogate motherhood and are best discussed under that heading below. Even so, it is emotionally, morally and legally important to distinguish unrelated embryo transfer of this type from surrogate motherhood – the intense relationship between mother and fetus occurs in both but, in normal circumstances, does not progress to that between mother and child in the latter procedure.

3.49 Once again, the 1990 Act has cleared the legal air; by virtue of ss 27 and 28, the child born of embryo donation is, for all purposes, the child of the carrying mother and her consenting husband.

The availability of IVF

3.50 We have discussed some of the moral issues surrounding assisted reproduction under the heading of donor insemination. Very much the same principles apply in the case of the infertile wife. There is, however, one major difference – while DI is a relatively simple process, IVF and its counterparts are both cost- and manpower-intensive. Problems of resource allocation are, thus, superimposed on those of ethical practice.

3.51 The response to the question of whether the effort applied to the alleviation of childlessness is well- or mis-directed is such a personal matter that specific discussion would be invidious; the general principles of resource allocation are outlined in chapter 11 below. Whether IVF, in its broad sense, should be available to fertile couples depends upon the motivation.[92]

3.52 Simplistically, one could classify the possible reasons into medical and non-medical, although we will see that this is not the easy division that might be supposed. In essence, the ethics of embryo selection mirror those of sperm selection which we have discussed above save for the fact that we are now dealing with an organism which, *of itself*, has the potential for human development; put at its lowest level, the human embryo is deserving of *some* respect and protection in law.[93] There may be good medical reasons, mainly in relation to the carriage of abnormal recessive genes, which the likely

92 K Dawson and P Singer 'Should Fertile People Have Access to In Vitro Fertilisation?' (1990) 300 BMJ 167. For a very controversial and critical early review of the cost-effectiveness of the IVF programme, see M G Wagner and P A St Clair 'Are In Vitro Fertilisation and Embryo Transfer of Benefit to All?' (1989) 2 Lancet 1027.
93 Warnock Committee at para 11.17. See para 3.58 below for further discussion.

majority of persons would see as justifying appropriate intervention on behalf of otherwise fertile couples; indeed, IVF combined with preimplantation genetic diagnosis (PGD), may offer the *correct* management.[94] Non-medical reasons may be of several types, the extreme being, perhaps, that of sex selection as a matter of parental choice. The issue arose as something of a *cause célèbre* in 2000 when a couple wished to ensure the birth of a girl, having lost their only daughter in tragic circumstances.[95] IVF as a method of sex selection is discouraged, but not wholly excluded by the HFEA.[96] In this particular instance, no clinic could be found which was willing to undertake the case and Mr and Mrs Masterton may yet plead their case in the Court of Session. It will, however, be seen that the case demonstrates the difficulties of categorisation. If the parents can show that they are suffering from, say, a demonstrable reactive depression as a result of their loss, selective replacement of their child *becomes* a medical treatment and the moral high ground has shifted – though perhaps not far enough to justify disregard for the interests of the resulting child. Even so, there is a tenable case for holding that we should not pass judgment in respect of a personal dilemma which affects no-one else.[97]

3.53 Other 'non-medical' reasons for 'fertile IVF treatment' include the early removal of ova for use in later life, thus circumventing the increased risk of chromosomal abnormalities in the child of a late pregnancy, or, secondly, the wholly hedonistic use of 'womb-leasing' for social reasons. The latter is discussed below.[98] As to the former, there are no legal objections in the United Kingdom to preserving embryos in the same way as sperm and a case for women deliberately delaying their pregnancies can be made out on grounds of social utility. There are, however, practical difficulties. The problems introduced by limitations on the storage times for embryos have been alleviated to an extent since the maximum time was raised to ten years provided the storage was for treatment purposes. Even so, there are important conditions as to the clinical status of the gamete providers which restrict the concession to genuine cases of medical need and storage cannot continue beyond the 55th birthday of the woman involved; the limit remains at five years if these conditions are not met. Secondly, the risks of pregnancy itself rise dramatically with age – the maternal mortality rate over the age of 40 is some ten times that in the case of women aged 20-24.[99] Thirdly, the pregnancy rate following

---

94 For an excellent review of the advantages and shortcomings of PGD, see J R Botkin 'Ethical Issues and Practical Problems in Preimplantation Genetic Diagnosis' (1998) 26 J L Med & Ethics 17.

95 See, for example, K Scott 'IVF Selection Still Off Limits' *Guardian*, 19 October 2000.

96 HFEA *Code of Practice* (2001) para 9.9 says that Centres *should* not select the sex of embryos for social reasons (our emphasis). PGD for medical reasons is, of course, accepted. This restrictive attitude is not held universally: S Gottlieb 'US Doctors Say Sex Selection Acceptable for Non-medical Reasons' (2001) 323 BMJ 828. Interestingly, a Scottish survey indicated that only 8% of persons favoured giving parents the right to choose the sex of their unborn children: V Hannah 'Scots Reject Creation of Designer Children' *Herald*, 8 November 2000.

97 It is, of course, equally possible to argue that the deontological problem involved *is* a matter for public decision. We return to the remarkable importance – both legal and ethical – of *naming* a medical condition in chapter 21.

98 See para 3.72.

99 Editorial Comment 'Too Old to have a Baby?' (1993) 341 Lancet 344.

embryo transfer deteriorates with age[100] and , finally, the indications are that older women require the implantation of more embryos than do the young in order to achieve the same implantation rate.[101]

3.54 We discuss the concept of ageism later[102] and there is no doubt that there is, at least, emotional discrimination against the old that is based on little more than societal conditioning. Have we any moral right to discriminate against an older woman in denying her access to motherhood when we would provide the facilities without qualm to her younger sister in otherwise identical circumstances? It is difficult to support such a policy when the woman herself is providing the scarce resource – the eggs – as is the case in IVF provided for the premenopausal woman. The counter-argument depends, of course, on the effect on the consequent child and it is not difficult to dream up circumstances in which an 'ageing' mother could be seen as a disadvantage to a young child. Nevertheless, given that we would not consider depriving 40-year-old women of natural pregnancy, it seems paternalistic in the extreme to deny them assisted reproductive services on the grounds of age alone. It is for these reasons that we find it hard to support judicial acceptance of a health authority's decision not to purchase infertility services for women above the age of 35[103] – an age which, to one of us at least, appears to be that of golden youth! We might add here, in parentheses, that the same may not apply to the post-menopausal woman. Quite apart from the fact that, here, we are dealing with ovum donation – and, hence, with a publicly scarce resource – treatment in this case is not that of an unfortunate abnormality but is, rather, an interference with the natural order. Paternalism is, thus, excluded from the equation and we are free to concentrate entirely on the resultant child – and with good reason when we hear of a 62-year-old Frenchwoman giving birth to a child derived from her brother's sperm.[104] None the less, the British Medical Association has declared its antagonism to an age based limitation.[105]

---

100 Figures are not available for the use of frozen embryos. Otherwise, this statement appears to be true only when the woman is using her own eggs. The live birth rate in the case of women aged 40-44 is then only 5.4% as opposed to 17.2% when donor eggs are used. There is a similar trend in the case of AID. See also A Templeton, J Morris and B Parslow 'Factors that Affect Outcome of In Vitro Fertilisation Treatment' (1996) 348 Lancet 1402.

101 M G R Hull, C F Fleming, A O Hughes and A McDermott 'The Age-related Decline in Female Fecundity' (1996) 65 Fertil Steril 783. Despite all this, the Dutch are, apparently, prepared to provide IVF for older women: T Sheldon 'IVF Could be Offered to Older Women in the Netherlands' (1996) 312 Brit Med J 1319.

102 See chapter 12.

103 *R v Sheffield Health Authority, ex p Seale* (1994) 25 BMLR 1. It is to be noted that HFEA imposes age limits for gamete donors. In respect of *treatment*, gametes should not be taken from women over 35 and men over 55. Gametes must not be taken for treatment from persons below the age of 18. These limits may be relaxed when the gametes are to be used for self-treatment or in exceptional circumstances: *Code of Practice* (2001) paras 4.20–4.22.

104 C Bremner 'French Woman Aged 62 Has Brother's Baby' *The Times*, 21 June 2001, p 13. The procedure was carried out in California.

105 (1994) 308 BMJ 723. There seems little limit to human ingenuity in the 'new reproductive era'; a mother has taken the Tees Health Authority to task for not providing an unmarried-17 year-old with IVF: P Wilkinson 'Mother Demands IVF for Teenager' *The Times*, 13 November 1999, p 3.

3.55 As in the case of DI, the question of the child's well-being raises the question of the potential mother's status – single, lesbian or of doubtful suitability. Here, in contrast to the DI situation, medical involvement in the procedure is essential if it is to be undertaken; it follows that the doctor cannot opt out of judgments, despite the fact that they involve purely social values. It is for this reason that the guidelines for assisted reproductive treatment centres included, from an early stage, the establishment, and use, of an ethical committee which has a wide remit as to the management of individual cases. No legally enforceable principles as to selection of candidates for the limited resource have been laid down, although the *Code of Practice*, as we have noted, contains a number of arguably intrusive conditions. In the only apposite case so far reported, refusal of treatment on the grounds that the patient had a history of prostitution and had been rejected as an adopter, was not considered so questionable as to provide grounds for judicial review of the decision.[106]

3.56 Nor is there, in our opinion, a great deal of help to be obtained from the 1990 Act, s 13(5). This, as noted above under DI, states that a woman shall not be provided with treatment services unless account has been taken of the welfare of any child born as a result of the treatment and of any other child who may be affected by the birth. Not only is this condition extremely wide – *any* child within the extended family might be said to be affected – but it is imprecise as to the quality and depth of account to be taken other than subtly indicating a covert disapproval of treatment outside the 'married' state. Moreover, it seems to us to have its own dangers. 'Taking account of' does not imply reaching a uniform conclusion; it is not too far-fetched to envisage 'shopping expeditions' on the part of unconventional would-be mothers to identify the most 'liberal' clinic as a source of treatment.

The legal position of the clinician

3.57 All procedures involving gamete donation carry the risk that the gametes themselves are defective and, as we have seen, this is a major justification for controlling the treatment of childlessness. Moreover, all those involving in vitro embryo transfer introduce the additional hazard that the embryo will be damaged either by the hormonal treatment required for superovulation or during manipulation and that an abnormal fetus will result. Animal experiments indicate that there is no higher incidence of abnormalities in live born neonates resulting from reimplantation than in those which are conceived normally and reports of an excess of human cases beyond the probability of chance are very rare.[107] The HFEA's Annual Report of 2000 quoted 120 children born as a result of IVF, DI or micromanipulation having developmental defects or syndromes – an occurrence of 1.3% of babies born, which does not indicate

---

106   *R v Ethical Committee of St Mary's Hospital (Manchester), ex p H (or Harriott)* [1988] 1 FLR 512, [1988] Fam Law 165. The possibility was not foreclosed – the greater part of the argument turned on whether the Committee was purely advisory or whether it had administrative responsibility. The case was also somewhat clouded by allegations of deceit.

107   A disturbing report has, however, come from Australia recently: M Hansen, J J Kurinczuk, C Bower and S Webb 'The Risk of Major Birth Defects after Intractyoplasmic Sperm Injection and In Vitro Fertilization' (2002) 346 New Engl J Med 725. The incidence of defects is said to be twice that following normal conception.

any increased risk.[108] The outcome of litigation following such a misfortune would depend very largely on proof of causation. However, the ground rules are clear. Section 44 of the 1990 Act applies the Congenital Disabilities (Civil Liability) Act 1976, s 1 to infertility treatments in that, if a child resulting from embryo transfer, GIFT,[109] micromanipulation or DI is born disabled and the disability results from an act or omission in the course of the selection, or the keeping or use outside the body, of the embryo or the gametes used by a person answerable to the child, then the child's disabilities are to be regarded as damage resulting from the wrongful act of that person and actionable at the suit of the child. This does not apply if one or both parents knew of the risk of their child being born disabled; particular importance is, therefore, likely to attach to the effectiveness of their consent in respect of the information given. Interestingly, this seems to open the door to an action for 'wrongful life'.[110]

THE SURPLUS EMBRYO

3.58 It is inevitable that surplus embryos will be produced whether IVF or ovum donation is being attempted. The status and disposal of such embryos have significance which is independent of the problems of successful implantation.

3.59 The criminal law can be considered only to be dismissed. We will see later[111] that the fetus, even if it has legal significance, has no legal status. It is, therefore, inconceivable that the unimplanted embryo could be accorded any greater standing. We cannot see that any criminal offence is committed by their disposal so long as the method accords with standards of public decency.

3.60 That being so, the problem can be seen as being ethical in nature and one which turns on the nature of the embryo. The US Ethics Advisory Board agreed that the 'human embryo is entitled to profound respect' but qualified this: 'but this respect does not necessarily encompass the full legal and moral rights attributable to persons.' Similarly, as already noted, the Warnock Committee (at para 11.17) recommended only that the embryo of the human species should be afforded *some* protection in law. Such general prevarication indicates the measure of the moral difficulties involved but is, at the same time, unhelpful; in the end, one must come to a decision – either the embryo is a full human being within the rigid theological, perhaps mainly Roman Catholic, doctrine or it is a laboratory artefact.

---

108 The occurrence differs according to the method used – 0.9% for fresh IVF and 1.4% for DI. The rates are of the same order whether IVF is 'fresh' (0.9%) or involves the use of frozen embryos (1.2%).

109 I Kennedy and A Grubb *Medical Law* (3rd edn, 2000) p 1530 point out that GIFT may not be included by reason of the precise wording of the Section. We believe that, should it be questioned, it would be decided on the basis of 'Parliamentary intention' as per *R (on the application of Quintavalle) v Secretary of State for Health* [2002] EWCA Civ 29, [2002] 2 All ER 625, (2002) 64 BMLR 72, CA.

110 See para 6.34 below.

111 See para 5.30 below.

3.61 We have argued previously that humanity is not established until implantation – this being largely on the grounds that it is only at implantation that the embryo achieves a capacity for meaningful development.[112] The acceptance of a 'specific moment' theory as to the acquisition of humanity is, however, by no means universal; an alternative approach suggested by Poplawski and Gillett[113] is to regard the process of becoming a human person as 'a progression through a series of linked developmental stages' and to attribute rights to the embryo because it represents a phase in the whole human form. The authors went on to base this moral value on the human capacity to react with others – a capacity which exists in modified form from implantation to death. We find this approach helpful, if only in a negative way, because, despite the authors' disclaimer, none of this perfectly valid analysis applies to the embryo in vitro. In the absence of implantation, there is no continuum and there is no human interaction; moreover, no moral value can be attributed to the embryo by virtue of its potential for personhood – for no such potential exists in the medium of the petri dish.[114]

3.62 It therefore seems acceptable – and both kinder and more practical – to liken the in vitro embryo to a culture of human tissue. If one accepts this premise, one simultaneously solves one's moral problem as to embryonic research which, when well done, must be valuable to the community as a whole. Nevertheless, this conclusion cannot be accepted without qualification – at the very least, the embryo must be accorded the respect due to any living human tissue. It could be replied that, in logic, there is no need to control laboratory interference with a research object that one believes has no moral status; but there *is* public disquiet over scientific involvement in the reproductive process and, on these grounds alone, it must be contained within a controlling framework. Most importantly, the morality of the argument rests upon the limitations of current technology. It is clear that our formula would be inadequate should technology advance to the state of being able to 'grow' fetuses to full term in vitro; were this to happen, we would be confronted with the production of non-humanised human beings, which would be intolerable.

3.63 But, whenever one considers technical limitation as representing a barrier on the theoretical 'slippery slope', one inevitably asks: 'for how long will we be able to do so?'[115] For the present, the interests of the embryo/fetus are protected from encroachment by the 1990 Act, s 3(3)(a) which, in essence, makes it a criminal offence, punishable by up to ten years' imprisonment, to keep or use an embryo in vitro that is more than 14 days old – excluding any time spent in suspended animation while frozen. Even so, this specific time limit has been attacked by purists, mainly on the grounds that a 13-day embryo

112 For the argument based on 'ensoulment', see N M Ford *When Did I Begin?* (1988).
113 N Poplawski and G Gillett 'Ethics and Embryos' (1991) 17 J Med Ethics 62.
114 However, even if one concludes that the unimplanted surplus embryo has no moral value *of itself*, it could be that we should accord it *some* value on the grounds that it has considerable moral importance for others. This approach is sometimes referred to as 'transitivity of respect' – on which, see M A Warren *Moral Status* (1997) p 170.
115 As this section is being written, it is reported that competent researchers anticipate the availability of artificial wombs within a few years: R McKie 'Men Redundant? Now We Don't Need Women Either' *Observer*, 10 February 2002.

is no less alive than is one of 15 days' gestation and that it is entitled to the same respect – as is the embryo formed at fertilisation.[116] The counter-argument is that controlled embryonic research is essential if the attack on genetic disease – which may well be the most important single factor dictating morbidity in humans – is to be carried on in a scientifically acceptable way.

3.64 Given that the undeveloped in vitro embryo merits a certain, albeit unspecified, respect, its treatment presents a dilemma which exists in three major parts. The first is that of the use and, indeed, the production of embryos for research purposes; this highly emotive issue is discussed in chapter 30. The second is closely related and concerns the pre-implantation selection of embryos as potential neonatal therapeutic agents.

3.65 This subject has assumed importance comparatively recently and arises from the very real possibility of treating blood dyscrasias, haemoglobinopathies and related conditions either by bone marrow donation (which we consider briefly below at para 14.19) or by the use of stem-cell – or toti-potent embryonal cell – implants. We will see later that the success of such treatment depends very much on genetic compatibility which is generally sought by way of sibling donation. The possibilities then arise, firstly, of creating siblings for the express purpose of providing a donor and this, of itself, although impossible to regulate, raises ethical issues. Pre-implantation diagnosis, however, introduces the possible secondary refinement of selecting the best-match sibling from a number of embryos created by in vitro fertilisation. While such a procedure must be seen to have important therapeutic possibilities, it does, at the same time raise the moral stakes very considerably. Can we be said to be respecting human embryos if we create a number and discard all but one on the grounds that they are 'not good enough'? Are we justified in creating embryos with the avowed intention of destroying them? Are we to re-select at the fetal stage if a multiple pregnancy develops? Most importantly, this procedure adds a new dimension to the inherent problems surrounding pre-implantation genetic diagnosis in that it involves the creation of a child – and not of a child per se but, rather, as a therapeutic tool for the benefit of its sibling. Quite how the resultant child will accept this in later life is a matter for conjecture. Suppose, however, the treatment fails – as it may well do? We find this scenario rather more disturbing in relation to the child's future. No-one can fail to sympathise with parents of a sick child who are seeking its cure. Nevertheless, this must be an area where the advances provided by modern technology must be balanced against the coincident inroads to public morality.[117]

---

116 T Inglesias 'In vitro Fertilisation: The Major Issues' (1984) 10 J Med Ethics 32. The same issue contains a contrary view from a moralist: G R Dunstan 'The Moral Status of the Human Embryo: A Tradition Recalled' (1984) 10 J Med Ethics 38. See also M Lockwood (ed) *Moral Dilemmas in Modern Medicine* (1985) ch 1; and the philosophical argument in A Holland 'A Fortnight of My Life is Missing' (1990) 7 J Appl Philos 25. See also Giesen (1989) 8 Med Law 553. Inevitably, much of the basic discussion of the topic is now somewhat dated.

117 The HFEA have, in fact, given authority for such a procedure: http://news.bbc.uk/hi/english/health/newsid, 27 February 2002. Some measure of the dilemma can be seen in the 1990 Act, s 13(6) which states that, before providing treatment, account must be taken of the welfare of any child who may be born as a result and of *any other child who may be affected by the birth* (our emphasis). A further American case, related to Alzheimer's disease, was reported at much the same time: N Hawkes 'Woman Has Designer Baby Free of Disease Gene' *The Times*, 27 February 2002, p 6.

3.66 The third main aspect of embryonal status relates to the practical problems surrounding the disposal of embryos that are surplus to immediate therapeutic needs. As already mentioned, overproduction of embryos is inseparable from the treatment of infertility by IVF; it is impossible to guarantee receptive wombs for those which remain unused in the individual case and, in many instances involving defective embryos, it could be wrong to attempt to do so. It follows that any new legislation that attempted to criminalise the necessary destruction of embryos would, at the same time, effectively shut the door on this form of treatment. The United Kingdom stands virtually alone within Europe in that current legislation allows for the production of embryos for the express purpose of non-therapeutic experimentation. In fact, the disposal of gametes and embryos depends almost entirely on the consent and, hence, the decision of those donating the gametes. It follows that whether or not an embryo can be used for treatment or research or whether it is to be destroyed at a certain time or in certain circumstances – eg on the death of the donor – depends upon the agreed consent of the two progenitors (1990 Act, Sch 3, para 6). The 1990 Act, however, makes no provision for the condition most likely to cause difficulty – that is, when there is disagreement between the two parties concerned.

3.67 The need for some form of legislation is exemplified in two American cases, the first of which arose in Tennessee in 1989. Here, a married couple who had provided stored embryos were divorced before the latter could be used. The father asked that they be destroyed while the mother wished to become pregnant by them. The judge at first instance ruled that the embryos were human beings – with all the rights attending that status – and that their fate should, therefore, be decided on the principle of their best interests; this meant that they should be implanted. This decision was reversed by the State Supreme Court, which held that the man's interest in not reproducing outweighed those of his spouse in procreating.[118] In a more recent case, the New York Court of Appeal came down firmly in favour of the enforceability of a valid preconception contract[119] – but this assumes, firstly, that there is a contract and, secondly, that it is unambiguous. Our feeling always has been that similar problems will result from the British legislation and that it would be better for 'consent to disposal' to be vested in the person for whom the embryos were intended – that is, the proposed woman recipient.[120] Parliament's remarkable concern for the embryo, in the face of some 180,000 abortions performed annually in Great Britain, is difficult to understand. Our preferred solution to embryo disposal would, at least, remove the anomaly which gives powers of disposal to the father of an embryo but allows him no rights as to the survival of his fetus (see chapter 5) – while this is explicable on the grounds that the equality of parental interest has altered dramatically in the transition, it seems unnecessary to

---

118 *Davis v Davis* 842 SW 2d 588 (Tenn Sup Ct, 1992). The case was, however, clouded by the fact that Mrs Davis now only wanted to donate the embryos; the court recognised that the issue would have been closer had she still wanted to become pregnant.

119 *Kass v Kass* 696 NE 2d 174 (NY, 1998) where the issue turned very much on the interpretation of the couple's instructions – an example of how difficult the drafting of 'advance directives' of all sorts can be.

120 This has, indeed, now come to pass: F Gibb 'Separated Women Seek Right to Use Frozen Embryos' *The Times*, 12 September 2002, p 9. The case, involving two women whose partners have withdrawn their consent, is due to be heard during preparation of this book.

have introduced a complication.[121] In practice, the power of both gamete donors to decide the fate of the embryo is limited by statute – stored gametes must be destroyed at the end of ten years and embryos must be allowed to perish after five years' preservation (1990 Act, ss 14(3) and (4)) unless they are to be used for treatment in the special circumstances outlined in para 3.53. This, at least, sets a limit to the difficulties in estate planning and the like that are inherent within a permitted policy of indefinite preservation of embryos.[122]

3.68 Uterine lavage represents a somewhat unusual extension of the technique of IVF through embryo transfer. In this process, a fertile woman is impregnated with semen; the resultant embryo is washed out of the uterus before implantation and is transferred to the infertile patient. While such a process might be seen as constituting an abortion, for reasons discussed below (chapter 5), it is improbable that it would be considered so in the United Kingdom. The Warnock Committee looked at the matter from the point of view of the donor and concluded (para 7.5) that the risks were such that the technique of embryo donation by lavage should not be used at the present time. The method seems to us to be so comparable to the practice of animal husbandry that there are good policy reasons for its proscription. Nevertheless, the current British legislation clearly allows for the use of embryos formed in vivo (1990 Act, Sch 3, para 7).

THE SURPLUS FETUS

3.69 The management of both infertility and childlessness due to abnormalities in the female provokes a particular problem of multiple pregnancies. Hormone treatment of primary infertility can be over-successful and result in pregnancies involving anything up to sextuplets – and, occasionally, beyond. As to childlessness, the chances of in vitro fertilisation ending in a live birth are improved by the insertion of 2-3 embryos and more than one of these then implants in about 30% of those transfers that result in pregnancy.[123] Few people can afford to bring up several children at the same time. Moreover, the common scenario of high order pregnancies which lead to live birth is that the infants are of very low birthweight; they occupy the facilities of a neonatal intensive care unit to a disproportionate extent; the parents face the spectre of their children dying one by one over a period of weeks and those

121 A scholarly discussion of this dichotomy within the US jurisdiction is to be found in J F Daar 'Assisted Reproductive Technologies and the Pregnancy Process: Developing an Equality Model to Protect Reproductive Liberties' (1999) 25 Amer J Law Med 455. The author drew attention to a further, though unreported, case which followed the principle adopted in *Davis* (para 3.67 above) that, in the absence of a contract, a non-reproductive option was to be preferred – provided that the dissenting party had a reasonable prospect of reproducing in another way: *JB v MB*, NY Superior Court, 1998.

122 Despite its antiquity, H Brown, M Dent, L M Dyer et al 'Legal Rights and Issues Surrounding Conception, Pregnancy, and Birth' (1986) 39 Vanderbilt LR 597 remains one of the best reviews of the many legal problems introduced by artificial reproductive methods. The relatively academic problems of succession of 'twin embryos' that are implanted at different times are settled by the elimination of 'storage time' from the age of an embryo (1990 Act, s 3(4)).

123 HFEA *Ninth Annual Report* (2000) Table 4.10.

that survive may well be brain damaged as a result of prematurity.[124] It is largely in order to circumvent this prospect that the current United Kingdom Code of Practice now decrees that no more than two eggs or embryos are to be transferred in any one cycle in any circumstances. Nevertheless, even triplets[125] may be an unwelcome result of a successful treatment and evidence has been adduced that more eggs are being used in the GIFT process leading to a multiple pregnancy rate of over 40%.[126] Moreover, the superfetation of hormone therapy is hard to control. Thus, the clinician may well be faced with the option of pregnancy reduction in utero.

3.70 This process, which is carried out at or earlier than the twelfth week of pregnancy, is generally known as selective reduction of pregnancy, but it has been pointed out that, as the individual fetal characteristics are unknown at the time, there is no 'selection' other than that dictated by operative convenience. We prefer the suggested alternative of reduction of multifetal pregnancy[127] – a description which serves to distinguish the process from the truly selective termination that may be used, say, when one fetus of twins is found to be compromised. The legality of the practice depends upon additions to the Abortion Act 1967 arising from the 1990 Act, s 37(5); its morality is inseparable from that of abortion and we return to the subject below.[128]

SURROGATE MOTHERHOOD

3.71 Surrogate motherhood requires the active co-operation of an otherwise uninvolved woman in the process of pregnancy and birth. It thus introduces a third party into marriage. The fact that the third party may have a financial interest in a medical treatment has led to a general antipathy to the procedure in the United Kingdom. Commercialism is, however, accepted in American medical practice – for example, blood is bought and sold – and there is considerable activity in this field in the United States.

3.72 At its simplest, and as the term is most commonly used, the infertile woman and her husband arrange with another woman that she will carry a

---

124 In a particularly publicised case, a woman conceived octuplets through a series of adventures and misadventures. She decided to maintain her pregnancy and all eight were stillborn at 19 weeks: Leading Article 'The Death of Babies' *Daily Telegraph*, 4 October 1996, p 25. At much the same time, a furore erupted when a woman carrying twins elected to have one of them aborted: C Dyer 'Selective Abortions Hit the Headlines' (1996) 313 BMJ 380; J Woods 'Mother's Dilemma over the Right to Choose Life' *Scotsman*, 6 August 1996.

125 Some 5% of clinical pregnancies derived from the transfer of three embryos will result in a triple pregnancy. Three embryos were inserted into Mrs Thompson, who had requested that only 2 embryos be used. She was delivered of triplets and was awarded £100,000 for loss of amenity. The case has not been reported: Leading Article 'Trouble with Triplets' *Scotsman*, 17 November 2000, p 15. The leader writer rather sadly visualised the grown-up children wondering which one of them their mother did not want.

126 *Sixth Report of the Interim Licensing Authority* (1991) p 15. Up to date figures are hard to come by as GIFT is currently not controlled under the 1990 Act. A very good case can be made that it should be so regulated.

127 R L Berkowitz and L Lynch 'Selective Reduction: An Unfortunate Misnomer' (1990) 75 Obstet Gynecol 873.

128 See para 5.81 et seq.

child conceived by donor insemination with the husband's semen and will surrender it to its genetic father after birth. The alternative, which also concludes with the return of the infant to its genetic parents, is that an embryo which is created in vitro from the gametes of a husband and wife is then implanted in the uterus of a 'surrogate'. There are several reasons for separating the two processes, which are often described as partial or complete surrogacy; we find it easier to refer to the latter technique more descriptively as 'womb-leasing'.[129] We return to this subject below but, for the present, we limit discussion to the more easily achieved objective of impregnating a fertile woman. That process, as defined, is akin to a pre-emptive adoption with the advantage that the 'adopted' baby shares at least half its genes with its 'adopting' parents. Since the practical possibility of following the normal process of adoption is decreasing steadily, there is much to be said, theoretically, in favour of surrogate motherhood as a treatment for the woman who is irrevocably childless – indeed, it is the *only* treatment for one who is childless by virtue of being both sterile and without a functional uterus. Yet the great majority of commentators and, possibly, the medical profession as a whole, shy away from accepting it as a means of satisfying an urge to parenthood – why?[130] The reason was summarised many years ago in the classic words of Winslade:[131] 'The practice has a potential for economic exploitation, moral confusion and psychological harm to the surrogate mothers, the prospective adoptive parents and the children.' This view crystallises the debate which has surrounded surrogacy since it first came to the attention of British courts some 25 years ago.

Statute law and surrogacy

3.73 Prior to 1990, the only way by which the prospective social parents – the 'commissioning couple' – could achieve their aim was through the medium of adoption and it is quite reasonable to regard a surrogacy arrangement as a form of adoption – albeit pre-arranged. The terms of the Adoption Act 1976 thus have at least an indirect bearing on surrogacy.[132]

3.74 The part of the Adoption Acts that is significant for present purposes relates to the prohibition of commercialism within the process – effectively banning 'baby selling' and the private placement of infants.[133] Thus, from the very beginning, there was a real possibility that surrogate motherhood – and particularly that which involved some form of monetary transaction – was illegal.[134] There is, however, much to be said for the view that surrogate

---

129   The technical term 'in vitro fertilisation surrogacy' is also used.
130   An opposing view was expressed by I Craft 'Surrogacy' (1992) 47 Brit J Hosp Med 728.
131   W J Winslade 'Surrogate Mothers: Private Right or Public Wrong?' (1981) 7 J Med Ethics 153.
132   And also, of course, the Adoption (Scotland) Act 1978. However, for ease of writing, we will refer here only to the 1976 Act.
133   Adoption Act 1976, s 57.
134   In the first American test, the court agreed on the fundamental right to include a third party in a pregnancy arrangement but excluded the right to carry a child for payment: *Doe v Kelly* 307 NW 2d 438 (Mich, 1981).

motherhood and adoption are distinct, albeit closely linked, processes.[135] In the first place, the surrogate mother is not pregnant, nor has she an existing child which she has to abandon at the time the proposition is put to her. She is under no pregnancy-related economic pressure and a main reason for prohibiting a trade in babies is, therefore, absent. Against this, it was pointed out[136] that, at least in the 1980s, 40% of volunteer surrogate mothers in the United States were unemployed or were in receipt of welfare;[137] surrogacy may, therefore, be one response to economic need but the element of urgency that is a hallmark of adoption is still lacking. The nature of any proposed payment is also different in the two cases. In one it is a matter of purchase of an existing commodity for sale; in the other it is a matter of expenses coupled with payment for services rendered[138] – not totally unlike a man paying for the support of the mother of his illegitimate child and supplementing this with a generous present on her bringing it to term. In the absence of specific legislation, the legality of surrogacy associated with exchange of money depends upon the acceptance of this distinction.

3.75 We will see later that the need to harmonise the statutory provisions of the Adoption Acts with the practicalities of surrogacy has been eliminated with the introduction of the parental order; it is, nevertheless, interesting to see how the courts struggled with the problem when it presented – *Re an adoption application (surrogacy)*[139] was just such a case and it was a remarkably amateurish affair. The principals met casually, the surrogate being motivated by a desire to help a childless couple, and she was impregnated naturally. A fee of £10,000 was agreed but half of this was returned by the surrogate on the grounds that she had obtained money from the sale of her story. All the principals, the judge said later, were supremely happy. They were also inexperienced and it was not for a further two and a half years that the 'parents' applied for an adoption order. The issue was simply whether or not this would be valid following such 'payment or reward'.[140] In summary, Latey J held that a surrogacy arrangement would not contravene the Adoption Act so long as the payments made did not constitute an element of profit or financial reward; he thought that the payments in the instant case did no more than compensate for the inconveniences of pregnancy. More significantly, he showed his faith in the commissioning parents by stating that, if necessary, he would apply his powers to allow some profit and reward[141] retrospectively in the interests of the child. An adoption order was made. Despite some doubts

135   I M Mady 'Surrogate Mothers: The Legal Issues' (1981) 7 Am J Law Med 323; I Davies 'Contracts to Bear Children' (1985) 11 J Med Ethics 61. The great majority of citations in this area result from the surge in interest in surrogacy in the 1980s. The dust has now settled and there is very little recent research.
136   P Parker 'Motivation of Surrogate Mothers: Initial Findings' (1983) 140 Am J Psychiat 117.
137   M Freeman, in a powerful exposure of the 'exploitation' theory, pointed out that a similar result would probably obtain were a matched sample of applications for a factory job to be considered: 'Is Surrogacy Exploitative?' in S A M McLean (ed) *Legal Issues in Human Reproduction* (1989) ch 7.
138   R Macklin 'Is There Anything Wrong With Surrogate Motherhood? An Ethical Analysis' (1988) 16 Law Med Hlth Care 57. For a strongly opposing view, see B Cohen 'Surrogate Mothers: Whose Baby Is It?' (1984) 10 Am J Law Med 243.
139   [1987] Fam 81, [1987] 2 All ER 826.
140   Adoption Act 1976, s 57(1).
141   Ibid, s 57(3).

being expressed at the time,[142] this relatively courageous decision has been followed without qualm.[143]

3.76 The conditions in the comparable, though more recent, Scottish case, *C v S*,[144] were something of an antithesis. The surrogate, who was unemployed, received £8,000 in expenses but then regretted her decision to give up the child. A parental order was, therefore, unavailable on the grounds of lack of consent by the legal mother and the commissioning couple sought to adopt the child a year after its birth. The sheriff, while holding that consent to adoption was being withheld unreasonably, none the less refused an adoption order because he considered the monetary transaction breached the terms of the statute;[145] a custody order was granted. On appeal to the Court of Session, however, it was held that the money had been paid in the expectation of a parental order rather than of adoption; the Act had, accordingly, not been contravened and an adoption order was substituted. While it is unclear to us why a provision for unreasonable withdrawal of consent should be available in respect of an adoption order but not of a parental order, *C v S* serves, at least, to harmonise policy as to the authorisation of 'reasonable' payments in respect of surrogacy on both sides of the Border.[146]

3.77 None the less, outside the United States, there appears to be a consensus which condemns the blatant commercialisation of child-bearing by way of intermediate, profit-making agencies and it was this which prompted the first relevant United Kingdom statute in the form of the Surrogacy Arrangements Act 1985.[147] The main purpose of the Act is to prohibit the making of a surrogacy arrangement on a commercial basis.[148] The principals involved are expressly excused from criminal liability (s 2(2)); moreover, payments made to or for the benefit of the surrogate are not regarded as being made on a commercial basis (s 2(3)). On the face of it, this hurried and somewhat ill-prepared measure is broadly acceptable. It removes the financially motivated entrepreneur from the scene and, at the same time, is at pains to exclude any suggestion of a criminal ancestry for the resulting children. Some aspects are, however, open to criticism. It does not involve non-commercial agencies who can, and do, operate without regulation; we will see later (at para 3.100) that

---

142 C Dyer 'Babies in the Courts' The Times, 13 March 1987, p 15.
143 *Re Q (parental order)* [1996] 1 FLR 369. The sum of £8,280 was authorised retrospectively.
144 1996 SLT 1387, sub nom *C and C v GS* 1996 SCLR 837.
145 Adoption (Scotland) Act 1978, ss 24(2) and 51.
146 Although this decision may seem a trifle contrived, it was clearly motivated by the best interests of the child. It is probable that an adoption order could, in any case, have been granted on these grounds alone: L Edwards and A Griffiths *Family Law* (1997) p 174.
147 This aspect has been the subject of legislation in many jurisdictions. In Australia, see Infertility Treatment Act 1995 (Victoria); Family Relationships Act Amendment Act 1988 (South Australia); Surrogate Parenthood Act 1988 (Queensland); Surrogacy Contracts Act 1993 (Tasmania). For the general approaches in the United States, see R A Charo 'Legislative Approaches to Surrogate Motherhood' (1989) 16 Law Med Hlth Care 96.
148 Advertising by way of newspapers, periodicals and telecommunications is proscribed in s 3, the criminal liability resting on the proprietor, editor, publisher etc. I Kennedy and A Grubb *Medical Law* (3rd edn, 2000) believe that the Act also criminalises the woman who advertises herself (at 1383).

this is a concession of, at best, doubtful value. By contrast, it appears to preclude the involvement of a remunerated professional lawyer in the making of a surrogacy arrangement; there is nothing in the Act to prevent the principals drawing up an understanding but it seems that it must be an amateur affair. For ideologists who disapprove of the idea of an experienced agency, it is worth noting that break-down of surrogacy arrangements is far less common in those clinics which require the intervention of professional expertise.[149] The doctor who merely assists in a pre-arranged surrogacy, however, commits no offence even if he or she is paid for the service.[150] The British Medical Association, while still regarding surrogacy as a reproductive option of last resort 'in cases where it is impossible or highly undesirable for medical reasons for the intended mother to carry a child herself', has recognised the widespread public acceptance of surrogacy and has softened its attitude to medical participation in the procedure.[151] The HFEA also allows for surrogacy to be initiated in licensed clinics subject to a similar medical restriction.[152]

3.78 Even so, a system which depends upon the vagaries of the courts cannot be satisfactory and some formula must be evolved if the commissioning couple is to have a legal right to receive the child – for the surrogate, at least in the United Kingdom, is clearly its legal mother irrespective of whether or not it is the product of her own ovum and, if she is married and conception was via consensual donor insemination, her husband is its father (1990 Act, ss 27 and 28); moreover, neither can simply surrender their parental duties.[153] Adoption could provide the solution, but the procedure is often tedious and the issue of an adoption order certainly cannot be guaranteed.[154] The 1990 Act, s 30 now offers an alternative by which the court may make a parental order which provides for a child carried by a surrogate to be treated in law as the child of the commissioning couple, provided that the gametes of one or both have been involved and that they are married and have attained the age of 18. This is subject to the consent of the surrogate and, where applicable, the father of the child – including a man who is the father by virtue of the 1990 Act, s 28 – if they can be found;[155] moreover, the agreement of the woman who carried the child is ineffective if made less than six weeks after the child's birth. The application must be made within six months of the birth

---

149 See P R Brinsden, T C Appleton, E Murray et al 'Treatment by In Vitro Fertilisation with Surrogacy: Experience of One British Centre' (2000) 320 BMJ 924.

150 I Kennedy and A Grubb *Medical Law* (3rd edn, 2000), p 1381. A minor difficulty as to confidentiality has been eradicated in the Human Fertilisation and Embryology (Disclosure of Information) Act 1992.

151 BMA *Changing Conceptions of Motherhood – the Practice of Surrogacy in Britain* (1996). At least two surrogacies have been funded through the NHS: 'NHS Pays for Sister's Surrogacy' *The Times*, 10 April 1996, p 11. For the evolution of medical attitudes, see L Foxcroft 'Surrogacy – Warnock and After' (1997) 2 Med L Internat 337.

152 *Code of Practice* (2001), para 3.16. The courts have, however, disallowed the funding of a surrogacy as part of the damages for negligence resulting in a woman's childlessness: *Briody v St Helens and Knowsley Area Health Authority* [2001] EWCA Civ 1010, [2001] 2 FLR 1094, (2001) 62 BMLR 1, CA.

153 Children Act 1989, s 2(9).

154 S M Cretney and J M Masson *Principles of Family Law* (6th edn, 1997) regard these cases as 'in family' – though the concept seems to involve an uneasy mix of genetic, legal and social relationships.

155 For some of the difficulties, see *Re Q (parental order)* [1996] 1 FLR 369.

and the child must be living with the commissioning couple. Applications are heard in private and a guardian ad litem is appointed to watch over the child's interests. It is a stipulation that no money, other than reasonable expenses, has been given to the surrogate other than that authorised by the court.[156] It is exceptional for a parental order to be refused if these conditions are fulfilled.[157]

3.79 The question of consent to a parental order leads to consideration of the validity of any contract made between a commissioning couple and the surrogate and to the final current piece in the jig-saw of statutory control of surrogacy in the United Kingdom. Section 36 of the 1990 Act inserts section 1A into the Surrogacy Arrangements Act 1985, by virtue of which no surrogacy arrangement is enforceable by or against any of the persons making it. In so legislating, the United Kingdom Parliament has followed the majority trend of those countries that have addressed the subject; whether it is the correct approach is open to argument. Undoubtedly, it is the nature of the contract which poses the greatest complications for surrogate motherhood. Non-commercial surrogacy is not illegal in the United Kingdom and is not, therefore, a practice which is fundamentally against public policy. To introduce deliberately the uncertainties of a breakable agreement seems to do little more than reflect an ambivalence in a Parliament which, while unable to follow the German model in outlawing the practice,[158] seems determined to oblate any signs of approval – surrogacy is to be seen as a form of legal liberty. A surrogate arrangement is clearly a difficult contract to draw up – it must allow for changes of heart on either side, illness in the surrogate, abnormalities in the resultant child and other imponderables, some of which, such as an abortion within the terms of the Abortion Act 1967, can be seen as basic rights. Nevertheless, it can be done; indeed, the judicial decision at first instance in the celebrated American case of *Baby M*[159] was based very largely on the law of contract. Rather than, in effect, hiding the issues, we feel it would be better to grasp the nettle and lay down what a surrogacy arrangement could *not* include – for example, a contract to pay an unreasonable sum of money, an undertaking not to accept a therapeutic abortion and the like. The rights and wrongs of an individual case should be subject to more than individual judicial interpretations – a point which was taken up by the judge in *Re an adoption application (surrogacy)*.[160] Given, however, that this is the present de facto position, there is much to be said for the encouragement of non-contractual memoranda of understanding which can be available in the event of later disagreement – a point to which we return below (para 3.104).

---

156 Parental Orders (Human Fertilisation and Embryology) Regulations 1994, SI 1994/2767; Parental Orders (Human Fertilisation and Embryology) (Scotland) Regulations 1994, SI 1994/2804. For analysis, see A Grubb 'Surrogate Arrangements and Parental Orders' (1995) 3 Med L Rev 204; K McK Norrie 'The Parental Orders (Human Fertilisation and Embryology) (Scotland) Regulations 1994' (1995) Fam LB 13-3. The first 'order' was, in fact, made pre-emptively: *Re W (minors) (surrogacy)* [1991] 1 FLR 385.
157 Cretney and Masson, para 3.78 above, p 947. The very great advantages of the parental order system are illustrated by the parallel US cases: *Doe v Doe* 710 A 2d 1297 (Conn, 1998) and *Doe v Roe* 717 A 2d 706 (Conn, 1998), the gist of which was to apply parental rights in the best interests of a child who had been accepted into a family.
158 Embryonenschutzgesetz (Embryo Protection Act) 1990, s 1(1)(vii).
159 *Re Baby M* 525 A 2d 1128 (NJ, 1987).
160 [1987] Fam 81 at 85, [1987] 2 All ER 826 at 829, Latey J.

The British cases

3.80 The development of judicial attitudes can be traced through a brief review of what are, by now, well-known cases.

3.81 The earliest example, *A v C*,[161] arose in 1978 – some time before 'assisted reproduction' became widely acceptable. The gist is that an unmarried couple arranged for a prostitute's friend to be inseminated on the understanding that the resultant child was returned to them; a fee of £3,000 was involved. The mother changed her mind and the father applied for access; this was granted in the child's best interests. Nevertheless, on appeal, Ormrod LJ described the agreement as 'pernicious and void' and the father as being 'a constant reminder of the whole sordid story'; the Court of Appeal unanimously reversed the decision and decreed that the father should not be allowed to see his son.

3.82 *Re C (a minor)*[162] was the first case to be fully covered but was, essentially, a matter of wardship. An American couple arranged a surrogacy in England through a commercial agency. As soon as the child was born, the local authority obtained a place of safety order under the Children and Young Persons Act 1969, s 28, in the belief that it would be abandoned by its mother; the father then initiated wardship proceedings. Latey J refused to discuss the rights and wrongs of surrogacy and concentrated solely on the welfare of the child – how she had been born was irrelevant. On these grounds, he considered that no one was better equipped than the commissioning couple to care for her; accordingly, he gave them care and control while, at the same time, continuing the wardship – even so, permission was given for the baby to live outside the jurisdiction. For present purposes, the most important aspect of the case is that the judge rejected suggestions that the commissioning couple were unfit parents because they had entertained a commercial surrogacy arrangement.

3.83 Surrogacy itself, and particularly the relationship between that process and adoption, was more directly considered in *Re an adoption application (surrogacy)*.[163] The facts and the outcome – including the liberal stance of the trial judge – have been discussed above.[164]

3.84 *Re P (minors) (wardship: surrogacy)*[165] was heard contemporaneously with the adoption case. In this instance, the surrogate declined to hand over the twins she had conceived by a married professional man. The children were made wards of court and were allowed to stay with their natural mother; the court action was essentially a matter of custody. By the time the case came to be heard, the twins had been with their natural mother for five months

---

161 (1984) 14 Fam Law 241, [1985] FLR 445. Commentators at the time saw the case as of interest from the DI aspect only.
162 [1985] FLR 846.
163 [1987] Fam 81, [1987] 2 All ER 826.
164 See para 3.75. A similar attitude to the rules governing both payment and maternal objection was followed in *Re AW (adoption application)* [1993] 1 FLR 62 and *Re MW (adoption: surrogacy)* [1995] 2 FLR 789, [1995] Fam Law 665. In both cases, the welfare of the child was the determining factor although the decision must have been difficult in the former.
165 [1987] 2 FLR 421.

and the judge was strongly influenced by the degree of maternal bonding that had already arisen. Accordingly, he found 'nothing to outweigh the advantages to these children of preserving the link to the mother to whom they are bonded, and who has exercised a satisfactory degree of maternal care'. Once again, it is to be noted that there was no criticism of either the commissioning parents or of the surrogate for having entered into a surrogacy agreement.[166]

3.85 One further case merits mention – *Re W*[167] – in which, as noted above, the judge was prepared to pre-empt the law in order to ensure bonding of 'womb-leased' twins with their genetic parents. Following this, there was a comparative dearth of new cases until the leading Scottish case of *C v S*[168] which has been discussed already.[169] One wonders at the reason for the hiatus; the probability is that surrogacy is now so well established that cases are now no longer regarded as meriting report unless there are special circumstances. This situation may not, however, last; there have been recent newspaper reports of examples which have had a less than happy ending.[170]

The American scene

3.86 The American comparison is, perhaps, becoming less important as the United Kingdom and Europe develop their own medical jurisprudence. Surrogacy is, however, far more common in the United States and, as a result, there are lessons still to be learnt from across the Atlantic. It would be impossible in a book of this size to undertake a comprehensive review and we must, perforce, be selective. It is also true that cases come to public notice only when there is conflict; reported cases should be considered on the understanding that, as in the UK, the great majority of arrangements proceed smoothly; cases such as that of *Re Baby M*[171] are instructive but not necessarily typical.

3.87 In that case, the surrogate, who had agreed to a fee of $10,000, refused to relinquish her child and, in fact, absconded with it contrary to a court order. When the matter came to trial, the judge was concerned to limit the issues to those of strict law and, in this respect, he rejected any relevance of the adoption laws. He concluded, on the one hand, that a valid contract had been made and broken and, on the other, that the state's interest in the welfare of its children dictated that the child be adopted by the commissioning couple. The Supreme Court of New Jersey, however, had no hesitation in overturning

---

166 For contemporary discussion of these cases see J Montgomery 'Constructing a Family – After a Surrogate Birth' (1986) 49 MLR 635; S P de Cruz 'Surrogacy, Adoption and Custody: A Case Study' (1988) 18 Fam Law 100.
167 *Re W (minors) (surrogacy)* [1991] 1 FLR 385.
168 1996 SLT 1387, sub nom *C and C v GS* 1996 SCLR 837.
169 See para 3.76 above.
170 In one, the surrogate was thought to be acting on behalf of two families at the same time: C Dyer 'Surrogate Mother Refuses to Give Up Baby' (1997) 314 BMJ 250. In the other, there were allegations that the surrogate had fabricated an abortion in order to keep the child: D Kennedy 'Minister Hints at Change in the Law' *The Times*, 16 May 1997, p 2.
171 525 A 2d 1128 (NJ, 1987).

this decision – and doing so forcibly.[172] The surrogacy contract was found to be against public policy and, as such, invalid; both the termination of the mother's parental rights and the adoption order were voided. None the less, the Supreme Court could find nothing in law against voluntary, non-commercial surrogacy, provided that the arrangement did not include any clause binding on the surrogate to surrender her baby. As a result, the court was able to dissociate the contractual aspects of surrogacy and the 'best interests' of the child and followed the lower court in awarding custody to the commissioning parents.[173]

3.88 A contrast is to be seen in the Californian case of *Johnson v Calvert*.[174] In this case, the surrogate was paid $10,000 to carry the embryo of a commissioning couple. After gestating for six months, she changed her mind as to handing over the child and the court was asked to decide on its parentage. The trial court held that a surrogate contract was both legal and enforceable and that the commissioning couple were the child's genetic, biological and natural parents; no parental rights attached to the surrogate. This disposition was upheld on appeal. In dismissing a further appeal, the Supreme Court of California held that it was the intention of the parties at the time of making the arrangement which decided the issue when there were conflicting grounds on which parentage could be established – in the present case, the surrogate had done no more than 'facilitate' the procreation of the commissioning couple's child. The court further stated that surrogate contracts did not violate any existing public policy as to adoption; any payments in the former were, effectively, made for services rendered and not as compensation for the transfer of parental rights.[175] Needless to say, this opinion has been severely criticised as fundamentally misunderstanding the biological realities of the surrogate's contribution.[176]

3.89 The significance of the apparent inconsistency between *Re Baby M* and *Johnson v Calvert* is explained to some extent by *Re Marriage of Moschetta*.[177] Here, the 'parents' of a year-old child, born by standard surrogacy, separated and the surrogate then claimed legal parentage. The Court of Appeal was, then, able to distinguish the case from *Johnson* because there was no conflict as to maternity – the surrogate was both the genetic and the gestational mother and was to be regarded as such. It is, however, to be noted that the court distinguished the definition of status from the allocation of custody.

---

172   537 A 2d 1227 (NJ Sup Ct, 1988).

173   See G P Smith 'The Case of Baby M: Love's Labor Lost' (1988) 16 Law Med Hlth Care 121.

174   851 P 2d 776 (Cal, 1993) discussed by A Grubb 'Surrogate Contract: Parentage' (1994) 2 Med L Rev 239. See also G Annas 'Using Genes to Define Motherhood: The California Solution' (1992) 326 New Engl J Med 417 discussing the decision in the lower court. Others may, however, feel as strongly as to the importance of the genetic affiliation: D R Bromham 'Surrogacy: The Evolution of Opinion' (1992) 47 Brit J Hosp Med 767.

175   The situation as to commercialism of surrogacy in the United States is hard to unravel. It seems that, while *Johnson v Calvert* clears the way in California, at least five states have passed statutes restricting the practice: R A Charo 'Legislative Approaches to Surrogate Motherhood' (1988) 16 Law Med Hlth Care 96.

176   R B Oxman 'California's Experiment in Surrogacy' (1993) 341 Lancet 1468.

177   30 Cal Rep 2d 893 (1994), discussed in detail by A Grubb 'Surrogate Contract: Parentage' (1995) 3 Med LRev 219.

Australia

3.90 In view of that country's leading position in the early development of medical jurisprudence, it is surprising that a surrogacy case was not litigated in Australia until 1998. *Re Evelyn*[178] was an interfamilial, altruistic case that 'went wrong' and resulted, ultimately, in a residency dispute in the Full Court of the Family Court. The final decision was in favour of the surrogate mother, a conclusion based largely, but not entirely, on the assumption that the child's best long-term interests lay in preservation of her natural bonding with her biological mother – this despite the fact that she had lived with the commissioning couple for the first year of her life. Both the trial judge and the Full Court also considered that the ambience of the surrogate's family was preferable for the child. Nevertheless, some residual determinative rights were granted to the commissioning couple.

The cases assessed

3.91 The British cases indicate that the public, as represented by its judiciary, are sympathetic to surrogate motherhood – an attitude which probably derives more from the *fait accompli* nature of the proceedings than from any basic empathy with the practice. It can be taken that no future decisions will be driven by antagonism.

3.92 Accordingly, it is very unlikely that a parental order will be withheld in the event of application by the commissioning parents and consent on the part of the surrogate and the legal father – if there is one. While it would always be possible for the court to override agreement by the parties, it is difficult to see how the motivation of the couple and their almost inevitable material status could be irrelevant to the child's 'best interests' – which is not to say that economic advantage will always take precedence.[179] In so far as it is possible to apply pre-1990 standards to the present day conditions, the indications are that the prime factor in the court's thinking in the event of disagreement between the parties would be the extent of family bonding – we suspect that much would depend on where, and for how long, the child was living at the time of adjudication. It would, however, be impossible to generalise. The single common feature would lie in the search for the child's best interests and it is this which would determine the direction and method of disposal of each case and it has to be remembered that what constitutes best interests is determined by an individual judge. There is no indication of what would result if the commissioning couple were to refuse to accept the infant; the precise details of each case would, again, be all-important, but it is difficult to see, in general, an alternative to intervention by the local authority by way of care proceedings. The position of the surrogate's husband under the terms of the 1990 Act, s 28(2) might then be problematical.

---

178 (1998) FLC 92. The case is examined in depth in M Otlowski '*Re Evelyn* –Reflections on Australia's First Litigated Surrogacy Case' (1998) 7 Med L Rev 38. The author points out that, despite the varying, but generally antipathetic, attitudes to surrogacy shown by the States' legislatures, surrogacy arrangements are acceptable in Australia.
179 See eg *Re P (minors) (wardship: surrogacy)* [1987] 2 FLR 421.

3.93 While there is no evidence on the point, we fancy that much the same approach would be taken whether the surrogate had incubated her own egg or that of the commissioning woman. This, however, might well not be the case in the United States where, judging from the Californian cases, major significance would be attributed to genetic status. As Grubb has put it:

> Infertile couples who seek surrogacy linked with IVF treatment can be reasonably certain they will come out of the arrangement ... as the child's parents. By contrast, couples who resort to traditional surrogacy ... will have no such reassurance.[180]

And, if it is possible to discern a trend from a single case, the same might well be true in Australia.

The morality of surrogate motherhood

3.94 What, then, is so special about the morality of surrogacy? Clearly, the most important difference lies in the inclusion of a third party to procreation – and in such a way as to provoke not only serious moral but also important socio-political questions; and, since the surrogate is, by definition, a woman, the latter are gender-based. Stripped to its essentials, surrogacy can be viewed from this perspective as being one way of exploiting women for the benefit of men[181] – a matter to which we have alluded above. The alternative is to see the outlawing of the practice as outright paternalism which denies a woman a chance to use her body as she pleases. It seems fair to say that the feminist movement is divided in its approach;[182] the argument is one which we will not take further here save to note the difficulties that arise from generalising in personal and individual affairs.

3.95 The second major objection lies in the suggestion that surrogacy is 'baby-selling'.[183] It is possible, however, to maintain that a baby is 'sold' only if persons with no genetic association purchase an infant that is already in being. It seems more logical to regard any monetary transaction in respect of surrogacy as payment for gestational expertise and, as the British cases indicate, the critical distinction lies between reasonable recompense and inducement to gestate.[184] The great majority of assisted reproduction is centred on private

---

180 (1995) 3 Med LRev 219 at 221. Other cases tend to support this view: eg *Soos v Superior Court of Arizona* 896 P 2d 1356 (Ariz, 1994), *Belsito v Clark* 644 NE 2d 769 (Ohio, 1994) – though the latter case is far less convincing.

181 G J Annas 'Fairy Tales Surrogate Mothers Tell' (1988) 16 Law Med Hlth Care 27.

182 L B Andrews 'Surrogate Motherhood: The Challenge for Feminists' (1988) 16 Law Med Hlth Care 72 and, by the same author: 'Beyond Doctrinal Boundaries: A Legal Framework for Surrogate Motherhood' (1995) 81 Va L Rev 2343. A further example of the debate is to be found in S Dodds and K Jones 'Surrogacy and Autonomy' (1989) 3 Bioethics 18.

183 So far as is known, only Israel positively encourages a commercial element in surrogacy arrangements: D A Frankel 'Legal Regulation of Surrogate Motherhood in Israel' (2001) 20 Med Law 605.

184 The court in *Johnson v Calvert* 851 P 2d 776 (Cal, 1993) considered many of these points and rejected the suggestion that surrogacy arrangements violated public policy. For a relatively recent debate, see A van Niekerk and L van Zyl 'Commercial Surrogacy and the Commodification of Children: An Ethical Perspective' (1995) 14 Med Law 163.

health care and, even within a public health service, there is indirect payment for obstetric expertise. Looked at in this way, either both surrogacy and embryo transfer are 'baby purchasing' or neither is – and there is no suggestion that sophisticated reproductive techniques are immoral on this score.[185] Thirdly, it is widely believed that surrogacy must have an ill-effect on children in general or on the individual resultant child. The former, represented by a fear that children may become 'objects for barter', is valid only so long as surrogacy itself is categorised as objectionable; the premise disappears once it is regarded as a legitimate treatment for childlessness. Any effect on the individual child by way of confusion as to parentage is comparable to that which we have discussed in relation to other forms of assisted reproduction. Whether or not there is a detriment seems to us to be unproven but if there is, it should not be insurmountable – certainly no more than in other examples of the unconventional family.[186] Even so, there is little doubt that the provisions of the 1990 Act, s 13(5) – discussed above[187] – are likely to discourage professional implication in surrogacy outside licensed clinics.

3.96 In favour of surrogacy, it must be remembered that, as noted above, it *is* a treatment for some forms of childlessness. Such cases may be rare, yet to encourage treatment by way of ovum donation for the woman who is childless because of ovarian inadequacy and, at the same time, to forbid surrogacy for the one who has no uterus, smacks of unfair discrimination.[188]

3.97 Surrogacy could, however, be used for purely selfish reasons – for example, a desire to have a child without interference with a career – although the prospect may be given exaggerated importance.[189] Such hedonistic womb-leasing is so comparable to nineteenth-century wet-nursing that the process as a whole has become suspect. This is unfortunate because there are, in fact, far more conditions in which IVF-linked surrogacy would be the preferred treatment of childlessness than there are those in which standard surrogacy would be indicated. Abnormality of the uterus or other causes of persistent miscarriage are commoner than loss of both uterus and ovaries; moreover, womb-leasing is the logical answer to an inability to carry, rather than to conceive, a baby – say, by virtue of heart disease, diabetes and the like. The other, and obvious, important difference is that, in womb-leasing, the commissioning couple are the genetic parents. Thus, one would imagine that the surrogate, having no such relationship to her fetus, would be less exposed to psychological trauma on surrendering it; the receiving parents are in

---

185 M Freeman 'Does Surrogacy Have a Future after Brazier?' (1999) 7 Med L Rev 1 suggests that remuneration is inevitable and is better in the open rather than underground.

186 It has been pointed out that, to be a parent, one must have some, but not necessarily all, of the defining features of parenthood: L van Zyl and A van Niekerk 'Interpretations, Perspectives and Intentions in Surrogate Motherhood' (2000) 26 J Med Ethics 404.

187 See para 3.56.

188 We agree, however, that the regulation of surrogacy is very unlikely to offend against the Human Rights Act 1998: R Ramsey 'Regulating Surrogacy – A Contravention of Human Rights?' (2000) 5 Med Law Internat 45.

189 Since both the HFEA and the BMA regard surrogacy as a last resort to be used only on medical grounds, it is unlikely that the procedure would be carried out by practitioners responsible to the GMC.

precisely the same end position as natural coital parents; and the child suffers no 'genetic insecurity'. Certainly, womb-leasing involves the use of high-grade technology – but even this serves to remove some of the intuitive distaste provoked by standard surrogacy. Neither the Warnock Committee nor the resultant legislation have distinguished between partial and full surrogacy; we feel, however, that the better argument lies in favour of clearly separating the two.[190]

3.98 There is, however, one aspect of womb-leasing that merits special attention – that is, the use of intrafamilial surrogates. Not only does this seriously disturb familial relationships but the procedure opens the door to emotional coercion. It appears to be a practice which should be made unlawful – as it is in many jurisdictions – although not everyone would agree.[191]

The future

3.99 The one thing that this rather extensive analysis has shown is that both the ethics and the law relating to surrogacy are still in an uncertain state and that the latter, at least, has been applied in piecemeal fashion. Many would say that it is right that customs so private as reproductive choice should be allowed to evolve by way of public opinion as represented by the common law. We have seen, however, that the United Kingdom has opted for statutory regulation and there is a good argument, to which we subscribe, for harmony across the board.

3.100 At present, while IVF-associated surrogacy clearly lies within the framework of the Human Fertilisation and Embryology Act 1990, standard surrogacy does not do so unless it involves artificial insemination that is provided *as a public service* (ss 2 and 4) other than in the form of AIH or AIP (for discussion of which, see para 3.8 et seq above). That being so, DI in the context of surrogacy is lawful only if performed privately or under cover of a licence – and we have seen that the involvement of licensed clinics as, as best, not encouraged by the HFEA. This leaves an unsatisfactory dichotomy, the solution of which is central to the repute of the process. Most people would now agree with the minority of the Warnock Committee[192] that it should remain available as a treatment option.[193] Nevertheless, most would also agree that it must be controlled.[194] It was against this background that the

---

190 Theoretically, womb-leasing should be the preferred surrogacy method for those of the Jewish faith as 'jewishness' is transferred through the female line. In fact, current Israeli law states that surrogacy is legal in that country only if the ovum does not come from the surrogate: R H B Fishman 'Surrogate Motherhood Becomes Legal in Israel' (1996) 347 Lancet 756.

191 In response to an English case involving a post-menopausal woman acting on behalf of her childless daughter, Lady Warnock is reported as saying 'It is a wonderful idea': D Kennedy 'Surrogacy Attempt Divides Experts' The Times, 3 July 1995, p 8. The baby was successfully delivered by caesarian section.

192 Cmnd 9314, para 3.2 above, 'Expression of Dissent A'.

193 So far as we know, in the English-speaking world, only Queensland has criminalised the procedure in all its forms: Surrogate Parenthood Act 1988 (Qd).

194 For an appraisal of the early attitudes, see D Morgan 'Who to Be or Not to Be: The Surrogacy Story' (1986) 49 MLR 358.

Brazier Review Team was set up in 1997, intending to ensure that the law continued to meet public concerns.[195]

3.101 Briefly,[196] the team recommended, first, that payments to surrogate mothers should cover only genuine expenses associated with the pregnancy and that additional payments should be prohibited in order to prevent surrogacy arrangements being entered into for financial benefit; reasonable expenses should be defined by the Ministers. Second, it was recommended that agencies to oversee surrogacy arrangements should be established and registered by Health Departments which would be required to operate within a Code of Practice; an advisory code would be drawn up to provide guidance for the registered agencies and also for those acting in a private capacity. Thirdly, current legislation dealing with surrogacy should be repealed and replaced by a consolidated Surrogacy Act which addressed the whole subject rather than specific aspects. In this respect, it was recommended that surrogacy arrangements should remain unenforceable, that the ban on commercial agencies and advertising should remain in force and that the prohibition should include the operation of unregistered agencies.

3.102 These proposals have been carefully researched and have much to commend them; nevertheless, we would take issue with some of them. Prominent in this respect is the question of payment – the rejection of which is central to the Brazier position. The concepts of provision of a service and recompense for that service are so closely linked that, save in unusual circumstances, the majority of persons would expect them to go hand in hand. Given that the demand for surrogates will not abate and given that private surrogacy arrangements are not prohibited, we have to agree with Freeman[197] that the effect of prohibiting paid arrangements in the registered field must be to force the process onto the 'back-streets', which would be to overturn the whole purpose of regulation. Of perhaps more immediate concern, as we have already said, it would take a very great deal of argument to convince us that payments to a surrogate mother are any less moral than payments to an IVF clinician. We support the case for reasonable payments provided these are determined by an overall authority.

3.103 As to the status of the regulatory authority, we prefer a policy of centralisation rather than regionalisation if for no reason other than to avoid the possibility of availability by 'post-code'. The concept of a State Surrogacy Board has been mooted for some time.[198] This, we feel, would involve the establishment of yet another, and probably superfluous, quango. It is certainly true that surrogate motherhood introduces problems additional to those involved in the provision of a treatment for childlessness; nevertheless, it is central to our view of surrogacy that, at base, it is precisely that and we remain unconvinced that the responsibility for its regulation is not best invested in a distinct Committee of HFEA.

---

195 M Brazier (Chairman) *Surrogacy: Review for Health Ministers of Current Arrangements for Payment and Regulation* (1998, Cm 4068).
196 For a very detailed critique see Freeman, para 3.95 above.
197 Para 3.95 above.
198 P Singer and D Wells *The Reproduction Revolution* (1984) at p 118.

3.104 Finally, we are unrepentant in our antipathy to declaring all surrogacy arrangements unenforceable. Very little attention is paid by commentators to the situation in which the commissioning couple wish to avoid their responsibilities and it is this that, in our opinion, constitutes the main potential mischief attached to surrogate motherhood; as we have already stated, it seems to be far preferable to establish the *conditions* of an arrangement that are unenforceable rather than its whole.[199]

3.105 Overall, we feel strongly that the procedure should be unlawful unless it is undertaken for a bona fide medical reason, other options having been considered and properly rejected. Effectively, then, we are making a plea for medicalising surrogacy – thus emphasising our view that surrogacy is the treatment of choice for a specific group of causes of childlessness and is, therefore, comparable to any other 'treatment services' provided under cover of the 1990 Act. In support of this, we suggest that a new Surrogacy Act does no more than insert its provisions as a new part in that Act.

199 A relatively minor recommendation of the Brazier team is that judges should be unable to authorise otherwise impermissible payments. There will always be exceptional circumstances and the adoption and surrogacy procedures are so close to one another that it should not be possible to play one off against the other. Similarly, there seems no reason why it should not be possible to overrule an unreasonable objection to a parental order such as can be done in relation to an adoption order.

4 The control of fertility

STERILISATION

4.1 The aim of sterilisation is to end the patient's ability to reproduce. A number of surgical procedures may be used to achieve this. In males, the most common method is vasectomy, in which the vas deferens is cut and tied. Sterilisation in females is usually achieved by division or clipping of the fallopian tubes, which carry the ova between the ovary and the womb.[1] An important feature of both operations from the legal and ethical standpoint is that they are generally intended to be irreversible; although it may be possible to repair the operation, prospective attempts to allow for reversibility are likely to result in procedures which fail in their primary purpose. Modern microsurgery has improved on this position – a development which may account for some of the apparently disparate court decisions that have been taken;[2] nevertheless, it is generally held that sterilisation will, or at least may well, bring a basic human function to an end.[3]

4.2 Ethical objections to sterilisation usually focus on this aspect of irreversible interference with the ability to reproduce. Those who object on these grounds would argue that such interference is unjustified, in that the individual may later undergo a change of mind and may wish to return to a position which is probably now closed. They would also stress that the decision to sterilise is one which is taken in the midst of subtle social and personal pressures; the likelihood of the decision being entirely free is, thereby, diminished – yet it is

---

1 Reviews of the literature indicate that vasectomy is the more successful and less expensive of the two procedures. Nevertheless, sterilisations involving the woman are more common than are those performed on men: N W Hendrix, S P Chauhan and J C Morrison (1999) 54 Obst Gynec Survey 766. Tubal ligation is also frequently complicated by ectopic pregnancy: C Westhoff and A Davis 'Tubal Sterilization: Focus on the U.S. Experience' (2000) 73 Fertil Steril 913.
2 See para 4.4 et seq below.
3 Current methods also allow for reversal of vasectomy – a success rate of up to 40% successful pregnancies is claimed. See A K Banergee and A Simpson 'Reversing Vasectomy' (1992) 304 BMJ 1130.

one that cannot easily be retracted.[4]   The objection of the Catholic Church is more direct.   In Catholic teaching, sterilisation is a mutilation of the body which leads to the deprivation of a natural function and which must, therefore, be rejected.   Sterilisation can only be accepted if it is carried out for strictly therapeutic purposes – that is, where it is necessary for the physical health of the patient; the performance of hysterectomy in the treatment of menorrhagia, for example, is admissible.[5]   The secular counterpart lies in the concept of maim; although, historically, this refers to injuries which limit a man's capacity for military service, the courts might well take exception, say, to castration on non-therapeutic grounds.[6]   In so far as it is possible to identify a lay consensus on the matter, it is that sterilisation is an acceptable method of contraception provided that the person undergoing the operation is adequately informed of the implications.   Very strong objections may be voiced, however, when there is any question as to the reality of the patient's consent and we return to the subject below.[7]

4.3   The legality of contraceptive sterilisation in the United Kingdom is now beyond doubt and only a small minority of other countries continue either to forbid the process altogether or to allow it only in narrowly defined circumstances.   Not infrequently, there is a minimum age below which sterilisation on request will not be available; under United States federal requirements it is 21 years, in Denmark, as a European example, it is 25.   Some jurisdictions, such as Japan, require spousal consent but there is general resistance to this on the grounds that the decision is a personal matter to be decided by the individual.   There is no doubt that this is the case in the United Kingdom; the Medical Defence Union has always emphasised that the doctor owes a duty of care to the patient and not to his or her spouse[8] and the courts would never grant an injunction to stop sterilisation or vasectomy.[9]   On the other hand, the very term 'family planning' implies a shared responsibility; the British Medical Association regards it as good medical practice to encourage potential patients to discuss such procedures with their partners[10] and we would certainly endorse such a policy.   On purely practical grounds, the surgeon may wish to avoid involvement in divorce proceedings and the like.

4   See an excellent letter: E Tuddenham 'Sterilise in Haste: Repent at Leisure and at Great Expense' (2000) 321 BMJ 962.

5   For a sensitive view from a Catholic clinician of this and other dilemmas, see J Poole *The Cross of Unknowing* (1989); 'Time for the Vatican to Bend' (1992) 339 Lancet 1340.   On a world scale, the attitude of orthodox Islam is just as rigid: D A R Verkuyl 'Two World Religions and Family Planning' (1993) 342 Lancet 473.   The growing debate between modern medical ethics and orthodox Catholicism is well illustrated by D M Cowdin and J F Tuohey 'Sterilization, Catholic Health Care, and the Legitimate Autonomy of Culture' (1998) 4 Christ Bioeth 14; J E Smith 'Sterilizations Reconsidered?' (1998) 4 Christ Bioeth 45.

6   A similar legislative attitude is to be found in the Prohibition of Female Circumcision Act 1985.   This raises the general question of self-inflicted injury, for which, see *R v Brown* [1994] 1 AC 212, [1993] 2 All ER 75, HL, discussed at para 15.1 below.

7   See para 4.8.

8   (1987) 3 J Med Def Union (3) 24.

9   *Paton v British Pregnancy Advisory Service Trustees* [1979] QB 276 at 280, [1978] 2 All ER 987 at 990, per Sir George Baker P.

10   A Somerville (on behalf of the Working Party) *Medical Ethics To-day: Its Practice and Philosophy* (1993) p 110.

Bravery[11] is no longer an acceptable authority but Lord Evershed MR may still be regarded as correct in saying:

> It would not be difficult ... to construct in imagination a case of grave cruelty on a wife founded on the progressive hurt to her health caused by an operation for sterilisation undergone by her husband in disregard of, or contrary to, the wife's wishes or natural instincts[12]

– and the alternative proposition would apply with equal force.

Liability for a failed sterilisation – the action for 'wrongful pregnancy'[13]

4.4 This question of divided responsibility finds its counterpart in the first limb of legal liability – was there a duty of care and to whom was it owed? Clearly, if a man or woman seeks sterilisation independently, the doctor's duty of care is limited to that man or woman. By contrast, the doctor owes a duty to both partners if they come to him together seeking a limitation of fertility that is of benefit to both. It follows from either premise that the doctor cannot be held liable to a potential present or future sexual partner of his patient of whom he has no knowledge. While this would seem to be a relatively simple proposition, it has been the subject of extensive argument in the Court of Appeal. Here, it was confirmed that a woman who became pregnant by a man who had been told three years previously that he need take no contraceptive precautions had no cause of action against those who had given the advice.[14]

4.5 Given, however, that a duty of care has been established, liability for a so-called wrongful or uncovenanted pregnancy[15] resulting from a failed sterilisation will not be imposed unless it can be established that the surgeon failed in that duty. Such failure can, in turn, be attributable either to incompetent clinical expertise or, more controversially, to inadequate explanation of the shortcomings of the procedure – in particular, as to the inherent possibility that conception might still occur after the operation due purely to the vagaries of nature. There are a number of important United Kingdom, Commonwealth and United States decisions which deal with these problems.

---

11   *Bravery v Bravery* [1954] 3 All ER 59, [1954] 1 WLR 1169, CA.
12   [1954] 3 All ER 59 at 62, [1954] 1 WLR 1169 at 1173.
13   Many writers use the term 'wrongful conception' rather than 'wrongful pregnancy'. We prefer the latter on the grounds that no damage is sustained by conception; the potential for damage arises only at implantation.
14   *Goodwill v British Pregnancy Advisory Service* [1996] 2 All ER 161, (1996) 31 BMLR 83.
15   The expression 'uncovenanted' was used by Kennedy J in *Richardson v LRC Products Ltd* (2001) 59 BMLR 185, [2000] Lloyd's Rep Med 280 to describe such a situation. In Scots law, the word has been used to describe not so much an unexpected happening as one which was not contemplated by the parties concerned. It is, therefore, apt to describe a failed sterilisation or 'wrongful pregnancy'. We believe that it is preferable to use the expression in place of the more commonly used but, still, distasteful, and often inaccurate, description 'unwanted pregnancy'.

4.6 The question of what constitutes a breach of any duty of care is addressed in detail in chapter 9. For the present, we need only draw attention to the fact that breach of duty is largely governed by the *Bolam*[16] principle, under which it is held that a doctor's action will not be held to be negligent if it conforms to a practice which would have been adopted by a responsible body of medical opinion. Thus, in *Venner*[17] a gynaecologist who accepted the patient's word that she could not be pregnant at the time of the operation was held to be not negligent on the grounds that others would have omitted a precautionary curettage in similar circumstances. As a result, it has come to be supposed that a judge cannot make a choice presented with two divergent expert opinions as to what was the correct procedure to adopt. A distinction has to be made, however between preferring an opinion – as in *Maynard*[18] – and preferring an interpretation of the facts. This was neatly explained in *Fallows v Randle*.[19]   In this case of failed female sterilisation, the rings occluding the fallopian tubes had either been placed negligently or had slipped off through no one's fault. In preferring the former sequence of events, Stuart Smith LJ had this to say:

> [The *Bolam* principle] has no application when what the judge has to decide is, on balance, which of the explanations [of failure] is to be preferred. This is a question of fact which the judge has to decide on the ordinary basis of a balance of probabilities.[20]

4.7 We suspect that the majority of actions based on the negligent *performance* of a sterilising operation will generally be of this relatively simple type and that liability may well be acknowledged prior to any hearing. An exception might lie when the patient has insisted on a modified operation in the anticipation of reversal at some time in the future – but such cases must be rare.[21]

4.8 Rather more interest centres on those actions in negligence and in contract which have been based on the grounds of inadequate provision of information as to the possibility of failure. In such cases, the supposed deficit has proved to be no more than a matter of communication between doctor and patient.

16 *Bolam v Friern Hospital Management Committee* [1957] 2 All ER 118, [1957] 1 WLR 582.
17 *Venner v North East Essex Area Health Authority* (1987) Times, 21 February. This might well, however, not apply now. In the virtually identical case of *Allen v Bloomsbury Health Authority* [1993] 1 All ER 651, (1993) 13 BMLR 47, the authority admitted liability and the only matter in issue was the quantum of damages. In a still later case, damages of over £88,000 were awarded against a gynaecologist who failed to explain to a patient that she might be pregnant at the time of operation: *Crouchman v Burke* (1997) 40 BMLR 163.
18 *Maynard v West Midlands Regional Health Authority* [1985] 1 All ER 635, [1984] 1 WLR 634.
19 [1997] 8 Med LR 160.
20 Ibid at 165. Moreover, two techniques may each pass the *Bolam* test for professional acceptability but it is for the court to decide which is in the patient's best interests: *Re S (adult patient: sterilisation)* [2001] 3 Fam 15, [2000] 3 WLR 1288, CA.
21 As exemplified in the very early twin Canadian cases of *Doiron v Orr* (1978) 86 DLR (3d) 719 and *Cataford v Moreau* (1978) 114 DLR (3d) 585. Liability for a subsequent pregnancy was not imposed in the former in which the operation had been modified; the surgeon was found to have been negligent in the latter where there were no such extenuating conditions.

Thus, in the interesting case of *Thake v Maurice*,[22] the issue turned eventually on the definition of the word 'irreversible' – the defendant claiming that it implied no more than that the procedure could not be reversed by surgery while the plaintiff contended that it represented a contract to provide absolute sterility which was beyond recall by natural processes. After something of a *volte face* between the trial court and the Court of Appeal as to breach of contract, it was held that the surgeon had been negligent in his failure to warn of the possibility of natural reversal of vasectomy. A rather similar case turned on the interpretation of the words on the form signifying consent to operation which stated 'We understand that this means we can have no children' and which the plaintiffs contended amounted to a representation that the operation was foolproof; the trial judge, however, held that the words merely acknowledged that the intended effect of the operation was that the couple should not have more children and found for the defendants.[23] Such semantic difficulties had been foreseen in the important Australian case of *F v R*[24] when King CJ specifically drew attention to the need not only to warn of the possible complications of surgery but also of the risk of failure as to the intended end result. There have been further English cases involving much the same issues[25] – one of which concerned a woman who became pregnant while her husband was producing persistently negative seminal specimens[26] – but these are better discussed together under the heading of consent.[27]

4.9 Thus far, we have accepted that a surgeon and/or his employers can be liable in the event of a wrongful pregnancy. What we have not broached is the *extent* of that liability and it is here that we run into considerable analytical difficulty – indeed, it might be said that this represents the major medical jurisprudential shift since the last edition of this book. Even so, we must still look at some relatively old cases in order to maintain an historical perspective.

4.10 Damages following a wrongful pregnancy can be sought under two main heads. First, there are those that derive from the pregnancy itself including damages for the pain and suffering of gestation and childbirth together with recompense for loss of earnings or additional expenses resulting from pregnancy

22 [1986] QB 644, [1984] 2 All ER 513; revsd [1986] QB 644, [1986] 1 All ER 497. It was later said of the trial stage of this case: 'I, for my part, think that ... the less we say about that decision, the better' (per Slade LJ in *Eyre v Measday* [1986] 1 All ER 488 at 492).

23 *Worster v City and Hackney Health Authority* (1987) Times, 22 June. As a further hurdle, the plaintiffs may have to convince the court that they would have continued contraceptive methods if they had been informed of a risk: *Newell v Goldenberg* [1995] 6 Med LR 371.

24 (1983) 33 SASR 189, SC.

25 Eg *Eyre v Measday* [1986] 1 All ER 488, CA; *Gold v Haringey Health Authority* [1986] 1 FLR 125; revsd [1988] QB 481, [1987] 2 All ER 888.

26 *Stobie v Central Birmingham Health Authority* (1994) 22 BMLR 135. The case drew attention to the fact that the common law interpretation of paternity may be challenged by way of laboratory tests. The phenomenon is said to occur in about 1:80,000 cases – see J C Smith, D Cranston, T O'Brien et al 'Fatherhood without Apparent Spermatozoa after Vasectomy' (1994) 344 Lancet 30.

27 See chapter 10 below. It is possible to discern an incremental shift towards judicial reliance on the patient's understanding rather than on what the surgeon said: *Gowten v Wolverhampton Health Authority* [1994] 5 Med LR 432; *Lybert v Warrington Health Authority* (1995) 25 BMLR 91, [1996] 7 Med LR 71.

and its convalescence. So far as we know, such damages have never been denied in any jurisdiction. Second, and far more controversial, is the claim for the upkeep of the resulting child until maturity – and it is here that the law has followed a course of sine wave appearance over the last two decades. Put at its simplest, the questions to be resolved are whether damages for the upkeep of an uncovenanted child should ever be awarded and, if so, whether the condition of the child should affect the quantum.

4.11 On the face of things, the issue is reasonably clear. A surgeon owes a duty of care to a couple; he has failed in that duty and, as a result, the very circumstance it was intended to avert has, in fact, occurred; ergo, the couple are entitled to restitution.[28] The fact that a child – and, particularly, a healthy child – is involved, however, introduces complications which are more of a moral than a legal nature; in essence, objection to *any* award in such a context is based on the view that a child is a blessing and that the gift of a child should never be regarded as a matter for compensation. The question was first fully addressed many years ago by the court in *Doiron v Orr*; the judge stated that he would have been prepared to award damages for mental anguish caused to the plaintiff, but was adamant in his refusal to accept that there could be liability for the cost of bringing up an unwanted child:

> I find this approach to a matter of this kind which deals with human life, the happiness of the child, the effect upon its thinking, upon its mind when it realised that there has been a case of this kind, that it is an unwanted mistake and that its rearing is being paid for by someone other than its parents, is just simply grotesque.[29]

4.12 Such rejection concentrates on the effect which an award might have on the child; in other cases, the focus has been more on the entitlement of the parents to damages. Basically, there are four possibilities in the solution of actions for wrongful pregnancy: damages should never be awarded; damages should always be awarded; the blessing of parenthood should be offset against the economic loss and the damages adjusted accordingly; a distinction should be made between healthy and disabled children and damages awarded only for the *extra* costs involved in the upkeep of the latter. Actions for wrongful pregnancy originated in America where the courts have taken a less than uniform approach to the problem. There are certainly several cases in which redress has been refused, the view, again, having been that parents cannot be held to have been damaged by the blessing of children.[30] Elsewhere, a middle view has prevailed, the assumption being that it is illogical to suppose that a benefit – that of parenthood – can derive from failure to provide proper medical care.[31] The majority of states has allowed recovery for all losses excluding those attributable to bringing up a healthy child.[32] In still other instances,

---

28   See, for example, Waller LJ in *Rees v Darlington Memorial Hospital NHS Trust* [2002] EWCA Civ 88, [2002] 2 All ER 177 at [44], (2002) 65 BMLR 117, quoting previous concurrence.

29   (1978) 86 DLR (3d) 719 at 722, per Garett J.

30   *Terrell v Garcia* 496 SW 2d 124 (Tx, 1973); *Public Health Trust v Brown* 388 So 2d 1084 (Fla, 1980); *Sutkin v Beck* 629 SW 2d 131 (Tx, 1982). It has been agreed, however, that damages are recoverable for the birth of a defective child.

31   *Kingsbury v Smith* 422 A 2d 1003 (NH, 1982); *Ochs v Borelli* 445 A 2d 883 (Conn, 1982).

damages have been awarded not only in respect of the pain and suffering involved in an unwanted pregnancy but also to offset the cost of rearing the child to maturity.[33] By and large, it is possible to extract virtually any 'solution' to the problems involved by a judicious section of opinions within the various US jurisdictions – and, wherever one looks, it is generally possible to find a powerful dissenting argument.[34] As we will see, the relevant jurisprudence in the United Kingdom has had to evolve without much precedental assistance from other common law countries.

4.13 The first comparable English case was that of *Scuriaga v Powell*[35] which was concerned with abortion rather than with sterilisation but which, none the less, provides some authority. Here, a healthy child was born by caesarean section subsequent to a negligent failure to terminate a pregnancy lawfully. The court held that there was no public policy reason preventing a claim against the doctor in such a case and damages were awarded in respect of the diminution of the plaintiff's marriage prospects, pain and suffering, and anxiety and distress. There was no claim for damages in respect of the child's upbringing but the trial judge, Watkins J, foreshadowed future developments in saying:

> Surely no one in these days would argue [that damages were irrecoverable] if the child was born defective or diseased. The fact that the child born is healthy cannot give rise to a different conclusion save as to a measure of damages

and this view was supported in the Court of Appeal.

4.14 The validity of the wrongful pregnancy action was upheld in *Udale v Bloomsbury Area Health Authority*[36] in which, while damages were given for pain and suffering along with loss of earnings following a negligently performed operation, an award in respect of the cost of bringing up the child was firmly rejected. In his judgment, Jupp J reiterated that the joy of having the child and the benefits it brought in terms of love should be set off against the inconvenience and financial disadvantages resulting from its birth – 'It is an assumption of our culture', he suggested, 'that the coming of a child into the world is an occasion for rejoicing'.[37]

---

32   *Cockrum v Baumgartner* 447 NE 2d 385 (Ill, 1992).
33   *Lovelace Medical Center v Mendez* 805 P 2d 603 (NM, 1991). The offset rule was followed in *Sherlock v Stillwater Clinic* 260 NW 2d 169 (Min, 1977); *Burke v Rivo* 551 NE 2d 1 (Mass, 1990). This 'balancing' approach was criticised in *Public Health Trust v Brown*, n 30 above. J H Scheid 'Benefits vs. Burdens: The Limitation of Damages in Wrongful Birth' (1984-5) 23 J Fam Law 57. For a comparative review, see A Stewart 'Damages for the Birth of a Child' (1995) J Law Soc Scot 298.
34   This is also the case within the Commonwealth. See the intense debate in *CES v Superclinics (Australia) Pty Ltd* (1995) 38 NSWLR 47 at 77, where the concept of 'offset' was well described by Kirby A-CJ.
35   (1979) 123 Sol Jo 406.
36   [1983] 2 All ER 522, [1983] 1 WLR 1098. Similar sentiments were expressed in an unreported negligence case, *Jones v Berkshire Area Health Authority*, quoted in *Gold v Haringey Health Authority* [1986] 1 FLR 125; revsd [1988] QB 481, [1987] 2 All ER 888.
37   [1983] 2 All ER 522 at 531, [1982] 1WLR 1098 at 1109.

4.15 The Court of Appeal criticised this view in the later case of *Emeh v Kensington and Chelsea and Westminster Area Health Authority*;[38] in addition, there was a strong rejection of the trial judge's view that the plaintiff's refusal of abortion was so unreasonable as to eclipse the defendant's wrongdoing.[39] Equally significantly, however, the Court of Appeal awarded damages for the cost of rearing the child and rejected the policy objections voiced in *Udale*.

4.16 The stage was thus set for *Emeh* to be established as the leading case in England and the practice of allowing damages for the upkeep of an uncovenanted, albeit healthy, child was followed in a succession of cases – and these included special damages for the costs associated with any defect and, conspicuously, for the costs of private education when that seemed appropriate.[40]   None of these cases was taken to appeal. Indeed, the only remaining difficulty appeared to lie in the relationship between the two heads of damage – were they distinct or did one flow from the other? The Court of Appeal subsequently held that a wrongful pregnancy is a personal injury which cannot be separated from its consequences.[41]

4.17 Meantime, Scottish policy was evolving in its own way. Earlier reports are, for the most part, concerned with procedural matters and do not deal with the arguments or their outcomes.[42] Two unreported cases[43], both based on lack of warning of the risk of failure rather than on operative negligence, caught the attention of the media. Both were settled out of court; but the substantial sum of £50,000 was offered in compensation in *Lindsay*,[44] suggesting that the Scottish courts might well recognise the unexpected birth of a healthy child as a suitable matter for 'damages'. This appeared to be confirmed in *Allan v Greater Glasgow Health Board*,[45] in which the court explicitly accepted that there were no grounds – of principle or of policy – to

---

38   (1983) Times, 3 January; revsd [1985] QB 1012, [1984] 3 All ER 1044, CA.
39   More recently, see *Crouchman v Burke* (1997) 40 BMLR 163, where a woman who would have had an early termination refused one at 15 weeks 'for understandable reasons' (per Langley J at 176). The possibility that refusal of an *early* abortion might be regarded as unreasonable still remains open. For early discussion of the relationship between abortion and wrongful pregnancy, see K McK Norries 'Damages for the Birth of a Child' 1985 SLT 69; A Grubb 'Damages for "Wrongful Conception" ' (1985) 44 CLJ 30. We have discussed the problem in the light of later cases in J K Mason 'Unwanted Pregnancy: A Case of Retroversion?' (2000) 4 Edin LR 191. Abortion and wrongful birth are considered at para 6.31.
40   *Benarr v Kettering Health Authority* [1988] NLJR 179; *Robinson v Salford Health Authority* [1992] 3 Med LR 270; *Allen v Bloomsbury Health Authority* [1993] 1 All ER 651, (1993) 13 BMLR 47; *Crouchman v Burke* (1997) 40 BMLR 163.
41   *Walkin v South Manchester Health Authority* [1995] 4 All ER 132, (1995) 25 BMLR 108. Which meant, in passing, that actions for wrongful pregnancy would be subject to the Limitation Act 1980, s 11.
42   *Smith, Petitioner* 1985 SLT 461; *Jones v Lanarkshire Health Board* 1990 SLT 19, 1989 SCLR 542; affd 1991 SLT 714, 1991 SCLR 806; *Teece v Ayrshire and Arran Health Board* 1990 SLT 512.
43   *Pollock v Lanarkshire Health Board* (1987) Times, 6 January; *Lindsay v Greater Glasgow Health Board* (1990) Scotsman, 14 March.
44   N 43 above.
45   (1993) 17 BMLR 135, 1998 SLT 580, OH. The court found, however, that there had been no negligence in this case. See also *Cameron v Greater Glasgow Health Board* 1993 GWD 6-433, (Lexis transcript available), in which damages of £40,000 were agreed; again, however, the action was unsuccessful.

prevent an award of damages for the upbringing of a child born in such circumstances. There is, of course, much force in the argument that such compensation amounts to a rejection of a fundamental value in our society – that of family love. On the other hand, it is implicit that the patient undergoing consensual, non-therapeutic sterilisation does not want any more children and that this may be for economic reasons. That being so, it is hard to refute the words of Peter Pain J: 'Every baby has a belly to be filled and a body to be clothed.'[46]

4.18 The relatively still waters of cross-border agreement were, however, to be rudely disturbed when this fundamental contradiction was authoritatively addressed in *McFarlane v Tayside Health Board*.[47] Here, the Lord Ordinary in the Outer House of the Court of Session held that a normal pregnancy culminating in a healthy child was a natural event which could not be regarded as an injury – hence, it could not form a basis for damages. He also decided that the joys of the child's existence wholly compensated the financial cost of bringing up the child – he rejected the concept of 'off-set', or a balancing of some benefit against some disadvantage, in that it involved placing a specific value on the life of the child. This decision, which was, in the circumstances, surprising, was reversed in the Inner House, where the Lord Justice-Clerk declined to discuss the relationship of pregnancy to personal injury and, rather, addressed the problem in terms of the basic principles of Scots law.[48] Injuria or the invasion of a legal right – in this case the right not to become pregnant – was sustained at conception of the child. Damnum, or prejudice suffered in respect of a legally recognised interest, was manifested in the effects of pregnancy and childbirth on the woman's bodily integrity. An obligation to make reparation arises when there is concurrence of injuria and damnum – and these conditions were satisfied in the instant case once the pregnancy was established.[49] The Inner House rejected the proposition that the blessing of a child was an overriding benefit, pointing out that the couple were relying on sterilisation in order to avoid the additional expenditure which the birth of another child would entail and, having decided the issue by way of principle, went on to conclude that there was no overriding consideration of public policy which the awarding of damages would contravene.

4.19 Most commentators then assumed that the equilibrium of English and Scots law had been re-established but, again unexpectedly, *McFarlane* was appealed to the House of Lords,[50] presumably so as to ensure that this was so; equally unexpectedly, the appeal was unanimously upheld – at least in part. The House decided by a 4:1 majority that the 'mother's claim' in respect of pain and suffering due to pregnancy and childbirth should stand; the major issue, however, concerned reparation for the costs of bringing up a healthy child.

46 In *Thake v Maurice* [1984] 2 All ER 513 at 526, [1985] 2 WLR 215 at 230.
47 1997 SLT 211, (1996) Times, 11 November.
48 *McFarlane v Tayside Health Board* 1998 SC 389 at 393, 1998 SLT 307 at 310.
49 Reiterated by Lord McCluskey 1998 SC 389 at 398. The House specifically held that the deliberate continuation of the pregnancy did not affect the chain of causation: cf Slade LJ in *Emeh v Kensington and Chelsea and Westminster Health Authority* (1983) Times, 3 January; revsd [1985] QB 1012, [1984] 3 All ER 1044, CA.
50 *McFarlane v Tayside Health Board* [2000] AC 59, 2000 SC 1, HL.

4.20 The reasoning behind the rejection of the latter claim, which undoubtedly represents a U-turn in the development of the jurisprudence, has never been easy to unravel, given that the defender's duty of care to the pursuers was admitted and acknowledged by way of the 'mother's' claim; each of the five Lords of Appeal gave different reasons for his decision and there is neither the space nor, perhaps, the need to detail these here.[51] In summary, Lord Slynn concluded that it would be neither just nor reasonable to impose on the doctor liability for the upkeep of a child until maturity and this is the theme which is adopted most often in the derivative cases; Lord Steyn took refuge in some rather tenuous concepts of distributive justice; Lord Hope thought that, since the benefits associated with a healthy child were incalculable, it was illogical to attempt an assessment of the net economic loss sustained by the child's parents; Lord Clyde was struck by the disproportion between the damages available when based on the full costs of upbringing and the surgeon's culpability; while Lord Millett eventually returned to the reasoning in the index English case[52] in holding that the law must accept the birth of a healthy baby as a blessing, not a detriment.[53]

4.21 We find none of these reasons to be entirely satisfactory. The argument is not about the value of a child – it is simply one of whether or not two persons should be compensated if their financial resources are diverted as a result of the negligence of the agent engaged to avert that outcome.[54] Moreover, the House in *McFarlane* deliberately left open the possibility of recompense for the upkeep of an unexpected *disabled* child – since this was, apparently, still available by way of existing precedent, the lacuna had to be filled with some urgency. Efforts both to circumvent the decision and to clarify the situation were, therefore, to be expected.

4.22 Attempts to undermine the 'healthy child/no maintenance' rule were disposed of summarily. In *Richardson v LRC Products Ltd*[55] – a burst condom case brought under the Consumer Protection Act 1987, s 3 – it was clearly held that the rule applied whether the claim was laid in negligence or in breach of a statutory duty. *Greenfield v Irwin (a firm)*[56] was another case of missed pregnancy rather than failed sterilisation; otherwise, the conditions were very similar to those in *McFarlane*. The plaintiff, however, sought to distinguish her case on the grounds that her loss was consequent on the physical injury of the pregnancy rather than on negligent advice; she also rather ingeniously attempted to demonstrate a difference between expenditure on a child and loss of earnings due to caring for that child. The Court of Appeal

---

51 One of us has analysed the case in greater detail elsewhere: see Mason, para 4.15 above.
52 *Udale v Bloomsbury Area Health Authority*, para 4.14 above.
53 Although the matter was discussed in depth only by a minority of the House, a refusal to terminate the pregnancy was not regarded as a *novus actus interveniens*. The circumstances surrounding 'wrongful pregnancy' are such that a termination would be lawful under the Abortion Act 1976, irrespective of the health of the fetus (see chapter 5 for discussion).
54 The decision was, in general, badly received by academic lawyers – eg E Cameron-Perry 'Return of the Burden of the Blessing' (1999) 149 NLJ 1887; J Thomson 'Abandoning the Law of Delict?' 2000 SLT 43; O Radley-Gardner 'Wrongful Birth Revisited' (2002) 118 LQR 11.
55 (2001) 59 BMLR 185, [2000] Lloyd's Rep Med 280.
56 [2001] EWCA Civ 113, [2001] 1 WLR 1279, (2001) 59 BMLR 43.

found both distinctions to be irrelevant; the suggestion that failure to provide financial support would contravene the Human Rights Act 1998, Sch 1, Article 8 (respect for family life) was also dismissed.

4.23 Attempts to entrench the possible exception for disabled children firmly within the law have, in general, been successful – albeit misapplied in that the great majority of cases in which this aspect of *McFarlane* has been argued have been, in fact, instances of wrongful birth. As is discussed below, these have a wholly different foundation; accordingly, they are considered in chapter 5.[57]

4.24 The only true comparator in our view is *Parkinson v St James and Seacroft University Hospital NHS Trust*.[58] Here, a woman gave birth to a disabled child following an admittedly negligent sterilisation operation. Brooke LJ pointed out that parents in a similar position had been able to recover damages for some 15 years following *Emeh*[59] and that both the 'fair, just and reasonable' test and the principles of distributive justice would be satisfied if the award was limited to the special costs associated with the disability. He was supported in a powerful speech by Hale LJ, who was, incidentally, the first female judge to express a view on the *McFarlane* judgment. Hale LJ started from the premise that to cause a woman to become pregnant against her will was an invasion of her bodily integrity; she then listed an impressive catalogue of the consequences of pregnancy which, she insisted, retained an invasive nature despite the fact that they derived from a natural process. She could find nothing unusual or contrary to legal principle in awarding damages in such a case. Admitting damages limited to the restitution of costs beyond those involved in bringing up a normal child gave no offence to those with disability and simply acknowledged that the costs in the event of disability were greater than in the case of normality – put another way, the 'deemed equilibrium' between the benefits derived from and the costs of maintaining an uncovenanted healthy child that underpins the *McFarlane* decision is distorted to an extent that is determined by the degree of disability in an unhealthy child.[60] In our view, however, the importance of Lady Hale's opinion is that her arguments based on bodily invasion can be applied almost verbatim to the birth of an uncovenanted normal child; it not only clearly justifies the award of damages in the event of the birth of a disabled child but it opens the way for a review of the *McFarlane* decision itself should the opportunity arise. It does, of course, leave open the question of what constitutes abnormality or disablement but, so long as these are measured in terms of extra costs, the courts should have no difficulty in deciding the individual cases.

4.25 Lady Hale is not yet done, however. In a further variation on the long-running saga of the wrongful pregnancy action, she has extended the potential

---

57 For a fuller consideration of the post-*McFarlane* cases, see J K Mason 'Wrongful Pregnancy, Wrongful Birth and Wrongful Terminology' (2002) 6 Edin LR 46.
58 [2001] EWCA Civ 530, [2002] QB 266, [2001] 3 All ER 97. *Taylor v Shropshire Health Authority* [2000] Lloyd's Rep Med 96 is a comparable case but pre-dated *McFarlane* and is likely to go to appeal.
59 Para 4.15 above.
60 It is important to note that the apparently attractive concept of 'deemed equilibrium' was rejected in *Rees*, para 4.25 below in both the concurring and dissenting judgments.

McFarlane exception from disability in the resultant child to disability in its mother.[61]   In *Rees*, a healthy child was born, as a result of a negligently performed sterilisation operation, to a woman who was severely visually handicapped. Hale LJ could see no essential difference between compensating for the extra costs of bringing up a disabled child vis à vis his or her normal counterpart – as in *Parkinson* – and compensating a woman for the extra costs in supporting a normal child that were dictated by her own disability – thus continuing and extending the concept of a *persisting* injury that she developed in *Parkinson*. Hale LJ thought that this did no more than put the mother in the same position as her 'able bodied fellows' who, by contrast, had no *need* for additional help in attending to a child's basic needs. Walker LJ, while rejecting the argument based on 'deemed equilibrium', nevertheless agreed that the circumstances of the case were not covered by *McFarlane* and represented a legitimate extension of *Parkinson*. Waller LJ, however, in a dissenting judgment, pointed to the unfairness of compensating a woman by virtue of her physical disability when other mothers in as great a need could not benefit. While many have considerable intuitive sympathy for the majority in *Rees*, it has to be admitted that it raises its own problems and, in doing so, casts further doubt on the *McFarlane* decision. As to the former, while we have suggested that the courts are well able to judge the additional costs associated with disability in a child, it is, pace Lady Hale's disclaimer, far less easy to assess the *costs* resulting from a degree of disability in its mother. Moreover, we must ask what constitutes disability? and what is so special about physical disability? Presumably, *Rees* would extend quite naturally to mental handicap and, if so, why not to economic pressures? Waller LJ found these to be good reasons for dissenting in *Rees* – for our part, we prefer to see them as being among the basic reasons for rejecting *McFarlane*. As to our doubts, *Rees* re-emphasises the convoluted and disparate reasoning behind the *McFarlane* decision. Walker LJ was happy that the decision did not interfere with the 'blessings of a healthy child' line adopted, in particular, by Lord Millett;[62] Waller LJ, by contrast, considered that it *was* contrary to the principles of fairness and justice espoused by Lord Slynn[63] and, in his unique way, by Lord Steyn.[64]   *McFarlane* was, certainly, concerned only with the uncovenanted birth of a healthy child to healthy parents but, somehow, the true ratio behind that decision must be established. Waller LJ in *Rees* reminded us that the House in *McFarlane* recognised that a claim for damages for bringing up a healthy child born as a result of the negligence of a surgeon would succeed in normal circumstances;[65] a case that was decided otherwise on what were, largely, unrelated moral principles, provides a less than satisfactory base from which to explore its variations. The answer might be found were *Rees* to be heard in the House of Lords. Even better, the House might, then, be able to take the opportunity to reconsider its whole position as to wrongful pregnancy – and, hopefully, conclude that restitution on the grounds

61   *Rees v Darlington Memorial Hospital NHS Trust* [2002] EWCA Civ 88, [2002] 2 All ER 177, (2002) 65 BMLR 117.
62   2000 SC 1 at 44.
63   2000 SC 1 at 11.
64   2000 SC 1 at 16. Even so, one wonders if the reasoning in *Caparo Industries plc v Dickman* [1990] 2 AC 605, which was concerned with fairness inter partes, should be extended to include the interests of third parties.
65   At para 44. See also Thomson, para 4.21 above, for similar criticism.

of corrective justice should be available in *all* cases of wrongful pregnancy. As a coda to this section on failed sterilisation, we note what must be the ultimate in negligence actions backed by support from the legal aid fund.[66] A Mr and Mrs Danns, who became parents seven years after the husband's vasectomy, sued the Department of Health for failure to publicise information about the risk to them and to others in their situation.[67] The research on which they depended indicated a risk of recanalisation of the vas of some 0.05% – which would seem to lay a heavy burden on the protective arm of the civil service! In the event, and almost inevitably, the action failed on the grounds that, in general, how a minister's statutory duties are exercised is a matter for his or her discretion. By no stretch of the imagination could the civil servants and advisers to the department be regarded as being sufficiently proximate to the various members of the public who might have an interest in the topic of male sterilisation by vasectomy – and the learned judge gave several further trenchant reasons why the action could not succeed.

Non-consensual sterilisation

4.26 If consensual sterilisation raises ethical misgivings, then non-consensual sterilisation can be seen as a minefield of powerful objection. This form of sterilisation has been carried out in some countries as an official or unofficial part of programmes of eugenic improvement or birth control. In the United States, for example, the enthusiasm for eugenics which was the feature of the earlier part of the last century led to legislative measures in a number of states providing for the sterilisation of mental defectives, those suffering from certain forms of genetically transmissible diseases and, in some cases, criminal recidivists.[68] Such laws were declared unconstitutional in some states and, in others, the number of operations carried out was small; nevertheless, compulsory sterilisation measures still remain on the statute books in a few jurisdictions. Interest now centres on the management of individual cases and here, despite some inevitable inconsistencies, a consensus has evolved in favour of non-consensual sterilisation given very specific criteria of justification. The seminal case is *Grady*,[69] where the power of the court to exercise jurisdiction as to the sterilisation of an incompetent minor in the absence of statute was firmly upheld. The problem in all such cases is to strike a balance between the individual's right to bodily integrity and the right to choose an operation which, in the case of the mentally handicapped, may carry with it greater freedom of access to community life and relationships.[70] To make such a choice in surrogate fashion, however, is to invoke a 'substituted

---

66   *Danns v Department of Health* (1995) 25 BMLR 121.
67   Relying on the archaic Ministry of Health Act 1919, s 2, which spelled out the duties of the minister in general terms – including ' ... to secure the ... effective carrying out ... of measures conducive to the health of the people ... '
68   D W Meyers *The Human Body and the Law* (1970) pp 28ff; P R Reilly 'Eugenic Sterilization in the United States' in A Milunsky and G Annas (eds) *Genetics and the Law – III* (1985), ch 17. The almost unavoidable comparison with developments in Europe is discussed by A N Sofair and J C Kaldjian 'Eugenic Sterilization and a Qualified Nazi Analogy: The United States and Germany, 1930-1945' (2000) 132 Ann Intern Med 312.
69   *Re Grady* 405 A 2d 851 (Md, 1979).
70   In the US, see *Conservatorship of Valerie N* 707 P 2d 760 (Cal, 1985).

judgment' test. The great majority of courts have recognised the near impossibility of doing this in the face of congenital mental illness and have, accordingly, opted for a 'best interests' test, which is also central to the welfare principle on which the United Kingdom medical jurisprudence related to treatment of the incompetent is founded.[71] A most important United States case in this respect is that of *Hayes*,[72] in which it was laid down that the courts could authorise sterilisation in the absence of consent so long as, inter alia, the subject was incapable of forming a judgment, was physically capable of procreation, was likely to engage in sexual activity and there was no reasonable alternative to sterilisation.

4.27 The root problem of non-consensual sterilisation, overshadowed as it is by the ghost of the eugenic movement, lies in the fact that it raises starkly the subject of what has been named the basic human right to reproduce – to which we return for general discussion below.[73] The phrase seems to have originated in the American case of *Skinner v Oklahoma*[74] – which, in fact, concerned the punitive sterilisation of a man – and has, since, come into common usage throughout the English-speaking world. In the United Kingdom, the concept was first articulated in the very significant case *Re D (a minor) (wardship: sterilisation)*.[75] The minor in this case was an 11-year-old girl who suffered from a rare condition known as Sotos' syndrome. Her IQ was roughly 80, a rating which need not necessarily make it impossible for the person in question to cope reasonably well in everyday life or even to marry and raise a child. There was medical evidence to the effect that her condition showed some signs of improvement and that this improvement could continue.

4.28 In her judgment in this case, Heilbron J was strongly influenced by the evidence given to the court to the effect that sterilisation was not always appropriate in such cases and that such a decision was not within the scope of the clinical judgment of a single doctor dealing with the case. Also to be taken into account was the irreversibility of the operation and the significance of carrying it out on so young a person:

> A review of the whole of the evidence leads me to the conclusion that in a case of a child of 11 years of age, where the evidence shows that her mental and physical condition and attainments have already improved, and where her future prospects are as yet unpredictable, where the evidence also shows that she is unable as yet to understand and appreciate the implications of this operation and could not give valid or informed consent, that the likelihood is that in later years she will be able to make her own choice, where, I believe, the frustration and resentment of realising (as she would one day) what happened could be devastating, an operation of this nature is, in my view contra-indicated.[76]

71   See *Re F*, para 4.41, discussed in detail below.
72   *Re Hayes* 608 P 2d 635 (Wash, 1980).
73   See para 4.37.
74   316 US 535 (1942).
75   [1976] Fam 185, [1976] 1 All ER 326.
76   [1976] Fam 185 at 196, [1976] 1 All ER 326 at 335.

4.29 Heilbron J has been criticised for not having addressed the general issues involved;[77] she did, however, refer to the 'basic human right of a woman to reproduce' and concluded that it would be a violation of that right if a girl were sterilised without her consent for non-therapeutic reasons. *Re D* remained the English authority for more than a decade and was quoted with approval in the Canadian case of *Re Eve*.[78] *Eve* is an important case because, among other reasons, the Supreme Court of Canada took several years to deliberate and, in so doing, canvassed a large number of opinions; moreover, by the time the trial had gone through all its stages, virtually every variant had been supported in the judgments.

4.30 Eve was the mentally retarded adult daughter of a mother who asked that she be sterilised, a major plank supporting the request being that, in the event of Eve becoming pregnant, neither she nor her mother would be able to care for the baby. The Supreme Court was in no doubts as to its having a parens patriae jurisdiction through which to authorise sterilisation should the need arise. That power was, however, limited by the principle of its being exercised in the best interests of the girl. In the light of this, the judgment was concerned to distinguish between therapeutic and non-therapeutic reasons for sterilisation; La Forest J concluded:

> The grave intrusion on a person's rights and the certain physical damage that ensues from non-therapeutic sterilization without consent ... have persuaded me that it can never safely be determined that such a procedure is in the best interests of that person ... [I conclude that non-therapeutic sterilization] should never be authorised ... under the *parens patriae* jurisdiction.[79]

He appreciated that there could be difficulty in drawing a line between a therapeutic and a non-therapeutic operation, but was content to emphasise that: 'the utmost caution must be exercised commensurate with the severity of the procedure.' In essence, it was this problem which provoked the apparent conflict between the court in *Eve* and that involved in the comparable English case of *Re B*,[80] which was the first of its kind to reach the House of Lords.

4.31 Having been reported at much the same time, it is inevitable that the approaches in *Eve* and *Re B* have been contrasted. It is unfortunate that the English case concerned a girl aged 17 and she would, therefore, shortly have passed out of the English wardship jurisdiction and it was considered that there was no parens patriae authority on which to fall back in the case of an adult such as was available to the Canadian courts.[81] A speedy decision was, thus, dictated, and there is no doubt that Lord Hailsham LC, on it being

---

77 A Bainham 'Handicapped Girls and Judicial Parents' (1987) 103 LQR 334.
78 (1986) 31 DLR (4th) 1.
79 The extant case at the time, *Re K and Public Trustee* (1985) 19 DLR (4th) 255, in which the main therapeutic ground for sterilisation was a phobic aversion to blood which would be accentuated with the onset of the menses, was regarded as 'at best, dangerously close to the limits of the permissible' – this despite the fact that an Appeal Court judge in *Re K* thought that the case should never have come to the court (per Anderson JA at 277). See also the later New Zealand case *Re X* [1991] 2 NZLR 365.
80 *Re B (a minor) (wardship: sterilisation)* [1988] AC 199, [1987] 2 All ER 206, HL.
81 See G T Laurie '*Parens Patriae* Jurisdiction in the Medico-legal Context: The Vagaries of Judicial Activism' (1999) 3 Edin LR 96.

suggested that the girl's progress could well be observed for a year, laid open his defences when he said: 'We shall be no wiser in twelve months than we are now.'[82]   A massive literature was built up around the case and we are able to refer here only to those aspects that we regard as essential to the understanding of the seminal decision.

4.32 B was a mentally handicapped epileptic with a mental age of five to six years. She had never conceived and was not pregnant but, absent being fully institutionalised, she was in danger of becoming so. Medical opinion – which, in contrast to that given in *Re D (a minor) (wardship: sterilisation)*,[83] was scarcely challenged – was that she would either have to be maintained on hormonal contraceptives for the rest of her reproductive life or her fallopian tubes could be occluded – and the court recognised this as being an irreversible procedure; it was common ground that any pregnancy that occurred would have to be terminated.

4.33 In authorising sterilisation, the House of Lords upheld the decisions of both the court of first instance and the Court of Appeal. The basic principle involved was the welfare of the girl; Lord Oliver, in particular, emphasised that there was no question of a eugenic motive, no consideration was paid to the convenience of those caring for the ward and no general principle of public policy was involved. Lord Hailsham LC made some specific comments aimed, in the main, at explaining any apparent variances from other relevant decisions. With particular reference to *Eve*,[84] he said:

> [The] conclusion that the procedure of sterilisation should 'never be considered for non-therapeutic purposes' is totally unconvincing and in startling contradiction to the welfare principle ... [The] distinction [drawn] between 'therapeutic' and 'non-therapeutic' purposes of this operation in relation to the facts of the present case ... [is] irrelevant ...

4.34 Lord Oliver also found, in effect, that there was no logic in distinguishing preventive medicine from therapy directed to the ward's interest and we would certainly agree with this. It is, however, possible to argue that 'non-therapeutic' in terms of La Forest J's judgment in *Eve* referred only to treatment designed for the benefit of others. If this be so, *Eve* and *Re B* are not greatly in conflict.[85]

4.35 The *Re B* decision has been widely criticised in the British academic literature.[86] We wonder, however, how much the *medical* aspects of the case

---

82 [1987] 2 All ER 206 at 212. The interesting point has been made that, since the procedure is prophylactic in nature, there can be no such thing as an 'emergency' sterilisation. See G B Little 'Comparing German and English Law on Non-consensual Sterilisation: A Difference in Approach' (1997) 5 Med L Rev 269.

83 [1976] Fam 185, [1976] 1 All ER 328.

84 *Re B* [1987] 2 All ER 206 at 213.

85 K McK Norrie 'Sterilisation of the Mentally Disabled in English and Canadian Law' (1989) 38 Int & Comp LQ 387.

86 See eg M Freeman 'For Her Own Good' (1987) 84 LS Gaz 949; S P de Cruz 'Sterilization, Wardship and Human Rights' (1988) 18 Fam Law 6; R Lee and D Morgan 'Sterilisation and Mental Handicap: Sapping the Strength of the State?' (1988) 15 J Law & Soc 229; J Montgomery 'Rhetoric and "Welfare" ' (1989) 9 OJL Stud 395 – a particularly trenchant attack. It is fair to remark that the decision in *Eve* has not been applauded everywhere in Canada: see M A Shone 'Mental Health – Sterilization of Mentally Retarded Persons' (1987) 66 Can BR 635.

have been taken into account. The speed with which the decision was taken has been questioned;[87] but this is, we suspect, no more than a reflection of the unanimity of professional opinion – there can be no doubt that pregnancy *is* contraindicated in some patients with mental handicap and that B was one of them. Medically speaking, *Re B* and *Re D* are poles apart. Norrie, for example, was among those who felt that the former was a case that should never have occupied the courts' time; sterilisation was always legal by way of the doctrine of necessity – or, simply, it was a necessary part of the management of the child's health.[88] We suggest that the major conceptual difference between *Eve* and *Re B* is that the former attempts to generalise on principles, whereas the latter is determined to particularise on the facts – and we see no objection to the latter line of thinking so long as it is accepted as such.

4.36 Lord Hailsham, however, also addressed the question of rights and it is this issue that has so occupied the commentators. He said: 'The right [of a woman to reproduce] is only such when reproduction is the result of informed choice of which the ward in the present case is incapable'[89] and, again:

> To talk of the 'basic right' to reproduce of an individual who is not capable of knowing the causal connection between intercourse and childbirth ... [or who] is unable to form any maternal instincts or to care for a child, appears to me wholly to part company with reality.[90]

4.37 The concept of the right to reproduce is one which deserves discussion in depth but which, again, we cannot provide in the space available; suffice it to say that the existence of an absolute right is by no means certain. Simplistically, it is difficult to envisage a right that requires the co-operation of another person who is under no obligation to provide it; moreover, an absolute right to reproduce would entail access by right to all means of assisted reproduction including surrogate motherhood by way of womb-leasing – and this is clearly untenable.[91] Grubb and Pearl[92] argued very convincingly that the only such right currently recognised in English law is the right to choose whether or not to reproduce – this being grounded in the principle of individual autonomy.[93] If this be so, given the inability of a subject to make a rational choice, there can be little objection to the courts assuming this right on his or her behalf.

---

87 I Kennedy and S Lee 'This Rush to Judgment' *The Times*, 1 April 1987, p 12.

88 (1989) 38 Int & Comp LQ 387. But this definition of necessity would not always be agreed: see J E S Fortin 'Sterilisation the Mentally Ill and Consent to Treatment' (1988) 51 MLR 634. For assistance, see the opinion of Neill LJ in *Re F (mental patient: sterilisation)* [1990] 2 AC 1 at 32.

89 [1987] 2 All ER 206 at 213.

90 Ibid at 213.

91 Per Hale LJ in *Briody v St Helens and Knowsley Area Health Authority* [2001] EWCA Civ 1010, [2002] 2 WLR 394 at 404–405, [2001] 2 FLR 1094 at 1104.

92 A Grubb and D Pearl 'Sterilisation and the Courts' (1987) 46 C LJ 439. See also Nicholson CJ in the Australian case *Re Jane* (1989) FLC 92-007. The reasoning in this case was very similar to that in *Re B*.

93 The possibility that a refusal to provide fertility treatment or an enforced sterilisation could offend the Human Rights Act 1998, Sch 1, Article 12 does not seem to have been tested.

4.38 An alternative approach is to regard the 'right' as one to retain the capacity to reproduce.[94]   While this is still subject to the individual's ability to choose, it does, at first sight, make the justification for court interference with that right more difficult. In our view, the resolution of the dilemma rests upon the definition of reproduction which, surely, cannot be limited and impersonalised to the single aspect of giving birth – it must include an element of after-care;[95] some mentally handicapped persons may not be able to supply this, although some can – it is, again, a question of degree and a matter of the individual medical status.[96] Moreover, the practical significance of this relative right disappears when, as in *Re B*, it is acknowledged that any pregnancy would have to be subject to therapeutic abortion.

4.39 A final criticism of *Re B* has been based on the suggestion that it, and others like it, are sex discriminatory – 'Would the court', asked Freeman,[97] 'have sterilised a boy of 17?' The answer is certainly 'no' – and has been shown later to be so[98] – but this only proves the rule. Unfair it may be, but it is a fact of life that reproduction can have no immediately adverse medical effect on a man. The only bases for intentional, non-consensual, non-therapeutic sterilisation of a man would be punitive or eugenic, which is what all would agree should be avoided; the fact that decisions such as *Re B* are gender-based actually contributes to their justification.

4.40 Two very similar wardship cases were reported shortly after *Re B*.[99]   In both, sterilisation was approved at first instance and neither was appealed. Medical evidence was given at both hearings to the effect that the proposed operation was reversible[100] – in up to 75% of cases, according to the gynaecologists in *Re M* who, in disclaiming the emotive overtones of 'sterilisation', preferred to regard the operation as contraceptive in nature. We suspect that this greatly influenced the judges because the evidence in favour of early sterilisation was less than fully agreed in both cases; indeed, a change of mind on the part of one medical expert had to be specifically explained as not having been made for eugenic reasons. The most interesting feature of both *Re M* and *Re P* is that they can well be regarded as sterilisations which were authorised on social grounds for the benefit of the wards – a matter of protecting their life-styles – with a strong hint of regard for the benefit of their carers; the decisions are certainly open to criticism.[101]

---

94   S A M McLean and T D Campbell 'Sterilization' in S A M McLean (ed) *Legal Issues in Medicine* (1981).
95   For full – and prophetic – discussion, see J A Robertson 'Procreative Liberty and the Control of Conception, Pregnancy, and Childbirth' (1983) 69 Va L Rev 405; A Thomas 'For Her Own Good – A Reply' (1987) 84 LSG 1196.
96   See L Appleby and C Dickens 'Mothering Skills of Women with Mental Illness' (1993) 306 BMJ 348.
97   (1987) LS Gaz R 949.
98   *Re A (medical treatment: male sterilisation)* [2000] 1 FLR 549, (2000) 53 BMLR 66, [2000] Lloyd's Rep Med 87. This is an odd decision as males with Down's syndrome are characteristically sterile.
99   *Re M (a minor) (wardship: sterilisation)* [1988] 2 FLR 497, [1988] Fam Law 434; *Re P (a minor) (wardship: sterilisation)* [1989] 1 FLR 182, [1989] Fam Law 102.
100 It was said, in somewhat unusual phraseology: 'The situation to-day is that the operation is not irreversible although it is the current *ethical* practice to tell the patients that it is an irreversible operation' [our emphasis] (per Eastham J, *Re P* [1989] 1 FLR 182 at 189).
101 Eg M Brazier 'Sterilisation – Down the Slippery Slope' (1990) 6 PN 25.

4.41 Thus far, we have been dealing only with minors concerning whom there was no doubt, at the time of the courts' authority under the wardship jurisdiction. The problem of the adult who was incapable of consent to treatment was yet to come and was first addressed by Wood J in *T v T*,[102] a case which involved an adult incompetent who was found to be pregnant; medical opinion was consistent that the pregnancy should be terminated under the terms of the Abortion Act 1967 and there was an additional application from the subject's mother for leave to sterilise her at the time of the termination. In the course of his determination, which had to be made in the absence of precedent, Wood J found that the Mental Health Act 1983 provided no solution to non-consensual treatment other than as to that which was aimed directly at the psychiatric condition; that even if the prerogative powers of the Crown as *parens patriae* in respect of adults still existed, there was no one who could now exercise it; that to perform an operation without consent and in the absence of a defence was tortuous irrespective of hostile intent,[103] and that it was not possible to rely on implied consent in such a case. The judge was unhappy with the defence of necessity, mainly on account of its ill-defined limits, and preferred to rely on the demands of good medical practice – not, in itself, the most unambiguous yardstick. In the circumstances, he fell back on the expedient of an anticipatory declaration that the performance of the two operations would not be unlawful.[104] This solution was later approved in the House of Lords in the important case *Re F*.[105]

4.42 *Re F* was concerned very largely with administration; nevertheless, it forms the basis for the 'best interests' test which is now such an integral part of British medical jurisprudence; it, therefore, still merits consideration in some detail. F was an adult with arrested mental development who was not pregnant; the conditions of *Re B* were, effectively, duplicated save that F was now beyond the protection of wardship. The trial judge, Scott Baker J, was prepared to see all treatment for physical conditions that was given to mental patients in good faith and in their best interests as lying within the exceptions to the law of battery which had been created so as to allow for the exigencies of everyday life.[106] His declaration that the operation would not be unlawful was upheld by the Court of Appeal where Lord Donaldson MR, likewise, saw nothing incongruous in doctors and others who had a caring responsibility being required to act in the interests of an adult who was unable to exercise a right of choice.[107] The Master of the Rolls was, understandably, reluctant to accept that serious medical treatment could be subsumed under the umbrella of actions acceptable in everyday life and preferred the formula of it falling 'within generally acceptable standards'. Neill LJ, approaching the problem from principle, concluded that the performance of a necessary, albeit serious, operation, including an operation for sterilisation, on a patient who could not consent would not be a trespass to the person or otherwise unlawful.[108] The

102 [1988] Fam 52, [1988] 1 All ER 613. Discussed in depth by J E S Fortin 'Sterilisation, the Mentally Ill and Consent to Treatment' (1988) 51 MLR 634.
103 Cf *Wilson v Pringle* [1987] QB 237, [1986] 2 All ER 440, CA.
104 RSC Ord 15, r 16.
105 *Re F (mental patient: sterilisation)* [1990] 2 AC 1, sub nom *F v West Berkshire Health Authority* [1989] 2 All ER 545.
106 *Collins v Wilcock* [1984] 3 All ER 374 at 378, [1984] 1 WLR 1172 at 1177, per Goff LJ.
107 [1990] 2 AC 1 at 18.
108 [1990] 2 AC 1 at 32.

court was, however, unanimous as to the need for approval of the High Court before a sterilisation operation was undertaken.

4.43 The correctness of the decision to sterilise was not challenged in the House of Lords, which was, rather, concerned with the resolution of questions of law and of legal procedure. The House, inter alia, confirmed that the parens patriae jurisdiction no longer existed in England, and that, if it were to be recreated, it would be for the legislature to do so – something which the majority of commentators would approve. Their Lordships also ruled that the procedure by way of declaration was appropriate and satisfactory in cases of this kind,[109] the court having no power to consent to the operation. Undoubtedly, however, the most important aspect of the decision for our purposes was that the common law provides that a doctor can lawfully give surgical or medical treatment to adult patients who are incapable of consenting – provided that the operation or other treatment is in their best interests; it would be in their best interests if, but only if, it was carried out in order to save their lives or to ensure improvement, or prevent deterioration, in their physical or mental health[110] – a rather curious juxtaposition of the major emergency with mild palliation. The House went even further in indicating that it might be the common law *duty* of the doctor to provide treatment in the case of adults suffering from mental disability who were in the care of a guardian or who were detained in mental hospitals. Lord Brandon argued pragmatically that this must be so – otherwise the workload on the courts would be unbearable. Logically, this authority would also apply to sterilisation but six reasons were given for distinguishing that operation – including its general irreversibility which would almost certainly deprive the woman of 'what was widely, and rightly, regarded as one of the fundamental rights of a woman, the right to bear a child'.[111] The House considered, however, that the involvement of the court in cases of this kind was not strictly necessary as a matter of law; it was, nevertheless, highly desirable as a matter of good practice.

4.44 Most people would have regarded this as an unfortunate result. Apart from providing no positive guidance, the House of Lords further held[112] that whether the 'best interests' test had been met would be judged on *Bolam*[113] principles. The application of a test for negligence to a question of clinical practice has been criticised.[114] In any event, it seems to us that, having made a bid for judicial supervision, the court, in so stating, effectively handed back control of the decisions to the doctors.[115] In fact, Lord Griffiths' dissent on

---

109 The current procedural guidelines are to be found in *Practice Direction (declaratory proceedings: incapacitated adults)* [2002] 1 WLR 325, (2002) 65 BMLR 72.
110 Per Lord Brandon.
111 [1990] 2 AC 1 at 55, 56.
112 [1990] 2 AC 1 at 68.
113 *Bolam v Friern Hospital Management Committee* [1957] 2 All ER 118, [1957] 1 WLR 582.
114 D Ogbourne and R Ward 'Sterilization, the Mentally Incompetent and the Courts' (1989) 18 Anglo-Am L Rev 230.
115 We do, however, appreciate that this depends to some extent on whether 'a matter of good practice' refers to good *medical* or good *legal* practice. Our interpretation has been the former, but that may be taking a blinkered view.

this point seems to have won the day[116] and, although it is jumping ahead in time, it should be noted here that the current directive makes it clear that sterilisation of a person who cannot consent to the operation is one of two categories of case that will in virtually all cases require the prior sanction of a High Court judge.[117]

> Although there is little doubt that many people distrust unbridled powers of doctors – particularly in the field of social medicine – we have never shared Lord Brandon's fears that, but for the courts, there is a risk of sterilisations being carried out for improper reasons or with improper motives. There is always the General Medical Council.

4.45 The precedent set by *Re F* is that decisions of this nature will continue to be made on a case-to-case basis and it is because the details of each case differ, and because only the doctors in clinical charge of a case can possess all the facts, that we approve the process; calls for specific legislation[118] should, we believe, be resisted because it would, inevitably, lead to generalisation in an area where the individual is paramount. With that in mind, it will be useful to follow the fate of some of the cases that have been decided since *Re F* and the publication of its consequent practice note.[119]

4.46 Two cases were heard in 1992. *Re HG*[120] was another case which was heard in something of hurry due to the imminence of the subject's 18th birthday. The girl was an epileptic who suffered from an unspecified chromosomal abnormality; there was no dispute that pregnancy would be disastrous for her and that long-term hormonal contraception was contraindicated. In making the order, the deputy judge said:

> [My conclusion is that] a sufficiently overwhelming case has been established to justify interference with the fundamental right of a woman to bear a child. I am certainly satisfied that it would be cruel to expose [her] to an unacceptable risk of pregnancy and that that should be obviated by sterilisation in her interests.[121]

This case had some administrative significance in indicating that declarations could be made as specific issue orders under the Children Act 1989, s 8,[122] although an appeal to the inherent jurisdiction of the court is the preferred route.

4.47 The adult patient in *Re W*[123] was also an epileptic who, again, was at small risk of becoming pregnant. Nevertheless, sterilisation was held to be

116 In *Re F* [1990] 2 AC 1 at 70.
117 *Practice Note (Official Solicitor: Declaratory Proceedings: Medical and Welfare Decisions for Adults who Lack Capacity)* [2001] 2 FLR 158, (2002) 65 BMLR 72; it is to be remarked that this note deals only with adults. The other situation is the discontinuation of nutrition and hydration of a person in a vegetative state (see chapter 17).
118 In the US, see *Re Guardianship of Joan I Eberhardy* 307 NW 2d 881 (Wis, 1981); in Canada, *Re Eve* (1986) 31 DLR (4th) 1; in the UK, Shaw (1990) 53 MLR 91, Fortin (1988) 51 MLR 634, Bainham (1987) 103 LQR 334.
119 *Practice Note (Official Solicitor: Sterilisation)* [1990] 2 FLR 530.
120 *Re HG (specific issue order: sterilisation)* [1993] 1 FLR 587, (1992) 16 BMLR 50.
121 Ibid at 592.
122 A new *Practice Note* [1993] 2 FLR 222 was then issued to cover this line of approach.
123 *Re W (mental patient: sterilisation)* [1993] 1 FLR 381, [1993] Fam Law 208.

in her best interests and a declaration was granted. A feature of the case was the reliance on *Bolam* as a measure of 'best interests'; the decision was, thus, dominated by medical, rather than judicial, opinion – a feature that was severely criticised.[124]

4.48 The 1993 *Practice Note*, however, specifically advised that a declaration in favour of non-consensual sterilisation should be granted only if there was a real danger rather than a mere chance of pregnancy resulting – and this was reflected in *Re LC*.[125] *LC* seems to have been the first case since *Re D* in which sterilisation was refused in the face of medical opinion. The danger to the woman was, however, not so much that of pregnancy as of sexual assault – and the latter risk was present irrespective of her fertility. One notable feature was that the care afforded her was exceptional, and this, of itself, was thought to provide good grounds for not imposing the risks of a surgical intervention.

4.49 There was, then, a hiatus in reported cases until 1998, when two further cases were heard. In the first of these,[126] Johnson J found the circumstances to be indistinguishable from those in *Re LC* in that the risk of pregnancy was speculative rather than real. This aspect of the case was independent of any 'right to reproduce' which, it was agreed, was irrelevant in *Re B* terms.[127] The freedom from risk, however, was, again, due to the care expended by the woman's parents; it is probably this factor which mainly caused the judge to reach his conclusion and to follow *Re LC* 'with reluctance'.

4.50 Thus, it seemed that a group of cases were being separated which depended on the immediacy of the risk of pregnancy. This was confirmed from the other side of the coin in *Re X*,[128] in which the woman concerned actually wanted to have a baby – sterilisation was authorised when it was agreed that she would have been incapable of looking after it.

4.51 All the cases thus far discussed have been related to the incompetent's way of life or, put another way, to her social best interests. At the same time, however, a line of cases was developing which referred to the subject's medical interests. The solution of some such cases will be obvious – clearly, it would not be necessary to obtain court approval before undertaking a hysterectomy in the treatment of carcinoma of the uterus despite the fact that she would be rendered infertile as a secondary effect. Rather more difficulty arises when the disability is associated with menstruation – a very real problem in the case of the incompetent who may well be confused and disturbed even by normal periods. On the other hand, sterilisation is a high price to pay for treating what may well have been, in ordinary circumstances, a comparatively simple menstrual disorder. In the first such case to come before the British

124 See I Kennedy 'Commentary' (1993) 1 Med L Rev 234.
125 *Re LC (medical treatment: sterilisation)* [1997] 2 FLR 258, [1997] Fam Law 604 (judgment in the case was given in October 1993).
126 *Re S (medical treatment: adult sterilisation)* [1998] 1 FLR 944, [1998] Fam Law 325.
127 [1988] AC 199, [1987] 2 FLR 314. See paras 4.33–4.34 above for dicta of Lord Oliver and Lord Hailsham in that case. Johnson J did not, however, feel the same way about the House of Lords' somewhat cavalier attitude to the risks of surgical operation.
128 *Re X (adult patient: sterilisation)* [1998] 2 FLR 1124, [1998] Fam Law 737.

courts, *Re E*,[129] concerning a 17-year-old, Sir Stephen Brown held that no formal consent of the court was necessary and that the parents were in a position to give a valid consent: 'A clear distinction is to be made between an operation to be performed for a genuine therapeutic reason and one to achieve sterilisation.'[130]   Sir Stephen's easy assurance in the face of the difficulties encountered in Australia (see para 4.57 below) is a little difficult to accept. Nevertheless, in a second case, *Re GF*,[131] which concerned a 29-year-old woman, the President underlined his opinion and declined to grant a declaration of lawfulness on the grounds that it was unnecessary when an operation was designed to improve the health of the patient. He did, however, lay down the conditions under which no application to the court was needed. These were that two doctors agreed: first, that the operation was necessary for therapeutic purposes; secondly, that it was in the patient's best interests; and, thirdly, that no practicable less intrusive treatment was available.

4.52 It was probably this last condition that brought a third case to the Family Court – that of *Re Z*,[132] which involved a 19-year-old woman with Down's syndrome. There was essentially no dispute as to the facts that Z suffered from painful and excessive periods and that a pregnancy would be disastrous; however, the experts disagreed as to how these conditions were to be managed – was it to be by way of the insertion of a Mirena intra-uterine device (see para 4.77 below) or by hysterectomy? Bennett J, relying on Lord Goff in *Re F*,[133] clarified the position of experts vis à vis the court:

> Experts are what they are – experts. They must be listened to with respect, but their opinions must be weighed and judged by the court.[134]

In the end, Bennett J concluded that Z's best interests were served by hysterectomy, the risks of which were offset by the certainty that it would eliminate her periods and would, at the same time, protect her totally from pregnancy; the use of a coil was unacceptably uncertain on both counts.

4.53 The problem of treatment of menstrual 'phobias' has also arisen in Scotland, where it provided a part basis for the only reported case so far in which sterilisation of an incapax has been opposed. In *L, Petitioner*,[135] it was held in the Outer House of the Court of Session that sterilisation of an autistic woman would not be justified by the avoidance of pregnancy alone – other methods of contraception were available, although these had their inbuilt risks.[136] The fact that these would not prevent menstruation, with which she was unable to cope, tipped the balance in favour of sterilisation by way of partial hysterectomy. It is to be noted that Scots law as to the treatment of

129 *Re E (a minor) (medical treatment)* [1991] 2 FLR 585, (1992) 7 BMLR 117.
130 (1992) 7 BMLR 117 at 119.
131 [1992] 1 FLR 293, [1993] 4 Med LR 77, sub nom *F v F* (1992) 7 BMLR 135.
132 *Re Z (medical treatment: hysterectomy)* [2000] 1 FLR 523, (1999) 53 BMLR 53.
133 [1990] 2 AC 1 at 80.
134 (2000) 53 BMLR 53 at 64.
135 1996 SCLR 538. Other, unopposed, sterilisation applications have been granted: A Ward 'Tutors to Adults: Developments' 1992 SLT 325.
136 For further discussion, see para 4.64 below.

those who cannot consent will be revolutionised with the introduction of the Adults with Incapacity (Scotland) Act 2000.[137]

4.54 In England, the various threads of 'social' and therapeutic sterilisation have now been drawn together in *Re S*[138] – the first relevant case to reach the Court of Appeal since *Re F*. Here, the conditions and the problems were very similar to those in *Re Z* save that the risks of pregnancy were rather more proximate in the latter – indeed, Wall J at first instance confirmed that the only reason a declaration was sought was that alternative methods of treatment were available and had been advocated. Wall J, in fact, regarded S's menstrual problems as more important than the risk of pregnancy and followed Bennett J in *Re Z* in concluding that S's best interests lay in a sub-total hysterectomy rather than in the insertion of a coil which, of itself, did not require court approval. Having declared the hysterectomy to be lawful, he then adopted the rather innovative strategy of leaving the choice of treatments to S's mother and her medical advisers in consultation.

4.55 In the event, the Court of Appeal were highly, and perhaps unfairly, critical of this decision, pointing out that the judge had run contrary to unanimous medical opinion; the declaration in favour of hysterectomy was reversed in favour of the insertion of a coil with the option of a further hearing should this not prove an effective remedy. The details of the individual case are not, however, as important as are the wider implications as to the relationship between the *Bolam* test[139] and the 'best interests' test. As Thorpe LJ put it: 'There can be no doubt that the speeches in *Re F* determine that the *Bolam* test is relevant to the judgment of the adult patient's best interests when a dispute arises as to the advisability of medical treatment'. There can, however, be a number of courses which might be followed by responsible doctors; the function of the *Bolam* test is, therefore, of a preliminary nature, doing no more than to establish the propriety of the options on offer. By contrast, there can be only one 'best interest' – a phrase which the court considered to be synonymous with the patient's welfare – and it is the function of the doctor or of the court to establish this as the paramount precondition to providing treatment for the incompetent. Moreover, the welfare of the patient will be decided on more than medical grounds – ethical, social, moral and welfare considerations must also be weighed in the balance.[140] The *Bolam* test, thus, has no place in the second or determinative phase of what is, effectively, a two-stage test for the lawfulness of non-voluntary treatment. It will be seen in chapter 9 that *Bolam* is coming under increasing attack as a modern legal principle; in our view, *Re S* provides a particularly strong barrier to any extension of its application.

---

137 For the avoidance of confusion with previous editions of this book, note that the 2000 Act, s 80 abolishes the office of tutor-dative.
138 *Re S (adult patient: sterilisation)* [2000] 1 FLR 465, [2000] Fam Law 322, revsd [2001] 3 Fam 15, [2000] 3 WLR 1288.
139 Discussed in detail in chapter 9. In brief: The doctor is not negligent if he follows a course which would be regarded as acceptable by a responsible body of medical opinion.
140 Per Butler-Sloss P [2000] 3 WLR 1288 at 1288, 1296. The President also noted that she had expressed similar views in *Re A*, para 4.39 above.

4.56 A final and important comment on *Re S* is to note that the Court of Appeal was unanimous in holding that any interpretation of Sir Stephen Brown's ruling on the need for involvement of the courts in cases such as these[141] should 'incline towards the strict and avoid the liberal' – a form of words which carries a ring of euphemism!

The Australian experience

4.57 No discussion of the role of the courts and of parents in this very particular area of medical jurisprudence would be complete without a short review of the Australian experience which, when the cases are taken in sequence, brings the problems into clear focus. In considering the need for involvement of the courts in non-voluntary sterilisation decisions, a surprisingly generous view of the medical profession was taken by Cook J in the first Australian case to be decided[142] when he said:

> It is not conceivable to this court that medical advisors would prostitute their Hippocratic Oath to perform unnecessary or ill-advised or untimely operations, particularly of a major kind.

4.58 *Re a Teenager* was a complex case and was at first thought to be solvable within the confines of the family acting in concert with the family medical practitioner; it reached court in an unusual way. The child, aged 14, had not yet started menstruating and the issue was that of the fear of the effects of menstruation on a girl who had a 'phobic reaction to blood'. Cook J took considerable note of the effects on others than the subject, ignored some powerful opposing opinions and held that consent to a hysterectomy lay within parental powers.

4.59 It is unsurprising that this decision was soon challenged in the very similar – even to the extent of both being pre-menstrual – case of *Re Jane*,[143] in which Nicholson CJ pointed to the difficulties of leaving matters in the hands of the medical profession in saying 'it is also possible that members of that profession may form sincere but misguided views about the appropriate steps to be taken'. Consequently, he held that the consent of the court was required when the prime purpose of the procedure was non-therapeutic and, in the event, a sterilisation was authorised in the best interests of the girl – best interests being judged in respect of her total environment.[144] The court demonstrated its obvious concern in recognising that the question of whether menstruation constituted a medical or social problem presented considerable difficulty. It is, in fact, clear from what has already been said that, whereas the English courts tend to regard 'menstrual' cases as being medical in nature, the Australian courts prefer not to compartmentalise their reasons and confine

---

141 Para 4.51 above.
142 *Re a Teenager* [1989] FLC 92-006.
143 (1989) FLC 92-007, sub nom *Re Jane, Re Elizabeth* (1989) 13 Fam LR 47.
144 For discussion of these and other cases, see K Petersen 'Private Decisions and Public Scrutiny: Sterilisation and Minors in Australia and England' in S A M McLean (ed) *Contemporary Issues in Law, Medicine and Ethics* (1996) ch 4.

'medical sterilisation' to those cases in which sterilisation is no more than incidental to treatment.

4.60 Judicial uncertainty on this point was settled, at least to a large extent, by the High Court of Australia in *Secretary, Department of Health and Community Services (NT) v JWB and SMB (Marion's case)*,[145] a case involving a 14-year-old epileptic girl with serious behavioural problems. Space does not admit of an analysis of the opinions delivered by the seven judges.[146] Suffice it to say that the majority of the court acknowledged that a distinction was to be drawn between therapeutic and non-therapeutic non-consensual sterilisation. They were, however, reluctant to use that precise wording because of its uncertainty. Nevertheless, the basis for their interpretation can be inferred from the fact that they made it clear that 'in speaking of sterilisation in this context, we are not referring to sterilisation which **is** a by-product of surgery appropriately carried out to treat some malfunction or disease'[147] – thus confirming the trend we have noted above. It will be seen, however, that this construct evades the issue of psychological trauma and, indeed, the case amplifies the difficulties in classifying 'menstruation' for, when it was remitted to the Family Court,[148] Nicholson CJ remarked:

> This case probably falls into the category where the court's consent is unnecessary ... since the procedure was required for medical and therapeutic reasons.

Within these parameters, it was held that non-therapeutic sterilisation always required the consent of the court; and, significantly, that a non-therapeutic operation could be authorised so as to enable her to 'lead a life in keeping with her needs or capacities'.[149]

4.61 Difficulties and doubts still remain, however, despite the careful exploration of their nature. The Australian courts have been at some pains to emphasise the dangers of generalising in such a highly personalised area;[150] that being the case, anomalies are bound to occur. Thus, in a later case,[151] involving severe disability following birth trauma, Warnick J appeared to interrupt the steady development of a jurisprudence when he said:

> To make a decision in this case in favour of sterilisation would be virtually equivalent to establishing a policy that all females with profound disabilities ... should be sterilised.

4.62 This apparently maverick case has, however, been distinguished on the grounds that Sarah had been institutionalised since early childhood; the judge was of the opinion that the real purpose of the application in the case lay in

145 (1992) 175 CLR 218, (1992) 66 ALJR 300.
146 The case is thoroughly explored by N Cica 'Sterilising the Intellectually Disabled' (1993) 1 Med L Rev 186.
147 (1992) 175 CLR 218 at 250.
148 *Re Marion (No 2)* (1992) 17 Fam LR 336.
149 At CLR 260.
150 See, particularly, the extensive discussion of the principles in the appeal stage of *P v P* (1994) 19 Fam LR 1.
151 *Re L and M (Sarah's case)* (1993) 17 Fam LR 357.

the convenience of her professional carers – to an extent, therefore, *Sarah's case* serves only to confirm the 'best interests' principle. It was followed by the last Australian case we intend to discuss – *P v P*[152] – which was, perhaps, unique in being one in which sterilisation was refused at first instance but was authorised on appeal. In support of their decision, the Full Court of the Family Court gave seven reasons which they found compelling and, at the same time, drew up guidelines to be followed in future cases. Thus, the majority of 'Western' jurisdictions have now evolved Codes of Practice which closely follow the current English *Practice Note*.[153]

4.63 It is clear from what has been said already, that we believe the solution of ethical problems in medicine is very much a matter of the evaluation of the individual case. If, however, one seeks a general solution to the problem of non-consensual sterilisation of the incompetent, it seems that, in reaching a position which lies somewhere between the rigid stance of the Supreme Court of Canada and the early paternalistic approach of the House of Lords, the High Court and the Family Court of Australia has reached a compromise which is probably as good as is obtainable and which seems to have influenced the more recent English decisions.[154] Two features of the Australian approach seem to us to stand out. First, the Australian courts tend to concentrate on menstruation as being something strongly to be avoided in persons who can neither understand nor manage the condition; the avoidance of pregnancy, although always considered, takes a relatively secondary role in the deliberations. Second, the judicial approach is essentially practical. Although it is the rule that all cases should be heard by the Family Court, the concept of a 'right to reproduce' in persons whose pregnancy would inevitably result in therapeutic termination is scarcely addressed – and a 'rights discourse' was virtually rejected in *Marion's* case. Having said which, it has to be admitted that there has been very little conflict as to the capacity of the Australian subjects. Nevertheless, perhaps the most important general feature to be extracted from the cases is their pragmatic acceptance that non-therapeutic or social considerations – which we are happy to see as aspects of preventive or holistic medicine – can properly be prayed in aid of the incompetent minor. The words of Pashman J in *Re Grady*, which provide a suitable coda to the discussion:

> [She] should have the opportunity to lead a life as rewarding as her condition will permit. Courts should cautiously but resolutely help her achieve the fullness of that opportunity. If she can have a richer and more active life, only if the risk of pregnancy is permanently eliminated, then sterilisation may be in her best interests [and] it should not be denied to her.[155]

152 *P v P* (1994) 19 Fam LR 1, Full Court of the Family Court.
153 Fn 131 above.
154 It is of interest that both the English and the Australian courts are content to leave representation of the incompetent to the Public Advocate or other equivalent of the Official Solicitor although the latter may require a separate representative in selected cases. The obligatory appointment of a special guardian – or sterilisation carer – in Germany as described by Little, para 4.31 above, may be an intuitive reaction to that country's unfortunate history in respect of sterilisation.
155 *In the matter of Lee Ann Grady* 426 A 2d 467 (NJ, 1981) at 486.

OTHER FORMS OF CONTRACEPTION

4.64 It may well be thought that many of the problems posed in the foregoing discussion of sterilisation – and particularly those of non-consensual sterilisation – could be obviated by the use of an alternative form of contraception[156]. Few long-term contraceptive methods can, however, be applied without some risk – and the risk may be serious. Oral hormonally based contraception has been greatly refined over the years but there is no doubt that compounds with a high oestrogen content will predispose to intravascular thrombosis;[157] progestogens increase the liability to cardiovascular disease when combined with smoking;[158] 'depot' preparations may cause menstrual disturbances;[159] and a possible association between contraceptive therapy and an increased incidence of carcinoma of the breast or cervix is still debated.[160] Although the evidence is ambiguous, the probability is that the risk of using the newer, or 'third generation', progestogen pills is some 1.7 times that when using the earlier preparations;[161] against this, it must be remembered that, on a world-wide scale, the risk of death associated with pregnancy is several hundred times that of death associated with contraception.[162]

156 For an update, see D T Baird and A F Glasier 'Contraception' (1999) 319 BMJ 969.
157 While we have no intention of discussing such matters in detail, it has to be remembered that the causes of intravenous and intra-arterial thrombosis differ; the harmful effect of a given type of contraceptive on one form must be balanced against its possible beneficial effect on the other: K McPherson 'Third Generation Oral Contraception and Venous Thromboembolism' (1996) 312 BMJ 68. So far as we are aware, contraceptives have been blamed for death in only one reported litigation case; *Coker v Richmond, Twickenham and Roehampton Area Health Authority* [1996] 7 Med LR 58; the action failed on the grounds that the risks had been properly explained – which probably accounts for the dearth of reports. Similarly, an allegation that a second generation contraceptive was responsible for a tragic case of brain stem stroke, failed on its facts and on the grounds of causation – an association between the drug and the event could not be shown on the balance of probability: *Vadera v Shaw* (1999) 45 BMLR 162, CA. The case, which has considerable significance in relation to statistical evidence, is discussed by R Goldberg 'The Contraceptive Pill, Negligence and Causation: Views on *Vadera v Shaw*' (2000) 8 Med L Rev 316.
158 Indeed, smoking increases the associated risks of thrombosis almost irrespective of the type of oral contraceptive in use: B V Stadel 'Oral Contraceptives and Cardiovascular Disease' (1981) 305 New Engl J Med 612.
159 D R Bromham 'Contraceptive Implants' (1996) 312 BMJ 1555; *Blyth v Bloomsbury Health Authority* [1993] 4 Med LR 151, discussed at p 283 below. Insertion and removal also requires expertise and may be a source of litigation: J Roberts 'Women in US Sue Makers of Norplant' (1994) 309 BMJ 145.
160 J O Drife 'The Contraceptive Pill and Breast Cancer in Young Women' (1989) 298 BMJ 1269. For a succinct analysis of the whole field, see A Szarewski and J Guiilebaud 'Contraception' (1991) 302 BMJ 1224.
161 J M Kemmeren, A Algra and D E Grobbee 'Third Generation Oral Contraceptives and Risk of Venous Thrombosis: Meta-analysis' (2001) 323 BMJ 131. The annual death rate due to idiopathic venous thromboembolism in users of contraceptives in general is of the order of 1:100,000: L Parkin, D C G Skegg, M Wilson et al 'Oral Contraceptives and Fatal Pulmonary Embolism' (2000) 355 Lancet 2133.
162 J O Drife 'The Third Generation Pill Controversy ("Continued")' (2001) 323 BMJ 119. A major class action, brought on behalf of seven women who have died from thrombotic disease, found that the risk from third generation contraceptives was not significantly greater than that of the second generation: *XYZ v Schering Health Care Ltd* [2002] EWHC 1420 (QB), [2002] All ER (D) 437 (Jul). The difference of a factor of 1.7 was accepted but it had been agreed that the action would fail if the increased risk was less than x 2. The issue cannot be said to be settled as yet.

4.65 The very effective interceptive methods are also suspect in that, although any association is certainly not a simple one, they may cause pelvic inflammation and permanent infertility. A few years ago, the fear of litigation would have deterred many physicians in the United States from fitting an intrauterine device.[163] The formulation of IUDs is, however, changing – in particular, the customary copper base is being replaced by physiological progestogens; the latter are effective for at least seven years – and have the additional advantage of significantly reducing the menstrual flow – while the reputation of the former is being re-established.[164] In general, IUDs offer rather better protection against pregnancy than do depot hormonal contraceptives. These are, however, mainly aspects of clinical medicine; they are introduced here only to emphasise that non-surgical contraception also has its pitfalls and cannot be imposed without forethought – it will have been noted above that several of the non-consensual sterilisation cases were precipitated by the wish to discontinue contraceptives.

4.66 The main legal and ethical issues relate to the provision of contraceptives for minors; although this was once a burning issue, it has now lost its urgency and the historic case of *Gillick*[165] is probably best discussed under 'Consent' below.[166] Nevertheless, the dilemma confronting the doctor who is consulted by a female minor requesting contraceptive advice and treatment still merits consideration.

4.67 The problem is essentially that of deciding whether the physician should do anything which might facilitate her engaging in sexual activity. If the patient is, say, aged 14 or 15, he may well be of the view that that is too young an age for sexual intercourse. This disapproval is more likely to be based on the view that sexual activity at such an age may lead to emotional trauma and a risk of disease – including iatrogenic disease – rather than on social or moral grounds. On the other hand, a refusal to prescribe contraceptives may ultimately be more damaging to the patient in that sexual activity may result in pregnancy – and giving birth to a child or abortion at such an age are likely to be severely disruptive of the patient's life.

4.68 The ethical dilemma by no means disappears once the decision is taken to provide contraception; the doctor then has to make the difficult decision whether or not to inform the patient's parents. This is really an issue of medical confidentiality which is discussed in detail in chapter 8, below. The decision in each case might, however, depend on the circumstances. A doctor who informed parents of the fact that their 13-year-old daughter had

163 G R Thornton 'Intrauterine Devices: Malpractice and Product Liability' (1986) 14 Law Med Hlth Care 4 provides a good overview.
164 Useful recent reviews include J A Fortney, P J Feldblum and E G Raymond 'Intrauterine Devices: The Optimal Long-term Contraceptive Method?' (1999) 44 J Reproduct Med 269; D Hubacher, R Lara-Ricalde, D J Taylor et al (2001) 345 New Engl J Med 561. Note that the Court of Appeal in *Re S*, para 4.54 above, preferred the use of the Mirena coil to sterilisation.
165 *Gillick v West Norfolk and Wisbech Area Health Authority* [1984] QB 581, [1984] 1 All ER 365; on appeal [1986] AC 112, [1985] 1 All ER 830, CA; revsd [1986] AC 112, [1985] 3 All ER 402, HL.
166 See chapter 10.

taken to prostitution could surely claim that it was in the best interests of the child to do so; this may not be the case when a 15-year-old girl is doing no more than engaging in occasional sexual activity with one partner. Two distinct legal issues are raised in this connection. The first is the general question as to whether a doctor can properly treat a minor without consent of the parents and, more specifically, whether he may give advice and treatment as to birth control; the second raises the possibility that, in so doing, he may attract criminal liability as being a party to the offence committed by the man who has sexual intercourse with his female minor patient. Both these issues were partially resolved by the decision in *Gillick*.

4.69 This controversial case resulted from the publication of a circular by the Department of Health stating that practitioners could, in strictly limited circumstances, discuss and apply family planning measures to minors without the express consent of their parents; Mrs Gillick sought, inter alia, to have the instruction declared unlawful. In the absence of any binding authority, the trial judge relied heavily on the common law and on the Canadian case of *Johnston*.[167] While distinguishing between physical or surgical and medical treatment, he concluded that a person below the age of 16 was capable of consent to contraceptive therapy provided she was of sufficient mental maturity to understand the implications. The Court of Appeal, however, concentrated on the duties and rights of parents, which they considered inseparable. The trial judge's decision was overturned unanimously and the Authority, strongly backed by the BMA, appealed to the House of Lords. This final court of arbitration reverted to what might be loosely termed the 'mature minor' principle – and has come to be known as '*Gillick*-competence' – and decided against Mrs Gillick by a majority of 3:2.

4.70 We return to *Gillick* below;[168] for the present we can note the overall tenor of the judgment as expressed by Lord Scarman:

> If the law should impose upon the process of growing up fixed limits where nature knew only a continuous process, the price would be artificiality and a lack of realism in an area where the law must be sensitive to human development and social change.[169]

4.71 The thrust of the case is, however, to be found in Lord Fraser's speech, in which he said that the doctor would be justified in proceeding with contraceptive advice without the parents' consent or even knowledge provided that he was satisfied that:

(i)   the girl would, although under 16, understand his advice;
(ii)   he could not persuade her to inform her parents or to allow him to inform the parents that she was seeking contraceptive advice;
(iii)   she was very likely to have sexual intercourse with or without contraceptive treatment;
(iv)   unless she received contraceptive advice or treatment her physical or mental health or both were likely to suffer; and

---

167 *Johnston v Wellesley Hospital* (1970) 17 DLR (3d) 139.
168 See chapter 10.
169 [1985] 3 All ER 402 at 421.

(v) her best interests required him to give her contraceptive advice, treatment or both without parental consent.[170]

4.72 Lord Fraser emphasised that the judgment was not to be regarded as a licence for doctors to disregard the wishes of parents whenever they found it convenient to do so and he pointed out that any doctor who behaved in such a way would be failing to discharge his professional responsibilities and would be expected to be disciplined by his own professional body accordingly.

4.73 The House also considered the second question posed and, despite a dissenting opinion, ruled that it was unlikely that a doctor giving contraceptive advice to a female minor would be committing an offence under the Sexual Offences Act 1956, s 28. It was pointed out that, were the contrary to be so, an offence would be committed irrespective of parental consent. In essence, only if the doctor actually intended to facilitate unlawful sexual intercourse could he be regarded as abetting an offence under s 6 of the 1956 Act – and this must be a condition which borders on the inconceivable. Moreover, as Woolf J explained in the trial stage of the case, an accessory before the fact must know the material circumstances of the offence, not merely, for example, that sexual intercourse might take place at an unidentified time with an unidentified man.[171]

4.74 The medical response to the House of Lords decision in *Gillick* was generally one of relief. Yet it is possible that it is something of a Pyrrhic victory; in the event of a complaint being laid, it may be very much harder for a doctor to show that he or she conformed to all five of Lord Fraser's conditions than merely to convince his peers that he was following his reasonable medical judgment. The General Medical Council has now modified its original attitude to confidentiality and the minor patient – possibly because the implications of *Gillick* are so widely appreciated. The doctor undoubtedly has a difficult task in assessing whether or not his young patient has sufficient understanding and intelligence for him to treat her with equanimity. The GMC's guidelines now state that, if the doctor considers the patient to be incapable of giving consent because of immaturity, he or she may disclose relevant information to an appropriate person or authority if it is essential to do so in the patient's medical interests. This, however, is subject to the incapax having been told of the intention. Furthermore, the GMC follows Lord Fraser in emphasising that the judgment of whether patients are capable of giving or withholding consent to treatment or disclosure must be based on an assessment of their ability to appreciate what the treatment or advice being sought may involve, and not solely on their age.[172]

4.75 The narrowness of the decision in *Gillick* cannot be overlooked – it is noteworthy that, on a simple head count, more judges supported the plaintiff

---

170 [1985] 3 All ER 402 at 413.
171 A vast literature was built on *Gillick*. An interesting objective Australian view of the whole case is to be found in J Morgan 'Controlling Minors' Fertility' (1986) 12 Monash Univ LR 161.
172 General Medical Council *Confidentiality: Protecting and Providing Information* (2000) para 3.8. See also General Medical Council *Seeking Patients' Consent: The Ethical Considerations* (1998) para 2.3.

than opposed her. It is certainly true that the consequences of a medical refusal of contraception would probably be worse for the girls in question than would be the circumvention of parental control. Yet, despite the evident progressive development of the public mood in the last 20 years, the warnings of those who supported Mrs Gillick should not be summarily dismissed as the protests of a latter-day Mrs Grundy; there is an undoubted tendency at present to undermine the concept of the innocence of childhood. There are many pressures which increasingly encourage the young to seek the status of miniature adults and a readiness for sexual activity is essential to this identity – to quote Lord Templeman: 'There are many things which a girl under 16 needs to practise, but sex is not one of them.'[173] All of this has an effect on the social and psychological well-being of children and the corresponding medical evidence – particularly of the increase in cervical cancer in those who have shown early sexual promiscuity and the disturbing increase in the incidence of sexually transmitted disease – should not go unnoticed. Mrs Gillick was, perhaps, less villainous than she was painted at the time. She has now passed from the public eye as a defender of sexual mores; nevertheless, we will see as we go through the pages of this book that her place in history is assured as the woman who, albeit unwittingly, changed the face of adolescent medical treatment.

Post coital contraception

4.76 Certain types of contraception are designed to – or, in practice, do – work after the embryo has formed. These are referred to as interceptive methods – or emergency contraception – of which the intrauterine device and the misnamed 'morning after' pill are prime examples.[174] Such methods are, essentially, designed to prevent implantation rather than to be contraceptive and the question has arisen as to whether they offend against the Abortion Act 1967. Much of the discussion turns on the interpretation of the word 'miscarriage' and whether or not this relates only to the displacement of the implanted embryo. The Attorney General of 1983 is quoted as having said that: 'the phrase "to procure a miscarriage" cannot be construed to include the prevention of implantation.'[175] Despite this, an argument can be developed to show that the processes are legally similar;[176] we, however, find it illogical to suggest that there can be miscarriage in the absence of true carriage. In any event, to argue that interceptive methods of contraception are illegal is, in practice, unrewarding. The use of an intrauterine device (IUD) must surely be morally preferable to the legal destruction of a recognisable human fetus and it is a matter for satisfaction that the issue has now been put beyond doubt. It is currently legal for a pharmacist to dispense 'emergency

173 [1985] 3 All ER 402 at 432.
174 It has been pointed out that the term 'morning after' implies a spurious sense of urgency; in fact, emergency hormonal contraception need only be instituted within 72 hours of sexual intercourse: F C Reader 'Emergency Contraception' (1991) 302 BMJ 801.
175 41 Official Report (6th series) col 239, 10 May 1983.
176 I J Keown '"Miscarriage": A Medico-legal Analysis' [1984] Crim LR 604.

contraception' without a doctor's prescription[177] and an application for judicial review of the relevant order has been dismissed on the grounds that we have outlined above – interceptive methods of contraception, it was said, were plainly excluded from the operation of the 1861 Act.[178]

4.77 We do, however, see a clear legal distinction between interception and the use of displanting methods that are specifically designed to displace the implanted embryo – the technique that is euphemistically termed 'menstrual extraction' is a common example of the latter while an IUD may be used for both purposes – its intended function being largely a matter of timing. Although this comes squarely within the definition of abortion – and is, therefore, unlawful either under the terms of the Offences Against the Person Act 1861, s 58[179] and/or may well constitute a technical offence under the Abortion Regulations 1968[180] so far as we know, only one apposite prosecution has succeeded; the case did, however, concern the insertion of an IUD into a woman who was certainly pregnant.[181]   Rather more help can be gained from the media in an otherwise unreported case[182] which involved a charge under the Offences Against the Person Act 1861, s 58 against a doctor who fitted a contraceptive coil to his secretary some 11 days after they had had intercourse. The judge, having heard gynaecological evidence that implantation would not have occurred, withdrew the case from the jury on the grounds that the woman could not have been pregnant 'in the true sense of the word'. It is unfortunate that this case was disposed of so summarily, as there are certain aspects which give rise to doubt as to its value as a precedent – not the least being an apparent rejection of a charge under the 1861 Act on the grounds that 'the modern techniques of interference [with reproduction] were not [then] available'.[183]   The judge is also reported as saying: 'Only at the completion of implantation does the embryo become a fetus. At this stage, she can be regarded as pregnant.'[184]   Which leaves open the question of what would be

---

177 As a result of relatively intense lobbying – see for example J O Drife 'Deregulating Emergency Contraception' (1993) 307 BMJ 695 – the Prescription Only Medicine (Human Use) Amendment (No 3) Order 2000, SI 2000/3231 came into force in January 2001. 'Over the counter' emergency contraception is available in the United States in Washington and California.

178 *R (on the application of Smeaton) v Secretary of State for Health* [2002] EWHC 610 (Admin), (2002) 66 BMLR 59. This provides an exhaustive review of the relevant literature.

179 A number of jurisdictions define the point at which legal pregnancy begins – usually as at implantation. For details, see K McK Norrie 'Post Coital Anti-pregnancy Techniques and the Law' in A A Templeton and D Cusine (eds) *Reproductive Medicine and the Law* (1990).

180 SI 1968/390.

181 *R v Price* [1969] 1 QB 541, [1968] 2 All ER 282. The conviction was quashed on the grounds of a misdirection.

182 *R v Dhingra* (1991) Daily Telegraph, 25 January.

183 We wonder if this is a correct interpretation of the law. See D J Hurst 'The Problem of the Elderly Statute' [1983] LS 21. Such judicial legerdemain has been employed in respect of the Human Fertilisation and Embryology Act 1990: see *R (on the application of Quintavalle) v Secretary of State for Health* [2002] EWCA Civ 29, [2002] QB 628, (2002) 64 BMLR 72 and was firmly relied on in *Smeaton*, n 178 above.

184 He may have been attentive to the terms of the Human Fertilisation and Embryology Act 1990, s 2(3) which states that '*For the purposes of this Act*, a woman is not to be treated as carrying a child until the embryo has become implanted.' The emphasis is added but the wording could be persuasive in other branches of the law.

the result if an IUD were to be fitted after the eleventh day following intercourse. It seems unlikely that a prosecution would succeed – the difficulty of proving intent would be almost insurmountable – and, pragmatically, this is probably a good thing.

4.78 Whatever may be the true situation in England, it is apparent that in Scotland a prosecution for the common law crime of abortion could not succeed, as proof of pregnancy is an essential element of that offence. None the less, the possibility of a prosecution for attempted abortion remains open.[185]

185 *Docherty v Brown* 1996 SLT 325.

5   Abortion

5.1   The current interest in legal abortion[1] in Great Britain is not whether it should be allowed; lawful termination of pregnancy has been with us since the passing of the Abortion Act 1967 and it is here to stay. In our view, a major significance of abortion in the context of medical ethics lies in the effect it has had on the medical ethos. Once the Act was accepted by doctors, the profession abrogated a main tenet of its Hippocratic conscience – as recently as 1994, the Declaration of Geneva, as amended in Stockholm, was advising: 'I will maintain the utmost respect for human life from its beginning'.[2] The Declaration of Oslo, however, while retaining this moral principle, modifies it to accord with modem attitudes: 'Diversity of response to this situation [the conflict of vital interests of the mother with vital interests of the child] results from the diversity of attitudes towards the life of the unborn child. This is a matter of individual conviction and conscience.'[3] This ethical watershed has spilled over to influence attitudes of and towards doctors in relation to all aspects of life and death. Modem medicine now shows no embarrassment in toying with the concept of the wanted and the unwanted.

5.2   This is, however, something of a narrow view. In the wider context, attitudes to abortion depend almost entirely on where the holder stands in respect of, on the one hand, the fetal interest in life and, on the other, a woman's right to control her own body[4] and it is this which perpetuates a near intractable moral conflict. The trial of strength has been waged at a relatively low key in Britain; whether this has been due to tolerance or to indifference is a matter for argument. Passion has, however, run high in the United States, where the

---

1   In our view, a great deal of emotion would be avoided if this were described as 'termination of pregnancy' leaving the term 'abortion' to signify non-medical or otherwise unlawful activity – and this was probably the intention of Parliament in the 1960s (see below). 'Abortion' is, however, now vernacular English and cannot readily be displaced. It is a question of 'What's in a name?'

2   There is, however, a subtle change of wording from the original 'from the time of conception'. See Appendix B.

3   World Medical Association (as amended 1983).

4   The absolute nature of such a right is seldom questioned. The view that it is, in fact, restricted by correlative duties is put by H V McLachlan 'Bodies, Rights and Abortion' (1997) 23 J Med Ethics 176.

protagonists have not been above resorting to serious crime in order to advance their cause;[5] moreover, the issue has been debated at an overtly political level. The political significance has been no less important nearer to home in the European Union, where it bid fair to forestall the reunification of Germany; there, it is possible to follow the arguments through the more staid deliberations of the legislature and the courts. We return to these examples later; meanwhile, we look briefly at the development of the law on abortion in the United Kingdom.

THE EVOLUTION OF THE LAW ON ABORTION

5.3 The evolution of legislation to decriminalise abortion is so well known as to merit only brief description. The fundamental law in England and Wales lies in the Offences Against the Person Act 1861, ss 58 and 59. The Act proscribes procuring the miscarriage of a woman by a third party, self-induced miscarriage, attempted procurement of miscarriage and supplying the means to do so – it is to be noted that the word 'abortion' appears only in the marginal note to the sections.[6] The Act makes no distinction between criminal and therapeutic activity and, although currently under scrutiny, these sections have not been repealed. The proscription prior to 1967 was so strong that, in addition to being punished by the courts, a doctor involved in an abortion was extremely likely to have his name erased from the Medical Register. As a result, and because of the attitudes adopted to extra-marital pregnancy, a large number of abortions were performed by persons of varying skill and in varying conditions. The extent of this type of abortion has never been established satisfactorily: suffice it to say that, 40 or so years ago, it provided an appreciable contribution to the work of forensic pathologists.

5.4 The first statutory break in this chain is to be found in the Infant Life (Preservation) Act 1929, which introduced the offence of child destruction or causing the death of a child capable of being born alive before it has an existence independent of its mother. The offence was not committed, however, if the act was done in good faith for the purpose only of preserving the mother's life. This slight concession to the needs of therapy was still highly restrictive both as to reason and as to time – effectively, in the present context, it served only to decriminalise feticide in the event of an impacted labour. It was left to the case of *R v Bourne*[7] to temper the legal influence on medical practice in the field. Mr Bourne performed an abortion, with no attempt at secrecy, on a 15-year-old girl who was pregnant following a particularly unpleasant rape.[8]

5   See Lancet 'This Is a Deadly Game' (1993) 342 Lancet 939 – and the legal battle continues: F Charatan 'US Judges Rule in Favour of Abortion "Hit list"' (2001) 322 Brit Med J 818. For an excellent study of the development of the conflict in the US, see L H Tribe *Abortion: The Clash of Absolutes* (1992).
6   The distinction, if any, between 'miscarriage' and 'abortion' is of academic interest in relation to pre-implantation methods of contraception (see paras 4.76, above and 5.39, below). Some writers believe the terms to be interchangeable: see, eg I J Keown '"Miscarriage": a Medico-legal Analysis' [1984] Crim LR 604.
7   [1939] 1 KB 687, [1938] 3 All ER 615.
8   There is a particularly instructive review of the trial and its ambience in B Brookes and P Roth '*Rex v Bourne* and the medicalization of abortion' in M Clark and C Crawford (eds) *Legal Medicine in History* (1994) ch 13.

Although Mr Bourne was indicted under the Offences Against the Person Act 1861, the trial judge, Macnaghten J, took the opportunity to link the 1861 and 1929 statutes and ruled that, in a case brought under the 1861 Act, the burden rested on the Crown to satisfy the jury that the defendant did not procure the miscarriage of the girl in good faith for the purpose only of preserving her life: the word 'unlawful' in the 1861 Act 'imports the meaning expressed by the proviso in section 1(1) of the Infant Life (Preservation) Act 1929'.[9] Mr Bourne was acquitted, the summing-up essentially recognising that a woman's life depended upon her physical and mental health and that an abortion was not illegal if it was performed because these were in jeopardy.[10] The law and the medical profession then lived in harmony for many years; the *Bourne* decision was undoubtedly stretched to the limits of interpretation by many doctors but the authorities turned a sympathetic eye.

5.5 But it is never a good thing for any section of the public, no matter how well intentioned, to flirt with illegality; moreover, there was still no authority for termination of the pregnancy in the event of probable malformation or other handicap of the potential neonate – a proposition which many would regard as being of the first importance. The situation was resolved when the Abortion Act, which started out, more aptly, as the Medical Termination of Pregnancy Bill,[11] was put into law in 1967; despite repeated attack, it remained unchanged until 1990.

5.6 It is interesting to compare the historic attitudes in England with those prevailing in Scotland where abortion, either self- or otherwise induced, has always been a common law offence without being defined by statute. The whole subject, including a review of the 1967 Act, occupies less than three pages in *Gordon*.[12] The difference in concern lies in the emphasis laid in Scots law on 'evil intent', which leads to a greater interest in the moral background to action; by and large, doctors are assumed to be acting in good faith and there is little doubt that Mr Bourne would have been unlikely to provoke a test case in Scotland. It is, in fact, arguable that there was no need to extend the Act to Scotland; its inclusion was only justified in that it removed any doubt as to the limits of therapeutic abortion in that country where, in effect, a legal policy similar to that recognised in *Bourne* had been openly followed for decades.

The Abortion Act 1967

5.7 The Abortion Act 1967[13] has been significantly amended by the Human Fertilisation and Embryology Act 1990, s 37.[14] In summary, it now states that

---

9   [1939] 1 KB 687 at 691, [1938] 3 All ER 615 at 617.
10   [1939] 1 KB 687 at 694, [1938] 3 All ER 615 at 619. The Australian courts have also used the word 'unlawful' as indicating that there must be a 'lawful' reason for termination of pregnancy. See para 5.24 below.
11   The title was changed on the last day of the debate – almost, it seems, in a desperate effort to conclude the proceedings (Official Reports HC, vol 751, col 1780).
12   G H Gordon *The Criminal Law of Scotland* (2nd edn, 1978) ch 28.
13   Hereafter 'the 1967 Act'.
14   Hereafter 'the 1990 Act'.

a person shall not be guilty of an offence under the law of abortion when termination is performed by a registered medical practitioner and two registered medical practitioners have formed the opinion in good faith that the continuance of the pregnancy would involve risk, greater than if the pregnancy were terminated, of injury to the physical or mental health of the pregnant woman or any existing children of her family (s 1(1)(a)); these therapeutic and social grounds are subject to the pregnancy not having exceeded its twenty-fourth week. The remaining justifications are now free of gestational restriction. These are that there is a risk of grave permanent injury to the physical or mental health of the pregnant woman (s 1(1)(b)); that the continuance of the pregnancy would involve risk to the life of the pregnant woman greater than if the pregnancy were terminated (s 1(1)(c)) – accounting for 141 cases in 2000; and, finally, that there is a substantial risk that, if the child were born, it would suffer from such physical or mental abnormalities as to be severely handicapped (s 1(1)(d)) – 1% of the total in 2000.[15] Subsections (b) and (c) are, additionally, not restricted by requiring the opinion of two registered medical practitioners; single practitioners may operate on their own initiative in such circumstances.[16] Termination under the Act may be carried out in National Health Service hospitals or in places approved for the purpose by the Minister or the Secretary of State (s 1(3)). It is this clause which legalises abortions performed privately and for a fee. The demand for termination is, however, so great that, since 1981, a compromise position has been achieved whereby the private sector acts as an agency for the NHS. Twenty-seven per cent of terminations were dealt with in this way in 2000 when a further 24% were performed independently of the NHS – the relative decrease in privately arranged terminations as compared with those undertaken on an 'agency' basis is a comparatively new development. The advent of medical methods for the termination of pregnancy has dictated a change in the location rules, which are now relaxed for this purpose.[17]

5.8 The great majority of legal abortions are performed under s 1(1)(a) of the 1967 Act for minor therapeutic or social reasons (97% of cases in England and Wales in 2000). It is arguable that the risks of an abortion to the health of a woman are always less than those of a full-term pregnancy – particularly if the termination is carried out in the first trimester.[18] Equally, it is obvious that the mental health of a woman who is carrying an unwanted pregnancy must suffer more damage if she is forced to carry her fetus than it would is she were relieved of her burden. It can also be argued that simple economics dictate that a *risk* to the well-being of any existing members of the family is

15 Abortion Statistics (2001).
16 It is to be noted that s 1(1)(b) contains no comparative element – there simply has to be a risk.
17 Section 1(3A), inserted by the 1990 Act, s 37(3). There were 19,491 terminations involving the use of antiprogesterones in 2000, some twice the number performed in 1996.
18 The risks of pregnancy and childbirth are not constant. Overall, they are about equal but the risk of pregnancy increases with age. Conversely, the risks of abortion in young nulliparae are greater than of pregnancy unless the procedure is completed in the first eight weeks of pregnancy (PR Myerscough (1975) 1 J Med Ethics 310). Abortion methods have become much safer in the last 25 years but the complication rates still alter with gestation.

occasioned by the advent of another mouth to feed. The indications are, therefore, that it is impossible for a doctor to perform an abortion in Great Britain[19] that can be shown to have been unlawful provided that all the administrative conditions are met.[20] As a corollary, the doctor who applies the letter of the law must always be acting in good faith – indeed, possibly the only way in which a termination can be carried out in *bad* faith is when it is done without the woman's consent.[21] We have been able to find only one conviction under the Act[22] and this appears to have arisen mainly because of the way the operation was performed.

5.9 In any event, the medical profession as a whole tends to look on the Act as a success[23] – witness the opposition to change which continued to the last days of the Parliamentary debate on the 1990 Act. Occasionally, however, issues arise which strain the constancy even of the medical establishment – abortion on the basis of fetal sex selection provides such an example. The problem being put to him, Dr John Dawson, spokesman on medical ethics for the British Medical Association at the time, is reported as saying:

> To terminate a pregnancy solely on the grounds of the sex of the foetus is an abuse of medical skills. It is unethical and I believe the GMC should take a serious view . . . [of] a doctor who undertakes that sort of work.[24]

Which may well be so – the issue is of a different dimension from pre-conception selection which we have discussed above[25] or, indeed, pre-implantation selection (see para 6.26); nevertheless, it is difficult to see it as illegal. The 1967 Act, at s 1(2), specifically states that, in making a determination as to the risk of injury to the woman's or her existing children's health, 'account may be taken of the pregnant woman's actual or reasonably foreseeable environment'. Given the right ethnic ambience – most particularly within Asian and Muslim cultures

---

19 The Abortion Act 1967 does not extend to Northern Ireland, where the Infant Life (Preservation) Act 1929 is preserved in the Criminal Justice Act (Northern Ireland) 1945, s 25; conditions as to the latter are unaffected by the Human Fertilisation and Embryology Act 1990, s 37 (see 'Northern Ireland' below). The Channel Islands have adopted legislation which is similar to, although rather more strict than, that of Great Britain – eg Termination of Pregnancy (Jersey) Law 1997.

20 One could, in fact, apply much the same reasoning to s 1(1)(c) though we fancy that this section is intended to cover terminations once the life-threatening condition has arisen – most commonly in late pregnancy when the dangerous toxaemias of pregnancy may arise and the risks associated with termination are, correspondingly, greater.

21 And, even then, the charge would be under the Offences Against the Person Act 1861 rather than under the 1967 Act. See C Dyer 'Gynaecologist Acquitted in Hysterectomy Case' (1996) 312 BMJ 11.

22 *R v Smith (John)* [1974] 1 All ER 376, [1973] 1 WLR 1510, CA.

23 D Munday, C Francome and W Savage 'Twenty-one Years of Legal Abortion' (1989) 298 BMJ 1231.

24 'Babies of Wrong Sex Aborted, Claims Report' Scotsman, 4 January 1988, p 2. It is noteworthy that it may well become a criminal offence in Germany for the doctor to reveal the sex of the fetus prior to abortion: D van Zyl Smit 'Reconciling the Irreconcilable? Recent Developments in the German Law on Abortion' (1994) 2 Med L Rev 302. It has to be acknowledged, however, that a case can be made for sex selection based on the concept of procreative autonomy: J Savulescu 'Sex Selection: The Case For' (1999) 171 Med J Austral 373.

25 See para 3.18.

– there can be no doubt that the birth of a female child could affect a woman's mental health and, possibly, her physical well-being, and there is nothing in the Act which limits such risks to those directly associated with the condition of pregnancy.[26] Even a person with a Western background may be mentally disturbed by the thought of a third male (or female) child and, while gender abortion may not constitute a major problem in our society, it serves to illustrate how wide is the facility for termination within the wording of the 1967 Act.

5.10 The availability of lawful termination has been further extended by s 37(4) of the 1990 Act, which amends s 5(1) of the 1967 Act so as to read:

> No offence under the Infant Life (Preservation) Act 1929 shall be committed by a registered medical practitioner who terminates a pregnancy in accordance with the provisions of this Act.

The criminal associations with 'viability' of the fetus[27] and the living abortus (which we discuss briefly below[28]) are, therefore, now almost, although not quite, entirely dispelled.

5.11 There are still some who would regard abortion in Great Britain as being unreasonably restricted as compared with other jurisdictions;[29] even so, the scope of the Abortion Act 1967 probably exceeds that envisaged by its originators. The number of terminations carried out in England and Wales reached a peak in 1998, when 187,402 abortions were performed. The first fall since 1976 occurred in 1991 and the trend continued until 1995. There was, however, a sharp rise in 1996 and, since then, the upward trend has resumed; the crude abortion rate among women resident in England and Wales in the age group 15-44 years was 16.1/1000 in 2000 – this arising from a total of 175,542 terminations. The comparable figures for Scotland, where both the number and the rate of abortions have continued to rise steadily, were 12,862 terminations involving 11.8/1000 women in 1998.

5.12 The number of terminations provided for foreign women in England and Wales in 2000 – 9,833[30] – represented 5.3% of the total. This shows a marked decline from the peak in 1973 when 33.8% of legal abortions were for patients from overseas. Clearly, there have been policy changes in other countries and it is worth considering some of these briefly.

---

26 Similar views were expressed by D Morgan 'Foetal Sex Identification, Abortion and the Law' (1988) 18 Fam Law 355.
27 See para 5.42 et seq below. For review of attitudes to late terminations, see J Savulescu 'Is Current Practice around Late Termination of Pregnancy Eugenic and Discriminatory?' (2001) 27 J Med Ethics 165.
28 See para 5.46 et seq.
29 For a global view of trends, see R J Cook, B M Dickens and L E Bliss 'International Developments in Abortion Law from 1988 to 1998' (1999) 89 Amer J Pub Hlth 579. It has been suggested that some 42% of the British public would support availability of abortion without any reason other than the woman's choice: J Wise 'British Public Supports Legal Abortion for All' (1997) 314 BMJ 627.
30 9,767 or 99% were under s 1(1)(a) of the 1967 Act.

THE COMPARATIVE POSITION

Northern Ireland

5.13 We have, thus far, spoken only in terms of Great Britain as far as domestic law is concerned. The position in Northern Ireland is particularly sensitive, due to its close association with the Republic of Ireland.[31] As a result, the Abortion Act 1967 does not run to the Province, where the law is still governed by the 1861 Act; this has, however, been modified by some important court decisions. In *Re K (a minor)*,[32] it was held that the law lay in the 1861 Act as modified by the charge to the jury in *R v Bourne*;[33] termination of a 13-week pregnancy in a severely handicapped ward of court was authorised. Again, in *Re A*,[34] the court used the reasoning in *Bourne* to apply the Criminal Justice Act (Northern Ireland) 1945, s 25 to the 1861 Act; a termination was held to be in the handicapped woman's best interests. It will be seen, below, that a very similar situation – albeit one that could be regarded as confusing – exists in New South Wales, where a particularly liberal approach to abortion has evolved. Thus, it may well be that the potential exists for homologation of abortion practice throughout the component parts of the United Kingdom. However, such a potential has not yet been realised; 1,528 women from Northern Ireland obtained terminations in England and Wales during 2000.

The Republic of Ireland

5.14 The Republic of Ireland, along with Germany within the European Union, confers a constitutional right to life on the fetus while, at the same time, paying due regard to the equal right to life of the mother.[35] The definitive law on abortion is derived from the UK's Offences Against the Person Act 1861 which is incorporated in the Health (Family Planning) Act 1979. As a consequence, a maternal/fetal conflict of interests may arise and, in recent years, this potential – exaggerated by the proximity of the Republic to mainland Britain – has been considered by both the Court of Justice of the European Communities and the European Court of Human Rights. The results indicate a slow but significant erosion of the previously rigid position.

5.15 In 1991, the Irish High Court sought a ruling from the CJEC on the legality of prohibiting the distribution of information relating to the availability of abortion facilities for Irish citizens in the United Kingdom; the answer was that, as a matter of morality, the Irish government was entitled to follow its own public policy.[36] The following year, the Supreme Court of Ireland extended the grounds on which a termination was permissible from circumstances in

---

31 The position is under review at the time of writing: D Payne 'Abortion in Northern Ireland to be Reviewed' (2001) 322 Brit Med J 1507.

32 *Re K (a minor), Northern Health and Social Services Board v F and G* (1991) 2 Med LR 371.

33 [1939] 1 KB 687, [1938] 3 All ER 615.

34 *Re A (Northern Health and Social Services Board v AMNH)* (1991) 2 Med L Rev 274.

35 Irish Constitution, Article 40.3.3. A detailed description of the basic Irish law is in A Sherlock 'The Right to Life of the Unborn and the Irish Constitution' (1989) 24 (NS) Irish Jurist 13.

36 *Society for the Protection of Unborn Children Ireland Ltd v Grogan* [1991] 3 CMLR 849, (1992) 9 BMLR 100.

which there was an inevitable or immediate risk to the life of the mother to those where there was a real and substantial risk to her life – represented in the instant case by the possibility of suicide. In obiter remarks, however, the court indicated that the right of an unborn child to life would, were the conflict to arise, take precedence over the right of the mother to travel.[37]

5.16 Later in the year, the twin problems of providing information and arranging travel to another jurisdiction were again aired, this time before the European Court of Human Rights[38] when an injunction of the Supreme Court restraining such counselling was challenged. On this occasion, while agreeing that the purpose of the injunction was to protect the national morality, the European Court decided that the degree of restraint imposed was disproportionate to the aim pursued. Accordingly, Article 10 of the European Convention on Human Rights was infringed. Two referenda supported this view and, as a result, the Regulation of Information Act 1995 was passed and held to be constitutional; the injunctions against the provision of information concerning the availability of abortion in Great Britain were subsequently lifted. A further rape-associated case, very similar to that involving X, arose in 1997; here it was confirmed that a 'suicide risk' came within the definition of a substantial risk to the mother's life, by reason of which an abortion carried out in Ireland would not be unlawful.[39]

5.17 Abortion law in the Irish Republic is, therefore, in an evolutionary phase and a further amendment to the Constitution intended to embody a proposed Protection of Human Life in Pregnancy Act 2002 is being debated as this book goes to press.[40] The Act cannot, however, come into force unless it is approved in a further referendum. Meantime, the practical effect of the current situation is of some interest. 3,650 Irish women had terminations in Great Britain in 1982; by 2000, this figure had risen to 6,381.

The United States

5.18 Practice in the United States has been profoundly modified as a result of persistent intervention through the courts which has been notable for its absence in Great Britain. It is, in fact, arguable that transatlantic experience now has little relevance to the United Kingdom. Nevertheless, as we have already pointed out, the United States remains one of the few jurisdictions where abortion remains an active political issue. It is, therefore, worth taking a brief look at its development.

5.19 Abortion laws in the mid-twentieth century differed in the various States of the United States. Some, as in New York, were wholly liberal; some, in Texas, corresponded roughly to the English Infant Life (Preservation) Act; but the majority followed variations on the United Kingdom Abortion Act. Then,

---

37   *A-G v X* [1992] 2 CMLR 277, (1994) 15 BMLR 104.
38   *Open Door Counselling and Dublin Well Woman v Ireland* (1993) 15 EHRR 244, (1994) 18 BMLR 1.
39   *A and B v Eastern Health Board* [1998] 1 IR 464. An interesting feature of the case is that the Health Board applied for, and obtained, authority to arrange a termination against the wishes of the 13-year-old girl's parents.
40   In fact, the referendum came down to a decision as to whether the threat of suicide would justify a termination. The vote was so close that it can have no effect of itself.

in 1973, the Supreme Court altered the whole picture in the historic twin decisions of *Roe v Wade*[41] and *Doe v Bolton*. [42] The effect of these well-known cases can be summarised: it is an invasion of a woman's constitutional right to privacy to limit her access to abortion by statute – and this applies also to schoolchildren, although their parents may still be informed of the circumstances;[43] the expression 'to preserve the life' of a woman is unconstitutionally vague, although 'to preserve the life or health' is acceptable – which raises an intriguing conflict. It was suggested at the time of the decision[44] that health is inclusive of convenience and that this effectively allows for abortion on demand – and although the Supreme Court specifically stated that there was no such absolute constitutional right, there is no doubt that the result of *Roe* is that abortion during the first trimester is an inalienable prerogative of the American woman and is grounded in the right to individual privacy. To confirm the essential nature of privacy, the court also ruled that an appeal on the grounds that wholly liberal laws were invalid – because they deprived unborn children of the right to life – was not available to an individual. Nevertheless, the court did give some weight to the rights of the developing fetus. In the first trimester, the question of abortion was to be decided solely between the woman and her physician; during the second trimester, the State could intervene by reason of its interest in the health of the mother, no such interest being vested in the fetus – interference of this type could include stating where and by whom an abortion could be done. After 'viability', which the court assessed as somewhere between the twenty-fourth and twenty-eighth week of pregnancy, it was agreed that the State had a compelling interest in the health of the fetus and could, therefore, constitutionally intervene on its behalf excepting when the conditions threatened the life or health of the mother.

5.20 The decision in *Roe v Wade,* which has resulted in nearly one-third of pregnancies in the United States being terminated legally, has been a subject of controversy ever since its pronouncement.[45] In the first place, it satisfies virtually no one; the anti-abortionists have been, inevitably, outraged, while the feminist lobby sees the result as being still too restrictive of women's rights. Secondly, the trimester rule is unreliable in that it rests upon fluctuating medical expertise and medical technology.[46] This was well put by O'Connor J:

> The lines drawn [in *Roe*] have now become 'blurred' ... The state can no longer rely on a 'bright line' that separates permissible from impermissible regulation. . . . Rather, the State must continuously and conscientiously study contemporary medical and scientific literature in order to determine whether the effect of a particular regulation is to "depart from accepted medical practice".[47]

41   93 S Ct 705 (1973).
42   93 S Ct 739 (1973).
43   *HL v Matheson* 101 S Ct 1164(1981).
44   J H Ely 'The Wages of Crying Wolf: A Comment on *Roe v Wade*' (1973) 82 Yale LJ 920.
45   It is poignant to find that 'Ms Roe' has been converted to the 'pro-life' cause and that, in fact, she never obtained her own termination: N McCorvey 'My Legal Fight Helped Start a Generation of Child Slaughter and That Makes Me Weep' Daily Telegraph, 20 January 1998, p 4.
46   N K Rhoden 'Trimesters and Technology: Revamping *Roe v Wade*' (1986) 95 Yale LJ 639.
47   In *Akron v Akron Center for Reproductive Health* 462 US 416 (1983) at 455-456.

5.21 There are, however, additional practical reasons why American attitudes have little influence on British thinking in this area. Fundamentally, and despite the emotions it engenders, abortion in the United States is not so much a philosophical issue as it is one of constitutional law.[48] Moreover, the subject has become highly politicised and the composition of the Supreme Court is subject to political adjustment. Thus, the Supreme Court firmly repelled a major attack on *Roe* which was mounted in the mid-1980s.[49] However, a change in personnel encouraged a further sally towards the end of the decade[50] which was rather more successful in that, although the court was unwilling to overturn the principles laid down in *Roe,* it upheld a Missouri statute which certainly limited the availability of abortion; the implication is that other States may be able to introduce similar restrictions. Apart from some considerations as to fetal viability, the central issue in *Webster* turned on the State's right to restrict the reasons for which pregnancies could be terminated at public expense. Indeed, it has been held for some time[51] that federal funding in the form of 'Medicaid' is available for abortions only in limited circumstances – such as preserving the life of the mother or terminating pregnancies resulting from rape or incest – and that, accordingly, the individual State health systems need not contribute towards expenses incurred on other grounds.

5.22 The struggle, however, continued. In 1992 the Supreme Court was, again, asked to pronounce on the legality of a State statute – in this case, the Abortion Control Act of Pennsylvania, which created a number of obstacles in the way of abortion 'on demand'.[52] The issue, here, as in many of the United States cases, was not so much related to a maternal/fetal conflict as to one involving, on the one hand, the woman's right to bodily privacy and, on the other, the State's interest in the protection of life and a preference for childbirth over abortion.[53] Put simply, the Supreme Court introduced an 'undue burden' test – which meant that the State was empowered to impose financial, medical or emotional barriers to abortion provided that these did not become a substantial obstacle, or undue burden, to choosing to terminate a pregnancy; the basic premise of the woman's liberty of conscience and bodily integrity was, in this way, upheld. Even so, some fetal rights were maintained, in that States could restrict abortion of the 'viable' fetus save in relation to a medical emergency threatening the mother. Needless to say, this decision was by the barest of

---

48   See I Loveland 'Abortion and the US Supreme Court' (1992) 142 NLJ 974.
49   *American College of Obstetricians and Gynaecologists v Thornburgh* 476 US 747 (1986).
50   *Webster v Reproductive Health Services* 109 S Ct 3040 (1989). For extensive and critical discussion, see W Dellinger and G B Sperling 'Abortion and the Supreme Court: The Retreat from *Roe v Wade*' (1989) 138 U Penn LR 83 and related papers. In J Bopp and R E Coleson 'What Does *Webster* Mean' (1989) 138 U Penn LR 157, the authors maintain, inter alia, that 'the trimester scheme may be considered *defacto* and *sub silentia* overruled'.
51   *Harris v McRae* 100 S Ct 2671 (1980).
52   *Planned Parenthood of Southeastern Pennsylvania v Casey* 112 S Ct 2791 (1992). See A Charo 'Undue Burden of Abortion' (1992) 340 Lancet 44.
53   However, the government is not required to finance the latter simply because it prefers, and supports, the former: *Rust v Sullivan* 111 S Ct 1759 (1991).

majorities and powerful dissenting opinions were handed down – including a rejection of the whole concept of a fundamental women's liberty to choose abortion. The opinion has been said to please no lobby[54] and there is every indication that the abortion debate will continue in the United States in an atmosphere of increasing acrimony and increasing subservience to political exigency.[55]

The Commonwealth

5.23 Turning to the Commonwealth, the most interesting, and hard fought, abortion battles have been waged in Canada where, until the last 15 or so years, the law was not outstandingly liberal. Control of legal terminations was vested in hospital abortion committees under the Criminal Code 1971, s 251; in the long-running case of *R v Morgentaler,*[56] however, the Supreme Court held that this section violated the security and liberty of the pregnant woman. The Chief Justice expressed his reasons for this conclusion as follows:

> Forcing a woman, by threat of criminal sanction, to carry a fetus to term unless she meets certain criteria unrelated to her own priorities and aspirations, is a profound interference with a woman's body and thus a violation of security of the person.[57]

In parallel litigation, the Canadian Charter of Rights and Freedom, Article 7 of which guarantees the 'right to life, liberty and security of the person', was held to be inapplicable to the fetus.[58] Those opposed to abortion gained a surprise victory in *Tremblay v Daigle*[59] – in which a father gained an interlocutory injunction to prevent the abortion of his child; the decision rested on the Provincial Charter of Rights and the case was held under the civil law jurisdiction of Quebec. The situation was, however, short-lived, the full Supreme Court of Canada reversing the decision unanimously.[60] It is to be noted that neither the Supreme Court of the United States nor that of Canada will allow of 'trade-off' or balancing act between fetal and maternal rights to life or health – it is the latter which is to be safeguarded.

5.24 The innate tendency towards liberal abortion law is also demonstrated in Australia where, other than in South Australia, the Northern Territories and, now, Western Australia, which have enabling statutes, the basic law corresponds to that in the Offences Against the Person Act 1861. Several landmark judicial interpretations of the word 'unlawful' in relation to medical

---

54 See Loveland (1992) 142 NLJ 974.
55 More recently, the problem of the control of the method of abortion – in the form of 'partial birth abortion' – has been before Congress. When a Bill to ban the method was eventually passed, the President vetoed the measure. For commentary, see G J Annas 'Partial-birth Abortion, Congress, and the Constitution' (1998) 339 New Engl J Med 279 and G J Annas '"Partial-birth" Abortion and the Supreme Court' (2001) 344 New Engl J Med 152.
56 [1988] 1 SCR 30.
57 Ibid at 56, per Dickson CJ. For discussion of this decision, see M L McConnell 'Abortion and Human Rights: An Important Canadian Decision' (1989) 38 ICLQ 905.
58 *Borowski v A-G of Canada* (1987) 39 DLR (4th) 731 (Sask, CA).
59 (1989) 59 DLR (4th) 609.
60 (1990) 62 DLR (4th) 634.

practice have resulted in a very wide availability of terminations.[61] The so-called 'Kirby ruling'[62] suggests that, in the same way as we see the position in Great Britain, it would be very difficult to establish that any termination performed by a medical practitioner was unlawful. However, two doctors were charged in 1998 with procuring abortion in contravention of the Criminal Code of Western Australia. The result was the rapid passage of the Acts Amendment (Abortion) Act 1998 (WA) which established the most liberal legislative control of abortion in Australia. While the lawfulness of the procedure was wholly medicalised, [63] the grounds included what is virtually abortion on request up to the 20th week of pregnancy. Interestingly, termination after the 20th week is rather more restricted than it is in other Australian jurisdictions.[64]

The German experience

5.25 The recent history of German legislation is instructive and is of practical importance in the light of current attempts to unify abortion law throughout the European Community.[65] Here, abortion legislation was isolated as the only exception to the general reunification formula that Western institutional and legislative experience should be extended to the East.[66] In brief, the existing situation was that, whereas abortion during the first 12 weeks of pregnancy was controlled solely by the free choice of the pregnant woman in the East, abortion was illegal in the West save in specific circumstances dependent, in large part, on 'stage of the fetus' provisions – a situation analogous to that in Britain with 'general hardship' substituted for s 1(1)(a) in the 1967 Act. Approximately 33% of pregnancies were terminated in East Germany but, very interestingly, abortions were at least as frequent in the West. Controversy, therefore, rested on a purely ideological base. The conflict was fuelled by a resurgence of activity by both conservative and liberal elements in West Germany but was, at the same time, dampened by an increasingly wide perception of abortion as a potentially dangerous piece of social engineering rather than a woman's right.[67]

---

61 Originating with *R v Davidson* [1969] VR 667 which introduced the concepts of necessity and proportionality of termination of pregnancy to offset potential harm; *R v Wald* (1972) 3 DCR (NSW) 25 in which the social and economic effects of pregnancy were taken into consideration; for a 'Code jurisdiction', see *Veivers v Connolly* [1995] 2 Qd R 326.

62 *CES v Superclinics (Australia) Pty Ltd* (1995) 38 NSWLR 47 per Kirby AC-J. For commentary, see K Petersen 'Medical Negligence and Wrongful Birth Actions: Australian Developments' (1997) 23 J Med Ethics 319. The same author provides a very useful comparison of abortion laws in 'Abortion Laws: Comparative and Feminist Perspectives in Australia, England and the United States' (1996) 2 Med Law Internat 77.

63 By amendments to the Health Act 1911, s 334 (WA).

64 An outstanding overview of the Australian scene is to be found in N Cica 'Abortion Law in Australia' *Australian Parliamentary Library Research Paper 1 1998-99* at http://www.aph.gov.au/library/pubs/rp/1998-99/999rp01.htm.

65 Where some countries have exceptionally liberal laws – eg Denmark, where women have a right to first trimester abortions.

66 Treaty on German Unity (31 August 1990), Article 31 *Family and Women*, para 4, Bundesgesetzblatt (BGbl) II, 1990, p 885.

67 E Kolinsky 'Women in the New Germany' in G Smith et al (eds) *Developments in German Politics* (1992) ch 14.

5.26 The compromise was that the issue would be settled on a free vote in the Bundestag two years after reunification. The federal parliament duly passed a law under which a pregnant woman could choose to have an abortion in the first three months of pregnancy provided she had undergone social counselling at least three days before the termination was carried out.[68] After long deliberation, the Constitutional Court declared that the new legislation was contrary to the Basic Law in certain respects – in particular, the new law failed to meet the minimum standards for the protection of unborn human life as set out in the Constitution; these could only be satisfied if the state placed a fundamental legal duty on the woman to carry her fetus to term.[69] As an interim measure, procedures were laid down which, if followed, would render consensual abortion within the first three months of pregnancy still illegal but not subject to criminal sanction.[70] The court's decision was founded on the premise that abortion offends against that part of the German Constitution which 'guarantees the right to life and freedom from bodily harm' – a right which extends, even if in modified form, to the fetus. These provisional measures continued in force until 1996, when a new law came into effect.[71] Abortion now remains illegal, but no criminal sanctions will be applied if it is performed within specified limits. Abortion is freely available on request in the first 12 weeks of pregnancy provided the woman has been counselled by her own doctor and by staff from an independent counselling centre. In providing this counselling, the doctor must give priority to the protection of the fetus. Abortion is available after 12 weeks' gestation when the life or the health of the woman is threatened or if the fetus suffers from a serious defect.

5.27 Compromise, albeit an imperfect solution, depolarises attitudes and fosters less violent confrontation.[72] The German experience, however, reinforces the view that, in the context of abortion, it dictates some acknowledgment of fetal rights and, here, one senses a wind of change blowing against a well-established screen in several jurisdictions.[73]

---

68 A Tuffs 'Germany: Abortion, the Woman's Choice' (1992) 340 Lancet 43.
69 H Karcher 'Abortion Law Diluted Again in Germany' (1993) 306 BMJ 1566; A Tuffs 'Germany: Illegality of Abortion' (1993) 341 Lancet 1467.
70 A form of prevarication which seems to be part of the Continental jurisdictions: for a controversial appraisal of the situation, see A Simon 'A Right to Life for the Unborn? The Current Debate on Abortion in Germany' (2000) 25 J Med Philos 220. Other 'compromises' were introduced – eg an illegal abortion could not be funded from statutory medical insurance but the woman could, subsequently, enjoy the social welfare and unemployment benefits. See the very full commentary by D van Zyl Smit 'Reconciling the Irreconcilable? Recent Developments in the German Law on Abortion' (1994) 2 Med L Rev 302.
71 Schwangeren-und Familienhilfänderungsgesetz (1995).
72 But cannot eliminate it – see the dogged opposition from the Bavarian Government: S Goldbeck-Wood 'Bavaria Threatens to Reduce Abortion Access' (1996) 312 BMJ 1118.
73 The European Court of Human Rights has steadfastly refused to pronounce on fetal 'personhood'. Nevertheless, the court held in *Bruggemann and Scheuten v Federal Republic of Germany* [1977] 3 EHRR 113 that not every aspect of the regulation of termination of pregnancy constitutes an interference with a woman's private life. The State had not done so by prohibiting abortion on demand.

THE RIGHTS AND VALUES OF THE FETUS

5.28 *Roe v Wade* highlights the fundamental ethical issue in abortion: at what point, and in what circumstances, does a fetus become a person, and at what point, if any, does that person have rights to an existence? This, however, is only a part of the package of what might loosely be called 'fetal rights' and which should, logically, be considered as an integrated whole. We intend to follow that concept in this chapter save that, so far as is possible, we prefer to eschew the language of rights which is unavoidably tainted with confrontational overtones. What is at stake here is respect for fetal values and these must vary, at least, with time. What follows is, therefore, related to abortion only in part; nevertheless, this chapter is a convenient place in which to consider the wider spectrum of fetal/maternal relationships.

5.29 The value that we place on human life is intimately linked with respect for personhood but what constitutes personhood is a matter of moral supposition and not one of scientific fact. The conservative view, as exemplified, particularly, by the Roman Catholic Church, lies at one extreme; this holds that personhood, and its consequent right to protection, exists from the moment of conception. We suggest that there are few who would support this view; there are, in fact, relatively good reasons, based, inter alia, on the totipotential capacity of the early embryonic cells, for regarding the pre-implantation morula as being, also, pre-embryonic. At the other end of the scale, there are those who would equate personhood with intellect and with the power to make decisions.[74] We reject such an extreme, if for no reason other than that it would deprive even young infants of a right to be valued as persons. Many attempts have been made to define the point at which the fetus is morally entitled to, at least, consideration within these brackets – the Jewish rabbinical law, for example, sets the time as when pregnancy is recognisable externally;[75] the early Christian moralists were attracted to the evidence of life exhibited by quickening;[76] and, currently, there is an increasing tendency to accord 'human rights' to the fetus at viability, the definitional complications of which are discussed later in this chapter.[77] At this point, we would only remark on the well appreciated fact that the limits of viability in terms of gestation periods will be steadily lowered to their physiological baseline as neonatal medicine improves and becomes more widely available. As O'Connor J put it in *Akron*:[78] 'The [*Roe v Wade*] framework is on a collision course with itself'; it is this inevitable trend that has sustained the several attempts to amend the British Abortion Act – and there are few indications that the conflict between the value attached to the developing fetus and the promotion of increasingly permissive abortion laws is likely to abate.

---

74   M Tooley 'A Defense of Abortion and Infanticide' in J Feinberg (ed) *The Problem of Abortion* (1973) and H Kuhse and P Singer *Should the Baby Live?* (1985), in particular, ch 6.
75   A Steinberg 'Induced Abortion in Jewish Law' (1980) 1 Int J Law Med 187.
76   See G R Dunstan 'The Moral Status of the Human Embryo: A Tradition Recalled' (1984) 10 J Med Ethics 38 for a comprehensive review.
77   A Peterfy 'Fetal Viability as a Threshold to Personhood' (1995) 16 J Leg Med 607 provides a most interesting overview.
78   462 US 416 (1983).

5.30 Even today, the law itself is inconsistent. Tort, criminal and constitutional law all have their own working definition of 'person' and the protection to which the fetus is entitled. Even so, it is everywhere accepted that, although fetal interests and rights may be established while in utero – or even before conception – they cannot be realised unless the fetus is born alive;[79] moreover, the legal concept of a separate existence is still further limited in England and Wales in the Congenital Disabilities (Civil Liability) Act 1976, under which the neonate must survive for 48 hours before being able to recover damages in negligence. 'There can be no doubt, in my view', said Sir George Baker,[80] 'that in England and Wales the foetus has no right of action, no right at all, until birth' and the same is equally true in Scotland – Scots law recognises no right of the fetus to continue to exist in its mother's womb.[81] From Canada, we have: 'There is no existing basis in law which justifies a conclusion that foetuses are legal persons',[82] from which it follows that a stillbirth cannot benefit. No suit for wrongful fetal death is recognisable in the United Kingdom[83] and we are left with an apparent paradox – as Pace[84] has put it: 'Liability is incurred for negligent injury to the foetus but not – or, at least, not necessarily – for its deliberate destruction.' There is, however, evidence that some jurisdictions are moving towards the recognition of such suits. Thus, in the United States, we read in very similar vein:

> To deny a stillborn recovery for fatal injuries during gestation while allowing such recovery for a child born alive would make it more profitable for the defendant to kill the plaintiff than to scratch him.[85]

The tone in this case, and in others that have both preceded it and followed it, indicates not so much a shift in jurisprudential reasoning as a search for punitive sanctions against the person who negligently destroys the child in utero – another form of expression of an intrinsic concern for the status of the fetus.[86]

79   An exception probably lies in the criminal law of California, where an offence of feticide has been established: *People v Davis* 872 P 2d 591 (Cal 1994). The courts in other states seem to be resisting such a move: eg *State v Green* 781 P 2d 678 (Kan 1987). Closer to home, see the Republic of Ireland, para 5.14 above.
80   *Paton v British Pregnancy Advisory Service Trustees* [1979] QB 276 at 279, [1978] 2 All ER 987 at 989.
81   *Kelly v Kelly* 1997 SC 285, 1997 SCLR 749, per Cullen LJ-C.
82   *Borowski v A-G of Canada and Minister of Finance of Canada* (1984) 4 DLR (4th) 112 at 131, per Matheson J. See also *Winnipeg Child and Family Services (Northwest Area) v G(DF)* (1997) 3 SCR 925.
83   Damages have been given for a stillbirth resulting from negligent treatment: *Bagley v North Herts Health Authority* [1986] NLJ Rep 1014. These were, however, to the mother; damages in respect of bereavement under the Fatal Accidents Act 1976 were expressly disallowed on the grounds that the negligence had caused the child to die in utero. The court was, however, at pains to ensure adequate compensation notwithstanding. See also *Grieve v Salford Health Authority* [1991] 2 Med LR 295, where only the quantum of damages for negligence leading to stillbirth was considered.
84   P J Pace 'Civil Liability for Pre-natal Injury' (1977) 40 MLR 141.
85   *Amadio v Levin* 501 A 2d 1085 (Pa, 1985).
86   It seems that, while 'wrongful fetal death' statutes are in place throughout the US, judicial interpretation varies – an action for wrongful death was dismissed in *Milton v Cary Medical Center* 538 A 2d 252 (Me, 1988) and, in general, most States operate a 'viability' limitation with recovery available only to the viable fetus. For further discussion, see B Dickens 'Wrongful Birth and Life, Wrongful Death before Birth, and Wrongful Law' in S A M McLean (ed) *Legal Issues in Human Reproduction* (1989) and Peterfy, para 5.29 above.

5.31 There are unmistakeable signs that the United Kingdom courts are also anxious to invest the fetus with as positive an identity as is possible within current legal constraints. In general terms, we have the Master of the Rolls stressing the right of an adult to refuse life-saving treatment but, at the same time, acknowledging that there might well be an exception to the rule were a viable fetus to be involved[87] – this was, however, an obiter statement that has been put to the test and rejected.[88] In England, it has been held that the fetus has common law rights irrespective of the Congenital Disabilities (Civil Liability) Act 1976[89] and, in Australia, this has been extended to an acceptance of a child's right to sue its mother for negligent injury in utero.[90] The trial judge in that case said:

> I would hold that an injury to an infant suffered during ... its journey through life between conception and parturition is not injury to a person devoid of personality other than that of the mother-to-be. Nicole's personality was identifiable and recognisable.

5.32 A similar trend has been evidenced in Scotland, where a fetus has been recognised as a person when criminally injured under the Road Traffic Act 1972,[91] while an extension of the statutory 'person' beyond a being 'with legal personality' has been approved under the Damages (Scotland) Act 1976:[92]

> It is perfectly common in ordinary speech to refer to a child in the womb as 'he', 'she', 'him' or 'her' ... it was this child who sustained injuries to his person and who died in consequence of personal injuries sustained by him.[93]

5.33 But, despite the evident tone of judicial concern, all these later examples depend upon the fetus being born alive and it can be said with confidence that there is no civil action available to the fetus in the United Kingdom for its negligent death.[94] Nevertheless, the cases demonstrate a clear intention to acknowledge – or even create – a persona in the fetus when it is possible to do so,[95] a tendency which has caused some difficulty in the field of criminal law.

---

87 *Re T (adult: refusal of medical treatment)* [1992] 4 All ER 649 at 653, (1992) 9 BMLR 46 at 50.
88 See para 5.63 below for further discussion. See *Re MB (adult: medical treatment)* [1997] 2 FCR 541, (1997) 38 BMLR 175 and *St George's Healthcare NHS Trust v S* [1998] 3 All ER 673. The problem of the enforced caesarian operation is dealt with at some length in chapter 10.
89 *Burton v Islington Health Authority, de Martell v Merton and Sutton Health Authority* [1993] QB 204, [1992] 3 All ER 833.
90 Reported by D Brahams 'Australian Mother Sued by Child Injured in Utero' (1991) 338 Lancet 687. This being a road traffic accident, there seems no reason why such an action should not be available in England under the 1976 Act (see para 5.53 below).
91 *McCluskey v HM Advocate* 1998 SCCR 629, [1989] RTR 182. The importance of subsequent live birth was acknowledged in the Sheriff Court in *HM Advocate v McDougall* 1994 Crim LB 12-3.
92 *Hamilton v Fife Health Board* 1993 SLT 624. The 1976 Act must now be read in conjunction with the Damages (Scotland) Act 1993.
93 Ibid Lord McCluskey at 629.
94 A Whitfield 'Common Law Duties to Unborn Children' (1993) 1 Med L Rev 28.
95 But the Canadian courts are still resolute: see the criminal case *R v Sullivan* (1991) 63 CCC (3d) 97.

5.34 Strictly speaking, it could be said that *A-G's Reference (No 3 of 1994)*[96] has little relevance to abortion. Nevertheless, it is of major significance as to judicial attitudes to fetal status and this seems the most appropriate place to discuss the case. In essence, it concerned the stabbing of a pregnant woman who gave birth to a severely premature baby two weeks later; it transpired that, contrary to what had been supposed, the fetus had been injured in the assault and the infant died 120 days after birth. The attacker was charged with murder and the trial judge directed an acquittal on the grounds that no conviction for murder or manslaughter was possible under the existing law. The Attorney General then sought a ruling from the Court of Appeal, asking whether the crimes of murder or manslaughter could be committed where unlawful injury was deliberately inflicted to a child in utero or to a mother carrying a child in utero, where the child was born alive and died having existed independently of the mother, the injuries in utero having caused or made a substantial contribution to the death; the court was also asked whether the fact that the child's death was caused solely as a consequence of injury to the *mother* could remove any liability for murder or manslaughter in those circumstances.

5.35 We are concerned here not with the niceties of the criminal law but, rather, with those aspects of the judgment which relate to the status of the fetus in utero. In this respect, Lord Taylor LCJ developed a two-stage argument. First, it was held that, in the eyes of the law, the unborn fetus is deemed to be part of the mother – an intention to cause serious harm to the fetus is, therefore, an intention to cause severe injury to a part of the mother; and, this being the case, malice directed at the mother can be transferred to the fetus once it is born.[97]

5.36 This decision was greeted by many lay commentators as another step towards the recognition of a fetal right to life. In fact, it is nothing of the kind, in so far as it deprives the fetus of any individual personality it previously enjoyed. The concept of an intention directed towards a child capable of becoming a person in being was summarily rejected – as Lord Taylor put it:

> An intention to cause serious bodily injury to the foetus is an intention to cause serious bodily injury to a part of the mother just as an intention to injure her arm or her leg would be so viewed,[98]

thus glossing over several differences, including the not unimportant fact that an arm is incapable of developing into an individual human being. And, in fact, the House of Lords would have nothing to do with that view when the case was referred to them,[99] Lord Mustill believing it to be wholly unfounded in fact.[100] Pointing to the truism that mother and fetus were unique human beings once the latter was born, his Lordship emphasised that the maternal-fetal relationship was one of bond, not of identity. In effect, the fetus was neither a 'person' nor an adjunct of its mother – it was a unique organism.

---

96 [1996] QB 581, [1996] 2 All ER 10, CA.
97 For an analysis of this decision, see M Seneviratne 'Pre-natal Injury and Transferred Malice: The Invented Other' (1996) 59 MLR 884.
98 [1996] 2 All ER 10 at 18.
99 *A-G's Reference (No 3 of 1994)* [1998] AC 245, [1997] 3 All ER 936, HL.
100 Ibid at AC 255.

Unfortunately, the House never defined the nature of that unique organism save in the negative sense that it is not a person in being while in utero – there is no offence of feticide and there never has been. At the same time:

> For the foetus, life lies in the future, not the past. It is not sensible to say that [the foetus] cannot ever be harmed or that nothing can be done to it which can ever be dangerous ... It may also carry with it the effects of things done to it before birth which, after birth, may prove to be harmful.[101]

Thus, the fetus remains a person-in-waiting – or a thing which will, in due course, become something; *A-G's Reference (No 3 of 1994),* in the end, does nothing to improve its status.[102]

5.37 Even so, the movement towards such improvement is fuelled by two developments which cannot be ignored – the availability of fetal therapy and an increasing recognition of risks to the health of the fetus which may be taken by pregnant women. Neither affects the abortion issue directly but each may have a profound effect on instinctive reactions to the debate;[103] we discuss the relevant cases later.[104] For the present, we note only that both offend against the extreme view, adopted by Lord Taylor,[105] which can be paraphrased as holding that the fetus is no more than a complex cellular appendage to its mother. There cannot be many who would sustain this interpretation – and it was firmly rejected by the House of Lords, where Lord Mustill[106] noted that the reason for the uniqueness of the fetus lies in the fact that its genome differs from that of its mother. Life is a constructive continuum from conception to birth and from infancy to adulthood and the so-called fetal-maternal conflict can be well-expressed in moral terms in two quotations:

> The increasing tendency to view the fetus as an independent patient or person occurs at the cost of reducing the woman to the status of little more than a maternal environment.[107]

and

> The developing human life has a great intrinsic value. It cannot be viewed purely as a part of the woman's body.[108]

---

101 Ibid at AC 271, per Lord Hope.
102 Which is unfortunate as, in the circumstances prevailing, the mother is being deprived of a child she actively desires. For commentary, see J K Mason 'A Lords' Eye View of Fetal Status' (1999) 3 Edin L R 246.
103 See the searching article by D Callahan 'How Technology is Refraining the Abortion Debate' (1986) Hastings Center Report, February, p 33.
104 See para 5.56 et seq below.
105 Para 5.36 above.
106 Para 5.36 above at AC 255. In the same case, Lord Hope showed that the theory becomes untenable once one admits of in vitro fertilisation (at AC 267).
107 J Bensehol 'Reasserting Women's Rights, in 'Late Abortion and Technological Advances in Fetal Viability' (1985) 17 Fam Plan Perspect 162, quoted by Callahan (1986) Hastings Centre Report, February p 33.
108 Swedish Government Official Report 'The Pregnant Woman and the Fetus – Two Individuals' SOU 1989.51. The aborted pre-viable fetus which is recognisable as such must now be given a respectful cremation in Sweden. See K Kallenberg, L Forslin and O Westerborn 'The Disposal of the Aborted Fetus – New Guidelines: Ethical Considerations in the Debate in Sweden' (1993) 19 J Med Ethics 32.

5.38 Some middle view has to be reached if we are not to drift into accepting the principle that the unwanted should be destroyed simply because they are unwanted. Many years ago, Ely[109] remarked, in relation to the right to privacy, that there is not a wide difference between being inconvenienced by a fetus and being inconvenienced by an unwanted infant. There is much to commend the concept of the maternal-fetal unity[110] – or symbiosis – which forces attention on the individual pregnant woman rather than simply on a woman or on a fetus, a dichotomy which serves only to polarise opinion.

5.39 The fetal status does, however, have additional important practical legal connotations at the beginning of and towards the end of pregnancy. The 1967 Act deals with the termination of pregnancy but certain procedures, in particular menstrual extraction and post-coital insertion of intrauterine devices, are performed partly because a pregnancy might exist before any definite diagnosis can be made. In the absence of any relevant amendment of the Act, it is doubtful if menstrual extraction, which deals with a problematical implantation, can be legal under the terms of the statute, which is concerned with the assessment of an established pregnancy. Nevertheless, displanting contraception is among those forms of 'after the fact' action to prevent the birth of an unwanted baby which are less likely to offend the public conscience than is frank fetal destruction; it seems illogical that they could be uniquely liable to censure under the Offences Against the Person Act 1861, s 58. The acquittal in *R v Dhingra* on just such a charge has been discussed already.[111] In withdrawing the case from the jury, the judge said:

> It is highly unlikely any ovum became implanted and only at the completion of implantation does the embryo become a fetus. At this stage she can be regarded as pregnant.[112]

5.40 This is now a true statement of the law.[113] We have argued the importance of implantation on general ethical grounds already;[114] happily, the law as represented by the Offences Against the Person Act 1861, the Abortion Act 1967 and the Human Fertilisation and Embryology Act 1990 now seems to be harmonised on the issue.

5.41 Consideration of early termination techniques must now include 'medical' abortion. There has been surprisingly little overt opposition to the method in Britain[115] – although, by contrast, the introduction of mifepristone in France

---

109 (1973) 82 Yale U 920.
110 Originally expressed in R F R Gardner 'A New Ethical Approach to Abortion and its Implications for the Euthanasia Dispute' (1975) 1 J Med Ethics 127.
111 See para 4.77.
112 *R v Dhingra*: T Shaw 'GP Cleared of Procuring His Secretary's Miscarriage' Daily Telegraph, 25 January 1991, p 5. It is difficult to see why, even so, there was no offence in so far as an offence is created by s 58 'whether [the woman] be or be not with child'.
113 See *R (on the application of Smeaton) v Secretary of State for Health* [2002] EWHC 610 (Admin), (2002) 66 BMLR 59.
114 See para 3.61.
115 Almost 20,000 terminations using antiprogesterones were carried out in England and Wales in 2000 (Abortion Statistics, 2001).

resulted in pressure sufficient to force the manufacturers to withdraw the product until the government, as a major shareholder, insisted on the resumption of research and clinical evaluation. Emotional accusations such as 'the launching of chemical warfare against unborn children' were met by emollient attempts to recategorise the process as 'contragestation' rather than abortion. [116] The treatment is to be distinguished from post-coital contraception[117] in that it is clearly abortifacient; it can, therefore, be administered only within the terms of the 1967 Act – interestingly, a company attempting to patent a similarly acting product was forced to include a disclaimer to this effect over two decades ago.[118] We view the introduction of 'contragestation' therapy with some concern as, in the same way as the 'morning after pill' it will inevitably come to be regarded as a safe form of contraceptive back-up. The result must be to blur the distinction, which we regard as essential, between contraception and abortion; while the two processes may be comparable in that they both *prevent* new life, it is only abortion that can be seen as *taking* life.

5.42   At the other end of fetal life, the possibility of the doctor being accused of child destruction by way of aborting a 'viable' fetus has now been removed.[119]   None the less, the offence can still be committed by those outwith the protection of the Abortion Act while other practical and moral implications still surround the late gestation fetus.   A brief consideration of 'viability' is still apposite – if only to assist understanding of the comparative law.

5.43   Viability is something of a legal fiction, originating in the United States, designed to define some point at which the state accepts a compelling interest to protect the lives of its unborn citizens; conceptually, therefore, viability is a term of American constitutional law and it probably has no place in English law.[120] The attainment of American viability coincides with the gestational age at which the fetus can be presumed to be capable of an existence separate from its mother and, as has been seen, the US Supreme Court has set this as lying between the twenty–fourth and twenty–eighth weeks of pregnancy.[121] Apposite United Kingdom legislation has, however, concentrated on the concept of being born, or being capable of being born, alive. Live birth is undefined and has generally been interpreted as the converse of stillbirth – effectively, a certificate of stillbirth cannot be issued if, having fully proceeded from its mother, the neonate breathed or showed any other sign of life. This carries no time limitation and, furthermore, leaves open what are 'other signs of life'. Williams[122] believed that they included a beating heart – in which case, every

---

116 A whole issue of Law, Medicine and Health Care was devoted to the subject. R Macklin 'Antiprogestin Drugs: Ethical Issues' (1992) 20 Law, Med Hlth Care 215 is of particular interest.
117 Discussed at para 4.76 et seq above.
118 *Upjohn Co (Kirton's) Application* [1976] RPC 324. The way is now cleared for medicinal abortion by the Abortion Act 1967, s 1(3A) (inserted by Human Fertilisation and Embryology Act 1990, 37(3)) which extends the types of premises in which a legal abortion can be performed.
119 1990 Act, s 37(4).
120 K McK Norrie 'Abortion in Great Britain: One Act, Two Laws' [1985] Crim LR 475.
121 *Webster v Reproductive Health Services* 109 S Ct 3040 (1989).
122 G Williams *Textbook of Criminal Law* (2nd edn, 1983), p 290. In this, he is supported by the World Health Organisation: see *C v S* [1988] QB 135 at 142, [1987] 1 All ER 1230 at 1236.

normally developed fetus delivered after 18 weeks' gestation could be said to be born alive. While we believe that this never could have held, it is obvious that the standards set require very little of the neonate; in theory, it need only have managed one breath, which may well have been unproductive, to have been 'born alive'. By contrast, viability implies an ability to live – at least for a reasonable time. Thus, viability is a product not only of fetal maturity but also of the motivation and resources of any medical attendants at the birth. As the Supreme Court of the United States pointed out in *Webster,* viability cannot be defined legally and is a matter for medical determination.

5.44 Considerable confusion existed at one time in England and Wales as a result of the apparently interchangeable use of the words 'born alive' in the Infant Life (Preservation) Act 1929, s 1(1) and 'viable' in the original Abortion Act 1967, s 5(1) but the issue now has little more than academic interest. In the most widely publicised of the relevant cases, *C v S,*[123] it was held that a fetus born following 18-21 weeks' gestation was not capable of being born alive because it was incapable of breathing by the use of its own lungs – with or without the use of a ventilator; live birth and viability were, thus, approximated, although the use of the ventilator maintained a medical resource element in the definition. The obverse decision was reached in *Rance,*[124] which, like its closely analogous case *Gregory,*[125] was a matter of 'wrongful birth' (see below); there it was held that a child was born alive if, after its birth, it existed as a live child, that is to say was breathing and living through the use of its own lungs alone. From the point of view of the law of homicide, therefore, the meaning of being born alive remains as it was decided more than a century ago.[126] 'Live birth' is clearly defined by the capacity to breathe and the confusing phrase 'any other sign of life' is, correspondingly, irrelevant.[127]

5.45 The case of Mrs Rance demonstrates vividly the unsatisfactory state of the law prior to 1990. Her child was known to be physically abnormal but, by the time the diagnosis was established, the gynaecologists were unable to terminate the pregnancy for fear of transgressing the Infant Life (Preservation) Act. But while that concern has now been removed, it has been replaced by moral considerations which are, if anything, exaggerated by the 1990 amendments to the 1967 Act.

5.46 Those who support the interests of the fetus have always been concerned to prevent the abortion, or feticide, of those capable of a free existence by lowering the fetal age above which termination is impermissible so as to keep pace with medical capabilities. They can be said to have succeeded to an

---

123 [1988] QB 135, [1987] 1 All ER 1230.
124 *Rance v Mid-Downs Health Authority* [1991] 1 QB 587, [1991] 1 All ER 801.
125 *Gregory v Pembrokeshire Health Authority* [1989] 1 Med LR 81.
126 *R v Handley* (1874) 13 Cox CC 79.
127 But it may still have significance in some circumstances. Based on this definition, a case can be made out for the disabled Siamese twin in the well-known case of *Re A (children) (conjoined twins: surgical separation)* [2001] Fam 147, [2000] 4 All ER 961 having been stillborn. See J K Mason 'Conjoined Twins: A Diagnostic Conundrum' (2001) 5 Edin L R 226 and further discussion at para 16.65.

extent by having this set at 24 weeks for the relatively slight medical and social reasons described in s 1(1)(a) of the 1967 Act.[128] The offset is that it may be difficult, particularly in the face of human error, to make a prognosis of serious neonatal handicap within that timescale. Accordingly, the 1990 Act removed the pre-existing 28 weeks' legal limit and imposed no other time restrictions on abortions performed by reason of fetal abnormality. Similar derestriction applies in the event of risk or grave injury to the pregnant woman – and such conditions are likely to arise particularly in late gestation. The *need* for late abortion thus remains and the Act is silent as to what is to be done with a live abortus. It has to be remembered that a living abortus is a creature in being; to kill such a being or to allow it to die without good reason may be murder or manslaughter – and s 37(4) of the 1990 Act absolves the gynaecologist of child destruction only.

5.47 One practical solution is to ensure that no mature abortus is given the opportunity to live. Not only may this involve the use of feticidal methods which are, at the same time, relatively dangerous to the pregnant woman but such methods may also be repugnant to all associated with the procedure – it is difficult to visualise a process which offends the Hippocratic and intuitive conscience more than the dismemberment of a relatively well-formed fetus.[129] This is precisely the situation the 'pro-life' parliamentary lobby sought to avoid and a clause designed to ensure that reasonable steps were taken to assist a mature abortus to live was introduced at a late stage in the debate on the 1990 Bill.[130] The motion was defeated, largely as a result of advice that doctors carrying out terminations after the twenty-fourth week of pregnancy 'would make every conceivable effort ... to make sure the baby was capable of living ..., a normal and independent existence'.[131] Lord Ennals quoted a letter from 20 gynaecologists:

> If the fetus is mature enough to have a reasonable chance of survival with intensive care, all possible steps are taken to optimise the recovery of both mother and fetus. Delivery then is usually by Caesarean section.[132]

5.48 Since the avowed purpose of the clause was to control the maverick, it is surprising that the medical profession was so antipathetic to a measure approved by its senior practitioners. Moreover, the stated practice raises some interesting issues. What distinction, if any, is made between the normal and handicapped fetus? Could the doctor be required to use a process which might result in a damaged neonate and possible litigation?[133] Can a woman in such a condition give a valid consent to a serious operation? Is it right to subject a

---

128 In passing, s 37 of the 1990 Act brings the law, as well as the practice, of abortion in Scotland into line with that of England.

129 R J Lilford and N Johnson 'Surgical Abortion at Twenty Weeks: Is Mortality Determined Solely by the Outcome?' (1989) 15 1 Med Ethics 82.

130 Such a condition has been declared unconstitutional in the United States: *Colautti v Franklin* 439 US 379 (1979); *American College of Obstetricians and Gynecologists Pennsylvania Section v Thornburgh* 106 S Ct 2169 (1986). Attempts by States to ban the 'partial birth' technique (para 5.22 above) have also been declared unconstitutional: eg *Planned Parenthood of Greater Iowa, Inc v Miller* (1998) 30 F Supp 2d 1157.

131 Official Reports (Lords) vol 522, col 1043, 18 October 1990, per Lord Walton at 1050.

132 Ibid at 1052.

133 For discussion, see R P S Jansen 'Unfinished Feticide' (1990) 6 J Med Ethics 61.

woman to an invasive procedure on behalf of the fetus and would she, in fact, consent? – a matter to which we return in chapter 10. Above all, parliament gave no indication of how the doctor was to dispose of his or her new patient.

5.49 The gynaecologist is certainly in a difficult position. On the one hand, he has effectively contracted to relieve a woman of her fetus. On the other, he is confronted by an infant who, on any interpretation, is entitled to a birth certificate and, if necessary, a certificate as to the cause of death.[134] Considerations as to the proper use of limited resources must also colour any decision-making. The principles of selective non-treatment of a defective neonate (see chapter 16) might well apply but, otherwise, we can see no theoretical objection to the view that failure to attempt to sustain a living infant could result in a charge of manslaughter or, in Scotland, of culpable homicide.

5.50 Legal precedents are slender in Great Britain and, what few there are, are inconsistent. In one case, an area health authority inquiry concluded that allowing an aborted fetus to die was an action which was fully within the law. In another, where an infant lived for 36 hours after having been aborted at 23 weeks, the coroner found that death was due to prematurity and that there was no culpability on the part of the medical staff. So far as we know, only one coroner, faced with such circumstances, has brought in a conclusion of death due to want of attention at birth to a premature infant;[135] no further action seems to have been taken. One prosecution is known to have been mounted by the DPP against a doctor who was alleged to have left a living abortus to die in the sluice-room; the magistrates took the unprecedented step of deciding there was no case to answer.[136] There was a further instance of a supposedly 21-week-old fetus, breathing and with a heart beat, being left to die without assistance for three hours; neither the birth nor the death were registered and the body was incinerated. In the absence of a cadaver, the coroner applied to the Home Office for authority to hold an inquest but this was refused for reasons which were not given publicly.[137] Similar uncertainty has been noted in America, where Dr Waddill, who ordered 'oxygen only' for a 26-week delivered fetus, was brought to trial for murder; two juries failed to agree, whereupon all criminal charges were dismissed.[138]

5.51 We find it illogical to distinguish in legal terms between abandonment of the newborn infant and abandonment of the living abortus. Morally, it is hard to divert further from the Hippocratic ethos than to leave to die a normal infant which is crying for the incubator simply on the grounds that it is unwanted.[139] The coroners' courts are, however, apparently happy to maintain a pragmatic approach to the problem. It was reported in 1996 that a normal

---

134 See Lord Wells-Pestell HL Official Reports (5th series) col 776 (12 December 1974).
135 Inquest on Infant Campbell, Stoke-on-Trent, 19 October 1983.
136 *R v Hamilton* (1983) Times, 16 September.
137 Reported by M Fletcher, *The Times*, 25 February 1988, p 2. The case was raised in Parliament on a motion for the adjournment: Official Reports (HC), 8 June 1989, vol 154, col 460.
138 B Towers 'The Trials of Dr Waddill' (1979) 5 J Med Ethics 205.
139 Ms Anne Widdicombe, a Parliamentary 'pro-life' activist, put the issue as lying between 'I perceive this to be a human being because I want it' or 'I perceive this not to be a human being because I do not want it': Official Reports (HC) 24 April 1990, vol 171, col 192.

infant, wrongly suspected of having severe physical abnormality and aborted at 27 weeks, survived for 45 minutes without active resuscitation. The coroner recorded a verdict of death due to legal termination[140] – which, on the face of things, is a surprisingly innovative finding and a further example of the reluctance of the law to interfere in medical practice if it can avoid doing so; it seems very unlikely that any similarly grounded actions against the doctor will be raised in the future.

5.52 We admit to some disappointment that the 'pro-abortus' motion in the House of Lords was lost and we deprecate any movement towards equating late abortion with deliberate feticide.[141] There is, in fact, no certainty that all women seeking a termination of pregnancy also seek the destruction of their fetus – indeed, the longer a woman has carried her fetus, the more likely it is that she would wish to preserve it. McLean, while insisting on the woman's right to control her whole pregnancy, has enlarged this concept and has suggested that much of the current rancour could be dispelled if women were given encouragement and the *opportunity* to undergo late, and salvageable, abortions.[142] We still hold to the view that, in general, 'viable' fetuses should be given a chance to live – there is no reason why such as can and do survive should not be regarded as parentless infants and offered for adoption on that basis. It is unlikely that there would be any shortage of adopting parents – particularly if the process was simplified to accord with the unusual circumstances.

MATERNAL RESPONSIBILITY TO THE FETUS

5.53 Thus far, we have considered the fetal/maternal relationship mainly within the context of abortion; the general topic of maternal responsibility for the well-being of the fetus remains to be discussed. In general, to allow actions by children against their mothers in respect of damage resulting from negligence during pregnancy must compromise the parent-child relationship and might also lead to their being used as a weapon in matrimonial disputes. Accordingly, the English Congenital Disabilities (Civil Liability) Act 1976 excludes such claims except as to injuries sustained during traffic accidents; here, special policy grounds and the availability of insurance were held to justify the admissibility of such claims.[143] The matter remains open in Scotland because there is no legislation on the subject and there is no reason in law to exclude a claim by a child against its mother in respect of prenatal injuries. It is possible, however, that the courts would be unsympathetic to such claims on policy grounds.

---

140 (1996) 119 Bull Med Ethics 4.
141 In fact, it has long been government policy that abortions beyond the twentieth week of pregnancy should be carried out only in hospitals having appropriate facilities including resuscitation equipment: Barbara Castle, Official Reports (HC), 21 October 1975, vol 898, col 245.
142 S A M McLean 'Women, Rights and Reproduction' in S A M McLean (ed) *Legal Issues in Human Reproduction* (1989) see the same author 'Abortion Law: Is Consensual Reform Possible?' (1990) 17 J Law & Soc 106. But would it not be both medically and economically more logical to encourage the woman to carry her fetus to term?
143 An apposite case, possibly the prototype, has been reported by C Dyer 'Boy Wins Damages after Injury in Utero' (1992) 304 BMJ 1400.

5.54 Discussion along these lines relates, largely, to injury to the fetus due to negligence as it is commonly understood. We have to look a degree deeper to determine the extent to which the mother's duty of care towards her unborn child might be held to limit her freedom of personal behaviour during pregnancy. Interest in this aspect of the fetal-maternal relationship reached its peak some two decades ago.[144] Major attention has since focussed on the use of alcohol and other drugs, including tobacco, on fetal morbidity and mortality – and the debate is by no means over. There was a time – and not so long ago – when it would have been well-nigh impossible to hold that social smoking and drinking of alcohol should be regarded in law as negligence. Yet there is virtually irrefutable evidence of their harmful effect on the fetus[145] and the issues of responsibility and liability for any consequent negligent injury have been the subject of widespread debate.[146]

5.55 Scrutiny of the interplay of fetal rights and maternal lifestyle has been nowhere more intense than in the United States, where well over 6,000 children are born each year suffering from fetal alcohol syndrome and where the occurrence of drug withdrawal symptoms in neonates has been escalating.[147] There, the state has not only a right but also a duty to protect its children under the parens patriae jurisdiction and there is strong support for the view that this extends to an interest in the well-being of the 'viable' fetus.[148] Cases of fetal neglect that have come before the courts have been assessed both under the common law and through the federal and state legislation prohibiting child abuse and neglect; as might be expected, the outcomes have not been entirely consistent and depend, to a large extent, on how the charges were framed and on the States' attitudes to feticide.[149] The case most widely publicised in the United Kingdom concerned Ms Stewart, who was found to have ingested amphetamines and cannabis before her infant was born brain damaged. The mother was charged in the criminal court with omitting to furnish necessary medical attendance or other remedial care; the case was

---

144 See eg E W Keiserlingck 'A Right of the Unborn Child to Pre-natal Care – the Civil Law Perspective' (1982) 13 Rev de Droit 49; P L Hallisey 'The Fetal Patient and the Unwilling Mother: A Standard for Judicial Intervention' (1983) 14 Pac LI 1065; J L Lenow 'The Fetus as a Patient: Emerging Rights as a Person' (1983) 9 Amer I Law Med 1.

145 For review: K O Haustein 'Cigarette Smoking, Nicotine and Pregnancy' (1999) 37 Int J Clin Pharmacol Therap 417; American Academy of Pediatrics 'Fetal Alcohol Syndrome and alcohol-related neurodevelopmental disorders' (2000) 106 Pediatrics 358.

146 N Macready 'Fetal Homicide Charge for Drinking while Pregnant' (1996) 313 Brit Med J 645.

147 For relevant data, see E J Larson 'The Effects of Maternal Substance Abuse on the Placenta and Fetus' in G B Reed (ed) *Diseases of the Fetus and Newborn* (2nd edn, 1994). The problem is, however, world-wide. Closest to home, approximately 13% of all neonatal discharges from hospital in Scotland demonstrate withdrawal symptoms due to maternal use of drugs of addiction: Scottish Executive, Written Parliamentary Answers, 2 May 2001 (Mr Malcolm Chisholm).

148 For an early exhaustive review of the US scene, see J E B Myers 'Abuse and Neglect of the Unborn: Can the State Intervene?' (1984) 23 Duquesne LR 1.

149 Currently, it seems that specific punitive legislation is in place in Wisconsin, South Carolina and South Dakota but other States may be following suit.

dismissed on the grounds that there was no statutory basis for the charge.[150] This has been the general fate of most criminal charges.[151] A number of civil actions have, however, been officially reported; these suggest that the fetus enjoys an enhanced standing in such courts and, having been born, may be able to sue on its own behalf.[152]

5.56   The courts in Canada have also appreciated the concept of intra-uterine child abuse and have immediately placed in care and protection neonates who have been subjected seriously to drugs or alcohol during pregnancy.[153] However, the courts will not go so far as to restrict the freedom of a woman to live her life as she would please while she is pregnant. In *Winnipeg Child and Family Services (Northwest Area) v G (DF)*[154] the Supreme Court ruled on a case involving an order which had been granted at first instance requiring that a five-month pregnant woman who was addicted to glue sniffing be detained in a health centre until the birth of her child. One of the grounds for the order was the parens patriae jurisdiction in respect of the fetus. It was argued that this inherent jurisdiction of the courts to protect the vulnerable – normally incapax adults and minors – should be extended to protect the fetus in utero. The Supreme Court refused, however, to sanction such a major change to the law. Noting that this would involve conflicts of fundamental rights and interests and difficult policy issues, the court recognised that the unique relationship which a woman has with her fetus is such that 'the court cannot make decisions for the unborn child without inevitably making decisions for the mother herself'. Such a power, if it were thought desirable, had to be introduced by the legislature.[155]

5.57   A ruling to the same effect has already been given in England in *Re F (in utero)*,[156] a case in which the local authority sought to make the fetus a ward of court so that it could be protected from its mother, who was leading a nomadic existence and who, shortly before the child was due, again went missing. The application was refused both at first instance and in the Court of Appeal on the grounds that, until the child was actually born, there would be an inherent incompatibility between any projected exercise of the wardship jurisdiction and the rights and welfare of the mother. Relying heavily on

---

150 See Solomon (1991) 17 Amer J Law M 411.
151 Eg *State v Gray* 584 NE 2d 710 (Ohio, 1992); *State v Carter* 602 So 2d 995 (Fla, 1992; *Commonwealth v Kemp* 643 A 2d 705 (Pa, 1994). Successful prosecution and imprisonment appears to have been reported in only one truly apposite case: *Whitner v South Carolina* 492 SE 2d 777(SC, Sup Ct, 1995). Routine neonatal testing for drugs has been found unreasonable on account of its penal connotations: *Ferguson et al v City of Charleston* 121 S Ct 1281 (2001).
152 *Grodin v Grodin* 301 NW 2d 869 (Mich, 1981). See also *Re Vanessa F* 351 NYS 2d 337 (1974).
153 *Re Children's Aid Society of Kenora and JL* (1982) 134 DLR (3d) 249; *Re Superintendent of Family and Child Service and McDonald* (1982) 135 DLR (3d) 330.
154 [1997] 2 SCR 925. See, also, an earlier case, *Re Baby R* (1989) 53 DLR (4th) 69 – powers to interfere with the rights of women must be given by specific legislation.
155 For a wide-ranging review of the whole field, see R Scott 'Maternal Duties to the Unborn? Soundings from the Law of Tort' (2000) 8 Med L Rev 1.
156 [1988] Fam 122, [1988] 2 All ER 193. Other Commonwealth jurisdictions have attempted rather similar protection of the viable fetus: *Re Baby P (an unborn child)* [1995] NZFLR 577. The absence of fetal/maternal conflict was a feature of this case in which the mother was taken into care in the interests of the fetus.

Paton,[157] the Court of Appeal first concluded that the fetus had no individual personality and that, therefore, there could be no jurisdiction in wardship; and, secondly, it was made clear that, in practice, it would be impossible to follow the principle of the paramountcy of the child's welfare in wardship if that conflicted with the liberty and legal interests of the mother.

5.58 The preferred course of action in such cases is to make the child a ward of court on its birth. The authority for this is the decision of the House of Lords in *D (a minor) v Berkshire County Council*,[158] in which the court upheld a decision to make a care order in respect of a child born prematurely and suffering from drug dependency. The House held that the words: '[The child's] proper development is being avoidably prevented or neglected' in the Children and Young Persons Act 1969, s 1(2)(a) referred to a continuing, rather than an instant, situation. Thus, while the court would not go so far as to make a fetus a ward of court, conditions both before birth and in the hypothetical future could be taken into account when assessing a neonate's need for care and control, the important point being that there is a genuine continuum. The decision caused considerable concern; first, on the grounds that its application to family law might be extended to the criminal field and, secondly, because it denied the drug addicted mother the right to prove her capacity for motherhood. For ourselves, we see *D (a minor)* as yet another case that was decided on its own facts; there is no reason to suppose that a similar decision would be taken in every instance – only that the remedy is there should it be needed in serious cases.[159]

5.59 *D (a minor)* is an example of fetal 'rights' maturing at birth. The reasons for seeking fetal protection in *Re F* were, we feel, far less pressing than were those in, say, *Re D;* the nature of any maternal improbity differed and it is possible to explain the two decisions in that simple light.[160] None the less, *Re F* is the more significant in that it lays down a principle which is likely to be followed in the absence of parliamentary intervention. Any rights vested in the fetus are strictly circumscribed. Whether or not one agrees with such a loading of the odds, there is little doubt that it has to be accepted on pragmatic grounds. There is simply no way in which the criminal law could be invoked so as to control a pregnant woman's smoking, eating or sexual habits, nor is it desirable – amongst other ill-effects, doctors would be turned into police informers. We can also foresee great difficulty in proof of causation: teratogenic effects are maximal in the first trimester of pregnancy and the further in time that the cause is removed from the visible effect, the more difficult it becomes to associate the two.

---

157 *Paton v British Pregnancy Advisory Service Trustees* [1979] QB 276, [1978] 2 All ER 987.
158 [1987] AC 317, [1987] 1 All ER 20, HL.
159 The court will certainly use its power. In *Re P (a minor) (child abuse: evidence)* [1987] 2 FLR 467, CA a place of safety order was granted on the day of a child's birth into a family which had a history of sexual abuse. For US examples involving drug abuse, see *Re Ruiz* 500 NE 2d 935 (Ohio, 1986); *Re Valerie D* 613 A 2d 748 (Conn, 1992).
160 It is noteworthy that the Court of Appeal was unable to see any logical difference between the early and the 'viable' fetus as regards a need for protection ([1988] 2 All ER 193 at 199, per Balcombe LJ).

Maternal/fetal conflict

5.60 The topic of parental neglect in the form of refusal of treatment in the fetal interest is becoming more controversial as the opportunities become ever more feasible. Until recently, this has had comparatively little impact in Britain. We suspect that the great majority of women who have carried a fetus long enough for it to be available for treatment are anxious that it should survive to childhood – most fetal treatments, or other interventions in the pregnancy on behalf of the fetus, are carried out in a consensual medical environment. The greater publicity attracted in the United States may reflect no more than a stiffer polarisation of attitudes; this leads to more conflicts of conscience which can be resolved only in the public courtroom.[161]

5.61 A subset of this problem lies in refusal, not of treatment for the fetus itself, but of maternal treatment which, if not undertaken, will lead to fetal damage or death. In such circumstances, a paradigm of conflict arises which is frequently seen as involving a choice either to respect the wishes of the woman or to disregard those wishes and treat the woman in a way which does not jeopardise the fetus.[162] The classic situation is to be found in refusal of caesarian section in the fetal interest. There are a number of relatively old precedents from the United States in which a mother has been ordered to undergo such treatment[163] and, occasionally, such directions have ended disastrously.

5.62 The exemplar case is *Re AC*,[164] where a caesarian section was ordered against the wishes of a moribund woman suffering from malignant disease in an attempt to salvage a 26-week-old fetus – the mother survived only long enough to see her baby die in a matter of hours. Brahams noted that the case should sound a warning bell to all interventionists in Britain; the majority of commentators adopted a similarly cautious approach to the subject on the grounds, among others, that it is nearly impossible to balance the benefits to the fetus against the reasonableness of withheld consent,[165] that unwanted

---

161 There has been some disagreement as to how often this occurs. L J Nelson and N Milliken 'Compelled Medical Treatment of Pregnant Women: Life, Liberty and Law in Conflict (1988) 259 J Amer Med Ass 1060 is at some odds with *V E B Colder, J Gallagher and MT Parsons* 'Court-ordered Obstetrical Interventions' (1987) 316 New Engl J Med 1192. See also N Rhoden 'The Judge in the Delivery Room: The Emergence of Court-ordered Cesarians' (1986) 74 Calif LR 1951. For a contrary view, see E-H W Kluge 'When Caesarian Operations Imposed by a Court are Justified' (1988) 14 J Med Ethics 206.

162 One need not, however, always approach the problem as one which necessarily involves a conflict: see J Mair 'Maternal/Foetal Conflict: Defined or Diffused?' in S A M McLean (ed) *Contemporary Issues in Law, Medicine and Ethics* (1996) ch 5.

163 Eg *Raleigh Fitkin-Paul Morgan Memorial Hospital v Anderson* 201 A 2d 537 (NJ, 1964); *Jefferson v Griffin Spalding County Hospital Authority* 274 SE 2d 457 (Ga, 1981).

164 533 A 2d 611 (DC, 1987). For discussion, see D Brahams 'A Baby's Life or a Mother's Liberty: A United States Case' (1988) 56 Med-leg J 156; M A Field 'Controlling the Woman to Protect the Fetus' (1989) 17 Law Med Hlth Care 114.

165 There is, none the less, a tide in favour of some sort of balancing act. Thus, in *Taft v Taft* 446 NE 2d 395 (Mass, 1983) the court refused surgical intervention but might have been prepared to accept medical treatment of the fetus. See F A Chervenak and L B McCullough 'Perinatal Ethics: A Practical Analysis of Obligations to Mother and Fetus' (1985) 66 Obst Gynecol 442. The views of F H Miller 'Maternal-Fetal Ethical Dilemmas: A Guideline for Physicians' (1991) 10 Seminars Anaesth 157 are particularly attractive.

intervention must injure the maternal doctor-patient relationship and that the standards of enforcement would be inequitable. This view was vindicated by the District of Columbia Appeal Court, where the court vacated the judgment in *Re AC* and, by a 7:1 majority, held that the right to informed consent encompassed a right to informed refusal of treatment; a fetus cannot have rights in this respect superior to those of a person who has already been born. Even so, the door was not quite shut:

> We do not quite foreclose the possibility that a conflicting State interest may be so compelling that the patient's interest must yield but we anticipate that such cases will be extremely rare and truly exceptional.[166]

The circumstances in *Re AC* were special – involving a dying woman carrying a barely viable fetus – and, although it will be clear that we support some notion of fetal rights, we would align ourselves with the view of the Court of Appeal on the particular facts of the case.

5.63 More recently, there has been something of a spate of cases in England where the issues have been less clear cut; the history of these cases provides a remarkable example of the evolution of a national jurisprudence. The first of these was *Re S*,[167] in which a woman who had been in labour for several days with the fetus impacted in a transverse lie steadfastly refused to undergo caesarian section. The clinicians appealed to the court and a declaration was granted to the effect that, the operation being in the vital interests of the patient and the unborn child, it could be performed lawfully despite the woman's refusal to give consent. Again, this decision was greeted with a volley of academic criticism.[168] It was, perhaps, unfortunate that Sir Stephen Brown P was not apprised of the Appeal Court decision in *Re A C* and, certainly, no analysis of the issues was contained in the decision handed down. Even so, the judge was faced with the need for an immediate answer and, apparently paradoxically, we support his decision – *Re AC* and *Re S* provide a near perfect example of circumstances altering the case. While Sir Stephen Brown P emphasised that the life of the unborn child was at risk, there was also no question but that the mother would die in great pain in the absence of surgical intervention; by contrast, there was no way in which maternal death could be avoided in *Re A C*. We believe that the declaration represented the correct humane – albeit possibly not the correct jurisprudential – solution in the circumstances.

5.64 The courts, however, then went further in their concern for the state's interest in the preservation of life. In *Norfolk and Norwich Healthcare (NHS) Trust v W*[169] and *Tameside and Glossop Acute Services Trust v CH (a patient)*[170]

---

166 *Re AC* 573 A 2d 1235 (DC, 1990), per Terry J. See D Brahams 'Enforced Caesarian Section: A US Appeal' (1990) 58 Med-leg J 164.

167 *Re S (adult: refusal of medical treatment)* [1992] 4 All ER 671, (1992) 9 BMLR 69.

168 See eg M Thomson 'After *Re S*' (1994) 2 Med L Rev 127.

169 [1996] 2 FLR 613, (1997) 34 BMLR 16. See also *Rochdale Healthcare (NHS) Trust v C* [1997] 1 FCR 274. Both cases were decided, effectively, on the basis of 'what a reasonable person would decide', given that the women were incapable of weighing up the considerations that arose.

170 [1996] 1 FLR 762, (1996) 31 BMLR 93.

the High Court upheld forced caesarean section, even justifying its action in *Tameside* by deeming the section to be 'treatment' for the woman's schizophrenia under the Mental Health Act 1983, s 63. We discuss these cases further in the more appropriate context of consent,[171] together with the Court of Appeal judgment in *Re MB (an adult: medical treatment)*.[172] It is sufficient to note here that the court in *Re MB* registered something of a *volte face*, holding that the courts have no jurisdiction to require a competent woman who refuses medical treatment to undergo that treatment *even if* the refusal might have adverse or fatal consequences for the fetus she bears. A woman carrying a fetus is entitled to the same degree of respect for her wishes as anyone else. That having been said, the court drew back. The paramountcy of the woman's autonomy was accepted but she was deemed to be incapax because of a fear of needles which had led her to refuse the operation. It was accepted that it was in the woman's own best interests to undergo the procedure and, faced with such a *fait accompli,* she 'consented'. The Court of Appeal had not, however, said its last word; this was to come in *St George's Healthcare NHS Trust v S*.[173] We discuss this case, which was indisputably mismanaged at first instance, more thoroughly at para 10.68. For present purposes, it needs only to be said that the Court of Appeal confirmed that:

> a competent woman, who has the capacity to decide, may for .... rational or irrational reasons, or for no reason at all, choose not to have medical intervention, even though the consequences may be the death or serious handicap of the child she bears, or her own death.[174]

And the Court emphasised that the Mental Health Act 1983 cannot be deployed for the detention of an individual against her will merely because her thinking process is unusual and contrary to the views of the majority of the community at large.

5.65 Such was the tone of the decision in *St George's* that one can say with near certainty that the day of the non-consensual caesarian section is now over in England and Wales. Indeed, we suggest that prudence should dictate a very cautious approach to fetal therapy of any sort, the great majority of which could, save on rare occasions, be properly withheld until birth.[175]

OTHER PEOPLE'S RIGHTS

5.66 The rights of those who participate as third parties receive comparatively little attention in the abortion debate as compared with that devoted to the woman and her fetus.

---

171 See chapter 10 below.
172 [1997] 2 FLR 426, (1997) 38 BMLR 175, CA.
173 [1998] 3 All ER 673; (1998) 44 BMLR 160, CA.
174 Per Butler-Sloss LJ in *Re MB*, n 172 above.
175 For   review of the issues involved, see A D Lyerly, E A Gates, R C Cephalo and J Sugarman 'Toward the Ethical Evaluation and Use of Maternal-fetal Surgery' (2001) 98 Obstet Gynecol 689. An interesting proposal is that, currently, such procedures should be regarded as research with all that that entails (see chapter 19).

Conscientious objection

5.67 This unconcern may well spring from the fact that the Abortion Act 1967 (at s 4) excuses the conscientious objector from participating in treatment by abortion unless that treatment is directed towards the saving of life or of preventing grave permanent injury to the health of the mother. But, while this would seem to be perfectly clear, the doctor's situation is not uncomplicated. The curious provision which stipulates that the English doctor must prove his conscience while his Scottish counterpart's sworn word will be accepted at face value is illogical but is of minor significance. The most important and unfortunate result of the 1967 Act is that some discrimination takes place against doctors, and especially those seeking to become gynaecologists, who are unable to accept its wide terms.[176] It is to be noted that, while a doctor may, in general, refuse to take part in the abortion procedure, he remains under an obligation to advise. Such advice is subject to the normal rules of medical negligence and the conscientious objector's only recourse is, therefore, to refer his patient to another practitioner, a practice which is only marginally compatible with a strong conscience and which must damage the essential bond of trust between doctor and patient.[177] The facts that the woman may well be unaware of her practitioner's attitude and that a second referral inevitably delays the termination provide one of the most powerful arguments put forward by those who would demedicalise early abortion.[178] It is often forgotten that a doctor's objection to abortion may be Hippocratic rather than, say, religious in origin and a logical case can be made, and a major ground for confrontation thereby removed, for delegating abortions which have no immediate therapeutic dimension to trained abortionists. The doctor's conscience does not absolve him from treating a woman when the continuation of the pregnancy is life-threatening and there is, of course, no right to conscience in treating the *results* of a legal abortion; these considerations apply equally to the nursing staff.

The nursing staff and others involved

5.68 The role of the nurse in therapy of all sorts is becoming more significant; this is exemplified in the sphere of abortion by the widespread use of prostaglandin infusions for induction of premature labour. Nurses have so great a part to play in this process that some doubt was raised as to whether they were, in fact, thus guilty of performing illegal abortions in the sense that they were not 'registered medical practitioners' as required by the 1967 Act; the Royal College of Nursing accordingly sought a declaration to the effect that the advice in a departmental circular[179] stating that, irrespective of the precise action taken, an abortion was legal provided that it was initiated by and was the responsibility of a registered medical practitioner, was wrong in

---

176 J Warden 'Abortion and Conscience' (1990) 301 BMJ 1013.
177 *Barr v Matthews* (2000) 52 BMLR 217 provides an interesting commentary. In this case, it was held that the doctor did not prevent the plaintiff obtaining a termination.
178 For a powerful argument on these lines, see S McLean *Old Law, New Medicine* (1999), chapter 4.
179 CMO (80) (2).

law. The complexities were such that the Royal College lost its case in the High Court, won it in the Court of Appeal and, finally, lost it in the House of Lords.[180] Effectively, therefore, abortion, no matter how it is performed, is a team effort and is no different in this respect from any other form of treatment. It is, nevertheless, interesting that, in total, five out of nine judges involved took the view of the nurses.

5.69 It is easy to believe that the sensibilities of the nursing staff are inadequately recognised within the abortion debate. The damage that conscientious objection causes to their career prospects may well be greater than that sustained by doctors – a doctor does not *have* to practise gynaecology but, as Lord Denning emphasised, nurses are expected to be mobile throughout the hospital system.[181] Moreover, current methods of termination beyond the twelfth week of pregnancy involve the nursing staff in an uncompromising way – whether it be in the delivery of what is comparable to a premature birth or in counting the fragmented parts of a formed fetus;[182] there can be no doubts as to their *rights* to special consideration even if these are not always respected.

5.70 Valid conscientious objection within the terms of the Abortion Act 1967, s 4 is, however, limited by a proximity test – that is, that it covers only those involved in the therapeutic team effort. The case of Mrs Janaway, who regarded herself as having been unfairly dismissed following her refusal to type a letter referring a patient for termination of pregnancy, was considered so important that it was taken to the House of Lords.[183] In the event, Mrs Janaway failed at every step, essentially on the grounds that participation in treatment, as applied to s 4, referred to actual participation in treatment administered in a hospital or other approved place; the suggestion in the Court of Appeal that the conscience clause applied to activities which would have been criminal absent the 1967 Act was rejected in the House of Lords – and, at any rate, a typist could not be held to be an accessory in the criminal sense. Mrs Janaway was clearly well distanced from the actual treatment but one can only guess whether others more closely involved – eg hospital porters – would be similarly excluded; the dividing line might be fine.[184] The advent of medical termination raises the unusual position of the conscientiously objecting pharmacist who is asked to fill the necessary prescriptions; in our view, the proximity test would be satisfied, although much depends on how the relationship between the pharmaceutical and medical professions is viewed.[185]

180 *Royal College of Nursing of the United Kingdom v Department of Health and Social Security* [1981] AC 800, [1981] 1 All ER 545, HL.
181 [1981] AC 800 at 804-805, [1981] 1 All ER 545 at 555.
182 See R J Lilford and N Johnson 'Surgical Abortion at Twenty Weeks: Is Morality Determined Solely by the Outcome? (1989) 15 J Med Ethics 82. J Glover *Causing Death and Saving Lives* (reprinted 1986) p 142 points to the effects on the health carers as providing a major moral distinction between, say, contraception and abortion.
183 *R v Salford Health Authority, ex p Janaway* [1989] AC 537, CA; affd sub nom *Janaway v Salford Area Health Authority* [1989] AC 537, [1988] 3 All ER 1079, HL.
184 It is interesting that, whereas the 'conscience clause' in the 1967 Act refers to participation in 'any treatment' authorised by the Act, s 38 of the Human Fertilisation and Embryology Act 1990, which 'governs' abortion by way of s 37, refers to participation in 'any activity' governed by the Act. The latter is, arguably, open to wider interpretation.
185 For analysis, see B D Weinstein 'Do Pharmacists Have a Right to Refuse to Fill Prescriptions for Abortifacient Drugs?' (1992) 20 Law Med Hlth Care 220. This is from the American view, where the matter is not addressed by statute – but the principles remain the same.

The father

5.71 The anomalous position of the father in the right to life debate also falls to be considered. It is clear from current worldwide decisions that, in so far as abortion is concerned, he has, for practical purposes, *no* rights. It seems incongruous that this should be so, irrespective of the reason for the abortion, and that it should apply even in cases which do not relate to the health of the mother; a father could not, for example, save the existence of a *potentially* haemophiliac son.

5.72 The English position was established in *Paton*,[186] where it was clearly laid down that a husband cannot by injunction prevent his wife from undergoing a lawful abortion. The decision was upheld by the European Court of Human Rights; the European Court, however, was clearly worried by the possible complication of fetal 'viability' – the matter was not decided and it remains an area of potential doubt.[187] It was clarified no further in *C v S*,[188] in which the unmarried father's locus standi was firmly rejected – and was not appealed – but in which the main thrust of the hearing was to establish that the fetus in question was *not* viable. It was, at one time, mooted that the fetus in Scotland might be able to petition through its tutor – ie its father – for interdict of any threatened harm;[189] any such remote possibility has now been excluded. In *Kelly v Kelly*,[190] the Inner House of the Court of Session agreed that the remedy of interdict would be available to prevent damage being caused to a person which, if it occurred, would sound in damages to that person. However, a review of the extensive Commonwealth decisions supported the view that the fetus had no rights for the protection of which the remedy of interdict might be invoked. It followed, therefore, that the father, as the guardian of the fetus, had no standing by which to prevent his wife's abortion. Although this result was predictable, permission to appeal to the House of Lords was granted; no further action was, however, taken.[191]

5.73 Attitudes elsewhere in the English-speaking world are diverse. The firm English stance would seem to be accepted in New Zealand but the reasoning there is based more on statute than on common law.[192] It is unlikely that an injunction to prevent a maternally-desired abortion would ever be granted in Australia but the position there is, again, complicated – this time by considerations of legality.[193] There is, perhaps, more flexibility in the United States, where it has been said that the state courts believe the father to have a

---

186 *Paton v British Pregnancy Advisory Service Trustees* [1979] QB 276, [1978] 2 All ER 987.

187 *Paton v United Kingdom* (1980) 3 EHRR 408.

188 [1988] QB 135, [1987] 1 All ER 1230.

189 D M Yorke 'The Legal Personality of the Unborn Child' 1979 SLT 158.

190 1997 SC 285, 1997 SCLR 749.

191 Interestingly, the European Commission on Human Rights has held that the father has standing in such circumstances. He would, however, be very unlikely to succeed before the Court in the face of the justifications in Article 8(2) which include the protection of the rights of others – and the woman's rights are substantially greater than the man's: *X v United Kingdom* (1980), application no 8416/79.

192 *Wall v Livingston* [1982] 1 NZLR 734, NZCA. The code of decision-making is laid down in the Contraception, Sterilisation, and Abortion Act 1977.

193 *A-G of Queensland (ex rel Kerr) v T* (1983) 46 ALR 275 indicates the difficulties.

real interest in the fate of his fetus but that the woman's interest in her health and her freedom from unwanted pregnancy must prevail.[194] Relevant cases denying paternal rights to veto abortions are now very old[195] and the door seems, now, to have been closed in *Casey*.[196] It is, however, in Canada that the fetus has come nearest to success in obtaining paternal representation. Thus, in *Medhurst*[197] a husband was given standing to seek an injunction against abortion and in *Tremblay*[198] it was considered that a potential father had as much right to speak on behalf of the fetus as anyone; neither of these cases succeeded and they probably represent no more than the general willingness of the Canadian courts to grant a locus standi to interested parties.[199] Caldwell has drawn attention to the increasingly caring role of the husband in the upbringing of his children. But it is doubtful if this will affect his future control over a pregnancy, for nothing can alter the fact that it is the woman who carries the fetus for nine months and whose health is mainly at risk during that time – and it is almost certainly this factor which explains the difference in legal attitudes to the father's interest in his fetus and in his in vitro embryo.[200] In our view, while acknowledging that the woman's right to control her body must take precedence, the interests of the father still deserve more consideration than is currently afforded them. The potential harm or wrong done to the father by the destruction of his unborn child ought not to be ignored.

The nature of the doctor's duty

5.74 The nature of the doctor's duties in relation to the fetus itself, rather than to the mother, is not completely solved – and this is particularly so in the case of the fetus that is known – or, better, should be known – to be disabled. It is clear that the doctor then, in either case, owes a duty of care to the mother under the terms of the Abortion Act 1967, s 1(1)(d) – indeed, it has been held that the existence of the Act is sufficient to introduce into the relationship between the health authority caring for a pregnancy and the parents, a duty to take reasonable steps to ensure that the parents can exercise their choice under the Act.[201] The health professional who fails, as a result of negligent antenatal care, to offer the opportunity to terminate a pregnancy because of fetal abnormality is, therefore, liable in tort to the parents.[202]

194 J L Caldwell 'Abortion: The Father's Lack of Standing' [1988] NZLR 165. For Europe, see *X v UK*, para 5.72 above.
195 *Coe v Gerstein* 41 L Ed 2d 68 (1973); *Doe v Doe* 314 NE 2d 128 (Mass, 1974); *Planned Parenthood of Missouri v Danforth* 428 US 52 (1976).
196 112 S Ct 2791 (1992).
197 *Medhurst v Medhurst* (1984) 9 DLR (4th) 252.
198 *Tremblay v Daigle* (1989) 59 DLR (4th) 609.
199 See nn 197 and 198 above. See also *Re Simms and H* (1980) 106 DLR (3d) 435.
200 See para 3.67.
201 *Rand v East Dorset Health Authority* (2000) 56 BMLR 39 per Newman J at 57, [2000] Lloyd's Rep Med 181. It is to be noted that any woman finding herself unwillingly pregnant could seek termination under s 1(1)(a) of the 1967 Act, a fact which might explain the apparent anomaly of an action for the wrongful birth of a normal child. See, for example, *Greenfield v Irwin (a firm)* [2001] EWCA Civ 113, [2001] 1 WLR 1279, [2001] 1 FLR 899.
202 The availability of such an action was accepted in England in *Salih v Enfield Health Authority* [1991] 3 All ER 400, (1991) 7 BMLR 1 and established in Scotland in *Anderson v Forth Valley Health Board* 1998 SLT 588, (1998) 44 BMLR 108 and *McLelland v Greater Glasgow Health Board* 1999 SC 305, 1999 SLT 543; on appeal 2001 SLT 446.

There has been a recent flurry of such actions which are known as actions for wrongful birth.[203] The main result has been to establish liability for the consequent upkeep of a disabled child which cannot be imposed following the birth of an uncovenanted, normal child; such damages will, however, be limited to the difference between the costs involved in the two circumstances.[204] We return to the subject in chapter 6.

5.75 It could, however, be held that the doctor has a similar duty to the fetus in protecting it from a life of pain and suffering or from one which is diminished for other reasons.[205] Actions for the dereliction, if any, of the latter duty are known colloquially as suits for 'wrongful life', which are discussed in greater detail in chapter 6. For the present, it need only be said that the British position is summed up in the words of Stephenson LJ, who asked how there could be imposed upon a doctor a duty towards the child to take away life by means of abortion:

> to impose such a duty towards the child would be to make a further inroad – in addition to that created by the Abortion Act 1967 – into the sanctity of human life which would be contrary to public policy.[206]

This rather old view is not easy to accept in light of the positive decisions in respect of wrongful birth actions discussed above. Moreover, apart from the saving of the mother's life, the so-called 'eugenic' clause[207] of the Abortion Act is probably that part which offends the Hippocratic conscience least.[208]

5.76 Even so, Stephenson LJ agreed that a wrongful birth action could be available to the mother in such circumstances. That cause has been widely

---

203 Eg *Hardman v Amin* (2000) 59 BMLR 58; *Lee v Taunton and Somerset NHS Trust* [2001] 1 FLR 419. *Parkinson v St James and Seacroft University Hospital NHS Trust* [2001] EWCA Cov 530, [2002] QB 266, [2001] 3 All ER 97 is particularly important as being a case of combined wrongful pregnancy (see chapter 4) and wrongful birth. We have discussed these cases and other relevant ones in J K Mason 'Wrongful Pregnancy, Wrongful Birth and Wrongful Terminology' (2002) 6 Edin LR 46. The same article also discusses the case of *Groom v Selby* [2001] Lloyd's Rep Med 39 at first instance in which a healthy, albeit uncovenanted, fetus became infected during parturition. It was confirmed in the Court of Appeal as being a case of wrongful birth: (2002) 64 BMLR 47. We respectfully suggest that this is a misnomer insofar as the 'failure' lay in the sterilisation procedure and the child was 'born' physically normal.
204 As a result of the House of Lords ruling in *McFarlane v Tayside Health Board* 2000 SC (HL) 1, [2000] 2 AC 59 (see para 4.19).
205 The possible justifications for s 1(1)(d) are well discussed in S Sheldon and S Wilkinson 'Termination of Pregnancy for Reason of Foetal Disability: Are There Grounds for a Special Exception in Law?' (2001) 9 Med L Rev 85.
206 *McKay v Essex Area Health Authority* [1982] 2 WLR 890 at 902, CA.
207 It is to be noted that s 1(1)(d) is there for the benefit of the mother rather than the fetus. For discussion, see J Gillott 'Screening for Disability: a Eugenic Pursuit? (2001) 27, supp.II J Med Ethics 21.
208 Which is not to deny that there is a powerful disability rights movement that demands much respect. See J Wyatt 'Medical Paternalism and the Fetus' (2001) 27 supp.II J Med Ethics 15.

upheld in the United States[209] and, as we have seen above, is now well established in the United Kingdom. It is, however, to be noted that, even if negligence is proved, cases may well fail on the grounds of causation.[210] (See para 6.30 for further discussion.)

ABORTION AND THE INCOMPETENT

5.77 We have no reason to believe that termination of pregnancy in minors is to be regarded as different from any other aspect of medical treatment; the principles involved are, therefore, best considered within the whole spectrum of consent which is addressed in chapter 10. In theory, any concerns for the fetus must be added to the equation but, in practice, the courts will always put the interests of a young mother above those of her fetus in the event of conflict – indeed, they *must* do so.[211]

5.78 Specific problems as to confidentiality are, however, likely to arise in the unique context of under-age pregnancy and these merit consideration. These have caused particular concern in the United States, where a distinction has been drawn between a duty to inform the parents of an impending procedure[212] and a need to obtain their authority;[213] there have been a number of conflicting decisions[214] but the matter has now probably been put beyond dispute in *Casey*,[215] where the need for parental consent was confirmed.

5.79 In Britain, the concept of the 'understanding child' has gone unchallenged since it was first mooted by Butler-Sloss J in 1982.[216] There can, however, be no doubt that to perform an operation without parental permission on a child too young to understand the issues – and, hence, to give a valid consent – would constitute an assault and, clearly, this applies to an abortion. In practice,

209 *Curlender v Bio-Science Laboratories* 165 Cal Rptr 477 (1980); *Robak v United States* 658 F 2d 471 (1981); *Noccash v Burger* 290 SE 2d 825 (Va, 1982); *Reed v Campagnola* 630 A 2d 1145 (Md, 1993). For a good overview, see J R Boitkin and M J Mehlman 'Wrongful Birth: Medical, Legal and Philosophical Issues' (1994) 22 J Law Med & Ethics 21. Success is far more likely in a wrongful birth action: eg *Viccaro v Milunsky* 551 NE 2d 8 (Mass, 1990). See also the South African case *Friedman v Glicksman* 1996 (1) SA 1134 – a spina bifida case in which a wrongful life action failed but a wrongful birth action was accepted.
210 *Rance v Mid-Downs Health Authority* [1991] 1 QB 587, [1991] 1 All ER 801; *Gregory v Pembrokeshire Health Authority* [1989] 1 Med LR 81.
211 Children Act 1989, s 1(1). See the specific criticism of an expert witness in *Re B (wardship: abortion)* [1991] 2 FLR 426 at 431 per Hollis J.
212 *HL v Matheson* 101 S Ct 1164 (1981).
213 *Hallmark Clinic v North Carolina Department of Human Resources* 519 F 2d 1315 (1975).
214 In *Re T W* 551 So 2d 1186 (Fla, 1989), the court was unable to discern a compelling state interest in overriding a minor's right to privacy only when abortion was concerned. In *Hodgson v Minnesota* 110 S Ct 2926 (1990) and *Ohio v Akron Center for Reproductive Health* 110 S Ct 2972 (1990), the Supreme Court held that only one parent need be notified. In both cases, however, it was noted that a judicial process to bypass parental consent was sufficient protection for the minor. For discussion of the early cases, see H L Hirsch 'The Law Protecting Children in the United States' in J K Mason (ed) *Paediatric Forensic Medicine and Pathology* (1989).
215 *Planned Parenthood of Southeastern Penysvania v Casey* 112 S Ct 2791 (1992). The importance of the judicial bypass was re-emphasised.
216 *Re P (a minor)* [1986] 1 FLR 272, (1982) 80 LGR 301.

short of strongly held religious views, it must be very rare for the parents of an unmarried girl below the age of 16 not to consent to termination of pregnancy[217] but the question remains – *must* the parents be informed prior to legal termination of a minor's pregnancy? The Abortion Act itself makes no distinction between age groups and, by implication, gives no grounds for supposing that the special conditions of abortion give rise to special rights to privacy. Yet it is hard to believe that all the 3,748 terminations carried out on girls aged 15 or under in 2000 (representing 2.1% of the total) were carried out with parental knowledge. Again, we can turn to practical considerations among which it is reasonable to assume that the majority of children who are old enough to *become* pregnant are also old enough to understand the consequences; the conditions laid down in *Gillick*[218] would, then, apply. Thus, although the knowledge and agreement of the parents are clearly desirable, it is likely that a doctor who has made reasonable efforts to induce his patient to confide in her parents and is still faced with an adamant refusal of consent to disclosure and who goes on to terminate a minor's pregnancy would be secure from action in the courts or before the General Medical Council. The trend in medical, legal and societal attitudes towards children's rights over the last two decades gives added support to this view.

5.80 Almost certainly, many abortions have been carried out on the mentally handicapped under the twin cover of good medical practice and legal necessity; authority for termination of pregnancy has probably also been obtained in camera on more than one occasion.[219] The legal uncertainties arising from the abolition of the English courts' parens patriae powers to care for adult incompetents have now been largely dispelled in respect of termination of pregnancy. Abortion is to be distinguished from, say, sterilisation in that the former is governed by statute which gives sufficient protection to doctors provided they comply with its terms; a formal declaration of lawfulness by the High Court, is not, therefore, needed.[220] Ethical problems, however, linger on. Thus, although the very wide terms of the 1967 Act would be met in virtually any of the circumstances under consideration, one might, on occasion, question whether the termination was being undertaken for the benefit of society rather than for the genuine good of the pregnant woman – for any supposed 'right to procreate' is violated by non-consensual abortion in the same way as it is by non-consensual sterilisation.[221] We can only suggest that this is an area where clinical judgment is all important; given that the Abortion Act and Regulations are followed, we would agree that the routine involvement of the High Court serves no useful purpose in the uncontested case.

---

217 For a case in which a mother opposed a termination for her 12-year-old daughter, see *Re B (wardship: abortion)* [1991] 2 FLR 426.
218 *Gillick v West Norfolk and Wisbech Area Health Authority* [1986] AC 112, [1985] 3 All ER 402, HL. The position in Scotland would be covered by the Age of Legal Capacity (Scotland) Act 1991, s 2(4). See para 10.25 et seq below for a full discussion.
219 F Gibb 'Judge Orders Abortion on Woman, Aged 25' *The Times*, 28 May 1987, p 1 records the surprise of a judge when his decision was publicised.
220 *Re SG (adult mental patient: abortion)* [1991] 2 FLR 329, sub nom *Re SG (a patient)* (1992) 6 BMLR 95; superseding *Re X* (1987) Times, 4 June.
221 M J Gunn 'Sex and the Mentally Handicapped: A Lawyer's View' (1986) 5 Med Law 255. The author believed that non-consensual abortion contravenes Article 12 of the European Convention on Human Rights (the right to marry and to found a family) – but it seems difficult to apply this if the woman concerned is unmarried.

REDUCTION OF MULTIPLE PREGNANCY AND SELECTIVE REDUCTION

5.81 The need for a reduction in the number of fetuses carried at one time has been discussed in chapter 3. Original doubts as to the legality of the process were based mainly on terminological grounds – first on whether the phrase 'termination of pregnancy' in the 1967 Act relates to the pregnancy as a whole and, if this strict interpretation is inappropriate, whether individualised feticide in situ can be regarded as an abortion.[222] Whatever the solution of this interesting academic argument may be, the situation has now been resolved in practice – both selective reduction and reduction of multiple pregnancy in utero are legal when the requirements of the Abortion Act 1967, as amended, are fulfilled in relation to the individual fetus.[223]

5.82 Thus, there is no legal difficulty in justifying pregnancy reduction on the grounds that continuance of a multiple pregnancy would have an adverse effect on a woman's foreseeable environment and, hence, would involve a risk of injury to the mental health of the pregnant woman; the conflict of economic and moral values was exposed vividly in a much-publicised case in England in which a woman insisted on reduction of a twin pregnancy involving two normal fetuses.[224] It might be equally appropriate to plead risk to the physical or mental health of the existing family – particularly if the intended remaining fetus or fetuses were regarded as 'existing children of the family'; the death of all octuplets following refusal of fetal reduction in another recent *cause célèbre* provides an extreme example.[225] Selective destruction of an abnormal fetus is, of course, justified under the serious handicap clause of the 1967 Act. Whether there is tort liability in the event of damage to a surviving fetus is arguable; the probability is that the doctor would not be liable in the absence of negligence in the operation.[226]

5.83 It scarcely needs emphasising that all the foregoing relates to legal justification – the morality of the procedure remains in doubt.[227] For our part, we find it hard to adopt a 'blanket' approach to this question.[228] There is, clearly, a marked moral difference between reducing a twin pregnancy and reducing one involving sextuplets. To say that both are wrong in that they offend against the principle of respect for human life is to ignore the similarly valid argument that ensuring the death of all six fetuses by inaction is, equally,

---

222 For somewhat opposing views, see J Keown 'Selective Reduction of Multiple Pregnancy' (1987) 137 NLJ 1165; D P T Price 'Selective Reduction and Feticide: The Parameters of Abortion' [1988] Crim LR 199.

223 Human Fertilisation and Embryology Act 1990, s 37(5) adding to the 1967 Act, s 2.5(2).

224 R L Berkowitz 'From Twin to Singleton' (1996) 313 BMJ 373.

225 Leading Article 'The Death of Babies' *Daily Telegraph*, 4 October 1996.

226 M Brazier 'A Legal Commentary' (1990) 16 J Med Ethics 68 in discussion of Jansen (1990) 6 J Med Ethics 61.

227 Conservative Roman Catholic opinion remains implacably opposed to the process, which is regarded as 'embryonicide' rather than abortion. See the Official Statement of the Centre of Bioethics, Catholic University of the Sacred Heart, Rome 'Against So-called Embryo Reduction' (1997) 127 Bull Med Ethics 8.

228 How, for example, can one accommodate the case of Mrs Thompson who, contrary to her instructions, was implanted with three embryos and, later, refused a reduction of pregnancy? (para 3.69 above).

disrespectful of the value of human life. The subject opens up the age-old question of whether it is permissible to use unacceptable means to achieve a desirable end – at which point, one can only retire behind the defence that each case must be judged on its particular merits.

6 Prenatal screening and wrongful life

6.1 The importance of genetically dependent diseases has risen as the control of those due to infection has increased. Currently, the proportion of childhood deaths attributable wholly or partly to genetic factors runs at about 50%. And it is becoming increasingly clear, as work continues on the Human Genome Project to map the genetic code of the human species, that a genetic component may well operate in many illnesses and conditions which were previously thought to be controlled by non-genetic factors. The social, ethical and legal implications which advances in genetics have for all of us expand by the day; correspondingly, genetic considerations increasingly breathe new life into the study of medical jurisprudence. The purpose of this introductory chapter is to outline the nature of genetic disease and to discuss the role of the genetic counsellor and liability for any negligent failure to diagnose, disclose or treat genetic abnormalities.

TYPES OF GENETIC DISEASE

6.2 Genetic diseases are of three main types. Some are chromosomal – the structure or the number of chromosomes is altered and typical disease states arise, many of these being associated with learning disability. The classic example is Down's syndrome – technically known as trisomy-21. The occurrence of some chromosomal abnormalities in the neonate increases markedly with maternal age. Approximately 2% of women aged 40, left to uncontrolled pregnancy, will produce a chromosomally defective child, half of these suffering from Down's syndrome; by the age of 45, the risk of trisomy-21 rises to about 4%. It is possible that advanced paternal age may also be a risk factor.

6.3 The second group includes those conditions described as unifactorial in origin. Genes are positioned on chromosomes which exist in the cells in pairs, one member of each pair being derived from each parent. Unifactorial disease results from the presence of a specific abnormal gene and, since either of a pair of genes can be donated at random by either parent to their offspring, it is a simple calculation to determine the statistical probability of an infant being so endowed (see Figure 6.1). The genes may be 'autosomal dominants'

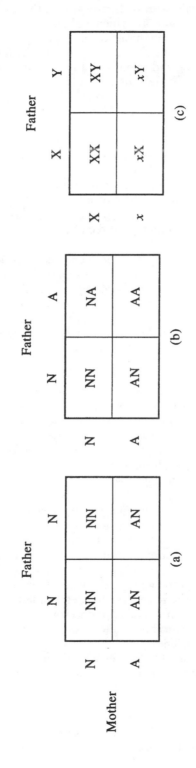

Figure 6.1 Unifactorial disease

(a) The mother has an abnormal gene (A). If this is dominant, half the children will have the disease; if it is recessive, half the children will be carriers.

(b) Both the mother and the father have one deleterious recessive gene (A); half the children will be carriers and one in four will suffer from the disease.

(c) The mother is a carrier of an abnormal X-linked gene (x). Half the male children will have the disease and half the female children will continue to carry the disease.

185

– in which case they will express themselves, in this case as a disease, when the pair of genes contains only one which is abnormal. Normal natural selection should lead to the eradication of dangerous dominant genes. They may arise by mutation, or spontaneous change – a process which is greatly augmented by, for example, ionising radiation – or the gene may possess some special attribute. Huntington's disease, for example, persists because the symptoms associated with the responsible gene often do not appear until beyond the time when the subject has attained procreative age – a situation known as late onset genetic disease. Alternatively, the gene may be an 'autosomal recessive', in which case its expression is repressed by its normal dominant partner. Those persons possessing a single abnormal recessive gene will be 'carriers' of – and are unlikely to show any evidence of – the disease with which it is associated. Frank disease will result only if an individual inherits the same two recessive genes – which means that both parents must have been carriers or one was a carrier and the other diseased; this, incidentally, provides the genetic basis for discouraging inbreeding.

6.4 Unifactorial disease may also be 'sex-linked' – or, better, 'X-linked'. Simplistically, this implies that the abnormal gene is present on part of the X chromosome which has no counterpart on the Y chromosome, the possession of which determines maleness. An abnormal recessive X-linked gene will be suppressed in the female by the dominant normal gene on the other X chromosome; it will, however, be free to express itself when coupled in the male XY configuration. Haemophilia is a classic example of such a disease.

6.5 It almost goes without saying that this description of unifactorial disease is grossly simplified. The picture must be painted on a background of penetrance – that is, the ability of the gene to express itself. Some may be so powerful that they cause some symptoms or signs in the recessive state; other dominant genes may be virtually asymptomatic. The degree of penetrance in individuals probably depends mainly on the total genetic environment – that is, the penetrance of a gene depends, to an extent, on the company it keeps.

6.6 The result is that very few genetic diseases can be regarded as truly unifactorial. The great majority of genetic disorders result from multifactorial traits which are believed to be the result not only of the effects of one or several genes but also of a combination of genetic and environmental factors. It is, therefore, generally impossible to predict mathematically the occurrence of this commonest type of genetic disorder. Coronary heart disease, for example, is to some extent genetically determined but the occurrence of symptoms will depend upon a number of uncertain features such as the potential patient's job, diet, recreation and smoking habits or the genetic control of blood cholesterol levels. The appearance of such conditions, however, lies in the individual's unpredictable future; we are, here, concerned with defects which can be demonstrated in utero and, in that respect, neural tube defects – spina bifida and anencephaly – are the most important multifactorial diseases.

6.7 Some form of behavioural or surgical treatment is available for those suffering from multifactorial disease and the same is true for a few unifactorial conditions. But there is no curative treatment for most of the more serious genetic disorders,[1] the control of which then depends on prevention. As the House of Commons Science and Technology Committee pointed out:

> While genetics is likely eventually to transform medicine, it may take some while before treatments based on genetic knowledge become available ... [i]n the short term, the most widespread use of medical genetics will be, as now, in diagnosis and screening.[2]

6.8 This 'public health' objective is a central function of the genetic counsellor; its relative importance, however, poses one of the major ethical problems of modern medicine – and one which is likely to increase.[3]

GENETIC COUNSELLING

6.9 Assessed as an arm of public health, the task of genetic counselling seems easy; in practice, it abounds with practical, ethical and, inevitably, legal problems; the Nuffield Council on Bioethics chose to make genetic screening the subject of its first report for just such reasons.[4] Modern genetic counselling involves more than merely quoting risks. The ideal is to avoid a directive approach but, rather, to concentrate on the psychological circumstances so that couples can be led to make decisions which are right for them rather than right for the scientists. Almost inevitably, however, the counsellor's opinion will be sought and how this is reached depends particularly on whether the counselling is retrospective or prospective – are parents seeking advice because they already have an affected child or is the need for consultation prior to parenting based on information derived from other sources? Patient-clients who know that genetic disease might affect their family come, in the main, with a degree of preparedness and an appreciation of their future options. The role of the counsellor assumes an entirely different mantle, however, if he is privy to information of which his clients know nothing – perhaps as a result of a confidential discussion with another health care professional; the question then arises as to whether and how such information should be imparted. These complex issues are discussed in detail in chapter 7.

6.10 In assisting clients towards a particular reproductive decision, the counsellor can virtually never make a firm statement as to having or not having a further child. He can take extraneous circumstances – eg religious or financial status – into consideration but, in the end, he is down to speaking about probabilities. In the case of unifactorial disease, he can give accurate figures – eg the chances of an overtly affected child are one in four pregnancies if both the mother and father carry recessive deleterious genes. The position

1   N A Holtzman et al 'Predictive Genetic Testing: From Basic Research to Clinical Practice' (1997) 278 Science 602.
2   House of Commons Science and Technology Committee *Human Genetics: The Science and its Consequences* Third Report, 6 July 1995, pp 36-37, paras 71, 72. As the report makes clear, *diagnosis* is aimed at individuals; genetic *screening* is routine screening of populations, or identifiable subsets of populations (for example, men or women only, or ethnic groups at increased risk for particular diseases).
3   While 95% of the more common genetic disease can now be tested for, the number of available cures remains very low.
4   Nuffield Council on Bioethics *Genetic Screening: Ethical Issues* (1993).

as to chromosomal disease is rather more complicated. In the usual circumstance, the condition is due to trisomy, in which three similar chromosomes are present in the cells rather than a pair; this is a chance occurrence which cannot be predicted mathematically. Males with trisomy-21 or Down's syndrome are commonly sterile but there is the theoretical risk that half the children of a female sufferer will also have the chromosomal defect; in practice, not only is such a pregnancy unlikely but, also, more than half of any affected fetuses would miscarry naturally. However, rather under 5% of Down's syndrome patients are not trisomic but, instead, demonstrate a chromosomal abnormality known as translocation – parts of chromosome-21 are exchanged for those of another.[5] This may also occur sporadically but, once it has done so, a carrier state can develop and affect one in three children – passage to later generations is, thus, possible and its occurrence will be independent of maternal age. The counsellor must, therefore, consider each sub-type of chromosomal disorder separately.[6]

6.11 In the event of a multifactorial condition, the probabilities can only be derived in an empirical fashion. Even then, the prospects are subject to interpretation. Thus, presented with a child with spina bifida, one can say there is a 10% chance that the couple will have a further child with developmental abnormality; it will sound quite different when expressed as a 90% chance of a normal infant. Moreover, nine to one are acceptable odds to many; others might regard anything less than 99 to 1 as an unacceptable risk. In the end, the choice rests with the couple and this choice is a product of their ability to understand and the skill of the counsellor.

6.12 Which is, perhaps, an easy enough thing to say but is, at the same time, a statement fraught with underlying ethical difficulty – and this is particularly so when the patient is already pregnant and we enter the field of prenatal diagnosis.[7] One has to ask, first, whether the goal of free patient choice is possible, given the fact that, once genetic counselling has been offered and accepted, a likely chain of events has already been set up in the minds of all those involved.[8] Clarke also asks whether the objective is, itself, morally defensible – or have we, for fear of being labelled eugenists, 'fled so far from medical paternalism that we deny ethical responsibility for our professional activities'? Moreover, the whole concept of genetic counselling can be

---

5   Some readers may require a more detailed explanation than we have space for. A very easily understood description is to be found in R F Mueller and I D Young *Emery's Elements of Medical Genetics* (9th edn, 1995) ch 3.

6   The risk is 1:3 rather than the anticipated unifactorial 1:4 because a quarter of the conceptuses will be monosomic and will die in utero. The significance of translocation disease was noted in *Gregory v Pembrokeshire Health Authority* [1989] 1 Med LR 81.

7   B Biesecker 'Prenatal Diagnosis of Sex Chromosome Conditions' (2001) 322 BMJ 441. The author makes the interesting point that, once a genetic abnormality is diagnosed in a fetus, the woman has suffered a loss – the loss of the healthy fetus she hoped she carried.

8   See, particularly, A Clarke 'Is Non-directive Genetic Counselling Possible?' (1991) 338 Lancet 998. On genetic counselling in general, see the major reference: A Clarke *Genetic Counselling: Practice and Principles* (1994). Not only may the patient accept or reject the advice given but so may her general practitioner: G H de Bock, C J van Asperen, J M de Vries et al 'How Women with a Family History of Breast Cancer and their General Practitioners Act on Genetic Advice in General Practice: Prospective Longitudinal Study' (2001) 322 BMJ 26.

questioned, in so far as it increasingly involves the systematic selection of fetuses and, hence approaches children as consumer objects subject to quality control.[9] The increasing 'need' for genetic counselling can be seen as being based on the increasing number of disorders which can be diagnosed and, as Lippman has said, before long, the definition of fetal imperfection will come to mean any condition which can be diagnosed in utero. The social and economic pressures on a woman to terminate a pregnancy once an abnormality is discovered in her fetus are such that her autonomous choice is severely prejudiced. These pressures would escalate were the somewhat bizarre suggestion adopted that the cost-efficiency of a genetic counselling service could be gauged by the number of abortions performed.[10] It is astonishing to read, for example, that the House of Commons Science and Technology Committee found that, in Edinburgh, a prenatal test for late onset Huntington's disease will not be offered to a woman who is herself afflicted unless she agrees to terminate if the test proves positive.[11] The rationale is that the child is otherwise burdened by the knowledge of its early death. Yet, such a policy betrays an underlying attitude towards those affected by such a condition and ignores the fact that they can enjoy many happy asymptomatic years of life. One thing is, however, certain: no woman can be forced to destroy her fetus. There is no legislative basis for such a suggestion which has strong overtones of positive eugenics.[12]

6.13 But the counsellor has several advisory options: he can dismiss the risks, he can advise sterilisation of either partner, he can put the options of artificial insemination by donor or of ovum donation, or he can arrange for a suitably controlled pregnancy coupled with the alternatives of live birth or abortion as conditions indicate.

CONTROLLED PREGNANCY

6.14 The counsellor may have advised a pregnancy or he may be presented for the first time with a couple in which the wife is already pregnant. In either event, should he feel that a risk exists, he now has at his disposal a considerable technical armamentarium to help in closing the gap between probability and certainty. His methods may be non-invasive or invasive.

Non-invasive techniques

6.15 X-rays of the fetus are contra-indicated save in an emergency. The modern alternative is visualisation by means of ultrasound. This is accepted as being innocuous as far as the fetus and mother are concerned and is widely used in

---

9 See A Lippman 'Prenatal Genetic Testing and Screening: Constructing Needs and Reinforcing Inequities' (1991) 17 Am J Law Med 15.
10 For discussion, and rejection, see A Clarke 'Genetics, Ethics, and Audit' (1990) 335 Lancet 1145.
11 House of Commons Science and Technology Committee, Third Report, para 90.
12 D J Galton and C J Galton 'Francis Galton: and Eugenics Today' (1998) 24 J Med Ethics 99; D J Kevles 'Eugenics and Human Rights' (1999) 319 BMJ 435. See also *Emeh v Kensington and Chelsea and Westminster Area Health Authority* [1985] QB 1012 at 1024, [1984] 3 All ER 1044 at 1053, per Slade LJ, CA.

obstetric management – so much so that testing may well be considered to be governed by implied consent alone;[13] moreover, its use in locating the placenta is an essential prerequisite to amniocentesis, chorionic villus sampling and fetoscopy.[14] Ever-increasing technical and interpretative skills have transformed ultrasonography from a fairly crude diagnostic tool to one which is capable of demonstrating not only the sex of the baby and major external abnormalities, such as spina bifida or anencephaly, but also congenital disease of the internal organs, and minor defects such as cleft lip – indeed, the identification of Down's syndrome is often based on the appearance of relatively subtle fetal anomalies.[15] The processes of obstetric management and genetic counselling are, therefore, irrevocably entwined and it is important that the woman is aware of the implications, which are similar to those we discuss below under amniocentesis. The clinician who discovers a fetal abnormality as a by-product of management can scarcely conceal his knowledge while the woman, for her part, may be ill-prepared to receive it; the case for 'informed consent'[16] to ultrasonography is strong. It is an interesting psychological side-effect of the process that many parents regard the sonogram as their first 'baby-picture' – something which tends to endow the fetus with a recognisable personality; this, in itself, has some influence on the management decision.[17]

Maternal invasion

6.16 Fetuses with neural tube defects – spina bifida or anencephaly – secrete an excess of the protein α-fetoprotein into the amniotic fluid and some of this is transferred to the maternal circulation. Testing the maternal serum thus offers a simple and risk-free method of diagnosing abnormality in the fetus and is very acceptable to mothers. While 80-90% of neural tube defective fetuses can be diagnosed in this way, the test is probably best regarded as a major indication of the need for amniocentesis. Conversely, it has been recognised for some time that a low maternal concentration of α-fetoprotein is associated with Down's syndrome in the fetus. Other maternal serum constituents – eg unconjugated oestriol, human chorionic gonadotrophin and the protein inhibin A – are also influenced. A very effective rate of diagnosis of Down's syndrome can be achieved by combining such analyses with consideration of the mother's age[18] and the use of ultrasonography – a detection rate of 85% is claimed or this integrated test with, equally importantly, a low

---

13 See Lippman, (1991) 17 Am J Law Med 15. It is difficult to know how seriously we should take suggestions such as ultrasound predisposing to, eg, left-handedness: K A Salvesen, L J Vatten, S H Eik-Nes et al 'Routine ultrasonography in utero and subsequent handedness and neurological development' (1993) 307 BMJ 159 – perhaps they should serve as gentle reminders.

14 See para 6.18 below.

15 Ultrasonography of the fetal neck tissues now has an 80% chance of detecting Down's syndrome (see below): J Wise 'Nuchal Test Detects 80% of Down's Syndrome Pregnancies' (1998) 317 BMJ 368.

16 See further chapter 10.

17 D Callahan 'How Technology is Reframing the Abortion Debate' (1986) Hastings Center Rep, February, p 33.

18 N J Wald, A Kennard, J W Densem et al 'Antenatal Maternal Serum Screening for Down's Syndrome: Results of a Demonstration Project' (1992) 305 BMJ 391.

false positive rate of 1%.[19] Most practitioners, however, probably would still wish to offer amniocentesis or chorionic villus sampling to women aged over 35 years and at, generally, higher risk. None the less, the introduction of a relatively cheap and effective test raises the possibility of extending routine testing to all pregnant women rather than to the older group alone. Here, however, we enter the realm of resource allocation – a subject dealt with in detail in chapter 11. For the present, we only draw attention to the conflict which arises between those who would hold to the assumption that 'because a test is possible, testing should be implemented as a service'[20] and those who emphasise the importance of cost-effectiveness before a new policy is established – in itself, often a source of contention.[21] All those involved in the field of prenatal screening would, however, agree that the provision of a test without adequate back-up counselling as to the significance of the results is likely to introduce as much harm as good.[22] We also question the ethical propriety of making available a plethora of tests for conditions, such as Down's syndrome, for which no treatment or cure is available. In these circumstances, the availability of such tests can *only* be justified to facilitate an abortion decision – otherwise, offering them can be seen as little more than a waste of resources. By contrast with what is, arguably, a dubious justification, it is possible to mount a *strong* ethical argument justifying tests which will identify illnesses, such as spina bifida, that are likely to expose a child to physical suffering and major surgical interventions.

6.17 Serum tests are generally performed in the second trimester; reliance on maternal serum for diagnosis thus leads to late terminations when one is indicated, whereas the current emphasis is on identifying chromosomal abnormalities in early pregnancy.[23]

Uterine invasion

6.18 The commonest invasive techniques for prenatal diagnosis which involve the fetus or its environment are amniocentesis and chorionic villus sampling. The former is technically easier and carries a lesser risk to the pregnancy; despite the theoretical advantages of the latter, amniocentesis is still probably the more popular method of direct investigation in the United Kingdom.

---

19   N J Wald, H C Watt and A K Hackshaw 'Integrated Screening for Down's Syndrome on the Basis of Tests Performed during the First and Second Trimesters' (1999) 341 New Engl J Med 461.
20   Editorial Comment 'Screening for Fetal Malformations' (1992) 340 Lancet 1006. And see Wald et al, para 6.16 above.
21   Eg M Connor 'Biochemical Screening for Down's Syndrome' (1993) 306 BMJ 1705. The original article sparked a massive correspondence, most of which was doubtful of the justification for extended screening. There is still considerable doubt as to the scientific basis for widespread serum testing; it is suggested that the use of maternal age combined with analysis of the routine ultrasound scan has been much underrated: D T Howe, R Gornall, D Wellesley et al 'Six-year Survey of Screening for Down's Syndrome by Maternal Age and Mid-trimester Ultrasound Scans' (2000) 320 BMJ 606.
22   S Vyas 'Screening for Down's Syndrome' (1994) 309 BMJ 753.
23   See para 6.19 below.

6.19 A significant number of British mothers undergo amniocentesis. The process consists of needling the sac surrounding the fetus and withdrawing fluid which contains excretions and metabolites of the fetus together with representative cells; the latter can be grown in culture for chromosomal studies and to detect certain metabolic diseases; the fluid can also be used for biochemical testing.

6.20 Biochemical tests can be made rapidly and can directly diagnose some rare diseases of defective metabolism of the gargoylism type. The onset of 'rhesus disease' can also be detected. But by far the most important test in the present context is that for α-fetoprotein, by means of which an efficient laboratory can now diagnose all neural tube lesions. Cell culture can indicate the presence of chromosomal disorder in some 10-20 days. In expert hands, the presence of what are termed 'inborn errors of metabolism' can be detected after some six weeks' culture.

6.21 On the face of things, therefore, amniocentesis provides very powerful means of preventing genetic disease but, at the same time, it presents both technical and ethical problems. First, a 'defensive' policy of amniocentesis for all would offer little or no benefit in terms of the proportion of positive results. In practice, it is used selectively on approximately 8% of the population[24] and almost exclusively for the diagnosis of chromosomal abnormalities, especially Down's syndrome. In the past, amniocentesis was commonly used where routine screening of maternal serum α-fetoprotein had shown a raised level which might indicate a structural abnormality of the fetus, notably a neural tube defect; such abnormalities are now, however, readily diagnosed by the use of ultrasound. As has been discussed above, the maternal α-fetoprotein level and other biochemical parameters are widely used in conjunction with the mother's age to calculate a risk score on which a decision to recommend amniocentesis may be more robustly based.[25] Having decided to test, however, it is to be noted that, even in the best hands, an adequate amount of fluid can only be obtained after about the fourteenth week of pregnancy – although the use of sophisticated ultrasonography may reduce this to 12 weeks; no fluid is obtained in some 5-10% of cases and the test must then be repeated; add to this the time required for effective cell culture and it will be seen that one is close to producing a viable infant – and a consequently more hazardous operation – in the event that termination of pregnancy is indicated.[26]

6.22 These concerns can be reduced by the use of chorionic villus sampling – or removal and study of the early placental cells; used in conjunction with recombinant DNA techniques, it can revolutionise the diagnosis and management of genetic disease. Chorionic villus sampling suffers in being of

---

24 Based on data from the Simpson Memorial Maternity Pavilion, Edinburgh 1998 – A A Calder, personal communication.
25 For full details, see H S Cuckle and N J Wald 'Screening for Down's Syndrome' in R Lilford (ed) *Prenatal Diagnosis and Prognosis* (1990).
26 The Human Fertilisation and Embryology Act 1990, s 37(4) has eliminated the legal concern here; the aesthetic distaste for, and the comparative danger of, late abortions remains.

no value in the identification of neural tube defects; the incidence of doubtful chromosomal analyses is some four times greater than that following amniocentesis; it is more expensive; and, currently, the risk of miscarriage following the procedure is certainly greater – occurring in some 2-3% of examinations. Against this, chorionic villus sampling provides a good source of fetal DNA. Perhaps the most important practical consideration lies in the fear that early villus sampling may result in facial or limb abnormalities in an otherwise normal fetus.[27] For all these reasons, the early enthusiasm with which the procedure was greeted has waned somewhat. It is probably best reserved for those women who are at greatest risk – and, therefore, most likely to seek an early termination – or for cases where there is a single gene defect likely to require diagnosis.[28]

6.23 Amniocentesis itself is said to carry a fetal mortality rate of up to 0.5%; slight though this may be, it is still not inconsiderable and, again, indicates the need for case selection – particularly if fertility is already low. It, too, cannot be used in a 'blanket' fashion – only specific diseases can be sought and discovered; moreover, irrespective of negligence, some false positive or false negative tests are inevitable and will increase with the complexity of the tests undertaken.

6.24 Such limitations of technique give rise to ethical, as well as practical, problems. Although modern techniques of gene marking have reduced the toll,[29] a proportion of normal male children at risk of X-linked disease are still legally aborted. Again, a raised α-fetoprotein level does not give a clear indication of the degree of neural tube defect and, although the additional use of high quality ultrasonography greatly improves the position, the routine abortion of fetuses with any detectable spinal abnormality will result in the destruction of some salvageable – and lovable – children. On the other hand, 10-20% of 'missed' cases will have a severe defect and will require much corrective surgery. Similarly, the mere presence of the typical chromosomal abnormality does not indicate the likely severity of Down's syndrome. There are other problems of interpretation. For example, given a chromosomal abnormality, what does it mean? Certain arrangements are well known to be associated with severe disease but in others – notably the 'XYY syndrome' – the evidence is by no means clear.[30] XYY boys are said to be prone to vicious behaviour but 'prone' is a very relative concept.[31] Should a doctor, on the one hand, recommend abortion of such a fetus as a 'precaution' or, on the other, say nothing and risk leaving the parents with an inexplicably 'difficult' child; alternatively, should he inform the parents, allow the pregnancy to run normally and possibly expose the family unnecessarily to an atmosphere of

27 H V Firth, P A Boyd, P Chamberlain et al 'Severe Limb Abnormalities after Chorionic Villus Sampling at 56-66 Days' Gestation' (1991) 337 Lancet 762.
28 R J Lilford 'The Rise and Fall of Chorionic Villus Sampling' (1991) 303 BMJ 936.
29 Eg markers are already available for cystic fibrosis, Duchenne muscular dystrophy and Huntington's disease.
30 See L Taylor 'Genetically Influenced Antisocial Behaviour and the Criminal Justice System' (1982) 33 NILQ 215.
31 On the supposed link between genetics and criminality see, generally, Ciba Foundation *Genetics of Criminal and Antisocial Behaviour* (1996).

distrust? What is one to do when one of the other common aberrations of the sex chromosomes – for example Klinefelter's (XXY) or Turner's (XO) syndrome – is discovered? Such abnormalities are often, but by no means always, associated with a degree of infertility or learning disability. The variations are so many that it is impossible to generalise. The essential point is that patients who request or consent to antenatal diagnoses of this type must fully understand the extent of their consent and must be aware of the potential consequent decisions to be made.[32] Some might wish to be apprised of every item of information which has come to light, while others might require to know only of conditions which have a fully understood and significant prognosis; much subsequent searching of conscience can be avoided by preparatory discussion of the issues.

6.25 At the same time, as we have already intimated, the doctor's own motivation, prejudices and failings cannot be discounted. Much will depend upon whether, and to what extent, he sees himself as a community rather than a personal physician – and how he sees his duty to be apportioned between the woman and her progeny. We have already concluded that it is well-nigh impossible to perform an illegal therapeutic abortion in Great Britain but the clinician is still confronted with the moral problems inherent in the interpretation of 'severe handicap' in the Abortion Act 1967, s 1(1)(d) – it is, for example, even possible to construct an argument which casts doubt on the ethical justification for abortion in such a serious condition as Huntington's disease.[33] What seemed, at first sight, to be an uncomplicated and thoroughly desirable procedure presents, in the end, as a Pandora's box of moral uncertainties.

6.26 Some of the difficulties can be overcome by more modern techniques. Fetoscopy, for example, allows for direct inspection of the fetus and, thence, an assessment of the degree of abnormality; at the same time, fetoscopy carries with it a fetal mortality of about 1%. Fetal blood sampling, originally developed for the diagnosis, inter alia, of haemophilia has had a relatively short life as the need for such relatively dangerous investigations recedes with the availability of recombinant DNA techniques.[34] Mention must also be made of the very different potential of in vitro fertilisation (for which see chapter 3) combined with embryo biopsy as an answer to the very high risk pregnancy and/or for those who find feticide morally unacceptable but who can tolerate embryocide. The technique of pre-implantation diagnosis involves removal and genetic analysis of single cells from eight-cell embryos, followed by selection of those embryos found to be normal for implantation. This immediately raises the question of the status of the surplus embryo which we discuss in detail below.[35] Aside from such moral implications, the procedure

32 An interesting survey was reported by H Statham and J Green 'Serum Screening for Down's Syndrome: Some Women's Experiences' (1993) 307 BMJ 174.

33 S G Post 'Huntington's Disease: Prenatal Screening for Late Onset Disease' (1992) 18 J Med Ethics 75. There is also a semantic problem as to whether the words 'if the child were born it would suffer from ....' (Abortion Act 1967, s 1(1)(d)) exclude conditions that are not present at birth – but any discussion is surely no more than academic pedantry.

34 N M Fisk and S Bower 'Fetal Blood Sampling in Retreat' (1993) 307 BMJ 143.

35 See chapter 19.

also carries with it the many difficulties associated with in vitro fertilisation of itself (see chapter 3) and we tend to doubt whether its benefits outweigh the imposed emotional and financial costs.[36] That having been said, however, it is impossible to ignore the speed with which this branch of science moves forward. The range of pre-implantation diagnoses is growing such that the technique is referable to an ever widening body of patient-clients. It is now possible to screen for a large number of conditions, including cystic fibrosis, Tay Sachs disease, Duchenne muscular dystrophy and even dominant disorders such as Marfan's syndrome. Anecdotal evidence suggests that, while families affected, for example, by hereditary cancers show little interest in prenatal diagnosis, couples at risk of passing on a dominant condition generally prefer prenatal diagnosis to the option of aborting an otherwise normal pregnancy.[37]

6.27 But increasing sophistication to some extent only serves to underline the fundamental moral issue of prenatal screening which is – how far is one to go in defining abnormality? Is the 'perfect baby' to be encouraged?[38] The concept of parents obtaining a termination on the grounds of, for example, the sex of the child may seem frivolous – or unprincipled – to many; but, as we discuss above,[39] it may be both medically defensible and legally acceptable. One can foresee more generally applicable dilemmas of conscience. Cases of Down's syndrome or of spina bifida which have not been discovered through prenatal screening are already candidates for neonaticide or local authority care. Is such disposal to run parallel with an increasing prenatal diagnostic capability when, as a result, more parents reject what will be regarded as imperfect children on increasingly demanding criteria? It is for such reasons that we argue later[40] in favour of legislation which ensures that, whatever may be the legal situation of the fetus, the best interests of the neonate are paramount.

6.28 On the other side of the coin, it is clear that genetic counsellors should not overemphasise the interests of the state in reducing the incidence of genetic disease and, as clinicians, should not join with the scientists in welcoming the genetic issue as 'unstoppable'.[41] Rather, the aim should be to concentrate on the particular circumstances and interests of the parents in wanting a child. The Nuffield Council on Bioethics,[42] the House of Commons Science and Technology Committee[43] and the British Medical Association[44] have all stressed the importance of accepting the ethical principle that screening or testing is justifiable only if based on free and informed consent. Similarly, in the United States, the National Institutes of Health Task Force on Genetic Testing has

---

36 A very good discussion is to be found in M Michael and S Buckle 'Screening for Genetic Disorders: Therapeutic Abortion and IVF' (1990) 16 J Med Ethics 43.
37 J D A Delhanty and J C Harper 'Genetic Diagnosis Before Implantation' (1997) 315 BMJ 828.
38 R F Chadwick 'The Perfect Baby: An Introduction' in R F Chadwick (ed) *Ethics, Reproduction and Genetic Control* (1987) p 93. See also E Yoxen *Unnatural Selection* (1986).
39 See para 5.9.
40 See chapter 16 below.
41 Editorial Comment 'Ethics and the Human Genome' (1991) 351 Nature, Lond 591, quoted by Clarke (1991) 335 Lancet 1145.
42 *Genetic Screening: Ethical Issues* paras. 4.6–4.16.
43 Third Report (1995) paras 81-105, esp paras 88, 97.
44 BMA *The BMA's Views on Genetic Testing* (21 November 1995).

stated that '[it] is unacceptable to coerce or intimidate individuals or families regarding their decision about predictive genetic testing'.[45] An elderly couple, for example, might see a pregnancy as their last possibility and might prefer to take their chance in the ignorant way of natural parenthood – and they should be allowed to do so; a woman who has managed to conceive by assisted means may rightly refuse to take the risks involved in subsequent chorionic villus sampling or amniocentesis. A refusal to accept information must be respected just as much as must the desire to receive information. To an extent, the wishes of patient-clients dictate the parameters of the duties of genetic counsellors and, indeed, of all health care professionals. In practice, the precise boundaries of such duties are established and maintained by the law through the actions for wrongful life and for wrongful birth, which are, essentially, actions for negligence brought over genetic counselling. We turn to consider these now and stress that what is said must be viewed in the light of this complex and, sometimes, conflicting moral background.

COUNSELLING AND NEGLIGENCE

6.29 The parents of an afflicted child may choose to raise an action in negligence against a genetic counsellor or doctor who has failed either to advise them of the risk of genetic illness in their children or to carry out, and interpret correctly, appropriate diagnostic procedures which would have disclosed abnormality in the fetus. The counsellor or doctor owes them a duty of care in which he or she has been found wanting; the parents may contend that, as a result, they have been deprived of the opportunity to terminate the pregnancy and they are now burdened with a sick or handicapped child. Such an action, brought by and on behalf of the parents, is generally known as one for 'wrongful birth'.[46] Damages may be sought in respect of the distress occasioned by the parents in respect of the existence of the defect in their child and for the extra costs which are entailed in bringing up the child.

6.30 The courts in the United States, which can be seen as the pathfinders in this particular area, have had something of a roller-coaster ride on their way to recognising damages for the birth of a handicapped child as a legitimate claim. In the early case of *Becker v Schwartz*[47] the New York Court of Appeals allowed a parental claim for damages in respect of the cost of the institutional care of a child suffering from Down's syndrome. The negligence in question was the failure of the doctor to recommend amniocentesis to a 37-year-old

---

45 N A Holtzman and M S Watson (eds) *Promoting Safe and Effective Genetic Testing in the United States* (1997).
46 Other related actions include an action for 'wrongful pregnancy', which we define as a claim that an unwanted implantation or pregnancy occurred because of another's negligence. Some authors distinguish an action for 'wrongful conception' which is raised on the rather narrower ground that a failed sterilisation operation has resulted in a conception: see B Dickens 'Wrongful Birth and Life, Wrongful Death before Birth and Wrongful Law' in S A M McLean (ed) *Legal Issues in Human Reproduction* (1989) ch 4. Such a distinction may be useful in limited circumstances but we prefer to use the umbrella term 'wrongful pregnancy' to encompass both. We discuss the action for 'wrongful life' at para 6.34 below.
47 386 NE 2d 807 (NY, 1978).

mother who, by virtue of her age, had a relatively high risk of bearing a handicapped child. Later, however, they found difficulty as to the conflict of interests. On the one hand, there is the question of public policy which should, in theory, favour birth over abortion.[48] On the other, the woman's prerogative to control her own body, and the consequent acceptability of abortion, have been increasingly recognised. The general rule which seems to have emerged is that, while wrongful life actions[49] will fail, the corresponding claim for wrongful birth will succeed.[50] Even so, the causation problem remains. In *Noccash*,[51] for example, widely based damages were awarded for the birth of an infant with Tay-Sachs disease but costs concerned with the child's funeral were disallowed on the grounds that the fatality was the result of hereditary factors rather than of the defendant's negligence. Other difficulties relate to the fact that pregnancy has been actually sought in these cases. Should the damages awarded then reflect the full costs of rearing a defective child or should they be limited to the difference in financial burden posed by a normal and a handicapped infant? Should they extend to compensation for emotional distress? These questions seem to be very finely balanced in the American courts[52] and, while, as has been noted, they will accept a wrongful birth action in principle in most cases, some state legislatures have enacted laws stating clearly their preference for denying such causes of action.[53] Moreover, the constitutionality of a prohibition on such actions has been upheld, as we see in the judgment of the Supreme Court of Minnesota in *Hickman v Group Health Plan Inc*.[54]

6.31 Comparable cases have been rare in the United Kingdom but the courts have shown an increased willingness to address the problems in recent years. There is no doubt that damages will be awarded in respect of negligent counselling; in other words, a wrongful birth action is available in the United Kingdom and we suspect that many cases are settled out of court;[55] the case of *Salih*,[56] involving the congenital rubella syndrome, is apposite in this connection

---

48 See eg *Azzolino v Dingfelder* 337 SE 2d 528 (NC, 1985); *Siemieniec v Lutheran General Hospital* 512 NE 2d 691 (Ill, 1987).
49 See para 6.34 below.
50 *Smith v Cote* 513 A 2d 341 (NH, 1986); *Proffitt v Bartolo* 412 NW 2d 232 (Mich, 1987) – where the inconsistency of dissociating the two types of action was vented. For a more recent discussion of these actions, see P M A Beaumont 'Wrongful Life and Wrongful Birth' in S A M McLean *Contemporary Issues in Law, Medicine and Ethics* (1996) ch 6.
51 *Noccash v Burger* 290 SE 2d 825 (Va, 1982).
52 See G G Sarno 'Recoverability of Compensatory Damages for Mental Anguish or Emotional Distress for Tortiously Causing Another's Birth' (1989) 74 ALR 4th 798.
53 As an example, consider this provision from the Utah Code Ann para 78-11-24: '[a] cause of action shall not arise, and damages shall not be awarded, on behalf of any person, based on a claim that but for the act or omission of another, a person would not have been permitted to have been born alive but would have been aborted.'
54 369 NW 2d 10 (1986).
55 *Rawnsley v Leeds Area Health Authority* (1981) Times, 17 November is an early example of an otherwise unreported case. For general discussion of the liability of genetic counsellors, see M L Lupton 'The Impact of Genetics on Society: The Law's Response' (1991) 10 Med Law 55.
56 *Salih v Enfield Health Authority* [1990] 1 Med LR 333; on appeal (1991) 7 BMLR 1, CA. It is to be noted that, while the trial judge awarded damages which included the basic costs of maintaining a child, the Court of Appeal, however, held that the family had been spared the cost of a normal child and this head of damages was extinguished.

in that liability was admitted without question. In *Gregory v Pembrokeshire Health Authority*[57] the trial judge found that the doctors' neglect to inform of the failure of an amniocentesis was a breach of the duty of care; the action failed, however, on grounds of causation, the plaintiff being unable to convince the court, or the Court of Appeal, that she would have had a second investigation had she been offered one. In *Anderson v Forth Valley Health Board*,[58] a couple sought damages in respect of the alleged negligence of a health board which led to their two sons being born suffering from muscular dystrophy. The pursuers averred that, had they been referred for genetic counselling and testing, a genetic disorder carried by the wife would have been discovered and the couple would have chosen to terminate both pregnancies. As it was, no tests were ever offered or carried out, despite the fact that the hospital had been informed of a history of X-linked Duchenne muscular dystrophy among the male members of the wife's family. The children's condition only came to light when one of the boys injured himself in a fall. After a very comprehensive review of the case law, Lord Nimmo Smith held that he could see 'no good reason' not to treat the pursuers as having suffered personal injuries 'in the conventional sense' and he accordingly awarded damages under the heads of both solatium and patrimonial loss.[59]

6.32 The decision of the Scottish courts in *McLelland v Greater Glasgow Health Board*[60] should be noted as to the matter of damages for solatium. In this case, a father was, for the first time, awarded damages for the shock and distress he suffered as the result of the birth of a son suffering from Down's syndrome – as in *Anderson*, the hospital had been made aware of a family history suggestive of genetic disease but had failed to offer an amniocentesis. This ruling is unprecedented because it is normally only the mother of the child who will receive damages for pain and suffering. The closest analagous authority we can find in England is *Newell v Goldenberg*,[61] in which a couple were awarded £500 for the anxiety and distress suffered when they discovered that Mrs Newell had become pregnant following the failure of her husband's vasectomy. Normally, the plaintiff must prove an element of psychiatric disturbance or illness in order to recover damages for 'nervous shock'. In *McLelland*, however, Lord MacFadyen was persuaded that this criterion goes only to the question of the existence of a duty of care; no question of a duty of care arises if the only harm suffered is anxiety and distress and there is no evidence of harm of a psychiatric nature. However, in the circumstances of the particular case, the defenders admitted to a duty of care to the father. Thus, an award of damages for the father's upset fell to be considered as would be any other head of damage when the pursuer has suffered material prejudice as a result of the defender's negligence.[62]

---

57 [1989] 1 Med LR 81.
58 (1998) 44 BMLR 108, 1998 SLT 588.
59 Wrongful pregnancy was also regarded as a personal injury in England: *Walkin v South Manchester Heath Authority* [1995] 4 All ER 132, [1996] 7 Med LR 211.
60 1999 SC 305, 1999 SLT 543.
61 [1995] 6 Med LR 371.
62 The McLellands, in fact, fell into the *McFarlane* trap (see below) between the Outer and the Inner Houses. Solatium was still awarded but the 'ordinary' costs of maintaining their child were deducted from the previously awarded full costs at the appeal which was heard after *McFarlane*: *McLelland v Greater Glasgow Health Board* 2001 SLT 446.

6.33 So far, so good, but the United Kingdom courts' attitudes were to be markedly affected by the House of Lords' ruling in *McFarlane v Tayside Health Board*[63] which we have discussed in some detail at para 4.18. It will be remembered that, while the House rejected the concept of compensation for the undesired normal child, it left open the position were such a child to be born disabled – thus raising the possibility that the well-established action for wrongful birth might no longer be available or, at best, might only be available in a modified form.[64] As we have seen in Chapter 5, this resulted in a rash of cases anxious to settle the matter. As a result,[65] the underlying validity of the wrongful birth action has been fully upheld; damages have, however, been modified in the light of *McFarlane* in that the costs of rearing a healthy child must, now, be deducted from the gross costs of caring for one who is disabled.[66]

DIMINISHED OR WRONGFUL LIFE ACTIONS

6.34 The basis of a parental claim may be clear enough, but what is the juristic nature of a claim brought on behalf of the child itself? The status of the fetus in utero is legally established – the fetus has a general right not to be injured by the wrongful act of a third party. This right was recognised at common law in Canada and in Australia in two important decisions, *Duval v Seguin*[67] and *Watt v Rama*.[68] Similar recognition is afforded to the fetus by the common law in Scotland[69] and has been held retrospectively to have existed in England prior to the Congenital Disabilities (Civil Liability) Act 1976.[70]

6.35 The most important aspect of these rights in the present context relates to the responsibilities of the mother to her fetus. The Law Commission considered this question and decided that an action against its mother in respect of damage resulting from her negligence during pregnancy should not be available to a child. It was felt that a claim of this type would compromise the parent-child relationship and might also be used as a weapon in matrimonial disputes. Accordingly, the English legislation excludes claims by a child against its mother except as to injuries sustained during traffic accidents; here, special policy grounds and the availability of insurance were held to justify the admissibility of such

---

63 2000 SC (HL) 1, [2000] 2 AC 59.
64 When one applies the reasoning of the individual Lords of Appeal in *McFarlane*, it becomes apparent that that might well have been the case: J K Mason 'Wrongful Pregnancy, Wrongful Birth and Wrongful Terminology' (2002) 6 Edin L R 46. For further analysis of the proposition, see G Hughes-Jones 'Commentary on *Taylor v Shropshire HA*' [2000] Lloyd's Rep Med 107.
65 *Rand v East Dorset Health Authority* (2000) 56 BMLR 39, [2000] Lloyd's Rep Med 181; *Hardman v Amin* (2000) 59 BMLR 58, [2000] Lloyd's Rep Med 498; *Lee v Taunton and Someset NHS Trust* [2001] 1 FLR 419, [2001] Fam Law 103.
66 T Weir 'The Unwanted Child' (2002) 6 Edin L R fears that this may result in the courts 'finding' disability where none exists; we doubt if this would arise in cases of wrongful birth though might be possible in the event of wrongful pregnancy.
67 (1973) 40 DLR (3d) 666.
68 [1972] VR 353.
69 *Hamilton v Fife Health Board* (1993) 13 BMLR 156, 1993 SC 369, 1993 SLT 624.
70 See *Burton v Islington Health Authority*, *de Martell v Merton and Sutton Health Authority* [1992] 3 All ER 833, (1992) 9 BMLR 69.

claims.[71] The matter remains open in Scotland because there is no legislation on the subject and there is no reason in law to exclude a claim by a child against its mother in respect of prenatal injuries. It is possible, however, that the courts may be unsympathetic to such claims on policy grounds.

6.36 It is also difficult to determine the extent to which the mother's duty of care towards her unborn child might be held to limit her freedom of action during pregnancy. Interest in this aspect of the fetal-maternal relationship has escalated in recent years[72] and has been discussed already at para 5.53 et seq. It is almost certain that the last word on the subject has not been said and it seems only a matter of time before the neonate – who could not even protest at the passive smoking to which he was subjected in utero – will be able to sue for the damage done although, admittedly, success would be difficult if not impossible in England by virtue of the Congenital Disabilities (Civil Liability) Act 1976, s 1(1).

6.37 Apart from the straightforward case of an injury to the fetus in utero, a child born with an abnormality may argue that some other sort of wrong has been done to it. First, he or she may claim that there was negligence prior to its conception, and that this negligence has resulted in its being born with certain abnormalities. An example of such a claim is provided by the American case of *Yeager v Bloomington Obstetrics and Gynecology, Inc.*[73] This concerned a child born suffering from brain damage due to haemolytic disease of the newborn which occurred because the hospital negligently failed to treat rhesus immunisation of the mother during a previous pregnancy; the court held it to be reasonably foreseeable that subsequent children would be injured as a result. Such a claim would also be competent in English law provided that, at the time of conception, the parents were not aware of the risk that their child would be born disabled. This exemption does not apply if, in an action by the child against its father, it is established that the father knew of the risk while the mother did not.[74]

6.38 The child may also bring a claim in respect of its *wrongful life*. The basis of this claim is that, through the negligence of the defendant, the child's parents were not afforded the opportunity to terminate the pregnancy; as a result, the child seeks damages for the impaired existence he or she is now being forced unwillingly to lead – put brutally, he or she would rather have not been born. The negligence in question may occur either before the child's conception – as, for example, in a case of negligent genetic counselling – or after conception – as when a doctor fails to detect an abnormality in the fetus. A high proportion of such cases result from laboratory errors which are, in general, clearly recognisable as negligent.

---

71   An apposite case, possibly the prototype, has been reported by C Dyer 'Boy Wins Damages after Injury in Utero' (1992) 304 BMJ 1400. At least one Australian case has been successful: D Brahams 'Australian Mother Sued by Child Injured in Utero' (1991) 338 Lancet 687. The contribution of a seat-belt to injury to the fetus – or to its protection – would be an interesting discussion in many cases.
72   For a recent review, see S McLean *Old Law, New Medicine* (1999), chapter 3.
73   585 NE 2d 696 (Ind, 1992). For earlier examples, see *Lazevnick v General Hospital of Monro County Inc* 499 F Supp 146 (Md, 1980); *Jorgensen v Meade-Johnson Laboratories* 483 F 2d 237 (1973); *Renslow v Mennonite Hospital* 367 NE 2d 1250 (Ill, 1977).
74   Congenital Disabilities (Civil Liability) Act 1976, s 1(4).

6.39 The early history of the wrongful life action can be traced through the United States courts. Attempts to extend the cause of action to merely being born have, not unnaturally, received short shrift.[75] Suits brought by defective children, however, pose difficulties with which the American legal system has been struggling for many years. In *Gleitman v Cosgrove*,[76] the plaintiff was born deaf, mute and nearly blind as a result of his mother's exposure to German measles during pregnancy. The Supreme Court of New Jersey dismissed the plaintiff's claim for damages against the doctors who were alleged to have told the mother that there was no risk of German measles harming her child.

6.40 The basis for dismissal was that its acceptance would amount to a statement that it was better not to be born at all than to be born handicapped; it was logically impossible, the court felt, to weigh the value of a handicapped life against non-existence. As it was expressed:

> It is basic to the human condition to seek life and to hold on to it however heavily burdened. If Jeffrey [the plaintiff] could have been asked as to whether his life should be snuffed out before his full term of gestation could run its course, our felt intuition of human nature tells us he would almost surely choose life with defects against no life at all 'For the living there is hope, but for the dead there is none ...'

6.41 A year later, the claim of a child similarly damaged by its mother's illness was rejected on the grounds that to allow a claim based on failure to abort the plaintiff would be the antithesis of the principles of the law of tort, which is directed towards the protection of the plaintiff against wrongs. The greatest wrong, it was pointed out by the court, is to cause another person's death.[77] In other cases, the courts have chosen to reject the claims of handicapped children on the grounds that it is impossible to assess the child's damages.[78]

6.42 There is no indication that the courts, in refusing the children's claims, have intended to limit compensation for this type of negligence. Actions by the parents for emotional shock, expenses incurred in rearing a defective child and the like have been successful and the trend has been – as explained in *Robak*[79] – to focus on the family as the true object of the claim. This was emphasised in *Prokanik v Cillo*,[80] which was a rare instance of a wrongful life action being accepted; a main reason for so doing was that the parents were time-barred and could not sue on their own behalf. In line with other common law jurisdictions, the American courts will, where it is possible, allow the neonate a suit for prenatal injury while denying one for wrongful life.[81]

---

75 *Beardsley v Wierdsma* 650 P 2d 288 (Wyo, 1982).
76 296 NYS 2d 687 (1967).
77 *Stewart v Long Island College Hospital* 296 NYS 2d 41 (1968).
78 Eg *Dumer v St Michael's Hospital* 233 NW 2d 372 (Wis, 1975); *Blake v Cruz* 698 P 2d 315 (Idaho, 1984); *Smith v Cote* 513 A 2d 341 (NH, 1986); *Cowe v Forum Group Inc* 575 NE 2d 630 (Ind, 1991).
79 *Robak v United States* 658 F 2d 471 (1981).
80 478 A 2d 755 (NJ, 1984). A similar option has been left open more recently: *Viccaro v Milunsky* 551 NE 2d 8 (Mass, 1990).
81 Eg, *Cowe v Forum Group Inc* 575 NE 2d 630 (Ind, 1991).

6.43 To our knowledge, there exists only one straightforward instance of a wrongful life action being allowed in full in the United States.[82] This case was effectively overturned by the Supreme Court of California in *Turpin*,[83] when it adopted the principle of allowing the suit to proceed and accepting a claim to special damages – ie those incurred as a result of the congenital defects – but not to general damages; the basis for the latter restriction lay in the still insoluble problem of comparing an impaired existence with not being born at all. The movement towards acceptance of the suit has, however, been arrested and there is now a definite trend in favour of rejecting such claims in toto.[84] When the plaintiff in *Bruggeman v Schimke*[85] averred that actions for wrongful life were being increasingly recognised, the court replied that this was simply not true and that any theory sustaining a legal right to be dead rather than to be alive with deficiencies was one completely contrary to the laws of the state. In practical terms, children are unlikely to be disadvantaged when an action for wrongful life fails. Since the courts allow the parents to recover the medical expenses in rearing a defective child, the child's separate claim will apply only to expenses incurred after reaching majority; in most cases, the defect will be so serious that the damaged child will never achieve that age. Even so, both the United States courts and the state legislatures appear increasingly concerned to express their preference for birth over abortion – and this to the extent that not only wrongful life but also wrongful birth actions may be rejected.[86]

6.44 A similar judicial antipathy to abortion is to be seen in the only apposite English case – *McKay v Essex Area Health Authority*.[87] Prior to this Court of Appeal decision, the Law Commission had considered the merits of the wrongful life action in its Report on Injuries to Unborn Children[88] and had come to the conclusion that it should not be allowed. The gravamen of this recommendation lies in the belief that to allow such actions would place 'an almost intolerable burden on medical advisors', who might be under 'subconscious pressures' to advise abortions in doubtful cases. As a result of these recommendations, the Congenital Disabilities (Civil Liability) Act 1976, s 1(2)(b) appears to exclude the right of a child to sue in such circumstances.[89] The infant plaintiff in

---

82 *Curlender v Bio-Science Laboratories* 165 Cal Rptr 477 (1980).
83 *Turpin v Sortini* 182 Cal Rptr 377 (1982). Also followed in *Harbeson v Parke-Davis Inc* 656 P 2d 483 (Wash, 1983).
84 Eg *Ellis v Sherman* 515 A 2d 1327 (Pa, 1986); *Proffitt v Bartolo* 412 NW 2d 232 (Mich, 1987); *Cowe v Forum Group Inc* 575 NE 2d 630 (Ind, 1991).
85 718 P 2d 635 (Kan, 1986).
86 For evidence of this from state legislatures see para 6.30 above. Also, *Azzolino v Dingfelder* 337 SE 2d 528 (NC, 1985). For major reviews, see E H Morreim 'The Concept of Harm Reconceived: A Different Look at Wrongful Life' (1988) 7 Law & Philos 3; B R Furrow 'Actions for Wrongful Life' in J K Mason (ed) *Paediatric Forensic Medicine and Pathology* (1989) ch 26.
87 [1982] QB 1166, [1982] 2 All ER 771, CA.
88 Law Com No 60.
89 A good argument can, in fact, be made out that wrongful life actions are not excluded. We, for example, find it hard to accept that wrongly advising a woman as to the potential dangers for her fetus does not affect her ability to choose her options bearing on her ability to have a healthy child. The Law Commission's fear of encouraging abortion seems to have greatly influenced the interpretation of the 1976 Act. In any case, it can also be argued that an action for wrongful life is still available at common law: J E S Fortin 'Is the "Wrongful Life" Action Really Dead?' [1987] J Soc Welfare Law 306. See also the commentary on *Cowe*: A Grubb [1993] 1 Med L Rev 262.

McKay was, however, born before 22 July 1976 and, therefore, did not come within the ambit of the Act; the issue of wrongful life was, therefore, open to the court.

6.45 In this case, the mother of the handicapped child had been in contact with the virus of German measles and had consulted her doctor. A blood sample was taken but this was mislaid. A second sample of blood was taken and the mother was duly informed that neither she nor the infant had been infected with rubella; however, the infant girl was found to be severely handicapped when she was born. The plaintiffs alleged that there was negligence on the part of the defendants in that they either failed to carry out the necessary tests on the blood samples or failed to interpret them correctly. A number of claims were made as a result of this alleged negligence, including a claim by the child for damages in respect of entry into a life of distress and suffering.

6.46 The court discussed the major issues of legal policy to which this case gave rise in an extensive judgment. While recognising that there was no reason why a mother in such circumstances may not be able to claim in respect of the negligent failure to advise her of her right to choose abortion, the court was not prepared to recognise any claim by a child to damages for wrongful life. The grounds on which this decision was reached are similar to those which have appeared in the American cases.

6.47 The initial analysis is in terms of the duty of the doctor. The doctor clearly owes to the fetus a duty not to do anything to injure it, but what duty is owed to a fetus which has been damaged by some agency for which the doctor can bear no responsibility – in this case by the rubella virus? The only duty which the court could see would be an alleged duty to abort the fetus and the question then to be considered was whether this could ever be legal.[90] As to 'wrongful life', it was held that an *obligation* to abort:

> [W]ould mean regarding the life of a handicapped child as not only less valuable than the life of a normal child, but so much less valuable that it was not worth preserving, and it would even mean that a doctor would be obliged to pay damages to a child infected with rubella before birth who was in fact born with some mercifully trivial abnormality. These are the consequences of the necessary basic assumption that a child has a right to be born whole or not at all, not to be born unless it can be born perfect or 'normal', whatever that may mean.[91]

6.48 Having declined to find a duty basis of the claim, the court also cavilled at the difficulties of assessing damages in such a case. Here, the impossibility of comparison argument was seen as a strong one: how could a court compare the value of a flawed life with non-existence or, indeed, with any 'after life' which an aborted child was experiencing? – the court declined to undertake any judgment on the conflicting views of theologians and philosophers on the latter aspect. Even faced with this conceptual difficulty, Stephenson LJ was of

---

90 This attitude, particularly as related to rubella immunisation, is challenged by Morreim (1988) 7 Law & Philos 3.
91 [1982] 2 All ER 777 at 781, per Stephenson LJ.

the opinion that it was better to be born maimed than not to be born at all except, possibly, in the most extreme cases of mental and physical disability – which provokes the questions: 'what is extremity?' and 'by what right do the courts take the view that existence is always to be preferred to non-existence?' The decision is, surely, one which should be left to the handicapped child by way of an objective substituted judgment – given the degree of disability, what would the individual child have thought? Although the matter has not been tested directly, it is very probable that a Scottish court would following the ruling in *McKay*.[92]

6.49 The doubtful aspect of the wrongful life action lies in the fact that it requires that the court should say to the plaintiff: 'Yes, it would be better had you not been born.' This judgment, however sympathetic to the motives behind it, would seriously compromise the value of human life which the courts are more usually called upon to endorse. The disabled should be helped and, if possible, compensated for the suffering which their lives may entail, but the moral basis for such compensation should be the desire to make life more comfortable and bearable – not the notion that they should not be in existence at all.

6.50 In line with this argument, we believe that the conceptual difficulties would largely disappear if, first, the Abortion Act 1967, s 1(1)(d) – the 'eugenic clause' – were accepted as having been drafted in the fetal, rather than the maternal, interest.[93] The 'right' of the handicapped fetus to abortion is then comparable to the defective neonate's right to refuse treatment (see chapter 16); failure to respond to the interests of either, albeit necessarily expressed by proxy, then falls into the ambit of consent-based negligence (see chapter 10) – in effect, the fetus is saying: 'but for the negligent advice given to me through my parents, I would not have chosen a disadvantaged condition; I now have to be disadvantaged and, therefore, I am entitled to compensation.' Secondly, we favour abandoning the principle of 'wrongful life' in favour of 'diminished life'; we can then look not at a comparison, whether it be between the neonate's current existence and non-existence or with normality, but, rather at the actual suffering that has been caused. There would have been no suffering in the event of an abortion, there was no abortion as a result of negligence, and it follows that the negligence has produced suffering which should be compensated according to its degree. This carries the practical advantage that the courts can understand and accommodate this form of damage, which allows for a distinction to be made between serious and slight defect.[94] Lord

---

92 *Anderson v Forth Valley Health Board* 1998 SLT 588 at 604, per Lord Nimmo Smith, referring to Lord Osborne in *P's Curator Bonis v Criminal Injuries Compensation Board* 1997 SLT 1180, (1997) 44 BMLR 70.

93 For discussion, see J K Mason *Medico-Legal Aspects of Reproduction and Parenthood* (2nd edn, 1998) pp 157-158. It is noteworthy that Stephenson LJ adopted this view in *McKay* (at All ER 780). But, having done so, why disallow 'wrongful life' actions on the grounds that they would encourage abortion?

94 See also Ackner LJ in *McKay* (at All ER 786): 'Subsection (2)(b) [of the 1976 Act] is so worded as to import the assumption that, but for the occurrence giving rise to a disabled birth, the child would have been born normal and healthy, not that it would not have been born at all' – and that, having disposed of the phrase 'wrongful life', appeared to be acceptable.

Donaldson MR, in a comment on *McKay*, has explained that the child also claimed that, if her mother had received appropriate treatment, her disabilities would have been less. She therefore sought damages based on the different between her quality of life as it was and the quality of life which she would have enjoyed if her mother had been treated – and this claim was allowed to proceed.[95] This is very close to an action for diminished life and is an aspect of *McKay* which merits closer study – though there seem to be no reports of the action.

6.51 The legal and philosophical arguments in favour of rejecting the wrongful life action are powerful but can be challenged. The apparently insurmountable hurdle on the road to acceptance lies in the more prosaic form of causation – it is undeniable that, save in exceptional circumstances, such as direct injury,[96] no *person* has caused the disabilities. Yet, in an age when compensation for injury is so widely available, it is difficult to see why the faulty genetic counsellor should be thus protected and intuition urges that justice is, thereby, thwarted[97] – suffering, if not the cause of the suffering, has been created by the negligence and to suffer is to be injured.

6.52 It is surprising that courts across the world have been content to assume the irrelevance of the wrongful life action and, until recently we have been able to find only one jurisdiction that has accepted the infant plaintiff's cause when confronted with the problem de novo.[98] An interesting situation has, however, now arisen in France where a handicapped child was born as a result of negligent failure to interpret correctly a pregnant woman's positive tests for rubella antibodies; had she been correctly counselled, she would certainly have terminated the pregnancy.

6.53 In an action for breach of contract brought on behalf of the parents, the court of first instance found against both the physician and the laboratory; innovatively, it also found them liable to the child for the loss caused by his handicap.[99] The *cour d'appel* then followed precedent and, while confirming the decision in favour of Mme Perruche, overturned that in favour of the child on the grounds of causation[100] – the arguments being similar to those rehearsed

---

95 *Re J (a minor) (wardship: medical treatment)* [1990] 3 All ER 930 at 935, (1992) 6 BMLR 25 at 31, CA.

96 Section 1A of the 1976 Act (inserted by way of the Human Fertilisation and Embryology Act 1990, s 44) allows for an action by a disabled infant when the disability is attributable to wrongful acts or omissions – including embryo selection – arising during the provision of treatment for infertility. This seems indistinguishable from an action for wrongful life, in which case, many of the objections as to the difficulty of assessment of damages and the like are reduced to solvable difficulties.

97 Remembering, however, that an action for wrongful birth is, at the same time, available to the parents.

98 *Zeitzoff v Katz* [1986] 40(2) PD 85 (SC Israel). See J Levi 'Wrongful Life Decision in Israel' (1987) 6 Med Law 373; A Shapira '"Wrongful Life" Lawsuits for Faulty Genetic Counselling: Should the Impaired Newborn Be Entitled to Sue?' (1998) 24 J Med Ethics 369. It was, however, rejected at first hand in the Roman-Dutch jurisdiction of South Africa: *Friedman v Glicksman* 1996 (1) SA 1134, where the coincident claim for wrongful birth was upheld.

99 Tribunal de Grande Instance, Evry, 13 January 1992.

100 Casse Civ 1, 26 March 1996, Bull Civ, 1996.1.156.

in *McKay*. The case then went through a series of appeals and was eventually referred to full chamber of the *Cour de cassation* who held that causation in the child's case was demonstrated by the mother having been prevented from exercising her freedom to proceed to a termination of the pregnancy in order to avoid the birth of a handicapped child; the harm resulting to the child from such handicap was caused by that negligence and he could claim compensation for it. The court was, in addition, anxious to ensure that the child himself was compensated because there was no guarantee that his parents would always support him.[101] This very unusual case[102] has not only disturbed the accepted medical jurisprudence in this area but also caused something of a political uproar in France. At heart, the public rejection of the Perruche judgment was based on revulsion at the concept of being compensated for being born and came, in the main, from three sources. It was attacked by the anti-abortion lobby by virtue of the stress laid on the woman's right to choose a termination of pregnancy. Disabled support groups protested that it devalued the lives of the imperfect – criticism was especially loud in the case of the allied Down's syndrome decisions.[103] Most powerfully, the medical profession rebelled and, indeed, went on strike at the thought of being compelled to be 100% right in their pre-natal screening.

6.54 Given the medico-legal ambience existing at the time, it is not easy to see the reason for the furore; nevertheless, it was sufficient to force the government into emergency legislation. As a result, one cannot, in France, treat the mere fact of being born as constituting damage. The parents of a child born with a handicap which remained undiagnosed during pregnancy due to a *serious* professional fault can claim compensation for harm suffered by them personally but not for costs attributable to the child's being handicapped – these will be available through the social services.[104] Thus, the French government has gone one stage further than the House of Lords in *McFarlane* and has outlawed damages for the upbringing of an uncovenanted child whether that child be healthy or disabled. Moreover, not only is an action for wrongful life no longer available but neither is one for wrongful birth. The ruling of the Cour de Cassation has, in the end, had an effect opposite to that which was intended and *l'affaire Perruche* probably represents the death of wrongful life within the European Union – but we still wonder if that should be a matter for universal rejoicing.

---

101 Bull Civ 2000 No 9, 17 November 2000. See E Guigou 'Comprendre l'arrêt Perruche' (2002) *Le Monde*, 10 January. The case is discussed in detail, and the decision disapproved, by T Callus '"Wrongful Life" a la Francaise' [sic] (2001) 5 Med Law Internat 117. It is carefully analysed, and again disapproved, by T Weir 'The Unwanted Child' (2002) 6 Edin LR 244 where the German position is also reviewed.

102 A similar judgment was handed down in 2001 in the case of *L*, a child with Down's syndrome. See M Spriggs and J Savulescu 'The Perruche Judgment and the "Right not to be Born"' (2002) 28 J Med Ethics 63.

103 A third untraced case has been reported as a news item: http://news.bbc.co.uk/hi/english/world/europe/newsid_1752000/1752556.stm. Since persons with Down's syndrome are not suffering and are probably perfectly happy in their own environment, this particular resentment can be well appreciated.

104 Law adopted by the French Senate on 19 February 2002. We are indebted to Weir, para 6.53 above, for the translation on which this précis is based.

7 Genetic information and the law

7.1 The rather tired adage that 'information is power' has been rejuvenated with the advent of the so-called 'new genetics'. Developments in genetic medicine over the last few years now mean that access to genetic information through genetic testing is relatively cheap and easy but, as a result, this has given rise to serious concerns about access to, and the use of, test results.[1] While the sensitivity of medical data is an issue of general concern which we address in the context of confidentiality in chapter 8, matters are particularly complicated in the context of genetics because of certain features that are said to be particular to genetic information.[2] First, a test result has implications not only for the individual who has been tested (the 'proband') but also for blood relatives of that person who share a common gene pool.[3] Second, this information has implications also for *future* relatives, in the sense that genetic disease passes vertically through generations. Thus, genetic information impacts directly on reproductive decisions. Third, genetic test results can disclose a likelihood of *future* ill health in persons who are currently well. Fourth, because in most cases testing is carried out by analysing a person's DNA, which remains unchanged throughout their life, genetic testing can be done at any stage from the cradle to the grave – and, indeed, beyond.[4] Thus, a fetus can be tested in utero for a condition such as Huntington's Disease which might not manifest itself until middle age. Finally, underlying all of these factors is the perceived benefit which genetic testing can offer in the guise of predictability.

1 See generally, G T Laurie *Genetic Privacy: A Challenge to Medico-Legal Norms* (2002).
2 For a good account of the range of problems which can flow from this see T H Murray et al (eds) *The Human Genome Project and the Future of Health Care* (1996).
3 On this, see L Andrews 'Gen-Etiquette: Genetic Information, Family Relationships and Adoption' in M A Rothstein (ed) *Genetic Secrets: Protecting Privacy and Confidentiality in the Genetic Era* (1997) ch 14; R Deech 'Family Law and Genetics' (1998) 61 MLR 697; L Skene 'Patients' Rights or Family Responsibilities' (1998) 6 Med L Rev 1; and, generally, T Marteau and M Richards *The Troubled Helix: Social and Psychological Implications of the New Human Genetics* (1996).
4 For an explanation of the range of ways in which genetic tests differ from other medical tests, see Advisory Committee on Genetic Testing *Consultation Report on Genetic Testing for Late Onset Disorders* (1997) p 10.

7.2 While this is a standard account of the argument that genetic information is somehow 'unique', we point out that other examples can be found of non-genetic information which functions in one or more of these ways. As the report *Genetics and Health* states: '[h]igh cholesterol levels [are] known predictors of cardiovascular disease, and high blood pressure of cerebrovascular disease risk … [and] … without recourse to genetic testing familial aggregation [is] discernible not only in the monogenetic disorders but also in a range of common disorders including heart disease, cancers and diabetes'.[5] Moreover, the term 'genetic information' covers a broad spectrum, from highly predictive monogenic disorders through susceptibility genes and on to a simple family history. Even the colour of our eyes provides a form of genetic data. However, not every class of this information is predictive of future ill health in any significant way. Indeed, many examples of genetic information are no more predictive than general health information. These factors militate against the argument that genetic data are in some way different from other forms of medical data and, for these reasons, the Human Genetics Commission (HGC) has stated that 'we do not feel that all personal genetic information be treated in the same way in every set of circumstances'.[6] None the less, the debate about how law and ethics should respond to genetic advances has proceeded in large measure on the premise that genetic information is exceptional.[7] There is certainly a general perception that genetic information is especially private,[8] and the HGC was established partly in response to this. Its 2002 report, *Inside Information*, is an attempt to address the public concerns and 'to maintain public trust and confidence that personal genetic information is properly protected'.[9]

7.3 The belief that genetic data are highly predictive is a key element underpinning the view that genetic information is somehow different, and this has led a range of persons or bodies to claim an interest in genetic test results. For example, relatives might wish to know if they too will be affected by disease or, indeed, if their progeny will be so affected. Insurers have always taken family history as an index of risk in the assessment of insurance cover but, now, genetic testing offers a seemingly more accurate and more scientific means of predicting liability. Similarly, employers might harbour deep concerns about the future employability of persons likely to be struck down by genetic disease, and the state itself has an undeniable interest in promoting public health by reducing the incidence of genetic disease in its citizens. In light of this range of interests, the potential for conflict over access and control of genetic information is axiomatic and it is important to recognise that the impact of a genetic test result on an individual's life might well be felt long before they experience the

---

5   See, The Nuffield Trust, *Genetics and Health: Policy Issues for Genetic Science and their Implications for Health and Health Services*, (2000).
6   HGC *Inside Information: Balancing Interests in the Use of Personal Genetic Data* (2002), para 1.26.
7   Cf, L O Gostin and J G Hodge Jr, 'Genetic Privacy and the Law: An End to Genetics Exceptionalism' (1999) 40 Jurimetrics 21.
8   HGC *Public Attitudes to Human Genetic Information* (2001).
9   HGC, para 7.2 above, para 1.25. This report follows the HGC's consultation document *Whose Hands on Your Genes?* (2000). Similar consultation is being undertaken in Australia jointly by the Australian Law Reform Commission and the Australian Health Ethics Committee, see their comprehensive Discussion Paper *Protection of Human Genetic Information* (Paper 66, 2002).

onset of disease. In its struggle to respond adequately to the dilemmas posed by advances in genetics, the law turns to ethics for guidance.[10] It is, therefore, apposite to consider the nature and strength of the ethical arguments which both support and refute the claims of those in each of the above categories and to assess the responses of the law to date in the light of this.

INDIVIDUAL AND FAMILY INTERESTS IN GENETIC INFORMATION

7.4 The availability of genetic information is appealing because of its perceived utility: what does it allow one to do? Even so, we consider it preferable to begin our inquiry by asking the opposite question: what does genetic information *not* allow one to do? Probably the most important single factor bearing on this debate is that few cures or successful treatments for genetic illnesses exist at present. Thus, except in rare cases, genetic information does not necessarily allow us to avoid genetic disease. This is important because it bears on the motivation of those who seek access to genetic testing or test results. Let us begin by considering the claims of the proband and his or her relatives.

7.5 In the absence of treatment or cure, *preparedness* is often cited as the justification for offering or seeking genetic testing. Adults and children can ready themselves, both psychologically and in other ways, for the onset of disease and couples contemplating a family or who have a child on the way can make a more informed reproductive choice in light of all the available facts.[11] Such justification is, however, a double-edged sword for a number of reasons. First, it is by no means clear that pre-emptive knowledge of future ill health is necessarily 'a good thing'.[12] While there are indications that this can be so,[13] there is also a growing body of evidence which suggests that adverse psychological sequelae can flow from such knowledge.[14] For example, Almqvist et al.[15] found in an international study that the suicide rate among persons given a positive genetic test result for Huntington's disease was 10 times higher

---

10 See A Buchanan et al *From Chance to Choice: Genetics and Justice* (2000).
11 V English and A Sommerville 'Genetic Privacy: Orthodoxy or Oxymoron?' (1999) 25 J Med Ethics 144. Cf, T M Marteau and C Lerman, 'Genetic Risk and Behavioural Change' (2001) 322 BMJ 1056.
12 But knowledge in this context will be relative both as to occurrence and severity of disease.
13 M Hietala et al 'Attitudes towards Genetic Testing among the General Population and Relatives of Patients with a Severe Genetic Disease: A Survey from Finland' (1995) 56 Amer J Hum Gen 1493; M R Hayden 'Predictive Testing for Huntingon's Disease: Are We Ready for Widespread Community Implementation?' (1991) 40 Amer J Med Gen 515; J Brandt et al 'Presymptomatic Diagnosis of Delayed-Onset with Linked DNA Markers: The Experience with Huntington's Disease' (1989) 216 J Amer Med Ass 3108.
14 L Andrews *Future Perfect: Confronting Decisions about Genetics* (2001), chapter 3, esp pp 31–40.
15 E Almqvist et al, 'A Worldwide Assessment of the Frequency of Suicide, Suicide Attempts, or Psychiatric Hospitalization after Predictive Testing for Huntington Disease' (1999) 64 Amer J Hum Gen 1293. The authors surveyed 100 centres in 21 countries and gathered data on 4,527 individuals who had undergone predictive genetic testing for Huntington's disease. Of those reviewed, 1,817 people had received a positive result, of whom five had taken their own lives. This extrapolates to 138/100,000 suicides per year, compared to the United States average of 12–13/100,000 per year. See, T Bird, 'Outrageous Fortune: The Risk of Suicide in Genetic Testing for Huntington Disease' (1999) 64 Amer J Hum Gen 1289.

than the United States average.[16] The Danish Council of Bioethics has warned too of the possibility of *morbidification*:

> The risk of participants in screening programmes possibly suffering from some form or other of morbidification or the notion of 'falling victim' to some inescapable 'fate' uncovered by the genetic examination in itself furnishes a basis for ensuring the provision of adequate information, counselling and follow-up in connection with such programmes.[17]

7.6 While it is important to draw a distinction between genetic *testing*, which involves an individual patient being tested in his own medical interests, and genetic *screening*, which involves the testing of populations for public health or research reasons, the Danish Council's observation remains valid in both contexts. It is for reasons such as these the Advisory Committee on Genetic Testing (ACGT)[18] issued a code of practice to regulate the availability of 'over-the-counter' genetic testing.[19] The committee recommended strongly that only tests which reveal carrier status for inherent recessive disorders should be made available outside the NHS genetic services.[20] This is allowable because the discovery of carrier status has no direct health implications for the proband. By contrast, however, testing for adult onset dominant conditions and X-linked disorders should only be provided in a clinical setting.[21] The importance of full and proper counselling in this context cannot be over-emphasised.[22] But issues move quickly in genetics and, partly in response to an unexpectedly pressing public interest in gaining access to a wider range of tests than was originally envisaged,[23] the Human Genetics Commission (HGC) launched a further consultation document in July 2002 which was aimed at a reconsideration of the position of over-the-counter genetics tests.[24] The results of this consultation are awaited at the time of writing.

7.7 Knowledge of one's own genetic constitution and of possible future ill health can have profound effects on one's sense of 'self'.[25] And, while an

---

16 While this rate is no greater than that for the symptomatic Huntington disease population, it is significant that the survey primarily focused on the two years after test results were given. This would tend to indicate that the deaths were more directly related to the disclosure of the genetic information, rather than to some other factors, such as the onset of the disease itself.

17 Danish Council of Ethics *Ethics and Mapping the Human Genome* (1993) p 60.

18 The Advisory Committee on Genetic Testing was established in the UK in July 1996 with a remit to give full consideration to the ethical and social aspects of genetic testing and to advise the government accordingly. It has since been replaced by the HGC, as we discuss below.

19 The first such test made available in the UK was for cystic fibrosis: see ACGT *First Annual Report: July 1996 – December 1997* (1998).

20 ACGT *Code of Practice for Genetic Testing Offered Commercially Direct to the Public* (1997).

21 Ibid, p 12.

22 Similar caution is urged in the Code of Practice on Genetic Paternity Testing Services (2001) issued by the Ad Hoc Group on Genetic Paternity Testing Services, available at <http://www.doh.gov.uk/pdfs/geneticspaternity.pdf>.

23 For an account of international testing practices, see Organisation for Economic Co-operation and Development *Genetic Testing: Policy Issues for the New Millennium* (2001).

24 HGC *The Supply of Genetic Tests Direct to the Public* (2002).

25 M Levitt 'The Ethics and Impact on Behaviour of Knowledge About One's Own Genome' (1999) 319 BMJ 1283.

individual who seeks out genetic testing might have prepared himself for possible bad news, can the same be said of that person's relatives who might suspect nothing as to the presence of genetic disease in their family? Eighty-five per cent of high risk couples are reported as having no knowledge of their condition. In such circumstances, information must come to these persons in ways which may raise issues of confidentiality. Even so, while the prevention of genetic disease may well be seen as admirable community medicine, there are difficulties when the principles are applied to the individual.[26] Should one impose knowledge on someone who has not sought it and who may, perhaps irrationally, be disturbed as a consequence? At what stage should this knowledge be used? It is arguable that premarital advice is preferable to prenatal warning, but to implement such a policy has implications which are scarcely acceptable. On the other hand, has a doctor a moral duty to impose counselling? Here the roles of the genetic counsellor and the health care professional assume paramount importance. The general practitioner who is in possession of familial genetic information is in a particularly difficult position; he has a general duty of care to all his patients, but a specific duty of confidentiality to the proband. What should he do? It might be asked if there is a legal duty in so far as an action might be brought were parents to discover after the birth of an abnormal child that relevant information had been available but not disclosed.[27] Yet, as we discuss in chapter 8, the practitioner might find himself facing an action for breach of confidence if disclosure was made. In legal terms, no precedent exists in the UK to guide the way in such cases.[28] We must, therefore, rely on ethical argument.

A right to know and a right not to know

7.8 The origin of this polemic lies in the fact that various parties have valid claims to the same information because, in essence, it relates to each of them. One could, in the first instance, categorise the strength of any claim to information by straightforward reference to the degree of consanguinity: the chances of a second cousin being affected by the same genetic condition are statistically smaller than those of a first cousin and the strength of any claim by the former is correspondingly weaker. This is, however, an unsophisticated approach and unhelpful in the case of the nuclear family, where claims to the information are at their strongest. Matters are complicated by the additional problem of deciding what is the best thing to do – to disclose or not to disclose? While few would argue that the risk of genetic disease should be withheld from family members when an effective treatment or cure is available, the motivation for disclosure in the absence of treatment is, once again, called

---

26 For general discussion of the implications of imparting genetic knowledge, see I Pullen 'Patients, Families and Genetic Information' in E Sutherland and A McCall Smith (eds) *Family Rights* (1990) ch 3. But not everyone would see a contradiction between concern for the genetic health of the population and concern for the problems of the individual family: see eg R F Chadwick 'What Counts for Success in Genetic Counselling?' (1993) 19 J Med Ethics 43.

27 G T Laurie 'Obligations Arising from Genetic Information: Negligence and the Protection of Familial Interests' (1999) 11 CFLQ 109.

28 There is some US authority that supports disclosure, see *Safer v Estate of Pack* 677 A 2d 1188 (NJ, 1996), discussed in Laurie, para 7.1 above, pp 268–69.

into question. If the aim is to facilitate preparedness, then the health care professional must consider the possibility that a relative might not, in fact, wish to know that he might develop a genetic disease. Yet, even if the practitioner is confident that a relative would wish to know, he must justify any disclosing action in ethical terms if he is faced with the proband's refusal to authorise release of the information. Current ethical principles are tested to their limits in such circumstances. Why, for example, should the autonomy of the relative who wants to know trump the autonomy of the proband who wishes to keep the information private? As Ngwena and Chadwick rightly state:

> ... what has to be taken into account is the fact that respecting the autonomy of one person may have implications for the autonomy of others. As the Royal College of Physicians argue, 'Blood relatives have an interest in knowing the truth which has nothing to do with influencing their behaviour towards affected individuals in their families, but as a necessary means to finding out the truth about themselves' ... How is the choice between the autonomy of different people made? ... What is clear is that the decision cannot be taken *on autonomy grounds.*[29]

7.9 The ethical principle of respect for patient confidentiality assists the practitioner to a certain degree in that it constitutes one of his primary duties to the proband. Yet release of the information can be justified equally by reference to the principle of non-maleficence if he genuinely feels that harm to relatives (or even their progeny) can be averted through disclosure – neither in ethics nor law is the principle of confidentiality seen as absolute (see chapter 8).

7.10 If the avoidance of harm is, indeed, the paramount consideration, then the prospect of harming a relative who might be disturbed by unsolicited information must also be considered. For this and other reasons, we argue elsewhere that the interest or right not to know deserves recognition.[30] Moreover, the basis of this interest lies not in autonomy or confidentiality but, rather, in privacy. Privacy consists of two aspects: informational privacy and spatial privacy. Informational privacy is concerned with the control of personal information and with preventing access to that information by others. An invasion of informational privacy occurs when any unauthorised disclosure of information takes place. Confidentiality is a subset of this privacy interest and is breached when confidential information which is the subject of the relationship is released to parties outside the relationship without authorisation. Informational privacy is wider than this in that it requires no relationship to exist.

7.11 Spatial privacy protects the individual's sense of 'self'. It recognises the interest which each of us has in maintaining a sense of separateness from others. Our spatial privacy is invaded when others 'invade our space' and this includes invasion of our psychological privacy which occurs, inter alia, when unsolicited information about oneself is received. An interest in *not*

---

29 C Ngwena and R Chadwick 'Genetic Diagnostic Information and the Duty of Confidentiality: Ethics and Law' (1993) 1 Med Law Internat 73 at 77.
30 Generally, Laurie, para 7.1 above, esp chapter 5.

knowing about oneself has been recognised by the Convention for the Protection of Human Rights and Dignity of the Human Being with regard to the Application of Biology and Medicine,[31] Article 10(2) of which states:

> Everyone is entitled to know any information collected about his or her health. *However, the wishes of individuals not to be so informed shall be observed.* (Emphasis added.)

Similarly, the UNESCO Universal Declaration on the Human Genome and Human Rights[32] states in Article 5c that:

> The right of every individual to decide whether *or not* to be informed of the results of genetic examination and the resulting consequences should be respected. (Emphasis added.)

7.12 However, the efficacy of grounding such a 'right' *solely* in terms of choice is doubtful.[33] The principle of respect for autonomy requires that we see the individual as a 'moral chooser'.[34] In order to choose meaningfully we require full information about the range of options available and the consequences of any particular choice. Unfortunately, this paradigm breaks down in the context of an interest in *not* knowing genetic information. Here, the choice is about knowledge itself. As Wertz and Fletcher have put it:

> [t]here is no way ... to exercise the choice of not knowing, because in the very process of asking 'Do you want to know whether you are at risk ...?' the geneticist has already made the essence of the information known.[35]

The principle of respect for patient confidentiality is similarly unhelpful in protecting the interest in not knowing. It is simply not meaningful to talk of a breach of confidence when information about the party to whom the duty is owed is disclosed *to that party*.

7.13 How then is the interest in not knowing to be protected? It is argued in more detail elsewhere that the concept of spatial privacy – which requires that a degree of respect be paid prima facie to an individual's state of separateness or, in this case, state of 'ignorance' – provides a viable mechanism.[36]   Spatial privacy can be invaded legitimately, but only if good cause can be shown. The following criteria could be considered for use by any health care professional when deciding how to resolve competing claims to genetic information in the familial context:

31 Council of Europe *Convention for the Protection of Human Rights and Dignity of the Human Being with regard to the Application of Biology and Medicine: Convention on Human Rights and Medicine* Oviedo, April 1997.
32 Adopted unanimously on 11 November 1997 in Paris at the Organisation's 29th General Conference.
33 Cf J Husted 'Autonomy and A Right Not to Know' in R Chadwick, M Levitt and D Shickle *The Right to Know and the Right Not to Know* (1997) ch 6.
34 This expression is borrowed from Stanley Benn, who explores the ideas of the 'moral chooser' and 'private life', inter alia, in *A Theory of Freedom* (1988).
35 D C Wertz and J C Fletcher 'Privacy and Disclosure in Medical Genetics Examined in an Ethic of Care' (1991) 5 Bioethics 212 at 221.
36 Laurie, para 7.1 above.

- the availability of a therapy or cure
- the severity of the condition and the likelihood of onset
- the nature of the genetic disease
- the nature of any further testing which might be required
- the nature of the information to be disclosed
- the nature of the request (for example, testing for the individual's health or for diagnostic purposes for a relative)
- the question of whether disclosure can further a legitimate public interest
- the question of how the individual might react if offered unsolicited information (for example, whether any advance directive has been made)

7.14 A practitioner who is faced with a refusal by a proband to communicate test results to relatives when a cure or effective treatment is available would be justified in disrespecting the proband's wishes in order to protect other family members from harm. He might, however, be rightly less inclined to disclose information about a condition for which nothing can be done and which has relatively mild symptoms. This nuanced approach can be supplemented by taking a hierarchical attitude when testing families – the need to test members of the younger generation can be greatly clarified if the older generations are approached and tested first.[37] The HGC endorses such a balancing approach:

> Bearing in mind the principle of genetic solidarity and altruism,[38] we take the view that disclosure of sensitive personal genetic information for the benefit of family members in certain circumstances may occasionally be justified. This would arise where the patient refuses to consent to such disclosure and the benefit of disclosure substantially outweighs the patient's claim to confidentiality.

7.15 However, the HGC goes on to state that such disclosure should be subject to the provisos that '(1) an attempt has been made to persuade the patient in question to consent; (2) the benefit to those at risk is so considerable as to outweigh any distress which disclosure would cause the patient; and (3) the information is, as far as possible, anonymised and restricted to that which is strictly necessary for the communication of risk'.[39] Of course, the problem of controlling communication between family members always remains, and a particularly problematic scenario arises when members of the younger generations are tested for a genetic condition and found to be positive. This must mean that one or more parents or grandparents are also affected in some way, yet these persons may have no idea of their condition or may have chosen not to know. It can be very difficult to stem the tidal flow of information within the familial milieu.

---

37 See B S Wilfond et al 'Cancer Genetic Susceptibility Testing: Ethical and Policy Implementations for Future Research and Clinical Practice' (1997) 25 J Law Med & Ethics 243.

38 These principles remind us that: 'We all share the same basic human genome, although there are individual variations which distinguish us from other people. Most of our genetic characteristics will be present in others. This sharing of genetic constitution not only gives rise to opportunities to help others but it also highlights our common interest in the fruits of medically-based research.', see HGC, *Inside Information*, para 7.2 above, para 2.11.

39 HGC *Inside Information*, para 7.2 above, para 3.68.

7.16 It is in the case of children that an appreciation of these subtleties can be found among legislatures and governments. In the United States the Genetic Privacy Act was drafted in 1995 as part of the ELSI[40] division of the Human Genome Project. This is a piece of federal legislation designed for possible adoption by individual states. The draft explains the Act's remit:

> [T]he overarching premise of the Act is that no stranger should have or control identifiable DNA samples or genetic information about an individual unless that individual specifically authorizes the collection of DNA samples for the purpose of genetic analysis, authorizes the creation of that private information, and has access to and control over the dissemination of that information.

7.17 The Act gives an individual from whom a sample is taken (the 'sample source') a number of rights, including the right to determine who may collect and analyse DNA, the right to determine the purposes for which a sample can be analysed and the right to order destruction of samples. Those who collect samples have a number of corresponding duties. The Act also protects genetic information from a number of potential abuses by third parties, such as the state or employers and insurers, and we return to this below.[41] For present purposes we focus on the provisions of the Act which deal with testing minors for genetic conditions.

7.18 The Genetic Privacy Act provides that an individually identifiable DNA sample source shall not be taken from a minor under 16 to detect any genetic condition which, in reasonable medical judgment, does not produce signs or symptoms of disease before the age of 16 unless an effective intervention is available to delay onset or ameliorate the severity of the disease; the said intervention must be made before the age of 16 and written authorisation has to be given by the minor's representative. The rationale behind this has been explained by the authors of the Act:

> There are two reasons for this prohibition on the exercise of parental discretion. First, if someone learns that the child is a carrier of a gene that disposes the child to some condition later in life, this finding may subject the child to discrimination and stigmatization by both the parents and others who may learn of this fact. Second, a child's genetic status is the *child's* private genetic information and should not be determined or disclosed unless there is some compelling reason to do so. (Emphasis added.)[42]

7.19 The Act is clearly designed to protect the spatial privacy interests of children, and recognises that these should not be invaded without due cause. Arguably, however, it is deficient in not recognising such interests for *all* persons about whom genetic information is known but who have not sought it themselves. By March 1998, 16 states had introduced laws regulating the

40 Part of the Human Genome Project is to establish programmes examining the 'Ethical, Legal and Social Issues' which arise from mapping of the human genome (ELSI).
41 See para 7.23 et seq.
42 The Act was drafted by George Annas, Leonard Glantz and Patricia Roche of the Boston University School of Public Health. A text of the Act and the comments of the authors can be found at http://www.ornl.gov/TechResources/Human_Genome/resource/privacy/privacy1.html.

privacy of genetic information and some 150 bills had been proposed in state legislatures.[43] 110 bills seeking to protect genetic privacy were introduced in the 105th Session of the US Congress, although none was debated beyond the sub-committee stage.[44] Such frantic legislative activity reveals the depth of concern which surrounds genetic information.

7.20 In the United Kingdom, the House of Commons Science and Technology Committee, in its third report, alerted the public to the range of issues and problems which flow from the availability of genetic information.[45] The committee recommended the establishment of a Human Genetics Commission with the power, inter alia, to monitor the provision of genetic services in the United Kingdom, advise on testing and screening procedures, and prescribe the circumstances in which particular screening or diagnostic procedures are provided or proscribed. This body was eventually set up in 1999 whereupon it took over the responsibilities of the pre-existing Advisory Committee on Genetic Testing (ACGT), the Human Genetics Advisory Commission (HGAC), and the Advisory Group on Advances in Genetics (AGAG). Other bodies, such as the Gene Therapy Advisory Committee (GTAC),[46] and the Genetics and Insurance Committee (GAIC) are unaffected by the establishment of the HGC and we discuss their work below.[47] The House of Commons Science and Technology Committee has recommended most recently that the Government conduct a thorough review of the advisory and regulatory organisations in this field with a view to producing a more streamlined structure.[48]

7.21 Each of the existing bodies has produced guidelines which show great sensitivity in respect of genetic information. In particular, the ACGT strongly recommended that no pre-symptomatic testing for late onset disorders for which there are no clinical treatments should be carried out on minors under 16,[49] and this has been endorsed by the Human Genetics Commission.[50] The ACGT also recommended, and the HCG has also accepted, that no over-the-counter testing for late onset disorders be allowed.[51] For testing which *is* permissible, suitable pre- and post-testing consultation should be made available at no extra cost by the suppliers of tests.[52] The In Vitro Medical Device Regulations ensure that safety, quality and performance criteria are met before tests are placed on the market.[53] However, these provisions do not regulate the actual testing *service* that patients might receive.

---

43 The Gene Letter vol 2, issue 2, March 1998.
44 See J Colby, 'An Analysis of Genetic Discrimination Legislation Proposed by the 105th Congress' (1998) 24 Amer J Law Med 443.
45 House of Commons Science and Technology Committee *Human Genetics: The Science and its Consequences* Third Report, 6 July 1995.
46 This body was established on the recommendation of the Clothier Committee *Report of the Committee on the Ethics of Gene Therapy* Cm 1788, 1992.
47 See paras 7.30 and 7.60.
48 House of Commons Science and Technology Committee *Developments in Human Genetics and Embryology* HC791, July 2002, para 13.
49 ACGT Code of Practice (para 7.6 above) Pt 7. Note, too, the Committee's Report on Genetic Testing for Late Onset Disorders (1998).
50 HGC *Inside Information*, para 7.2 above, para 4.37.
51 Although this guidance is under review by the HGC, para 7.6 above.
52 ACGT *First Annual Report* (para 7.6 above) pp 4 and 6.
53 SI 2000/1315.

7.22 No specific legislation to regulate the control and use of genetic information has been introduced in the United Kingdom to date. The HGC has, however, recommended a number of specific reforms, including (i) the creation of a criminal offence of the non-consensual or deceitful obtaining and/or analysis of personal genetic information for non-medical purposes, (ii) the possible introduction of exemption from the notification requirements of data protection laws for clinicians who hold information about genetic relatives, (iii) stringent controls of the uses of data in genetic databases, and (iv) new legislation to address genetic discrimination.[54] We consider aspects of these recommendations below.

OTHER PARTIES' INTERESTS IN GENETIC INFORMATION

7.23 A number of parties outside the family context profess an interest in access to genetic information. These include insurers, current and prospective employers, researchers, and the state itself. In this section, the nature of the interests at stake is considered and their respective weights in light of the interests of the proband and his relatives are assessed. The important issue of protection against genetic discrimination is also addressed.

Insurance

7.24 The forms of insurance most relevant to genetic testing are life and health insurance. Private health insurance is currently less important in the United Kingdom than in other jurisdictions because of the existence of the National Health Service. Life insurance, however, is a prerequisite for certain types of loan, including, in most cases, mortgages for the purchase of property. Most individuals also take out life insurance to protect their families in the event of their own premature death and, as we face the growing needs of an increasingly aged population, long-term care insurance is becoming a necessity. Insurance thus touches the lives of most of us and its denial can have far-reaching consequences for both individuals and families.[55]

7.25 Genetic information is clearly important to the insurance industry in order to assess the risk of providing cover at all and to determine the level of premiums if an offer of insurance is made. The nature of the interest at stake is entirely financial, and it is one that the industry may legitimately seek to protect. An insurance contract is an example of a contract *uberrima fides*: of the utmost good faith. In practice, this means that any information having a bearing on the assessment of risk should be disclosed to the insurer; otherwise, the contract can be avoided at any future time. Two possible avenues are open to the insurer in the context of genetic information. First, a request can be made that all test results be disclosed. Second, the insurer can require that the prospective insured undergo genetic testing. In respect of the first of these, it might be argued that this is no different to any other form of medical

54 HGC Inside Information, para 7.2 above.
55 For an account of the respective approaches in the US and the UK, see O O'Neill 'Insurance and Genetics: The Current State of Play' (1998) 61 MLR 716.

history. A genetic test result should be disclosed in the same way as one would disclose the removal of a melanoma or a family history of high blood pressure. This having been said, a concern has been expressed in many quarters that individuals might be deterred from seeking testing if it were to be the case that all test results should be disclosed. As the Science and Technology Committee commented:

> We accept that the insurance industry has collectively tried to deal with genetics in a responsible way; nonetheless we are concerned there is a real danger that people could decide to decline testing, even when such testing would be advantageous to them, because of the possible insurance implications.[56]

7.26 This has been borne out by a recent MORI poll on public attitudes to human genetic information published in March 2001 which showed that the use of genetic information to set insurance premiums was thought to be the least appropriate of the possible uses of that information. Four out of five respondents said it should not be used for that purpose.[57]

7.27 As to insurers actively requiring prospective customers to be tested, there is a fear that the increased availability of tests will lead to the 'development and proliferation of predictive genetic testing'.[58] This is to be deprecated because of the serious implications which it has for the (spatial) privacy interests of individuals required to be tested. An unacceptable degree of coercion is brought to bear in such circumstances which might vitiate any 'consent' to undergo testing.[59]

7.28 The Council of Europe has issued a recommendation on the protection of medical data which are processed automatically;[60] genetic data are specifically included. The Council recommends that member states take steps to ensure that their laws and practices reflect certain key principles embodied in the recommendation. These provide, among other things, that medical data should, in principle, be collected only by health care professionals or their assistants and, in the context of genetic information, this should only be for preventive treatment, diagnosis or treatment of the data subject or for scientific research, judicial procedure or criminal investigation. The collection and processing of genetic data outside these categories should be permitted only for health reasons; it could be allowed in order to predict ill health, but only in the case of an overriding interest and subject to appropriate safeguards defined by law. The drafters of the recommendation make it clear in the explanatory memorandum that:

56　Third Report (para 7.20 above) para 242.
57　HGC, *Public Attitudes*, para 7.2 above, para 33.
58　R Chadwick and C Ngwena 'The Human Genome Project, Predictive Testing and Insurance Contracts: Ethical and Legal Responses' (1995) 1 Res Publica 115.
59　Massachusetts passed a law in 2000 prohibiting both disclosure of test results and the requirement of genetic testing as a condition of employment or insurance, see An Act Relative to Insurance and Genetic Testing and Privacy Protection, Chapter 254 of the Acts of 2000.
60　Council of Europe *The Protection of Medical Data*, Recommendation No (97) 5 and explanatory memorandum, 13 February 1997.

a candidate for employment, an insurance contract or other services or activities should not be forced to undergo a genetic analysis, by making employment or the insurance dependent on such an analysis, unless such dependence is explicitly provided for by the law and the analysis is necessary for the protection of the data subject or a third party.[61]

7.29 The Nuffield Council on Bioethics has opined that those individuals with a known family history who decide to take a test and test positive should not be treated by the insurance company any differently from other family members – that is, they should still be assessed at the same level of risk as those family members who have not been tested[62] – it was reasoned that, since the industry tends to interpret family history cautiously,[63] 'there is unlikely to be a major difference in insurability between an individual with a family history of a genetic disorder and an individual who has had a positive genetic test result'.   By corollary, the Council envisages that those who test negative should benefit from this result and be treated as persons with no family history. In this way the Council hopes that individuals will not be deterred from having genetic tests and also that insurers will not be adversely affected, since they can continue their present practice based on family history.   However, the recommendations of the Council are somewhat different in respect of population screening programmes. In such cases the majority of those taking part would not be aware of any family history of disease. The Council considers that:

> [i]f insurers were to demand access to the results of population screening for polygenic or multifactorial disease (for example, for genetic predisposition to breast cancer), and premiums were increased for those who tested positive, many people would clearly be discouraged from participating in such programmes. This could have adverse consequences both for the health of individuals and for the public health,[64]

and it concludes that it is not acceptable for insurers to have access to genetic test results which arise from such programmes. Furthermore, because of the principle of free and informed consent (discussed in chapter 10), genetic testing should not be made a prerequisite for obtaining insurance.   Thus, it can be seen that the Council is emphatic that genetic testing solely for the purposes of assessing insurance risk is unacceptable – and this is true both for those who have a family history and for those who do not.

7.30   In the absence of clear government guidelines or legislative intervention, the Association of British Insurers (ABI), whose representatives account for 95% of insurance business in the United Kingdom, affirmed in 1997 and 1999 that insurers will not require a genetic test as a prerequisite for insurance cover.[65] Subsequent to this, the Government established the Genetics and

---

61   Ibid, para 103.
62   Nuffield Council on Bioethics *Genetic Screening: Ethical Issues* (1993) para 7.28.
63   Eg the Council notes that (para 7.23): 'Tables used by the insurance industry show that insurers treat 5% risk of developing Huntington's disease in the same way as a 50% risk: such individuals may be declined insurance or offered insurance at an increased premium, depending on their age at the time of application. Insurance prospects for individuals with a family history of Huntington's disease only improve when the risk is below 5%.'
64   Ibid, para 7.31.
65   ABI *Genetic Testing: Code of Practice* (1999).

Insurance Committee (GAIC) – a body charged with the task of approving access to certain genetic test results that are thought to have a clear actuarial significance. So far, only the test for Huntington's Disease has been approved in the context of life insurance.[66] None the less, the House of Commons Select Committee on Science and Technology made a series of stringent recommendations in its Fifth Report in April 2001,[67] including reform of the membership of GAIC and a call for the reformed body to re-examine its approval of the use of Huntington's Disease test results. This has not happened. The Association of British Insurers agreed, however, to extend a self-imposed moratorium to a period of five years (until 2006), and it has instructed its members not to ask for any genetic test results from applicants for any insurance policies up to £500,000 for life insurance or £300,000 for other forms of insurance. Above that level, only tests approved by the Genetics and Insurance Committee will be taken into account.[68] The Human Genetics Commission has welcomed this move, and proposes to lead a fuller public debate of the issues within the period of the moratorium.[69]

7.31 Finally, some have suggested that no access to genetic information should be granted to insurers at all. For example, Harper has argued that insurers should not be allowed to require disclosure of genetic test results within the ordinary run of life insurance policies.[70] But, even so, the problem remains of deciding whether a family history – as a form of genetic information – should also be excluded in such circumstances. The HGC has expressed reservations on this matter, and has called for further research.[71] Whether it is right that the increased costs of such a scheme should be passed on to the 'normal' population is probably a matter for Parliament to decide; ultimately, we cannot escape the fact that insurance, like most social constructs, is a cultural phenomenon. The task, then, is to match the most appropriate legal response to the way in which we wish insurance to operate within our culture. An approach that is biased towards solidarity might be an acceptable price to pay for a gesture of support for those who, through no fault of their own, are likely to find themselves increasingly disadvantaged.[72]

66 Department of Health, 'Committee Announces Decision on Use of Genetic Test Results for Huntington's Disease by Insurers' (13 October 2000), see http://www.doh.gov.uk/ genetics/gaic.htm. For an account of the work of the Committee and its remit, see Genetics and Insurance Committee, *First Annual Report: April 1999 – June 2000* (Department of Health, London, 2000).
67 House of Commons Science and Technology Committee Fifth Report, *Genetics and Insurance* (2001 HC 174).
68 Government response to the report from the House of Commons Science and Technology Select Committee: Genetics and Insurance Cm 5286 (2001).
69 HGC *Inside Information*, para 7.2 above, para 7.7.
70 P S Harper 'Insurance and Genetic Testing' (1993) 341 Lancet 224. The author points to the doubt as to whether genetic counselling can be seen as part of a 'medical assessment'. The majority approach seems to be much the same in the US: B R Furrow 'Cystic Fibrosis and DNA Tests' (Book review) (1993) 19 Amer J Law Med 177. For experience elsewhere, see S Gevers 'Use of Genetic Data, Employment and Insurance: An International Perspective' (1993) 7 Bioethics 126.
71 HGC *Inside Information*, para 7.2 above, paras 7.16-7.18.
72 There are two basic models of insurance: mutuality and solidarity. The former provides that the contribution of individuals should approximately reflect their level of risk. The principle of solidarity, however, requires that the burden of bearing risks is spread throughout the general body of insured persons.

Employment

7.32 An employer might have two contrasting reasons for seeking access to genetic information about his employees or future employees. First, there is a financial interest in not employing persons who are likely to become debilitated through disease and so affect profits through days lost. Second, he might have a genuine concern that the working environment could affect an employee's health adversely, perhaps by exacerbating an existing condition or by provoking symptoms in an otherwise asymptomatic individual.[73] This concern might relate to the person's health *in se*, and/or to the fear that compensation could be sought by an individual so affected. The propriety of permitting an employer or prospective employer access to genetic information must be addressed in each case. As with the insurance industry, access could be granted either to existing test results or a genetic test could be made a condition of the employment contract. Moreover, a request for genetic information could be made either pre- or post-employment.

7.33 Pre-employment requests for genetic information are the most effective means of reducing costs for the employer. Little expenditure is incurred in obtaining the information; the prospective employee is asked either to reveal existing knowledge or to take a relatively inexpensive test. No future expenditure need be incurred because the employer has no obligation to do so in the absence of an employment contract.

7.34 An employer who seeks genetic information from a current employee is in a very different position. Time and money may have been spent training someone who now cannot do the job, and termination of the employment contract is subject to strict requirements. All of which means that it is very much in the employer's financial interests to seek genetic information from *potential* rather than from *actual* employees. And one might argue that *future* employees can (and should) be excluded from employment if information reveals either the actual presence of, or a predisposition to, genetic disease such as is likely to pose a risk to themselves and/or others if they are employed.

7.35 This advantage of pre-employment screening was considered further by the Nuffield Council on Bioethics, which stated:

> Employees would, in principle, be empowered to avoid occupations which would increase the risk of ill health and which in the long run might be life threatening. In this way they could protect the economic security of themselves and their families.[74]

7.36 A major difficulty with such an otherwise admirable approach lies in the fact that the predictive accuracy of genetic predictive information is far from assured, and the very factors which concern employers – such as the likely date of onset and degree of affliction – are unlikely to be known. Also, the sensitivity of such information and the apparent public misunderstanding

---

73 Eg an environment which is dense with heavy particles is very bad for individuals suffering from or prone to α1-antitrypsin deficiency because this can lead to emphysema.
74 See para 7.29, para 6.6.

which surrounds genetic information provoke the very legitimate fear that the information could be used to exclude individuals from employment, or to terminate employment, even when they are not affected by disease and are unlikely to be so for some time. The question thus arises as to whether access to genetic information is an acceptable way by which to ensure the interests of employers and of employees or job applicants.[75]

7.37 A number of bodies have recognised and appreciated the privacy implications of employer requests for genetic information.[76] Relying heavily on recommendations of the Nuffield Council, the Science and Technology Committee itself recommended that legislation to protect the privacy of genetic information be introduced and be drafted so as to prohibit employers testing for genetic conditions other than those which might put the public at direct and substantial risk. Furthermore, any genetic testing for employment purposes should be strictly limited to specific conditions relevant to the particular employment and samples provided for testing should not be examined for evidence of other conditions.

7.38 The clear message here is that employers' access to genetic information must be justified on the grounds that the knowledge can have a direct bearing on the job of work to be done.[77] In other words, it is unacceptable for an employer to seek access to another individual's genetic information simply to further his financial interests. This is especially true when that access is sought in order to identify some *future* risk when that possibility does not affect the individual's current ability to perform his or her work at the time.

7.39 What, however, of the argument that genetic information should be revealed in order to protect the interests of employees and job applicants themselves? The Science and Technology Committee concluded that:

> Genetic Screening for employment purposes should be contemplated only where:
> (i) there is strong evidence of a clear connection between the working environment and the development of the condition for which the screening is conducted;
> (ii) the condition in question is one which seriously endangers the health of the employee; and
> (iii) the condition is one for which the dangers cannot be eliminated or significantly reduced by reasonable measures taken by the employer to modify or respond to the environmental risks.[78]

Importantly, the Committee stresses that 'employees should have the right to decide whether or not to participate in such screening'. It is unclear, however,

---

75 It should be noted, however, that the Human Genetics Commission found no evidence that there is any systematic use of predictive genetic information in employment in the UK, see HGC *Inside Information*, para 7.2 above, para 8.9.
76 See Nuffield Council on Bioethics, para 7.29 above, paras 6.20–6.23, The House of Commons Science and Technology Committee (1995), para 7.20 above, paras 231–233, and the Human Genetics Advisory Commission *The Implications of Genetic Testing for Employment* (1999).
77 Science and Technology Committee Report quoting Memorandum (vol II) p 52.
78 See para 7.20 at 233.

whether the recommendations are intended to extend both to current employees and job applicants. No convincing argument could be put that this should not be the case, but the Committee only mentions 'employees'.[79] The HGC broadly agrees with this, but emphasises that employers must not demand that an individual take a genetic test as a condition of employment. There must be compelling medical or safety grounds for offering a genetic test in any other circumstances.[80] As regards future uses of personal genetic information, the HGC has recommended a voluntary undertaking by employers to inform HGC of any proposals to use genetic testing for health and safety or recruitment purposes and, also, the establishment of a joint committee to monitor developments in genetic testing in this field.[81]

7.40 In stark contrast, the position in the United States seems to be a cause of more concern. One study of 1,500 genetic counsellors and physicians found that 785 patients had reported having lost their jobs or insurance because of adverse reactions to genetic knowledge about them.[82] In February 2000, President Clinton signed an Executive Order which prohibits federal government agencies from obtaining genetic information from employees or job applicants and from using genetic information in hiring or promotion decisions.[83] Three bills were introduced in the 107th Congress in an attempt to extend this sort of protection to the private sector.[84]

Discrimination

7.41 Perhaps the single most important concern related to genetic information lies in the potential for discrimination that it generates.[85] This is relevant to both the employment and insurance scenarios, yet no specific legal regulation currently exists in the United Kingdom to control genetic testing or screening or the uses to which the results can be put.[86] The matter of discrimination must, therefore, be dealt with under the current anti-discrimination laws. More focussed efforts have occurred in the United States, however, where, as of February 2001, the National Human Genome Research Institute reported

---

79 For a criticism of the Nuffield Council's recommendations, and by implications those of the Science and Technology Committee, see M A Rothstein 'Genetic Discrimination in Employment: Ethics, Policy and Comparative Law' in O Guillod and P Widmer (eds) *Human Genetic Analysis and the Protection of Personality and Privacy* (1994).

80 HGC *Inside Information*, para 7.2 above, generally chapter 8.

81 Further policy guidance is offered by The Recruitment Society *Proposal for a Code of Practice for Genetic Testing for Employers* (2000).

82 D Martindale 'Pink Slip in Your Genes: Evidence Builds that Employers Hire and Fire Based on Genetic Tests' (2001) January Scientific American 19.

83 The Executive Order to Prohibit Discrimination in Federal Employment Based on Genetic Information (2000).

84 HR602 Genetic Nondiscrimination in Health Insurance and Employment Act, S318 Genetic Nondiscrimination in Health Insurance and Employment Act, and S382 Genetic Information Nondiscrimination in Health Insurance Act of 2001.

85 R Hubbard and E Wald *Exploding The Gene Myth: How Genetic Information is Produced and Manipulated by Scientists, Physicians, Employers, Insurance Companies, Educators and Law Enforcers* (1997).

86 A failed Discrimination (Genetic Information) Bill was sponsored by Anne Campbell MP in the parliamentary session 1994/95. For discussion of regulation generally, see J Black 'Regulation as Facilitation: Negotiating the Genetic Revolution' (1998) 61 MLR 621.

that 37 states had enacted legislation on genetic discrimination in health insurance and 24 states had enacted provisions against genetic discrimination in the workplace. Over 100 anti-discrimination bills were introduced into state legislatures in the legislative session for 2000.[87]

7.42 Anti-discrimination law in the United Kingdom is governed by three pieces of legislation: the Sex Discrimination Act 1975, the Race Relations Act 1976 and the Disability Discrimination Act 1995. The protection afforded against discrimination by the 1975 and 1976 Acts is restricted to their precise remits – that is, sexual or racial discrimination. Since many genetic conditions are sex-linked or affect particular ethnic and racial groups, differential treatment of afflicted individuals could amount to discrimination within the terms of these Acts, probably as examples of indirect discrimination. It is not clear, however, how successful such arguments would be, there being no cases on point.[88] More opportunities for redress lie with the Disability Discrimination Act 1995, which is the first piece of United Kingdom legislation to deal directly with discrimination against disabled people. The Act outlaws discrimination in a wide range of fields – such as employment, the provision of goods, facilities and services, the sale and let of property, education and public transport.

7.43 The Act defines 'disability' and 'disabled persons' in Pt I as follows:

1(1) Subject to the provisions of Schedule 1, a person has a disability for the purposes of this Act if he has a physical or mental impairment which has a substantial and long-term adverse effect on his ability to carry out normal day-to-day activities.

1(2) In this Act 'disabled person' means a person who has a disability.[89]

7.44 In the context of employment, the provisions of the Act ensure that it is unlawful for an employer to treat an individual less favourably than he would treat others for a reason which relates to the individual's disability and when he cannot show that the treatment in question is justified. Discrimination can occur, inter alia, in respect of: (a) the arrangements which an employer makes for the purpose of determining to whom he should offer employment; (b) in the terms in which he offers employment; (c) his refusal to offer, or deliberate not offering of, employment; (d) his refusal to afford an employee opportunities for promotion, a transfer, training or receiving any other benefit, or his treating the employee differently in such opportunities; (e) his dismissal of an employee, or subjecting the employee to any other detriment.

7.45 These provisions could clearly go a long way to preventing discrimination against individuals based on information about their genetic constitution[90] – note, particularly, how pre-employment discrimination is also outlawed. However, the question arises of whether the provisions of the Act extend to

---

87 National Human Genome Research Institute *Health Insurance and Employment Discrimination* (2001).
88 Note too the exceptions for insurance assessments under the 1975 and 1995 Acts.
89 This definition is retained in the current version of the Equality Bill 2002, cl 124.
90 One limiting factor is the exemption for small business. The provisions of the Act do not apply to an employer who has fewer than 15 employees. This is due to end by 2004.

persons whose genome contains defective genes which do, or can have, a bearing on their ability to do their job. The crucial term here is '*can have*'. Clearly, persons who are already affected by a genetic condition come within the definition of 'disabled person'. But what of a person who merely has a predisposition to ill health? A literal interpretation of s 1(1) excludes such a person for it speaks of one who '*has* a physical or mental impairment'. The section must, however, be read in conjunction with Schs 1 and 2, which allow for regulations to be made which will clarify the definitions in s 1. In particular, Sch 1, para 8 concerns 'progressive conditions'. The examples given of such conditions are cancer, multiple sclerosis, muscular dystrophy or infection with the human immunodeficiency virus. The paragraph provides that someone who suffers from such a progressive condition will be treated as 'disabled' provided that their condition results in an impairment which, at least, has (or had) an effect on their ability to carry out normal day-to-day activities, even if that effect is not a substantial adverse effect. Even so, the individual must still be in some way symptomatic, thus excluding those who have 'merely' a predisposition to disease at the relevant time. This means, by inference, that discrimination against persons in this last category is not unlawful under the Act. This disparity and the question of genetic testing were raised in the parliamentary debates but the minister in charge stated:

> ... except in a few well-publicised cases, genetic tests are not as yet a useful indicator of future actual disability. Their inclusion would open up the [Act] to large numbers of people who are clearly not, and may never become disabled ... we cannot wander into a situation whereby, for some reason or another, potentially the entire population could claim protection under the [Act].[91]

7.46 It is certainly true that genetic tests are by no means accurate at present, but that does not mean that such tests cannot be misused by employers and others, nor that they will not be used to exclude people from jobs and other services for irrelevant and irrational reasons. Legislation designed to outlaw discrimination on the grounds of disability should cover *all* forms of discrimination, whether the disability is actual or perceived, current or future. It is arguable that the provisions of the Act as they currently stand are inadequate and are potentially prejudicial to persons likely to develop genetic conditions later in life; the Secretary of State might, with advantage, use the powers given under the Act to expand the definition of disability to include such persons.

7.47 The fear that existing statutes will be interpreted to cover just such circumstances has led to out-of-court settlements in the United States in favour of employees. For example, the US Equal Employment Opportunity Commission (EEOC) settled its first court action in April 2001 in which it had challenged the conduct of an employer in using genetic information and requiring genetic testing of employees to handle claims for work-related injuries.[92] The Burlington Northern Santa Fe railway (BNSF) had implemented a programme of genetic testing of previously donated samples without the

---

91 Official Reports, HC, vol 257, col 887, 28 March 1995.
92 United States Equal Employment Opportunity Commission, Press Release, 18 April 2001: http://www.eeoc.gov/press/4-18-01.html.

knowledge or consent of employees to investigate worker claims for injuries based on carpal tunnel syndrome. At least one worker had been threatened with termination of employment for refusing to submit to testing. The settlement ensures that the employer shall not directly or indirectly require its employees to submit blood for genetic tests, nor shall it analyse any blood previously obtained. The settlement is enforceable by the relevant District Court, although the court in question was at pains to point out that it offered no ruling on the respective arguments of the parties under the Americans with Disabilities Act 1990.[93]

7.48 The anomalies in the current UK provisions were summed up by Baroness Jay in the House of Lords:

> The paradox which is possible in the present situation is that where genetic counselling, genetic testing and identifying genetic markers is potentially one of the most exciting and liberating developments in medical science at the end of the 20th century, if it becomes the case that people feel that identifying those markers in their own personal situation will lead to discrimination, they will be less likely to take advantage of those extraordinary scientific advances which may help their own condition and in which medical science may be able to help future generations of children.[94]

7.49 While recognising the validity of arguments concerning adverse treatment of asymptomatic persons, the Human Genetics Commission has recommended separate legislation to address genetic discrimination, rather than wholesale reform of the Disability Discrimination Act (DDA).[95] This is partly because reform of the DDA would require a significant alteration to the definition of 'disability', and because of the difficulty in defining those with a pre-symptomatic genetic condition. Instead, the HGC follows a growing international consensus that specific genetic discrimination legislation is required, and has called upon the Government to consider such a measure in the forthcoming review of genetics in employment in 2005 and before the end of the genetics in insurance moratorium in 2006.[96]

RESEARCH INVOLVING GENETIC MATERIAL

7.50 We lay our cards on the table at this point by admitting our full support for medical research that is ethically sound and subject to the rigorous checks and balances that we outline in chapter 19. To this extent, genetic research is no different to other forms of research in the health care sector although, once again, we find that perceptions do not always reflect this reality. The Medical Research Council conducted a survey on public attitudes towards the collection of human biological samples in October 2000 which found

---

93 See also, the Federal Health Insurance Portability and Accountability Act 1996 which has recently been interpreted as covering genetics in the workplace, see HGC *Inside Information*, para 7.2 above, para 6.36.
94 Official Reports, HL, vol 564, col 1713, 13 June 1995.
95 HGC *Inside Information*, para 7.2 above, paras 6.30-6.31.
96 HGC *Inside Information*, para 7.2 above, paras 6.32-6.41.

disparate knowledge and understanding of the meaning and the goals of genetic research.[97] There was considerable evidence of negative associations with this type of work where understanding was lacking[98] and this was so despite the fact that most people continued to find general medical research to be worthy and worthwhile.[99] As the report states:

> [u]nderlying these negative associations was a feeling that genetics research can make people feel vulnerable about themselves. It was believed to be about seeking to perfect the human body, for good or bad ends, and that it could induce concern about individuals' own imperfections ... [a]longside this was a feeling expressed by a few that genetics research, if put to these sorts of uses, conflicts with the (beneficial) diversity of the human race. Though it would be a good thing to attempt to eliminate genetically linked diseases and conditions, this is likely to go hand-in-hand with other developments that will make it possible to produce "perfect" people.[100]

7.51 The Human Genetics Commission's People's Panel Quantitative Study of March 2001 revealed similar results. Over one third of those surveyed considered genetics research to be 'tampering with nature' and so unethical.[101] The response of the Human Genetics Commission, in turn, has been to recommend that all genetic research on human non-anonymised tissue samples or bodily material should be subject to independent research ethics review and that clear policies should be established by all research bodies for compliance with ethical review.[102] Whether such measures will succeed in engendering more public trust and confidence remains to be seen.[103] As O'Neill has stated: '... reported public trust in science and even in medicine has faltered *despite* successes, *despite* increased efforts to respect persons and their rights, *despite* stronger regulation to protect the environment and *despite* the fact that environmental concerns are taken far more seriously than they were a few years ago'.[104]

7.52 The balance of interests is nowhere more delicately struck than between the concern to protect individuals' rights and the public interest in furthering research. Few would now deny that some compromises must be made with the former in order to accommodate the latter. Thus, for example, the HGC supports the view that it is acceptable to seek general consent to future research in cases where there will be anonymisation of data and samples involved in genetic research.[105] Repeated processes of re-consent may not only be impractical but also unnecessarily invasive. Some jurisdictions have gone further still. For example, the law establishing the Icelandic Health Sector Database – which is an electronic database containing anonymised details from the health records of the majority of the Icelandic people – provides only

---

97 Medical Research Council *Public Perceptions of the Collection of Human Biological Samples* (2000).
98 Ibid, para 2.2.
99 Ibid, para 2.1.
100 Ibid.
101 HGC *Public Attitudes*, pp 20–22.
102 HGC *Inside Information*, paras 5.33 and 5.37.
103 Laurie (2002), para 7.1 above, pp 166–67 and pp 296–98.
104 O O'Neill *Autonomy and Trust in Bioethics* (2002), p 11.
105 HGC *Inside Information*, para 7.2 above, paras 5.18–5.19.

for an opt-out system,[106] that is, the legal presumption is that every citizen agrees to have his or her medical data entered onto the database unless he or she states otherwise. The justification for this is the need to obtain as much data as possible for sound epidemiological purposes.[107] However, the Icelandic government has been strongly criticised for failing to pay sufficient respect to its citizens and their rights by not actively seeking informed consent.[108]

7.53 No such proposal has been advanced in the United Kingdom, although Biobank UK raises similar issues.[109] This is an ambitious long-term longitudinal study which will follow 500,000 subjects through various periods of good and ill health, examining genotypic and phenotypic data together with environmental factors to establish the relationships between diseases and genes and the interaction between genes and environment. While informed consent would form an essential feature of the study, and rightly so in the circumstances, the project remains in the planning stage while wider issues are addressed, among which are questions of security of data and privacy protection.[110] Both the Human Genetics Commission[111] and a Working Group of the World Health Organisation (WHO)[112] have recommended oversight by an independent body of any genetic databases which might result from this or similar research. Such a body would be responsible for scrutinising both the ethical credentials of the researchers and their proposed research projects.[113]

THE STATE INTEREST IN GENETIC INFORMATION

7.54 The above sections have identified many varied interests in genetic information which are held by both individuals and institutions. Two particular state concerns arise from these interests: an inclination to reduce the financial burden wherever possible and a desire to minimise or eliminate harm to its citizens. The state has a role in protecting and advancing 'the public good' – that is, the collective interests of society as a whole. To what extent, then, can the state legitimately request results of genetic tests or require genetic testing?

---

106 Act on a Health Sector Database No 139/1998.
107 For a history and review of the system see H Rose *The Commodification of Bioinformation: The Icelandic Health Sector Database* (2001).
108 See H Roscam Abbing 'Central Health Database in Iceland and Patients' Rights' (1999) 6 Euro J Hlth Law 363. For a discussion of the Iceland experience and similar measures in Estonia, see Laurie (2002), para 7.1 above, pp 287–293.
109 For a comparison of the UK proposal with the Icelandic experience, see J Kaye and P Martin, 'Safeguards for Research Using Large Scale DNA Collections' (2000) 321 BMJ 1146.
110 This is a joint venture between the Wellcome Trust, the Medical Research Council and the Department of Health, see http://www.wellcome.ac.uk/en/1/biovenpopsts.html.
111 HGC *Inside Information*, para 7.2 above, paras 5.38–5.51.
112 WHO Working Group of the European Partnership on Patients' Rights and Citizens' Empowerment *Genetic Databases: Assessing the Benefits and the Impact on Human and Patient Rights* (2001).
113 For further recommendations as to safeguards see House of Lords Select Committee on Science and Technology *Human Genetic Databases: Challenges and Opportunities* (2001, HL 57).

7.55 One of the most obvious state interests in the health care setting[114] is that of securing public health and, perhaps unsurprisingly, it has been argued that mandatory testing for genetic disorders might halt the spread of genetic disease.[115] Even if little or nothing can be done for those already afflicted, disclosure might prevent the transmission of defective genes to future persons. Set against this, however, is the potential infringement of privacy interests which such practices can represent although, in this connection, it can be argued further that the state has a positive interest in facilitating individual choice. It can adopt a more pastoral role towards individuals by providing them with information which may help them make important life decisions such as whether or not to have a child if both partners are carriers of cystic fibrosis. Not only does this make individuals more independent as moral choosers but it might also have the desired social end of curtailing the further spread of genetic disease.[116] For example, Ball et al have noted that this view is held by the Royal College of Physicians:

> [the] Royal College of Physicians report suggests that as long as individuals have the right to decide for themselves whether to bear children it could be argued that such individuals should have access to the fullest possible information, including genetic, pertinent to that decision and therefore this should not be withheld.[117]

7.56 This implies that the state should seek to further its interest in facilitating choice by providing comprehensive screening programmes, a plethora of genetic tests accompanied by suitable counselling services and other support mechanisms, such as easy access to abortion. Cost implications aside, this would certainly further both individual and state interests by making free choice a market commodity. The risk of a conflict of interests would be almost entirely eliminated if such programmes were provided free of any coercive measures.[118]

---

114 We do not deal with forensic uses of genetic information here. These are considered by the HGC in its report *Inside Information*, para 7.2 above, chapter 9.

115 See S M Suter 'Whose Genes Are These Anyway?: Familial Conflicts Over Access to Genetic Information' (1993) 91 Michigan L Rev 1854 at 1897, citing H P Green and A M Capron 'Issues of Law and Public Policy in Genetic Screening', in D Bergsma (ed) *Ethical, Social and Legal Dimensions of Screening for Human Genetic Disease* (1974). See also M Shaw 'Conditional Prospective Rights of the Fetus' (1984) 5 J Leg Med 63, in which it is argued that prospective parents should face mandatory screening for certain conditions.

116 For sound policy recommendations, see European Society of Human Genetics *Populations Genetic Screening Programmes: Recommendations of the European Society of Human Genetics* (2000).

117 D Ball et al 'Predictive Testing of Adults and Children' in A Clarke (ed) *Genetic Counselling: Practice and Principles* (1994) at 77 referring to the Royal College of Physicians of London *Ethical Issues in Clinical Genetics: A Report of the Working Group of the Royal College of Physicians' Committees on Ethical Issues in Medicine and Clinical Genetics* (1991).

118 However, as the Nuffield Council has pointed out (para 7.29 above at 8.11): '[i]t has been argued that the availability of prenatal screening and diagnosis, together with the termination of seriously affected pregnancies, both reflect and reinforce the negative attitudes of our society towards those with disabilities. Indeed medical genetics may add a new dimension if genetic disorder came to be seen as a matter of choice rather than fate.'

7.57 The moral basis for introducing population genetic screening programmes has been questioned when no appropriate medical intervention is possible in light of a positive result.[119] No such programmes exist in the United Kingdom for adults and the only routine screening of children relates to neonates in respect of phenylketonuria, haemoglobin disorders and hypothyroidism.[120] The availability of a plethora of tests for prenatal genetic diagnosis has been noted in chapter 6. While this can facilitate parental choices as to the continuance of a pregnancy, it still raises concern that such testing is open to abuse if parents are in any way pressurised to test for a range of conditions and to abort any affected fetuses. The prospect that parents who choose not to abort a child might come to be seen as irresponsible is deplorable.[121] We agree with the ACGT in this regard – the aims of any programme should be clearly articulated, including any public health-related agenda on the part of the state, all programmes should be subjected to strict scrutiny by the National Screening Committee and each programme should be accompanied by impartial pre- and post-testing counselling. While it can be accepted that the state may have legitimate reasons for encouraging individuals to act responsibly in their use of any available genetic information, such encouragement should be offered only in the most moderate of terms. The autonomy and privacy interests of each of us require prima facie respect and this should be borne in mind whenever the introduction of a population screening programme is being considered. It is very difficult to justify any screening programme of children or adults which is unaccompanied by an effective cure or treatment. The strength of the state interest in promoting public health per se is insufficient to justify compromising the interests of individuals in receiving or not receiving genetic information about themselves. The Human Genetics Commission is well aware of these issues and has undertaken to consider both the matter of prenatal testing and screening programmes as part of its work on genetics and reproductive choice.[122]

GENE THERAPY

7.58 Advances in screening constitute only one aspect of the progress which has been made in human genetics over recent decades. Perhaps more significantly from the scientific point of view, possibilities have opened up for manipulation of the genes of existing and future individuals. This is best known as genetic engineering; inevitably, it has given rise to considerable bioethical debate.[123]

7.59 Gene therapy is one such form of genetic engineering and this may be of two types – somatic or germ-line.[124] Somatic gene therapy is directed towards

---

119 See, inter alia, Advisory Committee on Genetic Testing (para 7.6 above) Annex A and the Science and Technology Committee Third Report (para 7.20 above) para 83.

120 Nuffield Council on Bioethics (para 7.29 above) at 27. Screening for cystic fibrosis has been introduced more recently in some areas.

121 M Grodin and G Laurie 'Susceptibility Genes and Neurological Disorders: Learning the Right Lessons from the Human Genome Project' (2000) 57 Arch Neurol 1569.

122 HGC *Inside Information*, para 7.2 above, chapter 4.

123 See eg P Wheale and P McNally *Genetic Engineering: Catastrophe or Utopia?* (1988).

124 For an up-to-date account of progress so far in gene therapy, see J Kinderlerer and D Longley 'Human Genetics: The New Panacea?' (1998) 61 MLR 603 at 614ff.

the remedying of a defect within the patient and involves the insertion of genetic material which will perform some function which the patient's own genetic material cannot achieve. Germ-line gene therapy can be visualised in two ways: the insertion of genetic material into the pre-embryo, which is pre-emptive treatment of the future being and his or her progeny, or as the insertion of a gene into the germ cells of an individual. The latter therapy has no direct bearing on the individual but is intended to ensure that any subsequent children are born with or without certain characteristics. The scientific techniques involved have spawned considerable – and emotional – debate; indeed, genetic engineering is one of the few modern medical technologies in which study of the moral aspects has preceded the practical realities.

7.60 The ethical implications of somatic gene therapy were considered by the Committee on the Ethics of Gene Therapy – the Clothier Committee – which reported in 1992.[125] The Committee thought that this form of treatment was uncontroversial, if novel, and felt that it gave rise to no new ethical challenges. The Group of Advisors on Ethical Implications of Biotechnology of the European Commission similarly reported in 1994 and encouraged somatic gene therapy at a number of levels, including basic research, clinical trials and biotechnology.[126] This having been said, the group considered that, because of certain unknown risks associated with the process, research into somatic gene therapy should be restricted to serious diseases for which there is no other effective available treatment. Similar views have been expressed in the United States and in international documents concerned with the bioethics of manipulation of the human genome.[127] We can accept these assessments; the goals of somatic gene therapy are identical to the goals of other forms of treatment and, provided that it does not involve undue risk to the patient or to others, it is as ethically acceptable as is drug therapy or surgical intervention. There may be a need for caution if somatic gene therapy is developed so as to combat behavioural disorders; even then, however, the ethical considerations will be similar to those which already arise from the use of psychotropic drugs or psychosurgery and which are discussed in greater detail in chapter 21.[128]

7.61 Trials involving gene therapy began in 1990 but suffered a real setback in 1999 when the first death attributable to the technique occurred.[129]

---

125 Report of the Committee on the Ethics of Gene Therapy (1992).
126 Opinion of the Group of Advisers on Ethical Implications of Biotechnology of the European Commission *The Ethical Implications of Gene Therapy* (1994).
127 For the US position, see Report and Recommendations of the Panel to Assess the National Institutes of Health Investment in Research on Gene Therapy (1995). The Council of Europe Convention for the Protection of Human Rights and Dignity of the Human Being with regard to the Application of Biology and Medicine: Convention on Human Rights and Biomedicine states, in Article 13: 'An intervention seeking to modify the human genome may only be undertaken for preventative, diagnostic or therapeutic purposes and only if its aim is not to introduce any modification in the genome of any descendants.'
128 Over 100 somatic gene therapy studies had been reviewed and approved in the US by late 1995. See L Walters 'Reproductive Technologies and Genetics' in R M Veatch (ed) *Medical Ethics* (2nd edn, 1997) p 229.
129 E Weiss and D Nelson 'Teen Dies Undergoing Gene Therapy' (1999) Washington Post 29 September, p A1.

None the less, it has been reported in the United States that 'in the year of the tragedy, ... the National Institutes of Health (NIH) approved a record 91 gene transfer protocols that year, as compared with only 2 in 1990 and 51 in 1998. In 2000, that number dropped to 71, but it edged up to 73 in 2001, according to the NIH's Office of Biotechnology Activities'.[130] Twenty-one gene therapy protocols were reviewed by the UK's Gene Therapy Advisory Committee (GTAC) in 2000. The GTAC also responded to the American experience by issuing stricter and clearer guidelines on making proposals to conduct gene therapy research on human subjects in its Seventh Report published in 2001.[131] By the end of 2000, a total of 60 gene therapy protocols had either been completed, were being undertaken or were under review by the Committee.

7.62 The controversial nature of germ-line gene therapy – whether directed to the pre-embryo or to an individual's germ cells – rests on its capacity to change future people. Some such changes will, in themselves, be unobjectionable; it is difficult, for example, to find grounds for objection to preventive medicine which will ensure that the bearers of a serious genetically transmissible disease will not pass the condition on to their children. Such medical practice is no different from other, long-accepted, efforts to eradicate disease within the human population which, arguably, interfere with the natural order to a comparable degree.

7.63 The difficulty that some have with any form of germ-line therapy is that of the 'slippery slope' which is encountered at a number of points in medical jurisprudence.[132] If we allow germ-line therapy in relation to, say, a seriously debilitating disease, then how are we to prevent its use to eliminate characteristics which we would not, currently, label as a defect but which may be considered undesirable? Rifkin put the problem as follows:

> Once we decide to begin the process of human genetic engineering, there is really no logical place to stop. If diabetes, sickle cell anaemia, and cancer are to be cured by altering the genetic make-up of an individual, why not proceed to other 'disorders': myopia, colour-blindness, left-handedness? Indeed, what is to preclude a society from deciding that a certain skin colour is a disorder?[133]

7.64 This is a bleak view of scientific ambitions, but the concern for possible abuse that it expresses has been potent enough to cause a number of governmental or other official bodies to proscribe germ-line gene therapy. The Council of Europe was, initially, sufficiently suspicious to recommend a complete ban on such practices – on the grounds of its insult to human dignity – but later modified this to allow germ cell manipulation for therapeutic purposes.[134] UNESCO has not ruled out germ-line therapies ab initio in its

---

130   T Ready 'Gene Therapy in Recovery Phase' (2002) 8 Nature Medicine 429.
131   GTAC Seventh Annual Report (January 2000–December 2000) (2001). This report also contains a summary of gene therapy research from 1993-2001.
132   N Holtug 'Human Gene Therapy: Down the Slippery Slope' (1993) 7 Bioethics 402.
133   J Rifkin *Algeny* (1983) p 232, quoted in Holtug (1993) 7 Bioethics 402 at 405.
134   Council of Europe Recommendation 934 on Genetic Engineering (1982); Recommendation 1100 on the Use of Human Embryos and Foetuses in Scientific Research (1989).

Universal Declaration on the Human Genome and Human Rights but, rather, prohibits 'practices which are contrary to human dignity'.[135] An arguable case can be made that germ-line research falls into this category. The total outlawing of germ-line therapy has been recommended in Germany – and this attitude was endorsed in a statement from the medical research councils of 11 European states in 1988.[136]

7.65 However, germ-line gene therapy is not without its supporters – as Harris has asked: is there anything really wrong in wanting to have a fine child?[137] The real difficulty lies in distinguishing between eugenically-motivated, or enhancement, germ-line manipulation on the one hand and truly therapeutic intervention on the other. It should be necessary to forbid *all* work in this area only if it is felt that the demarcation line can never be held. Unfortunately, science's bad record in keeping to a narrow, acceptable track lends some force to the arguments of those who would prevent such meddling altogether.[138] We agree with the Human Genome Organisation's Ethics Committee (HUGO) which has called for 'widespread discussion on the appropriateness of the possible future use of gene transfer technology for enhancement and for germ-line interventions'.[139]

CLONING

7.66 The birth of Dolly the lamb in 1997 sparked one of the most controversial furores to affect the discipline of medical law and ethics since its beginnings some 30 years ago. Dolly was the first example of an adult vertebrate cloned – that is, genetically copied – from another adult. She was created using a 'fusion' technique whereby the nucleus from an adult cell (in this case mammarian cells) was fused with an unfertilised egg from which the nucleus had been removed. This egg was then transplanted into another adult sheep for normal gestation to take place. The benefits of such a technique include the improvement of production of transgenic livestock which can be used to produce therapeutic agents involving human proteins. Most recently, the development of stem cell technology has made possible the creation of pluripotent cell lines from undifferentiated human cellular material taken from embryos and deceased fetuses. The potential therapeutic benefits of this form of cloning technique such as the cultivation of replacement cells and tissues for diseased body parts have proven very attractive to researchers and governments alike,[140] leading to the rapid moral and legal acceptance of the practice in many countries.

135   See para 7.11 above, Article 11.
136   M A M de Wachter 'Ethical Aspects of Human Germ-line Gene Therapy' (1993) 7 Bioethics 166. The tone of the Declaration of Inuyama and Report of a Working Group on Human Gene Therapy is cautious but not prescriptive: reproduced and discussed in J C Fletcher and W F Anderson 'Germ-line Gene Therapy: A New Stage of Debate' (1992) 20 Law Med Hlth Care 26.
137   J Harris 'Is Gene Therapy a Form of Eugenics?' (1993) 7 Bioethics 178.
138   For a range of informed views, see G Stock and J Campbell *Engineering the Human Germline: An Exploration of the Science and Ethics of Altering the Genes We Pass to Our Children* (2000).
139   HUGO Ethics Committee *Draft Statement on Gene Therapy Research* (2001).
140   For an account of the science and ethics of this technique, see Nuffield Council on Bioethics *Stem Cell Therapy: The Ethical Issues* (2000).

7.67 These developments, however, also raise the spectre of human cloning, and it is in this regard that much of the controversy has arisen.[141] The prospect that individuals could clone themselves and have children who share precisely the same genetic make-up is, for some, to go too far. There is serious concern that the use of such a technique would alter our perception of what it means to be human. Moreover, many fear that the potential for exploitation is too great and envisage the production of human clones to be used as sources of spare parts.[142] Others still have posited that the birth of a clone would distort beyond recognition traditional familial hierarchies and relationships.[143] While many of these fears must be unfounded, we cannot deny that the strength of the reaction to these developments dictates a very cautious approach to the future.[144]

7.68 Initial governmental responses to the birth of Dolly were swift and unanimously condemnatory. The United Kingdom government quickly confirmed its position that any work which was designed to produce cloned human beings was unethical and illegal[145] – a matter which we address further below. In the United States, the National Bioethics Advisory Commission (NBAC) reported in June 1997 and concluded that the risks of research into human cloning involving clinical trials were too great and that legislation should be passed to prohibit research into cloning 'complete people'. As a result, the Cloning and Prohibition Bill 1997 was sent to Congress, but the Bill was not introduced in the first session. Since then, at least seven other cloning prohibition Bills have been introduced, each of which has failed. In August 2001 President Bush announced that research using federal funds to study embryonic stem cells could only be done on stem cell lines or colonies that existed prior to the date of his announcement.[146] This, in effect, precluded federal funding for research into stem cells from cloned human embryos, and one year on it was reported that only three cell lines are available to researchers.[147] Note, that this does not preclude research using private moneys – and, indeed, other reports tell of actual attempted reproductive assistance through cloning in America and elsewhere.[148]

7.69 At the state level, 19 states had proposed 22 Bills by the end of 1997, and California passed a law in that year imposing a five-year moratorium on cloning of an entire human being.[149] Towards the end of this period the

---

141 For an up-to-date account, see Committee on Science, Engineering, and Public Policy *Scientific and Medical Aspects of Human Reproductive Cloning* (2002).
142 A fear that gathers some substance when we read R J Boyle and J Savulescu 'Ethics of Using Preimplantation Genetic Diagnosis to Select a Stem Cell Donor for an Existing Person' (2001) 323 BMJ 1240.
143 For a range of views and arguments see generally (1999) 25 Journal Med Ethics Issue 2.
144 For a measured proposal, see A L Bonnicksen 'Procreation By Cloning: Crafting Anticipatory Guidelines' (1997) 25 J Law Med & Ethics 273.
145 Official Reports, HC 26 June 1997, col 615ff.
146 A Goldstein and A Allen 'Bush Backs Partial Stem Cell Funding' *Washington Post* 10 August 2001, p A01.
147 J Gillis and R Weiss 'Stem Cell Research Not Yet Booming' *Washington Post* 6 August 2001, p A01
148 R Dobson 'Claims of Clone Pregnancy Could Threaten US Stem Cell Research' (2002) 324 BMJ 868.
149 SB 1344, 1997–98 Leg, Reg Sess (Cal 1997) (enacted) (Human Cloning).

California Advisory Committee on Human Cloning submitted a report which encapsulates perfectly the sophistic nature of debate and legal response in this field.[150] While it endorsed President Bush's prohibition on work for so-called 'reproductive cloning', the Committee also unanimously recommended that the state permit the creation of cloned embryos as a source of human cells that ultimately could be used to regenerate or replace diseased tissues and organs, ie for 'therapeutic cloning'. A Bill which reflects these recommendations was proceeding through the California state legislature at the time of writing. Reactions from elsewhere mirror this distinction. A protocol to the Council of Europe Convention on Human Rights and Biomedicine prohibits the cloning of human beings[151] and the UNESCO Declaration on the Human Genome and Human Rights specifically disallows cloning as being contrary to human dignity.[152] Moreover, incentives to carry out research in this field in Europe have been removed with the passing of the Directive on the Legal Protection of Biotechnological Inventions,[153] Article 6 of which expressly prohibits the granting of a patent for 'processes for cloning human beings'.[154] In contrast, the Westminster Parliament voted in December 2000 to legalise the creation of embryos purely for research purposes, including stem cell research,[155] while, on the reproduction side, there has been considerable dispute over whether a cloned human organism is an 'embryo' for the purposes of the Human Fertilisation and Embryology Act 1990.[156] This has been resolved in favour of a purposive interpretation that brings such an organism within the definition and, therefore, within the Human Fertilisation and Embryology Authority's (HFEA) regulatory regime. It is likely, therefore, that licences for cloning techniques done to a reproductive end will not be granted – at least in the short to medium term. However, it is far from clear how long the tide can be held. In what can only be described as an unprecedented move – and certainly one that could scarcely have been contemplated at the time of the last edition of this book – Baroness Mary Warnock has recently expressed regret about the absolute nature of the ban on reproductive cloning which has gripped most legislatures.[157] Is this another shift from deontological ethics in favour of utilitarianism? We suspect that the days of the outright prohibition on reproductive cloning are numbered.

---

150 California Advisory Committee on Human Cloning (2002), see <http:// www.sfgate.com/chronicle/cloningreport/>.

151 Additional Protocol to the Convention for the Protection of Human Rights and Dignity of the Human Being with regard to the Application of Biology and Medicine, on the Prohibition of Cloning Human Beings (Paris, January 1998).

152 Article 11.

153 Directive of the European Parliament and of the Council on the Legal Protection of Biotechnological Inventions No 98/44/EC of 6 July 1998, published at OJ L213, 30 July 1998, p 13.

154 It should also be noted that, inter alia, this article excludes processes for modifying the germ-line genetic identity of human beings from patentability. We discuss this directive further in chapter 15.

155 'MPs Give Go Ahead for Embryo Research', The Times, 19 December 2000. The House of Lords approved this vote of the House of Commons on 22 January 2001. See now, the Human Fertilisation and Embryology (Research Purposes) Regulations 2001, SI 2001/188.

156 *R (on the application of Quintavalle) v Secretary of State for Health* [2002] EWCA Civ 29, [2002] QB 628, (2002) 64 BMLR 72.

157 M Warnock *Making Babies: Is There A Right to Have Children?* (2002), pp 102ff, 'Would the cloning of human be intrinsically wrong?'

7.70 When responding to developments which have consequences as far-reaching as do so many of those subsumed in the discipline of medical law, it is essential that a broad cross-section of views are obtained and, where possible, taken on board. The final response of the law to the advent of cloning remains to be seen – but the means by which the final end is reached can be as important as the reaching of the end itself.

Medical practice

8 Medical confidentiality

8.1 A general common law duty is imposed on a doctor to respect the confidences of his patients.[1] The nature of this obligation – which applies to all confidential information and not only to medical material – was discussed by the Court of Appeal in *A-G v Guardian Newspapers Ltd (No 2)*,[2] in which it was affirmed that there was a public interest in a legally enforceable protection of confidences received under notice of confidentiality. There are three elements required to establish a breach of the obligation. First, the information divulged must have the necessary quality of confidence about it; secondly, that information must have been imparted in circumstances importing an obligation of confidence; and, thirdly, there must be an unauthorised use of that information,[3] probably also with some evidence of detriment to the party to whom the duty of confidence is owed. All these criteria would apply in a medical context where the duty of discretion has been endorsed judicially. Thus, in *Hunter v Mann*[4] the court accepted that:

> ... the doctor is under a duty not to [voluntarily] disclose, without the consent of the patient, information which he, the doctor, has gained in his professional capacity.

More recently, in the very significant case of *W v Egdell*,[5] which we discuss in greater detail below, the court accepted the existence of an obligation of confidentiality between a psychiatrist and his subject, an obligation which counsel submitted was based not only on equitable grounds but also on implied contract.

---

1 The doctor-patient and priest-penitent relationships were cited as classic examples in *Stephens v Avery* [1988] Ch 449 at 455, [1988] 2 All ER 477 at 482, per Browne-Wilkinson V-C.
2 [1990] AC 109, [1988] 3 All ER 545.
3 Per Megarry J in *Coco v A N Clark (Engineers) Ltd* [1969] RPC 41 at 47, repeated with approval in *Stephens v Avery* [1988] Ch 449, [1988] 2 All ER 477.
4 [1974] QB 767 at 772, [1974] 2 All ER 414 at 417 per Boreham J. For a general discussion of the duty of confidentiality in the medical context, see G T Laurie *Genetic Privacy: A Challenge to Medico-Legal Norms* (2002), pp 211ff.
5 [1990] Ch 359, [1990] 1 All ER 835.

8.2 Whatever may be the legal basis for the duty, its ethical content is considerable. Indeed, in the context of medical law in particular, it is difficult to dissociate the two disciplines – thus, we have Lord Coleridge CJ: 'A legal common law duty is nothing else than the enforcing by law of that which is a moral obligation without legal enforcement.'[6] We can, therefore, look not only at what the patient feels is his legal entitlement but also at the ethical requirements of the medical profession itself. Here there are a number of sources from which the doctor can seek guidance. The Hippocratic Oath[7] makes several demands which can scarcely be regarded as binding on the modern doctor; none the less, its stipulations as to professional confidentiality are still firmly endorsed. The translation cited in the *sponsio academica* at graduation ceremonials in the University of Edinburgh runs: 'Whatever things seen or heard in the course of medical practice ought not to be spoken of, I will not, save for weighty reasons, divulge'. The Declaration of Geneva (amended at Sydney)[8] imposes much the same obligation on the doctor, requiring him to 'respect the secrets which are confided in me, even after the patient has died'.

8.3 The great majority of commentators on medical ethics endorse a continued adherence to a strict principle[9] although some doubt the efficacy of an absolute rule and prefer a form of contractual obligation which, it is thought, would promote the individual patient's autonomy.[10] Most critics, however, see the concept as being something of a pretence in that bureaucracy, fired by modern administrative technology, is increasingly invasive of the principle; certainly, patients' records must circulate fairly widely – and among professionals who are less deeply indoctrinated as to confidentiality than are their medical colleagues. As a result, it has been suggested that institutions should take over custodianship of confidences and thus impose an overall standard of duty on all who work in, for example, the hospital.[11] Arguably, this standard has now been met both at common law[12] and through statute.[13]

8.4 Even so, the special position of the doctor is unlikely to change in the foreseeable future and he is currently bound by the authority of, and is subject

---

6   In *R v Instan* [1893] 1 QB 450 at 453.
7   See Appendix A.
8   See Appendix B.
9   Eg J M Jacob 'Confidentiality: The Dangers of Anything Weaker than the Medical Ethic' (1982) 8 J Med Ethics 18; M H Kottow 'Medical Confidentiality: An Intransigent and Absolute Obligation' (1986) 12 J Med Ethics 117. Indeed, Ngwena and Chadwick even suggested that the concept has '... been elevated to the status of a principle of Medical Ethics', see C Ngwena and R Chadwick 'Genetic Diagnostic Information and the Duty of Confidentiality: Ethics and Law' (1993) 1 Med L Int 73 at 74.
10 S J Warwick 'A Vote for No Confidence' (1989) 15 J Med Ethics 183.
11 D L Kenny 'Confidentiality: The Confusion Continues' (1982) 8 J Med Ethics 9; M Siegler 'Confidentiality in Medicine: A Decrepit Concept' (1982) 307 New Engl J Med 1518. See also D F H Pheby 'Changing Practice on Confidentiality: A Cause for Concern' (1982) 8 J Med Ethics 12; A W Macara 'Confidentiality: A Decrepit Concept?' (1984) 77 J Roy Soc Med 577.
12 *A-G v Guardian Newspapers Ltd (No 2)*, para 8.1 above imposes a duty on all those who receive confidential information in circumstances which objectively (and reasonably) import a duty of confidence. Communications in a hospital must surely be a paradigm example of this.
13 Data Protection Act 1998. For commentary, see M Earle *Data Protection in the NHS* (2002).

to the discipline of, the General Medical Council (GMC). Subject to certain exceptions, which we discuss further below[14] the GMC imposes a strict duty on registered medical practitioners to refrain from disclosing voluntarily to any third party information about a patient which he has learnt directly or indirectly in his professional capacity.[15] A breach of this duty will be a serious matter, exposing the doctor to a wide range of potential professional penalties. It is to be noted, however, that sanctions of this nature are purely intra-professional and it has long been questioned whether they give adequate protection to the aggrieved patient; thus, the Law Commission has suggested that the common law position should be strengthened by establishing a statutory offence of breach of confidence which would include those arising between doctor and patient.[16]

8.5 The passing of the Data Protection Act 1998, implementing a 1995 EC Directive,[17] has provided further protection for medical information. It is not necessary for the purposes of this book to examine the provisions of the Directive or the Act in any great depth.[18] It is sufficient simply to note certain key features.[19] The law protects the privacy rights of individuals in respect of their personal data. Personal data are defined as 'any information relating to an identified or identifiable natural person; an identifiable person is one who can be identified, directly or indirectly, in particular by reference to an identification number or to one or more factors specific to his physical, physiological, mental, economic, cultural or social identity'.[20] The law regulates the processing of such data by reference to a set of eight principles that ensure, inter alia, that data are only processed when it is fair and lawful to do so, that data are processed only so far as is necessary for the purposes for which they were obtained, that the data are accurate and kept up to date, and that they should not be transferred to any jurisdiction where there are inadequate data protection provisions.

8.6 The law makes only two attempts to categorise information into distinct groupings. These are (a) sensitive personal data, and (b) anonymous data.

---

14 See para 8.9 et seq.
15 GMC *Confidentiality: Protecting and Providing Information* (2000). The advice of the BMA has no disciplinary authority but provides invaluable background to the GMC's instructions: see BMA *Confidentiality and Disclosure of Health Information* (1999). Other BMA guidance includes *Confidentiality and People Under 16* (1994) and *Revised Interim Guidelines on Confidentiality for Police Surgeons in England, Wales and Northern Ireland* (1998).
16 *Breach of Confidence* (Cmnd 8388) para 6.1. There has as yet been no government action on this report, which was issued in 1981.
17 European Directive 95/46/EC on the *Protection of Individuals with Regard to the Processing of Personal Data and on the Free Movement of Such Data* (Data Protection Directive). There is a general and strong European interest in the subject which is reflected elsewhere in the Council of Europe's *Recommendation on the Protection of Medical Data* (1997). This recommendation includes not only general principles which should guide national laws on the confidentiality of medical information, but also embraces specific recommendations relating to such matters as storage of data, their transmission across borders, and the use of data in medical research.
18 The Data Protection Act 1998 came into force on 1 March 2000.
19 For a guide to the Act, see R Jay and A Hamilton *Data Protection: Law and Practice* (2002).
20 Data Protection Directive, Article 2.

Both are of relevance in the health care setting. Sensitive personal data are defined as data relating to racial or ethnic origin, political opinions, religious or philosophical beliefs, trade-union membership, and the processing of data concerning health or sex life.[21] Additional protection is afforded to such data and, as we have seen elsewhere in this book, the primary point of reference is the concept of consent. In most circumstances, the data subject's specific consent to processing must be obtained. However, a wide range of alternative justifications for processing accompanies this protection, of which the following are most pertinent. For example, it is lawful to process sensitive data to protect the vital interests of the data subject or of another person where the data subject is physically or legally incapable of giving his consent. Also, processing is lawful without specific consent if it is required for the purposes of preventive medicine, medical diagnosis, the provision of care or treatment or the management of health care services, and where those data are processed by a health professional subject to the obligation of professional secrecy or by another person also subject to an equivalent obligation of secrecy. Overarchingly, member states have the power to create exemptions on the basis of 'substantial public interest'.[22] What those public interests are, or may be, is discernible in large part from the general tenor of the Directive, which makes special provisions, among others, for national security, the investigation and prosecution of crimes, legitimate journalistic activities and research.[23]

8.7 In this latter regard, the law creates a number of important protections for scientific researchers using data obtained from individuals. First, there is no requirement to notify a data subject of the identity and purposes of those who will process the data, nor the identity of any further recipients of those data when the data have not been received directly from the data subject.[24] Normally, this requirement must be met. Moreover, member states have a discretion to waive rights of access for individuals in the context of scientific research.[25] Second, the subject access provisions of the Directive do not apply when data are anonymised, for the law is concerned solely with personal data – ie those from which an individual can be identified.[26] This having been said, patients must still be informed when data are to be processed and the purposes for which this is likely to occur.

8.8 The provisions are all encompassing of identifiable personal information and, to that extent, are to be welcomed. Consent has a role to play but it does not emerge as a trump card. Indeed, the broad and indistinct categories of justifications for processing without consent potentially weaken the protection that is afforded to informational privacy interests. The model, however, is, as always, a search for a balance and few could deny that privacy protection should sometimes bow to other interests. But the devil is in the detail of determining which interests should be weighed in the balance and how far

---

21 Ibid, Article 8.
22 Ibid, Article 8(4).
23 See further in England and Wales, the Health and Social Care Act 2001, s 60, discussed further below.
24 Ibid, Article 11(2).
25 Ibid, Article 13(2).
26 Ibid, Recital 26.

privacy should be compromised in any given case. The example of research is particularly apt. Is it meaningful, for example, to say from the theoretical standpoint that anonymisation of data is sufficient to address privacy concerns? We return to this question below in the context of recent common law developments and the provisions of the controversial s 60 of the Health and Social Care Act 2001.

RELAXATION OF THE RULE

8.9 All the classic codes of practice imply some qualification of an absolute duty of professional secrecy. Thus, the Hippocratic Oath has it: 'All that may come to my knowledge ... which ought not to be spread abroad, I will keep secret', which clearly indicates that there are some things which *may* be published. The Declaration of Geneva modifies this prohibition to: 'I will respect the secrets which are confided in me' and the word 'respect' is open to interpretation. The GMC, while always emphasising its strong views as to the rule dictating professional secrecy, still lists a number of specific possible exceptions to the rule which provide a sound basis for discussion.[27]

Consent to publish

8.10 The first, and most easily recognisable, exception is when the patient or his legal adviser consents to a relaxation of secrecy. The situation is simple when viewed from the positive angle. A positive consent to release of information elides any obligation to secrecy owed by the person receiving that consent;[28] equally, an explicit request that information should not be disclosed is binding on the doctor save in the most exceptional circumstances – a matter which is of major concern in relation to communicable disease.[29]

Sharing information with others providing care

8.11 However, the position is not so clear when looked at from the negative aspect – that is, when the patient has neither consented to nor dissented from disclosure – and it may, indeed, be frankly unsatisfactory. How many patients know whether the person standing with the consultant at the hospital bedside is another doctor, a social worker or just an interested spectator? Would they have consented to their presence if they had been informed? The consultant may be responsible if, as a result, there is a breach of confidence – but this is small consolation to the patient who feels his rights have been infringed. What patient at a teaching hospital out-patient department is likely to refuse when the consultant asks: 'You don't mind these young doctors being present, do you?' – the pressures are virtually irresistible and truly autonomous consent is well-nigh impossible, yet the confidential doctor-patient relationship which began with his general practitioner has, effectively, been broken.

27 *Confidentiality*, para 8.4 above, section 3.
28 *C v C* [1946] 1 All ER 562.
29 See para 8.23 et seq below.

8.12 It is obvious that such technical breaches must be, and generally are, accepted in practice – a modern hospital cannot function except as a team effort and new doctors have to be trained, the return for a technical loss of patient autonomy being access to the best diagnostic and therapeutic aids available. The GMC recognises this in permitting the sharing of information with other practitioners who assume responsibility for clinical management of the patient and, to the extent that the doctor deems it necessary for the performance of their particular duties, with other health care professionals who are collaborating with the doctor in his patients' management.[30] The exception notes that it is the doctor's responsibility to ensure that such individuals appreciate that the information is being imparted in strict professional confidence.[31] The doctor's duty is thereby restricted in a reasonable way; it is difficult to see how he can be expected to carry the onus for any subsequent actions by his associates. Any such infringement might form the basis of a complaint to the Health Service Commissioner.[32]

The patient's interests

8.13 It is ethical to break confidentiality without a patient's consent when it is in his or her own interests to do so and when it is undesirable on medical grounds to seek such consent. The recipient of the information may be another health care professional as above, or a close relative or, as in a case where the doctor suspects that the patient is a victim of neglect or physical or sexual abuse, an unrelated third party – but it remains the doctor's duty to make every reasonable effort to persuade the patient to allow the information to be given, and to make clear to the third party that the information is given in confidence. When these situations occur, decisions rest, by definition, on clinical judgment – a properly considered clinical decision cannot be *unethical* whether it proves right or wrong and, in the event of action being taken on the basis of breach of confidence, the fact that it was a justifiable breach would offer a complete defence both in the civil courts and before disciplinary proceedings of the GMC;[33] the GMC does, however, stress the need for caution when the patient has insufficient understanding, by reason of immaturity, of what the treatment or advice being sought involves; we return to this aspect later in the chapter.[34]

The doctor in society

8.14 In so far as it rests on subjective definitions, the doctor's overriding duty to society represents what is arguably the most controversial permissible exception to the rule of confidentiality. Society is not homogeneous, but consists of groups amenable to almost infinite classification – regional, political, economic, by age

---

30 *Confidentiality* (para 8.4 above) section 3, para 7.
31 Ibid, para 9.
32 The Health Service Commissioners Act 1993 (as amended by Health Service Commissioners (Amendment) Acts 1996 and 2000) consolidates the powers to investigate complaints against individuals or bodies within the National Health Service. The 1996 Act removes the veto on the Ombudsman to investigate matters of clinical judgment.
33 On which, see chapter 1.
34 See para 8.37 below.

and so on. It follows that what one person regards as a duty to society may be anathema to another. Individual doctors are bound to weigh the scales differently in any particular instance while, in general, all relative weighting must change from case to case – there is, for example, a great deal of difference in respect of confidentiality between being stung by a bee and suffering from venereal disease. While it is clear that no rules can be laid down, some aspects of this societal conflict are of sufficient importance to merit individual consideration.[35]

8.15 The most dramatic dilemma is posed by the possibility of violent crime. What is the doctor to do if he knows his patient has just committed rape – particularly if there is evidence that this is but one of a series of attacks on women? Perhaps even more disconcertingly, what if it becomes apparent that his patient is about to commit such an offence? Statute law is helpful here only in a negative sense – misprision of felony, other than as related to treason, is no longer an offence.[36] There is case law to the effect that the doctor need not even assist the police by answering their questions concerning his patients, although he must not give false or misleading information.[37] The obligation on the prosecution to disclose to the defence all unused material which might have some bearing on the offences charged has caused some difficulty for police surgeons. Generally speaking, an accused gives consent to disclosure of specific information only. Other information may, however, come to light during the course of the examination; once this is in the police notes, the police may feel it their duty to include it in their 'disclosure', despite the fact that there is no consent to their so doing. The police surgeon may, therefore, feel it his ethical imperative to conceal his knowledge – but the decision must, at times, be difficult to make.[38]

8.16 In the early part of the twentieth century, both medical and legal opinion was divided on the issue of disclosure of serious crime; discussion was, however, based largely on the subject of illegal abortion, which has emotional overtones of its own. Nevertheless, it was in that context that Avory J made his well-known observation:

> There are cases where the desire to preserve [the confidential relation which exists between the medical man and his patient] must be subordinated to the duty which is cast on every good citizen to assist in the investigation of serious crime,[39]

35 The GMC states: 'In cases where you have considered all the available means of obtaining consent, but you are satisfied that it is not practicable to do so, or that patients are not competent to give consent, or exceptionally, in cases where patients withhold consent, personal information may be disclosed in the public interest where the benefits to an individual or to society of the disclosure outweigh the public and the patient's interest in keeping the information confidential ... In all such cases you must weigh the possible harm (both to the patient, and the overall trust between doctors and patients) against the benefits which are likely to arise from the release of information.' See *Confidentiality*, para 8.4 above, section 3 paras 18 and 19.
36 Criminal Law Act 1967, s 5(5).
37 *Rice v Connolly* [1966] 2 QB 414, [1966] 2 All ER 649. See also P Schutte 'Medical Confidentiality and a Police Murder Inquiry' (1989) 5 J Med Def Union (Spring) 21.
38 For guidance, see British Medical Association *Revised Interim Guidelines for Police Surgeons*, para 8.4 above.
39 Birmingham Assizes, 1 December 1914, reported in (1914) 78 JP 604. The judge referred to a possible moral duty in the event that the patient was not dying; his views as to strict moral duty were mainly concerned with the loss of evidence in failing to take a dying declaration from a moribund patient.

and this probably represents the foundation of the doctrine of the public interest as applied to medicine. This crystallised in the case of *W v Egdell*.[40]

8.17   Here, a prisoner in a secure hospital sought a review of his case with a view to transfer to a regional secure unit. His legal representatives secured a report from an independent consultant psychiatrist which was, in the event, unfavourable to W; as a result, the application for transfer was aborted. W was, however, due for routine review of his detention and the psychiatrist, becoming aware that his report would not be included in the patient's notes, feared that decisions would be taken on inadequate information with consequent danger to the public. He therefore sent a copy of his report to the medical director of the hospital and a further copy reached the Home Office; W brought an action in contract and in equity alleging breach of a duty of confidence. The trial judge, Scott J, considered that, in the circumstances:

> The question in the present case is not whether Dr Egdell was under a duty of confidence; he plainly was. The question is as to the breadth of that duty.[41]

Attention was drawn to the advice of the GMC as to the circumstances in which exception to the rule of confidentiality is permitted. The GMC's guidelines which applied at the time were contained in the so-called 'Blue Book'. Para 79 stated:

> Rarely, cases may arise in which disclosure in the public interest may be justified, for example, a situation in which the failure to disclose appropriate information would expose the patient, or someone else, to a risk of death or serious harm.

8.18   Scott J based his conclusions on broad considerations – that a doctor in similar circumstances has a duty not only to the patient but also to the public and that the latter would require him to disclose the results of his examination to the proper authorities if, in his opinion, the public interest so required; this would be independent of the patient's instructions on the point.

8.19   The Court of Appeal unanimously confirmed the trial judge's decision to dismiss the action but did so with rather more reservation – particularly as expressed in the judgment of Bingham LJ. The concept of a private interest competing with a public interest was rejected in favour of there being a *public* interest in maintaining professional duties of confidence; the 'balancing' of interests thus fell to be carried out in circumstances of unusual difficulty. Doubts, which we share, were cast on the applicability of the provisions of the *Blue Book* (then para 78(b)) to a doctor acting in the role of an independent consultant; disclosure would have to be justified under the then para 78(g) and, here, it was for the court, not the doctor, to decide whether such a disclosure was or was not a breach of contract. Moreover, there was no doubt that the Mental Health Act 1983, s 76 showed a clear parliamentary intention that a restricted patient should be free to seek advice and evidence for specific purposes which was confidential in respect of the authorities. Only the most compelling circumstances could justify a doctor acting contrary to the patient's perceived

40   [1990] Ch 359, [1990] 1 All ER 835.
41   [1990] Ch 359 at 389, [1989] 1 All ER 1089 at 1102.

interests in the absence of consent. Nevertheless, in the instant case, the fear of a real risk to public safety entitled a doctor to take reasonable steps to communicate the grounds of his concern to the appropriate authorities.

8.20 Looked at superficially, it is easy to view *Egdell* as a serious intrusion into the relationship of confidential trust between doctor and patient; it is equally possible to perceive the principle as emerging relatively unscathed. W's case was clearly regarded as extreme and, although we cannot exclude some concern, there is no evidence in the judgment that the courts would condone a breach of confidence on less urgent grounds. The 'danger area' seems to be better deliminated by way of independent activity on the part of doctors – as anticipated by Bingham LJ in *Egdell*. In *R v Crozier*,[42] a psychiatrist called by the accused, concerned that his opinion should be available to the court, apparently handed his report to counsel for the Crown; the now sentenced accused appealed on the grounds that the breach of confidentiality between doctor and patient had denied him the opportunity of deciding whether medical evidence would be tendered. The Court of Appeal again thought that there was a stronger public interest in the disclosure of the psychiatrist's views than in the confidence he owed to the appellant; the psychiatrist was found to have acted responsibly and reasonably in a very difficult situation. But what if a doctor acts *un*reasonably in such circumstances? The damage to the patient is done and he will get little satisfaction from the fact that the doctor is censured; it is surely a thoroughly paternalistic practice that should be carefully restrained.

8.21 On a more mundane note, the importance of disease in drivers has increased and presents a major dilemma to the conscientious doctor. Driving licences are issued for the lifetime up to the age of 70 and responsibility for reporting health deficiencies is placed firmly on the licence holder. Heart disease is always thought of as being paramount in this context but, in practice, very few car accidents that result in serious personal injury are caused by cardiac conditions. Moreover, the majority of cardiac patients are mature and conscious of their responsibilities. Epilepsy is a far more apposite example. Nearly half the instances of unconsciousness at the wheel of a car are epileptic in origin and the condition is found to have been undisclosed in over three quarters of these – the public need seems clear, but what is the doctor to do? The standard answer is that he should either persuade the patient to report the disability or obtain the patient's consent to disclosure, but this does not help when, as is likely, both courses are rejected. It has been suggested[43] that a doctor who knew that an unsafe patient of his was continuing to drive and who then failed to take any action on the point might be liable in damages for negligence to anyone harmed by his patient on the road. This seems unlikely to happen in a United Kingdom context – case law relating to dangerous patients of other types (for which, see chapter 21) would probably apply – and has been rejected in the United States.[44] We conclude that doctors are not

42 (1990) 8 BMLR 128.
43 Anonymous 'Doctors, Drivers and Confidentiality' (1974) 1 BMJ 399.
44 In *Crosby v Sultz* 592 A 2d 1337 (Pa, 1991) a suit against a doctor who allowed a diabetic patient to drive was rejected on the grounds that injuries inflicted on a person who could not be notified of the driver's condition were not foreseeable.

only protected against any action for breach of confidence by qualified privilege but also that they have a positive moral duty to inform the medical authorities at the vehicle licensing centre of patients who are a danger on the road by virtue of their medical condition; in the unlikely event of it being needed, *Egdell* would almost certainly be applied. This conclusion is supported by the advice proffered by the GMC in Appendix 2 of its current guidance on confidentiality which states that a doctor should make every effort to ensure that a patient who is considered to be unfit to drive understands his or her duty to inform the DVLA. The guidelines continue:

> If patients continue to drive when they are not fit to do so, you should make every reasonable effort to persuade them to stop. This may include telling their next of kin...If you do not manage to persuade patients to stop driving, or you are given or find evidence that a patient is continuing to drive contrary to advice, you should disclose relevant medical information immediately, in confidence, to the medical adviser at the DVLA. [45]

8.22 An interesting example of the problems posed was reported from New Zealand. There, a bus driver underwent a triple coronary bypass operation and was subsequently certified as fit to drive by his surgeon. His general practitioner, however, asked that his licence to drive be withdrawn and, furthermore, warned his passengers of their supposed danger. The practitioner's activities resulted in a report to the Medical Practitioners' Disciplinary Committee and a finding that he was: 'guilty of professional misconduct in that he breached professional confidence in informing lay people of his patient's personal medical history'. Dr Duncan sought judicial review of this decision. The High Court accepted the propriety of breaching medical confidentiality in cases of clear public interest, but refused the application on grounds which can be summed up: 'I think a doctor who has decided to communicate should discriminate and ensure the recipient is a responsible authority.'[46] Seldom can there have been a case which demonstrates the 'need to know' principle so forcibly.

Confidentiality and HIV infection

8.23 The spread of the human immunodeficiency virus has given rise to a host of problems related to confidentiality. Sexually transmitted diseases are not new to the medico-legal arena, but HIV and AIDS can be set apart for several reasons – not the least of which is the current absence of a cure; its relatively specific sexual connotation, together with its serious association with drug addiction, also open the door to considerable stigmatisation. Those who are found to be HIV-positive may be disadvantaged in a number of practical ways which have been discussed in chapter 2 and to which we refer again below;[47] all serve to fuel the concern which many such persons harbour as to the confidentiality of their status.

45 *Confidentiality* Appendix 2, paras 4–5.
46 *Duncan v Medical Practitioners' Disciplinary Committee* [1986] 1 NZLR 513 at 521, per Jeffries J.
47 See para 10.77 et seq.

8.24 Such concerns attract great sympathy, yet there are also social interests to be considered. The crucial dilemma here is whether relaxation of the confidentiality rule would lead to failure to seek advice and treatment and hence to the spread of the disease, or whether the imposition of absolute secrecy improperly denies others the opportunity to avoid the risk of exposure to infection or the benefits of early therapy where exposure has occurred.[48] Should a sexual partner be told of the risk if the patient himself declines to pass on the information? What is the situation if a person known to be infected is employed in circumstances in which he might expose others to the virus? The problem of confidentiality cannot, however, be settled by the balancing of conflicting private interests alone – the public health dimension has to be taken into account. AIDS is not, at present, a notifiable disease[49] – a dispensation which certainly helps to maintain confidentiality. The rationale given for this is that notifiability would inhibit persons from undergoing testing;[50] while some would doubt the validity of this, any public health 'risk' is justified on the grounds that, in the conditions of everyday social contact, HIV is transmitted only with great difficulty – if at all. As a result, it is government policy, supported by the majority of informed opinion, that any departure from the strictest anonymity in respect of HIV-related information must be subject to intense scrutiny.[51]

8.25 The English courts long ago declared their hand in weighting the balance between a strongly supported public policy in favour of freedom of the press against the need for loyalty and confidentiality with particular reference to AIDS patients' hospital records. In *X v Y*,[52] the names of two doctors being treated in hospital for AIDS were improperly disclosed; the health authority sought, and obtained, an injunction to prevent their publication by a newspaper. While holding that the health authority had not made out a case for forced disclosure of the source of the information, Rose J stated that such luck a second time was highly unlikely and that prison would be the probable consequence if the informer repeated his or her betrayal of confidence:

> The public in general and patients in particular are entitled to expect hospital records to be confidential and it is not for any individual to take it upon himself or herself to breach that confidence whether induced by a journalist or otherwise.[53]

8.26 The authority's action was not, as has been suggested, a 'cover-up' operation – the basic reasons underlying absolute confidentiality in AIDS-

---

48 Early intervention with combination therapy can help prevent maternal to fetal infection, see D Wilkinson et al 'Short Course Antiretroviral Regimens to Reduce Maternal Transmission of HIV' (1999) 318 BMJ 479. It can also help health care workers who have been exposed to the virus, P Eastbrook and G Ippolito 'Prophylaxis after Occupational Exposure to HIV' (1997) 315 BMJ 557.
49 Under the AIDS (Control) Act 1987, health authorities must provide reports to the responsible minister. The minister can also order hospitalisation and, if necessary, detention of sufferers: Public Health (Infectious Diseases) Regulations 1985, SI 1985/434.
50 M W Adler 'HIV, Confidentiality and a "delicate balance"' (1991) 17 J Med Ethics 196.
51 For a general overview of the ethical position, see R Gillon 'AIDS and Medical Confidentiality' (1987) 294 BMJ 1675.
52 [1988] 2 All ER 648, (1992) 3 BMLR 1.
53 [1988] 2 All ER 648 at 665, (1992) 3 BMLR 1 at 21, per Rose J.

related cases should be applied irrespective of the patient's calling. The decision can be justified medically on the grounds that the risks of a well-counselled physician passing the disease to a patient are, at worst, slightly more than negligible.[54] This is, however, an area in which the media are insatiable. A decade ago a rash of cases occurred in which the names of infected doctors was widely publicised in the press;[55] a number of letters from the health boards concerned testified to the fact that, given that the previous government policy required the boards to notify all patient contacts of such practitioners, it was virtually impossible to preserve anonymity.[56] Matters came to a head in the case of *H (a healthcare worker) v Associated Newspapers Ltd*.[57] This case was unlike any other in so far as the provisions of the Human Rights Act 1998 were in force at the time when the press sought either to name the health authority (N) for which H worked, or to disclose H's speciality and the approximate date when he became HIV positive. A fundamental tension of rights and interests therefore arose between, on the one hand, H's right to respect for his private life (Article 8) and, on the other, the right of the press to freedom of expression (Article 10). The issues were complicated by the fact that H, having received expert advice that the risks of exposure given his discipline were negligible, had challenged the existing government policy[58] that required a health authority to undertake a 'lookback exercise' to identify patients who had come into contact with HIV positive health workers. He would not, therefore, grant access to his patient records and sought injunctory relief to prevent any disclosure of his identity, discipline or the name of the health authority for which he worked. In defiance of an order that was given, the *Mail on Sunday* published a story from which clues to H's identity could be gleaned. The injunction was then varied to allow greater disclosure and a challenge was lodged in the Court of Appeal by H and N. In balancing the delicately poised issues surrounding the tensions between Articles 8 and 10, the Court of Appeal found some measure of support for both sides of the argument. First, the court reiterated the strong public interest in maintaining the confidentiality of health workers infected with HIV – to do otherwise, it was held, would simply deter others from coming forward, and this could be in no-one's interests. The injunction against naming H or N was, accordingly, upheld. However, the risk of H being thereby identified was insufficient to justify a continuing restriction on disclosure of his speciality – he was, in fact, a dentist. Such a constraint inhibited the airing of aspects of the debate which were of important public interest. Moreover, the court recognised the public interest in the new policy guidelines on recontacting patients and, with this in view, to this end, ordered that H should hand over his patient records once new

---

54   Worldwide there are only two reported instances of patients being infected by health care workers during clinical procedures, and in only one of these was the transmission route clear, see F Lot, J C Seguier, S Fegueux et al 'Probable Transmission of HIV from an Orthopaedic Surgeon to a Patient in France' (1999) 130 Ann Int Med 1, and C Ciesielski, D Marianos, C Y Ou et al 'Transmission of Human Immunodeficiency Virus in a Dental Practice' (1992) 116 Ann Int Med 798.

55   See eg the banner headlines in a quality newspaper: B Christie 'Hunt for AIDS Scare Patients' *Scotsman*, 27 May 1993, p 1. It seems that the doctor's name was published by the paper despite the fact that the Health Board intended to preserve anonymity.

56   Although this information need not be given 'face to face': *AB v Tameside and Glossop Health Authority* (1997) 35 BMLR 79, [1997] 8 Med LR 91.

57   [2002] EWCA Civ 195, (2002) 65 BMLR 132.

58   Health Service Circular *Guidance on the Management of AIDS/HIV Infected Health Care Workers and Patient Notification* (HSC 1998/226).

guidelines were in place (although these records should not be used without his permission or that of the court).

8.27 It is interesting to note that, as a result, the government's new proposals support lookback exercises only in very rare circumstances.[59] A major factor in this decision, beyond the scientific evidence of negligible risk in most cases, was the disproportionate negative public effect that previous exercises have had by way of unduly distressing sectors of the public. And, once again, the importance of maintaining the confidentiality of those with HIV is recognised.

8.28 Anyone infected with HIV constitutes an undoubted danger to his or her sexual partner, although the risk of transmission depends upon the nature of the sexual activity, the frequency and diversity of exposure and the extent to which precautions are taken. Counselling of HIV cases includes such information routinely, and patients are advised as to the need to disclose their status to those whom they might have put at risk of infection. It is unsurprising that there will be some patients who are not prepared to do so nor, indeed, to inform their general practitioners; the doctor is then faced with the problem of whether or not he, himself, should inform those with 'a need to know'. The GMC has advised doctors that:

> You may disclose information about a patient, whether living or dead, in order to protect a person from risk of death or serious harm. For example, you may disclose information to a known sexual contact of a patient with HIV where you have reason to think that the patient has not informed that person, and cannot be persuaded to do so. In such circumstances you should tell the patient before you make the disclosure, and you must be prepared to justify a decision to disclose information.[60]

8.29 Thus, passing information to a patient's spouse or other sexual partner in the absence of consent is allowable so long as every effort has been made to persuade the patient to do so and there is a serious and identifiable risk to a specific individual. The GMC concludes that the responsibility for any action taken is entirely that of the individual doctor – which tells us nothing as to how to construct that responsibility.

8.30 The Institute of Medical Ethics has advocated a relationship of mutual empowerment based on a balance between, on the one hand, the patient's proper power of decision making and, on the other, the doctor's exercise of clinical skills and, most importantly, of effective communication of information.[61] The ideal is that the person at risk should be able to make an informed choice whether or not to accept the risk and that this choice will be offered by the patient. In the exceptional case where the patient frustrates this policy, the doctor should, in the Institute's view, base his decision as to whether or not to breach confidentiality on the strength of his judgment that, by maintaining confidentiality, he can encourage the infected patient to

59 Department of Health *HIV Infected Health Care Workers: Consultation Paper on Management and Patient Notification* (2002), chapter 8.
60 GMC *Serious Communicable Diseases* (1997), para 22.
61 K M Boyd 'HIV Infection and AIDS: The Ethics of Medical Confidentiality' (1992) 18 J Med Ethics 173.

acknowledge his or her responsibility to respect the interests of others. In this respect, great importance is laid on whether or not the person at risk is also a patient of the doctor – the implication being that, in the first case, disclosure would be justified fairly easily but that confidentiality would be the better choice in the latter.

8.31 This may be a pragmatic solution, but it appears to us to be morally ambivalent. If it is medical beneficence to inform one's *patient* of a risk, it is scarcely justifiable to bask in the safety-net of confidentiality when one's duty of care is no more than indirect. A discussion based on moral principles, however, takes little account of the legal issues involved and it is arguable that a patient would have a right of action against a doctor who warned his or her spouse or other sexual partner of their potential risk. Despite the prima facie breach of confidence, a court would almost certainly balance the two private interests involved and hold that disclosure was justified by the intention to protect others from a possibly fatal risk. It is difficult to imagine a court awarding damages to such a plaintiff and there has been no decision directly in point taken in the United Kingdom. Conversely, it seems that there is a general common law duty and a statutory duty on the doctor in some parts of the United States and Canada to inform those at risk[62] – and the *Tarasoff* decision[63] which we discuss in chapter 21, could be taken as a pointer. A curious twist to this issue emerged in the remarkable Californian case of *Reisner*.[64] A young girl had been exposed to HIV infection through the transfusion of tainted blood. Neither she nor her parents were informed of this. Some years later she became intimate with a boyfriend, whom she infected with the virus. He raised a successful action for damages against the doctors for their failure to inform her, thereby subjecting him, as a foreseeable victim, to the risk of infection. This decision did not invoke the suggestion that the doctor had a duty to warn. It is not clear how a British court might react to a similar situation. The inference of a duty to care in respect of endangered third parties might be difficult to reconcile with existing notions in the United Kingdom. No duty to warn exists in the absence of a special relationship between the parties and it is difficult to see why the AIDS situation should constitute an exception to the general common law rule, in both England and Scotland, that there is no duty to rescue.[65] It is, however, possible that a doctor might even be held to have a *duty* – as opposed to mere justification – to warn a third party *who was also his patient*, as in this case there is a relationship which is sufficiently proximate to give rise to a duty of affirmative action.

8.32 It is impossible to leave the subject of confidentiality in HIV infection without mention of the specific problem of prisons – the environment could

---

62 In a number of American states specific statutory provisions impose a duty of disclosure on HIV positive persons to disclose their status to their partners: see J W Rose 'To Tell or Not to Tell: Legislative Imposition of Partner Notification Duties for HIV Patients' (2001) 22 J Legal Med 107. See also, D I Casswell 'Disclosure by a Physician of AIDS-related Patient Information: An Ethical and Legal Dilemma' (1989) 68 Can BR 225.

63 *Tarasoff v Regents of the University of California* 529 P 2d 55 (Cal, 1974); on appeal 551 P 2d 334 (Cal, 1976). Decisions following upon this include the contrasting cases of *Brady v Hopper* 751 F 2d 329 (1984) and *Peterson v State* 671 P 2d 230 (Was, 1983).

64 *Reisner v Regents of the University of California* 37 Cal Rptr 2d 518, (1995).

65 For further discussion, see A McCall Smith 'The Duty to Rescue and the Common Law' in M Menlowe and A McCall Smith (eds) *The Duty to Rescue* (1993) p 55.

have been designed for the spread of the condition and the consequences of disclosure of a positive status could be disastrous for the individual. A policy of confidentiality exists but, clearly, it is difficult, if not impossible, to maintain so long as positivity is associated with segregation, provision of personalised eating utensils and the like; there has also been some limited purposeful breaching of confidentiality in respect of a 'need to know' on the part of the staff.[66] Such potentials for disclosure discourage voluntary testing and counselling and serve as barriers to effective public health measures; they have been phased out since 1991. It has been shown that a guarantee of confidentiality results in a marked increase in identified positive subjects.[67] Such evidence tends to support the general national policy on confidentiality and HIV; at the same time, it cannot be denied that more prisoners are infected than are identified – the issue is, indeed, delicately balanced.

8.33 Finally, we discuss the issue of criminalisation of HIV transmission in chapter 2, but its relevance to confidentiality is shown in the means employed by the prosecution in the *Kelly*[68] case to secure conviction. Kelly had given a blood sample while in Glenochil prison as part of a research study into HIV prevalence in the institution. On discovering this, the prosecution sought, and received, a Sheriff warrant to gain access to confidential data from which to prove that the strain of virus with which Kelly was infected was also that contracted by his girlfriend. Serious concern has subsequently been raised as to the impact of such practices on uptake by research subjects in prisons.[69] It is not hard to see how such draconian measures in the name of one public interest may finish by thwarting another.

Confidentiality within the family

8.34 A narrower area of societal privilege lies within the family, where the doctor may be the first to recognise the signs of violence. The police are, in general, disinclined to interfere in cases of marital violence because of the unsympathetic reception they are likely to get from both sides in so doing. But this may not always be the case, and the doctor cannot be content to watch his patient suffer not only physical injury but also intense mental trauma. In the end, however, it is clear that an adult woman of sound mind is entitled to her autonomy; she has the opportunity of reporting to the police or, often more usefully, she has access to one of the many voluntary shelters which operate. She now has considerable protection under the law.[70] All the doctor can effectively do is to advise, and in this he may be able to help by arranging for treatment of the offender – 'wife battering' is markedly associated with alcoholism and neurotic symptoms in the husband.

66 T Groves 'Prison Policies on HIV under Review' (1991) 303 BMJ 1354. See also M Beaupré 'Confidentiality, HIV/Aids and Prison Health Care Services' (1994) 2 Med L Rev 149. The vexed question of the police's 'need to know' was discussed in J K Mason 'Recording HIV Status on Police Computers' (1992) 304 BMJ 995.
67 S A M Gore and A G Bird 'No Escape: HIV Transmission in Jail' (1993) 307 BMJ 147.
68 *HM Adv v Kelly* (23 February 2001, unreported), HCJ. The case has been discussed at para 2.72 et seq.
69 C Dyer 'Use of Confidential HIV Data Helps Convict Former Prisoner' (2001) 322 BMJ 633.
70 Family Law Act 1996, Part IV; Matrimonial Homes (Family Protection) (Scotland) Act 1981.

8.35 The position is different in the case of child abuse. Here the victim is defenceless and the victim is the patient. Parental autonomy must be forfeited on the grounds of impropriety while the doctor is covered, legally, by the doctrine of necessity – in this case to assume consent to disclosure by one who cannot give consent – and, professionally, by the advice of the GMC that disclosure in such circumstances is justified.[71]

8.36 In addition to legal problems, however, the doctor faces a clinical dilemma which, although less publicised, is of greater importance. The introduction of registers for infants at risk from violence and the obvious merit in nipping violence in the bud act as servo-mechanisms to one another. There is a real possibility that truly accidental injuries are being misdiagnosed, with a consequent reluctance on the part of parents to seek help for fear of being 'branded';[72] children may, therefore, actually suffer despite the doctor's concern for their safety. A case misdiagnosed as child abuse will cause considerable distress for those accused;[73] but, equally, a missed case which ends in murder can bring great recrimination on the doctor. The concern of the profession as to possible actions for defamation was certainly eased by the decision that a recognised caring authority may refuse to disclose the name of an informant.[74] In the end, however, such a right to or privilege of non-disclosure depends not so much on principles of confidentiality as on what lies in the public interest.[75]

8.37 Confidentiality between parent and child becomes further involved at teen age. Consent to treatment is discussed in detail in chapter 10; in the present context, we are concerned only with confidentiality and, particularly, with the doctor's relationship with the family. It is possible to conceive of other medical conditions which a minor might wish to conceal from his or her parents but, in practice, such conditions are likely to be limited to their sexual affairs.[76] As has already been indicated, young persons of both sexes do have intercourse and the doctor may be confronted by requests as to contraception or abortion by young girls or for treatment of venereal disease by minors of either sex. It is therefore unsurprising that the leading case to address the question of minors' rights to confidentiality – *Gillick*[77] – should concern contraception and has, in

---

71 *Confidentiality* (para 8.4 above) para 37c.
72 D M Wheeler and C J Hobbs 'Mistakes in Diagnosing Non-accidental Injury: 10 Years' Experience' (1988) 296 BMJ 1233. The European Court of Human Rights has now held that a means of determining allegations of negligence in this respect against local authorities must be available: *Z v United Kingdom* [2001] 2 FLR 612, (2002) 34 EHRR 3, overturning *X and others (minors) v Bedfordshire County Council* [1995] 2 AC 633, [1995] 3 All ER 353.
73 See two 'at-risk register' cases: *R v Norfolk County Council Social Services Department, ex p M* [1989] QB 619, [1989] 2 All ER 359; *R v Harrow London Borough Council, ex p D* [1990] Fam 133, [1990] 3 All ER 12, CA.
74 *D v National Society for the Prevention of Cruelty to Children* [1978] AC 171, [1977] 1 All ER 589, HL. Protection of the informant is guaranteed by law in places having compulsory reporting (eg Child Welfare Act 1977 (NSW)).
75 Contrast this with the non-medical case of *Interbrew SA v Financial Times Ltd* [2002] 1 Lloyd's Rep 542 (public interest in discovering iniquity overrode privilege against disclosing sources).
76 But see the case of Emma Hendry discussed below. *Inquiry into the death of Emma Jane Hendry* (15 January 1998, unreported), Glasgow Sheriff Court.
77 *Gillick v West Norfolk and Wisbech Area Health Authority* [1984] QB 581, [1984] 1 All ER 365; on appeal [1986] AC 112, [1985] 1 All ER 533, CA; revsd [1986] AC 112, [1985] 3 All ER 402, HL.

fact, been discussed under that head.[78] The twin issues of consent to treatment and right to privacy in young people are inextricably interwoven and, again, further discussion will be found elsewhere.[79] Here, we will attempt to limit discussion to those issues in the case which are specific to confidentiality.

8.38 From this point of view, the background to the *Gillick* decision is relatively simple, yet it represents the core of the case. As we have already suggested, contraception must be seen as sociologically preferable to abortion; even so, only a few young girls are likely to consent to their parents being told they are 'on the pill' and refusal to supply is unlikely to deter those who want sexual intercourse. On this basis, the doctor who secretly supplies contraceptives on request to a girl under the age of 16 is performing a duty to society. On the other hand, most would agree that parents have a right to know what is happening to their children and should, ideally, give consent to medical treatment irrespective of the minor's capacity to understand the complexities. It is, therefore, apparent that any entitlement to consent carries with it a simultaneous entitlement to confidentiality and vice versa. The House of Lords' solution of the problem is to be found in Lord Fraser's five criteria which have been recapitulated above[80] and which can be summarised as granting a right of confidentiality to the mature minor when the exercise of that right was in her best interests. It must, however, be emphasised that, throughout the case, an obligation was firmly imposed on the doctor to attempt to persuade the girl to inform her parents or to allow him to do so – that, in itself, constituting an important qualification of the normal rules of professional secrecy. Thus, despite the case seeming to represent a victory for the autonomy of youth, reliance on *Gillick* can still lead to unease on the part of both the doctor and the patient. On the one hand, the latter cannot know the former's intentions until *after* the consultation; on the other, the doctor must be prepared to justify his decision – but to whom and in what circumstances is left unstated. The decision to respect a minor's right to confidentiality may be a delicate one, and this is particularly so when drugs are prescribed. In one Scottish Fatal Accident Inquiry concerning a 14-year-old girl's death from an overdose of tricyclic antidepressants, a doctor's decision not to inform her parents of her treatment was considered to be perfectly correct. The patient's maturity was held to be such that her desire for confidentiality in relation to her parents had to be respected.[81]

8.39 The longest established family relationship is that of the spouse – what are his or her rights in both the positive and negative aspects of confidentiality? If the treatment is for a medical condition, a married person has the same rights to confidentiality in respect of the spouse as in respect of anyone else and, since the Abortion Act 1967 refers only to medical indications, this must apply to abortion. This can be implied also on legal grounds in that, since the husband has no right of veto either in Great Britain or in the United States[82]

---

78 See para 4.69 et seq above.
79 See 'Consent', para 10.25 below.
80 See para 4.71.
81 *Inquiry into the Death of Emma Jane Hendry* (15 January 1998, unreported), Glasgow Sheriff Court.
82 *Paton v British Pregnancy Advisory Service Trustees* [1979] QB 276, [1978] 2 All ER 987; confirmed in the US in *Planned Parenthood of Southeastern Pennsylvania v Casey* 112 S Ct 2791 (1992).

he similarly has no right to information, and it is not hard to think of instances where disclosure of an abortion to the spouse could be construed as being malicious.

8.40 The conditions are not quite so clear, however, when treatment of an individual is not primarily based on medical considerations but, at the same time, affects the whole family – effectively, this is a matter of sterilisation. Lord Denning was in no doubt in an early, minority, opinion that the surgeon should 'approach the spouse in order to satisfy himself as to consent'.[83] This must certainly be the case when genetic considerations are involved. Either or both parties may be contributing to a multifactorial trait; genetic counselling is impossible unless both husband and wife are involved. There is, however, less certainty when sterilisation is purely a matter of convenient family planning. On the face of it, there ought to be a consensual decision, but the twenty-first-century couple are not certainly going to be together until parted by death, religious differences may prohibit agreement and there must be times when one spouse feels compelled to act for his or her individual reasons. The doctor may rightly refuse to sterilise in the absence of consent to spousal consultation but he would, we believe, be acting correctly both in law and in ethics were he to do so; adults have a right to privacy and it could probably be left to the Divorce Court, as in *Bravery*, to decide whether such unilateral action rendered marriage intolerable. The matter has been discussed in greater detail in chapter 4. The very particular conditions attaching to genetic counselling are, similarly, addressed in detail in chapter 6.

Other special groups

8.41 Finally, there are many special groups which can be conceived of as raising particular problems in relation to medical confidentiality – those which spring to mind most readily are accused persons, prisoners and members of the armed forces. Accused persons are legally innocent and therefore have the same rights as any member of the public. The police surgeon must state that the result of his examination will be reported to third parties and cannot proceed if, as a result, consent to examination is refused. In the interests of justice, however, he may make, and transmit the results of, observations which need not be confined to purely visual impressions.[84] The doctor-patient relationship is complicated in respect of prisoners and confidentiality is best considered as part of the whole spectrum of prison medicine (see chapter 1). The relationship of medical officers in the armed forces to their individual patients is precisely the same as in civilian practice, with the proviso that the doctor's duty to society is accentuated when this is formulated as a duty to a fighting unit; eventually, the lives of many are dependent upon the health of individuals. There is thus a wider justification for disclosure than exists in civilian life and the serviceman has tacitly accepted this in enlisting; nevertheless, the principle of justification remains valid. Similar considerations apply, for instance, to doctors in medical charge of sports teams; the discussion has come full circle in that, basically, one's ethical standards depend upon one's definition of society.

83   *Bravery v Bravery* [1954] 3 All ER 59 at 67, [1954] 1 WLR 1169 at 1177, CA.
84   *Forrester v HM Advocate* 1952 JC 28.

8.42 Doctors employed by companies or other institutions to act as medical advisers on staff health also occupy a special position. A workplace doctor who is employed to carry out regular examinations on staff is bound by the terms of her contract to deliver information to the employer if this might have a bearing on the employer's business.[85] Moreover, such a doctor is not under a duty of care to a job applicant when assessing suitability for employment, even although it is reasonably foreseeable that the applicant might suffer economic loss if a careless error in assessment leads to the loss of a chance of employment.[86] It must now be stated explicitly before carrying out a pre-employment medical examination, or for fitness to work, that the results of that examination may be communicated to the employer and the written consent of the examinee should be obtained in the light of that information. Likewise, in the case of examinations carried out for insurance purposes, the doctor must obtain the positive agreement of the patient to waive the normal obligations of confidentiality within a 'need to know' formula. In the absence of such agreement, it is unlikely that the doctor engaged in industrial or insurance medicine could justify, on either ethical or legal grounds, a breach of a patient's confidence on the grounds that he, the doctor, owed a duty as an employee to his employer.

For the purposes of medical research

8.43 Information may be disclosed if necessary for the purposes of a medical research project which has been approved by a recognised ethical committee. The matter is included in the general discussion of medical research in chapter 19. Most controversially, s 60 of the Health and Social Care Act 2001 allows the Secretary of State to make provisions requiring or regulating the processing of patient medical data in their own medical interests or in the public interest, including research interests.[87] Regulations made under this Act state that:

> 'Anything done by a person, that is necessary for the purpose of processing patient information in accordance with these Regulations shall be taken to be lawfully done despite any obligation of confidence owed by that person in respect of it.'[88]

8.44 Inter alia, the Regulations allow confidential patient information to be processed with a view to (a) diagnosing communicable diseases and other risks to public health; (b) recognising trends in such diseases and risks; (c) controlling and preventing the spread of such diseases and risks; or (d) monitoring and managing – (i) outbreaks of communicable disease; (ii) incidents of exposure to communicable disease; (iii) the delivery, efficacy and safety of immunisation programmes; (iv) adverse reactions to vaccines and medicines; (v) risks of infection acquired from food or the environment (including water supplies);

---

85 *Kapfunde v Abbey National plc and Daniel* (1998) 46 BMLR 176.
86 Ibid.
87 These provisions only apply in England and Wales. The Confidentiality and Security Group for Scotland (CSAGS) produced its report of recommendations in April 2002, *Protecting Patient Confidentiality: Final Report* (2002) in which a more even balance between protecting individual rights to privacy and public interests in research is sought.
88 Health Service (Control of Patient Information) Regulations 2002, SI 2002/1438, reg 4.

(vi) the giving of information to persons about the diagnosis of communicable disease and risks of acquiring such disease. Note how these terms cover both public health measures and research ends. The wide-sweeping discretion of the Secretary of State has been criticised as unduly preferential of the amorphous and ill-defined 'public interest' compared to individuals' private interests in confidentiality of their medical data.[89]

8.45 Yet, there is evidence at common law of similar trends. In *R v Department of Health, ex p Source Informatics Ltd* the Court of Appeal was asked to rule on the legality of disclosing anonymised prescribing data to a firm that wished to sell them to pharmaceutical companies to assist in the marketing of their products.[90] Pharmacists had been asked to provide details of general practitioners prescribing habits, and all data were stripped of patient identifiers before being passed on. None the less, the Department of Health issued a policy statement to the effect that this practice was a breach of patient confidentiality; there was no provision for obtaining patient consent, nor could this be implied from the circumstances in which the information was originally generated. The Court of Appeal held, however, that there could be no breach of confidentiality because: '[t]he concern of the law here is to protect the confider's personal privacy. That and that alone is the right at issue in this case'.[91] In the Court's view, patient privacy was not under threat because there was no realistic possibility that patient identity could be revealed. Moreover, because the obligation of confidence binds in conscience as an equitable doctrine, and because a reasonable pharmacist's conscience 'would not be troubled by the proposed use made of patients' prescriptions',[92] such treatment of patient information was a fair use and entirely legal.

8.46 This decision challenges the law of confidence at its very core. On extremely uncertain legal authority, it shifts the basis of the duty of confidence from the public interest to the question of fairness of use. Furthermore, the Court saw fit to re-assess the basis upon which a duty will arise and how far it will extend, thereby conflating the establishment of a duty with its scope. Yet, while the former is clearly founded in equity in English law – where a proper role for the question of fairness might arise – the latter has traditionally been treated as a logically subsequent issue and not one that is bound up with notions of equity.[93] But, in light of the decision in *Source Informatics*, the

89 D Beyleveld 'How Not to Regulate in the Public Interest' (2001) 2 Genetics L Montr 5.
90 [2000] 1 All ER 786, (2000) 52 BMLR 65. For crticicism of both the trial court's ruling ([1999] 4 All ER 185, (1999) 49 BMLR 41) which was overturned, and that of the Court of Appeal, see D Beyleveld and E Histed 'Anonymisation is not Exoneration' (1999) 4 Med L Internat 69 and 'Betrayal of Confidence in the Court of Appeal' (2000) 4 Med L Internat 277.
91 Ibid, at All ER 797a.
92 Ibid, at All ER 796f.
93 For a legally enforceable right of confidentiality to arise several factors must be satisfied. First, the information must have the necessary quality of confidence about it; second, the information must be imparted in circumstances which import a duty of confidence; and finally, the information must be disclosed or used by the confidant without authority from the confider or without lawful excuse, as per the classic dicta of Megarry J in *Coco v A N Clark (Engineers)* (1969) 86 RPC 41. It is also probably the case that a form of detriment must be shown, although in personal information cases it is sufficient that the individual would rather that the information not be disclosed.

position now seems to be that there is no breach of confidence where there is no unfairness to the confider in a possible use of information, and this is so even when that use is unauthorised. This, however, goes against a number of established principles in this area of law. Existing precedents have made it clear that the duty of confidence rests on the basis of public interest and that, in large part, this also dictates the exceptions to the rule. Normally, information provided in confidence should not be used for any purpose that transgresses the legitimate boundaries of the consent of the confider and the onus has lain on those who would use the information either to obtain appropriate consent or to demonstrate that the particular use envisaged is in a public interest. However, the decision in *Source Informatics* indicates that the onus has shifted to the confider to show unfairness of use before an action will lie. Moreover, it removed the public interest requirement from the equation, and this is particularly disturbing because it also led the court to ignore the wider and longer term impact of its decision on the generality of public interest in maintaining confidences. Major difficulties now lie in the way of those who would explicitly object to such uses. On what legal basis might they do so? Arguably, the effect of *Source Informatics* is to reduce the individual's legal interest in his or her own information to no more than an interest in ensuring that anonymity is maintained. In so doing, other fundamental issues are ignored, including the role of consent in legitimising otherwise unacceptable uses of information, the concept of reasonable expectations of use and the importance of maintaining a prima facie respect for confidences.

CONFIDENTIALITY AND THE LEGAL PROCESS

8.47 Disclosure of confidential medical information as part of the legal process can be looked at in two main categories: statutory and non-statutory. Statutory disclosure presents no problem to the doctor, but is nevertheless showing signs of encroachment on traditional values. Thus, the original requirements for reporting by the doctor of infectious disease[94] or industrial poisoning[95] are clearly directed to the good of society. More recently, however, compulsory notification has become required more for statistical purposes[96] or for the protection of individuals by the state.[97] The two latter examples also exemplify the increasing acceptance of state control of the medical profession itself. Despite occasional protests at 'interference', most people would accept such regulations.[98]

8.48 It is to be noted that no immunity is granted to the doctor when a statutory duty is imposed on 'a person' to provide information. Such a situation arises, for example, under the Terrorism Act 2000, s 19, which places every person under an obligation to disclose to the police information connected with acts

---

94 Public Health (Infectious Diseases) Regulations 1988, SI 1988/1546.
95 Reporting of Injuries, Diseases and Dangerous Occurrences Regulations 1995, SI 1995/3163.
96 Abortion Regulations 1991, SI 1991/499; Abortion (Scotland) Regulations 1991, SI 1991/460.
97 Misuse of Drugs (Supply to Addicts) Regulations 1997, SI 1997/1001.
98 But some powerful objections can be raised. See, in particular, M Brazier and J Harris 'Public Health and Private Lives' (1996) 4 Med L Rev 171.

of terrorism. Opinion is divided, however, as to the working of the Road Traffic Act 1988 when, by virtue of s 172,[99] the doctor must provide on request any evidence which he has which may lead to the identification of a driver involved in an accident. The patient can scarcely expect the doctor to breach confidentiality; yet the doctor's liability under the law has been confirmed.[100]

8.49 There may, of course, be other times when the police would have an interest in access to medical records. Police engaged in the investigation of a serious arrestable offence may obtain a warrant to search for material which is likely to be relevant evidence. Under the Police and Criminal Evidence Act 1984,[101] magistrates cannot, however, issue a warrant to search for 'excluded material' which includes personal records relating to a person's physical or mental health and which are held in confidence; medical records are, therefore, excluded material. However, a constable may still apply to a circuit judge for an order to obtain such records. Not only must the court be satisfied of the need for access, but there must have been some statutory authority passed before the 1984 Act which would have authorised such a search. The Act illustrates some of the difficulties in applying an ethical principle by way of statute. Hospital notes are clearly excluded material and can, therefore, be withheld from the police irrespective of the purpose of their search. Thus, the police cannot obtain them even though their sole purpose is, for example, to establish the whereabouts of a potential murderer at a given time[102] – as Morland J said in *R v Cardiff Crown Court, ex p Kellam*:[103]

> Presumably Parliament considered that the confidentiality of records of identifiable individuals relating to their health should have paramountcy over the prevention and investigation of serious crime.

But one wonders if this was really in the contemplation of the legislature or of those who lobbied them so assiduously. Even so, a doctor who sees it as a public duty to co-operate with the police may produce such records[104] – provided, of course, that he is prepared to justify this later in a court of law or before his peers.

8.50 Other than by regulations, courts of law can compel the disclosure of medical material either through the production of documents or during evidence and cross-examination.

Disclosure of documents

8.51 A patient contemplating negligence proceedings against a doctor or a health authority will usually need access to his medical records so that his claim can be evaluated by his legal and medical advisers. Those in possession

---

99   As substituted by Road Traffic Act 1991, s 21.
100   *Hunter v Mann* [1974] QB 767, [1974] 2 All ER 414.
101   Section 9(1).
102   *R v Cardiff Crown Court, ex p Kellam* (1993) 16 BMLR 76. The court set aside the order to produce the documents 'with considerable reluctance'.
103   (1993) 16 BMLR 76 at 80.
104   *R v Singleton* [1995] 1 Cr App R 431, [1995] Crim LR 236.

of such records have been enjoined by the courts to act in a spirit of candour and not to resist disclosure – a course of action which might have the effect of delaying the resolution of a dispute and preventing a just outcome.[105] Failure to put one's 'cards on the table' can be met with an order for the discovery of documents under ss 32 and 34 of the Supreme Court Act 1981. Disclosure may be made to a medical expert or to the applicant's legal advisers. A plaintiff cannot engage in a general 'fishing expedition' to see whether he has a cause of action – an application must disclose the 'nature of the claim he intends to make and show not only the intention of making it but also that there is a reasonable basis for making it'.[106]

8.52 A person in possession of documents may be entitled to refuse disclosure on the grounds that it is not in the public interest to make the documents available.[107] This will rarely arise in medical negligence cases, but the court may·have to consider whether disclosure should be denied when there is a public health dimension to a case. This was the position in *Re HIV Haemophiliac Litigation*,[108] where the public interest in question was the confidentiality of policy documents relating to blood products policy. Similarly, in *AB v Glasgow and West of Scotland Blood Transfusion Service*,[109] the Court of Session would not order disclosure of the identity of a blood donor in an action resulting from the donation of contaminated blood – the pursuer's right to claim damages was not of such magnitude that it should take precedence over a material risk to the sufficiency of the national supply of blood for transfusion.

8.53 Court directions may also be made for the disclosure before trial of expert medical reports which it is proposed to bring in evidence. The exception to this policy once lay in cases involving a suggestion of medical negligence – the rationale being that parties should not have to disclose experts' reports which were directed to establishing liability rather than to the prognosis and quantum of damages.[110] Largely as a result of the unsatisfactory trial in *Wilsher*,[111] alterations were made to the Rules of the Supreme Court so as to bring medical negligence cases into line with others involving personal injury – prior disclosure was to become the norm rather than the exception. In general, *all* the cards must now be put down, not just those obviously concerned with the action; the current view is that the court can deal with problems of confidentiality relating to irrelevant conditions – such as a past history of sexually transmitted disease – by limiting disclosure to the other side's medical advisers who must respect medical confidentiality except where litigation is affected.[112] The whole tenor of the medical negligence case and its management have been reformed by the Woolf Report[113] which, we suggest, should be

---

105 *Naylor v Preston Area Health Authority* [1987] 2 All ER 353, [1987] 1 WLR 958, CA.
106 *Dunning v United Liverpool Hospitals Board of Governors* [1973] 2 All ER 454 at 460.
107 *Re EC (disclosure of material)* [1996] 2 FLR 725; [1997] Fam Law 160.
108 [1990] NLJR 1349.
109 1993 SLT 36, (1989) 15 BMLR 91.
110 *Rahman v Kirklees Area Health Authority* [1980] 3 All ER 610, [1980] 1 WLR 1244, CA.
111 *Wilsher v Essex Area Health Authority* [1987] QB 730, [1986] 3 All ER 80, CA.
112 *Dunn v British Coal Corpn* [1993] ICR 591, CA.
113 Lord Woolf *Access to Justice* (1996), chapter 15 (www.lcd.gov.uk/civil/finalfr.htm).

consulted in the original – it gives a major insight as to how the wind is blowing in this area. Disclosure of documents and information is, in any case, subject to what is commonly known as 'legal professional privilege' – a doctrine designed to allow the client unfettered access to his advisers. The concept is not without difficulties, of which the doctor should be aware. First, legal professional privilege is tightly defined and is likely to be overridden, whenever this is possible, in the interests of legal fairness.[114] Thus, disclosure of reports which are designed primarily for accident investigation and prevention and only secondarily for the purpose of seeking legal advice is likely to be ordered. It is clear that this gives rise to a conflict of interests. On the one hand, it could be held that the public good of preventive medicine must take second place to the threat of private litigation;[115] on the other, the imposition of professional privilege has, on occasion, been granted only reluctantly in that secrecy is inequitable to the person who suffers medical mishap.[116] Secondly, while professional privilege is there in order to allow the client to be uninhibited when approaching his legal advisers, there is no corresponding privilege to encourage a patient to be equally open in relation to his medical advisers. This was demonstrated forcefully in *W v Egdell*,[117] where it was concluded that a clear and important distinction was to be made between, on the one hand, instructions given to an expert and, on the other, the expert's opinion given in response to those instructions; the former was covered by legal professional privilege, while the latter was not. We have some difficulty in understanding how a question can be subject to absolute confidentiality while the answer is not; nevertheless, the ruling given at first instance was fully supported in the Court of Appeal. Thirdly, a request for information from a solicitor is not the same as an order of the court even though the conditions – eg that litigation is in progress – may seem similar; medical practitioners have been found guilty of serious professional misconduct for making such a mistake in good faith but in ignorance.[118] Finally, it is worth noting that, while the legal representative may, of course, withhold any documents to which professional privilege applies, the adversary may have advantage of these if they are disclosed in error and it is not obvious that privilege has not been waived.[119]

8.54 The doctor in the witness box has absolute privilege and is protected against any action for breach of confidence. The Earl of Halsbury LC provides the highest possible authority: the immunity of the witness in court 'is settled

---

114 Professional privilege is, in a sense, a product of the adversarial system of presenting evidence and is less likely to be upheld when proceedings are more akin to inquisitorial. The classic example of the latter is the case brought under the Children Act 1989 or in wardship proceedings: *Oxfordshire County Council v M* [1994] Fam 151.

115 *Waugh v British Railways Board* [1980] AC 521, [1979] 2 All ER 1169. The order to disclose may extend to specific accident report forms which might well be thought to be privileged (*Lask v Gloucester Health Authority* (1985) Times, 13 December). Failures, mistakes and 'near-misses' must now be reported to the National Patient Safety Agency (www.npsa.org.uk). How the intended 'no blame' culture will meld with the growing taste for litigation has yet to be seen – and the Chairman of the Agency, himself, appears uncertain: G Watts 'Coaxing Doctors to Confess' (2001) 323 BMJ 890.

116 *Lee v South West Thames Regional Health Authority* [1985] 2 All ER 385, [1985] 1 WLR 845, discussed also in 'Disclosure of Documents by Doctors' (1985) 290 BMJ 1973.

117 [1990] Ch 359, [1989] 1 All ER 1089.

118 See 'Medical Confidence and the Law' (1981) 283 BMJ 1062.

119 *Pizzey v Ford Motor Co Ltd* [1994] PIQR P15, CA.

in law and cannot be doubted'.[120] This privilege extends to pre-trial conferences and Scottish precognitions, the exception being that a privileged communication must not be made maliciously.[121] Judges may go to great lengths to protect the witness but, when so ordered, the doctor is bound to answer any question which is put to him;[122] refusal to answer in the absence of the court's discretion to excuse a conscientious witness must expose the doctor to a charge of contempt – and the court will take precedence even when there is a statutory obligation of secrecy.[123] In some European countries, however, the obligation to maintain confidentiality extends to the courtroom.

PATIENT ACCESS TO MEDICAL RECORDS

8.55 The right to see one's own medical records has now been accepted, even though there was earlier opposition to the principle on the part of some medical practitioners. In the past, a patient has had no access to such records, although access could be obtained by a plaintiff in a legal action. Concern over the storage of information on computers gave rise to a movement for allowing public access to personal records, and it was this general development which led to the first dent in this specific form of medical secrecy. The Council of Europe's Data Protection Convention required the recognition of a right of access to personal data stored in computer banks; this gave rise to the Data Protection Act 1984, which has now been replaced by the Data Protection Act 1998. The 1998 Act was a response to the EU Data Protection Directive of 1995 and, significantly, covers not only computerised data but also data which is manually stored in filing systems. The subject has a right to information as to the purposes for which data about him are being processed and the persons who will have access to them. In other respects, the new scheme of protection is broadly similar to that which was introduced in 1984: the protection of those about whom computerised information is stored lies in preventing the holding of inaccurate information or of concealing the fact that information is stored at all. Subject to a fee, a patient has the right to be told by the 'registered data user' – who could be any health caring body holding records – whether any such information is held and to be supplied with a copy of that information; the patient may then ensure its accuracy. There is provision, which is generalised throughout this area of legislation, for doctors to prevent access to information that is 'likely to cause serious harm' – a condition which is left undefined.

8.56 Subsequent to the passing of the 1998 Act further regulations have been implemented that are designed to deal directly with the management of personal data in the health care context. The Data Protection (Subject Access

---

120 In *Watson v M'Ewan* [1905] AC 480 at 486, HL.
121 *AB v CD* (1904) 7 F 72, per Lord Moncrief. This is the Court of Session stage of *Watson v M'Ewan*. The same applies in other Commonwealth countries. See *Hay v University of Alberta Hospital* [1991] 2 Med LR 204 (QB, Alberta), in which it was held that the plaintiff had no right to withhold consent to pre-trial discussions by the defendants with his medical attendants.
122 The exception to this requirement being disclosure of a source of information for which special rules apply (Contempt of Court Act 1981, s 10).
123 *Garner v Garner* (1920) 36 TLR 196.

Modification) (Health) Order 2000 restricts patients' rights over their medical data in a number of respects.[124] For example, the Order provides further exceptions to the subject's access rights in the case of personal data consisting of information about the subject's physical or mental health or condition – which will include most information held by NHS bodies. These are: (a) where permitting access to the data would be likely to cause serious harm to the physical or mental health or condition of the data subject or any other person (which may include a health professional); and (b) where the request for access is made by another on behalf of the data subject, such as a parent for a child, access can be refused if the data subject had either provided the information in the expectation it would not be disclosed to the applicant or had indicated it should not be so disclosed, or if the data were obtained as a result of any examination or investigation to which the data subject consented on the basis that information would not be so disclosed.[125]

8.57 An important development in allowing patient access to personal medical information came with the Access to Medical Reports Act 1988. The relevant reports are limited to those prepared by a doctor who has clinical charge of the patient and intended for direct supply to the patient's employer, prospective employer or to an insurance company (s 2). Reports by doctors who have had only a casual, non-caring professional association with the patient are excluded. Such reports as are included have always been subject to the patient's consent but the applicant must now positively seek such consent and must inform him of his rights to access (s 3). The patient can see the report before it is sent and, unless he has done so, issue of the report must be delayed for three weeks (s 4). He has the right to ask the doctor to alter anything that he feels is inaccurate and he may add a dissenting statement should the doctor refuse to do so (s 5). Once again, access may be withheld if disclosure would cause serious harm to the patient's physical or mental health – or to that of any other person – but, in those circumstances, the patient may withdraw his consent. The Access to Health Records Act 1990 provided access rights to manual files subject to certain limits at the discretion of the health care professional. However, since the passing of the Data Protection Act 1998, the terms of this Act are now redundant except in so far as they relate to a deceased person.[126]

8.58 It was at one time feared that patients' access to their records would lead to less frank opinions being expressed in hospital notes and to greater reliance on oral communication between health carers; the potential disadvantage to the patient is, then, evident – in the event of a change of location, his accompanying medical documents will be of less value to his new health carers than ought to be the case.[127] There is, however, no hard

---

124 The Data Protection (Subject Access Modification) (Health) Order 2000, SI 2000/413.
125 Before deciding whether these exemptions apply a data controller who is not a health professional must consult the health professional responsible for the clinical care of the data subject; or if there is more than one, the most suitable available health professional. If there is none, a health professional with the necessary qualifications and experience to advise on the matters to which the information requested relates must be consulted.
126 Access to Health Records Act 1990, s 3(1)(f); Data Protection Act 1998, Sch 16.
127 For a relatively early debate, see A P Bird and M T I Walji 'Our Patients Have Access to Their Medical Records' (1986) 292 BMJ 595; A P Ross 'The Case Against Showing Patients Their Records' (1986) 292 BMJ 578.

evidence that rights of access have affected medical practice adversely and, certainly, an impressive body of research can be quoted which stresses their practical advantages. There is even a movement towards giving patients physical possession of their records,[128] a facility made all the easier with the advent of swipe-card technologies.[129] The ownership of the contained intellectual property – ie the copyright – is held by the person who has created the notes or his employer, and not by the subject of those notes. The patient is therefore unlikely ever to have a successful property claim over his or her notes.[130]

THE PATIENT'S REMEDIES

8.59 For many years the law was slow to develop a remedy for breach of confidentiality in spite of its clear recognition of such breaches as a proper basis for legal action. This latter was considerably clarified and its requirements set out in the House of Lords decision in *A-G v Guardian Newspapers (No 2)*.[131] It is likely that a patient would be able to claim damages for improper disclosure of information about his health even if he suffered no financial loss as a result; this is almost implicit from *X v Y*,[132] in which it was said that 'No one has suggested that damages would be an adequate remedy in this case' – the clear implication being that they were there for the taking in the absence of a better solution. They might, of course, be only nominal; on the other hand, they might be considerable were it possible to show loss of society, severe injury to feelings, job loss, interference with prospects of promotion or the like. However, a distinction has to be made between actions in contract and in tort. Thus, in the trial stage of *W v Egdell*,[133] Scott J discarded the possibility of damages for shock and distress – other than nominal – largely on the particular facts of the case but also because it was based on breach of an implied contractual term;[134] the decision has no relevance to an action in tort.

8.60 The matter first came before the courts in Scotland over a century ago in two similarly named and well-known decisions, the *AB v CD* cases. In the earlier *AB v CD*,[135] the Court of Session considered an action for damages brought against a doctor who had disclosed to a church minister that the pursuer's wife had given birth to a full-term child six months after marriage. The court held that there was a duty on the part of the doctor not to reveal confidential information about his patient unless he was required to do so in

---

128 See M L M Gilhooly and S M McGhee 'Medical Records: Practicalities and Principles of Patient Possession' (1991) 17 J Med Ethics 138.
129 G Eysenbach 'Recent Advances: Consumer Health Informatics' (2000) 320 BMJ 1713.
130 In *R v Mid Glamorgan Family Health Services, ex p Martin* [1995] 1 All ER 356, [1995] 1 WLR 110, the court accepted that medical records were owned by the health authority, and a similar view was taken by the High Court of Australia in *Breen v Williams* (1996) 138 ALR 259.
131 [1990] 1 AC 109, [1988] 3 All ER 545.
132 [1988] 2 All ER 648, (1992) 3 BMLR 1.
133 [1990] Ch 359, [1990] 1 All ER 835.
134 Quoting *Bliss v South East Thames Regional Health Authority* [1987] ICR 700.
135 (1851) 14 D 177.

court or if disclosure were 'conducive to the ends of science' – but, in that case, identification of the patient would be improper. In the second *AB v CD*,[136] the pursuer was seeking a separation from her husband. Having been examined by the defender at the suggestion of her lawyers, she was later examined by the same doctor who was then acting on behalf of her husband. The doctor disclosed to the husband certain information he had obtained in the course of his first examination and the wife argued that this constituted a breach of confidence. Once again, the court accepted that there was a duty on the part of a doctor not to disclose confidential information about his patient but stressed that not every disclosure would be actionable. As Lord Trayner pointed out,[137] some statements may be indiscreet but not actionable; there might be, for example, an actionable breach if the disclosure revealed that the patient was suffering from a disease which was a consequence of misconduct on his part.[138] In fact, disclosure of the background to the illness may be of greater importance than the disclosure of illness itself.

8.61 This really amounts to no more than saying that the patient is entitled to protection against defamatory statements, a protection which is hardly adequate. In both English and Scots law, the patient is not being defamed if what the doctor says is true.[139] Moreover, in England, the law of slander (spoken defamation) requires that the plaintiff should be able to prove special damage – which is, essentially, pecuniary damage – except in those limited cases of slander which are actionable per se. The protection provided by the law of defamation in cases where the doctor verbally reveals confidential information to another is, thus, unlikely to be significant.

8.62 Qualified privilege should, in the absence of malice or reckless unconcern as to the truth of the statement, be a defence against any action for breach of confidence, as it already is in the law of defamation – qualified privilege in this context being but another expression of the 'need to know' principle. This is the ultimate determinant of ethical disclosure. The profession is not, or should not be, so concerned with the niceties of intra-professional relationships or of communication in good faith with paramedical or other responsible groups; what really matters is irresponsible gossip – and, here, the ultimate deterrent is the Professional Conduct Committee of the General Medical Council. Punitive action against a doctor is unlikely to be of material benefit to a wronged patient, but it is still a very effective preventive weapon.

8.63 More immediately effective is injunctory relief – a common remedy in this area of law – and one which has been extended considerably in recent

---

136 (1904) 7 F 72.
137 (1904) 7 F 72 at 85.
138 Scots law provides a potential remedy in the form of the *actio iniurarium*. For comments on the possible application of this delict in cases of breach of confidence, see Scottish Law Commission, Memorandum No 40 *Confidential Information* (1977) p 28.
139 The doctor's most likely exposure to defamation is, of course, on an intra-professional basis. For a brief overview, see Legal Correspondent 'Doctors and Defamation' (1985) 290 BMJ 1342.

years.[140] Given that the real fear at the core of a breach of confidence action is public disclosure of private facts, the 'gagging order' may, in many cases, be more desirable to the plaintiff than damages. Often, of course, damage has already been done because information has been made public, but the utility of this remedy never the less endures, as cases such as *X v Y* and *H v Associated Newspapers* demonstrate.[141]

8.64 We have seen, particularly in *X v Y*, that the courts have no great love for the 'media mole' in the hospital and, while there is deep-rooted respect for freedom of the press, there is an equally strong realisation of the need for integrity within the whole of the hospital hierarchy – and not only from those governed by professional codes of conduct; *how* the press comes by its information may be of considerable relevance as to how the courts interpret the media's use of it. Matters came to a head recently in the House of Lords in *Ashworth Hospital Authority v MGN Ltd*.[142] Here, a newspaper published an article that included verbatim extracts from the medical records of a multiple murderer detained in a secure hospital who was, at the time, engaged in a well-publicised hunger strike. The hospital applied for, and obtained, an order to the newspaper to explain how they obtained their information and to identify any employee of the hospital or intermediary who was involved in its acquisition. The newspaper appealed, largely on the basis of the Contempt of Court Act 1981, s 10 which holds that no correspondent can be compelled to disclose his sources of information unless it is established that disclosure is necessary in the interests of justice; the order, it was contended, was neither proportionate nor necessary on the facts of the case. The House held, however, that security of hospital records – and particularly those of a security hospital – was of such importance that it was essential that the source should be identified and punished in order to deter similar wrongdoing in the future – that was what made the order necessary, proportionate and justified. The importance of the hospital informational security as opposed to the privacy concerns of the individual was emphasised in that the fact that the subject himself had been in contact with the press was immaterial to the House's decision. And Lord Woolf could not resist pointing to the fact that the disclosure was made worse by the fact that it had been purchased by a cash payment! From our point of view, perhaps the most important aspect of *Ashworth* lies in its clear message that every member of a hospital's staff is subject to the same duty of confidentiality to the patients.

Confidentiality and death

8.65 Final reflection might, appositely, be concerned with death. The Declaration of Sydney says: 'I will respect the secrets which are confided in me, even after the patient has died.' This view is also endorsed by the GMC in its guidance to doctors:

---

140 *Venables v News Group Newspapers Ltd, Thompson v News Group Newspapers Ltd*, [2001] 1 All ER 908 (indefinite injunction against the entire world in respect of the identification of child killers).

141 See *X v Y*, para 8.25 above, and *H (a healthcare worker) v Associated Newspapers*, para 8.26 above.

142 [2001] 1 All ER 991, [2001] 1 WLR 515, CA; affd [2002] UKHL 29, [2002] 1 WLR 2033, HL.

You still have an obligation to keep personal information confidential after a patient dies. The extent to which confidential information may be disclosed after a patient's death will depend on the circumstances. These include the nature of the information, whether that information is already public knowledge or can be anonymised, and the intended use to which the information will be put. You should also consider whether the disclosure of information may cause distress to, or be of benefit to, the patient's partner or family.[143]

8.66 In practice, this is incapable of fulfilment as to the cause of death since a death certificate, signed by a doctor, is a public document – albeit, available only on payment of a fee for a copy. Once again, the spectre of AIDS raises its head in so far as confidentiality may, here, be as important to the bereaved family as to the deceased during life. It is certain that death certification in the United Kingdom – and probably elsewhere – is inaccurate, but this can only be compounded if doctors take it upon themselves to 'sanitise' the diagnosis so as to spare the relatives distress and, maybe, harm. A government publication[144] suggested that certificates relating to recent deaths should be available only to those who may legitimately want them – but such measures are unlikely to achieve strict confidentiality.[145] The dilemma of conscience for doctors is acute in many types of death which carry a social stigma but, pending an alteration in the law, we find it hard to accept that doctors should be encouraged to falsify facts which are attested to be 'true to the best of my knowledge and belief'. Our major concerns here, however, are, first, with conditions discovered after death and, secondly, with the circumstances leading to death. The legal position is that, as the confidence is prima facie a personal matter, the legal duty ends with the death of the patient, although it has been suggested that 'Equity may impose a duty of confidence towards another after the death of the original confider ... the question is not one of property ... but of conscience'.[146] Elsewhere, as in the Netherlands, access to medical information is regarded as a personal right that is not inherited by the deceased relatives.[147] In the UK, however, as we have seen, the provisions of the Access to Health Records Act 1990 continue to apply to deceased persons.

8.67 In professional ethical terms, there can be no doubt that a post-mortem report merits the same degree of confidentiality as does the report of the clinical examination; insurance companies and the like have an obvious interest in its content but their right to disclosure is the same as the right to discovery of hospital records – in the absence of a court order, consent to disclosure from the next of kin of the deceased is essential.

---

143 *Confidentiality*, para 8.4 above, para 40.
144 *Registration: A Modern Service* (Cm 531).
145 M B King 'AIDS on the Death Certificate: The Final Stigma' (1989) 298 BMJ 734.
146 See *Morison v Moat* (1851) 9 Hare 241; affd (1852) 21 LJ Ch 248, quoted by R G Toulson and C M Phipps *Confidentiality* (1996), paras 13–17. However, any action for breach of confidence before the death of the patient could be transmitted to the executor.
147 C Ploem 'Medical Confidentiality after a Patient's Death' (2001) 2 Med Law 215.

8.68 But has the public any rights to details of the medical history of the dead?[148] While the principle remains irrespective of personalities, this is essentially a problem of public figures – and it is remarkable how rapidly professional ethics can be dissipated, say, in describing to the media the wounds of President Kennedy or the psychiatric history of the principals in any *cause célèbre*. The former physician to President Mitterand of France faced professional disbarment, a fine and up to one year's imprisonment for publishing his book, *Le Grand Secret*, immediately after the President's death in January 1996. The book detailed Mitterand's long battle with cancer throughout his Presidency which had been hidden from the French public. A Paris court banned further sales of the book only days after its release, but the affair caused a storm of controversy over the appropriate balance between the public's 'right to know' and the individual's 'right to privacy'.[149] It is easy to say 'History will out, let it be sooner than later' but it is less easy to decide at what point revelations become history. As we indicate above, the GMC has suggested that whether or not disclosure after death will be improper depends, inter alia, on the nature of the information given, the extent of previous publication and the time elapsed since death – as to the last, the Council rightly will not specify a number of years, merely remarking that a doctor who discloses such information without the consent of a surviving relative may be required to justify his action. Moreover, a bark in this context carries a bite – no less a person than a former editor of the British Medical Journal has been taken to task for reporting information concerning the health of a well-known, albeit controversial, general after his death.[150]

8.69 Respect for the privacy of the dead seems reasonable – particularly when children or, especially, spouses are alive.[151] The Human Genetics Commission, for example, has endorsed the principle of respect for persons, both living and dead. It advocates something akin to a balance of factors similar to that offered by the GMC in determining when, if ever, genetic information can be derived from a deceased person: 'The seeking of DNA information for a good reason may justify the intrusion into the privacy of the dead, whereas seeking it purely for the purposes of sensational disclosure would not provide justification.'[152] The Department of Health has adopted a similar sensitive approach in its draft guidance on the import and export of body parts, requiring that all samples, whether taken from persons alive or dead, be anonymised to preserve confidentiality.[153] The courts, for their part, may apply the principles of medical confidentiality by insisting that an order imposing anonymity in judicial proceedings should remain in force

---

148 See S E Woolman 'Defaming the Dead' 1981 SLT 29.
149 See A Dorozynski 'Mitterand Book Provokes Storm in France' (1996) 312 BMJ 201.
150 S Lock and J Loudon 'A Question of Confidence' (1984) 288 BMJ 123, 125.
151 The courts are, however, concerned for a balancing of interests between those of the bereaved and of freedom to publish. See *Re X (a minor) (wardship: restriction on publication)* [1975] Fam 47, [1975] 1 All ER 697.
152 Human Genetics Commission *Inside Information: Balancing Interests in the Use of Personal Genetic Data* (2002), para 4.71.
153 Department of Health *Draft Code of Practice on the Import and Export of Human Body Parts* (2002), para 15.

after the subject's death in cases of major sensitivity – such as those involving declarations as to the withdrawal of treatment from the incompetent.[154] Not only does this appear logical but post-mortem publicity may, in turn, raise questions as to the ethics of previous non-disclosure. It has, for example, been seriously argued that Lord Moran invited criticism not so much for his disclosures after the death of Winston Churchill[155] as for his failure to draw attention to the physical state of his patient during life. Which brings us back almost to where we started – to the dilemma of the doctor's relationship to his patient vis-à-vis society.

---

154 *Re C (adult patient: publicity)* [1996] 2 FLR 251 – though this may not hold if the public interest dictates otherwise. For the balance of private and public interest and the imposition of anonymity in general, see *Re G (adult patient: publicity)* [1995] 2 FLR 528.
155 Lord Moran *Winston Churchill: The Struggle for Survival, 1944-1965* (1966).

9 Medical negligence

9.1 Medical negligence is more than a matter between two parties – it is also a political issue. There is concern in both medical and governmental circles over the growing incidence of personal injury actions against doctors and over the cost to the health system of compensating the victims. It is pointed out that medical negligence actions are destructive of trust in a doctor-patient relationship and distort the practice of medicine in an over-cautious direction. From the doctor's point of view, the prospect of being sued in the event of making a mistake is stressful and demoralising. Many of those working outside medicine may face such a prospect in the course of exercising their profession but, in the case of the doctor, the fundamentally hazardous nature of the work, combined with the demanding and fraught conditions under which it has to be performed, makes the possibility of error and subsequent legal action very strong indeed. Legal action is, thus, a very real risk for the medical practitioner[1] and it would be surprising if litigation at this level did not seriously compromise medical morale. Funding bodies might expect to find the picture equally bleak. £373m was paid by the NHS in compensation for medical negligence in the year 1999-2000.[2] When one adds such correlates as the fact that, for settlements up to £50,000, the cost of reaching the settlement are greater than the damages awarded in over 65% of cases, it is unsurprising that the Heath Service is currently facing a bill for medical negligence of about £2.6bn. The rate of new claims rose seven-fold between 1995-96 and 1999-2000[3] and it seems that only radical methods can contain the flood. What lies behind this increase in litigation? First and foremost, modern medicine is intrusive and the chances of injury are therefore increased. Secondly, the current social climate encourages expectations of cure. When these are not met, the culture of consumerism – fuelled by a press eager to disclose wrongdoing – advocates the allocation of blame and the seeking of compensation. Finally, intolerance of error, and of the fact that any complex

---

1   38 claims were launched against GP members of the Medical Protection Society in 1989; the comparable figure in 1998 was 500: C Dyer 'GPs Face Escalating Litigation' (1999) 318 BMJ 830.
2   (2001) 170 Bulletin of Medical Ethics 2.
3   National Audit Office *Handling Medical Negligence Claims in England* (2001), HC-403.

human endeavour will inevitably involve the making of mistakes, means that the public increasingly insists on accountability and, if possible, the pinning of an adverse outcome on some identifiable human agency. The public's tolerance for accidents has been greatly reduced – somebody, somewhere must be made to answer for what has happened.[4] This has created a climate which is excessively stressful for social workers, teachers and, to a marked extent, health care staff.

9.2 The current system comes under attack from all quarters.[5] Patients, it is argued, have great difficulty seeking compensation for negligently inflicted medical injury and may face awesome hurdles in the process of suing a doctor. Only a relatively small proportion of the victims of medical negligence bring an action for damages and, currently, 76% of these fail.[6] Those claimants who do succeed may have to wait a considerable time before damages are paid; the average time from claim to payment of damages above £10,000 is now some five and half years. The current system thus seems to the patient to be flawed: he or she has suffered an injury and yet it may be difficult to recover what is seen as his or her due. Moreover, having failed to get any explanation as to what went wrong and having been offered no apology, the patient may have felt that there was no alternative to bringing an action. Both sides – if one should talk of sides in this matter – see the current system of compensation for medical injury as being slow, traumatic and socially expensive, one from which it is often only the lawyers who profit. There must be a better way of dealing with this issue – a way which provides reasonably efficient compensation without destroying the doctor-patient relationship and without diverting health-targeted funds from hospitals and patient care into legal fees and damages.

9.3 A widely canvassed alternative to negligence actions, which commands much support, is to introduce a system of no-fault compensation, which will provide for the making of awards to injured patients irrespective of the requirement of proving fault on the part of medical personnel.[7] Such a scheme has operated in New Zealand since 1974 as part of an overall no-fault compensation scheme and, even if it has had its opponents, it has now survived into its fourth decade – albeit in a scaled-down model.[8] In the medical context,

---

4   Compare the assessment in A Merry and A McCall Smith *Errors, Medicine and the Law* (2001).
5   Not least from the senior judiciary: Lord Woolf 'Clinical Negligence: What is the Solution? How Can We Provide Justice for Doctors and Patients?' (2000) 4 Med L Internat 133.
6   See n 3 above.
7   For early surveys of the alternatives to fault-based compensation, see the discussion of New Zealand, Swedish and German schemes, in D Giesen *International Medical Malpractice Law* (1988) p 529. The New Zealand scheme is discussed by J Fleming *The Law of Torts* (9th edn, 1998) p 449 et seq; see also, S A M McLean 'Liability Without Fault – the New Zealand Experience' [1985] J Soc Welfare Law 125. For the Swedish system, see C Oldertz 'The Swedish Patient Insurance System – 8 Years of Experience' (1984) 52 Med-Leg J 43.
8   Criticisms included those of unacceptably low levels of compensation, high cost to the taxpayer and the removal of deterrents to safety practices in the workplace. On the last of these, see A Lewis 'No Fault Liability – Thirty Years of Experience in New Zealand' (1996) 15 Med & Law 425. The current legislation is to be found in the Accident Rehabilitation and Compensation Insurance Act 1992 as amended in 1993.

however, the New Zealand claimant must still establish that the injury resulted from 'medical or surgical misadventure', a requirement which has caused difficulties in distinguishing between those conditions which result from the physiological progress of a medical condition and those which are genuinely the result of misadventure occurring in the course of treatment. A considerable body of case law is devoted to determining just when a complication following upon a medical procedure is so rare as to amount to a misadventure.[9] Thus, it will be seen that such schemes do not do away entirely with all the difficult issues of foreseeability and causation which dog the operation of conventional tort law. It is, perhaps, significant that organisations such as the British Medical Association, whose primary concern as a trade union is for the interests of the profession, have consistently supported the introduction of a no-fault based system into the United Kingdom.[10] Under the scheme proposed by the BMA, compensation would be available for medically-induced injury but would exclude those injuries which were not avoidable through the exercise of reasonable care. The concept of negligence is therefore effectively preserved, although it would undoubtedly be easier to establish; moreover, there would be no inference of 'fault' of quite the same nature as arises in a tort-based system. A no-fault system of compensation has also been the preferred option in the Report of the Royal College of Physicians on the subject.[11]

9.4 For a variety of reasons, predominantly those of cost, the government has not supported the movement and a Private Member's Bill aimed in that direction was defeated in Parliament.[12] The government's attitude has not, however, been one of total inaction and the Department of Health has encouraged discussion of ways by which to make compensation more readily available and less costly.[13] The role of arbitration in helping to reduce the time and expense involved in meeting a claim for medical injury has attracted official attention.[14] A suggested scheme involved a panel of three arbitrators – composed of one doctor nominated by each litigant and a lawyer chairman – which would work entirely on paper and which would, therefore, avoid the cost of court proceedings and witnesses' time. Some objections to this are foreseen; in particular, it might be difficult to avoid the need for the examination of experts in certain cases of special complexity.

9   The issue was fully discussed by K Oliphant 'Defining "Medical Misadventure": Lessons from New Zealand' [1996] 4 Med L Rev 1. Oliphant suggested that in a possible British scheme, medical misadventure should be equated with 'treatment error', a concept which should include errors which have occurred in spite of the exercise of reasonable skill on the practitioner's part.

10 BMA *Report of the BMA No Fault Compensation Working Party* (1987); since when, the Representative Body has recommended a no-fault scheme annually.

11 *Compensation for Adverse Consequences of Medical Intervention* (1990).

12 National Health Service (Compensation) Bill 1991. The case against no-fault compensation is summarised by B Capstick, P Edwards and D Mason 'Compensation for Medical Accidents' (1991) 302 BMJ 230.

13 The administration of civil justice was, of course, thoroughly considered and overhauled as a result of Lord Woolf's Report *Access to Justice* (1996). The application to medical negligence is discussed further below.

14 Department of Health *Arbitration for Medical Negligence in the National Health Service* (Discussion Paper, 1991).

9.5 The argument in favour of retaining the present system for compensating the victims of medical accident or negligence can be couched in positive as well as negative terms. One is based on the deterrent value of the law of tort, the view being taken that to remove the threat of litigation will affect adversely the care with which doctors treat their patients. There is certainly some evidence that doctors are more cautious when they are aware of the Damoclean possibility of legal action; surveys undertaken in the United States indicate that successful litigation provokes greater care – at least in the realm of diagnosis.[15] Yet there are other ways of deterring carelessness. It may be that the extensive powers of the General Medical Council to deal with doctors who fail to live up to an expected standard of competence which are now under consideration will prove a more effective incentive to maintain high standards of practice.[16] Until such time as the new regulations come into force, the GMC's power to protect the public against sub-standard practice remains grounded in the Medical (Professional Performance) Act 1995.[17] A major invocation of these powers was evident in the proceedings against the Bristol thoracic surgeons who were found to have had what can only be described as an unacceptable mortality rate in paediatric operations.[18] One of the surgeons involved was removed from the register and the other was banned from paediatric heart operations for a period of three years.[19] The political ramifications of this case have been extensive and self-regulation of the medical profession is now, itself, subject to supervision.[20] The establishment of a clear, effective and patient-friendly system of investigating grievances might do more than satisfy those potential litigants whose principal goal is to find out what went wrong and to get an apology; it might also form a valuable base in a system of professional audit.

9.6 The power of deterrence is also qualified by the financial realities of the system in the United Kingdom. In this country, outwith private practice, the doctor has no direct contract with the patient and medical damages are usually underwritten by the state;[21] if one adds to these the surrealistic conditions surrounding legal aid – under which it may be economically preferable to settle an action out of court rather than to win a contested action – it becomes possible to raise an argument that the doctor in the United Kingdom is exposed to too little by way of stricture.

9.7 The question of compensation for medical injury in the United Kingdom has had a number of official airings. It was discussed many years ago as a

---

15   P M Danzon *Medical Malpractice* (1985) esp ch 1.
16   The subject has been discussed in Chapter 1. Basically, the only grounds for removing a doctor from the medical register will be that his or her fitness to practice is impaired: Draft Medical Act (Amendment) Order 2002, c 10.
17   Explained in GMC *GMC's Performance Procedures* (1997).
18   For which, see Bristol Royal Infirmary Inquiry (I Kennedy, chairman) *Learning from Bristol: The Report of the Public Inquiry into Children's Heart Surgery at the Bristol Royal Infirmary 1984-1995* (2001) (www.bristol-inquiry.org.uk/).
19   C Dyer 'Bristol Doctors found Guilty of Serious Professional Misconduct' (1998) 316 BMJ 1924.
20   National Health Service Reform and Health Care Professions Act 2002, ss 23-27.
21   Health Service Trusts are now insured through the National Health Service Litigation Authority. See National Health Service Litigation Authority Regulations 1995, SI 1995/2801.

special issue by the Royal Commission on Compensation for Personal Injury (The Pearson Commission),[22] which concluded that there were insufficient grounds for introducing no-fault compensation schemes. More recently, Lord Woolf addressed the matter in his wide-ranging investigation into the operation of the system of civil justice. Lord Woolf singled out medical negligence as an area for special consideration on the grounds that it was in respect of these claims that civil justice was 'failing most conspicuously'.[23] This failure was demonstrated by a variety of factors, including an unacceptable delay in the resolution of cases and a success rate which was lower than that in other personal injury litigation. The report suggested that the system could be improved by a better complaints procedure and by extending the jurisdiction of the Health Service Ombudsman to include complaints against the clinical expertise of NHS staff, both of which suggestions have been acted upon.[24] Lord Woolf was also concerned to establish what he described as a 'climate of change' that is marked by greater openness. One possible way of achieving this would be by making it incumbent upon doctors to inform patients if there has been an act or omission on their part which may have caused injury. It was questioned whether this duty already existed at common law, but Lord Woolf did not favour the imposition of this obligation on the grounds that the sensitive nature of the relationship between doctor and patient precluded it. He did, however, suggest that the GMC might explore ways of clarifying the responsibilities of the doctor in terms of candour,[25] and he also favoured the wider use of mediation schemes. It would seem, though, that, in spite of tinkering at the margins of the problem, the victims of medical negligence will have to continue to seek compensation through a fault-based tort system. Their ability to do so, however, currently depends to a very great extent on the availability of legal aid. There are indications that this may eventually be withdrawn in favour of a contingency fee system – a development attributable to the reluctance of the government to continue to fund what it sees as a cost ineffective system of compensation.[26] In the following sections, we analyse the operation of the existing system and the rules it has developed for the adjudication of such claims.

9.8 Placing a limit on medical accidents – if that were possible – would, of course, simultaneously limit their costs, even if no change were made to the system of compensation or to the rules surrounding the bringing of claims. There has been a greatly increased awareness of the scale of medical accidents in recent years and this has been accompanied by a more sophisticated approach to their understanding and prevention.[27] Studies of the occurrence of such

---

22 Cmnd 7054-1, 1978.
23 *Access to Justice: Final Report to the Lord Chancellor on the Civil Justice System in England and Wales* (1996) 15.2.
24 For the increased powers of the Health Service Ombudsman, see Health Service Commissioners (Amendment) Act 1996.
25 See L Beecham 'GMC approves new Ethical Guidelines' (1998) 316 BMJ 1556.
26 Lord Chancellor's Department Consultation Paper *Access to Justice with Conditional Fees* (1998) 3.15. The 1998 cost of legal aid in England and Wales for medical negligence cases was £27m.
27 See, for example, Institute of Medicine *To Err is Human* (2000), a document which sets ambitious targets for the reduction of the number of adverse events resulting in patient injury. This is an American study, and rather different considerations apply in the United Kingdom. For a United Kingdom perspective, see K G Alberti 'Medical Errors: a Common Problem' (2001) 322 BMJ 501.

events have concluded that the incidence of medical errors is unacceptably high and that many of these errors are potentially avoidable.[28] In the United Kingdom, this new approach has resulted in a number of initiatives within the NHS, including the setting up of a National Patient Safety Agency, the aim of which will be to enable safe systems to be installed and to encourage a system of error reporting which will assist in the avoidance of future accidents.[29] The shift to a safety-orientated approach to medical injury will require the placing of less emphasis on blame, in favour of an approach which encourages safer practices. The proponents of such systems believe that in the long run this approach will reduce the level of patient injury and control the cost of medical error far more effectively than will litigation or any system of punishment of those who make errors.

THE BASIS OF MEDICAL LIABILITY

9.9 Most claims in respect of medical injury are brought in tort, that is, on the basis of a non-contractual civil wrong. The reason for this is that, within the NHS, patients are not in a contractual relationship with the doctor treating them. In the private sector, by contrast, there will be a contractual relationship and it is, therefore, possible to bring an action for damages in contract. In practice, there is very little difference between the two remedies,[30] although the law of contract may provide a remedy for an express or implied warranty given by a doctor.[31] In a Canadian case, *La Fleur v Cornelis*,[32] the court held that a plastic surgeon was bound to an express contractual warranty that he had made to the patient. This warranty arose when he was unwise enough to say: 'There will be no problem. You will be very happy.' This sort of case will be comparatively unusual and, for all practical purposes, any discussion of medical negligence can confine itself to liability under the law of torts, in which the first question to be asked is: whom do we sue?

9.10 A medical injury may have been caused to the plaintiff by any one or more of the health care personnel who have treated him. Locating negligence may be simple in some cases but, in others, the patient may have to choose the responsible party from a fairly large group, which may include a general practitioner, a hospital consultant, other hospital doctors and the nursing staff. Locating the specific act of alleged negligence which caused the injury may also involve a degree of disentanglement.

---

28 R M Wilson, W B Runciman, R W Gobberd et al 'The Quality in Australian Healthcare Study' (1995) 163 Med J Australia, 458. On reporting considerations, see W Runciman, A Merry and A McCall Smith 'Improving Patients' Safety by Gathering Information' (2001) 323 BMJ 298

29 The direction of official thinking was indicated by the Department of Health document, *An Organisation with a Memory. Report of an Expert Group on Learning from Adverse Events within the NHS* (2000).

30 For a useful discussion of the distinction between contractual and tortious remedies in this context, see M A Jones *Medical Negligence* (2nd edn, 1996) pp 19–21.

31 An issue which arose in *Thake v Maurice* [1986] QB 644, [1984] 2 All ER 513; revsd [1986] QB 644, [1986] 1 All ER 479.

32 (1979) 28 NBR (2d) 569, NBSC; discussed by Jones, n 30 above.

The plaintiff may proceed directly against the doctor in question if an allegation is made of negligence on the part of a general practitioner. The general practitioner in the United Kingdom is solely responsible for the treatment of his patients and there can be no question of responsibility being imposed on a health authority unless the authority has intervened in the practitioner's treatment of his patient – all partners in a practice may, however, be liable for the actions of one of their number. The general practitioner must have approved indemnity cover,[33] which will normally be by way of membership of a medical defence society, to whom he will refer any claim against him; the society then advises him and undertakes the defence or settlement of the claim. General practitioners are not covered by the NHS indemnity which applies to hospital doctors[34] unless a claim arises in respect of work undertaken under a health authority contract. A general practitioner will be vicariously liable for the negligence of staff employed by him – nurses, receptionists etc – but not for the acts of a locum tenens or a deputising doctor who will, normally, be insured independently.[35]

9.11 The position is different if the alleged negligence occurs after the general practitioner has referred the patient for further treatment within the NHS. If the negligent act is committed by a health service employee, the patient then has the choice of proceeding either against the individual he feels has been negligent, or against the health authority or trust, or against both in a joint action. In practice, many actions are brought against the health authority or trust on the grounds of convenience. The liability of the authority or trust may be based on either of two grounds: (1) the duty of a hospital to care for patients; or (2) the vicarious liability of a health authority for the negligence of its employees.

9.12 There has been some doubt as to whether a hospital owes a non-delegable duty to use skill and care in treating its patients.[36] This has been addressed in some Commonwealth jurisdictions which have a somewhat different form of health care delivery to that existing in the United Kingdom. Thus, in the Australian case of *Ellis v Wallsend District Hospital*,[37] the majority held that there was a non-delegable duty in those cases where patients were permitted to go directly to the hospital for treatment and advice; no such duty would exist where the hospital merely provided services which a doctor could use to treat his own patients.[38] By contrast, the Ontario Court of Appeal has found that the hospital's duty extends no further than employing competent staff.[39] The minority view was, however, that hospitals, to a growing extent, hold out to the public that they provide medical treatment and emergency services

---

33 National Health Service Act 1977, s 43C inserted by Health Act 1999, s 9.
34 See para 9.15 below.
35 There was no vicarious liability for the negligence of a locum tenens in the Canadian case of *Rothwell v Raes* (1988) 54 DLR (4th) 193.
36 For discussion, see A M Dugdale and K M Stanton *Professional Negligence* (3rd edn, 1998) para 22.20; M Jones *Medical Negligence* (2nd edn, 1996) p 404.
37 (1989) 17 NSWLR 553, CA.
38 The matter was also pronounced upon, obiter, by the High Court of Australia in *Commonwealth v Introvigne* (1982) 56 ALJR 749 and *Kondis v State Transport Authority* (1984) 154 CLR 672, 55 ALR 225.
39 *Yepremian v Scarborough General Hospital* (1980) 110 DLR (3d) 513.

– and that the public increasingly relies upon them to do so; Blair JA, in expressing this view, drew upon the evolution of the law in England which he thought supported the view that the hospital could be personally liable for negligent treatment in certain circumstances.[40] The English case of *Wilsher*[41] could have provided an ideal ground to decide the matter but the issue was not raised by the plaintiffs; nevertheless, the possibility clearly remains open – it was said that:

> I can see no reason why, in principle, the health authority should not be [directly] liable if its organisation is at fault.[42]

9.13 The point is of some importance, particularly in respect of staff whose group or personal cover may be less comprehensive than is that of the professions, and the issue does, in fact, seem to have been decided in the ratio of *Re R (a minor) (No 2)*. Here it was said:

> Although it is customary to say that a health authority is vicariously liable for breach of duty if its responsible servants or agents fail to set up a safe system of operation in relation to what are essentially management as opposed to clinical matters, this formulation may tend to cloud the fact that in any event it has a non-delegable duty to establish a proper system of care just as much as it has a duty to engage competent staff and a duty to provide proper and safe equipment and safe premises.[43]

9.14 The discussion is, however, relatively sterile in the case of hospital doctors, the vast majority of whom are direct employees of the NHS. The health authority is, therefore, clearly liable for their negligence under the principle of vicarious liability. This provides that an employer is liable for his employee's negligent acts, provided that the employee is acting within the scope of his employment. It should be borne in mind that the employer may still be held vicariously liable even if the employee acts in direct contradiction of his employer's instructions or prohibitions.[44] The vicarious liability of hospitals throughout their hierarchy has been clearly established for half a century[45] and requires no further discussion.

9.15 The costs, especially to young doctors, of being members of a defence society have increased so dramatically that those who are working in the National Health Service have had to be subsidised by the authorities. Crown immunity has been extended to NHS doctors, dentists and community physicians since January 1990[46]

---

40 (1980) 110 DLR (3d) 513 at 579.
41 *Wilsher v Essex Area Health Authority* [1987] QB 730, [1986] 3 All ER 801, CA; revsd [1988] AC 1074, [1988] 1 All ER 871, HL, discussed below at para 9.52.
42 [1987] QB 730 at 778, [1986] 3 All ER 801 at 833, per Browne-Wilkinson V-C.
43 *Re R (a minor) (No 2)* (1997) 33 BMLR 178 at 197, CA, per Brooke LJ – a case including inadequate hospital communications.
44 R F V Heuston and R A Buckley *Salmond and Heuston on the Law of Torts* (20th edn, 1992) p 460.
45 *Roe v Minister of Health; Woolley v Ministry of Health* [1954] 2 QB 66; *Hayward v Board of Management of the Royal Infirmary of Edinburgh* and *Macdonald v Glasgow Western Hospitals Board of Management* 1954 SC 453. For discussion, see M A Jones *Medical Negligence* (2nd edn, 1996) pp 392 et seq.
46 See now Department of Health *NHS Indemnity – Arrangements fo Clinical Negligence Claims in the NHS* (1996) Cat No 96 HR 0024.

and, as a result, the entire costs of negligence litigation are now borne by the Health Service itself – though there is, of course, nothing to stop a plaintiff suing an individual doctor. One consequence is that health authorities may feel obliged to settle cases on the grounds that this is the cheapest, if not the fairest, option; moreover, there is a strong suspicion that compensation for the injured may be bought at the expense of limitations in treatment facilities for other patients – but this is, perhaps, to take too pessimistic a view and, in practice, the load is now spread in that all trusts are encouraged to make use of the mutual insurance offered by the Clinical Negligence Scheme for Trusts operated by the National Health Service Litigation Authority.[47]   It is to be noted that the scheme as it relates to individual doctors applies *only* to services provided within the NHS; doctors should, therefore, retain cover for any private or 'good Samaritan' work – and, indeed, for medico-legal activity.

WHAT CONSTITUTES NEGLIGENCE?

9.16 In determining whether there has been negligence in medical treatment, the courts pursue the same line of inquiry as they pursue in any other similar claim: did the conduct of the defendant amount to a breach of the duty of care which he owed to the injured plaintiff? Expressed somewhat differently, this amounts to asking whether the standard of the treatment given by the defendant fell below the standard expected of him by the law and whether there was, therefore, any fault in the legal sense. Fault remains the theoretical underpinning of the law in this area until such time as strict liability may be imposed.

9.17 It is scarcely necessary to point out that the concept of medical negligence has undergone a dichotomy over the last 20 years. On the one hand, we have the standard line of cases in which there has been a technical failure or misadventure – in other words, those that are associated with medical treatment in one form or another. There has, however, been a rapid growth in accusations of negligence arising before treatment was started – these have become known as information disclosure cases which are based on the rights of the patient to make an informed choice as to his or her treatment. The principles underlying the tort of negligence are similar in both situations. None the less, the latter has developed a jurisprudence of its own which is best discussed under the heading of 'consent' – for which, see chapter 10. Here, for the moment, we confine discussion to the established field of medical misadventure.

9.18 In either situation, a major difficulty for any plaintiff lies in the burden which falls upon him to prove that the defendant's negligence caused his injury. This is often a difficult burden to discharge and, indeed, suggestions have been made that the patient attempting to succeed in an action against a doctor should face a heavier burden in establishing his case than is required in any other personal injury litigation. There is an indication that this occurs in practice in so far as payment is made in some 30-40% of medical cases as compared with 86% in the general run;[48] the figures may, however, conceal

---

47   NHS (Clinical Negligence Scheme) Regulations 1996, SI 1996/251 made under National Health Service and Community Care Act 1990, s 21.
48   M A Jones 'Medical Negligence – the Burden of Proof' (1984) 134 NLJ 7, quoting the Pearson Report (para 9.7).

more than a simple cause and effect phenomenon. The legal foundation for this view, which was put forward by Lawton LJ,[49] may be tenuous and it was, in fact, strongly opposed in *Ashcroft*;[50] nevertheless, it is certainly true that there has been a degree of policy-based judicial reluctance to award damages against doctors.[51] In *Dwyer v Roderick*,[52] May LJ suggested that it would be:

> to shut one's eyes to the obvious if one denied that the burden of achieving something more than the mere balance of probabilities was greater when one was investigating the complicated and sophisticated actions of a qualified and experienced [inter alia] doctor than when one was enquiring into the inattention of the driver in a simple running down action.[53]

9.19 At the same time, the courts have not been insensitive to the plaintiff's difficulties in a medical negligence case. The correctives applied have been the occasional invocation of the principle of res ipsa loquitur or, as in *Clark v MacLennan*,[54] an attempt to shift the burden of proof to the defendant. The observations of Kilner Brown J in *Ashcroft* on this point are revealing:

> When an injury is caused which never should have been caused, common sense and natural justice indicate that some degree of compensation ought to be paid by someone. As the law stands, in order to obtain compensation an injured person is compelled to allege negligence against ... a person of the highest skill and reputation.[55]

We return to res ipsa below.[56]

The reasonably skilful doctor

9.20 There have been many judicial pronouncements by the courts on the standard of care which is expected of the doctor. As early as 1838 we see Tindall CJ ruling that:

> Every person who enters into a learned profession undertakes to bring to the exercise of it a reasonable degree of care and skill. He does not undertake, if he is an attorney, that at all events you shall gain your case, nor does a surgeon undertake that he will perform a cure; nor does he undertake to use the highest possible degree of skill.[57]

An echo of this is to be found in *R v Bateman*,[58] where the court explained that:

---

49 In *Whitehouse v Jordan* [1980] 1 All ER 650 at 659.
50 *Ashcroft v Mersey Regional Health Authority* [1983] 2 All ER 245 at 247, per Kilner Brown J.
51 See, now, the Lord Chief Justice, writing extra-judicially: Lord Woolf 'Are the Courts Excessively Deferential to the Medical Profession?' (2001) 9 Med L Rev 1.
52 (1983) 127 Sol Jo 805, CA.
53 But one doubts if this would, or should, apply 20 years later.
54 [1983] 1 All ER 416.
55 [1983] 2 All ER 245 at 246.
56 See para 9.61 et seq.
57 *Lanphier v Phipos* (1838) 8 C & P 475 at 478.
58 (1925) 94 LJKB 791 at 794, [1925] All ER Rep 45, CCA.

If a person holds himself out as possessing special skill and knowledge, by and on behalf of a patient, he owes a duty to the patient to use due caution in undertaking the treatment ... The jury should not exact the highest, or very high standard, nor should they be content with a very low standard.

9.21 The doctor is thus not expected to be a miracle-worker guaranteeing a cure or a man of the very highest skill in his calling. What standard then is he expected to meet? McNair J provides us with the classic answer to this question in *Bolam v Friern Hospital Management Committee*:[59]

The test is the standard of the ordinary skilled man exercising and professing to have that special skill. A man need not possess the highest expert skill at the risk of being found negligent. It is a well-established law that it is sufficient if he exercises the ordinary skill of an ordinary man exercising that particular art.

Nevertheless, he *is* professing a particular skill and, in the immortal words of McNair J, the test of that skill 'is not the test of the man on the top of the Clapham omnibus because [that man] has not got this special skill'.[60]

9.22 The doctor having that degree of competence expected of the ordinary skilful doctor sets the standard. He is the practitioner who follows the standard practice of his profession – or, at least, follows practices that would not be disapproved of by responsible opinion within the profession; he has a reasonably sound grasp of medical techniques and is as informed of new medical developments as the average competent doctor would expect to be. The circumstances in which a doctor treats his patient will also be taken into account. A doctor working in an emergency, with inadequate facilities and under great pressure, will not be expected by the courts to achieve the same results as a doctor who is working in ideal conditions.[61] This was alluded to by Mustill J in *Wilsher*, where he said that, if a person was forced by an emergency to do too many things at once, then the fact that he does one of them incorrectly 'should not lightly be taken as negligence'.[62]

9.23 The reasonably skilful doctor has a duty to keep himself informed of major developments in practice but this duty obviously cannot extend to the requirement that he should know all there is to be known in a particular area of medicine. In the case of *Crawford v Board of Governors of Charing Cross Hospital*[63] the plaintiff had developed brachial palsy as a result of his arm being kept in a certain position during an operation. Six months prior to the operation an article had appeared in the *Lancet,* pointing out just this danger but the anaesthetist against whom negligence was being alleged had not read the article in question. The Court of Appeal eventually found in favour of the anaesthetist, Lord Denning stating that:

---

59 [1957] 2 All ER 118 at 121, [1957] 1 WLR 582 at 586.
60 A test approved by the Privy Council: *Chin Keow v Government of Malaysia* [1967] 1 WLR 813.
61 This is in accordance with the general principle in the law of torts that errors of judgment are more excusable in an emergency: *The Metagama* (1927) 138 LT 369 at 370.
62 [1987] QB 730 at 749, [1986] 3 All ER 801 at 812.
63 (1953) Times, 8 December, CA.

it would, I think, be putting too high a burden on a medical man to say that he has to read every article appearing in the current medical press; and it would be quite wrong to suggest that a medical man is negligent because he does not at once put into operation the suggestions which some contributor or other might make in a medical journal. The time may come in a particular case when a new recommendation may be so well proved and so well known, and so well accepted that it should be adopted, but that was not so in this case.[64]

9.24 Failure to read a single article, it was said, may be excusable, while disregard of a series of warnings in the medical press could well be evidence of negligence. In view of the rapid progress currently being made in many areas of medicine, and in view of the amount of information confronting the average doctor, it is unreasonable to expect a doctor to be aware of every development in his field. At the same time, he must be reasonably up to date and must know of major developments. Hindsight is, of course, a harsh judge; yet, in a number of HIV-related cases, the courts have indicated that doctors could not have been expected to have known of a risk at a time when its significance was only just being established.[65] The practice of medicine has, however, become increasingly based on principles of scientific elucidation and report – the so-called 'evidence based medicine' – and the pressure on doctors to keep abreast of current developments is now considerable. It is no longer possible for a doctor to coast along on the basis of long experience; such an attitude has been firmly discredited not only in medicine but in many other professions and callings.

Usual practice

9.25 The 'custom test' – the test whereby a defendant's conduct is tested against the normal usage of his profession or calling – is one that is applied in all areas of negligence law. The courts have given expression to this test in the medical context in a number of decisions. In the important Scottish case of *Hunter v Hanley*, for example, there was a clear endorsement of the custom test in Lord Clyde's dictum:

> To establish liability by a doctor where deviation from normal practice is alleged, three facts require to be established. First of all it must be proved that there is a usual and normal practice; secondly it must be proved that the defender has not adopted that practice; and thirdly (and this is of crucial importance) it must be established that the course the doctor adopted is one which no professional man of ordinary skill would have taken if he had been acting with ordinary care.[66]

---

64   (1953) Times, 8 December, CA.
66   *Dwan v Farquhar* [1988] Qd R 234. In this case the risk of HIV transmission through blood transfusions was discussed in an article published in March 1983; there was no negligence in respect of a transfusion given in May of the same year. See also *H v Royal Alexandra Hospital for Children* [1990] 1 Med LR 297; M A Jones *Medical Negligence* (2nd edn, 1996) p 117.
66   1955 SC 200 at 206. The rigid simplicity of Lord Clyde's definition was defended in an anonymous article, 'Medical Negligence: *Hunter v Hanley* 35 Years On' 1990 SLT 325. *Hunter* was specifically approved by Lord Scarman in *Maynard v West Midlands Regional Health Authority* [1985] 1 All ER 635, [1984] 1 WLR 634. For a useful discussion of custom in a medical context, see *E v Australian Red Cross Society* (1990–91) 99 ALR 601 at 647 et seq.

9.26 This attractively simple exposition of the law, however, conceals a hurdle at the outset. It may, in many cases, be possible to prove that there is a 'usual and normal practice' – this is particularly so if there are guidelines covering a procedure, a ploy which is increasingly used in UK legislation[67] and which might be seen as being helpful to the plaintiff.[68] On the other hand, there will obviously be disagreement as to what is the appropriate course to follow in a number of medical scenarios. In some circumstances, the existence of two schools of thought may result in more than one option being open to a practitioner. If this is so, then what are the liability implications of choosing a course of action which a responsible body of opinion within the profession may well reject? Precisely this question arose in *Bolam*,[69] where the plaintiff had suffered fractures as a result of the administration of electro-convulsive therapy without an anaesthetic. At the time, there were two schools of thought on the subject of anaesthesia in such treatment, one holding the view that relaxant drugs should be used, the other being that this only increased the risk. In this case, the judge ruled that a doctor would not be negligent if he acted 'in accordance with the practice accepted by a responsible body of medical men skilled in that particular art'. Negligence would not be inferred merely because there was a body of opinion which took a contrary view. Subsequent cases confirmed this approach. In *Maynard v West Midlands Regional Health Authority* the trial judge had preferred an alternative medical approach to that which had been chosen by the defendant, notwithstanding the fact that this latter course found support in responsible medical opinion; both the Court of Appeal and the House of Lords confirmed that this was an unsatisfactory way of attributing negligence.[70] As a corollary to this, the plaintiff will have failed to discharge the burden of proof if the court is unable to select between two possible explanations.[71]

9.27 *Bolam* has been the object of sustained criticism from those who object to the implication that the medical profession itself determines what is an acceptable level of care.[72] Critics persistently argue that doctors themselves should not determine whether conduct is negligent; this should be a matter for the courts. In fact, courts had on occasion made precisely this point themselves[73] and a number of judges in the English High Court have not been afraid to attack the traditional view. In *Smith v Tunbridge Wells Health Authority*,[74] an action based on failure of information disclosure, for example, the judge applied *Bolam* but, despite the existence of a competent body of opposing

---

67 B Hurwitz 'Clinical Guidelines and the Law' (1995) 311 BMJ 1517.
68 These have not proved to be as productive of litigation as might be expected: A I Hyman, J A Brandenburg, S R Lipsitz et al 'Practice Guidelines and Malpractice Litigation: a Two-Way Street' (1995) 122 Ann Int Med 450.
69 [1957] 2 All ER 118, [1957] 1 WLR 582.
70 [1985] 1 All ER 635, [1984] 1 WLR 634. *Maynard* was followed in *Hughes v Waltham Forest Health Authority* [1991] 2 Med LR 155, in which the court emphasised that the fact that a surgeon's decision was criticised by other surgeons did not amount *in itself* to an indication of negligence.
71 *Harrington v Essex Area Health Authority* (1984) Times, 14 November.
72 Particularly in the Commonwealth: *Reibl v Hughes* (1980) 114 DLR (3d) 1; *Rogers v Whittaker* (1992) 109 ALR 625, [1993] 4 Med LR 79. And see, in general, 'informed consent' para 10.99 below.
73 See Lord Irvine 'The Patient, the Doctor, their Lawyers and the Judge: Rights and Duties' (1999) 7 Med L Rev 255.
74 [1994] 5 Med LR 334.

opinion, held that the decision not to do so was neither reasonable nor responsible. Nevertheless, there had been no high level judicial attack on the *Bolam* custom test in the Commonwealth until the High Court of Australia broke down the doors in the controversial information disclosure case of *Rogers v Whittaker*:[75]

> In Australia, it has been accepted that the standard of care to be observed by a person with some special skill or competence is that of the ordinary skilled person exercising and professing that special skill. But that standard is not determined solely or even primarily by reference to the practice followed or supported by a responsible body of opinion in the relevant profession or trade.

9.28 The High Court of Australia has a reputation for creativity; would the English courts, with their rather more conservative reputation, follow suit? An answer – even if a hesitant one – came in the House of Lords decision in *Bolitho v Hackney Health Authority*,[76] a case regarded by some commentators as representing a significant nail in *Bolam*'s coffin. *Bolitho* arose out of a failure on the part of a hospital doctor to examine and intubate a child experiencing respiratory distress. Negligence derived from a failure to attend was not disputed; however, the problem of causation still remained. Expert evidence was led by the plaintiff to the effect that a reasonably competent doctor would have intubated in such circumstances. The defendant, however, had her own expert witnesses prepared to say that non-intubation was a clinically justifiable response. The defendant argued that, had she attended the child, she would not have intubated her and her failure to attend would not, therefore, have made any difference to the outcome. The House of Lords accepted the truth of this evidence. The causation issue, here, is important from the jurisprudential aspect in so far as it was made clear that, while the *Bolam* test had no relevance as to the doctor's intention, it was central to the collateral question – would she have been negligent in failing to take action? – in other words, *Bolam* was attached to the question of causation when, in reality, it is concerned only with standards of care. As a result, given that she had responsible support, the action failed on both counts. However, the particular significance of *Bolitho* lies in the House of Lords's support for the Court of Appeal's departure from the certainties of *Bolam*. Rather than accepting a 'body of opinion' simply because it was there, Lord Browne-Wilkinson held that the court must, in addition, be satisfied that the body of opinion in question rests on a logical basis:

> In particular, in cases involving, as they so often do, the weighing of risks against benefits, the judge before accepting a body of opinion as being responsible, reasonable or respectable, will need to be satisfied that, in forming their views, the experts have directed their minds to the question of comparative risks and benefits and have reached a defensible conclusion on the matter.[77]

9.29 This appears to be a clear rejection of the *Bolam* rule simpliciter, but it must be read in the light of the strong caveat which Lord Browne-Wilkinson attached:

---

75   (1992) 109 ALR 625 at 631, [1993] 4 Med LR 79 at 82.
76   [1998] AC 232, [1997] 4 All ER 771, HL.

In the vast majority of cases the fact that distinguished experts in the field are of a particular opinion will demonstrate the reasonableness of that opinion ... But if, in a rare case, it can be demonstrated that the professional opinion is not capable of withstanding logical analysis, the judge is entitled to hold that the body of opinion is not reasonable or responsible ... I emphasise that, in my view, it will very seldom be right for a judge to reach the conclusion that views genuinely held by a competent medical expert are unreasonable.[78]

9.30 Thus, *Bolitho* undoubtedly devalues the trump card which *Bolam* presented to the medical profession, but only in limited circumstances. And, as to that, it is arguably undesirable to undermine the standard test beyond a certain point. *Bolam* provides some protection for the innovative or minority opinion. If this protection is removed, then the opinion which the cautious practitioner will wish to follow will be that which involves least risk. This may have an inhibiting effect on medical progress: after all, many advances in medicine have been made by those who have pursued an unconventional line of therapy. Such doctors may quite easily be regarded as negligent by a judge given to favouring conventional medical opinion.

9.31 In this respect, we can look to the decision in *De Freitas v O'Brien*,[79] which, rather than bolstering a conservative approach in assessing the acceptability of a body of opinion, gives comfort to the so-called 'super-specialist' who may, perforce, undertake procedures which others might regard as being inappropriate or even too risky. In this case, a spinal surgeon – said to be one out of only 11 such specialists in the country – maintained that the surgery he performed was in line with what his fellow spinal surgeons would have considered clinically justified. The plaintiffs, by contrast, claimed that run of the mill orthopaedic surgeons would not have operated in the circumstances. The Court of Appeal confirmed that the *Bolam* test did not require that the responsible body of opinion be large, thus endorsing the acceptability of acting within limits defined by a sub-speciality. One criticism of the decision in *De Freitas* is that it licenses the taking of risks. Yet, the court clearly retains its ability to declare an opinion to be unreasonable, a power which is firmly endorsed by *Bolitho*.

9.32 The Court of Appeal in *Bolitho* has been hailed as ushering in the 'new-*Bolam*'[80] although there were many who viewed it with a modicum of distrust.[81] It is, therefore, interesting to consider its progress since its birth – and, certainly, the case has attracted its fair share of attention. Maclean has scoured the data bases and has unearthed 64 post-*Bolitho* medical negligence cases involving a standard of care;[82] he concludes that, prior to November 2001, *Bolitho* was referred to in four cases in the Court of Appeal and in 25 at

77 [1997] 4 All ER 771 at 778, (1998) 39 BMLR 1 at 9.
78 [1997] 4 All ER 771 at 779, (1998) 39 BMLR 1 at 10.
79 (1995) 25 BMLR 51, [1995] 6 Med LR 108, CA.
80 A phrase which we would attribute to A Grubb 'Commentary' (1998) 6 Med L Rev 378.
81 A most searching review is that of M Brazier and J Miola 'Bye-Bye Bolam: A Medical Litigation Revolution?' (2000) 8 Med L Rev 85. See also J Keown 'Reining In the *Bolam* Test' (1998) 57 CLJ 248, H Teff 'The Standard of Care in Medical Negligence – Moving on from *Bolam*' (1998) 18 OJLS 473.
82 A Maclean 'Beyond Bolam and Bolitho' (2002) 5 Med L Internat 205.

first instance. [83] There is no way in which all these cases could be aired in a book of this size and several of them were 'consent-based' and are considered under that heading. Some do, however, merit mention – if only briefly.

9.33 *Wisniewski v Central Manchester Health Authority*[84] seems to us to be the most apposite case in that the 'logic' underlying the expert evidence was specifically considered. The case concerned a child who was born brain-damaged following 13 minutes' hypoxia during the birthing process; it was alleged that the midwife over estimated her ability and, as a result, the doctor failed to attend in appropriate time. As in *Bolitho*, negligence in relation to non-attendance was not in dispute; the problem, again, lay in causation – and in the two-stage definition of causation developed in *Bolitho* as to what would and should have happened in the absence of negligence. The establishment and the status of a 'responsible body of supporting opinion' was, therefore, of major importance and the conflict is illustrated in two quotations. Thomas J, at first instance, had this to say:

> [W]here analysis of the expert evidence on the facts relating to a particular case shows that a decision made by a doctor and supported by experts cannot be justified as one that a responsible medical practitioner would have taken, then a judge should not preclude himself from reaching [a] conclusion simply because clinical judgment is involved.[85]

However, Brooke LJ said in the Court of Appeal:

> [I]t is quite impossible for a court to hold that the views sincerely held by doctors of such eminence cannot logically be supported at all ... and the views of the defendants' witnesses were views which could be logically expressed and held by responsible doctors.[86]

9.34 The clear inference is that, had the doctor survived the first hurdle as to what he would have done had he attended, *Bolam* would have prevailed and the *Bolitho* exception would not have applied. Logic is, however, a somewhat unusual criterion on which to assess what is, essentially, a matter of clinical judgment and it seems unlikely that the courts will be able to retain control over health care standards if they rely on 'logic' alone.

9.35 It is, therefore, useful to turn to *Marriott*,[87] where a man sustained severe intracranial injury allegedly aggravated by his practitioner's failure to refer him back to hospital when his condition deteriorated. The health authority called expert evidence in support of the doctor but the trial judge considered this not to be reasonably prudent and found for the plaintiff. The Court of Appeal dismissed the appeal on two main grounds. First, the court questioned the acceptability of the evidence for both sides – 'it is questionable whether either had given evidence from which it was reasonable to infer that their

---

83   At the same time, there was judgment explicitly by way of the *Bolam* test in eight Court of Appeal and ten High Court cases; the author remarks that 'it would seem that *Bolam* is far from dead'.
84   [1998] Lloyd's Rep Med 223, CA.
85   Quoted [1998] Lloyd's Rep Med 223 at 235.
86   [1998] Lloyd's Rep Med 223 at 237.
87   *Marriott v West Midlands Regional Health Authority* [1999] Lloyd's Rep Med 23.

individual approaches were shared by a responsible body of others in their profession'[88] – a statement which seems to eliminate the single maverick from the *Bolam* equation. Even so, the judge was effectively dismissing the evidence of *both* sides – the court's opinion suggests that the result might have been different had she chosen one expert's evidence in preference to the other rather than substitute her own analysis. Secondly, however, the court affirmed her entitlement to question whether an opinion was reasonably held given an analysis of the risks involved in following that opinion. On the face of things, then, *Marriott* moves the *Bolitho* test from one of logic to one of reasonableness, which is much more akin to the reasoning applied in other, non-medical standard of care decisions. Unfortunately, the situation is still not clear as, while the Court of Appeal supported the trial judge's approach, it still retained the language of 'logic'. *Marriott* does, however, open an alternative route to 'New *Bolam*'.

9.36 The final case that we select for discussion in the present context is that of *Penney v East Kent Health Authority*,[89] which concerned three women who developed cancer of the cervix following a reported negative screening test. In the event, *Penney* is probably not as important a case as might be supposed in so far as it involved a limited remit. As with all screening tests, that for potential cervical cancer inherently involves both false positive and false negative tests, the latter being estimated as occurring in between 5% and 15% of cases examined. It was not, therefore, argued that a false negative report indicated negligence on the part of the screener per se; the issue was confined to what should have been done, in 1993, given the agreed fact that there were abnormalities in the claimants' slides. The health authority maintained that the unusual abnormalities present were open to interpretation and disposal and that the outcome of the case should be decided on *Bolam* principles. The trial judge considered, and the Court of Appeal agreed, however, that the *fact* was that abnormal cells were present which no screener, acting with reasonable care, could have been certain were not pre-cancerous; the slides should, therefore, have been labelled at least as borderline – he found 'the *Bolam* principle ill-fitting to Mrs Penney's case'. It is not easy, however, to see why that should be so in respect of 'excusability'. Pepitt J was clearly conscious of this and further held that, in the event that he was wrong, he would revert to *Bolitho* in that, given the facts, the contention of the health authority's experts that the slides could well have been reported as negative was inconsistent with the accepted principle of 'absolute confidence' and was, consequently, illogical – a conclusion with which it is difficult to disagree.

9.37 While it is unwise to generalise from a small number of selected cases, the impression gained is that, while the courts are increasingly determined to see that the *Bolam* principle is not extended,[90] they still have an innate reluctance to abandon it in respect of medical opinion; there is a sense that

---

88   Per Beldam LJ at 27. There is an interesting aside here – does it imply that there *is* a difference between the *Bolam* and the *Hunter v Hanley* tests?
89   (2000) 55 BMLR 63, [2000] Lloyd's Rep Med 41.
90   As, for example, into judging the patient's best interests: *Re S (adult patient: sterilisation)* [2001] 3 Fam 15, [2000] 3 WLR 1288.

Bolitho, although welcome, is being used mainly in a 'back-up' position. What seems certain is that *Bolam* can no longer be regarded as impregnable.

Innovative techniques

9.38 Resort to an innovative therapeutic technique may be appropriate in certain cases but should be made with caution. Whether or not the use of such a technique could amount to negligence would depend on the extent to which its use was considered justified in the case in question. In assessing this, a court would consider evidence of previous trials of the treatment and would also, no doubt, take into consideration any dangers which it entailed. It is possible that a court would decline to endorse the use of an untried procedure if the patient was thereby exposed to considerable risk of damage. Other factors which might be taken into account would be the previous response of the patient to more conventional treatment, the seriousness of the patient's condition and the attitude of the patient himself towards the novelty and risk. The standard of care to be applied in such circumstances would be expected of a doctor who is reasonably competent in the provision of *such treatment*. A doctor should not, therefore, undertake procedures which are beyond his capacity.[91]

9.39 A relevant case was heard recently in Scotland.[92] Here, the pursuer had suffered from abdominal pain for more than a year. In something of a last ditch attempt, her doctor prescribed chloramphenicol as a result of which she developed aplastic anaemia from which she recovered only after receiving a bone marrow transplant. She sued her doctor in negligence on the grounds that he could have chosen another drug which was not known to carry the 1:8000 to 1:30000 risk of bone marrow dysplasia which was associated with chloramphenicol – it was claimed that the treatment given was, in effect, a 'shot in the dark'.

9.40 In the event, Lord Johnston was not prepared to hold as negligent a decision which had been carefully arrived at, the doctor having weighed up all the possibilities. Drawing from Lord Browne-Wilkinson in *Bolitho*, the Lord Ordinary held:

> Within the framework of a balanced judgment, I consider that the decision of Dr Todd can be rationally and responsibly supported ... whatever may have been his alternatives. Furthermore, I consider that it should not be categorized even as an error of judgment ... I am prepared to hold that, within the options reasonably available to him ... it was a reasonable course to adopt.[93]

---

91   In *Tomkins v Bexley Area Health Authority* [1993] 4 Med LR 235, the patient's lingual nerve was damaged in the course of an operation for the removal of wisdom teeth. Wilcox J observed: 'When fine movements and fine judgments are the order of the day, with surgery being conducted in the confined space of the mouth, a high degree of care is needed.'
92   *Duffy v Lanarkshire Health Board* (1998, unreported).
93   As a postscript, Ms Duffy's claim under the Administration of Justice Act 1982, s 8 for remuneration in respect of her sister's marrow donation was also rejected (1998 SCLR 1142, 1999 SLT 906).

Misdiagnosis

9.41 A doctor is expected by the law to use the same degree of care in making a diagnosis that is required of him in all his dealings with his patients. A mistake in diagnosis will not be considered negligent if this standard of care is observed but will be treated as one of the non-culpable and inevitable hazards of practice.[94] Liability may, however, be imposed when a mistake in diagnosis is made because the doctor failed to take a proper medical history,[95] failed to conduct tests which a competent practitioner would have considered appropriate, or simply failed to diagnose a condition which would have been spotted by a competent practitioner. As a minimum, the doctor must examine his patient and pay adequate attention to the patient's medical notes and to what the patient tries to tell him.[96] Telephone diagnosis is hazardous, especially if the facts as related by the patient are such as to raise in the doctor's mind a suspicion that can only be allayed by proper clinical examination.[97]

9.42 One of the problems in determining whether there has been a mistake in diagnosis turns on deciding what investigative techniques need to be used in a particular case. Ordinary laboratory tests must be used if symptoms suggest their use[98] but elaborate and expensive investigative procedures would not be expected other than in complicated or puzzling cases. Failure to X-ray, for example, might well be negligence – but even that might not be so, particularly in the light of both public and professional awareness of the major contribution made by diagnostic radiography to the background radiation in developed countries. We can turn again to Lord Denning:[99]

> In some of the earlier cases, the doctor has been criticised for not having taken X-rays with the result that they have sometimes been taken unnecessarily. This case shows that the Courts do not always find that there has been negligence because a patient has not had an X-ray; it depends upon the circumstances of each case.

9.43 Only some 1% of radiographs taken of the ankle in casualty departments demonstrate a fracture and, of these, a high proportion would have healed in the absence of identification. The somewhat archival views of Lord Denning might be supposed to have lost their force in these days of 'high-tech'

---

94 In *Crivon v Barnet Group Hospital Management Committee* (1959) Times, 19 November, the judge said of misdiagnosis: 'Unfortunate as it was that there was a wrong diagnosis, it was one of those misadventures, one of those chances, that life holds for people.' Courts – and patients – might be less inclined to take such a view today.

95 *Chin Keow v Government of Malaysia* [1967] 1 WLR 813 (failure to inquire as to the possibility of penicillin allergy); *Coles v Reading and District Hospital Management Committee* (1963) 107 Sol Jo 115 (failure to consider possibility of tetanus).

96 *Giurelli v Girgis* (1980) 24 SASR 264, discussed in M A Jones *Medical Negligence* (2nd edn, 1996) p 171.

97 *Barnett v Chelsea and Kensington Hospital Management Committee* [1969] 1 QB 428, [1968] 1 All ER 1068; *Cavan v Wilcox* (1973) 44 DLR (3d) 42. A number of 'failure to attend' cases have been discussed above.

98 *Gardiner v Mounfield and Lincolnshire Area Health Authority* (1989) 5 BMLR 1, [1990] 1 Med LR 205.

99 In *Braisher v Harefield and Northwood Hospital Group Management Committee* (13 July 1966, unreported), CA. See H Jellie [1966] 2 Lancet 235.

investigative medicine. None the less, the approach to such problems is never easy and the truth of what was said in 1966 has been demonstrated as recently as 1999.[100]   In *Lakey*'s case, the patient fell and it was agreed that she had sustained a fracture of the pelvis when she attended hospital. The casualty officer found no evidence of fracture and, since the patient had been exposed to X-irradiation on several previous occasions, he decided against X-ray examination before sending her home; the presence of fracture was, however, confirmed on re-admission. The trial judge found that the original decision was taken after conscious deliberation and was not negligent – a ruling affirmed in the Court of Appeal. The case was, however, stated to have been close-run and we doubt if the outcome would be followed in any other than special circumstances in the future.

9.44 *Langley v Campbell*[101] and *Tuffil v East Surrey Area Health Authority*[102] provide good examples of successful actions against doctors on the basis of failure to diagnose correctly the nature of the patient's complaint. In *Langley*, the patient had returned from East Africa shortly before the development of symptoms. The general practitioner failed to diagnose malaria and negligence was found, the judge accepting the evidence of a relative who said that the family had suggested such a diagnosis to the doctor. In *Tuffil*, the patient had spent many years in a tropical climate; the doctor failed to diagnose amoebic dysentery, which proved fatal. This failure to diagnose was held to be negligence on the doctor's part. The publicity given to 'exotic disease' is now such that, again, we doubt if such cases would be defensible today.

9.45 In cases where a doctor is doubtful about a diagnosis, good practice may require that the patient be referred to a specialist for further consideration. It may be difficult for a doctor to know when to seek specialist advice – a fact explicitly acknowledged in the case of *Wilsher v Essex Area Health Authority*[103] – but in case of doubt, it is certainly safer for a doctor to refer the patient.[104]

Negligence in treatment

9.46 The most important distinction here is that to be made between a medical mistake which the law regards as excusable and a mistake which would amount to negligence.[105] In the former case, the court accepts that ordinary human fallibility precludes liability while, in the latter, the conduct of the defendant is considered to have strayed beyond the bounds of what is expected of the reasonably skilful or competent doctor.

9.47 The issue came before the courts most classically in the case of *Whitehouse v Jordan*, which still remains the authoritative example.[106] In this case negligence

---

100 *Lakey v Merton, Sutton and Wandsworth Health Authority* (1999) 40 BMLR 18, [1999] Lloyd's Rep Med 119, CA.
101 (1975) Times, 6 November.
102 (1978) Times, 15 March.
103 [1987] QB 730 at 777, [1986] 3 All ER 801 at 833.
104 It is to be noted that access to a second opinion is now a matter of patient entitlement.
105 For discussion, see Merry and McCall Smith, para 9.1 above.
106 [1981] 1 All ER 267, [1981] 1 WLR 246, HL.

was alleged on the part of an obstetrician who, it was claimed, had pulled too hard in a trial of forceps delivery and had thereby caused the plaintiff's head to become wedged, with consequent asphyxia and brain damage. The trial judge held that, although the decision to perform a trial of forceps was a reasonable one, the defendant had in fact pulled too hard and was therefore negligent. This initial finding of negligence was reversed in the Court of Appeal and, in a strongly worded judgment, Lord Denning emphasised that an error of judgment was not negligence.[107] When the matter came on appeal before the House of Lords, the views expressed by Lord Denning on the error of judgment question were rejected. An error of judgment could be negligence if it is an error which would not have been made by a reasonably competent professional man acting with ordinary care. As Lord Fraser pointed out:

> The true position is that an error of judgment may, or may not, be negligent; it depends on the nature of the error. If it is one that would not have been made by a reasonably competent professional man professing to have the standard and type of skill that the defendant holds himself out as having, and acting with ordinary care, then it is negligence. If, on the other hand, it is an error that such a man, acting with ordinary care, might have made, then it is not negligence.[108]

In the event, the House of Lords held that there had not, in any case, been sufficient evidence to justify the trial judge's finding of negligence.[109]

9.48 Gross medical mistakes will almost always result in a finding of negligence. Operating mistakes such as the removal of the wrong limb or the performance of an operation on the wrong patient are usually treated as indefensible and settled out of court; hence the paucity of decisions on such points.[110] Use of the wrong drug or, often with more serious consequences, the wrong gas during the course of an anaesthetic will frequently lead to the imposition of liability, and in some of these situations the res ipsa loquitur principle[111] may be applied.

9.49 Many historic cases deal with items of operating equipment being left inside patients after surgery. In these, generally known as the 'swab cases', the allocation of liability is made according to the principle laid down in the locus classicus of the law on this point, the decision in *Mahon v Osborne*.[112]

---

107 [1980] 1 All ER 650 at 658, CA.
108 [1981] 1 All ER 267 at 281, (1980) 1 BMLR 14 at 30. See a very comparable case in which the obsterician was found to have pulled on the forceps with a force beyond that which would have been used by a competent practitioner. The difficult issue of causation in cases of neonatal brain damage was also well aired: *Townsend v Worcester and District Health Authority* (1995) 23 BMLR 31.
109 A misjudgment will also be negligent if it is in respect of something 'lying within the area where only a sound judgment measures up to the standard of reasonable competence expected': *Hendy v Milton Keynes Health Authority (No 2)* [1992] 3 Med LR 119 at 127, per Jowitt J.
110 An example is *Ibrahim (a minor) v Muhammad* (21 May 1984, unreported), QBD, in which a penis was partially amputated during circumcision; only the quantum of damages was in dispute.
111 See para 9.61 below.
112 [1939] 2 KB 14, [1939] 1 All ER 535, CA.

In this case, as in subsequent decisions, the courts have shown themselves unlikely to dictate to doctors in a hard and fast way the exact procedure that should be used towards the end of an operation in order to ensure that no foreign bodies are left in the patient. At the same time, however, it is clear that the law requires that there should be some sort of set procedures adopted in order to minimise the possibility of this occurring. Overall responsibility to see that swabs and other items are not left in the patient rests on the surgeon; he is not entitled to delegate the matter altogether to a nurse. This point was emphasised in *Mahon* by Lord Goddard, who said:

> As it is the task of the surgeon to put swabs in, so it is his task to take them out and if the evidence is that he has not used a reasonable standard of care he cannot absolve himself, if a mistake has been made, by saying, 'I relied on the nurse'.[113]

9.50 In the later case of *Urry v Bierer*[114] the Court of Appeal confirmed that the patient was entitled to expect the surgeon to do all that was reasonably necessary to ensure that all packs were removed and that this duty required more than mere reliance on the nurse's count.

The problem of the novice

9.51 The degree of expertise possessed by a medical practitioner obviously depends to a considerable extent on his experience and the argument has been put forward that the standard of competence of a newly qualified doctor will be less than that expected of an experienced practitioner. Although this may be the day-to-day expectation, it is not that of the law. The strict application of the *Bolam* principle[115] would lead the courts to expect the doctor to show that degree of skill which would be shown by the reasonably competent professional. This is an objective standard and it is therefore irrelevant whether the doctor has qualified the day before or ten years before the alleged incident of negligence – it should make no difference to the way in which his conduct is assessed.

9.52 The problem was considered in the case of *Wilsher v Essex Area Health Authority*.[116] The plaintiff had been born prematurely and had been admitted to a specialised neonatal intensive care unit. Extra oxygen was administered by junior hospital doctors, who made an error in monitoring the arterial oxygen tension. It was claimed that this could have caused the virtually blinding condition of retrolental fibroplasia which occurred. It was argued by the

---

113 [1939] 2 KB 14 at 47, [1939] 1 All ER 535 at 559. Scott LJ, however, qualified this by pointing out that it might be necessary to dispense with normal precautions in an emergency.
114 (1955) Times, 15 July, CA. For discussion of further swab (and forceps) cases see M A Jones *Medical Negligence* (2nd edn, 1996) p 202.
115 [1957] 2 All ER 118, [1957] 1 WLR 582.
116 [1987] QB 730, [1986] 3 All ER 801. A lower standard of care for novices was proposed in the Australian case of *Cook v Cook* (1986) 162 CLR 376, in which it was held that an inexperienced driver might not be judged on the same standard as others. In this case, however, there were special features in the relationship between the parties.

defendants that the standard of care expected of the junior doctor was not the same as that of his experienced counterpart. Extensive use, it was said, had to be made of recently qualified medical and nursing staff and it was unavoidable that such staff should 'learn on the job'; it would be impossible for public medicine to operate properly without such arrangements and to do otherwise would, ultimately, not be in the best interests of patients. The judgments in the Court of Appeal are not free of ambiguity. The majority of the judges maintained that the public were entitled to expect a reasonable standard of competence in their medical attendants. The decision of Mustill LJ, however, makes it clear that he, at least, was prepared to define the standard of care according to the requirements of the post. An inexperienced doctor occupying a post in a unit which offered specialised services would, accordingly, need that degree of expertise expected of a reasonably competent person occupying that post; the defendant's actual hospital rank – house officer, registrar etc – would not be relevant in the determination.

9.53 Glidewell LJ also stressed the importance of applying an objective standard which would not take account of an individual doctor's inexperience. The apparent harshness of this conclusion was, nevertheless, mitigated by his suggestion that the standard of care is very likely to be met if the novice seeks advice or consults with his more experienced colleagues when appropriate. Even so, this apparently simple solution does not answer the question which many juniors may ask – how am I to be so experienced as to know when I should be uncertain? And, if, I cannot tell this, am I to ask my seniors before I make any important decision? This question effectively forces us back to accepting a standard of care test which is based on the doctor of similar experience irrespective of the post in which he operates. Conversely, however, an experienced doctor occupying a junior post would be judged according to his actual knowledge rather than by the lower standard of the reasonably competent occupant of that post – the rationale being that, by reason of his superior expertise, he would be more able to foresee the damage likely to arise from any negligent acts or omissions.[117] It is important to bear in mind that *Wilsher* was very much concerned with specialist units and there is no certainty that the judgments are applicable, say, to the general practitioner in so far as delegation of responsibility, hierarchical organisation and the like are particular features of hospital practice.

9.54 Hospital authorities cannot, of course, rely too much upon junior employees; the principles of vicarious liability will, by themselves, prevent this. As Lord Denning said in *Jones v Manchester Corpn*:

> It would be in the highest degree unjust that the hospital board, by getting inexperienced doctors to perform their duties for them, without adequate supervision, should be able to throw all the responsibility on to those doctors as if they were fully experienced practitioners.[118]

Once again, this may reflect Lord Denning's concern for the practitioner at the coal-face and there is little doubt that delegation of responsibility to another

---

117 See *Wimpey Construction UK Ltd v Poole* [1984] 2 Lloyd's Rep 499.
118 [1952] 2 QB 852 at 871, [1952] 2 All ER 125 at 133, CA.

can amount to negligence in certain circumstances. A consultant could, for example, be held to be negligent were he to delegate responsibility to a junior in the knowledge that the junior was incapable of performing his duties properly.

9.55 A junior to whom responsibility has been delegated must carry out his duties as instructed by his superior in order to avoid liability. If he chooses to depart from specific instructions, he will be placing himself in a risky position in the event of anything going wrong.[119] At the same time, there may be circumstances in which he is entitled to depart from instructions; obedience to manifestly wrong instructions might, itself, be construed as negligence in some cases.

PROTECTING PATIENTS FROM THEMSELVES

9.56 In certain circumstances, it is part of the duty of care of doctors and nurses to predict that patients may damage themselves as a result of their medical condition. The extent of the duty to safeguard against such damage is problematical and the decisions have not all gone the same way. In *Selfe v Ilford and District Hospital Management Committee*,[120] the plaintiff had been admitted to hospital after a drug overdose. Although he had known suicidal tendencies, he was not kept under constant observation and climbed on to the hospital roof while the two nurses on duty were out of the ward; he fell and was injured. Damages of £19,000 were awarded against the hospital.

9.57 By contrast, the plaintiff in *Thorne v Northern Group Hospital Management Committee*[121] failed to win an award of damages for the death of his wife who had left a hospital in suicidal mood. In this case, the patient had slipped out of the hospital when the nurses' backs were turned, returned home and gassed herself. The court took the view that, although the degree of supervision which a hospital should exercise in relation to patients with known suicidal tendencies is higher than that to be exercised over other patients, they could not be kept under constant supervision by hospital staff.

9.58 In *Hyde v Tameside Area Health Authority*[122] the Court of Appeal overturned a High Court award of substantial damages to a plaintiff who, believing he had cancer, made a suicide attempt in hospital. Not only did the court take the view that there had been no breach of duty on the part of the defendants, but Lord Denning stressed in his judgment that there were strong policy grounds why damages should not be awarded in respect of attempted suicide. Nowadays, that would probably be a minority view.

9.59 In *Kirkham v Chief Constable of Greater Manchester*[123] an appeal to the ex turpi causa principle – which may exclude liability where the plaintiff's

---

119 *Junor v Inverness Hospital Board of Management and McNicol* (1959) Times, 26 March, HL.
120 (1970) 114 Sol Jo 935.
121 (1964) 108 Sol Jo 484. A similar decision was taken in the Scottish case *Rolland v Lothian Health Board* (1981) unreported, OH, per Lord Ross.
122 [1981] CLY 1854, CA; (1986) 2 PN 26, CA.
123 [1990] 2 QB 283, [1990] 3 All ER 246. Other police cases are discussed in para 1.60 above.

act is in some way immoral – was rejected. It was held that the award of damages in respect of a suicidal death caused no affront to the public conscience – at least when the mind of the suicide was in some way unbalanced.

9.60 Finally, in *Hay (Gill's curator bonis) v Grampian Health Board*, [124] a voluntary psychiatric patient, who was known to be a high suicide risk, hanged herself in a bathroom while two nurses were attending other patients. She suffered serious and irreversible brain damage as a result. In a negligence action against the Health Board, it was claimed that the doctrine of res ipsa loquitur applied because the patient was supposedly under a regime of close observation. We now turn to a consideration of that principle.

RES IPSA LOQUITUR

9.61 Because it may be difficult in many personal injury actions to establish negligence on the part of the defendant, plaintiffs occasionally have recourse to the doctrine of res ipsa loquitur. This doctrine does not shift the onus of proof to the defendant, as is sometimes suggested; what it does achieve is to give rise to an inference of negligence on the defendant's part. [125] If the defendant cannot then rebut this inference of negligence, the plaintiff will have established his case. It follows from this that it is considerably easier for the plaintiff to succeed in his claim when res ipsa loquitur applies.

9.62 The classic case is probably that of *Cassidy v Ministry of Health*, [126] in which the plaintiff went into hospital for an operation to remedy Dupuytren's contracture of two fingers and came out with four stiff fingers. Denning LJ (as he then was) expressed the view that the plaintiff was quite entitled to say:

> I went into hospital to be cured of two stiff fingers. I have come out with four stiff fingers and my hand is useless. That should not have happened if due care had been used. Explain it if you can. [127]

9.63 The doctrine is most useful in cases where damage has occurred in an incident involving machinery or in the context of damage suffered while the plaintiff was involved in some sort of complex process. It can apply only where the plaintiff is unable to identify the precise nature of the negligence which caused his injury and where no explanation of the way in which the injury came to be inflicted has been offered by the defendant. The injury itself must be of such a kind as 'does not normally happen' in the circumstances

---

124 (1995) 25 BMLR 98.
125 There has been some debate as to the precise effect of res ipsa loquitur, but the current weight of opinion favours the view outlined here: see *Ng Chun Pui v Lee Chuen Tat* [1988] RTR 298, PC. For discussion, see J Fleming *The Law of Torts* (9th edn, 1998) p 353; D Giesen *International Medical Malpractice Law* (1988) p 515.
126 [1951] 2 KB 343, [1951] 1 All ER 574, CA.
127 [1951] 2 KB 343 at 365, [1951] 1 All ER 574 at 588. Other medical cases in which res ipsa loquitur has applied include: *Saunders v Leeds Western Health Authority* (1984) 129 Sol Jo 225; *Cavan v Wilcox* (1973) 44 DLR (3d) 42 and *Holmes v Board of Hospital Trustees of the City of London* (1977) 81 DLR (3d) 67.

unless there is negligence. Thus, in a case of neurological damage following difficult aortography,[128] the plea of res ipsa loquitur was rejected on the grounds that the injury sustained was of a kind recognised as an inherent risk of the procedure.

9.64 The doctrine's application in medical cases may still be particularly apt because of the difficulty that the ordinary plaintiff sometimes experiences in unravelling the cause of an injury sustained during technical procedures of which he has little understanding; indeed, he may well have been unconscious at the relevant time. It may also be seen as a potential corrective to the tendency of the medical profession to 'close ranks' when one of their number is accused of negligence. However, it is possibly of less importance in a climate of increasing openness – or, in today's usage, transparency. It must also be borne in mind that the courts are in general reluctant to apply the res ipsa loquitur principle and that this is certainly evident in medical negligence cases. As Megaw LJ said:

> [if one were to accept the view that negligence was inevitably proved if something went wrong and it was unexplained], few dentists, doctors and surgeons, however competent, conscientious and careful they might be, would avoid the totally unjustified and unfair stigma of professional negligence probably several times in the course of their careers.[129]

9.65 An unsuccessful attempt to raise the doctrine of res ipsa loquitur was made in *Ludlow v Swindon Health Authority*,[130] in which it was stressed that the plaintiff had to establish facts which, if unexplained, would give rise to an inference of negligence. In this case the plaintiff claimed to have regained consciousness during a caesarian section operation and to have experienced intense pain. She failed, however, to establish that the pain arose at a stage during which halothane should have been administered; there was, accordingly, no inference of negligence in the administration of the anaesthetic. Nevertheless, there are cases where the injuries sustained by the patient are of such a nature that there is an inescapable inference of negligence. In *Glass v Cambridge Health Authority*[131] the patient suffered brain damage as a result of suffering a heart attack under a general anaesthetic. The court held that this was not an event which normally would be expected to happen in the circumstances and that the onus therefore transferred to the defendant to provide an explanation of the event which was consistent with the absence of negligence.

9.66 The courts' general antipathy to res ipsa has been emphasised more recently. In *Ratcliffe v Plymouth and Torbay Health Authority*,[132] a case involving paraesthesia following a spinal anaesthetic, the plaintiff's appeal was based largely on the trial judge's dismissal of the maxim. In a very extensive and carefully explanatory judgment, the Court of Appeal affirmed that it could not be inferred that the untoward symptoms could not have occurred in the absence of negligence. The courts, it was said, would do

---

128 *O'Malley-Williams v Board of Governors of the National Hospital for Nervous Diseases* (1975, unreported), cited in [1975] 1 BMJ 635.
129 *Fletcher v Bench* (1973, unreported), CA cited in [1973] 4 BMJ 117.
130 [1989] 1 Med LR 104.
131 [1995] 6 Med LR 91.
132 (1998) 42 BMLR 64, [1998] Lloyd's Rep Med 162, CA.

medicine a considerable disservice if, because a patient suffered a grievous and unexpected outcome, a careful doctor was ordered to pay him compensation as if the doctor had been negligent:

> If the untoward outcome was extremely rare, or was impossible to explain in the light of the current state of medical knowledge, the judge will be bound to execise great care in evaluating the evidence before making such a finding, but if he does so, the prima facie inference of negligence is rebutted and the claim will fail.[133]

9.67 In effect, and as expressed by Hobhouse LJ, the court pointed out that res ipsa loquitur is no more than a convenient phrase to describe the proof of facts which are sufficient to support an inference – based on ordinary human experience with no need for expert evidence – that a defendant was negligent and, therefore, to establish a prima facie case against him. Hobhouse LJ may, indeed, have ended the matter once and for all by pointing out that res ipsa loquitur is not a principle of law; it is an expression that should be dropped from the litigator's vocabulary and replaced by the phrase 'a prima facie case'.[134]

9.68 And, as something of a coda, we note that in *Hay (Gill's curator bonis) v Grampian Health Board*[135] the use of the res ipsa doctrine was rejected although it was held that negligence had occurred. It was stated that the doctrine can only be used in cases where no explanation for events is available. Here, there was a clear explanation of how the patient came to attempt suicide – she had been allowed to go to the bathroom unsupervised.

CAUSATION

9.69 As if the problems of fault were not enough, it will do the plaintiff no good to establish negligence on the part of a defendant doctor unless he is able to prove that the damage he has suffered was caused by that negligence. This may be particularly difficult in the context of medicine, where there may be a variety of possible independent explanations for the occurrence of a condition. Thus, if a person brings an action for 'nervous shock', it may well be arguable that the symptoms complained of are those of a psychiatric state which existed before the claimed precipitating event.[136] Some assistance in this respect was provided to the plaintiff through the Scottish case of *McGhee v National Coal Board*,[137] in which it was held that liability will be imposed if it can be established that the negligence of the defender materially increased the risk of the plaintiff being damaged in the way in question.[138]

---

133 Per Brooke LJ at BMLR 80.
134 *Ratcliffe* was followed in *Gray v Southampton and South West Hampshire Health Authority* (2000) 57 BMLR 148.
135 (1995) 25 BMLR 98.
136 For modern examples, see *Abada v Gray* (1997) 40 BMLR 116, CA (schizophrenia could not be precipitated by a road traffic injury); *Gates v McKenna* (1998) 46 BMLR 9, [1998] Lloyd's Rep Med 405 (it was improbable that taking part in a stage hypnosis programme could precipitate schizophrenia and the possibility was unforeseeable).
137 [1972] 3 All ER 1008, [1973] 1 WLR 1.
138 [1972] 3 All ER 1008 at 1011, per Lord Reid, [1973] 1 WLR 1 at 4, per Lord Reid.

9.70 This principle was endorsed in *Clark v MacLennan*,[139] in which it was held that, where there was a precaution which could have been taken to avoid the precise injury which occurred, the onus was then upon the defendant to establish that his failure to take this precaution did not cause the plaintiff's injury. This 'recognised risk avoidance' concept brings us very close to that of res ipsa loquitur which, as we have seen, the courts are reluctant to apply. This antipathy was demonstrated in the very comparable case of *Ashcroft v Mersey Regional Health Authority*,[140] which was heard at much the same time as *Clark*. Here, the plaintiff underwent a relatively straightforward and commonplace operation to remove granulation tissue – the result of chronic infection – from the ear; she sustained a severe paralysis of the facial nerve. Opinion was divided as to whether the surgeon had negligently pulled too hard on the nerve or whether the injury was an unfortunate accident. In the result, Kilner Brown J was, with obvious reluctance, unable to shift the burden of proof and found that, on a balance of probabilities, there was no negligence. The correctness of this view was later confirmed in *Wilsher*,[141] where the House of Lords went so far as to reverse the opinion of the Court of Appeal and to order a retrial on the grounds that the coincidence of a breach of duty and injury could not, of itself, give rise to a presumption that the injury was so caused: 'Whether we like it or not, the law … requires proof of fault causing damage as the basis of liability in tort.'[142]

9.71 The difficulty for the plaintiff in *Wilsher* lay in the fact there were five possible causes for the condition with which he was afflicted. One of these was medical negligence but it could not be established that this *possible* cause actually made a material contribution to the injury. It might have done so, but this fact still required to be proved by the plaintiff. The House of Lords discarded the notion that *McGhee v National Coal Board*[143] constituted an authority for transferring the onus of proof to the defendant. *McGhee* was to be distinguished from *Wilsher* in that there were several agents which could have caused the injury in the latter but only one in the former.[144] This provided an exceptional inference as to cause and, as a result, *McGhee* positively affirmed that the onus of proving causation lies on the pursuer or plaintiff.

9.72 A similar point as to proof of causation was made in the lengthy and complicated litigation over pertussis vaccination. In *Loveday*[145] the court held that establishing a mere chance that the vaccine might cause brain damage in children did not discharge the obligation on the plaintiff. It is to be noted, parenthetically, that the decision in *Loveday* was not the last word on pertussis

---

139 [1983] 1 All ER 416.
140 [1983] 2 All ER 245.
141 *Wilsher v Essex Area Health Authority* [1988] AC 1074, [1988] 1 All ER 871, HL. For a useful summary of the complicated post-*Wilsher* landscape, see M A Jones *Medical Negligence* (2nd edn, 1996) p 250.
142 [1988] AC 1074 at 1092, [1988] 1 All ER 871 at 883, per Lord Bridge.
143 [1972] 3 All ER 1008, [1973] 1 WLR 1.
144 See the dissenting opinion of Browne-Wilkinson V-C in *Wilsher v Essex Area Health Authority* [1987] QB 730 at 779, [1986] 3 All ER 801 at 834. For discussion of the issue, see J Fleming 'Probabilistic Causation in the Tort Law' (1989) 68 Can BR 661.
145 *Loveday v Renton* [1990] 1 Med LR 117.

vaccine; in *Best v Wellcome Foundation Ltd*,[146] the Supreme Court in Ireland awarded £2.75m to a young man who had suffered brain damage after its administration. The ground for the award was, however, that the particular batch of vaccine used was sub-standard and should not have been released on the market – future litigants will still have to prove that, on the balance of probabilities, their injuries were caused by the vaccine per se.

9.73 In a rather similar causation problem, both the Court of Session and the House of Lords have declared that a judge was not entitled to propound his own theory of a causative link between an overdose of penicillin and deafness; the weight of the evidence in *Kay* was that the causative factor was the meningitis for which the penicillin had been prescribed.[147]

9.74 An interesting look at the obverse in vaccination cases was provided by *Thompson v Blake-James*.[148] Here, a child developed post-measles encephalitis and the parents sued their general practitioner for having given negligent advice as to vaccination. The child was subject to suspected seizures which, in the practitioner's view, contraindicated vaccination; he did not, however, mention a special protocol for vaccination in such circumstances which had been issued by the DHSS and, for that and other reasons, the trial judge later found against the first practitioner. Meantime, the parents had moved and had received very similar advice, with additional explanation, from a second practitioner; when they approached a third general practitioner, they informed him they had decided against vaccination. The claims against the second and third practitioners were dismissed at first instance. On appeal, the court distinguished between general and specific advice. In so far as the vaccination could not, at any rate, be undertaken for several months, Dr Blake-James was providing the former and the court decided that failure to mention alternatives would not necessarily constitute a breach of duty in such circumstances. Moreover, the parents had received further advice from the other practitioners; Dr Blake-James's advice was not, therefore, definitive and was not the cause of the child's disability.

9.75 An important variation on the causation theme was reintroduced in *Hotson*.[149] Here, the plaintiff was, admittedly, negligently treated following traumatic avulsion of the head of the femur and developed avascular necrosis. However, there was a 75% chance that this lesion would develop even in the event of correct diagnosis and treatment. The trial judge concluded that the matter was simply one of quantification of damages and the Court of Appeal upheld the view that the mistreatment had denied the plaintiff a 25% chance of a good recovery; damages were awarded and reduced accordingly. The

---

146 [1994] 5 Med LR 81, Ir SC; see D Brahamas 'Court Award for Pertussis Brain Damage' (1993) 341 Lancet 1338; C Dyer 'Man Awarded damages after Pertussis Vaccination' (1993) 306 BMJ 1365.
147 *Kay's Tutor v Ayrshire and Arran Health Board* [1987] 2 All ER 417, 1987 SLT 577, HL.
148 (1998) 41 BMLR 144, [1998] Lloyd's Rep Med 187, CA.
149 *Hotson v East Berkshire Area Health Authority* [1987] AC 750, [1987] 2 All ER 909, HL. A similar claim was dismissed in the early Scottish case of *Kenyon v Bell* 1953 SC 125. For discussion, see D T Price 'Causation – The Lords' "Lost Chance"' (1989) 33 ICLQ 735.

House of Lords, however, declined to measure statistical chances[150] and concluded that it was the original injury which caused the avascular necrosis. Lord MacKay expressed the true situation:

> ... the probable effect of delay in treatment was determined by the state of facts existing when the plaintiff was first presented at the hospital ... If insufficient blood vessels were left intact by the fall, he had no prospect of avoiding complete avascular necrosis whereas if sufficient blood vessels were left intact ... he would not have suffered the avascular necrosis.[151]

or, as put in *The Times* transcript,[152] what was meant by a chance was that if 100 people had suffered the same injury, 75 would have developed avascular necrosis and 25 would not. Thus, on the balance of probabilities, the plaintiff fell into the larger group – there being no evidence that he was one of the fortunate 25% who could benefit from treatment – and, consequently, his injury could not be attributed to the negligence of the defendants. It would be different if 51% of people sustaining the sort of injury which the plaintiff suffered could be treated with, say, a 20% chance of success. Then, on the balance of probabilities, the plaintiff would have fallen into that group of 51%, and, if a hospital negligently failed to offer him the treatment, he would have personally lost that 20% chance of a successful outcome. Whether that 20% loss is something which should attract compensation in the form of 20% damages is left open by the decision in *Hotson*.

9.76 Damages for a loss of chance have been awarded in the United States. In *Falcon v Memorial Hospital*,[153] the Supreme Court of Michigan awarded damages for the wrongful death of a woman who would have had a 37.5% chance of survival had she been treated effectively. The court held that the physician's inaction had elided any chance of survival and that the appropriate measure of damages was equal to the chance of survival multiplied by the total damages available for wrongful death.

9.77 The increased attention paid in recent years to what might loosely be termed 'psychosomatic' diseases has led to some interesting developments in the field of causation. Repetitive strain injury (RSI) – now more specifically referred to as Prescribed Disease A4[154] – is one such condition. Medical opinion differs as to whether it is organic or psychiatric in origin or whether it results from a combination of causes. Thus, it is not surprising that litigation has led

---

150 Statistical chances and personal chances are quite different matters: T Hill 'A Lost Chance for Compensation in the Tort of Negligence by the House of Lords' (1991) 54 MLR 511. The author regrets the fact that the House of Lords appears to leave open the possibility of future successful actions based on a *personal* loss of chance.
151 [1987] AC 750 at 785, [1987] 2 All ER 909 at 915.
152 (1987) Times, 6 July.
153 462 NW 2d 44 (Mich, 1990). See also the earlier case of *Herskovits v Group Health Co-operative of Puget Sound* 664 P 2d 474 (Wash 1983), in which the court allowed a claim for damages in respect of a cancer patient's loss of a 14% chance of survival for more than five years.
154 Social Security (Industrial Injuries) (Prescribed Diseases) Regulations 1985, SI 1985/967, Sch 1, Pt 1. There is nothing to stop an employee suing his employers in negligence despite the fact that the condition sustained is recognised as a work hazard (for which see Social Security Contributions and Benefits Act 1992, s 108(2)).

to some confusing results – ranging from large out of court settlements[155] to judicial comments such as: '[I agree] that RSI is, in reality, meaningless ... Its use by doctors can only serve to confuse.'[156] In what is probably the most important judicial airing of the subject,[157] the House of Lords overturned the Court of Appeal in holding that the fact that the trial judge was unwilling to accept that the plaintiff's condition was simply that of conversion hysteria was not, of itself, sufficient ground to sustain her claim in negligence; it was essential to the success of her case that she proved that her condition had been caused by repetitive movements while typing. If it was impossible to decide what was the cause of the condition from the medical evidence alone, the court was entitled to consider all the other evidence in concluding that the plaintiff had failed to prove her case.

9.78 Other conditions that raise similar problems include post-traumatic stress disorder,[158] myalgic encephalomyelitis[159] and the purely psychiatric condition of so-called 'nervous shock'.[160] We believe that a full discussion of the law in this area, a proportion of which is based on policy considerations, is beyond the scope of a book of this size.

9.79 A discussion of causation in medical negligence should not, however, omit specific mention of the increasingly common form of 'what if?' causation problem – given that a negligent or potentially negligent situation arises, what would have happened if it had not done so? We have seen that this may be exemplified in the actions of the tortfeasor – what would have happened, for example, if the doctor had attended her patient as she should have done in *Bolitho*?[161] We will also see in the next chapter that it applies equally to the plaintiff – what would have happened if the patient had been given advice and information consistent with reasonable care and skill rather than inadequate information? In either case, there is a breach in the duty of care – the question then is: 'would it have made any difference?' If the answer is 'yes', causation is proved; if it is 'no', the negligent action is not the cause of the injury and the action fails. This has disturbing connotations in so far as the judge can only make the distinction on the basis of his own interpretation of the evidence and the presentation of that evidence. His position is doubly difficult in that much must depend on whether or not a person is a 'good witness'. Moreover, it is axiomatic that the Court of Appeal, not having heard the evidence cannot alter the original opinion. While admitting that we see no alternative to the status quo, we are concerned that a whole action should, on occasion, turn upon such a single spindle. Perhaps it is another argument in favour of no-fault compensation?

---

155 'Revenue to Pay £79,000 to RSI Victim' *The Scotsman* 19 January 1994, p 5.
156 *Mughal v Reuters Ltd* (1993) 16 BMLR 127 at 140, per Prosser J.
157 *Pickford v Imperial Chemical Industries plc* [1998] 3 All ER 462, [1998] 1 WLR 1189.
158 *Frost v Chief Constable of South Yorkshire Police* [1997] 1 All ER 540, (1996) 33 BMLR 108, CA.
159 *Page v Smith* [1995] 2 All ER 736, (1995) 28 BMLR 133, HL.
160 *Alcock v Chief Constable of South Yorkshire Police* [1992] 1 AC 310, (1991) 8 BMLR 37.
161 Para 9.28 above.

INJURIES CAUSED BY MEDICAL PRODUCTS

9.80 The extensive use of drugs and other medical products in modern medical practice, coupled with the wide variety of available substances and devices, inevitably leads to a high incidence of injuries for which they are held responsible. The number of persons affected will be small in some instances due to the speedy detection of the dangers and the rapid withdrawal of the products concerned. In others, the scale of the claims may be astronomic, an example being the series of actions brought against manufacturers of intrauterine devices.[162] For these reasons, the question of compensation becomes an intensely political issue, as it has done in relation to HIV-contaminated blood and certain tranquillisers.

9.81 Compensation for injury caused by products is now largely regulated in the United Kingdom by the Consumer Protection Act 1987. This derives from the EU Council Directive on product liability,[163] the aim of which was to create strict liability for most injuries which were caused by defective products; this policy had long been advocated by commentators on compensation for personal injury. Under the terms of the Act, strict liability is borne primarily by the manufacturer of a defective product, although the suppliers will also be held liable if the manufacturer cannot be identified. Products include the components and raw materials from which a product is made and, in certain circumstances, a doctor may be a supplier of a drug. Despite strong protests from the industry, pharmaceutical products are not exempted from the system of strict liability. A drug will now be regarded as defective if it fails to measure up to that degree of safety which 'persons generally are entitled to expect' (s 3(1)).

9.82 In some circumstances, the manufacturer will be able to call on a development risk – or, in American terms, a 'state of the art' – defence.[164] Section 4(1)(e) of the Act provides that the manufacturer will not be liable if he can show:

> that the state of scientific and technical knowledge at the relevant time was not such that a producer of products of the same description as the product in question might be expected to have discovered the defect if it had existed in his products while they were under his control.

9.83 The aim of this defence is to relieve manufacturers of liability if the existence of a defect was undiscoverable at the time.[165] Expert evidence will be important in deciding whether a manufacturer has attained this goal within the limitation that the Act does not require the highest possible standards.

---

162 G R Thornton 'Intrauterine Devices: Malpractice and Product Liability' (1986) 14 Law Med Hlth Care 4.
163 Council Directive 85/374/EEC.
164 For a full exposition of the subject, see P R Ferguson *Drug Injuries and the Pursuit of Compensation* (1996).
165 C Newdick 'The Development Risk Defence of the Consumer Protection Act 1987' (1988) 47 CLJ 455. See also C J Stolker 'Objections to the Development Risk Defence' (1990) 9 Med Law 783.

Is a manufacturer entitled to market a drug which will be beneficial to many but which he knows may cause harm to a minority – in other words, is there such a thing as a socially acceptable risk? The traditional approach to this issue is by way of balancing the prospective benefit and risk. In general, sensitive users will have no claim to compensation if it is in the public interest that the drug should be available; much would then depend upon the presentation of the product and the nature of any warnings given. In this respect, s 3(2)(b) of the 1987 Act stipulates that, in assessing what constitutes defect, consideration must be given to what might reasonably be expected to be done with, or in relation to, the product. Thus, for example, it might reasonably be expected that children could gain access to drugs intended for adult use only. It is, however, unlikely that, say, suicide could be reasonably anticipated by the manufacturer.

9.84 The litigation relating to transmission of HIV infection through contaminated blood products has been taken in breach of a statutory duty under the National Health Service Act 1977 and in negligence.[166] Although it was, for some time in doubt due to the absence of any authoritative interpretation, any argument as to whether or not strict liability applies to human blood and its derivatives is now settled – blood is a naturally occurring substance which has not been manufactured but which has been won or abstracted; it, therefore, comes within the scope of the Act.[167] Moreover, as we shall see, the production of blood for transfusion is regarded as an industrial process. In terms of the Act, the National Blood Authority would normally be the producer of the 'product' but the hospital, or even the individual doctor, responsible for its transfusion would be the supplier. The application of strict liability to blood transfusion has, inevitably, been considered at greatest length in the United States, where the principle has been applied in some courts but where, in general, transfusion has been looked upon rather as the provision of a service than of a product,[168] thereby attracting potential actions in negligence – which would, of course, still be available outside the Act in the United Kingdom.[169] Clark[170] says that the majority of the United States have legislated to the effect that the supply of human blood is a service rather than a sale; the introduction of an element of 'sale' perhaps makes the distinction more urgent there than it is in the United Kingdom.

9.85 The matter has, however, at last come to the United Kingdom courts in the shape of *A v National Blood Authority*.[171] The judgment is, unfortunately, a High Court decision only, which is almost certain to go to appeal. Moreover, it is extremely thorough and it is difficult to do it justice in a book of this title. For these reasons, we do no more than attempt to extract the more important points. The case was brought as a class action by a group who had been

---

166 D Brahams 'Confidential Documents in HIV/Haemophilia Litigation' (1990) 336 Lancet 805.
167 1987 Act, ss 1(2) and 45(1). See, in particular, A M Clark *Product Liability* (1989) ch 3.
168 Eg *Coffee v Cutter Biological* 809 F 2d 191 (1987).
169 The supply of HIV-infected blood was the subject of common law-based litigation in the Australian case of *H v Royal Alexandra Hospital for Children* [1990] 1 Med LR 297.
170 *Product Liability* p 62.
171 (2001) 60 BMLR 1.

infected with hepatitis C virus (HCV) during routine blood transfusion. HCV[172] was discovered in May 1988 – although its presence had been suspected since 1975; a test for the presence of the virus was not developed until September 1989 and an improved test was not approved for use in the United Kingdom until April 1991. Prior to 1988, however, the occurrence of cases of post-transfusion hepatitis of uncertain origin had prompted the introduction of so-called 'surrogate tests' in the United States in September 1986; these tests did not identify a virus but, rather, the effects of viral contamination or, alternatively, a suspect life-style on the part of the donor. Surrogate tests were not supported, nor introduced, in the United Kingdom.

9.86 The group action was brought under the Consumer Protection Act 1987 by the relatively small number of persons who were infected between the coming into force of the Act and the introduction of a screening test for blood in 1989. Claims were lodged notwithstanding the facts that HCV was not identified at the time the claims commenced nor was a screening test available. The defendants agreed that the risk was known but asserted that avoiding the risk was impossible and that it could not be legitimate to expect the unattainable. The public was not entitled to expect 100% clean blood – the most that could be expected was that every reasonable precaution had been taken or carried out. In the event, arguments for both sides were based on the Council Directive rather than the 1987 Act – largely on the grounds that the latter *had* to be interpreted so as to be consistent with the former.[173] The issues were, therefore, concentrated on Articles 6 (which defines 'defective') and 7(e) (which describes the 'development risk' defence in much the same terms as s 4(1)(e) of the 1987 Act, above) of the Directive. It is to be noted that negligence was not a feature of this particular litigation.

9.87 In essence, the court found that the blood was defective, liability being 'defect-based' rather than 'fault-based'; avoidability was not a factor which could be taken into account in so far as it is 'outwith the purpose of the Directive'; the public at large was entitled to expect that the blood would be free from infection; and it was not material to consider whether any further steps could have been taken to avoid or reduce the risk that the blood would be infected. As to Article 7(e), the development risk defence was not available on the grounds that, if there is a known risk, then the producer who continues to produce and supply the product does so at his own risk. The court concluded that it is a lack of opportunity to discover the defect in the particular product that is essential to Article 7(e). Known risks do not qualify, even if they are unavoidable, and the problem came down to whether such 'testing' as was available, but not used, would have been able to identify a risk in an individual bag of blood. The court concluded that, whereas surrogate testing on its own would not, on the balance of probabilities, have done so, the combination of surrogate testing and screening once the virus had been identified would have been effective. A

172 Burton J, who tried the case, made a passionate plea for the abandonment of the abbreviation HCV; none the less, it is accepted medical terminology.
173 The European Commission had previously lodged a complaint with the European Court of Justice, later dismissed, that the United Kingdom's implementation of the 1987 Act did not comply with the Directive: *EC Commission v United Kingdom* [1997] ECR I-2649, [1997] All ER (EC) 481.

defence under Article 7(e) thus failed. So, as things stand at present, it seems that strict liability means what it says – strict liability; and manufacturers or producers will find it increasingly hard to plead a 'state of the art' defence.

9.88 *A v National Blood Authority* was a case fought at an exceptionally high level of responsibility and one wonders how much it will affect the individual doctor or pharmacist. Probably their major concern in respect of strict liability laws lie in the need to ensure that the manufacturer can be adequately identified in order to avoid claims being made against the individual supplier. An interesting American twist was shown in *Oskenholt v Lederle Laboratories*,[174] where a doctor, having been successfully sued for prescribing a faulty drug, himself brought an action against the manufacturers for damage to his professional reputation – a fair example of the worm turning!

CRIMINAL NEGLIGENCE

9.89 Medical negligence is predominantly a civil matter, but a spate of prosecutions in the early 1990s served to remind doctors that the loss of a patient may sometimes lead to criminal prosecution. Such prosecutions used to be rare; their increase points to heightened interest in the external regulation of medicine and to a diminution in the professional immunity which doctors may previously have enjoyed. In some respects, this process is healthy; in others, it is a matter for regret. The principle that doctors, and indeed all professionals, should be accountable for their failures is entirely acceptable; what is more dubious is that the criminal law, and particularly manslaughter prosecutions, should be the instrument chosen to perform that task. We believe that the concept of criminal liability for negligence involving a breach of duty is, at best, tenuous and that the minimum threshold for the invocation of criminal sanctions should be recklessness. We explore the implications of this below.

9.90 Criminal liability for negligence is effectively limited to prosecutions for manslaughter.[175] The level of negligence which the doctor must have manifested is considerably above that at which civil liability may be incurred. Traditionally it has been defined as 'gross' or 'extreme' negligence and sometimes, somewhat tautologically, as 'criminal negligence'; the essential concern is that it surpasses the civil test, as was stressed in *R v Bateman*:

> In order to establish criminal liability, the facts must be such that ... the negligence of the accused went beyond a mere matter of compensation between subjects and showed such disregard for the life and safety of others as to amount to a crime against the State and conduct deserving punishment.[176]

This, of course, does not answer the question of when conduct goes beyond the compensation level but it is probably impossible to be much more specific.

---

174 656 P 2d 293 (Ore 1982).
175 R E Ferner 'Medication Errors that have led to Manslaughter Charges' (2000) 321 BMJ 1212 was able to find 17 British cases between 1970 and 1999 – 13 of these arose in the third decade. Seven cases resulted in conviction excluding those where an appeal was successful.
176 [1925] All ER Rep 45 at 48, 19 Cr App Rep 8 at 11, per Lord Hewart LCJ.

It is clear that what is required is conduct which gives rise to a sense of outrage – or to the conclusion that the accused deserves *punishment* for what he did. Such a conclusion, though, is likely to be articulated in terms of a lack of regard for the patient's welfare or safety – and therein lies the problem. If criminal negligence is defined in terms of a deliberate exposure of the patient to some form of risk, then we are in the realms of recklessness rather than negligence.[177] It is one thing to punish a person for subjective recklessness; it is quite another to punish for objective negligence. In the former case the accused has effectively said: 'I knew of the risk of harm but did not care'; in the latter, he may have been quite unaware of any risk at all – the damage caused may have been the result of incompetence or ignorance, neither of which qualities necessarily deserve punishment.

9.91 The conduct involved in the relevant cases has ranged from, at one extreme, an apparent indifference with all the features of recklessness to mere incompetence at the other. In *Saha and Salim*,[178] two doctors administered an astonishing cocktail of drugs to a remand prisoner who died as a result. They were both convicted and sentenced to a term of imprisonment. By contrast, the conviction of two young and relatively inexperienced doctors for the manslaughter of a patient to whom they had incorrectly administered cytotoxic drugs was greeted with concern in medical circles and was, in due course, quashed by the Court of Appeal.[179] Somewhere in between lies the case of *R v Adomako*,[180] in which an anaesthetist failed to notice the fact that his patient was in distress when this would have been glaringly obvious to any competent practitioner. There was conflicting evidence on the question of whether the accused was out of the theatre at the time; if he had been, and if there had been a failure on his part to make adequate arrangements for the monitoring of the patient, then that would surely have amounted to a degree of recklessness which was strongly deserving of punishment. If, however, he was merely incompetent, it might be more difficult to argue for his conviction of manslaughter – although, undoubtedly, professional sanctions would still be needed. These cases were heard together on appeal,[181] when it was held that the proper test in manslaughter cases based on breach of duty was that of gross negligence rather than recklessness.[182] In contrast to that of the two young doctors, Dr Adomako's appeal failed. He did, however, carry his case to the House of Lords where his conviction was upheld.[183] It was further clarified that, in cases of manslaughter by criminal negligence involving a breach of duty, it was a sufficient direction to the jury to adopt the gross

---

177 A difficulty which the courts have acknowledged in those decisions where gross negligence manslaughter appears to have been replaced by reckless manslaughter: *R v Seymour* (1983) 76 Cr App Rep 211; *Kong Cheuk Kwan v R* (1985) 82 Cr App Rep 18.
178 (1992, unreported); see D Brahams 'Death of Remand Prisoner' (1992) 340 Lancet 1462.
179 *R v Prentice, R v Adomako* [1993] 4 All ER 935, (1993) 15 BMLR 13, sub nom *R v Holloway, R v Adomako, R v Prentice and Sulman* [1993] 4 Med LR 304. See C Dyer 'Manslaughter Verdict Quashed on Junior Doctors' (1993) 306 BMJ 1432.
180 [1991] 5 Med LR 277.
181 (1993) 15 BMLR 13, [1993] 4 Med LR 304.
182 (1993) 15 BMLR 13 at 21, [1993] 4 Med LR 304 at 310, per Lord Taylor, following *Andrews v DPP* [1937] AC 576, [1937] 2 All ER 552, HL and *R v Stone, R v Dobinson* [1977] QB 354, [1977] 2 All ER 341.
183 *R v Adomako* [1995] 1 AC 171, (1994) 19 BMLR 56, HL.

negligence test set out by the Court of Appeal; it was not necessary to define recklessness, although it was open to the judge to use the word 'reckless' in its ordinary meaning as part of his exposition of the law.

9.92 Thus, as the criminal law now stands, a grossly incompetent doctor is liable to conviction despite the fact that there is no element of subjective wrongdoing on his part. This might well be considered inappropriate.[184] The alternative view is that the law should protect the public and that prosecution represents one way of controlling those who cannot meet minimal professional standards. Surely, however, the law should, at the same time, recognise the difference between the reckless and the inadequate practitioner. There is, indeed, some evidence that the House of Lords was prepared to concede the inherent dangers of the gross negligence test. Thus, we have Lord MacKay commending the words of the trial judge in *R v Adomako*:

> You should only convict a doctor of causing death by negligence if you think he did something which *no reasonably skilled* doctor should have done. (Emphasis added)[185]

which is a very severe definition.

9.93 But are the criminal courts the appropriate guardians of conditions in the operating theatre? The General Medical Council has been widely criticised in the past for its ineffective control of clinical standards. It now appears prepared to use its newly erupted teeth.[186] It could well be that the better route to the protection of the public from clinical error lies along the development of the investigative and restrictive powers of the GMC and the Royal Colleges, leaving only the subjective wrongdoer where he belongs – in the criminal courts.

9.94 If concern is felt in the United Kingdom over the prosecution of, often junior, doctors for causing of the deaths of patients, it was considerably multiplied in New Zealand where, under the Crimes Act 1961, criminal liability was imposed on a doctor who merely failed to show 'reasonable knowledge, skill and care' in the treatment of his patients. This extraordinarily low threshold of liability was applied in *R v Yogasakaran*[187] and confirmed on appeal.[188] In this case, an anaesthetist had not checked the label on an ampoule of a drug which he injected into a patient. The ampoule was of the appropriate shape and size and was in the right place on the trolley but, for some reason unconnected with the anaesthetist, contained the wrong drug. Presumably, the same result would have been achieved if the anaesthetist had, in fact, read the label but had read it wrongly. Such a common mistake can hardly be seen as justification for convicting a person of a crime which carries with it a very great deal of moral opprobrium – it would surely be better investigated by the Medical Practitioners' Disciplinary Committee. Concerted medical opposition

---

184 For expansion of this argument, see A McCall Smith 'Criminal Negligence and the Incompetent Doctor' (1993)1 Med L Rev 336.
185 (1994) 19 BMLR 56 at 64-65.
186 See para 1.33, above.
187 [1990] 1 NZLR 399.

to the use of the criminal law in this fashion led, in fact, to a government-sponsored amendment to the Crimes Act, which required that there should be a substantial departure from the normally expected levels of care before liability for manslaughter could be imposed.[189] This effectively raised the standard in New Zealand to the gross negligence standard applied elsewhere. Most of the New Zealand doctors or nurses who were found guilty under the old legislation would not be convicted under the new standard.[190]

188 See D B Collins 'New Zealand's Medical Manslaughter' (1992) Med Law 221. The Privy Council refused to consider what it regarded as matters of policy.

189 Now enacted in the Crimes Act 1961, s 150A, inserted by Crimes Amendment Act 1997, s 2. On the background, see A Merry and A McCall Smith 'Medical accountability and the criminal law' (1996) Hlth Care Anal, and, by the same authors, 'Medical Manslaughter' (1997) Med J Austral 342.

190 P D G Skegg 'Criminal Prosecutions of Negligent Health Professionals: the New Zealand Experience' (1998) 6 Med L Rev 220 describes eight such cases. Five of the prosecutions failed partly or wholly because of the difficulty of proving that the defendant's conduct was a cause of death. A recent trial in Wales, which concerned the removal of a man's only healthy kidney, was halted for the same reason: C Dyer 'Surgeons Cleared of Manslaughter after Removing Wrong Kidney' (2002) 325 BMJ 9.

10 Consent to treatment

10.1 The paternalist might argue that there are many examples in medical practice of situations in which treatment is justified in the teeth of the patient's objection. Arguing from such a position – that the patient may be unable to appreciate that a particular treatment is in his best interest – the decision of the doctor to impose it is seen as serving the patient's interest in spite of what may turn out to be short-term objections. This, a paternalist would hold, cannot be wrong. Good health and physical comfort are preferable to ill health and physical discomfort: a patient will thus be happier treated than untreated.

10.2 Such arguments can, however, be sustained only in very limited conditions, such as when the patient is in an irrational state because of impaired or disturbed consciousness. Restraining a delirious patient is an instance of justifiable paternalism, as is the action of clearing the air passages of one who is about to choke to death. The intervention is justified by the conviction that this is what the patient would want, were he fully rational, or that such treatment is needed to restore him to a position in which he can make up his own mind.

10.3 The case for imposed treatment can also be couched in social terms. Illness is costly to the community and the individual is not entitled to refuse treatment which may minimise that cost. The community may have to support the family of a person who dies as a result of refusing treatment. Non-voluntary intervention is thereby justified. This argument is, however, also weak. Society may, indeed, be saved certain costs if a life is preserved, but it can be argued that the damage resulting from coercion convincingly outweighs that which it seeks to avert. Thus, for example, in *Davis v Hubbard*[1] the US District Court of Ohio rejected out of hand an argument that it had the power to authorise treatment of incompetent patients with psychotropic drugs on the grounds that the state had a legitimate interest in maintaining its institutions in the cheapest and most efficient manner. A coercive society can be most cost-effective – but this does not mean it is most desirable.

---

1   506 F Supp 915 (1980).

10.4 A possible, although uncommon, exception to this rejection of the social cost argument exists when a person is found to be suffering from a highly infectious and dangerous illness; few would then argue that he should be allowed to refuse treatment if such treatment is the sole way to reduce the risk of spreading the disease. Here, the only caveat to the application of imposed treatment is that it should be as non-coercive as is compatible with containment of the threat.[2]

NON-CONSENSUAL TREATMENT

The legal justification

10.5 The common law has long recognised the principle that every person has the right to have his bodily integrity protected against invasion by others. Only in certain narrowly defined circumstances may this integrity be compromised without the individual's consent – as where, for example, physical intrusion is involved in the carrying out of lawful arrest. The legal consequences of an unauthorised invasion of bodily integrity include civil actions for damages and, in theory at least, criminal liability for assault. In practice, non-consensual medical interventions would be unlikely to result in criminal charges, although this could be so in extreme cases.

10.6 The seriousness with which the law views any invasion of physical integrity is based on the strong moral conviction that everyone has the right of self-determination with regard to his body. Unless there is consent to an act of touching by another, such an act will – subject to the principle *de minimis non curat lex* – constitute a battery for which damages may be awarded. Consent can make physical invasion lawful, but the reality of such consent may be closely scrutinised by the law and is, anyway, subject to certain policy limitations. Consent will not normally render legitimate a serious physical injury; thus, it was held by Swift J in *R v Donovan*:

> As a general rule to which there are well established exceptions, it is an unlawful act to beat another person with such a degree of violence that the infliction of bodily harm is a probable consequence and, when such an act is proved, consent is immaterial.[3]

10.7 This being so, it is nevertheless important to note that the degree of harm suffered goes simply to the question of damages and does not operate in constituting the tort or delict. It is the affront to bodily integrity which makes the conduct actionable. No actual physical harm need, therefore, arise. In the same way, the motive of the aggressor is irrelevant. Thus, it matters not that the touching is designed to 'help' the person and, as a consequence, every touching of a patient by way of medical treatment is potentially a battery. The classic expression is that of Cardozo J:

> Every human being of adult years and sound mind has a right to determine what shall be done with his own body; and a surgeon who performs an operation without the patient's consent commits an assault.[4]

2   See M Brazier and J Harris 'Public Health and Private Lives' (1996) 4 Med L Rev 171.
3   [1934] 2 KB 498 at 507: endorsed in *R v Brown* [1996] 1 All ER 545.
4   *Schloendorff v Society of New York Hospital* 105 NE 92 (NY, 1914).

10.8 It is the patient's consent – either implied or expressed – which makes the touching legally innocuous and there is no doubt that surgical intervention is covered by this principle.[5] The theory, then, is quite simple – the reality is somewhat different. Much jurisprudence in common law countries has focused on the consent issue and, as a result, the so-called doctrine of informed consent has assumed a significant role in the medical negligence debate. As will be seen later in the chapter, it is a doctrine which lies surprisingly uneasily in the medico-legal ambience of the United Kingdom.

Is consent always necessary?

10.9 As a general rule, medical treatment, even of a minor nature, should not proceed unless the doctor has first obtained the patient's consent. This consent may be expressed or it may be implied, as it is when the patient presents himself to the doctor for examination and acquiesces in the suggested routine. This principle applies in the overwhelming majority of cases but there are limited circumstances in which a doctor may be entitled to proceed without this consent. Essentially, these can be subsumed under the heading of 'non-voluntary therapy', which has to be distinguished from involuntary treatment. The latter implies treatment against the patient's expressed wishes; the occasions on which this would be ethical are, indeed, very few, although, as already noted, a case can be made out when the interests of a third party or of society itself are involved. Non-voluntary treatment is that which is given when the patient is not in a position to have or to express any views as to his or her management. Treatment in the absence of consent is clearly more easily justified in such circumstances. These include, first, when the patient is incapable of giving consent by reason of unconsciousness; second, when the patient is a minor; and, finally, when the patient's state of mind is such as to render an apparent consent or refusal invalid.

The unconscious patient

10.10 It is possible to see non-voluntary treatment as proceeding with consent, although that consent has not been expressed. Thus, when an unconscious patient is admitted to hospital, the casualty officer may argue that his consent could be implied or presumed on the grounds that if he were conscious he would probably consent to his life being saved in this way. This may be true but, while the majority of patients could be expected to endorse the decision to treat in such circumstances, it is something of a fictitious approach to the problem.[6]

---

5   *A-G's Reference (No 6 of 1980)* [1981] QB 715, [1981] 2 All ER 1057. The Scots equivalent, albeit indirect, lies in *Smart v HM Advocate* 1975 SLT 65.

6   Although old, P D G Skegg *Law, Ethics and Medicine* (1984) remains a most valuable reference; the particular point is discussed at p 99. A rather mundane example involved a dental anaesthetist who inserted an analgesic suppository while the patient was anaesthetised in order to minimise the pain from multiple extractions. He had not discussed this particular treatment before the operation. The GMC found him guilty of serious professional misconduct: see J Mitchell 'A Fundamental Problem of Consent' (1995) 310 BMJ 43.

10.11 An alternative route is to apply the necessity principle. It is widely recognised in both criminal and civil law that there are times when acting out of necessity legitimates an otherwise wrongful act. The basis of this doctrine is that acting unlawfully is justified if the resulting good effect materially outweighs the consequences of adhering strictly to the law. In the present context, the doctor is justified, and should not have criminal or civil liability imposed upon him, if the value which he seeks to protect is of greater weight than the wrongful act he performs – that is, treating without consent.

10.12 Necessity will be a viable defence to any proceedings for non-consensual treatment where an unconscious patient is involved and there is no known objection to treatment. The treatment undertaken, however, must not be more extensive than is required by the exigencies of the situation – we do well to remember what Lord Devlin said, albeit in a rather different context: 'The Good Samaritan is a character unesteemed in English law.'[7] A doctor cannot, therefore, 'take advantage' of unconsciousness to perform procedures which are not essential for the patient's immediate survival or well-being. This was established in two well-known Canadian cases where the courts explored the distinction between procedures that are justified by necessity and those which are merely 'convenient', a distinction which is also applied by the British courts.[8]

10.13 In the first of these, *Marshall v Curry*,[9] the plaintiff sought damages for battery against the surgeon who had removed a testicle in the course of an operation for a hernia. The surgeon's case was that the removal was essential to a successful operation and that, had he not done so, the health and life of the patient would have been imperilled because the testis was, itself, diseased. Taking the view that the doctor had acted 'for the protection of the plaintiff's health and possibly his life', the court held that the removal of the testicle was necessary and that it would have been unreasonable to put the procedure off until a later date. By contrast, in *Murray v McMurchy*,[10] the plaintiff succeeded in an action for battery against a doctor who had sterilised her without her consent. In this case, the doctor had discovered during a caesarian section that the condition of the plaintiff's uterus would have made it hazardous for her to go through another pregnancy and he tied the fallopian tubes although there was no pressing need for the procedure to be undertaken. The court took the view that it would not have been unreasonable to postpone the sterilisation until after consent had been obtained, in spite of the convenience of doing it on the spot.[11]

10.14 The principle that emerges from these two cases is that a doctor is justified by necessity in proceeding without the patient's consent if a condition is discovered in an unconscious patient for which treatment is necessary in the sense that it would be, in the circumstances, unreasonable to postpone the

7 Lord Devlin *Samples of Law Making* (1962) p 90.
8 Per Lord Goff, *Re F* [1990] 2 AC 1, esp 74-77.
9 [1933] 3 DLR 260.
10 [1949] 2 DLR 442. *Devi v West Midlands Regional Health Authority* [1981] CA Transcript 491 provides an almost exact British parallel.
11 Such cases seem still not infrequent and a number of pressure groups exist in the UK, including the Hysterectomy Legal Fighting Fund and Action Against Unnecessary Hysterectomies, set up with the aid of Labour MP Diana Organ in 1997.

operation to a later date. Postponement of treatment is, however, to be preferred if it is possible to wait until the patient is in a position to give consent. A relatively recent English example arose in *Williamson v East London and City Health Authority*[12] in which the plaintiff consented to removal and replacement of a leaking breast implant. The condition was, however, found at operation to be more serious than had been anticipated and a subcutaneous mastectomy was performed. Although the evidence was conflicting, Butterfield J ruled that consent to the more serious procedure had not been given and that the plaintiff would not have agreed to it had she been given the opportunity. Damages of £20,000 were awarded despite the fact that the court agreed that the operation would have been needed at some time in the future.

10.15 The distinction between necessity and convenience is, nevertheless, often delicately balanced – particularly in the light of the sometimes vague terms of written consent forms. In an unreported Scottish case[13] the patient signed to the effect: 'I hereby give permission for myself to have a general anaesthetic and any operation the surgeon considers necessary.' The operation proposed was the comparatively simple removal of a supposed branchial cyst but, on exploration, the 'cyst' was found to be a carotid body tumour. Removal of such a mass is a far more difficult procedure and the patient, in fact, sustained paralysis of half his body. The Inner House concluded that permission was not limited by seriousness and that the patient had consented to any operation to the end of removing the swelling: 'Consent must be read as covering any operation considered by the surgeon at the time to be in the patient's interest' (per Lord Robertson). None the less, the three judges concerned could all foresee different conclusions if the operation lay outside the procedure contemplated by the patient. It is less certain that such a decision would be reached elsewhere, particularly in the United States, where it has been considered for many years that: 'the so-called authority [of such consent forms] is so ambiguous as to be almost completely worthless.'[14] Guidance on obtaining consent in the UK was provided to all health care professionals by the Department of Health in 2001.[15] Uniform model consent forms have been used in the NHS since 1990 and have recently been updated.[16]

10.16 It is possible that a member of the family, a partner or a close friend may be at hand when a patient is unconscious. In such a case, it may be wise for the doctor to obtain the agreement of that person largely in order to discover any anticipatory choice on the part of the patient or other details which might affect a clinical decision.[17] It is, however, now clear that, in the case of an

---

12 (1997) 41 BMLR 85, [1998] Lloyds's Rep Med 6. The case reads as a model moral as to the importance of filing adequate clinical notes.
13 *Craig v Glasgow Victoria and Leverndale Hospitals Board of Management* (22 March 1974, unreported) 1st Division. One has to note that this case is thirty years old – does it, together with *Williamson*, provide an example of changing public mores?
14 *Rogers v Lumbermen's Mutual Cas Co* 119 So 2d 649 (La, 1960).
15 Department of Health *Reference Guide to Consent for Examination or Treatment* (2001).
16 HSC 2001/023 *Good Practice in Consent* (www.doh.gov.uk/consent/hsc) followed by a guide to implementation (www.doh.gov.uk/consent/implementationguide.pdf).
17 Note that the World Medical Association *Declaration on the Rights of the Patient* (1981, amended 1995) speaks of the need in such cases to obtain the consent of a 'legally entitled person'. This Declaration also states that the physicians 'should always try to save the life of a patient unconscious due to a suicide attempt' (Principle 4(c)).

adult patient, no other person, not even the next of kin, has an automatic *legal* right to consent to or refuse treatment in England and Wales.[18] Indeed, the doctor who delays unreasonably while seeking the support of family or significant others is misconceiving the law. In Scotland, a welfare attorney may have been appointed under the Adults with Incapacity (Scotland) Act 2000 with power to consent to medical treatment under Part V of that Act. If so, such a person should be consulted by medical staff prior to treating an incapable adult, provided that it is practicable to do so. None the less, in no case is the doctor's position easy and, provided that it involved no adverse effects, the fact that the spouse's, parents', partner's or friend's agreement had been obtained could be of value in that it would diminish the likelihood of the patient feeling aggrieved at the invasion of his or her bodily integrity.[19] In those common law countries which retain the parens patriae jurisdiction, the courts have the power to consent or refuse on behalf of an incapax, whether they be in that state temporarily or otherwise. This is a wide-ranging discretion which is limited only by one principle: all decisions must be taken in the best interests of the patient. We discuss this jurisdiction in more detail below.

Proxy consent and the consent of minors

10.17 Proxy consents are truly valid only when the patient has given express authority to another person to give or withhold consent on his behalf or when the law invests a person with such power. The commonest example of the latter would be that of parent and child. When proxy consent of this sort is available, the person vested with the power must use it reasonably; a third party may be justified in ignoring an unreasonable withholding of consent. In Scotland, the proxy decision-maker does not have the right to refuse – only to consent to – proposed medical treatment.[20] Specific court authority, either to consent on behalf of a minor or to declare a particular course of conduct or non-conduct in respect of an adult incapax lawful, can be sought when there is dispute between carer and health care professional.[21]

10.18 A common occasion on which parents refuse to give consent to the medical treatment of their children is when they disapprove of it for religious reasons. The capacity of the 'mature minor' to consent to treatment on his or her own behalf is discussed in some detail below;[22] here, we are concerned only with the child who is evidently too young to take important decisions about his or her own medical treatment. A doctor taking steps to administer

---

18 *Re T (adult: refusal of medical treatment)* [1992] 4 All ER 649 at 653, (1992) 9 BMLR 46 at 50, CA, per Lord Donaldson MR.
19 Many United States have enacted 'good Samaritan' legislation aimed at protecting the doctor giving emergency roadside treatment; however, these vary in terms of protection and may not provide liability protection during or after disasters. In some states, malpractice insurance policies do not cover out-of-office care, and generally a physician is not covered if there is any payment for services or an accusation of gross negligence.See also Australian legislation: Emergency Services Amendment Act 2001; Ambulance Services Act 1990, s 26 (NSW).
20 Adults with Incapacity (Scotland) Act 2000, s 50.
21 See *Re F (adult: court's jurisdiction)* [2001] Fam 38, (2000) 55 BMLR 81, CA.
22 See para 10.25.

life-saving treatment such as a blood transfusion to the child against the wishes of its parents could rely upon the common law as above – and the current judicial climate is such that we believe a decision taken in good faith in the best interests of a child would, save in very unusual circumstances, be upheld by the courts[23]. It is also technically possible for the medical advisers to initiate care proceedings[24] or to apply for a specific issue order.[25] An alternative approach would be to invite the High Court to exercise its inherent jurisdiction and to negate the parental decision because that power had been exercised unreasonably. There has been some confusion as to the priority to be given to these possible tactics. In *Re O*,[26] it was held that the inherent jurisdiction of the High Court – by way of the Children Act 1989, s 100 – was the most appropriate legal framework within which to consider a contested issue relating to emergency treatment for a child. Only a few months later, however, another judge of the Family Division opted for the invocation of a specific issue order.[27] The difference is, however, largely a matter of the interpretation of a statute and its more subtle limitations; it was admitted in *R* that the inherent jurisdiction of the court was always available should its statutory jurisdiction be found wanting.[28] It is to be noted that neither court was in any doubt that blood transfusion should be authorised when medical considerations dictated the need.[29] Procedural guidance is now available in the guise of Practice Notes.[30]

10.19 Although there would be little public sympathy for parents who refuse on religious grounds to consent to blood transfusion for a perilously ill child, it would be a mistake to reject their position out of hand. The refusal of blood in such circumstances may seem to many to be irrational and pointless, but there is no doubt that it is a strongly held minority position. Ignoring it involves overriding religious convictions and this is a major step in a free society. Such action also entails a significant interference with the principle that parents should have freedom to choose the religious and social upbringing of their children. Strongest confirmation of this has come most recently from the Supreme Court of Ireland which has upheld the 'family autonomy' of parents to refuse a simple heel prick test on their new-born son for the eminently manageable condition of phenylketonuria, even although such refusal could lead to serious and irremediable brain damage.[31] While respect for parental

---

23 By extrapolation from *Re F (mental patient: sterilisation)* [1990] 2 AC 1, sub nom *F v West Berkshire Health Authority* [1989] 2 All ER 545, HL (the *Bolam* principle, see para 10.111 below, would, presumably, dictate the outcome).
24 Children Act 1989, s 31; Children (Scotland) Act 1995, s 57.
25 Children Act 1989, s 8(1).
26 *Re O (a minor) (medical treatment)* [1993] 2 FLR 149.
27 *Camden London Borough Council v R (a minor) (blood transfusion)* (1993) 91 LGR 623.
28 *Re R (a minor) (wardship: medical treatment)* [1992] Fam 11, (1991) 7 BMLR 147.
29 See also *Re S (a minor)(medical treatment)* [1993] 1 FLR 376: blood transfusion was authorised by the court in the case of a four-year-old boy whose parents objected on religious grounds – notwithstanding that it was a non-emergency situation. In the American case of *In re Brown* 689 NE 2d 397 (Ill, 1997), however, the court refused to order a blood transfusion for a pregnant woman in order to save the life of her fetus.
30 *Practice Note (Official Solicitor: Appointment in Family Proceedings)* [2001] 2 FLR 155 and *Practice Note (Officers of CAFCASS Legal Services and Special Casework: Appointment in Family Proceedings)* [2001] 2 FLR 151.
31 *North Western Health Board v W (H)* [2001] IESC 70. For commentary see GT Laurie 'Better to Hesitate at the Threshold of Compulsion: PKU Testing and the Concept of Family Autonomy in Eire' (2002) 28 J Med Ethics 136.

freedom certainly suggests caution, it is more often outweighed in the UK by the counter-arguments that there has been a redefinition of the role of the parents in respect of control of their children and that it is no longer possible to regard them as having an almost absolute power: 'Parental rights to control a child', said Lord Fraser, 'exist not for the benefit of the parent but for the child.'[32] The community interest in the welfare of children is demonstrated in a number of ways, some more draconian than others. Society is prepared to remove a child from its parents if it is in moral or physical danger; the child whose life is endangered by parental refusal of consent to medical treatment may be removed from its home on precisely the same grounds as may be the battered child. Any difference in the two cases lies in motives. The parent withholding consent may be doing so for what he sees as good reasons and in the interests of the child; the parent who neglects his child is unlikely to feel the same. In spite of this difference, however, there must be few who will see the parents' good faith as justifying the imperilling of the child's life; the death of a child in such circumstances might result in prosecution of the parents for manslaughter[33] – as was said in a well-known American case: 'Parents may be free to become martyrs themselves. But it does not follow that they are free in identical circumstances to make martyrs of their children.'[34] Thus, in *Re C (a child) (HIV testing)*,[35] Wilson J held that notwithstanding the opposition of both parents who rejected contemporary medical thinking on the causes and treatment of HIV and AIDS, it was overwhelmingly in the interests of the child that her HIV status be known. Accordingly, he ordered that a blood sample should be taken from the child.[36]

10.20 The Supreme Court of Canada has ruled that to allow parents to refuse blood transfusions for their child for religious reasons 'undermines the ability of the state to exercise its legitimate parens patriae jurisdiction'.[37] Indeed, the court continued: '[a]s society becomes increasingly aware of the fact that the family is often a very dangerous place for children, the parens patriae jurisdiction assumes greater importance.'[38]

10.21 More recently, the Family Division of the English High Court in *Re C (a minor) (medical treatment)*[39] refused to respect the wishes of parents to continue treatment of their 16-month-old child, who was suffering from spinal

32 In *Gillick v West Norfolk and Wisbech Area Health Authority* [1986] AC 112, [1985] 3 All ER 402 (see para 10.25 below). Following Lord Denning MR in *Hewer v Bryant* [1970] 1 QB 357 at 369: 'Parental rights start with the right of control and end with little more than advice.'
33 *R v Senior* [1899] 1 QB 283. A Rastafarian couple who had refused to allow their diabetic child to be given insulin wee convicted of manslaughter in 1993 – see D Brahams 'Religious Objection versus Parental Duty' (1993) 342 Lancet 1189; the author wondered why the child was not made a ward of court.
34 *People (ex rel Wallace) v Labrenz* 104 NE 2d 769 (Ill, 1952).
35 [2000] Fam 48, [1999] 2 FLR 1004.
36 Yet, while the principle of law may be well established, this can have little impact on the practical outcome in many circumstances. In the instant case the parents fled the country with the child before the sample could be taken.
37 *B v Children's Aid Society of Metropolitan Toronto* [1995] 1 SCR 315 at 433.
38 But the Supreme Court will not extend the jurisdiction to the child in utero: *Winnipeg Child and Family Services (Northwest Area) v G (DF)* [1997] 2 SCR 925.
39 [1998] 1 FLR 384, (1997) 40 BMLR 31.

muscular atrophy. Medical assessment of the infant's condition was to the effect that continued ventilation was futile, it only being a matter of time before she suffered a fatal collapse. The parents agreed that ventilation should be discontinued but were unwilling, on religious grounds, to stand idly by and watch a life wither away when further intervention could delay death. They insisted that the child be ventilated in the event of further collapse. We discuss this case below in the general context of withdrawal of treatment from handicapped neonates.[40] Its significance here lies in the attitude of the court in determining the point at which parental powers of consent fall away to be replaced by the court's power to exercise its inherent jurisdiction, and the extent to which parental power is subjugated to the clinical judgment of health care professionals. Importantly, whether we are concerned with the powers of the parents or the court, or with the duty of the medical profession towards the patient, the determining factor which limits interventions in each case is that of the subject's best interests. What exactly was in the best interests of this child? As orthodox Jews, the parents of C firmly believed that life should always be preserved where possible and could not accept the conclusion that it was in her best interests not to be reventilated if she was subsequently unable to breathe independently. The contrary attitude of the medical profession was unequivocal. Overwhelming clinical evidence testified to the 'futile' nature of continued intervention; the carers, in their turn, were unable to contemplate such a course of action in the best interests of the child. The court, in refusing to interfere with the medical assessment of the case, assiduously followed existing precedents which have eschewed all interference with the clinical judgment of health care professionals by the courts in cases such as this.[41] There was, however, no direct mention in this case of the place for the parents' religious views. The decision was presented as involving an objective assessment of best interests and, indeed, of what counts as futility, yet as we discuss below,[42] these notions are, in reality, highly subjective. Whichever way one looks at a case such as *Re C*, one cannot avoid the conclusion that it involves a value judgment. That the values of the parents in consenting on behalf of their child are completely ignored is at best paternalistic and, at worst, culturally imperialistic.[43] We have yet to encounter a case in the United Kingdom which displays a significant degree of sensitivity to the cultural and religious mores of parents.[44]

10.22 Nor would a human rights challenge assist parents in such circumstances. In *A NHS Trust v D*[45] it was argued that a clinical decision to withdraw and withhold life-sustaining treatment from an irreversibly brain damaged child contrary to parental wishes would be a breach of Article 2

---

40 See chapter 16.
41 *Re J (wardship: medical treatment)* [1991] Fam 33, [1990] 3 All ER 930; *Re J (a minor) (medical treatment)* [1993] Fam 15, [1992] 4 All ER 614; *Re R (a minor) (wardship: medical treatment)* [1992] Fam 11, (1991) 7 BMLR 147. We discuss these cases in detail in chapter 16.
42 See chapters 16 and 17.
43 For an account of the importance of cultural and religious tenets in withdrawal cases, see M F Morrison and S G DeMichele 'How Culture and Religion Affect Attitudes toward Medical Futility' in M B Zucker and H D Zucker *Medical Futility* (1997).
44 For a useful overview, see P Morgan and C Lawton (eds) *Ethical Issues in Six Religious Traditions* (1996).
45 [2000] 2 FLR 677, (2000) 55 BMLR 19.

(right to life) and Article 3 (prohibition on cruel and inhuman treatment) of the European Convention on Human Rights. However, Cazalet J held that there could be no such breach if the proposed action was in the best interests of the patient – and the unanimous medical opinion that it was so, arrived at in good faith, satisfied this test. Subsequent case law relating to negative treatment of both minors and incapable adults has similarly refuted any claim that this course of action is a breach of the Human Rights Act 1998. We consider these decisions more fully elsewhere.[46] This having been said, there is judicial authority to the effect that any serious dispute between health care professionals and parents, particularly one involving a threat to a child's life, should always be settled before a court.[47]

10.23 In contrast to these cases the Court of Appeal issued an unprecedented ruling in *Re T (a minor) (wardship: medical treatment)*[48] that parents of a child suffering from biliary atresia, a life-threatening liver defect, could legally refuse a liver transplant on behalf of the infant, even although there was firmly held medical opinion that a transplant would give the child a number of years of life beyond his current prognosis. We discuss this case in depth below.[49] Suffice it to say here that the significance of the court's ruling from the perspective of the law of consent lies in its willingness, indeed, determination, *not* to equiparate the concept of best *medical* interests with the far broader notion of *overall* best interests.

10.24 In many respects, the decision in *Re T* was easier for the Court of Appeal to achieve than was that in *Re C* for the High Court.[50] While both involved a rejection of received medical wisdom, the parents in the latter case sought to force health care professionals to treat against their will, while in the former, the parents simply requested to be left alone. *Re C* was therefore, to all intents and purposes, founded on a 'right to health care' argument. For ethical, pragmatic and economic reasons, no such right has ever been held to exist.[51] Thus, whilst parents do not have a right to demand continuous care on behalf of their child, there is scope for argument that their right to refuse on behalf of their child has been strengthened judicially. The focus in *Re T* on the effect of forced treatment on the relationship between the child and the parents may prove to be useful in the future for parents who seek to refuse medical care for their child because of their personal beliefs. It could, for example, be legitimately argued that they, too, would come to see their child differently if treatment were imposed without their consent. They may regard their child as 'tainted' or 'soiled' by medical treatment which is administered against their conscience, leading them to reject the child or treat him or her adversely. In such cases, the argument could be put that it is in the child's

---

46 See chapters 16 and 17.
47 See *R v Portsmouth Hospitals NHS Trust, ex p Glass* [1999] 2 FLR 905, (1999) 50 BMLR 269 and *Re J (child's religious upbringing and circumcision)* [2000] 1 FLR 571, (2000) 52 BMLR 82.
48 [1997] 1 All ER 906, (1996) 35 BMLR 63.
49 See chapter 16.
50 For discussion and comparison of these two cases, see J Loughrey 'Medical Treatment – The Status of Parental Opinion' [1998] Fam Law 146.
51 Compare *R v Cambridge Health Authority, ex p B (a minor)* (1995) 25 BMLR 5 (first instance) with the Court of Appeal ruling at (1995) 23 BMLR 1, discussed below in chapter 16.

overall best interests *not* to receive the said treatment.[52] This would be in keeping with a more recent trend in the British courts that acknowledges *overall* best interests as the proper measure of legal authority over an incompetent person.[53]

Mature minors

10.25 The questions of positive consent to and refusal of medical and surgical procedures by relatively mature minors in the absence of parental authority – or, indeed, knowledge – is one of the more controversial issues in this field. The status of the minor between the ages of 16 and 18 is now almost settled and we return to it briefly below; discussion is, here, confined to the child below the age of 16. The common law does not exclude such a child giving consent but the validity of that consent still falls to be considered in the light of the pivotal case of *Gillick v West Norfolk and Wisbech Area Health Authority*.[54] Although, as is well known, that case was specifically concerned with the provision of contraceptives (and is also discussed both under that heading and under confidentiality[55]), many of the points made in the majority opinions can be taken as relating to the consent of minors to medical treatment as a whole – indeed, the term '*Gillick* competent' is now part of medico-legal lore.[56]

10.26 The dominant opinion[57] was that the parental right to determine whether or not their minor child below the age of 16 years will have medical treatment 'terminates if and when the child achieves a significant understanding and intelligence to enable him or her to understand fully what is proposed' but, until the child attains such a capacity to consent, the parental right to make the decision continues save only in exceptional circumstances.[58] Despite the general tenor of his judgment, Lord Scarman affirmed that: 'Parental rights clearly exist and do not wholly disappear until the age of majority.' It can be taken as being now accepted that a doctor treating a child should always attempt to obtain parental authority but that, provided the patient is capable of understanding what is proposed and of expressing his or her wishes, the doctor may, in exceptional circumstances, provide treatment on the basis of the minor's consent alone. The decision to do so must be taken on clinical grounds and, clearly, must depend heavily on the severity and permanence of

52 A D Lederman 'Understanding Faith: When Religious Parents Decline Conventional Medical Treatment for their Children' (1995) 45 Case Western Res L Rev 891.
53 For minors see, *A (Children) (Conjoined Twins: Surgical Separation)* [2001] Fam 147, [2001] 2 WLR 480, and for adults see, *Re SL (adult patient: sterilisation)* [2001] Fam 15, (2000) 55 BMLR 105; *Re A (male sterilisation)* [2000] 1 FLR 549, (2000) 53 BMLR 66 and *Practice Direction (Declaratory Proceedings: Incapacitated Adults)* [2002] 1 All ER 794, [2002] 1 WLR 325.
54 [1986] AC 112, [1985] 3 All ER 402, HL.
55 See chapter 8 above.
56 *Re R (a minor) (wardship: medical treatment)* [1992] Fam 11, (1992) 7 BMLR 147 at 156, CA, per Lord Donaldson.
57 [1985] 3 All ER 402 at 423, per Lord Scarman.
58 A similar approach by Lord Denning MR in *Hewer v Bryant* [1970] 1 QB 357, [1969] 3 All ER 578 was strongly approved and the common law position in Canada, as expressed in *Johnston v Wellesley Hospital* (1970) 17 DLR (3d) 139, was also quoted.

the proposed therapy.[59] The concurrence of Scots law on this question has scarcely been disputed and is enshrined in the Age of Legal Capacity (Scotland) Act 1991, s 2(4).

10.27 The court in *Gillick* took the view that it would be a question of fact to be decided in each case whether a child seeking advice had sufficient understanding to give a consent valid in law. An illustration of this is provided by a case in which the court agreed that a schoolgirl aged 15 should be allowed to have an abortion against the wishes of her parents. Butler-Sloss J said: 'I am satisfied she wants this abortion; she understands the implications of it.'[60]

10.28 Thus, the problem of consent to treatment by minors is, to all intents, settled and is well understood. We have not, however, yet touched on refusal of treatment. This is an issue which has aroused considerable controversy. We return to it in a discussion of recent cases below.[61]

The mentally incompetent

10.29 A proportion of non-consensual treatment which can be provided for involuntary mental patients is proscribed by statute and is discussed elsewhere.[62] Such therapy is, however, specifically limited to treatment of the mental condition. Treatments of unrelated physical conditions are excluded and a therapeutic lacuna remains – how can treatment be provided legitimately to persons who are unable to consent to it?

10.30 We have already seen some of the difficulties entailed in the series of sterilisation operations which have come to the notice of the courts[63] and it is these very cases which have served to clarify the overall medical position. In *Re F*[64] it was clearly stated that a doctor can provide treatment for a mentally handicapped person in the absence of consent so long as that treatment is in the patient's best interests – a line of decisions has supported that view and, indeed, has extended its scope. It is, however, doubtful if this professionally orientated approach acts to the advantage of the mentally handicapped; this is despite the fact that the confusion arises, at least in part, from progressive changes on mental health legislation which have been designed, with the best of intentions, to restore autonomy to the mentally impaired – not the least significant of these being the removal of the parens patriae jurisdiction from the courts of England and Wales by the Mental Health Act 1959.

---

59 For a critical review of the *Gillick* decision with particular reference to the doctor's situation, see G Williams 'The *Gillick* Saga' (1985) 135 NLJ 1156, 1179.
60 *Re P (a minor)* [1986] 1 FLR 272, 80 LGR 301.
61 See para 10.41.
62 See chapter 21.
63 See chapter 4.
64 *Re F (mental patient: sterilisation)* [1990] 2 AC 1, sub nom *F v West Berkshire Health Authority* [1989] 2 All ER 545.

Parens patriae jurisdiction

10.31 The parens patriae jurisdiction – literally 'parent of the country' – is an ancient jurisdiction dating from as early as the thirteenth century. A product of the feudal system, it was originally held by the English monarch and allowed him to take care of those of his vassals who were unable to look after themselves. Through time, the jurisdiction came to be vested in the High Court, the prerogative being passed from the monarch to the Lord Chancellor by means of the Sign Manual – a regnal order authorising the Officer to exercise the jurisdiction on behalf of the Sovereign. Parallel developments occurred in a number of common law countries including Australia, Canada, Ireland and the United States, each taking its authority from English law.[65] The essential importance of the jurisdiction in the medical law context is that it permits a court to consent to or refuse medical treatment on behalf of an 'incapax', whether a minor or an incapable adult.

10.32 By something of a twist of fate, however, the jurisdiction was lost to the English and Welsh courts by the coincidence of two events in 1960. These were the passing of the Mental Health Act 1959 and the revocation by warrant under the Sign Manual of the last warrant authorising the Lord Chancellor to exercise the jurisdiction. The 1959 Act swept away previous legislative provisions dealing with incapable adults and reduced the power to treat adults suffering from mental illness to a single statutory footing. The effect of the revocation of the Sign Manual was to remove the jurisdiction from the common law completely. The net result was that no one, not even a court, can now consent to or refuse medical treatment on behalf of an incapable adult which does not fall within the provisions of the mental health legislation. The position of the minor remained unaffected, however, being governed by the courts' wardship jurisdiction. This disparity remains today – subject to the restrictions imposed by the Children Act 1989. In practice, however, the Court of Appeal has minimised any potential for adverse outcomes – such as a court finding itself in the invidious position of being unable to intervene on behalf of an incapacitated adult – by ruling that recourse to the inherent jurisdiction of the High Court to grant declarations on the lawfulness of interventions is both valid and in accordance with the terms of the European Convention on Human Rights.[66]

10.33 The loss of the parens patriae power has not occurred in other jurisdictions[67] where it provides a very wide-ranging prerogative. Thus, for example, in *Re Eve*[68] the Supreme Court of Canada confirmed the persistence of its parens patriae role, and that of the Canadian Supreme Courts, but refused

---

65 For comment see G T Laurie 'Parens Patriae in the Medico-legal Context: The Vagaries of Judicial Activism' (1999) 3 ELR 95 and J Seymour '*Parens Patriae* and Wardship Powers: Their Nature and Origins' (1994) 14 OJLS 159.

66 *Re F (adult: court's jurisdiction)* [2001] Fam 38, (2000) 55 BMLR 81.

67 Principally because the Sign Manual is a procedure unique to England.

68 [1986] 2 SCR 388. In a later case, *Winnipeg Child and Family Services (Northwestern) v GDF* [1997] 3 SCR 925, the court declined to extend the parens patriae jurisdiction so as to protect a fetus being carried by a glue-sniffing woman.

to exercise the jurisdiction to authorise a non-therapeutic sterilisation of an incapax adult woman.[69] The Australian Family Court also has the jurisdiction and has authorised the harvesting of bone marrow from a 12-year-old boy to help in the treatment of his aunt.[70] However, a high-ranking Australian State court has stressed the limits to the use of the doctrine. In *MAW v Western Sydney Area Health Service*,[71] the Supreme Court of New South Wales would not use the parens patriae jurisdiction to authorise the removal of sperm from an unconscious man for later fertilisation of his wife. The court held that it was not intended that this power should be invoked for the benefit of others. The jurisdiction has, however, also been used in Ireland[72] and in Scotland[73] to authorise the removal of artificial nutrition and hydration from severely and permanently incapacitated adults. This particular use of parens patriae is discussed further in chapter 17.

10.34 The loss of the parens patriae jurisdiction to England and Wales was confirmed by the House of Lords in *Re F*,[74] who then proceeded to develop a necessity test – based, again, on the patient's best interests – to legitimise the medical treatment of incapable adults. We believe that this form of best interests test should be distinguished from that which lies at the heart of the parens patriae jurisdiction in other countries. This is so for two reasons. First, the use of the test in England and Wales serves merely to support the lone authority of the court to declare a particular course of conduct as being lawful or unlawful and does not represent a consent on behalf of the incapax. This leads to the second point of distinction – summed up in the question: 'Who decides what constitutes best interests, and how?' For a long time, the answer in England and Wales has been the medical profession. Indeed, in *Re F*, the House of Lords ruled that the profession could so decide by reference to the standard of care required by the law of negligence:[75] what would a responsible body of medical opinion consider to be in the best interests of the patient? We have always found this to be doubtfully acceptable, because it places the focus not on the patient's interests as such, but on the views of the medical profession as to those interests. Such views could be arrived at by any number of means and need not represent a consensus – indeed, there is authority that the view of a *single* body of medical opinion is enough to satisfy the standard of care[76] and, hence, to establish what are the patient's best interests. Furthermore, the court is effectively excluded from that determination. Although the lower English courts have retrenched from this position more recently, holding that

---

69 But see the opposite result in the Australian High Court in *Secretary, Dept of Health and Community Services v JWB* (1992) 106 ALR 385.

70 *Re GWW and CMW* (1997) 21 Fam LR 612. A similar decision was reached in *Re Y (adult patient) (transplant: bone marrow)* [1997] Fam 110, (1996) 35 BMLR 111, in which it was held to be in the best interests of a 25-year-old incapax woman to donate bone marrow to her sister. We, however, have some concerns with such a use of the best interests test in England and Wales, as we discuss below at para 10.59.

71 [2000] NSWSC 358.

72 *Re a Ward* [1996] 2 IR 79, (1996) 50 BMLR 140.

73 *Law Hospital NHS Trust v Lord Advocate* 1996 SLT 848, (1998) 39 BMLR 166.

74 [1990] 2 AC 1, [1989] 2 All ER 545.

75 Laid down in *Bolam v Friern Hospital Management Committee* [1957] 2 All ER 118, [1957] 1 WLR 582.

76 See chapter 9 for discussion of the *Bolam* principle.

they are the ultimate arbiters of best interests,[77] we remain sceptical of their willingness in practice to challenge medical authority. They also face the weighty authority of the House of Lords in *Re F*. This is to be contrasted with the test as it is applied by courts exercising the parens patriae jurisdiction. Here the only question to be determined, by the court, is that of the *overall* best interests of the patient – of which the medical opinion as to the treatment proposed and the patient's reaction to it will be only one facet. This is a far more principled approach to the question of the treatment of the incapax and one which is more easily justified on ethical grounds.

Reforming measures

10.35 Even so, we cannot fully endorse either the parens patriae approach to consent or the concept of the best interests test as we have outlined it in respect of England and Wales. It is difficult to escape the fact that a test couched in the terms of either is inherently paternalistic. It is partly for these reasons that Scots law has recently abandoned the best interests test in the context of treatment decisions involving incapable adults with the introduction of the Adults with Incapacity (Scotland) Act 2000, the terms of which we discuss below.

10.36 Reforming measures have been on the horizon in England since the Law Commission's paper on Mental Incapacity in 1995.[78] Currently, the Government is sitting on a policy statement that outlines its proposals for change.[79] This draws heavily on responses arising from the Lord Chancellor's Department consultation process in 1997.[80] The policy addresses three main principles: (1) capacity, (2) best interests and (3) the general authority to act reasonably. We comment on capacity below in relation to case law.[81] In respect of best interests, it is recommended that the concept be retained as the test for ensuring lawful and ethical treatment of incapax persons. The Government now takes the view that, in determining what constitutes 'best interests', regard should be paid to a number of factors and statutory guidance as to implementation is promised. The factors to be considered include the past and present uncoerced wishes and feelings of the person concerned, the need to permit and encourage the person to participate as fully as possible in decision-making, a consideration of the views of other appropriate people and whether the purpose for which any intervention is required can be achieved by some other, less intrusive, means. Consideration should also be given to the likelihood of the person recovering capacity sufficiently to be able to make the decision in the reasonably foreseeable future. In addition, there are plans to introduce

---

77 *Re A (male sterilisation)*, para 10.24 above.
78 Law Commission, *Mental Incapacity,* No 231, 1995; For comment on the Law Commission's work, see P Alldridge 'Consent to Medical and Surgical Treatment – The Law Commission's Recommendations' (1996) 4 Med L Rev 129 and P Wilson 'The Law Commission's Report on Mental Incapacity: Medically Vulnerable Adults or Politically Vulnerable Law?' (1996) 4 Med L Rev 227.
79 *Making Decisions,* 1999, Cm 4465.
80 *Who Decides? Making Decisions on Behalf of Mentally Incapacitated Adults,* 1997, Cm 3803.
81 See para 10.49.

a general legal authority for carers to intervene and act reasonably in a patient's best interests relating to general day-to-day matters of care, such as giving medication, providing help with feeding or other matters of personal management. This will not include access to financial assets. There will also be provision for a court to appoint a welfare manager or other person with Continuing Power of Attorney, whose consent would be required before the general legal authority could be exercised by carers. Matters of dispute should be settled by a court. Certain types of medical intervention which are particularly invasive or which are of doubtful benefit to the health of the incapax – such as sterilisation, transplant donations and research – will require specific court approval, as will any question of treatment where the patient has made an advance statement. A new single court jurisdiction will be created to deal with all areas of decision-making for adults without capacity. This will be based at the Court of Protection. These reforms are not in force at the time of writing. In the interim, the Lord Chancellor's Department has produced a consultation paper containing a pack of leaflets designed to provide guidance for relatives, carers, medical practitioners and other professionals involved in the care of adults with mental incapacity. These make the most of the current common law position while setting the scene for the new legislation.[82]

10.37 As we have already seen, new legislation has already appeared in Scotland in the guise of the Adults with Incapacity (Scotland) Act 2000, Part V of which deals with medical treatment and research and came into force on 1 July 2002. Unlike its English counterpart, the Scottish Law Commission had expressed far more concern as to the best interests test and rejected an express reference to best interests in setting out the general principles governing its recommendations.[83] Instead, the Scottish Commission preferred to list a number of factors to be considered before treating an incapable adult. Although these reflect to a large extent the factors proposed in England,[84] the rejection of best interests is, nevertheless, significant. As a 'vague concept',[85] best interests permits of wide-ranging discretion even when, as the English proposals would have it, the test is tempered by 'factors' to be taken into account. Nonetheless, the position of the incapable adult in Scotland remains strongly influenced by health care professionals. The 2000 Act grants a 'general authority to treat' for any practitioner primarily responsible for a patient who – in the practitioner's certified opinion – is incapable in relation to a treatment decision. This is an authority to do all that is reasonable in the circumstances 'to safeguard or promote the physical or mental health of the adult'.[86] And,

---

82 *Making Decisions: Helping People who Have Difficulties Deciding for Themselves*, April 2002.
83 *Report on Incapable Adults*, 1995, para 2.50.
84 They include eg: seeking previously expressed wishes of the incapax; consultation with relatives and other carers; and the need to show a benefit for the incapax except in the most exceptional of circumstances.
85 The Scottish Office accepted the SLC's rejection of best interests, *Managing the Finances and Welfare of Incapable Adults*, 1997, at para 2.41.
86 2000 Act, s 47(1) and 47(2). Note, however, certain treatments such as neurosurgery, sterilisation and surgical implantation of hormones to reduce sex drive must first receive the approval of the Court of Session, while others such as electro-convulsive therapy, abortion, drugs to reduce sex drive or other procedures likely to result in sterilisation, must be cleared by the Mental Welfare Commission, see the Adults with Incapacity (Specified Medical Treatments) (Scotland) Regulations 2002, SSI 2002/275.

while the Act makes provision for the appointment of proxy decision-makers who should be consulted prior to any action where it is practicable to do so, these persons only have a power to consent on behalf of the incapable adult – that is, to accede to medical opinion; there is no correlative power to refuse. If a dispute arises, a second medical officer must be appointed from a list held by the Mental Welfare Commission and his or her agreement with the initial medical opinion provides the legal authority to proceed. The only course then left for the proxy is to appeal to the Court of Session. The primary carer can also do so in cases where the second medical officer agrees with the proxy. Codes of practice have been issued both for proxy decision-makers[87] and for those authorised to carry out treatment or research under the Act.[88] We have commented more fully on the terms of this legislation elsewhere.[89]

10.38 It is important to note that the 2000 Act does not displace the common law in its entirety. The common law still governs the position in emergencies and negative treatment decisions, that is, those relating to the withholding or withdrawal of treatment. Moreover, the common law clearly prevails in England and Wales where statutory reform is still awaited. For these reasons we must now turn to consider court-based jurisprudence.

The cases

10.39 We noted in the fifth edition of this book that the interval between the third and fourth editions had provided a remarkable series of cases which had served to draw together, and indicate judicial attitudes to, non-voluntary treatment involving minors, mature minors and doubtfully incompetent adults. This trend has continued beyond the last edition to the present day. Several of these cases have far-reaching implications; here, we consider only those aspects which are directly related to refusal of and consent to treatment.

10.40 The first, albeit not chronologically, which is of importance in the present context is *Re J*.[90] This case concerned a 16-month-old brain damaged child whose condition was such that his medical attendants considered it inappropriate to provide invasive intensive care in the event that he suffered a life threatening event. The boy's mother sought, and obtained, an order that such treatment should be given if it served to prolong his life. This order was immediately stayed and this stay was, later, upheld on appeal. The significance of *Re J* is that, in restating[91] in the clearest terms that the medical profession could not be required to undertake treatment against its clinical judgment, it

---

87 *Code of Practice for Continuing and Welfare Attorneys*, March 2001, SE/2001/90 (effective 2 April 2001), and *Code of Practice for Persons Authorised Under Intervention Orders and Guardians*, March 2002, SE/2002/65 (effective 1 April 2002).

88 *Code of Practice for Persons Authorised to Carry Out Treatment or Research Under Part Five of the Act*, April 2002, SE 2002/73, effective 1 July 2002.

89 G T Laurie and J K Mason 'Negative Treatment of Vulnerable Patients: Euthanasia By Any Other Name? (2000) Jurid Rev 159.

90 *Re J (a minor) (wardship: medical treatment)* [1992] 2 FLR 165, (1992) 9 BMLR 10.

91 The proposition had been previously stated in *Re J (a minor) (wardship: medical treatment)* [1991] Fam 33 at 41, (1990) 6 BMLR 25 at 30 and in *Re R (a minor) (wardship: medical treatment)* [1992] Fam 11 at 22, (1992) 7 BMLR 147 at 154, both per Lord Donaldson MR. The trial judge in the present case interpreted these remarks as not binding.

lays a base-line that, while *consent* to treatment is essential, there is no concurrent right to *demand* treatment – in short, there are 'checks and balances of consent and willingness and ability to treat'. We saw above how this ruling has been applied without question in *Re C (a minor) (medical treatment)*.[92]

10.41 *Re R*[93] is something of a landmark case as it constituted the first time that the concept of the mature – or *Gillick*-competent – minor had been tested in the United Kingdom courts; it also raised, but scarcely resolved, the relationship between consent to and refusal of treatment. Briefly, the case concerned a 15-year-old girl whose increasingly disturbed behaviour required sedative treatment. However, during her lucid phases – in which she appeared rational and capable of making decisions – she refused her medication and the local authority instituted wardship proceedings, the intention being to seek authority to provide anti-psychotic treatment whether or not she consented; R appealed against an order to that effect which had been obtained.

10.42 The Court of Appeal first disposed of the distinction, if any, between parental powers and those of the court in wardship and concluded that the latter were wider; the court could override both consent and refusal of treatment by the ward if that was considered to be in his or her best interests. The court then further distinguished *Gillick,* which was concerned with the developing maturity of normal children; the test elaborated in that case could not be applied to a child whose mental state fluctuated widely from day to day. But the aspect of the case having by far the most general significance lay in its definition of parental powers. Essentially, Lord Donaldson MR considered that the parental right which *Gillick* extinguished was to *determine* the treatment of a mature minor – and determination was considered to be wider in its implications than a right to consent, in so far as it included the right of veto. In explanation, Lord Donaldson introduced the concept of consent providing the key to the therapeutic door and of there being, in the case of the mature minor, two keyholders – the minor and its parents; consent by either *enabled* treatment to be given lawfully but did not, in any way, *determine* that the child should be treated. Lord Donaldson was later to regret his keyholder analogy in so far as keys can lock as well as unlock doors. It seems to us to be acceptable so long as it is modified to imply that refusal on the part of the child effectively means that the child has thrown away its key to a locked door; it is then only prudent that there should be a second key available as a fire precaution.

10.43 *Re R* raised a storm of academic protest. This was not, primarily, as to the assessment of mental incompetence, which the court considered should be based on the general condition of the patient rather than that at a given moment in time; nor was there great exception to the definition of the court's authority in wardship – which will, in any event, be less commonly invoked since the coming into force of the Children Act 1989. Rather, the criticism was directed at the retention of the parental right to give consent in the face of the child's refusal – an interpretation of the law which Kennedy described as

92 [1998] 1 FLR 384, (1997) 40 BMLR 31.
93 [1992] Fam 11, (1991) 7 BMLR 147.

'driving a coach and horses through *Gillick*'.[94] But is this, in fact, so? Lord Donaldson's distinction between a parental ability to determine a minor's treatment – which Lord Scarman considered to be overtaken by the child's developing maturity[95] – and to consent to treatment is a legitimate one and, as we have seen, a corresponding obligation to apply that treatment was firmly rejected. Moreover, the Master of the Rolls was, arguably, doing no more than interpreting the statute law of England. The Family Law Reform Act 1969, s 8(1) gives the minor aged 16-18 powers of consent to medical and surgical treatment equivalent to those of an adult. Section 8(3), however, goes on to say:

> Nothing in this section shall be construed as making ineffective any consent which would have been effective if this section had not been enacted.

10.44 It has been widely assumed that this section does no more than confirm the common law right of competent minors to decide these questions for themselves. We have always doubted this, largely because, if this is the correct interpretation, there was never any need for s 8(1) – a view which was endorsed by the absence of any such statute in Scotland prior to the Age of Legal Capacity (Scotland) Act 1991.[96] The better view, in our opinion, is that a parental right to consent on behalf of a child existed before 1969 and that s 8(3) preserves that right in the case of all those below the age of 18; this seems to have been the basis of Lord Donaldson's opinion.[97] The academic response to *Re R* demonstrates, above all, the difficulties which arise when attempting to apply general philosophical principles to particular medical cases. The opinion may have further muddied the murky waters of *Gillick* but what was the alternative? This could only have been to accede to the minor's right to refuse treatment when competent and to treat her when incompetent under the mantle of necessity. This is not only bad medicine; it also smacks of a 'cat and mouse' approach which cannot be ethically sustainable. It might have been better to confine the ratio to such narrow issues and to regard the remainder of Lord Donaldson's speech as obiter; but the Master of the Rolls, albeit with some reservations, consolidated his position in the next case – *Re W*.[98]

10.45 *Re W* takes us one step further down the road of consent in that it concerned a 16-year-old girl who, therefore, came within the provisions of s 8(1) of the Family Reform Act 1969 which states:

---

94 I Kennedy 'Consent to Treatment: The Capable Person' in C Dyer (ed) *Doctors, Patients and the Law* (1992) ch 3. See also A Bainham 'The Judge and the Competent Minor' (1992) 108 LQR 196, which is concerned more with the Family Law Reform Act 1969, s 8(1) rather than with s 8(3).

95 In *Gillick* [1986] AC 112 at 188, [1985] 3 All ER 402 at 423.

96 The Age of Legal Capacity (Scotland) Act 1991, s 2(4) gives statutory power, which is rather wider even than that envisaged in *Gillick*, to the mature minor under the age of 16 to consent to medical or dental treatment. The section is, however, *enabling* in that it provides an exception to the general rule that a person under 16 has no capacity to enter into any legal transaction. For the application of the English case law to Scotland, see L Edwards 'The Right to Consent and the Right to Refuse: More Problems with Minors and Medical Consent' [1993] JR 52.

97 (1992) 7 BMLR 147 at 156.

98 *Re W (a minor) (medical treatment)* [1992] 4 All ER 627, (1992) 9 BMLR 22. For a comparable Australian case, see *DoCS v Y* [1999] NSWSC 644.

> The consent of a minor who has attained the age of sixteen years to any ...
> medical ... treatment which, in the absence of consent, would constitute a
> trespass to the person, shall be as effective as it would be if he were of full age;
> and where a minor has by virtue of this section given effective consent to any
> treatment it shall not be necessary to obtain any consent for it from his parent
> or guardian ...

10.46 W was suffering from anorexia nervosa and was refusing all treatment
despite a rapid deterioration in her health. The Court of Appeal supported an
order that she be treated in a specialist unit but, in essence, did so on the
clinical grounds that the disease is capable of destroying the ability to make
an informed choice – the wishes of the minor thus constituted something which,
of themselves, required treatment. In the course of the judgments, however,
several general issues were either clarified or reinforced. First, it was reiterated
that the court had extensive powers in wardship and that these existed
irrespective of the provisions of the Family Law Reform Act 1969, s 8(1);
moreover, Lord Donaldson held that the exercise of the court's power to make
a specific issue order did not conflict with those sections of the Children Act
1989 which give a mature minor the right to refuse psychiatric or medical
treatment in defined circumstances.[99] All the opinions emphasised that this
attitude did not conflict with *Gillick* which was concerned with *parental* powers
only. Secondly, the court disposed in clear terms of the relationship of consent
to refusal of treatment with particular reference to the 1969 Act. Lord Donaldson
said:

> No minor of whatever age has power by refusing consent to treatment to
> override a consent to treatment by someone who has parental responsibility
> for the minor and a fortiori a consent by the court.[100]

Balcombe LJ said:

> I am quite unable to see how, on any normal reading of the words of the
> section, it can be construed to confer [an absolute right to refuse medical
> treatment] ... That the section did not operate to prevent parental consent
> remaining effective, as well in the case of a child over 16 as in the case of a child
> under that age, is apparent from the words of sub-s (3).[101]

10.47 This is, of course, a legal decision and it is true, as Balcombe LJ himself
said, that, in logic, there can be no difference between an ability to consent to
treatment and an ability to refuse treatment. But is there not a clear practical
distinction to be made? It is reasonable to suppose, paternalistic though it
may sound, that a qualified doctor knows more about the treatment of disease
than does a child. Thus, while consent involves acceptance of an experienced
view, refusal rejects that experience – and does so from a position of limited

---

99   This has been clearly restated in *South Glamorgan County Council v W and B* [1993]
     1 FLR 574, (1993) 11 BMLR 162.
100 [1992] 4 All ER 627 at 639, (1992) 9 BMLR 22 at 36.
101 [1992] 4 All ER 627 at 641, (1992) 9 BMLR 22 at 37, 38. Kennedy para 10.43 above
     at 60-61 regarded Lord Donaldson's refusal in *Re R* to accept refusal and consent as
     twin aspects of the single right to self-determination as bordering on the perverse; this
     was because he had no stated support. The presence of such support in *Re W* serves to
     fill the lacuna.

understanding. Furthermore, a refusal of medical treatment may close down the options – and this may be regretted later in that the chance to consent has now passed. The implications of refusal may, therefore, be more serious and, on these grounds refusal of treatment may require greater understanding than does acceptance. A level of comprehension sufficient to justify refusal of treatment certainly includes one to accept treatment but the reverse does not hold; the two conditions cannot be regarded as being on a par.[102] We accept, of course, that the same could also be true for most adults. But we have no difficulty with the courts deeming the distinction to be necessary in the case of vulnerable persons – be they minors or incapax adults. Indeed, as we show below,[103] just such an approach has been adopted in the case of the latter by the courts after the decision of *Re C (adult: refusal of medical treatment).*[104]

10.48 What is clear from both *Re R* and *Re W* is that, rather like Lord Denning before him, Lord Donaldson was concerned to protect the medical profession from the fire of litigation – his reference to consent providing a flak-jacket for the doctor demonstrates this vividly. It is, therefore, possible to criticise the two decisions as concentrating on this aspect and taking insufficient notice of the developing autonomy of adolescence. None the less, all the speeches in both cases are at pains to emphasise the importance of respecting the minor's wishes – and of giving them increasing value with increasing maturity. They emphasise that those wishes are not binding; but their tenor is such as to retain the concept of the mature minor very firmly and to insist that this is breached only in exceptional circumstances. It might, however, be posited that matters have changed with the introduction of the Human Rights Act 1998, and that a failure to respect a refusal by a mature minor would now be a breach of a considerable number of her fundamental rights, including those under Articles 2, 3, 5, and 8.[105] We doubt that this will be so, and would point to both the doctrine of proportionality – requiring a balance of community and individual interests – and the margin of appreciation that countries enjoy under the European Convention on Human Rights. The English courts have made a concerted effort to demonstrate their desire to find balance in these cases and there is little in ECHR jurisprudence that would lead them to upset that delicate equilibrium.

10.48a None the less, the ease with which this balance might be thought to be upset is very clearly illustrated by *Re M (child: refusal of medical treatment)*[105a] in which a 15½-year-old girl who had sustained acute heart failure was denied the right to refuse a heart transplant operation. While the High Court emphasised the need to take account of a mature minor's wishes as to her own medical treatment, it also endorsed the legal view that those wishes are in no way determinative. Johnson J was keen that his ruling be very clearly laid out for M to read for herself but, interestingly, he did not, himself, ascertain her views before passing judgment. Instead, these were gleaned by a local solicitor and the Official Solicitor who, together, formed the view that M was

---

102 For a contrary clinico-legal view, see J A Devereux, D P H Jones and D I Dickenson 'Can Children Withhold Consent to Treatment?' (1993) 306 BMJ 1459.
103 See para 10.54.
104 [1994] 1 All ER 819, [1994] 1 WLR 290.
105 See A Hockton, *The Law of Consent to Medical Treatment* (2002), paras 8.016–8.021.
105a [1999] 2 FLR 1097, (2000) 52 BMLR 124.

overwhelmed by her circumstances. She had said that she did not wish to die. By the same token, she had also indicated that she did not want someone else's heart, nor did she relish the thought of taking medicine for the rest of her life. In the final analysis Johnson J held that it was in M's best interests to receive a new heart and authorised her surgeons to perform the procedure. This must surely represent the outermost reaches of acceptable paternalistic practices. While it seems that she finally acquiesced, was the court really countenancing a forced transplantation if M had continued her resistance? More broadly, we question if it is ethically correct to earmark a scarce and expensive resource for someone who does not want it. Small wonder that Johnson J expressed concern at the gravity of his decision.

REFUSAL OF TREATMENT BY ADULTS

10.49 The Court of Appeal considered the adult who refuses treatment in *Re T*.[106] *Re T* appears to have been the first adult Jehovah's Witness case to have come before a British court. The case itself was fairly unexceptional. A pregnant woman was involved in a car accident and, after speaking with her mother, signed a form of refusal of blood transfusion. Following a caesarian section and the delivery of a stillborn baby, her condition deteriorated and a court order was obtained legalising blood transfusion on the grounds that it was manifestly in her best interests; the declaration was upheld by the Court of Appeal. The fundamental decision was to the effect that an adult patient who suffers from no mental incapacity has an absolute right to consent to medical treatment, to refuse it or to choose an alternative treatment[107] – 'it exists notwithstanding that the reasons for making the choice are rational, irrational, unknown or even non-existent'.[108] How, then, did the court reach its decision to support the provision of apparently involuntary treatment?

10.50 First, of course, it had to transform involuntary treatment into non-voluntary. This it did by finding that T's mental state had deteriorated to such an extent that she could not make a valid choice as between death and transfusion – and if there was doubt as to how the patient was exercising her right of self-determination, that doubt should be resolved in favour of the preservation of life.[109] But an additional factor of great importance to the doctors was added when it was stated that the effects of outside influence on a patient's refusal have to be taken into consideration; in short, the question of whether the patient means what he or she says has to be posed – and whether the decision was reached independently after counselling and persuasion or whether the patient's will was overborne is a matter to be decided by the

---

106   *Re T (adult) (refusal of medical treatment)* [1992] 4 All ER 649, (1992) 9 BMLR 46, CA.
107   The only possible qualification mentioned by Lord Donaldson – where the choice might lead to the death of a viable fetus – is discussed below at para 10.63.
108   [1992] 4 All ER 649 at 653, (1992) 9 BMLR 46 at 50, per Lord Donaldson.
109   For an example of the difficulty given a patient of marginal mental capacity, see C W Van Staden and C Kruger 'Incapacity to Give Informed Consent owing to Mental Disorder' (2002) J Med Ethics forthcoming. See, too, M A Jones and K Keywood 'Assessing the Patient's Competence to Consent to Medical Treatment' (1996) 2 Med Law Internat 107.

doctors. At first glance, this looks suspiciously like opening the door to involuntary treatment – that is, until one comes to Staughton LJ, who said:

> I cannot find authority that the decision of a doctor as to the existence or refusal of consent is sufficient protection, if the law subsequently decides otherwise. So the medical profession ... must bear the responsibility unless it is possible to obtain a decision from the courts.[110]

10.51 Since this will be possible only rarely in an emergency, *Re T* seems to place a well-nigh intolerable burden on the doctors, not all of whom in the middle of the night will be of consultant status. What, for example, is the young houseman to make of Lord Donaldson:

> ... what the doctors *cannot* do is to conclude that, if the patient still had the necessary capacity in the changed situation [he being now unable to communicate], he would have reversed his decision ... What they *can* do is to consider whether at the time the decision was made it was intended by the patient to apply in the changed situation.[111]

10.52 One of us, at least, is grateful that he is no longer likely to be faced with an uncompleted suicide attempt in a busy casualty department! Even the law is undecided on the definition of undue influence and, again, neither Lord Donaldson[112] nor Butler-Sloss LJ[113] made it any easier by including parents and religious advisers among those who might, as a result of their relationship, lend themselves more readily than others to overbearing the patient's will. The law, in fact, seems to have comparatively little difficulty in discounting religious belief. T was considered to be, at best, an uncommitted Jehovah's Witness and we have Ward J in *Re E*[114] saying of a 15-year-old '*Gillick* competent' boy who was refusing blood transfusion: 'I respect this boy's profession of faith, but I cannot discount at least the possibility that he may in later years suffer some diminution in his convictions.'

10.53 Yet, as we have already intimated, one feels that parents ought to be able to take seriously their duty to look after not only the physical but also the spiritual well-being of their children free from the potential accusation of exercising undue influence. *Re T* is, in our opinion, the least satisfactory of this series of cases and it is to be noted that, in contrast to *Re R* and *Re W*, leave to appeal to the House of Lords was granted – however, it was never taken up.

10.54 The authority of *Re T* was applied shortly afterwards in the very interesting conditions of the case of *Re C*.[115] Despite being a decision at first

---

110 [1992] 4 All ER 649 at 670, (1992) 9 BMLR 46 at 68. For an excellent analysis of undue influence, see *Centre for Reproductive Medicine v U* (2002) 65 BMLR 92, [2002] Lloyd's Rep Med 93; supported on appeal: [2002] EWCA Civ 565.
111 [1992] 4 All ER 649 at 662, (1992) 9 BMLR 46 at 60.
112 [1992] 4 All ER 649 at 664, (1992) 9 BMLR 46 at 62.
113 [1992] 4 All ER 649 at 667-668, (1992) 9 BMLR 46 at 65-66.
114 *Re E (a minor)* (1990) 9 BMLR 1 at 8. Ward J did say he wished to avoid notions of undue influence. Perhaps feelings are not as strong as they once were: 'of all influences religious influence is the most dangerous and powerful' – *Allcard v Skinner* (1887) 36 Ch D 145, [1886-90] All ER Rep 90 at 99-100, per Lindley LJ, referred to by Butler-Sloss LJ in *Re T* [1992] 4 All ER 649 at 667, (1992) 9 BMLR 46 at 65.
115 *Re C (adult: refusal of medical treatment)* [1994] 1 All ER 819, (1993) 15 BMLR 77.

instance only, the case is, nevertheless, extremely important in that it was the first in which the right to refuse treatment has been respected by the United Kingdom courts. The case concerned a 68-year-old patient suffering from paranoid schizophrenia who had developed gangrene in a foot while serving a term of imprisonment in Broadmoor. On removal of the patient to a general hospital, a consultant prognosed that he had only a 15% chance of survival if the gangrenous limb was not amputated below the knee.[116] The patient, however, refused the operation, saying that he preferred to die with two feet than to live with one. The hospital questioned C's capacity to exercise his autonomy in this way and an application for an injunction restraining the hospital from carrying out the operation without his express written consent was lodged with the court on C's behalf.

10.55 Thorpe J held that C was entitled to refuse the treatment even if this meant his death. Quoting with approval the dicta of Lord Donaldson in *Re T*, he stated that, prima facie, every adult has the right and capacity to accept or refuse medical treatment. He acknowledged that this might be rebutted by evidence of incapacity but this onus must be discharged by those seeking to override the patient's choice. When capacity is challenged, as in this case, its sufficiency is to be determined by the answer to the question: has the capacity of the patient been so reduced (by his chronic mental illness) that he did not sufficiently understand the nature, purpose and effects of the proffered medical treatment? This depends on whether the patient has been able to comprehend and retain information, has believed it and has weighed it in the balance with other considerations when making his or her choice. As Thorpe J said:

> Applying that test to my findings on the evidence, I am completely satisfied that the presumption that C has the right to self-determination has not been displaced. Although his general capacity is impaired by schizophrenia, it has not been established that he does not sufficiently understand the nature, purpose and effects of the treatment he refuses. Indeed, I am satisfied that he has understood and retained the relevant treatment information, that in his own way he believes it, and that in the same fashion he has arrived at a clear choice.[117]

10.56 Several points of interest arise from this judgment. First, it reaffirms the commitment of the law to the principle of respect for patient autonomy. There is a prima facie presumption of its existence and value which can only be overridden in established circumstances.[118] Furthermore, the particular facts of the case show that incapacity in one or several areas of one's life does not preclude autonomous behaviour in others, nor does it remove the presumption of competence to refuse. Indeed, the injunction obtained by the plaintiff extended not only to the particular operation contemplated by the hospital but to *all* future attempts to interfere with his bodily integrity without his express written consent. The importance of this should not be

---

116 This was, however, averted by intervention short of amputation: [1994] 1 All ER 819 at 821, (1993) 15 BMLR 77 at 78-79.
117 [1994] 1 All ER 819 at 824, (1993) 15 BMLR 77 at 82.
118 For a critique of the decision which doubts that it pays proper respect to patient autonomy, see M Stauch 'Rationality and the Refusal of Medical Treatment: A Critique of the Recent Approach of the English Courts' (1995) 21 J Med Ethics 162.

underestimated. In effect, it is tantamount to judicial recognition of the validity of advance refusals of treatment.[119] If, however, incapacity can ever be established, then, as we have seen, the patient must be dealt with in a manner which furthers his or her own best interests.[120]

10.57 The judgment in *Re C*, however, suffers from its vagueness. A patient's competence can be successfully challenged if it can be shown that he does not comprehend or absorb information to the extent that he understands it or if he is thought not to believe the information or if he cannot balance this information against other considerations when making his choice. In this way, hurdles are placed in the path of those seeking to exercise their autonomy but, at the same time, it remains uncertain how high they must jump in order to clear these hurdles. For example, the requirement that the patient must actually comprehend the information is not easy to assess – it can depend as much on the amount of information which is given to the patient and the manner in which it is provided as on the capacity of the patient to understand. Yet, the test is not '*can* the patient understand?' but, rather, '*does* the patient understand?' This imposes an obligation on medical staff to ensure that actual understanding is reached and this, in itself, is paradoxical given that treatment staff might not want the patient to understand if they disagree with the nature of his or her decision – as in *Re C*.

10.58 Neither is it exactly clear *what* the patient must understand. The decision talks of the 'nature, purpose and effects' of the treatment. This is potentially very broad and can encompass elements ranging from the general aim of the procedure to the risks and the consequences of refusal and beyond. Arguably, as Grubb has pointed out, the category of 'autonomous persons' is reduced to only the most 'comprehending' individuals if excessive amounts of information are required to be disclosed and understood.[121]

10.59 Finally, *Re C* confirms the role of the best interests test in the medico-legal field. If self-determination is successfully challenged, then the only option left is to treat the patient in his or her best interests. However, as we have argued above, this concept is also vague and leaves considerable control and power in the hands of the health care professionals. Neither the precise nor the general nature of best interests is defined by the United Kingdom courts. Cases such as *Re T* and *Re C* demonstrate that the principle of respect for patient autonomy – and, therefore, patient choice – is, prima facie, prescribed

---

119 More recently reaffirmed in *Re AK (medical treatment: consent)* [2001] 1 FLR 129, (2001) 58 BMLR 151. See too, British Medical Association *Code of Practice: Advance Statements about Medical Treatment* (2000).

120 The Government will incorporate a new definition of incapacity in its reforming legislation, as detailed in *Making Decisions*, para 10.36 above. A person is without capacity if, at the time that a decision needs to be taken, he or she is 'unable by reason of mental disability to make a decision ... or unable to communicate a decision ... because he or she is unconscious or for any other reason'. Mental disability is 'any disability or disorder of the mind or brain, whether permanent or temporary, which results in an impairment or disturbance of mental functioning', and a person is unable to decide if he or she is 'unable to understand or retain the information relevant to the decision, or unable to make a decision based on that information'. A broadly similar functional definition is contained in the Adults with Incapacity (Scotland) Act 2000, s 1(6).

121 See A Grubb 'Commentary' (1994) 2 Med L Rev 92 at 95.

but the tests which have been laid down give us no more than a general idea of where the limits of the principle lie.

10.60 All of this has been confirmed most recently in *Re B (adult: refusal of medical treatment)*.[122] Ms B was a 43-year-old patient who was paralysed from the neck down and sustained only by means of a ventilator. Ms B refused this intervention shortly after it was introduced but she was adjudged incompetent to do so by two psychiatrists in April 2001. She was, however, declared competent by an independent clinician in August of that year and, thereafter, the hospital treated her as such. Nevertheless, her attending physicians refused to remove the ventilator, advocating instead that their patient attend a rehabilitation unit which offered a slim chance of improvement in her condition. Ms B rejected this course of action and repeated her refusal on several occasions. Ultimately, the President of the Family Division attended Ms B's bedside to hear her story. In a poignant ruling, Butler-Sloss P reiterated the fundamental principles that now govern this area, namely, that a competent patient has an absolute right to refuse treatment irrespective of the consequences of her decision, and she issued very clear guidance to health care professionals as to their responsibilities in such cases. These include keeping the patient as involved in the decision-making process as possible, moving to resolve any dispute as promptly as practicable and finding other clinicians to undertake the course of action if the primary carers feel unable to do so. Perhaps most striking of all, notional damages of £100 were awarded in recognition of the technical assault that the health carers had committed by continuing to treat Ms B against her wishes.[123]

10.61 Straightforward as this may seem, these cases have to be read in conjunction with others in which the autonomy of the patient has been overridden and their right to choose for themselves has been denied.

REFUSAL OF TREATMENT IN LATE PREGNANCY

10.62 The decision of the Court of Appeal in *Re T* was not without its caveats. Lord Donaldson said:

> An adult patient who ... suffers from no mental incapacity has an absolute right to choose whether to consent to medical treatment, to refuse it or to choose one rather than another of the treatments being offered. *The only possible qualification is a case in which the choice may lead to the death of a viable foetus.*[124]

10.63 This 'possible qualification' was tested in the soon-to-follow decision of *Re S*,[125] in which a health authority applied for a declaration to authorise

---

122 Sub nom *Ms B and An NHS Hospital Trust* [2000] EWHC 429 (Fam), [2002] 2 All ER 449, (2002) 65 BMLR 149. We return to this case in chapter 18.
123 For general comment see, Special Clinical Ethics Symposium: 'The Case of Ms B, (2002) 28 J Med Ethics 232.
124 [1992] 4 All ER 649 at 652-653, (1992) 9 BMLR 46 at 50, emphasis added.
125 *Re S (adult: refusal of medical treatment)* [1992] 4 All ER 671, (1992) 9 BMLR 69. This case was decided only two and a half months after *Re T*.

the surgeons and staff of a hospital to carry out an emergency caesarian section on a 30-year-old woman who was in spontaneous labour with her third child. The woman refused to submit to a section on religious grounds. The surgeon in charge was adamant that both patient and baby would die without such intervention. After six days of Mrs S's labour, the health authority sought a judgment from the High Court. The decision of Sir Stephen Brown is approximately one page in length, one half of which is concerned with relating the facts, and there is little or no legal argument or analysis in the judgment whereby the declaration was agreed. As the President said:

> I [make the declaration] in the knowledge that the fundamental question appears to have been left open by Lord Donaldson MR in *Re T* ..., and in the knowledge that there is no English authority which is directly in point.

10.64 But it was precisely this lack of precedental authority which provoked major criticism in *Re S* in so far as the case, with all its jurisprudential limitations, bid fair to *provide* that authority. But the problems thus generated are both manifold and manifest. First, the decision was based wholly on the medical evidence. There was no discussion of how the competency of a woman to make such a choice is to be assessed. How is the choice by a woman in Mrs S's position to be validated? Secondly, when Lord Donaldson spoke of a 'viable' fetus, he was speaking in relative rather than absolute terms – for viability results from a combination of gestational age and obstetric expertise.[126] At what stage, therefore, is it regarded as legally acceptable to enforce the operation? Thirdly, we have to ask what importance is the court to place on the danger to the life of the woman herself. Strictly speaking, this should have no influence for, as was said in *Re T* and now confirmed in *Re B*, the right to decide whether or not to accept treatment persists even if refusal will lead to premature death. Yet we still believe that it is asking a great deal of the health care team to stand by and watch their patient die a painful death and it is probable that such considerations were in the mind of the President when he was confronted with an emergency situation.[127] Finally, the decision depends on very doubtful logic in that it is well established law that the fetus in utero has no rights of its own and has no distinct human personality;[128] moreover, there is no offence of feticide in the United Kingdom. If, then, we look upon an enforced caesarian as a means of resolving a conflict between a woman who is refusing treatment and a fetus who seeks it, there is, in sporting terms, effectively 'no contest' – there can be no valid reason behind isolating this particular situation as the one occasion on which the fetus achieves legal dominance over its mother. While we have considerable sympathy with the President in the particular circumstances of *Re S*, it is hard to see his decision as other than logically untenable.

126 See eg the American case *Re AC* 573 A 2d 1235 (DC, 1990) where the enforced caesarian section of a 26-week-old fetus ended, almost predictably, with the death of the neonate within hours. The case, which is discussed further in chapter 17, seems to have been unfortunately wrongly interpreted in *Re S*.
127 For some judicial sympathy, see Major J dissenting in *Winnipeg Child and Family Services (Northwestern) v GDF* [1997] 2 SCR 925: 'Where the harm is so great and the temporary remedy so slight, the law is compelled to act ... Someone must speak for those who cannot speak for themselves.'
128 Most recently expressed in *A-G's Reference (No 3 of 1994)* [1998] 1 Cr App Rep 91, HL.

10.65 None the less, it appeared for a time as though *Re S* had, indeed, set a precedent and, despite fierce criticism of *Re S*,[129] the English courts proceeded in *Norfolk and Norwich Healthcare (NHS) Trust v W*[130] and *Tameside and Glossop Acute Services Trust v CH (a patient)*[131] to impose caesarian sections on women against their wills. Indeed, in the latter case it was held that the performance of a caesarian section on a schizophrenic woman could be 'treatment' of her mental disorder within the terms of the Mental Health Act 1983.

10.66 The relationship between a pregnant woman and her fetus was, however, fully reconsidered by the Court of Appeal in *Re MB*.[132] The court was adamant in its ruling that a woman carrying a fetus is entitled to the same degree of respect for her wishes as is anyone else and reiterated the general principle that a person of full age and sound mind cannot be treated against his or her will without the door being opened to civil and criminal legal consequences. It also endorsed strongly the view that a refusal of medical treatment can be for any reason, rational or irrational, or for no reason at all. In particular, it was stressed that circumstances in which non-voluntary treatment is permissible arise only when the patient cannot give consent and when treatment is in the *patient's* best interests. The court has no jurisdiction to declare medical intervention lawful when a *competent* pregnant woman decides to refuse treatment, *even though* this might result in the death or serious handicap of the fetus she is bearing. The question of the woman's own best interests *does not arise* in such circumstances. On the facts of the particular case, the pregnant woman was declared incompetent because of a fear of needles which had led her to refuse the operation – but, at the end of the day, she consented and a healthy child was delivered.

10.67 This decision clearly places the autonomy of the woman above any interests of the fetus, including an interest in being born alive.[133] Yet, it is important to bear in mind that all of this is subject to the woman being competent when she makes her refusal. If she is not, she must be treated in her best interests. In the particular circumstances of *Re MB*, the assessment that the operation was in her best interests is open to little question; both the woman and her husband wanted the child to be born – subject to her needle phobia. However, it still remains open to speculation how the patient's best interests should be assessed if there is no clear indication of how the mother feels about the birth. In the final analysis, *Re MB* does little to remove from the medical profession the discretion and power to decide on a patient's

---

129 See eg A Grubb 'Commentary on *Re S*' (1993) 1 Med L Rev 92.
130 [1996] 2 FLR 613, (1996) 34 BMLR 16. The same judge made a similar decision in the less well reported *Rochdale Healthcare (NHS) Trust v C* [1996] 3 Hempson's Lawyer 505.
131 [1996] 1 FLR 762, (1996) 31 BMLR 93. For analysis see A Grubb 'Commentary' (1996) 4 Med L Rev 193. An interesting selection of views is to be found under the general heading 'Caesarian Section: A Treatment for Mental Disorder?' (1997) 314 BMJ 1183.
132 *Re MB (an adult: medical treatment)* [1997] 8 Med LR 217, (1997) 38 BMLR 175, CA.
133 For consideration of whether a human rights analysis might strengthen the legal position of the fetus, see G T Laurie, 'Medical Law and Human Rights: Passing the Parcel Back to the Profession?' in A Boyle et al (eds) *Human Rights and Scots Law: Comparative Perspectives on the Incorporation of the ECHR* (2002).

capacity to act autonomously – and ultimately, in cases of incapacity, to decide on the patient's best interests.

10.68 This discretion was not removed by the last case in this current line of authority,[134] although the Court of Appeal's ruling in *St George's Healthcare NHS Trust v S (No 2), R v Collins, ex p S (No 2)*[135] does provide helpful guidance for health care professionals who must decide on the capacity of a patient to consent to or refuse treatment. The case concerned S, a 36-year-old pregnant woman with pre-eclampsia who was advised that she would require to be admitted. Fully cognisant of the risks, and wishing her baby to be born naturally, S refused. As a consequence, she was seen by a social worker and two doctors and admitted to a mental hospital for assessment. On her transfer to another hospital a declaration was sought and granted to dispense with S's consent and the baby was delivered by caesarian section. S discharged herself and appealed against the declaration.

10.69 The Court of Appeal upheld its ruling in *Re MB* to the extent that a mentally competent pregnant woman has the absolute right to refuse medical intervention. The actions of the hospital were a trespass and the former declaration was set aside accordingly. Moreover, the court castigated the use of the mental health legislation to treat an otherwise healthy woman:

> The Act cannot be deployed to achieve the detention of an individual against her will merely because her thinking process is unusual, even apparently bizarre and irrational, and contrary to the views of the overwhelming majority of the community at large.

10.70 Thus, the position of the pregnant woman of sound mind has been brought into line with the 'adult of sound mind' referred to in *Re T*. More significantly, the Court of Appeal sought to prevent a repeat of this case and, indeed, others involving the treatment of patients of doubtful capacity, and issued guidelines for future reference. These are of considerable importance and we repeat them here for the sake of completeness:

(i)   The guidelines have no application where the patient is competent to accept or refuse treatment. In principle, a patient may remain competent notwithstanding detention under the Mental Health Act 1983.

(ii)   An application to the High Court for a declaration will be pointless if the patient is competent and refuses consent to the treatment. In this situation the advice given to the patient should be recorded. For their own protection, hospital authorities should seek unequivocal assurances from the patient (to be recorded in writing) that the refusal represents an informed decision: that is that she understands the nature of and reasons for the proposed treatment and the risks and likely prognosis involved in the decision to refuse or accept it. If the patient is unwilling to sign a written indication of this refusal, this too should be noted in writing. Such a written indication is merely a record for

---

134   *St George's Healthcare NHS Trust v S, R v Collins, ex p S* [1998] 3 All ER 673, (1998) 44 BMLR 160.
135   [1999] Fam 26, (1998) 44 BMLR 194.

      evidential purposes. It should not be confused with or regarded as a disclaimer.

(iii)   If the patient is incapable of giving or refusing consent, either in the long term or temporarily (eg due to unconsciousness), the patient must be cared for according to the authority's judgment of the patient's best interests. Where the patient has given an advance directive, before becoming incapable, treatment and care should normally be subject to the advance directive. However, if there is reason to doubt the reliability of the advance directive (eg it may sensibly be thought not to apply to the circumstances which have arisen), then an application for a declaration may be made.

(iv)   The authority should identify as soon as possible whether there is concern about a patient's competence to consent to or refuse treatment.

(v)   If the capacity of the patient is seriously in doubt, it should be assessed as a matter of priority. In many such cases, the patient's general practitioner or other responsible doctor may be sufficiently qualified to make the necessary assessment but, in serious or complex cases involving difficult issues about the future health and well-being or even the life of the patient, the issue of capacity should be examined by an independent psychiatrist, ideally one approved under s 12(2) of the Mental Health Act 1983. If, following this assessment there remains a serious doubt about the patient's competence, and the seriousness or complexity of the issues in the particular case may require the involvement of the court, the psychiatrist should further consider whether the patient is incapable by reason of mental disorder of managing her property or affairs. If so the patient may be unable to instruct a solicitor and will require a guardian ad litem in any court proceedings. The authority should seek legal advice as quickly as possible. If a declaration is to be sought, the patient's solicitors should be informed immediately and, if practicable, they should have a proper opportunity to take instructions and apply for legal aid where necessary. Potential witnesses for the authority should be made aware of the criteria laid down in *Re MB* and this case, together with any guidance issued by the Department of Health and the British Medical Association.

(vi)   If the patient is unable to instruct solicitors, or is believed to be incapable of doing so, the authority or its legal advisers must notify the Official Solicitor and invite him to act as guardian ad litem. If the Official Solicitor agrees he will no doubt wish, if possible, to arrange for the patient to be interviewed to ascertain her wishes and to explore the reasons for any refusal of treatment.

(vii)   The hearing before the judge should be inter partes. A declaration granted ex parte is of no assistance to the authority as the order made in her absence will not be binding on the patient unless she is represented either by a guardian ad litem, if incapable of giving instructions, or, if capable, by counsel or solicitor. Although the Official Solicitor will not act for a patient if she is capable of instructing a solicitor, the court may in any event call on the Official Solicitor, who has considerable expertise in these matters, to assist as an amicus curiae.

(viii)   It is axiomatic that the judge must be provided with accurate and all the relevant information. This should include the reasons for the proposed treatment, the risks involved in the proposed treatment, and in not proceeding with it, whether any alternative treatment exists, and the reason, if ascertainable, why the patient is refusing the proposed treatment. The judge will need sufficient information to reach an informed conclusion about the patient's capacity and, where it arises, the issue of best interest.

(ix)   The precise terms of any order should be recorded and approved by the judge before its terms are transmitted to the authority. The patient should be accurately informed of the precise terms.

(x)   Applicants for emergency orders from the High Court made without first issuing and serving the relevant applications and evidence in support have a duty to comply with the procedural requirements (and pay the court fees) as soon as possible after the urgency hearing.

10.71 Detailed though these guidelines are, it is noteworthy that they concern, primarily, procedural matters – the court was clearly disinclined to interfere in clinical matters. Indeed, it emphasised that the guidelines were, at the end of the day, guidelines only and advised that rigid compliance with them was inappropriate if to do so would put the patient's health or life at risk. The ball thus remains firmly in the health carers' court – subject, of course, to its being played according to the rules. A significant feature of the case, however, lies in its challenge to the use of mental health legislation as a means of legitimising involuntary treatment. There has been a recent increase in such cases, not only in relation to pregnant women, but also in the context of anorexics – who are discussed below.[136]

10.72 The experience of other jurisdictions in this respect has varied. In the United States, the issue has been affected by political pressure for the symbolic protection of the fetus – in the fiercely contested context of abortion – but this has been met by strong libertarian objections to interfering with maternal freedom during pregnancy.[137] These objections carried the day in Canada in the important decision of the Supreme Court in *Winnipeg Child and Family Services (Northwest Area) v GDF*,[138] the effect of which has been to dampen enthusiasm for intervening on behalf of the fetus.

OTHER VULNERABLE GROUPS

10.73 It is everywhere agreed that, to be valid, consent should be free, rational and unfettered; thus, prisoners constitute a further group which deserves special consideration.

10.74 The status of prisoners has been referred to briefly in chapter 1. It will be seen from this that it could be held that the incarcerated can never give a

---

136   See para 10.75.
137   For a comparative survey, see B J Glass 'A Comparative Analysis of the Right of a Pregnant Woman to Refuse Medical Treatment for Herself or her Viable Fetus: the United States and the United Kingdom' (2001) 11 Indiana Int Comp L Rev 507.
138   Para 10.20 above. For discussion, see L Shanner 'Case Comment and Note' (1998) 36 Alberta L Rev 751.

valid consent to treatment in that an element of coercion is implicit in the prison doctor-patient relationship. This proposition was considered in *Freeman*,[139] the decision in which greatly restricts this line of argument. The case turned in large measure on its own facts but the suggestion that the position of the prison psychiatrist vis-à-vis his patient voided a general consent was rejected; it was further stated that 'it was not open for it to be argued for the plaintiff that"informed consent" was a consideration which could be entertained by the courts'. While we believe that this latter opinion derived from a semantic misinterpretation of the concept which is discussed in detail below, the judgment clearly indicates that, in the absence of overt coercion, the restricted circumstances in which a prisoner's consent to treatment is given will be unlikely to affect the validity of that consent in law. An action for trespass is open to those in detention when consent to treatment has not been given[140] but mere negligence in obtaining that consent[141] will not brand the trespass as being coercive or oppressive. As an example of a valid refusal on the part of a prisoner, we have the judgment in *Secretary of State for the Home Department v Robb*,[142] a case which raised the question of whether the decision of a prisoner to go on hunger strike should be respected by the prison authorities. Somewhat unorthodoxly, the court applied a medical law approach to the case, even although the prisoner was not a patient, and upheld the individual's 'right to self-determination' to refuse food. In contrast, the attempt by the multiple murderer Ian Brady to starve himself to death was thwarted by the High Court when it refused his application for judicial review of the medical decision to force-feed him on the grounds that his personality disorder made him refuse food and therefore 'feeding' was treatment for his mental condition within the terms of the Mental Health Act 1983.[143]

10.75 In keeping with this last approach, a series of cases has similarly sanctioned the force-feeding of persons such as anorexics and depressives who refuse food. The rationale in each case has been that the feeding is *treatment* for the individual's *mental disorder*, this being the sole criterion under the legislation which permits health care professionals to forego consent.[144] Thus, for example, the trial judge in *Riverside Mental Health Trust v Fox*[145] held that an adult who was being treated for anorexia nervosa could be force-fed as a part of treatment for her mental condition. The Court of Appeal later overturned this decision but did so on procedural grounds and did not question the validity of the application of the 1983 Act to such a case. As if to endorse this line of reasoning, the Court of Appeal in *B v Croydon Health Authority*[146] authorised force-feeding under the 1983 Act of a woman with a borderline personality disorder, and feeding of a depressive and suicidal quinquagenarian was similarly ordered in *Re VS (adult: mental disorder)*.[147] In *Re C (detention:*

139   *Freeman v Home Office (No 2)* [1984] QB 524, [1984] 1 All ER 1036.
140   *Barbara v Home Office* (1984) 134 NLJ 888.
141   See paras 10.88–10.93 below.
142   [1995] 1 All ER 677.
143   *R v Collins, ex p Brady* (2000) 58 BMLR 173, [2000] Lloyd's Rep Med 355.
144   In particular, Mental Health Act 1983, s 63.
145   [1994] 1 FLR 614, (1993) 20 BMLR 1.
146   [1995] 1 All ER 683, CA.
147   [1995] 3 Med L Rev 292.

medical treatment)[148] an anorexic 16-year-old was detained using the High Court's inherent protective jurisdiction in order that she receive 'medical treatment' including, inter alia, force-feeding. This unusual procedure was justified as being in the child's best interests on the grounds that, because it was in her best interests to receive 'treatment' for her condition, it was also a part of those interests that she be detained – using reasonable force if necessary – so that the treatment could be carried out. It is to be noted that this order was not based on the detention provisions of the 1983 Act but, rather, on the common law powers of the High Court – which suggests that this jurisdiction is potentially very wide-ranging. Another interesting point is the use by Walls J of the three stage test for competency laid down in *Re C (adult: refusal of medical treatment)*.[149] That case concerned the competency of an adult. As we have seen, the capacity of a minor to agree to or refuse medical treatment has relied up until now on the concept of *Gillick* competence, the evaluation of which lies within the discretion of the health care professional. This equiparation of the test for competency in adults and minors is, in our view, correct, and adds judicial weight to our earlier argument that refusal of treatment by minors requires a higher standard of competency than does a decision to consent.[150]

10.76 All of this, however, must now be seen in light of the Court of Appeal decision in *R (on the application of Wilkinson) v RMO, Broadmoor Hospital Authority*[151] which revisits these decisions in the shadow of the Human Rights Act, and emphasises procedural requirements before such treatment can be embarked upon properly. As Hale LJ said:

> Whatever the position before the Human Rights Act 1998, the decision to impose treatment without consent upon a protesting patient is a potential invasion of his rights under article 3 or article 8. Super-*Wednesbury* is not enough. The claimant is entitled to a proper hearing, on the merits, of whether the statutory grounds for imposing this treatment upon him against his will are made out: ie whether it is treatment for the mental disorder from which he is suffering and whether it should be given to him without his consent 'having regard to the likelihood of its alleviating or preventing a deterioration of his condition'.[152]

---

148 [1997] 2 FLR 180, [1997] Fam Law 474.
149 Para 10.54 above.
150 In the context of minors the Scottish courts would not appear to agree with us. In *Re Houston, Applicant* (1996) 32 BMLR 93 Sheriff McGown interpreted s 2(4) of the Age of Legal Capacity (Scotland) Act 1991 in respect of a 15-year-old boy suffering from mental illness to mean that capacity to consent encompassed a capacity to refuse and, furthermore, it brings to an end the power of a parent to consent on behalf of the minor.
151 [2001] EWCA Civ 1545, [2002] 1 WLR 419, (2001) 65 BMLR 15.
152 Ibid, at para 83. See also, *R (on the application of Wooder) v Feggetter* [2002] EWCA Civ 554, [2002] 3 WLR 591, in which it was held that adequate written reasons to give a detained patient medication against his will must be produced by a second opinion doctor under the Mental Health Act 1983, and that these should be disclosed to the patient except in the rare circumstances where this would have an adverse effect on his physical or mental health.

CONSENT TO TESTING FOR HIV INFECTION

10.77   The question of whether tests for HIV infection can be undertaken without the consent of the patient has always been controversial.[153] There may be times when a doctor would wish to carry out such tests as part of a responsible diagnostic routine but, at the same time, be reluctant to alarm or embarrass his patient by disclosing his intention. Equally, the HIV status of a patient might be an issue after a needle-stick injury or blood contamination of medical personnel; the need to know could be urgent, yet the patient might refuse to consent to testing. Indeed, as we go to press the Royal College of Surgeons is demanding the right to test patients for HIV.[154] The legal problem is the same in each instance: does HIV testing exceed the bounds of any consent which the patient has already given to therapeutic or diagnostic investigation?

10.78   The GMC believes that specific consent to testing for HIV infection is required because of the serious social and financial consequences that may follow a positive diagnosis; every patient should have the opportunity to evaluate these consequences as they affect him personally. The Council has, accordingly, firmly rejected HIV testing in the absence of specific consent save in the 'most exceptional circumstances'.[155] At the same time, the GMC is quite clear that non-consensual testing is permissible if it is in the patient's medical interests to do so. It is more vague on the position regarding testing in the interests of others, urging simply that a practitioner should 'reconsider the severity of risk' to himself or others. The Council does agree, however, that the best interests of a child may dictate testing even in the face of parental objection.

10.79   Advice from such a source carries great ethical weight but does not help as to the legality of such testing. Here, conflicting advice has been offered to doctors in the United Kingdom. Legal opinion sought by the Council of the British Medical Association was to the effect that, not only was non-consensual testing impermissible but also, to do so, might well constitute an assault;[156] by contrast, the Central Committee for Hospital Medical Services was advised that the doctor may exercise his clinical judgment unless the patient asks specifically about HIV testing;[157] finally, the Medical Defence Union obtained an opinion which eliminated the possibility of assault once permission for venepuncture had been given but, nevertheless, thought that, save in exceptional circumstances – as, for instance

---

153   See K M Boyd 'HIV Infection: The Ethics of Anonymised Testing and of Testing Pregnant Women' (1990) 16 J Med Ethics 173. The position in the US, where AIDS is a notifiable disease, and elsewhere, may well be different and is not considered here; see D H J Hermann 'Liability Related to Diagnosis and Treatment of AIDS' (1987) 15 Law Med Hlth Care 36. For general discussion of blood testing, see A Grubb and D S Pearl *Blood Testing, AIDS and DNA Profiling: Law and Policy* (1990).

154   A Browne 'Surgeons Demand Right to Test Patients for HIV Infection' *The Times*, 29 July 2002, p 3.

155   General Medical Council *Serious Communicable Diseases* (1997).

156   M Sharrard and I Gatt 'Human Immunodeficiency Virus (HIV) Antibody Testing' (1987) 295 BMJ 911.

157   HMSC *Advice re HIV Testing* (1988) discussed by C Dyer 'Another Judgment on Testing for HIV Without Consent' (1988) 296 BMJ 1791.

when the expectation of a positive result was very low – specific consent for HIV should always be obtained.[158]

10.80 It is significant that much has changed in relation to HIV and AIDS since these advices were proffered.[159] Where once HIV was untreatable, combination therapy now provides significant hope for many people infected with the virus. Moreover, there is less evidence of a special case being made of the disease, as is demonstrated by the GMC's Guidance which relates to serious communicable diseases generally whereas once it spoke only of HIV and AIDS.[160]

10.81 We take the view that a patient who consults a doctor gives tacit consent to the carrying out of those diagnostic tests that the doctor considers necessary – the patient's consent to each and every test to be performed on a blood sample need not be obtained and it is unreal to speak of 'informed consent' in this context. This is not a unique view – as Dyer has reported: 'some lawyers have suggested that patients with a "perplexing presentation" might be taken to have given an implied consent to any tests designed to find out what was wrong with them.'[161] The essential question is whether the HIV test is of such a nature as to remove it from the scope of those tests to which the patient may be said to consent implicitly – reportedly, it would not be excluded, say, in Germany.[162] It is true that HIV tests carry major emotional, financial and social significance; moreover, the disease to be diagnosed is currently probably incurable – which distinguishes the test from one for, eg, syphilis. The same could, however, be said for a hypothetical test which demonstrated the presence of incurable malignant disease. It would not be necessary for the doctor to obtain specific consent to undertake such a test, yet it could have consequences similar to a test for HIV infection. The similarity is, however, not absolute – the major distinction being that, irrespective of the result, the mere fact that an HIV test has been undertaken carries serious insurance implications and has to be disclosed as a condition of many policies. We would raise, too, the potential psychological sequelae of an unexpected positive result. There is no escaping the fact that our society has constructed a stigma around this disease which makes the confirmation of a positive result all the more difficult to accept. Moreover, if such a result comes 'from the blue' when no specific consent was given, the question of the patient's right *not* to know arises.[163] These factors certainly

158 Medical Defence Union *AIDS: Medico-Legal Advice* (1988). These three opinions are discussed in detail by J Keown 'The Ashes of AIDS and the Phoenix of Informed Consent' (1989) 52 MLR 790.
159 Although not the legal position: A J Pinching, R Higgs and K M Boyd 'The Impact of AIDS on Medical Ethics' (2000) J Med Ethics 3.
160 For support for this process, see K M De Cock and A M Johnson, 'From Exceptionalism to Normalisation: A Reappraisal of Attitudes and Practice Around HIV Testing' (1998) 316 BMJ 290.
161 C Dyer 'Testing for HIV: The Medicolegal View' (1987) 295 BMJ 871. D Brahams 'Human Immunodeficiency Virus and the Law' [1987] 2 Lancet 227 shared our view so long as consent to test for HIV infection had not been specifically withheld. The issue of HIV testing is discussed extensively in R Bennet and C Erin (eds) *HIV and AIDS: Testing, Screening and Confidentiality* (1999)
162 H L Karcher 'Doctors and HIV: An International Perspective. 1 – Germany' (1991) 302 BMJ 195.
163 Discussed in the context of genetic information in chapter 7.

constitute grounds for treating the HIV test with special care but it is doubtful if it is a sufficiently powerful argument to exclude absolutely all testing for which no specific consent was given. None the less, the patient could argue that, had he been informed of the doctor's intention, he would not have consented to giving the sample; in such circumstances, an action for negligence might be available under the general terms of the consent doctrine.[164] The critical condition, here, is that he was informed – insurance and comparable complicating factors do not arise if the patient is ignorant of the facts. The professional attitude is summed up in a recent case in which a doctor was found guilty of serious professional misconduct for testing five patients for HIV without consent.[165] The GMC found that there was insufficient clinical evidence of infection in each patient, indicating, perhaps, that matters might be different were it otherwise. However, the practitioner must be prepared to justify his action, both in court and before his peers, in all cases of non-consensual testing.

10.82 All the above discussion relates to consent within the clinical setting and the patient's advantage; there can, in our opinion, be no vacillation if the advantage of testing is to another party – express consent would have to be obtained in such circumstances and action in its absence would have to be defended on the grounds of necessity or public interest.

10.83 In the earlier days of the pandemic, there were calls in some quarters for mandatory HIV testing; these were largely rejected, although a number of jurisdictions have introduced compulsory testing programmes for sections of the public. The World Health Organisation has been firm in its condemnation of such measures, pointing out that there are 'no benefits either to the individual or for public health arising from testing without informed consent that cannot be achieved by less intrusive means, such as voluntary testing and counselling'[166]. In spite of this, and similar endorsements of the voluntary approach to HIV testing, there has been a creeping tendency in some countries to allow compulsory testing of particular groups – such as military recruits or applicants for certain posts. In some US jurisdictions, for example, legislation allows testing to be carried out in the health care environment (for the protection of health care staff) or in prisons (for the protection of prison officials).[167] Some countries have also allowed compulsory testing of prostitutes.

10.84 Measures designed to protect health care staff from infection raise difficult issues, as do measures to protect patients themselves. Would the public interest justify coercive routine testing of some or all health carers? There has been an historical tendency in this direction in the United States,[168] which has been resisted in the United Kingdom, by both the government and the medical profession. In practice, it would be an ineffective way of solving a problem which is, to all intents, insignificant. Between 1988 and 2001 there were 22 patient

---

164 See paras 10.88 et seq below.

165 C Dyer, 'GP reprimanded for testing patients for HIV without consent' (2000) 320 BMJ 135.

166 World Health Organisation *Statement from the Consultation on Testing and Counselling for HIV Infections* (1992), 3.

167 See L O Gostin and D W Webber 'HIV Infection and AIDS in the Public Health and Healthcare System' (1998) 279 J Amer Med Ass 1108.

168 M Morris 'American Legislation on AIDS' (1991) 303 BMJ 325.

notification exercises in the UK following concerns of infection from health care workers. There was no detectable transmission of HIV from an infected worker despite around 7,000 patients having been tested.[169] It is more than doubtful if it would be morally defensible to spend millions of pounds of health service money[170] on exorcising such an ephemeral spectre. Indeed, the tendency in the UK is towards less interventionist practices. In July 2002 the Department of Health issued a consultation paper which laid out new guidance and policy on patient notification.[171] It follows expert advice from the Expert Advisory Group on AIDS that it is no longer necessary to notify every patient who has undergone an exposure prone procedure by an infected health care worker because of the very low levels of risk of transmission and the likelihood of wider public anxiety. Each decision should be made on a case-by-case basis and subject to clear guidelines contained in the paper. The paper itself was provoked in part by the Court of Appeal's judgment in *H v Associated Newspapers*[172] in which the very strong interests in confidentiality were stressed and weighed against the arguments in the name of freedom of expression and public safety that were mounted in support of a claim to identify an HIV-positive health care worker. The balance there was tipped most determinedly in favour of the public and private interests in maintaining confidentiality, and we discuss these in more detail in chapter 8.

10.85 The issue of contamination of the health carer has been raised on several occasions by the Royal Colleges of Surgeons of England and of Edinburgh.[173] Indeed, evidence indicates that the risk of transmission is greater *from* an HIV-positive patient *to* a health care worker. Data to June 1999 show that there have been 102 such cases worldwide, five of which were in the UK.[174] The principle of the need to obtain consent to testing before operation, even in an emergency, from a high-risk patient has been emphasised but the Colleges have agreed to support any surgeon who undertook non-consensual testing in the interests of seriously contaminated theatre staff – serious contamination and high-risk being, again, left to the individual surgeon's interpretation. It was said that testing before the patient had recovered from the anaesthetic could count as an assault; we confess to some difficulty in accepting this – it is hard to see where would be the element of assault provided no special invasion were made for the express purpose of obtaining the blood sample. In the current climate, however, it would be hard to justify a failure to wait the few minutes needed for the patient's recovery in order to carry out a relatively lengthy test; the situation, however, seems to be one of more theoretical than practical importance.

---

169 Department of Health, *HIV Infected Health Care Workers: A Consultation Paper* (2002), para 2.4.
170 K Tolley and J Kennelly 'Cost of Compulsory HIV Testing' (1993) 306 BMJ 1202.
171 Para 10.84 above.
172 *H (a healthcare worker) v Associated Newspapers Ltd; H (a healthcare worker) v N (a health authority)* [2002] EWCA Civ 195, (2002) 65 BMLR 132.
173 A Walker 'Surgeons and HIV' (1991) 302 BMJ 136 and most recently in 2002, see para 10.77 above.
174 Public Health Laboratory Service et al *Occupational Transmission of HIV: Summary of Published Reports* (1999).

10.86 Anonymised HIV testing, which may be of great epidemiological importance, is less controversial but still raises ethical issues.[175] Such tests involve either taking blood or saliva from random groups of patients who have not necessarily engaged in high-risk practices or using blood samples that have been obtained for other purposes. The morality of random testing for a specific condition depends, to a large extent and as discussed in chapter 8, on what would be done in the event of a positive result. The dilemma can be overcome by total anonymisation but this only substitutes one potential immorality by another – the knowledge obtained cannot now be used for the benefit of the individual or of his or her contacts. In general, however, the positive advantages of investigation seem to outweigh such objections provided that those tested are informed that their blood may be subjected to anonymised testing of any sort and that they will not be informed of the results. The Unlinked Anonymous Prevalence Monitoring Programme has, in fact, been in operation since 1990, providing a vital service for public health by generating data which could not be ascertained in any other way. Its work showed that, by the end of 1999, 33,200 adults were infected with HIV in the UK, over a third of whom were unaware of their infection.[176] Such figures are of major value in respect of public health and treatment planning, as well as for further research into the disease and its spread.

10.87 The question of whether it is ethically acceptable to carry out testing of this nature without the consent of the donors remains unresolved.[177] There is a strong argument for allowing it on the grounds of public interest. In this view, such testing cannot possibly harm the donor of the sample, who may well be unaware that his or her sample is being used in this way. A contrary view – which has been discussed in detail in respect of genetic testing in chapter 7 – is that a wrong is done even if the donor is unaware of it, and that a person who discovers that a personal sample has been used in this way is entitled to feel that his or her privacy has been infringed, irrespective of what protections against de-anonymisation were in place.

PROCEEDING WITHOUT CONSENT – THE CONSEQUENCES

10.88 Non-consensual medical treatment entitles the patient to sue for damages for the battery which is committed. It is also possible to base a claim on the tort of negligence, the theory being that the doctor has been negligent in failing to obtain the consent of the patient. There are important differences between the two forms of action which have given rise to much legal debate. The issue is, however, now settled and the law is clear.

10.89 An action for battery arises when the plaintiff has been touched in some way by the defendant and when there has been no consent, express or implied, to such touching. All that the plaintiff need establish in such an

---

175 See Boyd para 10.77 above.
176 Department of Health *Prevalence of HIV and Hepatitis Infection in the United Kingdom* (2001), p 1.
177 At the time of writing, public views are being sought on whether anonymised epidemiological testing should be allowed without consent. See: Department of Health and Welsh Assembly Government, *Human Bodies, Human Choices: A Consultation Report* (2002).

action is that the defendant wrongfully touched him. It is unnecessary to establish loss as a result and, therefore, there is no problem as to the causation of damage to be overcome. By contrast, in an action based on the tort of negligence, the plaintiff must establish that the defendant wrongfully touched him and that the negligence of the defendant in touching him without consent has led to the injury for which damages are sought. There is thus a problem of factual causation to be tackled and, for this reason, the action for battery is an easier option from the plaintiff's point of view. The measure of damages recoverable will also be different. All direct damages are recoverable in battery; only those damages which are foreseeable and which it is fair and just to compensate may be recovered in an action for negligence. Thus, an unforeseen medical complication arising from the procedure in question may give rise to something for which damages are recoverable in battery but not in negligence. Clarification of the circumstances in which each action is available was provided by the Supreme Court of Canada in *Reibl v Hughes*[178] and in the first apposite English case of *Chatterton v Gerson*.[179]

10.90 An action for battery is appropriate where there has been no consent at all to the physical contact in question. Thus, an action for battery is the suitable remedy if a patient has refused to submit to a procedure but the doctor has, nevertheless, gone ahead in the face of that refusal. A number of historic Canadian cases illustrate the typical circumstances. Actions were sustained in *Mulloy v Hop Sang*,[180] where the plaintiff's hand was amputated without his consent; in *Allan v New Mount Sinai Hospital*,[181] where the plaintiff had an anaesthetic injected into his left arm in spite of his objection to this procedure; and, as a final illustration, in *Schweizer v Central Hospital*,[182] in which the surgeon performing an operation on the back of a plaintiff whose consent was related to an operation on his toe was held liable for battery. It will be seen that, in all of these cases, what the doctor actually did was quite unconnected with the procedure to which the patient had consented. There was no consent to an operation of the 'general nature' of that which was actually performed – thus, they lay within the courts' policy of restricting battery actions to acts of unambiguous hostility.

10.91 A claim based on negligence is apt when the plaintiff has given his consent to an act of the general nature of that which is performed by the defendant but there is a flaw in this consent and, as a result, there has been no consent to certain concomitant features of the act of which he was unaware. The negligence lies in a failure to apprise the patient of such features as a result of which he has sustained damage; the damage is not due to negligent performance but results from a mishap which, in this instance, was a recognised potential hazard of the procedure. The distinction between the two forms of action was sharply outlined in *Reibl v Hughes* by Laskin CJC, who remarked in his judgment:

178 (1980) 114 DLR (3d) 1 at 10, per Laskin CJ.
179 [1981] QB 432, [1981] 1 All ER 257. See also *Hills v Potter* [1983] 3 All ER 716, [1984] 1 WLR 641.
180 [1935] 1 WWR 714.
181 (1980) 109 DLR (3d) 634.
182 (1974) 53 DLR (3d) 494.

I do not understand how it can be said that the consent was vitiated by the failure of disclosure of risks as to make the surgery or other treatment an unprivileged, unconsented to and intentional invasion of the patient's bodily integrity. I can appreciate the temptation to say that the genuineness of consent to medical treatment depends on proper disclosure of the risks which it entails, but ... unless there has been misrepresentation or fraud to secure consent to the treatment, a failure to disclose the attendant risks, however serious, should go to negligence rather than battery.[183]

10.92 Similarly, it was emphasised in *Chatterton v Gerson* that an action for trespass to the person is inappropriate once the patient is informed in 'broad terms' of the nature of the procedure and consent is given; an action for negligence is the proper remedy if there is a failure to disclose risks.

10.93 This, however, is not to say that an action in assault or battery is entirely irrelevant to medical law. In *Appleton v Garrett*[184] the High Court awarded both exemplary and aggravated damages against a dentist who had actively deceived patients as to their need for treatment over a number of years. Any consent offered by the patients was vitiated by the fraudulent misrepresentation of the practitioner. The court held that information had been deliberately withheld and the defendant had acted throughout in bad faith, making an action in battery, rather than in negligence, appropriate. This having been said, there need not be a nefarious purpose behind the touching for an assault to be committed, as the case of *Ms B* shows.[185] However, only notional damages are likely to be awarded in such cases in recognition of the affront to bodily integrity that the unauthorised touching represents.

The negligence action – causation problems

10.94 When there is a failure to disclose risks, the aggrieved patient is, in essence, claiming: 'You did not inform me of the risk which has eventuated; but for your failure, I would not have consented to the procedure; you have failed in your duty of care and, as a result, I have sustained injury.' The problem in negligence actions based on a lack of consent is, therefore, that of causation – the court must be satisfied that the defendant's failure to obtain the valid consent of the patient was, in fact, the cause of the patient's injury. To satisfy this requirement, the patient must prove that he would not have given his consent had he had the information of which he was allegedly deprived.

10.95 There are several ways by which the strength of the plaintiff's case can be assessed. The first involves a purely subjective judgment – that is, what would that particular patient have considered to be adequate information? This is clearly open to the abuse of hindsight. It will be only

---

183 For an interesting example of a British case following *Reibl*, see *Ardant v Smith* [1996] 7 Med LR 108.
184 (1995) 34 BMLR 23. See also [1996] 4 Med L Rev 311.
185 Discussed above at para 10.60. £100 in token damages was awarded.

too easy for a plaintiff, once he has suffered damage, to allege that he would not have given his consent when, in reality, he may well have been quite prepared to do so, even with full knowledge of the risks entailed – as a Californian court had it: 'Subjectively he may believe [he would have declined treatment] with the 20/20 vision of hindsight but we doubt that justice will be served by placing the physician in jeopardy of the patient's bitterness and disillusionment.'[186] The subjective standard is weighted overwhelmingly in favour of the plaintiff and only a few jurisdictions have accepted it.[187]

10.96 An alternative objective approach is to postulate a standard based on a reasonable patient. Would the reasonable patient have given his consent when confronted with full information of the risks and difficulties of the procedure in question? If the answer is 'yes', then it may be inferred that the plaintiff himself would have consented. This, like all objective tests, has the disadvantage of being potentially unfair to the plaintiff. There may be specific circumstances which are unique to the individual and it may well be that he or she genuinely would not have consented. To apply the objective standard might, then, be equally unsatisfactory: 'if it is Utopian to think one must concentrate on the particular patient, the law should surely be aiming at Utopia.'[188] The reasonable patient test has practical value in that judges are, themselves, patients and can, therefore, assess the evidence at first hand rather than by proxy; at the same time, this introduces the element of personal prejudice and, in *Maynard*,[189] the trial judge was considered to have been in error in preferring one body of medical opinion to another.

10.97 A third, compromise, possibility exists. The court may opt for an objective approach but qualify it by investing the hypothetical reasonable patient with the relevant special peculiarities of the individual plaintiff. In this way the edge is taken off the objective test, while the pitfalls of the purely subjective approach are avoided.

10.98 The courts in Canada vacillated for some time between the alternatives of the objective and subjective approaches.[190] Finally, in *Reibl v Hughes*,[191]

---

186 *Cobbs v Grant* 104 Cal Rptr 505 (1972).
187 The subjective standard was certainly used by the New Zealand Court of Appeal in *Smith v Auckland Hospital Board* [1964] NZLR 241, SC; revsd [1965] NZLR 191, NZCA, but there was no argument on the point in this very early case; a clear Antipodean preference for the subjective standard is to be found in the New South Wales Court of Appeal decision: *Ellis v Wallsend District Hospital* [1990] 2 Med LR 103. For full exposition, see D Giesen *International Medical Malpractice Law* (1988) pp 252 et seq.
188 K McK Norrie 'Informed Consent and the Duty of Care' 1985 SLT 289. Or achieving 'the ethical optimum of patient autonomy' as put by M Brazier 'Patient Autonomy and Consent to Treatment: The Role of the Law?' (1987) 7 LS 169.
189 *Maynard v West Midlands Regional Health Authority* [1985] 1 All ER 635, [1984] 1 WLR 634, HL. A rather similar judicial foray into medical decision-making was rejected on appeal in *Gold v Haringey Health Authority* [1988] QB 481, [1987] 2 All ER 888, CA. *Maynard* has been widely followed but is now under scrutiny in the light of *Bolitho v City and Hackney Health Authority* [1997] 4 All ER 1, (1997) 39 BMLR 1.
190 See eg *Male v Hopmans* (1967) 64 DLR (2d) 105; *Kelly v Haslett* (1976) 75 DLR (3d) 536.
191 (1980) 114 DLR (3d) 1.

the Supreme Court came down in favour of the compromise solution. The effect of this is that one's starting point is to determine the extent to which the balance of risks was, medically speaking, in favour of the treatment in question. This allows a decision to be made as to whether a reasonable patient would have consented and, that done, the court can proceed to look at the particular patient's condition. Here the judgment in *Reibl v Hughes* emphasised the importance of taking into account the patient's questions to the doctor, as these will demonstrate his concerns and will better enable the court to assess what a reasonable patient in the plaintiff's position would have done.

The concept of informed consent

10.99 The discussion thus moves inexorably to the issue of 'informed consent' – one which will always remain a classic example of the importation of a medical philosophy from across the Atlantic. Its progress has, in fact, been remarkably slow. Thus, while the first mention of 'informed consent' in the English courts seems to have been as late as 1981,[192] the seed was sown in America in 1957 in the case of *Salgo*.[193] Here, the court concluded that the doctor had a duty to disclose to the patient 'any facts which are necessary to form the basis of an intelligent consent by the patient to the proposed treatment'.[194] It is unfortunate that the phrase 'intelligent consent' was replaced in a later passage related to therapeutic privilege:[195]

> In discussing the element of risk, a certain amount of discretion must be employed consistent with full disclosure of facts necessary to an *informed* consent (our emphasis).[196]

10.100 Informed consent was later made a requirement for all state-funded research work following a series of allegations that potentially dangerous experiments were being conducted without the consent of the experimental subjects.[197] Silverman maintains that there are, thus, two distinct forms of 'informed consent' and, certainly, this must be so as to the assessment of the quality of the information provided. Such a review *must* be prospective in the case of research whereas it can only be retrospective, for example by way of litigation, in respect of day-to-day patient management.

10.101 In either event, informed consent introduced a new element to medical treatment. It is no longer a simple matter of consent to a technical assault; consent must now be based on a knowledge of the nature, risks, consequences and alternatives associated with the proposed therapy. Bray J's definition has gone relatively unchallenged[198] across the United States but it is still no more than a

---

192 *Chatterton v Gerson* [1981] QB 432, [1981] 1 All ER 257.
193 *Salgo v Leland Stanford Junior University Board of Trustees* 317 P 2d 170 (Cal, 1957).
194 Per Bray J.
195 See para 10.105 below.
196 We are indebted to W A Silverman 'The Myth of Informed Consent: In Daily Practice and in Clinical Trials' (1989) 15 J Med Ethics 6 for many of the historical facts.
197 Surgeon General's Memorandum *Clinical Investigations Using Human Subjects* (1966). It is, of course, now an integral part of research on a global scale (see chapter 19).
198 Eg *Harnish v Children's Hospital Medical Center* 387 Mass 152 (1982) where the phrase 'intelligent decision' was used.

broad expression of principle. It goes no way to explaining either what counts as informed consent or how we tell that the circumstances surrounding a given event satisfy the requirements.[199] In so far as it defines a doctor's duties rather than the patient's reaction, the phrase is a misnomer[200] which, we believe, has been applied in medical writing and, indeed, now almost inevitably, in official publications with inadequate exploration of its meaning. Moreover, the phrase is tautologous – to be ethically and legally acceptable, 'consent' must always be 'informed'. It is interesting to note that, although the English text of the Council of Europe's *Convention on Human Rights and Biomedicine* speaks of 'informed consent' in Article 5, the French text refers merely to 'consentment' *tout simple*.[201]

10.102 The topic recalls the aphorism of Frankfurter J, albeit in a completely different context:

> A phrase begins life as a literary expression; its felicity leads to its lazy repetition; and repetition soon establishes it as a legal formula indiscriminately used to express different and sometimes contradictory ideas.[202]

10.103 Thus, we suggest that, when Dunn LJ said in the fundamental United Kingdom case of *Sidaway*: 'The concept of informed consent forms no part of English law',[203] he may well have been referring to consent based on a subjective patient test – for no one would deny that 'information' must nowadays be passed from doctor to patient in the United Kingdom. Yet, similar disclaimers have been repeated both in England[204] and in Scotland[205] – and have been echoed in Australia[206] – and the legal definition has become no clearer. The phrase 'informed consent' is, however, now part of the lore of medical ethics; we must, therefore, accept it and consider the basic nature of the information that has to be given in order to validate consent to medical treatment.

---

199   G R Gillett 'Informed Consent and Moral Integrity' (1989) 15 J Med Ethics 117.

200   T K Feng 'Failure of Medical Advice: Trespass or Negligence' (1987) 7 LS 149.

201   Council of Europe, *Convention for the Protection of Human Rights and Dignity of the Human Being with regard to the Application of Biology and Medicine* (1997), Article 5.

202   *Tiller v Atlantic Coast Line Railroad Co* 318 US 54 at 68 (1943).

203   *Sidaway v Board of Governors of the Bethlem Royal Hospital* [1984] QB 493 at 517, [1984] 1 All ER 1018 at 1030, CA.

204   'English law does not accept the transatlantic concept of informed consent' per Lord Donaldson in *Re T (adult) (refusal of medical treatment)* [1992] 4 All ER 649 at 663, (1992) 9 BMLR 46 at 61, CA. The use of the words 'transatlantic concept' is, itself, misleading, as probably the majority of the United States still hold to a professional standard.

205   '[T]he law ... has come down firmly against the view that the doctor's duty to the patient involves at all costs obtaining the informed consent of the patient to specific medical treatments': *Moyes v Lothian Health Board* [1990] 1 Med LR 463, 1990 SLT 444 at 449, per Lord Caplan.

206   '... nothing is to be gained by reiterating ... the oft-used and somewhat amorphous phrase "informed consent"': *Rogers v Whittaker* (1992) 109 ALR 625 at 633, (1994) 16 BMLR 148 at 156 (High Court of Australia), per Mason CJ et al.

What needs to be disclosed?

10.104 Looked at from the ethical point of view, the matter is one of self-determination. A person should not be exposed to a risk of damage unless he has agreed to that risk and he cannot properly agree to – or, equally importantly, make a choice between – risks in the absence of factual information. The twin problems to be resolved are, therefore, by what general standard should the information be judged and, within that, to what extent must or should particular details be divulged?

10.105 The general standards available are conveniently described as the 'patient standard' and the 'professional standard'. The former has already been described above in the wide context of consent to battery. Precisely the same principles apply to counselling. Thus, the extreme of this school of thought would hold that, given a rational patient, the doctor must reveal all the relevant facts as to what he intends to do. It is not for him to determine what the patient should or should not hear. Obviously, there must be some medical assessment of what is or is not significant but, apart from the exclusion of irrelevant material, the patient should be as fully informed as possible so that he or she can make up his or her mind in the light of all the relevant circumstances. This approach most fully satisfies the requirements of self-determination but can be criticised on the grounds that it leaves little scope for the exercise of clinical judgment by the doctor. It is for this reason that even those most dedicated to patient autonomy will allow the doctor the 'therapeutic privilege' to withhold information which would merely serve to distress or confuse the patient.

10.106 This concession applies only to specific items selected by the doctor for specific reasons. It does not run as far as acceptance of the alternative ethical approach to disclosure of information – that is, one based on the professional standard. Here, counselling and informing are regarded as an integral part of clinical management; the extent and detail of the information supplied is a matter for decision by the doctor who is, therein, subject to the same duty of care as when prescribing or operating. It follows that, whichever standard is adopted, litigation based on inadequate information must be taken in negligence. Any difference lies in the test to be applied. Given a patient standard, the quality of information will be judged from the viewpoint of the prudent – or the particular – patient; under the professional standard, it will be that of the prudent doctor.

10.107 The choice between a 'patient standard' and a 'professional standard' is a difficult one. There must be respect for the patient's legitimate interest in knowing to what he is subjecting himself but, at the same time, there will clearly be cases where a paternalistic approach is appropriate. In addition, the practicalities of the situation must be borne in mind. Although it might be ethically desirable for patients to be as fully informed as possible, the time spent in explaining the intricacies of procedures could be considerable, particularly if a doctor is expected to deal with remote risks. Doctors – and, particularly, doctors operating in a NHS – simply do not have the time to spend on unduly lengthy explanations of all the ramifications of treatment and many would regard the practice as unnecessarily disturbing for the patient.[207] It has also been pointed out that adherence to a professional standard provides a coherent body of principles;[208] courts that are subject to this standard are, therefore, at least less likely to be inconsistent in their judgment of disputes. This clarity of approach is likely to continue with the release of detailed guidance both by the Department of Health[209] and the General Medical Council[210] as to what patients should be told in order to obtain valid consent.

10.108 A final point about the nature of the doctrine of informed consent relates to 'patient understanding'. The focus of the concept is on information given, supposedly to further the autonomy of the patient. But the consequent implication is that the health care professional has fulfilled his duty once he has proffered the information. Such a narrow interpretation, however, ignores consideration of the patient's ability to assimilate and analyse the information. If it is not also part of the doctor's duty to ensure at least a degree of understanding on the part of the patient, he can discharge his duty by offering information in a way that results in no enhancement of the patient's autonomy – the ethical basis of the doctrine is, accordingly, undermined. It is a fallacy to make consent forms longer and more detailed in an attempt to meet the requirements of the law for at least two reasons. First, this is likely to hinder rather than promote patient understanding, and, second, because a signed consent form has, in any case, no binding validity. It merely serves as *some* evidence that consent has been obtained, but this can always be rebutted if contrary evidence demonstrates that the patient was uncomprehending and did not truly provide his or her voluntary assent. This is confirmed by *Williamson v East London and The City Health Authority*,[211] which we have already looked at (see para 10.14). The surgeon maintained that she had explained that an extensive breast operation might be likely. The plaintiff did not accept that she was told this before the operation. The form which was signed related to silicon replacement, but was subsequently altered to read 'Bilateral replacement. Breast prosthesis. Right subcutaneous mastectomy'. There was no evidence that the patient had re-signed the form or initialled the amendments. The judge was satisfied that, on the balance of probabilities, the surgeon did not properly or sufficiently explain her intention to alter the operation.

The cases

10.109 Whatever standpoint one takes on information disclosure, a decision of some court can be found to endorse one's preferred approach. Within the Commonwealth, there are decisions ranging from the endorsement of the deliberate medical lie to the acceptance of the extreme patient-orientated

---

207 This, and other aspects, have been researched in Sheffield: D D Kerrigan, R S Thevasagayam, T O Woods et al 'Who's Afraid of Informed Consent?' (1993) 306 BMJ 298 and was found to be unmerited. The study, however, concerned the relatively innocuous repair of inguinal hernia – the authors concede that the results could be different in more serious circumstances.
208 C Newdick 'The Doctor's Duties of Care Under *Sidaway*' (1985) 36 NILQ 243.
209 Department of Health *Reference Guide to Consent for Examination or Treatment* (2001).
210 General Medical Council *Seeking Patients' Consent: The Ethical Considerations* (1998).
211 (1997) 41 BMLR 85, [1998] Lloyd's Rep Med 7.

approach which emphasises complete disclosure of risk. The United States, with its 51 independent jurisdictions, provides a useful overall view. Although a majority of the States still apply a professional standard, there is a recognisable national drift towards that of the prudent patient; it is worth recapitulating the reasons given for this in a typical case in which the onus was transferred.[212] These included:

(a)   that conditions other than those that are purely medical will influence the patient's decision;
(b)   that following the whim of the physician is inconsistent with the patient's right to self-determination; and
(c)   that the professional standard smacks of anachronistic paternalism.

10.110 In addition, the court in *Largey*[213] specifically ruled out the criticism that the prudent patient test obliges the doctor to list every possible complication of the proposed procedure. While this appears superficially disarming, it does, in fact, serve to emphasise that the professional is bound to be unsure of his precise position; as Margaret Brazier put it: 'the doctor is left to "second-guess" the courts.'

10.111 The way ahead in the United Kingdom is, now, clear. The starting point must be found in the complementary cases of *Hunter v Hanley*[214] in Scotland and *Bolam v Friern Hospital Management Committee*[215] in England, both of which define the essence of medical negligence. Most of the discussion of informed consent has been couched in *Bolam* terms and we will, for the moment, confine ourselves to that case – always with the caveat that we are following the loose thinking which surrounds that concept; for, as the High Court of Australia has pointed out,[216] consent is relevant to actions framed in trespass or battery, not in negligence which is simply a matter of standards of care. For present purposes, the essential part of the *Bolam* dictum runs: 'a doctor is not negligent if he acts in accordance with a practice accepted at the time as proper by a responsible body of medical opinion.'[217] Since it is agreed that actions based on lack of consent to medical treatment should be taken in negligence, it follows that any argument as to what needs to be disclosed in British medical practice hinges upon whether or not the *Bolam* principle applies equally to both diagnosis and treatment and to the giving of information.

10.112 That it did so was upheld both in *Chatterton v Gerson*[218] and in *Hills v Potter*.[219] The acid test, however, came in the seminal case of *Sidaway*[220]

---

212   *Largey v Rothman* 540 A 2d 504 (NJ, 1988). The prudent patient standard was set in *Canterbury v Spence* 464 F 2d 772 (DC, 1972). For retention of the professional standard, see *Wooley v Henderson* 418 A 2d 1123 (Md, 1980).
213   M Brazier 'Patient Autonomy and Consent to Treatment: The Role of the Law?' (1987) 7 LS 169.
214   1955 SC 200, 1955 SLT 213.
215   [1957] 2 All ER 118, [1957] 1 WLR 582.
216   In *Rogers v Whittaker* (1992) 109 ALR 625 at 633, [1993] 4 Med LR 79 at 83.
217   Per McNair J [1957] 2 All ER 118 at 122.
218   [1981] QB 432, [1981] 1 All ER 257.
219   [1983] 3 All ER 716, [1984] 1 WLR 641.
220   *Sidaway v Board of Governors of the Bethlem Royal Hospital* [1984] QB 493 at 517, [1984] 1 All ER 1018 at 1030, CA; affd [1985] AC 871, [1985] 1 All ER 643, HL.

where the proposition was accepted in the court of first instance but was received rather less enthusiastically in the Court of Appeal; there, Sir John Donaldson MR did not regard it as self-evident that the standards applied to diagnosis and treatment should be the same as those applied to disclosure. Concern was expressed that the definition of the duty of care was a matter for the law which 'could not stand by if the profession, by an excess of paternalism, denied their patients a real choice'.[221] Although the Master of the Rolls' colleagues were unable to follow him all the way, Browne-Wilkinson LJ also believed that there was a prima facie duty on the doctor to inform the patient – the assumption of the role of adviser carried with it the duty to disclose material and unusual risks.

10.113 The House of Lords, while maintaining a professional standard of disclosure, was, similarly, prepared to modify the existing law in certain respects. Thus, Lord Bridge held:

> A judge might, in certain circumstances, come to the conclusion that the disclosure of a particular risk was so obviously necessary to an informed choice on the part of the patient that no reasonably prudent medical man would fail to make it ...[222]

while Lord Templeman considered that:

> ... the court must decide whether the information afforded to the patient was sufficient to alert the patient to the possibility of serious harm of the kind in fact suffered.[223]

10.114 Lord Scarman, however, delivered what was, effectively, a dissenting judgment in which he indicated that: 'it was a strange conclusion if our courts should be led to conclude that our law ... should permit doctors to determine in what circumstances ... a duty arose to warn.' He found great merit in the American case of *Canterbury v Spence*,[224] in which it was held that, while medical evidence on this matter was not excluded, it was the court which determined the extent of, and any breach of, the doctor's duty to inform. Information includes warning. King CJ, for example, specifically instructed that the doctor's duty extends not only to disclose any real risks in the treatment but also to warn of any real risk that the treatment may prove ineffective.[225]

10.115 Two specific aspects of the information issue are confirmed as a result of *Sidaway*. The first is that material risks of a procedure must be disclosed, subject only to therapeutic privilege which a doctor might be required to justify. Following *Canterbury*, a risk can be defined as material if a reasonable person in the patient's position, if warned of the risk, would be likely to attach

221 [1984] QB 493 at 513, [1984] 1 All ER 1018 at 1028, CA.
222 [1985] AC 871 at 900, [1985] 1 All ER 643 at 663, HL.
223 [1985] AC 871 at 903, [1985] 1 All ER 643 at 665.
224 464 F 2d 772 (DC 1972).
225 *F v R* (1983) 33 SASR 189, SC. Alternative treatments should also be canvassed – particularly if there is a choice between medical and surgical procedures: *Haughian v Paine* (1987) 37 DLR (4th) 624, cited in (1987) 137 NLJ 557.

significance to it. Similarly, it is material if the medical practitioner is, or should reasonably be, aware that the particular patient, if warned of the risk, would be likely to attach significance to it.[226] Quite what that means in relation to chance is impossible to assess and, indeed, generalisations may be inappropriate as the test relates to the circumstances of the particular case. Moreover, significance in this field is a function not only of incidence but also of severity; thus, in *Hopp v Lepp*,[227] it was stated that a risk, even if it is a mere possibility, should be regarded as material if its occurrence causes serious consequences. As to incidence, it was agreed in *Sidaway* that a risk of 10% of a stroke resulting – as was established in *Reibl v Hughes*[228] – was one which a doctor could hardly fail to appreciate as necessitating a warning; but non-disclosure was considered proper in Mrs Sidaway's case when the risk of damage to the spinal cord was of the order of 1% or less. We have to admit to some concern that odds shorter than 100:1 might be regarded as immaterial in the eyes of the law.[229] A great deal will, however, hang on the *patient's* requirements as expressed by way of questioning and we return to this below.

10.116 Secondly, *Sidaway* confirmed the 'therapeutic' or 'professional' privilege to withhold information that might be psychologically damaging to the patient. This, again, follows the direction in *Bolam*, in which the judge said in his charge to the jury:

> You may well think that when a doctor is dealing with a mentally sick man and has a strong belief that his only hope of cure is submission to electroconvulsive therapy, the doctor cannot be criticised if he does not stress the dangers, which he believed to be minimal, which are involved in the treatment ...[230]

This principle has since been widely adopted.

10.117 It is also clear from *Sidaway* that, by way of exception to this rule, there must be particularly good reasons, which the doctor would have to justify, for failing to answer such questions as the patient puts and that there may, indeed, be a strict obligation to do so.[231] Thus, Lord Bridge held, albeit obiter, that:

> When questioned specifically by a patient of apparently sound mind about risks involved in a particular treatment proposed, a doctor's duty must, in my opinion, be to answer both truthfully and as fully as the questioner requires.[232]

10.118 'The fact that the patient asked questions revealing concern about the risk would make the doctor aware that this patient did, in fact, attach significance

---

226 Mason CJ et al in *Rogers v Whittaker* (1992) 109 ALR 625 at 634, [1993] 4 Med LR 79 at 83, Aus HC.
227 (1979) 98 DLR (3d) 464. But in the Australian case *Battersby v Tottman and State of South Australia* (1985) 37 SASR 524, the risk of blindness was considered a subject for obligatory disclosure only in a minority opinion – this may, however, have been because there was a strong possibility of suicide.
228 (1980) 114 DLR (3d) 1.
229 King JC accepted 200:1 as not being material in *F v R* (1983) 33 SASR 189, SC.
230 [1957] 2 All ER 118 at 124, [1957] 1 WLR 582 at 590, per McNair J.
231 Confirmed most recently in *Chester v Afshar* [2002] EWCA Civ 724, [2002] 3 All ER 552, CA.
232 [1985] AC 871 at 898, [1985] 1 All ER 643 at 661, HL.

to the risk'[233] – and, hence, affect its materiality; it was certainly this fact which served to turn a 1:14,000 chance of blindness into a risk which it was found negligent not to disclose in the Australian case of *Rogers v Whittaker.*

10.119 This inference was, however, disturbed in England in *Blyth v Bloomsbury Health Authority.*[234] Here, the trial judge's decision in favour of the plaintiff was reversed on appeal. He was found to be in error in holding that there was an obligation, when asked, to pass on *all* the information available to the hospital; the question of what a patient should be told in response to a general inquiry could not be detached from the *Bolam* test any more than when no such enquiry was made (per Kerr LJ). Neill LJ went further:

> I am not convinced [from *Sidaway*] that the *Bolam* test is irrelevant even in relation to the question of what answers are properly to be given to specific enquiries or that Lords Diplock and Bridge intended to hold otherwise.[235]

10.120 However, the argument in *Blyth* centred largely on some rather obscure therapeutic notes written in the hospital and there has been no judicial enthusiasm to follow its line.

10.121 The House of Lords' approach in *Sidaway* has been subject to academic criticism[236] largely because of the uncertainties it left behind. A strong impression remains that the House was not at ease with *Bolam* – only Lord Diplock was prepared to carry it to its conclusion. Yet ranks continued to be closed whenever the principle was directly questioned. Thus, in *Gold,*[237] Schiemann J at first instance attempted to distinguish counselling from treatment and was firmly overruled by the Court of Appeal.[238] The House of Lords has somewhat grudgingly confirmed that the courts retain the power to establish standards of care,[239] but, as we point out elsewhere, their Lordships find it acceptable to challenge medical opinion only when the latter has no rational basis. This attitude is now becoming almost unique in face of the current universal acceptance of a patient's right to decide on his or her own treatment. The writing was already on the wall 20 years ago in Canada where, in *Reibl,* it was held:

> [The] scope of the duty of disclosure ... is not a question that is to be concluded on the basis of the expert medical evidence alone ... What is under consideration here is the patient's right to know what risks are involved in undergoing or forgoing certain surgery or other treatment.[240]

---

233   Mason CJ et al in *Rogers v Whittaker* (1992) 109 ACLR 625 at 631, [1993] at 4 Med LR 79 at 82.
234   (1985) Times, 24 May; on appeal [1993] 4 Med LR 151, CA. *Blyth* reminds us that the principles derived from surgical cases can apply equally to medication – implied consent to taking a drug cannot be assumed: *Crichton v Hastings* (1972) 29 DLR (3d) 692.
235   [1993] 4 Med LR 151 at 157, Neil LJ concurring at 160.
236   For full discussion see I Kennedy and A Grubb *Medical Law* (3rd edn, 2000) pp 691 et seq.
237   *Gold v Haringey Health Authority* [1988] QB 481, [1987] 2 All ER 888, CA.
238   The integral nature of medical attendance has been emphasised in other contexts, eg in the management of the mentally incompetent: *Re H (a patient)* [1993] 1 FLR 28, [1993] 4 Med LR 91.
239   *Bolitho v City and Hackney Health Authority* [1997] 4 All ER 771, (1997) 39 BMLR 1.
240   (1980) 114 DLR (3d) 1 at 13.

and, in 1983, it was said of warning of therapeutic failure in the Supreme Court of South Australia:

> The ultimate question ... is ... whether the defendant's conduct ... conforms to the standard of reasonable care demanded by the law. That is a question for the court and the duty of deciding it cannot be delegated to any profession or group in the community.[241]

10.122 The strongest attack on *Bolam* to date has, however, come from the High Court of Australia where its application to counselling has been firmly rejected in *Rogers v Whittaker*. In that case, we have the majority opinion saying:

> There is a fundamental difference between, on the one hand, diagnosis and treatment and, on the other hand, the provision of advice or information to the patient ... Because the choice to be made calls for a decision by the patient on information known to the medical practitioner but not to the patient, it would be illogical to hold that the amount of information to be provided by the medical practitioner can be determined from the perspective of the practitioner alone or, for that matter, of the medical profession.[242]

and even more trenchantly, Gaudron J:

> [E]ven in the area of diagnosis and treatment, there is, in my view, no legal basis for limiting liability in terms of the rule known as 'the *Bolam* test' ... [It] may be a convenient statement of the approach dictated by the state of the evidence in some cases. As such, it may have some utility as a rule-of-thumb in some jury cases, but it can serve no other useful function.[243]

10.123 The ripples of *Rogers* have reached distant shores, including those of South Africa, where negligence is subsumed under a general heading of 'wrongfulness' for which the defence of *volenti non fit injuria* – ie voluntary assumption of risk – is available. In *Castel v De Greef* [244] the Cape Provincial Division of the Supreme Court endorsed not only the Australian High Court's patient-orientated disclosure test, but also that court's definition of material risk. It was held that, for a defence of *volenti non fit inuria* to be successful, the consenting party must have knowledge, awareness, appreciation and understanding of the nature and extent of the harm or risk involved, this being on the grounds that the patient has otherwise not voluntarily assumed the risks in question, ie is not *volens*. The juxtaposition of *volenti* and consent

---

241 *F v R* (1983) 33 SASR 189 at 194, per King CJ.

242 (1992) 109 ALR 625 at 632, [1993] 4 Med LR 79 at 83. For a full discussion of the case, see D Chalmers and R Schwartz '*Rogers v Whittaker* and Informed Consent in Australia: A Fair Dinkum Duty of Disclosure' (1993) 1 Med L Rev 139; R C Pincus 'Has Informed Consent Finally Arrived in Australia?' (1993) 159 Med J Austral 25; and B McSherry 'Failing to Advise and Warn of Inherent Risks in Medical Treatment: When Does Negligence Occur?' (1993) 1 J Law Med 5.

243 (1992) 109 ALR 625 at 635-636, [1993] 4 Med LR 79 at 84. This decision was reaffirmed by the High Court in *Chappel v Hart* [1998] HCA 55. However, in *Rosenberg v Percival* [2001] HCA 18, a case which was primarily concerned with information and causation, the High Court was not entirely dismissive of *Bolam*; the objection was not so much to the relevance of medical opinion as to its conclusiveness in assessing the necessary extent of disclosure.

244 1994 (4) SA 408.

suggests that, pace *Chatteron v Gerson*,[245] an action in trespass may still be available, at least in South Africa; the fact that *Castell* was taken in negligence was dictated by the nature of the pleadings. Thus, we see how a common concept of informed consent can be recognised in legal systems with varying traditions.

10.124 In the United Kingdom, however, habits die hard and the position in Scotland has been resolved in a way that leaves little room for doubt.[246] Lord Caplan had this to say:

> In my view ... the appropriate tests to apply in medical negligence cases are to be found in *Hunter v Hanley* and *Bolam* ... As I see it, the law in both Scotland and England has come down firmly against the view that the doctor's duty to the patient involves at all costs obtaining the informed consent of the patient to specific medical treatments ... I can read nothing in the majority view in *Sidaway* which suggests that the extent and quality of warning to be given by a doctor to his patient should not in the last resort be governed by medical criteria.[247]

10.125 But, despite this, there is no doubt that a movement away from *Bolam* has developed in the years since the previous edition of this book and there is now evidence that the British courts will not always adhere rigidly to the *Bolam* standard in disputes over information disclosure. In *Smith v Tunbridge Wells Health Authority*,[248] for example, the failure of a consultant surgeon to inform a 28-year-old man of impotence and bladder dysfunction following an operation to treat rectal prolapse was held to be negligent, despite medical support for the decision. Indeed, it was considered that disclosure of the risk was the *only* reasonable course of action.

10.126 Negligence was established in *McAllister v Lewisham and North Southwark Health Authority*,[249] when a senior consultant neurosurgeon failed to disclose the risks surrounding an operation to alleviate a weakness in the patient's leg which was linked to a neurological malformation. Among other lapses, a risk of hemiplegia was not disclosed. The trial judge held that:

> I have come to the conclusion that those who say that the warnings given ... were inadequate are right and there has not been shown to me on the evidence any reputable body of responsible opinion to the contrary.

10.127 *Newell and Newell v Goldenberg*[250] was in essence a wrongful pregnancy case, involving a vasectomy which reversed and led to a fourth conception for the plaintiffs. The undisclosed risk of this happening was 1:2,300 and the plaintiffs argued that, had they been informed, Mrs Newell

---

245 [1981] QB 432, [1981] 1 All ER 257.
246 *Moyes v Lothian Health Board* 1990 SLT 444, [1990] 1 Med LR 463. Two further Scottish cases are known to have failed but are very poorly reported: *Comber v Greater Glasgow Health Board* 1992 SLT 22n, *Hsuing v Webster* 1992 SLT 1071n. They are reported as news items in *The Scotsman*, 24 April 1991, p 4.
247 1990 SLT 444 at 449, [1990] 1 Med LR 463 at 468.
248 [1994] 5 Med LR 334.
249 [1994] 5 Med LR 343.
250 [1995] 6 Med LR 371.

would also have been sterilised. Mantell J found for the plaintiffs in holding that a patient about to undergo elective or voluntary surgery is entitled to be told about its effectiveness. He opined that, although some doctors might not have disclosed the risk at the relevant time, they would not, in so doing, have been acting reasonably or responsibly: '[t]he Bolam principle provides a defence for those who lag behind the times ... It cannot serve those who know better'.[251]

10.128 Turning to the Court of Appeal, a plaintiff's action for negligent failure to disclose the risk that a hysterectomy might not provide protection against conception was upheld in *Lybert v Warrington Health Authority*.[252] Without referring explicitly to *Bolam*, the court none the less decreed that part of the duty of care owed was to ensure that a proper and effective system existed for giving sufficient warning of failure. Ideally, that warning should be oral *and* in writing and could be given either on admission of the patient, before she agreed to the operation or before her discharge. Here the court is effectively laying down the acceptable standard of care for such cases and, in this respect, the decision represents a tentative incursion into near-virgin territory.

10.129 Most significant of all, however, is the Court of Appeal decision in *Pearce v United Bristol Healthcare NHS Trust*,[253] in which an action in negligence was brought by a couple whose child died in utero almost three weeks after reaching term. The mother had pleaded with the consultant two weeks after her delivery date either to induce the birth or to carry out a caesarian section, but he advised against it citing the high risks of induction and the long time for recovery from caesarian section. He did not disclose the risks of fetal death in the womb as a result of delay in delivery. In deciding whether the consultant was negligent in this regard, the court endorsed *Sidaway* as the law and accepted *Bolam* as the relevant test, but also followed Lord Bridge's caveat concerning the need to warn of 'significant risks'. Lord Woolf MR felt that Lord Templeman's views in *Sidaway* best summed up the position, whereby the patient was entitled to such information as was needed to make a balanced judgment in the circumstances. Moreover, Lord Woolf quoted with approval the passage from *Bolitho* concerning the role of the court in questioning medical opinion lacking a logical basis, which we discuss in chapter 9.[254] All of this led him to the following ratio:

> In a case where it is being alleged that a plaintiff has been deprived of the opportunity to make a proper decision as to what course of action he or she should take in relation to treatment, it seems to me to be the law...that if there is a significant risk which would affect the judgment of a reasonable patient, then in the normal course it is the responsibility of the doctor to inform the

251 Yet, as recently as 1998, we have Ebsworth J in a disclosure case: '[I]t was not open to the court, while probably preferring the evidence of one expert from that of another, to choose between genuine, equally competent and logically justifiable difference of opinion as to whether decisions made about treatment, including the obtaining of consent, had been professionally justifiable': *Newbury v Bath District Health Authority* (1998) 47 BMLR 138 at 149.

252 [1996] 7 Med LR 71.

253 (1999) 48 BMLR 118.

254 Note, however, that Lord Browne-Wilkinson in *Bolitho* made it clear that he was not dealing with an information disclosure case.

patient of that risk, if the information is needed so that the patient can determine for him or herself as to what course he or she would adopt.

10.130 This endorses Lord Bridge's views in *Sidaway*, and indeed, Lord Woolf cites with approval Lord Bridge's case of a 10% risk of stroke as an example of a 'significant risk'. Beyond that he does not say how the significance of a risk is to be determined. However, in one, possibly significant, regard Lord Woolf shifts the emphasis of this concept. He talks of the effect of a significant risk on the judgment of a *reasonable patient*, while Lord Bridge spoke of 'disclosure ... so obviously necessary to an informed decision on the part of the patient that no *reasonably prudent medical man* would fail to make it'. Does this represent a doctrinal shift towards a prudent patient test for Britain? It is arguable. But Lord Woolf only generated hope in half-measure, for he went on to apply his test to the facts of the case. In doing so, he concluded that there was no 'significant risk' because '[t]he doctors called on behalf of defendants did not regard that risk as significant; nor do I'. Moreover, he stated that the consultant could not be criticised when dealing with a distressed patient for not informing her of 'that very, very small additional risk' – one in the order of 0.1–0.2%. In this sense, the risk was 'small' in statistical terms. However, and importantly, there is little evidence that 'significance' is determined by reference to patient-orientated criteria. While the language used by the Court of Appeal is suggestive of a movement away from the precedents of the past, and while 'the doctor, in determining what to tell a patient, has to take into account all the relevant considerations',[255] the outcome and the reasoning may simply locate the decision within the existing paradigm – namely, the *Bolam* test. A possible exception lies where there is a 'significant risk' – ie a self-evidently high statistical risk of serious harm occurring, which *no* reasonable person, professional or otherwise, would find it acceptable to withhold. Even so, there is little doubt that the tenor of debate surrounding these matters has been veering to the side of the patient and her right to choose for many years now. Precedents such as this can be taken either way and the future direction of the law lies as much in the attitude with which the individual courts approach such cases as in the ratio of *Pearce*.[256] Movement away from *Bolam*, as the High Court of Australia so readily accepted in *Rogers v Whittaker*, is due to recognition of the fact that the advice-giving aspect of medical practice is not entirely a matter of medical knowledge and expertise. This must be correct for, unlike diagnosis and treatment, the question of whether a patient wishes to consent to a particular procedure is bound firmly to the notion of patient autonomy – the choice of the patient is crucial and a choice can only be real and valid if it is based on adequate information. This brings us full circle and back once again to the nature of the doctrine of informed consent and its future.

255 (1998) 48 BMLR at 125 – 'which include the ability of the patient to comprehend what he has to say to him or her and the state of the patient at the particular time, both from the physical point of view and an emotional point of view...' These matters go to the capacity of the individual patient to absorb the information. They tell us nothing about what the patient is entitled to know as a matter of law. Moreover, they are determined by medical judgment, nor patient need.

256 The problems involved are explicit in *O'Keefe v Harvey-Kemble* (1999) 45 BMLR 74, CA, a case involving cosmetic rather than therapeutic breast surgery. The warnings given were considered insufficient.

The consent doctrine in the future

10.131 Few would deny that the progress of the consent doctrine in the United States has shown signs of overreaction leading, in some instances, to the undue encouragement of malpractice litigation.[257] There is also little doubt that such fears have had their influence on the British courts – Dunn LJ, for example, considered that the acceptance of 'informed consent' would be damaging to the relationship of trust and confidence between doctor and patient and might have an adverse effect on the practice of medicine.[258] Two judges in the House of Lords in *Sidaway* admitted their reliance on an article by Robertson[259] in which an American opinion was quoted:

> The requirement of informed consent to medical treatment has, for at least the past two decades, been used as a cloth from which courts slowly have begun to fashion a no-fault system for compensating persons who have suffered bad results from medical treatment.[260]

10.132 Robertson, himself, concluded that 'it is judicial policy, rather than the importance of the patient's rights, which will dictate the future development of the doctrine in the United Kingdom'. We would hope that this cynical analysis is untrue – although it is certain that, so long as *Bolam* holds sway – in whatever measure – it is unlikely that the consent-based action will be used as widely in the British courts as it has been in those of the United States.

10.133 Nevertheless, the wind of change continues to blow and the question remains not so much 'is the doctrine of informed consent coming to the United Kingdom?' as 'what can we do to improve on the American model?'

10.134 In our view, a start might well be made by dropping the phrase 'informed consent' in favour of 'rational consent' – or, perhaps better, using the word 'understanding', for a competent adult has every right to make a decision which may appear irrational to others. Both are terms which pay due deference to patient autonomy and, at the same time, provide the doctor with a yardstick as to what is expected of him.[261] We need to ensure that any emerging spirit of confrontation between the medical profession and the public is halted and abandoned in favour of the concept of what Teff described as a therapeutic alliance.[262] Some time ago, Diana Brahams[263] expressed the issue well when she said:

---

257 In *Truman v Thomas* 611 P 2d 902 (Cal, 1980) a doctor was, effectively, held liable for failing to convince a reluctant patient of the importance of a screening test for cancer.
258 [1984] 1 All ER 1018 at 1030.
259 G Robertson 'Informed Consent to Medical Treatment' (1981) 97 LQR 102.
260 A Meisel 'The Expansion of Liability for Medical Accidents: From Negligence to Strict Liability by Way of Informed Consent' (1977) 56 Neb L Rev 51.
261 The use of other ill-defined terms such as 'effective consent' (Human Fertilisation and Embryology Act 1990, Sch 3) do little more than compound the difficulties.
262 H Teff 'Consent in Medical Procedures: Paternalism, Self-determination or Therapeutic Alliance?' (1985) 101 LQR 432.
263 D Brahams '"Informed Consent" – the Thin End of the Wedge' (1985) 135 NLJ 201.

it is up to us to persuade doctors to alter their practice so as to divulge more information routinely and bring their standards up to what a prudent patient would like to know – without intervention of law.

10.135 This is undoubtedly happening. The prudent patient and the prudent doctor standards are approximating de facto even if not de jure. A glance at the literature, and a glance at the views of the profession's leaders, clearly show that, even if the courts may still be doubtful as to the doctrine of informed consent, the medical profession now accepts it as a *fait accompli*. Increasingly, the gap between what *is* revealed and what *should be* revealed to the patient is closing.

11 Health resources and dilemmas in treatment

11.1 No resources are infinite. Even if a basic material is widely available, the costs of harvesting, treating or assembling it put some restraint on its use; moreover, the manpower required for distribution and exploitation of the finished product is also going to be limited. Applying these to medicine, it is clear that it is well-nigh impossible to provide every form of therapy for everyone – some sort of selective distribution is inevitable.

11.2 The logistics of medicine get no easier despite – or, more probably, because of – the massive technological advances of the last half century. Costs of all types are rising while even comparatively affluent countries face persistent economic difficulties. The average span of life is increasing – at least in the developed countries – and, as a result, people need treatment for longer; this treatment is not the 'easy-cure' type appropriate to infectious diseases but is rather a matter of sophisticated care for the results of degenerative change. In addition, members of the public are better informed on medical matters and are better able to assimilate the information they are given; they are subjected to a barrage of advice of varying quality on the Internet and, as a result, the choice of treatment is increasingly influenced by the patient's demands, with proportionate erosion of the doctor's discretion – in effect, while the latter may wish to treat on a productivity basis, the former views therapy in terms of feasibility.[1]

11.3 Somehow, a compromise must be achieved between demand and supply; the distribution of scarce resources poses some of the more complex ethical problems of modern medicine and permeates every aspect of its provision. They are not confined to the higher administrative echelons nor to the more esoteric departments of major hospitals. They may, indeed, arise and be answered subconsciously – every time a doctor travels to visit a patient he is

---

1   It is only fair to say that these widely held views can be criticised in that the evidence for their influence is virtually untested: S Frankel, S Ebrahim and G D Smith 'The Limits to Demand for Health Care' (2000) 321 BMJ 40. None the less, we accept the fact that ever-increasing financial provision for the health service has failed to close the gap between supply and demand.

distributing his resources in favour of one priority and this is possibly at the expense of others with which he could have dealt during his non-productive driving time.[2]

11.4 Such an example relates to the treatment of individuals. But the ethics of health service distribution can also be considered on a global scale; the problems arising at a national level occupy an intermediate position. We propose examining these as three separate issues.

GLOBAL DISTRIBUTION OF RESOURCES

11.5 It is beyond question that the world's medical resources are distributed unevenly both in material and in human terms. The money to buy the expensive paraphernalia associated with modern hospital medicine is simply not available in the developing countries; at the same time, there are inadequate facilities for the local training of doctors who must, therefore, travel to obtain experience. The result is a vicious circle in which doctors accustomed to the sophisticated methods of the developed nations return to their own countries only to depart again dissatisfied with what they have found; permanent emigration of doctors and, in particular, nurses adds to the problem.

11.6 All this occurs in the face of increasingly destructive pandemics of infectious disease – in particular HIV infection, tuberculosis and malaria – and the effect is amplified by a shortage of public health resources. Requests are then made of developed countries for medical assistance in the form of rapid response and the supply of cheap drugs.[3] The response, such as it is, is not necessarily entirely altruistic. Along with the development of international travel, we have created ideal conditions for the spread of such diseases and action at source may be a matter of self-preservation.

11.7 But the nature of aid provided to the developing countries cannot avoid being politically influenced and is certainly a matter beyond the scope of our current discussion.[4]

THE ALLOCATION OF NATIONAL RESOURCES

11.8 We come closer to personal reality when discussing resource allocation on a national scale and, here, a mass of relevant literature has built up in recent years – much of which admits the near impossibility of a wholly just solution.

2 This aspect is amplified in R Klein 'Dimensions of Rationing: Who Should Do What?' (1993) 307 BMJ 309.
3 J Frenk and O Gómez-Dantés 'Globalisation and the Challenges to Health Systems' (2002) 325 BMJ 95. Note: World Health Organization *Macroeconomics and Health: Investing in Health for Economic Development* (2001).
4 For a philosophical approach, see R Attfield 'The Global Distribution of Health Care Resources' (1990) 16 J Med Ethics 153. Attitudes are, in fact, changing and far more effort is being put into providing resources at the level of primary and paramedical care.

11.9 The primary problem, which is essentially political, is to establish what share of the national resources is to be allocated to health – and it is the open-endedness of claims to health care that leads to particular difficulties. These claims can never be met in full. Moreover, issues of justice between claimants will inevitably arise after the broad budgetary decisions have been made. Ideally, resource allocation should provide equal access to health care for those in equal need. Attempts have been made in recent years to achieve this by systematically correlating the revenue given to the health authorities with their needs. These needs were originally based by the Resource Allocation Working Party on the standardised mortality rates which were taken as representing the underlying morbidity. This, in itself, is open to criticism, as it reflects the needs at hospital level rather than those of the provision of primary care which is particularly affected by external factors such as the degree of social deprivation. Nevertheless, RAWP, as the process came to be known, appeared to provide an objective, albeit rough, formula which could be readily understood; inevitably, it was subject to criticism and the major discrepancies were ironed out slowly.[5] A new formula was introduced in 1991 which weights the age adjusted population of each region by the square root of its standardised mortality rate for those under 75 years old;[6] this was based on empirical findings. One effect is, as pointed out by Sheldon, to open the doors to differential interpretation at sub-regional level and to political lobbying by health authorities who can gain from some of the many variables which can, legitimately, be fed into the resultant equation – moreover, by their nature, empirical data are unlikely to be fully contemporary. Some explicit measure of macroallocation of national resources is clearly needed – it has been suggested that one result of its use is that vote maximising policies become more obvious and are, thus, more difficult to carry out.[7] Even so, it may well be that it is better left at a relatively unsophisticated level and that further research is directed to how the allocations, once made, are actually used.

11.10 When allocation is considered at sub-regional level, equity becomes a less significant factor and gives way to the dictates of demand. This inevitably involves a choice and this choice must be, to some extent, arbitrary. The ethical control of resources then depends, first, upon the broad base of representation on the allocation committee and, secondly, on the willingness of the constituent members not to press their own interests too hard – a process which has been described, and, to an extent, approbated, as shroud waving;[8] the lay influence of community health councils has been important at this point.[9]

---

5   N Mays 'Measuring Morbidity for Resource Allocation' (1987) 295 BMJ 703; G Bevan and J Charlton 'Making Access to Health Care More Equal: The Role of General Medical Services' (1987) 295 BMJ 764; J Smith 'RAWP Revisited' (1987) 295 BMJ 1015.
6   Department of Health *Funding and Contracts for Health Services, Working Paper 2* (1989). For discussion, see T A Sheldon, G D Smith and G Bevan 'Weighting in the Dark: Resource Allocation in the New NHS' (1993) 306 BMJ 835 – particularly for the mathematical analysis which is beyond the ambit of this book.
7   See eg A Maynard and A Ludbrook 'Applying Resource Allocation Formulae to Constituent Parts of the UK' (1980) 1 Lancet 85.
8   J Rawles 'Castigating QALYs' (1989) 15 J Med Ethics 143.
9   Community Health Councils are to be abolished (National Health Service Reform and Health Care Professions Act 2002, s 22) but patient and public involvement at all levels of health care is a cornerstone of current government policy (see also chapter 1).

11.11 In any event, a change in policy was laid down in the National Health Service and Community Care Act 1990 which established the district health authorities as purchasers of health services on behalf of the local population. In this role, they are required to act as good housekeepers and not only to provide what the people want but also to do this in the most cost-effective manner.[10] The choices can never be easy – is it possible to decide the relative importance between, say, strict economy, the avoidance of suffering or the prolongation of life? And how is one to identify the best route to the intended goal? If, for example, morbidity as a whole is taken as the yardstick, the alleviation of bronchitis and asthma has been found to take precedence; if, on the other hand, one considers total hospital in-patient days, mental health may be the single most important consideration. But to say that mental health and respiratory disease constitute the most serious burdens on the health service is not necessarily to say that they merit the greatest allocation of resources. There is a strong economic incentive to apply some sort of 'productivity test' in distributing the resources of society; the question is – is it ethical to do so? Analysis of the problem raises some stark and disturbing answers. Thus, it has been said that to reject opportunities to allow natural dying is costly in financial terms – in a health care service with finite resources, it is neither harsh nor unethical to accept the consequences of a financial limit.[11] And the same article expresses the grim reality of political power in the suggestion that to spend a lot on the elderly might not be supported by public opinion if it became known that younger lives were being lost because of inadequate finance.

11.12 This immediately draws attention to one major difficulty encountered in any such evaluation based on public opinion – which is that the welfare of unproductive citizens is likely to be regarded as secondary to that of the productive unless the views of voluntary organisations with specific interests are given particular consideration; the mentally handicapped and the elderly are, in fact, in double jeopardy – not only may they be seen as less deserving of resources, but they are less likely to be invited to subscribe to the opinion-making process. Geriatric patients, it is said, would not and should not expect priority over younger patients. Which is true enough – but they *would* expect equal consideration. Harris's argument,[12] which sees the saving of life as the main medical objective, is at its strongest when we are considering the use of life years as a parameter for the assessment of the disposal of scarce resources. The choice between a 20-year-old and an 80-year-old may be straightforward to the outsider. But, at the moment of decision, each patient values his or her life equally – and the problem, then, is how to measure that equality; a productivity test, for example, demands that treatment should be both beneficial *and* effective whereas an evaluation on the basis of social good may conclude that benefit alone is sufficient to justify the resultant costs to the community.[13]

10 See C Newdick 'Rights to NHS Resources after the 1990 Act' (1993) 1 Med L Rev 53.

11 G S Robertson 'Dealing with the Brain-damaged Old – Dignity Before Sanctity' (1982) 8 J Med Ethics 173.

12 J Harris 'Unprincipled QALYs' (1991) 17 J Med Ethics 185.

13 The rather dated paper by M A Somerville '"Shall the Grandparents Die?": Allocation of Medical Resources with an Ageing Population' (1986) 14 Law Med Hlth Care 158 remains one of our favourites. For a contemporary analysis, see J Hurley 'Ethics, Economics, and Public Financing of Health Care' (2001) 27 J Med Ethics 234.

11.13 It is inevitable that, so long as there is a restriction on resources – and there must be a limit even in Utopia – some principle of maximum societal benefit must be applied; the individual's right to equality must, to some extent, be sacrificed to the general need. The precise determination of a maximum benefit policy is difficult to make, but the decision is societal rather than medical and involves a 'cost-benefit' analysis and all that that entails as to the quality of life.[14] Essentially, there are three potential measures of a free health service – comprehensiveness, quality and availability – and the situation is that the goal of fully comprehensive, high quality medical care that is freely available to all on the basis of medical need is unattainable in the face of steadily increasing costs;[15] the temptation is to lower one standard in favour of the other two. The difficulties are formidable because what we are discussing at this level is essentially 'horizontal resource allocation', or priority setting between different types of service, which depends not so much on professional medical assessment and advice as on public opinion and on evidence as to cost and effectiveness[16] – and the former, at least, is a fickle measuring instrument. Not only can polls be grossly distorted by the way in which questions are put but also opinion is very subject to political and other extraneous influences; you do not sell newspapers by agreeing that treatment for varicose veins has a low priority – sales are improved by emphasising the injustice in regarding varicose ulceration as less debilitating than the peptic variety. Attempts that have been made in the past to sacrifice comprehensiveness in favour of 'core care' by way of translating societal attitudes into standardised decision-making[17] seem to achieve less than satisfactory results. The essential dilemma stems from the fact that the categories of choice on which a consensus may be sought are indefinable save at the margins of health care.[18] However, the new emphasis on explicitness in rationing strategies is an increasingly important development and may lead to surprising results; resource allocators, it has been said, should not take it for granted that their own values are shared by the general public.[19]

11.14 Given the absence of any obvious set of principles on which to act and given that the function of district health authorities is, on the one hand, constrained by the regional or higher authority[20] and, on the other, is to

---

14 A particularly poignant example is to be found in the salvage of extremely premature infants. The cost of intensive care has been put at £20,000 for each baby weighing less than 1.5kg and some 50% of these may sustain brain damage sufficient to require life-long support. Would the money be better spent on research into the prevention of prematurity? Office of Health Economics *Born Too Soon* (1992). See L Hunt 'Cost "Dilemma" Posed by Premature Babies' (1993) Independent, 20 January, p 6.
15 A Weale 'Rationing Health Care' (1998) 316 BMJ 410.
16 M Cochrane, C Ham, C Heginbotham and R Smith 'Rationing: At the Cutting Edge' (1991) 303 BMJ 1039.
17 P A Lewis and M Charny 'Which of Two Individuals Do You Treat When Only Their Ages Are Different and You Can't Treat Both?' (1989) 15 J Med Ethics 28.
18 See reply to Lewis and Charny, para 11.13 above: D Lamb 'Priorities in Health Care' (1989) 15 J Med Ethics 33; also B A Stoll 'Choosing Between Cancer Patients' (1990) 16 J Med Ethics 71.
19 E Nord 'The Relevance of Health State after Treatment in Prioritising between Different Patients' (1993) 19 J Med Ethics 37. It is to be noted that the deliberations of NICE (see para 11.22 below) are now held in public.
20 See Klein para 11.3 above.

provide what the public wants, it is unsurprising that the distribution of the scarcer resources is uneven and that the principles invoked in decision-making are uncertain – the factors given most weight have been found to range from the availability of other funding (eg the private sphere) for the service to the more obviously laudable potential for health gain in terms of length and quality of life.[21] In a survey of six districts, Ham found that there was a general reluctance to exclude some services entirely from their contracts. But it is from a review of a service which was *not* provided by some authorities – in this case, in-vitro fertilisation – that some of the clearest evidence of the factors likely to be considered influential is to be found. These included:

(a)   the presence of a prominent lobbyist for the service and the ready availability of the service;

(b)   whether or not a competent public health department could be used to interpret the effectiveness of and need for the service;

(c)   whether it represented a true health need;

(d)   having decided that there was a need, whether the particular service offered the best way of meeting that need;

(e)   notwithstanding the effectiveness of the service, whether it should be purchased at the expense of another unrelated service;

(f)   whether valid reasons could be given for selective treatment when supply fell short of demand; and

(g)   whether it was right to introduce a service which could not be given to everyone.[22]

11.15 Despite the obvious difficulties, we see it as self-evident that some form of cost evaluation in health care is essential at the resource purchasing level, if only to ensure impartiality – pressure groups are bad advocates in that they take no account of the deprivation elsewhere which is the concomitant to success in their own particular sphere. We agree with those who believe that there are no intrinsic ethical problems in applying economic considerations to health resource allocation. It should, rather, be accepted that without such control there is likely to be an unethical maldistribution of resources; as Williams put it, anyone who says no account should be paid to costs is, in reality, saying no account should be paid to the sacrifices thereby imposed on others – and there are no *ethical* grounds for ignoring the effect of an action on other people.[23] Surely, everyone would agree with this – but it still leaves open the question of in which group's favour is a marginal change in resource allocation to be tilted.

11.16 We must also not lose sight of the fact that there are more reasons than cost for limiting the availability of drugs and other treatments. A health authority may, for example believe that a given therapy is useless and,

---

21 See the analysis provided by C Ham 'Priority Setting in the NHS: Reports from Six Districts' (1993) 307 BMJ 435.

22 S Redmayne and R Klein 'Rationing in Practice: The Case of In Vitro Fertilisation' (1993) 306 BMJ 1521.

23 A Williams 'Cost-effectiveness Analysis: Is It Ethical?' (1992) 18 J Med Ethics 7. See also G Mooney 'QALYs: Are They Enough? A Health Economist's Perspective' (1989) 15 J Med Ethics 148.

accordingly, refuse to sanction its purchase. Such situations arise most commonly in those conditions for which there is, currently, no effective treatment. Sufferers from multiple sclerosis, for example, will clutch at any straw and will be unimpressed by the need for statistical evaluation of a drug before they can be given the chance to use it. So long as the adoption of a new drug remains a matter of individual advisory medical opinion, the result will be an inequality of distribution which breeds consumer dissatisfaction.[24] Alternatively, the condition itself may be questioned as to its nature – is its alleviation a truly medical matter or is it one of 'life-style enhancement' only? Here, we could place, for example, assisted reproduction and gender reassignment, both of which are discussed in some detail elsewhere in this book, in the 'grey' area of the black and white scale where we are likely to get different answers from different authorities.[25] At the more extreme, we could consider the supply of sildenafil (Viagra) through the NHS. There are occasions when impotence – as opposed to sexual inadequacy – can be seen as a proper medical concern. But this is a far cry from supplying a drug with no intention other than to improve sexual performance. Consequently, the government foresaw an exceptional demand for sildenafil which could have had an adverse effect, both financial and healthwise, on the rest of the community; accordingly, it issued Circular no. 1998/158 which advised doctors not to prescribe sildenafil and Health Authorities not to support the provision of the drug at NHS expense other than in exceptional circumstances. The circular was, however, declared unlawful in the High Court in that its 'blanket' nature was interfering with doctors' professional judgments.[26] It is, therefore, clear that the courts will strongly uphold the right of a patient to individual consideration in the face of attempted 'rationing' – but only when it is agreed that it is the treatment of a *disease* that is in issue.

11.17   Finally, it must, of course, be conceded that societies differ and, while some form of resource rationing is, as we believe, inevitable, no single system will be universally acceptable. Britain has been described as an original sin society[27] in which tribulation in the form of ill-health is expected – a view which, incidentally, is becoming less and less acceptable as the years pass. The United States, on the other hand, are seen as a society striving for perfectibility of man and dominated by consumerism; the demand for and the use of medical resources are bound to differ. That being so, it is, perhaps, anomalous that the first experiment in health care rationing to come into

---

24 At the same time, a national policy for the provision of a service may result in *local* decisions as to collateral economies; uniformity may, as a result, be even further compromised: R Cookson, D McDaid and A Maynard 'Wrong SIGN, NICE Mess: Is National Guidance Distorting Allocation of Resources?' (2001) 323 BMJ 743.

25 Even so, once the condition is classified as a disease, the authority must consider the individual's condition before refusing to fund treatment: *R v North West Lancashire Health Authority, ex p A, D and G* [2000] 1 WLR 977, (2000) 53 BMLR 148.

26 *R v Secretary of State for Health, ex p Pfizer Ltd* [1999] Lloyd's Rep Med 289, (2000) 51 BMLR 189. Note that it would have been lawful, given the time, for the Secretary of State to 'blacklist' sildenafil under the National Health Service (General Medical Services) Regulations 1992, SI 1992/635, Schs 10 and 11.

27 R Klein 'Rationing Health Care' (1984) 289 BMJ 143. For an updated comparative review, see R G Lee and F H Miller 'The Doctor's Changing Role in Allocating U.S. and British Medical Services' (1990) 18 Law Med Hlth Care 69.

force as a result of statute should have its origins in the United States.[28] The State of Oregon has, as a result of research including extensive public debate, arrived at an adaptable prioritised list of treatments which will and will not be available under Medicaid and business-related private insurance arrangements. Inevitably, the plan has had its difficulties – one of which lies in the constantly changing list of priorities and the consequent inflation of the basic health care package that is available.[29] Its success or failure also depends to a large extent on extraneous factors such as the strength of the state economy as a whole, which leads to fluctuation in the number of those covered. We doubt, however, if the Oregon experiment has any direct relevance to the United Kingdom. Quite apart from the disparate populations involved, the Oregon plan is directed at those who cannot, for financial and other reasons, obtain private medical insurance, whereas the NHS is open to all in the United Kingdom as a right.

11.18 The American experience of rationing within the private sector has been fraught with difficulty. The proportion of the domestic national product spent on health is substantial and people have come to expect a high level of medical attention. In an attempt to contain costs, the insurers introduced managed health care systems under which plans they undertook to provide necessary health care, the question of what is necessary being determined by the insurers themselves. These schemes have been widely criticised as limiting consumer choice and as constituting disguised rationing. The political and legal controversy surrounding them demonstrates the difficulty of imposing rationing on those whose expectations are high.[30]

11.19 There may well be valuable lessons to be learnt from the United States but, New Zealand, being, so far as we know, the only Commonwealth country to have overtly adopted a rationing policy in a fully tax-funded health system, perhaps offers a more useful comparator.

11.20 The New Zealand National Advisory Committee on Core Health and Disability Support Services appears to have rapidly abandoned the Oregon model of a list of treatments that are and are not available and, instead, has decided to issue a series of guidelines as to how restricted, publicly funded resources are to be allocated.[31] Guidelines were developed for the treatment of specific conditions and there is little doubt that the resulting compartmentalisation of resources gives rise to some uncomfortable,

---

28 M J Garland 'Justice, Politics and Community: Expanding Access and Rationing Health Services in Oregon' (1992) 20 Law Med Hlth Care 67; S Rosenbaum 'Mothers and Children Last: The Oregon Medicaid Experiment' (1992) 18 Am J Law Med 97; J Dixon and H G Welch 'Priority Setting: Lessons from Oregon' (1991) 337 Lancet 891. The New Zealand experience is referred to below at para 11.20.

29 C Ham 'Retracing the Oregon Trail: The Experience of Rationing and the Oregon Health Plan' (1998) 316 BMJ 1965.

30 A C Enthoven, H H Schauffler and S McMenamin 'Consumer Choice and the Managed Care Backlash' (2001) 27 Amer J Law Med 1.

31 The majority of our information is derived from the authoritative authorship of C M Feek, W McKean, L Henneveld et al 'Experience with Rationing Health Care in New Zealand' (1999) 318 BMJ 1346. See also C M Feek 'Rationing Healthcare in New Zealand: The Use of Clinical Guidelines' (2000) 173 Med J Austral 423.

albeit salutary, reading. The reasons for this discomfort are not easy to define. Probably no country in the world surpasses New Zealand in its dedication to human rights and to fair treatment for all, yet the fact that the guidelines as to eligibility for treatment of end stage renal failure included recommendations that, in usual circumstances, persons aged over 75 should not be accepted and that other serious diseases or disabilities that are likely to affect survival or the quality of life are reasons for exclusion clearly opens the door for discrimination on the basis of value-laden judgments which may well be beyond the medical remit; we return to this problem at para 11.37.

11.21 The seminal test of the guidelines[32] concerned a man, W, in end-stage renal failure who also suffered from diabetes and dementia.[33] A decision was taken to discontinue interim dialysis – first, on the grounds that W's moderate dementia left him outside the group of persons considered suitable for inclusion in the treatment programme but, later, on a pure clinical and 'best interests' standard. The decision was forcefully contested and the matter was ultimately heard by the New Zealand Court of Appeal. There, the Court refused to accept the case as a test of the guidelines, and, hence, as a question of rationing, and determinedly held it to be a matter of the exercise of clinical judgment within good medical practice – even to the extent of stating that the case raised no significant ethical issues; accordingly, the decision of the High Court that it was totally inappropriate for the Court to attempt to direct a doctor as to what treatment should be given to a patient was upheld.[34] None the less, despite its restricted scope, *Shortland* is still relevant to the 'rationing' debate in that it shows the difficulties inherent in making subjective clinical decisions once general guidelines have been laid down for the use of resources in specific conditions. As Feek et al put it: 'Explicit rationing will work only when clinicians accept the link between clinical decision making and resource allocation' – and one has to ask: which comes first? Moreover, whatever may be the logic that drives informed professional opinion, the public are unlikely to distinguish between the two. Feek et al quote the following press comment:

> [T]he reality is that [W's] case was not a priority. First concerns have to be for patients who are not terminally ill, who do not have other complications and who have a better chance of rehabilitation.[35]

None of which provides much comfort for the elderly, amnesic reader!

---

32 *Shortland v Northland Health Ltd* [1998] 1 NZLR 433, (1997) 50 BMLR 255.

33 Richardson P described this as brain damage (at BMLR 256) and his general practitioner as mild dementia. W had expressed a wish to remain alive – cf the English case of *Re D (medical treatment: consent)* [1998] 2 FLR 22, (1998) 41 BMLR 81 in which it was held that dialysis need not be imposed on a patient who could neither accept nor refuse treatment.

34 Salmon J at BMLR 257 relying heavily on *Re J (a minor)* [1993] Fam 15, [1992] 2 All ER 614.

35 From the *Nelson Mail*, 13 October 1997. The authors also refer to W's continued treatment as futile.

The National Institute for Clinical Excellence

11.22 The current United Kingdom parallel approach rests on the National Institute for Clinical Excellence which was established as a special health authority within the NHS in 1999;[36] its remit was described as being to carry out such functions in connection with the promotion of clinical excellence in the health service as the Secretary of State may direct. In essence, this wide remit crystallises into providing advice and guidance as to what treatments are best for patients on a national scale. Such guidance for 'best practice' can be divided into three categories: clinical guidelines, recommendations as to audit and the appraisal of the clinical- and cost-effectiveness of new and existing health technologies;[37] we are, here, concerned only with the last of these functions. In this respect, the Institute was hailed as a rational response to the existing situation, already outlined above, whereby individual health authorities determined whether, or in what circumstances, a given treatment would be provided – a system which had come to be popularly known as 'post-code prescribing'. Ideally, NICE's decisions were intended to be based on pure clinical need and efficiency but, inevitably, they had to include consideration of what was best for the health service itself; as we have already seen, clinical efficiency and cost-effectiveness cannot be dissociated in a tax funded service – the conclusion, as a leading article in *The Times* put it, is that: 'The National Institute for Clinical Excellence is rationing made plain.'[38]

11.23 As a consequence, NICE is, to an extent, living a lie[39] and is subject to not only commercial and political pressures but also to massive influence from the media – it becomes very much easier to approve a new or expensive treatment than to refuse its use. NICE has, to date, provided guidance on some 23 projected interventions.[40] One of the most illustrative has been in relation to the use of interferon beta for the treatment of multiple sclerosis. In June 2000, as a result of a breach of confidentiality, the Chairman of NICE confirmed that the Institute was considering a recommendation that interferon beta should not be prescribed to new patients on account of its low success rate and very high cost. Media speculation then prompted confirmation of this – but with the added rider that the Department of Health might consider ways in which the drug might be made available on a cost-effective basis.

36 National Institute for Clinical Excellence (Establishment and Constitution) Order 1999, SI 1999/220. Meetings of NICE must be open to the public (SI 1999/2219). The Scottish equivalent is the Health Technology Board for Scotland but a second organisation, the Scottish Intercollegiate Guidelines Network, which is concerned mainly with the clinical appraisal of new treatments, has also been operating within the NHS since 1993. We will confine our observations to NICE.
37 K Syrett 'Nice Work?' Rationing, Review and the 'Legitimacy Problem' in the 'New NHS' (2002) 10 Med L Rev 1.
38 Leading Article 'Not a Nice Habit' *The Times*, 12 April 2002, p 23. It is fair to say that at least one major survey suggests that NICE is more concerned with the clinical effect of a treatment than with the cost per QALY: J Raftery 'NICE: Faster Access to Modern Treatments? Analysis of Guidance on Health Technologies' (2001) 323 BMJ 1300.
39 R Smith 'The Failings of NICE' (2000) 321 BMJ 1363.
40 T H S Dent and M Sadler 'From Guidance to Practice: Why NICE is not Enough' (2002) 324 BMJ 842.

NICE issued its final guidance in February 2002 by which time the Department of Health had embarked on a risk-sharing scheme in which interferon beta would be funded only if treatment trials in individual patients showed it was effective – an attitude to research that was severely criticised by academic scientists.[41] Confusion reigns; meantime, full guidance on the treatment of multiple sclerosis is not expected until 2003.

11.24 The difficulties are not over, even when such finality is achieved. Currently, guidance is what it says and it is not mandatory on Heath Authorities. While this is likely to be changed, it still poses the question of where do the Health Authorities find the money to fund NICE's guidelines? In the absence of specific provisions, it can only come from a reduction in other, less media sensitive, forms of heath care; in short, we are back to the self-perpetuating dilemma in which limited funds strive to finance expanding demands for medical excellence. NICE is something of a brave attempt to rationalise, and nationalise, the response – but it cannot eliminate the underlying problems.[42]

The legal situation

11.25 Financial restraints clearly place the Secretary of State in some difficulty in discharging his statutory duty to provide, to such extent as he thinks necessary to meet all reasonable requirements including, inter alia, hospital accommodation.[43]

11.26 In some ways it is surprising that there have not been more actions brought by patients who feel that he has failed in these duties but, on reflection, it is probable that the dearth of cases results from the extreme improbability of a successful outcome. Cases are, however, reported sporadically and the classic action is that of *Hincks*.[44] In that case, patients in an orthopaedic hospital complained that they had waited an unreasonable time for treatment because of a shortage of facilities arising, in part, from a decision not to add a new block to the hospital on the grounds of cost; accordingly, they sought a declaration that the Secretary of State and the health authorities were in breach of their duty. In dismissing the application, Wien J said it was not the court's function to direct Parliament what funds to make available to the health service nor how to allocate them. The duty to provide services 'to such extent as he considers necessary' gave the minister a discretion as to the disposition of financial resources. The court could only interfere if the Secretary of State acted so as to frustrate the policy of the Act or as no reasonable minister could have acted; and no such breach had been shown in the particular case. Moreover, even if a breach was proved, the Act did not admit of relief by way of damages.

---

41 S Mayor 'Health Department to Fund Interferon Beta despite Institute's Ruling' (2001) 323 BMJ 1087.
42 NICE, in the form of a National Council for Health Priorities, was forecast in an exceptionally thorough analysis of the position at the time by C Newdick 'Resource Allocation in the National Health Service' (1997) 23 Amer J Law Med 291.
43 National Health Service Act 1977, s 3.
44 *R v Secretary of State for Social Services, ex p Hincks* (1979) 123 Sol Jo 436.

11.27 The case went to appeal[45] where, as might be expected, the judgment turned on the interpretation of 'reasonable requirements'. Lord Denning MR considered this to mean that a failure of duty existed only if the minister's action was thoroughly unreasonable. It was further thought that we should be faced with the economics of a bottomless pit if no limits in respect of long-term planning were to be read into public statutory duties; the further the advances of medical technology, the greater would be the financial burden placed upon the Secretary of State.

11.28 Since 1980, however, health authorities have been required to balance their individual budgets.[46] Inevitably, major decisions as to the provision of health care have been moved down one hierarchical step, thus bringing the decision-makers into closer contact with those affected. Society, in the form of the Patients' Forums, has a statutory place in the process[47] and, as a corollary, is entitled to judicial review of decisions thought to have been taken improperly. Nevertheless, attempts to extend this privilege to individuals seeking improved access to treatment have foundered consistently on the rock of the reasonableness inherent in the adverse decisions taken.

11.29 The paradigmatic case is that of *Walker*,[48] which concerned a baby whose surgery had been postponed five times because of a shortage of skilled nursing staff. The trial judge, Macpherson J, deprecated any suggestion that patients should be encouraged to think that the court had a role in cases which sought to compel the authority to carry out an operation that was not urgent; and the Court of Appeal confirmed his refusal of the application for review. Within two months, the same health authority was involved in a comparable case, the only major difference being that the child was possibly in greater immediate danger.[49] Reiterating that, to be so unreasonable as to come within the jurisdiction of the court, the Authority would have had to make a decision that no reasonable body could have reached,[50] Stephen Brown LJ said:

> In the absence of any evidence which could begin to show that there was [such a failure] to allocate resources in this instance ... there can be no arguable case ... It does seem to me unfortunate that this procedure has been adopted. It is wholly misconceived in my view. The courts of this country cannot arrange the lists in the hospital ... and should not be asked to intervene.

---

45 *R v Secretary of State for Social Services, ex p Hincks* (1980) 1 BMLR 93, CA. The case was discussed in J D Finch *Health Services Law* (1981) pp 38-39 and in 'Rationing of Resources' (1985) 290 BMJ 374 and by D Brahams 'Enforcing A Duty to Care for Patients in the NHS' [1984] 2 Lancet 1224. See also C Newdick 'Rights to NHS Resources after the 1990 Act' (1993) 1 Med L Rev 53. F H Miller 'Denial of Health Care and Informed Consent in English and American Law' (1992) 18 Am J Law Med 37.
46 National Health Service Act 1977, s 97A, inserted by Health Services Act 1980, s 6.
47 Established under the National Health Service Reform and Health Care Professions Act 2002, s 15.
48 *R v Central Birmingham Health Authority, ex p Walker* (1992) 3 BMLR 32, CA.
49 *R v Central Birmingham Health Authority, ex p Collier* (6 January 1988, unreported, available on Lexis). The case is discussed by D Brahams 'Seeking Increased NHS Resources Through the Courts' (1988) 1 Lancet 133. See also Newdick para 11.27 above; Miller para 11.27 above for this case and *Walker*.
50 *Associated Provincial Picture Houses Ltd v Wednesbury Corpn* [1948] 1 KB 223 at 229, [1947] 2 All ER 680 at 683, per Lord Greene MR, CA.

11.30 While expressing great sympathy with the parents, Stephen Brown LJ suggested that it might have been hoped that the publicity would bring pressure to bear on the hospital and there is no doubt that this effect could and does, materialise – particularly in a life-saving situation. Dyer reported a case of a woman suffering from end-stage renal failure who was refused dialysis facilities; on her being granted legal aid to take the authority to court, an extra £250,000 was made available to the local renal units.[51] Whatever one thinks of the morality of the process, it seems to have been a very successful exercise in 'shroud waving' – and it is to be noted that the money was not 'new' but was plucked from the waiting list fund. The circumstances were such, however, as to raise a real possibility of *Wednesbury* unreasonableness. An even more spectacular 'success' concerned Laura Davies, who received, and rejected, a liver and small intestine transplant; she was then given a second transplant involving seven organs at a cost estimated as £1m, which is said to have been defrayed by a Middle Eastern potentate.[52] Perhaps the most publicised relevant incident in recent years has been that of 'Child B', in which funding for an essentially ineffective treatment was refused.[53] This case is discussed in detail below;[54] for the present, it is appropriate only to quote the chief executive, who was, as the mouthpiece of the health authority, taken to be responsible for the decision:

> [The] case took on a symbolic importance, helping people to grasp the reality that expectation and demand had now outstripped their publicly funded systems' ability to pay without regard to the opportunity cost.[55]

11.31 It is, perhaps, worth noting that the NHS has not been singled out for judicial cheese-paring. In a case brought under the Chronically Sick and Disabled Patients Act 1970, it was held that the costs of the arrangements and the authority's resources were proper considerations in assessing whether a person had a need and whether it was necessary to make arrangements to meet it.[56] The case concerned the *removal* of social services from a disabled man; some of the difficulties involved are crystallised in the dissenting opinion of Lord Lloyd:

> How can resources help to measure [the man's] need? ... It cannot, however, have been Parliament's intention that local authority B should be able to say "because we do not have enough resources, we are going to reduce your needs". His needs remained exactly the same. They cannot be affected by the local authority's inability to meet those needs.[57]

Even so, as in the medical cases, the court was not minded to interfere with the tactics of resource allocation.

51 C Dyer 'Going to Law to Get Treatment' (1987) 295 BMJ 1554.
52 For a critical lay view of such disposal of both financial and organic resources, see K Muir 'Can Saving the Life of Little Laura Really Be Worth £1 million?' *The Times*, 22 September 1993, p 15.
53 *R v Cambridge Area Health Authority, ex p B (a minor)* (1995) 25 BMLR 5; revsd (1995) 23 BMLR 1, CA.
54 See chapter 16.
55 S Thornton 'The Child B Case – Reflections of a Chief Executive' (1997) 314 BMJ 1838.
56 *R v Gloucestershire County Council, ex p Barry* (1997) 36 BMLR 69, HL.
57 (1997) 36 BMLR 69 at 96.

11.32 It is to be noted, however, that resort to human rights and constitutional arguments has introduced a new element into resource allocation cases. The full impact of the Human Rights Act 1998 on the health service in the United Kingdom is still uncertain but it will, at the very least, require decisions to be made with regard to due process requirements and to claims to equality. It is unlikely, however, that Article 2 of the European Convention on Human Rights, which protects the right to life, will provide an automatic entitlement to treatment in any particular case; it could, however, prevent the evolution of any policy which denied reasonable access to readily available resources. Such human rights arguments have been made in a number of other jurisdictions. In South Africa, for example, the Constitutional Court held that the provision in the constitution which states that 'everyone has the right to have access to health care services ...' did not give an absolute entitlement to any particular treatment, and that hard decisions as to the availability of expensive treatments – in this case dialysis – would have to be made by the medical authorities.[58] This very supportable approach did not prevent the South African courts later ordering the Government to provide HIV-suppressing drugs to pregnant women as a matter of constitutional entitlement.[59]

11.33 The indications are that more than half the British public favour unlimited funding of the NHS.[60] While this is clearly impossible, it can be argued that, once it is established that there is a reasonable requirement for a particular service, no further qualification of the Secretary of State's duty to provide it exists and that inadequate resources do not absolve him from this duty.[61] This may well be so but, in so far as one cannot make a pot of tea without tap water unless one takes the water from the coffee urn, it adds little to the solution of the inherent problems. Clearly, however, a further major ethical dilemma centres on the imposed medical limitations on treatment of the individual and it is to that aspect that we now turn.

TREATMENT OF THE INDIVIDUAL

11.34 In discussion of the medical treatment of the individual, we are faced not with the hypothetical patient who may become ill but with one who is actually at risk. Objectivity is no longer the main arbiter and is replaced by need – which, in a medical context, can be defined as existing 'when an individual has an illness or disability for which there is an effective and acceptable treatment'.[62] In practice, access to such treatments will be limited by their cost – for a limited budget will provide only a limited number of treatment units. As a result, some form of differential treatment is enforced and, in turn, the assessment of relative needs involves a value judgment.

---

58 *Soobramoney v Minister of Health KwaZulu-Natal* (1997) 12 BCLR 1696 (CC), (1997) 50 BMLR 224.
59 *Minister of Health v Treatment Action Campaign* (2002) Constitutional Court – CCT 8/02, 5 July.
60 T Groves 'Public Disagrees with Professionals over NHS Funding' (1993) 306 BMJ 673.
61 G P Morris 'Enforcing a Duty to Care: The Kidney Patient and the NHS' (1983) 80 Law Soc Gaz 3156. But an extrapolation of *R v Gloucestershire County Council, ex p Barry* (1997) 36 BMLR 69 suggests that this would be unlikely to be sustained.
62 N Bosanquet 'A "Fair Innings" for Efficiency in Health Services' (2001) 27 J Med Ethics 228.

11.35 How, then, is that judgment to be made? In practice, many decisions are made instinctively and without the need for profound analysis – thus, the single-handed doctor will unhesitatingly choose the patient in greater pain for treatment, despite the fact that this will simultaneously delay the treatment of those in lesser pain. There may well be moral arguments against such a policy – it does, for example, act to the detriment of the stoic – but the circumstances are acute and, the urgency being comparable, the doctor has selected a single criterion on which to base his judgment. Moral agonising is, in practice, reserved for the treatment of chronic, life-threatening diseases, not only because they offer the opportunity for analysis but because they attract the use of expensive resources and will consume these for a long time – at which point the dilemma extends not only to the allocation of resources but also to their withdrawal. The treatment of chronic renal diseases and of brain injury provide good examples on which to base discussion.

36 It is easy to say that enough dialysis machines should be made available to treat all cases of chronic renal failure but, in existing circumstances, this may merely mean that some other financially dependent resource must be curtailed. Costs can be cut by, for example, changing a policy of hospital dialysis to one of home treatment, but the fact of financial restraint is not thereby removed – only its degree is altered. But, at the same time, the modern patient undoubtedly regards access to high technology medicine as his individual right and such a view is readily tenable when there is an urgent or life-saving need. If the doctor is, perforce, to qualify those rights, his reason for so doing must be beyond reproach and therein lies the problem.

11.37 The case of Mr McKeown in New Zealand[63] is a classic of its type. James McKeown was a man aged 76 in end-stage renal failure. He also had coronary artery disease and prostatic cancer. Given dialysis, his expectation of life was about two years; nevertheless, he clearly failed the consensus guidelines for the treatment of renal failure and the head of the dialysis unit is quoted as saying: 'Given our resources, he had to fit into a group we said no to'. The patient's family then laid a complaint of age discrimination with the Human Rights Commission of New Zealand. As a result, the hospital authorities ordered a clinical review of the case, renal dialysis was started and Mr McKeown died 18 months later – presumably by way of his malignant disease. How, then, is this case to be analysed in retrospect? On one view, the treatment, at best, served no useful purpose and, at worst, may have deprived a more deserving claimant of therapy. In the alternative, one can hold that all persons who have lost their kidney function will die at the same rate; all are, therefore, equally entitled to life-saving intervention and their length of survival is immaterial.[64] Our inclination is to adopt the latter stance – but we freely admit that intuition does not solve the underlying problem.

11.38 Essentially, the New Zealand system involves allocating resources in terms of triage. Triage is a curiously derived expression meaning, in the present

---

63 Reported by Feek et al, para 11.20 above.
64 This is, roughly, the view of J Harris 'What is the Good of Health Care?' (1996) 10 Bioethics 269. The question of from whose viewpoint we are to judge the futility of an eighteen-month extension of life is discussed in chapter 12.

context, the separation of casualties into priority treatment groups. It is essentially a military concept, the current British policy being to allocate four categories of casualty, ranging from those whose slight injuries can be managed by self-care to those who cannot be expected to survive even with extensive treatment and who are, therefore, treated on a humanitarian basis only; the policy is closely associated with that of casualty evacuation. Triage in this sense is not only good emergency surgical practice but is also ethically acceptable because it is directed to a single discernible end – that is, to win the war or the battle, and we accept that this, in itself, is a morally acceptable objective with which the medical branch of the armed services can quite properly associate itself. But can we, in ethical terms, simply transfer the concept of triage, which is an emergency procedure, to elective civilian practice? It may be possible to do so in special circumstances – it is, for example, a recognised practice following a major disaster, when the single most pressing objective is to mitigate the effects of that disaster. But we are not dealing with a single issue in normal practice. The circumstances of and the circumstances surrounding each patient are so disparate that triage, and its underlying principles, cannot be used as a convenient substitute, or subterfuge, for resource allocation and should be abandoned for that purpose.[65] What, then, does one put in its place?

Alternative models

11.39 There have been many attempts to solve the dilemma[66] but none is satisfactory – all generalisations fail when applied to the particular but we will briefly outline some proposals which have been made. It is, perhaps, easiest to progress from those parameters which we consider to be least appropriate at the individual patient level.

11.40 We do not believe that cost-benefit should be a major influence here. It needs no profound philosophical analysis to make one appreciate instinctively that it is right to deploy a helicopter to rescue a man on a drifting pleasure raft, despite the fact that his danger is of his own making, despite the expense and despite the fact that the helicopter is designed to carry ten persons. The immediacy of the situation has placed a very high value on life which it would be quite immoral to ignore. The value cannot, however, be infinite – otherwise, faced with the choice of saving one man on a raft or ten men in a sinking dinghy, the grounds for the 'value choice' would be equal whereas, in practice, few would doubt the correctness of choosing the larger number – always provided the operational circumstances were similar. Such choices must, however, be very rare in practice. In the chronic situation, as exemplified by dialysis, we are effectively confronted with a one-to-one choice between

65 Not everyone would agree with this view: eg J Cubbon 'The Principle of QALY Maximisation as the Basis for Allocating Health Care Resources' (1991) 17 J Med Ethics 181. See also K M Boyd and B T Potter 'Priorities in the Allocation of Scarce Resources' (1986) 12 J Med Ethics 197.
66 An exhaustive analysis of the alternatives was given in a classic paper by H J J Leenen 'The Selection of Patients in the Event of a Scarcity of Medical Facilities: An Unavoidable Dilemma' (1979) 1 Int J Med Law 161. For a more recent appraisal, see M J Langford 'Who Should Get the Kidney Machine?' (1992) 18 J Med Ethics 12.

two individuals; at this point it might be possible to introduce a cost-benefit argument which takes the form of assessing the relative gain to society of saving one or the other. In practice, this would invoke the use of some formula such as 'earning capacity x (65 – age)'. We believe, however, that neither age nor income group should be primary criteria regulating choice per se – it might be that the aged respond less well to treatment than do others[67] but that would be a different consideration. Such an assessment would, in addition, offend 'moral' practices which have almost attained the force of common law and of which 'women and children first' is an obvious example; at least according to admittedly crude criteria based on earnings potential, women would come out worse if such objective cost-benefit criteria were to be applied. But this is not to say that some concern for quality or expectation of life should not be thrown into the prognostic balance as discussed below.

11.41 The corollary to this line of thought is that scarce resources should be distributed on the basis of the 'deserts' or basic merits of the recipients. One aspect of this is discussed further in chapter 14, where we note a United States experiment which attempts to distribute a very scarce resource – human kidneys – to those hospitals which have, themselves, provided organs; while such a system has much to commend it, any benefit accrues to the hospital rather than to the individual patient who still has to be 'chosen' by some other method. Others would look at this criterion from the opposite point of view and would exclude those who could positively endanger the treatment programme – a group that is exemplified by those carrying the virus of hepatitis. But such reasoning is a purely technical matter. A more moralistic variant on this theme would hold it to be acceptable for a society which was providing the facility to exclude persons who increased the cost of care through their own choice;[68] while this is certainly arguable, it is a concept that is probably more applicable to communities in which the health of only a proportion is being supported by the taxes paid by the remainder – the beneficiaries of a national health service are more likely to see themselves as all in the same leaky boat.

11.42 More often, the assessment of 'deserts' is taken to apply to the intrinsic worth of the subject to society – and, again, we may look at this from the negative or positive aspect. First, such a method of selection inevitably discriminates against those who have some additional disability – and particularly mental disability – which limits their perceived value in a societal sense; this group, however, is, perhaps, better included among those falling to be assessed under the 'medical benefit' test discussed below. The alternative, positive, approach in the event of shortage of facilities for treatment is to select those who offer the greatest contribution to society now and in the future. In our view, allocation tests which attempt to distinguish between, for example, the philanthropic mafia millionaire and the contestant for an international prize in applied mathematics serve no useful purpose in that they are hopelessly subjective. Choices so based are clearly beyond the capacity or function of the doctor and the 'principle' can be dismissed out of hand.

---

67 Hence, say, the relative acceptability of denying in vitro fertilisation to older women: *R v Sheffield Heath Authority, ex p Seale* (1994) 25 BMLR 1.
68 H T Engelhardt 'Allocating Scarce Medical Resources and the Availability of Organ Transplantation' (1984) 311 New Engl J Med 66.

11.43 The one 'deserts-related' issue which is most commonly raised is that of age. It is very widely held that the older a patient is, the less can he or she command equal opportunity in a competition for therapy. The reasons for this acquiescence differ. Some will rely on the argument 'he's had his innings' – but even this depends, to an extent, on one's position in the batting order; others, more rationally, will point to the fact that results of treatment are generally better in the young than in the old – but simply because the results of coronary surgery are commonly more satisfactory in the middle-aged patient does not mean that surgery is not worthwhile in the 75-year-old. There is, moreover, a tendency to forget that not every therapy is effective for a full life-span; if we anticipate a likely five-year survival, it matters not whether the patient is aged 20 or 60. We suspect that the reason underlying the common assumption is that those responsible for decision-making are, by definition, below retiring age; it has been said, rightly, that there is often a wide discrepancy between the optimum solution of a problem from the perspective of society as a whole and that of the individual within that society.[69] Lewis and Charny[70] tried, by means of an opinion poll, to establish the points at which the public would be prepared to accept age-based choices and, thus, to map out decision-making boundaries which will reflect the values of society as a whole. This is a praiseworthy effort which may, indeed, be widely copied in the future as the government inspired lay participation in medical decision-making gathers momentum; for ourselves, while appreciating the value of uniformity and accepting the attractions of the development of guidelines established by way of wide societal involvement, we find it difficult to support a cold actuarial basis for making what is still a human clinical decision.

11.44 Clearly, the most widely acceptable criterion of selection would be that determined by medical benefit.[71] But, once again, this is easier to accept in theory than to put into practice. Unless one is dealing with a recoverable condition – and dialysis, which is providing the main theme for discussion, is only palliative – medical benefit is a relative matter and, moreover, prognosis is unpredictable. It is also difficult to avoid the conclusion that the individual's social status may influence the outcome of any therapy – despite the ultimate medical basis for any decision, access to scarce resources is, then, governed by what are, essentially, non-medical considerations.

11.45 But, even if the clinician claims absolute responsibility for allocation of his expertise, he must consider the quality of the life he is extending and it is here that he may obtain guidance from – or suffer the interference of – the health economist. Perhaps the greatest influence in this field over the last decade has been the introduction of the concept of quality adjusted life years – or QALYs.[72]

---

69 Lewis and Charny, para 11.13 above.
70 Ibid.
71 The choice made, inter alia, by Professor Gillon's remarkably prescient daughter: see R Gillon 'Justice and Allocation of Medical Resources' (1985) 291 BMJ 266. It was also the implicit choice of the court in *Re J (a minor) (wardship: medical treatment)* [1992] 2 FLR 165, (1992) 9 BMLR 10.
72 A Williams 'The Economic Role of "Health Indicators"' in G Teeling-Smith (ed) *Measuring the Social Benefits of Medicine* (1983).

Quality adjusted life years

11.46 The principle of the QALY is simple enough. A year of healthy life expectancy is scored as 1 and a year of unhealthy life as less than 1, depending upon the degree of reduction in quality; while death is taken as zero, a life considered to be worse than death can be accorded a minus score. The 'value' of treatment in terms of 'life appreciation' can then be assessed numerically. Thus far, in fact, QALY's seem to be doing little more than expressing the intuitive findings of the competent clinician in a mathematical formula. And, therein lies the rub – for the 'quality scoring' will still be founded on a 'best interests' assessment made by a third party and the paternalistic element in that assessment has been scarcely modified. It is, for example, hard for a middle-class doctor not to see a middle-class life as being of higher quality than one sustained on social security; a young physician may see a short life on the golf course as preferable to a long one tied to the television set – but this may well not be the patient's evaluation. It is thus apparent that, at this level, a QALY can only be truly evaluated with the patient's co-operation; it can then be used to decide between two possible treatments for the same condition. Here, in what has been described as 'vertical priority setting', one is on more level ground insofar as one is comparing like with like.[73] Used in this way, QALYs may actually augment the patient's autonomy by explicitly involving him or her in the process of rational consent to therapy.[74] Even so, a note of caution may be sounded as it is not difficult to confuse the objectives. The easy phrase 'not clinically indicated' may mean either that the treatment is not considered to be of overall benefit to the patient or it may imply an inappropriate allocation of resources.[75] The distinction is conceptually important; in the latter case, the professional has a legitimate prior interest in decision making while, in the former, the choice is one for the individual patient.

11.47 There are other more specific objections to QALYs as they are currently developed. Clearly, they operate to the disadvantage of the aged; they measure only the end-point of treatment without considering the *proportional* loss or gain in the quality of life; and there are parameters other than simple health which need to be fed into the equation. Possibly the most important moral criticism is that the QALY sets no value on life per se.[76] Harris considers that we should be saving as many lives, not life years, as possible – a proposition which simplifies the argument by removing it from the ambit of life-saving treatment which should, then, be apportioned only on a 'first come, first served' basis;[77] we also suggest that the customary use of the term 'life-saving', when what is really meant is 'death-postponing', can lead to false reasoning. What this view certainly does, however, is to emphasise that QALYs can never be used to compare the value of 'life-saving' therapies with those which are

73 Cochrane et al para 11.13 above.
74 See para 10.99.
75 See T Hope, D Sprigings and R Crisp '"Not Clinically Indicated": Patients' Interests or Resource Allocation?' (1993) 306 BMJ 379.
76 See, in particular, J Harris 'QALYfying the Value of Life' (1987) 13 J Med Ethics 117; Rawles, para 11.10 above.
77 Cf the case of Mr McKeown, para 11.37 above.

merely life-enhancing. Indeed, we may well wonder whether we have any right to pronounce on the quality of other people's lives and, hence, whether abstract formulae should ever be used to compare the management of individual persons or different disease states. We should be very careful lest we find that we have unwittingly written into the equation a constant such as that the mentally handicapped, for example, are, by definition, possessed of less QALYs than are those with no inherent deficit.[78]

11.48 In view of these many criticisms, it is not surprising that alternatives to the QALY are being actively sought. One such system is the saved young life equivalent, in which saving the life of a young person and restoring him or her to full health is regarded as the unit of measurement – on the grounds that most people would regard that as the maximum benefit that a single individual can obtain.[79] The comparative values of treatments is then assessed in terms of how many expected outcomes of each treatment would be equivalent to one SAVE. Our specific criticism of such a system would be that, even by its title, it actively promotes 'ageism', which is little more than an unfortunate, though inevitable, incidental to the QALY concept. Moreover – and in common with all such formulae – it reduces persons to numbers and tends to dehumanise medical practice.

11.49 This criticism hardens when the health economists tie cost to their preferred process of analysis – something which they must do in order to guide those responsible for macroallocation of resources. It may well be salutary for physicians and surgeons to be forced into knowing the cost-effectiveness of any given procedure. What health economists should not do, in our view, is to attempt to dictate the resolution of clinical problems in financial terms – to allow this is, as Rawles has put it, to condone: 'the development by health economists of fairer methods of denying patients treatment.'[80] To which the economist would reply: 'The economic perspective is clear – to maximise health improvements from limited resources by targeting resources at those activities high in the cost-QALY league table.'[81] It is up to society to define its objectives.

11.50 To some, the answer to the resource allocation dilemma is simply to increase the resources;[82] others regard this as a dangerous assumption – Klein, for example, suggested that it is only a slight exaggeration to say that the demand for health care is what the medical profession chooses to make it.[83] We believe that the transfer of funds from, say, nuclear weapon production to health care, while being admirable in itself, does no more than move the problem one incremental stage further. The majority would agree that some form of structured distribution of facilities at microallocation level is essential

---

78 For something of an ethical defence of *in*equality, see J Savulescu 'Resources, Down's Syndrome and Cardiac Surgery' (2001) 322 BMJ 875.

79 E Nord 'An Alternative to QALYs: The Saved Young Life Equivalent (SAVE)' (1992) 305 BMJ 875.

80 J Rawles and K Rawles 'The QALY Argument: A Physician's and A Philosopher's View' (1990) 16 J Med Ethics 93.

81 A Maynard 'Ethics and Health Care 'Underfunding'' (2001) 27 J Med Ethics 223.

82 Rawles, para 11.10 above.

83 Klein, para 11.3 above.

even though equity and efficiency may, at times, lie together uneasily. Harris, for example, has made out a powerful case against the QALY[84] but this is insufficient to convince one that the best method of resource allocation is on the basis of 'first come, first served'. McKie and his colleagues, in a continuing debate with Harris, saw QALYs, on the other hand, as a sensitive and egalitarian method of distributing scarce resources among competing individuals.[85] We doubt if they should be used in this way. To say that 'the QALY approach is egalitarian because no one's QALYs count for more than anyone else's' takes no note of the fact that, when the chips are down, the QALYs available to each player are unequally stacked. McKie et al were at their fairest when they said that they would restrict the QALY method of assessment if it was shown in a particular case to have a 'divisive and corrosive effect on the sense of community'. But to do so is to reintroduce subjective preferences into what was intended to be an objective exercise and is, to that extent, self-defeating. In the end, QALYs as they stand are no more than aids to decision-making and they are but one of a number of possible models;[86] possibly their most useful common feature is that they trigger debate as to how priorities in health care should be set rationally.

11.51 We should exclude from this discussion, and treat as a special case, the patient who is using a scarce resource but who is obtaining no benefit. The most clear example of this is one who is brain damaged and is being maintained in intensive care – a situation discussed in detail in chapter below. We believe that, once treatment is clearly of no avail, it is not only permissible but positively correct to discontinue heroic measures.[87] Of the many reasons for taking this view, the one which is presently apposite is that a resource, even if couched in terms of man-hours only, is thereby released for someone who is likely to benefit.

Random selection

11.52 In our search for an equitable and efficient method of providing limited treatment, only the option of random selection of patients – or of lottery, or 'first come, first served' – remains for discussion.

11.53 Such a policy has the advantage of apparent objectivity and, as we have seen, it could be regarded as the morally desirable choice in the context of potentially fatal disease. It is, however, a bad medical option because it takes no account of the gravity of the patient's condition and no account of 'medical benefit' – it concentrates on justice and ignores 'welfare'; moreover, the sheer length of waiting lists may prevent the most acceptable cases from the physician's point of view from ever obtaining treatment. As an option, it is also socially suspect in that it treats human beings as 'things' and pays no

---

84 J Harris 'Would Aristotle Have Played Russian Roulette?' (1996) 22 J Med Ethics 209.
85 J McKie, H Kuhse, J Richardson and P Singer 'Double Jeopardy, the Equal Value of Lives and the Veil of Ignorance' (1996) 22 J Med Ethics 204.
86 For a useful summing up, see R Robinson 'The Policy Context' (1993) 307 BMJ 994.
87 The most recent example is that of *Re G (adult incompetent: withdrawal of treatment)* (2001) 65 BMLR 6. It is to be noted, however, that such cases are rarely, if ever, argued on a resource basis. We discuss this case further in chapter 17.

justice to human values and aspirations. And, finally, its acceptance may be a cloak for no more than abrogation of responsibility. Nevertheless, it may be the way of allocating scarce resources that the public prefer.[88]

11.54 It is surprising that there is no recent precedental case law on which to judge the attitudes of society in respect of allocation of resources at the micro, or individual, level. The most likely reason for this is that decisions are taken in good faith and are based on principles which would be acceptable to a responsible body of medical opinion – there is, therefore, no action available in negligence; moreover, there is a tendency for well-publicised and apposite instances to be solved pragmatically.[89] For any assistance, we suspect we must go back to the classic case of *US v Holmes*.[90] In this instance, a ship's officer ordered a number of passengers to be ejected from a sinking lifeboat; Holmes, who helped effect the instructions, was convicted of manslaughter. A main argument for the prosecution was that the passengers, at least, should have been chosen by lot. It seems fair to assume that this decision would lend support to a policy of randomisation in the event of competition for scarce medical resources; the inferred element of an 'appeal to God' adds some moral weight to the argument. A rather similar English incident is reported in relation to a ferry-boat disaster. Here, a passenger assumed a position of authority and may well have occasioned the sacrifice of one man in order to save the lives of several other passengers; the case never came to court and the coroner thought that such killing would not necessarily be criminal. The commentator, however, considered that such authority as exists is to the effect that the killing of one to save the lives of others cannot be justified or even excused.[91] But such precedents are, at best, only loosely applicable to the present discussion.

11.55 As to the withdrawal of resources from a patient already using them, both United Kingdom and United States law is discussed in chapters 17 and 18. It is to be noted, however, that nowhere is there any authority for such action on the grounds of competing medical benefit – that is, that a further latecomer to the scene would be likely to do better. Indeed, there are strong indications that the contrary holds. In *Re J*,[92] Balcombe LJ said:

> I would stress the absolute undesirability of the court making an order which may have the effect of compelling a doctor or health authority to make available scarce resources (both human and material) to a particular child, without knowing whether or not there are other patients to whom the resources might

---

88 There is, for example, no objection to 'waiting lists' for organ transplantation. Calls for more public participation and debate are increasing: R Smith 'Rationing Health Care: Moving the Debate Forward' (1996) 312 BMJ 1553 and, as we have seen, are an integral part of government policy.

89 For a good example, see the report by D Brahams 'When is Discontinuation of Dialysis Justified?' (1985) 1 Lancet 176.

90 26 Fed Cas 360 (1841), No 15383.

91 Our authority is J C Smith and B Hogan *Criminal Law: Cases and Materials* (4th edn, 1990), p 231. The well-known case of *R v Dudley and Stephens* (1884) 14 QBD 273, [1881–5] All ER Rep 61, CCR was essentially a matter of killing and cannibalism for self-preservation and is too far removed to be appropriate to the present discussion.

92 *Re J (a minor) (wardship: medical treatment)* [1992] 2 FLR 165 at 176, (1992) 9 BMLR 10 at 20.

more advantageously be devoted ... [It might] require the health authority to put J on a ventilator in an intensive care unit, and thereby possibly to deny the benefit of those limited resources to a child who was much more likely than J to benefit from them.

The implication is clear – withdrawal of treatment will only be condoned when the patient can receive no further benefit.

A solution of the insoluble?

11.56 We have thus reached a position where no single parameter seems entirely satisfactory. Gordon[93] in a discussion of the doctrine of necessity, speaks of it as offending 'against the feeling that no human being has a right to decide which of his fellows should survive in any situation'; but, while most would agree with this proposition in a general sense, doctors cannot opt out of such decisions. Some idea of the complexity of the dilemma was given in an interesting study of dialysis decisions.[94] In this, 40 specimen patients' records were sent to 25 renal units with the request that ten patients be rejected on the grounds of inadequate treatment resources. Only 13 patients would have been accepted in all the units, but, at the same time, none was rejected by all; in the event, it was discovered that six of the ten most commonly rejected cases had already been successfully treated by the authors! Something of a lottery must have been operating despite the most earnest endeavours of physicians to improve upon the system – and it has to be noted that far more sophisticated approaches to organ allocation are now being operated.[95] We should also note that the New Zealand consensus guidelines, which we have discussed above, were introduced specifically to eliminate such anomalies – right or wrong, uniformity may be preferable to confusion.

11.57 We have not discussed a final possible criterion of selection – that is, the ability to pay for a resource. The omission probably derives from a natural repugnance to such an idea, particularly among those accustomed to a national health service. But, on reflection, we wonder if a modified concept of this type does not have its attractions as a way of alleviating scarcity while still retaining moral respectability – indeed, Dworkin has suggested that one criterion for the allocation of resources might be based on what the public *would* pay for given the need.[96] There is no shortage of dialysis machines from the manufacturing point of view; it is the shortage of money to pay for them and the associated manpower within the confines of a 'free' medical service which lies at the root of the problem. In these circumstances, it might not be unreasonable to allow patients to contribute to the purchase of 'engineering hardware' according to their means, on the principle that a machine which is bought releases another for the use of others who cannot do so. Such a system operates in the United States as regards dialysis where, admittedly, it was

93 G H Gordon *The Criminal Law of Scotland* (2nd edn, 1978) p 422.
94 V Parsons and P Lock 'Triage and the Patient with Renal Failure' (1980) 6 J Med Ethics 173. In fairness, however, it should be remarked that this is a very dated reference.
95 R W S Chang 'How Should Cadaver Kidneys Be Allocated?' (1996) 348 Lancet 453 and associated papers.
96 For discussion, see R Smith 'Being Creative about Rationing' (1996) 312 BMJ 391.

introduced for precisely the opposite reasons – that patients with chronic renal disease would be destroyed financially unless public assistance was given; but whatever the reason, it is probable that the overall provision of dialysis resources is better when distributed as a joint private and public enterprise.

11.58 Such a policy would be, we admit, difficult to apply with absolute equity. In particular, it could be argued that it would draw off in an unequal manner the personnel required to operate the machines and who have been trained at public expense.[97] To which one could answer that one does not expect a university graduate in law to accept only legal aid cases; one could also point out that a greater number of cases – of dialysis cases, at least – would be treated at home and that, by and large, the efficiency of domiciliary treatment and the financial status of the patient are closely related. In short, in certain circumstances, there may be a logical case for including private medicine within the public sector with possible benefit to the latter. What does seem to becoming increasingly clear is that an ideological attachment to a monopolistic tax-funded health service is not necessarily the best approach to an ideal service. As Bosanquet[98] has argued, other options for choice and competition are available and it is, perhaps, a failing of modern health economics that these potentially dynamic forces for developing improved and cost-effective programmes have not been explored more fully.

11.59 We appreciate that, at the end of this fairly lengthy discussion, we have come to little in the way of firm conclusions. We have approached the issues from the position of doctor and lawyer and it is, in some ways, comforting to find that philosophers may be in much the same dilemma.[99] Gillon probably sums up the debate correctly when he implies that, provided decisions are made taking into account fundamental moral values and principles of equity, impartiality and fairness, and provided the bases for decision-making are flexible in relation to the times, then the underlying system is just and is likely to yield just results. Alternatively, we can simply be stoical and acknowledge that: 'to live with circumstances that are unfortunate but not unfair is the destiny of men and women who have neither the financial nor the moral resources of gods and goddesses'.[100]

The responsibility of the individual

11.60 No discussion of this type would be complete without a passing reference to the responsibility of the individual to avoid the need for medical resources. The argument that prevention is better than cure has been widely popularised. No one would deny the importance of the theory at all levels but, equally, it

---

97 An effective case can be made out for an 'all or nothing' policy for health service employees: D W Light 'The Real Ethics of Rationing' (1997) 315 BMJ 112.

98 Para 11.34 above. The formation of elite Foundation Hospitals free from direct management by the Department of Health, and representing the middle ground between the public and private sectors, seems a move in this direction: 'Foundation Hospitals to be Given Greater Freedom' http://www.pm.gov.uk/print/page5052.asp.

99 Gillon, para 11.44 above.

100 Engelhardt, para 11.41 above.

is difficult to decide when friendly persuasion ceases and restriction of liberty begins. It follows that a good case can be made out for a right to choose to be unhealthy – and this not only on Kantian but also on utilitarian grounds, for every sudden death in late middle age that is prevented is potentially a long-term occupation of a bed in a psychogeriatric ward; it could well be that the quest for dementia that is inherent in many of the currently popular limitations on habit are remarkably cost-inefficient.

11.61 What does *not* follow is that there is a concomitant right to health resources when the consequences of that choice materialise. It seems that the public have little sympathy for the cavalier approach – in Williams's experience, the least unacceptable reason for discrimination in prioritisation was that the prospective patients had not cared for their own health.[101] In making such value judgments, however, the public are not constrained by principles of professional ethics and the issue is certainly not so easily solved by health care providers. Various views were put forward in an interesting debate in the British Medical Journal on whether or not coronary bypass surgery should be offered to smokers.[102] The attitude of the surgeons was conditioned by the poor results obtained in smokers and the fact that they spent longer in hospital. Non-treatment could, therefore, be justified on the grounds that treatment of non-smokers deprived others of more efficient and effective surgery. An alternative medical view was that non-treatment of symptomatic patients is often less effective in terms of overall cost to society than is operation, that there are many other 'self-inflicted' conditions which one would not hesitate to treat and that, at least in some cases, smoking is an addictive disease which merits sympathy. A warning was also sounded that, in regarding those who have brought medical ills upon themselves as, somehow, less deserving, the doctor is coming perilously close to prescribing punishment. We would accept the view expressed that the patient should be offered the chance when a positive therapeutic advantage – albeit a less than ideal advantage – may be attainable. The solution to the problem thus comes down to the 'best interests' of the individual; we believe, moreover, that this is the route that would be taken by the courts were such a case to be litigated – but the matter would, now, more likely be resolved on *Re S* standards[103] than by reliance on *Bolam*.

101 Williams, para 11.45 above.
102 'Should Smokers Be Offered Coronary Bypass Surgery?' (1993) 306 BMJ 1047: M J Underwood and J S Bailey 'Coronary Bypass Surgery Should Not Be Offered to Smokers' at 1047; M Shiu 'Refusing to Treat Smokers Is Unethical and a Dangerous Precedent' at 1048; R Higgs 'Human Frailty Should Not be Penalised' at 1049; J Garfield 'Let the Health Authority Take the Responsibility' at 1050.
103 *Re S (adult patient: sterilisation)* [2001] 3 Fam 15, [2000] 3 WLR 1288, CA – the standard being the *overall* rather than the *medical* best interests.

12 Treatment of the aged

12.1 Old age used to present no particular medico-ethical problems – senescence carried with it an increasing susceptibility to infection and the majority of the aged died at home within the family circle, having strayed not too far from their biblical allocation of three score and ten years.

12.2 Fewer people die in middle age today than did so in the past, while the physical health of the elderly is steadily improving; thus, longevity itself and the expectation of longevity are both increasing. Thirteen per cent of the population of the United Kingdom were aged over 65 years in 1971; this proportion had grown to 16% by 1996 and is expected to increase steadily so as to reach 24% in 2061 – persons over the age of 65 will outnumber those below age 16 after 2015. The elderly population is also growing older – the greatest expected proportional rise in the population is in those over 90 years old who are likely to double in numbers between now and 2036 when there will about 800,000 very old people.[1] Of greater importance in the present context is the projection that the number of people aged 65 or over suffering from a long-standing illness is likely to rise from some 6 million to-day to over 9 million in 2036. Even so, it is encouraging to note that the anticipated number of aged persons who require help with conditions of ordinary living falls according to the year in which the projection was made. Thus, it was forecast in 1976 that there would be some 3 million such persons in 2036; by 1991, the figure was revised to 800,000. Thus, the functional health of old people is improving as their numbers increase[2] – the relationship of their total number and the consequent drain on the social services is, therefore, not that of simple parallelism. Improved physical status, however, is not necessarily paralleled by improved mental capacity; indeed, a longer life provides more time during which the inevitable wastage of a limited supply of brain cells can occur. The stage is then set for a swelling proportion of the population that is suffering from various degrees of dementia; this may, itself, be of

---

1   These figures are adapted from those described by K-T Khaw 'How Many, How Old, How Soon?' (1999) 319 BMJ 1350 which are based on Office for National Statistics *National Population Projections; 1996 based* (1999).
2   M R Bone, A C Bebbington, C Jagger et al *Health Expectancy and its Uses* (1995).

primary degenerative type or be secondary to disease of the cerebral vasculature. Long-stay is likely when such patients are admitted to hospital and the dilemma in respect of resource allocation scarcely needs emphasis[3] – up to 20% of all medical and surgical beds in the United Kingdom may be occupied by people over the age of 75 years, although the current government initiatives on behalf of the elderly may alter the picture.[4] Population projections are now sufficiently sophisticated to indicate the problems likely to be met in deciding on the means by which to cope with conditions in the future – those means cannot be determined on the basis of administrative convenience alone but must involve both ethical and legal considerations.

AUTONOMY AND PATERNALISM IN THE TREATMENT OF THE AGED

12.3 The conflict between autonomy – or the exercise of choice – and paternalism – or the efforts of others to protect those who they consider to be in need of protection – lies at the heart of modern-day medical jurisprudence and is far more complex in the context of geriatric medicine than it is, say, in the relatively simple field of consent to surgical treatment by a competent adult. The elderly person is constrained in his – or, more likely, her[5] – choice of action by many factors, some of which are endogenous – such as the effects of early dementia – but others of which are extraneous – for example poverty. The impetus to paternalistic protection of the aged, no matter how it is ultimately applied, is likely to come from that person's family and, although the factor may be minimised in individual cases, it is undeniable that, in general, it is easier to live without the burden of caring for one's ageing parents; children take on the mantle of paternalism when they seek institutional care for their parents and there is no way in which subjectivity can be wholly eliminated from such action. It is arguable that children have no obligation to support their parents[6] and, regrettable as it may seem, such an obligation has never existed in English law; moreover, the common law duty which existed previously in Scotland has been removed by statute.[7] The public is probably insufficiently aware of the extent of intrafamilial abuse of the elderly; the degree of ignorance – or, in this case possibly, of indifference – is comparable to that which applied to child abuse 40 years ago. There is little doubt that abuse is extensive and that it occurs in various forms including verbal, physical and by way of neglect or deprivation; figures of between 5% and 65% of elderly persons being at risk are quoted, the incidence depending on the criteria used by the reporting agencies.[8] In one prospective study in England, 45% of

---

3 See K Andrews 'Demographic Changes and Resources for the Elderly' (1985) 290 BMJ 1023 for an early analysis.

4 Department of Health *National Service Framework for Older People* (2001).

5 The life expectancy in the age group 65–74 is 14.2 years for men and 17.9 years for women: Khaw, para 12.2 above

6 N Daniels 'Family Responsibility Initiatives and Justice Between Age Groups' (1985) 13 Law Med Hlth Care 153. Also by the same author *Am I My Parents' Keeper?* (1988).

7 Family Law (Scotland) Act 1985, s 1(1). But this is not universal. A duty to care for one's indigent parents exists, say, in South Africa: P Q R Boberg *The Law of Persons and the Family* (1991) quoting *Re Knoop* (1893) 10 SC 198.

8 B Pitt 'Abusing Old People' (1993) 305 BMJ 968.

carers admitted to some form of 'elder abuse'[9] – and the situation does not seem to have altered greatly over the last decade.[10] It follows that any attempt to enforce a filial duty of care for the aged would be likely to exacerbate domestic violence or neglect and, thus, provoke further deterioration in the geriatrics' conditions. Much of the care of the elderly must, therefore, devolve on the medical and social services and both of these must be supported by the law.[11]

Institutional treatment

12.4 Medical treatment of the aged in the United Kingdom has, as in all advanced societies, moved a long way since the chronically sick, including those who were simply homeless, were almost arbitrarily assigned to hospital wards which have been described as little more than 'human warehouses'.[12] Attention is now concentrated on maintaining the old person's environment as far as is possible. Such a policy must include as a starting point a system of pre-admission home visits by specialists in geriatric medicine; the fact that an inability to appreciate one's disablement is a concomitant of dementia has also dictated positive case-finding.[13] Both these activities may raise problems of etiquette, if not of ethics, between specialists and general practitioners; moreover, there is a strong possibility that case finding imposes an excessively heavy load on general practitioners. Antipathy to institutionalising the psycho-geriatric patient, however, inevitably calls for concomitant improvements in home help. Given a good relationship, much of this can be provided by the family – particularly if they are given assistance. The local authority has a duty to assess the needs of anyone who appears to be in need of community care[14] and, once the authority is satisfied of that person's needs, it has a duty to make suitable arrangements.[15] These are available by way of rather complex legislation. In essence, a disability living allowance, divided into care and mobility components, is payable to a person who, inter alia, is so physically or mentally disabled as to require the constant attention of another person by day (or prolonged or repeated attention at night) to assist with his or her bodily functions or for his or her protection from danger. Disability living allowance is payable only if the disability arose before the age of 65; it is replaced by attendance allowance if it arose later – and there is no age limit applied to this benefit.[16] Elective and temporary admission to hospital,

---

9 A C Homer and C Gilleard 'Abuse of Elderly People by their Carers' (1990) 301 BMJ 1359. It is fair, however, to say that such figures do not always obtain: J Ogg and G Bennett 'Elder Abuse in Britain' (1992) 305 BMJ 998.

10 A Tonks and G Bennett 'Elder Abuse' (1999) 318 BMJ 278.

11 See A Griffiths and G Roberts *The Law and Elderly People* (2nd edn, 1995).

12 T Howell 'The Birth of British Geriatrics' (1983) 13 Geriat Med 791.

13 M Arcand and J Williamson 'An Evaluation of Home Visiting of Patients by Physicians in Geriatric Medicine' (1982) 283 BMJ 718.

14 National Health Service and Community Care Act 1990, s 47. The quality of such assessment and the consequent disposal of the subjects is open to criticism: E Dickinson 'Long Term Care of Older People' (1996) 312 BMJ 862.

15 Chronically Sick and Disabled Persons Act 1970, s 2.

16 Social Security Contributions and Benefits Act 1992, ss 71, 75 and 64. These benefits are to be distinguished from invalid care allowance which is paid to the carer (s 70). The rights of married daughters to invalid care allowance have been upheld by the European Court of Justice: *Drake v Chief Adjudication Officer* [1986] 3 All ER 65, [1986] ECR 1995.

thus allowing the carers time for relaxation, can be a most useful adjunct. By and large, however, home assistance must be a function of the social services and the local authority is under an obligation to provide such aid in a 'preventive' mode. This includes help with the design of the house and the provision of meals, facilities for recreation and home helps.[17]

12.5 It may be, however, that such treatment is cost ineffective and is difficult to apply. In a case brought under the Chronically Sick and Disabled Patients Act 1970, it was held that the costs of the arrangements and the distribution of the authority's resources were proper considerations in assessing whether a person had a need and whether it was necessary to make arrangements to meet it.[18] The case concerned the *removal* of social services from a disabled man; some of the difficulties involved are crystallised in the dissenting opinion of Lord Lloyd:

> How can resources help to measure the man's need? ... It cannot, however, have been Parliament's intention that local authority B should be able to say 'because we do not have enough resources, we are going to reduce your needs'. His needs remain exactly the same. They cannot be affected by the local authority's inability to meet those needs.[19]

12.6 Even so, as we have seen in the previous chapter in relation to the National Health Service, the courts are loath to interfere with the distribution of public funds – and much the same applies to the social services provided by the local authority. The House of Lords was not minded to dictate the tactical allocation of resources in Mr Barry's case.

12.7 The economic return from this type of management depends, to an extent, on the degree of dependency – the expense of domicillary care increases with increased dependency and, at some point, it will become inequitable for a disabled person to expect cost-ineffective support at the expense of others who are, thereby, deprived of care;[20] clearly, however, the wishes – or autonomy – of the subject must be fed into the balance, and this demands the provision of adequate information.[21] The current proliferation of privately run nursing homes makes it very difficult to generalise as to the comparative prognosis of those cared for at home and those institutionalised. Inevitably, much depends upon the degree and efficiency of supervision of residential and nursing homes and we return to the subject below.

12.8 Nevertheless, some old people, who are fit other than in the mind, must be institutionalised to an extent which will depend upon the severity of

17 For a useful, simple review, see P Wanklyn 'Homes and Housing for Elderly People' (1996) 313 BMJ 218. Boarding accommodation, which is something less than residential care, can also be provided under the Health and Social Services and Social Security Adjudications Act 1983, Sch 9, Pt II; Social Work (Scotland) Act 1968, s 14. A general duty to care for the welfare of the elderly also rests on the local social service authority (Health Services and Public Health Act 1968, s 45).
18 *R v Gloucestershire County Council, ex p Barry* [1997] AC 584, [1997] 2 All ER 1, HL.
19 AC 584 at 599, All ER 1 at 6.
20 J G Evans 'Institutional Care and Elderly People' (1993) 306 BMJ 806.
21 This aspect of duty to the aged is emphasised by K Lothian and I Philp 'Maintaining the Dignity and Autonomy of Older People in the Healthcare Setting' (2001) 322 BMJ 668.

dementia. The simplest form of such care is by way of sheltered housing – which may be provided by the local authority, housing associations or as a private venture – but the degree of available supervision is generally so low as to eliminate it as a resort for persons who are anything greatly less than fully independent; sheltered housing might, however, be the ideal refuge for the elderly person who is subject to domestic abuse and, thereby, eligible for priority accommodation.[22] Beyond this, it may be possible to arrange for residential care in accommodation which the local authority has a duty to provide by virtue of the National Assistance Act 1948, s 21. Practice, however, falls short of the theoretical ideal. The local authority has no obligation to provide specialist or hospital-type medical facilities in such institutions,[23] which are already accepting patients whose requirements exceed those for which this method of disposal was designed; so-called 'Part III accommodation' – ie provided under the National Assistance Act 1948, ss 21 to 26 – tends to revert to the conditions which are less than ideal.

12.9 The result has been a growth of private homes, which has been encouraged by government policy that the local authorities should utilise the private sector.[24] Homes which must be registered under the Care Standards Act 2000 are known as care homes and include those which provide either board and personal care to those in need of it[25] (residential care homes) and those which, in addition, provide nursing care (nursing homes). The 2000 Act makes no nominal distinction between the two but the nature of the building, the staff requirements and the like will be reflected in the grant of registration.[26] The extension of private nursing homes, with governmental assistance as to charge, has provided some sort of solution to the problem of the scarcity of residential accommodation although the situation is not as good as it once was due to the continuing closure of private homes on economic and commercial grounds. The cumulative result is that hospital beds are blocked by older patients who cannot be moved – not only are the elderly thus retained in conditions that were not designed for such use but those who would benefit most are deprived of hospital accommodation. The government's new initiative in this respect involves the creation of some 5000 intermediate care beds together with supported intermediate care places which will be used to expedite discharge from hospital, to prevent unnecessary admissions and, also, to avoid premature admission to long-term residential care.[27] Inevitably, this is regarded in some quarters as being less than satisfactory and even contrary to accepted

---

22 Housing Act 1985, s 59. Vulnerability can only be defined following wide-ranging inquiry: *R v Lambeth Borough Council, ex p Carroll* (1987) 20 HLR 142.
23 Health and Social Care Act 2001, s 49.
24 Community Care (Residential Accommodation) Act 1992, amending National Assistance Act 1948, s 26.
25 Personal care essentially means bodily care for those who cannot manage for themselves. The fact that a person is not receiving assistance with bodily functions does not, however, mean that he or she cannot be in need of personal care: *Harrison v Cornwall County Council* (1990) 11 BMLR 21.
26 The Care Standards Act 2000, s 6 also establishes a National Care Standards Commission the general remit of which is to ensure the adequacy of standards of care for the vulnerable.
27 National Health Service *The NHS Plan: A Plan for Investment, A Plan for Reform* (2000) (Cm 4818-1) para 15.14.

geriatric practice[28] – but there is little doubt that the health care of old people has assumed a new political significance in the early 21st century.[29]

12.10 At the same time, the pressure to empty 'blocked' hospital beds is increasing – and, indeed, may be the government's primary aim – and it is here that manifest inequity creeps in. So long as the old person remains in hospital, his or her needs are met free through the medium of the NHS. The use of a local authority's residential or nursing home is, however, subject to a means test.[30] Effectively, a person who has a capital of £18,500[31] or more, which includes the value of his or her own home, has to pay his or her charges in full; the local authority will pay the difference between their basic and the actual costs until the person's savings have been reduced to £3,000; the authority will then pay the full fee.[32]

12.11 Something of a conflict may, therefore, develop between the local health authorities, who are anxious to clear their bed-space, and the elderly, backed by their families, many of whom would, quite reasonably, wonder why they have been singled out as a group to whom the facilities of a comprehensive health service are denied when most needed – it is estimated that some 40,000 houses are sold each year in order to finance long-term nursing care.[33] Health authorities may, and do, claim that their duty of care is limited by the resources available and, as a result, policies on the limitation of long-term care are variable – in fact, very few Health Authorities provide nursing home care; at the same time, the social services cannot find places for an indefinite number of persons discharged from hospital. Thus, not only may the older patient be discharged from hospital prematurely, but he or she may be moved from NHS to local authority accommodation with corresponding financial penalty.[34]

12.12 An interesting example arose in the case brought by Mrs Coughlan in 1999.[35] Here, a paraplegic woman had been assured of a 'home for life' in a nursing home controlled by the NHS; she applied for judicial review of the

---

28 J G Evans and R C Tallis 'A New Beginning for Care for Elderly People?' (2002) 322 BMJ 807.
29 See para 12.2 above.
30 The assessment of whether or not a person is 'in need' is not resource dependant. It is only after the need has been established that means affect charging for the services provided – at least in Scotland: *Robertson (AP) v Fife Council* [2002] UKHL 35.
31 National Assistance (Assessment of Resources) (Amendment) (No 2) (England) Regulations 2001, SI 2001/1066, r 3.
32 Health and Social Services and Social Security Adjudications Act 1983, s 17; J Warden 'The Lottery of Long Term Care' (1994) 308 BMJ 742.
33 Leading Article 'The Age of Health' *The Times*, 24 July 2000; M Dean 'UK's Long-term Nightmare on Nursing-care Costs' (1996) 347 Lancet 681. Predictably, the NHS has denied that it is neglecting the long-term health care of the elderly: Community Care Unit, NHS Executive *NHS Responsibilities for Meeting Longterm Health Care Needs* (1994).
34 The near absurdity of the schizoid approach to management is exemplified by the proposal that elderly persons discharged from hospital will receive direct cash payments to provide services that the local authorities' budgets cannot meet: A Vass 'Elderly Patients to Receive Cash to Speed up Hospital Discharge' (2002) 325 BMJ 179.
35 *R v North and East Devon Health Authority, ex p Coughlan* [2001] QB 213, [2000] 3 All ER 850. For brief discussion, see A Loux, S Kerrison and A M Pollock 'Long Term Nursing: Social Care or Health Care?' (2000) 320 BMJ 5.

Health Authority's decision to close the home and transfer its inmates to local authority care where 'nursing care' would be paid for according to the patients' means. The Court of Appeal carefully considered the concept of 'nursing care' and, while admitting the difficulties involved in the marginal case, distinguished between that which might be expected from an authority providing 'social care' and that which was required by way of a primary health need – in essence, the test was both quantitative and qualitative. The Court considered that the Health Authority was at fault in imposing eligibility criteria for admission to its nursing home which were so severe as to force the local authority to accept responsibilities for which it was unsuited under the terms of the National Assistance Act 1948, s 21.[36] *Coughlan* can, thus, be said to have clarified, but not solved, the inequities of the current situation.

12.13 It is, however, fair to say that the government has, at last, recognised these and, largely as a result of the recommendations of the Sutherland Commission,[37] a number of initiatives have either been or are about to be launched at the time of writing.[38] Amongst these, arguably the most important is that nursing care is now provided free in nursing homes controlled by the local authority; personal care is, however, still means tested.[39] A second major concession is that the value of a person's house is not now counted against his or her capital assets for the first 12 weeks of residential care, thus allowing the old person time for reflection and adjustment.[40] Finally, though not exclusively, and although one views the establishment of yet more quangos with some scepticism, Commissions to oversee the provision of care have been authorised on both sides of the Border – and their remit will certainly include regulation of the care of the aged.[41] It is also to be noted that the difficulties associated with the placement of elderly people under the care of either the health or local authorities is to be eased by the introduction of a single assessment process that is governed by relatively strict guidelines.[42]

12.14 No-one expects that good intentions will always be crowned with success. The care of the disabled elderly is a relatively thankless task and, at the end of the day, the management and conditions within residential and nursing homes depends on a dedicated 'coalface' staff which is unlikely to be available in the numbers needed. Some years ago, institutional care was found

36 As amended by National Health Service and Community Care Act 1990, ss 42 and 66.
37 Royal Commission on the Funding of Long Term Care (Sir S Sutherland, chairman) *With Respect to Old Age: Long Term Care – Rights and Responsibilities* (1999) (Cmnd 4192-1).
38 See, in particular, National Health Service *The NHS Plan: The Government's Response to the Royal Commission on Long Term Care* (2000); Department of Health *National Service Framework for Older People* (2001).
39 It is, however, now free in Scotland – defined as concerned with day-to-day physical tasks and needs: Regulation of Care (Scotland) Act 2001, s 2(28). See Community Care and Health (Scotland) Act 2002, s 1. For a comparative review of alternative systems, including compulsory insurance see (2002) BMJ pp 1542–1543.
40 National Assistance (Assessment of Resources) (Amendment) (No 2) (England) Regulations, SI 2001/1066, r 5.
41 Care Standards Act 2000, s 6; Regulation of Care (Scotland) Act 2001, s 1.
42 Department of Health *Single Assessment Process* (2002), HSC 2002/001, LAC (2002) 1.

to be of less than ideal quality[43] – but this was probably so on a global scale. Methods of placement have become more sophisticated and more money is being made available for the general care of the aged. When we add to these the anti-discriminatory measures which are being introduced for the protection of the aged (see para 12.31 below), we can hope – and perhaps anticipate – that a new deal for this vulnerable group is on the way.

THE INDIVIDUAL PATIENT

12.15 So far, we have considered the problems of the aged in general terms only; they become even more acute when applied to the individual patient. Thus, in the conditions of Part III housing, injuries due to falls and other mishaps in an unsupervised situation are likely to arise; deaths which occur later, and which are no more than temporarily associated, are likely to be the subject of inquiry by either the Coroner or the Procurator Fiscal.[44] Many such incidents may be beyond the control of inadequate staff, notwithstanding their dedication; yet the fear of culpability can rebound to the overall detriment of the patient – 'defensive' action by the nurses may result in unnecessary restraint of their charges.[45] Of greater immediate importance are the ethical problems surrounding those old persons who want to retain their independence and who resist removal to an institution. The danger, then, is double-sided – either the 'cussedness' of old age may be designated as mental illness and the aged person be compulsorily restricted or, as has occurred in some of the United States, the senile dement may be determinedly excluded from the social benefits which are available to those who can lay claim to a recognisable mental illness.

12.16 Excluding the Mental Health Acts, the legal resolution of the problem of compulsory disposal of the inadequate aged person in the United Kingdom rests, primarily, on the National Assistance Act 1948, s 47 and the National Assistance (Amendment) Act 1951, s 1. The first allows the compulsory removal from their homes of persons who are not mentally ill but who are suffering from grave chronic disease or, being aged, infirm or physically incapacitated, are living in insanitary conditions and are unable to devote to themselves, and are not receiving from other persons, proper care and attention. Removal may be effected in the person's own interest or in order to prevent injury to the health of, or serious nuisance to, other persons. The district community physician, or community medicine specialist, can apply for a magistrate's order giving seven days' notice of removal. The order allows for detention in a 'suitable hospital or other place' for up to three months; emergency removal for a period of three weeks, thus avoiding the seven day

---

43   See, for example, E Dickinson 'Long Term Care of Older People' (1996) 312 BMJ 862. The situation is not eased by the continued separation of nursing and personal care which has been described as 'futile and destructive': I Heath 'Long Term Care for Older People' (2002) 324 BMJ 1534.

44   For a recent review of accidents in the home, see S M Cordner and J Ozanne-Smith 'Accidental Death and Injury in the Home' in J K Mason and B Purdue (eds) *The Pathology of Trauma* (3rd edn, 1999).

45   A very full discussion is to be found in S H Johnson 'The Fear of Liability and the Use of Restraints in Nursing Homes' (1990) 18 Law Med Hlth Care 263.

notification period, can be achieved on the recommendation of the community physician if this is backed by another practitioner – who is normally the person's general practitioner – and the removal is in the interests of the person concerned.[46] The fact that this accelerated procedure is used in the majority of cases is a cause of anxiety as to the operation of the legislation.

12.17 It is estimated that the powers under s 47 and its amendment are invoked annually less than some two hundred times in England[47] and 15 times in Scotland. The Act merely stipulates that the subject may be removed to 'a suitable hospital or other place' – and the seven day notification requirement applies to the manager of the premises unless he or she has agreed to receive the 'patient'. As to the place of removal, the order does not provide for compulsory treatment – a fact which must lead to some antipathy on the part of hospital managers.[48] If the subject is sent to hospital, it is likely to be to a geriatric hospital rather than to a geriatric unit; admission to a general hospital is likely to be looked on as a contradiction in terms unless the admission is on the grounds of grave chronic disease. The moral issues were elegantly argued by Gray[49] who, first, questioned the justification for removing an elderly person from his or her home for the benefit of 'other persons' – as he pointed out, powers of compulsory home cleaning and the like are already available under the Public Health Acts 1936-1961. Secondly, the arguments balancing paternalism against personal liberty, which have been discussed above, are raised in a particularly acute form. Thirdly, the use of statutory powers may be little more than a cloak for inadequate social services or family care – which, taken together, are to be preferred to institutionalisation. And finally, and perhaps of greatest importance, there is a strong implication that the powers may be based on disapproval of deviant rather than of dangerous behaviour.[50]

12.18 The contrary view was put by Greaves[51] who concluded that reference to the standard philosophical alternatives do not do justice to the moral issues at stake; he saw the answer to the problem as lying somewhere between the application of rational principles and personal prejudices. Greaves gave no firm answer as to how this level is to be achieved, but accepted that, in certain circumstances, a decision must be taken by proxy on behalf of the old person – and that this is best done by a doctor whose personal ethical sensitivity is unlikely to be suppressed by the blanket application of a principle. Gray[52] in fact, pointed out that s 47 and its forerunners was originally seen as a mechanism for protecting the elderly against the whims of officialdom and the Medical

---

46 National Assistance (Amendment) Act 1951, s 1(1).
47 P Nair and J F Mayberry 'The Compulsory Removal of Elderly People in England and Wales under Section 47 of the National Assistance Act and its 1951 Amendment: A Survey of its Implementation in England and Wales in 1988 and 1989' (1995) 24 Age and Ageing 180. This analysis is rather old but, since there is no requirement to report such removals, data are very hard to come by.
48 Refusal of treatment was given as the reason for removal in 19% of cases in the above study.
49 J A M Gray 'Section 47' (1981) 7 J Med Ethics 146.
50 For further criticism, see J D Fear, P Hatton and E B Renvoize 'Section 47 of National Assistance Act: A Time for Change?' (1988) 296 BMJ 860.
51 D A Greaves 'Can Compulsory Removal Ever Be Justified for Adults Who Are Mentally Competent?' (1991) 17 J Med Ethics 189.
52 J A M Gray 'Section 47 – Assault On or Protection Of the Freedom of the Individual?' (1991) 17 J Med Ethics 195.

Officer of Health was thought to be the best person to do this. While criticising the Draconian powers available under s 47, he did not believe that it should be repealed – but this is largely because other coercive or frankly immoral practices would evolve in order to persuade old people to resign their homes; there is an ingrained way of public thought that, given the same abnormality, old people 'must' be protected while others merely 'ought' to be so persuaded. There is, in fact, no easy solution. In a more recent attack on the current legislation, it was admitted that there are underlying problems involving individuals in need of care which cannot, at present, be answered in any way other than by the use of s 47 and it was asked whether it is right to deny what may be the best, albeit imperfect, option to one person in the hopes of improving the law for others. None the less, the author concluded that all suggested justifications for the use of s 47 fail.[53] For our part, perhaps the most damning aspect of the legislation is that there was no record of the outcome of 24% the compulsory removals recorded by Nair and Mayberry.

12.19   However, the alternative procedures available must also be considered critically. Foremost among these are the statutory provisions within the Mental Health Act 1983 and the Scottish equivalent of 1984. There are, first, the extensive powers available under s 135 (s 117 in Scotland) whereby a justice, acting on information from an approved social worker, can authorise the police to enter and remove to a place of safety a mentally disordered person who is at risk and living alone (this can only be done in Scotland after a mental health officer or a medical commissioner has been refused entry). The subject can then be detained for only 72 hours and, unsurprisingly, the section is used very rarely.[54] Very much more important are the powers relating to compulsory admission to hospital for assessment (s 2 (s 24(S)) or for emergency assessment (s 4 (s 26(S)). These are discussed in greater detail in chapter 21; for the present it is necessary only to note that it might not be difficult to invoke them in cases where s 47 was appropriate – indeed, the Mental Health Act has been seen as the preferred route in an emergency.[55] We take the view, however, that committal under the 1983 and 1984 Acts inevitably classifies the elderly and confused as being mentally abnormal – and, to many, such classification represents a stigma; despite the simultaneous provision of a recognised system of appeal, the use of what is, effectively, a ruse as a matter of administrative convenience seems to us to be more morally reprehensible than is the use of the more straightforward s 47. Moreover, use of the Acts depends upon proof of incompetence. As has been emphasised in the Court of Appeal:

> The Act[s] cannot be deployed to achieve the detention of an individual against her will merely because her thinking process is unusual, even apparently bizarre and irrational, and contrary to the views of the overwhelming majority of the community at large.[56]

53 S J Hobson 'The Ethics of Compulsory Removal under Section 47 of the 1948 National Assistance Act' (1998) 24 J Med Ethics 38. Repeal of s 47 was envisaged in the Law Commission's draft Mental Incapacity Bill 1995. See para 12.26 below.
54 Section 136, which refers to persons in public places, is used more commonly as the proportion of patients in community care increases.
55 E Murphy 'What to do with a Sick Elderly Woman Who Refuses to go to Hospital' (1984) 289 BMJ 1435.
56 *St George's Healthcare NHS Trust v S* [1998] 3 All ER 673 at 692, (1998) 44 BMLR 160 at 180, per Judge LJ.

Although stated in a different context, the principle cannot be changed simply on the grounds that the patient is elderly.

12.20 The possibility of an application for guardianship remains[57] – the purpose being to empower the guardian, who may be the local authority, to dictate the place of residence of the disordered person. Once again, the practice is seldom adopted due, largely, to the fact that the essential function of a guardian is to maintain the incompetent in the community; to order removal to residential care is, in its way, to defeat the object of the exercise. Moreover, the guardian has no power to order treatment and the guardianship can be challenged by the subject's next-of-kin.

12.21 Thus, no current way of achieving compulsory residential care of the elderly is wholly satisfactory. The result is that, in the majority of cases, legal process is avoided and the elderly person is 'talked into' abrogating his or her independent status.

12.22 The removal of an elderly person to a home or hospital does not, of course, solve all treatment dilemmas. He or she may, like any other, refuse to accept treatment. Compulsion from the legal point of view is out of the question so long as the subject is competent, although, in practice, relatives and others may resort to pressure of various sorts to ensure compliance. The position of the doctor, though, is clear: treatment against the will of the patient could constitute an assault in criminal law or an actionable civil wrong. Thought should also be given to the moral inappropriateness of compelling treatment in such cases; no matter what they feel about apparently irrational refusal, few doctors would now attempt to force treatment upon a patient who is mentally competent and who does not want it[58] – although this is not to say they should not use such persuasive powers as they feel to be appropriate. The position of one who is dementing will, however, be different. Almost by definition, such a patient is unlikely to understand fully the nature of her condition and the treatment available. It might be argued that an analogy with the unconscious patient is applicable and, in that case, a doctor may justify the non-consensual treatment of his patient on the grounds of necessity. Dementing patients, however, are not unconscious. Their comprehension may be affected but, equally, they may still be capable of holding and articulating views.[59] It might be better, then, to consider such treatment as an acceptable instance of paternalistic intervention of the sort under which children who are incapable of full understanding are treated. A 'best interests' argument – or even, in appropriate circumstances, a substituted judgment – could be advanced should specifically legal justification be called for.

12.23 The incompetent patient who is admitted to hospital under the Mental Health Acts may be treated compulsorily for the mental disorder which forms the basis of his admission. Treatment for other conditions is not permitted by

57 Mental Health Act 1983, s 7.
58 And they might well attract legal sanctions in so doing: *Re B (consent to treatment: capacity)* [2002] 2 All ER 449, (2002) 65 BMLR 149.
59 For a seminal study, see M J Gunn 'Treatment and Mental Handicap' (1987) 16 Anglo-Am L Rev 242.

the legislation unless it can be seen as being part of that which is appropriate for the mental disorder. This apparently restrictive attitude is compensated by the common law – the lawfulness of a doctor operating on, or giving other treatment to, an adult person disabled from giving consent would depend not on any approval or sanction of a court, but on the question whether the operation or other treatment was justified on the basis of necessity and was in the best interests of the patient concerned.[60]

Legal protection

12.24 Any demented person, and certainly anyone for whom compulsory admission to an institution is justified, is unlikely to be able to manage his or her affairs. The law has, therefore, made special provision to ensure that the interests of incompetent elderly people are protected. In English law, the task of administering the affairs of such people may be performed by the Court of Protection. This court, which is an office of the Supreme Court of Judicature, has powers under the Mental Health Act to act on behalf of those who are incapable as a result of mental disorder, a category which would include those suffering from dementia. Application for the appointment of a receiver may be made by a relative or by some other person with a legitimate interest in the matter, including a creditor.[61] During the period in which the receiver acts for the incapable person, the court exercises overall control and supervision of his or her activities.[62] In Scotland, the care of the incompetent adult is now controlled by the Adults with Incapacity (Scotland) Act 2000.[63] Essentially, the Act allows for the appointment of a guardian or a welfare attorney who can act on behalf of an adult who is deemed by the Sheriff to be incapable in relation to decisions about his or her property, financial affairs or personal welfare. The interests of the incapax are carefully protected throughout the Act and the activities of any guardian are subject to the supervision of the Public Guardian. The duties and limitations of the welfare attorney are discussed in greater detail in chapter 10. Outwith the context of these formal legal institutions, the law also takes some account of the particular situation of the elderly person. Contractual capacity may be denied in England and Wales to one who cannot understand the implications of a contract and contracts

---

60 *Re F (mental patient: sterilisation)* [1990] 2 AC 1, sub nom *F v West Berkshire Health Authority* [1989] 2 All ER 545 at 551 per Lord Brandon at AC 55, HL. It will be seen throughout this book that this case has been cited as the basis for treatment of the incompetent in a number of ways. This includes admission to hospital for psychiatric treatment: *R v Bournewood Community and Mental Health NHS Trust, ex p L* [1998] 3 All ER 289, [1998] 3 WLR 107. The subject is treated at length in chapters 10 and 21.

61 The Public Guardianship Office was set up in April 2002 as the administrative arm of the Court of Protection. Its functions include giving help to Receivers and might even take on the responsibility itself.

62 For powers of the Court of Protection, see *Re W (EEM)* [1971] Ch 123 at 143, per Ungoed-Thomas J. Statute, if ever enforced, will make a new provision for the appointment of an authorised representative with the power to negotiate on behalf of a disabled person with the local authority as to the general provision of welfare services (Disabled Persons (Services, Consultation and Representation) Act 1986).

63 Section 80 of the 2000 Act abolishes the appointment of a curator bonis, tutor-dative or tutor-at-law in respect of persons over the age of 16 years

which are entered into by persons whose mind is affected by dementia may, of course, be set aside. Similarly, testamentary capacity is restricted to those who can comprehend the nature and extent of their estate and the claims which people may have upon them. In assessing such capacity, however, the law is not so much concerned to place a psychiatric label on a testator as to determine the impact which an apparent specific delusion may have on the contents of the will.[64]

12.25 The rules of testamentary capacity were developed with the interests of others in mind. The same focus of attention can be detected in the other areas of the law in which special regard has been paid to the needs of the elderly. Continuance of the property control arrangements which the elderly person him- or herself has made may now extend beyond the onset of incompetence.[65]

12.26 The law protecting the elderly, dementing person is, thus, well-intentioned but seriously fragmented; as a result, it is unsatisfactory from the view of both the patient and society. This is, however, almost inevitable as it has to derive from an uncomfortable amalgam of mental health and social security law. Thus, while, as we have seen, the Scottish Executive has passed the Adults with Incapacity Act 2000, it is, nevertheless currently engaged in a new Mental Health Bill[66] which will apply to all forms of mental disorder including those associated with old age. Similarly, while the Mental Incapacity Bill 1995 is no longer before Parliament, the Westminster government is actively seeking to modify the mental health laws.[67] The English Law Commission, moreover, foresaw the establishment of a reorganised Court of Protection which has the power to appoint 'managers' to make decisions, including health care decisions, on behalf of incapable individuals; both jurisdictions are, therefore, moving in much the same way.[68] Both the English Law Commission and the Scottish Act of 2000 set great store by expressions of intent provided by advance statements or directives by the incapaces – but it is also to be noted that both still allow the medical profession considerable discretion as to their management.[69]

Ethical considerations

12.27 There remain for consideration the practical and ethical aspects of the treatment of geriatric patients. These are often discussed in the context of euthanasia which we deal with later in chapter 18. But, while it is true that

---

64 *Banks v Goodfellow* (1870) LR 5 QB 549.
65 Enduring Powers of Attorney Act 1985. For Scotland, see Adults with Incapacity (Scotland) Act 2000, s 15.
66 Based on Scottish Executive *New Directions*, Report on the Review of the Mental Health (Scotland) Act 1984 (B Millan, chairman) (2001).
67 Department of Health *Reforming the Mental Health Act* (2000). And see, now, the draft Mental Health Bill 2002.
68 Law Commission *Mental Incapacity* Law Com No 231 (1995).
69 In Scotland, for example, a single medical practitioner can, in the absence of a guardian or welfare attorney, provide a certificate that an adult is incapable which is valid for up to one year (2000 Act, s 47).

many old persons may be suffering from terminal or incapacitating physical disease, an equal or greater number may be the victims of no more than intellectual deterioration; the greater part of geriatric medicine relates, in fact, to the management of incurable, rather than of life-threatening, disease. If the patient's best interests represent the therapeutic yardstick – as they should – the inner world of the geriatric must be assessed subjectively and not related to the observer's own youthful or middle-aged experience. The demented but otherwise physically capable old person is not in pain and, for all we know, is passing a reasonably contented life. The parallel in controversial treatment issues is to be found in the uncomplicated Down's syndrome infant who, as we have already argued, is as entitled to medical treatment as is his mentally normal counterpart. Glib phrases such as 'pneumonia is the old man's friend' come easily to the lips in this discussion and can be dangerously emollient unless they are qualified; death may certainly be a blessed relief to the patient in severe pain but problems raised in the treatment, say, of intercurrent infection in the contented dement are of the same order as are those faced by the mentally competent – one wonders if the more honest aphorism is not that 'pneumonia in an old man is his associates' best friend'.

12.28 We would, therefore, disagree to an extent with those who, effectively, call for a policy which is generally biased towards non-treatment of the elderly demented patient on grounds of the 'quality of cognitive life'.[70] At one time, this was frequently expressed by including in the hospital notes the instruction 'do not resuscitate', the morality and practicality of which is discussed below.[71] Similar instructions to withhold resuscitative measures in the event of cardiorespiratory arrest are known as 'No-code orders' in the United States where their validity has been upheld.[72] The judicial reliance on good medical practice that is evident on both sides of the Atlantic emphasises the importance of considering each patient as an individual problem. Following our analogy with the newborn, there is a case to be made out for selective non-treatment of the aged – but selection must be based on the individual patient's circumstances. Guidelines for treatments are just that – they provide a useful setting in which to formulate a decision; they should not be seen as instructions which transcend the realities of the particular patient's condition.[73]

12.29 The issues crystallise in the place of the elderly in the allocation of resources which, as we have seen, is inevitable in an expanding medical technological ambience – and the arguments are finely balanced. The views of the authoritative commentator Callahan, although somewhat dated, are

---

70 G S Robertson 'Ethical Dilemmas of Brain Failure in the Elderly' (1983) 287 BMJ 1775 remains a most useful reference.
71 See para 18.92. For an excellent legal appraisal, see J Hendrick and C Brennan 'Do Not Resuscitate Orders: Guidelines in Practice' (1997) 6 Nottingham LJ 24.
72 *Re Dinnerstein* 380 NE 2d 134 (Mass, 1978). For attempts in the US to codify the process, see T E Miller 'Do-Not-Resuscitate Orders: Public Policy and Patient Autonomy' (1989) 17 Law Med Hlth Care 245.
73 See General Medical Council *Withholding and Withdrawing Life-prolonging Treatments* (2002); British Medical Association *Withholding and Withdrawing Life Prolonging Medical Treatment* (2001).

particularly interesting in this context.[74] In brief, Callahan saw the need for objective planning if the otherwise certain breakdown in resources is to be avoided. The aged, it was said, have some claim to public funds but these are not unlimited – the goal is a balanced, affordable system of care for the elderly which admits of a good balance between length and quality of life. Effectively, we should see ageing as an inevitable part of life and accept that society discharges its principal duty to the elderly by avoiding premature death. Callahan admitted that any serious form of setting limits to treatment will be unpleasant but, since the possibilities of spending money in an attempt to turn old age into permanent middle age are infinite, we should impose an age limit upon ourselves. These views, needless to say, have attracted opposition particularly from those who see the welfare of the individual as transcending a policy of general societal benefit[75] – the argument that we should *always* prefer a younger patient before an older one on the grounds that society's net life gain is, thereby, more evenly distributed is attractive but too dispassionate for comfort. While we would agree that difficult decisions may have to be taken, we prefer the egalitarian philosophy which will avoid positive discrimination against the elderly – expressed as the age-indifference principle which asserts that each person is entitled to the same concern, respect and protection of society as is accorded to any other person in the community.[76] Therapeutic decisions are intensely individual matters which cannot be covered by way of restrictive formulae; age, and the effect of age, may be one factor in the decision to treat but it cannot be the *only* factor. To quote Harris again:

> All of us who wish to go on living have something that each of us values equally although for each it is different in character ... This thing is of course 'the rest of our lives'. So long as we do not know the date of our deaths then for each of us the 'rest of our lives' is of indefinite duration. Whether we are 17 or 70 ... so long as we each wish to live out the rest of our lives ... we each suffer the same injustice if our wishes are deliberately frustrated and we are cut off prematurely.[77]

12.30 In short, the commonly voiced argument that the old person has 'had a good innings' and must make way for the young is incomplete; the elderly batsman is fully entitled to a respected rest in the pavilion. Such problems may confront the surgeon with particular force; the application of the productive/non-productive test[78] must always affect his decision whether or not to operate on the elderly. A negative response to advanced malignant disease may be a simple matter but the improvement in operative techniques is such that the results of elective general surgery in the aged, even of an advanced technological nature such as coronary artery replacement, may be

---

74 D Callahan *Setting Limits* (1987). This sort of view was well criticised by H R Moody 'Should We Ration Health Care on Grounds of Age?' in *Ethics in an Ageing Society* (1992) ch 9.

75 See eg R W Hunt 'A Critique of Using Age to Ration Health Care' (1993) 19 J Med Ethics 19. The obvious difficulties of involving the law in this area are summarised by M Rivlin 'Should Age Based Rationing of Health Care Be Illegal?' (1999) 319 BMJ 1379. Currently, there is no evidence of attempts to introduce, say, an Age Discrimination Act.

76 J Harris 'The Principle of Age Indifference' in Age Concern Millennium Paper *Values and Attitudes in an Ageing Society* (1998).

77 J Harris *The Value of Life* (1985) p 89.

78 See para 18.58.

both satisfactory and rewarding – the fact that results may be generally better in the young does not mean that the same procedure in the old is necessarily not worthwhile. It has, in addition, been suggested that relatively risky surgery, offering either good health or a quick death, may be particularly attractive to the old who should not be denied the choice.[79] In any event, it is relatively unlikely that considerations of productivity can be applied to an acute surgical emergency occurring in an elderly patient with no other mortal disease. The only acceptable test is then one of feasibility – there can seldom be an ethical alternative to treatment if it can be given but, inevitably, high morbidity and mortality rates must be accepted.

12.31 The dilemma remains as to what to do in the event that a geriatric patient refuses treatment. There can be no doubt as to the rights of the competent adult to refuse treatment and these rights would certainly include opposition to forced feeding. The difficulty, as we know, is that the borderline between competence and incompetence is often indistinct in old age.[80] Court judgments or decisions on the part of those responsible may well be sought in dramatic situations such as the removal of life-support but are unlikely to be invoked for apparently trivial matters such as the manner of oral feeding; it is probable that many old people, no matter what their situation, are fed with a varying degree of force but the action is taken on the assumption that refusal to eat is non-volitional. The process is degrading both to the staff and to the patient and, moreover, carries considerable medical hazard. It is, however, difficult to see the alternative to compassionate and moderate coercion in such cases. Positive refusal of treatment by the competent old person is a different matter and one which has attracted considerable attention in the courts of the United States. There, the right to be let alone has been described as 'the most comprehensive of rights and the right most valued by civilised men'[81] and the courts have, in general, upheld such rights – perhaps the most apposite case being that concerning an 85-year-old, yet alert, man who frankly chose suicide by self-starvation in preference to medical care.[82] The problem of the management of the partially competent geriatric who depends upon artificial feeding can be more difficult; this is well exemplified in the various stages of *Conroy*,[83] which we discuss in greater detail below.[84] Here, it need only be noted that, although the appellate courts disagreed on the definition of medical treatment, both had misgivings as to the possible impact that the decision to abandon nasogastric feeding might have on the general treatment of the elderly

79 T Hope, D Sprigings and R Crisp '"Not Clinically Indicated": Patients' Interests or Resource Allocation?' (1993) 306 BMJ 379.
80 In an interesting unpublished paper: C Heginbotham 'Mental Disorder and Decision Making: Respecting Autonomy in Substitute Judgments' (1992) Paper presented to the UK Forum on Health Care Ethics and the Law, London, the author drew attention to the distinction between capacity, which hinges on cognitive and volitional attributes of the individual, and competence. Capacity, being a necessary, though insufficient, condition for competence is, thus, the more important.
81 *Griswold v Connecticut* 381 US 479 (1965).
82 *Re Plaza Health and Rehabilitation Center of Syracuse* S Ct, Onandaga Cty, NY, 4 Feb 1984.
83 *Re Claire C Conroy* 464 A 2d 303 (NJ, 1983), CA, 486 A 2d 1209 (NJ, 1985), SC.
84 See para 18.73.

incompetent. Indeed, in attempting to resolve the ethical issues in this area, it has been rightly, and prophetically, said that: 'Society should be wary of moving from a recognition of an individual's right to die to a climate of enforcing a duty to die.'[85] We recall the words of Murphy[86] who remarked some time ago that loss of dignity in the elderly derives from the way that we care for our sufferers from dementia, not from the illness itself. The condition is a challenge to society's attitudes to the aged and is to be met by the provision of appropriate facilities. In our previous editions, we have been sceptical as to the likelihood of any political initiative designed to improve the lot of our oldest citizens and there is some evidence to suggest that that scepticism was not misplaced.[87] Currently, however, there seems to be something of a change of impetus. The *National Service Framework for Older People*[88] does appear as something of a watershed and the Age Equality Commission Bill 2001 – the primary purpose of which is to establish a body to advise the Secretary of State as to the reduction of age discrimination and the enhancement of age equality – is still before Parliament. The appointment of a Commission is one thing; acting on its recommendations is quite another. But, who knows? – perhaps we may have a less gloomy picture of the treatment of the aged to paint in our next edition.

85 M Siegler and A J Wiesbard 'Against the Emerging Stream' (1985) 145 Arch Int Med 129.
86 E Murphy 'Ethical Dilemmas of Brain Failure in the Elderly' (1984) 288 BMJ 61.
87 E Roberts, J Robinson and L Seymour *Old Habits Die Hard: Tackling Age Discrimination in Health and Social Care* (2002).
88 Para 12.13 above.

Death

13 The diagnosis of death

13.1 Death is defined in *Chambers Twentieth Century Dictionary* as 'the state of being dead; extinction or cessation of life'. *Steadman's Medical Dictionary* adds to this 'in multicellular organisms, death is a gradual process at the cellular level with tissues varying in their ability to withstand deprivation of oxygen'. There is, therefore, a conceptual conflict between layman and doctor. To the former, a person is either alive or dead, and this is generally based on the appearances in a *fait accompli*; the doctor, however, is involved in death as a process; he must, therefore, seek a definable end-point. Prior to the mid-twentieth century, death could be seen without qualm as being 'a permanent state of tissue anoxia'. Indeed, this remains the *ultimate* definition; we will see that the great majority of modern discussion is concerned solely with whether or not, and to what extent, we can pre-empt that truism and declare a *person* to be dead. Tissue anoxia arises naturally in two ways – either respiration ceases, in which case there is a failure to harvest oxygen, or the heart fails, when oxygen is no longer distributed to the tissues. In either case, the diagnostic problem lies in the definition of permanence.

13.2 In practice, it is astonishing how often the moment of 'death of the person' is perfectly clear. One can generally tell immediately when a loved one or a carefully observed patient 'dies' in cardiorespiratory terms.[1] The patient has 'breathed his or her last' and the heart stops beating; this is 'somatic' death. But the individual cells of the body are not dead; they will continue to function until their residual oxygen is exhausted. How long this takes depends upon their oxygen consumption which, in turn, is correlated with their specialised activity. Theoretically, therefore, there should be evidence of cellular death before the state of permanence is accepted but, in practice, the doctor can rely on his senses and on his stethoscope because death is to be expected and is accepted on the vast majority of occasions when it visits.[2] Even so, one

---

1   The words 'carefully observed' deserve emphasis. The distinction between death and 'suspended animation' may, in some circumstances, be difficult to make *post facto*.
2   Even so, some jurisdictions demand visible evidence of pooling, or non-circulation, of the blood – so-called hypostasis – before death is finally certified.

is left with the disquieting realisation that brain cells will withstand anoxia for a time, albeit for only a few minutes. If we are to accept the concept of 'brain death', as argued below, we should treat the patient in irreversible cardiorespiratory failure as dying rather than dead – for the true agonal period in natural death is that which lies between cardiac and cerebral failure.

13.3 But what if death is unheralded and unexpected? It is common knowledge that an apparently permanent cessation of the respiration or blood flow can, in many instances, be challenged by physical or mechanical intervention. Thus, sudden heart failure may, in suitable cases, be reversed by electrical stimulation (cardioversion) or by cardiac massage coupled, perhaps, with artificial respiration or ventilation. But, while the patient has been 'saved from the dead', the process of cellular death has been initiated by the temporary failure of oxygen distribution. The majority of organs will recover from such an insult but the cells of the brain are outstandingly the most sensitive in the body to oxygen deprivation and, moreover, they are irreplaceable. Thus, a situation may arise whereby the body as a whole is brought back to life but where it is now controlled by a brain which is damaged to an uncertain degree. The decision to restore an interrupted cardiac function is not, therefore, a simple choice between the good (life) and the bad (death). It poses serious and urgent ethical problems which provide a base from which to discuss the more measured, and in some ways more complicated, issues arising from ventilator deaths.

13.4 When death strikes unexpectedly on its second front – by way of acute respiratory failure – it may be countered by the use of artificial ventilation. This may be accomplished by a mechanical respirator which simulates the movements of the chest wall or, more commonly in the context of the present discussion, by a ventilator which forces air in and out of the lungs.

BRAIN FUNCTION AS A MEASURE OF DEATH

13.5 The mechanisms underlying acute heart failure and respiratory failure need to be distinguished. Given an adequate oxygen supply, the heart will continue to beat independently of higher control – it did, for instance, often beat for some 20 minutes following the broken neck of judicial hanging; the cause of acute cardiac failure, therefore, lies within the heart itself. Respiration, on the other hand, is controlled by the respiratory centre – a nervous 'battery' situated in the brain stem. Moreover, now that acute anterior poliomyelitis ('infantile paralysis') has been virtually eradicated, there are very few extra-cerebral causes of acute respiratory failure that cannot be corrected by the ventilator. Acute respiratory failure of the type which is important in the present context is almost invariably the result of central damage – that is, damage to the brain stem. Oxygenation of the tissues, or cellular life, is, thus, based on a servo-type mechanism: the heart depends for its own tissue oxygen on the lungs which, in turn, are useless without the heart; together they supply oxygen to the brain which, therefore, cannot function in the absence of competent heart and lungs; yet the lungs are, themselves, dependent upon a functioning brain stem. We have, however, seen that the only segment of this triad which cannot be substituted is the brain. There are, therefore, strong logical arguments for defining death in terms of brain death rather than in the generally accepted terms of cardiorespiratory failure; indeed, Pallis holds that all death is, and always has been, brain stem death and that circulatory arrest just happens to be the commonest way to bring such death about,[3] a point to which we have already alluded. We prefer, however, to visualise the brain, the heart and the lungs as forming a 'cycle of life' which can be broken at any point; looked at in this way, there is no need to speak of two *concepts* of death – that is, cardiorespiratory death or brain death; it is simply that different criteria, and different tests, can be used for identifying that the cycle has been broken.[4] Be that as it may, it is also clear that we *must* turn to the brain when the natural functional condition of the lungs – or, occasionally, of the heart – is obscured by the intervention of a machine.

13.6 The brain itself is not uniformly sensitive to hypoxia.[5] Simplistically, it can be divided into three main areas: the cortex, which is responsible for our human intellectual existence and is the least able to withstand oxygen deficiency; the thalamus, which roughly regulates our animal existence; and the brain stem, which controls our purely vegetative functions including breathing. The brain stem is least affected by hypoxia; if it is so damaged, it can be assumed, as near certainly as is possible, that the rest of the brain is damaged to a similar or greater extent.[6] Generalised hypoxia will affect all tissues of the body but to a varying extent – the brain being pre-eminently at risk. Conditions producing such hypoxia may be natural – eg heart failure or severe internal haemorrhage – or unnatural, of which drug overdose or a reduced oxygen intake, due, for instance, to a poorly given anaesthetic, are probably the most important in the present context. Violence may be such as to reduce the chest movement – as in conditions of overcrowding – or, more likely, will cause 'surgical shock', in which a lowered blood pressure results in inadequate oxygen perfusion of the tissues. Other causative lesions – which can be natural or associated with injury – may be localised within the skull and injure the brain in secondary fashion by occupying the confined space and, effectively, squeezing the vessels carrying the blood. Whatever the cause, hypoxic *anatomic damage* to the brain is irreversible; but further damage is prevented once an efficient oxygen supply is restored. In such a situation, therefore, one can speak of *degrees* of brain damage and resultant coma but not of *stages* of coma because, once the oxygen supply is restored, the condition is no longer progressive.

13.7 The clinical condition of a person who is brain damaged but treated will vary with the degree of hypoxic insult sustained. Four degrees of coma were recognised by the early French writers:[7] *coma vigile,* which represents

---

3   C Pallis 'Return to Elsinore' (1990) 16 J Med Ethics 10.
4   This was much the view taken by the original United States President's Commission for the Study of Ethical Problems in Medicine *Defining Death: Medical, Legal and Ethical Issues in the Definition of Death* (1981).
5   The relative term 'hypoxia' is used advisedly to emphasise that oxygen lack need not be absolute – 'anoxia' – in order to cause brain damage.
6   Lesions which affect the lower brain and leave the cortex intact are the result of local vascular damage – not of generalised hypoxia.
7   P Mollard and M Goulon 'Le Coma Depassé' (1959) 101 Rev Neurol 3.

no more than a blurring of consciousness and intellect; *coma type* and *coma carus*, which are characterised by increasing loss of relative functions followed by vegetative functions; and, finally, *coma depassé* – something beyond coma in which all functions are lost and the patient can only be maintained by artificial means.

13.8 Thus, while all appropriate cases may properly be given intensive care for the purposes of diagnosis and assessment, it would be well-nigh impossible to justify the initiation of long-term treatment for a patient who was likely to retain no cortical and only minimal thalamic function. The identification of such a case presents a formidable technical dilemma because some *functional* or *physiological* damage may be recoverable while some 'dormant' brain cells may have survived to become activated later. This potential for evidence of clinical recovery underlies the distinction between a persistent and a permanent stage of cerebral dysfunction; it also accounts, at least in part, for the fact that recovery of brain function is more likely when it has been lost as a result of direct head injury than when a comparable loss is due to pure hypoxic damage.[8]

13.9 The wholly decorticated patient falls into the category originally defined by Jennett[9] as the persistent vegetative state – in layman's terms, the 'human vegetable'. Such a person will have periods of wakefulness but is, nevertheless, permanently unconscious; the state has been described as eyes-open unconsciousness.[10] The definition and management of such persons is discussed in detail in chapter 17. For the present, it will be clear that a human who has lost cortical function has, simultaneously, lost his human personality but, in so far as he is capable of oxygenating his tissues without mechanical support, he is equally certainly not dead – indeed, he is in some ways more 'alive' than was the fully conscious sufferer from poliomyelitis who existed only by virtue of the respirator. There have been serious suggestions that the decorticated patient should be regarded as dead – may not *homo sapiens* be weakened in its own fight for survival if it devotes strength and resources to maintaining *homo* when he is no longer *sapiens*?[11] These were very advanced views at the time they were expressed, but the equation of permanent loss of personality with no longer being alive is a philosophy that is gaining relatively wide acceptance.[12] Such an attitude may be tenable in a general discussion on euthanasia but, when related to the definition of death, it can only confuse the issue and enhance the already strong public apprehension of premature disposal of the body; a particularly influential article, for example, concluded that, while neocortical death may be compatible with our current concepts of death, it ought not to be introduced as public policy simply because the general public would not understand the issues and it would be needlessly divisive for society.[13]

---

8   R S Howard and D H Miller 'The Persistent Vegetative State' (1995) 310 BMJ 341.
9   B Jennett and F Plum 'Persistent Vegetative State after Brain Damage' (1972) 1 Lancet 734.
10 R E Cranford and D R Smith 'Consciousness: The Most Critical Moral (Constitutional) Standard for Human Personhood' (1987) 13 Am J Law Med 233.
11 Lord Scarman 'Legal Liability in Medicine' (1981) 74 J Roy Soc Med 11.
12 For a comparatively early exposition, see D R Smith 'Legal Recognition of Neocortical Death' (1986) 71 Cornell L Rev 850. For continuation, see R M Veatch 'The Impending Collapse of the Whole-Brain Definition of Death' (1993) Hasting Center Report 23, no 4.
13 R J Devettere 'Neocortical Death and Human Death' (1990) 18 Law Med Hlth Care 96. This paper also summarises the views of others in the field.

Put another way, could a non-cognitive, decorticated person with continuing cardiopulmonary function be buried?[14] Death must remain an absolute; there is no place in medical jurisprudence for conditional phrases such as 'at death's door' or 'as good as dead'. The definition of death has not – or should not have – changed; and, if we are to alter our diagnostic methods, the diagnosis of death must be as sure as it was when we were using the heart and lungs as its sole parameters.[15]

13.10 It follows that, if we are to adjudge death by death of the brain, we must be certain that there is *permanent* physical destructive damage to the *whole* brain[16] – and, as we will see later, this must include the brain stem. This principle has been unintentionally confused semantically by the Harvard group, who introduced the term 'irreversible coma'.[17] One's first reaction would be to equate such a condition with the persistent vegetative state – or decorticated patient – or an even lesser degree of cerebral incompetence.[18] It is, however, clear that the committee was describing what other Americans and, later, the British Royal Colleges dubbed 'brain death'.[19] Even this term is capable of misinterpretation – in particular, it can be taken as including 'partial brain death'. The alternative is to speak only in terms of 'brain stem death', a term which derives from the logical assumption that somatic life is impossible in the absence of a functioning brain stem.[20] Conceptual difficulties still remain which are concerned, for the most part, with such differences as there may be between 'brain stem death' and 'whole brain death'.[21] We are very doubtful whether the distinction needs to be emphasised. Natural diseases in the form of destructive primary lesions of the brain stem – generally in the form of haemorrhage – which do not simultaneously affect the rest of the brain are rare and are either partial in type or, more commonly, rapidly fatal; the resulting 'locked in' syndrome is a terrifying example but its existence is

---

14 D J Powner, B M Ackerman and A Grenvik 'Medical Diagnosis of Death in Adults: Historical Contributions to Current Controversies' (1996) 348 Lancet 1219.
15 J M Stanley 'More Fiddling with the Definition of Death?' (1987) 13 J Med Ethics 21. It is disturbing to read in the modern literature '[This] reflects the medical community's use of the terms "brain dead" or "clinically dead" for persons who are unconscious, comatose, and terminally ill without any reasonable prognosis of recovery': G J Banks 'Legal and Ethical Safeguards: Protection of Society's Most Vulnerable Participants in a Commercialized Organ Transplantation System' (1995) 21 Am J Law Med 45.
16 We use the term in a gross anatomical sense. It does not imply, as many US writers have suggested, that a search must be made for residual pockets of cellular survival before death can be certified. See, as an example, R Hoffenberg 'Christiaan Barnard; His First Transplants and their Impact on Concepts of Death' (2001) 323 BMJ 1478.
17 H K Beecher (chairman) 'A Definition of Irreversible Coma', Report of the ad hoc Committee of the Harvard Medical School to examine the definition of brain death (1968) 205 J Amer Med Ass 337. It is still suggested that this may cause confusion: R Cohen-Almagor 'Language and Reality at the End of Life' (2000) 28 J Law Med Ethics 267.
18 An authoritative report in the UK emphasises the distinction to be made between coma and the permanent vegetative state: Working Group of the Royal College of Physicians 'The Permanent Vegetative State' (1996) 30 J R Coll Physicians Lond 119. Coma classically presents as eyes-closed unconsciousness.
19 Conference of Medical Royal Colleges and their Faculties in the UK 'Diagnosis of Brain Death' [1976] 2 BMJ 1187.
20 The concept originally introduced by A Mohandas and S N Chou (1971) 35 J Neurosurg 211.
21 C Pallis *ABC of Brain Stem Death* (1983).

well appreciated by neurologists.[22] The only unnatural ways in which death or destruction of the brain stem can reasonably be expected in the presence of a normal cerebrum are following accident, judicial hanging or beheading – none of which are germane to the present discussion. For the rest, it is well-nigh impossible to conceive of a generalised, fundamentally hypoxic condition destroying the brain stem while sparing the highly specialised tissue of the cerebral cortex; and, even were this possible, continued attempts to maintain such a body artificially would be hopelessly non-productive and positively unethical. We believe that the common terms used to define the irreversible cessation of all brain function – 'brain stem death' and 'whole brain death' – can be regarded as synonymous in both practice and theory.[23] But, since the tests devised for diagnosis are, essentially, tests of brain stem function, we prefer the former term which is, in addition, in general use in the United Kingdom.

13.11 We do, however, accept that many misconceptions are founded on misunderstanding of the British standards for the diagnosis of brain stem death. These include three equally important phases. First, there is the exclusion of coma being due to reversible causes including drug overdose, hypothermia and metabolic disorders while, at the same time, making a positive diagnosis of the disorder which has caused the brain damage and ensuring that this, in turn, is irremediable. Secondly, there is the carrying out of a number of tests specifically designed to demonstrate destruction of the several components of the brain stem – which include the respiratory centre and, hence, the ability to breathe naturally. Thirdly, there is a carefully controlled system whereby a patient's inability to breath spontaneously is proved. These tests should be repeated although the recommendations are, of necessity, somewhat open on this point and depend, mainly, on the nature of the precipitating condition.

13.12 These criteria have been criticised on the grounds that the patient is 'being asked to prove he is alive' rather than that the physician is proving death. Positive tests, such as an electroencephalogram (EEG) or an angiogram – by which cessation of the blood flow in the brain can be visualised – are, therefore, often sought and one or other is, indeed, mandatory in some countries of the European Union.[24] It is almost incredible that an EEG, which measures the surface electrical activity of the cerebral cortex, should be positive in the presence of properly performed confirmatory tests for brain stem death but there is no reason why such a test should not be added if it would serve to allay any fears among the next of kin as to the certainty of death.

---

22 J M S Pearce 'The Locked In Syndrome' (1987) 294 BMJ 198. For general discussion, see C M C Allen 'Conscious but Paralysed: Releasing the Locked-in' (1993) 342 Lancet 130.
23 This is often the case in practice. Victorian legislation, for example, speaks in terms of irreversible cessation of all function of the brain (Human Tissue Act 1982, s 41) while, at the same time assessing this by way of tests for death of the brain stem – and this is acceptable: J L Dixon (chairperson) Parliament of Victoria Social Development Committee *Report upon the Inquiry into Options for Dying with Dignity* (1987).
24 Pallis, para 13.10 above, quoted France, Greece and Italy as so requiring. The UK, Eire, Belgium, Germany and the Netherlands are said to accept medical criteria alone as being diagnostic of brain stem death. Among countries in which there is specific legal recognition of the brain as an indicator of death are at least 33 of the United States, Canada and the States of Australia although this relates only to transplantation procedures in Queensland and Western Australia.

13.13 There is little doubt that any residual public misgiving would be lessened if the purposes of defining brain stem death were more fully understood. Certainly, it is a valuable tool in the provision of high quality organs for transplantation (see chapter 14) but this is only part of the story. The major purpose of the procedure is to establish a consensus by which patients who can no longer benefit can be removed from ventilator support. This is essential if the patient is to die with dignity, if the relatives are to be spared wholly unnecessary suffering and if resources, both mechanical and human, are to be properly apportioned. Accepting brain stem death is not a way of 'hurrying death along'; rather, the ventilator allows the pace of investigation, assessment and prognosis to be slackened; when it comes to the point, the diagnosis of brain stem death is, in the great majority of cases, only confirming what is clear from clinical observation – that the patient is dead.

13.14 In view of the very widespread international agreement that exists, it came as something of a surprise to find the Danish Council of Ethics rejecting the principle of brain death in 1989.[25] It may well be that the Council has no political power, but its observations are useful to look at as an example of the complex thinking which sometimes attaches to the issue. Reduced to a summary, the Council's view was that death should be defined in terms of what a particular community regards as death – few people, it stated, would refer to a warm, pink body as a corpse; the loss of brain function should be regarded as the irreversible onset and that of cardiac function as the termination of the process of death. Clearly, such a formula can apply only when the patient is maintained on a ventilator and, even within that limited parameter, it positively excludes cardiac transplantation as an ethically acceptable procedure. More worryingly, it tends to perpetuate a suspicion that different concepts of death are being used by the profession and the public and that special criteria apply in association with transplantation.[26] Understanding, or its lack, lies at the root of the problem. Evans, who has been a major opponent of the brain stem death concept, has suggested that our moral convictions stand independent of rational account or explanation[27] – and has been criticised for, thereby, rendering philosophical inquiry superfluous.[28] Yet, in simply calling for better 'education' of the public, it is easy to overlook or to minimise the importance of religious and cultural traditions. Transplant operations involving brain dead donors have been legalised only recently in Japan and a major reason for this must lie in the unique attitude to death that is widely held in that

---

25 B A Rix 'Danish Ethics Council Rejects Brain Death as the Criterion of Death' (1990) 16 J Med Ethics 5.

26 For further commentary on the Danish recommendations, see R Gillon 'Death' (1990) 16 J Med Ethics 3 and D Lamb 'Wanting It Both Ways' (1990) 16 J Med Ethics 8. The issue has been reopened recently by I H Kerridge, P Saul, M Lowe et al 'Death, Dying and Donation: Organ Transplantation and the Diagnosis of Death' (2002) 28 J Med Ethics 89. The authors suggest that those who are brain dead are not 'dead' but are legally available as organ donors – a distinction that seems to us would do little more than compound the confusion. A rather similar criticism, particularly directed at the concept of neocortical death, has been expressed by J Fisher 'Re-examining Death: Against a Higher Brain Criterion' (1999) 25 J Med Ethics 473.

27 M Evans 'A Plea for the Heart' (1990) 3 Bioethics 227; 'Death in Denmark' (1990) 16 J Med Ethics 191.

28 D Lamb 'Death in Denmark: A Reply' (1991) 17 J Med Ethics 100.

country. The Western critic should be wary before suggesting that centuries of cultural tradition should be swept aside in the name of modern medical technology.[29]

13.15 Perhaps we *are* 'fiddling with definitions' and should, rather, concentrate on what it is or is not ethical to do with a dying or a dead body. Gillett[30] has summarised the situation in that we do not and cannot require to prolong a life that will never again be engaged with the world; that we require that life to be terminated decently; and that we require that human remains should be treated with respect – and there is much to commend this rationalisation. Within such a framework, the problems of removal from the ventilator become technical rather than ethical. It has been advised that the diagnosis of brain stem death should be made by two doctors, one of whom should be the consultant in charge of the case and the other suitably experienced and clinically independent of the first;[31] but, while the vast majority of practitioners would abide by authoritative guidelines, there is no United Kingdom law on the point.

THE LEGAL EFFECT OF APPLYING BRAIN STEM DEATH CRITERIA

13.16 The application of brain stem death criteria has obvious implications as to causation in cases of unlawful killing. But any difficulties disperse once it is conceded that brain stem death means somatic death.[32] It then becomes clear that the effect of intensive treatment has been simply to delay the inevitable result of the initial insult to the brain and there is no break in the chain of causation. This was accepted, first, in America in *People v Lyons*[33] where it was found that the victim of a shooting incident was legally dead before being used as a transplant donor. The British position has been summed up in two leading cases to which we return in chapter 18. Thus, in Scotland, it was held:

> Once the initial reckless act causing injury has been committed, the natural consequence which the perpetrator must accept is that the victim's future depended on a number of circumstances, including whether any particular treatment was available and, if it was available, whether it was medically reasonable and justifiable to attempt it and to continue it.[34]

---

29 For discussion, see K Hoshino 'Legal Status of Brain Death in Japan: Why Many Japanese Do Not Accept "Brain Death" as a Definition of Death' (1993) 7 Bioethics 234; J Wise 'Japan to Allow Organ Transplants' (1997) 314 BMJ 1298. The Muslim Law Council also accepts brain stem death as a proper definition of death: V Choo 'UK Shariah Council Approves Organ Transplants' (1995) 346 Lancet 303.

30 G Gillett 'Fiddling and Clarity' (1987) 13 J Med Ethics 23. For a rather similar US view, see D Wickler and A J Weisbard 'Appropriate Confusion over "Brain Death"' (1989) 261 J Amer Med Ass 2246.

31 Lord Smith (chairman of Working Party) *The Removal of Cadaveric Organs for Transplantation: A Code of Practice* (1979). There is such legislation, for example, in the Australian States and in South Africa (eg Transplantation and Anatomy Act 1983 (South Australia), s 24). A very useful protocol for the diagnosis of brain stem death is to be found in M D O'Brien 'Criteria for Diagnosing Brain Stem Death' (1990) 301 BMJ 108.

32 Conference of Royal Medical Colleges and their Faculties in the United Kingdom 'Diagnosis of Death' [1979] 1 BMJ 332.

33 Sup Ct No 56072, Alameda Co (Cal, 1974).

34 *Finlayson v HM Advocate* 1978 SLT (notes) 60 at 61, per Lord Emslie LJ-G.

13.17 The later English decision was fully confirmatory:

> Where a medical practitioner, using generally acceptable methods, came to the conclusion that the patient was for all practical purposes dead and that such vital functions as remained were being maintained solely by mechanical means, and accordingly discontinued treatment, that did not break the chain of causation between the initial injury and the death.[35]

It is therefore clear that the law has no intention of regarding doctors who remove a brain stem dead patient from the ventilator as being, thereby, responsible for his death.

13.18 Although it is doubtful if it was needed, there is now case law which confirms the medical view that persons whose brain stems are dead are, themselves, dead. In the unusual case of *Re A*[36] – in which the parents of a child sought to have him retained on a ventilator for medico-legal reasons – the judge made a declaration that A, who had been certified as brain stem dead, was dead for all legal as well as all medical purposes and that a doctor who disconnected the apparatus was not acting unlawfully; the fact of death was emphasised when the judge held that he had no inherent jurisdiction over a dead child who could not be made a ward of court for the same reason.

13.19 The major legal problem still outstanding relates to the precise time that death occurs in such circumstances; there are several issues which depend upon that determination, and it is surprising that none appears to have been brought to the courts.

13.20 Lawyers are inclined to dismiss the problem of when death occurs on the assumption that the time of death can be equated to the time the diagnosis is made or to the time the ventilator support is removed. But a moment's reflection makes it clear that the diagnosis of brain stem death, and the consequent ending of treatment, must be retrospective – death has already occurred and the precise time at which it occurred is unknown and unknowable. Moreover, the choice of the time at which the necessary tests are undertaken is as likely to be based on convenience as on anything else. It is difficult to see how the doctor can conscientiously certify the 'date and time of death' – which is not the same as the 'date and time of death certification' – but it is easy to think of occasions on which he might be called upon to do so urgently.

13.21 One very real difficulty lay in the 'year and a day' rule, under which death could not be attributed to murder, manslaughter, infanticide or suicide if it occurred more than a year and a day after the precipitating cause. This rule has now been repealed by the Law Reform (Year and a Day Rule) Act 1996 – a statute which was introduced for the specific reason that the time when 'death on the ventilator' occurs is largely in the hands of the intensive care team. Time-related factors in the payment, or withholding, of life or personal accident insurance policies remain as being possibly important; one

---

35 *R v Malcherek; R v Steel* [1981] 2 All ER 422 at 428-429, CA, per Lord Lane LCJ.
36 [1992] 3 Med LR 303. *Re A* is sometimes taken as establishing that brain stem death constitutes the *legal* definition of death in England. In our view, it does no more than confirm that a person who is brain stem dead is legally dead.

example could concern the application of a suicide clause which would be lifted on a given day. Problems as to the payment of estate duty might also arise.

13.22 But the most intractable issue would seem to be that related to succession and the possibility of disputed survival. What is to be said as to the deaths of a husband and wife who are injured in the same accident, who are both ventilated and who are both declared brain stem dead? One thing is certain – survivorship cannot be judged on the basis of the technical diagnosis because the order in which death is determined could well be purely arbitrary. To remove ventilator support from both simultaneously and measure the time for the individual heart to stop beating would be confusing and would raise considerable difficulties in those jurisdictions which allow for *alternative* means of diagnosing death (see below); it is essential to hold on to the premise that the patients have been certified as being *already* dead. It would be wholly illogical to vary one's criteria to accommodate a specific situation – alternative methods in diagnosis are acceptable but double standards of death are not.[37] The rules of succession are bound by statute and, accordingly, this is one aspect of brain stem death which could be subject to legislative action. It seems to us that a positive solution to 'ventilated commorientes' is currently impossible; but a negative direction on the lines that evidence as to the time of removal of ventilator support cannot, by itself, be regarded as sufficient to rebut the statutory presumptions might, at least, be equitable and, at the same time, relieve the doctor of one moral problem.

The ethical position of the doctor

13.23 Thus, while we have said that the act of terminating treatment once brain stem death is diagnosed is a technical problem which raises no ethical issues, the time at which this is done unfortunately may do so. It is facile merely to remark that the doctor's decisions should be uninfluenced by extraneous factors because, in practice, he can scarcely avoid being aware of them – and influence is inseparable from awareness. The problems posed, say, by insistent pressure from relatives concerned for an insurance policy could be insoluble.

13.24 Other dilemmas of a purely moral nature may also arise. Thus, some religious faiths – in particular, orthodox Judaism – still find the concept of brain stem death unacceptable. Is it, then, right to continue ventilation of a dead body in order to respect the cultural traditions of the deceased's family? Some would say – yes, and this largely on the grounds that the heart will, in any case, probably stop beating within a few days of death of the brain stem irrespective of continued support. For our part, we must prefer the view that it is more respectful of the dead, kinder to the staff and, in the end, probably kinder to the relatives and certainly less sophistic to support good medical practice – albeit with the maximum compassion.[38]

37 See P D G Skegg *Law, Ethics, and Medicine* (1984) ch 9; Lamb, para 13.14 above.
38 See D Inwald, I Jacobovits and A Petros 'Brain Stem Death: Managing Care when Accepted Medical Guidelines and Religious Beliefs are in Conflict' (2000) 320 BMJ 1266 and accompanying comment by M Fisher and R F Raper. See also the closely allied case *Re C (a minor) (medical treatment)* [1998] 1 FLR 384, (1998) 40 BMLR 31.

13.25 In recent years, however, doctors and the public have been confronted by the picture of brain dead women being retained on support for the sole purpose of bringing a fetus to viability.[39] A plethora of moral problems then arise, the answers to which, if there are any, depend, first, on the gestational age of the fetus and, second, on whether the individual woman has or has not expressed her wishes or intentions while alive.[40] The classic situation is illustrated by an instance from Germany which concerned an unmarried, brain stem dead 18-year-old who was only 15 weeks' pregnant; the hospital ethics committee (see chapter 19) recommended continuation of the pregnancy – a decision which was, in our view surprisingly, widely supported by all other than women's groups.[11] The fetus was still born after six weeks of intensive effort. The President of the Federal Chamber of Physicians is reported as commenting: 'Due to scientific advances, medicine will, again and again, have to infringe ethical borders';[42] the alternative view, which we share, sees such actions as incremental nudges which may, ultimately, push this branch of medicine into areas of doubtful morality. Even so, we wonder if we would have been so sceptical had the fetus been of, say, 24 weeks' gestation? In the absence of any indication as to the woman's wishes – which is the probable scenario – the temptation is to say that to maintain her as an oxygenated cadaver would be an unacceptable invasion of a dying person's dignity and privacy. On the other hand, it would certainly not be unreasonable to hold that the fetus now constituted a living patient who should be treated in his or her best interests. Arguments based on a potential fetal/maternal conflict, such as have been raised under the heading of 'Abortion', would be invalidated once the mother was declared dead – yet, in the alternative, could the doctor be seen as acting unethically in failing to treat an organism that has no legal personality?

13.26 The situation is not greatly eased if the woman has expressed her intentions. Suppose she wishes to be ventilated for the sake of her fetus – which might be regarded as an autonomous choice of a competent adult. Unfortunately, we will see in chapter 14 that a person has no control over his or her dead body – such control as there is, is vested in the person in 'lawful possession' of the body and, in the circumstances envisaged, it might be difficult to establish who that person is. It might be posited that she has used the Human Tissue Act 1961[43] to bequeath her body for therapeutic purposes[44] but, again, it will be seen that the person in lawful possession of the body is under no obligation to follow the wishes of the deceased. And what if the woman has expressed a wish not to be maintained after death and the fetus is

---

39 For an exceptionally thorough discussion, see N S Peart, A V Campbell, A R Manara et al 'Maintaining a Pregnancy Following Loss of Capacity' (2000) 8 Med L Rev 275

40 Peart et al, para 13.25 above, also discuss the situation in which the woman is unconscious and we return to that problem briefly in chapter 14.

41 For full discussion, see C Anstötz 'Should a Brain-dead Pregnant Woman Carry her Child to Full Term? The Case of the "Erlangen Baby"' (1993) 7 Bioethics 340.

42 A Tuffs 'Keeping a Brain-dead Pregnant Woman "Alive"' (1992) 340 Lancet 1029.

43 See para 14.37 below.

44 And this might, in fact, be almost the only time that the *whole body* could be used for therapeutic purposes and, accordingly, come within the scope of the Act. Even so, the Act speaks in terms of *removal* of parts of the body – which leaves open the definition of Caesarian section!

viable? Is it impossible that the doctor who causes its death by following its mother's dictates could be charged under the Infant Life (Preservation) Act 1929?[45]

13.27   Fortunately, the conditions envisaged must arise extremely rarely and we suggest that, should the issues be raised, the courts would decide on the common sense aspects of the individual case and these, bearing in mind the best interests of the proposed neonate, would include the wishes and intentions of the woman's partner or close relatives. What is far more important in the context of the diagnosis of death is how such cases can occur. Jennett has said that, even with intensive care, cardiac function can be maintained for a few days at most once the brain stem is dead.[46] Many of these cases are said to have been ventilated for more than 50 days – which must suggest the possibility of a misdiagnosis.[47] This being so, attempts to incubate a fetus to viability in a woman who has been declared dead may not only be unethical but may also contribute to the confusion and distrust which, even today, colour the concept of brain stem death.

THE CASE FOR LEGISLATION

13.28   It is because of this latent unease that the case for a modern statutory definition of death has been widely canvassed and is applied in many jurisdictions.

13.29   The main difficulty in framing legislation is to allow for all modes of death – from the elementarily obvious to the complex ventilator case; it would be absurd to demand that criteria designed for the latter be applied to the former. As a result, most statutes, either existing or proposed, have applied some form of dual criteria of proof of death.[48] A typical expression is to be found in the United States Uniform Determination of Death Act 1980, which reads:

> An individual who has sustained either (1) irreversible cessation of circulatory and respiratory functions, or (2) irreversible cessation of all functions of the

---

45 Peart et al cite *R v Woollin* [1999] 1 AC 82, [1998] 4 All ER 103 in support of this but we are doubtful if the law of murder can be easily extrapolated to that of child destruction. Similarly, should the fetus be incapable of a separate existence at the time, we wonder if it is possible to 'procure the miscarriage' of a dead woman (Offences Against the Person Act 1861, ss 58 and 59).

46 B Jennett 'Brain Death 1981' (1981) 28 Scott Med J 191. It is fair to say that this is not agreed by all nor is it invariable: J F Parish, R C Kim, G H Collings *et al* 'Brain Death with Prolonged Somatic Survival' (1982) 306 New Engl J Med 14.

47 Yet there was, apparently, no doubt in the case of Ms Marshall who was maintained for 105 days before being delivered of an approximately 32 weeks' fetus which survived – quoted by Fisher, para 13.24 above.

48 D W Meyers *Medico-Legal Implications of Death and Dying* (1981) divided state statutes in the USA into three categories: those which provide for brain death as an express alternative to heart-lung orientated death, those which admit the use of brain-based criteria when a cardiorespiratory diagnosis is obviated by artificial maintenance; and those which recognise brain death simply as a means of determining or defining death. All states have now adopted brain death either by statute or by court recognition.

entire brain, including the brain stem, is dead. A determination of death must be made in accordance with accepted medical standards.

13.30 And, as an example of Commonwealth legislation, we quote the Human Tissue Act 1982 (Victoria), s 41:

A person has died when there has occurred:
(a) Irreversible cessation of the circulation of the blood in the body of the person, or
(b) Irreversible cessation of all functions of the brain of the person.

There are similar provisions in the Human Tissue Act 1983 (NSW), s 33.

13.31 But, in essence, all these measures do is to spell out good medical practice within a legal framework – and many would feel this to be unnecessary. They lay down no specific methods; these being relegated to codes of practice – and this, we believe, is rightly so. We would certainly agree with the great majority of commentators that any statutory definition of death must be limited to an enabling concept. Medical facilities and expertise alter and do so faster than can the law; it is, therefore, essential that the evaluation of diagnostic techniques remains in the hands of the medical profession. In fact, the ethical, philosophical and social problems inherent in the definition of death seem to have been largely solved in recent years;[49] definitive legislation might do little more than reanimate concerns which have, at least to a large extent, been put to rest and might, as a result, be self-defeating. The stethoscope and the CT scanner have it in common that both depend upon the expertise of their user – no Act of Parliament can alter that basic fact.

49 Pallis, para 13.10 above.

14 The donation of organs and transplantation

14.1 The juxtaposition of chapters on the diagnosis of death and on transplantation of organs should not be taken to indicate that they are *necessarily* associated. It is again emphasised that the concept of brain stem death is as important to neurosurgeons, who can, as a result, allow their hopeless patients to die in peace, and to the relatives, who can now accept the fact of death in a ventilated body with good conscience, as it is to the transplant surgeon. Nevertheless, and despite the introduction of new techniques to which we refer later, optimum transplantation – and, with it, maximum saving of lives – depends upon the acceptance of brain stem death; furthermore, the two conditions are closely linked in the public mind. This is, therefore, a not inappropriate point at which to discuss the ethics and legality of a procedure which, although now firmly established as accepted medical treatment, nevertheless still provokes some public disquiet.

TECHNICAL ASPECTS OF TRANSPLANTATION

14.2 There are three major biological hurdles to be overcome in successful transplantation therapy: neutralising the 'tissue immunity' reaction; ensuring that the donated organs are healthy; and preserving the viability of those organs in the period between their becoming available and their reception.

14.3 A tissue immunity reaction results from the recognition by the body of antigenically foreign material which it will then reject with a degree of determination that depends, to a large extent, on *how* different is the donated tissue from that of the recipient. From this point of view, we can distinguish three main forms of transplantation therapy:

(a)   Autotransplantation, or the resiting of portions of the same body. This is effectively limited to skin or bone grafting and poses only the difficulties of highly complex surgery. It is of no concern in the present context.

(b)   Homotransplantation or allografting, which involves the transfer of viable tissue from one human being to another.

(c)   Heterotransplantation or xenotransplantation – that is, the successful transplantation of organs from one species to another.

Xenotransplantation

14.4 Clearly, xenotransplantation is that form of organ grafting which will stimulate the maximum immune reaction. The reaction will be quantifiably different between so-called concordant species – for example, within the primates – and when the species are widely unrelated, or discordant, as in pig to man transplants; the reaction is then of a quite different order to that seen with the customary allograft and is known as hyperacute rejection of the donated organ. As a result, xenografting – xenografting and xenotransplantation are interchangeable terms – is a highly complex and experimental procedure; it will be convenient to discuss it and to dismiss it before proceeding to the major topic of homotransplantation.

14.5 There is not doubt that, although it is not, as yet, a practical, possibility, xenotransplantation has moved relatively rapidly towards realisation in the last five years. As we have suggested above, the major *clinical* barrier to xenografting lies in the intense immune reaction that is established when organs from different species share the same blood supply. The increasing sophistication of immunosuppressant drugs and of immunosuppressant techniques – in particular that of genetic replacement whereby transgenic animals, modified so as to contain human genetic material, are produced and, thus, take xenografting closer to allografting[1] – are, however, changing the scene to the extent that a man has survived for 70 days following the transplantation of a baboon's liver.[2] These rapid advances precipitated precautionary governmental action which has, thus far, culminated in the establishment of a Xenotransplantation Interim Regulatory Authority (UKXIRA); the Authority oversees the development of xenotransplantation and its co-ordination pending the introduction of primary legislation. The government's approach to this new therapy is, therefore, very similar to that it adopted in respect of assisted reproduction (see chapter 3). One of the first actions of the UKXIRA was to declare a moratorium on clinical trials of xenografting pending further research. Thus, consideration of the subject can still be pitched at a relatively superficial level in a book of this type. This, however, should not cloud the fact that xenotransplantation stimulates a host of ethical problems in addition to those which are severely practical.

14.6 As to the latter, in addition to the establishment of an immune response in the individual case, the community-based possibility of transmitting animal micro-organisms – in particular, viruses – to humans, and of their becoming

---

1   A James 'Transplants with Transgenic Pig Organs?' (1993) 342 Lancet 45.
2   T E Starzl, J Fung, A Tzakis et al 'Baboon-to-human Liver Transplantation' (1993) 341 Lancet 65. Even so, we remain unconvinced that such a result should be classified as a success. For more recent analysis from the US, see J K Fredrickson 'He's All Heart ... and a Little Pig Too: A Look at the FDA Draft Xenotransplant Guidelines' (1997) 52 Food Drug LJ 429; J M Kress 'Xenotransplantation: Ethics and Economics' (1998) 53 Food Drug LJ 353.

adapted to the new environment and of consequent human to human spread, is very real and constitutes one of the main reasons why xenotransplantation is suspect.[3] A corollary to this, which crosses the ethical/practical boundary, is that animals destined to be donors would have to be reared in 'pathogen-free' environments which are hard, if not impossible, to define and maintain but which would also involve much animal suffering – and the morality of xenotransplantation depends on there being a positive balance in favour of human advantage over animal disadvantage.[4] Given that it is acceptable to use animals in this way, one has to ask – what sort of animals? Clearly, tissue rejection would be minimised if non-human primates were used. It is, however, widely accepted that primates have special characteristics and constitute such a natural resource as to exclude them as organ donors.[5] Current interest, therefore, centres on the pig – an animal which has no antigenic but remarkable physiological affinities with man. Modern molecular biological techniques have already produced transgenic pigs in which at least one of the mechanisms leading to graft rejection appears to have been eliminated; there is little doubt that clinical trials using such organs are on the horizon, albeit not just around the corner.

14.7 All of which may be good scientific medicine but, like so many such 'advances', it raises both intuitive and philosophical doubts. Undoubtedly, there is a 'gut' distaste for being maintained by a porcine heart. More importantly, one must wonder at the morality of maintaining and, worse, breeding animals for the express purpose of substituting human body parts. The simple response that this is no different from eating pork in order to avoid starvation seems unsatisfactory – Downie,[6] for example, sees a moral difference between 'natural' feeding and 'unnatural' organ substitution. We feel, however, that the subject – which should include an analysis of the philosophy of speciesism – is too wide to be tackled here.[7] In fact, while very much appreciating the potential human advantages of xenotransplantation, we are equally concerned as to the possible ill effects on our human society. It

---

3   See Nuffield Council on Bioethics *Animal-to-Animal Transplants* (1996) ch 6 and its follow up: D A Muir and G E Griffin *Infection Risks in Xenotransplantation* (Prepared for the Department of Health, 2001). Also M Fox and J McHale 'Regulating Xenotransplantation' (1997) 147 NLJ 139 and F H Bach, A J Ivinson and C Weeramantry 'Ethical and Legal Issues in Technology: Xenotransplantation' (2001) 27 Amer J L Med 283 where the global nature of the risks are emphasised. It is fair to say, however, that no evidence of a severe threat to public health can be derived from a study of those who have already been treated with porcine tissues: J H Tanne 'Study Gives Reassurance on Safety of Xenotransplantation' (1999) 319 BMJ 533.
4   That such a balance exists was accepted by both the government appointed Advisory Group on the Ethics of Transplantation *Animal Tissue into Humans* (1996) and the Nuffield Council. Individuals are less convinced: see R Downie 'Xenotransplantation' (1997) 23 J Med Ethics 205.
5   While stating this firmly, the Advisory Group, considered that primates could, in strictly circumscribed conditions, be used for research into xenotransplantation. They would, of course, be protected by the Animals (Scientific Procedures) Act 1986.
6   Others are less convinced: eg J Hughes 'Xenografting: Ethical Issues' (1998) 24 J Med Ethics 18. For a comprehensive analysis, see M Fox and J McHale 'Xenotransplantation: The Ethical and Legal Ramifications' (1998) 6 Med L Rev 42. We also wonder at what stage of modification does a transgenic pig become human?
7   This aspect is well considered by W Cartwright 'The Pig, the Transplant Surgeon, and the Nuffield Council' (1996) 4 Med L Rev 250.

is not wholly unreal to foresee human organs being replaced by those of animals as they fail in sequence; we are then left with the unedifying picture of replacement therapy being continued until the irreplaceable and paradigmatic human organ, the brain, wears out. Moreover, since no health service could contain the costs of such a programme, longevity would become the prerogative of the rich; the structure of human society could be altered dramatically.

14.8 In addition to these relatively practical concerns, we have to ask if xenotransplantation can be accommodated within our existing medical jurisprudence. Writing from within the strongly consent-orientated Canadian jurisdiction, Caulfield and Robertson[8] have pointed out that the needs for continued surveillance and for mandatory autopsy following xenografting must lead to concepts of 'contracts to undergo treatment' rather than consent to do so. Moreover, is the public not entitled to consent or dissent to a programme which undoubtedly threatens its well-being? The appointment of a supervisory authority is, of course, a step in the right direction but a strong case can be made out for insisting on a wide-based popular expression of agreement before all moratoria are lifted.[9] In practical terms, no xenografts have, as yet, been performed in the United Kingdom; it is to be noted, however, that current government policy on the subject is very cautious but is by no means exclusive.[10]

14.9 Even so, the great majority of commentators would prefer to see improvements in the existing homotransplantation programme rather than the development of xenografting and the remainder of this chapter is devoted to organ replacement as it is generally understood.

Homotransplantation

14.10 Here, despite the fact that we are dealing with tissues from the same species, an immunity problem persists because, for practical purposes, no two persons other than monovular twins are genetically identical; the body can still recognise, and will reject, tissues of the same species which are 'non-self'.[11] This intra-species immune reaction can be increasingly well suppressed by the use, inter alia,[12] of the cyclosporine group of drugs and monoclonal

---

8 T A Caulfield and G B Robertson 'Xenotransplantation: Consent, Public Health and Charter Issues' (2001) 5 Med L Internat 81.

9 This line of argument is well expressed by M A Clark 'This Little Piggy Went to Market: The Xenotransplantation and Xenozoonose Debate' (1999) 27 J Law Med Ethics 137. The paper should, however, be read in conjunction with its sibling written by a member of the FDA's Subcommittee on Xenotransplantation: H Y Vanderpool 'Commentary: A Critique of Clark's Frightening Xenotransplantation Scenario' (1999) 27 J Law Med Ethics 153.

10 Official Reports HC, 15 February 1993, vol 219, col 80. See also *Government Response to "Animal Tissue into Humans"* (1997).

11 The alternative – where the transplanted material attacks the host – is a difficulty of bone marrow transplantation. See A M Denman 'Graft versus Host Disease: New Versions of Old Problems?' (1985) 290 BMJ 658.

12 A considerable body of new drugs is currently in the development stage: P A Andrews 'Recent Developments: Renal Transplantation' (2002) 324 BMJ 530.

antibodies. The general principle remains, however, that such suppression will be effective – and will have less adverse side effects – in proportion to the genetic similarity of donor and recipient. Thus, sibling donation will be especially satisfactory and intrafamilial exchanges in general are likely to show less antigenic discrepancies than are those between random strangers. Other variables, however, intrude and complicate the picture. Immunosuppression is non-specific; therefore, while the graft rejection process is being controlled, other desirable immune reactions – such as the body's defence against microbiological invasion – are also affected. Moreover, the greater the *quantity* of foreign material transplanted, the greater will be the need for immunosuppression and, as a corollary, micro-organisms that are normally resisted with ease will be increasingly able to establish themselves in the vulnerable body – the most specifically significant of these are viruses which are responsible for certain forms of malignant disease of the lymphoid system. Enhanced success of transplantation therapy is not, therefore, simply a matter of discovering more powerful immunosuppressants.

14.11 It is axiomatic that an organ intended as a replacement for a diseased tissue must be normal itself. The practical result is that donors should be relatively young and they must either be living or have died from accident or from localised natural disease which has no effect on the donated tissue. This implies a pragmatic limitation on the age of the donor but this is higher than might be expected – 70 in the case of kidneys, 50 for livers and 40 for donors of hearts[13] – and may be extended as the general health of the aged steadily improves.

14.12 Viability of the donated organ is that essential element which combines most clearly the technical and ethical problems of transplantation surgery. As has been discussed in chapter 13, the cells of the body will deteriorate when deprived of oxygen; the process of deterioration can be slowed markedly by chilling the organ, the viability, or competence, of which then depends on the 'warm anoxic time' – that is, the interval between cessation of the circulation and chilling of the specimen. In terms of practical transplantation, it becomes increasingly pointless to transplant a kidney after more than one hour's warm anoxia. Even so, the acceptable cold anoxic time is also finite and varies with the tissue involved – not only as regards its metabolic activity but also as to the urgency with which it must assume full function after transplantation; the heart and lungs can be used up to four hours after harvesting, the liver up to 8–12 hours and the kidneys can be maintained in vitro for more than 24 hours.[14] Imposed delays must, therefore, jeopardise the validity of the operation.[15]

---

13 W B Ross 'Increasing Organ Donation – A Review' (1989) 34 Scott Med J 451. The Exeter Protocol (see Feest et al, para 14.53 below) includes no overriding age limitation.
14 J Wallwork 'Organs for Transplantation' (1989) 299 BMJ 1291.
15 Cold perfusion of the whole body or of individual organs in situ is now used to reduce these difficulties. The non-heart beating donor may be returning and improving the supply of organs. J P Cachera, D Y Loisance, O Tavolaro et al 'Hypothermic Perfusion of the Whole Cadaver: A Response to the Question of the Multiple-organ Donor' (1986) 18 Transplant Proc 1407; G Kootstra, R Wijnen, J P van Hooff and C J van der Linden 'Twenty Percent More Kidneys through a Non-heart Beating Program' (1991) 23 Transplant Proc 910.

14.13 It will be evident that organs can be provided for transplantation by the living or by the dead. Living donation offers many technical advantages – tissue compatibility can be measured at leisure, the operation can be elective and the warm anoxic time can approach zero.[16] In theory, potential cadaver donors are widely available but, in practice, their recovery is capricious and both donor and recipient operations must often take on the character of emergency surgery. The recognition of brain stem death, however, offers the possibility of a variation on cadaver donation – the 'beating heart donor' – which bridges the gap between the living and the conventionally dead and carries with it many of the advantages of both types of donor. The legal and ethical limitations of all three methods must be considered.

THE LIVING DONOR

14.14 The donation of tissues which can be replaced rapidly – such as blood and bone marrow – presents, in practice, few technical or ethical problems other than that of commercialism to which we refer below.[17] We are concerned here only with non-regenerative tissues.

14.15 The legal regulation of living donations in the United Kingdom lies in both common and statute law. As to the former, the starting-point must be the principle that no person is to be deemed capable of consenting to his being killed or seriously injured. The living donation of a heart is, thereby, precluded. This, of course, is the extreme case and, beyond it, legality would depend upon the presumed risk-benefit ratio involved in the procedure – and assessment of this is difficult because the technological boundaries of medicine are always expanding. A few years ago, one would have said the same about the liver as about the heart; today, the use of segments of adult liver in paediatric transplantation therapy is recognised as part of the norm while partial liver transplantation between adults is also widely practiced[18] – in fact, since the liver regenerates both anatomically and functionally,[19] it may be that live liver donation is more akin to bone marrow donation than to organ transplantation.[20] The same is now true of donation of lobes of the lung – a matter of great importance in the treatment of the relatively common, life-threatening genetic condition of cystic fibrosis.[21] Given that the relative risks

---

16 The 1 year survival rate following live transplantation is 95% as compared with some 88% in the case of cadaver donations: P A Andrews 'Renal Transplantation' (2002) 324 BMJ 530. The Royal College of Surgeons has called for a doubling of the number of live transplants in the UK: *Report of the Working Party to Review Organ Transplantation* (P Morris, chairman) (1999) www.rcseng.ac.uk/services/publications/publications/pdf/rep_orgt.

17 Though bone marrow donation is certainly a procedure which cannot be undertaken light-heartedly.

18 A Marcos, R A Fisher, J M Ham et al 'Right Lobe Living Donor Liver Transplantation' (1999) 68 Transplantation 798.

19 S Kawasaki, M Makuuchi, S Ishizone et al 'Liver Regeneration in Recipients and Donors after Transplantation' (1992) 339 Lancet 580.

20 The Human Organ Transplants Act 1989, s 7 defines an organ as any part of the human body consisting of a structured arrangement of tissues which, *if wholly removed*, cannot be replicated by the body (our emphasis). This would include a liver but not necessarily a segment of liver.

21 The mortality associated with lung lobe donation is said to be approaching that of live kidney donation. However, two donors are needed to treat a single child. M E Hodson 'Transplantation using Lung Lobes from Living Donors' (2000) 26 J Med Ethics 419.

and benefits of a given procedure are both assessable and acceptable, the common law legality and the morality of live organ donation is now settled; consent to a surgical operation which is, in itself, non-therapeutic will be valid so long as the consequent infliction of injury can be shown not to be against the public interest.[22]

14.16   The statutory regulation of live donation is to be found in the Human Organ Transplants Act 1989,[23] which creates an offence if a live organ transplant between persons who are not genetically related is undertaken without the agreement of the Unrelated Live Transplant Regulatory Authority (s 2).[24] Genetically related transplantation is not subject to statutory control. Section 2(2) defines a genetic relationship. This can be so wide – it includes, for example, uncles and aunts by half blood – as to raise the suspicion that Parliament was concerned more with family loyalties than genetic niceties;[25] even so, it is surprising that interspousal donations, and donation by 'in-laws' or God-parents, are still subject to restriction.   Authority for an unrelated donation is, however, subject to very strict rules as to the absence of commercial involvement and as to the consent of the donor and counselling of both parties – additionally, the Authority must be informed of any difficulties in communication between the counsellor and the donor and/or recipient.[26] An interesting variation on the normal conditions for consent (for which see chapter 10) is that the donor *must* understand the processes involved – there is no scope here for 'professional privilege' in providing information; live organ donations involving unrelated incompetents are, therefore, very nearly legally impossible – the position as regards minors is discussed below. These rules, other than those associated with non-payment, are waived in the event that the donation is part of the treatment of the donor[27] – a circumstance which arises most commonly in what is known as the 'domino transplant'. Thus, in the treatment of cystic fibrosis by cadaver donation, for example, it is clinically more satisfactory to use a heart/lung preparation obtained from the dead donor than to implant a lung alone; this leaves the live recipient's heart available for donation in what will almost certainly be a non-related context. A large proportion of unrelated donations are, in fact, of this type.[28]

---

22 *R v Coney* (1882) 8 QBD 534. The obiter remarks of Denning LJ in *Bravery v Bravery* [1954] 1 WLR 1169 at 1180 have been endorsed: *A-G's Reference (No 6 of 1980)* [1981] QB 715, [1981] 2 All ER 1057.

23 An Order in Council made under the Northern Ireland Act 1984 extends the conditions to Northern Ireland.

24 See also particularly Human Organ Transplants (Establishment of Relationship) Regulations 1989, SI 1989/2107 and Human Organ Transplants (Unrelated Persons) Regulations 1989, SI 1989/2480.

25 Human Fertilisation and Embryology Act 1990, ss 27–29 do not apply for the purposes of the section. It is, however, fair to say that, consequent upon the major improvements in immunosuppression, not everyone is uncritical of the current restrictions which are not applied in some other European jurisdictions – eg Germany. It is probable that the only genetic match that is *essential* to, say, kidney donation is the ABO grouping – transplants between spouses and partners are, therefore, not only emotionally indicated but are also as technically satisfactory as are those between genetic relations.

26 Human Organ Transplants (Unrelated Persons) Regulations 1989, SI 1989/2480 reg 3(2)(e).

27 SI 1989/2480, 3(1)(c).

28 B New, M Solomon, R Dingwall and J McHale *A Question of Give and Take: Supply of Organs for Transplantation* (1994), p 35.

14.17 The proportion of live/cadaver renal transplants in the United Kingdom has been rising since 1992. In 1994, it was 7%; the comparable figure in 2000 was 18%.[29] This compares with present day figures of 15% in Germany and a remarkable 44% in the United States where, in both cases, the proportion has, again, been rising.[30] Despite the fact that there is no statutory protection for the *related* donor, there can be no doubt as to the legality of the removal of a kidney from a live adult for the purpose of saving the life of a seriously ill patient – subject, of course, to free and rational consent to the operation. Living donation by children, however, raises a number of thorny issues.

The minor as a donor

14.18 The donation of organs is required surprisingly often from children and, clearly, the advantages of live donation will apply here as well as they will in the adult situation. The legality of such operations on children below the age of 16 has not been decided by British courts and the issue must thus be considered in the light of the general legal principles applied to the medical treatment of minors. As discussed in chapter 10, consent to an operation on a minor below the age of 16 years should normally be obtained from the parents, subject only to the possible common law rights of the child.[31] Valid parental consent, however, refers to treatment for the advantage of the child; troublesome questions arise in relation to procedures which are not calculated to be to his or her benefit – does parental consent in such circumstances constitute an abuse of parental power?

14.19 It has been argued that the principle that a minor – or an incompetent adult with the mental age of a minor – cannot legally be subjected to any procedure which is not to his or her advantage is not an absolute one. It is also possible that a court might consider that the donation of an organ is not only in the public interest but is also in the interest of the minor donor, who will, almost certainly, be a sibling of the recipient. In such circumstances it might be supposed that it is in the interests of the minor that a member of his family should be saved rather than that his relative should die. This line of argument was successfully pursued in the index American decision in *Strunk v Strunk*.[32] In this case, the donor, who, although adult, had a mental age of six, was chosen to donate a kidney to his brother, who was critically ill. The court came to the

---

29 UK Transplant, www.uktransplant.org.uk. The figures include the Republic of Ireland. The annual total of renal transplants has remained remarkably steady over the decade but the waiting list in 2000 stood at an all time high of 6284.

30 N Biller-Andorno and H Schauenburg 'It's Only Love? Some Pitfalls in Emotionally Related Organ Donation' (2001) 27 J Med Ethics 162. The very high proportion of live transplants in the Scandinavian countries is remarkable (50% in Norway). It should be noted that live donation is the preferred method in some societies. In Japan, for example, the concept of brain stem death has only recently become acceptable, some 70% of donations were of live type. Virtually all transplants in India are 'live' but this is probably an administrative rather than cultural consequence (see para 14.36 below).

31 P D G Skegg 'English Law relating to Experimentation on Children' (1977) 2 Lancet 754 took the view that the Family Law Reform Act 1969, s 8 has no application to non-therapeutic procedures and that the rules of non-statutory law do not vary with different categories of persons. See Lord Donaldson in *Re W (a minor) (medical treatment)* [1992] 4 All ER 627, (1992) 9 BMLR 22, discussed para 14.22 below.

32 445 SW 2d 145 (Ky, 1969).

conclusion it would be in the donor's best interests for his brother's life to be saved after hearing evidence of the close relationship which existed between the two boys. Consequently, the operation was allowed although the donor was not in a position to give consent. *Strunk* has not, however, had an easy ride.[33] There is no assurance that it represents the general rule in the United States; indeed, it has been rejected in a more recent case involving a bone marrow transplant between three-year-old twins.[34] Again, this decision can be compared with that in the English case *Re Y* which, this time, concerned an adult *incapax* rather than a child.[35] Here, a bone marrow transplant was authorised between siblings largely on the grounds that, absent treatment for the lymphomatous child, the mother would have less time to devote to the incapax; the procedure was, accordingly in the best interests of the donor. It is clear that no rule can be anticipated – each case will stand on its own merits. A review of the Anglo-American cases suggests, however, that whether there is agreement or disagreement among the parties will be a major determining factor.

14.20 In practice, most jurisdictions are reluctant to allow the taking of organs from minors. In Canada, for instance, the Ontario Human Tissue Gift Act provides an example of statutory prohibition of donation by minors.[36] A policy of limitation was advised by the Australian Law Reform Commission in their report on transplantation. The Commission took the view that the donation by minors of non-regenerative tissue should not be forbidden without exception but that the circumstances in which it should be allowed should be circumscribed. The enabling conditions were suggested as being: when the donor and recipient are members of the same immediate family; when there is independent medical evidence that the prospective recipient will die unless the transplant is carried out; where the parents of the donor (or those in loco parentis) agree to the donation; where the donor has sufficient mental capacity and agrees to the donation; and, finally, when an ad hoc committee consisting of a judge and two other persons comes to the conclusion that the donation is desirable and in the interests of the donor. In the event, none of the individual states accepted this proposal and, indeed, some of those qualifications were applied to the donation of *regenerative* tissue; it is not lawful in Australia to remove non-regenerative material from the body of a living child for the purpose of transplantation.[37] A blanket ban on the use of minors as organ donors has been advocated by the World Health Organization.[38]

---

33 It was followed in *Hart v Brown* 289 A 2d 386 (Conn, 1972) (identical twins) and in *Little v Little* 576 SW 2d 493 (Tex, 1979) (14-year-old incompetent) but rejected in *In re Richardson* 284 So 2d 185 (La, 1973) (17-year-old incompetent) and in *In re Guardianship of Pescinski* 226 NW 2d 180 (Wis, 1975) (adult incompetent). It is interesting that, despite attempts to apply a substituted judgment test, all the relevant cases have been decided on the basis of the donor's best interests.
34 *Curran v Bosze* 566 NE 2d 1319 (Ill, 1990).
35 *Re Y (adult patient) (transplant: bone marrow)* [1997] Fam 110, (1997) 35 BMLR 111 (remarked on at para 10.33). Connell J was at pains to emphasise that the case should not be taken as a precedent for more invasive techniques which would, presumably, imply organ transplantation.
36 B M Dickens *Medico-legal Aspects of Family Law* (1979) p 96.
37 See eg Human Tissue and Transplant Act 1982, ss 12, 13 (Western Australia). The Human Tissue Act 1983, s 10 (NSW) forbids it by omission.
38 World Health Organization *Guiding Principles on Human Organ Transplantation* (1994) principle 4, discussed by M N Morelli 'Organ Trafficking: Legislative Proposals to Protect Minors' (1995) 10 Am U J Int Law Pol 917.

14.21 While the complete exclusion of minor donors would seem to many to be too extreme, there are powerful reasons why some limits should be placed on the use of children as donors of non-regenerative tissue and very great caution should be exercised in the case of young children in whom there is unlikely to be any significant understanding of what the donation entails. Even if a minor shows a reasonable degree of understanding of the donation and of the risks involved, a sharp distinction is to be made between instances when the recipient is a member of the immediate family and when he is not. It might be regarded as ethically acceptable for a minor to be used as a donor in the former case; generosity towards a brother or sister is to be encouraged and may even be regarded as a social duty.[39] The situation is less clear with relatives other than siblings. Should one apply the same rule to a situation where the prospective recipient is a cousin in the first degree? It is possible that the minor donor may be as fond of such a cousin as he is of a brother or sister and the illness of the cousin may be as distressing to him as would be the illness of a sibling. Nevertheless, a policy of limiting approved donation by minors to the immediate family has the attraction of certainty. The law in France[40] illustrates an acceptable compromise statutory position. There, a living minor may only donate to his brother or sister; consent must be given by the donor's legal representative; and the procedure must be authorised by a committee composed of at least three experts two of whom must be doctors and one of whom must have practised for 20 years. If the minor can be consulted, refusal on his part must be respected in all cases. The caution shown by countries subject to both common and civil law jurisdictions is noteworthy and, while statute is either ambivalent or silent on the matter in the United Kingdom, some clarification of the current legal position here has come from the Court of Appeal.

14.22 The case of *Re W*[41] dealt with consent to treatment by a 16-year-old and was concerned, in the main, with the application of the Family Law Reform Act 1969, s 8(1).[42] The problem of organ transplantation was not in issue but was touched upon by the Master of the Rolls; his views must, we feel, be regarded as obiter but are, nevertheless, persuasive. Lord Donaldson first disposed of the statute on the grounds that the section related to treatment and diagnosis; it could not, therefore, extend to the donation of organs as this did not satisfy either condition in respect of the donor. He went on:

> Organ donations are quite different and, as a matter of law, doctors would have to secure the consent of someone with the right to consent on behalf of a donor under the age of 18 or, if they relied on the consent of the minor himself or herself, be satisfied that the minor was '*Gillick* competent' in the context of so serious a procedure which would not benefit the minor.[43]

39 L F Ross 'Moral Grounding for the Participation of Children as Organ Donors' (1993) 21 J Law Med & Ethics 251 introduces the interesting concept of the family as an autonomous unit which can aspire to a collective purpose. Intrafamilial donation by a child advances the family's interests, which is a means of promoting the child's own interests. None the less, the author is extremely chary of exposing minors to risks they do not understand.
40 Law of 22 December 1976.
41 *Re W (a minor) (medical treatment)* [1992] 4 All ER 627, (1992) 9 BMLR 22.
42 Already discussed in greater detail at para 10.45 above.
43 [1992] 4 All ER 627 at 635, (1992) 9 BMLR 22 at 31.

14.23 As to the latter, he added, somewhat equivocally: 'This would be a highly improbable conclusion.' The whole passage is, in fact, a trifle confusing as, logically, '*Gillick*-competence' applies only to the under 16-year-old, whereas s 8(1) of the Act relates to the 16–18-year-old. However, Lord Donaldson continued:

> It is inconceivable that [the doctor] should proceed in reliance solely upon the consent of an under-age patient, however '*Gillick*-competent', in the absence of supporting parental consent and equally inconceivable that he should proceed in the absence of the patient's consent. In any event he will need to seek the opinions of other doctors and may be well advised to apply to the court for guidance ... [44]

which seems clear enough until we look at the summary provided by the Master of the Rolls:

> A minor of any age who is *Gillick*-competent in the context of a particular treatment has a right to consent to that treatment which again cannot be overridden by those with parental responsibility, but can be overridden by the court. Unlike the statutory right this common law right extends to the donation of blood or organs. [45]

14.24 We can only suggest that, however this is interpreted, it would be a brave surgeon who ignored Lord Donaldson's advice-in-chief. The minor's right to refuse is, however, clearly preserved.

14.25 That is, the minor's right to refuse to donate. But what of the minor's rights to refuse to receive a transplant? We discuss the case of *Re M (child: refusal of medical treatment)*[46] in chapter 10. Here, it need only be said that to authorise a non-consensual heart transplant on a determinedly reluctant 15½ year-old girl seems to be a remarkable example of the power of the 'best interests test'.

14.26 It appears, in fact, that, in respect of donation, transplant surgeons in general have developed their own jurisprudence. Our inquiries indicate that no currently practising British transplant surgeon would accept a live child as an organ donor; only one such instance, involving an identical twin aged 17 years, has arisen in the United Kingdom in the last 15 years. Only five living minor donors have been used in the Eurotransplant catchment area and none has been recorded in France, despite the enabling legislation; similarly, none is recorded by Scadiatransplant.[47] Discussion of the matter thus lies at the academic rather than the practical level.

14.27 Nothing, however, is static in modern medicine. At one time, there were reports that couples were having children for the express purpose of providing genetically compatible sibling donors of, at present, regenerative

---

44 [1992] 4 All ER 627 at 635, (1992) 9 BMLR 22 at 31.
45 [1992] 4 All ER 627 at 639, (1992) 9 BMLR 22 at 35.
46 [1999] 2 FLR 1097, (2000) 52 BMLR 124. Johnson J fully expressed the difficulty and the gravity of his decision.
47 J K Mason 'Legal Aspects of Organ Transplantation' in C Dyer (ed) *Doctors, Patients and the Law* (1992).

tissue only.[48] Whatever one feels about such a practice, the pragmatic answer is that, unlike the more sophisticated technique of employing in vitro fertilisation in conjunction with pre-implantation genetic diagnosis (discussed above at para 6.26), it cannot be prevented. Medico-legally, any such child, when born, would be protected by the rules governing donation by living minors. But, speaking ethically, it cannot be denied that the process does little credit to the doctrine of free consent – there is a strong impression that human life is, thereby, being used as a means to an end.

Patients in the permanent vegetative state

14.28 The current pressure to accept cognitive death as equivalent to somatic death[49] is such as to dictate a brief word on the permanent vegetative state. It is, perhaps, necessary to do no more than recapitulate our view that, tragic as their state may be, persons in the persistent vegetative state are existing by means of their own cardiovascular system and are not dead – and none of the standard defences of lawful killing could be applied to them. There is, of course, no reason why permanently vegetative patients should not be used as organ donors within the existing framework of the law when they die – although the manner of their dying may cast doubt on the quality of the organs thus made available;[50] but there can be no question of killing them – or limiting their existence – for the express purpose.[51] Predictably, this view is shared by the British Medical Association.[52] Times, however, change and an authoritative paper published on behalf of an International Forum for Transplant Ethics infers that to exempt PVS patients from the normal legal prohibitions against 'killing' would be humanitarian in that it would obviate the futile use of resources and would release organs that were suitable for transplantation.[53] We have to admit to strong doubts as to such a policy. To confuse the concept of brain stem death and to associate the permanent vegetative state with transplantation could only fan any embers of public distrust for 'premature grave robbing' which still remain. Burke and Hare attracted much sympathy in their role of exhumers; it was when they became pre-emptive that they fell from grace!

The donor as vendor

14.29 The commercialisation of transplant surgery remains one of the most urgent issues in the context of living organ donation. It is, essentially, a matter of consent and, on this score, it is to be distinguished from payment for cadaver organs – the latter being better considered as an aspect of the availability of organs.

---

48 For discussion, see J Rachels 'When Philosophers Shoot from the Hip' (1991) 5 Bioethics 67. No later cases have been reported – possibly because the novelty has worn off.
49 See para 13.9 above.
50 See para 14.61 below for further discussion.
51 Discussed by J Downie 'The Biology of the Persistent Vegetative State: Legal, Ethical, and Philosophical Implications for Transplantation' (1990) 22 Transplant Proc 995.
52 BMA 'Guidelines Relating to the Persistent Vegetative State' reproduced in (1993) 3 Bull Med Ethics, 8, para 9.
53 R Hoffenberg, M Lock, N Tilney et al 'Should Organs from Patients in Permanent Vegetative State Be Used for Transplantation?' (1997) 350 Lancet 1320.

14.30 Inevitably, a British view on donation for recompense must be coloured by one's experience of a national health service. Within that framework, it is difficult to see the sale of organs as other than a way for the rich to obtain priority essential care, the inequity being compounded by the corollary that the poor, who would form the pool of such donors, would be positively disadvantaged in the role of supplier. But it is only fair to remark that those working in a health care system that is governed by a market economy could see the situation as one in which an anxious buyer meets a willing seller. It is not easy to occupy an objective middle ground.

14.31 The problem may have existed in England before 1989 but it was then that it presented acutely. It transpired that impoverished Turkish donors were being recruited and paid to donate their kidneys to genetically and ethnically unrelated recipients; there were wide-ranging repercussions at both legislative and professional levels and these, of themselves, provoked further ethical debate.

14.32 The response of the legislature was to rush through the Human Organ Transplants Act 1989, which prohibits the exchange of money, other than legitimate expenses, for the purpose of organ donation by the living (s 1(1));[54] it is also an offence to advertise for the purpose (s 1(2)). Clearly, the legislative intention is to distinguish altruism from commercialism and to approve the former while condemning the latter. The distinction is dictated by the consent doctrine in that it is assumed that a free, uncoerced consent is impossible in the face of financial inducement. To which one might add the widely held moral objection to *any* commercialisation of the human body (see chapter 15).[55]

14.33 The great majority would accept these restrictions on the individual's power over his or her own body – and yet: cannot this be seen as unacceptable paternalism? Is it impossible that a commercial donor could make his decision in a reasoned manner and on his own altruistic grounds?[56] And who, in quest of unfettered consent, is to distinguish between external financial pressure and moral pressure exerted within the family?[57] It is at least arguable that, in closing the door on the use of an inessential part of one's body for gain, Parliament is striking at the individual publican's autonomy in favour of the corporate pharisee's inner virtue.[58]

---

54 And also from the dead – qv para 14.55. Interstate commerce in organs is illegal in the United States – National Transplantation Act 1984, Public Law 98–507 – and this has been followed within many States: Joralemon, para 14.56 below.

55 We are unconvinced by the philosophical argument that the wrong lies in the invasion of bodily integrity – a wrong which is offset by the good of altruism but which finds no such exculpation in the commercial situation: S Wilkinson and E Garrard 'Bodily Integrity and the Sale of Human Organs' (1996) 22 J Med Ethics 334. The money that accrues can be put to good use.

56 It is reported that one of the donors intended to devote the proceeds to the medical treatment of his daughter. See a sympathetic contribution by J Harvey 'Paying Organ Donors' (1990) 16 J Med Ethics 117.

57 For an interesting review of the subtle intrafamilial pressures that can be exerted, see Biller-Andorno and Schauenburg, para 14.17 above.

58 A powerful argument against a blanket prohibition of reward is mounted by A S Daar 'Paid Organ Donation – the Grey Basket Concept' (1998) 24 J Med Ethics 365 – among other writings by the same author.

14.34 The professional reaction to the 'Turkish affair' was no less positive. The name of one of the doctors concerned was erased from the Medical Register while the professional freedom of two others was severely curtailed.[59] The GMC has now issued definitive guidelines, which include:

> In no circumstances may doctors participate in or encourage in any way the trade in human organs from live donors. They must not advertise for donors nor make financial or medical arrangements for people who wish to sell or buy organs ... Doctors must also satisfy themselves that consent to a donation has been given without undue influence of any kind, including the offer of financial or material benefit.[60]

14.35 It has been said that to allow payment would be to open up a traffic in organs. Yet it is difficult to see why this could not be obviated by legalising paid donations by way of the Unrelated Live Transplant Regulatory Authority only. There is some empirical evidence that public opposition to payment is not as strong as might be supposed – between 40% and 50% may find the practice permissible[61] and it has been noted that: 'As long as there are adequate safeguards, any ethical or legal fastidiousness demanding that donation be only gratuitous could condemn the sick.'[62] In any event, a traffic in organs cannot now be confined within one jurisdiction. Networks for the commercial provision of organs already exist;[65] clearly any restrictions on the practice must be international if they are to be effective and the European Parliament has asked the Council of Ministers to ban the sale of organs throughout the European Community.[63] A British minister has said that: 'the concept of kidneys for sale is entirely unacceptable in a civilised society'[64] and many would undoubtedly agree – but, at the same time, it is difficult to identify the precise moral basis for so doing. As the International Forum has said:

> [F]eelings of outrage and disgust that led to an outright ban on kidney sales ... typically have a force that seems to their possessors to need no further justification. Nevertheless, if we are to deny treatment to the suffering and dying we need better reasons than our own feelings of disgust.[65]

14.36 Moreover, the fact that this antipathy is a specifically Western view merits repetition. It is at least arguable that, in a country such as India, where there is no cadaver transplant programme and where long-term dialysis is impracticable, paid organ donation may be not only ethical but also desirable.[66]

59 C Dyer 'GMC's Decision on "Kidneys for Sale"' (1990) 300 BMJ 961.
60 GMC 'Guidance for Doctors on Transplantation of Organs from Live Donors' (1992) News Review, December, Supplement.
61 A Guttmann and R D Guttmann 'Attitudes of Health Care Professionals and the Public towards the Sale of Kidneys for Transplantation' (1993) 19 J Med Ethics 148.
62 I Davies 'Live Donation of Human Body Parts: A Case for Negotiability?' (1991) 59 Med-Leg J 100.
63 A Dorozynski 'Europe Condemns Sale of Organs' (1993) 307 BMJ 756.
64 See J Warden 'Kidneys Not for Sale' (1989) 298 BMJ 1670.
65 J Radcliffe-Richards, A S Daar, R D Guttmann et al 'The Case for Allowing Kidney Sales' (1998) 351 Lancet 1950. It is to be noted that the possibility of payment for organs is still alive in the United States: D Josefson 'AMA Considers whether to Pay for Donation of Organs' (2002) 324 BMJ 1541 and has support in the United Kingdom: J Harris and C Erin 'An Ethically Defensible Market in Organs' (2002) 325 BMJ 114.
66 The Indian Government has outlawed payment for organs but the ban is not watertight. See: A K Singh, P A Srivatsava and A Kumar 'Current Status of Transplant Coordination and Organ Donation' (1998) 30 Transplant Proc 3627.

As has been said, the ethical distinction between allowing one poor and needy citizen to run the risk of brain damage in the boxing ring and denying another the right to sell a kidney may be hard to define.[67]

CADAVER DONATIONS

14.37   The deceased has very limited rights as to the disposal of his body in common law and the wishes of the executors would normally be supported rather than those of the dead person in the event of conflict. Statute law has, however, largely replaced common law and the collection and use of cadaver organs and tissues is now regulated in Great Britain by the Human Tissue Act 1961.[68] We note that, as a result of the exposure at the turn of the century of what had been, undoubtedly, widespread breaches of the law – and which are discussed in greater detail in chapter 15 – revision of this Act is under active consideration in both the English and Scottish jurisdictions; we can, however, only analyse the situation as it exists at the time of writing. At present, the 1961 Act provides, in s 1(1), that removal of an organ is authorised if there has been a specific request to this effect by the deceased; the removal may be for therapeutic, educational or research purposes. In the absence of such a request, s 1(2) provides for the authorisation of organ removal if the person 'lawfully in possession of the body' has, after making such 'reasonable enquiry as may be practicable', no reason to believe that the deceased had expressed any objection to organ removal or that the surviving spouse or 'any surviving relative' of the deceased objects to the body being so dealt with.

14.38   The somewhat loose wording of the Act has caused occasional difficulty in its implementation. This was particularly so as to the definition of the person in lawful possession. For some time it was considered that the term implied one with a right to possession, that is, the executors. The alternative view is that it refers to the person who has physical possession of the body who is, in practical terms, the hospital administrative officer. This latter interpretation is supported by the wording of other sections of the Act and is now widely accepted but the point has not been tested in the courts.[69] Clarity on the point is important in that, were the executors to be in lawful possession, they could overrule any specific request made by the deceased. Even allowing for the fact that the relatives have no locus standi to object to the removal of organs under s 1(1), which clearly expresses the law, the doctor is in a difficult position in the event of their objections being voiced. On the one hand, he has legal justification to proceed and he may, rightly, be thinking of the potential recipients. On the other, it would be extremely hard to justify in ethical terms

---

67   J Bignall 'Kidneys: Buy or Die' (1993) 342 Lancet 45.
68   The Anatomy Act 1984 is specifically limited to dissection of a body for the purposes of studying morphology – ie examination in an anatomy school. Post-mortem examinations for medico-legal or clinical purposes are excluded (s 1(4)). The Human Tissue Act 1961 takes precedence when authority for study derives from both Acts (s 1(5)). Although donation of the body under the 1984 Act is not uncommon, it raises no ethico-legal problems and is not considered further in this Chapter.
69   In fact, the Transplant of Human Organs Bill 2001 proposed substituting the words 'health authority or NHS Trust' for 'person lawfully' but the Bill lapsed with the dissolution of Parliament.

a decision to add further suffering to the bereaved. It is fortunate that such conflicts are very rare in practice but we return to the point when considering the shortfall in organs available for treatment. It should be noted, in passing, that the coroner or procurator fiscal may veto any authorisation if the death comes within their jurisdictions and it is concluded that organ retrieval might jeopardise their inquiries (s 1(5) and (9)).

14.39 The concept of 'such reasonable enquiry as may be practicable' is also vague, reasonableness being a matter of highly subjective judgment. The partial solution is to consider what is *un*reasonable – and it would clearly be unreasonable to prolong one's enquiries until the intended donor organ was non-viable. Such a pragmatic approach is, however, less tenable in the context of the beating heart donor, which is discussed below. Finally, the wording 'any surviving relative' is confusingly open-ended and must again be interpreted in a practical sense – the phrase must be taken to mean 'any relative who can reasonably be contacted within the limited time available', which effectively limits one to the immediate next of kin. This difficulty has been anticipated in Australia, where 'next of kin' are specified in order of 'seniority'; responsibility for consent is then vested in the most senior next of kin who can be contacted.[70]

14.40 The Human Tissue Act 1961 is unusual in that it details no sanctions in the event of its non-observance. That being the case, it is unsurprising that the question of whether any offence was committed thereby was soon raised;[71] the same authority went so far as to suggest that an apparently unauthorised action to save the life of a recipient might be justified on the basis of necessity. From the civil aspect, there seems no reason in principle why an action in tort for nervous shock should not be available to relatives who think that the conditions of reasonable inquiry have not been met. Success in such actions is notoriously difficult to achieve; we believe that the necessary conditions of proximity might well be satisfied if a close relative was confronted with what he or she regarded as a mutilated corpse but the additional hurdle of demonstrating a true psychiatric injury would be hard to overcome – mere shock or disgust would be insufficient grounds on which to found recompense.[72] Certainly, judicial support for such an action is not easy to find. The only authority that we have discovered lies in the old case of *Hughes v Robertson* in which it was said:

> I have no doubt that the cutting up or dissecting or otherwise unauthorised mutilation of a near relative's body constitutes a wrong of which a near relative has a title to complain.[73]

14.41 Even so, the majority opinion is that, while such actions have succeeded in the United States, they would be unlikely to do so in the United Kingdom.[74]

---

70 Eg Human Tissue Act 1983, s 4 (NSW).
71 P D G Skegg 'Liability for the Unauthorized Removal of Cadaveric Transplant Material' (1974) 14 Med Sci & L 53.
72 *Fraser v State Hospitals Board for Scotland* 2001 SLT 1051, 2001 SCLR 357.
73 1913 SC 349 per Lord Kyllachy
74 I Kennedy and A Grubb *Medical Law* (3rd edn, 2000), p 2250.

Beating heart donors

14.42 It is apparent that the major practical criticisms levelled at the Human Tissue Act 1961 derive from the prolongation of the warm anoxic time entailed in strict adherence to its terms. But such objections arise only when death is measured by the irrevocable failure of the cardiovascular system. In practice, the overwhelming proportion of cadaver-donated material will come from patients who have been maintained on ventilator support and in whom it will be appropriate to reach a diagnosis of death by means of brain stem criteria. There is no logical reason why ventilation should not be continued after death and the heart beat be maintained during an operation for organ donation. The ideal situation of the living donor is thus achieved in a cadaver.

14.43 The technical advantages of a beating heart donation are not in dispute and the process is essential to the success of some transplantations.[75] Why, then, is there continuing antipathy to the procedure? Much must stem from an inherent revulsion at performing what is a lethal operation amid the conditions pertaining to a living patient, but this is irrational once the concept of brain stem death has been accepted – any emotional bias should be directed towards the recipients. Perhaps the major problem lies in the fact that there are still those who, in all good conscience, cannot accept the technical criteria advocated for the diagnosis of brain stem death – doubts which affect both doctors and relatives;[76] some surgeons, while accepting a ventilated donor, will not operate until the patient is disconnected from the machine and shows a flat electrocardiogram. While fully accepting that every doctor is entitled to his own clinical judgment, we do suggest that the subject would be, so to speak, defused were it to be made compulsory for a death certificate to be issued, and the notification handed to the next of kin, before any donation could be effected. This would serve, first, to ease matters for the professionals involved – it is not entirely satisfactory for the surgeon undertaking a beating heart donation to have to 'satisfy himself by personal examination of the body that life is extinct' (Human Tissue Act 1961, s 1(4)) from a mere perusal of the hospital notes; secondly, we feel the process would set the minds of the relatives at rest. An alternative is to dissociate the problems of the definition of death from those of transplantation and to legislate purely for the latter contingency. Thus, the Human Tissue and Transplant Act 1982, s 24(2) of Western Australia makes no mention of death but ordains that two medical practitioners with specific qualifications must certify that irreversible cessation of all functions of the brain has occurred before organs can be removed from the body of a person whose respiration and circulation are being maintained artificially.

14.44 In any event, relatives must be confused and distraught unless given sympathetic counselling and, in practice, this should always be possible in

---

75 Eg heart transplants.
76 A recent review is to be found in J M A Swinburn et al and associated papers 'Discontinuation of Ventilation after Brain Stem Death' (1999) 318 BMJ 1753. For theoretical scepticism, see H Jonas 'Against the Stream: Comments on the Definition and Redefinition of Death' in T L Beauchamp and R M Veatch (eds) *Ethical Issues in Death and Dying* (2nd edn, 1996).

modern circumstances when, as a result of ventilator support, relatives will have been aware of the impending death for some time and will, no doubt, have been attending at the hospital – transplant co-ordinators are now widely established and can assist in the task to great advantage. Relatives should be given every available assistance. Thus, while we accept the view that an electroencephalogram is not necessary to establish the fact of death, we also believe that the relatives should have the right to such evidence should they ask for it. It is only by such pragmatic adaptations of the statutory law that beating heart donation will become universally accepted and that, as a consequence, the maximum proportion of high quality organs will be harvested.[77]

The availability of suitable organs

14.45 It has been calculated that there are enough suitable cadaver kidneys available in America to satisfy the demand but that the requirements are still not met because only one in eight potentially useful organs are obtained in practice.[78] An unsatisfactory situation also persists in the United Kingdom. Some 6284 patients were awaiting kidney transplants in 2000 – an all-time high;[79] by the same year, the number of cadaver transplants performed had fallen from 1766 in 1991 to1487. Nearly half the potential donors fail to become actual donors[80] and it is this deficit which needs to be corrected. The problem has been addressed by a Government Working Party[81] and new initiatives have been promised but, despite the urgency of the situation, no satisfactory solution has emerged as yet. In the meantime, the International Forum have stated: '[I]t is morally unjustified to perpetuate a system that falls short of increasing the availability of organs to people who might benefit from transplantation.'[82]

14.46 There are essentially two avenues to explore: to reform the law or to change professional and public attitudes. As to the former, it is clear that a

---

77 Since the last edition of this book, the Japanese Parliament has officially recognised the concept of brain stem death so long as transplantation is involved; this has resulted in a dual definition of death: J R McConnell 'The Ambiguity about Death in Japan: An Ethical Implication for Organ Procurement' (1999) 25 J Med Ethics 322. It is also to be noted that Muslim law now allows donation and receipt of organs using a brain stem death approach: V Choo 'UK Shariah Council Approves Organ Transplants' (1995) 346 Lancet 303. The major pockets of resistance to the concept have, therefore, been eliminated and only Pakistan and Poland among the major countries of the world do not now designate brain death as actual death (J Wise 'Japan to Allow Organ Transplants' (1997) 314 BMJ 1298).
78 For an overview of US attitudes, see H S Schwartz 'Bioethical and Legal Considerations in Increasing the Supply of Transplantable Organs: From UAGA to "Baby Fae"' (1985) 10 Amer J Law Med 397.
79 Para 14.17 above. The cost of hospital dialysis averages £25,000 per year and of home dialysis £15,000; following an initial operative cost of between £10,000 and £15,000, the follow-up treatment of the transplant recipient costs around £3,000 per year.
80 This is also true in America: P H Berry 'Organ Donation: Can the US Do Better?' (1999) 319 BMJ 1445.
81 R Hoffenberg (chairman) *Report of the Working Party on the Supply of Donor Organs for Transplantation* (1987).
82 I Kennedy, R A Sells, A S Daar et al 'The Case for "Presumed Consent" in Organ Donation' (1998) 351 Lancet 1650.

main source of cadaver organs under the Human Tissue Act 1961 results from a system of 'contracting in' to the transplant service, something which dictates a conscious effort that many healthy persons – and particularly young persons – find difficult to make.[83] It is widely suggested that the Act could profitably be altered so as to adopt a 'contracting out' position – that is, one in which consent to donation is presumed unless it is specifically withheld.[84] Such a system operates in several European countries, although with varying rigidity. Thus, a right of veto is still vested in the next of kin in Italy and Spain, while the sensitivities of the relatives are deeply respected in Belgium – very few transplant centres would apply the law in that country in the face of their opposition. The views of the next of kin are held at a minimum in Austria where, interestingly, the cadaver kidney donor rate is the highest among the leading 'transplant countries'.[85] Thus, a good case for 'presumed consent' can be made out – and contracting out on the Belgian model is clearly the preferred choice of the International Forum;[86] nevertheless, it carries with it a hint of coercion and it is hard to foresee a British government making such a major policy change. We believe that the following statement – admittedly made by a different administration and, admittedly, a decade ago – probably still represents the view of the major political parties in the United Kingdom:

> We must accept that nobody has a right to anybody else's organs. If something untoward happens, our organs may be of value to someone else but that should be the result of an altruistic decision about how we want our bodies to be used when we die. It should not be as a result of a right of the recipient ... It is the responsibility of the living whose organs may be of use to someone else; it is not anyone else's job to claim the organs.[87]

14.47 Whether objections from the next of kin would remain at the same level given a change of policy is uncertain. Kennedy et al[88] have pointed out that there is a difference for the relatives between making a decision and simply confirming the fact that the deceased had not registered an objection, but many doctors would still find the resulting pressure on relatives to be

83 Even so, it does not seem to deter them in Holland where what is possibly the most advanced and comprehensive legislation is to be found. Under the Organ Donation (Wet op de Orgaandonatie) Act 1998, everyone over the age of 18 is invited to register with a central registry. The individual can register one of four options as to post-mortem donation – a consent to donate any or specified organs, a refusal to donate, delegation of consent to the next of kin or delegation to a nominated person. The choice may be altered at any time. Access to the Central Register is available 24 hours a day. Living donation of organs and bone marrow is also covered by the Act. The Act is also fully acceptable on ethical grounds in so far as a coercive element is avoided by providing an equal opportunity to consent or refuse.
84 C A Erin and J Harris 'Presumed Consent or Contracting Out' (1999) 25 J Med Ethics 365 maintain, correctly, that there is a distinction to be made between the two. Rather than speak in terms of consent, they prefer to look upon both approaches as being morally right.
85 New et al, para 14.16 above, fig 11.
86 See para 14.28 above.
87 Official Reports, HC, 28 March 1991, vol 188, col 1142 per Stephen Dorrell. Nevertheless, another private member's Bill calling for 'presumed consent', and which has the support of the BMA, is due to be presented to Parliament as we write: BMA News, 23 February 2002, p 2.
88 See para 14.45 above. Much the same point was made by S Eaton 'The Subtle Politics of Organ Donation: A Proposal' (1998) 24 J Med Ethics 166.

distasteful. At the same time, this fear may be being exaggerated to the detriment of the programme. It is now quite clear that signing a donor card is a legally effective written expression in life of a request that one's body should be used for therapeutic purposes, yet the great majority of transplant surgeons will be reluctant to press the matter if the relatives express an objection. While this may be very good and sympathetic medicine, it is, paradoxically, doubtful medical ethics – effectively, the last autonomous wish of the individual is being thwarted simply because he or she is in no position to object. Whether or not a firmer attitude would result in significantly more donations is uncertain, but it is scarcely fair to blame the law for any shortcomings if the law is being disregarded; it has been said, in a slightly different context, that the kidney donor card is not dead but may require intensive care to restore it to more robust health.[89]

14.48 Such professional antipathy to or apathy in seeking the co-operation of relatives may be an important factor; this has led to a movement in favour of 'required request' for organ donation – a format which imposes a legal obligation on doctors to seek permission from the relatives for the removal of tissues from suitable dead persons. This is now the subject of federal law in the United States;[90] a Transplant Notification Bill having the same objectives was introduced in the House of Commons in 1988 but made no progress. There is, in fact, considerable debate in the United Kingdom as to the efficacy of this type of legislation.[91] Moreover, 'required request' undoubtedly compromises the clinical autonomy of the medical staff concerned. It has to be appreciated that, in addition to the difficulties associated with grieving relatives, maintaining a brain dead beating heart donor is effort-intensive, particularly as regards multi-organ donation, and facilities may simply not be available in the acute care unit.[92] Even so, it is significant that failure to ask about donation constitutes the second most important reason for the loss of useable organs.[93]

14.49 The final word rests with Parliament:

> We have no plans at this time to introduce legislation to change the way in which organs are donated for transplant. Our current publicity campaign ... is ongoing and encourages people to join the National Health Service Organ Donor Register, carry the donor card and, most importantly, discuss their wishes with their friends and family.[94]

89 R M R Taylor 'Opting In or Out of Organ Donation' (1992) 305 BMJ 1380. The Scottish *Independent Review Group on Retention of Organs at Post-mortem* (Professor S McLean, Chairman) was particularly emphatic on this point: Final Report (2001), para 58.
90 US Public Law 99-509 9318.
91 G D Chisholm 'Time to End Softly Softly Approach on Harvesting Organs for Transplantation' (1988) 296 BMJ 1419 regarded it as 'positive'; R M R Taylor and J H Salaman 'The Obligation to Ask for Organs' (1988) 1 Lancet 985 saw it as the only answer to a dialysis 'crisis'; A Bodenham, J C Berridge and G R Park 'Brain Stem Death and Organ Donation' (1989) 299 BMJ 1009 were doubtful.
92 But some writers would see these merely as difficulties to be overcome. For particularly trenchant support of required request, see Taylor and Salaman, para 14.48 above.
93 S M Gore, D J Cable and A J Holland 'Organ Donation from Intensive Care Units in England and Wales: Two Year Confidential Audit of Deaths in Intensive Care' (1992) 304 BMJ 349.
94 Official Reports, HC, 4 July 2000, col 144W.

Non-heart beating donation

14.50 An alternative – or, perhaps, complementary – approach to reducing the 'wastage' of organs would be to acknowledge the layman's possible distrust of brain stem death and revert to a cardio-respiratory definition of death. To do so, or to use the definitions of death in parallel,[95] takes us into the realm of what is now known as non-heart beating donation. Such donors can be used in two main ways. In the first, mechanical support is removed from a 'brain dead' ventilated patient whose heart will then cease to function as a result of respiratory failure. This is little more than a matter of raising public confidence and we have already seen that many surgeons adopt this procedure as a routine. Alternatively, suitable patients who have died suddenly and who have not been ventilated can be used as donors[96] and this raises a number of both legal and ethical questions.

14.51 First, the questions arise as to whether the use of a 'second-best' organ is better than no transplant and, collaterally, whether it is an either ethically or legally appropriate procedure. As to the first part, there is little doubt that transplantation is almost always the preferred treatment of end stage renal failure so long as the organ has a reasonable chance of survival; nevertheless, a discussion of any likely shortcomings in the procedure would be an essential part of informed consent to operation. As to the latter, the current attitude of transplant surgeons would be essential to the resolution of any dispute as to negligence; the *Bolam* principle, which is discussed in chapter 9, would undoubtedly apply both as to disclosure of information and the operative technique. The problem may, however, be exaggerated; in practice, any differences in outcome between non-heart beating and beating heart donations appear to be of a subtle nature only.[97]

14.52 More importantly, however, in returning to the use of unventilated, non-heart beating donors we have come full circle and we are, at the same time, returning to the 'race against time to save a life'. Moreover, the pressures to reduce the warm anoxic time are even greater than they were now that we are fully aware of, at least, the theoretical advantages of the beating heart donation.[98] This being so, major significance attaches to what can be regarded as the true 'agonal period' – that is, the so-far undefined period between the beginning and the end of the somatic death process. In our view, this is classically limited by, on the former hand, irrevocable cardiorespiratory failure and, on the latter, by irrevocable failure of cerebral cortical function. We do not know how long this period lasts – indeed, it almost certainly varies with the individual – but it may be the most profound period of a person's existence

---

95 This approach is adopted in the United States' Uniform Determination of Death Act – see chapter 13 above for discussion.
96 G Kootstra, R Wijnen, J P van Hooff and C J van der Linden 'Twenty Percent More Kidneys through a Non-heart Beating Program' (1991) 23 Transplant Proc 910.
97 R M H Wijnen, M H Booster, B M Stubenitsky et al 'Outcome of Transplantation of Non-heart-beating Donor Kidneys' (1995) 345 Lancet 1067.
98 Cold perfusion of the whole body or of individual organs in situ is used to reduce these difficulties: J P Cachera, D Y Loisance, O Tavolaro et al ' Hypothermic Perfusion of the Whole Cadaver: A Response to the Question of the Multiple-organ Donor' (1986) 18 Transplant Proc 1407.

and deserving of the greatest respect. It is, therefore, surprising to find that, at least in the United States, there is no standard imposed delay between cessation of cardio-respiratory function and the harvesting of organs – the Institute of Medicine suggests five minutes[99] but it seems it can be anything from ten minutes to being discounted altogether.[100] It is at least possible that such discrepancies are founded on misconceptions. Those who support the shorter times do so on the assumption that death may be defined as the irreversible failure of the cardiorespiratory system only when the heart beat has stopped for such a period as precludes the possibility of cardiac autoresuscitation – and this could well be five minutes. But the fact that the body is irreversibly dead does not mean that the persona, as represented by cerebral function, is also dead; hypoxic death of the brain cells – and, with it, a total loss of mind – cannot be assumed for a longer period.[101] In our view, death should not be regarded as complete until some fifteen minutes have elapsed since cessation of cardiac and pulmonary function – and, in parentheses, we believe that this should be a matter of hospital routine independent of the transplant programme.

14.53 Ethical consideration of this 'agonal period' thus assumes major practical importance in the context of the suggested introduction of 'elective ventilation' as a means of widening the supply of organs. Essentially, the concept involves extending the source of donors from accident and emergency departments so as to include the medical wards. Deeply comatose patients dying from strokes or other cerebral medical conditions are transferred to the intensive care unit and are there supported until brain stem death supervenes and organ retrieval can be arranged. The procedure was pioneered in Exeter,[102] where the original research involved between three and 41 hours' intensive care for eight donors who would, otherwise, have been missed. A rigid protocol was drawn up but, while appreciating that great care had been put into the drafting of the protocol – and accepting the caution expressed by the authors – we believe that the procedure raises a number of legal and ethical difficulties.[103] As to the former,

---

99   As reported in an extremely critical article by J Menikoff 'Doubts about Death: The Silence of the Institute of Medicine' (1998) 26 J Law Med Ethics 157. The author implies that the better limit would be 15 minutes. Members of the Institute of Medicine's Committee on Non-Heart-Beating Organ Transplantation refute his criticisms in a follow-up article at p 166.

100   J M DuBois 'Non-Heart-Beating Organ Donation: A Defense of the Required Determination of Death' (1999) 27 J Law Med Ethics 126.

101   We are, thus, side-stepping a metaphysical argument as to 'what is death'. We would, however, support the expressed view that to allow for both cardio-respiratory and cerebral definitions of death is, essentially, measuring different manifestations of the same phenomenon: A M Capron and L R Kass 'A Statutory Definition of the Standards for Determining Human Death: An Appraisal and a Proposal' (1972) 121 Univ Penn L Rev.

102   T G Feest, H N Riad, C H Collins et al 'Protocol for Increasing Organ Donation after Cerebrovascular Deaths in a District General Hospital' (1990) 335 Lancet 1133. The protocol was also used elsewhere: M A M Salih, I Harvey, S Frankel et al 'Potential Availability of Cadaver Organs for Transplantation' (1991) 302 BMJ 1053. These authors suggested that, realistically, including potential medical donors aged 50-69 would have provided a harvest of 36 kidneys per million population per year, which is coming somewhere near the need for 48 kidneys per million population per year.

103   For similar misgivings, see J V McHale 'Elective Ventilation – Pragmatic Solution or Ethical Minefield?' (1995) 11 Prof Neg 23; S A M McLean 'Transplantation and the "Nearly Dead": The Case of Elective Ventilation' in S A M McLean (ed) *Contemporary Issues in Law, Medicine and Ethics* (1996).

we doubt if the authority vested in the hospital and the surviving relatives by the Human Tissue Act 1961, s 1(2) can be assumed before a person is dead. That is, perhaps, a minor point and it could be argued that no *authority* is being claimed by consenting to removal to the intensive care unit. Ethically, however – and despite the precondition of deep coma – we wonder if it is right to alter radically the mode of death, and, perhaps, to prolong the dying process, purely for the benefit of others.[104] The concurrent problem of whether intensive care beds should be utilised in this way is, in our view, a purely practical matter to be resolved by the doctors in charge. In the event, it has been agreed that the procedure is unlawful given the current regulations[105] – it cannot be in the *patient's* best interests and, thus, cannot be undertaken without valid consent; elective ventilation has been discontinued, at least for the time being. Despite the obvious advantages to the organ harvest, we believe this to be correct – one cannot exorcise a feeling that death is being pre-empted and it is certain that this form of organ husbandry must be very carefully controlled if a backlash of public reaction – and a return to a public fear of 'pre-empted death' – is to be avoided.[106]

14.54 This is of immense overall importance as it is probable that British policy in the quest for more donated organs will depend upon public education for the foreseeable future. One still has to wonder at the basic reasons underlying the refusal of some 30% of relatives to consent to donation[107] – the same public will flock to donate their blood at the sight of a poster advertising an appropriate time and place. Ignorance may be one factor, antipathy on the part of the entertainment media another and, undoubtedly, the suggestion of ambivalence, as regards both techniques and ethics, among the medical profession play their parts. Attitudes may, however, be changing as the results of the more exotic transplant operations improve.[108] We believe that the best way forward is to maximise the concept of the multiple organ donor. It is not easy to enthuse about a treatment whereby one family's joy at the availability of a donor must be balanced against another's tragedy; the public's imagination might well be fired were it generally appreciated that one regrettable death could be compensated by the salvage of four or more lives. This process will undoubtedly be reinforced as increasingly experienced transplant co-ordinators are established as major points of contact with the public.

---

104 This is denied on the grounds that it is a corpse that is being ventilated: A Nicholls and H Riad 'Organ Donation' (1993) 306 BMJ 517. But are the patients dead when the ventilation is instituted? The Exeter group have put up a strong defence of their procedure, only to be contradicted: see H Riad and A Nicholls 'Elective Ventilation of Potential Organ Donors' (1995) 310 BMJ 714 and associated debate.

105 NHS Executive *Identification of Potential Donors of Organs for Transplantation* HSG (94) 41. For support for changing the law to accommodate elective ventilation, see A B Shaw 'Non-therapeutic (Elective) Ventilation of Potential Organ Donors: The Ethical Basis for Changing the Law' (1996) 22 J Med Ethics 72.

106 G Routh 'Elective Ventilation for Organ Donation – The Case Against' (1992) 8 Care Crit Ill 60. For the opposite view, see C H Collins 'Elective Ventilation for Organ Donation – The Case in Favour' (1992) 8 Care Crit Ill 57.

107 Gore et al, para 14.48 above.

108 Eg N Brousse and O Goulet 'Small Bowel Transplantation' (1996) 312 BMJ 261.

Payment for tissues

14.55 Any discussion on the availability of organs must take into account the possibility of their provision on a commercial basis. We have discussed the ethics of donation for reward by the living and have concluded that this is essentially a matter of valid consent by the donor. But the selling of cadaver organs is, at root, directed to the enticement of the next of kin. Put this way, the proposition can be seen as appealing to the baser human instincts and as something with which the medical profession should have no truck – typically put:

> A shift into any form of commercialism or its currently more fashionable cousin 'rewarded gifting' holds the potential of threatening the entire spiritual structure upon which organ transplantation is based at present.[109]

14.56 The possibility is, however, by no means excluded and seems to be gaining momentum in the United States. Manoeuvres to avoid ethical restrictions such as wholesale to kidney banks rather than to individuals have been mooted; standardised cash awards in various forms – such as payment of donors' funeral expenses[110] – have been suggested; and an 'insurance policy' in the form of preferred status is, perhaps surprisingly, the top-ranked option in the United States, where over half those responding to a survey approved the introduction of incentives to improve the supply of organs.[111] Commenting on this, Peters, who supported payment of a fixed death benefit to donors through an organ procurement organisation, suggested that those in the transplant field have wrongly adhered to certain moral values of their own – values which are not necessarily accepted by those at the giving and receiving end of the process;[112] Sells has also pointed out that antagonism to incentive represents an essentially Western view of ethics as we think they ought to be practised:

> Western societies have prescribed for the rest of the globe without giving much thought, evidently, to the differing ethical and medical circumstances in which our less-affluent colleagues have to operate.[113]

109 F T Rapaport 'Progress in Organ Procurement: The Non Heart-beating Cadaver Donor and Other Issues in Transplantation' (1991) 23 Transplant Proc 2699.
110 The so-called 'Pennsylvania Plan': for discussion, see D Joralemon 'Shifting Ethics: Debating the Incentive Question in Organ Transplantation' (2001) 27 J Med Ethics 30.
111 D S Kittur, M M Hogan, V K Thukral et al 'Incentives for Organ Donation?' (1991) 338 Lancet 1441. The 'carrot' of preferred treatment for registered donors is discussed and approved by R Jarvis 'Join the Club: A Modest Proposal to Increase Availability of Donor Organs' (1995) 21 J Med Ethics 199, but is rejected in the same issue by R Gillon 'On Giving Preference to Prior Volunteers when Allocating Organs for Transplantation' (1995) 21 J Med Ethics 195.
112 T G Peters 'Life or Death: The Issue of Payment for Cadaveric Organ Donation' (1991) 265 J Amer Med Ass 1302. For criticism of his arguments, see E D Pellegrino 'Families' Self-interest and the Cadaver's Organs: What Price Consent?' (1991) 265 J Amer Med Ass 1305. Opposition also comes from R W Evans 'Incentives for Organ Donation' (1992) 339 Lancet 185; 'Organ Procurement Expenditures and the Role of Financial Incentives' (1993) 269 J Amer Med Ass 3113. For support from an unlikely source of payment for cadaveric organs, see G P Smith 'Market and Non-market Mechanisms for Procuring Human and Cadaveric Organs: When the Price is Right' (1993) 1 Med Law Internat 17.
113 R A Sells 'Commerce in Human Organs: A Global Review' (1990) 19 Dialysis Transplant 10.

14.57 This is not to say that we approve of a traffic in human organs – in fact, we find payment for the organs of the dead far less easy to justify than payment to the living donor.[114] Given, however, that the process was strictly controlled – say, through a restructured Unrelated Live Transplant Regulatory Authority – and supposing that it *succeeded* in providing life-saving treatment for those dying on the waiting list, reward for donation of cadaver organs appears in a less scandalous light than it did at first sight. The following observation from America is, perhaps, indicative of the trend in that country:

> It is only a matter of time before this country will be forced to decide on *the type of commercial system* which should be adopted in order to meet the demand of transplantable human organs. (Emphasis added.)[115]

THE FETUS OR NEONATE AS A TRANSPLANT DONOR

14.58 Transplantation therapy in the neonatal period is now a standard part of paediatric surgery. Suitable organs, such as the liver, may become available from other newborn infants suffering from fatal conditions; such opportunities are rare but no new issues are then involved because the infant is subject to the conditions of the Human Tissue Act 1961 in just the same way as is the adult or the minor. This, however, is not always so in the case of the fetus who may be involved as an organ donor at maturity or as a cell donor at an early stage of development.

14.59 In the former circumstance, the fetal organs must be both mature and viable if they are to be used to good purpose. One potential source of mature organs is the stillbirth which, by definition, must be of more than 24 weeks' gestation.[116] Equally by definition, however, the stillbirth must neither have breathed nor shown any other sign of life once separated from its mother. It follows that its organs must have been anoxic for an uncertain, but almost certainly significant time; the chances of their being viable in the sense of being transplantable are, therefore, very slight and, save in the exceptional circumstances hypothesised below, the stillbirth can be ignored as a possible source of *organs*. The exception lies in the stillbirth who was known to be alive shortly before a catastrophe during birth; in our view, the practicalities of dealing with a distraught mother, coupled with the absence of a ready recipient, preclude even these stillbirths as donors. It follows that the 'fetal' donor must be alive when born and we are, in fact, considering the neonate as a donor. None the less, it is convenient to retain the term 'fetal donor' in order to distinguish him or her from the neonate that has been under treatment for a significant time.

14.60 The 'live fetal' donor might then derive from a therapeutic abortion – a possibility which is rendered more real by the 1990 amendments to the

---

114   A very suspicious attitude is adopted by Joralemon, para 14.56 above.
115   G J Banks 'Legal and Ethical Safeguards: Protection of Society's Most Vulnerable Participants in a Commercialized Organ Transplantation System' (1995) 21 Am J Law Med 45.
116   Still-Birth (Definition) Act 1992.

Abortion Act 1967 which, inter alia, permit an abortion on the grounds of fetal abnormality without limit of gestational age (s 1(1)(a)) and absolve the doctor from liability under the Infant Life (Preservation) Act 1929 when terminating a pregnancy within the provisions of the 1967 Act (s 5(1)). The use of a living abortus as a transplant donor would be constrained by the terms of the Polkinghorne Report and is best regarded as an aspect of fetal research.[117] Ultimately, therefore, discussion of the fetal organ donor is limited to that of the anencephalic fetus; new ethical ground is, thereby, broken.

14.61 The status of the anencephalic neonate is considered further in chapter 16. Here, it need only be said that treatment of the infant who exists only by virtue of a residual brain stem is, perhaps, the quintessential example of medical futility.[118] On the other hand, the anencephalic is, by existing standards, legally a 'creature in being' to whom the existing rules of homicide apply. Thus, the neonate must be allowed a natural death which, save in exceptional circumstances, will occur within about one week.[119] Two major difficulties arise from this – first, as to the diagnosis of death in such circumstances and, secondly, as to the unpalatable corollary that the dead neonate or abortus must be reanimated if it is to provide undamaged organs. As to the former, the Royal Colleges and their Faculties in the United Kingdom have concluded that: 'organs for transplantation can be removed from anencephalic infants when two doctors who are not members of the transplant team agree that spontaneous respiration has ceased.'[120] On the face of things, this seems to be doing no more than restating a diagnostic test for death which has been, and still is, the norm – moreover, the test is equally applicable to fetuses who have been fatally brain damaged during delivery and who might, exceptionally, be considered as donors. More importantly, perhaps, it pre-empts suggestions that anencephaly per se should carry a presumption of death[121] – for the surviving anencephalic neonate is in the same position as is the adult in the persistent vegetative state.[122] It is, therefore, both unnecessary and impracticable to attempt to introduce a brain death standard. There is, however, a further practical difficulty in that fetal tissues – and particularly the heart – are extremely sensitive to 'warm anoxia' – the best results from the small number of cases reported are said to have come from those infants who were placed on life support and the organs used as soon as possible without regard to the existence of brain stem activity.[123] The time required to satisfy the Royal Colleges' criterion of cessation of respiration may, therefore, dictate an unacceptable deterioration in the quality of the donor organs which,

---

117 For which see para 20.26 below.
118 See para 16.78 below for the important US case *In the matter of Baby K* 16 F 3d 590 (4th Cir, 1994). The findings at first instance are recapitulated in T L Beauchamp and R M Veatch *Ethical Issues in Death and Dying* (2nd edn, 1996), chapter 8, p 376.
119 P A Baird and A D Sadovinich 'Survival in Infants with Anencephaly' (1984) 23 Clin Pediat 268. Interestingly, an exception arose in the high profile case of Baby K, above, who survived for over two years.
120 Report of the Working Party of the Conference of Medical Royal Colleges and their Faculties in the United Kingdom on Organ Transplantation in Neonates (1988).
121 D Brahams 'Transplantation, the Fetus and the Law' (1988) 138 NLJ 91.
122 See chapter 17.
123 The Medical Task Force on Anencephaly 'The Infant with Anencephaly' (1990) 322 New Engl J Med 669.

in general, must be recovered from a 'beating heart' donor. But this practice depends, as we have seen, on the acceptance of 'brain stem death' and the transplant surgeon is left with a well-nigh insoluble dilemma – so much so that at least one authoritative commentator has questioned whether it is possible to establish death legally in an anencephalic and, at the same time, preserve the best interests of the recipient of its organs.[124] Attempts to redefine death in the anencephalic as a state of 'brain absence' or to regard such a neonate as 'not being a reasonable creature in being' seem to us to be examples of semantic juggling which should be resisted; the same applies to the more extreme suggestion that the definition of death should be extended so as to include anencephalics as a group[125] – as McCullagh has observed:

> Classification as 'dead' will not cause an anencephalic who is breathing to cease doing so ... One would require also to accept the burial of a spontaneously breathing patient.[126]

14.62 The more honest approach is to accept that, at the least, the legality and morality of anencephalic donations are matters for concern and that it is probable that their eventual solution will be founded on strongly utilitarian rather than strict deontological principles.

14.63 The implicit result of using the Royal Colleges' criteria is that anencephalic donation must involve some form of 'reanimation ventilation'. This inevitably introduces moral qualms – not the least being that the period of 'deanimation' will be unacceptably short – and, at the end of the day, one has to ask whether the manifest invasion of normal ethical standards is justified by results. It has been estimated that the use of anencephalic neonates would result in the availability of not more than 20 suitable donors each year in the United Kingdom;[127] the surprisingly low yield of organs which would accrue in the United States has been emphasised[128] as has their poor quality and associated distressingly bad therapeutic success rate.[129]

14.64 All these factors were considered in what appears to be the only extant judicial consideration of the status of the anencephalic – at least in the English speaking jurisdictions.[130] The circumstances of T's birth were widely publicised. She was born anencephalic and, during her life of nine days, her parents sought to have her declared dead so that her organs could be used to save other lives. The circuit court judge held that she was not brain dead but, nevertheless, gave permission for a single kidney to be removed on the grounds

124 S McLean 'Facing the Dilemma of a Life and Death Issue' (1991) Scotsman, 26 August, p 9. For a similar US view, see J L Peabody, J R Emery and S Ashwal 'Experience with Anencephalic Infants as Prospective Organ Donors' (1989) 321 New Engl J Med 344.
125 For review, see W F May 'Brain Death: Anencephalics and Aborted Fetuses' (1990) 22 Transplant Proc 885.
126 P McCullagh *Brain Dead, Brain Absent, Brain Donors* (1993) p 168.
127 See J R Salaman 'Anencephalic Organ Donors' (1989) 298 BMJ 622.
128 See May, para 14.61 above, reporting the findings, in particular, of Shewmon.
129 D A Shewmon, A M Capron, W J Peacock and B L Schulman 'The Use of Anencephalic Infants as Organ Sources' (1989) 261 J Amer Med Ass 1773.
130 *Re T A C P* 609 So 2d 588 (Fla, 1992).

that this was not harming her. This ruling was upheld in the District Court of Appeal but, despite the fact that the baby was now dead, the Supreme Court of Florida then agreed to accept the case as one which 'raised a question of great public importance requiring immediate resolution'. Much of the court's deliberation concerned the common and statute law of Florida but questions of principle were also addressed. Having established that T was legally alive at the relevant time, the parents' request that an additional common law standard of death applicable to anencephalics was considered in the light of current technology. It was held:

> Our review of the medical, ethical, and legal literature on anencephaly discloses absolutely no consensus that public necessity or fundamental rights will be better served by granting this request. [131]

and, later:

> We acknowledge the possibility that some infants' lives might be saved by using organs from anencephalics who do not meet the traditional definition of 'death' we affirm to-day. But weighed against this is the utter lack of consensus, and the questions about the overall utility of such organ donations. The scales clearly tip in favor of not extending the common law in this instance. [132]

14.65 Thus, the essential ethical problem is to decide whether the utilitarian advantages stemming from anencephalic organ donation are sufficient to offset the inherent deontological doubts raised by the procedure.[133] A 'cost-benefit' analysis inclines us to the view that the price is too high. The balance is, however, finely adjusted;[134] there might well be a case for further consideration should transplantation techniques improve to the extent that it can be shown clearly that, once obtained, organs from anencephalics offer a genuine prospect of life to those who are otherwise condemned to death.

14.66 The question would then remain whether a woman can properly choose to carry an affected baby close to term purely to provide transplantable organs. Such a programme appears, at first sight, to be unethical on the grounds that a human being is being used as a means. Yet, to prevent it could be seen as unreasonable paternalism. A veto not only *might* deprive potential recipients of life but it would also strike a direct blow at a woman's right to control her body. We would not support a total ban on what may be a truly altruistic endeavour – but it is an aspect of transplantation therapy which must merit very careful scrutiny.

---

131 Ibid at 594.
132 Ibid at 595.
133 M Harrison 'Organ Procurement for Children: The Anencephalic Fetus as Donor' (1986) 2 Lancet 1383. For criticism of the utilitarian view, see A Davies 'The Status of Anencephalic Babies: Should Their Bodies Be Used as Donor Banks?' (1988) 14 J Med Ethics 150.
134 For an international assessment, see L S Rothenberg 'The Anencephalic Neonate and Brain Death: An International Review of Medical, Ethical and Legal Issues' (1990) 22 Transplant Proc 1037.

FETAL BRAIN IMPLANTS

14.67 Normal adult nerve cells cannot replicate, whereas fetal cells are actively growing and multiplying; theoretically, therefore, an implanted fetal nerve cell will grow and provide a source of important cellular metabolites that are often deficient in the aged. The use of fetal neural tissue for the treatment of Parkinsonism[135] in the elderly – and its extension to the treatment of other degenerative diseases of the ageing brain – was, at one time, a burning issue. Much of the urgency has now been dispelled as a moratorium has been agreed as to further clinical trials. Moreover, enthusiasm for the procedure has been, to a large extent, diverted to the more fashionable quest for stem-cell therapy (for which, see chapter 20). None the less, the procedure raises a number of legal and ethical problems which should be kept in mind – and we see four of these as being of major importance.

14.68 In contrast to fetal organs, fetal brain cells must be immature and are ideally harvested at 10-14 weeks' gestation. Thus, the first problem is that, excluding the rare opportunities derived from natural spontaneous miscarriage – and all commentators accept that there is a clear moral distinction to be made – the process is inextricably linked to abortion. The legal consequence is that fetal brain therapy is largely governed by the Abortion Act 1967; morally speaking, those who are opposed to abortion can accept fetal brain implantation only on the basis that it is desirable to extract some good from an intrinsically bad action if it is possible to do so[136] – and by no means all moralists would agree to such a proposition.[137] Certainly, virtually everyone would agree that a termination of pregnancy and any subsequent transplantation must be dissociated; the prospect of a woman becoming pregnant in order to provide therapeutic material for an aged relative is scarcely acceptable – as Nolan has put it, it involves seeing fetuses as valuable primarily for their medicinal properties rather than for their stunning developmental potential. Secondly, it is obvious that the individual brain cells must be viable in themselves; can it then be said that the fetus is dead when subjected to surgery? Here, we must rely to an extent on semantic and pragmatic arguments. A 10-14 week-old fetus is not viable – it has no organised heart beat, its lungs cannot conceivably function as oxygenators and, once delivered, it is so clearly not born alive that its existence will go unrecorded save in respect of the abortion regulations; it follows that it is born dead. Moreover, in practice, the technique of abortion will have been so traumatic to the fetus as to preclude

135   Note that there is a clinical distinction to be made between idiopathic Parkinson's disease and the signs of Parkinsonism which occur in several other conditions: Editorial Comment 'Parkinson's Disease: One Illness or Many Syndromes?' (1992) 339 Lancet 1263.

136   J A Robertson 'The Ethical Acceptability of Fetal Tissue Transplants' (1990) 22 Transplant Proc 1025 argues, persuasively, that the physician using the material has no complicity in obtaining it. The discussion is continued by K Nolan 'The Use of Embryo or Fetus in Transplantation: What There Is to Lose' (1990) 22 Transplant Proc 1029, who concludes that the use of fetal tissues obtained after elective abortion is justified only as a last resort.

137   See R Gillon 'Ethics of Fetal Brain Cell Transplants' (1988) 296 BMJ 1212 for a brief report of expressed attitudes. For extended analysis, see D G Jones 'Fetal Neural Transplantation: Placing the Ethical Debate Within the Context of Society's Use of Human Material' (1991) 5 Bioethics 23.

any form of life as it is generally accepted. But, be that as it may, it is still very difficult to answer the question: 'Is it brain dead?' in the affirmative.

14.69 Thirdly, we cannot overlook the revulsion with which most people view any form of tampering with the brain and particularly the idea of 'brain transplants' – as well they might when it is seriously argued that a severed and perfused head might exist more happily than one attached to an aching body.[138] There is, of course, no suggestion that such developments are remotely upon us; nevertheless, the BMA's recommendation that nervous tissue should only be used for transplantation in the form of isolated neurones or tissue fragments[139] should be fully endorsed.[140] Finally, there is some moral repugnance to the use of tissues from the very young to sustain the aged. This is unfair in the present context for the aged are just as entitled to available treatment as is any other population group. But we must ensure that it is true treatment designed to ameliorate specific disease processes. Dr Faustus, in his quest for eternal youth, is scarcely admirable but there are few who have passed middle age who could honestly deny at least a touch of sympathy for his objectives; it is important that we do not seek to force the role of Mephistopheles upon the neurosurgeon.[141]

138 C Fleming 'If We Can Keep a Severed Head Alive ...' (1988) 297 BMJ 1048.
139 Medical Ethics 'Transplantation of Fetal Material' (1988) 296 BMJ 1410.
140 The question of the persona and brain tissue transplants is discussed in G Northoff 'Do Brain Tissue Transplants Alter Personal Identity? Inadequacies of some "Standard" Arguments' (1996) 22 J Med Ethics 174. See the associated editorial comment R Gillon 'Brain Transplantation, Personal Identity and Medical Ethics' (1996) 22 J Med Ethics 131.
141 For an excellent review of the agonies of a Research Review Committee, see A S MacDonald 'Foetal Neuroendocrine Tissue Transplantation for Parkinson's Disease: An Institutional Review Board Faces the Ethical Dilemma' (1990) 22 Transplant Proc 1030.

15 The body as property

15.1 We have encountered examples of moral, ethical and legal recognition of the relationship between the concept of 'self' and the physical entity known as 'the human body' at many junctures in the discussion thus far. In particular, the central position in medical law of the principle of respect for the patient's autonomy determines that the individual patient has the ultimate right to control his or her body and what is done with or to it. Primarily, that control is exercised through the concept of consent to and its correlate, refusal of treatment. Thus, we have seen in chapter 10 that disrespect of a refusal to an invasive procedure can result in actions in negligence or for assault and the use and storage of gametes is strictly controlled according to the written consent of the donor under the Human Fertilisation and Embryology Act 1990 (see chapter 3). That said, it is by no means the case that we have an absolute right, either ethically or legally, to do whatever we want with our bodies – we have noted how the Human Organ Transplants Act 1989 prohibits 'trade' in organs and the House of Lords was categoric in *R v Brown*[1] that ritual physical abuse of the body for sexual pleasure remains criminal even when undertaken within the envelope of full and informed consent by the parties involved. The question therefore arises as to what limits are set to the right to control our bodies. In recent years, this debate has centred around the very important issue of the status of the body as property. This chapter will consider three aspects of that debate: property in material taken from living persons; property in material taken from cadavers; and the granting of intellectual property rights in human material.

PROPERTY IN LIVING HUMAN MATERIAL

15.2 Intuitively, it is perfectly natural for us to talk of 'my body' and to infer that, because it is 'my' body, I can determine precisely what is done to it or its parts. Moreover, for most people, this feeling is inherently bound up with the proprietary notion that, because my body is my own, I 'own' my body. However,

---

1   *R v Brown* [1994] 1 AC 212, [1993] 2 All ER 75.

it is far from clear that there is support for this in either legal or ethical terms. No ethical principle or imperative exists on which one can ground a property right in oneself.[2] And, as Harris has pointed out, it is a 'spectacular non sequitur' to deduce that, because no one can make a slave of me and own my body, I necessarily own my body myself.[3] Indeed, the idea of property is primarily a legal one. It is a construct which allows us to order our society according to a chosen value system which, in turn, greatly facilitates the achievement of certain of our social goals – in our case, those of most Western states which encourage commerce and sanction commodification. The role of ethics lies not in grounding a property right but in determining whether it is appropriate to commodify something such as the human body which, for reasons we have already discussed in chapter 1, has a particular moral status deserving of respect. Thus, for many, the idea that one can buy or sell body parts is repugnant in that it shows disrespect for the status of 'the human body'.[4] Trade in body parts also gives rise to the spectre of exploitation, which is ethically questionable because it has the potential to harm those who are exploited. The counter to this, of course, is that, while no one would sanction forced participation in the trade of body parts, it is unduly paternalistic to eschew the consent of individuals who would willingly sell their tissues.[5] It is on just such a basis, amongst others, that the Human Organ Transplants Act 1989 has been criticised as being an unsophisticated knee-jerk reaction to a serious problem open to a workable solution.[6]

15.3 Matters are further complicated by the opaqueness of the law as to the actual status of body parts in property terms. Thus, while there is evidence in the case law which suggests that regenerative body material such as hair,[7] blood[8] and urine[9] can be the subject of property,[10] the United Kingdom courts and legislatures have been, on the whole, reluctant to address this issue directly.[11] The Human Organ Transplants Act 1989 says nothing about property in organs as such and merely criminalises those who would attempt to trade in the material. Similarly, in controlling the use and storage of gametes, the Human Fertilisation and Embryology Act 1990 relies on the expressed written wishes of the donor of gametes but falls far short of acknowledging a property right in any sample. This should be compared with the Court of Appeal of California's

---

2   However, for argument to this effect, see D Beyleveld and R Brownsword *Human Dignity in Bioethics and Biolaw* (2001), ch 8.
3   J W Harris 'Who Owns My Body' (1996) 16 OJLS 55 at 71.
4   L Skene 'Arguments Against People Legally 'Owning' Their Own Bodies, Body Parts and Tissue' (2002) 2 MacQuarie LJ 165. Also cf, S R Munzer 'An Uneasy Case Against Property Rights in Body Parts' (1994) 11 Soc Philosoph Pol 259, and A Ryan 'Self-Ownership, Autonomy and Property Rights' (1994) 11 Soc Philosoph Pol 241.
5   M M Friedlaender 'The Right to Sell or Buy a Kidney: Are We Failing Our Patients?' (2002) 359 Lancet 971.
6   J Radcliffe-Richards et al 'The Case of Allowing Kidney Sales' (1998) 351 Lancet 1950.
7   *R v Herbert* (1961) 25 JCL 163.
8   *R v Rothery* [1976] RTR 550, (1976) 63 Crim App Rep 231.
9   *R v Welsh* [1974] RTR 478.
10 In each of these criminal cases, the accused was convicted of theft for removing the 'property' of another without permission. Eg in *Rothery* the accused gave a sample of blood to be tested for alcohol levels and then 'stole' it by removing it from the police station.
11 Cf, the Supreme Court of Western Australia ruled in *Roche v Douglas* [2000] WAR 331 that human tissue taken from a deceased person was 'property' for the purposes of its court rules; this allowed the court then to claim dominion over the sample to authorise testing to settle a familial paternity dispute.

decision in *Hecht v Kane*,[12] in which the court held that a deceased man who had previously deposited sperm for the use of his partner had an interest 'in the nature of ownership' of the samples such as to render them 'property' within the meaning of the Probate Code and, accordingly, disposable property on his death.[13] Similarly, the German Bundesgerichtshof has ruled that excised body parts that are not intended for another (such as transplant organs) or for return to the individual (such as stored sperm), are subject to the normal rules of personal property.[14] These decisions should be contrasted with the French case of *Parpalaix v CECOS*,[15] in which the court ordered the return of frozen sperm to the wife of the depositor on the basis of an agreement which had been made between him and the sperm bank. It refused, however, to go so far as to recognise any property interest in the sperm.[16]

The embryo in vitro

15.4 The Human Fertilisation and Embryology Authority is equally indecisive as to the disposal of embryos which are created for assisted reproduction but which are not used for the purpose. Once again, the 1990 Act avoids any recognition of property rights and control over the use and disposal of the frozen embryos falls to be determined by the will of the parties contributing to their formation. However, unlike gametes, two parties provide the genetic material contained in embryos. Who, then, has the power to dispose of them?

15.5 In this respect, Sch 3 to the 1990 Act provides that effective written consent must be given by each person whose gametes have contributed to the embryo.[17] In practice, this gives either contributor a veto over its use but it provides neither with rights of disposal – the embryos must be allowed to perish if the gamete providers cannot agree and the storage time for the embryo has exceeded the statutory limit.[18]

15.6 The regulations which govern storage of gametes and embryos provide that the initial storage period of five years may be extended up to ten years,

---

12   16 Cal App 4th 836 (1993).
13   Similarly, the Tennessee Supreme Court held in *Davis v Davis* 842 SW 2d 588 (1992) that the embryo occupied an 'interim category' as neither 'person' nor 'property', yet which entitled it to a special respect. While the parties were denied 'a true property interest' they retained an interest, 'in the nature of ownership' in relation to the use and disposal of their pre-embryos.
14   Bundesgerichtshof, 9 November 1993, BGHZ, 124, 52.
15   JCP 1984.II.20321. In subsequent cases the French court struggled to find a valid basis in law for dealing with embryos and sperm, vacillating between the law of obligations on the one hand and the principle of 'the established family' on the other: see (1996) *La Semaine Juridique* Ed G, No 27, 22666.
16   The current position in France is embodied in Law No 94-653 of 29 July 1994, which was incorporated into the public health code. Article 16 excludes the human body, its products and its parts from being the subject of property law. See also, the National Consultative Ethics Committee for Health and Life Sciences (CCNE) *Opinion that the human body should not be used for commercial purposes* (Opinion No 21, 1990).
17   Schedule 3, para 6(3).
18   Human Fertilisation and Embryology (Statutory Storage Period for Embryos) Regulations 1996, SI 1996/375, r 14(1)(c). As we go to press, two women are contesting the veto powers of their partners who have changed their minds: F Gibb 'Separated Women Seek Right to Use Frozen Embryos' *The Times*, 12 September 2002, p 9.

and in some cases longer, so long as the gamete providers do not lodge an objection when asked to reaffirm their consent to storage. It is important to note here that actual written reconfirmation of such consent is required. This can be problematic at a number of levels, particularly if a couple who have provided gametes has separated or if gametes have been supplied by a donor who is no longer traceable. In each case, the embryos will be allowed to die if no reconfirmation is obtained.[19]

15.7 We view this system of consents with a degree of concern. In the absence of any property right in embryos, the aim for which they have been created can be thwarted easily by the withholding of consent by a potentially disinterested, bitter or uncontactable contributor. Thus, the person for whom they were intended, that is the woman who was to carry one or more of them, will be denied the opportunity to benefit from the original treatment proposed. While we do not suggest that a property system would be problem-free, we believe that to recognise a property right in embryos which vests, in the first instance, in the woman who is to receive treatment would go a long way to resolving the current controversies surrounding these issues. It should not be forgotten that a considerable number of embryos had to be destroyed at the end of the first five-year period of storage precisely because of the difficulties outlined above.[20] The mere creation of a facility to extend the storage period will not make the problems go away.

The fetus in vivo and fetal materials

15.8 Whatever may be said about the embryo in vitro, there should be no support for extending a woman's property right to an implanted fetus. A clear moral distinction is to be made between the in vitro and the in vivo human organism, not least because of the immediate potentiality of the latter to become a complete human being.[21] It is to be noted that the Polkinghorne Committee[22] suggested that provision be made in any consent to fetal research procedures for the relinquishment of property rights 'if, indeed, there be any' (para 8.4). This clearly refers to maternal rights in respect of the fetus. Times have, however, changed since 1989. While the Polkinghorne Committee regarded the dissociation of the use of fetal tissues and abortion as the overriding consideration, others might now see it as anomalous if a 'profit sharing' agreement were enforceable between a biotechnological institute and the donor when the tissues of a living person were used but the institute could escape any duty of financial recompense by using tissues from a fetus.

15.9 But what of a non-viable or stillborn fetus and/or fetal material that is discharged from the mother as result of either a medical termination or a spontaneous miscarriage? The potentiality for viable human life has clearly ended in such a case[23] and we must consider the possibility of property rights

19 Schedule 3, para 6(3).
20 K D Hopkins 'First Batch of Human Embryos Destroyed in UK' (1996) 348 Lancet 399.
21 Although the fetus is not a legal person, the concept of it being 'property' is too close to that of slavery for comfort.
22 *Review of the Guidance on the Research use of Fetuses and Fetal Material* (Cm 762, 1989).
23 The possible exception to this is the living abortus which we discuss in chapter 5.

afresh. The Polkinghorne Committee refused to address this issue and preferred, instead, to recommend that the full and informed consent of the woman be obtained concerning the use and/or disposal of the material. While we acknowledge that, in moral terms, a dead fetus might command greater respect than fetal material *in se*, we do not consider that the recognition of a property interest in either necessarily involves such a degree of disrespect as would lead us to refuse to recognise any such interest. The potential value of any tissue is,[24] nowadays, uncertain but is surely increasing and we suggest that the mother of the fetus should retain any available property claim not only in respect of the fetus itself but also of its associated materials. Of course, the matters of ownership and disposal should be approached cautiously and with sensitivity at such an emotional time.

The Nuffield Report

15.10 The themes of abandonment and consent figured large in the April 1995 report of the Nuffield Council on Bioethics, which addressed the question of property in body parts generally – including gametes, embryos and fetal material.[25] After reviewing the legal and ethical position on human tissue, the Council made its recommendations in light of the provisions of the Human Tissue Act 1961, the Human Organ Transplants Act 1989 and the Anatomy Act 1984, from which it is clear, first, that any tissue given or taken from individuals is received free of all claims and, second, that the common law position is, as yet, unsettled. It recommended that any disputed claim over material should be settled with regard to the nature of the consent given to the initial procedure for removal. Moreover, it was the Council's view that it should be implied in any consent to medical treatment which involves the removal of tissue that the tissue has been abandoned by the person from whom it was removed.[26] It was recommended that tissue removed from an individual who is unable to give valid consent should not be the subject of any claim, either by the incapax or by his or her representatives.[27]

15.11 The Council's recommendations are certainly in keeping with the trend which has emerged in the United Kingdom to date.[28] Yet, we cannot help but feel that the Council, like the courts and legislature before it, was reluctant to face the real issues concerning body ownership head-on.[29] Stark et al studied

---

24 See para 15.12 below.
25 Nuffield Council on Bioethics *Human Tissue: Ethical and Legal Issues* (1995).
26 Ibid, ch 9, in particular para 9.14.
27 Para 15.10 above, paras 9.15–9.17.
28 Eg, the Medical Research Council has stated that: 'The human body and its parts shall not, as such give rise to financial gain. Researchers may not sell for a profit samples of human biological material that they have collected as part of MRC funded research, and research participants should never be offered any financial inducement to donate samples', see MRC *Human Tissue and Biological Samples for Use in Research: Operational and Ethical Guidelines* (2001), Part 2. This reflects the terms of Article 21 of the Council of Europe Convention on Human Rights and Biomedicine, although it is important to note that both the Convention and the MRC draw a distinction between no property in the body and its parts *as such* and 'inventions' using human material which may be subject to intellectual property rights. We discuss this further below.
29 For a full discussion, see P Matthews 'The Man of Property' (1995) 3 Med L Rev 251.

the attitudes of a small sample of in-patients but this sheds little light on the major current ethical debate over body parts and does not help us as to the actual or potential legal position.[30] It is telling, for example, that few of those surveyed had been told about the possible uses of the material. Indeed, more recent evidence suggests a shift in cultural attitude towards self-ownership among certain sectors of the community. The Medical Research Council's survey on the perceptions of the public on the collection and use of human biological samples found that of those surveyed, younger people tended to view payment for such samples as a matter of right – or they were, at least, open to the prospect.[31] This was especially so when research was likely to generate income for commercial organisations. In contrast, members of the older generation tended to adhere to the classic gift paradigm, expecting nothing in return for altruistic and public spirited donations.[32] However, support for allowing volunteers to retain a degree of ownership in donated samples was also found among GPs and nurses who took part in the survey.[33]

15.12 The Nuffield Council's report was based, in the main, on the premise that people see no value in their excised body parts; this premise has long dominated this area of debate, yet it is one which has always been questionable and is easily challenged today. 'Value' exists in a variety of forms. Consider the value which we attach to fetal tissue and the controversy which has surrounded proposed research and therapies using such tissue (see chapter 16). Consider, too, the fact that we find it meaningful to continue to talk about '*my* appendix' and '*my* gall stones' even when these materials have been removed from our bodies. Perhaps most significantly of all, the advent of the biotechnological age has meant that there can be considerable economic value which accrues to biotechnological products produced using human material. Thus, to assert, as the Council does, that patients should be deemed to abandon their tissues, is to ignore the potential values which those very persons may well hold in retaining control over such material. A system of consents does not permit that control to be exercised as fully as might be desirable.

Commercialism and human material

15.13 Gold has noted, for example, that, because the courts tend to ignore sociological, psychological and anthropological attitudes towards the body and, instead, reduce everything to economics, they ignore signs of people's ambiguity about technological advancement.[34] It is widely assumed that the

---

30 The survey showed that only 10% of hospital patients believed that they retained ownership of tissue removed after surgery, while 47% thought that the material belonged either to the hospital (27%) or to the laboratory (20%). Only 27% of those surveyed were of the opinion that no one owned the material: R D Start et al 'Ownership and Uses of Human Tissue: Does the Nuffield Bioethics Report Accord with Opinion of Surgical Inpatients?' (1996) 313 BMJ 1366.
31 Medical Research Council, *Public Perceptions of the Collection of Human Biological Samples*, (2000).
32 At para 6.12.
33 At para 17.
34 E R Gold *Body Parts: Ownership of Human Biological Material* (1996).

interposition of commercial interests between the source of valuable material and its user is unacceptable because it leads necessarily to exploitation. At the same time, it is accepted that the encouragement of commercial profit-making by users, primarily by the biotechnology industry, can only bring benefits to the community in the guise of more therapies and cures. But, as Gold correctly observes, giving property rights to biotechnology researchers focuses the medical industry primarily on cure and shifts attention away from the equally, or more, important pursuit of determining – and eradicating – the underlying causes of illness and disease.[35] Similarly, as we discuss in the context of surrogacy (see chapter 3), it is not necessarily exploitative *in se* to offer financial incentives or rewards to individuals to use their bodies in certain ways. As Andrews has said in the context of that debate, it may be more devaluing to persons not to recognise their worth in monetary terms for the contributions they can make to society from the use of their bodies than it is to protect them from potential predators – provided, always, that the value that they represent is not entirely reducible to those terms.[36] That something is potentially exploitative does not mean that it must always be so, and it certainly does not justify the courts' refusing to deal directly with the real interests and issues.

15.14 The case which most clearly betrays the skewed attitude of the judiciary towards these matters is *Moore v Regents of the University of California*.[37] John Moore suffered from hairy cell leukaemia and his spleen was removed at the Medical School of the University of California at Los Angeles. His doctor, Dr Golde, discovered that cells from the spleen had unusual and potentially beneficial properties and developed an immortal cell-line from them without his patient's knowledge or consent. Moreover, Dr Golde sought, and obtained, a patent over the cell-line which he subsequently sold to a drug company for $15m – and it has been reported that the drugs and therapies which were developed from the patented product are now worth in excess of $3b.[38] Moore brought an action against the researchers, the university and the drug company when he discovered the truth about his cells. He filed 13 causes of action in total but those concerning the questions of property and consent are of most direct interest. In particular, he alleged *conversion* – that, as the 'owner' of the cells, his property right had been compromised by the work carried out on the cells by the defendants. He also alleged breach of fiduciary duty and lack of informed consent because he had never been told of the potential use of his cells and, correspondingly, he had never given his full and informed agreement to the initial operation. The Californian Supreme Court upheld these two last claims but rejected the argument in conversion. The court opined that it was inappropriate to recognise property in the body, first, because no precedent could be found on which to ground such a claim and, secondly, because to recognise individual property rights in body parts would be to hinder medical research 'by restricting access to the necessary raw materials' – a pure utilitarian consideration. Moreover, the court was concerned that a contrary decision would '[threaten] to destroy the economic

---

35 Ibid, p 37.
36 L B Andrews 'Beyond Doctrinal Boundaries: A Legal Framework for Surrogate Motherhood' (1995) 81 Virginia Law Rev 2343.
37 793 P 2d 479 (Cal, 1990). See also, *Brotherton v Cleveland* 923 F 2d 661 (6th Cir, 1991).
38 B Merz, 'Biotechnology: Spleen-Rights' *The Economist*, 11 August 1990, p 30.

incentive to conduct important medical research' because '[i]f the use of cells in research is a conversion, then with every cell sample a researcher purchases a ticket in a litigation lottery'.[39] The irony of this decision is pointed out in the dissent of Broussard J:

> ... the majority's analysis cannot rest on the broad proposition that a removed part is not property, but ... on the proposition that a *patient* retains no ownership interest in a body part once the body part has been removed. (Emphasis added.)

15.15 Thus, while each of us is denied recognition of a property interest in excised parts of our bodies, third parties may not only gain such an interest but can go on to protect such an interest using forms of property law such as the law of patents.

15.16 But does not such an example demonstrate precisely the kind of value which individuals could retain in their excised parts? The properties of the patient's cells are a *sine qua non* of the ultimate invention. And, while no one would deny that much time and money would need to be expended in turning the natural material into a patentable product, is the view of the Supreme Court in *Moore* not something of an over-reaction to the *possible* consequences of applying property law to the human body? It is entirely reasonable to hold that some financial reward should also be given to the source of the valuable sample while, at the same time, accepting that the majority of the spoils should return to those who have done the work in creating a patentable product. It is *not* reasonable to exclude completely from the equation the one person who can make everything possible. Furthermore, policy is not always on the side of the researchers, as another on-going American dispute demonstrates very well. In *Greenberg et al v Miami Children's Hospital Research Institute Inc*,[40] a law suit has been brought by parents of children affected by a rare, fatal and incurable genetic disorder called Canavan disease against researchers who developed and patented a test for the disease using samples donated by the families. The defendants had worked closely with afflicted families receiving samples and gaining access to registers containing details of other affected groups around the world. However, when the Canavan gene was eventually identified the researchers sought a patent over it and a related test and proceeded to restrict access to the latter save through tightly controlled exclusive licences. The plaintiffs objected strongly and, in much the same way as happened in *Moore*, have mounted an action on a number of grounds, including lack of informed consent, breach of fiduciary duty and conversion. In this last respect, the plaintiffs claim a property interest in their samples, the genetic information therein and information contained in the Canavan Register. Paradoxically, however, this case stands in stark contrast to *Moore*, for here policy favours the plaintiffs: the families want information about the disease and the test to be freely available, while it is the patent holders who wish to

---

39 For comment on *Moore*, see B Hoffmaster 'Between the Sacred and the Profane: Bodies, Property, and Patents in the *Moore* Case' (1992) 7 Intellect Prop J 115 and E B Seeney, 'Moore 10 Years Later – Still Trying to Fill the Gap: Creating a Personal Property Right in Genetic Material' (1998) 32 New England Law Rev 1131.

40 At the time of writing the proceedings were tied up in a complicated jurisdictional dispute, see Illinois (Eastern Division) District Court, (2002) WL 1483266 (ND Ill).

restrict access and so potentially hinder research. It seems, then, that policy is finely balanced on either side.

15.17 We have argued elsewhere that the time has now come to recognise a modified form of property rights for individuals in their own (excised) body parts.[41] We should not to be distracted from the property debate by the illusion that consent is the sole, or optimal, ethico-legal solution to the dilemmas thrown up by modern medicine, as many official bodies would have us believe.[42] A consent model disempowers individuals to the extent that the single 'right' that it gives is a right to refuse. How does this help the person who is willing to participate in medical research but has qualms about the subsequent use of his samples towards undesirable ends? It does not, for his only option is not to participate.[43] A property right would, at least, allow an element of continuing control over such samples after surrender and would allow for a legally recognised voice in how they are used. The same is not true once an initial consent has been obtained, for so long as the requisite information is disclosed at the time the sample is provided the sample source's 'rights' have, thereby, been exhausted. It is uncertain how far these views would be accepted in the courts in the United Kingdom.

15.18 This does not, however, take us very far with the question of disposal of the commercially valueless specimen. We suggest that a consent-based action in negligence would be available if, for example, a patient's susceptibilities were outraged by his tissues being used for demonstration purposes but this is by no means certain. Fortunately, the question is of no more than academic interest in the overwhelming majority of cases.

Tissues at molecular level

15.19 As a final point, we bring the reader's attention to the United States federal Genetic Privacy Act 1995, which we discuss in the context of control over genetic information in chapter 7. In an unprecedented move, this piece of legislation vests a right of property in a DNA sample in the source of that sample. Thus, in addition to requiring clear written consent from the donor in respect of the gathering and use of any DNA material, the Act puts him in a stronger bargaining position in respect of any potentially profitable research work which might be carried out on his sample. Lin argues that this approach promotes, rather than hinders, research because those previously hesitant to provide samples now have an incentive to do so.[44] We would agree, and add

---

41   K Mason and G Laurie 'Consent or Property? Dealing with the Body and its Parts in the Shadow of Bristol and Alder Hey' (2001) 64 MLR 711. Cf C H Harrison 'Neither Moore nor the Market: Alternative Models for Compensating Contributors of Human Tissue' (2002) 28 Am J L and Med 77.
42   See, eg, Nuffield Council, para 15.10 above, and Human Genetics Commission, *Inside Information: Balancing interests in the Use of Personal Genetic Data* (2002), para 5.25: '... best practice requires that the question of commercial involvement in research or access to genetic databases should be fully explained at the time of obtaining participants' consent.'
43   Nor could he seek to impose conditions on his donation as there is no obvious legal right to have those conditions respected.
44   M M J Lin 'Conferring a Federal Property Right in Genetic Material: Stepping into the Future with the Genetic Privacy Act' (1996) 22 Am J Law Med 109.

that it also clarifies the legal position substantially and makes for a more principled approach to the question of ownership of body parts. While the full impact of this model law remains to be seen, we believe that the Act could be but the first step on the road to full recognition of ownership of one's own body and its parts. However, the experience in Oregon does not augur well. There a property right in genetic samples was granted to citizens in 1995, but after several years of intensive lobbying by the pharmaceutical industry and research institutes, a reforming Bill was passed in June 2001 that removed this right and replaced it with more stringent privacy protection.[45] The claim is that Oregon will now have the most far-reaching privacy legislation of its kind in the United States to protect citizens' interests, but we remain convinced that the Oregon experiment was not given sufficient time for the promise and the pitfalls of a property paradigm to be and addressed and explored. More openness of spirit prevails elsewhere. The Australian Law Reform Commission is currently undertaking a consultation on whether individuals should have a form of property right in their own genetic material. It is pointed out in the Issues Paper, for example, that: '[t]he recognition or creation of donor property rights might allow donors to negotiate with researchers for the use of their genetic samples and contract to share in any resulting commercial benefits'.[46] This consultation was partly prompted by the Genetic Privacy and Anti-discrimination Bill 1998 which was based on the 1995 American Act and which appeared before the Australian Parliament but was defeated. Although the Australian Bill did not go as far as to recognise a property right in samples, it did require individuals' authorisation either to waive or to receive economic benefits deriving from their samples.[47] In the UK, the Human Genetics Commission did not address the issue directly, preferring instead to fall back, once again, on the familiar consent model.[48]

PROPERTY IN CADAVERS AND CADAVER TISSUES

15.20 The concept that third parties can own body parts while the person from whom those parts are taken cannot do so, is also to be found in the law relating to cadavers.[49] For a long time the 'no property in a corpse' rule was thought to exclude all possibility of property in a dead body or its parts in England and Wales[50] – although there is some authority in Scotland that property can exist in a corpse, at least until it is buried or otherwise disposed of.[51] The case of *R v Kelly*[52] established, however, that there are serious limitations to any such rule which may have important consequences for the users of human tissue removed from cadavers. In *Kelly* the Court of Appeal was faced with the question

---

45 Senate Bill 114 was before the 71st Oregon Legislative Assembly (8 January – 7 July 2001).
46 ALRC *Protection of Human Genetic Information* (Issues Paper 26, 2001) para 7.47.
47 See Senate Legal and Constitutional Legislation Committee, *Provisions of the Genetic Privacy and Non-discrimination Bill 1998* (1999). There was also a right that records and samples be returned or destroyed.
48 Human Genetics Commission, para 15.17 above.
49 See, Mason and Laurie, para 15.17 above.
50 Nuffield Report, para 10.2. The Australian case *Doodeward v Spence* (1908) 6 CLR 406 is frequently cited in this regard.
51 *Dewar v HM Advocate* 1945 JC 5 at 14.
52 [1998] 3 All ER 741.

of whether it was theft for a junior technician of the Royal College of Surgeons to remove body parts for use, and ultimate disposal, by an artist who was interested in using them as moulds for his sculptures. The defendants relied on the 'no property' rule as their defence. The court held that the rule refers only to a corpse or its parts which remain in their natural state, but that:

> ... parts of a corpse are capable of being property... if they have acquired different attributes by virtue of the application of skill, such as dissection or preservation techniques, for exhibition or teaching purposes.[53]

15.21 So it was in the *Kelly* case. Work had been done on the body parts in question, such that they became specimens owned by the Royal College. To remove them without authority was, therefore, theft. The court opined, however, that the 'no property' rule is so deeply entrenched in English jurisprudence that legislative action would now be required for it to be changed *in se*. That having been said, the court went on to speculate that the common law might recognise property in human body parts even when those parts had not acquired different attributes, but if they had attracted a 'use or significance beyond their mere existence'.[54] What we are not told is who would be the holder of any such right. An answer may be found, however, in an earlier ruling by the Court of Appeal, which was approved of in *Kelly*.

15.22 In *Dobson v North Tyneside Health Authority*[55] the relatives of a woman who had died from brain tumours brought an action in negligence against the health authority for failure to diagnose the nature of the deceased's condition properly and in time. In order to succeed, however, it was important to establish whether the tumours were malignant or benign and this could only be done by examining samples from the deceased's brain. The brain had been removed by the hospital at autopsy and preserved in paraffin[56] but it had been disposed of later. The relatives therefore brought a further action against the hospital alleging that it had converted 'property' to which the relatives were entitled and that, at best, it acted as a bailee having no right of unauthorised disposal. In rejecting these claims, the Court of Appeal held that no right of possession or ownership of the brain, or indeed of the corpse, vested in the relatives. At best, a limited possessory right to a corpse is enjoyed by the executor or administrator of a deceased person but this right is only to possess the corpse with a view to its burial or disposal.[57] More importantly, the court held that the next of kin have no such legal right unless they assume the role of executor or administrator. Secondly, the court held that property rights could arise in respect of body parts where some work or skill differentiates the body or its parts from a corpse in its natural state. It quoted, with halting approval, the following passage from the Australian decision *Doodeward v Spence*,[58] which involved a dispute over the 'ownership' of a two-headed fetus:

53 At 749–750.
54 At 750.
55 [1996] 4 All ER 474, (1996) 33 BMLR 146.
56 One of us finds this hard to understand. Normal procedure would be to preserve the brain in formaldehyde and to remove small pieces which would be processed into small 'paraffin blocks' for examination. The latter would present a negligible storage problem.
57 No executor or administrator had been appointed in the present case until after the body had been disposed of.
58 (1908) 6 CLR 406 at 414, per Griffith CJ.

... when a person has by lawful exercise of work or skill so dealt with a human body or part of a human body in his lawful possession that it has acquired some attributes differentiating it from a mere corpse awaiting burial, he acquires a right to retain possession of it, at least as against any person not entitled to have it delivered to him for the purposes of burial.

15.23 Two elements from this passage are worth noting. First, any such property right which accrues, accrues to the person who does the work. Second, the property right which springs into existence is subject to the right of those with the right to possession for burial. We have already seen that no possessory right for burial purposes existed in *Dobson*. But had the brain become property? Gibson LJ did not seem to think so. The brain had not been preserved for the purposes of teaching or exhibition, nor was the case analogous to a stuffing or an embalming, which displays an intention to retain the part as a specimen. The brain had been removed and preserved only under the obligation to remove material bearing on the cause of death imposed by the Coroners Rules 1984.[59] The hospital intended to abide by these rules and was at liberty to destroy the brain once the material was no longer required by the coroner.

15.24 *Dobson* is as interesting for the questions that it does not answer as it is for those that it does. For example, as to the possessory right of executors, must the body and *all* of its parts be returned? Similarly, what is the role of intention in creating property rights? Reading *Dobson* and *Kelly* in conjunction, it seems that property rights can arise if work is done on a tissue *with the intention* of retaining the sample as a specimen or for some other purpose. But just how much, or little, work needs to be done? In *Kelly* the court indicates that dissection or preservation techniques are enough to make a sample 'property'.[60] If so, then merely to carry out an autopsy or to place a sample in formaldehyde is enough to create 'property'.[61] And, as we have seen from *Dobson*, that property belongs to he who would 'use' the goods and certainly not to the source or his/her significant others. Thus, if the Court of Appeal in *Kelly* is correct and the common law does one day move to the position that property rights may arise because of the 'inherent' valuable attributes in tissue samples, it is undoubtedly the case that such rights will vest in the 'discoverer' of those properties. Current proposals for long-overdue reform of the law relating to cadavers, which we discuss in more depth in chapter 14, leave open the position on accrual of property rights, but seem to favour the continuation of the 'no property' rule.[62] At the same time, the reforms would extend the consent model by allowing third parties, such as next-of-kin, parents or partners, to authorise, or veto, dealings with the remains of a loved one.[63] We simply

---

59 Coroners Rules 1984, SI 1984/552, r 9.
60 [1998] 3 All ER 741 at 749–750.
61 The Nuffield Council is of the view that 'a hospital which has tissue in its possession, for example for transplant, has such property rights over the tissue as to exclude any claim of another to it, as does a coroner or pathologist who has carried out a post-mortem and retains body parts for examination': Report at para 10.6. Without wishing to labour the point, there is a world of difference between placing a brain in preservative and preparing blocks for microscopic examination; the precise conditions obtaining in *Dobson* are, therefore, of some significance.
62 Department of Health, *Human Bodies, Human Choices: The Law on Human Organs and Tissue in England and Wales* (2002), para 7.19.
63 Ibid, ss 6–8.

point out that consent and property are not mutually exclusive concepts; indeed, to the extent that they are both a means of furnishing respect, they should perhaps be made to work together towards a common end.[64]

INTELLECTUAL PROPERTY LAW AND THE HUMAN BODY

15.25 We end this section with a consideration of intellectual property rights in the human body. We have already seen how in *Moore* a patent was granted over the 'Mo' cell-line produced using Mr Moore's cells. Certainly, patent law has had to adapt rapidly in the last few decades to meet the demands of the biotechnology industry. Astronomical sums are invested in research and development by drug companies and the industry has fought long and hard to ensure that its products receive patent protection. This, it is thought, assures a degree of return on the investment. The earning potential of the industry is tremendous. It is estimated that the world revenue for biotechnology products exceeded £70 billion in 2000, £9 billion of which was concentrated on the UK market.[65]

15.26 A patent offers an absolute monopoly for up to 20 years over an invention to the extent that all others can be excluded from competing in the marketplace with the same, or a similar, product. Strict criteria must be met to obtain protection but, once secured, a patent can protect a commercial enterprise against all comers. Yet patenting is not a morally neutral exercise and the biotechnology industry has faced considerable problems in obtaining protection for itself.[66] These problems have been particularly acute in Europe and arise because the work of the industry involves the manipulation of living organisms. Thus, for many, to patent a biotechnological invention is to patent 'life' itself.[67]

15.27 Standard criteria for patentability are accepted in most countries of the world.[68] To be patentable, an invention must be new, it must involve an 'inventive step' – in the sense that the development should not be obvious to a person skilled in the particular field – and it must have utility or be made or used in any kind of industry. In the United States, there is no provision in the law to refuse registration of a patent on the grounds of morality. Thus, while it was argued in *Diamond v Chakrabarty*[69] that a patent for a genetically hybridised oil-eating bacterium should be revoked on the grounds that no patent should be

---

64 Mason and Laurie, para 15.17 above.
65 Department of Trade and Industry, *Biotechnology Clusters* (1999), para 2.1.
66 For a useful historical account, see: Nuffield Council on Bioethics *The Ethics of Patenting DNA* (2002), Appendix 2.
67 Compare A J Wells 'Patenting New Life Forms: An Ecological Perspective' (1994) 3 Euro Intellect Prop Rev 111 and S Crespi 'Biotechnology Patents: The Wicked Animal Must Defend Itself' (1995) 9 Euro Intellect Prop Rev 431.
68 In the US the law is contained in 35 USC paras 101, 102 and 103. The UK equivalent is found in the Patents Act 1977, s 1(1). A degree of harmonisation of patent criteria was achieved with the establishment of the TRIPS Agreement (Trade Related Aspects of Intellectual Property Rights) at the Uruguay Round of GATT in 1994. The Agreement is administered by the World Trade Organisation which had 144 member countries as of 1 January 2002.
69 447 US 303, 66 L Ed 2d 144 (1980).

given over 'life', this was rejected by the Supreme Court which held that 'Congress intended statutory subject matter to include anything under the sun that is made by man'. Similarly, when, in 1988, Harvard University sought a patent for its *ONCOmouse* – a mouse genetically engineered with a human cancer gene in such a way that it develops cancer as a matter of course – the US Patent and Trademark Office granted the patent without question.

15.28 Harvard faired significantly less well in Europe. Although an application for a patent over *ONCOmouse* was filed in 1985, this was not granted until 1991,[70] and even then its validity was in constant doubt until November 2001, when it was eventually upheld in a modified form.[71] In essence, the problem of patent protection faced by the biotechnology industry in Europe stems from the 'morality provisions' of the European Patent Convention 1973 (EPC), which embodies the patent law of 24 European countries as of 1 July 2002. Article 53 of the EPC states:

> European patents shall not be granted in respect of:
> (a) inventions the publication or exploitation of which would be contrary to *ordre public* or morality, provided that the exploitation shall not be deemed to be so contrary merely because it is prohibited by law or regulation in some or all of the Contracting States;
> (b) plant or animal varieties or essentially biological processes for the production of plants or animals; this provision does not apply to microbiological processes or the products thereof.

15.29 The Harvard patent was challenged both on the grounds that it was inherently immoral to patent 'life' under Article 53(a) and because it was an attempt to patent an 'animal variety' under Article 53(b).[72] Yet, in *HARVARD/ ONCOmouse*,[73] the Examining Division of the European Patent Office allowed the patent in respect of (a) because it held that the morality question is to be tested by balancing, on the one hand suffering of the animal, with, on the other, the potential benefits to humanity. The 'carrot' of a potential cure for cancer tipped the scales in favour of patentability. In respect of (b) it was held that the 'invention' being claimed was a 'non-human mammal' and this was much broader than a mere 'animal variety'; therefore, no problem arose under Article 53(b).[74] Neither of these interpretations has been disturbed by the latest edict from the Opposition Division. Such linguistic gymnastics are clearly driven by policy concerns as to the attractiveness of Europe to the investor in biotechnology. Laws which are too strict act as a disincentive and encourage more investment in the United States where morality in this field is, seemingly, not a problem.

15.30 Patents over human material have been granted for a number of years. For example, over 1,175 human DNA patents were granted in the period 1981-95, mainly in the United States. Yet, as with ONCOmouse, the European

---

70 [1991] EPOR 525.
71 A Abbott 'Harvard Squeaks Through Oncomouse Patent Appeal' (2001) 414 Nature 241. The scope of the original patent covered all non-human mammals; now it is reduced to 'transgenic rodents'.
72 *HARVARD/ONCOmouse* [1990] EPOR 4.
73 [1991] EPOR 525.
74 Opposition proceedings were immediately started by 16 groups after this decision.

Patent Office (EPO) has had to deal with moral objections to such patents. The invention in dispute in *HOWARD FLOREY/Relaxin*[75] concerned H2 Relaxin, a protein produced naturally by women at the time of childbirth which softens the pelvis and so eases the passage of the child. Howard Florey genetically engineered this protein and sought a patent for the artificial chemical. It was argued before the Opposition Division of the EPO, first, that it would be tantamount to slavery to grant a patent for such a product, in that it involved the sale of human tissue; secondly, that this too was exploitative and an offence to human dignity; and, finally, that any patent over DNA is inherently immoral because DNA is 'life'. Each of these arguments was rejected out of hand by the Division. It held that there can be no question of slavery because no woman is forced to surrender material – all the subjects consented. Similarly, it was not necessarily exploitative to use human material because free and informed consent was given; the Division pointed out that human material is used in a variety of contexts without the question of exploitation arising. Finally, it was held that DNA is not 'life' but a chemical substance which carries genetic information: 'no woman is affected in any way by the present patent.'[76] The general policy of the EPO is to interpret the exceptions to patentability narrowly and to presume that the protection criteria are satisfied unless a strong contrary case can be shown.[77]

15.31 The controversy surrounding the morality of patenting DNA and genetically engineered products has also been addressed by European law, primarily in the name of protecting the EU's Single Market. After a very difficult passage lasting 10 years, a European Directive was eventually adopted in July 1998 in an attempt to clarify the legal position in respect of biotechnological patents.[78] Guidance is given on the kinds of invention which will never receive patent protection,[79] and the morality provision as defined in *ONCOmouse* is incorporated in a modified, although still relatively imprecise, form.[80] Indeed, a number of member states have yet to implement the Directive because of general uncertainty about its terms,[81] while others

---

75 [1995] EPOR 541.
76 At 550-551.
77 See, eg, *PLANT GENETIC SYSTEMS/Glutamine Synthetase Inhibitors* [1995] EPOR 357 and *LELAND STANFORD/Modified Animal* [2002] EPOR 2 (immuno-compromised chimera mouse was patentable – controversial technology not in itself a bar to patenting).
78 Directive of the European Parliament and of the Council on the Legal Protection of Biotechnological Inventions, No 98/44/EC of 6 July 1998.
79 Under Article 6 the following are unpatentable: (a) processes for cloning human beings; (b) processes for modifying the germ line genetic identity of human beings; (c) uses of human embryos for industrial or commercial purposes; (d) processes for modifying the genetic identity of animals which are likely to cause them suffering without any substantial medical benefit to man or animal, and also animals resulting from such processes.
80 Article 6 requires that a *substantial medical* benefit accrue to humanity or animals before the morality test will be satisfied.
81 The French government is in negotiations with the European Commission over the meaning of Article 5, alleging that there is inconsistency between the meaning of paras 1 and 2. Article 5 states: '1. The human body, at the various stages of its formation and development, and the simple discovery of one of its elements, including the sequence or partial sequence of a gene, cannot constitute patentable inventions. 2. An element isolated from the human body or otherwise produced by means of a technical process, including the sequence or partial sequence of a gene, may constitute a patentable invention, even if the structure of that element is identical to that of a natural element.'

have unsuccessfully challenged its validity alleging, inter alia, that it entails a breach of the principle of legal certainty and a breach of the fundamental right to respect for human dignity.

15.32 Once again, however, the interpretative authority in charge – this time the European Court of Justice – has taken a narrow view of the circumstances, and has upheld the Directive both as to its legitimacy as an instrument of European law and as to its substantive content of European patent law.[82]

15.33 We consider that, well-intended as it is, the morality provision in European patent law is ill-placed. Primarily, this is because it can never attain to that which it was designed to achieve. The crucial point is that the refusal of a grant of a patent does nothing directly to prevent the creative process from continuing. Thus, Harvard could continue to produce the mouse for sale on the open market even if ONCOmouse had never been given a patent – all that would be lost would be a chance to monopolise that market. If one is concerned by the act of creation itself, and this must be the main concern in these cases, then attention should be turned not to the point at which protection is offered, but to the point at which the creation takes place.[83] This cannot be done through the law of patents but, rather, through other mechanisms such as the introduction of regulatory schemes or the creation of authorities which can monitor the industry. Making morality part of patent law does nothing to regulate the biotechnology industry.

15.34 Other features of patent law are problematic for the health care sector, especially in the realm of pharmaceuticals.[84] The monopolistic right that a patent gives to an inventor potentially prevents many individuals from gaining access to vital medicines, as the recent South African AIDS drugs debacle demonstrated only too well.[85] The European Parliament issued a Resolution in October 2001 calling on the EPO to reconsider the grant of patents to Myriad Genetics over the genes for breast cancer, BRCA1 and BRCA2,[86] and at the time of writing opposition proceedings instigated by the Institut Curie, the Assistance Publique-Hôpitaux de Paris and the Institut Gustave-Roussy

---

82 *Netherlands v European Parliament (C377/98)* [2002] All ER (EC) 97. Note, the Directive only harmonises the law in the 15 member states of the European Union, but the implementing regulations of the European Patent Convention have been amended to reflect the terms of the morality provisions of the Directive to ensure consistency of approach across the 24 signatory countries to the EPC. This was applied most recently in relation to the 'Edinburgh' patent belonging to the University of Edinburgh which initially was granted over 'animal transgenic stem cells' but this raised controversy when it was suggested that this might lead to human cloning. In opposition proceedings before the EPO in July 2002 the patent was amended to exclude human or animal embryonic cells, although it still covers modified human and animal stem cells, see <http://www.european-patent-office.org/news/pressrel/pdf/backgr_3.pdf>.

83 This is argued more fully in G T Laurie 'Biotechnology: Facing the Problems of Patent Law' in H L MacQueen and B G M Bain (eds) *Innovation, Incentive and Reward: Intellectual Property Law and Policy* (1997) Hume Papers on Public Policy 46.

84 B Domeij 'Patent Claim Scope: Initial and Follow-on Pharmaceutical Inventions' [2001] EIPR 326.

85 In which the companies sought, quite legally, to forestall the production of cheaper generic drugs 'Drug Giants Bow to AIDS Campaign' *The Times*, 20 April 2001, p 23.

86 European Parliament *Resolution on the Patenting of BRCA1 and BRCA2 ('Breast Cancer') Genes* (4 October 2001, B5-0633, 0641, 0651, and 0663/2001).

are before the EPO in respect of these patents. The concern is summed up by the Nuffield Council on Bioethics in its recent discussion paper on the ethics of patenting DNA:

> The opposition is aimed at curtailing any possible deleterious consequences which might stem from sanctioning the monopoly conferred on Myriad Genetics, including the possible threat to the development of research and the identification of new tests and diagnostic methods. It has also been argued that the patent will have a serious impact on equitable access to testing. It is suggested that the monopoly is antithetical to an approach to public health that is based on a commitment to the comprehensive care of patients at high-risk.[87]

15.35 Moreover, and as the Council goes on to point out, there are currently no other methods of diagnosing the presence of the breast cancer susceptibility gene BRCA1 that can be used without infringing the patents because of the way in which Myriad Genetics has used its patent monopolies world-wide.[88]

15.36 There are numerous responses that we might have to this. One could be to deny patent protection altogether, but this is an unrealistic prospect and may be counter-productive if the venture capitalists are to be believed – they would simply cease funding the research necessary to produce the products in the first place.[89] More realistically, there is much that can be done to work within and to improve the current patent system. For example, standards of drafting patent applications should be strengthened to ensure (i) that inventions are properly described and (ii) that unsustainable claims to protection are not made. This, in turn, would facilitate a more rigorous examination process that should ensure that protection is granted only to innovations that are truly inventive and which have never been made available to the public. Indeed, the Nuffield Council has argued that patents over gene sequences themselves would become the exception not the norm if the criteria for patentability were more properly applied.[90] Ultimately, patent offices and courts must work together more closely so as to limit the effects of overly broad patents, by restricting protection to the precise contribution that an invention makes to human knowledge and no further.[91]

15.37 Most radically, however, the grant of a patent could be made conditional on the assumption of certain attendant responsibilities to the community. For example, the Human Genome Organisation's Ethics Committee (HUGO)

---

87 Nuffield Council, para 15.26 above, para 4.6.
88 At para 5.4.
89 This consideration influenced the European Group on Ethics in Science and New Technologies (EGE) in its report on patenting human stem cells wherein it concluded that it would not be in the public interest to exclude patent protection altogether. Instead the Group recommended more rigorous ethical evaluation of controversial patent applications, see EGE *Opinion No 16: Ethical Aspects of Patenting Inventions Involving Human Stem Cells* (2002), paras 2.1 and 2.10.
90 A similar view is expressed by the British Medical Association *Gene Patenting: A BMA Discussion Paper* (2001). A key feature of the argument is the assertion that much of the work of the biotechnology industry to produce gene sequences is 'obvious' ie lacks 'inventive step' and so would not attract patent protection.
91 Another option is to make more use of compulsory licences, but there is a significant cultural resistance to this in many quarters, especially in the United States.

recommended in April 2000 that: 'profit-making entities dedicate a percentage (eg 1–3%) of their annual net profit to healthcare infrastructure and/or to humanitarian efforts'.[92] There is no reason why this quid pro quo should not become part of patent law, provided that there is sufficient political will to make it so. It is a form of benefit-sharing that could go a long way to restoring public trust in privately-funded research, and it might give a more acceptable face to the prospect of patenting the human genome.[93]

CONCLUSION

15.38 It seems that whether we are dealing with living or dead human tissue, whether we are looking at humanity at the structured or the molecular level, or whether we are considering domestic or international regulation, we are faced with a schizoid approach to property rights in human material. On the one hand, there is an innate antipathy to the concept; on the other, we accept the inexorable march of 'science' knowing that, if something is there to be discovered, someone will discover it – and with little concern for the consequences. Governments may set up regulatory authorities as the significance of each scientific advance becomes apparent but they are relatively powerless in the face of global international pressures. What does seem clear is that, so far as the domestic scene is concerned, our courts must appreciate that this is a field in which technology and societal attitudes are advancing and being fashioned rapidly – and the common law must keep pace and accelerate as is necessary. Put in a nutshell, the legal issues involving the DNA double helix can no longer be resolved by way of authority derived from the exhibition of an anatomical aberration in a nineteenth-century fairground.

---

92 HUGO Ethics Committee, *Statement on Benefit-Sharing* (2000).
93 At least one governmental advisory body has recommended the adoption of such a scheme, see Canadian Biotechnology Advisory Committee *Patenting of Higher Life Forms and Related Issues: Report to the Government of Canada Biotechnology Ministerial Coordinating Committee* (2002), p 18.

16 Medical futility (or non-productive medical treatment): I The beginning of life

16.1 It is probably fair to say that the health care professional will, intuitively, seek to prolong life so long as it is possible to do so. The massive technological advances of the last half century have increased our capabilities in this respect and, perhaps because of this, we have become more and more aware that, occasionally, the preservation of life can be a negative blessing. Such an assessment may come from the patient him- or herself – in which case we are in the field of euthanasia, which we discuss in chapter 18. Alternatively, the health carers may, themselves, raise the question, not so much as to whether it is in the patient's interest that he or she should live or die but, rather, whether his or her death should be prolonged by medical treatment. In other words, there are times when we must ask ourselves if treatment should be considered futile and should be abandoned – and such moments will arise with patients of any age. Even so, there are two situations in which life and death decisions become fundamental and unavoidable – when we are born and when we are dying. It is for this reason that we have divided the discussion into two sections dealing, respectively, with the beginning and the end of life while, at the same time, recognising that the principles derived can be applied at any intervening time.

16.2 When the first edition of this book was written, selective non-treatment of the newborn and, most particularly, withholding the means of survival from mentally handicapped infants were burning issues; it is fair to say that the legal and ethical standards in this area are, now, relatively stabilised. In the interim, however, a comparable flurry of interest developed around the management of the incompetent adult, with greatest importance attaching, in this instance, to the patient in the persistent or permanent vegetative state. Categories have become blurred in the process. Much as we predicted originally, selective non-treatment of the newborn progressed to the selective non-treatment of the defective child, while the infant whose brain has been destroyed by meningitis can be used as a model for the adolescent who is similarly affected. It is somewhat ironic that the long and careful deliberations of the House of Lords in *Bland*[1] can trace their origins to the thoroughly unsatisfactory case of *Arthur.*[2]

1   *Airedale NHS Trust v Bland* [1993] 1 All ER 821, (1993) 12 BMLR 64, Fam D, CA, HL.
2   *R v Arthur* (1981) 12 BMLR 1.

16.3 All such situations, which form a continuum from neonatal deformity, through the persistent vegetative state, to the catastrophically afflicted adult, have it in common that treatment may be contraindicated on the grounds either that it is achieving no medical effect or that continued treatment can be seen as being against the patient's best interests. These can be subsumed together under the general heading of futility. Simple as this analysis appears to be, attempts to reach a universally satisfactory definition of 'futility' do little more that open a Pandora's box of conflicting moral values – for it cannot be denied that it raises the curtain on what is no less than the first act in the wider drama of euthanasia. Thus, while we find the concept useful, albeit in a restricted way, we cannot introduce it without some consideration of its limitations.

THE CONCEPT OF MEDICAL FUTILITY

16.4 Before starting the discussion, however, it is well to clear up what may become a source of trans-Atlantic misconception. The term in the United States is seen generally as a shorthand way to describe the situation in which a patient demands and a physician objects to the provision of a particular medical treatment on the ground that the treatment will provide no medical benefit to the patient.[3] This definition, in introducing an element of conflict, is restrictive and, we believe, self-defeating. Conflict there may be, but an essential aspect of the regime is that it should be carried out, so far as is possible, in an atmosphere of mutual understanding and agreement – and it is with this aim in mind that we address the subject.

16.5 The basis for the concept of futility is certainly not new. More than a quarter of a century ago, it was said:

> The whole resources of an advanced medical service are currently deployed in the pursuit of the preservation of life. It is becoming obvious that the costs of this policy are becoming insupportable ... We must face an inescapable duty to let some patients die.[4]

16.6 The philosophy behind this approach was widely accepted during the 1980s but has since been challenged on several grounds. First, it confuses futility or non-productivity of treatment with rationing of resources; secondly, it suggests that doctors can and should select their patients for treatment by way of their own judgments as to their relative worth; thirdly, the statement, as it stands, conflicts head-on with the rapidly evolving respect for the principle of patient autonomy; and, finally, it speaks in the language of duty while, at the same time, failing to identify the beneficiary of that duty. All of which lead us directly to the question – what do we mean by futility?

16.7 Even then, this question can be formulated in a number of ways. Who is to make the definition – the patient, his surrogate or the doctor? And, if it is

---

3   J F Daar 'Medical Futility and Implications for Physician Autonomy' (1995) 21 Am J Law Med 221.
4   E Slater 'Severely Malformed Children: Wanted – A New Approach' (1973) I BMJ 285.

the last, what is his objective standard – for one man's futility is another's courageous effort.[5] Equally, reliance on, say, the surrogate is bound to end in conflict because, as we will see later – and despite some moral doubts on the part of respected American bioethicists[6] – no doctor in the United Kingdom can be compelled to provide a particular treatment against his better judgment.[7]

16.8 Can we refine this choice more closely by considering the quality of the decision to be made? We could, for example, define futile treatment as care that does not accomplish its intended purpose – in which case, a respirator that kept a person breathing could never be classed as providing futile treatment irrespective of the status of the patient. Despite later legal intervention,[8] this is clearly not how the medical profession intended the term to be used; Jecker and Pearlman[9] reviewed the literature and identified four major alternative definitions of futility:

(a)   treatment which was either useless or ineffective;
(b)   that which fails to offer a minimum quality of life or a modicum of medical benefit;
(c)   treatment that cannot possibly achieve the patient's goals; or
(d)   treatment which does not offer a reasonable chance of survival.

16.9 This mix demonstrates very well the fundamental distinction which must be made between, on the one hand, the *effect* of a treatment – which is no more than an alteration in some bodily function – and, on the other, the *benefit* of a treatment – which is something that can be appreciated by the patient.[10] Put another way, the need is to distinguish between physiological and normative futility[11] – in which case, it is arguable that the former is to be decided on purely medical grounds while the latter involves a quality or value judgment which is the prerogative of the patient or his surrogates.[12]

---

5 See, eg, the case of *Baby Nguyen* referred to in W Prip and A Moretti 'Medical Futility: A Legal Perspective' in M B Zucker and H D Zucker *Medical Futility* (1997) ch 13. One hospital was prepared to treat aggressively an infant with kidney failure, bowel obstruction and brain damage who had been rejected for treatment by another. A very similar case is discussed by J J Paris, R K Crone and F Reardon 'Physicians' Refusal of Requested Treatment: The Case of Baby L' (1990) 322 New Engl J Med 1012.

6 Eg R M Veatch and C M Spicer 'Futile Care: Physicians Should Not Be Allowed to Refuse to Treat' in T L Beauchamp and R M Veatch *Ethical Issues in Death and Dying* (1996) p 392. It is to be noted that the vast majority of analysis of 'futility' currently derives from America.

7 The situation in the US is complicated by the varying conditions in 'advance directive' or 'living will' legislation. Thus, in 11 States, there is provision for indicating what treatment persons wish to receive in the event of permanent unconsciousness. See Prip and Moretti, para 16.7 above. On the other hand, a line of decisions justifying withdrawal of futile treatment in the face of objection is developing – culminating in *Gilgunn v Massachusetts General Hospital* No 92-4820 (Mass Super Ct, Suffolk Co, 22 April 1995), see T Rutter 'US Doctors Win Life Support Lawsuit' (1995) 310 BMJ 1223.

8 See para 16.78 below.

9 N S Jecker and R A Pearlman 'Medical Futility: Who Decides?' (1992) 152 Arch Intern Med 1140.

10 L J Schneiderman and N S Jecker 'Futility in Practice' (1993) 153 Arch Intern Med 437.

11 Veatch and Spicer, para 16.7 above.

12 The major part of an issue (1992) 20 Med Law Hlth Care was given over to the problem. See, in particular, R Cranford and L Gostin 'Futility: A Concept in Search of a Definition' at 307.

Against which, it has been said that medical judgments are never value-free and that to abandon such judgments at the behest of the patient is to subvert the core of medical professionalism.[13] The doctor's dilemma can, perhaps, best be appreciated in terms of objective. When the primary aim of the health carer is to preserve life, futility only has a role to play when life can no longer be preserved. This is a relatively straightforward issue – either life can be saved or it cannot. However, matters become altogether more complicated when the doctor assumes the role of quality of life provider – futility then assumes a role which is far less clear cut and this is particularly so when decisions are made as to life or death. In such cases, medical intervention *may* keep the patient alive but, none the less, futility is advanced as a justification for allowing him or her to die. Futility then becomes not futility in the face of death – which is an easily appreciated absolute – but, rather, futility in the face of an unacceptable quality of life, which is a far more subjective construct.

16.10 Thus, the whole topic of medical futility – when seen as a concept rather than as a series of problem-solving exercises – is fraught with difficulties and contradictions. It has been said that futility is not only a word which is foreign to the families of handicapped neonates but it is also one which is unacceptable because of its hopelessness; its use militates against achieving the proper societal response.[14] Gillon believed that 'when judgments are to be used as a basis for withholding or withdrawing potentially life prolonging treatment, they had better be made rather precisely and preferably expressed in terms that are less ambiguous, complicated and distressing'.[15] While it is clear that we accept the *medical* principles behind selective non-treatment of the newborn,[16] of 'do-not-resuscitate' orders and of withdrawal of treatment from persons in the permanent vegetative state, we have great sympathy with those who object to *futility* on semantic and philosophical grounds. We much prefer to speak of non-productive treatment, which places the problem firmly in the medical field and, as a result, carries the added advantage of clarity of intention.[17] Meantime, it is suggested that non-productivity and futility can be reconciled if the latter concept is confined to Schneiderman and Jecker's summary definition:

> A treatment which cannot provide a minimum likelihood or quality of benefit should be regarded as futile and is not owed to the patient as a matter of moral duty.[18]

---

13 J F Drane and J L Coulehan 'The Concept of Futility: Patients Do Not Have a Right to Demand Medically Useless Treatment' (1993) 74 Hlth Prog 28; H Brody 'Medical Futility: A Useful Concept?' in Zucker and Zucker, p 364, para 16.7 above, ch 1.
14 B Anderson and B Hall 'Parents' Perceptions of Decision Making for Children' (1995) 23 J Law Med & Ethics 15; C Weijer and C Elliott 'Pulling the Plug on Futility' (1995) 310 BMJ 683.
15 R Gillon '"Futility" – Too Ambiguous and Pejorative A Term?' (1997) 23 J Med Ethics 339.
16 We have retained this expression because it is well established. Paediatricians will, however, point out that it covers a period of care which demands particular clinical and nursing skills. Everyone should read I Laing 'Withdrawing from Invasive Neonatal Intensive Care' in J K Mason (ed) *Paediatric Forensic Medicine and Pathology* (1989).
17 We discuss this concept in greater detail at para 18.58 below.
18 See para 16.8 above.

16.11 Schneiderman and Jecker have also reminded us that there are *positive* dangers of abuse if the term 'futile treatment' is adopted uncritically within the medical vocabulary. These include the resurgence of inappropriate paternalism, the erosion of patient autonomy, the unjustified avoidance of the duty to treat – or, we might add, the creation of an ephemeral duty *not* to treat – and the introduction of disguised and arbitrary rationing of resources. Many of these pitfalls are revealed in the cases which follow.

Selective non-treatment of the newborn

16.12 It is apparent that we regard the problem of non-productive treatment as one that is common to all ages; nevertheless, selective non-treatment of the newborn retains some unique features. First, it is intimately bound up with the subject of abortion – in so far as a large proportion of conditions which call for 'futile' neonatal treatments were present and were diagnosable in utero and, as such, constituted grounds for legal termination of pregnancy by way of the Abortion Act 1967, s 1(1)(d). What, then, of those affected fetuses which come to full term undiagnosed? Where do public opinion and the law stand between the opposite extremes, on the one hand, of upholding an absolute right to life and, on the other, of supporting a positive policy of elimination of the imperfect? There has to be a middle road but, in the case of the neonate, we must find it without the aid of statute.

16.13 Second, treatment decisions taken immediately after birth concern human beings who are at the most vulnerable period of their lives – human beings, moreover, who cannot express their feelings for the present or the future and who clearly cannot have indicated their preferences to their surrogates. This may explain the relative dearth of court decisions concerning treatment of the neonate. Parents faced with decision-making at this point are likely to agree with their medical advisers simply because they have no evidence on which to *disagree*. It is only when the bonds of adversity have been cemented between the parents and the disabled infant that the former are likely to have developed strong independent opinions as to which treatments are appropriate. As a result, the majority of cases in which the court is called upon to adjudicate concern disabled infants rather than neonates.

16.14 In either case, however, the 'futility' debate is, as discussed above, likely to be conducted at the 'quality of life' level. We have, however, not yet considered whether this is, of itself, a morally tenable level. Have we the right to place relative values on lives or is all life sacrosanct? This question represents the foundation stone of the futility argument and, while it is applied throughout the spectrum of selective treatment, it is convenient to discuss it in the context of the early stages of human development.

Sanctity or quality of life?

16.15 The doctor's dilemma is self-evident – is he or she practising truly 'good' medicine in keeping alive a neonate who will be unable to take a place in society or who will be subject to pain and suffering throughout life? In short, is one to displace a concept of the sanctity of life based on a Hippocratic and theological foundation by a standard related to the quality of life which is, essentially, justified by a utilitarian ethos?[19] The situation gives rise to a catalogue of questions – of which the first might well be to ask if there is, in fact, any solid basis for what has become known as the 'sanctity of life doctrine'. This seems to us to be, at least, doubtful, particularly if the doctrine is to be interpreted in terms of vitalism – or 'the sanctity of life at any price'. The Hippocratic Oath proscribes euthanasia but neither it, nor the more contemporary Declaration of Geneva impose an obligation to provide treatment at all times; rather, the emphasis is on doing no harm – an approach which clearly allows for pragmatic interpretation. A persuasive case can also be made out for there being no theological imperative to regard human life as sacrosanct.[20]

16.16 Even so, while vitalism has been largely rejected, a modified concept of the sanctity of life is widely endorsed; the debate continues as to the acceptable extent of that modification and, in its turn, raises a number of derived questions, many of which are unanswerable in the abstract. Who is to determine the minimum quality of life? Whose life are we considering – the infant's? or are we also taking into account that of the parents or, indeed, the well-being of society? Do we, in fact, *want* a society in which the right to life depends upon achieving a norm which is largely measured in material terms? Should the disabled infant whose dying is needlessly prolonged be helped on its way? – and, if so, is this help to be a matter of omission or should positive steps be taken to end life? And, behind all these, now lies the Human Rights Act 1998 with its implications under Article 2 (the right to life) and Article 3 (the right not to be subjected to inhuman or degrading treatment) of the European Convention.

16.17 In the discussion of euthanasia which follows in chapter 18, stress is laid on the relationship between the quality of life and the proportionate or disproportionate treatment which is needed to maintain that quality. But the quality of the therapeutic environment at the beginning of life is very hard to assess. Not only can the patient express no opinion but, were it possible, he or she has no yardstick by which to judge; as put by McKenzie J in Canada:

> ... he would not compare his life with that of a person enjoying normal advantages. He would know nothing of a normal person's life having never experienced it.[21]

16.18 As an inevitable result, parents must be invited to make 'life or death' decisions on behalf of their abnormal offspring – and they will be guided by the doctor whose advice is likely to be on the lines that consideration for the preservation of life is secondary to that of preventing suffering. Medical leadership supports this parental responsibility – 'in the absence of a clear code to which society adheres, there is no justification for the courts usurping

---

19 A classic review is to be found in L Gostin 'A Moment in Human Development: Legal Protection, Ethical Standards and Social Policy in the Selective Non-treatment of Handicapped Neonates' (1985) 11 Am J Law Med 31.
20 K Boyd 'Euthanasia: Back to the Future' in J Keown (ed) *Euthanasia Examined* (1995) ch 7.
21 *Re Superintendent of Family and Child Services and Dawson* (1983) 145 DLR (3d) 610 at 621.

the parents' rights'[22] – and it has been backed by influential academic legal thought – 'the criminal law should stay its hand. The decision of the parents should prevail'.[23] These are, however, generalisations and the cases which follow demonstrate that generalisations provide no easy answers to individual problems.

16.19 In particular, the early cases fail to address the solution of conflict between the medical carers and the parents. As we have seen, this underlies the concept of medical futility which, as a result, can be seen as developing in the United Kingdom only since the 1980s. Thus, we have the evidence of Dr Dunn at the trial of Dr Arthur: 'no paediatrician takes life but we do accept that allowing babies to die is in the baby's interest at times'[24] – and the wealth of distinguished supporting evidence showed that this paediatric practice was clearly acceptable at the time. It does, however, involve a number of assumptions:

(a)   that there is an essential difference between activity and passivity when the same end – death – is realised by either and, arising from this, that passivity does not conflict with the doctor's duty to 'maintain life from the time of conception';[25] moreover, it presupposes that passivity is clinically preferable from the patient's viewpoint;

(b)   that there is a point at which death is preferable to life; and

(c)   that some, as yet unidentified, person can decide that point in surrogate fashion and that it is right and proper for others to follow that judgment through.

16.20 Yet this seems to come perilously close to breaking the law. To kill a living human being deliberately is murder and, except as to the specific crime of infanticide,[26] the age of the victim has no relevance. Killing a child by omission could be prosecuted under the Children and Young Persons Act 1933, s 1;[27] it is more likely to be charged as manslaughter although it could be murder[28] – the paramount considerations being whether or not there is a duty of care and, if there is, what is the extent of that duty.[29] It is difficult to see how the consultant in charge of the paediatric ward could be seen as not having a duty of care to his patients. Yet, anything up to 30% of deaths in a neonatal intensive care unit follow the deliberate withdrawal of life support[30] and we have Farquharson J charging the jury in the leading apposite criminal case:

22 Editorial Comment 'The Right to Live and the Right to Die' (1981) 283 BMJ 569.

23 G Williams 'Life of a Child' Correspondence, *The Times*, 13 August 1981.

24 *R v Arthur* (1981) 12 BMLR 1 at 18. Dr Dunn would now limit withholding life-saving treatment only in three groups of neonate: those with severe malformations, those with severe hypoxic/traumatic brain damage; and those of extreme prematurity with major problems such as brain haemorrhage: P M Dunn 'Appropriate Care of the Newborn: Ethical Dilemmas' (1993) 19 J Med Ethics 82.

25 Declaration of Geneva (see Appendix B).

26 Infanticide Act 1938.

27 The section probably applies only to parental obligations. If this be so, it would not constitute a potential sanction against the health care team. See I Kennedy and A Grubb *Medical Law* (3rd edn, 2000), p 2165.

28 *R v Gibbins and Proctor* (1918) 13 Cr App Rep 134, CCA.

29 *R v Stone; R v Dobinson* [1977] QB 354, [1977] 2 All ER 341, CA.

30 A Whitelaw 'Death as an Option in Neonatal Intensive Care' [1986] 2 Lancet 328; C H M Walker '… Officiously to Keep Alive' (1988) 63 Arch Dis Child 560.

I imagine that you will think long and hard before concluding that doctors, of the eminence we have heard ... have evolved standards that amount to committing a crime.[31]

16.21 Moreover, we have not yet fed the rights of the neonate into the equation. In our view, the newly born baby has the same rights to respect as has every human being. This proposition is, however, increasingly under attack as the definition of personhood in terms of intellect is developed. We have already observed that, if it is valid to treat the fetus as a non-person, it is also valid to use the same parameters by which to deny personhood to the neonate; there are, indeed, those who are prepared to equate the status of 'infanticide' with that of 'feticide'[32] – or even of contraception. It is against this conflicting legal and ethical background that we can trace the absorption of the concept of medical futility into the medical jurisprudence of the United Kingdom as, first, related to the neonate and infant.

Futility or a duty not to treat?

16.22 Although *R v Arthur*[33] was, chronologically speaking, not the first instance of selective non-treatment of the newborn to come before the English courts, it was undoubtedly that which brought the whole subject before the public conscience. In so far as it was taken through the criminal courts, it is an unsatisfactory prototype; nevertheless, it has been said that there are surprisingly few substantive issues in medical ethics that Dr Arthur's case does not raise[34] and it remains an important landmark.

16.23 Put briefly, the salient features of the case are that a baby was born with apparently uncomplicated Down's syndrome and was rejected by his parents; Dr Arthur, a paediatrician of high repute and impeccable professional integrity, wrote in the notes 'Parents do not wish it to survive. Nursing care only'; the baby died 69 hours later. Dr Arthur was charged with murder but, during the course of the trial, medical evidence was adduced to the effect that the child had not been physically healthy; accordingly, the charge was reduced to one of attempted murder and Dr Arthur was acquitted.

16.24 The central question raised by the trial is why, in the light of the acknowledged developments in neonatal intensive care, was Dr Arthur singled out for prosecution?[35]

16.25 In our view, the most logical answer lies in the application of a 'treatability' test. Dr Arthur's patient was in no physical pain and, so far as

31 *R v Arthur* (1981) 12 BMLR 1 at 22.
32 See in particular H Kuhse and P Singer *Should the Baby Live?* (1985) ch 6. Other observations along the same lines include J G Bissenden 'Ethical Aspects of Neonatal Care' (1986) 61 Arch Dis Child 693; C Wells 'Whose Baby Is It?' (1988) 5 J Law & Soc 323.
33 (1981) 12 BMLR 1.
34 R Gillon 'An Introduction to Philosophical Medical Ethics: The Arthur Case' (1985) 290 BMJ 1117.
35 Only a few weeks previously, the Director of Public Prosecutions had decided that no action would be taken against a doctor who had allegedly refused to sustain a baby, Stephen Quinn, who was suffering from spina bifida: *The Times*, 6 October 1981, p 1.

was known prior to autopsy, he required no treatment. Death in such circumstances depends on the withholding of nourishment and to take away such a life is to make a social rather than a medical decision – the fact that it was taken by a doctor rather than a member of the public should be irrelevant. The prosecution of Dr Arthur led to a storm of resentment on the part of the leaders of the medical profession but this was almost entirely due to a failure to appreciate that there is a world of difference between withholding treatment from a dying patient and refusing sustenance to one who shows firm evidence of a will to live.[36] Any confusion as to the doctor's role is dispersed once it is appreciated that there is a fundamental distinction to be drawn between physical defect – for which invasive treatment remains an option – and mental defect for which no curative treatment is available. The failure of the medical establishment in this respect is exemplified in the statement of the President of the Royal College of Physicians:

> Where there is an uncomplicated Down's case and the parents do not want the child to live ... I think there are circumstances where it would be ethical to put it upon a course of management that would end in its death ... I say that with a child suffering from Down's and with a parental wish that it should not survive, it is ethical to terminate life.[37]

16.26 By any standards, this is a remarkable interpretation of both medical and parental responsibilities and powers. In the light of later judicial decisions, which are discussed below, it is unlikely that Dr Arthur's regime would be acceptable today and the case has lost any credibility as a precedent. In our view, the management pattern disclosed in *R v Arthur* is best seen as an example of the dangers of extrapolating the concept of 'futility' to one of an obligation not to treat in the face of parental pressure.

Case law other than *Arthur*

16.27 With, perhaps, one major exception,[38] the law in this area has shown a remarkably steady development in the last 20 years. None the less, the template was undoubtedly established in the prototype case of *Re B (a minor)*,[39] the judgment in which has been said still to represent the law in this particular field.[40] Thus, despite its antiquity, *Re B* still merits close consideration.

16.28 In essence, B was an infant suffering from Down's syndrome complicated by intestinal obstruction of a type which would be fatal per se but which was

---

36 Eg Editorial Comment 'Paediatricians and the Law' (1981) 283 BMJ 1280.
37 (1981) 12 BMLR 1 at 21-22. See also the leading article at the time, 'After the Trial at Leicester' (1981) 2 Lancet 1085. It is possible that a similar attitude persists even now: Z Kmietowick 'Down's Children Received "Less Favourable" Hospital Treatment' (2001) 322 BMJ 815 commenting on R Evans (chairwoman) *The Report of the Independent Inquiries into Paediatric Cardiac Services* www.rbh.nthames.nhs.uk.
38 *Re T (a minor) (wardship: medical treatment)* [1997] 1 All ER 906, discussed in greater detail at para 16.52 et seq below.
39 (1981) [1990] 3 All ER 927, [1981] 1 WLR 1421, CA.
40 *Re J (a minor) (wardship: medical treatment)* [1990] 3 All ER 930, (1990) 6 BMLR 25, CA paraphrasing Lord Donaldson MR [1990] 3 All ER 930 at 938, (1990) 6 BMLR 25 at 34.

readily amenable to surgical treatment. The parents took the view that the kindest thing in the interests of the child would be for her not to have the operation and for her to die – in passing, a decision which was later described by Dunn LJ as 'an entirely responsible one'. The infant was made a ward of court and, in the face of both judicial indecision and medical disagreement, the question 'to treat or not to treat?' came before the Court of Appeal.

16.29 The summary answer to the basic question was provided by Dunn LJ in saying: 'She should be put in the position of any other mongol child and given the opportunity to live an existence.'[41] For the major analysis, however, we must look to Templeman LJ who, adhering to the general principles relating to the affairs of minors,[42] concluded that the judge of first instance, in refusing to authorise the operation, had been too much concerned with the wishes of the parents; the duty of the court was to decide the matter in the interests of the child. In coming to the conclusion that these interests were best served by treatment, he said:

> ... it devolves on this court ... to decide whether the life of this child is demonstrably going to be so awful that in effect the child must be condemned to die or whether the life of this child is still so imponderable that it would be wrong for her to be condemned to die ... Faced with [the] choice, I have no doubt that it is the duty of this court to decide that the child must live[43]

and it was this that led Lord Donaldson to look upon *Re B* as close to a binding authority for the proposition that there is a balancing exercise to be performed in assessing the course to be adopted in the best interests of such children.

16.30 Templeman LJ did, however, clearly leave the door open for an alternative decision in saying:

> There may be cases ... of severe proved damage where the future is so certain and where the life of the child is so bound to be full of pain and suffering that the court might be driven to a different conclusion. [44]

16.31 Thus, the court clearly accepted that there is an essential prognostic difference between mental and physical handicap and, as to the latter, laid the foundations for a quality of life therapeutic standard rather than one based on a rigid adherence to the principle of the sanctity of human life.

16.32 Even so, the medical profession was now left in a cleft stick. Allowing for the fact that they relate to different jurisdictions, *Re B* and *Arthur* are virtually impossible to reconcile. Legally speaking, it is difficult to see why the parents' wishes as to the death of their offspring should be overruled when major surgery is involved, yet be regarded as ultimately decisive when it is

---

41 [1990] 1 All ER 927 at 929, [1981] 1 WLR 1421 at 1425.
42 Guardianship of Minors Act 1971, s 1. See, now, Children Act 1989, s 1.
43 [1990] 1 All ER 927 at 929, [1981] 1 WLR 1421 at 1424. The case was well discussed by
    D D Raphael 'Handicapped Infants: Medical Ethics and the Law' (1988) 14 J Med Ethics 5.
44 [1990] 3 All ER 927 at 929, [1981] 1 WLR 1421 at 1424.

not and, in a clarification which seems only to add to the confusion, the Attorney General said shortly after Dr Arthur's trial:

> I am satisfied that the law relating to murder and to attempted murder is the same now as it was before the trial; that it is the same irrespective of the age of the victim; and that it is the same irrespective of the wishes of the parents or of any other person having a duty of care to the victim. I am also satisfied that a person who has a duty of care may be guilty of murder or attempted murder by omitting to fulfil that duty, as much as by committing any positive act.[45]

16.33 This unsatisfactory situation persisted for almost a decade but has since been greatly clarified in the series of cases overseen by Lord Donaldson MR.[46] The decisions in these cases relate to treatment of infants rather than of the newborn. They can, therefore, be taken as early examples of the application of medical futility across the whole span of life.

Selective non-treatment in infancy

16.34 *Re C*[47] concerned a moribund child and the essence of the decision was that the hospital were given authority to treat her so as to allow her life to come to an end peacefully and with dignity; such treatment as would relieve her from pain, suffering and distress would be given but it was specifically said to be unnecessary to use antibiotics or to set up intravenous infusions or nasogastric feeding regimes. It was emphasised that the decision was based on the paramountcy of her welfare, well-being and interests. *Re C* thus represents the antithesis of *Re B* in respect of physical disability and, in retrospect, neither case was difficult to decide.

16.35 Baby J[48] was, however, not dying and the case illustrates more clearly the real dilemma presented by these cases. The situation was that the brain-damaged child suffered from repetitive fits and periods of cessation of breathing for which he required ventilation. There was no doubt that he could be rescued in the probable event that he sustained further episodes of respiratory failure but it was equally certain that he would die if the necessary treatment was withheld. Non-treatment in these circumstances cannot be dressed in such euphemisms as 'allowing a peaceful and dignified death' and the question before the court was what was to be done if he sustained a further collapse. The Court of Appeal had little difficulty in agreeing with the judge of first instance that:

> it would not be in J's best interest to reventilate him [by machine] in the event of his stopping breathing unless to do so seems appropriate to the doctors caring for him given the prevailing clinical situation.[49]

---

45 19 HC Official Reports (6th series) written answers, col 349 8 March 1982.
46 For review of these cases, see J K Mason 'Master of the Balancers: Non-voluntary Therapy under the Mantle of Lord Donaldson' [1993] JR 115.
47 *Re C (a minor) (wardship: medical treatment)* [1990] Fam 26, [1989] 2 All ER 782.
48 *Re J (a minor) (wardship: medical treatment)* [1990] 3 All ER 930, (1992) 6 BMLR 25.
49 [1990] 3 All ER 930 at 933, (1992) 6 BMLR 25 at 29.

16.36 In the course of his judgment, the Master of the Rolls made several observations which we see as being of particular importance. In the first place, he stressed that, while there was a strong presumption in favour of a course of action that will prolong life, nevertheless, the person who makes the decision must look at it from the assumed view of the patient.[50] Following on from this, consideration must be given to the prognosis in terms of pain and suffering – including the distress caused by any treatment of itself; in J's case, the quality of life, even without the added effect of further hypoxic episodes, was extremely low. Thirdly, the court held that decision making was a co-operative effort between the doctors and the parents – or, in the case of wardship, between the doctors and the court with the views of the parents being taken into consideration;[51] any choice must be made solely on behalf of the child in what was believed to be his best interests. Finally – and this we see as especially significant – it was emphasised that any decision taken was one which would affect death by way of a side-effect; the debate was not about terminating life but solely about whether to withhold treatment designed to prevent death from natural causes:

> The court never sanctions steps to terminate life. That would be unlawful. There is no question of approving, even in a case of the most horrendous disability, a course aimed at terminating life or accelerating death. The court is concerned only with the circumstances in which steps should not be taken to prolong life.[52]

16.37 *Re C* and *Re J* must, however, be looked at in conjunction with a third case which was unfortunately also named *Re J*[53] – and called here *Re J(2)*. In this instance, a mother attempted to enforce the intensive care of her child who had sustained severe brain damage as a result of a fall. The Court of Appeal, however, refused to entertain the suggestion that it should direct clinicians to provide treatment against their best clinical judgment:

> I agree with Lord Donaldson that I can conceive of no situation where it would be proper ... to order a doctor, whether directly or indirectly, to treat a child in the manner contrary to his or her clinical judgment. I would go further. I find it difficult to conceive of a situation where it would be a proper exercise of the jurisdiction to make an order positively requiring a doctor to adopt a particular course of treatment in relation to a child.[54]

50 Lord Donaldson demonstrated a sympathy with the 'substituted judgment' test throughout this series of cases (see para 16.40 below).
51 The nurses were singled out for praise in the Court of Appeal in *Re C*, where there were clear indications that their views should also be considered.
52 [1990] 3 All ER 930 at 943, (1990) 6 BMLR 25 at 40, per Taylor LJ. In *Re C*, the Court of Appeal would not even tolerate the expression 'treat to die'.
53 *Re J (a minor) (medical treatment)* [1993] Fam 15, [1992] 4 All ER 614. Two supportive decisions have been reached in Scotland. The determination in the fatal accident inquiry concerning the death of Rebecca Cassidy supported a decision not to treat an extremely low birth-weight premature infant: see S English 'Doctor was Right not to Resuscitate "Unviable" Baby' *The Times*, 27 June 1997, p 11. The decision not to provide a liver transplant for a teenage girl was accepted as good medical practice in the inquiry into the death of Michelle Paul: see G Bowditch 'Surgeon Right to Refuse Teenager a Liver Transplant' *The Times*, 23 July 1997, p 7.
54 [1993] Fam 15 at 29, [1992] 4 All ER 614 at 625, per Balcombe LJ.

16.38 Thus, this series of cases indicates a strong judicial belief in the doctor's clinical autonomy. It also shows a very determined stance in favour of a quality of life standard which is founded on the principle of the patient's 'best interests'.

16.39 The use of this standard is best considered under the management of the permanent vegetative state.[55] For present purposes, we consider only the relationship between 'best interests' and 'no interests' in which we are, in fact, reverting to the problem of distinguishing mental from physical disability. It may well be permissible to see death as a blessed relief from severe pain or unacceptable bodily invasion and, therefore, an outcome of a treatment that is in the patient's 'best interests'. By contrast, the patient who has sustained brain damage of such degree as to permanently deprive him or her of sensation and cognition has no immediate interests as between death or survival.[56]

16.40 We believe that some other test is called for in the latter circumstance and that it is there, in particular, that we can legitimately call on the concept of medical futility to guide our therapeutic programming. However, as we have seen, this can conflict with the respect due to *patient* autonomy and, to avoid this, it may be preferable to rely on the principle of substituted judgment – or, in other words, to follow the regime that one assumes the patient him- or herself would have opted for if given the chance.[57] The objections to such a test are discussed in greater detail below.[58] For the present, we will only observe that its acceptance relieves one of an element of hypocrisy that is inherent in the 'best interests' test. We are constantly assured that judicial treatment/non-treatment decisions are founded on the best interests of the patient alone and that the interests of the relatives, carers and, indeed, the state are irrelevant – yet, in all honesty, it is hard, if not impossible, to separate these extraneous interests. Substituted judgment allows us to take the latter into consideration with a relatively clear conscience. A competent patient may opt for non-treatment rather than treatment and the effects of the decision on his or her family can legitimately form part of its foundation; there is no reason why this should not be incorporated in the substituted judgment.

16.41 In fact, the English courts, in their anxiety to maintain the welfare principle, have tended to confuse the two tests. Thus, we have Lord Donaldson[59] quoting McKenzie J:[60]

> It is not appropriate for an external decision maker to apply his standards of what constitutes a liveable life ... The decision can only be made in the context

---

55 See para 17.5 et seq below.
56 Although Dworkin, for one, speaks in terms of critical interests which persist despite the loss of appreciative capacity: R Dworkin *Life's Dominion* (1993), discussed extensively by A Grubb 'Commentary on *Law Hospital NHS Trust v The Lord Advocate*' (1996) 4 Med L Rev 301. We see this, however, as having academic rather than practical consequences.
57 'Donning the mental mantle of the incompetent patient': see *Superintendent of Belchertown State School v Saikewicz* 370 NE 2d 64 (Mass, 1977).
58 See para 17.45.
59 In *Re J* [1990] 3 All ER 930, (1990) 6 BMLR 25.
60 In *Re Superintendent of Family and Child Services and Dawson* (1983) 145 DLR (3d) 610.

of the disabled person viewing the worthwhileness or otherwise of his life in its own context as a disabled person.[61]

16.42 Although it was taken as expressing the best interests of J, this is as clear a description of the principle of substituted judgment as one is likely to find. It also re-emphasises the mental/physical divide – a divide which has become even more apparent in some relevant cases which have been reported since the era of Lord Donaldson.

Important cases post-Donaldson

16.43 *Re C (a baby)*[62] concerned a premature infant who developed meningitis resulting in her being blind and deaf and suffering from repeated convulsions. She could survive only by virtue of artificial ventilation but, given that support, it was thought that she could live for months or even up to two years. Meantime, her pain and distress were expected to increase. She was described as not being in coma but as having 'a very low awareness of anything, if at all'; Sir Stephen Brown P summed up her condition as 'almost a living death'. Medical opinion was that she had no independent existence and that it was in her interests that ventilation should be discontinued – in which case she would die within hours. The President had no doubt that he should grant leave to the medical staff to adopt this recommended regime.

16.44 The President was invited to make observations as to when it would be appropriate for doctors placed in this position to seek the leave of the court; he thought, however, that it would not be right to make any general observation about that matter – medical and legal opinion concurred in believing that each case should be considered on its particular facts.

16.45 The parents in *Re C (a baby)* agreed with the recommendations of their medical advisers. In the second important case, *Re C (a minor)*,[63] however, the parents were orthodox Jews, who firmly believed that life should always be preserved. Their child, aged 16 months, suffered from spinal muscular atrophy – a progressive condition for which it was agreed there was no curative treatment. Nevertheless, she was conscious, able to recognise her parents and was able to smile. The recommended plan was to undertake a form of therapeutic test by removing her from supportive ventilation; if, as was probable, she suffered a further respiratory relapse, she would not be reventilated but would be allowed to die. The parents accepted the first part of the plan but were unable to consent to the second. The stage was, thus, set for the classic American 'futility' scenario.

16.46 In the event, the President relied heavily on Lord Donaldson's leading cases[64] in defining the legal limits of the doctor's duties. In particular:

---

61 [1990] 3 All ER 930 at 936, (1990) 6 BMLR 25 at 32.
62 *Re C (a baby)* [1996] 2 FLR 43, (1996) 32 BMLR 44.
63 *Re C (a minor)* (1997) 40 BMLR 31.
64 *Re J (a minor)* [1990] 3 All ER 930, (1992) 6 BMLR 25; *Re J (a minor)* [1993] Fam 15, [1992] 4 All ER 614; *Re R (a minor) (wardship: medical treatment)* [1992] Fam 11, (1991) 7 BMLR 147.

[To follow the wishes of the parents] would be tantamount to requiring the doctors to undertake a course of treatment which they are unwilling to do. The court could not consider making an order which would require them so to do. [65]

16.47 The situation was defined as one in which the hospital trust sought the court's consent in the absence of consent by the parents. The medical evidence was not in dispute and was backed by the general recommendations issued by the Royal College of Paediatrics and Child Health[66] – under which, spinal muscular atrophy would be regarded as a 'no-chance situation' in which medical treatment may be deemed inappropriate. Leave was granted to the hospital to withdraw treatment and to exclude resuscitation in the event of respiratory arrest – such a regime being justified as being in C's best interests.

16.48 Much the same situation underlay what is probably the latest apposite case. *A National Health Service Trust v D*[67] concerned a child who had been born with irreversible lung disease and multi-organ failure. Any therapeutic 'progress' could be measured no more than in terms of an occasional voluntary movement of a digit or hand. The Trust applied for a declaration that, in the event of a further cardio-respiratory arrest, it would be lawful not to resuscitate him but to initiate treatment designed to let him end his life peacefully and with dignity. Medical opinion was unanimously in favour of this approach which was strongly opposed by the parents on the grounds that it was premature. Cazalet J, relying heavily on the previous Donaldson judgments, granted the declaration on the grounds that it was in the child's best interests that he be so managed;[68] in so doing, the judge stated the law in clear terms:

[T]he court's prime and paramount consideration must be the best interests of the child. This of course involves ... consideration of the views of the parents concerned ... However, ... those views cannot themselves override the court's view of the ward's best interests.[69]

16.49 Cazalet J also considered the implications of compliance with the European Convention on Human Rights and concluded that there could be no infringement of Article 2 insofar as the order was made in the best interests of D. At the same time, he confirmed that Article 3 encompassed the right to die with dignity[70] – an increasingly commonly used phrase which seems to us to be becoming equivalent to 'without the encumbrance of invasive forms of treatment'.

16.50 Thus, while all the cases cited could be subsumed under the rubric of medical futility, we see them as illustrating a relatively steady – and significant

---

65 (1997) 40 BMLR 31 at 37.
66 Royal College of Paediatrics and Child Health *Withholding or Withdrawing Life Saving Treatment in Children: A Framework for Practice* (1997).
67 [2000] 2 FLR 677, (2000) 55 BMLR 19.
68 In *R v Portsmouth Hospitals NHS Trust, ex p Glass* [1999] 2 FLR 905, (1999) 50 BMLR 269, the Court of Appeal refused to consider a rather similar request for a pre-emptive declaration. *D* was distinguished in that it referred to one specific form of treatment – mechanical ventilation – whereas the declaration sought in *Glass* would have involved general directions as to how the doctors should treat a child.
69 [1992] 2 FLR 667 at 686, (2000) 55 BMLR 19 at 28.
70 Quoting *D v United Kingdom* (1997) 24 EHRR 423. Cazalet J did not enlarge on his interpretation of either article.

– extension of the conditions which render non-treatment lawful. Two common threads are to be seen. On the one hand, the courts will not, and are unlikely ever to, order doctors to provide treatment against their better judgment – especially for those who are severely brain damaged. As a corollary, it is clear that, no matter what may be the practical clinical situation, parents and other guardians have no *legal* right to insist on treatment which the doctors can justifiably regard as being inappropriate. This, however, depends upon the weight of the medical opinion expressed. It is to be noted that the medical evidence has never been seriously challenged by the amicus curiae in the reported cases and one wonders what would be the outcome were it to be otherwise. The general tenor of the decisions since *Re B* through the two *Re Js* suggests that the courts would opt for the salvaging of life – as Lord Donaldson put it: 'There is without doubt a very strong presumption in favour of a course of action which will prolong life' albeit adding the rider 'but … it is not irrebuttable'.[71] At the same time, the more recent *Re C* cases raise the possibility of a subtle change of emphasis leading to supremacy of the 'quality of life' as the basis of assessment. It is true that all life and death decisions – and the applications themselves – have been based on a 'best interests' test, but the facts of each successive case point to an incremental erosion of the pure concept – is it not, in fact, possible to discern the glimmers of a legal recognition of the 'personhood' construct? The *C* and *J* cases can also be distinguished in that, while the latter – together with *D* – are concerned with the non-provision of treatment that interferes with the natural process, the former relate to the withdrawal of treatment that is already in place; it is difficult in the extreme to deny that the *C* cases sanction a regime which will inevitably bring about a death which would not otherwise have occurred – barely distinguishable from that which Taylor LJ excluded in *Re J*[72] and which was foreseen by Balcombe LJ in *Re J (2)*.[73] Can this be looked on as a tentative step towards legalised euthanasia? We can understand how such a view might be taken.

16.51 Finally, the more recent cases illustrate vividly the difficulties surrounding the whole concept of futility. Continued treatment was futile from the perspective of the doctors in *Re C (a baby)*[74] and *Re C (a minor)*[75] and this constitutes the justification of its withdrawal; it is, surely, carrying sophistry too far to plead 'best interests' – we discuss the matter again at para 17.48 below but, meantime, we suggest that it is better to be honest. But, if a procedure is to be regarded as futile, it must be devoid of utility and, certainly, the 'futile' treatment of C in *Re C (a minor)* and the potential treatment of D in *National Health Trust* were of major utility to their parents. In other words, there is a practical as well as a theoretical distinction to be made between futile treatment and *medically* futile treatment. The doctor is entitled to assess the latter and to argue in favour of its non-provision or withdrawal. But, in the end, to do so is no more than a powerful contribution to the overall

---

71 *Re J (a minor) (wardship: medical treatment)* [1990] 3 All ER 930 at 938, (1990) 6 BMLR 25 at 34.
72 [1990] 3 All ER 930 at 943, (1990) 6 BMLR 25 at 40.
73 [1993] Fam 15 at 30, (1992) 9 BMLR 10 at 20, CA.
74 (1996) 32 BMLR 44.
75 (1997) 40 BMLR 31.

assessment of the former – which goes some way to supporting Sir Stephen Brown P in his resistance to generalising in this field.[76]

A reversal of the trend?

16.52 We have noted above the inclination of the courts to follow the medical opinion whenever it is possible to do so; the case of *Re T (a minor) (wardship: medical treatment)*,[77] in which the trend was reversed, is, therefore, of considerable interest.

16.53 Here, the child curiously designated as C, was born with biliary atresia – a condition likely to be fatal within 2½ years in the absence of transplantation therapy. Remedial surgery at the age of 3½ weeks produced no improvement but medical opinion was unanimous in believing that the chances of a successful transplant were good and that the operation was in C's best interests. This included the opinion of a consultant engaged on behalf of the mother who opposed a further operation on the grounds of the pain and suffering C had sustained following the first procedure and who even took her child abroad where there were no facilities for a liver transplant. The child's local authority then raised the matter as a special issue under the terms of the Children Act 1989, s 100(3). As a result, the trial judge found that the mother's conduct was not that of a reasonable parent and directed that C be admitted to a hospital that was prepared to undertake a transplant operation.

16.54 The Court of Appeal, however, unanimously reversed this decision, largely on the grounds that the judge had failed to give adequate weight in the necessary balancing exercise to the objections of the parents – which, it was said, were supported by qualities of devotion, commitment, love and reason. These included an assessment of the pain and suffering likely to be imposed by a second major operation and of the chances and consequences of failure. In addition, the court agreed with one expert opinion that passing back responsibility for parental care to the mother and expecting her to provide the essential commitment to the child after the operation in the face of her opposition was, in itself, fraught with danger for the child. How would the mother cope with having to remain in England? asked Butler-Sloss LJ. The mother and the child were one for the purposes of the case and the decision of the court to assent to the operation jointly affected the mother and son and also the father. Waite LJ went so far as to hold that the child's subsequent development could be injuriously affected if his day-to-day care depended upon the commitment of a mother who had suffered the turmoil of her child

---

76 *Re C (a baby)* (1996) 32 BMLR 44. See also Waite LJ: 'All these cases depend on their own facts and render generalisations … wholly out of place' in *Re T (a minor) (wardship: medical treatment)* [1997] 1 All ER 906 at 917, (1996) 35 BMLR 63 at 75. The Ethics Committee of the BMA has now published comprehensive guidelines covering all age groups: *Withholding and Withdrawing Life Prolonging Medical Treatment* (2001) www.bmjpg.com/withwith/ww.htm.

77 [1997] 1 All ER 906, (1996) 35 BMLR 63. For discussion, see M Fox and J McHale 'In Whose Best Interests?' (1997) 60 MLR 700; A Bainham 'Do Babies Have Rights?' (1997) 56 CLR 48; A Grubb 'Commentary' (1997) 4 Med LRev 315.

being compelled against her will to undergo a major operation 'against which her own medical and maternal judgment wholeheartedly rebelled'.[78] The appeal was upheld and the orders of the trial judge to the effect that surgery should be performed notwithstanding the refusal of the mother to consent were set aside.

16.55 *Re T* raises a number of questions – both general and particular. It is, first, reasonable to question whether it is right to place discussion of the case within a section devoted to medical futility. Our view is that it represents one side of the wide concept – albeit the rather unusual reverse in which the parents, on behalf of their child, are claiming treatment to be futile in so far as it is, on balance and in their view, offering minimal benefit. It will be seen below that we reject this prognostic assessment and it may be that the importance of the case lies in providing a measure of how far the concept of futility can be stretched without incursion into areas such as euthanasia – it is possible, but it is certainly not easy, to accommodate phrases such as: '... the prospect of forcing the devoted mother of this young baby to the consequences of this major invasive surgery ...'[79] within the envelope of the child's unaffected best interests. Equally to the point, one has to ask if the decision in *Re T* does, in fact, represent a watershed in the medico-legal symbiosis that has developed in this area. C's parents were described as health professionals; their status is unstated but the Court of Appeal was clearly impressed by their understanding of the situation – so much so that, at times, the mother's views appear to take on the significance of another expert medical opinion. Moreover, previous court decisions represent not so much a judicial submission to the medical will as, rather, a reluctance to impose a duty to treat on unwilling doctors. *Re T* was an antithetical proposition, the end result of which was to place an embargo on treatment which at least some experts were willing to provide. It may not, therefore, be a decision taken against the stream.

16.56 Whether it was a 'good' decision in medical jurisprudential terms is, again, questionable. Despite the protestations of all three judges, and despite the court's repeated assurance as to the responsibility and devotion of the parents, an unavoidable impression remains that their interests weighed heavily in the balance at the expense of the paramountcy of those of the child. Certainly, there is great good sense in the opinion of the trial judge. There are few fields of modern medicine in which progress is as fast as it is in transplantation therapy. It is at least possible that additional technology would become available during the several years of good quality life available within the current state of the art; not only might these then be extended beyond current expectation but, in the interim, the mother's attitude might well change. It is hard to dismiss such gains as *medically* futile objectives.

Futility or scarcity of resources?

16.57 We have suggested already that the concept of futility carries with it the real danger that it can be used as a means to the disguised and arbitrary

78 [1997] 1 All ER 906 at 917, (1996) 35 BMLR 63 at 75.
79 *Re T* [1997] 1 All ER 906 at 916, (1996) 35 BMLR 63 at 74, per Butler-Sloss LJ.

rationing of resources. This may well be so but, before accepting this as wholly pejorative, it is well to note the underlying practicalities.

16.58 In the first place, the one necessarily follows the other. Thus, if one patient is removed from futile treatment, that resource automatically becomes available to another for whom it will be useful – but the motive behind the exchange remains subject to interpretation. Secondly, given that resources are not infinite, therapeutic merit is a good candidate for the most acceptable basis for their distribution; as we discuss in chapter 11, the 'first come, first served' regime fails in principle because it dictates the provision of treatment in medically futile circumstances. Thirdly, the law clearly accepts that resource allocation forms a proper part of medical decision making. Thus, we have Balcombe LJ:

> [M]aking an order which may have the effect of compelling a doctor or health authority to make available scarce resources ... to a particular child ... might require the health authority to put J on a ventilator in an intensive care unit, and thereby possibly to deny the benefit of those limited resources to a child who was much more likely than J to benefit from them.[80]

16.59 None the less, the seeds of conflict are there to be sown and are well illustrated in *R v Cambridge Health Authority, ex p B*,[81] which concerned a 10-year-old child who had been suffering from lymphoma since the age of five. By the time of the action, she had received two courses of chemotherapy and had undergone whole body irradiation and received a bone marrow transplant before she suffered a further relapse. At this point, her doctors determined that no further treatment could usefully be given and estimated her life expectancy as between six and eight weeks. Her father had, meantime, obtained a second opinion from the United States which, effectively, suggested that further treatment carried an 18% chance of a full cure. Doctors who were prepared to continue treatment in the United Kingdom regarded this as unduly optimistic and set the chance of success at anything between 10% and 2.25% – which was, of course, to be set against the risk to the patient's life and the distress associated with the proposed treatment; due to a shortage of beds, this would have to be carried out in the private sector and the cost was estimated to be in the region of £75,000. Taking into account the judgment of their own clinicians, the nature of the treatment and its chances of success, the health authority declined to provide the funding, giving as its reasons, first, that the treatment would not be in B's best interests and, second, that the expenditure of so much money with so little prospect of success was an ineffective use of their limited resources bearing in mind the present and future needs of other patients. The father sought judicial review of this decision.

16.60 In the High Court hearing, Laws J began his determination with the words: 'Of all human rights, most people would accord the most precious place to the right to life itself.' Even if this is true, which it probably is, we doubt if it follows that there is a rights-based entitlement to any particular

---

80 *Re J (a minor) (wardship: medical treatment)* [1993] Fam 15 at 30, (1992) 9 BMLR 10 at 20.
81 (1995) 25 BMLR 5, QBD; revsd [1995] 2 All ER 129, (1995) 23 BMLR 1, CA.

treatment; the 'right to life' in this context means no more than the right not to have one's life taken away and this right is in no sense infringed if it is agreed that the available treatment is either futile or against the patient's best interests. In confronting such criticism, Laws J opined that, in contrast to the position in criminal law, public law allowed no difference of principle between act and omission and, accordingly, the decision of the health authority assaulted the child's right to life. He then considered the justification for such an assault and concluded that, while the doctors could rightly assess the chances of success of the proposed treatment and its objective disadvantages in terms of risk and suffering, the assessment of the patient's best interests was not, in the end, a medical question at all. Rather, it was a matter to be decided by the child's father acting as a surrogate responsible for her overall care. Thus, in the end, the issue turned on the provision of funds – and the learned judge considered that, when the question was whether the life of a 10-year-old might be saved, by however slim a chance, the authority should do more than 'toll the bell of tight resources'. In conclusion, while admitting that there might still be cogent reasons for withholding funding which had not been explored, Laws J ordered that the authority's decision be reconsidered in the light of his judgment.

16.61 Almost predictably in the light of previous decisions in which the allocation of resources formed a part,[82] the Court of Appeal reversed this order emphasising, in general, that its function was to rule upon the lawfulness of decisions – not to express opinions as to the merits of medical judgment. In particular, the court rejected the suggestion that the wishes of the parents had been inadequately considered; in fact, the authority was under great pressure from the parents and had taken its decision in response to that pressure. Secondly, Sir Thomas Bingham MR considered that, by any showing, the treatment was at the frontier of medical science. Thirdly, he held:

> I have no doubt that in a perfect world any treatment which a patient ... sought would be provided if doctors were willing to give it, no matter how much it cost ... It would, however, be shutting one's eyes to the real world if the court were to proceed on the basis that we do live in such a world.[83]

16.62 And, further, the court cannot make a judgment as to how a limited budget is to be best allocated. In the end, it was open to the health authority to reach the decision they had already reached. We should, as a coda, note that B's treatment was ultimately funded from both private and public sources; she died 14 months after the hearing. All the doctors involved agreed that B's life under treatment was likely to be oppressive; can one say that the gain of a year of such life negates the imprint of medical futility? – it is an arguable point but we have our doubts.

16.63 The case of Child B provided the perfect setting for 'shroud-waving' in the popular press; an in-depth analysis of the media coverage shows the extent of the pressures exerted.[84] It was, of course, unfortunate that clinical and

82 See para 11.26 et seq above.
83 (1995) 23 BMLR 1 at 8–9.
84 V A Entwistle, I S Watt, R Bradbury and L J Pehl 'Media Coverage of the Child B Case' (1996) 312 BMJ 1587.

economic considerations became entwined and, inevitably, the press saw the issue almost exclusively in financial terms; the situation was, however, bound to arise as the funding for what are known as 'extra-contractual referrals' – or the purchase of medical services outside the particular health authority – is subject to special regulation. But was *ex p B* an attempt to impose resource rationing under the cloak of medical futility? We think not. An authority must abide by the decisions of its expert advisers who were unanimous that the suggested treatment was contraindicated. In the circumstances, the authority might well have been regarded as behaving unreasonably if it *had* persisted with treatment. At the most, its attitude could be seen as part of the now familiar balancing exercise; we will never know what would have been the decision had the proposed regime not been quite so extravagant of public money – or, on the other side of the coin, had not involved quite such risk and discomfort to the patient.

16.64 *Re T* and *ex p B* may seem to be at odds, in that the Court of Appeal recognised the interests of the parents as having a high priority in the former and rejected them in the latter. The cynic might say that this is simply a matter of health care economics – that parental interests will be supported when they pose no threat to the pocket of the NHS. The alternative and, in our view, better approach is to see the two decisions as consistent. We do not disguise our suspicions as to the correctness of that taken in *Re T*. The fact remains that the court conducted a balancing act in both cases and, rightly or wrongly, concluded that the risks and suffering involved in treatment outweighed the chances of success. Certainly, the decisive evidence came from opposing corners but, at the end of the day, the lesson is that the courts will not impose what they, having heard the medical evidence, regard as medically futile – or, better, non-productive – treatment of children whose management is in dispute. Although they were stated in a rather different context, the words of Sir Thomas Bingham MR provide the foundation for our current jurisprudence:

> [T]he decision of a devoted and responsible parent should be treated with respect ... But the role of the court is to exercise an independent and objective judgment. If that judgment is in accord with that of the devoted and responsible parent, well and good. If it is not, then it is the duty of the court, after giving due weight to the view of the devoted and responsible parent, to give effect to its own judgment. That is what it is there for.[85]

Conjoined twins

16.65 Many of the cases of 'futile' medical treatment that have been considered by the courts relate to the withholding or withdrawal of mechanical means to oxygenate the tissues. Perhaps the most controversial case that has arisen since the last edition of this book concerned the management of conjoined twins.[86] One of the twins, Mary, was so disabled as to be incapable of an

---

85 In *Re Z (a minor) (freedom of publication)* [1997] Fam 1 at 32, [1995] 4 All ER 961 at 986.
86 *Re A (children) (conjoined twins: surgical separation)* [2001] Fam 147, (2001) BMLR 1, CA.

independent existence. Thus, it was possible to regard separation from her sister, Jodie, as akin to disconnecting her source of oxygen – or life support machine – when its continued use was medically futile.[87] We can pre-empt discussion of the case by quoting Walker LJ:

> If Mary had been born separated from Jodie but with the defective brain and heart and lungs which she has, and if her life were being supported, not by Jodie but by mechanical means, it would be right to withdraw that artificial life-support system and allow Mary to die.[88]

16.66 It is for this reason that we have chosen to discuss the case, which has multiple facets,[89] at this particular point.

16.67 In brief, *Re A (children) (conjoined twins: surgical separation)* concerned conjoined twins, one of whom, Jodie, had a normal heart and lungs. Mary, by contrast, had no functioning heart and her lungs were unusable; her tissues were oxygenated only because she shared a common aorta and venous return with her sister. Mary would die immediately were the twins to be separated whereas, in such circumstances, Jodie would be expected to live a near normal life; both would die in a matter of months if no action was taken. Since it was never disputed that the twins constituted two living individuals,[90] the medical alternatives were stark. Either the hospital could do nothing and accept 'the will of God' that both would die – which was the parents' strong preference and which would have been legally 'acceptable' practice[91] – or they could be separated, in which case, Mary's life of a few months would be sacrificed so as to ensure Jodie's survival.

16.68 It would be convenient to be able to see this as a purely moral problem. In practice, however, the undoubtedly far from satisfactory ruling of the Court of Appeal[92] was, throughout, overshadowed by considerations of the criminal law – before any decision involving the death of Mary could be accepted, it had to be cleansed of a suspicion of murder. A number of strategies were deployed to this end. These included self-defence or its support on behalf of Jodie, the necessity of avoiding an inevitable wrong[93] and absence of intention to kill. At least one of these factors was sufficient to convince all three judges of the lawfulness of the operation and it is beyond the scope of this book to argue these uncertain areas of the criminal law.

---

87 This reconstruction was not, however, accepted by the majority of the court.
88 (2001) 57 BMLR 1 at 109.
89 An entire issue of the *Medical Law Review* (2001) 9, no 3 was devoted to the case on which there is now a massive bibliography.
90 Though it is possible to see them as an integrated 'item' sharing common assets: B Hewson 'Killing Off Mary: Was the Court of Appeal Right?' (2001) 9 Med L Rev 281.
91 Per Ward LJ at BMLR 36. This was also the preferred option of R Gillon 'Imposed Separation of Conjoined Twins – Moral Hubris by the English Courts?' (2001) 27 J Med Ethics 3 and H Watt 'Conjoined Twins: Separation as Mutilation' (2001) 9 Med L Rev 237.
92 For a powerful step by step criticism, see J McEwan 'Murder by Design: The "Feel-Good Factor" and the Criminal Law' (2001) 9 Med L Rev 246.
93 The reasoning, which precluded a defence of necessity in *R v Dudley and Stephens* (1884) 14 QBD 273, was specifically rejected in *Re A*.

16.69 But, even when the problem of criminality is settled,[94] the case raises ethical questions of equivalent complexity. Fundamental to these is the problem of what constitutes 'best interests' in this and comparable cases. Here, Johnson J, at first instance, and Walker LJ on appeal were happy in the notion that it was not in Mary's best interests to be maintained alive – this being based on the quality of life she could anticipate. Other members of the Court of Appeal, however, could not accept this – Ward LJ holding that separation would bring her life to a close before it had run its natural span without providing any countervailing advantage. Thus, the difference of opinion clearly highlighted the distinction to be drawn between the concepts of the sanctity and the quality of life to which we have already drawn attention. The further distinction between commission and omission, or between activity and passivity, in end of life decision making is closely bound to this fundamental issue. We discuss the question of whether there is an *ethical* distinction to be made elsewhere (see para 18.49 et seq); whatever the answer may be, there certainly is an important *legal* difference which we address more fully in chapter 18. Suffice it to say, here, that, having accepted that Mary was receiving no treatment which could be withdrawn in passive fashion, the Court of Appeal in *Re A* concluded that the operation to separate the twins constituted an assault on Mary. Thus, it was a positive action that would end her life and, as such, was dangerously close to, if not actually, crossing the Rubicon of euthanasia – a journey that the court was unwilling to make.[95] Thirdly, *Re A* reopens the controversy surrounding the moral doctrine of double effect and its associated concept of intent (for which, see para 18.76). The case particularly asks whether the 'good' effect – in this instance, Jodie's long term survival – can be justified if the 'bad' accompaniment is at the expense of *another* non-consensual party as represented here by Mary's premature death. In the event, only Walker LJ was prepared to hold that Mary's death could be seen as an unintentional result of Jodie's survival. Given the proportionality provided by Mary's negligible advantage, if any, in remaining alive, it is difficult to see why the majority of the court rejected a not unreasonable escape route from a hideous moral dilemma.[96]

16.70 We have previously suggested that many of these difficulties could have been avoided by accepting Mary as a still-birth which, it seems, would have been possible given that she never had any lung function.[97] To do so would also have limited the effect of the ruling in *Re A* to separation of a still-birth which would be completely lawful; as things stand, many are concerned at the potential effect of the decision on the law of murder. None the less, the

---

94 And a case can be made out that it was not: S Uniacke 'Was Mary's Death Murder?' (2001) 9 Med L Rev 208.

95 Johnson J in the High Court was prepared to equate cutting off Mary's oxygen supply with withdrawing food from those in coma – see discussion of *Bland* at para 17.9 et seq below – which can be regarded as an omission; the Court of Appeal rejected this unanimously.

96 See, for example, Uniacke, para 16.69 above. Though, as the other members of the court noted, it is not certain that double effect will always survive following *R v Woollin* [1999] 1 AC 82, [1998] 4 All ER 103. Effectively, this says that a 'bad' result cannot be seen as unintentional if it was inevitable.

97 J K Mason 'Conjoined Twins: A Diagnostic Conundrum' (2001) 5 Edin LR 226. For the diagnosis of still-birth, see *Rance v Mid-Downs Health Authority* [1991] 1 QB 587, [1991] 1 All ER 801, discussed at para 5.44 above.

court rejected this solution unanimously and we suspect that this may have been because of the somewhat conflicting way in which much of the relevant medical evidence was presented. Walker LJ, for example, quoted the leading surgeon as saying; 'Mary was not still-born but she could not be resuscitated and was not viable'[98] which, by *Rance* standards, seems to be something of a contradiction in terms. Ward LJ was content to quote the then Brooke J's definition of live birth in *Rance* and to comment: 'I think I can guarantee that when my Lord said that, he did not relate his observations to Siamese twins' – which is scarcely a robust rejection of our hypothesis.

16.71 The Court of Appeal was, then, left to solve the almost insoluble and, in the end, very nearly acknowledged that. Faced with alternatives that could never satisfy everyone, it relied on a balancing act – which decision, it asked, contained the less wrong? The Court decided unanimously in favour of separation – with the proviso that the authority of the case was confined by its very unique circumstances – and, in strict utilitarian terms, this has to be seen as correct; one cannot be so certain when speaking deontologically.

16.72 A final comment on the ethical components of *Re A* relates, once again, to the question of parental rights and responsibilities in such cases. The Court of Appeal took full cognisance of the parents' wishes yet barely questioned its own right to have the final say. Looked at dispassionately, the reasons given by the parents for their opposition to the operation – including deeply held religious convictions and the anticipated difficulties in maintaining a family unity that would be imposed by a disabled child – are, essentially, based on parental interests. Whether or not one agrees with the logic of the decision, it was based on wide-ranging analysis and careful thought rather than on custom, and this must have been to the 'better' interests of the children; as Freeman put it: 'there are more important rights to confer upon children than the right to autonomous parents.'[99] Against this, one must also quote Harris: 'This is a finely balanced judgment, but perhaps just because it is, the justification for overturning the choice of the parents is absent.'[100] It is perhaps a sobering thought that a case which has provoked so much controversy and which may have a profound influence on the law might never have been heard had the twins not been in the care of an authority that was anxious to proceed in circumstances where many might not have done so.

Comparative experience in the United States

16.73 The American experience in this field of neonatal and paediatric medicine demonstrates a somewhat turbulent history. Twenty-five or so years ago, there was a strong legal bias in favour of a sanctity of life approach. Opinions were handed down such as: 'If there is any life-saving treatment available, it must be given regardless of the quality of life that will result'[101] or 'Children are not

98 (2001) 57 BMLR 1 at 105.
99 M Freeman 'Whose Life Is It Anyway?' (2001) 9 Med L Rev 259.
100 J Harris 'Human Beings, Persons and Conjoined Twins: An Ethical Analysis of the Judgment in *Re A*' (2001) 9 Med L Rev 221.
101 *Re McNulty* No 1960 Probate Court (Mass, 1980) following *Maine Medical Center v Houle* No 74-145, Sup Ct (Me, 1974).

property whose disposition is left to parental decision without hindrance'[102] and, in general, extensive surgery was ordered so long as it was feasible.

16.74 However, a change appeared in the next decade. In *Weber v Stony Brook Hospital*,[103] the Court of Appeal in New York would not overturn a judgment to the effect that, in refusing permission for surgery, the parents had 'elected a treatment which was within accepted medical standards'; 'to allow [a guardian]' it was said 'to bypass the statutory requirements would catapult him into the very heart of a family circle to challenge the parents' responsibility to care for their children'. The decision in *Re Infant Doe*[104] was that the value of parental autonomy outweighed the infant's right to live when 'a minimally adequate quality of life was non-existent' – this despite the fact that the anatomic abnormality present in association with Down's syndrome was amenable to relatively routine surgery; moreover, the case arose in Indiana, which was, at the time, the only state in which the life of the newborn was protected by statute. It has been described as a case: 'in which a baby whose life could almost certainly have been saved was starved to death under color of law'.[105]

16.75 The position then became even more turbulent. *Infant Doe* provoked presidential reaction on the grounds that selective non-treatment contravened federal laws protecting the handicapped; hospitals receiving federal aid were reminded that they were prohibited from withholding life-saving medical or surgical treatment from handicapped infants. Particular attention was paid to the provision of nourishment, fluids and routine nursing care – items which were not considered options for medical judgment: 'no health care provider should take it upon itself to cause death by starvation or dehydration.' Nevertheless, the United States District Court for the District of Columbia rapidly invalidated these rules by declaring, inter alia, that the Rehabilitation Act 1973, s 504, which protects the rights of the handicapped, 'could never be applied blindly and without any consideration of the burdens and intrusions which might result'.[106] The Federal regulations were, therefore, revised but were again struck down.[107]

16.76 The call for legislation was strong in the United States and was ultimately met by the Child Abuse Amendments of 1984 which amend the Federal Child Abuse Prevention and Treatment Act 1974.[108] The essential thrust is that, having defined medical neglect, the amendments lay down the circumstances in which withholding medically indicated treatment would not be so described. These include the presence of irreversible coma, when treatment would merely prolong dying and when treatment would be futile or inhumane – but correction of a simple complication of Down's syndrome is not included as an exception.

---

102 *Re Cicero* 421 NYS 2d 965 (1979).
103 456 NE 2d 1186 (NY, 1983).
104 (1982) GU 8204-004 A (Monroe County Cir, 12 April), cert denied 52 USLW 3369 (US, 1983). See G P Smith 'Defective Newborns and Government Intermeddling' (1985) 25 Med Sci & L 44.
105 N Lund 'Infanticide, Physicians and the Law' (1985) 11 Am J Law Med 1.
106 *American Academy of Paediatrics v Heckler* 561 F Supp 395 (DDC, 1983).
107 *American Hospital Association v Heckler* 105 S Ct 3475. The death knell was sounded in *Bowen v American Hospital Association* 106 S Ct 2101 (1986).
108 The onus of monitoring and enforcing the Act remains with the individual states.

16.77 There have been two notable developments in more recent years. First, the United States appears to be the only country in which xenotransplantation has been actually attempted as a treatment of last resort. Given the current state of the art, we would regard the procedure as an outstanding example of medical futility; the subject in general and the case of Baby Fae in particular are, however, discussed in chapter 19.[109] Second, and very much to the point in the present discussion, we have had the case of *Baby K*.[110]

16.78 Baby K was born an anencephalic and, accordingly had no cognitive abilities or awareness; she was, however, placed on a ventilator because of respiratory distress. Given a prognosis of death within a few days, the hospital doctors recommended supportive care only; in so far as there is no cure for anencephaly and, hence, there was no remedy for the child's mental state, treatment was considered futile and both medically and ethically inappropriate. However, her mother, who had already refused a recommended termination of pregnancy, had a firm belief in God's unique responsibility for human life;[111] accordingly, she insisted on mechanical ventilation when required – and this was, in fact, provided on at least three occasions. The hospital then sought a declaration that it was not required to provide respiratory support and this application was refused by the district court. It is, for present purposes, unfortunate that the Appeals Court was constitutionally unable 'to address the moral or ethical propriety of providing emergency stabilizing medical treatment to anencephalic infants' and the issue became one of the interpretation of statute – EMTALA[112] – which, effectively, requires hospitals to provide 'stabilising' treatment in an emergency situation to any person who comes to hospital and requests treatment.

16.79 In the event, the case was decided in favour of the mother on the narrow ground that the statute applied – but this was because the treatment requested was for respiratory distress rather than for anencephaly. But, in so concluding, a number of other problems were addressed. First, it was held that the parents have a constitutional right to make medical decisions on behalf of their children[113] and that no such right is accorded to physicians in their choice of treatments. At first glance, this seems entirely contrary to the British position

---

109 See para 19.51.
110 *Re Baby K* 832 F Supp 1022 (ED Va, 1993); affd 16 F 3d 590 (4th Cir, 1994); cert denied 1994 US App Lexis 5461. The greater part of the information on this case is taken from E J Flannery 'One Advocate's Viewpoint: Conflicts and Tensions in the *Baby K* Case' (1995) 23 Law Med & Ethics 7 and E W Clayton 'Commentary: What is Really at Stake in *Baby K*?' (1995) 23 Law Med & Ethics 13. For further commentary, see 'Anti-dumping Law: Application to Anencephalic Infants' (1993) 19 Amer J Law Med 548.
111 One wonders, then, whether the only acceptable treatment should not have been inactivity.
112 Emergency Medical Treatment and Active Labor Act 1992. Other statutes were cited including the Rehabilitation Act 1973, which prohibits health providers from discriminating on the basis of handicap or disability in the provision of medical care.
113 This cannot, however, be absolute, as argued by Clayton, para 16.77 above. It is to be noted that exceptions such as those associated with the management of children of Jehovah's Witnesses (see para 10.18 above) can be explained in that these may cause harm to the child who is, then, covered by the child abuse laws.

as expressed in *ex p B*;[114] it has to be remembered, however, that the court in *Baby K* was concerned only with statute and not the 'best interests' of K. Second, the courts in *Baby K* rejected the hospital's submission on the grounds that its proposals for non-treatment were based on the child's disability rather than on its respiratory condition. Although the reasoning was different, this is, to an extent, a reflection of the seminal English case of *Re B*; there is, however, a world of difference between Down's syndrome and anencephaly – there is little doubt that, were a *Baby K* case to come to the English courts, it would be treated as one of Templeman LJ's exceptions destined to a demonstrably awful life.[115] Finally, *Baby K*, again, leads us to the definition of futility. It is arguable that intensive care was 'useful' to K in that it restored her respirations. Equally, however, it can be seen as 'futile' in that to do so was not a worthwhile achievement from the patient's point of view. We are then faced with the recurring problem – ought we, and can we, isolate the patient's interests from those of other involved parties, including those of the state? And if we cannot, ought treatment decisions to be left solely in the hands of the physician? In the end, the *Baby K* decision was policy-based – the courts were unwilling to undermine a general statute in order to solve a particular dilemma; the outcome might have been very different had the courts been able to consider the patient's 'best interests' but there seem to have been no further developments.[116]

Is the treatment of infants a separate issue?

16.80 Thus far, we have concentrated mainly on the neonate and the infant. The discussion has been long and we must ask if there is good reason for this emphasis. There are at least two good reasons for isolating the issues in early life from those in adulthood or those which are essentially perimortal. In the first place, decisions in the first situation rest almost entirely on prognosis, which is another way of expressing an informed guess as to the future. This may, in any event, be difficult and, while we know that we are dealing with only short-term survival at the end of life, this is not the case at birth – we may be confident of what will be the state of affairs next week but we cannot say the same about the next decade. Moreover, the neonate is not passing from a settled norm into a progressively less satisfactory condition; he is developing in a sub-optimal milieu which is his norm – can one say with any certainty that the Down's syndrome child, who has never known anything different, is dissatisfied with his existence within himself? Thus, we would take issue with the reasoning of Professor Williams, who wrote: 'If a wicked fairy told me she was about to transform me into a Down's baby and would I prefer to die I should certainly answer yes',[117] because this is not the question

---

114 For discussion, see F H Miller 'Infant Resuscitation: A US/UK Divide' (1994) 343 Lancet 1584. *Baby K* is a very interesting case in the present context but is probably not a particularly influential US case in relation to parental rights – for which see *Weber v Stony Brook Hospital* 456 NE 2d 1186 (NY, 1983); *Bowen v American Hospital Association* 476 US 620, 106 S Ct 2101 (1986).

115 *Re B (a minor)* (1981) [1990] 1 All ER 927 at 929, [1981] 1 WLR 1421 at 1424.

116 For a wide-ranging review of the European situation, see H E McHaffie, M Cuttini, G Brölz-Voit et al 'Withholding/Withdrawing Treatment from Neonates: Legislation and Official Guidelines across Europe' (1999) 25 J Med Ethics 440.

117 G Williams 'Down's Syndrome and the Duty to Preserve Life' (1981) 131 NLJ 1020.

being asked of the infant. The better view is that of Lord Donaldson – that the starting point in analysing the defective's condition is not what might have been but what is.[118]

16.81 The second major distinction between life and death decisions at the extremes of life is that, while the adult sufferer is likely to be able to express an opinion or, save in a few cases, to have previously intimated his wishes, there is no way in which the neonate can consent to treatment, suffering or death. Consent must be parental and one then asks where, in fact, do lie the parents' rights that it is feared will be usurped by the courts? Have they any more right to reject a child than to abandon it? If it can be criminal to disbar an older child from treatment,[119] why is it less culpable to fail, or to connive at failure, to provide the minimum of neonatal treatment – infant feeding? How do these rights differ when exercised in the light of medical advice rather than by way of simple intuition in the privacy of the home? Is it likely that a blind eye would be turned on parents who, on their own initiative, decided to abandon their disabled child? And can the parents who are, in addition to their emotional involvement, economically and socially concerned, make a truly objective decision on behalf of the child?[120]

16.82 These questions have, in the main, an ethical or social dimension. *Re C* and the *Re J* cases have, we suggest, clarified the criminal aspects of neonaticide and there is little doubt that non-treatment decisions are now taken on a daily basis in the United Kingdom.[121] Campbell,[122] writing on severely brain damaged children, believed that anything, including feeding, that prolongs such non-human or artificial life is 'wrong for the child, wrong for the family and wrong for society'. This, however, clearly depends on a value evaluation of the quality of life and, consequently, on a largely undefined discretion.[123] While it may well be an expression of the current state of the law, we suggest that decision-makers in the field should be wary of extending the bounds of *Re J* with impunity – life clearly carried great weight in Lord Donaldson's balance pan and does so in those of his successors.

16.83 What we *have* seen, is that the English courts are resolute in distinguishing between non-treatment and euthanasia and, in this respect, the fundamental distinction to be made is between, on the one hand, infants with

---

118 In *Re J (a minor) (wardship: medical treatment)* [1990] 3 All ER 930 at 936, (1990) 6 BMLR 25 at 32, paraphrasing McKenzie J.

119 *R v Senior* [1899] 1 QB 283, CCR.

120 A useful overview is to be found in S Moor 'Euthanasia in Relation to Newborn Babies – A Comparative Study of the Legal and Ethical Issues' (1996) 15 Med Law 295 and 537. The problem of responsibility surfaced dramatically in England in 2002 when the parents of a baby suffering from the severely disfiguring Goldenhar's Syndrome refused a tracheostomy to alleviate the child's breathing difficulties. Their reason was not related to futility but, rather, to fears for the baby's safety. The operation was agreed after some seven hours' discussion in the Family Court: C Dyer 'Parents Agree to Surgery for Disfigured Baby' (2002) 324 BMJ 632.

121 See A G M Campbell and H E McHaffie 'Prolonging Life and Allowing Death: Infants' (1995) 21 J Med Ethics 339.

122 A G M Campbell 'Children in a Persistent Vegetative State' (1984) 289 BMJ 1022.

123 See, in particular, C Wells '"Otherwise Kill Me": Marginal Children at the Edges of Existence' in R Lee and D Morgan (eds) *Birthrights* (1989) ch 11.

pure mental defects and, at the other extreme, those with severe physical incapacity resulting, for example, from neural tube defects. Treatment of the latter is a matter of careful medical management which must incorporate an element of selection.[124] Many such handicapped children will inevitably die and many should be allowed to do so; the principle of 'allowing nature to take its course' on the basis of a shared decision between doctor and parents is acceptable in both a moral and a legal sense provided that the decision is taken in the best interests of the child.[125] By contrast, if the mentally handicapped child is not to live, it must be encouraged and guided towards death. There is no non-treatment for the anatomically normal Down's baby because it needs no treatment and failure to feed in the latter instance can only be categorised as neonaticide – ie *killing* of the neonate, which brings us back to the question of whether there is, in fact, any true difference between non-treatment and euthanasia. Kuhse[126] has argued most persuasively that there is no moral or legal distinction to be drawn between activity and passivity in this area of medical practice. Gillon[127] put it:

> While there may be some social benefit in distinguishing between actively 'allowing to die' and painlessly killing such infants, there is, I believe, no other moral difference and doctors who accept such 'allowing to die' of severely handicapped newborn infants should not deceive themselves into believing that there is such a difference.

16.84 Elsewhere, the same author emphasised that, while there is no *necessary* moral difference between killing and letting die, it does not follow that there is a moral equivalence.[128] Were this so, we would have to approve the spectre of the paediatrician armed with a lethal syringe – and the concept is quite unacceptable. As we discuss in chapter 17, in relation to the permanent vegetative state, it is hard to assail the logic which says that a quick death is preferable to one which depends upon the vagaries of nature; nevertheless, we believe that natural death is the only acceptable concomitant of a decision not to treat a severely physically defective infant – and we also believe that food and water should be provided for any child which is capable of taking nourishment by mouth. In so saying, we admit to being guided, to a very considerable extent, by moral intuition alone – as a well-respected medical philosopher once put it: 'We are, here, noting a deep human inhibition which it might be unwise to tamper with in the name of logic.'[129] Clinicians are similarly beset by the illogic of intuition:

124 For a philosophical assessment, see J Harris 'Ethical Problems in the Management of Some Severely Handicapped Children' (1981) 7 J Med Ethics 117. Recent results from the coalface are reported by I M Balfour-Lynn and R C Tasker 'Futility and Death in Paediatric Medical Intensive Care' (1996) 22 J Med Ethics 279.

125 D D Raphael 'Handicapped Infants: Medical Ethics and the Law' (1988) 14 J Med Ethics 5 was one of the first to point to the conceptual difficulty in attributing any *interest* in death – 'the most you can say is that someone would prefer to die'.

126 H Kuhse 'A Modern Myth. That Letting Die is not the Intentional Causation of Death: Some Reflections on the Trial and Acquittal of Dr Leonard Arthur' (1984) 1 J Appl Philos 21. The same point is made by Harris, para 16.83 above.

127 R Gillon 'Conclusion. The *Arthur* Case Revisited' (1986) 292 BMJ 543.

128 R Gillon 'Euthanasia. Withholding Life-Prolonging Treatment and Moral Differences between Killing and Letting Die' (1988) 14 J Med Ethics 115.

129 R S Downie 'Modern Paediatric Practice: An Ethical Overview' (1989) in Mason, p 366, para 16.10 above, ch 31.

There is a powerful psychological distinction [between 'killing' and 'allowing to die'] which is important to the staff of intensive care units. To them, there is a big difference between not using a respirator to keep an infant of 600 g alive and giving a lethal injection, although the end result is the same.[130]

16.85   And, whatever logic may tell us, *Re J* spells out clearly what is the law. The situation is one in which the most acceptable course is not, unhappily, the kindest.

16.86   Advances in modern medicine have, at the same time, brought their own problems to the neonatal period. It is increasingly possible to maintain and rear premature infants of low birth weight and evidence is accumulating that a number of such children are disadvantaged to an extent which is inversely proportionate to their birthweight. [131] The discussion of selective non-treatment is, accordingly, being extended to include attitudes to intensive care of the premature infant. It is trite medicine to say that premature births should be prevented by improved ante-natal care. The fact remains that they will continue and their numbers will be augmented not so much due to poor maternal care as by the improved medical management of high-risk pregnancies. In these circumstances, we can see little alternative but to agree with those who believe that, since an accurate prognosis is generally impossible, such infants should always be offered treatment until such time as it is clearly ineffective – the test for treatment is, on these terms, one of feasibility – not of futility. The difficulty of such a rule is that, while resuscitation may be successful, the end result may be a severely handicapped survivor; quite apart from the individual clinical result, there may also be a serious problem of resource distribution:

> The ability to preserve the lives of these infants must be weighed against the resultant increase in the numbers of impaired children, the distress and suffering caused by lengthy treatment and hospitalisation, their eventual expected quality of life, and the socio-economic consequences for society as a whole.[132]

16.87   We have discovered only one recent relevant case – and this from a Scottish fatal accident inquiry which was poorly reported. The case involved the death of a 23-week-old neonate which was not taken into intensive care. The sheriff ruled that 'the doctor's decision not to resuscitate was made in the best interests of the child and was a reasonable clinical decision in the circumstances ... The doctor's clinical judgment had to take precedence over the wishes of the parents'. Since this is one of the clearest judicial statements on the relative rights of the parents to come from Scotland, it is something of a pity that the case went no further.[133]

---

130   A G M Campbell 'Ethical Issues in Child Health and Disease' in J O Forfar (ed) *Child Health in a Changing Society* (1988).

131   L W Doyle, L J Murton and W H Kitchen 'Increasing the Survival of Extremely-immature (24–28 weeks' gestation) Infants – At what Cost?' (1989) 150 Med J Austral 558.

132   J Griffin, quoted by L Hunt 'Cost "Dilemma" Posed by Premature Babies' (1993) Independent, 20 January, p 6 in discussion of Office of Health Economics *Born Too Soon* (1993).

133   S English 'Doctor Was Right not to Resuscitate "Unviable" Baby' *The Times*, 27 June 1997, p 11.

A need for legislation?

16.88 Despite the reluctance of the courts to interfere with clinical judgments, it might still be thought that the medical practitioner needs more official guidance and legal protection when undertaking selective non-treatment decisions. The current vogue in the United Kingdom when the common or statute law is unclear as to detail is for the creation of 'guidelines' by an authoritative body. These generally do not have the force of law but their non-observance will reflect adversely on the person who fails to follow them. As we have already noted, documents relating to paediatric practice are now available.[134] Of the two publications we have quoted, that from the Royal College of Paediatrics and Child Health is the more practical and definitive. In summary, it outlines five situations where the withholding or withdrawal of curative medical treatment might be considered:

(a) *The brain dead child.* Once the diagnosis of brain death has been made, it is agreed within the profession that treatment in such circumstances is futile and withdrawal is appropriate.[135]

(b) *The permanent vegetative state.* We discuss this state below.[136]

(c) *The 'no chance' situation.* The child has such severe disease that life sustaining treatment simply delays death without alleviation of suffering. Medical treatment may, thus, be deemed inappropriate.

(d) *The 'no purpose' situation.* Although the patient may be able to survive with treatment, the degree of physical or mental impairment will be so great that it is unreasonable to expect them to bear it. The child in this situation will never be capable of taking part in decisions regarding treatment or its withdrawal.

(e) *The 'unbearable' situation.* The child and/or family feel that, in the face of progressive and irreversible illness, *further* treatment is more than can be borne. These wishes are irrespective of the medical opinion on its potential benefit.

16.89 In situations that do not fit these five categories, or where there is dissent or uncertainty about the degree of future impairment, the child's life should be safeguarded in the best possible way.

16.90 The guidelines from the British Medical Association are more general and, effectively, set the ethical framework within which to work. The basic presumption is that life-prolonging treatment should be initiated where there is reasonable uncertainty as to its benefit. On the other hand, best interests are not necessarily synonymous with prolongation of life and there are circumstances in which active intervention would be inappropriate. These are:

– that the child has no potential to develop awareness;

– he or she will be unable to interact or to achieve the capacity for sel-directed action; and that

– the child will suffer severe unavoidable pain and distress.

---

134 See para 16.47 above.

135 It will be seen from chapter 13 that we regard this as something of a contradiction; the child is dead and you cannot *treat* a corpse. There is specific case law to the effect that the health carers cannot be compelled to do so: *Re A* [1992] 3 Med LR 303.

136 See para 17.5 et seq.

16.91 If the child's condition is incompatible with survival or where there is broad consensus that the condition is so severe that treatment would not provide a benefit in terms of being able to restore or maintain the patient's health, intervention may be unjustified. Similarly, where treatments would involve suffering or distress to the child, these and other burdens must be weighed against the anticipated benefit, even if life cannot be prolonged without treatment.

16.92 The BMA firmly believes that parents are generally the best judges of their young children's, and the family's, interests; doctors take the lead in judging the clinical factors and parents the lead in determining best interests more generally. When a decision is reached to withhold or withdraw a particular treatment, it is the value of the treatment which is being assessed, not the value of the child – the overall objective of providing benefit does not change. While those with parental responsibility have the legal power to give or withhold consent to treatment for a child, this is provided they are not acting against his or her best interests; parental power to withhold consent for a child's treatment is likely to be curtailed where the treatment refused would provide a clear benefit to the child, where the statistical chances of recovery are good or where the severity and burdens of the condition are not sufficient to justify withholding or withdrawing life-prolonging treatment. Perhaps the only controversial statement from the BMA lies in para 15.1 where it is said: 'Where there is genuine uncertainty about which treatment option would be of most clinical benefit, parents are usually best placed and equipped to weigh the evidence and apply it to their child's own circumstances.' Clearly, this depends, and is so conceded, upon full discussion between doctors and parents, but the paragraph is, in our view confusing when it adds: 'the actual treatment decision will depend upon the medical assessment of benefit'.[137]

16.93 There is ample authority supporting the premise that there are some infants who *ought* not to be assisted to live by invasive methods. The incapacitated child has as much right to die in peace as has his grandfather and there are times when it is clear that that right should be exercised. Moreover, it is now clear that a responsible clinician who believes that to be the right course cannot be compelled to provide treatment with which he disagrees.[138] Nevertheless, while there is probably now sufficient case law to justify non-treatment decisions, many would hold that clarifying legislation is still desirable if only to do no more than relieve the clinician of an *accusation* of homicide in such circumstances. Moreover, legislation can anticipate and forestall the 'domino effect'. It does not need much imagination, for example, to envisage parental rejection of the newborn as being justified by a club foot or even unattractive features.

---

137 For a full empirical study of how decisions are made in practice, see H E McHaffie, I A Laing, M Parker and J McMillan 'Deciding for Imperilled Newborns: Medical Authority or Parental Autonomy?' (2001) 27 J Med Ethics 104.

138 *Re J (a minor) (medical treatment)* [1993] Fam 15, (1992) 9 BMLR 10. Interestingly, one of the reasons given was that to do so might require the health authority to use intensive care resources and, thereby, to deny them to someone who might derive greater benefit ([1993] Fam 15 at 29, (1992) 9 BMLR 10 at 20, per Balcombe LJ). The implication is that the courts see a difference between not starting a life-saving treatment and withdrawing it.

16.94 The case of *Baby K* has already demonstrated the difficulties that surround *positive* legislation in fields such as this and, in our view, statute law ought not to create new offences – it should do no more than lay down the conditions under which a doctor who withholds or withdraws treatment commits no offence. Furthermore, since legislation is always difficult to adapt to changing circumstances, it should be relatively non-specific and should allow for the free exercise of clinical decision-making in individual cases. If there were to be legislation – and we discuss the need further under the heading of the permanent vegetative state[139] – we suggest the inclusion of a clause to the effect:

> In the event of positive treatment being necessary for a neonate's survival, it will not be an offence to withhold such treatment if two doctors, one of whom is a consultant paediatrician, acting in good faith and with the consent of both parents if available, decide against treatment in the light of a reasonably clear medical prognosis which indicates that the infant's further life would be intolerable by virtue of pain or suffering or because of severe cerebral incompetence.

16.95 We believe that, on the one hand, this emphasises the interests of the infant while, on the other, it clarifies and protects the legal position of paediatricians who are forced into making particularly stressful clinical decisions.[140]

16.96 None of the published codes really addresses the critical dilemma of the infant who satisfies all the requirements but still survives without treatment. We find it difficult, if not impossible, to disagree with those who hold that normal feeding, not involving medical intervention, should be continued whenever the infant is capable of taking nourishment by mouth – yet we have to acknowledge that there are times when this does not seem to be in the neonate's best interests in terms of suffering. The status of normal feeding is, however, again best discussed under the heading of PVS, where the problem has been fully addressed in the courts.[141]

The interests of others

16.97 No practical solutions to the ending of life can be applied without giving thought to those who must participate in any process and, in particular to those who have a conscientious objection to the procedures. Were there to be any legislation which legalises the withholding or withdrawal of treatment in specified circumstances, it must, in our view, include a discretionary clause similar to that in the Abortion Act 1967, s 4. We emphasise the role of the

---

139 See para 17.52 below.
140 J K Mason and D W Meyers 'Parental Choice and Selective Non-treatment of Defective Newborns: A View from Mid-Atlantic' (1986) 12 J Med Ethics 67. Very similar conclusions are to be found in the amendments to the US Child Abuse Prevention and Treatment Act 1974 (see para 16.76 above). They are also compatible with the teaching of the Roman Catholic Church: *Care of the Handicapped Newborn: Parental Responsibility and Medical Responsibility* (1986).
141 See para 17.5 et seq below.

nursing staff and the importance of safeguarding their position both now and in the event of legislation. It is the nurses, not the doctors, who will bear the brunt of selective non-treatment; not only must they be spared responsibility for carrying out instructions but, also, their sensitivities must be fully respected. We strongly commend the increasingly accepted principle of a team approach to neonatal intensive care.[142]

16.98 We believe that current court decisions have done much to define parental powers in this area. No one would deny that the parents' views should be ascertained, nor that they should carry great weight – but they cannot be fully determinative. Common attitudes to the management of disabled infants are based on the assumption of marital harmony, in that they relate so firmly to the wishes of 'the parents' – what if there is disagreement? Fortunately, the situation must arise only rarely. There can, however, be little doubt that, while the birth of a handicapped child may uncover qualities of goodness in the parents that are beyond expectation, an opposite reaction can be provoked.[143] Certainly, there are always the courts – but who is to say that judges qua judges are uniquely fitted to decide controversial questions of the value of infant life?[144] and can they do any more than accept the views of those who are or are not to provide the treatment? It is essential that the medical and legal professions – as well as society at large – should make sure of the lines they intend to draw in the face of potential conflict, whether this be inter-professional of inter-parental. Perhaps, despite the best efforts of all the parties involved, the case for legislation in the field remains attractive.

142 The point was well taken in the judgment in *Re C (a minor) (wardship: medical treatment)* [1990] Fam 26, [1989] 2 All ER 782.
143 See B Shepperdson 'Abortion and Euthanasia of Down's Syndrome Children – The Parents' View' (1983) 9 J Med Ethics 152. And, for an interesting debate: 'Informed Dissent': M Simms 'The Views of Some Mothers of Severely Mentally Handicapped Young Adults'; A Davis 'The View of a Disabled Woman' (1986) 12 J Med Ethics 72, 75.
144 See Walker LJ in *Re A (children) (conjoined twins: surgical separation)* (2000) 57 BMLR 1 at 16, quoting Scalia J in *Cruzan v Director* (1990) 497 US 261 at 294.

17 Medical futility: II Later life

17.1 We have suggested in the previous chapter that the concept of medical futility can be applied as a continuum from the neonate to the terminally ill. The full picture is, however, not quite so simple, as the underlying reasons for, and the management of, non-treatment will vary according to age. Thus, non-treatment in infancy has been, at least in part, a matter of the management of physical disability. But this has been morally permissible only because treatment of itself would result in an intolerable life which it would be inhumane to enforce on the child who would, at the same time, die naturally if he or she were untreated. Such conditions are uncommon in adult life and, when they do occur – as, for example, in accidental quadriplegia – their management is more allied to euthanasia[1] than to selective non-treatment.

17.2 Disability due to brain damage is, however, common to both infancy and adulthood and we have seen that, while the courts will not tolerate the deliberate shortening of life, they are fully prepared to accede to non-treatment of associated lethal disease in the severely brain-damaged child – and to base this on an undeniably 'quality of life' standard as measured by a 'best interests' test. It is of some interest to speculate on why it is that this has been accepted relatively easily in the case of children while the legal attitude to the management of the brain damaged adult has taken so long to mature and has done so amid so much controversy. Is it that we give greater weight to life that has 'been lived' than to life which has no past? Do we see a sustainable distinction between starting on a life with handicap and continuing life in a disabled state? Are we less concerned with any residual cognitive ability in the infant than we are with comparable but expressible brain activity in the adult? And are we frightened of an ever-widening definition of what is perceived as intolerable in the adult? Possibly the most important delineator lies in the purely pragmatic reason that fatal intercurrent disease is simply less common in the brain damaged adult in whom, accordingly, non-treatment moves ever closer to euthanasia and, as a result, becomes less acceptable.

1   See chapter 18.

17.3 Yet we are constantly assured that we are *not* practising euthanasia in allowing such persons to die. Thus, we have Hoffmann LJ saying:

> This is not a case about euthanasia because it does not involve any external agency of death. It is about whether, and how, the patient should be allowed to die.[2]

17.4 It is for this reason that we have detached the management of the brain damaged adult – and, particularly, the adult in the permanent vegetative state – from our discussion of euthanasia. Legally – if less certainly logically – it sits easier under the heading of 'futile treatment'; as Lord Goff put it in the House of Lords in *Bland*, 'it is the futility of the treatment [of Anthony Bland] which justifies its termination'.[3]

THE PATIENT IN THE PERMANENT VEGETATIVE STATE

17.5 We have already discussed the effect of hypoxia on the various segments of the brain. In clinical terms, this means that depriving the brain of oxygen can result in anything from mild intellectual deterioration to death – the outcome being determined almost exclusively by how rapidly normal oxygenation can be established. How much consciousness or cognitive ability is retained then depends on the degree of cortical damage and this can be of very considerable moral and medico-legal significance. In any event, the brain stem – which controls our vegetative functions – will survive an hypoxic insult better than will the cortex, and the truly critical situation arises when the cortex is wholly destroyed but the brain stem continues to function. This is the condition which was originally described as the 'persistent vegetative state' by Jennett and Plum.[4] The patient then has no consciousness and the awesome nature of the condition is summed up in the phrase: 'Consciousness is the most critical moral, legal, and constitutional standard, not for human life itself, but for human personhood'[5] – the unconscious or comatose patient is incapable of fulfilling his human function in a way which transcends the loss of any other capacity; it follows that the whole status of the person in a position of persistent unconsciousness is in doubt.

17.6 It is notoriously difficult to identify a satisfactory definition of the persistent vegetative state. The distinguishing features include an irregular but cyclic state of circadian sleeping and waking unaccompanied by any behaviourally detectable expression of self-awareness, specific recognition of external stimuli, or consistent evidence of attention or inattention or learned responses.[6] It is important to note that patients in this state, while generally being in a spastic condition, are not immobile and, to a varying extent, retain both cranial-nerve and spinal reflexes, including those related to visual and auditory stimuli.

---

2 In *Airedale NHS Trust v Bland* [1993] 1 All ER 821 at 856, (1993) 12 BMLR 64 at 101, CA.
3 [1993] 1 All ER 821 at 870, (1993) 12 BMLR 64 at 116.
4 B Jennett and F Plum 'Persistent Vegetative State after Brain Damage' (1972) 1 Lancet 734.
5 R E Cranford and D R Smith 'Consciousness: The Most Critical Moral (Constitutional) Standard for Human Personhood' (1987) 13 Am J Law Med 233.
6 Multi-society Task Force on PVS 'Medical Aspects of the Persistent Vegetative State' (1994) 330 New Engl J Med 1499 (Pt 1), 1572 (Pt 2).

Again, this reflects the degree of brain damage; we can, therefore, speak in terms of degrees of vegetativeness, although it requires skilled neurological expertise to distinguish retained – or recovered – cortical function from sub-cortical reflex activity. In addition, the concept has its built-in semantic difficulties, the most urgent of which lies in the word 'persistent'. A persistent state is one which persists until it is relieved – from which it follows that the diagnosis of the persistent vegetative state envisages a potential for recovery; this was the understanding of those who coined the term.[7] It is, in our opinion, essential that discussion – and any legislation based upon it – should be devoted to the management of the permanent vegetative state (PVS).[8] Even then, the difficulties are not all eliminated. Permanence is a presumption rather than a certainty; whether or not that presumption is acceptable depends on empirical evidence which must, also, bow to practicality. Thus, the Multi-society Task Force in America defined the persistent vegetative state as a vegetative state present one month after acute traumatic or non-traumatic brain injury; it concluded that a permanent state can be assumed if the patient has been vegetative for one year.[9] But to say that a state is permanent if it has been present for a year[10] involves a balancing act between reasonableness and certainty. The compromise, no matter how high is the degree of clinical certainty, is unlikely to satisfy everyone and the possibility of exceptions to the rule cannot be denied; nevertheless, the advantages of establishing a cut-off point outweigh the disadvantages of prolonging the decision indefinitely. Of equal importance is the fact that, as we have already noted, the word 'vegetative' fails to define the degree of brain damage involved. Therapeutic decisions in PVS thus depend not only on its permanence but also on the definition of vegetative which must, to an extent, involve a value judgment.

17.7   Having reached a diagnosis, however, we are left with what may well be regarded as the ultimate tragedy in human life – a human being who is alive in the cardiovascular sense in that he or she can breathe and maintain a heart beat, and who is, equally, not brain stem dead, but who, at the same time, has no contact with the outside world and will never have such contact again. We have discussed the concept of neocortical death above.[11] At this point we need only reiterate that it has no place in the law of the United Kingdom. The law as to killing is unaffected by the mental state of the victim – dements and aments are still protected in so far as the term 'reasonable being' implies no more than 'human being' – and persons in the permanent vegetative state still represent 'persons in being'. They present an extra jurisprudential difficulty in that, being unconscious, they are free from pain – or, at least, pain cannot be expressed in a manner which makes it treatable; the doctrine of 'double effect' cannot, therefore, be applied within their management – and, in this respect, it is to be

---

7 See, S Laureys, M-E Faymonville and J Berre 'Permanent vegetative state and persistent vegetative state are not interchangeable terms' (2000) 321 BMJ letters, 17 October.

8 See, especially, 'The Permanent Vegetative State – Review by a Working Group Convened by the Royal College of Physicians and Endorsed by the Conference of Medical Royal Colleges and their Faculties of the United Kingdom' (1996) 30 J R Coll Physicians Lond 119.

9 See para 17.6 above.

10 Agreed by the BMA: *BMA Guidelines on Treatment Decisions for Patients in Persistent Vegetative State* (1996) and by the Working Party of the Royal College of Physicians, para 17.6 above.

11 See para 13.5 et seq.

noted that, absent an intercurrent infection or similar complication, well-managed PVS patients have a life expectancy that is to be measured in years. Lord Scarman,[12] while appreciating –

> that there are great social problems not only in the life support of the human vegetable but also in the survival of barely sentient people who cannot look after themselves,

also added:

> there are implications in the right to terminate another's existence of which it is well to be fearful in the absence of a more prolonged analysis of the problem than that which it has received.

17.8 These extra-judicial remarks were made some time ago; since then, the topic has been subject to intense moral scrutiny and, recently, to extensive legal analysis. We have spent some time on the definitional difficulties of the condition because, without an understanding of them, it is impossible to appreciate the distinctions which have been made in the various cases that have come before the courts in recent years and the reasons underlying them. All those that we discuss have it in common that the courts were being invited to pronounce on the lawfulness of withdrawing physiological support from severely brain-damaged patients.

THE ENGLISH CASES

17.9 The first, and most important case in which the matter was addressed in the United Kingdom was *Airedale NHS Trust v Bland*.[13] Anthony Bland was crushed in a football stadium in April 1989 and sustained severe anoxic brain damage; as a result, he relapsed into the persistent vegetative state. There was no improvement in his condition by September 1992 and, at that time, the hospital sought a declaration[14] to the effect that they might lawfully discontinue all life-sustaining treatment and medical support measures, including ventilation, nutrition and hydration by artificial means; that any subsequent treatment given should be for the sole purpose of enabling him to end his life in dignity and free from pain and suffering; that, if death should then occur, its cause should be attributed to the natural and other causes of his present state; and that none of those concerned should, as a result, be subject to any civil or criminal liability. This declaration – save for the final clause, which was considered inappropriate[15]

---

12 Lord Scarman 'Legal Liability and Medicine' (1981) 74 Proc Roy Soc Med 11.
13 [1993] 1 All ER 821, (1993) 12 BMLR 64, Fam D, CA, HL.
14 The English courts have been in something of a dilemma in such cases since their authority under the parens patriae jurisdiction was removed by way of the Mental Health Act 1959 and revocation of the last warrant under the sign manual. The court cannot now give effective consent to medical treatment on behalf of a mentally incompetent adult unless that treatment is directed to the cause of the incompetence. The court can, however, make an anticipatory declaration as to the lawfulness or otherwise of a proposed action: see discussion of *Re F* at para 10.30 et seq above.
15 This problem was considered in greater detail in the comparable Scottish case *Law Hospital NHS Trust v Lord Advocate* 1996 SLT 848, (1996) 39 BMLR 166, for which see para 17.31 below.

– was granted in the Family Division essentially on the grounds that it was in AB's best interests to do so; the court considered there was overwhelming evidence that the provision of artificial feeding by means of a nasogastric tube was 'medical treatment' and that its discontinuance was in accord with good medical practice. An appeal was unanimously dismissed in the Court of Appeal. From three exceptionally well-considered opinions, we extract only that of Hoffmann LJ:

> This is not an area in which any difference can be allowed to exist between what is legal and what is morally right. The decision of the court should be able to carry conviction with the ordinary person as being based not merely on legal precedent but also upon acceptable ethical values.[16]

and, later:

> In my view the choice the law makes must reassure people that the courts do have full respect for life, but that they do not pursue the principle to the point at which it has become almost empty of any real content and when it involves the sacrifice of other important values such as human dignity and freedom of choice. I think that such reassurance can be provided by a decision, properly explained, to allow Anthony Bland to die.[17]

17.10 The inherent difficulty of the declarator procedure is that it is concerned only with the *lawfulness* of an action[18] and, when the *Bland* case came to the House of Lords, Lord Browne-Wilkinson and Lord Mustill were at particular pains to emphasise that the ethical issues should be considered and legislated for by Parliament:

> [I]s this a matter which lies outside the legitimate development of the law by judges and requires society, through the democratic expression of its views in Parliament, to reach its decisions on the underlying moral and practical problems and then reflect those decisions in legislation? I have no doubt that it is for Parliament, not the courts, to decide the broader issues which this case raises.[19]

17.11 It was, therefore, not surprising that, although the House could not entirely avoid addressing the ethical and moral problems involved, it did so to a lesser extent than did the Court of Appeal. In this respect, the fundamental conflict lies in the inevitable distortion of the principle of the sanctity of life which would result from a decision to terminate the care on which life depended.[20] The majority of the House was able to dispose of this on the grounds that the principle was certainly not absolute. Moreover, since the right to refuse treatment – including life-sustaining treatment – is now firmly part of common law and medical ethics, the principle of the sanctity of life must yield to that of the right to self-determination and, of the many lines of argument considered, it

---

16 [1993] 1 All ER 821 at 850, (1993) 12 BMLR 64 at 95.
17 [1993] 1 All ER 821 at 855, (1993) 12 BMLR 64 at 100.
18 See J Bridgeman '"Declared Innocent?"' (1995) 3 Med L Rev 117.
19 [1993] 1 All ER 821 at 878, (1993) 12 BMLR 64 at 124, per Lord Browne-Wilkinson.
20 For major discussion, see J Keown 'Restoring Moral and Intellectual Shape to the Law after *Bland*' (1997) 113 LQR 481.

is this which seems to us to bind all five Law Lords most closely together. As Lord Goff put it,[21] the right to self-determination should not be eclipsed by the fact of incompetence – it must always be present. This also forms the basis of Lord Mustill's reasoning, which is summarised below and which, essentially, justifies the withdrawal or withholding of treatment. We are less happy with the alternative view taken, in particular, by Lord Lowry and Lord Browne-Wilkinson. In essence, this also started from the premise that non-voluntary treatment was lawful only so long as it was justified by necessity; but, once necessity could no longer be claimed – by reason of the futility of treatment – further invasion of the patient's body constituted either the crime of battery or the tort of trespass. On this view, any potential medical offence lies not in *withholding* treatment but in *continuing* it to no purpose. This argument seems to us to be dangerously open-ended in relation to conditions less clear-cut than the persistent vegetative state – a situation which Lord Mustill was clearly anxious to avoid. None the less, this concern has been borne out more recently in guidance from the British Medical Association which proposes extending the PVS ruling to other incapacitated patients.[22] We discuss this further below.[23]

17.12 The greater part of the opinions in *Bland* was concerned for the doctors' position vis-à-vis the criminal law. First, it was essential to elide the possibility of murder by classifying removal of support as an omission rather than as a positive act.[24] There was wide agreement that, while there was no moral or logical difference, a distinction was certainly to be made in law. The House came to a unanimous conclusion that discontinuance of nasogastric feeding was an omission; their Lordships achieved this in various ways but, in general, it was considered impossible to distinguish between withdrawal of and not starting tube feeding – and the latter was clearly an omission. Next, the problem of the duty of care had to be addressed. Lord Mustill's argument can be summarised:

(a)   Treatment of the incompetent is governed by necessity and necessity is, in turn, defined in terms of the patient's best interests.

(b)   Once there is no hope of recovery, any interest in being kept alive disappears and, with it, the justification for invasive therapy also disappears.

(c)   In the absence of necessity, there can be no duty to act and, in the absence of a duty, there can be no criminality in an omission.

17.13 This, however, leads to what was, perhaps, the major hurdle – can feeding be regarded as medical treatment and, therefore, a fit subject for medical decision-making, or is it always such a fundamental duty that it can never be wilfully withheld? The Lords in *Bland* had rather more trouble with this than have had their counterparts in the United States and we return to the subject in a little more detail below.[25] Eventually, however, a consensus was

---

21   [1993] 1 All ER 821 at 866, (1993) 12 BMLR 64 at 112.
22   British Medical Association *Withholding and Withdrawing Life-Prolonging Medical Treatment: Guidance for Decision Makers* (2nd edn, 2001).
23   See para 17.30.
24   For further discussion of which, see chapter 18 below.
25   See para 17.39 et seq.

reached that nasogastric feeding at least formed part of the general medical management. While it is certainly more difficult to see nasogastric feeding as medical treatment than it is to accept gastrostomy feeding as such, we do not share some of the academic distrust of the concept that has been expressed.[26]

17.14 At the end of the day, the House of Lords was able to justify their unanimous decision on the basis of the patient's best interests. All the opinions stressed that it was not a matter of it being in the best interests of the patient to die but, rather, that it was not in his best interests to treat him so as to prolong his life in circumstances where 'no affirmative benefit' could be derived from the treatment.[27] We confess to some difficulty in accepting a 'best interests' test in these circumstances and we return to the matter below.[28] For the present, we point out that its application dictates the concurrent acceptance of 'good medical practice' as the yardstick of assessment. This led the House of Lords to conclude that the *Bolam* test[29] – that the doctor's decision should be judged against one which would be taken by a responsible and competent body of relevant professional opinion – applied in the management of PVS. This gives considerable discretion to the medical profession to decide what amounts to the patient's best interests by reference to its own standards[30] and, in deciding that artificial feeding was, at least, an integral part of medical treatment, the House of Lords opened the door to the health carers to withdraw alimentation. Nevertheless, the requirement to seek court approval in every case was maintained[31] – subject to the hope that the restriction might be rescinded in the future – and there was, in fact, a strong undercurrent to the effect that the decision was specific to *Bland* rather than a general statement on the removal of alimentation from brain damaged persons.

English cases post-Bland

17.15 Consideration of the later cases suggests that a note of caution may not have been misplaced. Almost exactly a year later, we had the case of *Frenchay Healthcare NHS Trust v S*.[32] This concerned a young man who had been in apparent PVS for two and a half years as a result of a drug overdose. When it was discovered that his gastrostomy tube had become detached, a declaration was sought that the hospital could lawfully refrain from renewing or continuing alimentary and other life-sustaining measures and could restrict any medical treatment to that which would allow him to die peacefully and with the greatest dignity. The declaration was granted and the decision was upheld on appeal.

---

26   See, eg, J M Finnis '*Bland*: Crossing the Rubicon?' (1993) 109 LQR 329.
27   [1993] 1 All ER 821 at 883, (1993) 12 BMLR 64 at 130, per Lord Browne-Wilkinson.
     See also [1993] 1 All ER 821 at 865, (1993) 12 BMLR 64 at 115.
28   See para 17.39 et seq.
29   *Bolam v Friern Hospital Management Committee* [1957] 1 WLR 582, (1957) 1 BMLR 1.
30   See [1993] 1 All ER 821 at 883, (1993) 12 BMLR 64 at 130, per Lord Browne-
     Wilkinson: '... on an application to the court for a declaration that the discontinuance
     of medical care will be lawful, the courts *only* concern will be to be satisfied that the
     doctor's decision to discontinue is in accordance with a respectable body of medical
     opinion and that it is reasonable ...' (emphasis added).
31   *Practice Note* [1996] 4 All ER 766, (1996) 34 BMLR 20.
32   [1994] 2 All ER 403, (1994) 17 BMLR 156, CA.

17.16 *Frenchay v S* differs from *Bland* in a fundamental respect – that, although the prospect had been mooted, the actual decision to discontinue treatment was not a considered one but was one forced by events. As a corollary, the judicial inquiry was certainly hurried and this was the factor which most concerned Waite LJ in the Court of Appeal. The decision has also been subject to academic criticism on these grounds.[33] More importantly, Sir Thomas Bingham MR considered it plain that the evidence in *Frenchay* was neither as emphatic nor as unanimous as that in *Bland*'s case.[34] We must also consider the potential results of failing to make or countermanding the declaration sought – either the doctors would have been forced into an operation which was, in the opinion of the consultant in charge, of no benefit to the patient and which possibly verged on criminal intervention or they would have had to do nothing and take their chance with the law.

17.17 Sir Thomas accepted such medical opinion as was provided but was, himself, conscious of a qualitative difference between the two cases. The question thus arises as to whether *Frenchay* represents a 'slippery slope' on which we could descend from PVS to little more than physical or mental disability when assuming that the patient's 'best interests' lie in non-treatment; alternatively, is it a judicial effort to homogenise non-treatment decisions – during which process, PVS becomes merely the end-point for decision-making rather than a condition to be considered on its own? We discuss below[35] the difficulties in harmonising the 'specific-case' stance adopted in *Bland* with the relatively open-ended direction as to withholding 'futile' treatment that was provided in *Re J*.[36] Meantime, perhaps the main inference to be drawn is that each case is special and must be judged on its own facts.[37]

17.18 Later English cases have been reported only spasmodically. We comment briefly on some of these mainly to indicate the quality of the evidence.

17.19 *Re C*[38] concerned a 27-year-old man who had been in PVS for four years following an anaesthetic disaster. Clinically, the case was of great severity and the judge appears to have accepted without demur the evidence provided by the relatives as to the likely wishes of the patient.

17.20 *Re G*[39] related to a young man whose brain damage, sustained in a motorcycle accident, was intensified by a later anoxic episode. The case was

---

33 See eg A Grubb 'Commentary' (1994) 2 Med L Rev 206.
34 [1994] 2 All ER 403 at 411, (1994) 17 BMLR 156 at 163.
35 See para 17.50.
36 *Re J (a minor) (wardship: medical treatment)* [1990] 3 All ER 930, (1990) 6 BMLR 25.
37 A point which was emphasised in *Bland* and also in the even more doubtful Irish case of *In the matter of a Ward* (1995) 2 ILRM 401. Precisely the same result was achieved in this case although the reasoning was complicated by considerations of Irish constitutional law. For discussion, see J K Mason and G T Laurie 'The Management of the Persistent Vegetative State in the British Isles' [1996] JR 263; J Keown 'Life and Death in Dublin' [1996] CLJ 6.
38 R Ford 'Patient in coma may die in dignity' *The Times*, 18 November 1995, p 1. The importance of continued post-mortem anonymity was considered in *Re C (adult patient: restriction of publicity after death)* [1996] 2 FLR 251.
39 [1995] 3 Med L Rev 80. In passing, it was held that the public interest in these cases determined that they should be heard in open court: *Re G (adult patient: publicity)* [1995] 2 FLR 528.

of particular interest in that there was some dispute amongst the relatives as to the course to be adopted. Sir Stephen Brown P concluded that the dissenting views of the patient's mother should not be allowed to operate as a veto when his best interests – as defined by the surgeon in charge – favoured removal of nutrition. It seems likely, therefore, that the comments of Lord Goff in *Bland*[40] to the effect that the attitudes of relatives, while due great respect, should not be determinative will be followed in the event of conflict.

17.21 *Swindon and Marlborough NHS Trust v S*[41] was unique among reported cases in being concerned with a patient who was being nursed at home. Rather as in *Frenchay*, however, the issue was forced by blockage of the gastrostomy tube; further treatment would, therefore, have involved hospitalisation. Ward J held that, given the certain diagnosis of PVS, to discontinue life-sustaining measures would be in accordance with good medical practice as recognised and approved within the medical profession. Once again, as in *Re G*, the court firmly adopted *Bolam* as the benchmark – there is a strong suggestion that good medical practice is being seen as a test of lawfulness.

17.22 There was no doubt as to the diagnosis in any of these three cases. *Re D*,[42] however, concerned a 28-year-old woman who had sustained very severe brain damage following a head injury some six years before. Again, an emergency arose when her gastrostomy tube became displaced. All medical opinion was to the effect that D was totally unaware of anything or anyone but she did not fully satisfy the conditions laid down by the Royal College of Physicians for the diagnosis of the permanent vegetative state.[43] The President of the Family Division regarded her as suffering 'a living death' and was unable to accept that, because she did not fulfil one of the diagnostic criteria, she was not in a permanent vegetative state. He, therefore, did not believe he was extending the range of cases in which a declaration as to the removal of feeding and hydration might properly be considered. It was appropriate and in her best interests to make such a declaration.

17.23 *Re H*,[44] involved a 43-year-old woman who had existed for three years in a severely brain damaged state following a vehicular accident. She, too, was agreed to be wholly and unalterably unaware of herself or her environment but, equally, it was agreed that she did not fit squarely within one of the College of Physicians' diagnostic criteria. Sir Stephen Brown P thought that, in this instance 'it may be that a precise label is not of significant importance'. Indeed, the whole area is prey to semantic juggling – one expert, while agreeing that the case did not fit the criteria for the permanent vegetative state, nevertheless thought that H was in a vegetative state which was permanent. The court reiterated that, while it was aware of the consequences that would follow the suspension of treatment, it did not in any sense sanction anything which is *aimed* at terminating life:

40 [1993] 1 All ER 821 at 872, (1993) 12 BMLR 64 at 118.
41 [1995] 3 Med LR 84.
42 (1997) 38 BMLR 1.
43 See para 17.6 above.
44 *Re H (adult: incompetent)* (1997) 38 BMLR 11.

The sanctity of life is of vital importance. It is not, however, paramount and ...
I am satisfied that it is in the best interests of this patient that the life sustaining
treatment ... should be brought to a conclusion.[45]

17.24 Thus, while all these cases show distinctive variations, they also have
common features which may serve as pointers to the future. The first is that,
the precedents having been set, the baseline lies in the confirmed diagnosis of
PVS. Once that is made, the conclusion follows automatically that the patient's
best interests dictate the termination of assisted feeding and, indeed, there
may well be an obligation on the doctor to discontinue treatment.[46] Second,
and following from this, the Official Solicitor has been loath to oppose any
applications for withdrawal of support once the diagnosis is confirmed.
Complete medicalisation of treatment decisions in the condition may, then,
be only a short step away. This having been said, a Practice Direction now
makes it clear that High Court approval should be sought in almost all cases
where removal of feeding and hydration is contemplated.[47] The court is charged
with weighing the advantages and disadvantages for the patient of removal
in light of the available medical evidence, although it is difficult to see how
any conclusion other than withdrawal could be reached when faced with a
good faith assessment of medical futility by the care team. We say this in light
of most recent developments which – contrary to the expectations of some –
demonstrate that the provisions of the Human Rights Act 1998 make virtually
no difference to the position of patients in PVS.

17.25 In *NHS Trust A v Mrs M, NHS Trust B v Mrs H*[48] declarators of
legality were sought on the proposed withdrawal of feeding and hydration
from two patients in PVS. In authorising this the High Court not only endorsed
the pre-existing position under *Bland*, but went further in testing this precedent
against possible human rights objections under the 1998 Act, namely Article 2
(right to life), Article 3 (prohibition of cruel and inhuman treatment), and
Article 8 (right to respect for private life). Rather than considering the
particularised reasoning of Butler-Sloss P in respect of each of these provisions,[49]
a few points of principle and policy should be noted.

17.26 The court clearly adopted a *good faith* approach to the issue, focusing
on the fact that, because a 'responsible body of medical opinion' has reached
a conclusion as to futility, there is little more to be said on the matter. This,
however, makes professionalism rather than principle the measure of patient
protection. But, given that medical professionals are qualified only to comment
on the medical futility of any proposed course of action, it is unclear why this
should be determinative of the issue. It is true that the court retains for itself
the ultimate role as arbiter of best interests[50] but, as the Official Solicitor's

---

45 (1997) 38 BMLR 11 at 16.
46 Following the argument put forward by Professor Grubb in Commentary [1995] 3 Med
L Rev 83, 85.
47 *Practice Direction (Declaratory Proceedings: Incapacitated Adults)* [2002] 1 WLR 325,
65 BMLR 72.
48 [2001] 2 WLR 942, (2001) 58 BMLR 87.
49 For such an analysis, see A R MacLean 'Crossing the Rubicon on the Human Rights
Ferry' (2001) 64 MLR 775.
50 As we discuss further in chapters 9 and 10.

Practice Note of 2001 also makes clear,[51] an application to the High Court is little more than a confirmatory exercise in respect of the diagnosis of PVS from which a declarator of legality of withdrawal should follow.[52]

17.27 Second, in examining the content of the human rights laid before it, the court fixed on the principle of respect for personal autonomy and concluded that, because the PVS patient could not consent to continued intervention, to continue to intervene against his or her best interests – as determined by (medically qualified) others – would *violate* protection under Article 8. This, however, turns self-determination on its head. Indeed, why is this a relevant consideration in the context of someone who cannot meaningfully experience or exercise this state? It is precisely because the patient cannot do so that 'best interests' enters the equation. The error lies in the failure to appreciate that it is *respect* for the human being that is required, not only (or necessarily) respect for her 'right to choose'. The proper focus should be on respecting individual rights and interests as these are determined in a principled manner – not as they are determined by health care professionals. While policy may have driven the court to its particular interpretation, it does a great disservice to the broader obligation to uphold human rights.

17.28 The court also relied upon the incapacity of these patients to restrict their rights in another respect. It held that, because PVS patients are insensate and cannot appreciate their state of being, it is not cruel and degrading to subject them to the vagaries of withdrawal of feeding and hydration – thus adopting the excessively narrow interpretation of Article 3 that a victim must be able to experience the inhuman treatment before a violation will occur.[53] This, however, is a distorted view of European jurisprudence which has held only that a victim's own subjective reactions to treatment can impact on the question of whether violation has occurred.[54] In no way does it follow, however, that subjectivity is a pre-requisite to violation.

17.29 We see Lord Mustill's fears as to extending the precedent in *Bland* to other, non-PVS, cases being realized in the final English case to be considered. In *Re G (adult incompetent: withdrawal of treatment)*[55] the patient was a 45-year-old woman who had suffered serious anoxic brain damage after inhaling her own vomitus following surgery. She had been kept alive for nine months by means of artificial nutrition and hydration when the NHS trust responsible for her care brought the matter to court for a declaration of legality as to the withdrawal of her means of artificial sustenance. G's family supported the application, stating that she would not have wished to remain in such a state. One expert witness was enough to convince the court that there was no reasonable prospect of her ever recovering and that she should be allowed to 'die with dignity'. Moreover, it was held not to be inconsistent with her human

---

51 *Practice Note (Official Solicitor: Declaratory Proceedings: Medical and Welfare Decisions for Adults Who Lack Capacity)* [2001] 2 FLR 158.
52 Ibid, Appendix 2.
53 Article 3 states: 'No one shall be subjected to torture or to inhuman or degrading treatment or punishment.'
54 *Campbell and Cosans v UK* (1983) 7 EHRR 165, para 28.
55 (2001) 65 BMLR 6.

right to life that a decision be made to discontinue treatment, despite her inability to give a valid consent to its withdrawal. A declaration to this effect was granted.

17.30 We view this last decision with a degree of concern. It comes very close to the controversial guidance of the British Medical Association, already mentioned, which suggests that an assessment of futility leading to the withdrawal of feeding and hydration may be appropriate for patients with dementia or for those who have suffered serious stroke.[56] This is highly problematic as we have argued elsewhere,[57] not least because the heavy and continuing emphasis placed on medical assessment rather than on a robust and principled approach to individualised human and patients' rights may mean that an expansionist development of clinical discretion is inevitable.

THE POSITION IN SCOTLAND

17.31 The outcome of a case similar to *Bland* was awaited with some interest in Scotland, accentuated in part by some very real jurisdictional variations between the two countries. The difficulty of deciding what were, essentially, criminal matters in a civil court was common to both jurisdictions. The House of Lords, while being unanimously wary on the point,[58] was quite prepared to accept a fait accompli: 'This appeal', said Lord Mustill, 'has reached this House, and your Lordships must decide it'. There was, however, no certainty that such pragmatism would be available to the Scottish courts. On the other hand, the English court in *Bland* was undoubtedly hampered by the absence of any residual powers of parens patriae and, again, the issue was in some doubt in Scotland. This, then, was the uncertain position when Scotland's first PVS case to come to the Court of Session by way of *Law Hospital NHS Trust v Lord Advocate*,[59] in which authority was sought by relatives of a middle-aged woman in PVS (Mrs Johnstone), and by the hospital treating her, to discontinue feeding.

17.32 In the event, the Inner House confirmed that it was not competent to issue a declarator to the effect that a proposed course of action was or was not criminal – it could, however, authorise a declaration in the knowledge that it would not bar proceedings in the High Court but in the hope that it would, in practice, ensure that no prosecution was undertaken there.[60] The court did, however, find that, in contrast to the position in England, the parens patriae jurisdiction survived in Scotland and that any authority thus given would have the same effect in law as if consent had been given by the patient. In this respect, it is to be noted that the Scottish courts had further string to their bow,

---

56 BMA, *Withholding and Withdrawing Life-prolonging Medical Treatment*, para 17.11 above. See also GMC *Withholding and Withdrawing Life-prolonging Treatments: Good Practice in Decision-making* (2002) paras 22–24.

57 See G T Laurie and J K Mason 'Negative Treatment of Vulnerable Patients: Euthanasia by Any Other Name?' [2000] JR 159.

58 See [1993] 1 All ER 821 at 864–865, 876, 880, 886–887, (1993) 12 BMLR 64 at 110, 122, 127, 133–134, per Lord Goff, Lord Lowry; Lord Browne-Wilkinson and Lord Mustill respectively.

59 *Law Hospital NHS Trust v Lord Advocate* 1996 SLT 848, (1996) 39 BMLR 166. The case was reported by Lord Cameron from the Outer House to the Inner House without any preliminary judgment.

60 1996 SLT 848 at 855, (1996) 39 BMLR 166 at 176, per Lord President Hope.

which was not available to their counterparts in England, in that they could appoint a tutor dative to oversee the interests of an incompetent adult[61] – and this included the power to consent to medical treatment on behalf of the incapax.[62] In fact, there was no need to appoint a tutor dative to look after the long-term interests of the patient in PVS as the book is effectively closed once the decision to discontinue feeding and hydration has been taken – the Inner House held that the court, in so deciding, could act on its own initiative and would do so in the future.

17.33 The tutor dative procedure was, however, designed to overcome any difficulties as to *consent to treatment* on the part of the incompetent. The court in PVS cases is effectively refusing treatment and no authority existed as to the capacity of a tutor dative to authorise action which leads, inevitably, to the death of the patient. The Inner House considered the numerous rulings that had been reached in several common law jurisdictions as to the correct test for exercising the power of consent or refusal of treatment on behalf of incompetents and concluded that the common denominator is that the decision should be taken in the patient's best interests. It followed that if, as in Mrs Johnstone's case, treatment could be of no benefit, then there were no longer any best interests to be served by continuing it.[63] Accordingly, the Lord Ordinary was authorised to provide a declarator to the effect that removal of life-sustaining treatment from Mrs Johnstone would not be unlawful in respect of its civil law consequences.[64]

17.34 The Lord President also remarked that nothing in his opinion was intended to suggest that an application must be made in every case where it is intended to withdraw treatment:

> The decision as to whether an application is necessary must rest in each case with those who will be responsible for carrying that intention into effect, having regard in particular ... to any statements of policy which may, in the light of this case, be issued by the Lord Advocate.[65]

17.35 And it is here that we run into some difficulties following a statement by the Lord Advocate[66] to the effect that the policy of the Crown Office will be that no criminal prosecution will follow a decision to withdraw feeding but that this is subject to authority to do so having first been obtained by way of the civil law. This appears to pre-empt the direction by the Inner House. However, the Lord Advocate did not say he *would* prosecute in any case that was not so authorised and he went on to say, admittedly in an unofficial ambience:

---

61 See A Ward 'Tutors to Adults: Developments' 1992 SLT 325.
62 For commentary on the parens patriae jurisdiction in Scotland and elsewhere, see G T Laurie 'Parens Patriae in the Medico-legal Context: The Vagaries of Judicial Activism' (1999) 3 ELR 95.
63 1996 SLT 848 at 859, (1996) 39 BMLR 166 at 182-184, per Lord Hope.
64 It is clear that such a complex manoeuvre will be unnecessary in the future when the Inner House will use its parens patriae powers but it was convenient to use it in the instant case. See *Law Hospital NHS Trust v Lord Advocate (No 2)* 1996 SLT 869, (1996) 39 BMLR 166 at 197.
65 1996 SLT 848 at 860, (1996) 39 BMLR 166 at 184.
66 J Robertson 'Policy on right to die welcomed' *Scotsman*, 12 April 1996, p 1.

In Scotland, a decision to withdraw treatment in any case cannot be *guaranteed* immunity from [prosecution] unless the withdrawal has first been authorised by the Court of Session.[67] (Emphasis added.)

17.36 Thus, both the Lord President and the Lord Advocate of the time agreed that decisions could be made on medical grounds and independently of the courts – but neither gave any guidance as to when it would be either necessary or unnecessary to seek judicial approval. The latter concluded in his paper: '... it is for doctors and relatives involved in such tragic situations to decide which course of action they wish to adopt.'

17.37 We would hope, and expect, that good common sense would prevail but, meanwhile, we suggest that not many doctors will be prepared to trust to chance that they have 'got it right'. It is reasonable to expect the criminal law to set out the boundaries of impermissible conduct in advance. Vagueness in criminal law offends the widely recognised principle of legal certainty, which requires that crimes should be clearly defined. The situation has now arisen where the doctor may be required to second guess the criminal law – a position that is hardly defensible.

17.38 This common law position remains unchanged with the passing of the Adults with Incapacity (Scotland) Act 2000.[68] The Act is determinedly not about any form of 'negative treatment', ie treatment which results in the death of the patient. Indeed, the Scottish Executive made it very clear that withdrawal or withholding decisions are outside the remit of the legislation.[69] However, we have argued elsewhere[70] that it will be impossible to maintain a clear distinction between positive and negative treatment decisions involving incapable adults, not least because the courts will invariably become involved in settling disputes as to the best thing to do under the Act: to treat or not to treat? Thus, although the powers of a proxy decision-maker under s 50 do not include a 'right' to refuse as such,[71] his 'right' to a second opinion challenging a medical decision to continue intervention, and ultimately the 'right' appeal to court, will necessarily mean that a jurisprudence relating to negative treatment will develop around this new legislation.

THE BEST INTERESTS TEST

17.39 The best interests test has been widely accepted as the measure of good practice in surrogate medico-legal decision-making not only as to PVS but also as to allied problems confronting those caring for incompetent adults.[72]

67 Lord Mackay of Drumadoon 'Decision on the Persistent Vegetative State: Law Hospital' (1996), paper presented at the Symposium on Medical Ethics and Legal Medicine, Royal College of Physicians and Surgeons of Glasgow, 26 April 1996.
68 Note, however, that the office of tutor dative no longer remains. Instead, welfare guardians or other proxy decision-makers can be appointed under the terms of the 2000 Act.
69 Scottish Executive *Policy Memorandum*, 8 October 1999.
70 Laurie and Mason, para 17.30 above.
71 See further chapter 10, paras 10.37–10.38.
72 Eg in sterilisation of the mentally incompetent: *Re F (mental patient: sterilisation)* [1990] 2 AC 1; *L, petitioner* 1996 SCLR 538.

We have, however, to express our doubts as to its validity in respect of the removal of feeding and hydration from PVS patients. This is so for three main reasons.

17.40   First, it lends itself to interpretation. Certainly, Lord Goff in *Bland* was of the opinion that the correct framing of the question in these cases was of crucial importance. He said:

> The question is not whether the doctor should take a course which will kill his patient, or even take a course which has the effect of accelerating death. The question is whether the doctor should or should not continue to provide his patient with medical treatment or care which, if continued, will prolong his patient's life ... [T]he question is not whether it is in the best interests of the patient that he should die. The question is whether it is in the best interests of the patient that his life should be prolonged by the continuance of this form of medical treatment or care.[73]

17.41   Then, we have Lord Hope in *Law Hospital*[74] using the negative approach – 'there are no longer any best interests to be served by continuing treatment' – which can be compared with Lord Browne-Wilkinson's medical orientation in *Bland*:[75] 'unless the doctor has reached the affirmative conclusion that it is in the patient's best interest to continue the invasive care, such care must cease.' Our sympathies lie with Lord Clyde:[76]

> [W]hile in the context of some medical situations expressions [such as for the welfare of or in the best interests of] may be of value, I find less assistance in such language when the choice is between life of a sort and death.

17.42   Secondly, it is difficult to accept Lord Goff's argument in *Bland* as to the nature of the question to be asked: 'we are not saying that it is your best interests to die, just that it is in your best interests not to receive essential physiological support.' How can these two be separated?[77] How can one avoid the conclusion that to argue that it is in one's best interests to be starved is to say anything other than that it is in one's best interests to die? To ask the truly honest question fatally undermines the best interests test. How, then, can one depend upon such a test?

17.43   Thirdly, we believe that the concept of consent is of major importance to the jurisprudence of the vegetative state and it is difficult to fit 'consent' into the inherently paternalistic concept of 'best interests'. It is possible to hold that the best interests of the patient are best served by respecting his

---

73   [1993] 1 All ER 821 at 869, (1993) 12 BMLR 64 at 115.
74   1996 SLT 848 at 859, (1996) 39 BMLR 166 at 183.
75   [1993] 1 All ER 821 at 883, (1993) 12 BMLR 64 at 129.
76   In *Law Hospital* 1996 SLT 848 at 863, (1996) 39 BMLR 166 at 196. The case against reliance on 'best interests' in the context of PVS is argued by A J Fenwick 'Applying Best Interests to Persistent Vegetative State – A Principled Distortion?' (1998) 24 J Med Ethics 86. An alternative view is given in the same issue: R Gillon 'Persistent Vegetative State, Withdrawal of Artificial Nutrition and Hydration, and the Patient's "Best Interests"' (1998) 24 J Med Ethics 75.
77   Lord Lowry in *Bland* had similar reservations: [1993] 1 All ER 821 at 887, (1993) 12 BMLR 64 at 123.

autonomy but the argument has something of a hollow ring. We believe that an alternative basis on which to decide what an incompetent person would have consented to or refused must be found and, here, we suggest that the use of the 'substituted judgment' test might be a preferred alternative in the circumstances under consideration.

17.44 The English courts, at least, have consistently rejected this approach in favour of a best interests test but, like it or not, an element of substituted judgment pervades many of the relevant cases.[78] Our reasons for seeking what is, in effect, compliance with the patient's supposed wishes are several. In so far as substituted judgment acknowledges the autonomy of the patient, it is ethically preferable to a best interests test which is, at base, paternalistic. The absolute right of a competent adult to consent to or refuse treatment is now established in all common law jurisdictions; it is wrong to deprive a person of his or her rights to autonomy on the grounds that he or she is incompetent to express that freedom of choice.[79] Moreover, it eliminates many of the more obvious objections to the latter formulation – 'how can it be in the best interests of anyone to die?'; 'how can a person with no interests have any best interests?', and the like.

17.45 The main ground for objection to the concept of substituted judgment lies in its inapplicability to those who have never been competent to take such decisions.[80] But to limit its application to a subjective evaluation of the patient's previously expressed wishes – an interpretation that is very much a part of the doctrine as used in the United States – is, we believe, to take too narrow a view of the test. Judgments on which treatment decisions are made do not have to be substituted for written or clearly expressed preferences on the part of the patient; nor must they be rejected simply because no such declarations of intent are available. In the absence of indications of any sort, there seems no reason why an objective assessment cannot be made – what would a reasonable person of similar type and character have decided in the prevailing circumstances? It could be said that this is no more than semantic pedantry as, given no previous indications, it is almost impossible to conceive of a situation where the 'substituted judgment' and the 'best interest' tests would not coincide.[81] There is also the view that the best interests test – sensitively applied – may take the claims of autonomy into account. It is surely not in a person's best interests to have his explicit or implicit preferences ignored.[82]

---

78 See eg the reasoning of the Master of the Rolls in *Re J (a minor) (wardship: medical treatment)* [1990] 3 All ER 930 at 936, (1990) 6 BMLR 25 at 32, quoting McKenzie J in *Superintendent of Family and Child Services and Dawson* (1983) 145 DLR (3d) 610. Substituted judgment was quite clearly used in *Re D* (1997) 38 BMLR 1 on the evidence of her mother and in *Re G* (2001) 65 BMLR 6 on the evidence of the family.

79 See Lord Goff in *Bland* [1993] 1 All ER 821 at 866, (1993) 12 BMLR 64 at 112, quoting the Supreme Judicial Court of Massachusetts in *Superintendent of Belchertown State School v Saikewicz* 373 Mass 728 (1977).

80 But the test has academic support otherwise. See I Kennedy, and A Grubb 'Commentary on *Airedale NHS Trust v Bland*' (1993) 1 Med L Rev 359 at 362; D Tomkin and P Hanafin 'Medical treatment at life's end: the need for legislation' (1995) 1 Med-Leg J Ireland 3.

81 An exception could lie in the management of the mentally disabled neonate. See discussion of *R v Arthur* (1981) 12 BMLR 1 in chapter 16.

82 It is to be noted that the Government include the ascertainable past and present wishes and feelings of the person among the criteria of 'best interests' in its proposal for reform: *Making Decisions*, 1999, Cm 4465, discussed in chapter 10.

Even so, on balance, substituted judgment fits the concept of consent more closely and this is particularly so when considering how consent by proxy can be applied.

17.46   The PVS cases do, in fact, suggest that judicial antipathy to this approach is less rigid than it once was. The words of Lord Clyde in *Law Hospital* merit repetition:

> It seems to me that, in a case such as the present, the question for the court is whether ... it is or is not just and proper to grant the authorisation in the circumstances as viewed from the position of the patient.[83]

17.47   For many of the reasons we have outlined, the Scottish Executive chose to abandon the best interests test as a measure of legitimate dealings with incapable patients under the Adults with Incapacity (Scotland) Act 2000. Now, any person responsible for authorising or effecting an intervention on an incapable adult cannot lawfully do so unless he or she is satisfied that the intervention will benefit the adult and that such benefit cannot reasonably be achieved without the intervention.[84] Moreover, account should be taken of (i) the past and present wishes and feelings of the adult, so far as these can be ascertained; (ii) the views of the nearest relative and primary carer of the adult, as far as it is reasonable and practicable to do so; (iii) the views of any proxy-decision maker; and (iv) the views of any other person appearing to have authority to intervene, or who has been consulted by a Sheriff in this regard.[85] We welcome this change of approach, with the one caveat that the medical carer who must consult and take account of these views should be given clear guidance about how these views should be balanced, or prioritised, in the event of disagreement. The worst scenario would be that too many views would actually achieve nothing more than stalemate and inaction. Although we have already noted that the 2000 Act does not authorise negative treatment decisions, such as the withdrawal of artificial feeding and hydration from patients in PVS, we reiterate our belief that the Scottish courts will none the less have to rule on such decisions, as, for example, where the primary carer wishes to continue the intervention and there is evidence that the patient would not want this or a relative or proxy objects.[86]

A MORE HONEST APPROACH?

17.48   A further alternative is to approach the truth and to admit that the deliberate removal of sustenance from a vegetative patient is indistinguishable from euthanasia. In order to circumvent this, the courts in England, Scotland and the Republic of Ireland have been at pains to emphasise that the cause of death in PVS cases is the original injury. But, while it is true to say that this was the ultimate cause of death, the proximate cause, given that the patient

83   1996 SLT 848 at 863, (1996) 39 BMLR 166 at 196.
84   2000 Act, s 1(2).
85   2000 Act, s 1(4).
86   For a proposal for an ethical approach to this balancing process, see D T Wade 'Ethical Issues in Diagnosis and Management of Patients in the Permanent Vegetative State' (2001) 322 BMJ 352.

has survived for a minimum of a year, must be the results of starvation – otherwise, there would be no death and, hence, no cause of death. There would be no difficulty in certifying death as being due to (a) inanition due to lawful removal of support due to (b) severe brain damage due to (c) cerebral hypoxia. A further practical advantage would be that the mortality statistics should be maintained correctly – and it would be possible to discover how often such decisions are made.

17.49 The fears of the judiciary are summed up by Lord Goff in *Bland,* who declined to allow active steps to bring about death in PVS patients because this would be to authorise euthanasia and: 'once euthanasia is recognised as lawful in these circumstances, it is difficult to see any logical basis for excluding it in others.'[87] We question this view, first, on the grounds that, once the concept of substituted judgment is accepted, removal of sustenance from PVS patients equates, at most, to passive, voluntary euthanasia which is already practised widely under one name or another. PVS cases occupy a unique niche in the spectrum of euthanasia. All higher brain function has been permanently lost, there is no awareness and no sensation. There is no alternative of palliative care because there are no senses to palliate – as Lord Goff put it: 'there is no weighing operation to be performed.' Only the vestiges of the person remain as the breathing body and, once the patient's close relatives have come to terms with the situation, it is futile to maintain that respiration.

17.50 All this, however, depends upon the certainty of definition and diagnosis. Anthony Bland's and Mrs Johnstone's conditions were unequivocal but one cannot avoid the impression that the precedents laid down in their cases are being extended to include less well defined conditions than was intended at the time. The House of Lords distinguished *Bland* from other 'quality of life' cases such as *Re J.*[88] The two cases have very different ratios. In the former, a wholly insensate patient was deemed to have no interest in continued treatment which could, therefore, be discontinued as being futile. In the latter, it was accepted that some benefit could be derived from treatment of a patient who was not insensate but it was held that non-treatment was to be preferred when any supposed benefit was weighed against other considerations such as pain and suffering. *S,*[89] *Re D*[90], *Re H,*[91] and now *Re G*[92] in particular, demonstrate a shift in thinking from that adopted in *Bland* towards that involved in *Re J* and one wonders if this is not something of a move towards acceptance of active euthanasia; the cases provide the most impressive example to date of the willingness of the British courts to take 'quality of life' decisions and, in our view, represent a significant step in this area of law. At the end of the day, all the cases discussed, from *Bland* to *Re H* and beyond, represent variations on what is meant by 'best interests'; the fundamental question is, then, whether the jump from 'no interests' to 'a balance of interests' is acceptable in the management of the vegetative state or whether it represents a quantum leap onto the slippery slope of ending 'valueless lives'.

87 [1993] 1 All ER 821 at 867, (1993) 12 BMLR 64 AT 113.
88 [1990] 3 All ER 930, (1990) 6 BMLR 25, discussed in chapter 16.
89 *Swindon and Marlborough NHS Trust v S* [1995] 3 Med LR 84.
90 (1997) 38 BMLR 1.
91 (1997) 38 BMLR 11.
92 (2001) 65 BMLR 6.

17.51 It has to be remembered that all the post-*Bland* cases have been scrupulously examined and all were supported not only by respected medical opinion but also by the Official Solicitor. All the patients were, by any standards, existing in appalling conditions and we have the gravest doubts as to whether the failure of a single arbitrary clinical test should be allowed to distinguish them in any significant way – and it is at least arguable that the near-vegetative state is a more horrifying condition than is PVS itself.[93] In short, we submit that the approach adopted by the courts in *Re J* could properly be applied to the withdrawal of feeding (or other vital treatment) from severely damaged adult patients. *Re J* and its allied cases went a long way to medicalising the whole approach to termination of treatment decisions and, provided medical authority is tempered by the sensitive handling of close relatives, there seems to be no fundamental reason why it should not be applied irrespective of age – the courts would then be involved only in those cases in which there is serious dispute between or within the health caring and family groups. Public acceptance of this policy would be greatly eased by an open acceptance by the medical profession of the futility of treatment of vegetative patients.[94] This is already the position advocated by the BMA in respect of patients with severe dementia or who have suffered catastrophic stroke.[95]

17.52 Inevitably, however, one is reminded of the calls in the House of Lords and the Court of Session for Parliamentary intervention – and, while this has its attractions, the proposal is not of unquestionable merit. To legislate for PVS alone would be to concentrate on its particular clinical status and to segregate it from the general euthanasia debate – which is as it should be.[96] Other advantages of legislation could be that the limits of PVS were statutorily determined[97] and that a clear framework could be devised within which doctors withdrawing treatment could be seen to be acting lawfully without the need for routine approval by a court. A line could thus be drawn between unequivocal and doubtful cases and a barrier placed at the edge of any developing slippery slope. On the other hand, legislation of this type could be seen as disadvantageous in that it would be restrictive – while withdrawal of support from the *Bland*-type patient would be permissible, non-treatment options might be barred in many cases of brain damage in which only minimal cognitive function remained such as in *S, D, H* and *G*. To many, this would represent the primary function of the legislation; to others, it might seem an unacceptable price to pay for the loss of individual judgment – as we have already suggested, generalisations are difficult to apply in a medical context. It might, therefore, be thought preferable to introduce purely enabling legislation along much the same lines as we have suggested in chapter 16.

---

93 R Cranford 'Misdiagnosing the Persistent Vegetative State' (1996) 313 BMJ 5.
94 See K R Mitchell, I H Kerridge and T J Lovat 'Medical Futility, Treatment Withdrawal and the Persistent Vegetative State' (1993) 19 J Med Ethics 71.
95 BMA, *Withdrawing and Withholding Treatment*, para 17.11 above.
96 J K Mason and D Mulligan 'Euthanasia by Stages' (1996) 347 Lancet 810.
97 Perhaps based on the guidelines of the Royal College of Physicians, para 17.6 above.

17.53 To do so, however, would be to move towards the diametric alternative of complete medicalisation of the subject – something which was, admittedly, in the contemplation of Lord Goff in *Bland* and Lord Hope in *Law Hospital*.[98] This solution also makes sense in that it is the doctor who has to make the diagnosis and the doctor who is familiar with the associated difficulties[99] – as Lord Browne-Wilkinson said in *Bland*: 'In the past, doctors exercised their own discretion, in accordance with medical ethics, in cases such as these',[100] and he added that this was to the great advantage of society. Moreover, the courts are, ultimately, dependent on the medical evidence. Again, however, PVS decisions carry more than purely medical implications[101] and there is a powerful impression that the public is uneasy when confronted with unbridled autonomy of the medical profession:

> Although essentially the decision [to treat or not to treat] is one for the clinical judgment of responsible medical practitioners ... it is desirable as a safeguard and for the reassurance of the public that the court should be involved in the way I have indicated.[102]

17.54 It is impossible to deny that doctors vary in their intellectual abilities and moral application. The familiar ghost of *Bolam*[103] is, perhaps, not the ideal preceptor in such sensitive territory – it could well be a mistake to tamper with our current pragmatic resolution of the problems involved:

> Provided the legal process continues to provide solutions that accord with sound medical ethics and commonsense, there should be no tension between those who provide or withhold life-prolonging treatment and those who ultimately judge their decisions.[104]

PVS IN THE UNITED STATES

17.55 There are more than 50 jurisdictions in the United States where PVS decisions are, to an extent, governed by constitutional and statute law. This,

---

98 It is to be noted that the Americans find no difficulty in seeing artificial feeding as a medical matter: see eg B Brody 'Special Ethical Issues in the Management of PVS Patients' (1992) 20 Law Med Hlth Care 104. A Meisel 'A Retrospective on *Cruzan*' (1992) 20 Law Med Hlth Care provides a comprehensive list of apposite court decisions and statements from learned societies.

99 For discussion, see a series of papers: K Andrews 'Recovery of Patients after Four Months or More in the Persistent Vegetative State' (1993) 306 BMJ 1597, 'Patients in the Persistent Vegetative State: Problems in their Long Term Management' (1993) 306 BMJ 1600; R Gillon 'Patients in the Persistent Vegetative State: A Response to Dr Andrews' (1993) 306 BMJ 1602.

100 [1993] 1 All ER 821 at 880, (1993) 12 BMLR 64 at 126.

101 See M Angell 'After Quinlan: The Dilemma of the Persistent Vegetative State' (1994) 330 New Engl J Med 1524.

102 *Airedale NHS Trust v Bland* [1993] 1 All ER 821 at 833, (1993) 12 BMLR 64 AT 77, per Sir Stephen Brown P. This applied to all PVS cases but later judges were prepared to limit court hearings to those cases in which there was conflict: eg Lord Goff [1993] 1 All ER 821 at 874, (1993) 12 BMLR 64 at 120.

103 *Bolam v Friern Hospital Management Committee* [1957] 2 All ER 118, (1957) 1 BMLR 1.

104 D Collins 'Prescribing Limits to Life-prolonging Treatment' [1994] NZLJ 246.

together with the sheer volume of work involved,[105] makes it difficult to follow the more important cases and to identify a definite trend in the development of the relevant common law in that country.

17.56 In fact, this is not of major concern to the British reader, as this appears to be one area in which the United Kingdom courts are forging a particularly independent path. Due respect is paid to United States decisions[106] but, such is their diversity, that a selective approach is inevitable. The fundamental distinction between the two main jurisdictions seems, to us, to lie in the test by which to justify termination of treatment which, we have seen, is firmly held to be that of the best interests of the patient in the United Kingdom. By contrast, three standards for surrogate decision-making under this heading are available in the United States[107] – the subjective, substituted judgment and best interests standards, the inference being that these are adopted in descending order of acceptability. Thus, the substituted judgment test – in which the surrogate makes his or her best approximation of what management schedule the patient would have wanted – is adopted only if the subjective test, which is based on what wishes the patient actually expressed, is not available; contrary to the position in the United Kingdom, the best interests test is, then, to be regarded as something of a last resort. Clearly, the tests run into one another and the standards of proof can be manipulated – what, for example, constitutes an 'expression of intention'? The scope for interpretation is, therefore, very wide and, for that reason, we are limiting our discussion to only a few cases which are of comparative interest.

17.57 Consideration of the American scene must include a brief reference to the old, but fundamental, case of *Re Quinlan*;[108] this involved a 21-year-old girl who was in what was described at the time as a chronic persistent vegetative state and who existed on ventilator support. Given a hopeless prognosis, her parents sought to remove her from intensive care against the advice of the health care team. The Supreme Court of New Jersey found, however, that Ms Quinlan's right to privacy would allow her to refuse further ventilator therapy were she competent and that this right persisted when she was incompetent. It concluded that evidence from her friends was insufficiently probative to establish what her actual wishes would be but, interestingly, rescinded this assessment a decade later.[109] Her father was appointed her guardian with authority to act on her behalf and to withdraw treatment, subject to the agreement of the attending physicians and of the hospital ethics committee. The function of the ethics committee was seen as, first, effectively covering the physician against any subsequent challenge by a family member and, secondly, as protection against any 'less than worthy motivations of

---

105 It was estimated that, from 1975 to 1989, between 2,900 and 7,000 life-sustaining medical treatment cases were heard by the American judiciary and some 50 to 75 went to appeal. These derive from an estimated 13.6m apposite deaths: T L Hafemeister et al 'The Judicial Role in Life-sustaining Medical Treatment Decisions' (1991) 7 Issues in L & Med 53, quoted by Meisel para 17.53 above.

106 See eg Sir Thomas Bingham MR in *Bland* [1993] 1 All ER 821 at 836–837, (1993) 12 BMLR 64 at 80–81.

107 Meisel, para 17.53 above.

108 *Re Quinlan* 355 A 2d 647 (NJ, 1976).

109 *Re Claire Conroy* 486 A 2d 1209 (NJ, 1985).

family or physician' – indeed, the court was happy to turn over assessment of future cases to such tribunals.[110]

17.58 *Quinlan* was not appealed to the US Supreme Court and it was not until 1990 that Ms Cruzan's case was heard there.[111] *Cruzan* was, therefore, awaited with great interest but, in the end, the decision was disappointing in its depth and scope – it has been said that perhaps the chief problem with the majority decision was its almost complete lack of attention to medical reality.[112] Ms Cruzan's situation was very similar to that of Ms Quinlan, save that the former, while requiring tube-feeding in order to survive, had no need of ventilator support; after three years in PVS, her parents requested that feeding and hydration be discontinued – this being justified on the basis of their interpretation of her wishes when competent and in accordance with previous precedent.[113] The Supreme Court of Missouri overturned the trial judge's permissive order and the case went to the Supreme Court of the United States. The question before the Supreme Court, however, was simply whether the Constitution debars a State from requiring 'clear and convincing evidence' of a person's expressed decision while competent to have hydration and nutrition withdrawn in such a way as to cause death – that is, to insist on the highest subjective test for decision-making. The court decided, by the narrow majority of 5:4, that it had but it has been pointed out consistently that it did not dictate the use of such a standard which has, subsequently, been rejected by all States other than Missouri and New York. *Cruzan* thus made no effective change to the law as it had previously evolved and, in fact, the case withered away as the State did not contest a second hearing based on new evidence and Ms Cruzan was allowed to die.

17.59 Some observations in the Supreme Court are, however, significant even though they might be regarded as obiter. First, the majority opinion held that the principle that a competent person has a constitutionally protected liberty interest in refusing unwanted medical treatment can be accepted by inference.[114] Secondly, Justice O'Connor, who sided with the majority, agreed with the minority that artificial feeding cannot be distinguished from other forms of medical treatment; as a consequence, refusal of the artificial delivery of food and water is protected by the Constitution. In view of these, most commentators are agreed that, paradoxically, the power of the family and health care team to make agreed decisions as to withdrawal of treatment from the incompetent is, at least, unaltered and, possibly, strengthened by *Cruzan*.

17.60 Following from this, we have selected one further case which seems to us to be significant. *Re Fiori*[115] concerned a man who had been in PVS for some 15 years and was tube-fed but not ventilated. In allowing his mother's request to withdraw gastrostomy feeding, the Superior Court of Pennsylvania

110 For an appraisal of shared decision making, see B Spielman 'Collective Decisions about Medical Futility' (1994) 22 J Law Med & Ethics 152.
111 *Cruzan v Director, Missouri Department of Health* 110 S Ct 2841 (1990).
112 G J Annas 'Nancy Cruzan and the Right to Die' (1990) 323 New Engl J Med 670.
113 See Meisel, para 17.53 above.
114 110 S Ct 2841 at 2851. The question as to whether the 'right' is based on liberty or privacy interests is a very US-orientated argument.
115 652 A 2d 1350 (Pa, 1995).

specifically rejected the need for a prior express statement by the patient as the test. Indeed, in holding that the surrogate decision-maker can consider 'the patient's personal value system for guidance' in the absence of an expressed view as to the use of life support, the court positively approved the use of an objective standard much as we have suggested above.[116] Of greater general importance, it held that there is no need for a court to intervene in the decision-making process unless there is disagreement between the interested parties and, while limiting itself strictly to the permanent vegetative state of a patient who had never clearly expressed a preference for termination, the court concluded that the surrogate consent of a close family member, backed by the written approval of two physicians, protects the patient's interests sufficiently.

17.61 *Fiori* thus seems a major step towards accepting the family's ultimate responsibility for taking treatment withdrawal decisions in the United States. There are, however, two provisos to consider. First, the decision was strictly limited to the patient satisfying the PVS criteria. Secondly, despite the importance attached to the family, it is at least arguable that the concept of family decision-making is illusory, given the overwhelming power of the medical advisers – and the procedure envisaged by the Superior Court of Pennsylvania will only operate successfully when there is complete agreement. One suggested alternative method of decision-making is to *assume* that no one would wish to be maintained in the PVS and that, once the diagnosis was made, we could act on that assumption.[117] It would then be up to families seeking to continue treatment to justify their stance.[118] This has a ring of certainty about it but, at the same time, it re-introduces the image of unrestrained medicalisation which we have raised doubts about above. Perhaps the better way of looking at the dilemma of PVS is to remind ourselves that perhaps several hundred commonsense decisions are taken for every one that is argued in the courts.[119]

'DO NOT RESUSCITATE' ORDERS

17.62 The last aspect of medical futility that falls to be discussed is the so-called 'do not resuscitate' (DNR) order. There can be no doubt that it is often undesirable, effectively, to prolong the process of dying – irrespective of the competence of the patient at the time.[120] Nevertheless, in extending the concept of non-treatment to the incapacitated rather than the incompetent, it is possible that our attitudes are being moulded overly in favour of death, rather than

---

116 See paras 17.43–17.47.
117 C H Baron 'Why Withdrawal of Life-support for PVS Patients Is not a Family Decision' (1991) 19 Law Med Hlth Care 73.
118 A similar attitude to the burden of proof is shown by Angell, para 17.53 above.
119 Other jurisdictions have followed the general trend. In South Africa, for example, 'the feeding of the patient in PVS did not serve the purpose of supporting human life as it is commonly known' and it would not be acting wrongfully to discontinue artificial feedings: *Clarke v Hurst* [1994] 5 Med LR 177.
120 A particularly effective series of commentaries is to be found related to E L Schucking 'Death at a New York Hospital' (1985) 13 Law Med Hlth Care 261. See also the papers associated with R F Weir 'Betty's Case: An Introduction' (1989) 17 Law Med Hlth Care 211.

treatment, as a management option. Moreover, we have to ask ourselves whether the DNR option is a valid example of an exercise of the principle of futility – there is a physical and moral divide between the PVS patient and the patient who is reaching the end of life in a natural fashion, albeit often in a state of diminished competence. Where one places the DNR order is a matter of ethical importance. After much consideration, we doubt if it is correctly sited under 'futility' and will discuss the matter under the heading of euthanasia.[121]

121 See chapter 18.

18 Euthanasia

18.1 Thus far, we have looked at the ending of life in the general context of withdrawal of treatment that was regarded as inappropriate. The legal insistence that this did not constitute euthanasia has been a feature of all the cases discussed – and, indeed, it is this which underwrites their legality. In this chapter, we consider the occasions when the premature termination of life is the intended aim – and this is, at least, one definition of euthanasia. Euthanasia can, however, also be seen as providing a 'good' death or 'easing the passing' and we will, where necessary, include this in our discussion. We have already considered the infant or young child as a separate issue and have explained our reasons for isolating such cases; here it is proposed to discuss the subject only in relation to the adult patient.

18.2 Conditions at each end of life differ significantly from both the legal and ethical viewpoints. Unlike the infant, the adult patient may well be able to express his wishes as to the quality of his own life. In default of this, those responsible for the patient's management have a background of previous abilities and aspirations from which to measure the likely shortfall; clinical decisions can be based on history rather than on clairvoyance. On the other hand, the aged present a bewildering array of mental and physical variations which virtually preclude generalisations as to management – and attitudes to the elderly are inevitably coloured by the fact that their potential for meaningful relationships is waning rather than developing.

18.3 The prohibition on the taking of human life is based on fundamental and deeply held ethical convictions. These may have different roots, and may be expressed in a wide variety of ways, but whatever their basis, they form a fundamental part of our moral lives. Until recently, the prohibition against killing was most frequently expressed in religious terms, human life being seen as a gift over which we may have stewardship but no final control. That position is still widely supported in some societies but, even in societies where religious morality has been dethroned, the right to life is still accorded particular weight. This is reflected in the modern human rights debate, where the right to life is treated as being at the heart of the entire edifice of the liberal position. The European Convention on Human Rights, for example, provides in Article 2 that 'everyone's right to life shall be protected by law', a proposition which is similarly entrenched in many other statements of human rights. Nevertheless, few of those who recognise its value will deny that life may be taken in at least some circumstances. The principle of self-defence – either in the private context or in the course of a just war – may admit the killing of others. Similarly, some at least of those who would normally condemn murder might, none the less, see legal execution as an appropriate part of the process of criminal justice. In medicine, too, stout opponents of euthanasia may accept the legitimacy of abortion – a process which, by any standards, involves the taking of *some* form of life. Many people now admit the right of a person to commit suicide and do this on the grounds that, in general, the right to self-determination is the most fundamental of all human rights. The door is thereby opened to a debate on whether euthanasia in some forms might be a morally acceptable practice.[1]

VOLUNTARY AND INVOLUNTARY EUTHANASIA

18.4 The major thrust of those concerned to legalise the termination of life on medical grounds has always been concentrated on what is generally known as voluntary euthanasia. This form of words implies that the patient specifically requests that his life be ended. Most exponents of voluntary euthanasia agree that this request must come from one who is either subject to intolerable pain or disability or who is suffering from an illness which is diagnosed as terminal. It may be made prior to the development of the illness in question or during its course. In either case, it must not result from pressure of any sort from relatives or from those looking after the patient. We follow earlier authorities[2] in distinguishing non-voluntary euthanasia as a sub-variety of voluntary euthanasia. This involves the death, ostensibly for the avoidance of undue suffering, of someone who cannot express any views on the matter and whose position is therefore ascertained by reference to a proxy – be it the family or the actual medical attendant. In practice, non-voluntary euthanasia presents only as an arguable alternative to non-treatment which we have discussed in detail in the preceding chapters.

18.5 Involuntary euthanasia is a quite different concept and is one from which most groups pressing for reform of the law have been careful to distance themselves. An act of involuntary euthanasia involves ending the patient's life in the absence of either a personal or proxy invitation to do so. The motive – the relief of suffering – may be the same as that involved in voluntary

---

1 The literature on the moral status of euthanasia and of its legal implications is vast. A useful starting point in the modern literature is R Dworkin, *Life's Dominion: an argument about abortion and euthanasia* (1993). The fundamental issue of the moral status of human life is considered by M A Warren *Moral Status* (1997) and by J Finnis, 'A philosophical case against euthanasia' in J Keown (ed) *Euthanasia Examined* (1995) pp 23–35. See also, J McMahon *The Ethics of Killing: Killing at the Margins of Life* (2001). Works concerned with specifically legal issues include: M Otlowski, *Voluntary Euthanasia and the Common Law* (1997) and H Biggs *Euthanasia, Death with Dignity and the Law* (2001). John Keown is a consistent critic of the legalisation of euthanasia: see his *Euthanasia, Ethics and Public Policy: An Argument against Legalisation* (2002).
2 Notably, J Glover *Causing Death and Saving Lives* (1977, reprinted 1986) p 191.

euthanasia but its only justification lies in a paternalistic decision as to what is best for the victim of disease. In extreme cases, indeed, there may be no claim to individual advantage – or the patient's consent may be expressly withheld – and the grounds may be no more than those of social convenience. It is examples of this last type which provide the major armamentarium of those who oppose the legalisation of euthanasia – the inherent threat to the old or to the mentally or physically infirm scarcely needs emphasis.

18.6 Criminal cases are rarely reported unless they demonstrate some specific point of law. Even so, there have been surprisingly few relevant trials – and this despite the number of doctors who claim to have taken part in some form of euthanasia.[3] Including the remarkable Dr Adams,[4] whose case we discuss below,[5] the great majority of the few who have come to trial in these circumstances on charges of murder, manslaughter or culpable homicide have been accused of no more than using therapeutic drugs in overdose and all the relevant verdicts have indicated the reluctance of British juries to convict a medical practitioner of serious crime when the charge arises from what they see as his considered medical judgment. In *R v Carr*[6] a doctor was accused of attempted murder by injecting a massive dose of phenobarbitone into a patient whose lung cancer had been declared inoperable some seven months previously. He was acquitted of the charge but, in the course of the summing-up, Mars-Jones J had this to say:

> However gravely ill a man may be ... he is entitled in our law to every hour ... that God has granted him. That hour or hours may be the most precious and most important hours of a man's life. There may be business to transact, gifts to be given, forgivenesses to be made, 101 bits of unfinished business which have to be concluded

which is as good a comment on misplaced paternalism as is likely to be found. Nevertheless, the sympathetic attitude of the courts is deeply entrenched and was confirmed in the case of Dr Moor. This GP, who admitted in the course of a public debate to having used painkillers to bring about the easy deaths of patients, was charged with the murder of a terminally ill patient into whom he was alleged to have injected a lethal dose of diamorphine. The judge left the jury in no doubt as to his own view of the matter, saying:

> You have heard that this defendant is a man of excellent character, not just in the sense that he has no previous convictions but how witnesses have spoken of his many admirable qualities. You may consider it a great irony that a doctor who goes out of his way to care for [the deceased] ends up facing the charge that he does.[7]

The jury responded by acquitting Dr Moor within an hour.

3 And not only in the United Kingdom. See, eg, C Zinn, who reported that 'A Third of Surgeons in New South Wales Admit to Euthanasia' (2001) 323 BMJ 1268.

4 H Palmer 'Dr Adams' Trial for Murder' [1957] Crim LR 365.

5 See para 18.77.

6 *R v Carr* (unreported, but see *The Sunday Times*, 30 November 1986, p 1). In Scotland, a doctor who injected an elderly patient with ten times the normal dose of diamorphine was acquitted of culpable homicide – the defence was, however, one of accidental error: *HM Advocate v Watson* (1991) Scotsman, 11 June, p 8, 14 June, p 3.

7 C Dyer 'British GP cleared of murder charge' (1999) 318 BMJ 1306.

18.7 It will be remarked that, between these cases, Dr Cox, a consultant rheumatologist, was convicted of attempted murder.[8] *R v Cox*, however, demonstrates very well how the individual circumstances alter one's approach and the case is discussed in greater detail below.[9] We must also note the more recent case of Dr Harold Shipman, who was convicted in 2000 of the murder of 15 patients – an example of serial killing which has cast a long shadow over the medical profession in the United Kingdom and which bears indirectly on the euthanasia argument. [10] Dr Shipman, however, was quite different from other doctors who may have risked prosecution to end what they saw as the unbearable suffering of terminally ill patients; he killed patients for reasons which are not altogether apparent but which may have been connected with a pathological desire to exercise control over life and death. The case seriously dented trust in the medical profession and could be used as an argument against lifting the current strict prohibitions on the taking of life. Dr Shipman's imitators – if there are any – might find welcome opportunities in a system of legalised euthanasia in which they would play the role of dispatchers. [11]

ACTIVE AND PASSIVE EUTHANASIA

18.8 A patient's life may be terminated, or death accelerated, either actively or passively. This distinction – or whether there is, indeed, any true distinction – is one of the most hotly argued issues in the euthanasia debate and one which can be addressed on either the legal or the moral plane.

18.9 Despite the rarity of cases involving the medical profession, there is no ambiguity in the attitude of the law in the United Kingdom towards a positive act of euthanasia. It is summed up in the words of Devlin J:

> If the acts done are intended to kill and do, in fact, kill, it does not matter if a life is cut short by weeks or months, it is just as much murder as if it were cut short by years.[12]

18.10 While motive is irrelevant, intention is all-important. If a doctor intends to kill, he is as liable to prosecution as is the layman. There have been recommendations for the introduction of a specific offence of 'mercy-killing'[13] and, although these have not been translated into legislation – and although there is, apparently, no intention so to do – there is an innate reluctance on the part of the courts to convict the genuine 'mercy-killer' of an offence which carries a mandatory sentence of life imprisonment. This is particularly so when relatives have cared for the sick with great devotion and have ultimately decided to release them from misery. In such circumstances, the prosecutor may well exercise his discretion and accept a plea of

---

8 *R v Cox* (1992) 12 BMLR 38.
9 See para 18.43.
10 A public inquiry was set up to investigate the deaths of a further 459 of his patients.
11 H G Kinnell 'Serial Homicide by Doctors: Shipman in Perspective' (2000) 321 BMJ 1594.
12 Palmer, para 18.6 above.
13 See R Leng 'Mercy Killing and the CLRC' (1982) 132 NLJ 76.

manslaughter;[14] alternatively, the court may accept a plea of diminished responsibility on the grounds of mental abnormality[15] – psychiatrists are just as ready to diagnose or to infer a reactive depression in the accused.[16]

18.11   Until quite recently, one would have supposed that the public was content with such a practical solution and had little or no wish to see it extended. One might also have supposed that developments in palliative care, and greater interest in the hospice movement, might have led to a decreased demand for medical assistance in dying. Such assumptions have been shown to be wrong: the euthanasia debate has continued, and, if anything, has sharpened with each lowering of legal barriers to the practice. Lawful euthanasia has now arrived in more than one jurisdiction, and this has added a new dimension to a debate which, until recently, consisted mainly of unsuccessful attacks on a unanimous legal refusal to allow euthanasia.

18.12   One of the main focal points of the debate has been the Netherlands, where medically-practised euthanasia became lawful in November 2000. This ended the previous half-way house arrangement in Dutch law under which euthanasia remained illegal but, at the same time, doctors who carried out acts of euthanasia on their patients would not be prosecuted, provided they complied with certain requirements. The novelty of the current Dutch legislation warrants its examination in some detail.

18.13   The Termination of Life on Request and Assisted Suicide (Review Procedures) Act, Article 293 amends the Penal Code of the Netherlands to read as follows:

> (1) A person who terminates the life of another person at that other person's express and earnest request is liable to a term of imprisonment of not more than twelve years or a fine of the fifth category.
> (2) The offence referred to in the first paragraph shall not be punishable if it has been committed by a physician who has met the requirements of due care [referred to in Article 2 of this law] ... and who informs the municipal autopsist of this ...'

---

14   Eg *R v Johnson* (1961) 1 Med Sci Law 192. A typical Scottish case, *HM Advocate v Brady* (1996 unreported), involved a man who smothered his brother who was suffering from Huntington's disease; he was found guilty of culpable homicide and was admonished: B Christie 'Man Walks Free in Scottish Euthanasia Case' (1996) 313 BMJ 961. However, there are limits, and relatives who assume that the prosecution authorities and the courts will be sympathetic are running a major risk. An example of this is *R v Latimer* [2001] 1 SCR 3, in which the Supreme Court of Canada upheld the murder conviction of a father who had killed his 12-year-old daughter who suffered from a severe form of cerebral palsy. The father invoked a defence of necessity, arguing that the killing was the lesser of two evils. This was roundly rejected by the court, which pointed out: 'Killing a person – in order to relieve the suffering produced by a medically manageable physical or mental condition – is not a proportionate response to the harm represented by the non-life-threatening suffering resulting from that condition'.

15   See chapter 22.

16   S Dell *Murder into Manslaughter* (1984) p 35 et seq. In *R v Taylor* [1979] CLY 570, a man who battered his autistic child to death was placed on probation for 12 months. Perhaps the most remarkable example comes from the USA, where no charges were pressed against a man who held the staff at gun-point while disconnecting his son from the ventilator: see eg J D Lantos, S H Miles and C K Cassel 'The Linares Affair' (1989) 17 Law Med Hlth Care 308.

18.14 The concept of due care is defined in the legislation as requiring the doctor to believe that the patient's request was 'voluntary and well-considered' and that the patient's suffering was 'lasting and unbearable'. For his part the patient, having been informed about his situation, must believe that there is no other reasonable solution. The doctor must also have consulted an independent physician who has seen the patient and has given a written opinion on compliance with the due conditions.[17] In addition to setting out these criteria for the administration of euthanasia, the Act provides for the reporting of instances of euthanasia to regional review committees, which have power to refer non-compliance cases to the public prosecutor.[18]

18.15 The Dutch legislation allows for advance consent, thus recognising the validity of a living will. A written declaration of this nature has the effect of a concrete request for euthanasia which may be exercised when the patient is no longer capable of expressing his will. One consequence of this is that a patient who does not have the capacity to object, but who may, in fact, not now want to die, could be killed by a doctor who, possessing an earlier written authorisation, decides that it would be better for the patient to do so – or even to bring a slow and prolonged process of dying to a 'tidy end'.

18.16 The scale of the practice of euthanasia in the Netherlands, under both the earlier transitional provisions and now under the fully-legalised system, is a matter of dispute, although most studies suggest that it is extensive. In 1991, it was said that nearly 2% of deaths in the Netherlands resulted from euthanasia; these involved approximately 2,300 cases of euthanasia and 400 of assisted suicide each year.[19] This high incidence might, in itself, give rise to concern but the evidence which has emerged of the widespread disregard among doctors in the Netherlands of the formal requirements laid down in the transitional regime is even more disquieting.[20] Such failures suggest that administrative or internal medical control of the practice is unlikely to prevent abuses, a conclusion which robs the argument based on voluntariness of much of its force. It appears, in fact, that euthanasia has been practised in many cases without the consent of the patient.[21] This might provide grounds for asserting that it becomes far more difficult to control the practice once an absolute prohibition against killing is removed. This leads us to the famous slippery slope, a piece of moral terrain which has attracted much comment, even though its mere existence is a matter of fierce debate. If there is a slippery

---

17 Article 2.
18 Controversially, the Netherlands Act provides for the carrying out of euthanasia on minors (Article 2(3) and (4)). Children between 12 and 16 who are deemed to have a 'reasonable understanding' (the statute's language) of their interests may give consent to euthanasia, provided that their decision is agreed to by parents. Children aged 16 and 17 may opt for euthanasia, but this may only be carried out if the parents (or those exercising parental authority) have been involved in the decision process.
19 H Hellema 'Euthanasia – 2% of Dutch Deaths' (1991) 303 BMJ 877.
20 H Hendin, 'Euthanasia Consultants or Facilitators' (1999) 170 Med J Austral 351; P J van der Maas, G van der Wal, I Haverkate et al 'Euthanasia, Physician-Assisted Suicide, and other Medical Practices Involving the End of Life in the Netherlands, 1990-1995' (1996) 335 New Engl J Med 1699.
21 Indeed, specific studies have been made on the point: L Pijnenborg, P J van der Maas, J J M van Delden and C W M Looman 'Life-terminating Acts without Explicit Request of Patient' (1993) 341 Lancet 1196.

slope in the Netherlands, then there are certainly several prominent milestones on it, including the call by the Dutch Commission for the Acceptability of Life Terminating Action for public debate on whether the life of a patient suffering from severe dementia without serious physical symptoms might be terminated with or without he or she having executed an advance directive on the point.[22]

18.17   Opponents of the Netherlands approach of euthanasia have expressed concern that the grounds for its exercise will inevitably become more trivial until what matters is not the grounds for wanting to die, but the want itself. This could rapidly lead to an acceptance of euthanasia in the face of relatively minor discomfort or of conditions which, although distressing, are not necessarily either permanent or terminal. Such concerns do not appear ill-founded when one reads that a Dutch psychiatrist has been found to be medically justified in assisting the suicide of a physically healthy woman who was depressed[23] – precisely the situation foreseen by those who oppose legalising the termination of life. The Dutch experience could, in fact, be taken as an object lesson rather than as a paradigm.[24]

18.18   The pioneering legislation in the Netherlands has not led to a large number of other jurisdictions following suit; it would, however, be surprising if this situation were to persist, given that the acceptance of a practice in one jurisdiction often influences the decision to allow a practice elsewhere. Indeed, a similar measure has now been introduced in Belgium where, in 1997, the Council for Bioethics recommended that euthanasia be legalised, a recommendation which probably reflects what was, anyway, happening in practice.[25]

18.19   A major difficulty in assessing the Dutch experience lies in definition and this probably derives from their use of the term 'medical decisions concerning the end of life (MDEL).[26]   MDEL includes a wide spectrum of activity ranging from manifest euthanasia, through the concept of 'double effect',[27] to the most controversial, and hard to unravel, group involving termination of life without an explicit request.   Griffiths extrapolated the

---

22   H Hellema 'Dutch Doctors Support Life Termination in Dementia' (1993) 306 BMJ 1364.

23   'Mercy-killing Doctor Freed' (1993) Scotsman, 22 April, p 8.

24   For a major advocate of the Dutch system, see P Admiraal 'Voluntary Euthanasia' in S A M McLean (ed) *Death, Dying and the Law* (1996) ch 7.   A forceful opposition view is to be found in J Keown 'Some Reflections on Euthanasia in the Netherlands', 'Further Reflections on Euthanasia in the Netherlands in the Light of the Remmelink Report and the Van der Maas Survey' in   L Gormally (ed) *Euthanasia, Clinical Practice and the Law* (1994) chs 4 and 5.   For a good factual review, see J Griffiths 'The Regulation of Euthanasia and Related Medical Procedures that Shorten Life in the Netherlands' (1994) 1 Med Law Internat 137.   An interesting critique of the Dutch experience, which reveals how the availability of euthanasia can obscure other options, is H Henden *Seduced by Death: Doctors, Patients and the Dutch Cure* (1997).

25   In 2000, it was revealed that the incidence of euthanasia in the Flemish-speaking part of the country was similar to that revealed in the earlier Netherlands studies: L Deliens, F Mortier, J Bilsen et al 'End of Life Decisions in Medical Practice in Flanders, Belgium: a Nationwide Survey' (2000) 356 Lancet 1806.

26   Griffiths, para 18.17 above, supports the suggestion that this would be better expressed as 'medical procedures that shorten life'.

27   See para 18.76 below.

available data to suggest that, on these grounds, an MDEL is the immediate cause of death in more than half all the deaths in the Netherlands due to chronic disease. Nevertheless, only some 5% of MDELs are instances of true euthanasia and euthanasia in the Netherlands clearly includes both the active killing of the patient and assisting the patient to precipitate his or her own death – a procedure which is now widely known as physician-assisted suicide (PAS). Is there, in fact, a distinction to be made?

Physician-assisted suicide

18.20 The classic case of PAS involves the provision of the means of ending life to a patient who will complete the act; this is properly described as an act of suicide, albeit assisted. It is, however, doubtful if the same can be said if the doctor, in person, administers the *coup de grâce*; we are, then, in the realm of active euthanasia. But such a distinction will not always be that easy. Take, for example the doctor who responds to a request to disconnect the ventilator in a case of progressive neurological disease – is this to be classed as refusal of treatment by the patient or as assisted suicide? And what of the paralysed patient who wishes to die but is receiving no treatment that can be refused – is the ending of that life a matter of assisting suicide or of active euthanasia? Or, what is the position of the doctor who performs the venepuncture and then holds the syringe while the patient presses the plunger?[28] Clearly, there is no bright dividing line between refusal of treatment, suicide, assisted suicide and euthanasia yet, in practice and, perhaps, intuitively, most people would perceive a distinction. Sometimes this may be subtle – as between the first two, for example, we have Lord Donaldson saying:

> This appeal is not in truth about 'the right to die'. There is no suggestion that Miss T wants to die ... This appeal is about the 'right to choose how to live'. This is quite different, even if the choice, when made, may make an early death more likely[29]

which, taken in the context of refusal of a life-saving blood transfusion, attracts something of an aura of legal expediency. Again, we have the Court in the American case of *Vacco v Quill*:[30]

> [The] distinction between assisting suicide and withdrawing life-sustaining treatment in hopeless cases is logical, widely recognized and endorsed by the medical profession and by legal tradition

and we only wish it *were* always so. On other occasions, however, the difference may be obvious. In respect of assisted suicide and euthanasia, for example, it is not difficult to see a practical difference between the classic

---

28 These examples are taken from D W Meyers and J K Mason 'Physician Assisted Suicide: A Second View from Mid-Atlantic' (1999) 28 Anglo-Am L Rev 265 in which the comparative Anglo-American scene is discussed in detail.

29 *Re T (adult: refusal of medical treatment)* [1992] 4 All ER 649 at 652, (1992) 9 BMLR 46 at 49.

30 117 S Ct 2293 (1997).

ploy of 'leaving the pills' and undertaking a lethal injection – and it is this sort of comparison that most people have in mind when addressing the subject.[31]

18.21 There is also legislative precedent for distinguishing physician-assisted suicide as a separate entity. Having seen initiatives designed to decriminalise active voluntary euthanasia fail in both California and the state of Washington by narrow majorities,[32] Oregon introduced its Death with Dignity Act of 1994, which concerned assisted suicide only. This was passed by an even more slender majority but, after a series of stays on constitutional grounds, the measure was re-enacted by a majority of 60:40.[33] Under the Oregon Act, it is lawful for a doctor to prescribe a lethal dosage of a drug for a patient who wishes to end his or her life – but not to involve him- or herself in the suicidal act. Certain conditions must be satisfied, including those of competence on the patient's part to make the decision. The patient must make the request voluntarily and must be suffering from a terminal illness. Critics of the law have pointed out that it empowers the physician to determine matters such as competence and voluntariness, and it has been suggested that it naively accepts medical reassurances of compliance with the requirements.[34] The fact that Oregon's Medicaid Plan, which provides medical cover for indigent patients, will pay for physician-assisted suicide while it will not do so for certain other treatments is of particular interest. Those who believe that financial pressure has the potential to encourage dispirited and vulnerable people to take a convenient way out, might take particular note of this.[35] The Act's passage into law was, however, not the end of the issue. A number of challenges have been mounted, including the introduction into Congress of the Pain Relief Promotion Act of 1999, which would have directly banned the use of controlled drugs to end life, even where it was legal under assisted suicide legislation.[36] The failure of this Bill has not deterred the United States Government from further attempts to prevent assisted suicide through the use of drug

---

31 For commentary, see L R Churchill and N M P King 'Physician Assisted Suicide, Euthanasia, or Withdrawal of Treatment' (1997) 315 BMJ 137.

32 Only one jurisdiction has passed such legislation: Rights of the Terminally Ill Amendment Act 1996 (NT, Australia). Four persons died under its provisions before the Australian Senate declared the measure to be unconstitutional.

33 The foundations of the Act are described by C K Smith 'Safeguards for Physician-assisted Suicide: The Oregon Death with Dignity Act' in McLean, para 18.17 above, ch 5. Subsequently, the United States Supreme Court has decreed that statutes which *prohibit* assisted suicide – and which are in force in thirty-four States (Fraser and Walters, para 18.27 below) – are not unconstitutional; the arguments are, however, essentially based on US constitutional law and have very little relevance outside the US: *Vacco v Quill* 117 S Ct 2293 (1997); *Washington v Glucksberg* 117 S Ct 2258 (1997). For discussion, see V J Samar 'Is the Right to Die Dead?' (2000) 50 DePaul Law Rev 221.

34 S R Martyn and H J Bourguignon 'Now is the Moment to Reflect: Two Years of Experience with Orgeon's Physician-Assisted Suicide Law' (2000) 8 Elder LJ 1. For reports on the working of the law, see A Chin et al 'Legalized Physician-Assisted Suicide in Oregon – the First Year's Experience' (1999) 340 New Engl J Med 577; A D Sullivan et al, 'Legalized Physician-Assisted Suicide in Oregon – the Second Year' (2000) 342 New Engl J Med 598.

35 The economic implications are discussed by S Graboyes-Russo, 'Too Costly to Live; the Moral Hazards of a Decision in *Washington v. Glucksberg* and *Vacco v. Quill*' (1997) 51 U Miami L Rev 907.

36 D Orentlicher 'The Pain Relief Promotion Act of 1999' (2000) 283 JAMA 255.

administration regulations[37] – attempts which are largely motivated by a desire to avoid the use of Federal funds for the purpose.

18.22 The chances of legislation which legalises active euthanasia being accepted in the United Kingdom are very slim;[38] but opposition might be very much less were it possible to legislate for PAS alone – an electorate that, rightly, could not accept the doctor as an executioner might be less hostile to a doctor who could be regarded as a friend in need.[39] Whatever their reasons, there is some evidence that both doctors and the public will accept the distinction. In a major survey undertaken in Scotland, McLean and Britton[40] found that, given a change in the law, 43% of doctors across the United Kingdom would opt for the legalisation of PAS – defined as the person's action leading to their own death – and 19% for active euthanasia in which the actions of other persons leads to death; the high proportion of undecided respondents (38%) should be noted. As opposed to this, 42% of Scottish people would prefer voluntary euthanasia while 28% would choose PAS. It is difficult to avoid the conclusion that, in this very sensitive situation, most people would wish to pass the ultimate responsibility to others.

18.23 It is hard to define the public attitude to either euthanasia or PAS – indeed, the public itself can appear confused. Thus, in McLean and Britton's survey, 67% thought that human beings should have the right to choose when to die (with 20% opposed) but only 55% (with 30% opposed) agreed that PAS should be made legal in Great Britain.[41] Perhaps the most powerful evidence as to current opinion in Great Britain is to be found in the survey carried out by Social and Community Planning Research in 1996,[42] where 82% of the survey population thought that doctors should be allowed to end a person's life when requested. The opinion was, however, selective. Thus, while 86% supported the procedure in comatose, incurably ill patients who were on ventilator support, the proportion dropped to 42% when the patient had an incurable, painful but not fatal illness – the situation faced by Dr Cox.[43] It does seem that there is a groundswell in favour of a change in the law,[44] although it would be useful, were it possible, to survey the opinions of those

37 F Charatan, 'US Government Moves against Doctor Assisted Suicide' (2001) 323 BMJ 1149.
38 House of Lords *Report of the Select Committee on Medical Ethics* (HL Paper 21-1, 1994) – which, admittedly, would have no truck with physician-assisted suicide either. The Government's response to this aspect of the report was robustly supportive: 'The Government can see no basis for permitting suicide. Such a change would be open to abuse and put the lives of the weak and vulnerable at risk.' (May 1994, Cmnd 2553)
39 See para 18.101 below for further discussion.
40 S A M McLean and A Britton *Sometimes a Small Victory* (1996).
41 It was stated in *Compassion in Dying v State of Washington* 79 Fed 3d 790 (1996) that US opinion polls show majorities of between 64% and 73% in favour of physician-assisted suicide. In a study involving oncologists and oncology patients, the latter were consistently more in favour of PAS than were their physicians: E J Emanuel, D L Fairclough, E R Daniels and B R Clarridge 'Euthanasia and Physician-Assisted Suicide: Attitudes and Experiences of Oncology Patients, Oncologists, and the Public' (1996) 347 Lancet 1805.
42 See J Wise 'Public Supports Euthanasia for Most Desperate Cases' (1996) 313 BMJ 1423.
43 See para 18.43 below.
44 R Smith 'Euthanasia: Time for a Royal Commission' (1992) 305 BMJ 728.

who are close to death – even so, generalisations can never provide a satisfactory template in such intensely individualised conditions.[45]

18.24 There are also uncertainties as to the attitudes of the medical professions. McLean's survey disclosed only 30% of doctors opposed to a change in the law to allow physician-assisted suicide; by contrast, this rose to 57% in a study carried out at much the same time by the BMA.[46] Similarly, 55% of the BMA sample would not take part in PAS if asked while only 37% of McLean's study group would never do so. Whatever one is to make of these figures, it is interesting to note that the majority of Western anglophone medical 'establishments' – as represented by their national Associations – want nothing to do with either PAS or euthanasia.[47] Nor, one might perhaps reflect, are moral questions to be determined on the basis of straw polls. The fact that a majority believes that something is right does not *make it* morally right. There is ample evidence of considerable public enthusiasm in the United States for the death penalty; those who argue that public (or indeed professional) acceptance of physician-assisted suicide contributes weightily to its legalisation might consider whether consistency requires them to accept the morality of the death penalty in communities in which it is widely endorsed.

18.25 We are on equally difficult ground when we move from opinion to theory. There is a widely-held belief that assisting another to take his or her life is morally different from taking that life oneself. But where do the grounds of this difference lie? To assist in bringing about a result involves moral responsibility for that result on causal grounds, as is recognised in the criminal law doctrine of complicity. To argue that simply because one sets in motion, but does not complete a sequence of events, one is relieved of responsibility for the outcome is unconvincing. A rather more fruitful approach for the proponents of physician-assisted suicide is to defend the right to commit suicide and to characterise the provision of assistance as being legitimate in view of that right. This then shifts the debate to an examination of the moral significance of the act of suicide and to the issue of whether, if this right is acknowledged, there are counterbalancing conflicting interests. This raises questions of greater moral complexity than many proponents of physician-assisted suicide imagine to be necessary. There are, for example, real moral doubts about suicide itself, which in one view can be seen as a conscious

---

45 Although, in fact, a group of American oncology patients (ie with malignant disease) did not differ in any significant way from the general public: see Emanuel et al, n 41 above.
46 J Coulson 'Doctors Oppose Legal Mercy Killing for Dying' (1995) BMA News Review (March) p 15. The BMA sample was, however, small and, one suspects, relatively selected. However, in a poll taken by the BMA only six months later, the gap between the two series narrowed – eg 46% of doctors opted for a change in the law to allow active medical intervention to terminate life if asked as opposed to 44% who were against. The proportion who would not intervene if so requested fell to 48%: J Coulson 'Till Death Us Do Part?' (1996) BMA News Review (Sept) p 23.
47 Eg C-G McDaniel 'US Doctors Reaffirm Opposition to Euthanasia' (1996) 313 BMJ 11. A Working Party of the British Medical Association concluded, in 1988, that the deliberate taking of a human life should remain a crime and that the doctor who feels compelled by conscience to end a patient's life must take his chance with the scrutiny of the law.

rejection of the value of human personhood.[48] And, at the end of the day, there may be strong pragmatic reasons for the view that the medical profession simply should not involve itself in actions which confuse its role. In this respect, the classic words of Capron still merit consideration:[49]

> I never want to have to wonder whether the physician coming into my hospital room is wearing the white coat (or the green scrubs) of a healer, concerned only to relieve my pain and restore me to health, or the black hood of the executioner. Trust between patient and physician is simply too important and too fragile to be subjected to this unnecessary strain.

18.26 This concern over trust has been the subject of close scrutiny. Emanuel and his colleagues found, in their survey of cancer patients and members of the public in general, that 19% of the former and 26.5% of the latter would change doctors if their doctor spoke to them about euthanasia or physician-assisted suicide.[50] We suggested above that statistics as to what people think should not drive the debate – but these figures are not about moral attitudes, they are about the fears of, in some cases, very vulnerable people.

18.27 Trust is only one of many considerations which have to be borne in mind. In addition, there are the familiar issues of coercion and abuse, both of which may serve to render decisions to end life less than fully voluntary, as, indeed, may confusion. The concept of the entirely rational person deciding to take his or her life after due reflection, and with no pressure from others or idea as to the expectations of others, may well not fit the reality.[51]

SUICIDE AND ATTEMPTED SUICIDE – THE CURRENT LAW

18.28 Suicide and attempted suicide are no longer criminal offences.[52] Whether or not this implies a legal right to end one's life is debatable but it is, at least, now firm law that the refusal of life-sustaining treatment is not a matter of attempted suicide.[53] The major interest, here, lies in the residual offence of counselling, procuring, aiding and abetting suicide which remains an offence in England and Wales by virtue of the Suicide Act 1961, s 2(1). In passing, it may be mentioned that there is some doubt as to whether an offence

---

48 For a useful survey of the moral arguments surrounding suicide, see M P Battin, *Ethical Issues in Suicide* (1994). For an example of the rejection of a right to commit suicide, see D J Velleman, 'A Right fo Self-Termination?' (1999) 109 Ethics 606.

49 A M Capron 'Legal and Ethical Problems in Decisions for Death' (1986) 14 Law Med Hlth Care 141. See also the view of a hospice practitioner R C Twycross 'Assisted Death: A Reply' (1990) 336 Lancet 796. Practical implications (including statistical estimates of demand) are also considered by E J Emanuel 'What is the Great benefit of Legalizing Euthanasia or Physician-Assisted Suicide?' (1999) 109 Ethics 629.

50 Emanuel et al, para 18.23 above.

51 But for a contrary, well-argued view from America, see S I Fraser and J W Walters 'Death – whose Decision? Euthanasia and the Terminally Ill' (2000) 26 J Med Ethics 121.

52 Suicide Act 1961.

53 For a discussion of the relationship between suicide and the refusal of treatment, see J Fletcher 'The Courts and Euthanasia' (1987/88) 15 Law Med Hlth Care 223. D Lanham 'The Right to Choose to Die with Dignity' (1990) 14 Crim LJ 401, considers the subject in detail.

of abetting suicide exists in Scotland, where the Suicide Act never applied – it is difficult to imagine a common law offence of aiding an act which is not, itself, a crime.[54]   Concerning ourselves only with England, our current interest lies in the   relationship of outside agencies to the would-be suicide and, particularly, in the standing of the doctor.

18.29 As to the general outsider, it is now clear that, while counselling or assisting a suicide remains an offence, this can only be illegal if conducted on a basis of immediacy and intent – the impersonal distribution of advice or information is unlikely to attract legal sanction.[55]

18.30 We are unaware of any prosecutions of doctors in the United Kingdom. Whether such a prosecution would succeed depends, in our view, very much on the type of assistance given. It might, for example, be perfectly clear to a patient that he would die were he to use a conveniently located switch to disconnect an electrically operated life-sustaining apparatus; the fatal dose of a drug would be far less obvious and its 'successful' use might depend upon advice from the medical attendant – and, in law, counselling, procuring, aiding and abetting are taken as a whole. In practical terms – and, particularly, in view of the British jury's well demonstrated benign attitude to the medical practitioner – it would be very difficult to prove 'beyond reasonable doubt' an intent to commit a crime. 'Leaving the pills' could, certainly, be an offence but, equally, it could be one to which the law might turn, at least, an unseeing eye. The situation is, however, likely to be different when the doctor's assistance necessarily involves some activity.   Such instances involve, pre-eminently, cases of progressive neurological disease in which the patient may wish to commit suicide but is physically unable to do so without assistance. These cases constitute a very specific group which has its own special ethical problems.[56]

Progressive neurological disease

18.31 In so far as the right of the competent adult to refuse life-saving treatment is now universally established,[57] and that the legal right to control one's body has found expression in the decriminalising of suicide, it is but a short step to holding that to refuse assistance in dying to a person who is incapable of ending his or her own life is an affront to that person's rights of autonomy. It is important, though, to isolate two separate issues. One is the right to reject treatment, even if one is incapable of physically resisting the imposition of treatment. The second is more controversial and involves an attempt to assert a legal right to assistance in suicide.

54 By contrast, a case can be made out for believing that assisting a person to commit suicide would be considered to be culpable homicide: see R A McCall Smith and D Sheldon *Scots Criminal Law* (2nd edn, 1997) p 171.   The topic has been re-assessed by: P R Ferguson 'Killing "Without Getting into Trouble?" Assisted Suicide and Scots Criminal Law' (1998) 2   Edin L R 288.
55 *A-G v Able* [1984] QB 795, [1984] 1 All ER 277.
56 For a very comprehensive review of such cases, see J H Veldink, J H J Wokke, G van der Wal et al 'Euthanasia and Physician-assisted Suicide among Patients with Amyotrophic Lateral Sclerosis in the Netherlands' (2002) 346 New Engl J Med 1638.

The right to refuse treatment

18.32 The *general* right to refuse treatment is discussed in detail at para 18.59 below. Here, we are concerned only with that right as it applies to the extreme example of progressive neurological disease. The application of the right in these circumstances was first upheld in the very significant Canadian decision of *Nancy B v Hôtel-Dieu de Québec.*[58] Ms B, who suffered from the Guillain-Barré syndrome, was existing by virtue of ventilation; she sought to have her ventilator disconnected and was supported in this by her family and the hospital. In making the required order, Dufour J called upon the Civil Code of Lower Canada, which held:

> 19.1. No person may be made to undergo care of any nature whether for examination, specimen taking, removal of tissue treatment or any other act, except with his consent,

and concluded that this encompassed ventilation. He proceeded:

> What Nancy B is seeking … is … that nature may take its course; that she be freed from the slavery of a machine as her life depends on it. In order to do this, as she is unable to do it herself, she needs the help of a third person. Then, it is the disease which will take its natural course.

As a result, the person responsible for the actual cessation of treatment would not violate the criminal law in so doing. At the same time, however, the judge ruled that, not only would it not be homicide, it would also be neither suicide nor assisted suicide.

18.33 *Nancy B* has now been followed in England by the equally important, although rather confusingly named, case of *Ms B v An NHS Hospital Trust.*[59] The facts of the two were very similar in that the 'English' Ms B was suffering from progressive paralysis due to a haemorrhage into her spinal cord and was, at the time of the hearing, maintained by the use of a ventilator. She had already effected an advance directive (see para 18.64) and repeatedly asked that she be disconnected from her machine but the clinicians refused to do so, preferring an attempt to wean her from life support. Ms B then sought a declaration that the treatment she was being given was an unlawful trespass. Butler-Sloss LJ, who heard the case herself at first instance, made it clear that, in the circumstances, the case was not concerned with the patient's best interests but solely with her legal capacity to accept or refuse treatment.[60] Ms B's case

---

57 For the UK, see *Re T (adult: refusal of medical treatment)* [1992] 4 All ER 649, (1992) 9 BMLR 46; *Re MB (an adult: medical treatment)* [1997] 2 FLR 426, (1997) 38 BMLR 175; *Ms B v An NHS Hospital Trust* [2002] EWHC 429. For a Canadian decision, see *Ciarlariello v Schacter* [1993] 2 SCR 119. Examples of leading cases from the US include: *Re Kathleen Farrell* 529 A 2d 404 (NJ, 1987); *Bouvia v Superior Court of Los Angeles County* 179 Cal App 3d 1127 (1986).

58 (1992) 86 DLR (4th) 385, (1992) 15 BMLR 95.

59 Para 18.31 above. A very similar case had been heard before but had received little attention: *Re AK (adult patient)(medical treatment: consent)* [2001] 1 FLR 129, (2001) 58 BMLR 151.

60 The matter is discussed in detail in chapter 10. Effectively a medical assessment of 'best interests' is applicable only when the patient is incompetent. Guidelines were given in *Ms B* but originated in *St George's Healthcare NHS Trust v S* [1999] Fam 26.

can, therefore, be dealt with in précis at the moment. Suffice it to say that she was found to have full capacity; she was moved to another hospital that was willing to disconnect her and she died some four weeks later. Butler-Sloss LJ emphasised the importance of a competent patient's free choice by imposing nominal damages of £100 against the hospital for their unlawful trespass.

18.34 In one respect, the effect of *Ms B* is merely to rehearse the well-established proposition that the competent adult may reject treatment, even if this will result in death. But the case also demonstrates the limitation of the *doctors'* autonomy that is inherent in the doctrine and we return to this below at para 18.84.

18.35 We should also remind readers that there is abundant evidence that removal of life support mechanisms at the request of the patient is not only acceptable but may be obligatory in the United States. Thus, in *Farrell*,[61] a motor neurone disease case, not only was a request for disconnection from the ventilator agreed, but the right to professional assistance during the agonal phase was upheld. An equally emphatic case arose in California, where the health care team was instructed to provide full facilities in order to ease the patient's dying.[62] It is thus clear that the United States' jurisdictions recognise a practical as well as a theoretical distinction between refusal of treatment and assisted suicide.[63]

Assistance with suicide

18.36 The second issue – that of whether there is a legal right to assistance with suicide – was considered by the Supreme Court of Canada in *Rodriguez v A-G of British Columbia*.[64] The arguments in Ms Rodriguez's case, which concerned the setting up of a mechanism she could use to end her life should she become paralysed as a result of her motor neurone disease, were, in the main, based on Canadian constitutional law and, in particular, related to possible conflicts between the Canadian Charter of Rights and Freedoms and the Criminal Code; these are issues specific to Canadian law, but their relevance in the United Kingdom has greatly increased with the passage of the Human Rights Act 1998. It was held by a majority of 5:4 that, while the patient's autonomy was at stake in such cases, the deprivation of rights consequent on the refusal of such a request was not contrary to the principles of fundamental justice, which required a fair balance to be struck between the interests of the state and those of the individual; neither were the liberty and security of the person compromised – one reason being that the provisions in the Criminal Code, s 241 prohibiting assisted suicide were there as a *protection* for the terminally ill who were particularly vulnerable as to their life and will to live:

---

61 *Re Kathleen Farrell* 529 A 2d 404 (NJ, 1987).
62 *Bouvia v Superior Court of Los Angeles County* 179 Cal App 3d 1127 (1986).
63 See *Vacco v Quill* (1997) 117 S Ct 2293. For discussion of the position in the United States, see N L Cantor and G C Thomas 'The Legal Bounds of Physician Conduct hastening Death' (2000) 48 Buffalo L Rev 83.
64 *Rodriguez v A-G of British Columbia* (1993) 107 DLR (4th) 342, (1993) 50 BMLR 1.

[T]his protection is grounded on a substantial consensus among Western countries ... that, in order to effectively protect life and those who are vulnerable in society, a prohibition without exception on the giving of assistance to commit suicide is the best approach ... The formulation of safeguards to prevent excesses has been unsatisfactory and has failed to allay fears that a relaxation of the clear standard set by the law will undermine the protection of life and will lead to abuses of the exception.[65]

18.37 Despite the rather narrow basis for the judgment, some of the dissenting opinions express important general principles. In particular, the 'floodgates' argument was dismissed, not because it might not occur, but because a person should not be denied a choice which others have open to them simply on the grounds that, as a consequence, others may then abuse such powers as they have over the weak and ill[66] – effectively, each individual person must be treated fairly by the law and not made a scapegoat for the fallibility of others (per McLachlin J). Finally, the opinion of Cory J merits repetition:

[D]ying is an integral part of living ... It follows that the right to die with dignity should be as well protected as is any other aspect of the right to life. State prohibitions that would force a dreadful, painful death on a rational but incapacitated terminally ill patient are an affront to human dignity.[67]

Thus, the arguments for and against assisted suicide of this type are finely balanced but all the dissenting opinions in *Rodriguez* stressed that it was for Parliament, not the courts, to make such fundamental decisions.

18.38 The issue first came to the attention of the United Kingdom courts in the *Linsell* case,[68] in which a patient in the terminal stages of motor neurone disease sought a declaration that her doctor would not be prosecuted if he administered potentially lethal doses of analgesics when her condition deteriorated. The patient withdrew her application when she heard that a substantial body of medical opinion had endorsed her doctor's planned palliative management regime, which meant that no ruling was required. A similar plight was brought before the courts some four years later by Mrs Pretty,[69] whose application was, ultimately, heard in the European Court of Human Rights. In this case the patient, who was just able to communicate, sought the assurance of the Director of Public Prosecutions (DPP) that he would not bring charges against her husband under the Suicide Act, s 2(1) if the latter took steps to end her life at her own request but by unspecified

---

65 (1993) 107 DLR (4th) 342 at 410, per Sopinka J.
66 We do not intend, here, to discuss the bizarre case of Dr Kevorkian in America who is said to have invented and promoted a 'suicide machine' – he faced a Grand Jury and was acquitted of all charges. He then filmed his operation and, as a result, was tried and convicted of second degree murder. In 2002, the Michigan Supreme Court refused to review the rejection of his appeal by the State Court of Appeal.
67 (1993) 107 DLR (4th) 342 at 413.
68 E Wilkins 'Dying Woman Granted Wish for Dignified End' *The Times*, 29 October 1997, p 3.
69 *R (on the application of Pretty) v DPP* [2001] UKHL 61, [2002] 1 All ER 1, (2002) 63 BMLR 1, HL.

method.[70] The DPP declined to give this assurance, saying that it was improper for him to decline in advance to prosecute a breach of the criminal law.[71] This refusal was challenged by Mrs Pretty, by means of judicial review, on the grounds that the decision infringed rights which were protected under the Human Rights Act 1998.

18.39 Mrs Pretty based her claim on five Articles in the European Convention on Human Rights: Article 2 (the right to life); Article 3 (the prohibition of torture and cruel and degrading treatment); Article 8 (the right to respect for private life); Article 9 (the right to freedom of thought, conscience and religion) and Article 14 (the prohibition of discrimination). Although the court was clearly sympathetic to her plight, none of these Articles was deemed to be grounds on which to base a right to assistance with suicide. The court rejected the argument that Article 2 created a right of self-determination in relation to life and death, holding that the right was clearly concerned with preventing the unjustified taking of life. The appellant's argument in respect of Article 3 was that there was an obligation on the part of the state to provide assistance in the prevention of suffering – a positive rather than a negative duty. This was rejected by the court, which held that the state in this case was not in breach of its duty to prevent the infliction of suffering – and Mrs Pretty's suffering resulted from a disease rather than from the act of any person.

18.40 In dealing with the right to respect for private life (Article 8), the House of Lords did not consider a prohibition of assistance in suicide to amount to an infringement of autonomy for the purposes of the Article in question. The right of autonomy protected by the Article was the right to exercise autonomy while living one's life, and, as pointed out by Lord Bingham, there was nothing in the Article to suggest that it has any bearing on the choice to live no longer.[72] This narrow interpretation is open to criticism in that the concept of autonomy, as it is generally understood, includes decisions about dying. Dying is a part of life, even if death is not, and it is difficult to imagine how at least some decisions about the nature of one's death could be seen to have nothing to do with the exercise of self-determination.[73] The European Court did, in fact, appreciate the force of this argument but preferred to consider whether interference on the part of the state was justified under Article 8(2) which lists a number of exceptions that could be regarded as 'necessary in a democratic society'. In the event, the ECHR agreed with the House of Lords in finding that the 'blanket' application of the Suicide Act 1961, s 2(1) infringed none of the five Articles considered. In particular, Article 2 imposed a duty on the state to protect life and there was no implication that this created a right to die; the prohibition of assisted suicide was not disproportionate to the need to protect the state's vulnerable citizens (Article 8); and that to distinguish between

70 It will be seen from the discussion at para 18.20 above that, by our definition, assisted suicide was not a real possibility in that Mrs Pretty would have been unable to complete the act herself. This issue does not seem to have been considered in any of the judgments.
71 It was also constitutionally impossible – Lord Bingham in the House of Lords drew attention to the Bill of Rights 1688 which denies the Crown and its servants any power to alter laws without the consent of Parliament ((2002) 63 BMLR 1 at 44).
72 (2002) 63 BMLR 1 at 39.
73 Mrs Pretty's case is well argued by R English 'No Rights to Last Rites' (2001) 151 NLJ 1844. See also K M Boyd 'Mrs Pretty and Ms B' (2002) 28 J Med Ethics 211.

those who could and those who physically could not commit suicide – and, thus, to avoid any supposed discrimination against the latter contrary to Article 14 – would be to undermine the protection of life that the 1961 Act was designed to safeguard.

18.41 Both the House of Lords and the ECHR appreciated, and were much influenced by, the fear that permitting assisted suicide would open the door to abuse of the sick and the elderly, an attitude that was summed up well by Lord Bingham when quoting with approval the conclusions of the House of Lords Select Committee on Medical Ethics:

> The message which society sends to vulnerable and disadvantaged people should not, however obliquely, encourage them to seek death, but should assure them of our care and support in life[74]

ACTIVE EUTHANASIA

18.42 By contrast with the foregoing, there can be no doubt that active euthanasia is unlawful. This has been unequivocally restated in the landmark case of *Bland*, where we have Lord Mustill:

> [T]hat 'mercy killing' by active means is murder ... has never so far as I know been doubted. The fact that the doctor's motives are kindly will for some, although not for all, transform the moral quality of his act, but this makes no difference in law. It is intent to kill or cause grievous bodily harm which constitutes the mens rea of murder, and the reason why the intent was formed makes no difference at all.[75]

18.43 This, then, was the position when Dr Cox was charged with the attempted murder of Mrs Boyes, his patient of 13 years' standing.[76] Mrs Boyes was suffering from rheumatoid arthritis – not, of itself, a fatal condition but one causing intense pain; she had expressed a wish to die and was, indeed, already categorised as 'not for resuscitation'.[77] It was admitted that Dr Cox injected her with two ampoules of potassium chloride, which is known to be potently cardiotoxic but, at the same time, is a substance which the majority of practitioners would regard as having no analgesic value – and it is this which distinguishes Dr Cox's case from any other prosecutions of doctors of which we are aware.[78] The only issue at trial was, therefore, that of intent – as Ognall J put it at the outset of his summing up:

> If he injected her with potassium chloride with the primary purpose of killing her, of hastening her death, he is guilty of the offence charged.[79]

---

74 Report, para 239, p 49. Per Lord Bingham (2002) 63 BMLR 1 at 42.
75 *Airedale NHS Trust v Bland* [1993] 1 All ER 821 at 890, (1993) 12 BMLR 64 at 137.
76 *R v Cox* (1992) 12 BMLR 38. Dr Cox was charged with attempted murder presumably because Mrs Boyes had been cremated before her death was regarded as suspicious. Any arguments as to the cause of death would, therefore, have been speculative.
77 For which see para 18.92 below.
78 Another trial concerned with voluntary euthanasia by way of injection of potassium chloride and lignocaine was aborted when the prosecution offered no evidence: *R v Lodwig* (1990) Times, 16 March.
79 *R v Cox* (1992) 12 BMLR 38 at 39.

and later:

> If a doctor genuinely believes that a certain course is beneficial to his patient, either therapeutically or analgesically, then even though he recognises that that course carries with it a risk to life, he is fully entitled, nonetheless, to pursue it. If in those circumstances the patient dies, nobody could possibly suggest that in that situation the doctor was guilty of murder or attempted murder.[80]

18.44 Essentially, therefore, the problem for the jury was one of intention – did Dr Cox *intend* to kill his patient[81] or did he hope to grant her a short pain-free period during the process of dying? In the event, Dr Cox was found guilty of attempted murder.

18.45 So, what distinguished Dr Cox from Dr Carr or Dr Moor whose cases we have discussed above? Obviously, we can never know the precise reason for a jury verdict but we can extract some factors which they may have found important – even if only subliminally. First, Mrs Boyes was incurably but not terminally ill. It is interesting that none of the sporadic attempts to legalise 'euthanasia' – at least in the United Kingdom – have attempted to go beyond the confines of terminal disease. There may well be an intuitive distinction to be made which we suggest would be rightly founded on the difficulty of limiting the definition of incurable or intolerable disease. Secondly, Dr Cox injected a non-therapeutic substance and it is reasonable to assume that, while public opinion in the United Kingdom will give great latitude to the medical profession in its fight against suffering, it is not yet prepared to accept the use of a substance which has no analgesic effect and is known to be lethal when injected in concentrated form. Thirdly, and as a direct result of this, he was unable to plead 'double effect' or necessity – moral and legal concepts which we introduce below at para 18.76.

18.46 Even so, sympathy for Dr Cox was widespread.[82] No immediate custodial sentence was imposed; the vice-president of the Voluntary Euthanasia Society castigated what he saw as a supine jury; the General Medical Council was content to admonish him on the grounds that, although his actions had fallen short of the high standards which the medical profession must uphold, he clearly acted in good faith; and the responsible regional health authority offered continued employment subject to certain restrictions.[83] We believe that the jury decision was certainly right in law but that public dissatisfaction ultimately stems from the law's determination to dissociate motive from intent when faced with unlawful killing[84] – as in the case of Dr Arthur, whose case

---

80   (1992) 12 BMLR 38 at 41.
81   Whether or not it was 'an act of mercy' was a matter only for the judge in sentencing, motive being irrelevant to the jury.
82   It is reported that 11% of doctors in the USA who are closely associated with relevant cases had received requests for a lethal injection and 4.7% had complied with the request at least once: D E Meier, C-A Emmons, S Wallenstein et al 'A National Survey of Physician-Assisted Suicide and Euthanasia in the United States' (1998) 338 New Engl J Med 1193.
83   C Dyer 'GMC Tempers Justice with Mercy in Cox Case' (1992) 305 BMJ 1311.
84   This view is central to the persuasive argument in K Boyd 'Euthanasia: Back to the Future' in J Keown (ed) *Euthanasia Examined* (1995) ch 7.

is discussed in chapter 16, Dr Cox was certainly not a murderer as the word is commonly interpreted. None the less, for reasons which appear elsewhere in this chapter, we cannot accept that individual doctors should be given free rein in this field absent specific legislation.[85] Moreover, any such legislation must, itself, be suspect. It has been said that current attitudes to euthanasia are comparable to the attitudes to abortion in the early 1960s;[86] it is precisely the fear that current attitudes to abortion may become those to euthanasia in the twenty-first century that tempers our intuitive sympathy for both Dr Cox and his patient.

PASSIVE EUTHANASIA

18.47 By contrast with the positive action thus far discussed, passive euthanasia involves the shortening of life through an omission to act. Few people will find difficulty as to what is meant by active euthanasia. The definition of passive euthanasia, however, presents a number of problems in so far as death resulting from inaction of one sort or another is spread across the whole spectrum and includes, inter alia, non-treatment of a treatable condition, withdrawal of treatment and refusal of treatment – and we have already discussed this last variant. Sub-categories exist even within this framework. Thus, treatment can be withdrawn either because it is non-productive or because, based on an anticipated quality of life, it is in the patient's best interests to do so; alternatively, treatment can be refused because the competent patient wishes to die or, simply, because he or she has an aversion to a particular form of treatment.

18.48 What one regards as passive euthanasia, then, depends not only on whether one is speaking in legal, moral or medical terms but also on personal preference or prejudice. As to the latter, we have tended to use the death certificate as our benchmark – would the patient have died if the physician had not retreated into his passive mode or, put another way, could we certify death as being due to natural causes with a clear conscience? On this definition, passive euthanasia is confined to withdrawal of life-sustaining treatment in the incompetent and refusal of further treatment by the competent patient where death is the intended outcome – with the 'do not resuscitate order' providing a virtually distinct category. The concept of 'double effect' (see para 18.76) is also so bound to the subject of passive euthanasia that it cannot be ignored in this context. Such a classification will seem unsatisfactory to some; nevertheless, it forms the basis for the discussion that follows.

18.49 The question of whether allowing an event to happen through inaction is morally different from taking positive steps to bring it about has been extensively debated in moral philosophy. Criticism of the act/omission

---

85 For an interpretation of the relationship between the law and the medical profession see Hoffmann LJ in *Airedale NHS Trust v Bland* [1993] 1 All ER 821 at 858, (1992) 12 BMLR 64 at 103: 'The court [has been invited] to decide whether, on medical facts which are not in dispute, [the action] would be justified as being in the best interests of the patient. This is a purely legal (or moral) decision which does not require any medical expertise and is therefore appropriately made by the court.'

86 R Smith 'Euthanasia: Time for a Royal Commission' (1992) 305 BMJ 728.

distinction has been intense and sustained over recent decades. Thus, the position advanced by Philippa Foot in her classic paper 'The Problem of Abortion and the Doctrine of Double Effect' – that our duty not to harm others is stronger than our duty to assist[87] – finds fewer supporters today than it did when it was published in 1976. This change has even had its effect on the legal world, within which commentators – and occasionally judges – have expressed disquiet over the drawing of a sharp distinction between act and omission for the purposes of attributing liability for the consequences. In spite of this, there remain grounds for making this distinction in relation to euthanasia, even if its validity has been called into question elsewhere. One reason for arguing against the distinction is that it tolerates inconsistency and may merge into moral cowardice. In this view, a doctor who knows that his failure to treat will result in death should accept the same responsibility for that death as if he had brought it about through a positive act.

18.50 How, then, is this objection to be answered? One response is to say that the distinction reflects a widely held moral intuition which, even if it involves inconsistency, allows for the practical conduct of day to day moral life. Morality, like the law, needs to be rooted in daily experience. Doctors who engage in passive euthanasia need – and maybe are entitled to – the comfort of thinking they are not actually killing their patients. A sophisticated morality will recognise such ordinary human needs. A second response would be consequentialist in nature. The act/omission distinction plays an important role in the preservation of a near-absolute prohibition of killing. The weakening of this prohibition could have the effect of blunting the respect which we accord to human life. The combination of these two approaches is sufficient to tip the scales in favour of retaining the distinction.[88]

18.51 Selective non-treatment is practised fairly widely while only a very small number of physicians would work actively to end the life of a patient.[89] The medical profession as a whole accepts the distinction as argued above. As one commentator put it: 'Our gut intuition tells us that there is a difference between active and passive euthanasia and we are not going to be browbeaten into changing our minds by mere logic.'[90] – and it is not beyond the capacity of moral philosophy to support this: 'We cannot capture our moral judgments by appeal to argument alone ... in the area of dying; intuitions and conceptions formed by actual experience must be given weight.'[91]

---

87 P Foot in S Gorovitz et al (eds) *Moral Problems in Medicine* (1976).
88 The contrary argument, which, clearly, we find difficult to accommodate, has been put in an editorial article by L Doyal and L Doyal 'Why Active Euthanasia and Physician Assisted Suicide should be Legalised' (2001) 323 BMJ 1079.
89 In one of many such studies, this one undertaken by the BMA, 22 out of 750 doctors admitted to having actively ended the life of a patient on request although a surprising 46% believed that they should be legally permitted to do so. 90% supported passive euthanasia and 75% recognised a moral distinction between active and passive euthanasia: J Coulson 'Till Death Us Do Part?' (1996) BMA News Rev, Sept, p 23.
90 T B Brewin 'Voluntary Euthanasia' (1986) 1 Lancet 1085. See also D P Sulmany 'Killing and Allowing to Die: Another Look' (1998) 26 J Law Med & Ethics 55.
91 G Gillett 'Euthanasia, Letting Die and the Pause' (1988) 14 J Med Ethics 61. This attitude was challenged by M Parker 'Moral Intuition, Good Deaths and Ordinary Medical Practitioners' (1990) 16 J Med Ethics 28.

18.52 The legal position is, in one sense, clear. We can return to *Bland,* per Lord Mustill:[92]

> The English criminal law ... draws a sharp distinction between acts and omissions. If an act resulting in death is done without lawful excuse and with intent to kill it is murder. But an omission to act with the same result and with the same intent is in general no offence at all.

So far, so good, but Lord Mustill went on to say:[93]

> There is one important general exception at common law, namely that a person may be criminally liable for the consequences of an omission if he stands in such a relation to the victim that he is under a duty to act.

And there is Lord Keith:[94]

> In general it would not be lawful for a medical practitioner who assumed responsibility for the care of an unconscious patient simply to give up treatment in circumstances where continuance of it would confer some benefit on the patient. On the other hand, a medical practitioner is under no duty to treat such a patient where a large body of informed and responsible medical opinion is to the effect that no benefit at all would be conferred by continuance.

Lord Keith was, of course, speaking of the permanent vegetative state. There is, however, no doubt that, despite his obvious duty of care – and despite his potential liability – the doctor who discontinues treatment of an incompetent patient in the circumstances envisaged will not be prosecuted provided his inaction is covered by the doctrine of good medical practice.

18.53 An illustrative example of this comes from New Zealand.[95] The circumstances surrounding the case were very similar to those in *Nancy B,*[96] save that the patient, L – also suffering from the Guillain-Barré syndrome – was incapable of expressing his wishes. His existence depended on artificial ventilation and the question put to the High Court was in the rather stark terms: would the doctors' action in withdrawing ventilator support make them guilty of homicide?[97]

18.54 Thomas J approached this issue by asking whether a doctor is obliged to continue treatment which has no therapeutic or medical benefit notwithstanding that the withdrawal of the treatment may result in the clinical death of the patient. He commented that all natural life has ceased in such a case; it was the *manifestations* of life which were maintained artificially and which were brought to an end by the doctor's intervention. He proceeded on the twin principles of humanity and common sense. On this basis, he concluded that life support provided *only* for the purpose of deferring certain death could

---

92 [1993] 1 All ER 821 at 890, (1992) 12 BMLR 64 at 137.
93 [1993] 1 All ER 821 at 890, (1992) 12 BMLR 64 at 137.
94 [1993] 1 All ER 821 at 861, (1992) 12 BMLR 64 at 106-107.
95 *Auckland Area Health Board v A-G* [1993] 1 NZLR 235, [1993] 4 Med LR 239.
96 See para 18.32.
97 Crimes Act 1961, ss 151(1) and 164, NZ.

not be regarded as a necessity of life; moreover, doctors have a lawful excuse to discontinue treatment when there is no medical justification for continuing that medical assistance. Withdrawal of treatment would not be unlawful if it was carried out within the accepted confines of 'good medical practice' – or adhering to a procedure which provided safeguards against the possibility of individual error. Within this scenario, withdrawal of life support would not be the cause of death *as a matter of law* – and this would coincide with the common-sense perception.

18.55 Thomas J's admirable analysis attracted particularly favourable comment in the House of Lords in *Bland*. Jurisprudentially, it owes much to the reasoning in PVS cases and this is inevitable in that L's disease state was more advanced than was that of Ms Rodriguez or Nancy B. The judge was able, however, to medicalise the dilemma fully and thus avoid what is, in our view, the sophistry of the 'best interests' test.

18.56 It is to be noted that all these cases of 'assistance in dying' have it in common that the courts have been anxious to ensure that the cause of death was attributed to natural disease. We suggest, and have argued already in respect of PVS,[98] that the cause of death following withdrawal of any form of life support should depend on whether the support was removed before or after brain stem death has occurred. If the person is dead at that time, the cause of death is clearly the original anoxic or other insult sustained by the brain. When, however, a treatment is discontinued solely by reason of its futility, there is nothing to be lost – and much to be gained by way of intellectual honesty – in attributing death, correctly, to 'Lawful withdrawal of life support systems which were necessitated by [the disease]'.

Allowing the patient to die

18.57 While selective non-treatment has gained general acceptance as being a part of good medical practice, it is clear that it will not find moral endorsement in all its forms – much will depend on the nature of the treatment that is being withheld. The issue thus focuses on the distinction between what have become known as ordinary and extraordinary treatments. There is a general consensus, now established in both legal and medical opinion, that the doctor need not resort to heroic methods to prolong the life – or, perhaps better, to prolong the dying – of his patient; considerations of cost and of the distribution of other resources are important here, although they must be secondary to the well-being and the dignity of the patient.[99] These principles are embodied in the classic expression of the ordinary/extraordinary treatment test which is to be found in the directive issued by Pope Pius XII in 1957:[100]

> Man has a right and a duty in case of severe illness to take the necessary steps to preserve life and health. That duty ... devolves from charity as ordained by

98 See chapter 17.
99 It is clear from at least two speeches in *Bland* ([1993] 1 All ER 821 at 879, 893, (1992) 12 BMLR 64 at 125, 140, per Lord Browne-Wilkinson and Lord Mustill), that resources might be a legitimate concern of the clinician.
100 (1957) 49 Acta Apostolicae Sedis 1027.

the Creator, from social justice and even from strict law. But he is obliged at all times to employ only ordinary means ... that is to say those means which do not impose an extraordinary burden on himself or others.

18.58 This statement represents the core of Roman Catholic teaching on the matter and a similar approach has found widespread support in non-religious discussions of the issue, where the denial of the need to resort to extraordinary measures may be based on quite different grounds. Clearly, however, the difficulty about such a test lies in making the fundamental distinction between ordinary and extraordinary treatments and the Pope, himself, qualified 'ordinary' as 'according to personal circumstances, the law, the times and the culture'. Thus, the ordinary/extraordinary test should not and cannot be applied as a general, all embracing rule. Some have, accordingly, suggested that the comparison should be between proportionate and disproportionate therapy; we would take this concept one stage further in preferring the contrast of medically productive and non-productive means – the test being whether or not a particular treatment is doing the condition any good. Factors such as the physical and psychological pain involved in the treatment, its claim on scarce resources and the general prospects for the patient and his family may all be taken into account in deciding whether or not a treatment is productive. Clearly, non-productivity and medical futility have much in common as a treatment standard and, as we have already discussed, the arguments for and against their adoption are very similar. The scope for ethical and legal disagreement is wide and, in the long term, social consensus must be sought on ways to resolve the conflicts engendered by the notion of futility[101] – which we are convinced must come to be accepted in some way. Meantime, imperfect and value-laden as the concepts of futility and non-productivity may be, their practical value should not be discarded for fear of offending what Miles has described as an elitist view of 'autonomy'.[102]

Whose body is it?

18.59 The individual's right of self-determination, which we have discussed above within the confines of progressive neurological disease, is now established as the determining factor in *any* situation of therapeutic conflict – whether it is a problem of abortion, consent to treatment or euthanasia. Yet the question can still be properly asked – are there circumstances in which the wishes of the individual should be looked upon as being qualified by other considerations?

---

101 For a UK approach, see K R Mitchell, I H Kerridge and T J Lovat 'Medical Futility, Treatment Withdrawal and the Persistent Vegetative State' (1993) 19 J Med Ethics 71. Guidelines have been drawn up in New South Wales to cover cases in which life support treatment is deemed futile. Life supporting therapy is widely defined and includes chemotherapy, radiotherapy and renal dialysis: NSW Department of Health *Dying with Dignity* (1993) discussed by D John (1993) 306 BMJ 1363. In the United States the American Medical Association has issued guidance on the notion of futility. The Association accepted that it would be difficult to establish a consensus on this issue, and therefore recommended a process-based approach: Council on Ethical and Judicial Affairs, 'Medical Futility in End-of-Life Care: Report of the Council on Ethical and Judicial Affairs' (1999) 281 JAMA 937. For a wide-ranging overview, see M B Zucker and H D Zucker *Medical Futility* (1997).
102 S H Miles 'Medical Futility' (1992) 20 Law Med Hlth Care 310.

18.60 The theologian might well answer Yes; the Roman Catholic church, for example, allows no right to suicide and declining treatment might be regarded as suicide in certain circumstances. Others might hold that to diminish the seriousness and awe with which we view life is but a step towards the rejection of values which are of crucial importance to society. We would do well to reflect on the moral steps which are being taken when we pay homage to the cult of self-determination.[103]   None the less, the principle of self-control is now firmly established and is reflected legally in the offence of battery – the concept of informed refusal has achieved the same standing in medical jurisprudence as that of informed consent.[104]

18.61 The common law basis for these decisions lies in the assumption that the rights of the competent individual to self-determination will normally outweigh the interests of the state in the preservation of life.[105] In addition, there are human rights principles which underpin the proposition that treatment may not be imposed on the competent adult. This would almost certainly amount to an infringement of rights protected by the Human Rights Act 1998 should it ever be necessary to invoke that statute; Article 3 of the European Convention on Human Rights[106] prohibits the infliction of inhumane measures, into which category non-consensual treatment would be likely to fall.[107] To the same effect, the Council of Europe's Convention on Human Rights and Biomedicine provides in Article 5 that any intervention in the health field may only be carried out if the patient gives a free and informed consent. In some jurisdictions, the right to reject medical treatment has been specifically recognised in legislation. Pioneering statutory action in this field is to be found in the Medical Treatment Act 1988 of Victoria which, among other things, introduced the offence of medical trespass which is committed by a medical practitioner who knowingly treats contrary to the certified wishes of the patient; thus, the practitioner cannot plead his own ethos and there is no 'conscience clause'. Simultaneously, however, the Act exonerates the doctor who fails to treat in accordance with a certificate of refusal from professional, criminal and civil liability (s 9).[108]

18.62 The Victorian legislation is far-reaching. In particular, no distinction is made between terminal and other illness. Moreover, the right to refuse treatment is unqualified; it is subject neither to the interests of the state nor to those of third parties – non-consensual caesarian section on behalf of the

---

103   For a searching analysis, see O O'Neill *Autonomy and Trust in Bioethics* (2002). See also the Israeli Patients' Rights Act 1996 which, inter alia, permits a right to informed consent but, on communitarian grounds, refers refusals to a committee.

104   *St George's Healthcare NHS Trust v S, R v Collins, ex p S* [1998] 3 WLR 936, [1998] 3 All ER 673 is probably the strongest authority in the United Kingdom.

105   This is argued in a wide-ranging article by E Wicks 'The Right to Refuse Medical Treatment under the European Convention on Human Rights' (2001) 9 Med L Rev 17.

106   Now Sch 1 to the 1998 Act.

107   On the other side of the coin, a *failure* to provide treatment in the patient's best interests does not contravene the Convention: *A NHS Trust v D* [2000] 2 FLR 677, (2000) 55 BMLR 19; *NHS Trust A v M, NHS Trust B v H* [2001] Fam 348, (2001) 58 BMLR 87.

108   The power to appoint an agent in the event of supervening incompetence is granted in the Medical Treatment (Enduring Power of Attorney) Act 1990. For description of the 1988 Act, see D Lanham 'The Right to Choose to Die with Dignity' (1990) 14 Crim LJ 401.

fetus, for example, now has no place in Victorian medical practice.[109] The Act specifically excludes palliative treatment – or the provision of reasonable medical procedures for the relief of pain, suffering and discomfort (s 3) – from that which can be refused but, at the same time, preserves the patient's rights at common law in this respect. On the face of things, therefore, the Medical Treatment Act 1988 is a particularly firm expression of the doctrine of patient autonomy; it is also a remarkable example of the denial of a physician's autonomy – and, pace those who are untroubled by the distinction[110] – it is difficult to see it as other than legislative approval of passive euthanasia of either voluntary or non-voluntary type.

18.63 It is to be noted that informed lay and medical opinion[111] has rejected the need for a similar statute in the United Kingdom where the common law and the advance directive, an importation from the United States, offer alternative solutions. As we have seen, there is ample evidence that the right of the competent individual to refuse treatment is ingrained in the common law and human rights law – and this right persists even though it may result in the patient's death; moreover, a refusal can take the form of a declaration of intention never to consent in the future.[112] By contrast, the position of the advance directive or 'living will', which is designed to express the autonomy of the incompetent patient, has not been settled by statute, although case law in the United Kingdom now recognises its significance.[113]

18.64 In theory, the principle of the advance directive is simple – the individual executes a document expressing his or her wishes as to treatment in the event of being disabled from doing so verbally and the physician acts upon it when the occasion arises. It is important to remember that, while the advance directive commonly expresses a refusal of treatment, it may, equally, authorise that life-prolonging measures be maintained – though it cannot, of course, *require* that such treatment be given; looked at in this way, the advance directive becomes an aspect of the right to choose rather than the right to die.[114] There seems little doubt that an unambiguous directive being applied in unambiguous circumstances would have the support of common law.

109 Neither has it in England: *St George's Healthcare NHS Trust v S, R v Collins, ex p S* [1998] 3 WLR 936.
110 For example, Rehnquist CJ in *Vacco v Quill* (1997) 117 S Ct 2293 at 2298. For an interesting tour of the semantics of euthanasia, see D P T Price 'Assisted Suicide and Refusing Medical Treatment: Linguistics, Morals and Legal Contortions' (1996) 4 Med L Rev 270.
111 House of Lords *Report of the Select Committee on Medical Ethics* HL Paper 21-1 (1994).
112 *Re C (adult: refusal of medical treatment)* [1994] 1 All ER 819, sub nom *Re C (mental patient: medical treatment)* (1993) 15 BMLR 77 at 82. The question of the capacity to refuse has been dealt with in chapter 10. A recent poll of 300 UK doctors revealed that 96% accepted the right of the competent patient to refuse treatment. However, only 61% were prepared to end a patient's treatment knowing that it would kill them. Perhaps predictably, only 49% thought that the courts should decide on competence – the preferred alternative being a mixed tribunal: G Clews 'Doctors Back Patients' Right to Refuse Treatment' (2002) BMA News, 30 March, p 12.
113 *Re AK (adult patient)(medical treatment: consent)* [2001] 1 FLR 129, (2001) 58 BMLR 151.
114 An elegantly neutral consideration of advance directives is to be found in A Sommerville 'Are Advance Directives Really the Answer? And What was the Question?' in S A M McLean (ed) *Death, Dying and the Law* (1996).

18.65 The difficulty is, however, that, while the theory may be simple, practice has its complications. Perhaps the main concern lies in the fact that it is almost impossible to devise an intelligible document which will be unambiguous in all circumstances – in particular, who is to define words such as 'severe', 'advanced' or 'comparable gravity'. Secondly, there is the persistent concern that the patient has, during the critical phase, changed his or her mind; Dworkin, in his classic *Life's Dominion*,[115] points out that the person who drafts a 'living will' and the incompetent who benefits from it are, effectively, different persons and the one need not necessarily be empowered to speak for the other. Given these imponderables, the doctor's dilemma is summed up in the words of Lord Donaldson:

> ... what the doctors *cannot* do is to conclude that, if the patient still had the necessary capacity in the changed situation [he being now unable to communicate], he would have reversed his decision ... what they *can* do is to consider whether at the time the decision was made it was intended by the patient to apply in the changed situation,[116]

from which it is clear that the doctor should, and probably must, apply his own interpretation to an advance directive.

18.66 The legal status of the advance directive in the United Kingdom has, however, been slow to evolve. A practice note of 1994 gave some weight to such directives, although it was hardly dogmatic in its tone:

> The views of the patient may have been previously expressed, either in writing or otherwise. The High Court exercising its inherent jurisdiction may determine the effect of a purported advance directive as to future medical treatment ... In summary, the patient's expressed views, if any, will always be a very important component in the decisions of the doctors and the court.[117]

18.67 Two of the Law Lords in *Bland* indicated that the advance directive had legal status[118] but their comments were certainly obiter. However, in *AK (adult patient) (medical treatment: consent)*,[119] the court stated quite clearly that an advance declaration by a patient should be observed by those treating him, although it stressed that care should be taken to ensure that the declaration still represented the patient's wish. In this case a 19-year-old suffering from motor neurone disease had asked that artificial ventilation, nutrition and hydration should be discontinued two weeks after he lost all ability to communicate. The court was satisfied that the patient had had the capacity to make this request and that it should be observed.

---

115 R Dworkin *Life's Dominion* (1993).
116 In *Re T (adult: refusal of medical treatment)* [1993] Fam 95 at 115, (1992) 9 BMLR 46 at 60.
117 *Practice Note* [1994] 2 All ER 413. Note that considerable 'persuasive' importance has been put on the advance directive by the Court of Appeal in *St George's Healthcare NHS Trust v S (No 2)* [1998] 3 WLR 936.
118 Per Lord Keith and Lord Goff in *Bland* [1993] 1 All ER 821 at 860, 866, (1992) 12 BMLR 64 at 105, 112.
119 Para 18.63 above.

18.68 All in all, we believe that the case against legislating for an imperative living will is stronger than that in its favour, and this also appears to be the view of the United Kingdom Government, which has stated that it believes that existing common law rules and the BMA guidelines[120] on the issue provide sufficient grounds for the regulation of this matter.[121] As things stand, only a minority of adults have executed such directives. It would be asking too much of doctors presented with a comatose patient to be required to search for one before beginning treatment;[122] on the other side of the coin, we would hope that the possession of a 'Request for Treatment' card never becomes a prerequisite for admission to the intensive care unit.[123]

A limited concept?

18.69 We have already remarked on how blurred are the boundaries of 'passive euthanasia' and on the subjective nature of its definition. Thus, treatment of the patient in the permanent vegetative state is, in our opinion, best regarded as an example of medical futility and has been discussed under that heading.[124] At the other end of the scale, we find the removal of life support from the competent patient indistinguishable from physician-assisted suicide and continued treatment in the face of refusal has now been seen to constitute an assault.[125] Effectively, therefore, 'pure' passive euthanasia is limited to those relatively rare management decisions involving patients who have retained some cortical activity but are unable to make competent decisions and who, at the same time, are not known to have previously expressed an unequivocal preference as to treatment in the prevailing conditions.

18.70 So far as we know, there are no apposite legal precedents outside the neonatal field to look to in the United Kingdom, where the lawfulness of non-treatment in such circumstances would be very much determined by good medical judgment. The more frequent recourse to the law courts in the United States – particularly as represented by a flurry of activity in the 1980s – has, however, served to demonstrate certain principles and, at the same time, the difficulties which may be encountered.

18.71 Certain aspects of the individual circumstances have been given particular attention. In the first place, great emphasis is placed on intentions which have been expressed in life, not only specifically but also by words or attitudes. This is exemplified in the *Eichner/Storar* decisions.[126] In the first of these, the guardian's right to refuse treatment on behalf of an incompetent was upheld on the grounds that the latter had expressed his preferences, albeit

---

120 British Medical Association *Statement on Advance Directives* (1994).
121 Lord Chancellor's Department *Making Decisions* (1999).
122 But see the duties of the doctor to seek the views of a proxy under the Adults with Incapacity (Scotland) Act 2000, s 47.
123 Having said all of which, it has to be acknowledged that most of the American States have legislation giving legal status to the advance directive and there is no public outcry.
124 See chapter 17 above.
125 *Ms B v An NHS Trust*, para 18.33 above.
126 *Re Storar* 420 NE 2d 64 (NY, 1981) (Consolidating *Eichner v Dillon*).

only in conversation, when he was healthy. Mr Storar, on the other hand, had never been competent and the appellate court refused his mother's request to abandon blood transfusion therapy for his cancerous condition; it was thought that no one, not even a parent or a sibling, should decide that an incompetent should bleed to death. The authority of an advanced oral directive is, however, not absolute and may be subject to evidence of its being 'clear and convincing' – a condition which was first introduced in the important case of *Cruzan*,[127] which has been discussed in chapter 17. Secondly, some importance is attached to the imminence of death; in general, persons who are likely to survive for more than a year with treatment are maintained on therapy.[128] Thirdly, special provision is made for the permanent or persistent vegetative state, regarding which it has been held:

> Life expectancy analyses assume that there are still some benefits to be derived from the continued existence of an incompetent patient. That assumption ... is not appropriate in the case of persistent vegetative patients.[129]

18.72 It is, therefore, probably wrong to regard *Quinlan*[130] as the seminal case in the context of passive euthanasia and we have discussed it more appropriately under futile treatment. Although there were many other apposite examples,[131] perhaps the most instructive case remains that of Ms Conroy;[132] *Conroy* was, admittedly, concerned primarily with assisted feeding but we have established that feeding is, for current purposes, an aspect of treatment – and is certainly so regarded in the United States.[133]

18.73 Ms Conroy was an elderly incompetent diabetic, severely malformed and with an intellectual capacity above that of a person in the persistent vegetative state – even if only marginally so. Permission to remove her nasogastric tube was sought and granted by the trial court on the grounds that no valid purpose was served by needlessly prolonging such a life. Although the subject had, meantime, died, the finding was appealed and was reversed – the Court of Appeal considering that death following removal of the feeding tube would have been due to dehydration and starvation; this implied active killing and they were not prepared to condone active euthanasia. Great

---

127   *Cruzan v Director, Missouri Department of Health* 110 S Ct 2841 (1990). An analysis of the legal effects of *Cruzan* is given in A Meisel 'A Retrospect on *Cruzan*' (1992) 20 Law Med Hlth Care 340. The author cited some 75 'right to die' cases heard in the US courts since 1976. For a survey of these cases, N L Cantor and G C Thomas, 'The Legal Bounds of Physician Conduct Hastening Death' (2000) 48 Buffalo Law Rev, 83.
128   *Re Claire C Conroy* 464 A 2d 303 (NJ, 1983); on appeal 486 A 2d 1209 (NJ, 1985).
129   *Re Hilda M Peter* 529 A 2d 419 (NJ, 1987).
130   *Re Quinlan* 355 A 2d 647 (NJ, 1976).
131   Eg *John F Kennedy Memorial Hospital Inc v Bludworth* 452 So 2d 921 (Fla, 1984); *Re Bertha Colyer* 660 P 2d 738 (Wash, 1983); *Re Nancy Ellen Jones* 529 A 2d 434 (NJ, 1987); *Guardianship of Grant* 747 P 2d 445 (Wash, 1987) – particularly describing procedures to follow to avoid judicial involvement in such cases.
132   *Re Claire C Conroy* 464 A 2d 303 (NJ, 1983); on appeal 486 A 2d 1209 (NJ, 1985).
133   Eg *Re Severns* 425 A 2d 156 (Del, 1980); *Re Mary Hier* 464 NE 2d 959 (Mass, 1984); *Brophy v New England Sinai Hospital* 497 NE 2d 626 (Mass, 1986); *Corbett v D'Alessandro* 487 So 2d 368 (Fla, 1986). In *Re Requena* 517 A 2d 893 (NJ, 1986), a hospital was ordered to retain a patient who refused to consent to artificial feeding and to honour her decision.

concern was also expressed as to the knock-on effect which might seriously compromise the standards of treatment of the mentally retarded and of the senile demented. Even so, the Supreme Court of New Jersey reversed the appellate decision, holding that:

> artificial feeding by means of a nasogastric tube ... can be seen as equivalent to artificial breathing by means of a respirator. Both prolong life through mechanical means when the body is no longer able to perform a vital bodily function on its own,[134]

the extrapolation being that the patient has the right to refuse both. While the Supreme Court commended the appointment of a guardian to act as proxy for the incompetent, it still laid down very strict criteria – including investigation by an ombudsman – before such decisions could be taken by the medical staff and the guardian or relatives. In the absence of *any* indications of the patient's wishes – under what the court referred to as the 'pure objective test':[135]

> the net burdens of the patient's life with treatment should clearly and markedly outweigh the benefits that the patient derives from life. Further, the recurring, unavoidable and severe pain of the patient's life with the treatment should be such that the effects of administering life-sustaining treatment would be inhumane.

18.74 The court expressly declined to authorise decision-making based on the personal worth or social utility of another's life, or the value of that life to others:

> We do not believe that it would be appropriate for a court to designate a person with the authority to determine that someone else's life is not worth living simply because, to that person, the patient's 'quality of life' or value to society seems negligible.

18.75 *Conroy* is not an ideal authority, as the case was decided negatively because of the quality of the evidence. It does, however, provide a template by which decisions in similar cases can be measured. As we have seen, the American cases give great importance to the potential life-span of the patient. It is, therefore, appropriate to consider the effect this has on attitudes to euthanasia as a whole.

'Double effect'

18.76 We have seen that the law condemns active euthanasia on the grounds of intent. The terminally ill are beyond curative therapy by definition, and their management becomes a matter of the relief of suffering. Achieving this may, inevitably, involve some risk to life – but it is the patient's comfort, not his or her premature death, which is the intended outcome. The terminally ill

---

134   486 A 2d 1209 at 1236.
135   It should be noted that the Supreme Court regarded this as a 'best interests' test rather than one of substituted judgment.

patient thus most clearly sets the scene for the application of the philosophical concept of 'double effect'.[136]

18.77 The principle of double effect, as invoked in this context, is that an action which has a good objective may be performed despite the fact that the objective can only be achieved at the expense of a coincident harmful effect. This analysis has, however, to be qualified – the action itself must be either good or morally indifferent, the good effect must not be produced by means of the ill-effect and there must be a proportionate reason for allowing the expected ill to occur.[137] It is implicit in this doctrine that the good effect must outweigh the bad and this may involve a value judgment. Thus, it might well be ethically right to administer pain-killing drugs in such dosage as simultaneously shortens the life of a terminally ill patient; it would not be justifiable to give the same dose to a young man with identical pain who stood a reasonable chance of recovery. The seminal case in the United Kingdom is that of *R v Adams*.[138] Dr Adams was thought to have treated a patient, who was incurably but not terminally ill, with increasing doses of opiates. Following her death, he was tried for murder and was acquitted. In the course of his summing up, Devlin J said: 'The doctor is entitled to relieve pain and suffering even if the measures he takes may incidentally shorten life', which is a clear direction. Twenty years after the *Adams* verdict, Lord Edmund Davies commented: 'Killing both pain and patient may be good morals but it is far from certain that it is good law.'[139] Williams,[140] by contrast, found the proposition easily justified by necessity. Any conflict has now been resolved. Devlin J's classic direction was followed in *R v Cox*[141] and the charge to the jury in the latter case was cited with approval by the House of Lords in *Bland,* where we have Lord Goff:

> [It is] the established rule that a doctor may, when caring for a patient who is, for example, dying of cancer, lawfully administer painkilling drugs despite the fact that he knows that an incidental effect of that application will be to abbreviate the patient's life … Such a decision may properly be made as part of the care of the living patient, in his best interests; and, on this basis, the treatment will be lawful.[142]

And this is so whether the management regime is justified under the essentially moral doctrine of double effect or under the legal principle of necessity. However, since the judgment in *Bland,* the House of Lords has pronounced on intention in the case of *R v Woolin,*[143] in which a consequence was said to be

---

136 For a wide-ranging analysis of double effect, see D Price 'Euthanasia, Pain Relief and Double Effect' (1997) 17 LS 323. See also, D Mapel 'Revising the Doctrine of Double Effect' (2001) 18 Jnl of Applied Philosphy, 257; G Williams 'The Principle of Double Effect and Terminal Sedation' (2001) 9 Med L Rev 41. We regard 'double effect' as being synonymous in this context with the legal doctrine of necessity or with the European Continental concept of *'force majeure'*.

137 It will be seen that Dr Cox (see para 18.43 above) would have failed on at least two counts to establish a 'double effect' justification for his action.

138 H Palmer 'Dr Adams' Trial for Murder' [1957] Crim LR 365.

139 'On Dying and Dying Well – Legal Aspects' (1977) 70 Proc Roy Soc Med 73.

140 *Textbook of Criminal Law* p 416.

141 (1992) 12 BMLR 38.

142 [1993] 1 All ER 821 at 868, (1993) 12 BMLR 64 at 114.

143 [1999] 1 AC 82, [1998] 4 All ER 103.

intentional if the actor was 'virtually certain' that it would occur. In the Court of Appeal decision in *Re A (children) (conjoined twins: surgical separation)*,[144] Ward LJ said that it could be difficult to reconcile the doctrine of double effect with *Woolin* but, nonetheless, he could 'readily see' how the doctrine would work in cases where pain-killers are administered to deal with acute pain.

18.78 We can also look to the important cases in infancy discussed in chapter 16. The majority of these came to judicial notice only because the patient was a ward of court; indeed, the principle is now so well established that there would be very few occasions outside wardship in which the courts would expect to be involved. The interesting inclusion of the whole caring team in the decision-making process[145] might be thought to be confined to paediatric practice but there is no reason why such a routine should not be extended to hospitals for adults; to do so would not only ensure 'open' decision-making but would also serve to emphasise that the effects of any treatment decisions fall not upon the doctor but on the nursing staff who will care for the dying person.

THE INCURABLE PATIENT

18.79 The relative simplicity of the euthanasia debate has, thus far, depended upon the use of the adjective 'terminal', which defines a patient status which can only deteriorate – and, as we have already noted, attempts to legalise euthanasia in the English-speaking world have never extended beyond the concept of the management of the dying patient. The problems for the doctor, and for the ethicist, become more complex when discussion is extended to the incurably ill whose condition may certainly get worse but which is also likely to remain static, often for long times. Many variations on such a state can be envisaged and different therapeutic solutions adduced. There are, however, two overriding considerations likely to influence one's thinking – first, whether the patient is sentient or non-sentient and, secondly, whether or not the distinction between incurable illness and death depends upon the use of artificial means.

The incapacitated patient

18.80 Thus, at one extreme, we have the fully conscious, incapacitated patient able to breathe naturally, as exemplified by the paraplegic or tetraplegic whose condition results from an accident or localised brain-stem haemorrhage. The clinical and moral solutions here are based on the same principles as relate to the terminally ill but conscious patient – any differences are those of emphasis. Once again, we are at the grey interface of passive euthanasia, assisted suicide and refusal of treatment and, as a result, major weight must be given to patient autonomy. Much of the discussion in this area has been

---

144 [2001] Fam 147, [2000] 4 All ER 961.
145 *Re C (a minor) (wardship: medical treatment)* [1990] Fam 26 at 34, 37, [1989] 2 All ER 782 at 786, 788, per Lord Donaldson MR.

approached from the theoretical angle and concentrates on the right to die. By contrast, most of those who have been involved in the hands-on care of disabled persons have been impressed by their tenacity to life and their ability to adapt.[146] This was demonstrated vividly in an old, but emotionally influential, study of tetraplegia – a condition which must be as near to wholly intolerable as can be imagined; 18 out of 21 sufferers said that they wished to be resuscitated in the event of their degenerating into coma.[147]

18.81 Subject to the consent of a sentient patient, both the double effect doctrine and the productive/non-productive treatment test are available in the management of those who are incapacitated; their rationale needs to be just that much more firmly based than is so in the case of the terminally ill.

The conscious patient maintained artificially

18.82 The medico-legal response to a positive request for the doctor to disconnect the mentally competent patient from the mechanical respirator on which he or she depends has already been discussed in some detail. The international case law indicating that not to do so would constitute non-consensual treatment and, accordingly, battery is now overwhelming – but the underlying implications of compliance are disturbing. It is almost trite to say that the ethical difficulties concerning the removal of mechanical respiratory support from those who can no longer benefit originate from the *provision* of that support – the primary decision is more important than those which follow as a consequence of that action.[148] But the doctor presented with an accident or an acute neurological emergency has virtually no choice of initiative action. He is dealing with a conscious but suddenly paralysed patient and he must provide support because he cannot know whether an individual patient is going to respond either physically or emotionally to heroic treatment – and, if the doctor does not know, the patient cannot give or withhold his informed consent to setting the therapeutic train in motion. Can the doctor, then, accede to a later request to remove support?

18.83 It has been suggested that switching off a mechanical support is an omission and is, therefore, both morally and legally acceptable. This is, in our opinion, untenable in practical terms. It would be an omission not to switch *on* the emergency supply in the event of a central power failure; that is easily distinguished from a deliberate, premeditated decision to remove the power – one has to *act* to turn off the television and the same will apply to the respirator.[149] Kennedy[150] has pointed out that a well-wisher disconnecting a conscious patient from his respirator would be guilty of homicide or perhaps

---

146 The contrary impression given by the litigation involving Ms B and Mrs Pretty may well be due to the media exposure given to 'high profile' cases.
147 B P Gardner et al 'Ventilation or Dignified Death for Patients with High Tetraplegia' (1985) 291 BMJ 1620. See also M Siegler and A J Weisbard 'Against the Emerging Stream' (1985) 145 Arch Int Med 129 which remains an instructive read.
148 I M Kennedy 'Switching Off Life Support Machines: The Legal Implications' [1977] Crim LR 443.
149 For an authoritative alternative view see Williams para 18.77 above, p 282.
150 [1977] Crim LR 443.

of abetting suicide – and, in the United States, Mr Linares was, at least, brought before a grand jury.[151] The difference adduced by Lord Goff in *Bland*[152] was that, whereas the doctor was allowing the patient to die from his pre-existing condition, the interloper was actively intervening to stop the doctor from prolonging the patient's life. *Bland*, in fact, very nearly solves the problem – albeit indirectly. Thus, if, as was decided, the withdrawal of nasogastric feeding is an omission, it is but a short step to conclude that withdrawal of respiratory support is, likewise, an omission – and Lord Browne-Wilkinson, for one, was happy to see them as similar. The analogy admittedly involves some elasticity of conscience. So, while Lord Browne-Wilkinson further concluded that a nasogastric tube did nothing, of itself, to sustain life and that its removal could not be said to cause death, it is difficult to say the same of the ventilator of which the air-bag is an integral part. The main practical difference between the two must lie in the immediacy and the certainty of death when the respirator is turned off; the care team is, effectively, being asked to suffocate their patient.[153]

18.84 The modern doctor's dilemma was vividly exposed in the English case of *Ms B v an NHS Hospital Trust*[154] which we have discussed in some detail above. The clinicians in charge of Ms B may have been badly advised but, whether or not they misinterpreted their legal position, they clearly thought that medical options other than death of their patient were available. The frank admission by the responsible doctors that they could not bring themselves to take the step of withdrawing ventilation from a viable patient is a striking and significant aspect of the case. In the event, another hospital was found that was willing to do so – and the use of the phrase 'to do so' surely pulls the carpet from under those who would identify 'switching off' as an omission. The doctors' evidence, set out in some detail in the judgment, serves as a reminder of the difficulties which medical staff may experience if they are expected to act contrary to their impulses to preserve life rather than to extinguish it.[155]

The unconscious patient and the patient in intensive care

18.85 The management of the unconscious, breathing patient has been fully discussed in Chapter 16. There remain for consideration those comatose patients who are unable to sustain their cardiorespiratory functions without the aid of mechanical ventilation.

18.86 The vast majority, perhaps all, of living patients with severe brain damage must be offered such care when they present at hospital. Recourse is

151 Lantos et al, para 18.10 above.
152 [1993] 1 All ER 821 at 867-868, (1992) 12 BMLR 64 at 113-114.
153 It is very difficult to avoid the corollary – that Bland's carers were being asked to starve him to death.
154 Para 18.33 above.
155 The medical correspondent of *The Times* (T Stuttaford, 23 March 2002, p 5) indicated that 'Standard medical teaching remains that we should never willingly and deliberately shorten life'. Since removal from ventilation is clearly done deliberately and, equally clearly, shortens life, the determining issue is simply one of willingness – or, put another way, of autonomy.

automatic for the purposes of facilitating diagnosis and assessment; there is, then, no legal or ethical objection to regarding the ventilator as merely a part of the diagnostic machinery nor to dispensing with it once a diagnosis of irretrievable functional brain loss has been made. But a decision to treat, which, in this case, is within the doctor's clinical choice, is a different matter carrying with it the inescapable consequence that, at some time and for some reason, the treatment must be withdrawn. The critical point for applying the productive/non-productive ethical test is, as we have already indicated, at the beginning. With one exception, any later decisions are based on clinical or technical considerations alone.

18.87 This exceptional ethical decision relates to the allocation of scarce resources which include machines, beds, doctors and nursing staff, together with the necessary technical back-up. It may be necessary for a resource-based value judgment to be made at some point. Making a choice between patients may be among the doctor's most agonising moments and the weight to be given to economic and policy considerations can only be judged by the individual physician or surgeon on such factors as are outlined in chapter 11. There are now sufficient obiter statements from a variety of English cases to allow one to say with confidence that the courts will be sympathetic to resource-based management arguments. We do, however, suggest that this relates only to a competition for an *available* facility. There is nothing to support the suggestion that it would be acceptable to *remove* a patient from essential intensive care for no reason other than that a medically more rewarding case required the bed.[156]

18.88 Resources aside, the removal of a patient from intensive care depends, primarily, on a simple alternative – either he is dead or he is not dead. It can be taken that the whole brain is dead once the criteria for brain stem death have been met and we have the authority of the Conference of the Royal Medical Colleges and their Faculties[157] that the individual is dead when the whole brain is dead. In such circumstances, continued treatment is no more than treatment of a corpse – far from being unethical to withhold support, it would be positively immoral to continue other than to serve the purpose of beating heart organ donation or, conceivably, of post-mortem parturition (for which, see para 13.25). Withdrawal of treatment would also be legally indicated.[158]

18.89 However, it may still be proper to discontinue artificial ventilation even if death is not diagnosed. The closely allied considerations of productive/non-productive treatment and of 'death with dignity', untrammelled by tubes and wires, may be regarded by some as being related to the moral sphere and by others as being clinical in nature. Even so, the purely clinical consideration – that the treatment is doing, and will do, no good – will justify removal of support. One of two things may then happen – the patient will either continue to breathe of his own accord or he will die. In the former case, the patient has

---

156   See Balcombe LJ in *Re J (a minor) (wardship: medical treatment)* [1993] Fam 15 at 30, (1992) 9 BMLR 10 at 20, discussed previously at para 16.37 above.
157   'Diagnosis of Death' [1979] 1 BMJ 332. Legislation to this effect is generalised in the English-speaking world.
158   *Re A* [1992] 3 Med LR 303.

reverted to a state of irreversible coma, the management of which has already been discussed. No moral or legal problem arises in the latter situation; the outcome will have resulted from a clinical decision taken in good faith and after due deliberation based on a productive/non-productive treatment test. As we have already discussed, consent of the next of kin would be desirable but not essential to the question of lawfulness.

FEEDING AS A PART OF TREATMENT

18.90 We have already referred to feeding as a part of treatment in relation to *Bland* in chapter 17. The definition of artificial feeding was not, however, addressed in either *Bland* or *Re R (adult: medical treatment)* – or in any of the other relevant British cases. As Strong[159] has pointed out, when we speak of providing nourishment, we are referring to a continuum which runs from natural breast feeding through feeding by mouth to seriously invasive procedures which may even entail surgical operation. Once discomfort and danger are introduced, so too is balancing the advantages and disadvantages – or, in practice, applying a productive/non-productive treatment test.[160] The fundamental question is, therefore, at what *stage* does the act of feeding become medical treatment?

18.91 Increasing invasiveness carries increasing risk – it, therefore, seems logical to classify anything which involves invasion as medical treatment. At the other end of the scale, it is difficult to conceive of purely natural feeding as treatment and, so far as we are aware, no court in either the Commonwealth or America has ever suggested that normal feeding could properly be withheld on clinical grounds from someone able to accept it. None the less, even this distinction is over-simplistic. At one extreme, spoon feeding of a reluctant ament can be regarded as invasive and, accordingly, as medical treatment; at the other, the instillation of fluid through a tube can be seen as simple care involving no risk – but it can be done only as a *result* of invasion. The difficulties are exemplified in the drafting of the Victorian legislation which includes 'the reasonable provision of food and water' under the heading of palliative treatment – and, therefore, outwith the statutory control of the patient[161] – and, then, fails to define 'reasonable provision'. An all-embracing definitional solution seems impossible. We can only look to a minimum standard and suggest that any form of feeding which requires some *medical* training and expertise can be considered medical treatment and, accordingly, may properly be subject to selective provision. The insertion of a nasogastric tube involves a surprising degree of skill and, on this basis, nasogastric feeding would qualify as medical treatment; thus, the decision in *Bland* is, to us, unexceptional. By contrast, the provision of food and water by normal means – that is, by mouth and dependent on the patient's swallowing reflexes – is a

---

159   C Strong 'Can Fluids and Electrolytes be "Extraordinary Treatment"?' (1981) 7 J Med Ethics 83.
160   K C Micetich et al 'Are Intravenous Fluids Morally Required for a Dying Patient?' (1983) 143 Arch Int Med 975. The complication rate of intravenous hyperalimentation may approach 50%.
161   Medical Treatment Act 1988 (Vict), s 3.

matter of skilled nursing care. It may also be seen as the quintessential example of kindness and humanity.[162]

THE 'DO NOT RESUSCITATE' ORDER

18.92 There can be no doubt that it is often undesirable, effectively, to prolong the process of dying[163] – the problem, however, is to establish an acceptable general policy in an area that is so susceptible to subjective judgments. In a **very** influential document on the subject, the British Medical Association and the Royal College of Nursing have issued a set of guidelines which they stress can only be viewed as a framework on which policy can be based.[164] In essence, the guidelines emphasise that an informed, non-coerced, advance directive must be respected and that, in the absence of such information, the presumption should be in favour of attempting resuscitation. An advance decision that cardiopulmonary resuscitation (CPR) will not be attempted (providing a 'DNAR order') can only be made in the light of the likely outcome, the patient's ascertainable wishes and his or her human rights; adequate communication in respect of a decision is all important, but information should not be forced on patients who are unwilling to share it. The key question is whether CPR will provide any benefit to the patient but the wishes of one who wants to be resuscitated irrespective of the prognosis should be respected.[165] The views of the relatives of incompetent adults must be taken into account but it should be made clear that their role is not to take decisions on behalf of the patient.[166] The guidelines recommend recourse to the courts if there is disagreement in respect of the management of a child. It is appropriate to consider making a DNAR order when attempted CPR will almost certainly not restart the patient's heart, when there is no benefit in so doing or when the expected benefits are outweighed by the burdens. Decisions must always be made on an individual basis – blanket policies are regarded as being unethical and probably unlawful under the Human Rights Act 1998. The guidelines also stress the importance of adequate documentation of the decisions and of how they were reached.[167]

18.93 Well meaning though such guidelines may be, it is clear that they conceal a hornet's nest of moral dilemmas. Exclusion from resuscitation in British hospitals is said to be more likely in patients with a current diagnosis

162 *Airedale NHS Trust v Bland* [1993] 1 All ER 821 at 856, (1992) 12 BMLR 64 at 101, per Hoffmann LJ.
163 For a classic example, see the papers associated with R F Weir 'Betty's Case: An Introduction' (1989) 17 Law Med Hlth Care 211. For a recent American review assessing the moral grounds for providing or withholding treatment, see M Hilberman, J Kutner, D Parsons and D J Murphy 'Marginally Effective Medical Care: Ethical Analysis of Issues in Cardiopulmonary Resuscitation (CPR)' (1997) 23 J Med Ethics 361.
164 Resuscitation Council (UK) *Decisions Relating to Cardiopulmonary Resuscitation – A Joint Statement from the BMA, Resuscitation Council and RCN* (2001): www.resus.org.uk/pages/dnar.htm.
165 Subject to the proviso that the doctor cannot be required to provide treatment against his clinical judgment: *Re J (a minor) (medical treatment)* [1993] Fam 15.
166 The terms of the Adults with Incapacity (Scotland) Act 2000 must be honoured.
167 The latest advice from the GMC is to be found in *Withholding and Withdrawing Life-prolonging Treatments: Good Practice in Decision-making* (2002), paras 84-94. The GMC positively recommends the Resuscitation Council's guidelines at fn 26.

of malignancy, dementia or pneumonia or with a past or present history of stroke.[168] But at what stage of the disease is the patient with cancer to be regarded as not to be salvaged? How are we to assess what is the patient's idea of an acceptable quality of life? To what extent is dementia a contraindication imposed for the benefit of the carers?[169] Perhaps most importantly – who is to make the decisions and how deeply involved should the patient be in the process? Despite the Council's and the GMC's guidance that the patient's consent is highly desirable, one would have thought that obtaining such consent would raise intractable practical difficulties. Surprisingly, however, it is said that the majority of patients actually welcome appropriate consultation.[170]

18.94 Finally, we might revert to the question of age. There is little doubt that DNR orders are issued more often and more freely in older patients; irrespective of the diagnosis and prognosis – DNR orders were written in five major American medical centres for 22% of patients under 54 years old, rising to 56% for those aged more than 85.[171] In our opinion, it is particularly important to ensure that junior doctors in the prime of life are trained to understand the needs of the elderly disabled. The somewhat chilling observation of Rhoads, albeit from across the Atlantic and made some time ago, bears preservation: 'How large a factor is age in deciding to relax therapeutic efforts seems to depend somewhat on the age of the physicians making the decisions.'[172]

18.95 Cases involving DNR orders come to the attention of the courts only rarely. An exception lies in the significant case of *Re R*,[173] which concerned a 23-year-old man who could not sit up, chew food or communicate in any formal way. He was probably blind and deaf and other physiological disabilities indicated that his condition was appalling. Nevertheless, he could not be regarded as being in the permanent vegetative state. A DNR order in the event of cardiac arrest was signed by the consultant psychiatrist and agreed by the patient's mother. However, a member of the staff at the day centre at which he was treated arranged for an application for judicial review of the order. The health authority then sought a declaration that it would be lawful to withhold life-sustaining treatment – which included resuscitation and ventilation, nutrition and hydration by artificial means and the administration of antibiotics – and to treat the patient so that he suffered minimum distress until his death. The application was later amended so as to exclude withholding of nutrition and hydration – and, in fact, it was proposed to perform a non-consensual gastrostomy.

168 R M Keating 'Exclusion from Resuscitation' (1989) 82 J Roy Soc Med 402.
169 See *Re D (medical treatment)* (1997) 41 BMLR 81, [1998] 2 FCR 178, in which treatment was lawfully suspended in a man whose long-standing mental disability made it impossible for him to commit himself to co-operate in his haemodialysis.
170 M E Hill, G MacQuillan, M Forsyth and D A Heath 'Cardiopulmonary Resuscitation: Who Makes the Decision?' (1994) 308 BMJ 1677.
171 R B Hakim, J M Teno, F E Harrell et al 'Factors Associated with Do-Not-Resuscitate Orders: Patients' Preferences, Prognoses, and Physicians' Judgments' (1996) 125 Ann Int Med 284.
172 J E Rhoads 'The Right to Die and the Chance to Live' (1980) 6 J Med Ethics 53. A brief but informative review of patient and physician attitudes is to be found in R Morgan, D King, C Prajapati and J Rowe 'Views of Elderly Patients and their Relatives on Cardiopulmonary Resuscitation' (1994) 308 BMJ 1677.
173 *Re R (adult: medical treatment)* (1996) 31 BMLR 127, [1996] 2 FLR 99.

18.96 At the hearing, all the medical witnesses expressed the view that cardiopulmonary resuscitation (CPR) would not be appropriate in R's case, this being largely on the grounds that it was unlikely to be successful. Withholding antibiotics was, however, considered as a separate issue and was recommended subject to the approval of the patient's general practitioner and to the consent of one or both parents – and this distinction was recognised by the court in its determination.

18.97 In granting the declaration as sought, the President, Sir Stephen Brown repeated that there was no question of the court being. asked to approve a course aimed at terminating life or accelerating death. In tying *Re R* to *Re J*,[174] however, the President clearly admitted a 'quality of life' standard for decisions involving adults – approving Taylor LJ in *Re J*:

> [T]he correct approach is for the court to judge the quality of life [the patient] would have to endure if given the treatment and decide whether in all the circumstances such a life would be so afflicted as to be intolerable ... [175]

18.98 Approved management regimes thus seem to be following the course we anticipated in chapter 17. The case also strongly indicates that non-treatment decisions in the case of the incapacitated should normally be taken by health professionals in concert with people close to the patient; it is only in the event of serious challenge to the clinical opinion that court intervention will be required. At the same time, *Re R* raises the question as to whether feeding and hydration are to be seen as different in quality from other medical treatments.[176]   Our own tentative view is that any apparent divergence from the House of Lords decision in *Bland* derives from the rather specialised wording of the application in *Re R* and has no significant general application.

Criminal liability for withholding treatment

18.99 The case of *Quinlan*[177] settled the problem of criminal liability for ventilation withdrawal in the United States and there have been many later confirmations of this.[178]   The position in the United Kingdom was resolved, first through the Scottish case of *Finlayson*[179] and later in the English case of *Malcherek*,[180] both of which have been discussed in relation to causation in chapter 13. Although *Finlayson* was not cited in *Malcherek*, the two decisions have remarkable similarities in that, in excluding criminality, the judges, first, relied on the concept of good medical practice and, second, declined to define death in both cases. This latter omission might, at first glance, be interpreted as vacillation on the part of the law; in fact, it reinforces the

---

174   *Re J (a minor) (wardship: medical treatment)* [1991] Fam 33, (1990) 6 BMLR 25.
175   (1990) 6 BMLR 25 at 42.
176   As suggested by the BMA in their Discussion Paper, para 17.11 above.
177   *Re Quinlan* 355 A 2d 664 (NJ, 1976).   See chapter 16 for discussion.
178   Eg *Re Bertha Colyer* 660 P 2d 738 (Wash, 1983); *Re Nancy Ellen Jones* 529 A 2d 434 (NJ, 1987); *Barber v Superior Court* 147 Cal App 3d 1006 (1983).
179   *Finlayson v HM Advocate* 1978 SLT (Notes) 60.
180   *R v Malcherek* [1981] 2 All ER 422, [1981] 1 WLR 690, CA (*R v Steel* being heard simultaneously on appeal).

former principle in leaving the clinical decision firmly in the hands of the clinician.[181]

18.100 There is no reason to suppose that these decisions would not be applied in the civil courts and it would now be necessary to prove negligence – with all that entails – before a doctor could be considered culpable of a ventilator death. There are no United Kingdom authorities but a similar policy line has been adopted in the United States.[182]

A NEED FOR LEGISLATION?

18.101 It will be appreciated that, throughout this discussion, we have tended to the view that there is little need for legislation in respect of the incurably or terminally ill adult patient; the great majority of life or death decisions can be based on good medical practice which is contained by relatively clear legal and moral guidelines. The movement in favour of voluntary euthanasia is, however, maintaining its momentum, and the autonomy-based arguments advanced by its supporters merit a response. As will be apparent from our discussion above, we believe that there are persuasive reasons for rejecting the legalisation of voluntary euthanasia, not the least of these being the extent to which the policy of legalised euthanasia in the Netherlands has been inadequately policed and progressively more widely interpreted. The uncertainty of the common law has been used in the past as a justification for change in the law, but the law is now much clearer in the light of recent decisions. The decisions in *Pretty* and in *Ms B*[183] both clarify the boundaries of intervention in the case of a competent adult patient, and the legality and persuasiveness of advance declarations are, also, now well established. These decisions, together with the body of cases concerning treatment decisions in the case of children and adults without capacity, create a medico-legal landscape which is much more certain today than it was a decade ago. The law on euthanasia is now very clear: acts committed with the principal intention of bringing an end to life are legally impermissible, except where the patient himself or herself performs them. Treatment may be withdrawn after a request from a competent adult; this will not amount to homicide if death results. The legal prohibition of assisted suicide remains in place. All of this involves a restriction on the autonomy of the individual and, for some, that will be unacceptable. The restrictions are not, however, arbitrary – as the Canadian Supreme Court made clear in *Rodriguez*[184] and the House of Lords, and the European Court of Human Rights, reiterated in *Pretty*. It may be that, at some future date, the legislature, or the courts in applying principles of human

---

181 Some concern was shown in Scotland when the Solicitor General stated that the prosecuting authorities were not in a position to give an assurance that withdrawing life support would not lead to prosecution: G Duncan 'Doctors Warned about Decision to Withdraw Life Support' *Scotsman*, 1 April 1993, p 3. We believe, however, that this was no more than a reminder as to procedure, not as to principle.
182 Eg *Lovato v District Court* 601 P 2d 1072 (Colo, 1979).
183 *R (on the application of Pretty) v DPP* [2001] UKHL 61, [2002] 1 All ER 1, (2002) 63 BMLR 1; *Re B (adult: refusal of medical treatment)* sub nom *Ms v An NHS Hospital Trust* [2002] EWHC 429 (Fam), [2002] 2 All ER 449, (2002) 65 BMLR 149.
184 *Rodriguez v A-G of British Columbia* (1993) 107 DLR (4th) 342, (1993) 50 BMLR 1.

rights, will decide that the balance between the individual rights of autonomy and those of the public interest in defending the current virtually absolute prohibition of killing will be differently interpreted – but that will be a political decision which is difficult to predict. What is clear, though, is that recourse to the Human Rights Act 1998 will not necessarily provide a legal answer to moral dilemma.

18.102 If, however, the balance of legislative opinion were to swing in favour of allowing medical assistance in dying in hard cases such as those involving Mrs Pretty or Ms Rodriguez – and these are admittedly the most difficult to resolve – then, once again, we consider it could best be done by permissive action. The opportunity exists in England to insert a subsection in the Suicide Act 1961 amending s 2(1) – which criminalises aiding or abetting suicide. Suitable wording might be:

> The provisions of s 2(1) shall not apply to a registered medical practitioner who, given the existence of a competent directive, is providing assistance to a patient who is suffering from a progressive and irremediable condition and who is prevented, or will be prevented, by physical disability from ending his or her own life without assistance.[185]

Having said which, we concede that many would regard this as allowing too much discretion to the medical profession and that they would prefer a positive, and possibly restrictive, approach.[186] Either route would achieve the desired result of legislating for a specific, relatively uncontroversial aspect of assistance in dying and, for our part, we would go no further. Legalising active euthanasia compromises the duty of the state to protect its subjects and the integrity of the medical profession[187] too deeply for general acceptance at the present time. It is the prospect of a relentless progression that lies at the heart of the euthanasia resistance movement.

---

185 See J K Mason and D Mulligan 'Euthanasia by Stages' (1996) 347 Lancet 810.
186 For an example, see Professor McLean's draft Bill, para 18.22 above. Positive legislation would certainly be needed in the United States and, with this in mind, we have produced our own suggested Bill: see Meyers and Mason, para 18.20 above.
187 Most commentators anticipate the active involvement of doctors in carrying out any programme: M Otlowski 'Active Voluntary Euthanasia: Options for Reform' (1994) 2 Med L Rev 161; M Battin 'Voluntary Euthanasia and the Risks of Abuse: Can We Learn Anything from the Netherlands?' (1992) 20 Law Med Hlth Care 133.

Research and experimentation

19 Biomedical human research and experimentation

19.1 At one time, biomedical experimentation using human subjects proceeded almost as a routine. The researchers justified their activities as benefiting mankind; the subjects were generally happy to 'oblige' or to be reasonably recompensed; and research was of manageable quantity. Attitudes and conditions have, however, changed. The reaction against paternalistic medicine has gained momentum pari passu with an increasing concern for the rights of the individual; the potential investigations and the instrumental and other means for conducting them have greatly increased; and there has been something of an explosion not only in the production of new therapeutic agents but also in control of their distribution. But the greatest single impulse to regulate experiments on human beings sprang from a realisation of the appalling depths which were plumbed in the genocidal era of the Second World War when, undoubtedly, much valuable information was gathered but only at the cost of immense suffering. The awareness of what had happened in the medical laboratories of Nazi Germany and Japan led to a determination that medical research should never again be tainted by such callous disregard for the rights of the individual, and it is this determination which led to the promulgation of international codes on the ethics of research. Such endeavours were not everywhere supported, however, and the end of the Soviet era in Eastern Europe resulted in a frank acknowledgment in a number of countries that medical science in the Soviet Union and its satellite countries had been far from meeting the ethical standards expected it the West.[1] This has been translated into action in Poland, for example, by the introduction of a code of medical ethics which, in a remarkable judgment of the Polish Constitutional Court in 1992, was held to outrank contradictory provisions of the law.[2]

ETHICAL CODES IN HUMAN BIOMEDICAL EXPERIMENTATION

19.2 The first internationally accepted set of ethical guidelines in this context was known as the Nuremberg Code and was a direct result of the war-crimes

---

1   Z Szawarski 'Research Ethics in Eastern Europe' (1992) 82 Bull Med Ethics 13.
2   The English text of this code was published in (1992) 82 Bull Med Ethics 13; the decision of the Constitutional Court is discussed by E Zielinska at p 25.

trials.[3] It was, however, apparent that the medical profession itself should publicly endorse the principles expressed in the ten clauses of the Nuremberg Code; this movement culminated in the Declaration of Helsinki – drawn up by the World Medical Association in 1964 and revised several times between 1975 and 2000 – which is reproduced as Appendix E.[4] Many national authorities have attempted to explain or expand upon the basic principles established at Nuremberg and, for the British reader, the most important of these are the comprehensive set of guidelines issued by the Medical Research Council in 1992.[5] In the European context, a draft additional protocol to the Council of Europe's Convention on Human Rights and Biomedicine, opened for ratification in 1997,[6] has now been published for consultation. This sets out the broad principles under which research may be undertaken on human subjects – under which such research is justified only if there is no comparable effectiveness.[7] Of greater immediate importance, the Council of the European Union has issued a directive, which is binding on the member states, on the conditions under which research in the development of medicinal products is to be conducted.[8] The emphasis here is on good clinical practice which is defined in Article 1(2) as:

> [A] set of internationally recognised ethical and scientific quality requirements which must be observed for designing, conducting, recording and reporting clinical trials that involve the participation of human subjects. Compliance with this good practice provides assurance that the rights, safety and well-being of trial subjects are protected, and that the results of the clinical trial are credible.

19.3 The Directive does not apply to non-interventional trials which are, essentially, trials in which the recipient of the medicinal product is being treated in the normal way without assignment to treatment by way of an advance protocol.

19.4 All modern codes have it in common that they appreciate the need for human experimentation and, at the same time, accept that this can only be accomplished at the expense of some of the subjects' right to self-determination. It is, however, universally accepted that the morality of this sacrifice depends

---

3   There is a wide discussion of the problem of the significance of Nuremberg in G J Annas and M A Grodin (eds) *The Nazi Doctors and the Nuremberg Code: Human Rights in Human Experimentation* (1992).
4   Other international codes include the International Ethical Guidelines for Biomedical Research involving Human Subjects published in Z Bankowski and R J Levine *Ethics and Research on Human Subjects: International Guidelines* (1992). For discussion of the various guidelines, see K M King 'A Proposal for the Effective International Regulation of Biomedical Research Involving Human Subjects' (1998) 34 Stanford J Int Law 163.
5   Medical Research Council *Responsibility in Investigations on Human Participants and Material and on Personal Information* (1992). For clinical trials, see Medical Research Council *MRC Guidelines for Good Clinical Practice in Clinical Trials* (1998).
6   But not yet ratified by the United Kingdom.
7   Council of Europe *Convention for the Protection of Human Rights and Dignity of the Human Being with Regard to the Application of Biology and Medicine* (1997). The draft protocol is to be found in the Bulletin of Medical Ethics (2001) No 172, p 8.
8   European Parliament and the Council of Europe Directive 2001/20/EC of 4 April 2001. National legislation compatible with compliance with the directive must be effective from 1 May 2004 at the latest.

upon the grant of 'informed' consent – which we have discussed in detail in chapter 10. All codes contain specific instructions as to the inclusion of minor and incompetent research subjects. In addition, the doctor's classic ethical position must show some flexibility. The Hippocratic Oath states: 'I will follow that regimen which ... I consider for the benefit of my patients and abstain from whatever is deleterious and mischievous'; the absolutist could say that this precludes all experimentation on patients, yet it is clear that progress in medicine depends upon some form of trial in which the trialist him or herself is uncertain of the result – the so-called position of equipoise; in allowing his patients to be involved, the primary clinical carer commits himself to accepting a similar, more dubious, role. The commonest strategy adopted is that of the randomised control trial which, in turn, is the paradigm representation of the ethical problems in research. A balance determined by the interests of all the parties involved must be sought if the programme is to be regarded as ethical.[9]

WHAT IS RESEARCH?

19.5 Research and experimentation are commonly used as interchangeable terms – we, however, believe that there is a distinction to be made. Research implies a predetermined protocol with a clearly defined end-point. Experimentation, by contrast, involves a more speculative, ad hoc, approach to an individual subject. The distinction is significant in that an experiment may be modified to take into account the individual's response; a research programme, however, is, by definition, bound to tie the researcher to a particular course of action until such time as its general ineffectiveness is satisfactorily demonstrated.[10]

19.6 Research activities can be broadly categorised as clinical or therapeutic research, which is aimed at the improved treatment of a patient or a group of patients and as non-therapeutic – in which the essential object is the furtherance of purely scientific knowledge which may, eventually, have a wider application than patient care.[11] This distinction makes little conceptual difference to the general requirements for ethical research. The mere fact that the research subject, being a patient at the time, may receive benefit does not mean that the programme can be undertaken unregulated by research codes – indeed, the fact that a relatively vulnerable group is involved emphasises the care with which the project should be monitored.[12] Only the degree of risk to be permitted in proportion to the expected outcome is affected by the nature of the research.

---

9 For a simplified overview, see S J L Edwards, R J Lilford and J Hewison 'The Ethics of Randomised Control Trials from the Perspectives of Patients, the Public, and Healthcare Professionals' (1998) 317 BMJ 1209.

10 For an excellent, albeit dated, discussion, see B M Dickens 'What is a Medical Experiment?' (1975) 113 Can Med Assoc J 635.

11 The eminent researcher, Doll, rightly points out that there are other forms of research available that do not involve actual human subjects – eg research by questionnaire, study of records etc: R Doll 'Research Will Be Impeded' (2001) 323 BMJ 1421.

12 Edwards et al (para 19.4 above) emphasise the interesting observation that a high proportion of participants in a research programme enter because the think they have something to gain – and tie this to the question of how much they actually understand when consenting.

19.7 It follows from this classification that research subjects may be of four types: individual patients; a group of patients who are suffering from one particular condition; patients who have no association with the disease or process under review but who are readily available; and, finally, healthy volunteers – a heterogeneous group which is of importance because it may involve other 'captive' populations, including the researchers themselves.

19.8 The logical implication of this division of subjects is that researchers should also be categorised. Thus, the individual patient is under the care of a doctor. Any experimental procedure or treatment is, therefore, performed on a care-associated basis and, while there may be difficulties in a hospital setting where 'care' is very much a team concept, the essential doctor-patient relationship is, and should be, maintained. But it cannot be said with reference to any of the other types of research subject that 'the health of my patient [and the singular noun is to be noted] is my first consideration' and, consequently, the researchers should not include the patients' physicians. Even so, doctors must be involved when human subjects are subject to medical experimentation; the danger of non-medical researchers being, not so much callous, as uncomprehending of their subjects' reactions, is such that a situation excluding doctors would only be acceptable in the event that the researchers were their own experimental subjects.

The risks involved

19.9 All research involves some risk and it is the art of the good investigator to minimise that risk. But there are certain guidelines to be followed which are spelled out in the Declaration of Helsinki[13] and also in the draft protocol.[14] A risk/benefit analysis must be undertaken in each case and patients may be involved only when the benefit to them clearly outweighs the inconvenience, discomfort or possible harm which the protocol may impose. The Royal College of Physicians in their own report[15] distinguished between research involving 'less than minimal risk' and that involving 'minimal risk'. The former is the risk of the sort involved in giving a sample of urine or a single venous sample in an adult; the latter arises where there is a reasonable chance of a mild reaction – such as a headache or a feeling of lethargy – or where there is a remote chance of serious injury or death. If the level rises above that of minimal risk, then the College took the view that patients should be involved only if:

(a)   the risk is still small in comparison with that already incurred by the patient as a consequence of the disease itself;
(b)   the disease is a serious one;
(c)   the knowledge gained from the research is likely to be of great practical benefit;
(d)   there is no other means of obtaining that knowledge; and
(e)   the patient gives a fully informed consent

13 Paras 16–18.
14 Para 19.2 above.
15 Royal College of Physicians *Research Involving Patients* (1990).

and these still represent the views expressed in the very large number of comparable documents that have been produced in the last decade.

19.10 The question of whether healthy volunteers may ever be exposed to serious risks in the course of medical research is problematic. The Declaration of Helsinki states:

> Medical research involving human subjects should only be conducted if the importance outweighs the inherent risks and burdens to the subject. This is especially important when the human subjects are healthy volunteers. (para 18)

19.11 Thus, a project would have to be of exceptional importance before a substantial risk to the healthy volunteer would be acceptable. On the face of things, the draft protocol to the European Convention on Human Rights and Biomedicine allows more discretion in stating that research that does not have the potential to produce results of direct benefit to the health of the research participant may only be authorised if it 'entails acceptable risk and acceptable burden for the research participants' (Article 8); here, the accent appears to be more on risk taking than on assessment of risk. Both are, however, subjective exercises. What, for example, is one to say of the use of volunteers in, say, potentially harmful research into the development of vaccines against diseases that may affect the community? Indeed, one can interpolate a further question – at what stage does a prophylactic exercise directed against an unknown hazard become, or cease to be, a research project?[16] The ethics depend on an uncertain amalgam of necessity, altruism and courage, the contribution of each being difficult to quantify.

19.12 There will clearly be differing views as to what risks are justifiable; it is equally clear that there will be those who would accept risks of a very high order on communitarian grounds and it is questionable whether they should be prevented from so doing. There are legal limits to the extent to which consent decriminalises the infliction of harm[17] and it is interesting to speculate how far the consent of a volunteer to a dangerous medical experiment would serve as a defence to a charge of assault or homicide.[18]

19.13 The AIDS pandemic brought the issue of participation in risky research into focus. In one view, the threat which HIV poses justifies the suspension of normal controls on research. This would mean that the normal procedures for investigating the safety of promising drugs might be circumvented and volunteers would be allowed to run risks which would, in normal circumstances, be considered excessive. While it would be unwise, and scientifically inappropriate, to suspend all regulation of AIDS-related research, the necessity

---

16 For an interesting discussion of the development and use of a vaccine designed to protect against biological warfare, see T M Gibson 'A Shot in the Arm for the Military: Consent to Immunisation against Biological Warfare Agents' (2002) 5 Med L Internat 161.

17 *A-G's Reference (No 6 of 1980)* [1981] QB 715, [1981] 2 All ER 1057, CA; *Smart v HM Advocate* 1975 SLT 65; *R v Brown* [1994] 1 AC 212, [1993] 2 All ER 75. See also The Law Commission *Consent in the Criminal Law* (Law Com No 131, 1995).

18 It is to be noted, however, that no such charges were brought in something of a *cause-célèbre* at a noted US hospital: J Savulescu and M Spriggs 'The Hexamethonium Asthma Study and the Death of a Normal Volunteer in Research' (2002) 28 J Med Ethics 3.

of the situation undoubtedly justifies such measures as 'fast-track approval' of therapeutic drugs.[19] The same may well apply to research subjects in similar situations. Volunteers who accept high risks are likely to be regarded as scientific heroes if they are also researchers. In the case of patients, willingness to explore any avenue of hazardous treatment might be regarded as lying within the range of acceptable personal risk-taking. Why, then, should we refuse the help of the consenting research subject?[20]

THE DESIGN OF EXPERIMENTS

19.14 All experiments cost money and cause some inconveniences both to colleagues and subjects. Badly planned research loses all ethical justification if, as a result, the findings are scientifically useless. Although the evaluation of a project from this aspect encapsulates a strong ethical component, it is, essentially, a matter for the scientists themselves. It is not the task of the research ethical committee (see below) to undertake additional scientific review, nor is it constituted to do so, but it should satisfy itself that the review already undertaken is adequate for the purpose; the REC is empowered to require the researchers to resubmit their request after further review if it is not so satisfied.[21]

19.15 It is important to distinguish two major types of ethics committees. Hospital based clinical or hospital ethics committees are common and wield considerable power in the United States, where their function generally includes therapeutic and prognostic decision-making;[22] there is little doubt that they are being increasingly introduced elsewhere as an aid to ethical decision making in a clinical setting. The situation in the United Kingdom is, however, evolving. A number of such committees or variations have been established following a pioneer effort in 1993[23] and, currently, some 18% of NHS hospital trusts have some form of decision-making ethical back-up; only 17% of these, however, include established committees.[24] These arrangements result from unofficial initiatives. Official local research ethical committees (LRECs) are set up by Health Authorities purely to vet research projects and this mainly

---

19   L C Fentiman 'Aids as a Chronic Illness: a Cautionary Tale for the End of the Twentieth Century' (1998) 61 Albany LR 989.

20   The issue was discussed by C Levine 'Has AIDS Changed the Ethics of Human Subjects Research?' (1988) 16 Law Med Hlth Care 167.

21   Department of Health *Governance Arrangements for NHS Research Ethics Committees* (2001), paras 9.9, 9.10 (www.doh.gov.uk/research/documents/gafrec.pdf).

22   For a discussion of procedural aspects of American hospital ethics committees, see 'Ethics Committees' (1992) 20 Law Med Hlth Care 278 (S M Wolf 'Toward a Theory of Process' 278; J C Fletcher 'Ethics Committees and Due Process' 291; C B Cohen 'Avoiding "Cloudcuckooland" in Ethics Committee Case Review: Matching Models to Issues and Concerns' 294; B M Dickens 'Ethics Committees, Organ Transplantation and Public Policy' 300).

23   'UK's First Hospital Ethics Committee' (1993) 90 Bull Med Ethics 5, reporting the setting up of an ethics committee within an NHS trust hospital in Northwest London.

24   A Slowther, C Bunch, B Woolnough and T Hope 'Clinical Ethics Support Services in the UK: An Investigation of the Current Provision of Ethics Support to Health Professionals in the UK' (2001) 27 J Med Ethics, Supp I, i12. This paper forms part of a larger symposium – see, in particular, J Hendrick 'Legal Aspects of Clinical Ethics Committees' at p i50, which considers the uncertainties as to liability.

from the point of view of their moral implications as to the use of subjects and of resources. The need to extend research so as to include a number of departments has necessitated the establishment of multi-centre research ethics committees. The essential nature of such committees is emphasised in the Declaration of Helsinki and in European directives;[25] their composition in the UK, along with matters of procedure, are regulated by guidelines issued by the Department of Health by way of the newly created Central Office for Research Ethics Committees.[26] Each local committee should include both sexes and cover a range of ages; hospital staff and general practitioners should be represented and the committee must include a sufficiently broad range of expertise so that the scientific and methodological aspects of proposals can be reconciled with the ethical implications. A quorum consists of at least seven members of the committee which must not, itself, exceed 18 members. The Committee can, when indicated, seek the advice of specialist referees.

19.16 At least one-third of the membership must be lay members and at least half of these must be people who have never been associated with the health or social services and who have never undertaken research. The inclusion of 'average citizens' can be seen as no more than a necessary political gesture; on the other hand, lay members may be better placed than professionals to appreciate the effects of different treatments on the day-to-day lives of the patients and their inclusion may, therefore, have definite practical advantages. One such member must be present in a quorum as must one expert member in order to facilitate understanding of the clinical and/or methodological components of the project under review.[27] It is to be noted that Health Authorities can set up as many LRECs within their boundaries as is commensurate with the work-load.[28]

19.17 The guidelines are not governed by statute and, accordingly, it is not a *legal* requirement that prospective researchers submit their proposals to a local research ethics committee for approval, but there are several reasons why the carrying out of medical research will be effectively impossible without such approval. To begin with, it is not possible to use NHS patients or resources for an unapproved project.[29] Funding is also likely to be denied unless an ethics committee's imprimatur is obtained, and the results of unapproved research will not be accepted for publication by reputable scientific journals.

---

25 Para 19.2 above.
26 Obligatory guidelines are now embodied in Department of Health *Governance Arrangements for NHS Research Ethics Committees* (2001), para 19.14 above. Similar guidelines are available for Scotland (2001): www.show.scot.nhs.uk/cso. For notes on the relationship between LRECs and MRECs, see 'Research Ethics Committee Update' (1998) 138 Bull Med Ethics 13.
27 The government sees the need for, and will provide facilities for, education and training of REC members and administrators (paras 4.10 and 4.11).
28 Special guidelines for multi-centre research ethics committees, which are set up in relation to research projects involving five or more Health Authorities, are detailed in Chapter 8 of the governance arrangements. Applications for research involving gene therapy, xenotransplantation and human fertilisation must be made to the appropriate regulatory authorities. Co-ordination of LREC and MREC activity is now the responsibility of the Central Office for Research Ethic Committees.
29 The body conducting research is encouraged to submit its proposals to a LREC even when there is no NHS involvement.

There are also pragmatic grounds compelling compliance with the guidelines – which clearly represent 'good medical practice'; appeal to *Bolam* principles would be virtually unavailable in the event of misadventure associated with research undertaken without approval – the *Bolitho* limitations (see para 9.28 above) would almost certainly apply.[30]

19.18 The decisions of hospital ethics committees have been declared to be subject to judicial review;[31] in the same way, a researcher frustrated by a LREC could pursue a remedy by that route. The aggrieved research subject may also seek redress, in his case most obviously through an action against the researcher.[32] It could be argued that a relationship exists between the committee member and the research subject which is of sufficient proximity to give rise to a duty of care and that this might, in theory, lead to civil liability in a case where a committee member has failed to exercise due care in the scrutiny of a research proposal. The guidelines, however, make it clear that the appointing Authority will take full responsibility for all the actions of members in the course of carrying out their duties other than those involving bad faith, wilful default or gross negligence (para 4.14). The precise meaning of the last term in the context of an indemnity is uncertain.[33]

Randomised controlled trials

19.19 Biomedical research almost inevitably involves a randomised controlled trial at some time.[34] The principle is simple – in order to decide whether a new drug or other treatment is better than an existing one, or is preferable to none at all, the new treatment is given to a group of patients or healthy volunteers and not given to as similar a group as can be obtained. The subtleties of experimental design are critical to the success of the project and, as stated above, a badly conceived trial is fundamentally unethical. But even the best designed trial has its built-in moral problem – depending on how one looks at it, on the one hand, a relatively untried treatment which may do harm is being given to one group while, on the other, a treatment which may be of considerable benefit is being withheld from a similar group. In one view, this is ethically unacceptable, as there can be no grounds – other than, possibly, those of limited resources – for withholding a treatment which is believed to be beneficial. The doctor must do his best for patients but the problem is to know what is best and, in particular, to know whether the patient's recovery

---

30 We can, in addition, anticipate specific legislation to ensure compliance with the EC Directive 2001/20/EC by May 2003.

31 *R v Ethical Committee of St Mary's Hospital (Manchester), ex p H (or Harriott)* [1988] 1 FLR 512.

32 Those injured in the course of pharmaceutical trials may be compensated by the company sponsoring the trial, as recommended by the Association of the British Pharmaceutical Industry in its *Clinical Trial Compensation Guidelines* (1991).

33 Accountability prior to the recent guidelines was considered in a major review: J V McHale 'Guidelines for Medical Research – Some Ethical and Legal Problems' (1993) 1 Med L Rev 160.

34 Other forms of trial, which are beyond the scope of this book, can be used and may be preferable on ethical grounds. For a very full and useful description, see A L Avins 'Can Unequal Be More Fair? Ethics, Subject Allocation, and Randomised Clinical Trials' (1998) 24 J Med Ethics 401.

is being hindered by the restraints of the experimental protocol.[35] The first essential for any controlled trial is, therefore, that it must provide its answer as rapidly as possible and it must be terminable as soon as an adverse effect becomes apparent. Conflict may arise between statisticians and doctors, with the former possibly insisting on evidence from many more cases – and possibly observed for longer – than the latter may feel is necessary.

19.20 When, then, should randomised trials stop? At what point does the clinician say that enough is enough and that the evidence of benefit is sufficient to justify the conclusion that a treatment does, indeed, do good? Conversely, at what point does the apparent emergence of an adverse effect dictate that the project be abandoned? The patient involved in such a trial will have been informed that he is possibly being denied a potential benefit – yet his consent will have been based on his trust that there is genuine scientific uncertainty. Once this uncertainty is resolved to the extent of a belief – on, say, a balance of probabilities – that the treatment offers clinical benefit, then it becomes questionable whether it can still be denied to some in a continuing quest for statistical significance.[36] In deciding this question, it is important that the researcher bears in mind the fundamental precept which governs ethical medical research – that one does not use patients as a means to a scientific end but treats them as an end in themselves. Even so, the practical dilemma remains – the clinically orientated researcher stands to see his subsequent report criticised for want of scientific support while the more scientifically minded one sleeps uneasily because he worries that his research has reached an inadequate conclusion. Most good trials include plans for periodic analysis; there is a good case to be made for an independent observer, or the ethical committee itself, being responsible for monitoring the trial from this angle.[37]

19.21 The principle of randomisation lies at the core of clinical trials and of the ethical problems associated with their conduct. It is almost impossible for health professionals not to have some preference when there is a choice of treatments.[38] For this reason, if for no other, many doctors having care – and especially primary care – of patients distrust the randomised clinical trial. Most do so for fear that the doctor-patient relationship will be jeopardised; a significant number are, however, concerned with the problems of informed

---

35 The practical anxiety is outlined in simple terms in F Verdú-Pascual and A Castelló-Ponce 'Randomised Clinical Trials: A Source of Ethical Dilemmas' (2001) 27 J Med Ethics 177 – and the statisticians put the counter-argument: J Hilden and A Gammelgaard 'Premature Stopping and Informed Consent in AMI Trials' (2002) 28 J Med Ethics 188.

36 For an analysis, see N Johnson, R J Lilford and W Brazier 'At what Level of Collective Equipoise Does a Clinical Trial Become Ethical?' (1991) 17 J Med Ethics 30. The standards of proof have been compared to the different standards applied in the civil and criminal courts: The Lancet 'On Stopping a Trial before its Time' (1993) 342 Lancet 1311.

37 E Pickworth 'Should Local Research Ethics Committees Monitor Research They Have Approved?' (2000) 26 J Med Ethics 330. The author thinks not – mainly on the practical grounds that they could not accommodate the extra work-load but also because it would introduce an element of policing into what is an advisory role. The Declaration of Helsinki, however, acknowledges a Committee's right to do so (at para 13).

38 True 'equipoise', or indifference, may be impossible to attain for many reasons; at best, it will be unusual. Perhaps we should be looking for genuine disagreement among experts rather than genuine uncertainty. See Avins, para 19.19 above.

consent.[39] This is discussed in greater detail later[40] but here it can be said that it also has a profound effect on the patient's acceptance of a trialist status. Refusal may be on simple utilitarian grounds but is equally liable to stem from confusion. No randomised therapeutic trial can be ethical unless the professionals genuinely cannot agree as to which treatment yields the best results. Given that the doctors are unsure, it may be difficult for the patient to solve what appears to him to be an insoluble problem. The result of the cumulative adverse factors is that accrual rates to important trials are often very low[41] – it is reported that a fundamental research project intended to identify the best treatment for early breast cancer had to be closed after a very low recruitment because the insistence on full informed consent frightened off both surgeons and patients.[42] Researchers therefore seek devices which will circumvent the confrontation between clinicians and patient and most of these involve some form of pre-selection – or 'pre-randomisation' – prior to discussion of treatment.[43] There are specific ethical and practical objections to such manoeuvres but, in general, it seems doubtfully moral to use what is essentially a ruse in order to obviate an agreed ethical practice which is an integral part of the basic principles not only of the Declaration of Helsinki but also of all modern directives and guidelines. One does well, however, not to lose sight of the view from the other side. One perfectly arguable school of thought will hold that this is the penalty we have to accept: 'unless we wish to return to the dark ages when treatment was determined by conceptual rationalism rather than scientific method.'[44] Others would emphasise that care must be taken lest, by attenuating our commitments to present patients in favour of benefits to those of the future, we do not lose overall more than we gain.[45] Communitarian ethicists are currently consigned to the peripheral darkness – but they are still alive out there.

19.22 One further feature deserves mention before we leave the subject of randomisation – that is the 'double-blind' technique. This form of research, which is virtually confined to drug trials, attempts to reduce subjectivity in assessment by keeping the assigned therapeutic groups secret not only from the patients but also from the physicians involved. This clearly dictates that

---

39 Edwards et al (para 19.4 above) refer to three trials in which 47% of doctors concerned thought that few patients knew they were taking part in a controlled experiment, even though they had given written consent. The problem of consent may be particularly acute where the participants in a randomised trial are illiterate or where they do not share the scientific view of the researcher: see M Barry and M Molyneux 'Ethical Dilemmas in Malaria Drug and Vaccine Trials: a Bioethical Perspective' (1992) 18 J Med Ethics 189. See also, M Angell 'Investigators' Responsibilities for Human Subjects in Developing Countries' (2000) 342 New Engl J Med 967.
40 See para 19.38 below.
41 M Angell 'Patients' Preferences in Randomized Clinical Trials' (1984) 310 New Engl J Med 1385.
42 M Baum, K Zilkha and J Houghton 'Ethics of Clinical Research: Lessons for the Future' (1989) 299 BMJ 251. Professor Baum still stands as a 'hawk' in what he describes as the AK (after-Kant) age: *Reply to Rothman and Michels* (2000), para 19.31 below at 444.
43 S S Ellenberg 'Randomization Design in Comparative Clinical Trials' (1984) 310 New Engl J Med 1404. See, in particular, M A Zelen 'A new Design for Randomized Clinical Trials' (1979) 300 New Engl J Med 1242. For a simple explanation of pre-randomisation, see D J Torgerson and M Roland 'What Is Zelen's Design?' (1998) 316 BMJ 606.
44 Baum et al (1989) 299 BMJ 251.
45 Angell (1984) 310 New Engl J Med 1385.

the patient's doctor cannot be the researcher; it also makes it implicit that the ethical justification of the trial is agreed by the 'caring' physicians involved, for they must have perfect equipoise if they are to join in the trial and, at the same time, provide what is, to their mind, the 'best treatment' for their patients. This, further, leads to some form of conscious pre-selection in that it may be, for example, necessary to exclude patients on the grounds of the severity of their disease; the trial then becomes limited to establishing the effectiveness of a treatment for the milder forms of the disease and loses much of its validity. We find it hard to justify the 'ethics' of the 'double-blind' trial on several grounds; *The Times*, however, sees it as currently forming the bedrock of modern health economics.[46]

Groups of subjects

19.23 There may be clear advantages in using healthy volunteers as experimental subjects – the Declaration of Helsinki does not preclude their use (para 16) but, by definition, it must be limited to non-therapeutic research. Medical research may be combined with medical care (para 28) but we doubt if this could be extended to using patients as if they were healthy; we believe that the use of a group of persons who are already under stress, and who probably have a sense of obligation to the doctors, simply because of their accessibility, must bring such research close to unethical practice; non-therapeutic research in patients should be confined to a type which adds no extra burden – for example, through the use of existing blood samples as is discussed below.[47] It can be argued that the use of volunteers is, a priori, unjustifiable but we prefer the view that people have a right to exercise altruistic impulses, particularly in a society in which the benefits of free health care are extended to all. None the less, considerable caution is needed, particularly as to the repetitive volunteer who is particularly prone to exploitation even if the researchers are unconscious of this – they may, for example, be quite unaware of marital disharmony caused by frequent absences from home. Motivation of the ever-ready volunteer takes several forms, some good and others bad, and, among these, the problem of recompense looms large. Both the Declaration of Helsinki and the authoritative directive 2001/20/EC are silent on this aspect[48] but it is probable that, in the conditions of present-day society, few suitable volunteers would come forward in the absence of some inducement; large payments would, however, be clearly unethical and a reasonable balance must be set – if for no other reason than to satisfy the needs of randomisation. It might be noted that the Royal College of Physicians Report *Research*

---

46 Leading article 'Nice Decisions' *The Times*, 13 August 2002, p 17. The fact that it is well-nigh impossible to discover whether or not such a claim is true is among the reasons underlying calls for a national register of research projects: R Horton and R Smith 'Time to Register Randomised Trials' (1999) 319 BMJ 865.

47 See para 19.56. For what is, perhaps, the all time greatest example of the dangers of using patients in this way, see *Hyman v Jewish Chronic Disease Hospital* 206 NE 2d 338 (1965) where a group of hospital patients were injected with cancer cells as an active control for a group of cancer patients who were similarly treated.

48 The latter proscribes incentives and financial inducements other than compensation but only in respect of minors (Article 4(d)) and incapacitated adults (Article 5(d)). Otherwise, the matter would be considered by the responsible Ethics Committee.

Involving Patients described payments to patients as 'generally undesirable' but occasionally acceptable in the case of long and tedious studies.[49] Even in such cases, 'payments should not be for undergoing risk, and payments should not be such as to persuade patients to volunteer against their better judgement'.

19.24 The topic of inducement does, however, bring us to the problems of the use of specific populations who are special because of their easy access, malleability and the like. Students, and particularly medical students, provide an example about whom there is little difficulty; they are of an age to make legally valid decisions, they may well have an active interest in the trial and most, if not all, educational establishments have very stringently controlling 'ethical committees' to protect against, say, repetitive use. Much the same could be said for the armed forces, who may be particularly vulnerable to improper research in war or when war threatens – even in 1990, non-consensual trials were allowed on American troops engaged in the Gulf War[50] and we have discussed the use of experimental vaccines above (see para 19.11). The use of prisoners, however, exposes many ethical issues that are based, essentially, on the argument that some advantage, even if only imagined, must accrue to the prisoner participating in a trial; that advantage may be so great as to induce the prisoner to volunteer for research which involves greater discomfort or risk than would be accepted by a free man and, in particular, it may compromise his inalienable right to withdraw from the trial. The arguments are not, however, entirely one way – it is possible to be paternalistic in an attempt to preserve other peoples' autonomy. Thus, prisoners could well resent protective attitudes on the grounds that it is their right to dispose of their bodies and to take such risks as they please that is being compromised. This could be the subject of lengthy debate but we suggest that the conditions in today's prisons are such that any process which provides some relief deserves, at least, a sympathetic evaluation and, secondly, that many prisoners might be benefited therapeutically through helping society. But it is also felt that experiments on prisoners should be particularly rigidly controlled by ethical committees which should always contain lay members with experience in criminology. Nowhere is it more important to observe the maxim 'the aims do not justify the method – the method must be judged in its own right'.[51]

19.25 When comparing treatments, however, the use of patients is axiomatic. This is what the Declaration of Helsinki means by medical research combined with professional care which is admissible 'only to the extent that the research is justified by its potential prophylactic, diagnostic or therapeutic value' (para 28).

19.26 A clinical trial is rarely undertaken unless there is good reason to suppose that one therapy will show an advantage over others and particularly over those currently accepted as the best available. The advantage need not be direct; it could, for example, be collateral in that the results of the method

49 Royal College of Physicians *Research Involving Patients* (1990).
50 G J Annas and M A Grodin 'Treating the Troops: Commentary' (1991) 21 Hastings Center Rep (2) 24.
51 Specific governmental arrangements are said to be in place for ethical review of research on prisoners: *Governance Arrangements for NHS Research Ethics Committees*, Section B (in preparation).

were not better but were achieved with less disfigurement or with fewer side effects. Anticipation of advantage can, in general, only be based on laboratory or, where appropriate, animal experimentation[52] and, while the view is occasionally expressed that the latter is less moral than is human biomedical research, it is, still, generally acceptable given that the conditions are controlled. The corollary, as we have already emphasised, is that an experimental method must be immediately withdrawn if it is found to be positively deleterious and the patients involved must be transferred, whenever possible, to an alternative regime. The results of the experimental therapies may, however, take a considerable time to filter through and, by then, there may be no turning back. A typical example was provided by the study of the use of folic acid supplements in order to reduce the incidence of neural tube defects in infants. Two pilot studies were undertaken; both showed an apparent marked reduction in recurrence rates in affected families but neither stood up to statistical analysis. The problem then arose as to whether the study should be continued and, if so, whether the clinical impression was sufficient to render the use of placebos unethical. It was decided that the matter was so important that a major randomised trial was indicated, the intent being to study at least 2,000 pregnancies. In the event, after more than seven years, sufficient information had been gained from 1,195 informative pregnancies. Thus, the trial could now be ended, it being clear that folic acid supplements had no adverse effects but had a significant protective effect as regards fetal neural tube defect.[53]

The use of placebos

19.27 A placebo is an inert substance without pharmacological action. The mere taking of medicine may lead to subjective, or symptomatic, improvement; this is the 'placebo effect', which must be considered whenever a new drug or procedure is on trial. On the other hand, the trial drug may do more harm than inactivity; but, for psychological reasons, inactivity must involve apparent activity if the two regimens are to be properly compared. In either case, the controlled giving of a placebo necessarily involves the deception of patients and this raises some complex issues.

19.28 The extreme position is that placebos offend against the fundamental rightness of fidelity.[54] If, as is often the case, there is patient resistance to the use of such controls, this should not be regarded as an excuse for further deception but rather as an indication that such experiments are unacceptable to society. To which one could reply that a poor experiment is a worse affront to society and that the simple expedient is to leave out those who object – little is lost, other than, perhaps, absolute numbers, and, as previously discussed, experimental volunteers are, by nature, already a selected group.

52 The view is occasionally expressed that the latter is at least as, if not more, objectionable than is research on humans. The 2000 version of the Declaration is noticeably more sensitive in this respect than was its predecessors.

53 MRC Vitamin Study Research Group 'Prevention of Neural Tube Defects: Results of the Medical Research Council Vitamin Study' (1991) 338 Lancet 131.

54 For a seminal analysis, see B Simmons 'Problems in Deceptive Medical Procedures: An Ethical and Legal Analysis of the Administration of Placebos' (1978) 4 J Med Ethics 172.

19.29 More practical objections are based on the effect of the experiment on patient care; the circumstances in which it is ethical to deprive a patient of treatment must be strictly regulated. It would, for example, be improper to use placebo controls when pain was a feature of the condition under treatment, despite the fact that some patients might derive benefit; many pain killers are available and can be used as reference substances. The basic circumstances in which placebo trials are ethical and, perhaps, necessary are, first, and perhaps foremost, when there is no alternative to the experimental treatment available. Such a situation might arise in the treatment of degenerative neural disease – though, even here, *some* form of pharmacologically active substance might well be thought preferable. Second, the use of a placebo could be justified when the effect of adding a new treatment to an established one is under study. In the majority of instances, however, the purpose of their use is to analyse the effect of a treatment on subjective symptoms rather than on organic disease.[55]

19.30 The latest version of the Declaration of Helsinki has raised some interesting additional points as to the use of placebos. Para 29 states:

> The benefits, risks, burdens and effectiveness of a new method should be tested against those of the best current prophylactic, diagnostic and therapeutic methods. This does not preclude the use of placebo, or no treatment, in studies where no proven prophylactic, diagnostic or therapeutic method exists.

19.31 The European Agency for the Evaluation of Medical Trials criticises this on the grounds that the use of placebos is ruled out whenever an alternative exists; the Agency believes that comparison of a new method with an active control does not always give the same scientific satisfaction as does comparison with a passive control;[56] the argument, although not stated in precise terms, seems to be that an ideal trial might require the use of placebo as a comparator to both the old and the new alternatives. One can see why this might be so but it presupposes considerable understanding on the part of the research subjects. Perhaps more significantly in the ethical context, it has been pointed out that, although the clause is there to prohibit exploitation of vulnerable communities, the use of an established method as a control may be beyond the socio-economic means of many developing countries; a case can, indeed, be made for the general interpretation of universal principles in the context of specific situations.[57]

19.32 The WMA has, subsequently, modified its stance so as to allow placebo trials despite there being accepted treatment 'where for compelling and scientifically sound methodological reasons [their] use is necessary to determine the efficacy or safety of … a method'. The rules are also relaxed where the

---

55 For further criticism, see K J Rothman and K B Michels 'The Continuing Unethical Use of Placebo Controls' (1994) 331 New Engl J Med 384. A cautious but relatively benign attitude, which, to an extent, parallels our views, is adopted by P P De Deyn and R D'Hooge 'Placebos in Clinical Practice and Research' (1996) 22 J Med Ethics 140.

56 This seems to be very much the attitude of the Food and Drugs Administration in the United States which is said to insist on the inclusion of placebo in all circumstances – a view heavily criticised, again, by K R Rothman and K B Michels 'Declaration of Helsinki should be Strengthened' (2000) 321 BMJ 442.

57 S M Tollman 'Fair Partnerships Support Ethical Research' (2001) 323 BMJ 1417.

condition under investigation is a minor one and patients who receive placebo are not subjected to any additional risk of serious harm.[58]

19.33 All of which may seem trite and fairly easily accommodated within an ethical spectrum. But times move on and, since the last edition of this book, we have been confronted with the extension of the placebo concept into surgery – and especially, although not exclusively, into the surgery of those conditions in which symptoms and signs become intermingled; the paradigmatic example is in the use of fetal brain implants in the treatment of Parkinsonism (see para 14.67 above).[59] Essentially, we have here a randomised controlled trial in which some patients are implanted but in which the control group's brains are untouched. Space does not admit of further discussion. Suffice it to point out that, on top of the philosophical difficulties involved in the acceptance of medicinal placebo therapy, we must now impose deceptive target imaging by way of magnetic resonance imaging, an anaesthetic, a scalp incision and at least a token hole in the skull on a person who is to receive no additional therapy. Justification of the programme on utilitarian grounds is possible but certainly not easy.

Experimental treatment

19.34 Early in the chapter, we distinguished between research and experimentation – the latter being regarded as involving ad hoc and relatively – or entirely – untried treatment applied to an individual with little more scientific basis other than expediency. It follows that we see medical experiments – as opposed to research – on human beings as being morally justified only in extreme conditions.

19.35 The status of the experimental therapist has always been uncertain since 1797 when the unfortunate Dr Baker was pilloried in court for introducing what still remains the standard treatment for fractures of the limb bones.[60] To some extent this has been imposed as medical law has developed. The innovative doctor cannot depend upon *Bolam* if things go wrong since, by definition, no supportive body of medical opinion is available – the pioneer is alone in more senses than one.

19.36 Yet the patient who has no other hope is surely entitled to grasp an outside chance and, given the fact that he believes it to be a genuine chance, the doctor is entitled, and perhaps ought, to provide it. He must, however, believe that there is a chance – he cannot provide, nor can the patient consent

---

58 Bulletin of Medical Ethics 'News' (2001) No 173, p 7.
59 For which see: W Dekkers and G Boer 'Sham Neurosurgery in Patients with Parkinson's Disease: Is it Morally Acceptable?' (2001) 27 J Med Ethics 151. For uncompromising criticism, see P A Clark 'Placebo Surgery for Parkinson's Disease: Do the Benefits Outweigh the Risks?' (2002) 30 J Law Med Ethics 58. These papers particularly contrast and analyse those by T Freeman et al 'Use of Placebo Surgery in Controlled Trials of a Cellular-based Therapy for Parkinson's Disease' (1999) 341 New Engl J Med 988 and R Macklin 'The Ethical Problems with Sham Surgery in Clinical Research' (1999) 341 New Engl J Med 992.
60 *Slater v Baker and Stapleton* (1797) 95 ER 860.

to, treatment that is certain to result in serious bodily harm or death.[61] In this respect, the ruling in *Bolitho* (see para 9.28 above) may be greatly to the doctor's advantage; given the conditions envisaged, it could be relatively easy in the event of an action in negligence, to convince a court that his decision was logical *in all the circumstances* of the case. In practice, the Declaration of Helsinki supports the concept of experimental treatment:

> In the treatment of a patient, where proven prophylactic, diagnostic and therapeutic methods do not exist or have been ineffective, the physician, with informed consent from the patient, must be free to use unproven or new ... measures, if in the physician's judgement it offers hope of saving life, re-establishing health or alleviating suffering.[62]

19.37 Clearly, this aspect of research and experimentation is one where the informed consent of the patient is of paramount importance and it is to this universally accepted precept that we return briefly.

INFORMED CONSENT

19.38 The theoretical baseline for an ethical research programme or therapeutic experiment is drawn on free, autonomous participation by the subject and this, in turn, depends upon 'informed consent', the nature of which has been discussed in chapter 10.

19.39 The principles in relation to experimentation are similar to those governing therapy; most commentators would hold that the patient's rights are, if anything, greater in the former situation than they are in the sphere of pure patient management. The standard of information provided must certainly be that of the 'reasonable subject' – if not that of the actual subject – rather than that of the 'reasonable doctor'.[63] Even so, there are many and variable difficulties which make it almost impossible to lay down hard and fast rules – these include the essential need for some measure of ignorance in the trial, the seriousness of the condition being treated, the psychology of individual patients and the like. The complexity is such that some confrontation between the back-room and the coal-face is almost inevitable:

> The central dogma [of professional medical ethicists] seems to be that whatever is done for the sake of medical science is alien to the treatment of the individual, and should therefore be labelled an 'experiment', necessitating informed consent by the patient and adjudication by an ethics committee.[64]

61 *A-G's Reference (No 6 of 1980)*, para 9.12 above.
62 Para 32. The paragraph adds that the case should be included in a structured research project whenever possible.
63 For a short resumé of the debate, see L Doyal and J S Tobias 'Informed Consent in Medical Research' (1998) 316 BMJ 1000. Much of the current discussion centres on the ethics of publication; this is inevitable as research without publication is so much wasted effort.
64 Lancet 'Medical Ethics: Should Medicine Turn the Other Cheek?' (1990) 336 Lancet 846. But can one wonder at this when one reads of Dr Milhaud who seemingly used, and caused the death of, a patient in the permanent vegetative state in research on hypovolaemic shock: G Maio 'The Cultural Specificity of Research Ethics – or Why Ethical Debate in France is Different' (2002) 28 J Med Ethics 147. The author points to the difficulties in harmonising differing national cultures within an international framework.

19.40 Such general problems are amplified in practice. It is widely agreed that the patient's consent must be based on four main lines of explanation: the purpose of the experiment; the benefits to the patient and society; the risks involved; and the alternatives open to the subject. Who is to impart the information – the patient's physician or the researcher? Should the patient have the benefit of a 'friend' to interpret for him? Should there be confirmation of the consent procedure? It has been fairly widely mooted that, in fact, informed consent is a double-edged weapon – token consent may take the place of the genuine and relieve the researcher of responsibility. Might it not be better to burden the investigator with full responsibility rather than provide such a shield? Many of the states of the United States have enacted 'informed consent statutes', some of which lay down specific disclosure requirements for particular procedures. In the same spirit, United States courts, dealing with claims that inadequate information has been given to experimental subjects, have tended to stress the requirement that there be a considerably higher burden of disclosure in cases involving non-therapeutic research than in therapeutic cases,[65] a view shared by a Canadian court in the well-known case of *Halushka v University of Saskatchewan*.[66] Here the court said: 'There can be no exceptions to the ordinary requirements of disclosure in the case of research as there may well be in ordinary medical practice.'

19.41 These difficulties are highlighted in 'care associated' research when, effectively, the doctrine of informed consent implies that the patient has to choose for him- or herself whether to accept an experimental treatment or to be randomised in a comparative therapeutic trial. The philosophical basis of patient autonomy is perfectly clear, but is the ideal end attainable in practice? Ought a patient to be told of a 'last chance' effort? Is the medically naive patient capable of giving consent as required? Can he be expected to understand the risks when the medical profession itself is so divided?

19.42 A remarkable example of how such uncertainty may operate in practice – and which, despite its age, still merits keeping in memory – came before a coroner's court inquiring into the death of a female patient – a death due, interestingly enough, to a failure to inform a temporary house officer of the research in progress.[67] It came to light that 15 units were involved in a trial treatment of colonic cancer which involved infusing selected but randomised patients with a potent cytotoxic drug post-operatively; all units had submitted the trial protocol to their ethical committees and 11 had decided that 'informed consent' need not be obtained. *The Lancet*, while, admittedly, concluding that special consent should have been obtained on the grounds of both variance from standard procedures and the degree of risk involved, summed up the dilemma in a series of questions: when, if ever, can informed consent be dispensed with? If a trial is concerned with the treatment of cancer, how can

---

65 Eg *Whitlock v Duke University* 637 F Supp 1463 (NC, 1986); affd 829 F 2d 1340 (1987).
66 (1965) 53 DLR (2d) 436: K Morin 'The Standard of Disclosure in Human Subject Experimentation' (1998) 19 J Leg Med 157.
67 Coroner's Court, Birmingham, 19 September 1981. Discussed in Leading Article 'Secret Randomised Clinical Trials' (1982) 2 Lancet 78. See also D Brahams 'Death of Patient who was Unwitting Subject of Randomised Controlled Trial of Cancer Treatment' (1982) 1 Lancet 1028 and 'Clinical Trials and the Consent of the Patient' (1982) 226 Practitioner 1829.

consent be obtained without adding to the patient's distress? At what stage in the trial should consent be obtained? and, finally, have local ethical committees the authority to override national and international guidelines on the ethics of research? To which we would add – how can you possibly expect a patient to understand such a complex subject? – and *The Lancet* answers that the patient should not be included in the trial if he or she is not capable of understanding the basic plan of management.[68] One thing is certain – no such anomalous situation would be allowed to develop today.

19.43 A real problem here is that doubts as to patients' ability to understand complex medical information can very easily result in the striking of an unacceptably paternalistic attitude – sometimes with shocking consequences. Such a situation arose in New Zealand in the course of the Auckland cervical cancer campaign.[69] Here, a senior doctor, believing that cancer in situ would not spread, was strongly of the view that some women with abnormal cervical smear tests were best left untreated. These patients were denied treatment over a period of 15-20 years without being told that they were, in effect, involved in a therapeutic experiment. The doctor in charge of the experimental research believed honestly and firmly in his hypothesis, but his failure to obtain consent was severely criticised both by medical colleagues and by the judicial inquiry which was established to investigate the matter; the impact on medicine in New Zealand and, hopefully, elsewhere, has been profound.[70]

Research and the incompetent

19.44 Particularly difficult ethical and legal problems arise in relation to those patients who cannot give a valid consent to participation in clinical research by virtue of their mental condition. Such patients must be excluded automatically if informed consent is an absolute prerequisite for involvement in research, yet this would have the effect of halting valuable lines of inquiry into serious and debilitating diseases. One way round this difficulty is to accept that there are special groups of patients who cannot consent but whose involvement is vital if research into a condition from which they suffer is to make progress. Such patients may be used in research provided that certain safeguards are erected; these would be designed so as to ensure that they are not subjected to appreciable risk or inconvenience and would include the agreement of relatives and/or that of some independent supervisory party. Although the 'consent' of relatives is of no legal effect in these circumstances, it is an important check, in that they may be assumed to have the interests of members of their family at heart. The required approval of an independent authority would cover those instances in which it was suspected that uncaring relatives had been thoughtless.

68 (1982) 1 Lancet 1028.
69 Judge S Cartwright *The Report of the Cervical Cancer Enquiry* (1988); discussed by A V Campbell 'An "Unfortunate Experiment"' (1989) 3 Bioethics 59.
70 C Paul 'The New Zealand Cancer Study: Could it Happen Again' (1988) 297 BMJ 533; P McNeill 'The Implications for Australia of the New Zealand Report of the Cervical Cancer Inquiry: No Cause for Complacency' (1989) 150 Med J Austral 264; G Gillett 'NZ Medicine after Cartwright' (1990) 300 BMJ 893.

19.45 The Draft Additional Protocol to the Convention on Human Rights and Biomedicine has addressed the matter directly[71] and proposes that research on persons without the capacity to consent to research may be undertaken if:

(i)   the results of the research have the potential to produce real and direct benefit to the subject's health,

(ii)   research of comparable effectiveness cannot be carried out on persons able to consent,

(iii)   where possible, the persons undergoing the research have been informed of their rights and the safeguards prescribed,

(iv)   the necessary authorisation has been given specifically and in writing by the legal representative or an authority, person or body provided for by national law, taking into account any previously expressed wishes or objections by the subject,

(v)   the person concerned does not object to taking part.

19.46 Exceptionally, where condition (i) above is not satisfied, research may be authorised if it has the aim of contributing 'to the ultimate attainment of results capable of conferring benefit to the person concerned or to other persons in the same age category or afflicted with the same disease or disorder or having the same condition' provided, at the same time, that the research entails only minimal risk and minimal burden for the individual concerned. It is this latter criterion, not the ultimate value of the research, that constitutes the bench-mark.

19.47 The main additional, or alternative, condition provided in the EC Directive 2001/20/EC which, as we have seen, is concerned only with research involving medicinal products, is that 'the research is essential to validate data obtained in clinical trials on persons able to give informed consent or by other research methods and relates directly to a life-threatening or debilitating clinical condition from which the incapacitated adult concerned suffers'.[72]

19.48 Even so, the United Kingdom has not yet ratified the Convention on Bioethics and the EC Directive is not yet in force. The situation in England is not, therefore, entirely clear. As the law there stands, there can be no legal justification – other than, possibly, that of necessity – for any non-therapeutic invasion of the bodily integrity of an incapacitated person. It is, therefore, possible that research of this type is unlawful pending review of the Mental Health Act 1983 (for which, see chapter 21). On the other hand, the fact that Research Ethics Committees can allow incapacitated patients to be involved in research[73] indicates that there is at least de facto legal recognition of the procedure which has the approval of the Law Commission.[74] The situation is now quite clear in Scotland where research on incompetent adults is now regulated by statute.[75] The necessary conditions almost exactly parallel those

---

71 Para 19.2 above, Article 18. See also the general agreement with the Declaration of Helsinki, para 24.
72 Para 19.2 above, Article 5(e).
73 Guidelines, para 19.15 above at para 9.17(c).
74 Law Commission *Mental Incapacity* (Law Com No 231, 1995).
75 Adults with Incapacity (Scotland) Act 2000, s 51.

laid down in the Protocol to the Convention save that, in addition, authority for surrogate consent is specifically vested in a person appointed as the incapax' guardian or welfare attorney; where there is no appointed guardian welfare attorney, power to consent lies with the subject's nearest relative.[76]

THE UNETHICAL RESEARCHER

19.49 All that has gone before has assumed that the researcher is acting in good faith with the interests of the profession and of the public at heart. Occasionally, however, concern arises not so much as to research of poor quality – which is distinguished relatively easily – but, rather, as to the publication of frankly fraudulent studies.[77]

19.50 Modern doctors are under some pressure in this area. In high-profile areas of research, the competitive spirit may have a lamentable effect. The temptation to falsify results or to suppress the truth may be too much for some scientists, particularly when there is a prospect of high earnings from patents. Even in the more mundane reaches of medicine, the senior academic who publishes frequently is likely to attract more funding than his colleague who does not and the advantage of 'being first' encourages premature reporting. More importantly, advancement in hierarchical medicine now depends heavily on the number of publications to the junior's credit. Such influences lead to 'sloppy science' which is, perhaps, understandable. There is, however, no excuse for the deliberate falsification of results – which is less easy to identify and of which a number of examples were reported in the late 1980s and early 1990s.[78] The danger in these cases is that the public, often prompted by the news media, may be led to believe in therapeutic claims which are unsupported by the available data or that, as a result, they may be subjected to valueless or dangerous treatment schedules. The issue is also, understandably, of great interest to pharmaceutical companies, who may be wrongly deprived of profits if a drug is withdrawn from the market on the basis of fraudulent results.[79] This happened in the case of Debendox, which was withdrawn after claims by the Australian gynaecologist, William McBride, that the drug could cause deformities in a small proportion of the children of those women to whom it was administered. An inquiry by the New South Wales Medical Tribunal subsequently concluded that McBride claimed statistically significant results where none, in fact, existed.[80] McBride is reported as saying that he had

---

76 As defined in the Mental Health (Scotland) Act 1984, ss 53–57.
77 Ten cases of scientific fraud were processed through the disciplinary committee of the GMC between 1987 and 1993: S Kingman 'GMC may not pay legal costs for investigating Fraud' (1993) 307 BMJ 403. The penalties for scientific fraud are severe, and include that of being struck off the register for misconduct: 'Sex, Scandal and Fraud' (1992) 305 BMJ 272.
78 J Smith 'Preventing Fraud' (1991) 302 BMJ 362.
79 The effect of publication of results – genuine as well as fraudulent – on the stock-market has also to be considered. Researchers who also trade in the relevant pharmaceutical shares may find themselves in breach of the Company Securities (Insider Dealing) Act 1985: see D S Freestone and H Mitchell 'Inappropriate Publication of Trial Results and Potential for Allegations of Illegal Share Dealing' (1993) 306 BMJ 1112.
80 M Ragg 'Australia: McBride Guilty of Scientific Fraud' (1993) 341 Lancet 550.

changed his data in 'the long-term interests of humanity'.[81] The fraudulent researcher, of course, faces a variety of sanctions. He may be criminally liable for fraudulently obtaining research funds, and he could, also, face civil action for any loss incurred by drug manufacturers. In addition, there are powerful professional disciplinary procedures that can effectively end a scientific career.

19.51 We have already referred to the closely allied problem of experimental treatment where the difficulty may lie in distinguishing courageous innovation from unethical experimentation – and, human nature being what it is, the answer often depends on the outcome. The case which remains most vividly in the memory is that in which a baboon's heart was transplanted into a neonate with congenital heart disease.[82] The parents of the child were unmarried minors and doubts have been expressed as to whether they could give 'informed consent' in the true sense. A consultant summed up the procedure:

> I think this xenograft is premature because I am not aware of any finding in the clinical literature that suggests anything but the prevailing rule – the human body will reject a transplanted animal organ. Baby Fae will reject her baboon heart within the next week or two, and cyclosporine will not prevent it.[83]

19.52 Most would agree with this assessment – Baby Fae actually survived for two and a half weeks – but the procedure had been approved by the university's institutional research board and there was some further professional support for the operation. Nevertheless, it does appear to be an example of premature experimental treatment which fails the test of a reasonable chance.

19.53 We are left with the complex problem of whether or not information gained from frankly immoral research should be used for the general good – the classic, and ultimate, examples being data obtained in the concentration camps of the Second World War.[84] The arguments are finely balanced. In the end, we subscribe to the view that the fact that children do not, say, now die from certain forms of hypothermia is best regarded as a monument to those who suffered and died to make it possible; if the material is used, they will, at least, not have done so in vain.

COMPENSATION FOR PERSONAL INJURY IN RESEARCH

19.54 The research volunteer who is injured in the course of a medical experiment may resort to a claim for compensation under the law of tort.

---

81 N Swan 'Australian Doctor Admits Fraud' (1991) 302 BMJ 1421.
82 L L Hubband 'The Baby Fae Case' (1987) 6 Med Law 385.
83 Details taken from H S Schwartz 'Bioethical and Legal Considerations in Increasing the Supply of Transplantable Organs: From UAGA to "Baby Fae"' (1985) 10 Amer J Law Med 397.
84 A particularly poignant series of interviews with survivors was published in M Gwyther and S McConville 'Can Good Come from Evil' (1989) The Observer Magazine, 19 November, p 18.

Such a route, of course, may prove to be difficult: researchers may have taken every precaution to avoid injury and there may therefore be no evidence of negligence. A few years ago, one would have said that an action based on inadequate provision of information would be unlikely to succeed unless the failure of disclosure was of an obviously material nature; now, one would not be so sure. Lord Woolf's move towards increased attention to the expectations of the reasonable patient, expressed in *Pearce*,[85] has yet to work its way through the courts and consent in the context of research would be expected to attract particularly harsh inquiry. Nevertheless, although the odds against a plaintiff in such actions may not be as long as they were, the research subject could still be in a somewhat uncertain situation and it is, no doubt, for this reason that all modern guidelines or directives as to the management of research projects emphasise the importance of compulsory protection of subjects against the possibility of mishap. Thus, the mandatory EC Directive states unequivocally that a clinical trial may be undertaken only if, inter alia, provision has been made for insurance or indemnity to cover the liability of the investigator and sponsor (Article 3(2)(f)) while, before approving a proposal, a REC in the United Kingdom must, currently, be adequately reassured as to the insurance and indemnity arrangements for treatment and compensation in the event of injury, disablement or death of a research participant attributable to participation in the research.[86]

19.55 Quite what constitutes reassurance is, at present, undecided. It may be that the existing NHS indemnity scheme would suffice – but this would not cover research undertaken outside the NHS. The Association of the British Pharmaceutical Industry has recommended to its members that compensation be paid 'when, on the balance of probabilities, the injury was attributable to the administration of a medicinal product under trial or any clinical intervention or procedure provided for by the protocol that would not have occurred but for the inclusion of the patient in the trial'[87] but, again, this would by no means guarantee the research subject adequate compensation should anything go wrong. We suspect that most commentators would favour a form of no-fault compensation but the answer lies in the hands of government.

RANDOM SAMPLE TESTING

19.56 One aspect of research which has received little consideration concerns the use of samples which have been removed for defined, usually therapeutic, reasons. The use of such samples for other investigations subjects the patient to no further discomfort and, while a patient could undoubtedly make directions as to the disposal of any biological specimen he has provided, this would, as things stand, be by virtue of no more than an inchoate right.[88] It could be thought reasonable to assume from silence that the patient was indifferent in

85 *Pearce v United Bristol Healthcare NHS Trust* (1999) 48 BMLR 118 at 124.
86 Guidelines, para 9.15(l).
87 Association of the British Pharmaceutical Industry *Clinical Trial Compensation Guidelines* (1991).
88 For a recent review, see K Mason and G Laurie 'Consent or Property? Dealing with the Body and Its Parts in the Shadow of Bristol and Alder Hey' (2001) 64 MLR 710.

the matter, yet there is an element of invasion of the patient's privacy in 'finding out things' about him without his consent – no matter how much it might be felt that the geographic distribution of genes or any cultural alterations in body chemistry, for example, might provide useful research projects. But a balance has, again, to be struck – and now has to be struck in the shadow of the investigations at Bristol and Alder Hey into the disposal of body parts that we have discussed already in chapter 15.

19.57 The whole matter of the disposal of human tissues is currently sub judice and is likely to be the subject of extensive legislation throughout the United Kingdom. Meantime, we suggest that the justification of such projects rests on the consequences of a positive finding. At one extreme, a search for a particular blood group gene in a specific population could make no possible difference to the subjects and it is difficult to see why it should be impermissible. But, at the other, one would have to think carefully before embarking on, say, a survey of abnormal genetic markers with its consequent possible influences on marriage and having a family. The problem raised as a consequence of a positive finding would, in our opinion, be sufficiently grave to indicate that the project should never have started without explicit consent from the specimen donors.

19.58 But the indications will not always be so clear, while other surveys might be thought at the time to have been of no immediate consequence to the patient but, later, could be significant were the results to be published. Take, as an example, the routine estimation of blood alcohol as a community study. In the event of the samples deriving from accidents, the results could be of particular interest to the police or insurance companies and would normally be made available only by consent of the subjects. Serious consequences might, however, arise if the result of a research analysis was entered in the patient's notes and these were later subject to disclosure.[89] Such an outcome is sufficient to convince us that no research of potentially damaging type would be ethical in the absence of informed consent if there was a chance that the subject and the result could later be associated. And, since the potential is virtually unforeseeable, this effectively means that no non-consensual research using identifiable human material can ever be ethical.

19.59 What, then, of anonymised research of this type? The question, including that of whether *total* anonymisation is ever possible, is discussed in chapter 7. Here, we can leave ourselves wondering if the judgment in *R v Department of Health, ex p Source Informatics Ltd*[90] would apply in the conditions envisaged; it might – there is not all that difference between anonymised prescriptions and anonymised laboratory data – but, were it to do so, we would still wonder if the Court of Appeal so intended.

---

89 The evidence might be used in the United Kingdom (*R v Sang* [1980] AC 402, [1979] 2 All ER 1222, HL) but one could suppose that it could not be used specifically under the Road Traffic Act 1988, which requires that a blood specimen be taken by a medical practitioner with the consent of the subject. But, then, how are we to interpret the Road Traffic Offenders Act 1988, s 15(2), which says that evidence of the proportion of alcohol in the blood shall be taken into account in all cases 'including cases where the specimen was not provided in connection with the alleged offence'?

90 [2001] QB 424, [2000] 1 All ER 786, CA.

20 Research on children, fetuses and embryos

20.1 A child is by no means a miniature version of an adult. Children respond differently to drugs, as they do to a number of other treatments, and it is impossible to say that the effect of a particular therapy on an adult will be mirrored when applied to a child. Medical research on children is, therefore, necessary before a treatment can be approved for paediatric use. As in adults, such research may entail not only therapeutic research on sick children but also essential non-therapeutic research on normal control groups; it is this non-therapeutic research which poses the ethical and legal problems.[1] These should, however, be kept in perspective. Research involving children has lowered the rate of infant mortality considerably; for example, research on vitamin A deficiency in children in developing countries has made it possible to lower mortality rates among those affected by measles.[2] Similarly, research on mother/child transmission of HIV has reduced the incidence of infection in the children of infected mothers – an important matter in the control of the global pandemic.

20.2 Such research involves a variety of procedures, ranging from the completely benign – such as studies of weight and height – to those which are frankly invasive. As an example of the latter, the Institute of Medical Ethics cited a French project which involved lumbar punctures on newborn infants for non-therapeutic reasons.[3] There is also evidence that other dangerous procedures have been used with children being exposed to radiation and unproved vaccines.[4] Such investigations would not be approved by research ethics committees today, but the conclusions of the Alder Hey Inquiry into the

---

1 For general discussion of the issue, see J K Mason *Medico-Legal Aspects of Reproduction and Parenthood* (2nd edn, 1998) p 319 et seq.
2 Working Group on Women and Child Health, F Dabis, J Orne-Gliemann, F Perez et al 'Improving Child Health: the Role of Research' (2002) 324 BMJ 1444.
3 See R H Nicholson (ed) *Medical Research with Children: Ethics, Law and Practice* (1990) p 19.
4 The *Final Report of the Advisory Committee on Human Radiation Experiments* (Washington, 2000) contains a valuable account of the history of experimentation on children, as well as extensive information on radiation experiments (http://tis.eh.doe.gov/ohre/roadmap/achre/report.html).

post-mortem retention of children's organs remind us of the fact that research might still be conducted with scant regard to the rights and sensitivities of others.[5]

NON-THERAPEUTIC RESEARCH ON CHILDREN

20.3 The essential difficulty with non-therapeutic research on children lies, again, in the question of consent. An adult may be able to give an informed, and therefore valid, consent to participation in research – but can the same be said of a child? The Declaration of Helsinki specifically mentions the 'legally incompetent' participant in research, stating that the consent of the guardian should be procured;[6] this approach was also adopted in the guidelines on experimentation issued by the British Paediatric Association,[7] the Medical Research Council,[8] the Royal College of Physicians[9] and, in the United States, by the National Institutes of Health.[10] All these influential bodies accept that non-therapeutic research on children is justified in that it is intended to benefit other children – although it should not be carried out if it could be done equally well using adults. In the view of the Royal College of Physicians, parental consent is required in respect of children under 16 years old and also in the case of 'some older children'.

20.4 Parental consent will not be sufficient if proposed non-therapeutic research involves more than a minimal risk to the child – a condition which, inevitably, raises the issue of what risks are minimal. Federal Regulations in the United States hold that the risk is minimal where 'the probability and magnitude of harm or discomfort anticipated in the research are not greater in and of themselves than those ordinarily encountered in daily life or during the performance of routine physical or psychological examinations or tests.'[11] The Institute of Medical Ethics, which studied the question in depth,[12] defined a minimal risk as one which carried a risk of death lower than 1:1,000,000, a risk of major complications less than 1:100,000 and a risk of minor complications of less than 1:1,000. The American approach uses language; this approach uses figures. Both convey the same general message: where there is a risk that makes one stop and think, it has ceased to be minimal. In

---

5   H Bauchner and R Vinci 'What Have We Learnt from the Alder Hey Affair?' (2001) 322 BMJ 309.
6   World Medical Association *Ethical Principles for Medical Research Involving Human Subjects* (Revised, 2000), para 25. The Declaration is reproduced in Appendix E.
7   British Paediatric Association *Guidelines for the Ethical Conduct of Medical Research Involving Children* (1992).
8   Medical Research Council *The Ethical Conduct of Research on Children* (1991).
9   Report of the Royal College of Physicians of London *Research Involving Patients* (1990) p 19.
10 National Institutes of Health *Policy and Guidelines on the Inclusion of Children as Participants in Research Involving Human Subjects* (1998).
11 45 CFR Sec 46 (102.i) (1997).
12 Institute of Medical Ethics 'Medical Research with Children: Ethics, Law and Practice' (1986) Bull no 14, p 8. For discussion of the recommendations, see R J Robinson 'Ethics Committees and Research on Children' (1987) 294 BMJ 1243. See also M A Grodin, L H Glantz and A M Dellinger 'Children as Research Subjects: Science, Ethics and Law' (1996) 21 J Hlth Politics Policy Law 159.

addition, the Institute thought that the consent of the child should be obtained after the age of seven years. This concern was shared by the Royal College of Physicians, which felt that a child who is capable of giving a consent should also be allowed to refuse to participate in a research procedure – even if parental consent has been obtained. The College does not rule out proceeding with research involving a child who objects but is too young to give consent but it suggests that, in such circumstances, investigators should reconsider whether it is appropriate to go ahead.

20.5 Obtaining parental consent is clearly important, but the fact that it has been given does not, of itself, justify carrying out research on children. Our first concern here must be with the welfare of the child, and it need hardly be said that parental consent to something which is obviously to the detriment of the child is unacceptable. Parents do not have an absolute, unfettered right to regulate their children's lives; it is implicit in the modern concept of parenthood that the aim of such parental powers as there are is to protect and enhance the status of the child.[13] It follows that the researcher cannot simply say: 'The parents have consented and this means that I can go ahead'; parental consent may justify the involvement of children in non-therapeutic research but it will do so only because it points to the acceptability of the research in terms of some interest of the child.

20.6 One way of assessing parental consent is to see it as a substitute for the child's own judgment which cannot, as yet, be expressed. Under this theory, parental consent does no more than voice what the child would be expected to state, had he the ability to do so. Acceptance of this approach salves any qualms the researcher might have – in effect, the child consents to what is done, the only complication being that this cannot be expressed personally. Critics of theories of proxy consent point out that this involves a blatant fiction. It would be more honest, they argue, to accept that this constitutes non-consensual research and to admit the need to justify it on other grounds. The difficulty cannot be avoided by attempting to justify the child's involvement in terms of his 'future identification' with the decision made on his behalf.[14] It is difficult to see any distinction between 'identification' and 'consent' and, whatever terms one uses to imply future assent, there is no certainty that the child will, in fact, subsequently endorse what his parents have decided.

20.7 The matter may, however, be approached from an entirely different perspective – one which focuses not on any imagined consent of the child but on what is in that child's best interests. This test would allow the parents to involve the child in that which is in – or, alternatively, that which is not manifestly against – the child's best interests. The first of these would require that the non-therapeutic research secures some benefit for the child – a difficult, though not impossible, case to make. A child is a member of a class within the community – the class of children – and the individual can be said to be a

---

13   See B M Dickens 'The Modern Function and Limits of Parental Rights' (1981) 97 LQR 462; also A McCall Smith 'Is There Anything left of Parental Rights' in E Sutherland and A McCall Smith (eds) *Family Rights* (1991) ch 1.
14   R B Redmon 'How Children Can Be Respected as Ends Yet Still Be Used as Subjects in Non-therapeutic Research' (1986) 12 J Med Ethics 77.

potential beneficiary if research will benefit the class as a whole. It is also possible to extrapolate the reasoning used to justify organ donation (see chapter 14) and to argue that participation in research related to a disease from which, for example, a sibling is suffering will benefit the normal child – it being in his interests that his sibling should recover.

20.8 An allied benefit-based theory focuses on the altruistic nature of participation in non-therapeutic research.[15] Here, the issue is, at base, whether or not parents have the right to involve their children in projects by way of imposed unselfishness. Such co-operation is undoubtedly good for the subject, but this would apply only if the child were sufficiently mature to understand the philanthropic nature of what he was doing. An older child may later derive satisfaction from the fact that he helped others when younger, but the same objection applies here as to proxy consent – how can we be sure that this is what he would feel?

20.9 The alternative interpretation of the best interests test, which allows for measures which are not to the actual detriment of the child – or not against its interests – clearly licenses the child's involvement in non-therapeutic research so long as the risks involved are negligible.[16] This assessment gives a wider discretion to the parent, who may choose to interpret his duty to society as including a duty to engage his children in pro-social activities. Such parents act within their rights, and cannot be regarded as abusing their position until such time as the child suffers actual harm or runs an appreciable risk of harm.[17]

20.10 Even if this were not accepted, and the child's interest in non-participation were to be seen as being more significant than any parental social duty, the non-interventionists could still hold that this is an area of the family's activities in which the law has no right to interfere. State intervention may be justified if a child's life is threatened through neglect or through a parental decision which is going to lead to great danger – but these are not the stakes involved in comparatively harmless research. The protagonist of individual self-determination is unlikely to approve of a justification based on relative values but the inevitable consequence of the extreme individualistic position would be the suspension of all non-therapeutic medical research on children – which would benefit nobody, least of all the children themselves.

20.11 Discussion thus far has proceeded on the assumption that the child in question is not of an age to give any meaningful consent. Even so, many children of relatively tender age will be able to understand the issues involved and the question then arises as to the weight to be given to any agreement they might give. The age at which a child can appreciate the implications of

---

15 See A McCall Smith 'Research and Experimentation Involving Children' in J K Mason (ed) *Paediatric Forensic Medicine and Pathology* (1989) p 469.
16 For further discussion, see the wide-ranging recent analysis by A Plomer 'Participation of Children in Clinical Trials: UK, European and International Perspectives on Consent' (2000) 5 Med L Internat 1.
17 The test of acceptability then becomes one of the 'reasonable parent': see J K Mason *Medico-legal Aspects of Reproduction and Parenthood* (2nd edn, 1998) p 324 et seq.

what he is doing will obviously vary, but some generalisations may be made.[18] Children under the age of seven are usually considered to be incapable of that degree of morally sophisticated thought required to make consistent altruistic decisions but, above that age, a child may be perfectly able to understand that he is helping doctors to cure others by taking part in the research programme. A child who was not able to grasp the general idea of medical research by the age of 15 would probably be an exception today. This view is supported by a study which was designed to assess the ability of groups of nine- and 14-year-olds to make decisions relating to medical treatment. The 14-year-olds were shown to have the same general level of capacity to make this sort of decision as did adults and a surprising degree of competence was shown in the nine-year-old group.[19]

20.12 The ethical issues might be clarified to an extent if the law could give a clear answer to this question. Unfortunately, the law itself is uncertain in this area and this has not eased the difficulties of those involved in paediatric research. In 1962 the Medical Research Council stated that:

> in the strict view of the law, parents and guardians of minors cannot give consent on their behalf to any procedures which are of no particular benefit to them and which may carry some risk of harm.[20]

20.13 This was followed by a Department of Health circular which confirmed that interpretation in a negative way:

> Health authorities are advised that they ought not to infer [from a Royal College of Physicians' recommendation that children can be used in certain forms of research provided the consent of the guardian has been obtained] that the fact that consent has been given by the parent or guardian and that the risk involved is considered negligible will be sufficient to bring such clinical research investigation within the law as it stands.[21]

20.14 The advice of the Department of Health was roundly attacked by doctors. Lawyers were also critical of this strict view of the law, pointing out the paucity of authority on the point.[22] In these conditions – almost amounting to a legal vacuum – the proper way of approaching the issue is to look at general legal principles governing the parent/child relationship and to infer from these what a court might decide if the matter were to come before it.

---

18 See J Berryman 'Discussing the Ethics of Research on Children' in J van Eys (ed) *Research on Children* (1978) p 85. See discussion by P Alderson and J Montgomery *Health Care Choices: Making Decisions with Children* (1996); M Paul 'Informed Consent in Medical Research. Children from the Age of 5 should be Presumed Competent' (1997) 314 BMJ 1480.
19 L A Weithorn and S B Campbell 'The Competency of Children and Adolescents to make Informed Treatment Decisions' (1982) 53 Child Develop 285. For discussion, see R H Nicholson (ed) *Medical Research with Children* p 146.
20 Report of the Medical Research Council for 1962-3 (Cmnd 2382) pp 21–25.
21 Supervision of the Ethics of Clinical Research Investigations and Fetal Research HSC (5) 153.
22 See eg discussion by G Dworkin 'Law and Medical Experimentation: Of Embryos, Children and Others with Limited legal Capacity' (1987) 13 Monash Univ LR 189.

20.15 The judgment of the House of Lords in *Gillick v West Norfolk and Wisbech Area Health Authority*[23] confirmed the view that the consent of a minor to medical treatment may be adequate even without parental ratification provided that the child has sufficient understanding and intelligence to appreciate what is involved. 'Parental rights', said Lord Scarman, 'exist only so long as they are needed for the protection of the person and property of the child'. It is not certain, however, whether the *Gillick* principle, which is concerned with consent to treatment, would be applied to cases of non-therapeutic experimentation. Much would, of course, depend on the severity of the procedure – this being one of the factors to be balanced in the assessment of '*Gillick*-competence'. As to statute, it is clear that the Family Law Reform Act 1969, s 8 refers only to diagnosis and treatment[24] – the statutory age of 16 years has, therefore, no relevance as to consent to experimentation. To infer from this that consent to non-therapeutic investigations is impossible below the age of majority would be, again, to accept a total embargo on paediatric research. It is not unreasonable to extrapolate Lord Donaldson's interpretation of the law in *Re R*[25] and to infer that anyone who is capable of doing so may give consent but that demurral by the minor would be a very important consideration in judging whether to carry out the research. Moreover, this would be even more significant than it would be in relation to treatment – to such an extent that it would be improbable in the extreme that a responsible doctor would ignore the minor's negative attitude. The problem then becomes that of deciding whether there is any age below which a person is deemed incapable of consent and, while there is no law on the point, it would be unwise, in our opinion, for a researcher to accept the unendorsed consent of a child under the age of 16; indeed, the circumstances in which such a consent would be acceptable would be exceptional. Hazardous experimentation authorised by the consent of a minor alone might, in fact, be unlawful and actually *restrained* by statute.[26]

20.16 To say that a procedure is legal is not to say that it is necessarily morally acceptable; furthermore, there is no reason to assume that the court, if asked, would approve an action which was unethical. The position is, therefore, still delicately balanced. Anticipating a judicial reaction is a matter for ethical committees who may assume that the court would act as a wise parent would act – giving first consideration to the child but being, at the same time, hospitable to good research. Thus, the essential measure is the 'risk-benefit ratio' of the investigation – but, within this, the 'risk' factor must, without doubt, retain primary control. We also suggest that, notwithstanding what the true legal position may be, it would be, in practice, improper to proceed with an experiment involving a child against the wishes of its parents. The only exception might be when that refusal was clearly unreasonable and was jeopardising an otherwise essential trial to which a

23 [1986] AC 112, [1985] 3 All ER 402, HL.
24 It is problematic as to whether this limitation applies in Scotland in so far as the Age of Legal Capacity (Scotland) Act 1991, s 2(4) refers to consent by the understanding minor to 'any surgical, medical or dental *procedure* or treatment' (our emphasis).
25 *Re R (a minor) (wardship: medical treatment)* [1992] Fam 11, (1991) 7 BMLR 147.
26 Lord Donaldson distinguished between medical treatment and a severely damaging operation which gave no benefit to the subject: *Re W (a minor) (medical treatment)* [1992] 4 All ER 627 at 635, 639, (1992) 9 BMLR 22 at 31, 35.

child who was capable of understanding – the 'mature minor' of *Gillick* – had already consented. Such conditions must be extremely rare; in the event of their materialising, a decision to go ahead should be taken only after very careful consideration – and, probably, not even then.

20.17 It must not be thought that an ethical assessment of a project is always clear cut. A most apposite, albeit now historic, example was an experiment in preventive medicine which entailed the deliberate infection with the virus of hepatitis of children in a home for the subnormal. Although the chances of the children being infected naturally within six months of admission were as high as 60%, the project was castigated by some writers.[27] Others disagreed with such an analysis – one of Britain's most respected paediatricians at the time described the experiment as: 'a small, carefully controlled trial for which the director also deserves a great deal of credit for his scrupulous care in securing the truly informed consent of the children's parents.'[28] The legal implications of using children as research subjects have been aired more recently in the United States in *Grimes v Kennedy Krieger Inst Inc*,[29] a decision of the Maryland Court of Appeals. The facts of this case make disturbing reading. Families with children were encouraged to move into houses in which only partial lead-pollution controls had been implemented. The level of lead contamination in the blood of the children living in such houses was then measured against levels in a control group living in less polluted conditions. The court held that it would not be left to the researchers to determine what is an acceptable risk to the health of children, and that the consent of parents would not be sufficient where there was a real risk of harming the health of children.[30]

THERAPEUTIC RESEARCH ON CHILDREN

20.18 And that is an appropriate comment by which to lead us to a brief discussion of therapeutic research on children which, it might be thought, raises no more issues than does non-therapeutic research as we have discussed above.

20.19 A moment's thought, however, shows us that this is not true. To begin with, we cannot apply a substituted judgment test of any sort. We can make a reasonable assumption that a child would want to be cured of a disease or disability if that were possible. What we cannot know is *how* he or she would want to be cured – and we certainly cannot know if he or she would want to take a chance on a lottery choice of treatments.

20.20 As in the case of non-therapeutic research, we can appeal to the doctrine of autonomy when the child is old enough to be capable of making a decision

27 See, for a good review at the time, L Golman 'The Willowbrook Debate' (1973) 9 World Med (1)(79).
28 A W Franklin 'Research Investigation on Children' (1973) 1 BMJ 402 at 405.
29 782 A2d 807 (2001).
30 For discussion, see G Johnson, 'Recent Development: *Grimes v. Kennedy Krieger Inst Inc*' (2001) 9 U Balt J Environ Law 72. And for a spirited defence: L F Ross 'In Defense of the Hopkins Lead Abatement Studies' (2002) 30 J Law Med Ethics 50.

– although the assessment of capacity would surely have to be exceptionally rigorous in the conditions envisaged – but we have no such fall-back position in the case of the neonate or young child. The onus of consent falls squarely on the parents and we must ask if it is ever possible – or ever fair – to expect a fully informed consent as to therapeutic research from parents who are confronted by a sick, possibly newborn, child. The issue thus presents starkly as one of the child's welfare or 'best interests' and, in these special circumstances, responsibility for the decision is very largely that of the neonatologist or paediatrician.

20.21 This does still not resolve the dilemma. By definition, the doctor does not know which of the treatments on offer is the 'best' for the child – the research programme would be fundamentally unethical if he did; it follows that there is a 50 % chance of the decision *not* being in the child's best interests whichever choice is made – indeed, there is a 50 % chance of it failing a 'no detriment' test. Following this one step further, it becomes easy to conclude that therapeutic research on children can *never* be justified – or, at best, can be justified only in exceptional circumstances. Yet we all know that it must be done or paediatrics will become a static subject. Allmark et al have argued that every infant has a 'global' interest in medical progress and it is this which tips the scales in favour of ethical justification for participation in therapeutic research on children.[31] Admittedly, this carries the stamp of the advocate's last card – and it is scarcely a high trump card; nevertheless, it may well provide the escape from what is, essentially, a utilitarian cul-de-sac.

20.22 These problems, taken together, are sufficient to explain why paediatricians may be loath to seek parental consent to their children being involved in a dedicated programme of therapeutic research.[32] Failure to do so, however, involves following a dangerous road – consent is now accepted as providing both the key and the lock to medical interventions of any sort. A recent example of the difficulties in defining the ethical limits of research in children has been provided by the long-running investigation into the randomised controlled trial of the treatment of premature infants with breathing difficulties conducted in North Staffordshire in the past decade.[33] Eighteen parents of babies involved in the study complained to the General Medical Council that they had not been informed of the experimental nature of the treatment[34] and the matter is still sub judice. As a result, an official inquiry was established which was severely critical of the study from many aspects.[35] An interesting feature of this incident is the attention it draws not only to the ethical conduct of a research project – as, for example, in obtaining informed

31 P Allmark, S Mason, A B Gill and C Megone 'Is It in a Neonate's Best Interest to Enter a Randomised Controlled Trial?' (2001) 27 J Med Ethics 110.
32 Though it is possible that this is an area in which a Zelen protocol (see para 19.21 above) might be acceptable. For explanation, see D J Torgerson and M Roland 'What is Zelen's Design?' (1998) 316 BMJ 606.
33 M P Samuels, J Raine, T Wright et al 'Continuous Negative Extrathoracic Pressure in Neonatal Respiratory Failure' (1996) 98 Pediatrics 1154.
34 J Jones 'Doctors Suspended in Child Health Inquiry' (2000) 320 BMJ.
35 NHS Executive *Report of a Review of the Research Framework in North Staffordshire Hospital NHS Trust* (R Griffiths, chair) (2000) (www.doh.gov.uk/wmro/northstaffs.htm, updated 08/05/00).

consent – but also to the ethical component lodged in the *design* of a research project – is the design such that it will provide valid results? Clearly, this will often be controversial[36] and a main, and widely agreed, recommendation of the Griffith Report was to the effect that a new governance framework should be elaborated to cover research undertaken in the NHS. It remains to be seen whether this will be followed up at Government level.

FETAL EXPERIMENTATION

20.23 Several of the legal and moral attitudes to fetal life have already been discussed. The possibilities of fetal research and experiment, which are repugnant to many, extend the area of debate and merit further discussion. Research on the fetus is of considerable importance: just as children are, medically, more than little adults so, or rather more so, are fetuses not just immature children; the environment in which they exist is wholly different and, as has already been discussed, it is within that environment that something in the region of half the morbidity and mortality of infancy is fashioned.[37] Major areas of disease will never be properly understood in the absence of fetal research. Nor will the outstanding dilemma of drug therapy during pregnancy be fully resolved.

Sources of fetal material and the problems of consent

20.24 Other than those which are born alive prematurely and with which we are not currently concerned, fetuses become available either through spontaneous miscarriage or as a result of therapeutic abortion. It is axiomatic that any necessary consent to research can only be given by the mother and both her attitude and that of her physicians may be different in the two cases.

20.25 The position seems clear in the case of miscarriage. The mother is distressed and, normally, wants everything possible done for her offspring. It seems unlikely in the circumstances that a research project will be contemplated but, were it so, the informed consent of the mother would be required. The therapeutic abortion situation is rather different. In the majority of cases, the mother will have requested termination and it could be held that, in so doing, she has effectively abandoned her fetus. The Peel Committee made the following recommendation:

> There is no legal requirement to obtain the patient's consent for research but, equally, there is no statutory right to ignore the parent's wishes – the parent must be offered the opportunity to declare any special directions about the fetus.[38]

---

36 Compare, for example, E Hey and I Chalmers 'Investigating Allegations of Research Misconduct: the Vital Need for Due Process' (2000) 321 BMJ 752 with Anonymous 'North Staffs – a Progress (?) Report' (2001) Bull Med Ethics, no 172, p 3. The conclusions are at startling variance.

37 The Peel Committee, reporting in 1972, listed 53 ways in which fetal research could be valuable, a catalogue which will have increased in the interim: *Report of the Committee on the Use of Fetuses and Fetal Material for Research* (1972).

38 At para 42.

20.26 This recommendation would now be considered inadequate. The very strict rules as to consent to research on the abandoned embryo should, in theory, be extrapolated to the abandoned fetus.[39] Moreover, the Peel Report has been overtaken by that of the Polkinghorne Committee[40] which detected no material distinction between the results of therapeutic or spontaneous miscarriage.[41] It was firmly recommended that positive consent be obtained from the mother before fetal tissue is used for research or treatment in either circumstance[42] – for it was thought to be too harsh a judgment to infer that she has no special relationship with her fetus that has been aborted under the terms of the Abortion Act 1967;[43] the mother was entitled, at least, to counselling on the point. The Committee also recommended that her consent should include the relinquishing of any property rights – a recommendation which is discussed in greater detail below.[44] Interestingly, the Committee rejected the notion of any control by the father over the disposal of his child – this being on the grounds that paternal consent was not required for an abortion and that his relationship to the fetus is less intimate than is that of the mother.[45] We have already referred to the general denial of paternal interests in the fetus which we see as unreasonable;[46] this seems to be a further questionable extension of the principle of the woman's right to self-determination.

20.27 The recommendations of the Polkinghorne Committee have now been re-examined in the wake of the Bristol and Alder Hey reports into organ retention (see chapter 15). At the time of writing, the Government has issued a consultation report which examines all aspects of the use of human tissue.[47] This report endorses the Polkinghorne principles but suggests that, in certain areas, the climate of opinion has altered sufficiently to merit changes in approach. In relation to maternal consent, for example, a possible revised system is set out which would give the woman the right to information about anonymisation and about the circumstances in which tissue might be used in future for purposes other than those originally explained to her. The report also considers a role for the father and sets out a possible approach which would give the father a role in consenting to research on fetal materials provided that the woman is prepared to identify him for the purposes of obtaining his views. In those circumstances, any objection which he raised to the proposed research would be respected. It is important to note that in a case where the proposed research will be conducted on identifiable tissue, and where this could have personal implications for both the man and the woman, then the proposal would require the consent of both.

39 Human Fertilisation and Embryology Act 1990, Sch 3.
40 *Review of the Guidance on the Research Use of Fetuses and Fetal Material* (Cmnd 762).
41 At para 2.9.
42 At para 3.10.
43 At para 2.8.
44 See para 20.37.
45 At para 6.7. For this and several other criticisms of the recommendations, see J Keown 'The Polkinghorne Report on Fetal Research: Nice Recommendations, Shame about the Reasoning' (1993) 19 J Med Ethics 114.
46 See para 5.72 above.
47 Department of Health and Welsh Assembly Government, *Human Bodies, Human Choices: The Law on Human Organs and Human Tissue in England and Wales* (2002).

20.28 The Polkinghorne Committee was established mainly in response to concerns over fetal brain implants (which we discuss as a separate issue above[48]), and, as a consequence, one of its main concerns was that the research worker seeking consent should be wholly independent of the caring gynaecologist – every moral and public policy principle dictates that it be made absolutely clear that abortions are not being performed in order to provide research or therapeutic material; the timing of a therapeutic abortion should be subject only to considerations of care for the pregnant woman.

The status of the fetus

20.29 The Polkinghorne Committee was fully alert to the fact that conditions for fetal research are not uniform and, in particular, that the fetal subject may be alive or dead – or it may be killed during the process of abortion. The living human fetus should be accorded a profound respect – a conclusion which is based upon its potential for development into a fully formed human being.[49] In so saying, the Committee clearly differentiated the dead fetus but still thought that this commanded respect. Research on the living fetus should be considered in a way broadly similar to that pertaining to children and adults and it was, therefore, recommended that it should not be undertaken if the risk to the fetus was more than minimal; research or experimentation carrying a greater risk should be limited to that which was of direct benefit to the subject. Respect for the dead fetus was recognised by the belief that research in that area should also be considered by ethics committees.[50]

20.30 Somewhat surprisingly, the Committee did not seek that the law be used to impose their restrictions. Rather, fetal research was to be overseen by local ethical research committees[51] and here, as we discuss above,[52] conditions are not uniform. Definitions of minimal or of direct benefit are likely to differ – as, indeed, are doctors' interpretations of research and experimentation and of the need for reference to an ethics committee. The general ethical and legal principles involved still merit discussion.

20.31 Some useful research is non-invasive and may be coupled with patient care but even then there is no simple answer. Thus, the experimental use of X-rays, at least in the first trimester, would be unethical; ultrasonic investigations seem, by contrast, to be wholly safe – but we cannot yet know, for example, whether fetal ultrasonic investigations will affect the subject at retiring age. Our more immediate concern is with invasive investigations and these, once again, focus attention on the uncertainties surrounding the legal status of the unborn child (see chapter 5).

20.32 It is now clear that 'wrongful death' in utero of the fetus that is incapable of being born alive gives rise to no action in the United Kingdom; neither the

48 See paras 14.67–14.69 above.
49 At para 2.4.
50 At para 7.3.
51 At para 2.3.
52 See para 19.15.

dead non-viable fetus nor the stillbirth has any right of action of itself and the only redress available is to the parents on the grounds of distress, inconvenience and the like[53] – but this is not to deny the trend towards a moral and legal acceptance of fetal rights which are comparable to those of a self-existent child.[54] If the fetus were born deformed, it would clearly have right of action against a research worker whose defence, assuming causation to have been proved, would rest on the standard of reasonable care having been observed. The matter of consent then becomes paramount and must be judged in the same light as has been discussed in relation to children.

20.33 Assuming that the mother has a right of proxy consent to research procedures, the risk/benefit test would have to be very stringently applied, because, whereas the child has at least minimal understanding, the fetus can certainly have none. A negligence action based on a lack of informed consent would be more likely to succeed in these conditions than in many others; if, by contrast, parental consent is impossible, the damaged infant has a cause of action for trespass which will be virtually indefensible other than on issues of causation. In practice, the nature of any invasive experiment of this type is strictly limited on clinical grounds.

20.34 But what if the fetus should die? The fetus not being a legal person, there is no offence of feticide as such; but, should the fetus die prior to or during a resultant miscarriage, an offence may lie under the Offences Against the Person Act 1861, s 58 or under the Infant Life (Preservation) Act 1929, s 1 if the subject were capable of being born alive. Both these sections, however, include a requirement of intent, in the former to procure a miscarriage and in the second to destroy life. To prove an offence, it would then be necessary to show that the action amounted to constructive intent – that is, something was done when it was known that fetal death was a very high probability – and this seems a very doubtful proposition. It is, however, quite clear that intentional or reckless intra-uterine injury which results in neonatal death can attract a charge of manslaughter or of culpable homicide;[55] it is at least likely that disregard of the recommendations of the Polkinghorne Committee would give rise to an inference of recklessness. We do, however, see such eventualities as being extremely rare.

The pre-viable fetus

20.35 Perhaps it is the pre-viable fetus which attracts most emotion in the general issue of fetal research. Pre-viability implies that the fetus as a whole is incapable of a separate existence but that, nevertheless, there are signs of

---

53 See eg *Bagley v North Herts Health Authority* [1986] NLJ Rep 1014; *Grieve v Salford Health Authority* (1991) 2 Med LR 295. Actions for wrongful death of the fetus have, however, succeeded in the United States where some 37 States recognise an action for the death of a viable fetus and an additional six allow such an action in the case of a non-viable fetus. See *Santana v Zilog Inc* 95 F 3d 780 (1996).

54 The constitutional protection of the fetus may be less extensive than that provided by private law – particularly when the issue is that of abortion: M L McConnell 'Sui Generis: The Legal Nature of the Foetus in Canada' (1991) 70 Can BR 548.

55 *Kwok Chak Ming v R* [1963] HKLR 349; *McCluskey v HM Advocate* 1989 SLT 175; *A-G's Reference (No 3 of 1994)* [1996] QB 581, [1996] 2 All ER 10.

life in some organs. There can be no doubt that this is the fetal state which offers the greatest research potential; it is also true that the time available for such research is limited and so, therefore, is the opportunity for abuse. But, again, one must ask – is this an ensouled human being with the privacy rights of a human being? And, moreover, do we know that it has no feeling and is incapable of pain and suffering?[56] The Polkinghorne Committee was unable to discern any relevant ethical distinction between the pre-viable and the viable fetus – thereby diverging from the Peel Report. None the less, the status of the pre-viable fetus in relation to the criminal law needs consideration and the door is not quite closed on the moral concerns of the researcher.

20.36 We suggest that the criminal law is inadequate in this area. To destroy a fetus outside the terms of the Abortion Act is to destroy life. But, in doing so, what offence is being committed? No charge of murder or manslaughter can be raised in respect of a fetus absent its survival after birth;[57] the discussion may, therefore, seem sterile in present conditions. It is doubtful whether the Abortion Act 1967 would be an adequate safeguard in the event of an extension of techniques being coupled with a deterioration in professional standards; it might then be necessary to invent an offence of feticide. The moral dilemma is clear from the questions posed above and, equally, turns on the definition of 'life'. We suggest that the moral problem may be resolved by considering, first, whether or not a placenta is present and whether there is or is not a competent fetal-maternal connection. If there is, the fetus is, subject to normality, alive and destructive research or experimentation would be morally unacceptable; they should be disallowed on these grounds alone. If, however, the pre-viable fetus is separated from its mother, it is no longer capable of an existence; it is, therefore, possible to argue that its state is one of somatic death. Experiments or research conducted on the body are, by this reasoning, conducted during the interval between somatic and ultimate cellular death which has been described in chapter 13. Accordingly, we suggest that the processes involve neither moral nor legal culpability.

The dead fetus and fetal materials

20.37 Much useful research can be done on fetuses which are clearly dead or are incomplete; the major debate as to the morality of such research depends on how the fetus came to be dead – any objection on principle to the use of tissue from dead fetuses is almost certainly grounded on an overall objection to abortion.[58] Disposal of the dead fetus and fetal materials[59] must, ultimately,

---

56 The problem of fetal experience of pain seems unresolved and one wonders if it is capable of resolution: Z Kmietowicz 'Antiabortionists Hijack Fetal Pain Argument' (1996) 313 BMJ 188; I Murray 'Guidelines Will Ensure Foetuses Feel no Pain' *The Times*, 25 October 1997, p 2. The majority opinion seems to be that fetuses of less than 24 weeks' gestation feel no pain.
57 Para 20.34 above.
58 For discussion of attitudes and practices in relation to fetal tissue research in various countries, see 'Fetal Tissue Research around the World' (1992) 304 BMJ 591.
59 Ie, those parts of the products of conception which are discarded by both the mother and the fetus – the placenta and its membranes and the umbilical cord. The Polkinghorne Committee preferred the term 'other contents of the uterus'.

be subject to the mother's discretion but the extent of her authority is currently a matter of legal debate. Despite the strong reservations expressed by the Polkinghorne Committee, it is possible that property rights in respect of such tissues can arise, but recent case law indicates that such rights would vest in the researchers rather than the mother. We discuss this further in chapter 15. The Polkinghorne Committee condemned out of hand the sale of fetal tissues and materials for commercial purposes; this sentiment certainly persists in Article 21 of the European Convention on Human Rights and Biomedicine, which prohibits commerce in 'the human body and its parts, as such'.[60]

20.38 The rules concerning certification and disposal of stillbirths and of babies who die after birth do not apply to the fetus which is born dead at or before twenty four weeks' gestation.[61] Under Department of Health guidelines, such fetuses are normally incinerated unless any contrary wishes are expressed by parents. Comparable guidelines have also been issued by the Royal College of Nursing, which has expressed concerns as to the practical difficulties involved in providing for their sensitive disposal which is envisaged in official recommendations.[62] Hospital incineration is, after all, a functional process which is not easily modified.

EMBRYONIC AND EMBRYONIC STEM CELL RESEARCH

20.39 There are two quite distinct forms of research involving human embryos. The moral debate which preceded the passage of the Human Fertilisation and Embryology Act 1990 was concerned with research on the embryo with a view to understanding embryo development, reproductive issues, and genetic disease. In the final years of the twentieth century this form of research was somewhat eclipsed by strong enthusiasm for research into the therapeutic use of stem cells taken from embryos. In this form of research, the embryo is a potential source of material for use on others; it is not the embryo itself which is the object of interest. In this section we shall consider the two forms of research separately, because of this important moral and scientific distinction. At the same time, there are, of course, moral issues which are common to both of these fields of research.

Embryonic research

20.40 Research into human infertility and an understanding of embryonic development and implantation are inseparable. Embryonic research is also essential to the study and conquest of genetic disease. Systematic study in both these fields depends upon a supply of human embryos, for there always comes a time when animal models are inadequate for human research

60 See also, *Human Bodies, Human Choices*, para 20.27 above, which raises the possibility of legislation specifically excluding property rights in the body of a fetus or fetal tissue.
61 Although cremation authorities have discretion to permit the cremation of pre-viable fetuses.
62 Royal College of Nursing *Sensitive Disposal of All Fetal Remains – Guidance for Nurses and Midwives* (2001).

purposes. Essentially, there are two adoptable attitudes: either one can be totally opposed to research and experimentation on what are considered to be living human beings who cannot refuse consent to manipulation, or one can hold that the benefits to mankind are likely to be so great that the opportunity for study must be grasped if it is presented. Given that the case for human research is agreed – and we believe that it must be – the problem then arises as to how the necessary material is to be obtained within an acceptable moral framework. There are, again, two possibilities which are by no means mutually exclusive – either one can use the inevitable surplus of embryos that are produced for infertility treatments, or one can go one stage further and create embryos in vitro for the explicit purpose of using them for research. It is first necessary to look at the general proposition.

20.41 Arguments against a policy which prohibits embryo research rely, ultimately, on the view that, although the embryo may have human properties, it is not a human being invested with the same moral rights to respect as are due to other living members of the human community.[63] This approach has a familiar ring to it; indeed, it introduces the same concepts of personhood that have been so much a part of the abortion debate. There is, however, a crucial distinction to be made between lethal embryo research and abortion. The life of the aborted fetus is extinguished because its interests are outweighed by a more powerful and tangible set of interests – namely, those of the pregnant woman. The embryo subjected to experimentation, by contrast, dies because of the far less obvious interests of society in the pursuit of medical knowledge. The justification of feticide in abortion does not necessarily license the taking of in vitro embryonic life – and the legislative concern for the latter in the face of a liberal abortion policy may not be as unreasonable as is sometimes argued.[64]

20.42 Yet, if we consider, first, the surplus embryo, we have to ask: 'what is the alternative to embryocide?' The techniques in IVF and the welfare of the patient demand that more embryos are created than are strictly necessary; to say that all must be implanted[65] is to fly in the face of the reality that there are insufficient wombs available for the purpose. The alternatives then lie between embryocide and reduction of multiple pregnancy – of which the former is clearly the less objectionable. We have discussed elsewhere[66] the ethics of obtaining good from a morally poor or doubtful *fait accompli*. It is only the innate public fear of the 'scientist'[67] which stands against the acceptance of such a principle – one which we believe to be valid, perhaps particularly so in respect of the undifferentiated embryo.

---

63 For a statement of this position, see J Harris 'Embryos and Hedgehogs: On the Moral Status of the Embryo' in A Dyson and J Harris (eds) *Experiments on Embryos* (1990) p 65. The issue of the status of the embryo, and in particular the ethical and religious implications of using the embryo for research, are fully and clearly canvassed in the report of the US National Bioethics Advisory Commission *Ethical Issues in Human Stem Cell Research* (1999).
64 See eg Mason p 471, at para 20.9.
65 As seems to be the case in the Infertility (Medical Procedures) Act 1984 (Victoria), s 6(5). But the section can be read as being directed only at the creation of embryos for non-therapeutic research purposes, which is certainly unlawful in Victoria.
66 See chapter 19.
67 M Warnock *A Question of Life* (1985) p xiii.

20.43 But this can only hold so long as the basic tenet of the doctrine of double effect – that the good result must not be achieved by means of the ill-effect – is observed and it is this that distinguishes research on the surplus embryo from that undertaken on the embryo that has been created for the purpose; it follows that the latter needs further justification. The proponents of unrestricted research would reply that it is acceptable not only because the embryo fails to satisfy the requirements of personhood which the fetus, similarly, fails to satisfy but also because, at least in its earlier stages,[68] its cells are pluripotential. In other words, until the development of the primitive streak, the conceptus is not a single, identifiable individual; any of its cells can develop along a number of lines, into a placenta, a hydatidiform mole, a human being or, indeed, several human beings. The early embryo thus lacks the essential qualities which go to make the human individual unique and worthy of moral respect.

20.44 The counter-assertion is, of course, that the embryo is the first stage of the human being that is born at the end of pregnancy – and that this holds from the moment of syngamy. It has been pointed out that the embryo stage is an essential part of life and that it makes no sense to argue that a person's life begins only with the appearance of the primitive streak on about the fourteenth day after conception.[69] It follows that the use of an embryo for any purpose that does not bear upon its future good constitutes a wrong; the embryo is, otherwise, being treated as a means to an end rather than as an end in itself – a process which offends a fundamental principle governing the way in which we treat other persons. To create human life in the full knowledge that it can have only the most limited future is seen by many opponents of embryo experimentation as an example of amoral exploitation and a first step on yet another slippery slope.

20.45 Between the two 'extreme' positions – that of a total rejection of embryo research on the grounds of its inescapable immorality and that of its acceptance in the case of any embryo, however derived – lies the middle view that, whereas research on surplus embryos is acceptable, the creation of embryos for that purpose is not. This is a view which is held by many and one with which we have very great empathy. Even so, it is not easy to establish a valid moral basis for the claim – because, in so far as the ultimate outcome is their destruction, the harm done to the embryos is the same in each case. A possible philosophical solution depends on distinguishing harm from wrong. No *wrong* is done to the embryo at the time it is formed with a view to implantation; a later failure to achieve that goal is due to circumstances which are, to a large extent, beyond the control of the person who has brought it into being. By contrast, the embryo which is developed with the express intention of harming it is clearly *wronged* at the moment of its formation. Thus, while the harm done to each is the same, the wrong done is of a different quality. But do those who take the middle road adopt such reasoning in reality? It seems more probable that they accept instinctively that a utilitarian argument which holds that the benefit to mankind

---

68 The use of the term 'pre-embryo' is suggested for this stage of development. We feel, however, that this smacks of changing words to establish a moral bolt-hole.
69 A Holland 'A Fortnight of My Life is Missing: A Discussion of the Status of the Pre-embryo' (1990) 7 J Appl Philos 25.

exceeds the harm done to what are the unfortunate rejects of a legitimate therapeutic activity cannot be substantiated in the case of specially created research subjects. This problem has raised what has been, perhaps, the most difficult hurdle for the world's legislatures[70] – and the United Kingdom Parliament is, we believe, unique in having opted in favour of the similar moral status of in vitro embryos whether they be surplus or specific creations.

The legal response

20.46 The legal regulation of embryo research in the United Kingdom is embodied in the Human Fertilisation and Embryology Act 1990, by virtue of which, it is illegal to conduct any research on human embryos except under licence from the Authority. The Authority can only issue such a licence if the project is thought to be desirable for the purposes of advancing the treatment of infertility, for increasing knowledge of the causes of congenital disease, for studying the causes of miscarriage, for developing methods of contraception, or for developing methods of detecting the presence of genetic or chromosomal abnormalities in embryos before implantation; other reasons may be added by regulation.[71] In the absence of further regulation, no licence may authorise altering the genetic structure of a cell while it is part of an embryo[72] and, while the hamster test for the normality of human sperm is allowed, all products of such research must be destroyed not later than the two-cell stage. There are strict regulations as to the maintenance of experimental records.[73] Overall, licences cannot authorise keeping or using an embryo after the appearance of the primitive streak – taken as being not later than 14 days after the gametes were mixed – nor may any embryo be placed in any animal.[74] Most importantly, in decreeing that research may be carried out, Parliament placed no restrictions on the source of the embryos used; the Authority has no mandate to impose an overall embargo on the creation of embryos for that specific purpose.

Embryonic stem cell research

20.47 The framers of the 1990 legislation may have imagined that the issue of embryo research would no longer be controversial once Parliament had answered the fundamental moral question and a system of tight regulation was in place. If so, they were to be proved right, but only for a relatively short time. The successful production of stable cell lines from human embryonic stem cells in 1998 provoked major interest in the possible use of such cells in transplantation therapy.[75] Stem cells are self-perpetuating cells at an early

---

70 The UK debate is well summarised in R G Lee and D Morgan *Human Fertilisation and Embryology* (2001).

71 Schedule 2, para 3(2).

72 An organism formed by cell nuclear replacement is considered to be an embryo: *R (on the application of Quintavalle) v Secretary of State for Health* [2002] EWCA Civ 29, [2002] QB 628, (2002) 64 BMLR 72.

73 Section 15.

74 Section 3.

75 J A Thomson et al 'Embryonic Stem Cell Lines Derived from Human Blastocysts' (1998) 282 *Science* 1145.

stage of development which can transform themselves into different forms of specialised tissues. If such cells can be cultivated in the laboratory, then it may be possible to prompt them to differentiate into types of tissue found in particular organs which can be used to repair organ damage. In simple terms, this technology might be used to grow heart tissue, neural cells, bone cells and other forms of tissue. This could lead to major advances in the treatment of a wide range of diseases of which diabetes, cancer, stroke and spinal cord injury are only a few examples.

20.48 As we have already discussed, one of the main drawbacks in transplantion therapy is the rejection by the body of the implanted foreign tissue, autologous transplantation (such as a skin graft from one part of the body to another) does not involve this risk. Stem cell biology has developed its own way round the rejection problem through the removal of the nucleus of an embryonic cell and its replacement with a nucleus taken from the cell of the prospective patient. Stem cells are then taken from the resulting embryo and tissue is grown from them which can be transplanted back to the patient without risk of rejection. The process of creating such an embryo is known as therapeutic cloning. This is quite distinct from reproductive cloning, because the embryo is not allowed to develop beyond an early point and is not implanted in a uterus.

20.49 The ethical and legal issues surrounding human stem cell research of this nature differ from those addressed in the earlier debate on embryo research in that, whereas other forms of embryo research may be intended to assist reproductive medicine and future embryos, this type involves using embryos for the benefit of persons in general. This has invigorated the opposition of those who have a principled objection to any form of embryo research.[76] At the same time, arguments in favour of such research have been forcefully advanced, often on the grounds that the benefit to humanity of the resulting therapies outweighs the interests of the embryos, particularly if use is made of cells derived from embryos which were rendered surplus within the accepted IVF treatment programme.[77]

20.50 Scientific interest in the possibilities opened by embryonic stem cell research was accompanied by intense bioethical debate in Western Europe and the United States. Although the Human Fertilisation and Embryology Act 1990 allowed for research on human embryos in the United Kingdom, the purposes for which such research could be carried out were, as we have seen, limited by the conditions of Sch 2, para 3(2); the list of permitted projects does not embrace research on embryos with a view to using embryonic stem cells for therapeutic purposes; moreover, replacement of the cells of an embryo was specifically disallowed under s 3(3)(d) of the 1990 Act. Fresh regulations

---

76 For a recent expression of ethical opposition to embryo research, see C Tollefsen 'Embryos, Individuals, and Persons: An Argument Against Embryo Creation and Research' (2001) 18 J Appl Philosoph 65.
77 For an argument that the surplus status of the embryo does not necessarily make stem cell research more acceptable, see J-E S Hansen 'Embryonic Stem Cell Production through Therapeutic Cloning has Fewer Ethical Problems than Stem Cell Harvest from Surplus IVF Embryos' (2002) 28 J Med Ethics 86.

were, therefore, needed before any such work could be carried out in the United Kingdom. Public debate on the issue was initiated by the appointment by the Government of an expert group to advise on the ethical and scientific aspects of stem cell research. This group recommended that embryonic stem cell research should be permitted and that therapeutic cloning involving cell nuclear replacement should be allowed.[78] A similar conclusion was reached at about the same time by a group set up by the Nuffield Council on Bioethics.[79]

20.51 The parliamentary airing of the issue resulted in the approval of additions to the regulations in schedule 2. These additions permit embryonic research for the purpose of increasing knowledge about the development of embryos, increasing knowledge about serious disease and enabling such knowledge to be applied in developing treatments for serious disease. The Government, however, agreed to a review of these regulations by a select committee of the House of Lords which, in due course, reported in favour of the proposed additions.[80] Embryonic stem cell research for therapeutic purposes is thus now legal in the United Kingdom, provided a licence is obtained from the Human Fertilisation and Embryology Authority. There remain issues which will need attention, in particular the issue of the legal regime under which stem cell lines are handled. The Human Fertilisation and Embryology Authority may control the circumstances in which stem cells are obtained from embryos but, once cell lines are established, these do not appear to fall within the scope of the Authority's powers. This matter is currently under consideration as part of the overall review of the law relating to human tissue.

20.52 While the United Kingdom has proved ready to facilitate stem cell research, other countries have been either more cautious or, in some cases, frankly hostile to the process. There is an outright ban on all forms of embryo research in some jurisdictions; a compromise has been reached in others. There has been a particularly prolonged debate in Germany, both within and outside Parliament, and the resulting compromise allows the importation, for research purposes, of embryonic stem cell lines established prior to the date of passage of the legislation. A similar compromise had been suggested in the United States, where there has been strong political hostility to the use of Federal funds for this purpose. Federal funding controls, however, do not preclude the carrying out of research in a strictly privately-funded setting and it is, therefore, theoretically possible to carry out even more extensive embryo research than may be undertaken under the seemingly more liberal regimes of the United Kingdom or the Netherlands. In practice, however, major institutions will be severely inhibited by federal funding restrictions.

78 Department of Health *Stem Cell Research: Medical Progress with Responsibility* (2000).
79 Nuffield Council on Bioethics *Stem Cell Therapy: A Discussion Paper* (2000).
80 House of Lords *Stem Cell Research* (HL Paper 83(i) 2002).

Psychiatry and the law

21 Human rights, psychiatry and the law

21.1 The practice of psychiatry is one of the most controversial areas of medicine, the subject of endless public debate and of frequent political intervention. The reasons for this are complex; one factor, however, stands out: while treatment for physical conditions almost always depends upon the consent of the patient, the psychiatrist may be called upon to treat the unwilling. The associated powers may involve detention for a considerable time, something which is usually reserved to the judiciary in a state governed by law. In addition, psychiatric treatment is likely to be aimed at ameliorating a disturbance of mood or behaviour. In so doing, it sets out to alter the functioning of the human mind and this can be seen as an interference in human autonomy which will be justified only in the most exceptional circumstances. Thus, in the view of some critics,[1] the powers accorded to psychiatric medicine give rise to unnecessary and unwanted intervention in the lives of persons whose situation, although unusual, may be tolerable from their own point of view. Others have taken a quite different stand, and have argued that society has not been ready enough to intervene in this area, particularly where issues of public safety are involved. The tension between these positions has led to shifts in psychiatric and legal policy, as governments have wrestled with conflicting demands.

21.2 In the earlier part of the twentieth century society favoured the institutional or asylum approach to the management of mental illness. Those diagnosed as suffering from a psychiatric illness were usually sent to 'mental hospitals' where in-patient treatment would be provided. This system was inevitably both stigmatising and coercive, and in the United Kingdom in the late 1950s a fundamental change in emphasis was signalled with the

---

1 For classic examples of radical views of mental illness and society's response to it, see T S Szasz *The Myth of Mental Illness* (1972) and R D Laing *The Divided Self* (1965). A more recent critique is contained in C Unsworth *The Politics of Mental Health* (1987); see also T Mason and L Jennings 'The Mental Health Act and Professional Hostage Taking' (1997) 37 Med Sci & Law 58.

publication of the Percy Commission Report, which advocated the treatment of psychiatric patients as far as possible on a voluntary basis. The legislation which followed from this, the Mental Health Act 1959 and its Scottish counterpart, was seen as a liberalising measure, but over the following two decades concern grew up over the extent to which compulsorily detained patients could be compulsorily treated without any possibility of review or without any safeguards against the abuse of medical power. The mental health legislation which was introduced at the beginning of the 1980s, the Mental Health Act 1983 and the Mental Health (Scotland) Act 1984, was intended to boost patient rights while at the same time allowing for compulsory detention and treatment of those who were unable or unwilling to consent. Safeguards were also introduced to ensure that certain forms of treatment (such as ECT) could not be given without further consultation (see para 21.52 below).

21.3 Greater sensitivity to the rights of the mentally ill was accompanied by an enthusiasm for returning psychiatric patients to the community. This policy, which was founded on concern for patients and a desire to allow their re-integration, was welcomed by governments which were keen to contain hospital costs. The closure of psychiatric wards, however, had the effect of limiting opportunities for care and treatment, and was seen by many to be incompatible with patient welfare. At the same time, inadequate provision was made for treatment and supervision in the community, and this was exacerbated by public concern over safety. Against this background, the United Kingdom entered into a third period of legislative review at the very end of the twentieth century, resulting in the publication in 2000 of a major White Paper, *Reforming the Mental Health Act*. This document sets out the shape of the third great reform of mental health law in 50 years. Like its predecessors, it demonstrates how mental health policy involves the balancing of public protection, patient welfare, and human rights considerations.[2] The human rights elements in this equation are now more important than ever, and any legislative response or judicial interpretation has to take full account of the implications of the Human Rights Act 1998, and the Convention rights which this introduces into domestic law. Several articles of the European Convention have a direct bearing on mental health law, and in particular on the issue of detention and compulsory treatment. The most important of these is Article 5, which sets out the right to liberty in the following terms: 'Everyone has the right to liberty and security of person. No one shall be deprived of his liberty save in the following cases and in accordance with a procedure prescribed by law' (there then follow six exceptions, the relevant one in this context being: (e) the lawful detention of persons for the prevention of the spreading of infectious diseases, of persons of unsound mind, alcoholics or drug addicts or vagrants). The leading case on the interpretation of Article 5 as it applies to psychiatric treatment is *Winterwerp v Netherlands*,[3] in which the European Court of Human Rights set out certain minimum conditions which must be satisfied if detention under mental health legislation is to be justified. These are:

2   Since we went to press, the government has published a Draft Mental Health Bill 2002 (Cm 5538-1), which has been subject to criticism: Z Kmietowicz 'Organisations Unite against Draft Mental Health Bill' (2002) 325 BMJ 9. For a useful précis, see L Birmingham 'Detaining Dangerous People with Mental Disorders (2002) 325 BMJ 2. The exigencies of publication prevent a full appraisal in this edition.

3   (1979) 2 EHRR 387.

- the patient must be 'reliably shown' by 'objective medical expertise' to be of 'unsound mind';
- the disorder must be of a nature to justify detention; and
- the disorder must persist throughout the period in which the patient is detained.

21.4 These requirements are framed in broad terms, and there is obviously some leeway in which states may interpret them. The jurisprudence of the European Court of Human Rights, however, has established that patients should not be detained if nothing can be done for them medically. In *Aerts v Belgium*,[4] for example, the Court held it was a breach of Article 5 to detain a mentally disordered patient in a prison, without treatment, because a hospital bed was not available. Article 5 has also been found to require timely release on recovery (even if it is reasonable to stage release in the interests of the patient or the community)[5] and to require reasonably early and frequent reviews of detention decisions.[6] Article 8 recognises that: 'Everyone has the right to respect for his private and family life, his home and his correspondence.' This article, along with Article 3 ('no one should be subjected to torture or to inhuman or degrading treatment or punishment') might be used to question the legitimacy of compulsory treatment for mental disorder. However, even if Article 3 would disallow cruel treatment, the fundamental acceptability of non-consensual treatment would be supported by Article 8(2), which allows exceptions to Article 8(1) on the grounds, amongst others, of the protection of health.[7]

21.5 The protection afforded to psychiatric patients by the Human Rights Act 1998 was considered by the Court of Appeal in *R (on the application of Wilkinson) v RMO, Broadmoor Hospital Authority*.[8] The patient in this case had been detained in a high security hospital for over 30 years, having been convicted of the rape of a young girl. There was a difference of psychiatric opinion as to the diagnosis, most of the psychiatrists who had examined him over the years having diagnosed psychopathic personality disorder. Latterly the doctor in charge of his case had decided that treatment would be appropriate for psychotic symptoms – treatment which the patient was determined to resist. The issue then arose as to whether treatment by way of ss 63 and 58(3)(b) of the Mental Health Act 1983, which justify non-consensual treatment in such circumstances, was compatible in this case with the patient's Convention rights. It was argued for the patient in this case that the Convention permitted treatment in the face of refusal by a capacitated patient only where this was necessary to protect others from serious harm or possibly to ensure the safety of the patient himself. Such an interpretation would seriously limit the grounds of medical intervention in such circumstances and, in the result, it was not accepted by the court, although the propriety of judicial review of treatment decisions was accepted where differences of psychiatric opinion emerged. However, the judgment of Simon Brown LJ contains obiter remarks which suggest that it is 'increasingly difficult to justify' any exception to the

---

4   (1998) 29 EHRR 50, (1998) 53 BMLR 79.
5   *Johnson v United Kingdom* (1999) 27 EHRR 440.
6   *E v Norway* (1994) 17 EHRR 30.
7   *Herczegfalvy v Austria* (1992) 15 EHRR 437, (1992) 18 BMLR 48.
8   [2001] EWCA Civ 1545, [2002] 1 WLR 419, (2002) 65 BMLR 15.

proposition that a patient, voluntary or otherwise, should be entitled to refuse medical treatment. These remarks have caused some concern amongst psychiatrists, and such concern is well-founded. Indeed, a strong case can be made out that not treating a treatable and sufficiently serious mental disorder in the face of patient unwillingness to consent itself amounts to inhuman or degrading treatment under Article 3 of the Convention.[9]

THE GROUNDS FOR INTERVENTION

21.6 The mere presence of a psychiatric condition will not, of itself, be sufficient to justify compulsory treatment: a person may suffer from psychiatric illness and yet still be able to reach a reasoned decision as to whether or not to undergo therapy. Compulsory treatment is justified only if a person's remaining untreated poses a threat to his own health or safety or to the safety of others.

Danger to others

21.7 The detention of mentally disordered persons who pose a threat to others is a widely accepted practice and has become an increasingly important issue in mental health policy. The proportion of psychiatrically disturbed people likely to commit violent acts is actually very small, but such persons engender substantial concern. It is politically difficult for governments to resist pressure to make this form of detention easier, and yet there are serious civil liberties concerns over the too-ready use of mental health powers to deprive persons of their freedom. It would contribute little to the overall welfare of the psychiatrically ill if exaggerated concerns as to the risk of violence by mentally disordered persons were to reverse progress made in allowing psychiatric patients to lead their lives in as normal as possible conditions within the community.[10] It is salutary to ask why public safety considerations justify the detention of those who are mentally disordered and thought to be potentially dangerous, when those who seek to do so will not allow the preventive detention of persons who are not mentally disordered but are, perhaps, equally dangerous – or reckoned to be so on the basis of their past conduct or their disclosed intentions for the future. Attempts may be made to justify the preventive detention of the mentally disordered on the grounds that they are more dangerous than other potentially dangerous, but not mentally disordered, persons. In this view, the presence of mental disorder either makes the former group both less predictable and less amenable to deterrence – and, therefore, inherently more of a risk to others – or the presence of mental disorder may have a quite opposite result and make the risk of harm to others much more

---

9 Mental health law is, however, very specific. Shortly after *Wilkinson*, Lord Eassie in the Court of Session held that non-consensual treatment under s 26 of the Mental Health (Scotland) Act 1984 did not infringe Articles 6 and 8 of the Convention. The treatment concerned was not, however, a treatment requiring a second opinion (see para 21.52 below): *M, Petitioner* (2002) Times, 26 August, OH.

10 P J Taylor and J Gunn 'Homicides by People with Mental Illness: Myth and Reality' (1999) 174 Brit J Psychiat 174. The contribution of mental illness to the overall level of violence within society is thought to be small: E Walsh, A Buchanan and T Fahy 'Violence and Schizophrenia: Examining the Evidence' (2002) 180 Brit J Psychiat 490.

quantifiable.[11] Whatever justification is preferred, the prediction of dangerousness is an imprecise – and, perhaps, fruitless – exercise.[12] Many attempts have been made to determine an objective concept of dangerousness but none has succeeded sufficiently in allaying doubts as to the strong element of subjectivity that is inherent in such judgments.[13] Disparities are frequently detected; in one such study, 60% agreement between a group of assessors was achieved in only four out of 16 case appraisals.[14] Psychiatric assessment of dangerousness must not, therefore, be considered an exact science – although the fact remains that reliable prediction is exactly what courts, parole boards and tribunals may expect. It is, indeed, possible that dangerousness is best established retrospectively by way of a history of recidivism; the problem then becomes one for the criminologist rather than the psychiatrist.

21.8 It is not easy to second guess the Government's policy in this field. The 2000 White Paper, *Reforming the Mental Health Act,* signalled an intention to deal with the dangerously mentally disordered as a separate group within the category of those requiring compulsory treatment; such patients were to have a care and treatment plan which would be primarily designed to 'manage and reduce high risk behaviours which pose a significant risk to others'.[15] The tone of the draft Mental Health Bill, however, is significantly different; the protection of patients' rights is now the predominant theme and 'dangerous people with a severe personality disorder' are not described as such in the draft.[16] The definition of mental disorder is, however, now broadened (see para 21.38 below) so that such persons are by no means excluded from the legislation – indeed, it could be claimed that sexual deviants and drug dependents, who are currently dealt with as separate categories, could also find themselves in the ranks of those subject to statutory compulsory treatment.[17] The main management plan for those who have been remanded for medical treatment by the courts will now rest on the preparation and application of care plans under the aegis of clinical supervisors (draft Bill, s 68). The way is, therefore, still open to managing potentially dangerous persons by way of the widely canvassed option of placing them in institutions which are neither

11 For a discussion of the legal issues surrounding dangerousness, see J K Mason 'The Legal Aspects and Implications of Risk Assessment' (2000) Med L Rev 69.

12 For a discussion of the potential effect of risk assessments on the prevention of homicide, see E Munro and J Rumgay 'Role of Risk Assessments in Reducing Homicides by People with Mental Illnesses' (2000) 176 Brit J Psychiat 116.

13 P E Mullen 'Mental Disorder and Dangerousness' (1984) 18 Austral NZ J Psychiat 8; see later 'A Reassessment of the Link between Mental Disorder and Violent Behaviour' (1997) 31 Austral NZ J Psychiat 3. Opinions differ amongst psychiatrists as to the ethical implications of making predictions of dangerousness. Not all psychiatrists are reluctant to do so; see eg T Grisso and P S Applebaum 'Is it Unethical to Offer Predictions of Future Violence?' (1992) 16 Law and Hum Behav 621. Legislators might prove ready to act on such predictions: M A Bochnewich 'Prediction of Dangerousness and Washington's Sexually Violent Predator Statute' (1992) 29 Cal West Law R 277.

14 G Montadon and T Harding 'The Reliability of Dangerousness Assessments: A Decision-making Exercise' (1984) 144 Brit J Psychiat 149. This study is now rather old and some commentators believe that prognostic possibilities are improving: G T Harris ad M E Rice 'Risk Appraisal and Management of Violent Behavior' (1997) 48 Psychiat Serv 1168.

15 *Reforming the Mental Health Act,* Part 2, 1.4.

16 This is the currently preferred term for those commonly known as psychopaths or persons with psychopathic personality.

17 Birmingham, para 21.3 above.

part of the mainstream health nor prison services. Stress will be laid on the therapeutic benefit of care plans for individual patients – treatment authorised under the proposed legislation will, for example, be carried out under NHS auspices – but, where it is necessary, 'treatment' may be confined to managing behaviour that might lead to serious harm to other people. Human rights considerations are addressed in procedural proposals. These include the constitution of a new Mental Health Tribunal and Mental Health Appeal Tribunal (draft Bill, ss 3, 4) which will deal with applications by or in respect of all patients who will come under the auspices of the Act as well as those who have come to the attention of the courts. The lower courts cannot remand a person for medical treatment which continues for longer than 28 days. The Court of Appeal may do so but, in such circumstances, the person's clinical supervisor must apply to the Mental Health Tribunal for an order approving the plan.[18]

21.9 Whatever will be the eventual situation in England in respect of the mentally disordered criminal, it has, to an extent, been pre-empted in Scotland with the passing of the Mental Health (Public Safety and Appeals)(Scotland) Act 1999 – itself being said to be of an interim nature only.[19] This Act amends the Mental Health (Scotland) Act 1984, ss 64, 66, 68 and 74 so as, in the main, to empower the Sheriff to refuse an appeal for discharge from hospital by a patient who is subject to a restriction order[20] if he is satisfied that the patient is suffering from a mental disorder 'the effect of which is such that it is necessary, *in order to protect the public from serious harm*, that the patient continue to be detained in hospital, *whether for medical treatment or not*' (authors' emphasis). The history of the Act merits some description as it explains some of the difficulties surrounding the management of the dangerous psychopath, who can be seen as the paradigm of the 'dangerous patient'.

21.10 The complicating factor here has always lain in the problem of whether or not psychopathy is treatable – a question which is still open to debate.[21] The significance of this lies in the wording of the Mental Health Act 1983, ss 3 and 73.[22] The former, in effect, states that a person cannot be compulsorily admitted to a mental hospital for treatment unless the mental condition is treatable – which means that treatment is likely to alleviate or prevent a deterioration of his condition; the latter, which applies to the discharge of a person subject to a restriction order, holds that an appeal for discharge will be accepted if, at the time, the patient is not suffering from a psychopathic disorder which makes it appropriate for him to be detained in hospital. The House of Lords considered the relationship of the two sections in *Reid v Secretary of State for Scotland*[23] and held that the conditions determining an order for

18 Much of the language of the draft Bill owes its origin to the severe criticism meted out to the previous Green and White Papers: see P E Mullen 'Dangerous People with Severe Personality Disorder' (1999) 319 BMJ 1146.
19 In addition, the Scottish Executive has published its own document of intent *Renewing Mental Health Law* (2001).
20 See Mental Health (Scotland) Act 1984, s 62 or Mental Health Act 1983, s 41.
21 Indeed, many of the outstanding cases in this area rest on a fluctuating diagnosis between psychopathy and schizophrenia, which is a recognisedly treatable condition – eg *W v Egdell* [1990] Ch 359 (chapter 8 above) or *Reid*, n 23 below.
22 Or Mental Health (Scotland) Act 1984, ss 17 and 64.
23 [1999] 2 AC 512, [1999] 1 All ER 481.

discharge were to be interpreted by reference to the statutory criteria for detention in hospital – in other words, an order for discharge was inevitable once it was established that the psychopathic condition was unlikely to respond to treatment.[24] Just such a situation occurred shortly after this ruling when a dangerous psychopath was declared to be untreatable and, therefore, had to be discharged from a secure hospital.[25] The public furore which followed resulted in the 1999 Act which was passed as an emergency measure.

21.11 The 1999 Act was always considered to be of an interim nature[26] and a challenge to its terms by way of the Human Rights Act 1998 was inevitable – particularly in view of the fact that the relevant sections in the Mental Health Acts were designed to protect the individual from uncontestable detention. *A v The Scottish Ministers*[27] was first heard in the Inner House which, essentially, undertook an exercise balancing, on the one hand, the Government's duty under Article 2 to protect the lives of its citizens and, on the other, the individual's right to liberty embodied in Article 5. In addition to giving high priority to Article 2, the House depended heavily on the derogations permitted in Article 5(1)(e)[28] – that the detention of persons is lawful for reasons which we have already noted above and which, if used to their limits, allow the state a remarkably wide margin of appreciation.

21.12 *A* and its associated cases were then taken to the Privy Council[29] where, again, the safety of the public was considered paramount and the appeal was dismissed unanimously – the dictum of Lord Clyde sums up the position well:

> In principle, it cannot be right that the public peace and safety should be subordinated to the liberty of persons whose mental states render them dangerous to society.

Indeed, *A v The Scottish Ministers* appears to confirm a general impression that, in interpreting the Human Rights Act 1998, the United Kingdom courts tend not to use the rights of the individual as their benchmark but will, rather, concentrate on the reasonableness or unreasonableness of their infringement by the state. In any event, government and executive on both sides of the border were clearly anxious to avoid a repeat of the *Ruddle* case and it may be for this reason that 'treatability' has no part in the 2002 draft Bill. Paradoxically, this may contribute to the cumulative antipathy to the draft Bill in so far as it seems to open the door to compulsory 'hospitalisation' of many whose liberty is, currently, uncompromised.

---

24 Thus, the House of Lords overturned the contrary judgment of the English Court of Appeal in *R v Canons Park Mental Review Tribunal, ex p A* [1995] QB 60, [1994] 2 All ER 659. Both courts, however, ruled that the hospital environment did, of itself, alleviate the condition and that the patient could be detained legitimately.
25 *Ruddle v Secretary of State for Scotland* 1999 GWD 29-1395.
26 Although the tone of the *Report of the Committee on Serious Violent and Sexual Offenders* (2000) (Chairman, Lord Maclean) suggests that it is unlikely to be diluted.
27 2001 SC 1, [2000] UKHRR 439. The Inner House decision is considered and criticised by G T Laurie 'Medical Law and Human Rights: Passing the Parcel Back to the Profession?' in A Boyle et al (eds) *Human Rights and Scots Law* (2002).
28 Following, in particular, the European Court of Human Rights in *Litwa v Poland* (2001) 33 EHRR 53.
29 2001 SLT 1331.

Liability for premature release

21.13 Nevertheless, it is clear that the threat of harm to others as a result of premature release from hospital detention is very real and is likely to influence the medical officers who are responsible for the clinical decisions; yet it is equally clear that excessive caution may cause injustice to the patients themselves. This issue has provoked litigation in the United States where the courts have imposed civil liability upon psychiatrists when patients have been released and have subsequently harmed others.[30] Undoubtedly, *Tarasoff v Regents of the University of California*[31] remains the most significant case in this context. Here, a patient had confessed to a therapist that he intended to harm a woman who had rejected his advances. The therapist failed to warn her of the danger and she was later killed by the patient; her family then sued the therapist's employers successfully.

21.14 The important feature of *Tarasoff* – which has been both rejected and extended in later US cases – is to be found not so much in the failure to warn as in the failure to take preventive action which was available to the therapist by way of the unique power to control his patient that he held. This concept of derivative responsibility has been amplified in a relatively recent case in Ohio,[32] and it would be unsurprising if psychiatrists' judgments were to be clouded by the possible consequences of releasing a patient who might reoffend.[33]

21.15 In addition, considerable strains could be forced on a national health system if it had to bear the costs of harm caused by mentally disordered persons and it is interesting to speculate on how the United Kingdom courts are likely to react in similar circumstances. There have been a number of cases concerning the comparable responsibility of the police which provide pointers; the most important of these, in so far as it has gone to the European Court of Human Rights, is *Osman v Ferguson*.[34] Here, a known paedophile 'stalker' admitted that he might well do violence; the police took no action and he later injured a child and killed one of its parents. An action in negligence was dismissed, mainly on the grounds that it would not be just, fair or reasonable to hold that the general duty laid on the police to suppress crime included liability to unpredictable victims of crime.

21.16 The same issue arose in a medical context in *Palmer v Tees Health Authority*,[35] in which damages were sought by the mother of a child who had been abducted and murdered by a psychiatric out-patient under the defendant's

30 See, for example, *Perreira v State* 768 P 2d 1198 (Colo, 1989).
31 529 P 2d 55 (Cal, 1974); on appeal 551 P 2d 334 (Cal, 1976). The case and its significance are discussed by R D Mackay 'Dangerous Patients. Third Party Safety and Psychiatrists' Duties – Walking the *Tarasoff* Tightrope' (1990) 30 Med Sci Law 52.
32 *Estates of Morgan v Fairfield Family Counselling Center* 673 NE 2d 1311 (Ohio, 1997).
33 See T E Gammon and J K Hulston 'The Duty of Mental Health Care Providers to Restrain their Patients or Warn Third Parties' (1995) 60 Mo L Rev 749.
34 [1993] 4 All ER 344; *Osman v United Kingdom* [1999] 1 FLR 193. The ECtHR confirmed the findings of the Court of Appeal save as to freedom of access to the courts which it was thought had been compromised. See, now, *Barrett v Enfield London Borough Council* [2001] 2 AC 550, [1999] 3 All ER 193, HL.
35 (1998) 45 BMLR 88, QBD; [1999] Lloyd's Rep Med 151, CA.

care. The court was reluctant to impose a duty of care on the basis that the relationship of proximity between plaintiff and defendant had not been established. Not only was the identity of the potential victim unknown to the defendant, thus ruling out proximity – and, as Stuart-Smith LJ put it in the Court of Appeal, of the possibility of issuing a warning – but it was also suggested that to impose liability could lead to the practice of defensive medicine and could divert the attention of health authorities away from their primary function. *Palmer*, however, did not tell us what would happen in the event of a prospective victim being identifiable. For this, we can find some, albeit rather indirect, evidence from *Clunis v Camden and Islington Health Authority*.[36] In this case, the plaintiff, a psychiatric patient suffering from a schizo-affective disorder, had been discharged into community care but had missed four appointments made for him by the doctor who was responsible for his care. He was convicted of manslaughter on the grounds of diminished responsibility after he had attacked and killed an innocent stranger. He then sued the health authority responsible for his care[37], arguing that the authority's negligent failure to assess his mental state had resulted in his suffering losses resulting from conviction and imprisonment. The Court of Appeal upheld the authority's argument that to impose liability in this case would be to allow the plaintiff to profit from his own illegal act, which is contrary to the ex turpi causa rule preventing a wrongdoer from claiming damages in such circumstances. More importantly in the present context, it was held that, in this instance, the psychiatrist who certified that Clunis was fit for discharge was not liable to him by way of a duty of care. The arguments were, however, largely based on statute and, significantly, it was stated that the principle of a common law duty in such conditions was undecided – and it remains open for consideration in appropriate cases. Nonetheless, the evidence from various sources strongly suggests to us that public policy considerations, at least, would inhibit a *Tarasoff*-like decision in the United Kingdom. It is probable that a duty of care to a third party would only be established if there was some pre-existing relationship between the health care professional and the ultimate victim.

CONTROLLING TREATMENT

Paternalism and mental health

21.17 Non-voluntary treatment of the dangerous person can, as we have seen, be justified to an extent by concern for the safety of third parties. By contrast, the compulsory treatment of mental illness in those who pose no threat to others is based on the notion of justified paternalism.[38] A paternalistic act is one which is not sought by the patient but which is provided with the intention

36 [1998] QB 978, [1998] 3 All ER 180.
37 The limitations on liability provided by the Mental Health Act 1983, s 139(1) does not apply to health authorities and National Health Service Trusts (s 139(4)).
38 There is a major survey of paternalism in general in D Van De Veer *Paternalistic Intervention* (1976). Other contributions include: B Gert and C M Culver 'Paternalistic Behavior' in M Cohen, T Nagel and T Scanlon (eds) *Medicine and Moral Philosophy* (1981) p 201; A E Buchanan and D W Brock *Deciding for Others: The Ethics of Surrogate Decision Making* (1990) esp ch 7.

of protecting him from harm. Ordinarily, paternalistic action will be considered wrong because it offends the principle of autonomy. It may be justified, however, when the person for whose benefit the act is performed is unable to make an informed choice for himself. The intellectually impaired and the mentally ill may well fit into this category in that their ability to understand the reality of their situation is compromised by their mental state. The absence of rationality in such cases then warrants action directed towards preventing their being harmed. In such circumstances, it will be appropriate to take the frankly paternalistic route and apply a 'best interests' test.[39]

21.18 This is the way followed in the United Kingdom statutes whereby, subject to the safeguards discussed in detail below, treatment for the mental disorder that has occasioned compulsory admission to hospital may be given without specific consent. The courts are now, almost regularly, using a best interests rule to justify non-consensual treatment of a non-psychiatric nature and there is no doubt that doctors will continue to rely upon it. However, it cannot be denied that legitimating paternalism in this way carries the danger of licensing excessive interference in the lives of those afflicted by mental illness. There must, therefore, be limits both as to the determination of incompetence and the extent of treatment.

21.19 At the same time, just as it might be wrong in certain circumstances to force treatment upon an unwilling patient, so too might it be wrong in some cases to deny treatment out of respect for the patient's rights. If legislation goes too far in protecting the mentally ill from unwanted treatment, then the end result may be prolonged and avoidable suffering for this group of patients. In Canada, considerations of civil liberty have significantly eroded the paternalistic claim of society to treat those who are suffering from mental disorder. In *Fleming v Reid*,[40] the appellants, who had committed crimes of violence, had been diagnosed as suffering from schizophrenia. Their doctor had decided that they were incompetent and proposed to treat them with neuroleptic drugs, a proposal which was vetoed by the patients' substitute decision-maker. The latter pointed out that the patients had had previous experience of this form of treatment and had objected to it at a time when they were competent. Under the relevant mental health legislation, the Ontario Mental Health Act, the substitute decision-maker's refusal to consent could be overridden by a review board and it was the decision by a review board to do just this that led to the legal challenge. In due course, the Ontario Court of Appeal held that this decision contravened Article 7 of the Charter of Rights and Freedoms, which protects the right to bodily integrity and personal autonomy. It was only in the absence of any indication of the patient's previously expressed, competent rejection of treatment, that a best interest argument might be used to justify imposing involuntary treatment on an incompetent person. This means, in effect, that if one expresses an antipathy to any form of drug treatment, and if one subsequently becomes incompetent, psychiatric medicine may be powerless to attempt a cure. Psychiatric treatment is, thus, put on the same footing as the treatment of physical illness, an approach which fails to distinguish those features which make psychiatric disease a special case –

39 C W van Staden and C Kruger 'Incapacity to Give Informed Consent owing to Mental Disorder' (2002) J Med Ethics, in press.
40 (1991) 82 DLR 4th 298.

namely, that it distorts or destroys the ability to make a *rational* decision. It is this sort of dilemma that mental health legislation seeks to avoid.

Statutory control of treatment

21.20 As has been noted already, both the English and Scottish Parliaments have announced their intention of introducing new mental health legislation. Each has produced papers that are, effectively, expressions of intent.[41] We are, therefore, in something of an editorial limbo which has been deepened by the publication of the English draft Bill. As a result, what follows is a description of the law as it stands at the time of writing; we have, however, interspersed this where possible with brief notes addressed to some areas in which change seems likely.

21.21 The *current* framework for the treatment of mental illness in the United Kingdom is to be found in the Mental Health Act 1983, the Mental Health (Scotland) Act 1984,[42] and the Mental Health (Patients in the Community) Act 1995. The first two of these statutes introduced major reforms which related principally to the regulation and review of involuntary treatment and to consent to certain forms of treatment. The English Act also established a Mental Health Act Commission,[43] which was structured along the lines of the long-standing Scottish Mental Welfare Commission[44] – both have the general power to monitor procedures for admission to hospital and to scrutinise the conditions in which patients are detained. The 1995 Act is concerned in the main with the aftercare of patients who have been hospitalised.

Informal treatment

21.22 Treatment for mental illness is provided on either a voluntary or an involuntary basis. Informal – that is, voluntary – treatment may be provided by any registered medical practitioner or, indeed, by any layman provided that the provisions of the Medical Act 1983 as to impersonation are observed. Informal hospital treatment is regulated by s 131 of the Mental Health Act 1983, which states that a patient may enter hospital for psychiatric treatment without any order being made for that purpose and with freedom to leave at will. Informal patients can object to any particular treatment; they have unhindered access to the courts and enjoy certain other privileges which are denied to those who are detained compulsorily. The proportion of informal patients has increased markedly over the last three decades, this being an objective which was first expressed legislatively in the Mental Health Act 1959;

---

41 Department of Health and Home Office *Reforming the Mental Health Act* (2001); Scottish Executive *Renewing Mental Health Law* (2001). See, now, the draft Mental Health Bill 2002 (Cm 5538–1). The draft of the Mental Health (Scotland) Bill 2002 unfortunately appeared too late for consideration in this edition.
42 Discussion here is principally in terms of the Mental Health Act 1983. The 1984 Act is similar in many respects but has some important differences – eg in the role of the sheriff in compulsory admission (s 21). There is a full treatment of the Scottish provisions in J Blackie and H Patrick *Mental Health: The Law in Scotland* (2nd edn, 2002).
43 Mental Health Act Commission Regulations 1983, SI 1983/894.
44 Established by the Mental Health (Scotland) Act 1960, s 2.

current intentions in both England and Scotland are that voluntary treatment should continue to be the ideal.

21.23 Many seriously incapacitated psychiatric patients are looked after in nursing homes and other institutions without having any formal order made in respect of their care. In *R v Bournewood Community and Mental Health NHS Trust, ex p L*[45] the House of Lords considered the position of informal patients who lack the capacity to give a proper consent to treatment but who are, none the less, compliant. In this case, a profoundly autistic adult was admitted for in-patient treatment following an outburst of disturbed, self-harming behaviour. He was not detained compulsorily under the provisions of the Mental Health Act as he did not resist admission. Relations between the hospital and the plaintiff's carers deteriorated, with the result that an action was brought against the health trust for damages for unlawful detention. The Court of Appeal allowed damages, but the House of Lords overturned this decision after hearing argument that requiring such patients to be detained under the Act – rather than admitted informally – would pose an immense burden on existing arrangements. In effect, compulsorily detaining such patients would be a luxury which the system simply could not afford at current levels of funding. In the result, the House of Lords ruled that informal treatment of compliant patients who were, nevertheless, incapable of consenting was justified on the principle of necessity and was in accordance with the Mental Health Act's objective of facilitating informal treatment; the Act does not exclude the application of common law powers in the provision of treatment to psychiatric patients. What was seen by some to be a serious lacuna in the law had, in effect, been neatly filled by the flexible doctrine of necessity.

21.24 As emphasised by Lord Steyn, patients in this category who are detained – and both Lord Nolan and Lord Steyn, in particular, emphasised that they *are* detained – are denied the statutory protections afforded those who are compulsorily detained; in addition, they do not qualify for many of the benefits derived from supervision by the Mental Health Act Commission. These seem to be unfortunate legacies of the House of Lords' decision. None the less, it is clearly the intention of Parliament that hospital treatment should be available to all psychiatric patients and that this should not involve undue formality. What, is needed, then, is a system which allows for flexibility rather than a rigid separation of two classes of patient – and the avowed intention of the legislation proposed for 2002–3 is to focus on the needs and characteristics of individual patients.The draft Bill acknowledges this in Part 5 where, in addition, the rights of the informal patient are clearly established. Moreover, the informal patient who is likely to be hospitalised for more than 28 days will be entitled to safeguards which include the appointment of a nominated person who, in general, must be informed of the treatment the patient is receiving and, significantly, has the power of proxy veto.

21.25 The informal status of a patient in a psychiatric hospital may be changed to that of compulsory detention (s 5(1)). This can be effected by the 'doctor in charge' of the patient on the grounds that it appears to him that 'an application ought to be made' for compulsory admission (s 5(2)). Detention under this

45 [1998] 3 All ER 289, [1998] 3 WLR 107.

provision expires after 72 hours. Nurses may also restrain a patient from leaving hospital if this is deemed to be immediately necessary and if it is not practicable to secure the immediate attendance of the doctor in charge or his delegate (s 5(4)). This form of detention may last for only six hours or until a doctor entitled to act under s 5(2) is able to attend.

Compulsory admission

21.26 There are currently three routes to involuntary admission to hospital under the Mental Health Act 1983. These are, in brief:

(1) *Admission for assessment under section 2 (1984 Act, s 17)*

21.27 Application for such admission must be made either by the patient's nearest relative or by an approved social worker. The application must also be supported by two registered medical practitioners, one of whom must be qualified in psychiatry. Force may be used to transfer the patient to hospital provided it is not excessive.

21.28 The grounds for admission under s 2 are that a patient is suffering from a mental disorder of a nature or degree which warrants detention in hospital for assessment for at least a limited period and that he should be detained in hospital 'in the interests of his own health or safety or with a view to the protection of other persons'. Patients admitted for assessment may be kept in hospital for up to 28 days and such admissions cannot be renewed.[46]

21.29 Patients must be informed of their legal position and rights and may apply to have the case reviewed by a mental health review tribunal during the first 14 days of detention. The procedures for admission under s 3 (see below) must be invoked if it is proposed to detain the patient for a longer period.

(2) *Emergency admission*

21.30 A patient may be admitted in an emergency under s 4 (1984 Act, s 24). This form of admission can be effected on the recommendation of one doctor and is valid for only 72 hours. The doctor need not be a specialist in mental illness but he must, if practicable, have known the patient beforehand (s 4(3)). Emergency admission may be converted to admission for treatment (28 days) by obtaining an additional opinion from a specialist in mental illness.

(3) *Admission for treatment*

21.31 Longer-term compulsory detention for treatment is governed by s 3 (1984 Act, s 30). Application procedures are similar to those used for admission

---

46 For the common law power of detention in Scotland, see *Black v Forsey* 1988 SC 28, HL.

for assessment although, under s 3, the nearest relative must be consulted when admission is being sought by a social worker. Court authority for admission will be needed if the relative objects. The grounds for admission for treatment are that, in the opinion of the doctors recommending admission, the patient is: (a) suffering from mental illness, severe mental impairment, psychopathic disorder or mental impairment and his mental disorder is of a nature which makes it appropriate for him to receive medical treatment in a hospital; (b) in the case of psychopathic disorder or mental impairment, such treatment is likely to alleviate or prevent deterioration in his condition; and (c) it is necessary for the health or safety of the patient or for the protection of other persons that he should receive such treatment and it cannot be provided unless he is detained under this section. Treatment for sexual disorders is excluded.

21.32 Admission for treatment allows for detention for up to six months. This period is renewable for a second period of six months and, thereafter, for periods of a year at a time. Detention under s 3 can, therefore, last indefinitely subject to the responsible medical officer's bona fide belief that it is in the patient's best interests (s 20(4)(a) and (b)).

21.33 The route to compulsory treatment is much the same under the draft Bill although there are differences according to whether or not the patient is detained in hospital at the time. Essentially, the relevant conditions which must be present before any action is taken are that the patient must be suffering from mental disorder which warrants the provision of medical treatment; that it is necessary for the health or safety of the patient or for the protection of other persons that treatment is provided; and that treatment cannot be provided unless he is subject to the provisions of the proposed Act. Again, it is a three stage process which consists of:

(a)   *Examination* by two practitioners, one of whom must be a recognised specialist and an approved mental health professional. The opinion as to the relevant conditions being met must be unanimous (s 11) but, in an emergency, the case may proceed in the absence of a second medical opinion. The examination must normally be completed in 120 hours.

(b)   *Assessment.* Given that a need for assessment is determined, the mental health professional must explain the situation to the patient, inform him of his rights to advocacy and appoint a nominated person as above. The patient must then be registered with the appropriate hospital (s 17) and becomes liable to compulsion; his assessment, and interim treatment, is the responsibility of an appointed 'clinical supervisor'. In addition, the hospital management must prepare a 'care plan' for a registered patient. In general, the assessment period cannot exceed 28 days.

(c)   *Treatment.* Application for an order authorising treatment must be made to the Tribunal on completion of the assessment. Before making the application, the clinical supervisor must consult with the patient's nominated person and any carer of the patient (s 31). A treatment order is limited to a period of six months but further orders of six months may be made; the further order may be for 12 months if the patient has already been under treatment for more than 12 months (s 38).

21.34 The move to a community care philosophy in psychiatric treatment means that there is a number of relatively seriously ill patients living outside psychiatric hospitals. Even so, the Mental Health Acts are closely bound to the management of those who are *detained* in hospital. As a result, not only have some existing measures of supervision, such as guardianship, proved inadequate but other attempts at long-term community orientated control have been shown to be improper under statute. Thus, the practice of granting leave (permissible under the Act) and revoking the leave if the patient became non-compliant was expressly declared to be unlawful.[47] Section 46(10) of the draft Bill now proposes authorising the clinical supervisor to revoke leave if it is necessary for the patient's health or safety or for the protection of others; this does not apply once the patient has ceased to be liable to be provided with medical treatment. What appear to be extensive powers of enforcement to attend hospital when under orders to do so are provided by s 53(3) of the draft Bill. We have already noted above that lack of supervision has resulted in a number of crimes of violence which have contributed to a general sense of dissatisfaction with the existing system. As a result, there is little doubt that proposed legislation will provide for the application of care and treatment orders to patients outside hospital together with the introduction of measures to ensure compliance with their terms. The draft Bill takes account of these problems to the extent that a distinction is made between resident and non-resident patients throughout. It seems likely, however, that there will be extensive modification – in favour of both the patients and the public – of the Mental Heath (Patients in the Community) Act 1995.

21.35 Persons without physical illness who are compulsorily detained in hospital – and particularly those who are mentally disturbed – are likely to see themselves as victims of paternalistic injustice. The strong possibility exists that they may institute proceedings against those responsible for their committal to and/or detention in hospital. This was foreseen in s 139 of the 1983 Act, which states:

> No person shall be liable ... to any civil or criminal proceedings ... in respect of any act purporting to be done in pursuance of this Act ... unless the act was done in bad faith or without reasonable care.

Moreover, no civil proceedings may be brought against any person without the leave of the High Court. Although this section seems, at first sight, to limit the rights of the patient quite severely, it has been held that Parliament must have intended to retain the court's inherent power to protect the rights of the individual; application for judicial review does not constitute 'civil proceedings' for the purposes of the Act and remains open to an aggrieved patient.[48] As to power of the court to withhold leave to bring an action, the Court of Appeal in *Winch*[49] overturned the trial judge's ruling that leave to proceed depended upon there being a prima facie case to bring. The court was no longer required to establish that there were substantial grounds for the

---

47 *R v Hallstrom, ex p W; R v Gardner, ex p L* [1986] QB 1090, [1986] 2 All ER 306.
48 *Ex p Waldron* [1986] QB 824, sub nom *R v Hallstrom, ex p W* [1985] 3 All ER 775, CA. Discussed by Legal Correspondent 'Actions by Psychotic Patients' (1986) 292 BMJ 128.
49 *Winch v Jones, Winch v Hayward* [1986] QB 296, [1985] 3 All ER 97, CA. Discussed by Legal Correspondent 'Legal Proceedings by Mental Patients' (1986) 292 BMJ 820.

patient's contention; the issue was simply whether or not the complaint appeared to be such that it deserved the fuller investigation which would be possible if the applicant was allowed to proceed – in Miss Winch's case, the court went so far as to deny any suggestion that the proceedings were likely to succeed. In passing, it will be remembered that s 139 relates only to actions against individuals. No such protection is afforded, for instance, to a Health Authority.

21.36 It cannot be denied, however, that detention in hospital for long periods is open to abuse without some form of independent review. This is provided for in the establishment of mental health review tribunals, to which patients who wish to have their cases considered can apply.[50] The tribunals have been subject to considerable criticism – a low incidence of appeals has been alleged and patients are said to have experienced difficulty in obtaining adequate representation. It is, perhaps, for these reasons that new and independent Mental Health Tribunals are proposed for both England and Scotland. Hospital authorities are duty bound to explain to patients their right of appeal to a tribunal; a case is now referred automatically if this right is not exercised within the first six months' detention. Hospital managers are also obliged to refer patients to the tribunal when detention has been renewed and the case has not been considered for three years. In all of this, however, the onus lies on the patient to prove that his continued detention is unjustified, whereas it might be argued that the reverse should be the case.

Conditions justifying compulsory admission

21.37 A major civil rights concern in this area is that the boundaries of mental illness should not be drawn so widely as to embrace forms of behaviour that are no more than non-conformist and, indeed, any new legislation must be compatible with the Human Rights Act 1998. Compulsory admission should be limited to conditions which amount to an illness that can be said to compromise the mental health of the sufferer and, in this respect, the 1983 and 1984 Acts distinguish between admission for assessment and admission for treatment. In the former case, the patient may be admitted under compulsion if he is thought to be suffering from a 'mental disorder' which is a term so widely defined as to include almost any mental aberration. Admission for treatment is more closely controlled and the Act requires that the patient be suffering from one of four specifically identified disorders: mental illness, severe mental impairment, psychopathic disorder or mental impairment. Those suffering from the first two conditions may be admitted irrespective of the likely effect of treatment; those suffering from psychopathic disorder or mental impairment can be detained only if they are likely to benefit from treatment. The draft Bill definition of 'treatment' is of interest in view of the controversy

---

50 P F Mawson 'The Function of Mental Health Review Tribunals under the Mental Health Act' (1986) 26 Med Sci & Law 291. For an account of the way in which the tribunals interpret their role and of the supervision by the courts of the process of review, see G Richardson *Law, Process and Custody: Prisoners and Patients* (1993) p 278 et seq.

that has arisen in past cases.[51] For the purposes of the future Act, it follows that of 1983 (s 145) and includes:

(a) nursing;
(b) care;
(c) habilitation (including education, and training in work, social and independent living skills); and
(d) rehabilitation.

It does appear, then, that the Bill is making provision for the compulsory treatment of those who are likely to benefit from no more than their environment. Moreover, as we have already intimated, the concept of 'treatability' has been banished from the Bill; thus, there is no need to suppose that detention or supervision will, necessarily, succeed.

21.38 The English draft Bill now defines mental disorder as any disability or disorder of mind or brain 'which results in an impairment or disturbance of mental functioning' – which seems to include virtually any aberration of behaviour – and there are no sub-sets to this; for the purposes of the application of the Act, however, it must be of such a nature or degree as to warrant the provision of medical treatment. The Scottish Mental Health Bill, by contrast, is likely to define three categories of mental disorder: mental illness, learning disability and personality disorder. Whether or not persons with learning disability will be included in the legislation remains open for discussion.

21.39 Perhaps the most significant distinction lies in the fact that the term 'mental illness', while being dropped from the English White Paper, is retained in its Scottish counterpart; its meaning is, therefore, worth brief consideration.[52] There is a wide consensus that it includes psychoses such as schizophrenia – and also anorexia nervosa – but neurotic conditions may well be considered as being unlikely to warrant hospital detention and, therefore, to be beyond its scope. The problem was neatly put by Roth and Kroll,[53] who cited the case of a young man who courted disaster through compulsive risk-taking; this involved having dangerous masochistic sexual encounters with violent men and, ultimately, led to his death. Such conduct is an 'illness' in so far as it affects the subject's general health and is beyond his control much as an organic illness would be; it would be classified as illness were it due, say, to hormonal imbalance but not if it were psychological in origin – which, say the authors, is illogical.[54] Personality disorders may be distinguished from mental illness, as the Scottish Executive intends, on a variety of grounds. The

---

51 For discussion of 'treatability', see para 21.10 above. Note that the same view of 'hospitalisation' as a form of treatment as was taken in *R v Canons Park Mental Health Review Tribunal, ex p A* [1995] QB 60, (1994) 18 BMLR 94 and *Reid v Secretary of State for Scotland* (para 21.10) was adopted in the little-known case of *R v Mental Health Review Tribunal, ex p MacDonald* (1998) COD 205. And see, also, the earlier case *R v Mersey Mental Health Review Tribunal, ex p D* (1987) Times, 13 April.
52 In fact, the only legal definition within the UK jurisdiction is to be found in Mental Health (Northern Ireland) Order 1986, SI 1986/595 (NI 4), Article 3(1).
53 M Roth and J Kroll *The Reality of Mental Illness* (1986) p 79.
54 Interestingly, psychiatric harm is not 'bodily injury' – at least within the terms of the Warsaw Convention.

role of organic factors in the former is controversial;[55] moreover, if one of the criteria of illness is that it 'overlays' the normal self, this cannot be said of a personality disorder which lies at the core of 'self'. The condition of pschopathy, which was identified by psychiatrists of the nineteenth century,[56] is listed as a mental disorder in the American Psychiatric Association's DSM-IV. Yet its precise defining criteria are unclear[57] and there s some concern that the tendency to label a wide range of anti-social conduct as psychopathic may lead to an undue medicalisation of deviant behaviour. One Scottish judge, having listened to a description of its symptomatology, remarked:

> It is, to my mind, descriptive rather of a typical criminal than of a person ... regarded as being possessed of diminished responsibility.[58]

This is an unscientific view but, in a sense, it points to the difficulty which many people have with the concept – namely, how is psychopathy to be distinguished, if at all, from uncomplicated anti-social conduct?

21.40 As things stand at present, sexual deviancy is specifically excluded as a sole ground for intervention under both the 1983 and 1984 Acts. This means that a person may engage in outrageous sexual practices but will not be liable to compulsory treatment unless he also manifests one of the qualifying mental disorders discussed above. In *Clatworthy*,[59] the appellant had been detained by reason of psychopathic disorder. He argued, successfully, that the only ground for the diagnosis was his sexual behaviour and that this could not, by itself, constitute the basis for his detention by virtue of the explicit exclusion of sexual deviance as a statutory form of mental disorder. Contemporary psychiatry is understandably cautious on this subject.

CONSENT TO TREATMENT

21.41 Previous legislation made no direct reference to the conditions under which a person compulsorily admitted could be given hospital treatment. It is important to note that the Mental Health Acts refer only to treatment given for the mental condition itself and it will have been noted throughout this book that this can cause considerable difficulty – in particular as related to reproductive activity in the female. The rules evolved to regulate the treatment of physical illness in psychiatric patients have been discussed in chapter 10; occasionally, however, psychiatric and physical disease are so intimately

---

55 See M Dolan 'Psychopathy: a Neuro-biological Perspective' (1994) 165 Brit J Psychiat 151. A genetic factor may, however, be operating: M Roth 'Psychopathic (Sociopathic) Personality' in R Bluglass and P Bowden (eds) *Principles and Practice of Forensic Psychiatry* (1990). Roth also cites research revealing EEG abnormalities in psychopaths.
56 The historical background is discussed in N Walker and S McCabe *Crime and Insanity in England and Wales* (1973) at II, p 205. See also P Pichot 'Psychopathic Behaviour: A Historical Overview' in R D Hare and D Schalling (eds) *Psychopathic Behaviour: Approaches to Research* (1978).
57 The category of personality disorder is now more differentiated – and refined. For a survey of advances in the diagnosis of conditions of this nature, see P Tyrer, P Carey and B Ferguson 'Personality Disorder in Perspective' (1991) 159 Brit J Psychiat 463.
58 *Carraher v HM Advocate* 1946 JC 108 at 117, per Lord Normand.
59 *R v Mental Health Tribunal, ex p Clatworthy* [1985] 3 All ER 699.

associated that the courts may be called upon to decide what is and what is not 'treatment of the psychiatric condition'. Such a situation is exemplified in the condition of anorexia nervosa – a life-threatening eating disorder which affects teenage girls in particular. The subject has been addressed in relation to refusal of treatment in chapter 10; here we confine ourselves to the more specific aspect of the treatment of psychiatric disease.

Anorexia nervosa

21.42 In the seminal case of *Re W*,[60] the Court of Appeal was in no doubt that, in the exercise of its inherent jurisdiction, it had the power to overrule a minor's refusal of treatment. It went on to say, per Lord Donaldson MR, that it is a feature of anorexia nervosa that it is capable of destroying the ability to make an informed choice:

> It creates a compulsion to refuse treatment or only to accept treatment which is likely to be ineffective. This attitude is part and parcel of the disease and the more advanced the disease, the more compelling it may become.[61]

These are strong words which, we suggest, open the door to non-consensual treatment of *all* cases of anorexia nervosa, irrespective of age.

21.43 In respect of adults, the courts of England and Wales now have no parens patriae jurisdiction. Given, then, that the patient has the capacity to refuse treatment, the courts have to decide whether or not force-feeding constitutes a treatment for mental disorder which can be given without consent under the terms of the Mental Health Act 1983, s 63 or, alternatively, is justified within the broad envelope of s 145 (see para 21.37 above). The problem was addressed in the Family Division in *Re KB*,[62] which involved an 18-year-old suffering from anorexia nervosa who was detained under the Mental Health Act 1983, s 3. Interestingly, she was originally force-fed under s 58 of the Act[63] but this was found to be improper; the health authority, therefore, sought a declaration that it was lawful to do so under the terms of s 63. It was agreed by all that nasogastric feeding was medical treatment.[64] The problem was whether the feeding was given as treatment for her mental disorder or for her physical symptoms – that is, to increase her weight. Ewbank J was happy to accept the argument that she was suffering from anorexia nervosa, which is an eating disorder, and that relieving symptoms was just as much a part of treatment as relieving the underlying cause; it was clear that feeding by nasogastric tube in the circumstances of the type of case was treatment envisaged under s 63. By way of an obiter dictum, the judge also followed *Re W* in that the treatment she was refusing was

---

60 *Re W (a minor) (medical treatment: court's jurisdiction)* [1993] Fam 64, [1992] 4 All ER 627.
61 [1993] Fam 64 at 81, [1992] 4 All ER 627 at 637.
62 *Re KB (adult) (mental patient: medical treatment)* (1994) 19 BMLR 144.
63 See para 21.52 below.
64 Relying, perhaps a trifle dubiously, on *Airedale NHS Trust v Bland* [1993] 1 All ER 821, (1993) 12 BMLR 64.

related to her mental illness and that, accordingly, she did not have the capacity to refuse that treatment.[65]

21.44 The matter was put beyond doubt in *B v Croydon Health Authority.*[66] This was a slightly different case in that the patient was suffering from 'borderline personality disorder' which manifested itself in a compulsion to self-harm, including punishment by way of denying herself something she enjoyed; the problem, again, was whether she could be legally compulsorily fed as her life became increasingly at risk. Thorpe J, at first instance, concluded that the effect of s 63 was to limit the autonomy of a detained patient whose capacity is unimpaired to treatments that are not related to the mental illness for which he or she is detained. On appeal, Hoffmann LJ rejected the suggestion that every act which forms part of treatment as defined by s 145 must, in itself, be likely to alleviate or prevent a deterioration of the mental disorder; treatments designed to alleviate the consequences of the disorder are all capable of being ancillary to a treatment calculated to alleviate or prevent a deterioration of the psychopathic disorder. There was no conceptual vagueness about treating the symptoms or consequences of a mental disorder and there was no question of the exercise of arbitrary power. The appeal was dismissed.

21.45 Some of the reasoning in these cases may seem to lean towards sophistry.[67] The cases as a whole do, however, demonstrate a judicial anxiety to save lives when that is possible and some distrust of an autonomy which allows patients to take fatal treatment decisions in circumstances in which their competence to do so is, at least, doubtful.

Forced feeding of prisoners

21.46 The psychopathic overtones of *B* lead us to the other, largely peripheral, topic of compulsory feeding of prisoners, many of whom in which the situation arises will have a background of personality disorder but as many of whom will be acting from political or other non-medical motives. As a consequence of this mix, the position of the doctor who wishes to save the life of a subject who is actively resisting sustenance demands particularly careful assessment.

21.47 Current policy is that the doctor's role is to advise the prisoner of the dangers of starvation, to have treatment and hospital facilities available but, otherwise, to refrain from interference. While this policy accords with the Declaration of Tokyo,[68] the doctor must, at times, be concerned as to whether the prisoner can, in truth, form an unimpaired and rational judgment.

---

65 A similar approach was adopted at first instance in *Riverside Mental Health NHS Trust v Fox* [1994] 1 FLR 614, sub nom *F v Riverside Health Trust* (1993) 20 BMLR 1. The judge's order authorising force feeding was, in fact, set aside on appeal but this was on technical grounds – the possibility of a further application in the event of need was fully accepted.
66 [1995] Fam 133, [1995] 1 All ER 683.
67 Though A Grubb 'Treatment without Consent (Personality Disorder): Adult' (1995) 2 Med L Rev 191 regards them as being the most sensible solution.
68 See Appendix D.

Voluntary starvation leads to severe metabolic dysfunction and, consequently, to mental impairment. A major ethical dilemma then arises as to whether the doctor can or should adjust his attitude according to the subject's current mental state.

21.48 This clearly smacks of 'cat-and-mouse' treatment which would, by to-day's ethical standards be deemed improper; moreover, re-feeding after some three weeks of starvation carries a serious risk of cardiac failure.[69] One would, in fact, have thought that the question had been solved in *Secretary of State for the Home Department v Robb*[70] in which Thorpe J firmly held that the right of the defendant to determine his future was plain. That right was not diminished by his status as a detained prisoner and there was no countervailing state interest to be set in the balance. However, Kennedy, in a closely argued analysis,[71] has pointed out, first, that it was unusual for the case, which concerned a prisoner rather than a patient, to be considered on the basis of medical law rather than of human rights and, secondly, that the tenor of the judgment was permissive rather than obligatory – the authorities *need* not feed, not *may* not feed. In short, *Robb* rested on its own merits and laid down no over-arching principle.

21.49 This point was raised in the later case of *R v Collins, ex p Brady*[72] in which the prisoner, Brady, went on hunger strike, ostensibly in protest at an attempt to move him from his protected environment. His responsible medical officer decided to force feed him and he was granted judicial review of that decision. The court approached the question as one of human rights which was to be judged by way of reasonableness.[73] It was adjudged that Brady's going on hunger strike was a symptom of his admitted personality disorder and that, as a result, treatment of starvation was treatment of the underlying psychopathy; the decision to treat was perfectly reasonable. In addition, in so far as he was unable to weigh the contending issues as to risks and needs in his own mind,[74] he was incapacitated in relation to all his decisions about food; the doctors were legally entitled to supply medical treatment in his best interests. As an addendum, in an obiter statement, Kay J had this to say:

> It would seem to me to be a matter for deep regret if the law has developed to a point in this area where the rights of a patient count for everything and other ethical values and institutional integrity count for nothing.[75]

We have every sympathy with Kay J who was forced, regretfully, to concede that it was beyond the compass of a first instance judge to decide the point in the absence of a need to do so.

---

69 M Peel 'Hunger Strikes' (1997) 315 BMJ 829.
70 [1995] Fam 127, [1995] 1 All ER 677.
71 I Kennedy 'Consent: Force-feeding of Prisoners' (1995) 3 Med L Rev 189.
72 (2001) 58 BMLR 173, [2000] Lloyd's Rep Med 355.
73 In its turn, to be based on the principles laid down in *R v Ministry of Defence, ex p Smith* [1996] QB 517, [1996] 1 All ER 257 – a particularly high standard of 'reasonableness' is needed in cases involving fundamental human rights.
74 *Re C (adult: refusal of medical treatment)* [1994] 1 All ER 819, (1993) 15 BMLR 77.
75 (2001) 58 BMLR 173 at 193.

General criteria as to consent to treatment by mental patients

21.50 In general, however, we are mainly concerned with the treatment of what is commonly non-violent mental disorder occurring in involuntary patients. The 1983 and 1984 statutes go some way to clarifying the scope of acceptable intervention by, in particular, delimiting the degree of invasion which is permitted and by, at the same time, defining the nature of consent to the procedures.

21.51 As has already been intimated, non-consensual treatment of the underlying mental disorder – and, as has become apparent, *only* the mental disorder – is permitted by statute (s 63 of the 1983 Act, draft Bill s 117) but the extent of this is limited by the conditions imposed by ss 57 and 58. Section 57 refers to what are loosely known as irreversible procedures, which include destruction of brain tissue or of its function and the surgical implantation of hormones for the control of the male sex drive;[76] it applies to the treatment of both voluntary and involuntary patients.[77] Consent by the patient is needed before such treatment can be given and this must be verified and certified as real by an appointed doctor and two non-medical witnesses who have also been appointed for the purpose.[78] Furthermore, the appointed doctor must certify that the treatment is likely to benefit the patient; he can do this only after consultation with two persons concerned professionally with the patient, one of whom is a nurse and the other neither a doctor nor a nurse. It is apparent that this section presents some difficulties. First, consent is essential. It follows that a patient who cannot consent cannot have treatment even though it may appear appropriate; the regulations can be waived only when the treatment is regarded as life saving (s 62(1)(a)). Secondly, the two confirmatory opinion providers must be *professionally* involved and it may be difficult to find a professional who knows the patient and is, at the same time, neither a doctor nor a nurse. The fact and results of irreversible treatments must be notified to the Mental Health Act Commission, who may withdraw the certificate issued by the appointed doctor (s 61(3)). The whole scenario must, however, now be very rare.[79]

21.52 Section 58 controls 'hazardous' treatments which, currently, include electro-convulsive therapy and long-term drug treatment – the latter being defined as continuing for three months or more. These may only be given if the patient has consented and either his responsible medical officer or an appointed doctor has verified that consent or if an appointed medical practitioner has certified that the patient cannot give valid consent but that the treatment would be of benefit to him; again, the doctor must consult two other persons as above who have been professionally concerned with the patient. Hazardous treatment can be given in the absence of certification only if it is

---

76 The specific limitations of ss 57 and 58 are laid out in the Mental Health (Hospital, Guardianship and Consent to Treatment) Regulations 1983, SI 1983/893.

77 The equivalent legislation in the Mental Health (Scotland) Act 1984, s 97 applies only to detained patients but this is specifically targeted for change in the forthcoming legislation.

78 The procedures to be followed in such cases are laid out in the *Code of Practice* approved by Parliament in 1990, para 16.

79 An average of 4–5 patients receive psychosurgery (see below) per year in Scotland: Scottish Association in Mental Health *Looking at Psychosurgery* (1999) www.samh.org.uk.

needed to save the patient's life or, provided it is not irreversible, to prevent a serious deterioration in his condition (s 62(1)(b)). Treatment covered by s 57 or s 58 may be given in circumstances of urgency if it is neither hazardous nor irreversible and is either necessary to alleviate serious suffering on the patient's part or represents the minimum interference necessary to prevent the patient from behaving violently or being a danger to himself or others.[80] The patient may withdraw his consent to s 57 or s 58 treatments at any time – once he does so, the process of certification must start again (s 60).

21.53 There are significant differences from these regulations in the draft Bill. First, s 112, which deals with destruction of brain tissue, makes no mention of hormonal implants. Similarly, s 118 refers only to electro-convulsive therapy; long term drug treatment is not included. In each case, however, opportunity is provided for the addition of other treatments. Second, non-consensual psychosurgery will be available under s 115. The regulations are complex as to certification, the most significant condition, perhaps, being that a declaration of lawfulness from the High Court will be required. The difficulty of obtaining the required confirmatory opinions has not been recognised and the patient's nominated person must be involved at all stages.

SUMMARY OF PROPOSALS FOR REFORM

21.54 It might be convenient here to summarise the proposed wide-ranging changes anticipated in mental health law. There will be a new independent decision-making body, the Mental Health Tribunal, which will scrutinise and authorise treatment plans drawn up by clinical staff caring for the patient. Under the new system, there will be three stages to the compulsory treatment process. In stage one, there will be an initial examination of the patient – conducted by two doctors and a social worker – to decide whether compulsory powers for his or her care should be invoked. This can only be done if, without such treatment, the patient might be at risk of serious harm or might pose a risk of serious harm to others. In the second stage, the patient may be detained for a period of 28 days, during which a formal assessment will be made and treatment may be initiated under a formal care plan. In the third stage, the use of compulsion beyond 28 days will depend on a decision by the new Mental Health Tribunal. In the third stage, a care and treatment order may be made by the Mental Health Tribunal – or by a court in the case of a mentally disordered offender. This treatment order may specify treatment in the community or in a hospital. The first two orders may last for up to six months each; subsequent orders may last for up to twelve months. Steps may be specified in community orders to prevent patients, if they do not comply with the order, becoming a risk to themselves, their carers or the public. In addition, a new Patient Advocacy Liaison Service will provide access to information and legal representation.

21.55 The Scottish White Paper *Renewing Mental Health Law* follows a similar pattern although the existing broad framework of emergency detention (up to 72 hours), short-term detention (up to 28 days) and long-term compulsion is likely to be retained. The objective is a flexible system of management

---

80 Section 62(1)(c) and (d).

which combines community and hospital care. As in England, the patient will have the right appoint a Named Person to help with his or her interests in Mental Health Act proceedings which will also include a new Mental Health Tribunal. The Mental Welfare Commission for Scotland will continue to promote the principles of the Act. Importantly, the Mental Health (Public Safety and Appeals) (Scotland) Act 1999 will be reviewed in the light of the Privy Council decision in *A v The Scottish Ministers*.[81]

21.56 We confess to some difficulty in endorsing the degree of antipathy that the publication of the draft Bill has provoked, particularly among the medical profession.[82] Certainly, its wording suggests that a wider group of persons than previously could now be subject to compulsory regulation – and this could include those who are, basically, anti-social. Most would agree, however, that we are witnessing major social changes and it is difficult for the law to ignore these. Moreover, the tone of the Bill in relation to delimiting human rights is, at most, permissive – there is no compulsion to extend the catchment area of the legislation. Finally, the Bill follows the pattern of much modern social statute law in establishing a Code of Practice as a base on which it should be applied. How the new Acts operate will, therefore, be as much in the hands of the coal-face workers as in those of the bureaucrats of Westminster and Holyrood. If there is to be criticism, it seems that it is more properly aimed at yet another increase in the administrative burden that is being forced on the medical profession.

Behaviour modification

21.57 The focus of our discussion so far has been on treatment, the main purpose of which is to restore the patient – as far as is possible – to the pre-morbid state. Psychiatry and psychology may, however, make rather broader claims and offer to alter undesirable behaviour. The methods used to achieve this may be non-intrusive, in the sense that they involve no physical intervention, or they may be very invasive – brain surgery, commonly referred to as psychosurgery or neurosurgery for mental disorder (NMD) – being the most extreme example. Several ethical problems arise in either case: are coercive techniques ever acceptable? To what extent has the therapist the right to impose his model of desirable behaviour on the patient?[83] can consent ever be given to such treatments if they are offered in the form of an inducement – for example, as an alternative to punishment? These questions are posed most dramatically in relation to neurosurgery for mental disorder, which, as a result, merits separate discussion.

21.58 The essential claim of NMD is that it can change behaviour patterns in reasonably predictable ways. Modern techniques avoid the crudities of leucotomy and involve localised stereotactic interference with parts of the brain which influence feelings and sexuality – a process which involves destruction of

81 Para 21.11 above.
82 Z Kmietowicz 'Organisations Unite against Draft Mental Health Bill' (2002) 325 BMJ 9.
83 S Fairbairn and G Fairbairn (eds) *Psychology, Ethics and Change* (1987); A McCall Smith 'Changing the Offender: Ethical Issues in Behaviour Modification' (1988) Acta Juridica 169; J Holmes and R Linley *The Values of Psychotherapy* (1989).

brain tissue approximating in size to that of a garden pea. NMD may be offered for a variety of conditions, most frequently for affective illnesses such as depression; other indications have included aggressive behaviour, intractable pain and unacceptable sexual urges.[84] Any discussion of the effectiveness of the procedure raises, of course, the question of the standpoint from which success is measured. It is important to distinguish the concept of therapeutic success – removal of symptoms without incurring unacceptable side-effects – from that of manageability. It is hardly proper to regard a treatment as successful if its main effect is merely to render the patient passive and compliant. In one sense, this constitutes little more than the 'neutralising' of the patient and psychosurgery lies open to the challenge that it is primarily a method of social control. As one writer has put it, 'Life in "Brave New World" may be more pleasant for all, but only John the Savage is fully human'.[85]

21.59 The utility of NMD is debated. A number of surgeons have reported good results. It is, however, rarely used. There were 17 referrals for psychotherapy in England and Wales in the years 1997-99 and in all cases certificates of treatment were issued by the Mental Health Act Commission.[86] The Assembly of the United Nations has resolved that NMD should never be imposed on an involuntary patient and that, otherwise, its use should be subject to informed consent by the patient.[87] But, even if one accepts that the patient is capable of giving a consent which is valid, in that it is informed and uncoerced, that fact alone may not be sufficient to justify the treatment – a grossly maiming and irreversible operation which achieves only a doubtful therapeutic purpose could well be seen as a procedure which is unacceptable on grounds of public policy. As we have seen, the patient who is incapable of consenting may not, as things stand, be given irreversible and hazardous treatments. He may therefore suffer, and the alternative view might well be that there is no reason why patients should be denied a potentially effective treatment purely because it is open to abuse or is hazardous. Such treatments should, of course, be subjected to control – preferably control which embodies an element of outside, lay opinion – but they should not be excluded from the range of those available by virtue only of their nature. It is for this reason that proposals are before the Scottish Parliament to amend the regulations so as to allow non-consensual NMD subject to approval in each case by the Court of Session.[88] There is, however, considerable opposition to the proposal both inside and outside Parliament and its further progress is doubtful.[89]

84 E S Valenstein 'Who Receives Psychosurgery?' in E S Valenstein (ed) *The Psychosurgery Debate* (1980) p 89. Modern practice virtually confines the procedure to the treatment of depression, obsessive compulsive disorders and bi-polar affective disorder: Royal College of Psychiatrists Working Group *Neurosurgery for Mental Disorder* (2000) www.rcpsych.ac.uk/publications/cr/council/cr89.pdf.
85 J Kleinig *Ethical Issues in Psychosurgery* (1985).
86 D Chiswick 'Forensic Psychiatry' in J K Mason *Forensic Medicine for Lawyers* (4th edn, 2001), p 415.
87 General Assembly of the United Nations *Resolution A/RES/46/119* of 17 December 1991, principle 11(14).
88 Adults with Incapacity (Specified Medical Treatment) (Scotland) Regulations 2002, SI 2002/275. The proposal emanates from the CRAG Working Group on Mental Illness *Neurosurgery for Mental Disorder* (1996). See K Foster 'Executive to Allow Banned Brain Surgery' *The Scotsman*, 12 June 2002.
89 It is also difficult to reconcile with the contrary intention expressed in *Renewing Mental Health Law*, para 26 (para 21.55 above).

21.60 Controversy of almost equal intensity surrounds the use of chemical methods to control the behaviour of actual or potential sex offenders.[90] Opponents of these procedures have described them in such terms as 'chemical castration' and have been especially concerned as to their inherent coercive nature. Certainly, Parliament has expressed this view in specifically including surgical implantation of hormones to control the male sex drive in those 'irreversible' treatments controlled by s 57 of the 1983 Act. On the other hand, it is perfectly possible to see behaviour modification of this type in a properly therapeutic light. The person troubled by sexual inclinations which he cannot control may look upon drug treatment as his only hope of a normal life in the community.[91] On this analysis, the refusal of treatment to someone who genuinely seeks it can amount to unacceptable paternalism – and this may well be behind the proposal to delete them from the category of treatments to which special safeguards apply.

21.61 Just such an instance arose in *R v Mental Health Commission, ex p X*.[92] X was a compulsive paedophile who sought medical help. Standard antiandrogen treatment was unsuccessful and he was transferred to a new and relatively untried synthetic compound with the proprietary name of Goserelin; this was administered monthly by the subcutaneous insertion of a thin cylindrical implant. A satisfactory response was obtained with three insertions; however, the Mental Health Commission was now concerned as to the validity of his consent and withdrew its approval of the relevant certificates. X applied for judicial review – as a result of which, the Commission's decision was quashed. The court's opinion raised several interesting points; some were, to an extent, peripheral to the main question but they merit note. First, it was held that, despite its action, a synthetic chemical compound could not be described as a 'hormone'; secondly, the subcutaneous injection of a substance through a needle, albeit of wide bore, was not a 'surgical implant'. Most importantly, however, the court noted that sexual deviance is expressly excluded from the definition of mental disorder for the purposes of the 1983 Act (s 1(3)); Goserelin was used for the treatment of such deviance and, although success in this respect would inevitably lead to improvement in any associated mental condition, it was not a treatment for mental disorder and was not subject to the controls of s 57. The Commission's decision was unreasonable.[93] Once again, some of the observations made may be seen as bordering on the casuistic; nevertheless, we feel that the case demonstrates that, if it is possible to do so, the courts will disapprove a bureaucratic attempt to separate a patient from the treatment he genuinely seeks and that they will support the doctors who are supplying it in good faith.

90 Mental Health (Hospital, Guardianship and Consent to Treatment) Regulations 1983, SI 1983/893.
91 S L Halleck 'The Ethics of Antiandrogen Therapy' (1981) 138 Am J Psychiat 642.
92 (1988) 9 BMLR 77.
93 For discussion of the case see P Fennell 'Sexual Suppressants and the Mental Health Act' [1988] Crim LR 660.

22 Psychiatry and the criminal law

22.1 The psychiatrist – and also the clinical psychologist – may become involved with criminal law at a number of points in the process of trial. Most dramatically, he may be called upon to provide evidence to the court of the accused person's mental state; this intimately involves the psychiatrist in the essential function of any criminal trial – the determination of guilt or innocence. In addition to fulfilling this need, psychiatric evidence may be invoked to assist the court in the exercise of its sentencing power. Psychiatric reports on an offender may persuade the court to impose a more lenient custodial sentence or may point to what would be a more appropriate means of dealing with the offender; moreover, the court may ensure, as a result, that an offender gets further psychiatric or other medical treatment. The psychiatrist may be called upon to assist the court in other ways. Even when the sanity of the accused is not in question, evidence may be called as to the mental state of a witness, if that is relevant to the issue of the reliability of his or her evidence.[1] Attempts have been made to introduce psychiatric evidence which is aimed at demonstrating that an accused person's disposition was such that he could not have formed the necessary intention to commit the offence with which he is charged, but the courts have generally been reluctant to allow what they see as the usurpation of their exclusive power to decide such issues of mens rea.

22.2 The grounds for strictly limiting the scope of psychiatric evidence were spelled out in *R v Turner*, in which the Court of Appeal warned that:

> The fact that an expert witness has impressive scientific qualifications does not, by that fact alone, make his opinion on matters of human nature and behaviour within the limits of normality any more helpful than that of the jurors themselves; but there is a danger that they think it does.[2]

---

1 This was accepted in *Toohey v Metropolitan Police Comr* [1965] AC 595, [1965] 1 All ER 506, HL. See also *R v MacKenney* (1980) 72 Cr App Rep 78.
2 [1975] QB 834 at 841, [1975] 1 All ER 70 at 74, per Lawton LJ. For discussion, see D H Sheldon and M D MacLeod 'From Normative to Positive Data: Expert Psychological Evidence Re-assessed' [1991] Crim LR 811; D Sheldon 'The Admissibility of Psychiatric and Psychological Evidence' 1992 SLT 301. For an interesting analysis of the defects in the 'common sense' view of human conduct, see R D Mackay and A M Colman 'Excluding Expert Evidence: A Tale of Ordinary Folk and Common Experience' [1991] Crim LR 800.

This has meant, in English law at least, that there has been very little room for the insights of human psychology in interpreting an accused person's conduct. In *R v Hurst*,[3] for example, an attempt to introduce evidence of the accused's idiosyncratic reactions was unsuccessful. In this case a drug courier, who claimed that she had been coerced into committing the offence, sought to adduce expert evidence that, since she had been trained in her youth to fear men she was, as a consequence, likely to do as she was ordered. In *R. v Smith (Morgan James)*,[4] however, the House of Lords held that evidence of the appellant's depression should have been put to the jury so that they might consider this in judging the effect of the provocation in question. This injects an element of psychological subjectivity in which expert evidence may play a part, but the decision is limited in its effect to the plea of provocation. Other jurisdictions have shown themselves readier to invoke the insights of psychiatry and psychology. This has happened in Canada, for example, but even there, where the judiciary is more receptive to psychological evidence, concern has been expressed about the possible usurpation of the right of the court itself to determine issues of human conduct without resort to evidence of psychiatric or psychological syndromes.[5] If there is tension here between law and the behavioural sciences, this is because the law, in its judgment of human conduct, has traditionally adhered to objective standards. Psychology and psychiatry, by contrast, are inherently subjective disciplines; they seek to understand and explain how an individual mind has worked, a perspective which in many cases may have an exculpatory effect. This, of course, leads to concern that such evidence may destabilise the criminal law by weakening the objective standards to which people are expected to conform. Even if the courts were to become more receptive to the possibility that psychologists can throw light on obscure or abnormal aspects of human behaviour, such a development should not be allowed to introduce prejudice into a trial. The courts should be cautious, for example in admitting psychological profiling, a technique that has been widely used in the investigation of crime – particularly in the United States and not always with unequivocal results.[6] Psychological predictions as to what sort of person is likely to have committed an offence may help investigators but is not admissible as prosecution evidence and should not be available to the defence.[7] The part played by the psychiatrist in the criminal justice process still has its ethical snares even when thus limited. In theory, the psychiatric witness should be required to do no more than pronounce on the presence or absence of a mental abnormality but, in practice, the danger exists that he will be encouraged to address himself to the question of responsibility. There is also the risk that psychiatric questions will be unduly

---

3   [1995] 1 Cr App Rep 82. For comment, see (1995) 59 J Crim L 252.
4   [2000] 4 All ER 289.
5   A process heralded by the decision in *R v Lavallee* [1990] 1 SCR 852. For further discussion, see D M Paciooco 'Coping with Expert Evidence about Human Behaviour' (1999) 25 Queen's LJ 305.
6   Now extending to the psychological autopsy, of which possibly the most publicised example was the investigation into the explosion on the USS Iowa, in which 47 people died: see D Canter and M Cremer 'The Psychological Autopsy' in J K Mason and B Purdue (eds) *The Pathology of Trauma* (3rd edn, 1999) ch 30. It is to be noted that the psychological autopsy has been rejected in the English Court of Appeal: *R v Gilfoyle* [2001] 2 Cr App R 57, [2001] Crim LR 312.
7   For full discussion, see D C Ormerod 'The Evidential Implications of Psychological Profiling' [1996] Crim LR 863.

simplified in order to provide the 'key' to the unlocking of certain pleas. This has happened in relation to that of diminished responsibility,[8] in respect of which medical evidence frequently goes unchallenged; the court may be looking for a pretext for the exercise of leniency. It is doubtful if psychiatrists should lend themselves to procedures which might involve moral and professional compromise.[9] The psychiatrist gives evidence to the court as an expert. He does not provide an irrebuttable conclusion as to the state of mind of the accused but, rather, tenders an expression of opinion which will ultimately be decided upon by the judge or jury as the case may be. As a Scottish judge said of expert witnesses:

> Their duty is to furnish the judge or the jury with the necessary scientific criteria for testing the accuracy of their conclusions, so as to enable the judge or jury to form their own independent judgment by the application of these criteria to the facts proved in evidence.[10]

22.3 While a jury does not have to accept psychiatric evidence, it is not justified in discounting such evidence when it is not contradicted in any way. This has been clearly laid down in a number of cases[11] but forensic psychiatric evidence is sometimes ignored in spite of this legal acknowledgment.[12] Certainly, psychiatric evidence which is favourable to the accused is more likely to be accepted in a case where the accused attracts sympathy – where, for example, a woman is charged with the killing of a tormenting and violent husband – rather than in those where such sympathy is unlikely – as in a brutal murder committed for purposes of sexual gratification.[13]

MENTAL ILLNESS AND CRIME

22.4 At the heart of this issue is the question of the extent to which mental illness affects responsibility for criminal conduct. At one extreme is the view that a great deal of such conduct is explained by the psychopathological factors present in the offender's background – the 'crime as disease' position. At the other is the notion that the vast majority of mentally ill offenders are, in fact, responsible for their crimes, on the grounds that their mental abnormality does not necessarily impair their ability to understand the difference between right and wrong and to choose accordingly. Most supporters of the latter position would agree, however, that there can be no question of responsibility where illness is so severe as to distort fundamentally the offender's perception

---

8   See para 22.21 et seq below.
9   D Chiswick 'Use and Abuse of Psychiatric Testimony' (1985) 290 BMJ 975. See also J R Rappeport 'Ethics and Forensic Psychiatry' in S Bloch and P Chodoff (eds) *Psychiatric Ethics* (2nd edn, 1991) p 391.
10 *Davie v Edinburgh Magistrates* 1953 SC 34 at 40, per Lord Cooper.
11 *R v Matheson* [1958] 2 All ER 87, [1958] 1 WLR 474, CCA; *Taylor v R* (1978) 22 ALR 599.
12 Psychiatric evidence was discounted by the jury in the trial of Peter Sutcliffe, the so-called 'Yorkshire Ripper'. For discussion, see G Silverman 'Psychiatry after *Sutcliffe*' (1981) 125 Sol Jo 518. Also, H A Prins 'Diminished Responsibility and the Sutcliffe Case: Legal, Psychiatric and Social Aspects (A "Layman's" View)' (1983) 23 Med Sci & Law 17.
13 See para 22.23 below.

of reality. They may also be ready to accept the effect of organic brain changes on behaviour and, hence, on culpability; there appears, for example, to be convincing evidence of such a link in the case of Huntingdon's disease. [14] The controversial cases, then, are those which involve the less serious conditions, such as neuroses or personality disorders.

22.5 The problem here is essentially that of identifying a causal relationship between mental illness and crime. Such a relationship cannot be conclusively established, although the association of certain psychiatric conditions with criminal conduct appears to be strong.[15] This is particularly the case with psychopathy. As Hare and his collaborators observed on studying the careers of a group of men diagnosed with antisocial personality disorder: 'Psychopaths generally had significantly more convictions for assault, theft, robbery, fraud, possession of a weapon, and escaping custody than did non-psychopaths.'[16] Other conditions may underlie other instances of criminal conduct. A proportion of those suffering from depressive illness, for example, may engage in violent conduct directed against persons or property; the most likely explanation of this conduct lies not in any defect of character so much as in the irritability which stems directly from the illness. Similarly, a number of shop-lifting incidents, particularly those which are markedly out of character, are thought to be associated with depression.[17] Certain crimes attract a psychiatric explanation by virtue of their unusual nature. Arson may be motivated by a financial motive or by a desire for revenge but it is apparently motiveless in some cases. This suggests that there is a psychopathological explanation, a hypothesis which is borne out by the frequently abnormal psychiatric profile of arsonists – particularly younger ones.[18] In the case of sex offences, the nature of the crime may be so bizarre as to make sense only in terms of a psychiatric explanation. Once again, the backgrounds of many sex offenders reveal a range of defects and abnormalities, many of which are rooted in highly stressful experiences in early life. It is significant that many child abusers were themselves sexually abused as children and, in the midst of a widespread moral panic over the sexual abuse of children, it is salutary to reflect on the fact that paedophilia, the condition which may lead to such conduct, is a psychiatric disorder listed as such in the diagnostic manuals.[19] This fact may not exculpate the offender – it may not be unreasonable to expect people to control unacceptable drives and impulses – but it may be

---

14   P Jensen, K Fenger et al 'Crime in Huntingdon's Disease: A Study of Registered Offenders among Patients, Relatives, and Controls" (1998) 65 J Neurol Neurosurg Psychiat 467.
15   Numreous studies point to a high incidence of psychiatric conditions among offenders. An example is: S Hodgins, S A Mednick, P A Brennan et al 'Mental Disorder and Crime: Evidence from a Danish Birth Cohort Study' (1996) 53 Arch Gen Psychiat 489.
16   R Hare, L McPherson and A Forth 'Male Psychopaths and their Criminal Careers' (1988) 56 J Consult Clin Psych 710.
17   R Bluglass 'Shoplifting' in R Bluglass and P Bowden (eds) *Principles and Practice of Forensic Medicine* (1990) p 787; G H Gudjonsson 'Psychological and Psychiatric Aspects of Shoplifting' (1990) 30 Med Sci & Law 45.
18   H Prins, G Tennant and K Tirck 'Motives for Arson (Fire Raising)' (1985) 25 Med Sci & Law 275. Arson has also been associated with epileptic automatism: R Brook, M Dolan and P Coorey 'Arson and Epilepsy' (1996) 36 Med Sci & Law 268.
19   World Health Organisation *The ICD-10 Classification of Mental and Behavioural Disorders*, F 65.4 (1992); American Psychiatric Association *Diagnostic and Statistical Manual of Mental Disorders* (4th edn, 1994).

that a therapeutic response, rather than an unambiguously punitive one, is more appropriate in some cases of this nature.

22.6 The presence of psychiatric abnormality does not of itself provide grounds for exculpation unless it can be established that the abnormality caused the commission of the offence. Even then, the question of whether the defendant could have chosen not to do as he did remains. A person may have a strong urge to commit an antisocial act, but society may expect such urges to be controlled. Is it unreasonable to expect similar self-control on the part of the mentally abnormal person? It is certainly not such a person's fault if a desire to commit an offence is prompted by illness – but neither is it the fault of the mentally normal person if he experiences a similar strong antisocial desire, which may spring from his unconscious. In fact, society may expect both to conform to the provisions of the criminal law, provided that both are aware that these provisions exist. What lies at the heart of responsibility is the *ability* of a person to conform, because we do not (or, at least, should not) hold people responsible for that which they cannot do. If the condition from which the mentally abnormal person suffers is such as to prevent him from conforming to the provisions of the law, then it is wrong to hold him to account. The test, then, should not be whether a particular label can be put on the condition from which a defendant suffers, but whether the effect of his illness was to put him in a position where he either did not know what he was doing or could not help doing it. Such a test satisfies the criteria of a humane theory of criminal responsibility but, as will be seen below, the law has not found it easy to apply.

THE INSANITY PLEA

22.7 The belief that the insane should not be punished because they are not responsible for punishable acts lies at the root of the insanity defence in criminal law.[20] In simple language, the insane are not 'to blame' for what they do, and for many laymen that intuitive moral assessment will be sufficient. At a more theoretical level, a variety of grounds can be postulated as justifying acquittal in such cases. The insane offender may be ignorant of the fact that what he is doing is wrong, in either moral or legal terms, or he may be unaware of the consequences of his actions. His intentions or his motives in acting might, likewise, differ from those of the sane offender if they are affected by thought disorder. The acts of the insane may also be analysed in terms of involuntariness. That an act should be voluntary is a pre-requisite for the attribution of responsibility: if it is not willed by the actor, the law takes the view that there is no actus reus and that there can, then, be no criminal liability.[21] The insane offender can therefore be exculpated either on the

---

20 For a useful discussion of the theoretical basis of the insanity defence, see J Radden *Madness and Reason* (1985). There is an excellent survey in L Reznek *Evil or Ill* (1997), which succeeds in combining philosophical and psychiatric insights. Legal treatments of the issue include R D Mackay *Mental Condition Defences in the Criminal Law* (1995), F McAuley *Insanity, Psychiatry and Criminal Responsibility* (1993) and F Boland *Anglo-American Insanity Defence Reform* (1999). For a comparative survey, see: P Bal and F Koenraadt 'Criminal Law and Mentally Ill Offenders in Comparative Perspective' (2000) 6 Psychology Crime Law 219.
21 On voluntary acts, see A Ashworth *Principles of Ciminal Law* (3rd edn, 1999) pp 98 et seq.

grounds of lack of mens rea – in that he did not act with the requisite criminal intent – or because there was no actus reus.

22.8 Involuntariness, however, poses a difficult concept for the criminal law and is generally used to describe only those acts over which the actor has no muscular control. A nervous spasm is classically an involuntary act, as is an act performed while asleep. The status of acts falling into the category of irresistible impulses is, however, different. A mental disorder may well have prompted an accused to steal or set fire to property but, although this may be something over which he (or his reflective ego) really has no control, it would not be accepted as an involuntary act in terms of the criminal law if it were shown that the act was performed consciously. It is only in those states where somebody is so disturbed as to be 'out of control' that his actions might fit into the usual criminal law category of involuntary acts.

22.9 In many cases, a mentally abnormal offender may act in a way which would not exculpate him prima facie in terms of the mens rea and actus reus requirements. The accused may know exactly what he is doing and intend to achieve a very specific and intelligible objective in acting as he does, yet there are clear grounds for exculpation if the conduct in question is closely associated with a mental disorder. An example of such a case is *R v Oommen*,[22] a decision of the Supreme Court of Canada. Here a man who suffered from paranoid beliefs that he was being persecuted by a particular group integrated a woman with whom he was living into this delusional belief structure. He now saw her as being under instructions by his persecutors to kill him, and he killed her first, acting in what he saw as self-defence. It was held that, although he knew exactly what he was doing, he might not have thought that his act was wrong because, as a result of his delusional beliefs, he saw her as an immediate threat to his life. The accused was sent back for retrial on this basis.

22.10 The place of deterrence is also an important consideration. If it is accepted that deterrence is one of the principal purposes of the criminal law, then there is no point in convicting the insane because the deterrent effect is unlikely to have significant personal impact. As Barry J put it:

> It is useless for the law to seek to deter persons from committing crimes if they cannot be influenced by the possibility or probability of subsequent punishment because of their psychotic condition. The kind of mental awareness which justly exposes the person to punishment for a criminal act is thus sane awareness not the distorted or confused or unreal awareness of a diseased mind.[23]

The McNaghten Rules

22.11 Merely being insane does not, in itself, qualify as a defence to a criminal charge in English law. In order to benefit from the special verdict of 'not guilty by reason of insanity', an accused person must satisfy the test laid down in the McNaghten Rules, the controversial text which has dominated

22 [1994] 2 SCR 507.
23 *R v Weise* [1969] VR 953 at 964.

English law on the subject since the mid-nineteenth century. The rules originate in the pronouncement of the House of Lords in 1843 in the case of Daniel McNaghten,[24] who had been charged with the shooting of the Prime Minister's secretary in the belief that the secretary was the Prime Minister himself. The House of Lords laid down the basic test that acquittal on the grounds of insanity was appropriate if the accused 'was labouring under such a defect of reason, from disease of the mind, as not to know (1) the nature and quality of the act he was doing, or, if he did know it, (2) that he did not know he was doing what was wrong'. This test, variously formulated and interpreted, has since been applied throughout the Commonwealth as well as in the United States, where it has had mixed fortunes.

22.12 Criticism of the McNaghten Rules has been forceful and sustained. At the root of the problem is the very antiquity of the rules; nineteenth-century psychiatric notions differed from those of today in terminology and in substance, and it seems remarkable that Victorian concepts should still dominate the modern test of insanity (even the term 'insanity' has been abandoned in contemporary psychiatry). At the outset, the rules place too great an emphasis on reason as the controlling element in human behaviour. Secondly, the concept of disease of the mind, which forms a vital part of the rules, is one which is no longer favoured by psychiatrists. Nor is there an accepted legal definition of what constitutes such a disease – and this raises the question as to the status of a host of conditions, including psychopathy and other personality disorders. More important than the objections on the point of reason are those which refer to the emphasis in the rules on the knowledge of the accused. The controversy here has focused on the interpretation of the word 'know'. Narrowly interpreted – and the majority of the critics of McNaghten have assumed that it is the narrow interpretation which will be favoured by the courts – the word 'know' implies cognitive awareness rather than broader emotional understanding. As a result of this, many insane offenders might be held to fail the McNaghten test on the grounds that, in this sense, they would probably know what they were doing. In fact, courts have tended to take a broader view of the knowledge requirement and have often required something more than an intellectual knowledge of the nature and quality of the act in question. In Canada, s 16 of the Criminal Code essentially embodies the McNaghten test of insanity but states that a defence may be established if it is shown that the accused failed either to know or to appreciate the nature and quality of his act.[25] In interpreting this provision, the Canadian courts have ruled that, in order to be said to appreciate the nature and quality of his act, an accused person must not only know what he is doing but also must be able to understand the consequences of his act. This was taken even further by the Supreme Court of Canada in *Cooper v R*,[26] in which it was said that appreciation involves emotional as well as intellectual awareness and, thus, is not the same as knowledge as conceived in the McNaghten test. This

---

24 (1843) 10 Cl & Fin 200, HL. McNaghten experienced delusions of persecution and would probably be diagnosed today as suffering from paranoid schizophrenia.

25 The application of s 16 of the Canadian Criminal Code is discussed by S V Verdun-Jones 'Tightening the Reins: Recent Trends in the Application of the Insanity Defence in Canada' (1991) Med Law 285.

26 (1980) 110 DLR (3d) 46.

would clearly cause difficulties in the case of psychopaths, who typically lack this ability to appreciate matters emotionally. It is not surprising, then, that in *Kjeldsen v R*[27] the court should have opted for intellectual, as opposed to emotional, appreciation as the criterion for the application of the insanity test in the Criminal Code. Kjledsen was a sexually-motivated psychopath who cold-bloodedly killed his female victim. It was apparent that the killing left him unmoved and that he probably did not appreciate (in an emotional sense) the nature of what he was doing. But, if he were to be adjudged insane, then every person who committed a crime and simply felt no remorse or emotional distress over what he had done, or who was simply incapable of empathising with his victim, would be entitled to an acquittal on the grounds of insanity. The court therefore endorsed the view that the requirement that the accused appreciate the wrongfulness of his act did not refer to emotional appreciation.

22.13   There has also been some judicial debate over the significance of the term 'wrong' as it is used in the context of the McNaghten Rules. Does the accused have to know that his act is morally wrong or does he have to know that it is legally wrong? English courts have come down in favour of the latter; a successful defence must show that the accused did not know that the act was legally wrong.[28] In theory, at least, this might lead to the absurd result of the denial of the insanity defence to an accused who heard voices commanding him to commit murder and, although he knew murder to be illegal, thought that the voices came from the Prime Minister and acted accordingly.

22.14   One avenue of escape from the limitations of McNaghten is to adopt a test which emphasises the actor's control over action. This test concentrates not on the cognitive aspects of the matter but on volitional features – an accused is not to be held responsible if he is shown to be incapable by reason of mental disorder of conforming his conduct to the requirements of law. These theories have long enjoyed support, and indeed a control test is written into a number of statutory statements of the defence, sometimes alongside other criteria. The Criminal Code of Western Australia, for example, allows the defence where the accused can establish lack of capacity either to understand what he is doing, or to know that what he is doing is wrong, or to control his actions.[29] One form of the control test is the irresistible impulse doctrine, which was rejected in English law in *Sodeman v R*[30] and, again, in *R v Rivett*[31] and which has attracted little support elsewhere.[32] Control theories need not, however, always be tied to the irresistible impulse concept; this is demonstrated by some American decisions in which the suddenness of the prompting to act has not been regarded as significant.

---

27   [1981] 2 SCR 617.
28   *R v Windle* [1952] 2 QB 826, [1952] 2 All ER 1, CCA.
29   Section 27. For discussion of the Western Australian provisions, see Law Reform Commission of Western Australia *Report on the Criminal Process and Persons Suffering from Mental Disorder* (1991).
30   [1936] 2 All ER 1138, PC.
31   (1950) 34 Cr App Rep 87, CCA.
32   For the fate of the irresistible impulse concept in Canada, see *R v Wolfson* [1965] 3 CCC 304; *R v Borg* [1969] SCR 551.

22.15 A final, and wider ranging, difficulty associated with these tests of responsibility which focus on ability to control behaviour lies in the fact that such theories view the cognitive and volitional functions of the mind as being quite separate and isolated. Modern psychiatry rejects this and regards the human personality as an integrated whole – one cannot distinguish these functions and view them in isolation from other mental processes.

Alternative attitudes

22.16 The American experience of the insanity defence has been particularly interesting. Criticism of the McNaghten Rules in the United States has been intense and the courts have responded by experimenting with a variety of alternative approaches.[33] For some, however, such reforms have not gone far enough, and there have been attempts in a number of states to abolish the insanity defence altogether, leaving the matter to be decided through the application of ordinary mens rea rules. These moves have been prompted in large part by concern over the abuse of the defence by defence lawyers eager to exploit any possible avenue for their clients.[34]

22.17 The McNaghten Rules have never been part of Scots criminal law. The Scottish courts have, therefore, been tied to no specific formula and have developed a fairly simple test of insanity. In *HM Advocate v Kidd* [35] the judge's instruction to the jury, although couched in terms of reason and of alienation – which are not terms which would necessarily be accepted by psychiatrists today – stated quite simply that the defence would be available if the accused was considered to be of unsound mind at the time of the offence. That is language which anybody can understand and, although a psychiatrist might argue that it begs a lot of questions, at least the psychiatrist himself should find it quite possible to give an opinion to a court in terms of mental soundness or unsoundness.

22.18 Reform of English law was considered at length by the Butler Committee, which reported in 1975.[36] The committee accepted the fact that there were major flaws in the McNaghten Rules and proposed that a verdict of 'not guilty on evidence of mental disorder' should be introduced; this would be appropriate if there was adequate psychiatric evidence of the existence in the accused of a sufficiently severe degree of mental disorder at the time of the commission of the offence charged. This recommendation is embodied in the Draft Criminal Code, prepared by the Law Commission, which provides for a defence where the accused suffers from severe subnormality or, at the time of the offence, a severe mental illness.[37] It would also be a defence under this draft code if mental disorder is proved to negate the fault element in the

---

33 A Model Penal Code 4.01 was also introduced.
34 American developments have been surveyed by R D Mackay *Mental Deficiency Defences in the Criminal Law* (1995) p 127 et seq. See also the same author 'Post-Hinckley Insanity in the USA' [1988] Crim LR 88.
35 1960 JC 61. For an analysis of the development of the Scottish cases, see R A A McCall Smith and D Sheldon *Scots Criminal Law* (2nd edn, 1997) p 135.
36 Report of the Committee on Mentally Abnormal Offenders (Cmnd 6244).
37 *Codification of the Criminal Law* (Law Com no 143).

offence, the grounds upon which this is to be done being left open. Severe mental illness is defined in cl 38(e) of the draft and embraces those conditions which lead to significant thought disorder – particularly delusions.

22.19 Until the reform envisaged in the draft code is acted upon, the McNaghten Rules remain the governing test of insanity in English criminal law, although the Criminal Procedure (Insanity and Unfitness to Plead) Act 1991 allows a broader range of options to a court once the special verdict has been reached. Under this Act, except where the special verdict follows upon a charge of murder, a court is no longer obliged to order detention in a secure hospital under a restriction order (which had no limit of time); it may choose from a number of options, including a supervision or treatment order, guardianship or the absolute discharge of the defendant.[38] This removes the inflexibility of the previous system and will also help to avoid the absurdity of, say, detaining a diabetic or somnambulist in a psychiatric hospital under the draconian shadow of a restriction order – which is what would have happened following upon a successful defence of insane automatism under the previous system.[39]

Unfitness to plead

22.20 In addition to the criticism directed against the actual criteria of the insanity defence, there have also been frequent calls for reform of the rules governing fitness to plead. Until the implementation of the Criminal Procedure (Insanity and Unfitness to Plead) Act 1991, a person who was deemed incapable of standing trial by reason of mental disorder would be sent to hospital under a restriction order without any trial as to whether or not he committed the offence with which he was charged. Now there must be a trial of the facts in order that the jury may decide whether the accused actually committed the offence in question. The 1991 Act makes no changes in the grounds upon which there may be a finding of unfitness to plead. The basis of the plea is an inability to understand proceedings and to defend oneself, but the way in which the criteria for the plea are applied varies greatly.[40]

DIMINISHED RESPONSIBILITY

22.21 The plea of diminished responsibility was devised as a means of allowing the court to avoid a conviction for murder where the mental condition of the accused made the attribution of full responsibility inappropriate. The doctrine was first used in Scotland in the case of *HM Advocate v Dingwall*[41] in 1867 and was eventually introduced into English law in the Homicide Act 1957, s 2(1). This provides that, in cases of homicide, there should be no conviction for murder if the accused is found to be suffering from:

---

38 Similar powers are available under the Criminal Justice (Scotland) Act 1995.
39 See I Mackay 'The Sleepwalker is not Insane' (1992) 55 MLR 714.
40 D Grubin 'Unfit to Plead in England and Wales 1976-1988: A Survey' (1991) 158 Brit J Psychiat 540; 'What Constitutes Fitness to Plead?' [1993] Crim LR 748.
41 (1867) 5 Irv 466.

such abnormality of mind (whether arising from a condition of arrested or retarded development of mind or any inherent causes or induced by disease or injury) as substantially impaired his mental responsibility for his acts and omissions in doing or being a party to the killing.

The doctrine is justified because of the fixed penalty of life imprisonment for murder; it is not required elsewhere because the degree of culpability can be considered in sentencing. The reduction of the offence to one of manslaughter allows this discretion to be exercised in a homicide charge and the court can then choose a sentence ranging from the leniency of a probation order on the one hand to life imprisonment on the other.[42] Sentencing discretion already exists in respect of most other offences and, as a result, the case for extending the application of the plea is hardly strong. Some have criticised the whole concept of a diminished responsibility plea, arguing that we are either responsible or not responsible for our actions and that there should be no half-way house. It has been pointed out that the killing is both premeditated and intended in many cases where homicide occurs in conditions accepted as qualifying for diminished responsibility. Self-control in such circumstances is still a possibility; it is quite unlike the situation, say, where there is a disorder of thinking as a result of psychotic illness. Such iconoclasm discounts the fact that we do regularly make allowances which influence the extent to which we hold people to account for their acts. More usually, such allowances are described as mitigating circumstances rather than as factors influencing responsibility, but the ultimate effect will be the same. The usefulness of the concept of diminished responsibility lies in its flexibility; through its operation, those who are accused and for whom sympathy is felt can be treated in a lenient fashion on conviction without there being any condoning of their offence. A plea of diminished responsibility will, for example, enable the courts to look with equal mercy on cases of 'mercy-killing'. Inferring diminished responsibility in such circumstances does not involve any diminution of the seriousness with which the taking of life is viewed; what it does say is that some penalty other than a long prison sentence may be appropriate by virtue of the accused's mental condition.

22.22 The conditions which may give rise to a successful plea of diminished responsibility vary considerably.[43] General guidance as to what constitutes abnormality of mind for the purposes of the Homicide Act 1957, s 2(1) was given by Lord Parker CJ in *R v Byrne*,[44] where he stated that such abnormality existed when there was a state of mind 'so different from that of ordinary human beings that the reasonable man would term it abnormal'. This concept,

---

42 S Dell *Murder into Manslaughter* (1984); S Dell 'The Mandatory Sentence and Section 2' (1986) 12 J Med Ethics 28.

43 For an Australian survey which reveals the wide range of conditions on which pleas of diminished responsibility have been based, see K L Milte, A A Bartholomew and F Galbally 'Abolition of the Crime of Murder and of Mental Condition Defences' (1975) 49 A LJ 160 – in the cases studied, the conditions included epilepsy, paranoia, reactive depression and alcoholism.

44 [1960] 2 QB 396, [1960] 3 All ER 1, CCA. See also *Rose v R* [1961] AC 496, [1961] 1 All ER 859 and *R v Seers* (1984) 79 Cr App Rep 261, CA, where it was stressed that there need not be a condition 'on the borderline of insanity' in every case. The Court of Appeal in England has addressed the issue of what amounts to an abnormality of mind for purposes of s 2 of the Homicide Act 1957 in *R v Sanderson* (1993) 98 Cr App Rep 325.

it was stressed, was wide enough to cover 'the mind's activities in all its aspects', including both the ability to form a rational judgment as to right and wrong and the ability to control behaviour in accordance with that judgment.

22.23 The wording of s 2(1) excludes abnormality of mind that derives from the working of the emotions. A person who kills another in a state of rage, or who commits homicide out of passionate hatred or jealousy, will not succeed with a plea of diminished responsibility. Alcoholic intoxication may justify the plea but only if the intoxication (a) has caused an abnormality of the mind by way of organic damage or (b) it results from an uncontrollable compulsion to drink caused by the fact that the person is dependent on alcohol.[45] The evidence of mental abnormality may need only to be slight in 'meritorious' cases in which the courts may be prepared to clutch at whatever psychiatric straws are available to avoid the consequences of a conviction for murder. Yet such a process has its dangers and there have been occasional judicial reactions to what is seen as the over-extension of the concept. This has been a particular issue where diminished responsibility has been applied in domestic abuse cases. Such cases frequently involve conduct by people who have been subjected to intolerable treatment and which takes place in the context of extreme emotion. One possibility is to regard such persons as suffering from a specific psychiatric syndrome – and the controversial diagnosis of Battered Women's Syndrome is a case in point.[46] In Scotland, the nature of the diminished responsibility plea was thoroughly examined in the case of *Galbraith v HM Advocate*.[47] In a lengthy judgment, the Court of Criminal Appeal made it clear that it would not be necessary to establish that the accused was suffering from a mental illness or disease, as this would be unduly restrictive. What matters is that there should be an abnormality – recognised by the appropriate science – which results in a lessening of the accused's responsibility. This abnormality may be the product of one factor, or a combination of more than one, including physical or psychological trauma and organic conditions. This approach, which is receptive to changes in psychological and psychiatric thinking, should make it easier for the defence to be applied in Scotland in the future. It is significant, however, that the judgment excludes conditions caused by the voluntary taking of alcohol or drugs as bases for a plea of diminished responsibility. Psychopathic personality disorder is also specifically excluded.

The problem of psychopathy

22.24 There has been considerable disagreement among psychiatrists as to the condition of psychopathy, which has already been mentioned above in the

---

45 *R v Tandy* [1989] 1 All ER 267, [1989] 1 WLR 350, CA.
46 See the change of emphasis in *R v Thornton* [1992] 1 All ER 306 and *R v Thornton (No 2)* [1996] 2 All ER 1023 – in the latter, it was agreed that the syndrome was relevant in considering a defence of provocation. Cf *R v Ahluwalia* [1992] 4 All ER 889, in which the consideration was that of diminished responsibility. For a cynical view of 'syndromes' in general, see I Freckleton 'Contemporary Comment: When Plight Makes Right – the Forensic Abuse Syndrome' (1994) 18 Crim LJ 29.
47 *Galbraith v HM Advocate (No 3)* 2002 JC 1, 2001 SLT 953.

context of 'dangerousness'. Some deny the value of the concept altogether, arguing that it does no more than describe those who behave consistently in an antisocial fashion. The term appears, however, in diagnostic manuals and in mental health legislation and it has occasionally been accepted by the courts as grounds for a plea of diminished responsibility;[48] it is also widely accepted and used in criminology. What, then, is psychopathy and is the psychopath to be held legally responsible for his acts? According to the International Classification of Diseases, Injuries and Causes of Death of the World Health Organisation, psychopathy involves:

> deeply ingrained maladaptive patterns of behaviour, generally recognisable by the time of adolescence or earlier, and continuing throughout most of adult life, although becoming less obvious in middle or old age.[49]

22.25 The Mental Health Act 1983 defines psychopathic disorder as a:

> persistent disorder or disability of mind (whether or not including impairment of intelligence) which results in abnormally aggressive or seriously irresponsible conduct on the part of the person concerned.[50]

22.26 Views on the aetiology of the condition differ. There is a growing body of research which points to a biological explanation, and the implications of this as to responsibility for actions are considerable[51] – if psychopaths behave as they do because their biology is different, then we have to ask whether responsibility should be held to be the same for them as it is for normal people. Psychopathy, however, compromises moral abilities and the ability to empathise with others; even if a psychopath does not see the need to conform to rules, he can still do so – if he chooses. Biology does not affect his understanding of the existence of a rule, nor his ability to conform to it. It might alter the level of inclination to conform but the degree of a person's responsibility is not to be assessed on the basis of weak or strong inclinations.

22.27 Psychopathy has caused some difficulty for the criminal courts.[52] One response has been to deny its relevance to the question of criminal guilt, a sceptical approach based on the notion that all that a diagnosis of psychopathy does is to confirm that the patient behaves in a deviant fashion. Legal scepticism can be understood in the absence of more specific clinical features; while a judge or jury may be prepared to accept the presence of insanity when the condition of the accused is described in terms of delusions, hallucinations or blunting of affect, they may be less swayed by a general term such as personality disorder.

48 See G Williams *Textbook of Criminal Law* (2nd edn, 1983) p 691. Professor Williams summed up the doubts at p 654: 'The term [psychopathy] can be regarded as a declaration of interest in the subject of habitual criminality by the medical profession.'
49 World Health Organisation ICD 9 (1978).
50 Section 1(2). The Mental Health (Scotland) Act 1984 and the Mental Health (Public Safety and Appeals) (Scotland) Act 1999 refer to 'personality disorder', which is undefined.
51 Eg P A Arnett 'Autonomic Responsivity in Psychopaths: a Critical review and Theoretical Proposal' (1997) 17 Clin Psychol Rev 903; R J R Blair, L Jones, F Clark and M Smith 'The Psychopathic Individual: a Lack of Responsiveness to Distress Cues' (1997) 34 Psychophysiology 192.
52 For discussion, see M Roth 'Psychopathic (Sociopathic) Personality' in Bluglass and Bowden (eds) *Principles and Practice of Forensic Medicine* (1990) p 437.

22.28 As a result, the fate of the psychopath in the British criminal process has varied. Psychopathy would have to be accepted as a mental disease in order to justify an insanity plea in McNaghten terms in England or to satisfy the test of insanity in Scots law; the issue has not, however, been decided in a United Kingdom case.[53] In *R v Cooper*[54] the Supreme Court of Canada decided that a personality disorder could fit within the concept of a 'disease of the mind' for legal purposes but, even were this to be generally accepted, it is most unlikely that psychopathy would have such an effect on cognitive capacity as to relieve the accused of responsibility. Indeed, personality disorders are specifically excluded from the scope of the insanity defence in a number of jurisdictions.[55] This being so, the only practical implications psychopathy has for the criminal courts relate to the plea of diminished responsibility and, here, there has been occasional willingness to allow evidence of the condition to reduce murder to manslaughter. More usually, however, the courts have declined to accept it as grounds for the plea and the psychopath will most probably be sentenced in the same way as any other offender.[56] The Butler Committee concluded that 'the psychopath is, in general, untreatable, at least in medical terms'. That being so, he could expect to find little haven in the psychiatric hospital but whether this view is generally held is unclear since the Mental Health Act 1983, s 3(2)(b) now includes the psychopath amongst those who may be compulsorily admitted – subject, for the time being at least, to a treatability test (see para 21.37 above).

Automatism

22.29 The difficulty of reconciling legal requirements with medical insights into the nature of human action is also illustrated by the development of the automatism defence in criminal law. Like the insanity plea, this is a controversial defence which raises some awkward problems of balancing justice for the individual against the protection of society.

22.30 The basic principle of the criminal law that only voluntary acts will result in criminal liability clearly indicates acquittal if the accused has acted automatically. Automatic behaviour consists of acts of which an actor is not conscious or over which he has no control. Actions of somnambulistic type

---

53 The diagnosis was not clearly established in *A-G for Northern Ireland v Gallagher* [1963] AC 349, [1961] 3 All ER 299, HL.

54 (1979) 13 CR (3d) 97.

55 As in the American Law Institute's Model Penal Code, which provides that the term 'mental disease or defect' excludes an abnormality 'manifested only by repeated criminal or anti-social conduct' (s 4.01). For further discussion, see P A Fairall and P W Johnston 'Anti-social Personality Disorder (APD) and the Insanity Defence' (1987) Crim LJ 78.

56 See eg *R v Jennion* [1962] 1 All ER 689, [1962] 1 WLR 317, CCA. In *R v Aarons* [1964] Crim LR 484 a reduction to manslaughter was allowed by way of a diagnosis of psychopathy; none the less the accused was sentenced to life imprisonment. For the Scottish position, see D Chiswick 'Criminal Responsibility in Scotland' in Bluglass and Bowden, para 22.27. Chiswick suggests that the rejection of the term psychopathic disorder in favour of a synonymous description may increase the chances of this form of personality disorder being accepted as grounds for a plea of diminished responsibility.

provide a classic illustration of this sort of behaviour.[57] Sleep-related violence may take place within the context of night terrors, which occur during slow-wave sleep, or it may occur in the course of somnambulistic activity itself. In a night terror, the subject may awake to find his hands round the throat of his sleeping partner and he may have no recollection of events preceding this. The same type of amnesia will occur when he has been sleep-walking. He may have performed complicated actions – operated machinery, opened doors or even fired a gun – and yet none of these will have been executed consciously. It is obvious that there should be no responsibility for such behaviour although it has been observed that somnambulistic behaviour does, in fact, involve a higher level of consciousness than has been supposed previously. Automatic behaviour can result from a number of other causes. These may arise from well-established patho-physiological conditions such as hypoglycaemia, the encephalopathies and post-traumatic states. Cerebral function may also be affected by the state of the blood vessels (arteriosclerosis)[58] and by the ingestion of alcohol and drugs, but offences committed while intoxicated are usually considered in a different context. More legally – and, indeed, morally – controversial are states of dissociation resulting from acute emotional stress; these are sometimes categorised as non-organic automatism.

22.31 The main problem with the defence of automatism lies in the difficulty of establishing with certainty that a given physical condition actually produced automatic behaviour. Idiopathic epilepsy may be taken as an example. It is beyond question that complicated actions, of which the subject may later have no recollection, may be performed either during a seizure or in the post-ictal period. These actions are clearly unconscious and are therefore involuntary from the point of view of the law. That, unfortunately, is as far as certainty can go. There is very little concrete evidence of the occurrence of violence in such states[59] but automatism at least provides an explanation of otherwise inexplicable behaviour; its rejection in such circumstances would be substantially unfair to the accused. Whether an acquittal is appropriate in such cases or whether some other form of disposal is to be preferred involves complicated policy issues.

22.32 In principle, a finding that the criminal offence was committed automatically should result in an acquittal. This will, in fact, be the result in some cases but, in others, the reluctance of the courts to release potentially dangerous offenders has led to the development of two conceptual categories of automatism – insane and non-insane. If the automatic behaviour is classified as insane, the court will then be able to deal with the offender in the same way as it deals with other insane offenders and so ensure that society is protected from potential danger. In theory, at least, the non-insane automaton is also

---

57 The possibility of violence during sleep is discussed by I Oswald and J Evans 'Serious Violence during Sleep Walking' (1985) 147 Brit J Psychiat 688. See also P Fenwick 'Murdering while Asleep' (1986) 293 BMJ 574. For a full treatment of the issue, see C Shapiro and A McCall Smith *Forensic Aspects of Sleep* (1997).

58 *R v Charlson* [1955] 1 All ER 859, [1955] 1 WLR 317; *R v Kemp* [1957] 1 QB 399, [1956] 3 All ER 249.

59 The form of association between epilepsy and violent or aggressive behaviour is controversial. See P Fenwick 'Automatism' in Bluglass and Bowden, para 22.27 above; also P Fenwick 'Aggression and Epilepsy' in M Trimble and T Bolwiq (eds) *Aspects of Epilepsy and Psychiatry* (1986) p 31.

entitled to acquittal. The question which the courts have, thus, set for themselves is: in what circumstances will automatism count as insanity?

22.33 A useful starting point for discussion is Lord Denning's judgment in *Bratty v A-G for Northern Ireland*.[60] The accused in this case was charged with the murder of a girl whom he strangled when what he described as 'a feeling of blackness' came over him. The basis for deciding whether automatic behaviour should be classified as insane, according to Lord Denning, depended upon the question of whether or not it resulted from a disease of the mind. Clearly, if a criminal action derives from a disease of the mind it is appropriate to raise the question of insanity, with all that this entails. In *Bratty*, Lord Denning chose to define disease of the mind in terms of a mental disorder which had manifested itself in violence and which was prone to recur. These criteria indicate the main policy objective behind the distinction – the protection of the public. But the decision is open to criticism in that its logical corollary is that a non-recurrent disorder would not be a disease of the mind; the reasoning is also somewhat circular in that the definition of mental disease depends upon the inference of mental disorder which is, itself, not defined. The case of *R v Quick*[61] highlights the difficulties faced by the courts when trying to evaluate complex medical problems within the framework of a public protection policy. The appellant in *Quick* was a diabetic who, having injected himself with insulin and then failed to eat, went into a hypoglaecemic state during which he committed an assault. The court declined to hold that hypoglycaemia resulting from incorrect therapy was a disease of the mind and ruled that the defence of non-insane automatism was available. The injection of insulin, it was held, was an external factor in the same sense as a blow to the head is an external factor in those cases in which concussion leads to automatic behaviour. Recklessness in failing to eat could, of course, mean that the defence of non-insane automatism would not be available, a point which was stressed in the later case of *R v Bailey*.[62] In this case, the court, by implication, took the view that the defence of insane automatism would be appropriate in those cases where a state of hyperglycaemia[63] resulted from failure of the medical regime; in such cases the abnormal state is produced by disease and not by an external cause such as the injection of insulin. The Court of Appeal, however, stressed the role of recklessness and emphasised that what mattered was knowledge of the risks of what would happen in the event of non-compliance with medical advice. An attempt to circumvent the strictures of this rule was made in *R v Hennessy*,[64] a decision which, once again, denied the defence of non-insane automatism to a diabetic who failed to inject himself with insulin. The appellant in this case argued that his condition of automatism was caused not only by this failure but also by stress, anxiety and depression. It was held that these were not external causes for the purposes of the automatism defence but were states of mind that were prone

60 [1963] AC 386, [1961] 3 All ER 523, HL.
61 [1973] QB 910, [1973] 3 All ER 347, CA.
62 [1983] 2 All ER 503, [1983] 1 WLR 760, CA.
63 The attention of the non-medical reader is drawn to the difference between hypo- (too little) and hyper- (too much). The importance of this to the current discussion was stressed in *R v Bingham* [1991] Crim LR 433, CA.
64 [1989] 2 All ER 9, [1989] 1 WLR 287, CA.

to recur; they were, therefore, relevant to insane rather than to non-insane automatism.

22.34 The position of the epileptic is somewhat clearer.[65] In *R v Sullivan*,[66] the House of Lords dealt with the case of an epileptic who had been convicted of assault during an alleged seizure. The judgment of Lord Diplock in this case is unambiguous: any disease-induced state of mind which satisfies the requirements of the McNaghten Rules – in that it impairs the faculties of reason, memory and understanding – amounts to insanity for legal purposes. The permanence or transience of the impairment is irrelevant, as is the question of its having been caused functionally or organically. Acts performed as a result of an epileptic seizure amount, therefore, to insane automatism. This will be the case even if the offence in question is not one involving violence; in this respect the decision in *Sullivan* broadens the concept of insane automatism beyond Lord Denning's definition in *Bratty*, where the condition was required to manifest itself in violence.

22.35 The problem of somnambulistic automatism came before the Court of Appeal in *R v Burgess*.[67] The appellant had alleged that an attack he made on a friend was committed while he was asleep. The jury accepted that he was not conscious at the time of the attack but returned a verdict of insane automatism rather than non-insane, as was claimed. The Court of Appeal upheld this verdict on the grounds that the somnambulistic behaviour was a product of a disease of the mind rather than of any external cause. This decision maintains the principle that automatism will be treated as insanity if it results from a mental disorder that is prone to recur – with or without manifestations of violence. The concern of the courts over the acquittal of persons who might pose a future danger are understandable, but the difficulty will always be that of predicting dangerousness in such cases. One episode of somnambulistic violence may provide weak grounds for prolonged detention, particularly when the causative factors in relation to such behaviour are so difficult to identify – and the evidence given in *R v Parks*[68] was that there is no recorded instance of repeated violence during sleepwalking. In *Parks*, a case involving homicide, the Supreme Court of Canada reached the opposite conclusion to that in *Burgess* and held that the loss of mental faculties in somnambulistic automatism is caused by the normal condition of sleep rather than by disease of the mind – it was pointed out that, otherwise, all children and some 2.5% of adults could be said to be affected by mental disease.[69] The words of Watt J, the trial judge in this case, have a persuasive ring:

> There may be any number of appropriate responses ... in the control and treatment of those who have caused serious social harm while in a somnambulistic state, but a mischaracterization of the disorder as a disease of the mind and the use of the blunt instrument of indefinite confinement by warrant under a special verdict of not guilty by reason of insanity is not one of them.[70]

65 K J M Smith 'Epileptic Action and Criminal Responsibility' (1983) 99 LQR 506.
66 [1984] AC 156, [1983] 2 All ER 673, HL.
67 [1991] 2 QB 92, [1991] 2 All ER 769.
68 (1990) 78 CR (3d) 1, [1992] SCR 871.
69 (1990) 78 CR (3d) 1 at 5, per Brooke JA.
70 Quoted by Brooke JA (1990) 78 CR (3d) 1 at 5.

22.36 Following the ruling of the High Court in *HM Advocate v Cunningham*[71] in 1963, Scots law took a particularly harsh view of automatism, denying any defence in such cases other than that of insanity. This changed with the decision in *Ross v HM Advocate*[72] in which the court accepted that acquittal is the appropriate result where non-insane automatism is established. The automatic behaviour in *Ross* resulted from involuntary drugging. In later cases, however, the Scottish courts have sought to limit the scope of this defence by insisting that there should be clear evidence of a complete lack of consciousness on the part of the accused; they have also stressed that the accused should in no way be the author of his own state of impairment.[73]

22.37 Non-organic automatism, or psychogenic automatism, has been viewed very much more sceptically by some courts. Such automatism may occur when there is subjection either to prolonged stress or to a sudden shock. In each case, a state of dissociation may result in which actions are performed without the exercise by the subject of conscious control. In a series of decisions, the Canadian courts recognised what became known as 'psychological blow automatism' as being grounds for acquittal as non-insane automatism; more prolonged states of dissociation were treated as insanity.[74] In *R v K*,[75] for example, the accused, who had been undergoing treatment for a severe neurotic condition, killed his wife after the shock of hearing that she planned to leave him. Psychiatric evidence to the effect that the killing took place while he was in a state of automatism was accepted by the jury and the accused was acquitted. Similarly, in *R v Gottschalk*[76] the accused was acquitted of assault after psychiatric evidence was led of his state of depersonalisation which was productive of automatism. A reverse in the trend of the Canadian decisions occurred, however, with the decision of the Supreme Court of Canada in *Rabey v R*,[77] in which it was held that dissociation resulting from a psychological shock should be treated as insanity rather than as non-insane automatism. It is significant in this case that the accused, who assaulted a woman after she had rejected him, did not have a psychiatric record such as that which was produced by the defendants in *K* and *Gottschalk*. It may be suspected, too, that the court wished to restrict defences of psychogenic automatism for policy reasons, as the whole concept is an obvious candidate for abuse and the introduction of non-meritorious defences.[78]

22.38 The High Court of Australia considered the issue of psychogenic automatism in *R v Falconer*,[79] a case involving the killing by a woman of her violent and abusive husband. The High Court ruled that psychiatric evidence

---

71 1963 JC 80, 1963 SLT 345.
72 1991 SLT 564, 1991 SCCR 823.
73 *Ebsworth v HM Advocate* 1992 SLT 1161, 1992 SCCR 671; *Macleod v Napier* 1993 SCCR 303. See discussion in R A A McCall Smith and D Sheldon *Scots Criminal Law* (2nd edn, 1997) p 28.
74 See M E Schiffer *Mental Disorder and the Criminal Process* (1978) p 101.
75 (1971) 3 CCC (2d) 84.
76 (1974) 22 CCC (2d) 415.
77 (1981) 114 DLR (3d) 193.
78 For a criticism of *Rabey*, see R D Mackay 'Non-organic Automatism – Some Recent Developments' [1980] Crim LR 350.
79 (1990) 65 ALJ R 20.

of the dissociative state in which the accused had acted should have been admitted – and it was also observed that there was no reason in principle why the law should allow automatism following upon physical trauma and yet disallow it if it proceeds from a psychological cause. In England, the possibility of a non-insane automatism defence based on dissociation was rejected in the Court of Appeal decision in *R v Isitt*.[80] The accused in this case failed to stop after an accident and had attempted to evade the police. In considering his claim to have been in a state of shock, the court took the view that, although the accused's mind might have been 'shut to the moral inhibitions which control the lives of most of us', there was no suggestion that his mind was not working at all and the defence of automatism was, therefore, not available. This concept of 'diminished awareness' has, again, been rejected by the Court of Appeal in a driving case.[81] A vehicle user caused the death of two pedestrians while driving in a state in which his awareness of his surroundings was impaired due to fatigue. The court held that this failed to qualify as automatism, as some conscious control of his actions was still retained. On the other hand, a defence of automatism based on a claim that being raped three days before committing a robbery had resulted in post-traumatic stress disorder and a consequent dissociative state was allowed to go to the jury in the Crown Court.[82]

A delicate balance?

22.39 All forms of 'mental defence' give rise to the same general dilemma. While the non-punishment of the mentally disordered is seen as an attractive goal, the need both for a certain degree of scepticism and a measure of social defence have constantly to be borne in mind. A broad, sympathetic view of excusing conditions of this sort may prevent the unjust punishment of those who are truly not responsible for their actions, but it may also have the effect of blunting our conceptions of responsibility and of imposing upon psychiatric institutions a group of people who should not be there. At the same time, too fine a net will deny a defence to meritorious cases and that, too, is socially damaging. The inescapable task of the criminal law then becomes one of charting an acceptable middle course. To achieve this, the criminal law should adhere to a broad definition of insanity which allows maximum leeway for a court to take into account expert evidence while at the same time avoiding necessarily being bound to an acceptance of psychiatric notions of responsibility. The matter is thus ultimately left in lay hands which, although fettered to an extent by theoretical guidelines, may none the less exercise such discretion as the situation demands. In the final analysis, the question: 'Is the accused responsible for his acts?' is answered not in terms of a McNaghten-style dissection of mental states but in terms of our reaction to the question: 'Should the accused be punished?' Finding the answer to that question, of course, will, in many cases, be as perversely difficult and unsettling as ever.

80 (1977) 67 Cr App Rep 44, [1978] RTR 211, CA.
81 *A-G's Reference (No 2 of 1992)* [1994] QB 91, [1993] 4 All ER 683. The driver's reaction was attributed by the defence to the condition of 'driving without awareness'.
82 *R v T* [1990] Crim LR 256. The outcome of the trial is not stated.

Appendices

Appendices

Appendix A
The Hippocratic Oath

23.1

'I swear by Apollo the physician, by Aesculapius, Hygiea and Panacea, and I take to witness all the gods, all the goddesses, to keep according to my ability and my judgement the following Oath:

'To consider dear to me as my parents him who taught me this art; to live in common with him and if necessary to share my goods with him; to look upon his children as my own brothers, to teach them this art if they so desire without fee or written promise; to impart to my sons and the sons of the master who taught me and the disciples who have enrolled themselves and have agreed to the rules of the profession, but to these alone, the precepts and the instruction. I will prescribe regimen for the good of my patients according to my ability and my judgement and never do harm to anyone. To please no one will I prescribe a deadly drug, nor give advice which may cause his death. Nor will I give a woman a pessary to procure abortion. But I will preserve the purity of my life and my art. I will not cut for stone, even for patients in whom the disease is manifest; I will leave this operation to be performed by practitioners (specialists in this art). In every house where I come I will enter only for the good of my patients, keeping myself far from all intentional ill-doing and all seduction, and especially from the pleasures of love with women or with men, be they free or slaves. All that may come to my knowledge in the exercise of my profession or outside of my profession or in daily commerce with men, which ought not to be spread abroad, I will keep secret and will never reveal. If I keep this oath faithfully, may I enjoy my life and practice my art, respected by all men and in all times; but if I swerve from it or violate it, may the reverse be my lot.'

Appendix B
Declaration of Geneva

(As amended at Stockholm, 1994)*

24.1

At the time of being admitted as a member of the medical profession:
I solemnly pledge myself to consecrate my life to the service of humanity;
I will give to my teachers the respect and gratitude which is their due;
I will practise my profession with conscience and dignity;
The health of my patient will be my first consideration;
I will respect the secrets which are confided in me, even after the patient has died;
I will maintain by all the means in my power, the honour and the noble traditions of the medical profession;
My colleagues will be my sisters and brothers;
I will not permit considerations of age, disease or disability, creed, ethnic origin, gender, nationality, political affiliation, race, sexual orientation, or social standing to intervene between my duty and my patient;
I will maintain the utmost respect for human life from its beginning even under threat, and I will not use my medical knowledge contrary to the laws of humanity.
I make these promises solemnly, freely and upon my honour.

* The authors are grateful to the Medical Ethics Department of the British Medical Association for providing the current updated texts of Appendices B–E.

Appendix C

International Code of Medical Ethics

(As amended at Venice, 1983)

English text

25.1

Duties of Physicians in General

A PHYSICIAN SHALL always maintain the highest standards of professional conduct.

A PHYSICIAN SHALL not permit motives of profit to influence the free and independent exercise of professional judgement.

A PHYSICIAN SHALL, in all types of medical practice, be dedicated to providing competent medical service in full technical and moral independence, with compassion and respect for human dignity.

A PHYSICIAN SHALL deal honestly with patients and colleagues, and strive to expose those physicians deficient in character or competence, or who engage in fraud or deception.

THE FOLLOWING PRACTICES are deemed to be unethical conduct:

(a) Self advertising by physicians, unless permitted by the laws of the country and the Code of Ethics of the National Medical Association.
(b) Paying or receiving any fee or any other consideration solely to procure the referral of a patient or for prescribing or referring a patient to any source.

A PHYSICIAN SHALL respect the rights of patients, of colleagues, and of other health professionals and shall safeguard patient confidences.

A PHYSICIAN SHALL act only in the patient's interest when providing medical care which might have the effect of weakening the physical and mental condition of the patient.

A PHYSICIAN SHALL use great caution in divulging discoveries or new techniques or treatment through non-professional channels.

A PHYSICIAN SHALL certify only that which he has personally verified.

Duties of Physicians to the Sick

A PHYSICIAN SHALL always bear in mind the obligation of preserving human life.

A PHYSICIAN SHALL owe his patients complete loyalty and all the resources of his science. Whenever an examination or treatment is beyond the physician's capacity he should summon another physician who has the necessary ability.

A PHYSICIAN SHALL preserve absolute confidentiality on all he knows about his patient even after the patient has died.

A PHYSICIAN SHALL give emergency care as a humanitarian duty unless he is assured that others are willing and able to give such care.

Duties of Physicians to Each Other

A PHYSICIAN SHALL behave to his colleagues as he would have them behave towards him.

A PHYSICIAN SHALL NOT entice patients from his colleagues.

A PHYSICIAN SHALL observe the principles of 'The Declaration of Geneva' approved by the World Medical Association.

Appendix D
Declaration of Tokyo, 1975

26.1

Statement on torture and other cruel, inhuman or degrading treatment or punishment

Preamble
It is the privilege of the medical doctor to practise medicine in the service of humanity, to preserve and restore bodily and mental health without distinction as to persons, to comfort and to ease the suffering of his or her patients. The utmost respect for human life is to be maintained even under threat, and no use made of any medical knowledge contrary to the laws of humanity.

For the purpose of this Declaration, torture is defined as the deliberate, systematic or wanton infliction of physical or mental suffering by one or more persons acting alone or on the orders of any authority, to force another person to yield information, to make a confession, or for any other reason.

Declaration
1. The doctor shall not countenance, condone or participate in the practice of torture or other forms of cruel, inhuman or degrading procedures, whatever the offence of which the victim of such procedures is suspected, accused or guilty, and whatever the victim's beliefs or motives, and in all situations, including armed conflict and civil strife.

2. The doctor shall not provide any premises, instruments, substances or knowledge to facilitate the practice of torture or other forms of cruel, inhuman or degrading treatment or to diminish the ability of the victim to resist such treatment.

3. The doctor shall not be present during any procedure during which torture or other forms of cruel, inhuman or degrading treatment is used or threatened.

4. A doctor must have complete clinical independence in deciding upon the care of a person for whom he or she is medically responsible. The doctor's fundamental role is to alleviate the distress of his or her fellow men, and no motive whether personal, collective or political shall prevail against this higher purpose.

5. Where a prisoner refuses nourishment and is considered by the doctor as capable of forming an unimpaired and rational judgement concerning the consequences of such a voluntary refusal of nourishment, he or she shall not be fed artificially. The decision as to the capacity of the prisoner to form such a judgement should be confirmed by at least one other independent doctor. The consequences of the refusal of nourishment shall be explained by the doctor to the prisoner.

6. The World Medical Association will support and should encourage the international community, the national medical associations and fellow doctors to support, the doctor and his or her family in the face of threats or reprisals resulting from a refusal to condone the use of torture or other forms of cruel, inhuman or degrading treatment.

Appendix E

Declaration of Helsinki

(As amended at Edinburgh, 2000)

27.1

Ethical Principles for medical research involving human subjects

A. *Introduction*

1.   The World Medical Association has developed the Declaration of Helsinki as a statement of ethical principals to provide guidance to physicians and other participants in medical research involving human subjects. Medical research involving human subjects includes research on identifiable human subjects or identifiable material.

2.   It is the duty of the physician to promote and safeguard the health of the people. The physician's knowledge and conscience are dedicated to the fulfilment of this duty.

3.   The Declaration of Geneva of the World Medical Association binds the physician with the words: 'The health of my patient will be my first consideration', and the International Code of Medical Ethics declares that, 'A physician shall act only in the patient's interest when providing medical care which might have the effect of weakening the physical and mental condition of the patient'.

4.   Medical progress is based on research which ultimately must rest in part on experimentation involving human subjects.

5.   In medical research on human subjects, considerations related to the well-being of the human should take precedence over the interests of science and society.

6.   The primary purpose of medical research involving human subjects is to improve prophylactic, diagnostic and therapeutic procedures and the understanding of the aetiology and pathogenesis of the disease. Even the best proven prophylactic, diagnostic and therapeutic methods must continuously be challenged through research for their effectiveness, efficiency, accessibility and quality.

7.   In current medical practice and in medical research, most prophylactic, diagnostic and therapeutic procedures involve risks and burdens.

8.   Medical research is subject to ethical standards that promote respect for all human beings and protect their health and rights. Some research populations are vulnerable and need special protection. The particular needs

of the economically and medically disadvantaged must be recognized. Special attention is also required for those who cannot give or refuse consent for themselves, for those who may be subject to giving consent under duress, for those who will not personally benefit from the research and for those for whom the research is combined with care.

9.   Research investigators should be aware of the ethical, legal and regulatory requirements for research on human subjects in their own countries as well as applicable international requirements. No national ethical, legal or regulatory requirement should be allowed to reduce or eliminate any of the protections for human subjects set forth in this declaration.

B. Basic Principles for all medical research

10.   It is the duty of the physician in medical research to protect life, health, privacy, and dignity of the human subject.

11.   Medical research involving human subjects must conform to generally accepted scientific principles, be based on a through knowledge of the scientific literature, other relevant sources of information, and on adequate laboratory and, where appropriate, animal experimentation.

12.   Appropriate caution must be exercised in the conduct of research which may affect the environment, and the welfare of animals used for research must be respected.

13.   The design and performance of each experimental procedure involving human subjects should be clearly formulated in an experimental protocol. This protocol should be submitted for consideration, comment, guidance, and where appropriate, approval to a specially appointed ethical review committee, which must be independent of the investigator, the sponsor of any other kind of undue influence. This independent committee should be in conformity with the laws and regulations of the country in which the research experiment is performed. The committee has the right to monitor ongoing trials. The researcher has the obligation to provide monitoring information to the committee, especially any serious adverse events. The researcher should also submit to the committee, for review, information regarding funding, sponsors, institutional affiliations, other potential conflicts of interest and incentives for subjects.

14.   The research protocol should always contain a statement of the ethical considerations involved and should indicate that there is compliance with the principles enunciated in this Declaration.

15.   Medical research involving human subjects should be conducted only by scientifically qualified persons and under the supervision of a clinically competent medical person. The responsibility for the human subject must always rest with a medically qualified person and never rest on the subject of the research, even though the subject has given consent.

16.   Every medical research project involving human subjects should be preceded by careful assessment of predictable risks and burdens in comparison with foreseeable benefits to the subjects or to others. This does not preclude the participation of healthy volunteers in medical research. The design of all studies should be publicly available.

17.   Physicians should abstain from engaging in research projects involving human subjects unless they are confident that the risks involved have been adequately assessed and can be satisfactorily managed. Physicians should

cease any investigation if the risks are found to outweigh the potential benefits or if there is conclusive proof of positive and beneficial benefits.

18.   Medical research involving human subjects should only be conducted if the importance of the objective outweighs the inherent risks and burdens to the subject. This is especially important when the human subjects are healthy volunteers.

19.   Medical research is only justified if there is a reasonable likelihood that the populations in which the research is carried out stand to benefit from the results of the research.

20.   The subjects must be volunteers and informed participants in the research project.

21.   The right of research subjects to safeguard their integrity must always be respected. Every precaution should be taken to respect the privacy of the subject, the confidentiality of the patient's information and to minimise the impact of the study on the subject's physical and mental integrity and on the personality of the subject.

22.   In any research on human beings, each potential subject must be adequately informed of the aims, methods, sources of funding, any possible conflicts of interest, institutional affiliations of the researcher, the anticipated benefits and potential risks of the study and the discomfort it might entail. The subject should be informed of the right to abstain from participation in the study or to withdraw consent to participate at any time without reprisal. After ensuring that the subject has understood the information, the physician should then obtain the subject's freely-given informed consent, preferably in writing. If the consent cannot be obtained in writing, the non-written consent must be formally documented and witnessed.

23.   When obtaining informed consent for the research project the physician should be particularly cautious if the subject is in a dependent relationship with the physician or may consent under duress. In that case the informed consent should be obtained be a well-informed physician who is not engaged in the investigation and who is completely independent of this relationship.

24.   For a research subject who is legally incompetent, physically or mentally incapable of giving consent or is a legally incompetent minor, the investigator must obtain informed consent from the legally authorized representative in accordance with applicable law. These groups should not be included in research unless the research is necessary to promote the health of the population represented and this research cannot instead be performed on legally competent persons.

25.   When a subject deemed legally incompetent, such as a minor child, is able to give assent to decisions about participation in research, the investigator must obtain that assent in addition to the consent of the legally authorised representative.

26.   Research on individuals from whom it is not possible to obtain consent, including proxy or advance consent, should be done only if the physical/mental condition that prevents obtaining informed consent is a necessary characteristic of the research population. The specific reasons for involving research subjects with a condition that renders them unable to give informed consent should be stated in the experimental protocol for consideration and approval of the review committee. The protocol should state that consent to remain in the research should be obtained as soon as possible from the individual or a legally authorized surrogate.

27. Both authors and publishers have ethical obligations. In publication of the results of research, the investigators are obliged to preserve the accuracy of the results. Negative as well as positive results should be published or otherwise publicly available. Sources of funding, institutional affiliations and any possible conflicts of interest should be declared in the publication. Reports of experimentation not in accordance with the principles laid down in this Declaration should not be accepted for publication.

C. Additional principles for medical research combined with medical care
28. The physician may combine medical research with medical care, only to the extent that the research is justified by its potential prophylactic, diagnostic or therapeutic value. When medical research is combined with medical care, additional standards apply to protect the patients who are research subjects.
29. The benefits, risks, burdens and effectiveness of a new method should be tested against those of the best current prophylactic, diagnostic or therapeutic methods. This does not exclude the use of placebo, or no treatment, in studies where no proven methods exists.
30. At the conclusion of the study, every patient entered into the study should be assured of access to the best proven prophylactic, diagnostic or therapeutic methods identified by the study.
31. The physician should fully inform the patient which aspects of the care are related to the research. The refusal of a patient to participate in a study must never interfere with the patient physician relationship.
32. In the treatment of a patient, where proven prophylactic, diagnostic and therapeutic methods do not exist or have been ineffective, the physician, with informed consent from the patient, must be free to use unproven or new prophylactic, diagnostic and therapeutic measures, if in the physician's judgement it offers hope of saving life, re-establishing health or alleviating suffering. Where possible, these measures should be made the object of research, designed to evaluate their safety and efficacy. In all cases, new information should be recorded and, where appropriate, published. The other relevant guidelines of this Declaration should be followed.

Index

Index

Abortion—*contd*
religious objection to 1.8, 5.29
Republic of Ireland 5.14–5.17
Scotland 4.78, 5.6, 5.11, 5.72
selective non-treatment of neonate, and
  5.49, 16.12
selective reduction of pregnancy 3.69,
  3.70, 5.81–5.83
sex of fetus, on grounds of 3.18, 5.9
statistics 5.11–5.12, 5.17, 5.79
third party rights 5.66–5.76
  conscientious objection 5.67,
    5.69–5.70
  doctor, nature of duty 5.74–5.76
  father 5.71–5.73
  nurse 5.68–5.70
time limit 5.45–5.46
United States 5.2, 5.18–5.22
  Roe v Wade 5.19, 5.20, 5.21,
    5.28, 5.29
uterine lavage 3.68
viability of fetus 5.42–5.52
wrongful birth action 5.74, 5.76
wrongful life action 5.75
Abuse
child abuse 8.35–8.36
elderly person, of 12.3, 12.8
wife battering 8.34, 22.23
Accident
blood alcohol sampling as research 19.58
industrial 8.47
medical *see* MEDICAL NEGLIGENCE
road traffic *see* ROAD TRAFFIC ACCIDENT
Accused person
confidentiality, and 8.41
Adultery
doctor, by 1.36
donor insemination as 3.23–3.24
Advance directive 18.63–18.68
see also EUTHANASIA; LIVING WILL
Advertising by doctors 1.42–1.43
Advisory Committee on Genetic Testing
7.6, 7.20, 7.21, 7.57
Advisory Group on Advances in Genetics
7.20
Advocacy Service 1.38
Age
see also CHILD; ELDERLY PERSONS; INFANT
consent to medical treatment, for *see*
  CONSENT TO TREATMENT
'do not resuscitate' order, and 18.94
homosexual acts, consent to 2.15, 2.25
in vitro fertilisation 3.53–3.54
incest, and 2.11, 2.12
resource allocation, and 11.43
resuscitation, and 18.94
sterilisation, and 4.3
transplantation time limits 14.12
AIDS *see* HIV/AIDS
Alcoholic intoxication
automatism, and 22.30
diminished responsibility, and 22.23

Amniocentesis 6.18–6.19, 6.28
biochemical tests 6.19
defensive 6.21
Down's syndrome 6.15, 6.16, 6.21,
  6.24, 6.30
failure of 6.31
failure to recommend 6.30, 6.32
false positive/negative 6.23
fetal mortality rate 6.23
neural tube defects 6.16
time for 6.21
ultrasonography, and 6.15, 6.16
Anaesthetists
medical negligence 9.91, 9.94
Androgen insensitivity syndrome 2.38
see also TRANSSEXUALISM
Anencephaly 6.6, 6.15
transplant donation 14.61
United States, *Baby K* case
  16.78–16.79, 16.94
Animals
experimentation on 3.57, 19.26
transgenic, use in xenotransplantation
  14.6–14.7
Anorexia nervosa
consent to treatment 21.42–21.45
forced feeding 10.75
minor with 10.75
refusal of treatment 10.45–10.47, 10.75
Anti-social personality disorder *see*
  PSYCHOPATH
Arbitration
medical negligence cases 9.4
Armed forces, member of
confidentiality issues for medical
  officer 8.41
homosexuality 2.21–2.24
research, use for 19.24
Arson
criminal responsibility 22.5
Artificial insemination
see also DONOR INSEMINATION; HUMAN
  FERTILISATION AND EMBRYOLOGY
  AUTHORITY; IN VITRO FERTILISATION;
  SURROGATE MOTHERHOOD
abnormal fetus resulting 3.57
disability of resulting child 3.57
husband/partner, by 3.8, 3.9–3.19
  long-term prisoners 3.17
  nullity of marriage, and 3.16
  pre-implantation genetic selection
    3.10
  sex selection 3.11, 3.18–3.19
  sperm
    banked for use after death 3.12,
      15.3
    Blood case 3.13–3.15
    recovery from dead/comatose
      partner 3.13–3.15
  techniques 3.10
prisoners 3.17
transsexualism, and 2.66

674